OLIVIER BLANCHARD, MASSACHUSETTS INSTITUTE OF TECHNOLOGY
DAVID JOHNSON, WILFRID LAURIER UNIVERSITY

MACROECONOMICS

THIRD CANADIAN EDITION

Toronto

À Noelle
O.B.

To Susan
D.J.

Library and Archives Canada Cataloguing in Publication

Blanchard, Olivier (Olivier J.)
    Macroeconomics/Olivier Blanchard, David Johnson. — 3rd Canadian ed.

Includes index.
ISBN-10: 0-13-200328-7
ISBN-13: 978-0-13-200328-5

1. Macroeconomics. I. Johnson, David R., 1956 II. Title.

HB172.5.B556 2006339   C2006-903815-5

ISBN-10: 0-13-200328-7
ISBN-13: 978-0-13-200328-5

Editor-in-Chief: Gary Bennett

Acquisitions Editor: Laura Paterson Forbes

Marketing Manager: Eileen Lasswell

Developmental Editor: Paul Donnelly

Production Editor: Cheryl Jackson

Copy Editor: Rohini Herbert

Proofreader: Catharine Haggert

Production Coordinator: Christine Kwan

Composition: Joan M. Wilson

Art Director: Julia Hall

Cover and Interior Design: Jennifer Stimson

Cover Image: Patrick Doherty/Getty Images

1 2 3 4 5   11 10 09 08 07

Printed and bound in the United States of America

A B O U T   T H E   A U T H O R S

Olivier Blanchard

Olivier Blanchard is the Class of 1941 Professor of Economics at MIT. He did his undergraduate work in France, and received a Ph.D. in economics from MIT in 1977. He taught at Harvard from 1977 to 1982, and has taught at MIT since 1983. He has frequently received the award for best teacher in the department of economics.

He has done research on many macroeconomic issues, from the effects of fiscal policy, to the role of expectations, to price rigidities, to speculative bubbles, to unemployment in Western Europe, transition in Eastern Europe, and more recently, on labour market institutions. He has done work for many governments and many international organizations, including the World Bank, the IMF, the OECD, the EU commission and the EBRD. He has published over 150 articles and edited or written over 15 books, including *Lectures on Macroeconomics* with Stanley Fischer.

He is a research associate of the National Bureau of Economic Research, a fellow and a council member of the Econometric Society, a member of the American Academy of Arts and Sciences, and a past vice president of the American Economic Association. He is also a member of the French Council of Economic Advisers.

He lives in Cambridge, Massachusetts, with his wife, Noelle. He has three daughters, Marie, Serena, and Giulia.

David R. Johnson

David R. Johnson is Professor of Economics at Wilfrid Laurier University. His published research in macroeconomics includes studies of Canada's current account, the determination of the Canada–U.S. exchange rate, Canadian fiscal policy, and a number of studies of inflation targets both in Canada and around the world. His more recent research considers various aspects of the economics of education. His book "Signposts of Success: Interpreting Ontario's Elementary School Test Scores" was published in 2005 by the C. D. Howe Institute and was short-listed for both the Donner Prize and Purvis Prize.

David's undergraduate degree is from the University of Toronto. He has a masters degree in economics from the University of Western Ontario, and he obtained a Ph.D. in economics from Harvard University in 1983. Olivier Blanchard was one of the supervisors on his thesis. After working for two years in the Research Department of the Bank of Canada, David came to Wilfrid Laurier University. He has visited at the National Bureau of Economic Research in Cambridge, Massachusetts, and at the University of Cambridge in England.

When not doing economics, David plays Oldtimer's hockey in the winter and sculls at the Cambridge Rowing Club in the summer. He is an active member of First Mennonite Church in Kitchener, where he often teaches Sunday school. He lives in Waterloo with his wife, Susan, who is also an economics professor. They have shared, and nearly completed, the raising of two children, Sarah and Daniel, who more than occasionally think that there is too much discussion of economics over the dinner table.

BRIEF CONTENTS

C O N T E N T S

BOXES

PREFACE

We had two main goals in writing this book:

- To make close contact with current macroeconomic events.

  What makes macroeconomics exciting is the light it sheds on what is happening around the world, from the introduction of the euro in Western Europe, to the recent U.S. recession, to the long Japanese economic slump, to the inflation crisis in Argentina. These events—and many more—are described in the book, not in footnotes, but in the text or in detailed boxes. Each box shows how you can use what you have learned to get an understanding of these events. Our hope is that these boxes not only convey the "life" of macroeconomics, but also reinforce the lessons from the models, making them more concrete and easier to grasp.

- To provide an integrated view of macroeconomics.

  The book is built on one underlying model, a model that draws the implications of equilibrium conditions in three sets of markets: the goods market, the financial markets, and the labour market. Depending on the issue at hand, the parts of the model relevant to the issue are developed in more detail while the other parts are simplified or lurk in the background. But the underlying model is always the same. This way, you will see macroeconomics as a coherent whole, not a collection of models. And you will be able to make sense not only of past macroeconomic events, but also of those that unfold in the future.

Organization

The book has two central components, a core and the set of two major extensions. An introduction precedes the core. The two extensions are followed by a review of the role of policy. The book ends with an epilogue (the structure of the book is highlighted by the flowchart on page xiii).

- Chapters 1 and 2 introduce the basic facts and issues of macroeconomics.

  Chapter 1 offers a tour of the world, from Canada, to the United States, to Europe, to Japan. Some instructors may prefer to cover it later, perhaps after Chapter 2, which introduces basic concepts, articulates the notions of short run, medium run, and long run, and gives a quick tour of the book.

  While Chapter 2 gives the basics of national income accounting, we have put a detailed treatment of national income accounts to Appendix 1 at the end of the book. This both decreases the burden on the beginning reader and allows for a more thorough treatment in the appendix.

- Chapters 3 to 17 constitute the **core**.

  Chapters 3 to 8 focus on the **short run**. They characterize equilibrium in the goods market and in the financial markets, and they derive the basic model used to study short-run movements in output, the *IS-LM* model. The open economy material appears in Chapters 6, 7, and 8.

  Chapters 9 to 13 focus on the **medium run**. Chapter 9 focuses on equilibrium in the labour market and introduces the natural rate of unemployment. Chapters 10, 11, and 12 develop a model based on aggregate demand and aggregate supply and show how that model can be used to understand movements in activity and in inflation, both in the short run and in the medium run. Chapter 12, which looks at the dynamic relation between inflation and activity, is a bit harder and is optional. Chapter 13 looks at open economy issues in the medium run. In particular, there is an analysis of fixed and flexible exchange rates.

  Chapters 14 to 17 focus on the **long run**. Chapter 14 describes the facts, showing the evolution of output over countries and over long periods of time. Chapters 15 and 16 develop a model of growth, focusing on the determinants of capital accumulation and technological progress and the role of each in growth. Chapter 17 looks at growth in the open economy. It stresses the role of net immigration and foreign capital in creating economic growth. An appendix deals with the concept of an optimal current account deficit.

- Chapters 18 to 23 cover the two major **extensions**.

  Chapters 18 to 21 focus on the role of **expectations** in the short run and in the medium run. Expectations play a major role in most economic decisions and, by implication, in the determination of output. Chapter 18, which introduces basic tools, is simplified relative to the first edition. Also, many readers rightly suggested it was both easier and more natural to start with the role of expectations in financial markets.

  Chapters 22 and 23 focus on **pathologies**, times when (macroeconomic) things go very wrong. Chapter 22 looks at periods of high unemployment. Chapter 23 looks at episodes of hyperinflation.

- Chapters 24 to 26 return to **macroeconomic policy**.

  While most of the first 23 chapters discuss macroeconomic policy in one form or another, the purpose of Chapters 24 to 26 is to tie the threads together. Chapter 24 looks at the role and the limits of macroeconomic policy in general. Chapters 25 and 26 review monetary and fiscal policy. Some teachers may want to use parts of these chapters earlier. For example, it is easy to move forward the discussion of the government budget constraint in Chapter 26.

Structure of the Book

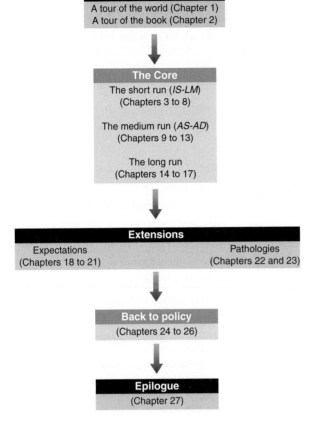

- Chapter 27 serves as an **epilogue**. It puts macroeconomics in historical perspective, showing the evolution of macroeconomics in the last 70 years and discussing current directions of research.

Alternative Course Outlines

Intermediate macroeconomics is typically taught as a single two-semester course with one instructor or as two one-semester courses, often with different instructors. The book's organization assumes two 12- or 13-week terms with some time used for evaluation and perhaps review. Some chapters are more difficult than others and would require more time in class.

If an instructor had a group of intermediate macroeconomics students for two consecutive semesters, it would make sense to use the book in order. The two extensions and the back-to-policy section apply the material learned in the core.

A first one-semester course could cover Chapters 1 through 13. This would bring the course to the end of the medium-run analysis. It might be possible to cover one or two topics in the extension chapters or the back-to-policy chapters.

The second one-semester course could cover the long-run material and the extensions and use the back-to-policy chapters as an opportunity to apply the core material and address the policy issues in more depth.

Features

We have made sure never to present a theoretical result without relating it to the real world. For this purpose, in addition to discussions of facts in the text itself, we have introduced three types of boxes:

- **Focus** boxes, which expand on a point made in the text.
- **In Depth** boxes, which look at a particular macroeconomic episode in detail.
- **Global Macro** boxes, which look at macroeconomic episodes from around the world.

The margin notes running parallel to the text create a dialogue with the reader, smoothing out the more difficult passages and allowing for a deeper understanding of the concepts and the results derived along the way.

For students who want to explore macroeconomics further, we have introduced the following three features:

- **Digging Deeper** notes, which expand on an argument in the text, often by indicating how an implicit assumption in the text could be relaxed and what the implications might be.
- **Short appendices** to some chapters, which show how a proposition in the text can be derived more rigorously or expanded.
- A **Further Readings** section at the end of each chapter, indicating where to find more information, including a number of key Internet addresses.

Each chapter ends with three ways of making sure that the material in the chapter has been thoroughly understood:

- A **summary** of the chapter's main points.
- A list of **key terms**.
- A series of **end-of-chapter exercises**, some of them requiring access to the Internet, some of them requiring the use of a spreadsheet program. More challenging exercises, Web-based or otherwise, are indicated by an asterisk (*).

The Teaching and Learning Package

The book comes with a number of supplements to help both students and instructors.

For instructors:

- **Instructor's Solutions Manual**. The *Instructor's Solutions Manual* provides answers to all end-of-chapter questions and exercises.

- **Test Item File**. The test bank is completely revised with an additional 25 new multiple-choice questions per chapter, for a total of over 1,200 questions.
- **PowerPoint Lecture Slides**. These electronic slides provide outlines, summaries, equations, and graphs for each chapter.

All of these instructor's supplements are available on an **Instructor's Resource CD-ROM** or can be downloaded from our online catalogue.

For students:

- **Spreadsheets**. Most of the chapters have one or more spreadsheets associated with the material in the chapter. These spreadsheets allow the student to work through a large number of calculations related to the chapter material. They can be downloaded from a protected site at www.pearsoned.ca/text/blanchard.
- **Study Guide**. Each chapter in the *Study Guide* begins with a presentation of objectives and a review. It is organized in the form of a tutorial, covering the important points of the chapter, with learning suggestions along the way. The tutorial is followed by quick self-test questions, review problems, and multiple-choice questions. Solutions are provided for all *Study Guide* problems.

Acknowledgments and Thanks

Any book owes much to many. A third edition begins with all those who worked on the first and second Canadian editions and then on the numerous American editions. However, for this third Canadian edition, I need to add special thanks to one person, Greg Lang, and then a whole group of students. The group of students who need to be thanked are the many students who have taken Economics 390 at Wilfrid Laurier University over the past three years. They are the testers for my ideas in this edition. In particular, they were the test group who used the spreadsheet-based problems that now cover most of the material in this third edition. I enjoyed creating the spreadsheets and I think most of the students enjoyed using the spreadsheets. Greg Lang was the skilled computer assistant in making huge improvements in the spreadsheets, providing answers to the questions, and then in carefully updating much of the other material in the book as we moved from the second Canadian edition to the third Canadian edition. Thank you very much, Greg.

Many thanks to Associate Professor David M. Gray at the University of Ottawa for his meticulous review of this manuscript. He did a wonderful job.

In addition to those already listed, a number of persons at Pearson Education Canada worked hard on this edition. They are: Acquisitions Editor, Laura Forbes; Developmental Editor, Paul Donnelly; Production Editor, Cheryl Jackson; Copy Editor, Rohini Herbert; Production Coordinator, Christine Kwan; and Composition Specialist, Joan Wilson.

We have benefitted from comments and suggestions of reviewers. They include:

Vettivelu Nallainayagam, Mount Royal College

Bill Marr, Wilfrid Laurier University

Richard Miles, British Columbia Institute of Technology

Sapan Dasgupta, Dalhousie University

Hamza Ali Malik, Lakehead University

Ajit Dyanandan, University of Northern British Columbia

Ryan Compton, University of Manitoba

Eric C. Howe, University of Saskatchewan

Carol Lau, Concordia University

Jean-Francois Tremblay, University of Ottawa

Finally, I would like to thank Angelo and Olivier for inviting me to join them on the second Canadian edition. I have known and liked both of these men for many years. Angelo and I became friends on the squash courts in graduate school. He is a wonderful colleague and always ready to lend econometric expertise. Olivier Blanchard taught a course in graduate macroeconomics that I took in my first year at Harvard. I often think Olivier is one of the best teachers from whom I have ever had the privilege to learn. Olivier's course and its companion course in macroeconomics, taught by Benjamin Friedman, convinced me to become a macroeconomist. I have much appreciated the leadership of these two men as teachers and mentors in my professional life. I hope the users of this edition find the same enjoyment from the study of macroeconomics that I have.

David Johnson
Waterloo, Ontario

INTRODUCTION

The first two chapters introduce you to the issues and the approach of macroeconomics.

CHAPTER 1

Chapter 1 takes you on a macroeconomic tour of the world, from Canada's recent macroeconomic history and policy issues, to the long U.S. expansion of the 1990s, to the introduction of a common currency in Western Europe, to the recession in Japan and the recent events in Asia.

CHAPTER 2

Chapter 2 takes you on a tour of the book. It defines the three central variables of macroeconomics: output, unemployment, and inflation. It then introduces the three concepts around which the book is organized: the short run, the medium run, and the long run.

CHAPTER 1
A TOUR OF THE WORLD

What is macroeconomics? The best way to answer this question is not to give you a formal definition but, rather, to take you on an economic tour of the world, to describe both the main economic changes and the issues that keep macroeconomists and macroeconomic policy makers up at night.

At the time of writing, macroeconomists and policy makers in Canada and around the world face new problems and can reflect on past success. In Canada and in other countries, the decades after 1990 saw a substantial reduction in inflation. This was viewed as a success. In Canada, federal and provincial budgets moved from deficit to surplus. This, too, was viewed as a success. In Canada, although unemployment was well over 10% from 1991 to 1994, it did eventually fall. Unemployment in Canada averaged 7.2% from 2000 to 2005. This was also viewed as a success. There was great uncertainty in the United States in 2001 following the terrorist attack on the World Trade Center in September. The stock market also fell in value by a large amount through 2001 and into 2002. Policy makers in both Canada and the United States wondered how the dramatic fall in stock prices would affect the North American economy. In Europe, they worry about unemployment, which has been high now for more than two decades. In Asia, after many decades of fast growth, Japan suffered a severe recession through much of the 1990s and even into the next decade. On the other hand, the Chinese economy averaged real growth of 8.5% per year from 1990 to 2003.

This chapter looks more closely at what is happening in Canada and then in these other three parts of the world. Read it as you would read an article in a newspaper. Do not worry about the exact meaning of the words or about understanding all the arguments in detail. Regard it as background, intended to introduce you to the issues of macroeconomics; the words will be defined and the arguments articulated in later chapters. Indeed, once you have read the book, come back to this chapter; see where you stand on the issues, and judge how much progress you have made in your study of macroeconomics.

1-1 | Canada

When macroeconomists look at an economy, they focus first on three measures. The first is *aggregate output* and its rate of growth. The second is the *unemployment rate*, the proportion of workers in the economy who are not employed and are looking for a job. The third is the *inflation rate*, the rate at which the average price of goods in the economy is increasing over time.

Figure 1–1 provides basic statistics for Canada and its neighbour, the United States. Output is measured for both countries in American dollars. How do Canada and the United States compare?

The United States is a much larger economic unit than Canada. Production is 10.5 times greater than in Canada, while the American population is only nine times greater. As a consequence, average output per person in the United States is 20% higher. This gap has been a great concern for Canadians. For two of the three variables listed above, the unemployment rate and inflation, the two countries were comparable in 2003. Both countries had inflation between 2 and 3%. Canada comes off slightly worse in the comparison of unemployment rates. The basic problem highlighted by the Canada–U.S. comparison in Figure 1–1 is the problem that will dominate the macroeconomic agenda in Canada over the next 10 years. How can we generate faster growth in output per person and thus catch up with the Americans?

It is fair to say that in Canada, inflation was not the macroeconomic problem on the policy horizon in the first decade of the twenty-first century. Table 1–1 gives some historical perspective on output growth, the unemployment rate, and inflation in Canada. Inflation has been low for the past seven years, certainly lower than in the period 1962–2000. Inflation did not rise very much even as unemployment fell and output growth increased in the latter portion of the decade of the 1990s. An average rate of real output growth of 4% per year from 1994 to 2000 was considered a very good outcome. Should policy makers have been satisfied with an unemployment rate between 7 and 8%? We need a historical perspective on this quite controversial question.

Figure 1–2 shows Canada's unemployment rate from 1950 to 2005. The figure shows Canada's unemployment rate increasing steadily from very low values in the 1950s to much higher values in the 1980s and 1990s. By historical standards, an unemployment rate of 7.7% is

The **Organization for Economic Cooperation and Development (OECD)** does a great deal of useful work to make national statistics comparable. Variation in collection methods across countries makes this work necessary.

Many have noted that while there is a large gap between average output per person in the United States and that in Canada, the gap between the median output per person in Canada and that in the United States is smaller. The implication: The higher incomes in the United States are also more unequally distributed.

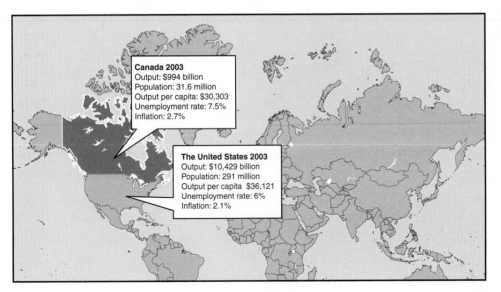

Canada 2003
Output: $994 billion
Population: 31.6 million
Output per capita: $30,303
Unemployment rate: 7.5%
Inflation: 2.7%

The United States 2003
Output: $10,429 billion
Population: 291 million
Output per capita $36,121
Unemployment rate: 6%
Inflation: 2.1%

FIGURE 1–1

Canada and the United States

You might ask why 2003. As of February 2006, these are the latest sets of comparable data for Canada and the United States produced by the OECD. More recent data for the two countries appear later.

Source: OECD Country Statistical profiles.
www.oecd.org

| TABLE | 1–1 | Growth, Unemployment, and Inflation in Canada, 1962–2005 |

The unemployment rate after 1976 is measured in a consistent manner. Prior to 1976, the estimates come from the *Historical Statistics of Canada* Series D233.

(in percent)	1962–2000 (average)	1994–2000 (average)	2001	2002	2003	2004	2005
Output growth rate	3.8	4.0	1.5	3.4	2.3	3.1	2.3
Unemployment rate	7.8	8.8	7.2	7.6	7.6	7.1	6.8
Inflation rate	4.7	1.6	2.5	2.2	2.7	1.8	2.2

Source: Growth rate: annual rate of real GDP growth, using CANSIM II variable V3862685; *Unemployment rate*: average over year, using CANSIM II variable V159752 after 1976 (Prior to 1976, *Historical Statistics of Canada*). *Inflation rate*: annual rate of change in consumer prices, using CANSIM II variable V735319.

quite high. However, by the standards of the last 25 years (and, as we shall see, in comparison with European unemployment rates), an unemployment rate of 7.7% is certainly a substantial improvement over the average unemployment rate of 10.5% from 1992 to 1996. Does unemployment remain a significant policy concern when it is at 7%? Eventually, we have to answer this question.

Budget Deficits

Reducing government deficits dominated much of the economic debate in the 1990s. The federal government had been running large deficits since the mid-1970s. In 1990, the federal government deficit was 5% of GDP. By contrast, until 1990, provincial governments were able to more or less balance their books. But both federal and provincial governments (especially Ontario and Quebec) went through the first half of the decade facing large and rapidly increasing deficits. Spiralling costs of financing this mountain of debt left many Canadians worried about the legacy that they were leaving to future generations. In response to these fears,

| FIGURE | 1–2 |

The Unemployment Rate in Canada, 1950–2005

The unemployment rate in Canada has been trending upward over time since the 1950s. However, the last 10 years have been characterized by falling unemployment rates.

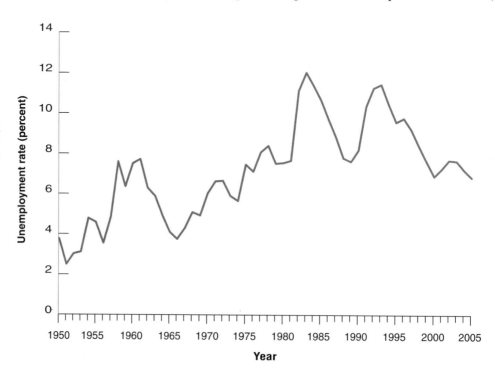

Source: Using CANSIM II variable V2062815 after 1976. Before 1976 series D233, *Historical Statistics of Canada.*

and to a shift in public opinion toward a taste for less government, politicians at all levels began to cut both expenditures and transfers. The results have been dramatic. In February 1995, the Minister of Finance, Paul Martin, announced that the federal government would achieve a balanced budget for its 1997 fiscal year, and he forecast a zero deficit until the end of the decade. In fact, as Figure 1–3 shows, the federal government swung into surplus in 1997 and into a large surplus (almost 2% of GDP) in 2000. After 2000, the size of the surplus has been much smaller. Does this matter? Should we worry if the budget goes back into deficit?

Government deficits in Canada are measured on both a public accounts basis (prepared by individual governments) and a national accounts basis (prepared by **Statistics Canada**). There are a number of differences, the most important being that loans from certain trust funds controlled by the federal government are not included in the national accounts estimates of the deficit. Basically, Statistics Canada measures government expenditures when they are made, whereas the public accounts attempts to measure expenditure obligations (such as pensions for civil servants) when they are incurred. Figure 1–3 is presented on a national accounts basis.

The sharp improvement in the finances of the federal government has opened up a new debate. Some argue that we should cut government spending more deeply. They point out that a string of large deficits has left Canadians with a large debt that makes us vulnerable to an increase in world interest rates and puts us in a poor position to handle a downturn in the economy. They also argue that individual taxpayers are better at spending their own money than are government bureaucrats. They propose using the savings from a smaller government to pay down the national debt and to cut taxes. Others argue that fiscal restraint has been excessive. They believe that the cutbacks have hurt the economic recovery and have had detrimental long-term consequences. They also believe that restraint has gutted many important government programs and that we should seize the opportunity to restore funding in important areas, such as health care and education. The debate is heated, but everyone agrees that it is nice to finally have a choice to make.

◀ From the public accounts, the federal deficit is sometimes reported on a financial requirements basis—literally a measure of the amount of borrowing in the market that is done to manage the government's cash flow. This measure is used less often in Canada, but it comes closest to the way that the U.S. federal deficit is reported.

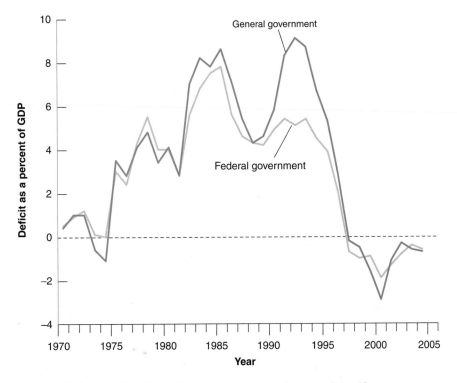

FIGURE 1-3

Canadian Government Deficits as a Proportion of Output since 1970

Large federal government deficits date back to the mid-1970s. These are deficits calculated on a national accounts basis.

Source: Fiscal Reference Tables, September 2005, Department of Finance. Table 46.

1-2 | The United States

Canadians spend a lot of time and energy looking at the behaviour of the U.S. economy. Americans are our biggest customers. We look at the same three variables: output, the unemployment rate, and the inflation rate.

By all three measures, the United States is doing well in the transition to the twenty-first century. Look at Table 1-2. As in Table 1-1, the first column gives the average value of output growth, unemployment, and inflation for 1960–2000; the next two columns give the numbers for 1994–2000 and then for individual years for 2001–2005.

In 2001, output growth in the United States was very low, only 0.5%. The unemployment rate increased in the next year. However, in 2002–2005, 2003, and 2004, more rapid economic growth halted the rise in unemployment, and in 2004 the unemployment rate was 5.1%. Inflation remained low through all these years. Two macroeconomic policy issues dominate the U.S. policy picture in 2006:

- Was the 1990s talk about the "New Economy" all hype, or was there some substance? In particular, can the United States hope to replicate the high rates of output growth that characterized the 1994–2000 period?

- Since 2001, the U.S. budget deficit has steadily increased, reaching 4.6% of U.S. output in 2003 and 2004. The federal deficit fell slightly to 2.6% of GDP in 2005 but still remains high. Should we worry about such large deficits? What are the costs likely to be?

Let us discuss both sets of issues in turn.

Has the United States Entered a New Economy?

Many of the New Economy claims had no basis in fact. Take, for instance, the valuation of the numerous dot-com companies, whose stock prices rose to astronomical heights in the late 1990s, only to collapse in the early 2000s. One claim, however—the claim that the U.S. economy had entered a period of faster technological progress and therefore could expect higher growth in the future—is more plausible and worth examining.

The way to examine this claim is to take a long-term view and plot the rate of growth of *output per worker* since 1960 in the United States. (Output per worker is also called *productivity*; the rate of growth of output per worker is called the rate of productivity growth.) This is done in Figure 1–4. A look at the figure suggests two conclusions:

- Although growth rates vary a lot from year to year, it appears that starting at some point in the 1970s, there was a decrease in the average rate of growth of output per worker.

TABLE 1–2 Growth, Unemployment, and Inflation in the United States, 1960–2005

(in percent)	1960–2000 (average)	1994–2000 (average)	2001	2002	2003	2004	2005
Output growth rate	3.2	3.9	0.5	1.9	3.0	4.4	3.5
Unemployment rate	6.1	4.9	4.8	5.8	6.0	5.5	5.1
Inflation rate	3.9	1.8	2.4	1.7	1.8	2.0	3.4

Output growth rate: annual rate of growth of output (GDP). *Unemployment rate:* average over the year. Inflation rate: annual rate of change of the price level (GDP deflator).

Source: OECD Economic Outlook Database; 2005 values from the Economic Report of the President.

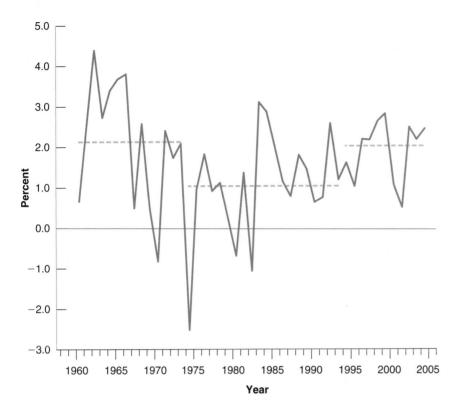

FIGURE 1–4

Rate of Growth of Output per Worker in the United States since 1960

The average rate of growth of output per worker de-creased in the mid-1970s. It appears to have increased again since the mid-1990s.

The average annual growth rate for the period 1960–1973 (represented by the dashed horizontal line from 1960 to 1973 in the graph) was 2.1%. The average annual growth rate for the period 1974–1993 (represented by the dashed horizontal line from 1974 to 1993) was a much lower 1%.

● In the recent past, however, the average rate of growth of output per worker appears to have increased again. The average annual growth rate for the period 1994–2004 (repre-sented by the dashed horizontal line from 1994 to 2004) was 2%—1% higher than the 1974–1994 average and roughly equal to the 1960–1973 average.

An annual 1% increase in the growth rate of output per worker might not seem like much—but it is. Think of it this way: A 1% higher annual growth sustained for 20 years means that at the end of 20 years, productivity will be 22% higher than it otherwise would have been; sustained for 50 years, productivity will be 64% higher. Other things being equal, an increase in productivity of 64% translates into a 64% increase in output per capita, a 64% increase in what economists call the *standard of living*—a very substantial increase.

Can we be confident that growth of output per worker will continue at the same higher rate in the future as it has since 1994? Figure 1–4 suggests caution: The rate of growth of out-put per worker fluctuates a lot from year to year. The high growth rates since 1994 might just be a series of "lucky" years that will not be repeated. Some economists believe that it is too early to tell. Other economists are more optimistic. They believe that the underlying rate of technological progress has, indeed, increased in the United States, largely as a result of the development and better use of *information technologies*, from computers to faster communi-cation networks. If they are right, it is, indeed, reasonable to expect faster productivity growth and a faster increase in the standard of living for some time to come.

Should You Worry about the U.S. Budget Deficit?

In 2003, the U.S. budget deficit—that is, the difference between what government spends and government revenues—was equal to 4.6% of output, a large number by historical standards.

$(1.01)^{20}$ – 1.0 = 22%; $(1.01)^{50}$ – 1.0 = 64%. For a review of exponents, see Appendix 2 at the end ◄ of the book.

◄ "per capita" means per person. (In Latin, capita means head.)

◄ This discussion might re-mind you of the controver-sies surrounding global warming. The world tem-perature varies a lot from year to year. We need to observe many unusually warm years to be certain that we are, indeed, seeing a trend toward global warming.

To put this number in perspective, Figure 1–5 shows the evolution of the budget deficit as a proportion of U.S. output since 1990.

At the start of the 1990s, the U.S. budget deficit was also very high, reaching nearly 6% of output in 1992. From 1992 onward, however, the deficit steadily fell. This reduction was the result of three main factors: a decrease in defence spending made possible by the end of the Cold War; strong output growth leading to strong growth of government revenues; and a program of deficit reduction put in place by the Clinton administration, mostly in the form of tight limits on government spending. By 1998, the deficit had turned into a surplus. In 2000, the budget surplus reached nearly 2% of GDP.

Things turned around sharply in 2001, though. The recession of 2001 led to lower revenue growth. The events of September 11, 2001, and, later, the wars in Afghanistan and Iraq led to an increase in security and defence spending. And deficits were made much larger by tax cuts introduced by the Bush administration in 2001 and 2002. Today, the effects of the 2001 recession on the budget are all but gone, but the increase in defence spending and the tax cuts continue to be the main factors contributing to the current deficits. Although George W. Bush's second term of administration has promised to cut the deficit in half by 2008, most forecasts state that in the absence of drastic changes in defence spending or substantial tax increases, the deficits will remain large for the rest of the decade.

Some economists argue that these U.S. budget deficits are no great concern. The tax cuts, they argue, have led to a faster and stronger recovery from the recession of 2001. And lower taxes are good for the economy, in that lower taxes mean fewer distortions and more motivation for people to work and for firms to invest.

Most economists, however, are more worried. They agree that temporary deficits were justified to help the economy recover from the recession in the early 2000s. But long-lasting deficits, they argue, are another matter altogether. For a given amount of private saving, the larger the amount government borrows, the smaller will be the amount left for private investment. In other words, deficits lead to lower capital accumulation and, by implication, to lower output in the future. Apart from this, the deficit cannot go on forever. Sooner or later,

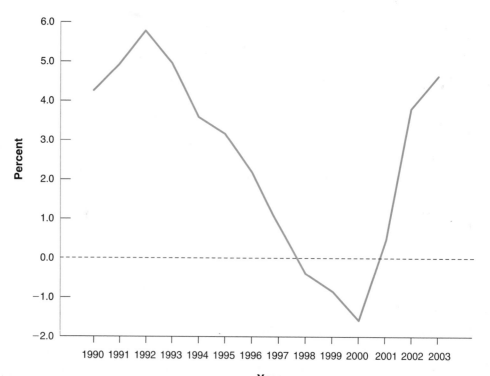

FIGURE 1–5

The U.S. Budget Deficit since 1990 (ratio to output, in percent)

The U.S. budget has gone from large deficits in the early 1990s, to surpluses in the late 1990s, and back to large deficits since 2001.

taxes will eventually have to be raised anyway. These costs, the economists argue, may not be large in the short run, but they may be very substantial in the long run.

At this stage, there seems to be little commitment on the part of government or on the part of Congress to reduce deficits. Whether, how, and when deficits will be reduced is one of the major issues facing the U.S. economy. Because of links between the U.S. economy and the rest of the world, the U.S. deficit is a concern for the whole world.

1-3 | The European Union

In 1957, six European countries decided to form a common European market—an economic zone where people and goods could move freely. Since then, 19 more countries have joined the group, with 10 of them joining in 2004. This group is now known as the **European Union**, or EU for short. (Until a few years ago, the official name was the *European Community*, or EC. You may still encounter that name.) The group of 25 countries is known as the EU25. (We will sometimes refer to the EU15, the group of 15 countries that constituted the European Union before the 2004 enlargement.) Together, the 25 countries form a formidable economic power. As Figure 1–6 shows, their combined output is equal to the output of the United States, and many of them have a standard of living—a level of output per capita—close to that of the United States.

The recent economic performance of the European Union is shown in Table 1–3. The numbers refer to the EU15, not the EU25; the reason is that data on growth and inflation for some of the new members are not available for the early years. The format of the table is the same format we used for Canada and the United States. The first two columns give the average value of the rate of growth of output, the unemployment rate, and the inflation rate for the period 1960–2000, and for the period 1994–2000. The next four columns give numbers for each year from 2001 to 2004. Numbers for 2005 are estimates.

The main conclusion to draw from the table is that the economic performance of the European Union over the last decade has been far less impressive than that of the United States or Canada over the same period:

● Average annual output growth from 1994 to 2000 in the European Union was only 2.3%. This was 1.6% below the average annual growth rate in the United States (1.7% below Canada) over the same period and 0.8% below the average growth rate in the European Union from 1960 to 2000. And although the European Union did not experience a recession in the early 2000s, its growth rate has remained low. In 2005, the EU15 growth rate was estimated to be only 1.4% compared with 3.6% in the United States and 2.3% in Canada.

TABLE 1–3 Growth, Unemployment, and Inflation in the European Union, 1960–2005

(in percent)	1962–2000 (average)	1994–2000 (average)	2001	2002	2003	2004	2005
Output growth rate	3.1	2.3	1.7	1.1	0.9	2.1	1.4
Unemployment rate	5.8	9.0	7.3	7.8	8.1	8.1	7.9
Inflation rate	5.4	2.0	2.3	2.6	2.2	1.9	2.2

Output growth rate: annual rate of growth of output (GDP). *Unemployment rate*: average over the year. *Inflation rate*: annual rate of change of the price level (GDP deflator).

Source: OECD *Economic Outlook* Database.

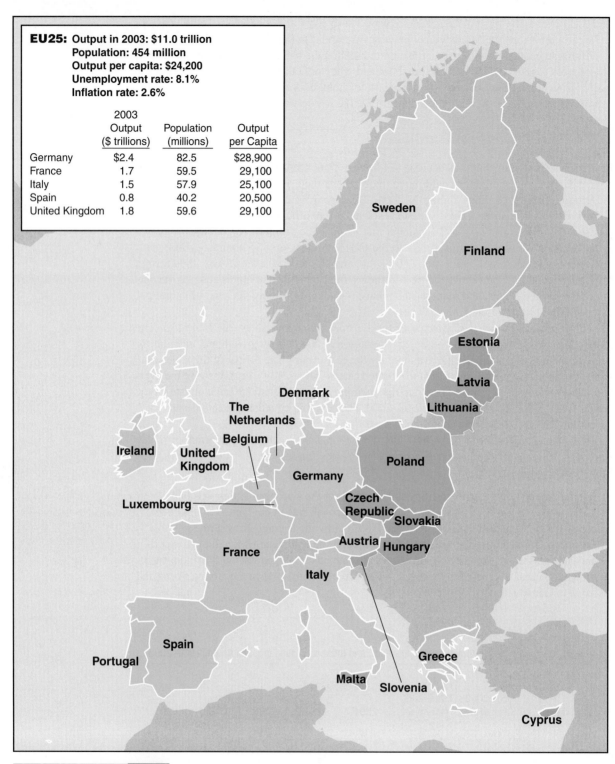

	2003 Output ($ trillions)	Population (millions)	Output per Capita
Germany	$2.4	82.5	$28,900
France	1.7	59.5	29,100
Italy	1.5	57.9	25,100
Spain	0.8	40.2	20,500
United Kingdom	1.8	59.6	29,100

EU25: Output in 2003: $11.0 trillion
Population: 454 million
Output per capita: $24,200
Unemployment rate: 8.1%
Inflation rate: 2.6%

FIGURE 1–6

The European Union, 2003.

- Low output growth has been accompanied by persistently high unemployment. The average unemployment rate from 1994 to 2000 was 9%. It has remained high since then, and in 2004, the unemployment rate was projected to be above 8%.

- The only good news is about inflation. Inflation had been high in the 1970s and 1980s. It decreased in the 1990s and has remained low since then. The inflation rate for 2004 was projected to be under 2%.

At this time, two issues dominate the agenda of European macroeconomists:

- The first is, not surprisingly, high unemployment. Although the unemployment rate has come down from its peak reached in the mid-1990s, it is still very high. Can it be reduced further, say, all the way down to the U.S. rate of unemployment? What reforms and what macroeconomic policies are needed to achieve this?

- In 1999, 12 European countries, all the largest countries with the exception of the United Kingdom, agreed they would use a common currency, the *euro*, in place of their national currencies. By January 1, 2002, the conversion process was complete. Other countries are deciding whether to adopt the euro. Even now, many questions remain. What is the euro doing for Europe? What macroeconomic changes has it brought about? How should macroeconomic policy be conducted in this new environment?

Let us discuss both issues in turn.

How Can European Unemployment Be Reduced?

High unemployment has not always been the norm in Europe. Figure 1–7, which plots the evolution of unemployment rates in the EU15 and in the United States since 1960, shows how low the European unemployment rate was in the 1960s. At that time, the talk in the United States was

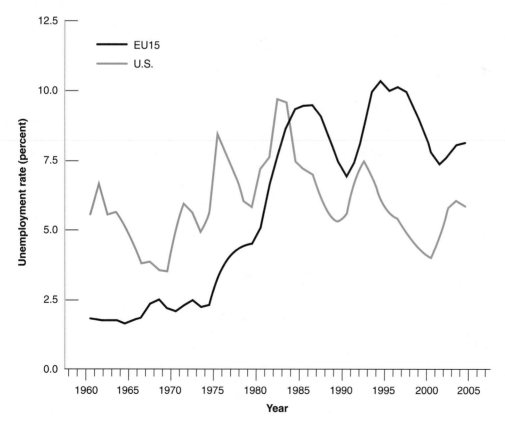

FIGURE 1–7

Unemployment Rates: Europe versus the United States since 1960

The European unemployment rate has gone from being much lower than the U.S. unemployment rate to being much higher.

about the European *unemployment miracle*; U.S. macroeconomists actually went to Europe hoping to discover the secrets of that miracle. In the late 1970s, however, the miracle vanished. Since the early 1980s, the unemployment rate in Europe has been much higher than that in the United States. Today, the unemployment rate stands at 8.1%. And in some of the larger countries of the European Union, such as France, Germany, Italy, and Spain, it is close to 10%.

Despite a large amount of research, there is still disagreement about the causes of high European unemployment:

- Some economists point to what they call *labour market rigidities*. Europe, they argue, suffers from unemployment benefits that are too high, minimum wages that are too high, and stringent regulations that protect workers' jobs to too great an extent. They argue that these high benefits, high minimum wages, and excessive job protection regulations are the causes of high unemployment. The solution, they conclude, is to remove these *rigidities*, to make European labour markets more like the U.S. labour market. When this is done, they argue, the European economies will soar, and unemployment will fall. In terms of labour market rigidities, Canadian labour markets seem to be between European and U.S. labour markets. The average Canadian unemployment rate seems to fall between U.S. and European unemployment rates (see Tables 1–1, 1–2, and 1–3).

- Other economists point out that many of these labour market rigidities were already in existence in the 1960s when European unemployment was very low. They point to other factors instead, such as bad labour relations and inadequate macroeconomic policies, particularly high interest rates in the 1980s and 1990s. They argue that better labour relations and better macroeconomic policies can lead to a steady decrease in unemployment without the need for dramatic reforms of the labour market.

Most economists stand somewhere in-between. They believe a sustained decrease in unemployment will require a combination of some labour market reforms, better labour relations, and appropriate macroeconomic policies. This leaves open many questions: What specific labour market reforms should be implemented? How can labour relations be improved? Finding the answers to these questions is one of the tasks facing European macroeconomists and policy makers today.

What Will the Euro Do for Europe?

In 1999, the European Union (EU) started the process of replacing national currencies with one common currency, the euro. Only 11 of the 15 EU countries participated at the start; they were joined in 2001 by Greece. The three remaining members of the EU15, Denmark, Sweden, and the United Kingdom, have decided to keep their currencies for the time being, but they may adopt the euro in the future. The 10 new members of the EU25 do not yet meet the criteria required for admission.

The transition took place in steps. On January 1, 1999, each of the 11 countries fixed the value of its currency to the euro. For example, 1 euro was set equal to 6.56 French francs, and 166 Spanish pesetas, and so on. From 1999 to 2002, some prices were quoted both in national currency units and in euros, but the euro was not yet used as currency. The euro started to be used as the common currency in 2002, when euro notes and coins replaced national currencies. These 12 countries of the euro area have now become a *common currency* area.

How will the euro change the European economy?

- Supporters of the euro point first to its enormous symbolic importance. In light of the many past wars among European countries, what better proof can there be that the page has definitely been turned than the adoption of a common currency? They also point to the economic advantages of having a common currency: no more changes in the relative price of currencies for European firms to worry about, no more need to change currencies when travelling between euro countries. Together with the removal of other obstacles to trade among European countries, which has taken place since 1957, the euro will

What to call the group of countries that have adopted ▶ the euro is not settled. "Euro zone" sounds technocratic. "Euroland" reminds some of Disneyland. "Euro area" seems to be winning, so this is how we refer to it in this book.

contribute, they argue, to the creation of a large, if not the largest, economic power in the world. There is little question that the move to the adoption of the euro is, indeed, one of the main economic events of the start of the twenty-first century.

- Others worry that the symbolism of the euro may come with some economic costs. They point out that a common currency means a common monetary policy, and that means the same interest rate for all euro countries. What if, they argue, one country plunges into recession, while another is in the middle of an economic boom? The first country needs lower interest rates to increase spending and output; the second country needs higher interest rates to slow its economy. If interest rates have to be the same in both countries, what will happen? Isn't there the risk that one country will remain in recession for a long time or that the other will not be able to slow its booming economy?

Throughout the 1990s, the question was: Should Europe adopt the euro? That question is now moot. The euro is here, and it is here to stay. So far, no member country has had to face a severe recession, so the system has not really been tested. The full costs and benefits of the euro remain to be assessed.

1-4 | Japan and China

Forty years ago, Japan and China would not have been included in our economic tour. Their outputs per capita were low compared with the United States and with those of Europe. Things are very different today. We will look at Japan first and then briefly at China. As the first column of Table 1–4 indicates, since 1960, Japan's output has grown at an average annual growth rate of 4.7%. This is 1.5% higher than the corresponding growth rate for the United States over the same period. As you can see from Figure 1–8, Japan's output per capita is now very close to that of the United States.

This is the good news. The bad news can be seen in the remaining columns of Table 1–4. Japan's economic performance over the last decade has been nothing short of dismal:

- The average annual rate of growth of output from 1994 to 2000 was only 1.4%. This is 3.3% below the average annual growth rate since 1960. Things were even worse in 2001 and 2002, two years of practically zero growth. This long period of low and sometimes negative growth is known as the *Japanese slump*. Growth has turned positive, however, since 2003, bringing hopes that the slump may be coming to an end.

- As a result of the long slump, the unemployment rate, which used to be very low in Japan, steadily increased. It reached 5.4% in 2002 and is now slowly declining. By U.S., and even more so, by EU standards, 5.4% would appear to be a very low unemployment rate. But for Japan, this is the highest unemployment rate it has ever experienced, and it reflects a very depressed labour market.

| TABLE 1–4 | Growth, Unemployment, and Inflation in Japan, 1960–2005 |

(in percent)	1962–2000 (average)	1994–2000 (average)	2001	2002	2003	2004	2005
Output growth rate	4.7	1.4	0.4	–0.3	2.5	3.0	2.4
Unemployment rate	2.0	3.7	5.0	5.4	5.3	4.8	4.4
Inflation rate	5.1	–0.1	–1.5	–1.2	–2.5	–2.0	–1.1

Output growth rate: annual rate of growth of output (GDP). *Unemployment rate*: average over the year. *Inflation rate*: annual rate of change of the price level (GDP deflator).

Source: OECD Economic Outlook Database; 2005 update from *OECD Economic Outlook*, December 2005.

FIGURE 1–8

Japan and China, 2003

Source: *The Economist.*

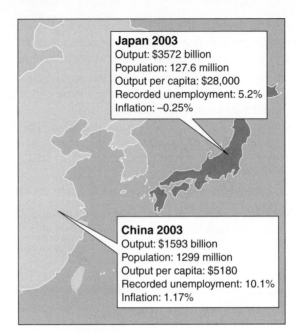

Japan 2003
Output: $3572 billion
Population: 127.6 million
Output per capita: $28,000
Recorded unemployment: 5.2%
Inflation: –0.25%

China 2003
Output: $1593 billion
Population: 1299 million
Output per capita: $5180
Recorded unemployment: 10.1%
Inflation: 1.17%

- As a result of high unemployment, the inflation rate decreased and eventually turned negative in the 1990s. It has remained negative since then. In other words, Japan is experiencing *deflation*—a decrease in the average price of goods over time. You might conclude that if inflation is bad, deflation must be good. But, as we will see later in the book, the evidence is that deflation—as opposed to low inflation—does not lead to a good economic outcome.

Given this description of where Japan stands, you can guess the two main issues confronting Japanese macroeconomists at this point:

- What triggered the slump?
- Why did it last so long? Will the current recovery last?

Let us look at both questions in turn.

What Triggered the Slump?

Just as there was talk of a "European unemployment miracle," there was talk of a "Japanese growth miracle." It would seem that being labelled a miracle is a mixed blessing. In both cases, the miracles abruptly ended.

Until the early 1990s, the main question on macroeconomists' minds was: Why is Japan doing so well? What explains its sustained high growth rate? Is it the rapid accumulation of capital generated by a high savings rate? Is it its high level of education, which allows it to adapt foreign technologies and achieve a high rate of technological progress? Is it the internal organization of Japanese firms, which leads them to become steadily more efficient?

Now the central questions are radically different: Why did Japan do so poorly for more than a decade? What broke down, and how can it be fixed?

Most economists believe that the trigger for the slump of the 1990s can be found in the striking movements in Japanese stock prices from the mid-1980s to the early 1990s. Figure 1–9 shows the behaviour of the *Nikkei* index—an index of stock prices in the Japanese stock market—since 1980. From 1985 to 1989, the Nikkei increased from about 13,000 to 39,000; in other words, the average price of a share in the Japanese stock market tripled in less than four years. This sharp increase was followed in the early 1990s by an equally sharp decrease. In less than two years, from 1990 to 1992, the Nikkei fell from 35,000 to 16,000! Since then, the Nikkei has further decreased, although by less.

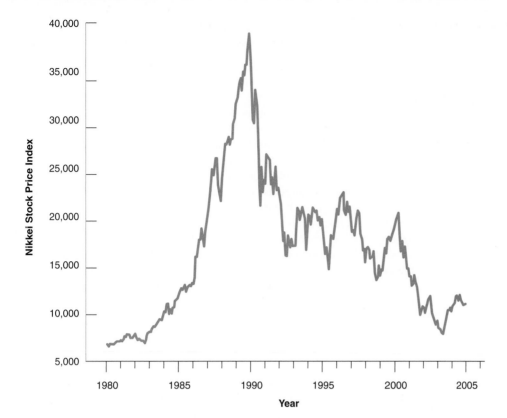

FIGURE 1-9

The Japanese Stock Market Index, 1980–2004

The large increase in the index in the second half of the 1980s was followed by an equally sharp decline in the early 1990s.

Why did the Nikkei go up and then down so much and so quickly? In general, stock prices can move for one of two reasons:

- One reason is what economists call *fundamentals*. For example, anticipations of higher profits in the future lead financial investors to be willing to pay more for shares today, so stock prices increase.

- The other reason is *speculative bubbles*, or *fads*, where investors buy stocks at high prices, hoping to resell them at higher prices in the future, whether or not this is justified by fundamentals.

Most observers interpret the rise and fall of the Nikkei as a speculative bubble, an excessive increase in stock prices in the 1980s, followed by a sharp decline and a return to reality in the early 1990s. They point to parallel movements in the prices of other Japanese assets, such as land and housing. Real estate prices increased in line with the Nikkei, and since 1990 have declined even more than stock prices. They argue that the result of the stock market boom was a boom in demand and output in the late 1980s and that the result of the stock market fall was a sharp drop in demand and output in the 1990s.

How Will Japan Recover?

When it became clear that the decline in the stock market in Japan had triggered a recession, both monetary and fiscal policies were used to increase demand and thereby increase output:

- The Japanese central bank decreased interest rates to very low levels. They have remained under 1% since the mid-1990s and are now literally equal to zero. Clearly, monetary policy cannot decrease them further.

Does this remind you of what happened to the NASDAQ (the U.S. stock market where shares of high-tech companies are traded)? The NASDAQ increased from 1000 in 1996 to nearly 5000 in 2000, only to fall back to 1200 in 2002. Broader market indexes, such as the Dow Jones or the Standard and Poor's index, fell, however, by much less, so the effect of the fall of the NASDAQ on the U.S. economy was much more limited.

- The Japanese government increased spending on public works and cut taxes to stimulate spending by consumers and firms. Both increased spending and lower taxes have led to persistently large budget deficits.

Nevertheless, despite low interest rates, lower taxes, and higher government spending, the slump continued throughout the 1990s. This led a number of economists to conclude that the problem could not be solved by macroeconomic policies alone and that the Japanese economy would not grow quickly again before a number of structural problems were identified and solved. They pointed to a long list of problems in the Japanese economy, including a very inefficient retail distribution system and political corruption.

Their argument, however, was not fully convincing. Most of the problems they pointed to were present even earlier when the Japanese economy was growing rapidly. But one problem—the state of the banking system—had clearly gotten worse and might well be a serious obstacle to recovery. With the sharp decline in growth in the 1990s, many firms that had taken out bank loans found themselves unable to repay them. Rather than writing off these loans, many banks preferred to hide their losses by lending more to those very same borrowers who could not repay the previous loans. Meanwhile, firms with good projects could not borrow. Without a healthy banking system, many economists argued, it would be difficult for Japan to return to steady growth.

Since 2003, however, output growth in Japan has turned positive. How much of this growth is due to improvements in its banking system and how much is simply due to other factors is not yet clear. On the one hand, the Japanese government has started taking steps to return the banking system to good health. It is a painful process, forcing many borrowers and a number of banks with bad loan portfolios into bankruptcy. But it is a necessary step to make room in the economy for better banks and better borrowers. On the other hand, part of the increase in Japan's output clearly reflects other economic factors, for example, higher exports to fast-growing China. How fast Japan can and will recover from its slump remains among the toughest questions confronting macroeconomists today.

Rapid Growth in China

It is difficult to take a macroeconomic tour of the world in 2005 without a brief stop in China. China has been the example of rapid economic growth in the last 25 years. In the mid-1980s, reasonable estimates of per capita real income in China were $1000 US. This value increased fourfold to $3980 US in 2000 and then rose by 25% between 2000 and 2003 to $5180 US (Constant dollar values are from *The Economist*, March 3, 2005). This is a massive increase in income per capita.

The reason this increase in income per capita is so important to the world is that China has such a huge population. Figure 1–8 makes the obvious point that the population of China, at 1.299 billion in 2004, dwarfs every other country and political unit in the world, except India. No other country is even close to China in population. If each of the one billion consumers in China consumes $1000 dollars more in just three years, this is a substantial increase in aggregate demand in the world economy. If the Chinese population were to consume and earn at North American levels, then the world economic picture would be dramatically changed. Even at a low level of per capita income, as Figure 1–8 shows, the total size of the Chinese economy is about one-third the total size of the Japanese economy.

There are at least two very interesting macroeconomic issues associated with the rapid growth of the Chinese economy. At the time of writing (March 2006), oil prices (and other commodity prices) had been rising for the past year or more. This run-up in the real price of oil and other commodities is being blamed on Chinese demand for those goods as the Chinese rapidly increase their imports of raw materials. Raw material producers, such as Canada and Australia, have benefitted from the boom in their exports, or Chinese imports. The second interesting macroeconomic issue relates to the Chinese exchange rate policy. Up to the time of writing, the Chinese government had fixed the value of the Chinese currency at 8.28 yuan to one U.S. dollar. At this exchange rate, the Americans perceive that the

Chinese have an unfair trading advantage. The low value of the yuan (it takes, in a sense, a lot of yuan to buy one U.S. dollar) means that Americans find Chinese exports inexpensive and Chinese find American exports expensive. There is a great deal of pressure from the Americans on the Chinese government to either allow the yuan to float in world foreign exchange markets or revalue the yuan. An example of revaluation would see the Chinese government change the fixed exchange rate from 8.28 yuan per U.S. dollar to 4.14 yuan per U.S. dollar. Such a change would, in the view of American politicians, solve all their problems. The new exchange rate would immediately double the prices for American consumers of Chinese goods and halve the prices for Chinese consumers of American goods. Many jobs would be created in the United States as imports from China to the United States fell and exports from the United States to China boomed. On July 22, 2005, China moved from fixing the yuan at 8.28 to the U.S. dollar to fixing its currency to a basket (a group) of currencies. The change involved a very small reduction in the number of yuan needed to buy a U.S. dollar. We will analyze exchange rate policy in much more detail at a number of places in the rest of this book, since it is a very important component of macroeconomic policy.

1-5 | Looking Ahead

This concludes our world tour. There are many other regions of the world we might have looked at:

- Latin America, which went from very high to low inflation in the 1990s. Some countries, such as Chile, appear to be in good economic shape. Some, such as Argentina, are struggling. A collapse of Argentina's exchange rate and a major banking crisis led to a large decline in output in that country in the early 2000s, from which it is emerging only now.

- Central and Eastern Europe, where most countries shifted from a centrally planned system to a market system in the early 1990s. Many economists expected this shift to a market economy to lead to a large increase in output. In most countries, the shift was characterized, instead, by a sharp decline in output at the start of transition. Only later did output growth become positive; in some countries, output is still below its pretransition level.

- Africa, which has suffered decades of economic stagnation, but where some countries are now starting to grow.

FOCUS   Gathering Macro Data

Where do the data we have examined in this chapter come from? For example, where does one find the number for inflation in Germany over the last two decades? Forty years ago, the answer would have been to learn German, find a library with German publications, find the page where inflation numbers were given, write them down, and plot them by hand on a nice clean sheet of paper. Today, improvements in the collection of data and the development of computers and electronic databases make the task much easier.

International organizations now collect data for many countries. For the richest countries, the most useful source is the **Organization for Economic Cooperation and Development (OECD)**, based in Paris. Most of the world's rich economies belong to the OECD. The complete list is Australia, Austria, Belgium, Canada, the Czech Republic, Denmark, Finland, France, Germany, Greece, Hungary, Iceland, Ireland, Italy, Japan, Korea, Luxembourg, Mexico, the Netherlands, New Zealand, Norway,

Poland, Portugal, the Slovak Republic, Spain, Sweden, Switzerland, Turkey, the United Kingdom, and the United States. Together, these countries account for about 70% of world output. The *OECD Economic Outlook*, which is published twice yearly, gives basic data on inflation, unemployment, and other major variables for member countries, as well as an assessment of their recent macroeconomic performance. The data, going back to 1960, are available on diskettes; they are on most macroeconomists' hard disks.

For those countries that are not members of the OECD, information is available from other international organizations. The main world economic organization, a sort of world economic club, is the **International Monetary Fund (IMF)**. The IMF publishes the monthly *International Financial Statistics (IFS)*, which contains basic macroeconomic information for all IMF members. It also publishes the annual *World Economic Outlook*, an assessment of macroeconomic developments in various parts of the world. Although its language is sometimes stilted, both the *World Economic Outlook* and the *OECD Economic Outlook* are excellent sources of information.

Because these publications sometimes do not contain sufficient details, you may need to turn to specific country publications. **Statistics Canada** has a user-friendly Web site, **www.statcan.ca**. The button "Canadian Statistics" gives a variety of up-to-date values for various measures of Canadian economic activity. These tables refer you to tables in CANSIM II. This is the Statistics Canada electronic database. The librarian at your university or college will be able to tell you if your institution has a subscription to CANSIM. Be warned, it does take some experience to find and download series from CANSIM. Most of the graphs and tables in this text give you CANSIM II identifier numbers for the series presented. This will make it easier for you to update these series or use them in other economics courses. The Bank of Canada also has an excellent Web site, **www.bankofcanada.ca**. It contains the *Monetary Policy Report*, a biannual publication that uses both words and graphs to describe the state of the Canadian economy and the policy actions taken by the Bank of Canada. By the end of this book, you should be able to read and understand the *Monetary Policy Report*.

Major countries now produce remarkably clear statistical publications, often with an English translation. In the United States, an extremely good buy is the *Economic Report of the President*, prepared by the Council of Economic Advisors and published annually. This report has two parts. The first is an assessment of current U.S. events and policy. The second is a set of data for nearly all relevant macroeconomic variables, usually for the entire post–World War II period.

A longer list of data sources, both for Canada and for the rest of the world, as well as how to access some of them through the Internet, is given at the end of Appendix 1 to this book.

SUMMARY

There is a limit to how much you can absorb in this first chapter. Think about the questions to which you have been exposed already:

- What determines expansions and recessions? Why did the United States experience such a long expansion in the 1990s? Why did Canada undergo such severe recessions in 1982 and again in 1991? How will the euro affect monetary policy in Europe? Could monetary and fiscal policies have prevented the Japanese slump?

- What are the interactions between the stock market and economic activity? Can the poor performance of Japan in the 1990s be attributed to the sharp decline in the Japanese stock market in the early 1990s?

- Why was inflation in Canada and elsewhere so much lower in the 1990s than it was in previous decades?

What is so bad about high inflation? What is so bad about the deflation we are now observing in Japan?

- Why is unemployment so high in Europe? How could the Japanese unemployment rate have been so low for so many years?

- Why do growth rates differ so much across countries, even over long periods of time? Why did Japan grow so much faster than the United States and Europe for so long? Have we in North America entered a "New Economy" in which growth will be much higher in the future? How will rapid growth in China change the world?

The purpose of this book is to give you a way to think about these questions. As we develop the tools you need, we will show you how to use them by returning to these questions and showing you the answers they suggest.

KEY TERMS

- European Union (EU), 9
- International Monetary Fund (IMF), 17

- Organization for Economic Cooperation and Development (OECD), 3
- Statistics Canada, 5

An asterisk denotes a harder question. [Web] indicates that the question requires access to the Internet.

1. TRUE/FALSE/UNCERTAIN

Using the tables and graphs in this chapter, label each of the following statements true, false, or uncertain. Explain briefly.

a. Recently, inflation has been below its historical average in Canada, the United States, the European Union, and Japan.

b. In the 1960s and early 1970s, the United States had a higher rate of unemployment than did Europe, but today, it has a much lower rate of unemployment.

c. The European "unemployment miracle" refers to the extremely low rate of unemployment that Europe has been enjoying since the 1980s.

d. If China maintains its growth rate at the magnitudes seen in the last 10 years, it will become the largest economy in the world.

2. ECONOMIC GROWTH IN THE RICHEST COUNTRIES

a. Use Tables 1–1, 1–2, and 1–3 to compare the recent growth experiences of Canada, the United States, and the EU in 2001–2005 with their growth experiences from 1960–2000.

b. Look at the unemployment rates in Canada, the United States, and the EU in the period 2001–2005. How do they relate to output growth?

c. Use Figure 1–4 to consider whether productivity growth has increased permanently since 1994.

3. CORRECT THE POLITICIANS

Politicians often tell only one side of the story. Consider each of the statements, and comment on the other side of the story.

a. There is no such thing as a rate of unemployment that is too low. Unemployment is bad. The lower it is, the better.

b. There is no slowdown in growth, just a slowdown in the ability of economists to measure output correctly.

c. There is a simple solution to the problem of high European unemployment: Reduce labour market rigidities.

d. The recession in Japan was well deserved because it was caused by corruption and poor regulation of the financial system.

e. What can be wrong about joining forces and adopting a common currency? The euro is obviously good for Europe.

4. WHEN WILL CHINA CATCH UP?

Suppose that from now on, the output of the People's Republic of China will grow at an annual rate of 9%, whereas the output of the United States will grow at an annual rate of 3%.

a. Using the latest data available from this chapter on the level of output in each country, how long will it be before China's output becomes larger than that of the United States?

b. Suppose also that the population of both China and the United States will remain constant from now on. How long will it be before China's output per worker becomes larger than that of the United States?

This book comes with a Web page (**www.pearsoned.ca/text/ blanchard**), which is updated regularly. For each chapter, the page offers discussions of current events and includes relevant articles and Internet links. You can also use the page to make comments on the book and engage in discussions with other readers.

The best way to follow current economic events and issues is to read *The Economist*, a weekly magazine published in the United Kingdom. The articles are well informed, well written, witty, and opinionated. Make sure to read the magazine regularly.

WHERE TO FIND THE NUMBERS

The purpose of this appendix is to help you find the numbers you are looking for, be it inflation in Malaysia last quarter, consumption in the United States in 1959, or youth unemployment in Ireland in the 1980s.

For a Quick Look at Current Numbers

- The best source for the most recent numbers on production, unemployment, inflation, exchange rates, interest rates, and stock prices for a large number of countries is the last four pages of *The Economist*, published each week (Web address: **www.economist.com**). This Web site, as most of the Web sites listed below, contains both information available free of charge and information available only to subscribers.

- There are several Web pages that collect and analyze recent data. One of the best is **www.yardeni.com**, the home page of Dr. Edward Yardeni, Chief Economist of a large bank, Deutsche Morgan Grenfell.

- A good summary of current developments in the Canadian economy is provided by the *Canadian Economic Observer,* published monthly by Statistics Canada, and on the Statistics Canada homepage. Your library probably has the *Canadian Economic Observer* in electronic form. If you cannot wait, information is released every day as it becomes available in *The Daily* on its Web site.

For More Detail about the Canadian Economy

- Statistics Canada provides a number of sources. Its Web page (www.statcan.ca) provides free access to all the main economic indicators for the past few years. In addition, you can download various guides detailing the construction of the Consumer Price Index (CPI), the Labour Force Survey, and so on.

  The main database of economic time series available from Statistics Canada is called CANSIM II. Finding what you want in CANSIM II is not easy. Related series are grouped in what are called *CANSIM tables*, but there is very little relationship between adjacent tables, so you will need some patience (and a good search engine!). Access to the CANSIM II database is on a subscription basis only (find out if your university has such access). CANSIM II gives yearly data as far back as 1926 and quarterly data as far back as 1947 on hundreds of thousands of economic time series.

- The Department of Finance publishes *Economic Reference Tables*, which give annual data on the main economic and financial aggregates over the past few years. Its Web site (**www.fin.gc.ca**) has a number of useful (and free) publications, including a detailed description of the federal budget and monthly statements about federal government revenues and expenditures (*The Fiscal Monitor*). *The Economy in Brief*, published quarterly, gives succinct summaries of major developments in the Canadian economy. The various provincial ministries also make similar information available online.

- On a quarterly basis, the Bank of Canada publishes the *Bank of Canada Review*. In addition to two or three articles related to monetary policy, it gives data at various frequencies on financial variables and monetary aggregates (the most recent data are reported by day or week; older data are reported by month or year). Its Web site (www.bankofcanada.ca) provides access to much of these data in *Weekly Financial Statistics*. In addition, there is now a small library of historical data series that can be downloaded, as well as *Bank of Canada Working Papers* and articles on monetary policy.

- Several of the large chartered banks provide daily and weekly summaries of developments in financial markets, including various interest rates for Canada and the United States. A few also provide current values of the main economic aggregates. Read their explanations of what is currently happening and what they expect will occur in the near future in financial markets. Ask yourself how it compares with what you have learned in this class.

- Recent data are much easier to obtain than earlier data. A good source for the latter is F. H. Leacy (ed.), *Historical Statistics of Canada*, 1983. This is available online from Statistics Canada.

For More Detail about the U.S. Economy

- For a detailed presentation of the most recent numbers, look at the *Survey of Current Business*, published monthly by the U.S. Department of Commerce, Bureau of Economic Analysis (Internet address: **www. bea.doc.gov**). A user's guide to the statistics published by the Bureau of Economic Analysis is given in the *Survey of Current Business*, January 1995, pages 36–52. It tells you what data are available, in what form, and at what price.

- Once a year, the *Economic Report of the President*, written by the Council of Economic Advisers and published by the U.S. Government Printing Office in Washington, gives a description of current evolutions, as well as numbers for most major macroeconomic variables, often going back to the 1950s. (The statistical tables in the report can be found at **www.access.gpo.gov/eop/**)

- The authoritative source for statistics going back as far as data have been collected is *Historical Statistics of the United States, Colonial Times to 1970*, Parts 1 and 2, published by the U.S. Department of Commerce, Bureau of the Census (Internet address: **www.census.gov/stat_abstract/**).

- The standard reference for national income accounts is *National Income and Product Accounts of the United States.* Volume 1, 1929–1958, and Volume 2, 1959–1988, published by the U.S. Department of Commerce, Bureau of Economic Analysis (Internet address: www.bea. doc.gov).

- For data on just about everything, including economic data, an excellent source is the *Statistical Abstract of the United States*, published annually by the U.S. Department of Commerce, Bureau of the Census (Internet address: **www.census.gov/statab/www/**).

Numbers for Other Countries

The OECD, located in Paris, publishes three very useful publications. The OECD includes most of the rich countries in the world. (The list is given earlier in this chapter.) (Internet address: www.oecd.org)

- The first is the *OECD Economic Outlook*, published biannually. In addition to describing current macroeconomic issues, it includes data for many macroeconomic variables. The data typically go back to the 1970s and are reported consistently, both across time and across countries.

- The second is the *OECD Employment Outlook*, published annually. It focuses more specifically on labour-market issues and numbers.

- Occasionally, the OECD puts together current and past data and publishes the *OECD Historical Statistics*. At this point in time, the most recent is *Historical Statistics, 1960–1993*, published in 1995.

The main strength of the publications of the International Monetary Fund (IMF, located in Washington, D.C.) is that they cover most of the countries of the world (Internet address: **www.imf.org**).

The IMF issues four particularly useful publications:

- The first is the *International Financial Statistics* (*IFS*), published monthly. It has data for member countries, usually going back a few years, mostly on financial variables but also on some aggregate variables (such as GDP, employment, and inflation).

- The second is the *International Financial Statistics Yearbook*, published annually. It has the same coverage of countries and variables as the IFS but gives annual data for up to 30 years.

- The third is the *Government Finance Statistics Yearbook*, published annually, which gives data on the budget of each country, typically going back 10 years. (Because of delays in the construction of the numbers, data for the most recent years are often unavailable.)

- The fourth, the *World Economic Outlook*, published biannually, describes major evolutions in the world and in specific member countries.

For long-term historical statistics for several countries, an excellent new data source is *Monitoring the World Economy, 1820–1992,* Development Centre Studies, OECD, Paris, 1995. This study gives data going back to 1820 for 56 countries.

Finally, if you still have not found what you are looking for, here are two useful sites: The Macroeconomics Resources site of the Harvard Business School (**www.hbs.edu/units/bgie/internet/**), which assesses the quality of—and provides links to—a large number of other potentially useful Web sites.

A site maintained by Bill Goffe at the University of Mississippi (**http://rfe.wustl.edu**) lists not only data sources but also sources for economic information in general, from working papers, to jokes, to jobs in economics, and so on.

CHAPTER 2
A TOUR OF THE BOOK

The words *output*, *unemployment*, and *inflation* appear daily in newspapers and on the evening news. So, when we used them in Chapter 1, you were familiar with them, at least to the extent that you knew roughly what they meant. Now they need to be defined precisely, and this is what is done in the first two sections of this chapter. In section 2-1, we focus on aggregate output and show how we can look at aggregate output both from the production side and from the income side. In section 2-2, we look at the unemployment rate and at the inflation rate. Having defined the major macroeconomic variables, we then take you, in section 2-3, on a tour of the book. On that tour, we introduce the three central concepts around which the book is organized:

- The *short run*—what happens to the economy from year to year.
- The *medium run*—what happens to the economy over a decade or so.
- The *long run*—what happens to the economy over a half century or more.

Building on these three concepts, we then give you a road map to the rest of the book.

2-1 | Aggregate Output

Economists studying economic activity in the nineteenth century or during the Great Depression had no reliable measure of aggregate activity (*aggregate* is the word macroeconomists use for *total*). They had to put together bits and pieces of information, such as the production of pig iron or sales at department stores, to infer what was happening to the economy as a whole.

It was not until the end of World War II that **national income and expenditure accounts** (or national income accounts, for short) were put together in major countries. Measures of aggregate output have been published on a regular basis in Canada since 1947. (You will find measures of aggregate output for earlier times, but these have been constructed retrospectively.)

Like any accounting system, the national income accounts define concepts and then construct measures corresponding to these concepts. One needs only to look at statistics from countries that have not yet developed such accounts to realize how crucial such precision and consistency are. Without them, numbers that should add up do not; trying to understand what is going on often feels like trying to balance someone else's chequebook. We shall not burden you with the details of national income accounting here. But, because you will occasionally need to know the definition of a variable and how variables relate to each other, Appendix 1 at the end of the book gives you the basic accounting framework used in Canada (and, with minor variations, in most other countries). You will find it useful whenever you want to look at economic data on your own.

> Putting the national income accounts together was a gigantic intellectual achievement. The Nobel prize was awarded in 1971 to Simon Kuznets, from Harvard University, and in 1984, to Richard Stone, from Oxford University, for their contributions to the development of the national income and product accounts.

GDP, Value Added, and Income

The measure of **aggregate output** in the national income accounts is **gross domestic product** (**GDP**). There are three ways of thinking about an economy's GDP. Let us examine each one:

> You may encounter another term, **gross national product** (**GNP**). There is a subtle difference between "domestic" and "national," and thus between GDP and GNP. We shall examine it in Chapters 6 and 17 (and also in Appendix 1). For the moment, you can ignore the difference between the two.

1. GDP Is the Value of the Final Goods and Services Produced in the Economy during a Given Period. The important word is *final*. To see why, consider the following example. Suppose that the economy is composed of just two firms.

- Firm 1 produces steel, employing workers and using machines. It sells the steel for $100 to Firm 2, which produces cars. Firm 1 pays its workers $80 and keeps what remains, $20, as profit.

- Firm 2 buys the steel and uses it, together with workers and machines, to produce cars. Revenues from car sales are $210. Of the $210, $100 goes to pay for steel and $70 goes to workers in the firm, leaving $40 in profit.

We can summarize this information in a table:

Steel Company		
Revenues from sales		$100
Expenses (wages)		$80
Profit		$20

Car Company		
Revenues from sales		$210
Expenses		$170
Wages	$70	
Steel purchases	$100	
Profit		$40

What is GDP in this economy? Is it the sum of the values of all production in the economy — the sum of $100 from the production of steel and $210 from the production of cars, $310? Or is it the value of the production of final goods, here cars, $210?

Some thought suggests that the right answer must be $210. Why? Because steel is an **intermediate good**, a good used in the production of the final goods, cars, and thus should not be counted in GDP — the value of *final* output. We can look at this example in another way. Suppose the two firms merged so that the sale of steel took place inside the new firm and was no longer recorded. All we would see would be one firm selling cars for $210, paying workers $80 + $70 = $150, and making $20 + $40 = $60 in profits. The $210 measure would remain unchanged — as it should.

This example suggests constructing GDP by recording and adding up the production of final goods — and this is indeed roughly the way actual GDP numbers are put together. But the example also suggests another way of thinking about and constructing GDP.

2. GDP Is the Sum of Value Added in the Economy during a Given Period. The term value added means exactly what it suggests. The value added by a firm in the production process is defined as the value of its production minus the value of the intermediate goods it uses in production.

In our two-firm example, the steel company does not use intermediate goods. Its value added is simply equal to the value of its production, $100. The car company, however, uses steel as an intermediate good. Thus, value added by the car company is equal to the value of the cars it produces minus the value of the steel it uses in production, $210 − $100 = $110. Total value added in the economy, or GDP, equals $100 + $110 = $210. Note that aggregate value added would remain the same if the steel and car firms merged and became one firm.

This definition gives us a second way of thinking about GDP. Put together, the two definitions imply that the value of final goods and services — the first definition of GDP — can also be thought of as the sum of the value added by all firms along the chain of production of those final goods — the second definition of GDP.

3. GDP Is the Sum of Incomes in the Economy during a Given Period. We have looked so far at GDP from the *production side*. A third way of looking at GDP is from the *income side*. Think about the revenues left to a firm after it has paid for intermediate goods.

- Some of the revenues are collected by government in the form of taxes on sales — such taxes are called *indirect taxes*.
- Some of the revenues go to pay workers — this component is called *labour income*.
- The rest goes to the firm — that component is called *capital income*.

In short, looking at it from the income side, value added is the sum of indirect taxes, labour income, and capital income.

Let us return to our example. There are no indirect taxes. Of the $100 of value added by the steel manufacturer, $80 goes to workers (labour income) and the remaining $20 goes to firms as profit (capital income). Of the $110 of value added by the car manufacturer, $70 goes to labour income and $40 to capital income. For the economy as a whole, value added is $210, of which $150 ($80 + $70) goes to labour income and $60 ($20 + $40) to capital income.

In this example, labour income accounts for 71% of GDP, capital income for 29%, indirect taxes for 0%. Table 2–1 shows the breakdown of value added among the different types of income in Canada in 1961 and 2005. The table shows that except for indirect taxes (which are equal to zero in our example), the proportions we have been using in our example are comparable with those of the Canadian economy. Labour income accounted for about 55% of Canadian GDP. Capital income, which includes depreciation, that portion of capital used

(in percent)	1961	2005
Labour income	62%	56%
Capital income	14%	19%
Depreciation	12%	13%
Indirect Taxes	12%	12%

Source: See Appendix 1.

up in production, totals either 26% in 1961 or 32% in 2005. Indirect taxes account for the remaining 12%. In 2005, corporate profits were relatively high by historical standards. The share of GDP accruing to labour was 56% instead of its more normal 60%. To summarize: You can think about aggregate output—about *GDP*—in three different but equivalent ways.

- From the output side: GDP is equal to the value of the final goods and services produced in the economy during a given period.
- Also from the output side: GDP is the sum of value added in the economy during a given period.
- From the income side: GDP is the sum of incomes in the economy during a given period.

Nominal and Real GDP

Canadian GDP was $1369 billion in 2005, compared with $41 billion in 1961. Was output 33 times higher in 2005 than in 1961? No. This leads us to the distinction between nominal GDP and real GDP.

Nominal GDP is the sum of the quantities of final goods produced times their current price. This definition makes it clear that nominal GDP increases over time for two reasons. First, the production of most goods increases over time. Second, the prices of most goods also increase over time. We produce more and more cars and their prices increase each year as well. If our intention is to measure production and its change over time, we need to eliminate the effect of increasing prices. That is why **real GDP** is constructed as the sum of the quantities of final goods times *constant* (rather than current) prices.

Let us look more closely at the construction of real GDP. If the economy produced only one final good, say, a particular car model, constructing real GDP would be easy. We could merely count the number of cars produced each year and call that number real GDP. Or, if we wanted to have a measure in dollars rather than cars, we could use the price of cars in a given year and then use it to multiply quantities in all years.

Suppose, for example, that the quantity produced and the price of cars in three successive years was as shown here:

> Warning! People often use "nominal" to denote small amounts. Economists use nominal for variables expressed in current prices. And economists surely do not refer to small amounts. The numbers you will see in this book are typically expressed in billions or millions of dollars.

Year	Quantity of Cars	Price of Cars	Nominal GDP
1991	10	$10,000	$100,000
1992	12	$12,000	$144,000
1993	13	$13,000	$169,000

Nominal GDP, which is equal to quantity of cars times their price, goes up from $100,000 in 1991 to $144,000 in 1992, a 44% increase, and from $144,000 in 1992 to $169,000 in 1993, a 16% increase.

How should we define real GDP, and by how much does it go up? We can define it as the number of cars: 10 in 1991, 12 in 1992, 13 in 1993. This implies a 20% increase in real GDP from 1991 to 1992 and an 8% increase from 1992 to 1993. Or we can define it by multiplying the number of cars in each year by a *common* price, say, the price of a car in 1992. This approach gives us, in effect, *real GDP in 1992 dollars*.

Using this approach, real GDP in 1991 (in 1992 dollars) is equal to $10 \times \$12,000 = \$120,000$. Real GDP in 1992 (in 1992 dollars) is equal to $12 \times \$12,000 = \$144,000$, the same as nominal GDP in 1992. Real GDP in 1993 (in 1992 dollars) is equal to $13 \times \$12,000 = \$156,000$. Note that because we multiply the number of cars in each year by the *same* price, the increase in real GDP, when measured in 1992 dollars, is the same as when measured in cars: Real GDP in 1992 dollars increases by 20% from 1992 to 1993 and by 8% from 1993 to 1994. If we had decided to measure real GDP in 1993 prices, the level of real GDP would be different (because the prices are not the same in 1993 as in 1992), but its increase from year to year would be the same as above.

Just to be sure: Compute real GDP in 1993 prices, and compute the rate of growth from 1991 to 1992 and from 1992 to 1993.

The main problem in constructing real GDP in practice is that there is more than one final good. Real GDP must be defined as a weighted average of the output of all final goods, which brings the question of what the weights should be. Relative prices of the goods would appear to be the natural weights. If a good costs twice as much per unit as another one, then it should clearly count twice as much in the construction of real output. But this raises other questions: What if, as is often the case, relative prices change over time? Should we choose the relative prices in a given year as weights, or should we change the weights over time? More discussion of these issues and of the way real GDP is constructed in Canada is left to an appendix to this chapter. What you should know is that the best measure of real GDP in the national income accounts is called **real GDP in chained (1997) dollars** ("1997" because, as in our example, 1997 is the year when, by construction, real GDP is equal to nominal GDP). It is a measure of the output of the Canadian economy, and its evolution shows how Canadian output has increased over time.

Figure 2–1 plots the evolution of both nominal and real GDP since 1961. By construction, the two are equal in 1997. The figure shows that real GDP in 2005 was 4.7 times its level of 1961—a considerable increase, but clearly much less than the 26-fold increase in nominal GDP over the same years. The difference between the two results from the increase in prices over the period.

Suppose that real GDP was measured in 1970 dollars rather than 1997 dollars. Where would the two graphs intersect?

The terms *nominal GDP* and *real GDP* each have many synonyms, and you are likely to encounter them in your readings:

- *Nominal GDP* is also called **dollar GDP** or **GDP in current dollars**.
- *Real GDP* is also called **GDP in terms of goods**, **GDP in constant dollars**, **GDP adjusted for inflation**, or **GDP in 1997 dollars**—if the year in which real GDP is set equal to nominal GDP is 1997, as is the case in Canada at this point.

This concludes your introduction to the main macroeconomic variable, GDP. In the chapters that follow, unless indicated otherwise, GDP will refer to real GDP, and Y_t will denote *real* GDP in year t. Nominal GDP and variables measured in current dollars will be denoted by a dollar sign in front—for example, $\$Y_t$ for nominal GDP in year t.

Similarly, **GDP growth** in year t will refer to the rate of change of real GDP in year t. GDP growth equals $(Y_t - Y_{t-1})/Y_{t-1}$. Periods of positive GDP growth are called **expansions**. Periods of negative GDP growth are called **recessions**. To avoid calling just one quarter of negative growth a recession, macroeconomists usually use the word only if the economy goes through at least two consecutive quarters of negative growth. The Canadian recession of 1990 to 1991, for example, was characterized by five consecutive quarters of negative growth, including all four quarters of 1990 and the first quarter of 1991.

Rate of output growth: $(Y_t - Y_{t-1})/Y_{t-1}$

rate of growth > 0: expansion

rate of growth < 0: recession

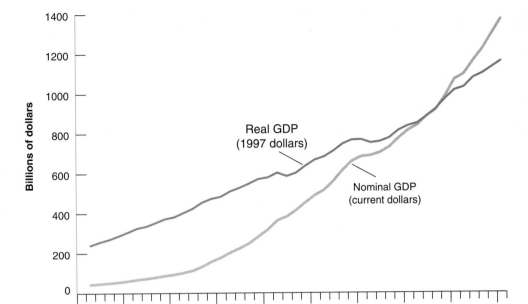

FIGURE 2–1

Nominal and Real GDP in Canada, 1961–2005

From 1961 to 2005, nominal GDP increased by a factor of 31.4. Real GDP increased by a factor of 4.7.

Source: Real GDP 1961–1980 using CANSIM II variable V3862685; 1981–2005 using CANSIM II variable V3860085; nominal GDP 1961–2005, using CANSIM II variable V646937.

FOCUS   Real GDP, Technological Progress, and the Price of Computers

A tough problem when it comes to computing real GDP is how to deal with changes in the quality of existing goods. One of the most difficult cases is computers. It would clearly be absurd to assume that the quality of a personal computer in 2004 is the same as the quality of a personal computer produced in 1981 (the year IBM first introduced the PC). The same amount of money clearly buys much more computing power in 2004 than it did in 1981. But how much more? Does a 2004 computer provide 10 times, 100 times, or 1000 times the computing services of a 1981 computer? How should we take into account the improvements in internal speed, RAM, and hard drive sizes, and the fact that 2004 computers can access the Internet, and so on?

The approach used by economists to adjust for these improvements is to look at the market for computers and how it values computers with different characteristics in a given year. Example: Suppose the evidence from prices of different models on the market show that people are willing to pay 10% more for a computer with a speed of 4 GHz (4000 megahertz) rather than 3 GHz. (The first edition of this book, published in 1996, compared two computers, with speeds of 50 and 16 megahertz, respectively. A good example of technological progress.) Suppose all new computers this year have a speed of 4 GHz compared with 3 GHz last year. And suppose the dollar price of new computers this year is the same as the dollar price of new computers last year. In this case, the economists in charge of computing the adjusted price of computers will conclude that new computers this year are, in fact, 10% cheaper than they were last year.

This approach, called **hedonic pricing**, puts an implicit price on each of a good's characteristics—in the case of a computer, its speed, memory, and so forth. ("Hedone" means "pleasure" in Greek.) Hedonic pricing is used by the Department of Commerce, which constructs real GDP, to estimate changes in the price of complex and fast-changing goods, such as automobiles and computers. Using this approach, the Department of Commerce estimates that for a given price, the quality of new computers has increased, on average, by 18% a year since 1981. Put another way, a typical personal computer in 2004 delivers $1.18^{23} = 45$ times the computing services a typical personal computer delivered in 1981.

Not only do computers deliver more services, they have become cheaper as well. Their dollar price has declined by about 10% a year since 1981. Putting this together with the information in the previous paragraph, it means that their quality-adjusted price has fallen at an average rate of 18% + 10% = 28% per year. Put another way, a dollar spent on a computer today buys $1.28^{23} = 292$ times more computing services than did a dollar spent on a computer in 1981.

2-2 | The Other Major Macroeconomic Variables

GDP is the main macroeconomic variable. Two others, unemployment and inflation, tell us about other important aspects of how an economy is performing.

The Unemployment Rate

The **unemployment rate** is defined from the ratio of the number of unemployed to the labour force and then expressed as a percentage:

$$u = \frac{U}{L} \times 100$$

unemployment rate = unemployed/labour force

The **labour force** is defined as the sum of those employed and those unemployed:

$$L \quad = \quad N \quad + \quad U$$

labour force = employed + unemployed

What determines whether a worker is counted as unemployed? Until 1945, in Canada, and more recently in other countries, the number of people registered at unemployment offices was the only available data on unemployment, and only those workers who were registered in unemployment offices were counted as unemployed. This system led to a poor measure of unemployment. How many of the truly unemployed actually registered varied both across countries and across time. Those who had no incentive to register—for example, those who had exhausted their unemployment benefits—were unlikely to take the time to come to the unemployment office, so they were not counted. Countries with less generous benefit systems were likely to have fewer unemployed registering and therefore smaller measured unemployment rates.

Today, most countries rely on large surveys of households to compute the unemployment rate. In Canada, this survey is called the **Labour Force Survey (LFS)**. It relies on interviews of 60,000 households every month. The survey classifies a person as employed if he or she has a job at the time of the interview; it classifies a person as unemployed if he or she does not have a job and has been looking for work in the last four weeks. Most other countries use a similar definition of unemployment. In Canada, estimates based on the LFS survey show that in 2005, on average, 16.1 million people were employed and 1.2 million people were unemployed, so the unemployment rate was 1.2/(16.1 + 1.2) = 6.9%.

Note that only those *looking for work* are counted as unemployed; those not working and not looking for work are counted as **not in the labour force**. When unemployment is high, some of those without jobs give up looking for work and therefore are no longer counted as unemployed. These people are known as **discouraged workers**. Take an extreme case: If all workers without a job gave up looking, the unemployment rate would equal zero. This would make the unemployment rate a very poor indicator of what is happening in the labour market. More typically, high unemployment is associated with more workers dropping out of the labour force. Equivalently, a higher unemployment rate is typically associated with a lower **participation rate**, defined as the ratio of the labour force to the total population of working-age persons. Since the start of economic reform in Eastern Europe in the early 1990s, unemployment has increased, often dramatically. But equally dramatic has been the drop in participation rates. In Poland, in 1990, for example, 70% of the decrease in employment was accounted for by early retirements—by people dropping out of the labour force rather than becoming unemployed.

Macroeconomists care about unemployment for two main reasons: The unemployment rate tells them something about whether an economy is operating above or below its normal level. And unemployment has important social consequences. Let us look at each in turn.

Unemployment and Activity. In most countries, there is a clear relation between the change in unemployment and GDP growth. This relation is known as **Okun's law**, after the economist Arthur Okun, who first identified and interpreted it in the 1960s. The relation between these two variables in Canada since 1962 is plotted in Figure 2–2, which shows the change in the unemployment rate on the vertical axis and the rate of GDP growth on the horizontal axis. Each point in the figure shows the growth rate and the change in the unemployment rate for a given year. (Figures, such as Figure 2–2, that plot one variable against another over time are called **scatter diagrams**.)

The figure shows that high output growth is typically associated with a decrease in the unemployment rate and low output growth associated with an increase in the unemployment rate. This makes sense: High output growth leads to high employment growth, as firms hire more workers to produce more. High employment growth leads to a decrease in unemployment.

The relation has a simple implication. If the current unemployment rate is too high (what constitutes *too high* or *too low* will be the topic many chapters later; we can leave this discussion until then), it will take a period of higher growth to reduce it. If, instead, the unemployment rate is about right, then output should grow at the rate that is consistent with an unchanged unemployment rate. The unemployment rate therefore provides macroeconomists with a signal of where the economy stands and what growth rate might be desirable. Return to our discussion of the unemployment rate around the world in Chapter 1: Those economists who believe that the unemployment rate is currently *too low* would like to have lower output growth for some time to allow unemployment to return to a higher level. This is why they advocate macroeconomic policies aimed at slowing down growth for a time. Other economists believe that the unemployment rate is too high and advocate macroeconomic policies to speed up output growth for a time.

Social Implications of Unemployment. Macroeconomists also care about unemployment because of its direct effects on the welfare of the unemployed. Although unemployment benefits are greater today than they were during the Great Depression, unemployment is still associated with financial and psychological suffering. How much depends on the nature of the unemployment. One image of the unemployed is that of a stagnant pool, of people remaining unemployed for long periods of time. As we shall see later in the book, this image does not reflect what happens in Canada or other Western economies. In reality, each month, many

Okun's law:

High output growth ⇒ unemployment rate ↓

Low output growth ⇒ unemployment rate ↑

From Figure 2–2, what is the rate of growth of output associated with roughly no change in the unemployment rate?

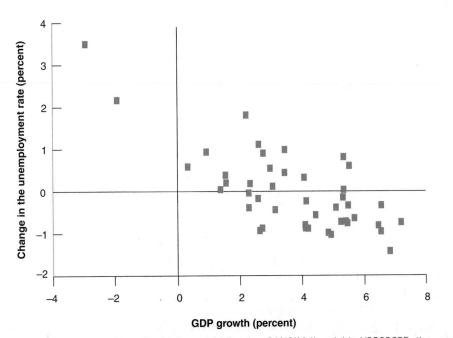

FIGURE 2-2

Change in the Unemployment Rate versus GDP Growth, 1962–2005

High output growth is typically associated with a decrease in the unemployment rate. Conversely, low output growth is typically associated with an increase in the unemployment rate.

Source: GDP growth is percent change in real GDP using CANSIM II variable V3862685; the unemployment rate 1976–2005 using CANSIM II variable V1 59752; prior to 1976 using *Historical Statistics of Canada*.

In 1994, the official unemployment rate in Spain reached 24%. (The rate has fallen since then, but it still stands above 10% today.) This was roughly the same unemployment rate as in the United States or Canada in 1933, the worst year of the Great Depression. Yet, Spain in 1994 looked nothing like the United States or Canada in 1933. There were few homeless, and most cities looked prosperous. Can we really believe that nearly one-fourth of the Spanish labour force was looking for work?

To answer this, we must first examine how the Spanish unemployment number is put together. Much like in Canada, unemployment numbers in Spain are determined by surveying 60,000 households monthly. People are classified as unemployed if they indicate that they are not working but are seeking work.

Can we be sure that people tell the truth? No. Although there is no obvious incentive to lie—answers to the survey are confidential and are not used to determine whether people are eligible for unemployment benefits—those who are working in the underground economy may prefer to play it safe and report that they are unemployed instead.

The size of the **underground economy**—that part of economic activity not measured in official statistics, either because the activity is illegal or because firms and workers would rather not report it to avoid paying taxes—is an old issue in Spain. Because of this, we actually know more about the underground economy in Spain than in many other countries. In 1985, the Spanish government tried to find out more about it and organized a detailed survey of 60,000 individuals. To try to elicit the truth from those interviewed, the questionnaire asked interviewees for an extremely precise account of the use of their time, making it more difficult for them to misreport. The answers were interesting. The underground economy in Spain—defined as the number of people working without declaring it to the social security administration—accounted for between 10 and 15% of employment. But it was composed mostly of people who already had a job and were taking a second or even a third job! The best estimate from the survey was that only about 15% of the unemployed were, in fact, working. This implied that the unemployment rate, which was officially 21% at the time, was, in fact, closer to 18%, still a very high number. In short, the Spanish underground economy was significant, but it just was not the case that most of the people unemployed in Spain were working in the underground economy.

How did the unemployed in Spain survive? Did they survive because Spanish unemployment benefits were unusually generous? No. Except for very generous unemployment benefits in two regions, Andalusia and Extremadura—which, not surprisingly, suffered even higher unemployment than the rest of the country—unemployment benefits were roughly in line with unemployment benefits in other OECD countries. Benefits were typically 70% of the person's previous wages for the first six months and 60% thereafter. The benefits were given out for a period of 4 to 24 months, depending on how long people had worked before becoming unemployed. The 30% of the unemployed who had been unemployed for more than two years did not receive unemployment benefits. So, how did they survive? The key lies with the Spanish family structure. The unemployment rate was highest among the young. In 1994, it was close to 50% for those between ages 16 and 19 and around 40% for those between ages 20 and 24. The young typically stay at home until their late 20s and have increasingly done so as unemployment has increased. Looking at households rather than at individuals, the proportion of households in Spain where no one was employed was less than 10% in 1994; the proportion of households that received neither wage income nor unemployment benefits was below 3%. In short, most of the unemployed received financial support from family members.

people become unemployed, and many of the unemployed (on average, 30% of them) find jobs. But even in this setting, some groups (often the young, the ethnic minorities, and the unskilled) suffer disproportionately from unemployment, remaining chronically unemployed and being most vulnerable to becoming unemployed when the unemployment rate increases.

Figure 1–2 in the previous chapter showed substantial variation in Canada's unemployment rate over time. Virtually everyone would agree that when the unemployment rate is at 9, 10, 11, or 12%, the unemployment rate is too high. Everyone is adversely affected when unemployment is too high. You may be unemployed. Your neighbour or your relative may be unemployed.

The Inflation Rate

Inflation is a sustained rise in the general level of prices, a sustained rise in the **price level**. The **inflation rate** is the rate at which the price level increases.

The practical issue is how to define this price level. Macroeconomists typically look at two measures of the price level, at two *price indexes*: the GDP deflator and the consumer price index.

The GDP Deflator. Suppose nominal GDP, $\$Y_t$, increases but real GDP, Y_t, remains unchanged. Then, the increase in nominal GDP must result from the increase in prices. This motivates the definition of the GDP deflator. The **GDP deflator** in year t, P_t, is defined as the ratio of nominal GDP to real GDP in year t:

$$P_t = \frac{\text{nominal GDP}_t}{\text{Real GDP}_t} = \frac{\$Y_t}{Y_t}$$

Index numbers are often set to 100 rather than 1 in the base year. 100 is short for 100%, which, in decimal terms, is equal to 1. If you look at the *Economic Report* (Table B3) you will see that the GDP deflator is equal to 100 for 1992 (the base year), to 102.6 in 1993, and so on.

Note that in the year in which, by construction, real GDP is equal to nominal GDP (1997 at this point in Canada), this definition implies that the price level is equal to 1. This is worth emphasizing: The GDP deflator is what is called an **index number**. Its level is chosen arbitrarily—here it is equal to 1 in 1997—and has no economic interpretation. But its rate of change has a clear economic interpretation: It gives the rate at which the general level of prices goes up over time—the rate of inflation.

Rate of inflation:
$$(P_t - P_{t-1})/P_{t-1}$$

One advantage to defining the price level as the GDP deflator is that it implies that a simple relation holds among nominal GDP, real GDP, and the price level. To see this, reorganize the previous equation to get:

$$\$Y_t = P_t Y_t$$

Nominal GDP is equal to the GDP deflator times real GDP.

The Consumer Price Index. The GDP deflator gives the average price of the goods included in GDP—the final goods *produced* in the economy. But consumers care about the average price of the goods they *consume*. The two prices need not be the same: The set of goods produced in the economy is not the same as the set of goods bought by consumers. This is true for two reasons. Some of the goods in GDP are sold not to consumers but to firms (machine tools, for example), to government, or to foreigners. And some of the goods bought by consumers are not produced at home but, rather, imported from abroad.

To measure the average price of consumption, or equivalently the **cost of living index**, macroeconomists look at another index, the **consumer price index (CPI)**. The CPI has been in existence since 1914 and is published monthly (in contrast, GDP numbers and the GDP deflator are published quarterly).

The CPI gives the cost in dollars of a specific list of goods and services over time. The list, which is based on a detailed study of consumer spending, attempts to represent the consumption basket of a typical urban consumer. It is revised approximately every five years. Each month, Statistics Canada employees visit stores to find out what has happened to the price of the goods on the list. Each month, about 60,000 price quotations are collected. These prices are then used to construct the price index.

Like the GDP deflator, the CPI is an index. It is set equal to 1 in the period chosen as the base period and thus does not have a natural level. The current base period is 1992 so that the average for the year 1992 is equal to 1. In 2004, the CPI stood at 124.6; thus, it cost 24.6% more in dollars to purchase the same consumption basket than in 1992.

Like the GDP deflator, the CPI is also typically set to 100 rather than to 1 in the base period (so, for example, equal to 163 rather than to 1.63 for 1998).

You may wonder how the rate of inflation differs depending on whether the GDP deflator or the CPI is used to measure it. The answer is given in Figure 2–3, which plots the two inflation rates since 1962 for Canada.

The plots on the graph yield two conclusions:

- The CPI and the GDP deflator move together most of the time. In most years, the two inflation rates differ by less than 1%.

- There are a few exceptions. The GDP deflator is the price of goods produced in Canada. The CPI is the price of goods consumed. These can be different goods. As an obvious example, Canada produces a lot more forest products than it consumes. If there is a boom in forest product prices, or other commodity prices, then the GDP deflator may rise more rapidly than the CPI. This happened in 1975 when oil and other commodity prices boomed and inflation measured using the GDP deflator was higher than inflation

FIGURE 2-3

Canadian Inflation Rate, Using the CPI and the GDP Deflator, 1962–2005

The inflation rates, computed using either the CPI or the GDP deflator, are largely similar.

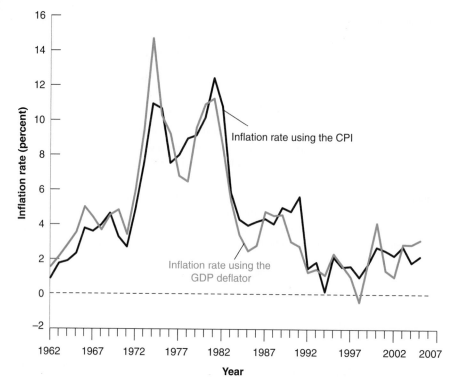

Source: GDP deflator using CANSIM II variable V646937 divided by CANSIM II variable V3862685; and consumer price index using CANSIM II variable V735319.

measured using the CPI. The reverse occurred in 1997 when commodity prices fell. In 1991, when Canada switched from a manufacturers' sales tax, which was hidden, to the Goods and Services Tax, which consumers paid directly, CPI inflation was higher than GDP inflation.

In what follows, we shall make no distinction between the two indexes unless the discussion requires us to focus on their difference. Thus, we shall simply talk about the *price level* and denote it by P_t, without indicating whether we have the CPI or the GDP deflator in mind.

Inflation and Unemployment. Is there a relation between inflation and either output or unemployment? Or does inflation have a life of its own? The answer: There is a relation, but it is far from mechanical—it varies across time and countries.

The relation between unemployment and inflation in Canada since 1970 is shown in Figure 2–4. The change in the inflation rate (using the CPI)—that is, the inflation rate this year minus the inflation rate last year—is plotted on the vertical axis. The unemployment rate is plotted on the horizontal axis. The figure gives the combinations of unemployment rates and changes in inflation rates for each year since 1970.

Figure 2–4 shows a negative relation between the unemployment rate and the change in inflation. When the unemployment rate is low, inflation tends to increase. When the unemployment rate is high, inflation tends to decrease. This negative relation is called the Phillips relation, and the curve that fits the set of points best is called the **Phillips curve**, named for the economist who first documented the relation between unemployment and inflation. Where this relation comes from, why it changes through time and place, and what it implies, will be the focus of many later chapters.

The Phillips curve:
Low unemployment ⟹ inflation ↑
High unemployment ⟹ inflation ↓ ▶

We will see in Chapter 8 that the nature of the Phillips curve has changed since Phillips first documented it in 1958, but the name is still used.

▶

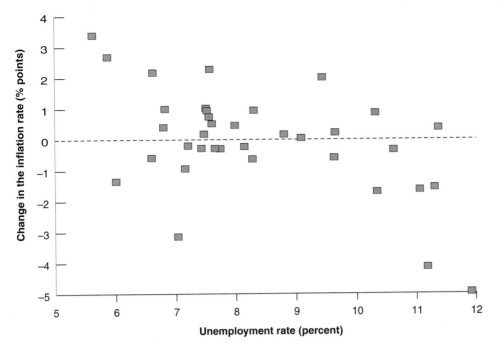

FIGURE 2-4

Change in the Canadian Inflation Rate versus the Canadian Unemployment Rate, 1970–2005

When the unemployment rate is low, inflation tends to increase. When the unemployment rate is high, inflation tends to decrease.

Source: Inflation is the percent change in the CPI using CANSIM II variable V735319; unemployment rate 1976–2005 using CANSIM II variable V159752; prior to 1976 using *Historical Statistics of Canada*.

Why Do Economists Care About Inflation? If higher inflation meant just a faster proportional increase in all prices and wages—a case called *pure inflation*—inflation would be only a minor inconvenience. Relative prices would not be affected by inflation. Take, for example, the workers' *real wage*—the wage measured in terms of goods rather than in dollars. In an economy with 10% inflation, prices would increase by 10% a year but so would wages—and real wages would remain the same. Inflation would not be entirely irrelevant; people would have to keep track of the increase in prices and wages in making decisions. But this would be a small burden, hardly justifying making control of the inflation rate one of the major goals of macroeconomic policy.

So, why do economists care about inflation? Precisely because there is no such thing as pure inflation. During periods of inflation, not all prices and wages rise proportionately. Because they do not, inflation affects income distribution. For example, retirees in many countries receive payments that do not keep up with the price level, so they lose in relation to other groups when inflation is high. This is not the case in Canada, where the various federal old age benefits automatically rise with the CPI, protecting retirees from inflation. But during the very high inflation that has taken place in Russia since the early 1990s, retirement pensions have not kept up with inflation, and many retirees have been pushed to near starvation.

Inflation also leads to distortions. Some prices, which are fixed by law or by regulation, lag behind the others, leading to changes in relative prices. Taxation interacts with inflation to create more distortions. If tax brackets are not adjusted for inflation, for example, people move into higher and higher tax brackets as their nominal incomes increase, even if their real incomes remain the same. Variations in relative prices also lead to more uncertainty, making it harder for firms to make decisions about the future, such as investment decisions.

To summarize: Economists see high inflation as affecting income distribution and creating both distortions and uncertainty. How important these problems are and whether they justify trying to achieve and maintain, say, zero inflation, are much debated questions. We shall take them up later in this book.

This ignores the changes in real wages that would occur even if there were no inflation. A more accurate statement is that under pure inflation, inflation would not affect the evolution of real wages.

This is known as *bracket creep*. In Canada, beginning in 2001, the tax brackets are adjusted automatically for inflation: If inflation is 5%, all tax brackets also go up by 5%—in other words, there is no bracket creep. However, there was bracket creep from 1994 to 2000.

2-3 | A Road Map

Having defined the main variables, let us now turn to the central question of macroeconomics. What determines the level of aggregate output?

- Reading newspapers suggests one answer: Movements in output come from movements in the demand for goods. You probably have read news stories that begin, "Production and sales of automobiles were higher last month, apparently due to a surge in consumer confidence, which drove consumers to showrooms in record numbers." Such explanations point to the role of demand in determining aggregate output as well as to factors ranging from consumer confidence to tax rates to interest rates.

- But, surely, no amount of consumers rushing to showrooms will increase India's output to the level of output in North America. This suggests a second answer. What must matter is the supply side: how advanced the technology of the country is, how much capital it is using, the size and the skills of its labour force. These factors, not consumer confidence, must be the fundamental determinants of the level of output.

- One may want to push this argument one step further: Neither technology and skills nor capital is a given. The technological sophistication of a country depends on its ability to innovate and introduce new technologies. The skills of workers depend on the quality of the education system. The size of its capital stock depends on how much people save. Other factors may also be important. If firms are to operate efficiently, they need a clear system of laws under which to operate and an honest government to enforce them. This suggests a third answer: The true determinants of output are such factors as the education system, the saving rate, and the quality of government. It is there that we must look if we want to understand what determines output.

Which of the three answers is the right one? The answer is all three. But each of them applies over a different time period.

- In the **short run**, say a few years or so, the first answer is the right one. Year-to-year movements in output are primarily driven by movements in demand. Changes in demand, which can arise from changes in consumer confidence or from any other source, can lead to a decrease in output (a recession), or an increase in output (an expansion).

- In the **medium run**, say, a decade or two, the second answer is the right one. Over the medium run, the economy tends to return to the level of output determined by supply factors: the capital stock, technology, and the size of the labour force. And over a decade or two, these factors do not move so much that it is a mistake to take them as given.

- In the **long run**, say, a half century or more, the third answer is the right one. To understand why Japan has grown so much faster than the United States and Canada over the last 50 years, we must explain why both capital and the level of technology have increased faster in Japan than in North America. We must, indeed, look at such factors as the education system, the saving rate, and the role of government.

This way of thinking about the determinants of output underlies macroeconomics, and it underlies the organization of this book.

A Tour of the Book

The book is organized in three main parts; first, the core; then, two extensions; and, finally, a look at the role of macroeconomic policy. This organization is shown in Figure 2–5. Let us now describe it in more detail.

The Core. The core is composed of three parts—the short run, the medium run, and the long run.

- Chapters 3 to 8 look at the determination of output in the short run.

  The focus is on the determination of the demand for goods. To focus on the role of demand, we assume that firms are willing to supply any quantity at a given price; in other words, we ignore supply constraints. Chapter 3 looks at the goods market. Chapter 4 focuses on financial markets. Chapter 5 puts goods and financial markets together. The resulting framework is known as the *IS-LM* model. Developed in the late 1930s, the *IS-LM* model still provides a simple way of thinking about the determination of output in the short run, and it remains a basic building block of macroeconomics. It also allows for a first pass at studying the role of fiscal policy and monetary policy in affecting output. Chapters 6 to 8 add the open economy into the short-run analysis. Chapter 6 looks at openness in goods and in financial markets. Chapter 7 looks at the effects of the open economy on the demand for goods. Chapter 8 looks at the *IS-LM* model in an open economy.

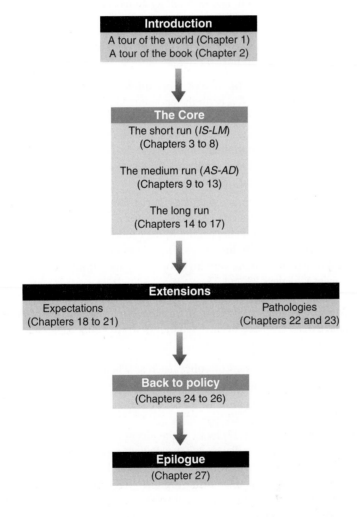

FIGURE 2–5

The Organization of the Book

- Chapters 9 to 13 reintroduce the supply side and look at the determination of output in the medium run.

  Chapter 9 focuses on the labour market. Chapter 10 puts together goods, financial, and labour markets and shows how one can think about the determination of output both in the short run and in the medium run. The model developed in that chapter is called the aggregate supply–aggregate demand (*AS-AD*) model of output. Chapters 11 and 12 show how the model can be used to think about several issues, such as the relation between output and inflation and the role of monetary and fiscal policy both in the short run and in the medium run. Chapter 13 analyzes the medium run in the open economy setting. When countries have different inflation rates there are important implications for exchange rate policy to consider.

- Chapters 14 to 17 focus on the long run.

  Chapter 14 introduces the facts and looks at the growth of output both across countries and across long periods of time. Chapters 15 and 16 then discuss the role and the determinants of both capital accumulation and technological progress in growth. Chapter 17 recognizes the role of the rest of the world in the process of growth. There are significant movements of people, capital, and technology across national borders.

Extensions. The core chapters give you a way of thinking about the determination of output (and unemployment, and inflation) over the short, medium, and long runs. But they leave out several elements. These are explored in two extensions.

- The core chapters did not include the role of *expectations*. But expectations play an essential role in macroeconomics. Nearly all the economic decisions people and firms make—to buy bonds or stocks, whether or not to buy a machine—depend on their expectations of future profits, of future interest rates, and so on. Fiscal and monetary policies affect activity not only through their direct effects but also through their effects on expectations. Chapters 18 to 21 focus on the role of expectations and their implications for fiscal and monetary policies.

- The core chapters on the short run and the medium run focus on fluctuations in output—on expansions and on recessions. Sometimes, however, the word "fluctuations" does not accurately capture what is happening in the economy. Something goes very wrong. Inflation reaches extremely high rates. Or, as was the case during the Great Depression, unemployment remains very high for a very long time. These two *pathologies* are the topics of Chapters 22 and 23.

Back to Policy. Monetary and fiscal policies are discussed in every chapter of the book. But once the core and the extensions have been covered, it is worth going back and assessing the role of policy.

- Chapter 24 focuses on general issues of policy, such as whether macroeconomists know enough to use policy at all and whether policy makers can be trusted to do what is right.

- Chapters 25 and 26 then assess the role of monetary and fiscal policies.

Epilogue. The final chapter, Chapter 27, looks at the recent history of macroeconomics and how macroeconomists have come to believe what they believe today. From the outside, macroeconomics often looks like a field divided, with different schools—Keynesians, monetarists, new classicals, supply-siders, and so on—hurling arguments at each other. The actual process of research is more orderly and more productive than this image suggests. We identify what we see as the main differences among macroeconomists and the set of propositions that define the core of macroeconomics today.

- We can think of GDP, the measure of aggregate activity, in three equivalent ways: (1) GDP is the value of the final goods and services produced in the economy during a given period; (2) GDP is the sum of value added in the economy during a given period; and (3) GDP is the sum of incomes in the economy during a given period.

- Nominal GDP is equal to the sum of the quantities of final goods produced times their current prices. This implies that changes in nominal GDP reflect both changes in quantities and changes in prices. Real GDP is a measure of output. Changes in real GDP reflect changes in quantities only.

- The labour force is defined as the sum of those employed and those unemployed. The unemployment rate is defined as the ratio of the number of unemployed to the labour force. A person is classified as unemployed if he or she does not have a job and has been looking for work in the last four weeks.

- The empirical relation between GDP growth and the change in the unemployment rate is called Okun's law. The relation shows that high output growth is associated with a decrease in the unemployment rate and, conversely, that low growth is associated with an increase in the unemployment rate.

- Inflation is a rise in the general level of prices, in the price level. The inflation rate is the rate at which the price level increases. Macroeconomists look at two measures of the price level. The first is the GDP deflator, which gives the average price of goods produced in the economy. The second is the consumer price index (CPI), which gives the average price of goods consumed in the economy.

- The empirical relation between the inflation rate and the unemployment rate is called the Phillips curve. This relation has changed over time and also varies across countries. In Canada today, it takes the following form: When the unemployment rate is low, inflation tends to increase. When the unemployment rate is high, inflation tends to decrease.

- Inflation leads to changes in income distribution and increases distortions and uncertainty.

- Macroeconomists distinguish among the short run (a few years), the medium run (a decade or two), and the long run (a half century or more.) They think of output as being determined by demand in the short run, by the level of technology, the capital stock, and the labour force in the medium run, and by such factors as education, research, saving, and the quality of government in the long run.

KEY TERMS

- aggregate output, 23
- base year, 40
- consumer price index (CPI), 31
- cost of living index, 31
- discouraged workers, 28
- dollar GDP, GDP in current dollars, 26
- GDP deflator, 31
- GDP growth, expansions, recessions, 26
- GDP in terms of goods, GDP in constant dollars, GDP adjusted for inflation, GDP in 1997 dollars, 26
- gross domestic product (GDP), 23
- gross national product (GNP), 23
- hedonic pricing, 27
- index number, 31
- inflation, 30
- inflation rate, 30

- intermediate good, 24
- labour force, 28
- Labour Force Survey (LFS), 28
- national income and expenditure accounts, 23
- nominal GDP, 25
- not in the labour force, 28
- Okun's law, 28
- participation rate, 28
- Phillips curve, 32
- price level, 30
- real GDP, 25
- real GDP in chained (1997) dollars, 26
- scatter diagrams, 29
- short run, medium run, and long run, 34
- underground economy, 30
- unemployment rate, 28

An asterisk denotes a harder question. [Web] indicates that the question requires access to the Internet.

1. TRUE/FALSE/UNCERTAIN

a. The share of labour income in GDP is much smaller than the share of capital income.

b. Canadian GDP in 2005 was 33 times higher than Canadian GDP in 1961.

c. If a high unemployment rate discourages workers from looking for work, then the unemployment rate can be a poor indicator of labour market conditions. To assess the situation, one must also look at the participation rate.

d. A reduction in the rate of unemployment requires high output growth.

e. If the Japanese CPI is currently at 108 and the U.S. CPI is at 104, then the Japanese rate of inflation is higher than the U.S. rate of inflation.

f. The rate of inflation computed using the CPI is a better index of inflation than the rate of inflation computed using the GDP deflator.

2. GDP AND ITS COMPONENTS

Suppose you are measuring annual GDP by adding up the final value of all goods and services produced in the economy. Determine the effect of each of the following transactions on the level of GDP. You may have to consult Appendix 1.

a. You buy from a fisherman $100 worth of fish, which you cook and eat at home.

b. A seafood restaurant buys $100 worth of fish from a fisherman.

c. CN Rail buys new railcars from Bombardier for $200 million.

d. The French national railway buys new railcars from Bombardier for $200 million.

e. WestJet sells one of its jets to Air Canada for $80 million.

*3. MEASURED VERSUS TRUE GDP

Suppose that instead of cooking dinner for an hour, you decide to work an extra hour, earning an additional $12. You then buy some Chinese food for $10.

a. By how much does measured GDP increase?

b. Does true GDP increase or decrease? Explain.

4. MEASURING GDP

During a given year, the following activities occur:

a. A silver mining company pays its workers $200,000 to mine 75 kilograms of silver. The silver is then sold to a jewelry manufacturer for $300,000.

b. The jewelry manufacturer pays its workers $250,000 to make silver necklaces, which it sells directly to consumers for $1,000,000.

   i. Using the "production of final goods" approach, what is GDP in this economy?

   ii. What is the value added at each stage of production? Using the "value added" approach, what is GDP?

   iii. What are the total wages and profits earned? Using the income approach, what is GDP?

5. NOMINAL AND REAL GDP

An economy produces three goods: cars, computers, and oranges. Production units and prices per unit for years 1998 and 1999 are as follows:

	1998 Quantity	1998 Price	1999 Quantity	1999 Price
Cars	10	$2000	12	$3000
Computers	4	$1000	6	$500
Oranges	1000	$1	1000	$1

a. What is nominal GDP in 1998 and in 1999?

b. Using 1998 as the base year (i.e., using 1998 prices), what is real GDP in 1998 and 1999? By what percentage does real GDP increase from 1998 to 1999?

c. Using 1999 as the base year (i.e., using 1999 prices), what is real GDP in 1998 and 1999? By what percentage does real GDP increase from 1998 to 1999?

d. The growth rate we obtain for real GDP depends on which year is used as a base year. Is this statement true or false?

6. THE GDP DEFLATOR

Use the data from problem 5 to answer the following:

a. Using 1998 as the base year, what is the GDP deflator for 1998 and 1999? What is the rate of inflation over this period?

b. Using 1999 as the base year, what is the GDP deflator for 1998 and 1999? What is the rate of inflation over this period?

c. Does the choice of base year affect the rate of inflation computed using the GDP deflator?

7. THE UNEMPLOYMENT RATE

Suppose that in a given month in Canada, there are 18 million working-age people. Of these, only 14 million have jobs. Of the remainder, 2 million are looking for work. 1.5 million have given up looking for work, and 0.5 million do not want to work.

a. What is the labour force?

b. What is the labour-force participation rate?

c. What is the official unemployment rate?

d. If all discouraged workers were counted as unemployed, what would be the unemployment rate?

8. CHAIN-TYPE INDEXES

As can be seen from problems 5 and 6, the use of base year prices to compute the rate of change of real GDP and the rate of inflation has some very unattractive properties. Every time a new base year is selected (e.g., to reflect the growing share of services in GDP), all past growth rates of real GDP and all past rates of inflation based on the GDP deflator have to be revised. To avoid these problems, virtually all statistical agencies around the world, including Statistics Canada, started using chain-type indexes in 1995. In this problem, we shall see, using the economy described in problem 5, how chain-type indexes are constructed. Further discussion of this method can be found in the appendix to Chapter 2.

a. Construct real GDP for years 1998 and 1999 for the economy described in problem 5 by using the average price of each good over the two years.

b. By what percentage does real GDP increase from 1998 to 1999?

c. What is the GDP deflator in 1998 and 1999? What is the rate of inflation using the chain-type deflator?

d. Do you find this method of construction of real GDP growth and of the inflation rate attractive? Why, or why not?

9. HEDONIC PRICING

As the first focus box of Chapter 2 explains, it is hard to measure the true increase in prices of goods whose characteristics change over time. Hedonic pricing offers a method of computing the quality-adjusted increase in prices.

a. Consider the case of a routine medical checkup. Name some reasons why you may want to use hedonic pricing to measure the increase in the price of this service.

Now consider the case of a medical checkup for a pregnant woman. Suppose that in the year a new ultrasound method is introduced, the price of this checkup increases by 20% and all doctors adopt the ultrasound simultaneously.

b. What information do you need in order to determine the quality-adjusted increase in pregnancy checkups?

c. Is that information available? Explain. What can you say about the quality-adjusted price increase of pregnancy checkups?

10. USING THE WEB TO GET THE MOST RECENT GDP INFORMATION [WEB]

Look up the value of "real gross domestic product" on the Statistics Canada Web site **www.statcan.ca**.

a. Do the changes over the most recent four quarters suggest that the economy was in a recession? An expansion? Neither? Explain briefly.

b. For each of the most recent two years, compute the percentage of total GDP consisting of consumption, investment, exports, and imports.

FURTHER READING

If you want to know more about the many economic indicators that are regularly reported on the news—from the help-wanted index to the retail sales index—a good reference is:

John Grant, *A Handbook of Economic Indicators* (Toronto: University of Toronto Press, 1992).

For more about the LFS or the CPI, see:

- Statistics Canada, *Guide to the Labour Force Survey*, January 1997.
- Statistics Canada, *Your Guide to the Consumer Price Index*, No. 62-557-XPB, December 1996.

Both publications can be downloaded from the Statistics Canada Web site www.statcan.ca.

THE CONSTRUCTION OF REAL GDP AND CHAIN-TYPE INDEXES

The example we used in the chapter had only one final good—cars—so constructing real GDP was easy. But how should one construct real GDP when there are two or more final goods? This is the question taken up in this appendix.

All that is needed to make the relevant points is an economy where there are two goods. So, suppose that an economy produces cars and potatoes.

- In year 0, it produces 100,000 kilograms of potatoes, at $1 a kilogram, and 10 cars, at $10,000 a car.
- One year later, in year 1, it produces 100,000 kilograms of potatoes, at $1.20 a kilogram, and 11 cars, at $10,000 a car.
- Nominal GDP in year 0 is therefore equal to $200,000, nominal GDP in year 1 is equal to $230,000. This information is summarized in the following table:

Nominal GDP in Year 0 and in Year 1

	Quantity	Year 0 $ Price	$ Value
Potatoes	100,000	1.00	100,000
Cars	10	10,000.00	100,000
Nominal GDP			200,000
	Quantity	Year 1 $ Price	$ Value
Potatoes	100,000	1.20	120,000
Cars	11	10,000.00	110,000
Nominal GDP			230,000

The increase in nominal GDP from year 0 to year 1 is equal to $30,000/$200,000 = 15%. But what is the increase in real GDP?

The basic idea in constructing real GDP is to evaluate quantities in both years using the same set of prices. Suppose we choose, for example, the prices of year 0; year 0 is then called the **base year**. The computation is then as follows:

- Real GDP in year 0 is the sum of quantities in year 0 times prices in year 0: (100,000 × $1) + (10 × $10,000) = $200,000.
- Real GDP in year 1 is the sum of quantities in year 1 times prices in year 0: (100,000 × $1) + (11 × $10,000) = $210,000.

- The rate of change of real GDP from year 0 to year 1 is thus ($210,000 − $200,000)/$200,000 = 5%.

However, this answer raises an important issue: Instead of using year 0 as the base year, we could have used year 1, or any other year for that matter. If, for example, we had used year 1 as the base year, then:

- Real GDP in year 0 would be equal to (100,000 × $1.2 + 10 × $10,000) = $220,000.
- Real GDP in year 1 would be equal to (100,000 × $1.2 + 11 × $10,000) = $230,000.
- The rate of change of real GDP from year 0 to year 1 would be equal to $10,000/$220,000 = 4.5%.

The answer using year 1 as the base year would therefore be different from the answer using year 0 as the base year. So, if the choice of the base year affects the constructed rate of change of output, what base year should one choose?

Until 2001, in Canada—and still today in most countries—the practice was to choose a base year and change it infrequently, say, every five years or so. The last two base years in Canada were 1992 and 1997. When 1992 was used as the base year, then real GDP was constructed using 1992 prices for all years going back. Then, after 1997, national accounts switched to a 1997 base year and real GDP for all years was recalculated using 1997 prices.

This practice was logically unappealing. Every time the base year was changed and a new set of prices was used, all past real GDP numbers—and all past rates of change of real GDP—were recomputed: History was, in effect, rewritten every five years! Starting in 2001, Statistics Canada (the government office that produces the GDP numbers) shifted to a new method, which does not suffer from this problem. The method requires three steps.

1. The rate of change of real GDP from each year to the next is computed using as the common set of prices the average of the prices for the two years. For example, the rate of change of real GDP from 1998 to 1999 is computed by constructing real GDP for 1998 and real GDP for 1999 using as the common set of prices the average of the prices for 1998 and 1999 and then computing the rate of change from 1998 to 1999.

2. An index for the level of real GDP is then constructed by linking—or chaining—the constructed rates of change for each year. The index is set equal to 1 in some arbitrary year. Right now, the year is 1997. Given that the constructed rate of growth for 1998 by Statistics Canada is 2.3%, the index for 1998 equals

(1 + 2.3%) = 1.023. The index for 1999 is obtained by multiplying the index for 1998 by the rate of growth from 1998 to 1999, and so on.

3. Finally, this index is multiplied by nominal GDP in 1997 to give real GDP in chained (1997) dollars. As the index is 1 in 1997, this implies that real GDP in 1997 equals nominal GDP in 1997. *Chained* refers to the chaining of rates of change described above. (*1997*) refers to the year where, by construction, real GDP is equal to nominal GDP.

This index is more complicated to construct than the indexes used before 2001. But it is clearly better. The prices used to evaluate real GDP in two adjacent years are the right prices, namely, the average prices for those two years. And because the rate of growth from one year to the next is constructed using the average prices in those two years rather than the set of prices in an arbitrary base year, history will not be rewritten every five years or so, as it used to be under the previous method for constructing real GDP: when the base year was changed all past growth rates were recomputed.

Figure 2A–1 presents growth rates of real GDP in Canada from 1982 to 2001. One set of growth rates is calculated using chained measures of real output and the other using 1997 constant dollars, that is, real GDP constructed in the less complicated manner. There is almost no difference between these two measures. Statistics Canada only constructed chained measures of real GDP back to 1981. Earlier measures of real GDP are not chained. A third measure of the growth rate of real GDP, which uses 1992 prices, shows slower growth after 1997.

FIGURE 2A–1

Comparing the Growth Rate of Real GDP: Chained and Nonchained Measures

The figure shows that the growth rate of real GDP is very similar whether a chained measure of real GDP is used or the more traditional base-year measure is used. The further back in time the base year, the greater is the variation. Growth in real GDP using 1992 prices is slower than growth in real GDP using 1997 prices after 1997.

Source: Gross domestic product, chained 1997 dollars, using CANSIM II variable V3860085; gross domestic product, 1997 constant prices, using CANSIM II variable V3862685; gross domestic product, 1992, constant prices, using CANSIM II variable V646962.

THE CORE: THE SHORT RUN

In the short run, demand determines output. Many factors affect demand, from consumer confidence to fiscal and monetary policies.

CHAPTER 3

Chapter 3 looks at equilibrium in the goods market and the determination of output. It focuses on the interaction among demand, production, and income. It shows how fiscal policy can be used to affect output.

CHAPTER 4

Chapter 4 looks at equilibrium in financial markets and the determination of the interest rate. Monetary policy affects the interest rate.

CHAPTER 5

Chapter 5 looks at the goods and financial markets together. It shows what determines output and the interest rate in the short run. The model developed in Chapter 5 is called the *IS-LM* model and is one of the workhorses of macroeconomics.

CHAPTER 6

Chapter 6 discusses the implications of openness in goods and financial markets. An important determinant of the choice between domestic and foreign goods is the real exchange rate—the relative price of foreign goods in terms of domestic goods. Openness in financial markets allows people to choose between domestic and foreign assets. This imposes a tight relation, the interest parity condition, among the exchange rates, current and expected, and domestic and foreign interest rates.

CHAPTER 7

Chapter 7 focuses on goods market equilibrium in an open economy. It shows how fiscal policy affects both output and the trade balance and discusses conditions under which a real depreciation improves the trade balance.

CHAPTER 8

Chapter 8 characterizes goods and financial market equilibrium in an open economy; the open economy version of the *IS-LM* model from Chapter 5. Under flexible exchange rates, monetary policy affects output not only through its effect on the interest rate but also through the exchange rate. Fixing the exchange rate implies giving up the ability to change the interest rate.

CHAPTER 3
THE GOODS MARKET

When economists think about year-to-year movements in economic activity, they focus on the interaction among *production*, *income*, and *demand*. Changes in the demand for goods lead to changes in production. Changes in production lead to changes in income. And changes in income lead to changes in the demand for goods. This interaction is summarized in Figure 3–1.

This chapter looks at this interaction and its implications.

FIGURE 3–1

Production, Income, and the Demand for Goods

3-1 | The Composition of GDP

Purchases of machines by firms, food by consumers, or new executive jets by the federal government depend on different factors. If we are to think about what determines the demand for goods, it makes sense to decompose aggregate production (GDP) from the point of view of the different goods being produced and the different buyers for these goods. The decomposition of GDP typically used by macroeconomists is given in Table 3–1. (A more detailed version for the year 2005, with more formal definitions, is given in Appendix 1 at the end of the book.)

"Output" and "production" are synonymous. There is no rule for using one or the other; use the one that sounds better.

- The first component of GDP is **consumption**, (C). These are the goods and services purchased by consumers, ranging from food to airline tickets, to vacations, to new cars, and so on. Consumption is by far the largest component of GDP, accounting for 56% of GDP in 2005.

- **Investment** (I) is sometimes called **fixed investment** to distinguish it from inventory investment. Investment is the sum of **nonresidential investment**, the purchase by firms of new plants or new machines (from turbines to computers), and **residential investment**, the purchase by people of new houses or apartments.

    The two types of investment (residential and nonresidential) and the decisions behind them have more in common than might first appear. Firms buy machines or plants to be able to produce more output in the future. People buy houses or apartments to get *housing services* in the future. This is the justification for lumping both under "investment." Together, the two components of investment accounted for 18% of GDP in 2005.

- **Government spending**, (G), represents the purchases of goods and services by the federal, provincial, and local governments. The goods range from airplanes to office equipment. The services include services provided by government employees. In effect, the national income accounts treat government as buying the services provided by government employees—and then providing these services to the public, free of charge.

    Note that G does not include **government transfers**, such as Employment Insurance or Old Age Security, or interest payments on the government debt. Although these are clearly government expenditures, they are not purchases of goods and services. That is why the figure for government spending on goods and services in Table 3–1, 22% of GDP, is smaller than the figure for total government spending, including transfers and interest payments. That figure, in 2005, was about 36% of GDP.

Warning! To the person on the street or the financial press, "investment" refers to the purchase of any asset, such as gold or shares of General Motors. Economists use "investment" to refer to the purchase of *new capital goods*, such as machines, buildings, or houses. When referring to the purchase of financial assets, economists say "financial investment."

| TABLE 3–1 | The Composition of Canadian GDP, 2005 |

		Billions of Dollars		Percent of GDP	
	GDP (Y)	1369		100	
1	Consumption (C)	762		56	
2	Investment (I)	225		18	
	Nonresidential		155		11
	Residential		90		7
3	Government spending (G)	298		22	
4	Net exports	+55		+4	
	Exports (X)		519		38
	Imports (Q)		−464		−34
5	Inventory investment (I_S)	+9		0	

Source: Statistics Canada, CANSIM II, Table 380-0017.

- The sum of lines 1, 2, and 3 gives the purchases of goods and services by consumers, firms, and government. To get to the purchases of goods and services, we must take two more steps.

  First, we must subtract **imports** (Q), the purchases of foreign goods and services by consumers, firms, and government. Second, we must add **exports** (X), the purchases of Canadian goods and services by foreigners.

  The difference between exports and imports, ($X - Q$), is called **net exports**, or the **trade balance**. If exports exceed imports, a country is said to run a **trade surplus**. If exports are less than imports, the country is said to run a **trade deficit**. In 2005, exports accounted for 38% of GDP. Imports were equal to 34% of GDP, so Canada was running a trade surplus of 4% of GDP.

- The sum of lines 1 through 4 gives the purchases (equivalently, the sales) of Canadian goods and services in 2005. To get to production in 2005, we need one last step. Some of the goods produced in a given year are not sold in that year but sold in later years. And some of the goods sold in a given year may have been produced in an earlier year. The difference between goods produced and goods sold in a given year—equivalently, between production and sales—is called **inventory investment** and is denoted I_S (subscript S for **stocks** of goods, another term for inventories). If production exceeds sales, firms accumulate inventories. Inventory investment is positive. If production is less than sales, firms decrease inventories. Inventory investment is negative. Inventory investment is typically small—positive in some years, negative in others. In 2005, inventory investment was positive, but not even one full percent of GDP.

With this decomposition of GDP, we can now turn to our first model of output determination. The first step is to think about what determines the demand for goods.

3-2 | The Demand for Goods

Denote the total demand for goods by Z. Using the decomposition of GDP we just saw in section 3-1, we can write Z as:

$$Z \equiv C + I + G + X - Q$$

Note that this equation is an **identity** (which is why it is written using the symbol " $\equiv$ " rather than an equal sign). It defines Z as the the sum of consumption, plus investment, plus government spending, plus exports, minus imports.

Assume now that all firms produce the same good, which can be used by consumers for consumption, by firms for investment, or by government. With this simplification, we need to look at only one market—the market for "the" good (thus the title of the chapter, "The Goods Market" rather than "The Goods Markets")—and think about what determines supply and demand in that market.

Assume further that firms are willing to supply any amount of the good at a given price, P. In other words, assume that the supply of goods is completely elastic at price P. This assumption will allow us to focus on the role of demand in the determination of output. As we shall see later in the book, this assumption is valid only in the short run. When we move to the study of the medium run (starting in Chapter 9), we will need to give up this assumption.

Assume finally that the economy is *closed*, that it does not trade with the rest of the world: Both exports and imports are equal to zero. The assumption is clearly counterfactual: Modern economies trade with the rest of the world. Later (starting in Chapter 6), we will abandon this assumption and look at what happens when the economy is open. But, for the moment, this assumption will simplify things: We will not have to think about what determines exports and imports.

Exports−imports ≡ net exports ≡ trade balance

Exports > imports ⇔ trade surplus

Exports < imports ⇔ trade deficit

Production − sales = inventory investment

A model nearly always starts with the word "assume" (or "suppose"). This is an indication that reality is about to be simplified in order to focus on the issue at hand.

Under this last assumption, $X = Q = 0$, and the demand for goods Z is the sum of consumption, investment, and government spending:

$$Z \equiv C + I + G$$

Let us discuss each of these three components in turn.

Consumption (C)

The main determinant of consumption is surely income, or more precisely **disposable income**, the income that remains once consumers have received transfers from government and paid their taxes. When their disposable income goes up, people buy more goods; when it goes down, they buy fewer goods. Other variables affect consumption, but for the moment we will ignore them.

Let C denote consumption, and Y_D denote disposable income. We can write:

$$C = C(Y_D)$$
$$(+)$$

This is just a formal way of stating that consumption is a function of disposable income. The function $C(Y_D)$ is called the **consumption function**. The positive sign below Y_D reflects the fact that when disposable income increases, so does consumption. Economists call such an equation a **behavioural equation**, to indicate that the equation reflects some aspect of behaviour—in this case, the behaviour of consumers.

We will use functions in this book as a simple but formal way of representing relations between variables. What you need to know about functions—which is very little—is described in Appendix 2 at the end of the book. This appendix develops the mathematics you need to go through this book. Do not worry: We will always describe a function in words when we introduce it for the first time.

It is often useful to be more specific about the form of the function. Here is such a case. It is reasonable to assume that the relation between consumption and disposable income is given by:

$$C = c_0 + c_1 Y_D \tag{3.1}$$

In words: It is reasonable to assume that the function is a **linear relation.** The relation between consumption and disposable income is then characterized by two **parameters**, c_0 and c_1.

The parameter c_1 is called the **propensity to consume**. (It is also called the *marginal propensity to consume*. We will drop "marginal" for simplicity.) It gives the effect of an additional dollar of disposable income on consumption. If c_1 is equal to 0.6, then an additional dollar of income increases consumption by $\$1 \times 0.6 = 60$ cents. A natural restriction on c_1 is that it be positive: An increase in disposable income is likely to lead to an increase in consumption. Another natural restriction is that c_1 be less than 1: People are likely to consume only part of any increase in income and to save the rest.

The parameter c_0 has a simple, literal interpretation. It is what people would consume if their disposable income in the current year were equal to zero: If Y_D equals zero in equation (3.1), $C = c_0$. A natural restriction is that if current income is equal to zero, consumption is still positive: People must eat! This implies that c_0 is positive. How can people have positive consumption if their income is equal to zero? The answer is by dissaving—by selling some of their assets or by borrowing.

The relation between consumption and disposable income implied by equation (3.1) is drawn in Figure 3–2. Because it is a linear relation, it is represented by a straight line. Its intercept with the vertical axis is c_0; its slope is c_1. Because c_1 is less than 1, the slope of the line is less than 1: The line is flatter than a 45-degree line. (A refresher on graphs, slopes, and intercepts is also given in Appendix 2.)

FIGURE 3-2

Consumption and Disposable Income

Consumption increases with disposable income, but less than one for one.

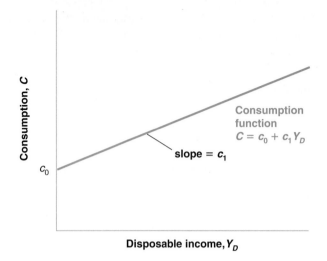

Consumption, C

c_0

slope = c_1

Consumption function
$C = c_0 + c_1 Y_D$

Disposable income, Y_D

Next, we need to define disposable income. Disposable income is given by:

$$Y_D \equiv Y - T$$

where Y is income and T is taxes paid minus government transfers received by consumers. This equation is an identity; thus the use of the symbol " $\equiv$ ". For short, we will refer to T simply as taxes—but remember that it is equal to taxes minus transfers.

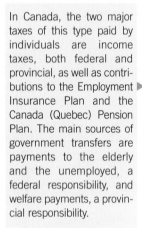

In Canada, the two major taxes of this type paid by individuals are income taxes, both federal and provincial, as well as contributions to the Employment Insurance Plan and the Canada (Quebec) Pension Plan. The main sources of government transfers are payments to the elderly and the unemployed, a federal responsibility, and welfare payments, a provincial responsibility.

Replacing Y_D in equation (3.1) gives:

$$C = c_0 + c_1(Y - T) \tag{3.2}$$

Consumption is a function of income and taxes. Higher income increases consumption, although less than one for one. Higher taxes decrease consumption, also less than one for one.

Investment (*I*)

Two types of variables:

Endogenous variables— explained by the model

Exogenous variables— taken as a given

Models have two types of variables. Some variables depend on other variables in the model and are therefore explained within the model. Such variables are called **endogenous**. This is the case for consumption here. Other variables are not explained within the model but are instead taken as a given. Such variables are called **exogenous**. This is how we will treat investment here. We will take investment as a given, and write:

$$I = \bar{I} \tag{3.3}$$

Putting a bar on investment is a simple typographical way to remind us that we take investment as a given.

The reason for taking investment as a given is to keep our model simple. But the assumption is not innocuous. It implies that when we look at the effects of changes in production later, we will do so under the assumption that investment does not respond to such changes in production. It is not hard to see that this implication may be quite bad as a description of reality: Firms that experience an increase in production may decide that they need more machines and increase their investment. We will leave this mechanism out of the model here, but we will introduce a more realistic treatment of investment in Chapter 5.

Government Spending (*G*)

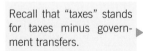

Recall that "taxes" stands for taxes minus government transfers.

The third component of demand in our model is government spending, G. Together with taxes T, G describes **fiscal policy**—the choice of taxes and spending by government. Just as we just did for investment, we will take G and T as exogenous. But the rationale for this assumption is different from that for investment. It is based on two considerations.

First, governments do not behave with the same regularity as do consumers or firms, and so there is no reliable rule we could write for G or T corresponding to the rule we wrote for consumption. This consideration is not fully convincing, however. Even if governments do not follow simple behavioural rules as consumers do, a good part of their behaviour is predictable. We will look at these issues later, in particular in Chapters 25 to 27, but we leave them aside until then.

Second, and more importantly, one of the tasks of macroeconomists is to advise governments on spending and tax decisions. That means we do not want to look at a model in which we have already assumed something about their behaviour. We want to be able to say, "If you were to choose these values for G and T, this is what would happen." The approach in this book will typically treat G and T as variables chosen by government and not try to explain them within the model.

Because we will (nearly always) take G and T as exogenous, we will not use a bar to denote their value. This will keep the notation lighter.

3-3 | The Determination of Equilibrium Output

Let us collect the pieces we have introduced so far. Assuming that exports and imports are both zero, the demand for goods is the sum of consumption, investment, and government spending:

$$Z \equiv C + I + G$$

If we replace C and I from equations (3.2) and (3.3), we get:

$$Z = c_0 + c_1(Y - T) + \bar{I} + G \tag{3.4}$$

The demand for goods (Z) depends on income (Y), taxes (T), investment ($\bar{I}$), and government spending (G).

Let us now turn to **equilibrium** in the goods market. Assume that firms do not hold inventories so that the supply of goods is equal to production Y. Then, **equilibrium in the goods market** requires that the supply of goods (Y) equals the demand for goods (Z):

$$Y = Z \tag{3.5}$$

This equation is called an **equilibrium condition**. Models include three types of equations: identities, behavioural equations, and equilibrium conditions. We now have seen examples of each: The equation defining disposable income is an identity, the consumption function is a behavioural equation, and the condition that supply equals demand is an equilibrium condition.

Replacing demand (Z) using equation (3.4) gives:

$$Y = c_0 + c_1(Y - T) + \bar{I} + G \tag{3.6}$$

Equation (3.6) represents algebraically what we described informally at the beginning of this chapter. Production, Y, (the left side of the equation) must be equal to demand (the right side). And demand, in turn, depends on income, Y. Note that we are using the same symbol Y for production and income. This is no accident! As we saw in Chapter 2, production and income are identically equal: They are the two ways of looking at GDP—one from the production side, the other from the income side.

Having constructed a model, we can solve it to look at what determines the level of output, how output changes in response to, say, a change in government spending. Solving a model means not only solving it algebraically but also understanding why the results are what they are. In this book, solving a model will also mean characterizing the results using graphs—sometimes skipping the algebra altogether—and describing the results and the mechanisms in words. Macroeconomists always use these three tools:

1. Algebra to make sure that the logic is right
2. Graphs to build the intuition
3. Words to explain the results

Make it a habit to do the same.

If firms hold inventories, then the supply of goods need not equal production all the time: Firms can supply more than they produce by decreasing their inventories. Conversely, firms can increase inventories by producing more than they supply. It is easier to start thinking about the equilibrium by ignoring this possibility. (Think of an economy that produces only haircuts. There cannot be inventories of haircuts— haircuts produced but not sold? Equilibrium requires that production of haircuts be equal to demand for haircuts.)

Three types of equations:
  identities
  behavioural equations
  equilibrium conditions

See Figure 3–1: Demand determines production (the equilibrium condition). Production is equal to income. And income determines demand (equation [3.4]).

Using Algebra

Rewrite the equilibrium equation (3.6):

$$Y = c_0 + c_1 Y - c_1 T + \bar{I} + G$$

Move $c_1 Y$ to the left side and reorganize the right and the left sides:

$$(1 - c_1)Y = c_0 + \bar{I} + G - c_1 T$$

Divide both sides by $(1 - c_1)$:

$$Y = \frac{1}{1 - c_1}[c_0 + \bar{I} + G - c_1 T] \qquad (3.7)$$

Autonomous means independent—in this case, ▶ independent of output.

If $T = G$

$G - c_1 T = G - c_1 G$
$\qquad\quad = G(1 - c_1)$
$\qquad\quad > 0$ if $c_1 < 1$

Equation (3.7) characterizes equilibrium output, the level of output such that supply equals demand. Let us look at both terms on the right, beginning with the second one.

The second term, $[c_0 + \bar{I} + G - c_1 T]$, is that part of the demand for goods that does not depend on output. This term is called **autonomous spending**. Can we be sure that autonomous spending is positive? We cannot, but it is very likely to be. The first two terms in brackets, c_0 and $\bar{I}$, are positive. What about the last two, $G - c_1 T$? Suppose that government is running a **balanced budget**—taxes equal government spending. If $T = G$, and the propensity to consume (c_1) is less than 1 (as we have assumed), then ($G - c_1 T$) is positive and so is autonomous spending. Only if government ran a very large budget surplus—if taxes were much larger than government spending—could autonomous spending be negative. We can safely ignore that case here.

Turn to the first term, $1/(1 - c_1)$. Because the propensity to consume (c_1) is between 0 and 1, $1/(1 - c_1)$ is a number greater than 1. This number, which multiplies autonomous spending, is called the **multiplier**. The closer c_1 is to 1, the larger is the multiplier.

What does the multiplier imply? Suppose that for a given level of income, consumers decide to consume more. More precisely, assume that c_0 in equation (3.2) increases by $1 billion. Equation (3.7) tells us that output will increase by more than $1 billion. For example, if c_1 equals 0.6, the multiplier equals $1/(1 - 0.6) = 2.5$ so that output increases by $2.5 \times$ $1 billion = $2.5 billion. We have looked here at an increase in consumption, but clearly, any increase in autonomous spending—from an increase in investment to an increase in government spending to a reduction in taxes—will have the same qualitative effect: It will increase output by more than its direct effect on autonomous spending.

Where does the multiplier effect come from? Looking back at equation (3.6) gives the beginning of a clue. An increase in c_0 increases demand. The increase in demand then leads to an increase in production and income. But the increase in income further increases consumption, which further increases demand, and so on. The best way to strengthen this intuition is to use a graphical approach.

Using a Graph

Equilibrium requires that the production of goods (Y) equals the demand for goods (Z). Figure 3–3 plots both production and demand as functions of income; the equilibrium is the point at which production and demand are equal.

First, look at the plot of production as a function of income. Production is measured on the vertical axis, and income is measured on the horizontal axis. Plotting production as a function of income is straightforward, as production and income are always equal. Thus, the relation between the two is simply the 45-degree line, the line with a slope equal to 1, in Figure 3–3.

Second, look at the plot of demand as a function of income. The relation between demand and income is given by equation (3.4). Let us rewrite it here for convenience, regrouping the terms for autonomous spending together in the term in parentheses:

$$Z = (c_0 + \bar{I} + G - c_1 T) + c_1 Y$$

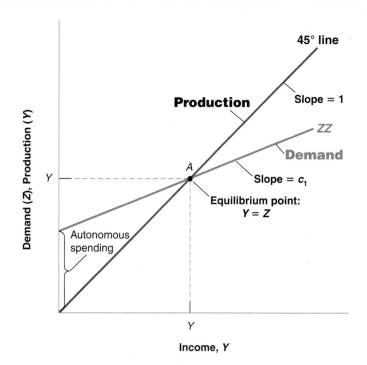

FIGURE 3-3

Equilibrium in the Goods Market

Equilibrium output is determined by the condition that production be equal to demand.

Demand depends on autonomous spending and on income—through its effect on consumption. The relation between demand and income is drawn as ZZ in the figure. The intercept with the vertical axis—the value of demand when income is equal to zero—equals autonomous spending. The slope of the line is the propensity to consume, c_1: When income increases by 1, demand increases by c_1. Under the restriction that c_1 is positive but less than 1, the line is upward sloping but with slope less than 1.

Equilibrium holds when production equals demand. Thus, equilibrium output, Y, is given by the intersection, at point A, of the 45-degree line and the demand relation, ZZ. To the left of A, demand exceeds production; to the right, production exceeds demand. Only at A are the two equal.

Now, return to the example we looked at earlier. Suppose that c_0 increases by $1 billion. At the initial level of income (the level of income associated with point A), consumers increase their consumption by $1 billion. What happens then is shown in Figure 3–4, which builds on Figure 3–3.

For any value of income, demand is higher by $1 billion. Before the increase in c_0, the relation between demand and income was given by the line ZZ. After the increase in c_0 by $1 billion, the relation between demand and income is given by the line ZZ', which is parallel to ZZ but higher by $1 billion. In other words, the demand relation shifts up by $1 billion. The new equilibrium is at the intersection of the 45-degree line and the new demand relation, at point A'. Equilibrium output increases from Y to Y'. It is clear that the increase in output, $(Y' - Y)$, which we can measure either on the horizontal or the vertical axis, is larger than the initial increase in consumption of $1 billion. This is the multiplier effect.

With the help of the graph, it becomes easier to tell how and why the economy moves from A to A'. The initial increase in consumption leads to an increase in demand of $1 billion. At the initial level of income, Y, the level of demand is now given by point B: Demand is $1 billion higher. To satisfy this higher level of demand, firms increase production by $1 billion. The economy moves to point C, with both demand and production higher by $1 billion. But this is not the end of the story. The higher level of production leads to an increase in income of $1 billion and to a further increase in demand so that demand is now given by point

The distance between Y and Y' on the horizontal axis is larger than the distance between A and B— which is equal to $1 billion.

FIGURE   3–4

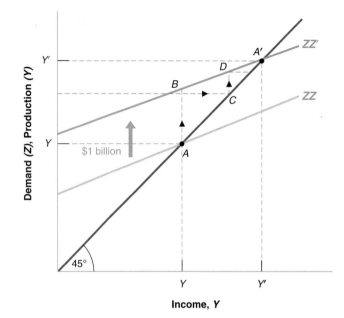

The Effects of an Increase in Autonomous Spending on Output

An increase in autonomous spending has a more than one-for-one effect on equilibrium output.

D. Point D leads to a higher level of production, and so on, until the economy is at A', where production and demand are again equal, and which is therefore the new equilibrium.

We can pursue this line of thought a bit more, and this will give us another way of thinking about the multiplier. The first-round increase in production (the distance AB in Figure 3–4) equals $1 billion. The second-round increase in production (the distance CD), in turn, equals $1 billion (the increase in income in the first round) times the marginal propensity to consume out of income, c_1—hence, $\$c_1$ billion. Following the same logic, the third-round increase in production equals $\$c_1$ billion (the increase in income in the second round), times c_1, the marginal propensity to consume out of income; it is thus equal to $\$c_1 \times c_1 = \$c_1^2$ billion. Following this logic, the total increase in production after, say, n rounds equals $1 billion times the sum:

$$1 + c_1 + c_1^2 + \cdots + c_1^n$$

Such a sum is called a **geometric series**. Geometric series will come up often in this book. A refresher on their properties is given in Appendix 2. The main property of such series is that when c_1 is less than one (as it is here) and as n gets larger and larger, the sum keeps increasing but approaches a limit. That limit is $1/(1 - c_1)$, making the eventual increase in output $\$1/(1 - c_1)$ billion.

The expression $1/(1 - c_1)$ should be familiar: It is the multiplier, derived another way. This gives us an equivalent but more intuitive way of thinking about the multiplier. We can think of the original increase in spending as triggering successive increases in production, with each increase in production implying an increase in income, which leads to an increase in demand, which leads to a further increase in production, which leads . . . and so on. The multiplier is the sum of all these successive increases in production.

A trick question: Think about the multiplier as the result of these successive rounds. What would happen in each successive round if c_1, the propensity to consume, was larger than one?

Using Words

How can we summarize our findings in words?

Production depends on demand, which depends on income, which is itself equal to production. An increase in demand, such as an increase in government or in consumer spending, leads to an increase in production and a corresponding increase in income. This increase in income leads to a further increase in demand, which leads to a further increase in production, and so on. The end result is an increase in output that is larger than the initial shift in demand, by a factor equal to the multiplier.

The size of the multiplier is directly related to the value of the propensity to consume: The higher the propensity to consume, the higher is the multiplier. What is the value of the propensity to consume in Canada today? To answer this question, and more generally to estimate behavioural equations and their parameters, economists use **econometrics**, the set of statistical methods used in economics. To give you a sense of what econometrics is and how it is used, Appendix 3 at the end of the book gives you a quick introduction, using as an application the estimation of the propensity to consume. The conclusion from the appendix is that in Canada today, the propensity to consume is around 0.6. An additional dollar of disposable income leads on average to an increase in consumption of 60 cents. This implies a multiplier equal to $1/(1 - c_1) = 1/(1 - 0.6) = 2.5$.[1]

How Long Does It Take for Output to Adjust?

Let us return to our example one last time. Suppose that c_0 increases by \$1 billion. We know that output will increase by an amount equal to the multiplier $1/(1 - c_1)$ times \$1 billion. But how long will it take for output to reach this new higher level?

Under the assumptions we have made so far, the answer is: Right away! In writing the equilibrium condition (3.5), we have assumed that production is always equal to demand—in other words, production responds to demand instantaneously. In writing the consumption function (3.1), we have assumed that consumption responds to disposable income instantaneously. Under these two assumptions, the economy goes instantaneously from point A to point A': The increase in demand leads to an increase in production right away, the increase in income associated with the increase in production leads to an increase in demand right away, and so on. We can think of the adjustment in terms of successive rounds as we did earlier, but all these rounds happen at once.

This instantaneous adjustment does not seem very plausible. And, indeed, it is not. A firm that faces an increase in demand may decide to wait before adjusting its production, drawing down its inventories to satisfy demand. A consumer who gets a raise at work may not adjust her consumption right away. And these delays imply that the adjustment of output will take time.

Describing formally this adjustment of output over time—what economists call the **dynamics** of adjustment—would take us too far. But it is easy to do it in words.

Suppose that firms make decisions about their production level at the beginning of each quarter; once the decision is made, production cannot be adjusted for the rest of the quarter. If purchases are higher than production, firms draw down inventories to satisfy purchases. If purchases are lower than production, firms accumulate inventories.

Now, let us return to our example and suppose that consumers decide to spend more, that they increase c_0. During the quarter in which this happens, demand increases, but—because of our assumption that production was set at the beginning of the quarter—production does not yet change. Therefore, income does not change either. In the following quarter, firms having observed an increase in demand in the previous quarter are likely to set a higher level of production. This increase in production leads to a corresponding increase in income and a further increase in demand. If purchases still exceed production, firms further increase production in the following quarter, and so on. In short, in response to an increase in

---

[1]**DIGGING DEEPER.** In reality, the multiplier is smaller than 2.5, for two reasons.

We have assumed that taxes, T, are a given. But in reality, when income increases, taxes increase. This means disposable income increases less than one for one with income, and this implies that consumption increases less than we have assumed here. (This is explored in more detail in problem 6 at the end of the chapter.)

We have assumed that imports and exports were equal to zero. But in reality, when income increases, some of the increase in demand falls not on domestic goods but on foreign goods. In other words, the demand for domestic goods increases by less than we have assumed here. We will explore this in more detail in Chapter 7.

Canada's last severe recession occurred from 1990 to 1991. Table 1 shows that real GDP fell from $771.8 billion in 1990 Quarter 1 to $745.6 billion in 1991 Quarter 1 before real GDP began to increase. As we saw in Chapter 2, a recession is sometimes defined as two consecutive quarterly decreases in real GDP. This episode had four consecutive quarterly decreases in real GDP.

The second column of Table 1 gives all the values of real GDP from 1989 Quarter 1 to 1991 Quarter 4. Note that GDP is measured at an annual rate so that the numbers are equal to four times their true value for that quarter. Reporting monthly or quarterly values at an annual rate may at first appear confusing. But reporting all variables (whether daily, monthly, or quarterly) at an annual rate—and thus at a common rate—makes comparison among them easier. Thus, in 1990:2, 1990:3, 1990:4, and 1991:1, the change in real GDP is negative.

How bad was this recession? The total reduction in real GDP was $26.2 billion from the 1990:1 peak to the 1991:1 trough. This reduction is calculated at an annual rate. In 1990, there were roughly 28 million Canadians. The income of each Canadian fell by $936 or, for an average family of four, their income fell by $3,744. This is a substantial amount of money for most families.

TABLE	1	Real GDP, 1989–1991
Quarter (1)		**Real GDP (2) (in Billions)**
1989:1		760.0
1989:2		763.6
1989:3		765.2
1989:4		766.3
1990:1		771.8
1990:2		768.5
1990:3		763.6
1990:4		757.2
1991:1		745.6
1991:2		747.8
1991:3		750.4
1991:4		753.2

Column (2)—Real GDP seasonally adjusted at annual rates (SAAR)
Billions of 1997 dollars (chained)
Source: Using CANSIM II variable V498943.

consumer spending, output does not jump to the new equilibrium but rather increases over time from Y to Y'. How long this adjustment takes depends on how and how often firms revise their production schedule. The more often firms adjust their production schedule and the larger the response of production to past increases in purchases, the faster is the adjustment.

We will often do in the book what we just did in the last two paragraphs. Having looked at changes in equilibrium output, we will then describe informally how the economy moves from one equilibrium to the other. This will not only make the description of what happens in the economy feel more realistic, but it will often reinforce our intuition about why the equilibrium changed in the first place.

We have focused in this section on *increases* in demand. But the mechanism is symmetrical: Decreases in demand lead to decreases in output. The In Depth box on this page describes the last recession in Canada. It is important to understand the causes of recessions.

3-4 | Investment Equals Saving: An Alternative Way of Thinking about Goods-Market Equilibrium

Thus far, we have thought about equilibrium in terms of equality between the supply and the demand for goods. An alternative—but equivalent—way of thinking about equilibrium focuses on *investment* and *saving* instead. This is how John Maynard Keynes first articulated this model in 1936, in *The General Theory of Employment, Interest and Money.*

By definition, **private saving** (*S*), saving by consumers, is equal to their disposable income minus their consumption:

$$S \equiv Y_D - C$$

As we grow up, we are told of the virtues of thrift. Those who spend all their income are doomed to end up poor. Those who save are promised a happy life. Similarly, governments tell us, an economy that saves is an economy that will grow strong and prosper! Equation (3.7), however, tells a different and quite surprising story.

Suppose that at a given level of disposable income, consumers decide to save more. In terms of equation (3.2), the equation describing consumption, they decrease c_0, therefore decreasing consumption and increasing saving at a given level of disposable income. What happens to output and to saving?

Equation (3.7) makes it clear that equilibrium output decreases when c_0 decreases. As people save more at their initial level of income, they decrease their consumption. But this decreased consumption decreases demand, which decreases production.

Can we tell what happens to saving? Return to the equation for private saving (by assumption, there is no change in public saving, and so saving and private saving move together):

$$S = -c_0 + (1 - c_1)(Y - T)$$

On the one hand, $-c_0$ is higher: Consumers are saving more at any level of income; this tends to increase saving. But,

on the other hand, Y is lower: This decreases saving. The net effect would seem to be ambiguous. In fact, we can tell which way it goes. Remember that we can think of the equilibrium condition as the condition that saving equals investment, equation (3.8). By assumption, investment does not change. So, the equilibrium condition tells us that in equilibrium, saving does not change either. Although people want to save more at a given level of income, income decreases by an amount such that saving is unchanged. This means that attempts by people to save more lead both to a decline in output and to unchanged saving. This surprising pair of results is known as the **paradox of saving**.

So, should you abandon the old wisdom? Should government tell people to be less thrifty? No. The results of this simple model are of much relevance in the *short run*. But—as we shall see later in this book when we look at the *medium run* and the *long run*—other mechanisms come into play over time and an increase in the saving rate is likely to lead to higher saving and higher income. An important warning remains, however: Policies that encourage saving may be good in the medium and the long run, but may lead to a recession in the short run.

Using the definition of disposable income, we can rewrite private savings as income minus taxes minus consumption:

$$S \equiv Y - T - C$$

Now, return to the equation for equilibrium in the goods market. Production must be equal to demand, which, in turn, is the sum of consumption, investment, and government spending:

$$Y = C + I + G$$

Subtract taxes (T) from both sides and move consumption to the left side:

$$Y - T - C = I + G - T$$

The left side of this equation is simply private saving (S) so that:

$$S = I + G - T$$

Or equivalently,

$$I = S + (T - G) \qquad (3.8)$$

The term on the left is investment. The first term on the right is *private saving*. The second term is **public saving**—taxes minus government spending.

Equation (3.8) thus gives us another way of looking at equilibrium in the goods market. Equilibrium in the goods market requires that investment equals **saving**—the sum of private and public saving. This way of looking at equilibrium explains why the equilibrium condition for the goods market is called the **IS relation**, for "**I**nvestment equals **S**aving." What firms want to invest must be equal to what people and the government want to save.

> If taxes exceed government spending, the government is running a budget surplus—public saving is positive. If taxes are less than government spending, the government is running a budget deficit—public saving is negative.

The two equivalent ways of stating the condition for equilibrium in the goods market:

Supply of goods
= demand for goods ▶

Investment = Saving

To strengthen your intuition for equation (3.8), think of an economy where there is only one person who has to decide how much to consume, invest, and save—a "Robinson Crusoe" economy. For Robinson Crusoe, the saving and the investment decisions are one and the same: What he invests (say, by keeping rabbits for reproduction rather than eating them), he automatically saves. In a modern economy, however, investment decisions are made by firms, whereas saving decisions are made by consumers and the government. In equilibrium, equation (3.8) tells us all those decisions have to be consistent: Investment must be equal to saving.

We can study the characteristics of the equilibrium using equation (3.8) and the behavioural equations for saving and investment. Note first that *consumption and saving decisions are one and the same*: Given their disposable income, once consumers have chosen consumption, their saving is determined, and vice versa. The way we specified consumption behaviour implies that private saving is given by:

$$S = Y - T - C$$
$$= Y - T - c_0 - c_1(Y - T)$$

Rearranging, we get:

$$S = -c_0 + (1 - c_1)(Y - T)$$

In the same way that we called c_1 the propensity to consume, we can call $(1 - c_1)$ the **propensity to save**. The propensity to save tells us how much people save out of an additional unit of income. The assumption we made earlier that the propensity to consume (c_1) is between zero and one implies that the propensity to save $(1 - c_1)$ is also between zero and one. Private saving increases with disposable income but by less than one dollar for each additional dollar of disposable income.

In equilibrium, investment must be equal to savings, the sum of private and public saving. Replacing private saving in equation (3.8) by its expression from above,

$$I = -c_0 + (1 - c_1)(Y - T) + (T - G)$$

Solving for output,

$$Y = \frac{1}{1 - c_1} [c_0 + \bar{I} + G - c_1 T]$$

This is exactly the same expression as equation (3.7) earlier. This should come as no surprise. We are looking at the same model, just in a different way. This alternative way will prove useful in various applications later in the book. Such an application is given in the Focus box, "The Paradox of Saving" on page 55.

3-5 | Is Government Omnipotent? A Warning

Equation (3.7) implies that government, by choosing the level of spending (G) or the level of taxes (T), can choose the level of output it wants. If it wants output to increase by, say, $1 billion, all it needs to do is to increase G by $(1 - c_1)$ billion; this increase in government spending, in theory, will lead to an output increase of $(1 - c_1)$ billion times the multiplier $1/(1 - c_1)$, thus $1 billion.

Can governments really choose the level of output they want? The existence of recessions makes clear the answer is no. There are many aspects of reality that we have not yet incorporated in our model. We will do so in due time. But it is useful to list them in brief here:

You may want to have a glimpse at the longer list given in the Focus box ▶ "Fiscal Policy: What Have We Learned and Where?" in Chapter 26.

- The effects of spending and taxes on demand are much less mechanical than equation (3.7) makes them appear. They may happen slowly, consumers and firms may be scared of the budget deficit and change their behaviour, and so on (Chapters 5 and 21).

- Maintaining a desired level of output may come with unpleasant side effects. Trying to achieve too high a level of output may, for example, lead to accelerating inflation and may become unsustainable in the medium run (Chapters 11 and 12).
- Cutting taxes or increasing government spending may lead to large budget deficits and an accumulation of public debt. Such debt will have adverse implications in the long run (Chapters 17 and 26).

As we refine our analysis, the role of government in general and the successful use of fiscal policy in particular will become increasingly difficult. Governments will never again have it so good as in this chapter.

SUMMARY

What you should remember about the components of GDP:

- GDP is the sum of consumption, plus investment, plus government spending, plus exports, minus imports, plus inventory investment.
- Consumption (C) is the purchase of goods and services by consumers. Consumption is the largest component of demand.
- Investment (I) is the sum of nonresidential investment—the purchase of new plants and new machines by firms—and of residential investment—the purchase of new houses or apartments by people.
- Government spending (G) is the purchase of goods and services by federal, provincial, and local governments.
- Exports (X) are purchases of Canadian goods by foreigners. Imports (Q) are purchases of foreign goods by Canadian consumers, Canadian firms, and the Canadian government.
- Inventory investment (I_S) is the difference between production and purchases. It can be positive or negative.

What you should remember about our first model of output determination:

- In the short run, demand determines production. Production is equal to income. And income determines demand.
- The consumption function shows how consumption depends on disposable income. The propensity to consume describes how much consumption increases for a given increase in disposable income.
- Equilibrium output is the point at which supply (production) equals demand. In equilibrium, output equals autonomous spending times the multiplier. Autonomous spending is that part of demand that does not depend on income. The multiplier is equal to $1/(1 - c_1)$, where c_1 is the propensity to consume.
- Increases in consumer confidence, in investment demand, or in government spending or decreases in taxes all increase equilibrium output in the short run.
- An alternative way of stating the goods-market equilibrium condition is that investment must be equal to saving, the sum of private and public saving. For this reason, the equilibrium condition is called the *IS* relation (*I* for investment, *S* for saving).

KEY TERMS

QUESTIONS AND PROBLEMS

An asterisk denotes a harder question. [Web] indicates that the question requires access to the Internet.

1. TRUE/FALSE/UNCERTAIN

a. The largest component of GDP is consumption.

b. Government spending, including transfers, was equal to 22% of GDP in 2005.

c. The propensity to consume has to be positive, but beyond that it can take on any positive value.

d. Fiscal policy describes the choice of government spending and taxes and is treated as exogenous in our goods-market model.

e. The equilibrium condition for the goods market states that consumption equals output.

f. An increase of one unit in government spending leads to an increase of one unit in equilibrium output.

2. A SIMPLE ECONOMY

Suppose that the economy is characterized by the following behavioural equations:

$$C = 160 + 0.6Y_D$$
$$\bar{I} = 150$$
$$G = 150$$
$$T = 100$$

Solve for

a. equilibrium GDP (Y).

b. disposable income (Y_D).

c. consumption spending (C).

3. THE CONCEPT OF EQUILIBRIUM

For the economy in question 2,

a. Assume output is equal to 900. Compute total demand. Is it equal to production? Explain.

b. Assume output is equal to 1000. Compute total demand. Is it equal to production? Explain.

c. Assume output is equal to 1000. Compute private saving. Is it equal to investment? Explain.

4. USING THE MULTIPLIER

a. Consider a decline in real GDP of 2%. For the simple economy in question 2, how many units of real GDP equal 2% of equilibrium GDP?

b. If the 2% decline in real GDP were caused by a reduction in $\bar{I}$, how many units would $\bar{I}$ fall?

c. If the government wanted to return real GDP to its equilibrium level after the fall in $\bar{I}$, would it increase or decrease G? By how many units would it increase or decrease G?

5. THE BALANCED BUDGET MULTIPLIER

For both political and macroeconomic reasons, governments are often reluctant to run budget deficits. Here, we examine whether policy changes in G and T that maintain a balanced budget are macroeconomically neutral. Put another way, we examine whether it is possible to affect output through changes in G and T so that the government budget remains balanced. Start with equation (3.7).

a. By how much does Y increase when G increases by one unit?

b. By how much does Y decrease when T increases by one unit?

c. Why are your answers to (a) and (b) different?

Suppose that the economy starts with a balanced budget: $T = G$. If the increase in G is equal to the increase in

T, then the budget remains in balance. Let us now compute the balanced budget multiplier.

d. Suppose that both G and T increase by exactly one unit. Using your answers to parts (a) and (b), what is the change in equilibrium GDP? Are balanced budget changes in G and T macroeconomically neutral?

*e. How does the propensity to consume affect your answer? Why?

*6. AUTOMATIC STABILIZERS

So far in this chapter, we have been assuming that the fiscal policy variable T is independent of the level of income. In the real world, however, this is not the case. Taxes typically depend on the level of income, and so tax revenue tends to be higher when income is higher. In this problem, we examine how this automatic response of taxes can help reduce the impact of changes in autonomous spending on output.

Consider the following model of the economy:

$$C = c_0 + c_1 Y_D$$
$$T = t_0 + t_1 Y$$
$$Y_D = Y - T$$

G and $\overline{T}$ are both constant.

a. Is t_1 greater or less than one? Explain.

b. Solve for equilibrium output.

c. What is the multiplier? Does the economy respond more to changes in autonomous spending when t_1 is zero or when t_1 is positive? Explain.

d. Why is fiscal policy in this case called an "automatic stabilizer"?

*7. BALANCED BUDGET VERSUS AUTOMATIC STABILIZERS

It is often argued that a balanced budget amendment would actually be destabilizing. To understand this argument, consider the economy of question 6.

a. Solve for equilibrium output.

b. Solve for taxes in equilibrium.

Suppose that the government starts with a balanced budget and that there is a drop in c_0.

c. What happens to Y? What happens to taxes?

d. Suppose that government cuts spending in order to keep the budget balanced. What will be the effect on Y? Does the cut in spending required to balance the budget counteract or reinforce the effect of the drop in c_0 on output? (Do not do the algebra. Give the answer in words.)

CHAPTER 4
FINANCIAL MARKETS

The **Bank of Canada**, the Canadian central bank, operates monetary policy. About every six weeks, the Bank announces whether interest rates will increase, decrease, or stay the same. The model of economic activity we developed in Chapter 3 did not include interest rates. This was a strong simplification, and it is time to relax it. This requires that we take two steps. First, we must look at what determines interest rates and the role of the Bank of Canada in this determination. This is the topic of this chapter. Second, we must look at how interest rates affect economic activity. This is the topic of the next chapter.

To understand what determines interest rates, we must look at **financial markets.** The task appears daunting: In modern economies, there are thousands of financial assets and thousands of interest rates—interest rates on short-term bonds, on long-term bonds, on government bonds, on corporate bonds, and so on. To make progress, we must simplify. Just as we assumed, in looking at the goods market in Chapter 3, that there was only one type of good, we assume in this chapter that there is just one type of bond, and therefore just one interest rate. We can then think about the determinants of *the* interest rate. As we shall see, one way to solve this problem is to have the interest rate determined by the condition that the demand for money is equal to the supply of money. And because the central bank can change the supply of money, monetary policy has a direct effect on the interest rate.

The chapter has three sections. Section 4-1 looks at the demand for money. Section 4-2 looks at the determination of the interest rate under the assumption that the supply of money is directly under the control of the central bank. Section 4-3 (which is optional) introduces banks as suppliers of money and revisits the determination of the interest rate and the role of the central bank.

Before we start, a warning: Discussions of financial markets and financial issues are fraught with semantic traps. Such words as "money" or "wealth" have very specific meanings in economics, and these are often not the same meanings as in everyday conversations. The purpose of the Focus box "Semantic Traps: Money, Income, and Wealth" is to help you avoid some of these traps. Read it carefully, and come back to it once in a while.

Semantic Traps: Money, Income, and Wealth

In everyday life, we use the word "money" to denote many things. We use it as a synonym for income: "making money." We use it as a synonym for wealth: "She has a lot of money." In economics, you must be more careful. Here is a basic guide to some terms and their precise meanings.

Income is what you earn from working plus what you receive in interest and dividends. It is a **flow**—that is, it is expressed per unit of time: weekly income, monthly income, or yearly income. J. Paul Getty was once asked what his income was. Getty answered, "$1000." He meant but did not say: per minute.

Saving is that part of after-tax income that is not spent. It is also a flow. If you save 10% of income and your income is $3000 per month, then you save $300 per month. **Savings** (plural) is sometimes used as a synonym for wealth—the value of what you have accumulated over time. To avoid potential confusion, we will not use it in the book.

Your **financial wealth**, or simply **wealth**, is the value of all your financial assets minus all your financial liabilities. In contrast to income or saving, which are flow variables, financial wealth is a **stock** variable. It is the value of wealth at a given moment of time. At a given moment of time, you cannot change the total amount of your financial wealth. You can do this only over time, as you save or dissave, or as the value of your assets

change. But you can change the composition of your wealth; you can, for example, decide to pay back part of your mortgage by writing a cheque on your chequing account. This leads to a decrease in your liabilities (a smaller mortgage) and a corresponding decrease in your assets (a smaller chequing account balance); but it does not change your wealth.

Financial assets that can be used directly to buy goods are called money. Money includes currency and chequable deposits, deposits against which you can write cheques. Money is also a stock. Someone can have a large wealth but small money holdings, for example, $1,000,000 worth of stocks but only $500 in his chequing account. Or someone can have a large income but small money holdings, for example, be paid $10,000 a month but have a very small positive balance in her chequing account.

Investment is a term economists reserve for the purchase of new capital goods, from machines to manufacturing plants to office buildings. When you want to talk about the purchase of shares or other financial assets, you should refer to **financial investment**.

Learn how to be economically correct: Do not say "Mary is making a lot of money"; say "Mary receives a high income." Do not say "Joe has a lot of money"; say "Joe is very wealthy."

4-1 | The Demand for Money

Assume that you have the choice between only two financial assets:

- **Money**, which can be used for transactions but pays zero interest. In reality, there are two types of money: **currency**, the coins and bills issued by the central bank, and **chequable deposits**, the bank deposits on which you can write cheques. The distinction between the two will be important later when we look at the supply of money. But for the moment, it does not matter.

◄ Chequable deposits often pay a small interest rate. We ignore this here.

- **Bonds**, which cannot be used for transactions but pay a positive interest rate, i. In reality, there are many assets other than money and, in particular, many types of bonds, each associated with a specific interest rate. As discussed earlier, we shall also ignore this aspect of reality for the moment.

Suppose that as a result of having steadily saved part of your income in the past, your financial wealth today is $50,000. You may intend to keep saving in the future and to increase your wealth further, but its value today is a given. The choice you have to make today is how to allocate this $50,000 between money and bonds.

Think of buying or selling bonds as implying some cost, for example, a phone call to a broker and the payment of a transaction fee. How much of your $50,000 should you hold in money and how much in bonds?

Holding all your wealth in the form of money is clearly very convenient. You will never have to call a broker or pay transaction fees. But it also means you will not receive interest income. Holding all your wealth in the form of bonds implies receiving income as interest on all your wealth. But having to call your broker whenever you need money to take the subway or pay for a cup of coffee is a rather inconvenient way of living. Therefore, it is clear that you should hold both money and bonds. In what proportions? This depends mainly on two variables:

Make sure you see the difference between the deci-
◄ sion about how much to save (a decision that determines how wealth changes over time) and the decision about how to allocate a given stock of wealth between money and bonds.

- Your *level of transactions*. You want to have enough money on average to avoid having to sell bonds to get money too often. Say that you typically spend $5000 a month. You may want to have, on average, say, two months' worth of spending on hand, or $10,000 in money, and the rest, $50,000 − $10,000 = $40,000, in bonds. If, instead, you typically spend $6000 a month, you may want to have $12,000 in money and thus only $38,000 in bonds.

- The *interest rate on bonds*. The only reason to hold any of your wealth in bonds is that they pay interest. If bonds paid no interest, you would hold all of your wealth in money: Bonds and money would pay the same interest rate (namely, zero), and money, which can be used for transactions, would therefore be more convenient.

  The higher the interest rate, the more you will be willing to incur the hassle and the costs associated with buying and selling bonds. If the interest rate is very high, you may decide to squeeze your money holdings to an average of only two weeks' worth of spending, or $2500 (assuming your monthly spending is $5000). This means you will be able to keep, on average, $47,500 in bonds, getting more interest as a result.

Let us make this last point more concrete. Most of you probably do not hold bonds directly; few of you have a broker. But you or your parents may hold bonds indirectly, through a money market account. **Money market funds** receive funds from people and firms and use these funds to buy bonds, typically government bonds. Money market funds pay an interest rate close to the interest rate on the bonds that they hold—the difference coming from the administrative costs of running the funds and from their profit margin.

In the early 1980s, with the interest rate on money market funds reaching 14% per year, people who had previously kept all of their financial wealth in their chequing accounts (which paid no interest) realized how much interest they could earn by holding part of those funds in a money market account instead. Money market funds became the rage. Since then, however, the interest rate has decreased. In 2001, the interest rate paid by money market funds was down to about 2%. This is better than zero—the rate paid on many chequing accounts—but much less attractive than the rate in 1981. As a result, most people put less in their money market fund and more in their chequing account than they did in 1981.

Let us formalize this discussion. Denote the amount of money people want to hold—their *demand for money*—by M^d (the superscript d stands for *demand*). We just argued that an individual's money demand depends on two variables: his level of transactions and the interest rate. The demand for money for the economy as a whole is just the sum of all individual demands for money. Thus, money demand for the economy as a whole depends on the overall level of transactions in the economy and on the interest rate. The overall level of transactions in the economy is hard to measure. But it is reasonable to assume that it is roughly proportional to nominal income: If nominal income increases by 10%, it is reasonable to think that the amount of transactions in the economy also increases by roughly 10%. So, we write the relation between the demand for money, nominal income, and the interest rate as:

$$M^d = \$Y\,L(i) \tag{4.1}$$
$$(-)$$

where $\$Y$ denotes nominal income. This equation says that the demand for money is equal to nominal income times a function of the interest rate, denoted $L(i)$. The minus sign under i in $L(i)$ captures the fact that the interest rate has a negative effect on money demand: An increase in the interest rate *decreases* the demand for money.

This equation summarizes what we have learned so far:

- The demand for money increases in proportion to nominal income. If income doubles, increasing from $\$Y$ to $\$2Y$, then the demand for money increases from $\$Y\,L(i)$ to $\$2Y\,L(i)$; it also doubles.

Revisit Chapter 2's example of an economy composed of a steel company and a car company. Calculate the total volume of transactions in that economy and its relation to GDP. If the steel company and the car company double in size, what happens to transactions ▶ and to GDP?

What matters here is nominal income—income in dollars, not real income. If real income does not change but prices double, leading to a doubling of nominal income, people will need to hold twice as much money to buy the same consumption basket. ▶

- The demand for money depends negatively on the interest rate. This is captured by the function $L(i)$ and the negative sign underneath: An increase in the interest rate decreases the demand for money.

The relation between the demand for money, nominal income, and the interest rate implied by equation (4.1) is represented graphically in Figure 4-1. The interest rate, i, is measured on the vertical axis. Money, M, is measured on the horizontal axis.

The relation between the demand for money and the interest rate, for a given level of nominal income, is represented by the M^d curve. The curve is downward sloping: The lower the interest rate (the lower i), the higher the amount of money people want to hold (the higher M).

At any interest rate, an increase in nominal income increases the demand for money. In other words, an increase in nominal income shifts the demand for money to the right, from M^d to $M^{d'}$. For example, at interest rate i, an increase in nominal income from $\$Y$ to $\$Y'$ increases the demand for money from M to M'.

Money Demand and the Interest Rate: The Evidence

How well does equation (4.1) fit the facts? In particular, how much does the demand for money respond to changes in the interest rate?

To get at the answer, first divide both sides of equation (4.1) by $\$Y$:

$$\frac{M^d}{\$Y} = L(i) \tag{4.2}$$

The term on the left side of the equation is the ratio of money demand to nominal income—in other words, how much money people want to hold in relation to their income. Thus, if equation (4.1)—and by implication equation (4.2)—is a good description of reality, we should observe an inverse relation between the ratio of money to nominal income and the

$L(i)$ is a decreasing function of the interest rate i. Equation (4.2) predicts that when the interest rate is high, the ratio of money to nominal income should be low. When the interest rate is low, the ratio of money to nominal income should be high.

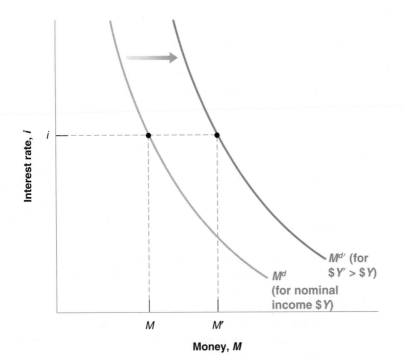

FIGURE 4-1

The Demand for Money

For a given level of nominal income, a lower interest rate increases the demand for money. For a given interest rate, an increase in nominal income increases the demand for money.

$M^{d'}$ (for $\$Y' > \$Y$)

M^d (for nominal income $\$Y$)

Interest rate, i

Money, M

FIGURE 4-2

The Ratio of Money to Nominal Income and the Interest Rate, 1968–2005

The interest rate and the ratio of money to nominal income typically move in opposite directions.

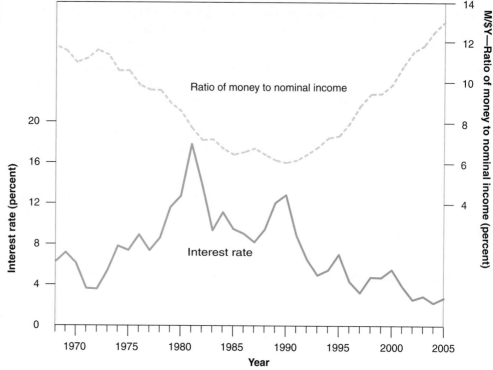

Source: Nominal income (nominal GDP using CANSIM II variable V498086); money supply (*M*1 using CANSIM II variable V37141); interest rate (three-month Treasury bill rate using CANSIM II variable V122484).

interest rate. This provides the motivation for Figure 4–2, which plots the ratio of money to nominal income and the interest rate against time, for the period 1968 to 2005.

The ratio of money to nominal income is constructed as follows: Money, *M*, is the sum of currency outside banks plus personal chequing accounts plus current accounts plus adjustments to *M*1 described in the notes to Table E1 (*Bank of Canada Banking and Financial Statistics*). This measure of money is called **M1**. Nominal income is measured by nominal GDP, $Y. The interest rate, *i*, is the average interest rate paid by government bonds during each year.

Figure 4–2 has two characteristics:

(1) The first is the decline in the ratio of money to nominal income exactly when nominal interest rates peak in the entire period from 1980 to 1990. Households and firms reduced their holdings of money when higher interest returns were available on assets, such as money market funds.

Economists sometimes refer to the inverse of the ratio of money to nominal income—that is, to the ratio of nominal income to money—as the **velocity** of money. The word "velocity" comes from the intuitive idea that when the ratio of nominal income to money is higher, the number of transactions for a given quantity of money is higher, and it must be the case that money is changing hands faster; in other words, the *velocity* of money is higher. Therefore, another equivalent way of stating the first characteristic of Figure 4–2 is that the velocity of money is highest when nominal interest rates are highest.

Velocity was slightly higher in 2005 than in 1968, even though interest rates were similar. Why might this be? One reason is that many innovations in financial markets have made it possible to hold lower money balances or lower currency balances for a given amount of

More precisely, the interest rate is the average over the year of the three-month Treasury bill rate. A precise definition of Treasury bills is ▶ given in section 4-2.

$$\frac{1}{(M/\$Y)} = \frac{\$Y}{M}$$

$$= velocity$$

transactions. Perhaps the most important development is the increased use of credit cards. At first glance, credit cards would appear to be money: When we go to a store, aren't we asked whether we want to pay with cash, cheque, credit card, or debit card? But, despite what they may seem, credit cards are not money. You actually do not pay when you use your credit card at the store; you pay when you receive your bill and send your monthly payment. What credit cards allow you to do is to concentrate many of your payments in one day and thus to decrease the average amount of money you need to have during the rest of the month. You would expect the introduction of credit cards to reduce money demand in relation to nominal income over time.

Some (but not all) credit cards also allow you to defer payment and thus to borrow, often at a high interest rate. This is a separate service and not one that is relevant here.

Similarly, debit cards can be used to pay for goods. However, a debit card is used when you have money in your bank account, balances that are included in the money supply. Thus, debit cards did not change the velocity of money very much. Figure 4–2 suggests that use of credit cards was about the same in 1970 as in 2005.

(2) The second is the negative relation between year-to-year movements in the ratio of money to nominal income and the interest rate. A better way to look at year-to-year movements is with a scatter diagram. Figure 4–3 plots the *change in the ratio of money to nominal income* versus the *change in the interest rate* from year to year. Changes in the interest rate are measured on the vertical axis. Changes in the ratio of money to nominal income are measured on the horizontal axis. Each point (shown as a square) in the figure corresponds to a given year. The vertical and horizontal lines give the mean values of the change in the ratio and in the interest rate for the period 1969–2005. The figure shows a negative relation between year-to-year changes in the interest rate and changes in the ratio. The relation is not tight, but if we were to draw a line that best fits the cloud of points, it would clearly be downward sloping, as predicted by our money demand equation.

Note that most of the points lie either in the upper-left quadrant (increases in the interest rate, decreases in the ratio) or the lower-right quadrant (decreases in the interest rate, increases in the ratio).

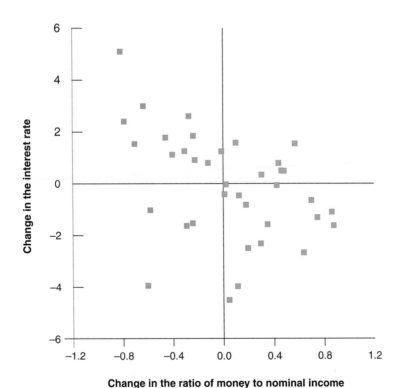

FIGURE 4–3

Changes in the Ratio of Money to Income and Changes in the Interest Rate, 1969–2005

Increases in the interest rate are typically associated with a decrease in the ratio of money to nominal income; decreases in the interest rate are typically associated with an increase in that ratio.

Source: See Figure 4–2.

4-2 | The Determination of the Interest Rate: I

Throughout this section, "money" stands for "central bank money" or "currency." ▸

We have looked at the demand for money. We now need to look at the supply of money. In reality, there are two suppliers of money: banks supply chequable deposits, and the central bank supplies currency. In this section, we will assume that all money is currency, supplied by the central bank. In the next section, we will reintroduce chequable deposits and look at the role of banks. Introducing banks makes the discussion more realistic. But it also makes the mechanics of money supply more complicated, and it is better to build the intuition in two steps.

Money Demand, Money Supply, and the Equilibrium Interest Rate

Suppose that the central bank decides to supply an amount of money equal to M. (Let us leave aside for the moment the issue of how the central bank chooses and changes the amount of money in the economy. We will return to it in a few paragraphs.)

The name of the relation (LM) is more than 50 years old. L stands for liquidity: Economists use liquidity as a measure of how easily and how cheaply an asset can be exchanged for money. Money is fully liquid, other ▸ assets less so; we can think of the demand for money as a demand for liquidity. M stands for money. The demand for liquidity must equal the supply of money.

Equilibrium in financial markets requires that money supply be equal to money demand, that $M^s = M^d$. Using equation (4.1) for money demand, the equilibrium condition is:

$$\text{Money supply} = \text{Money demand}$$
$$M = \$Y\, L(i) \qquad (4.3)$$

This equation tells us that the interest rate must be such that people are willing to hold an amount of money equal to the existing money supply. This equilibrium relation is called the **LM relation.**

This equilibrium condition is represented graphically in Figure 4–4. Just as in Figure 4–1, money is measured on the horizontal axis, and the interest rate is measured on the vertical axis. The demand for money, M^d, drawn for a given level of nominal income, is downward sloping: A higher interest rate implies a lower demand for money. The supply of money is drawn as the vertical line denoted M^s: The money supply equals M and is independent of the interest rate. Equilibrium is at point A, with interest rate i.

With this characterization of the equilibrium, we can then look at the effects of changes in nominal income or in the money stock on the equilibrium interest rate.

Figure 4–5 shows the effects of an increase in nominal income on the interest rate. The figure replicates Figure 4–4, and the initial equilibrium is at point A. An increase in nominal

---

FIGURE 4–4

The Determination of the Interest Rate

The interest rate must be such that the supply of money is equal to the demand for money.

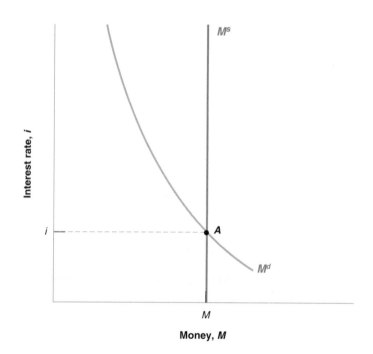

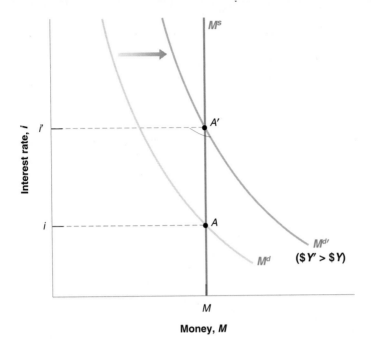

FIGURE 4-5

The Effects of an Increase in Nominal Income on the Interest Rate

An increase in nominal income leads to an increase in the interest rate.

income increases the level of transactions, which increases the demand for money at any interest rate. The demand curve shifts to the right, from M^d to $M^{d'}$. The equilibrium moves along the fixed money supply, from A to A', and the equilibrium interest rate increases from i to i': *An increase in nominal income leads to an increase in the interest rate.* The reason: At the initial interest rate, the demand for money exceeds the unchanged supply. An increase in the interest rate is needed to decrease the amount of money people want to hold and re-establish equilibrium.

Figure 4–6 shows the effects of an increase in the money supply on the interest rate. The initial equilibrium is at point A, with interest rate i. An increase in the money supply, from M

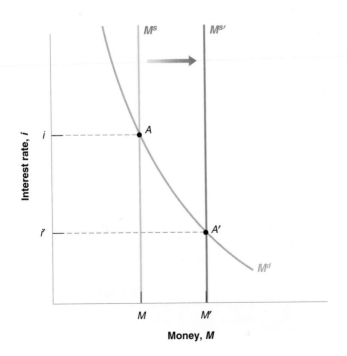

FIGURE 4-6

The Effects of an Increase in the Money Supply on the Interest Rate

An increase in the supply of money leads to a decrease in the interest rate.

to M', leads to a shift of the supply curve to the right, from M^s to $M^{s'}$. The equilibrium moves from A to A', and the interest rate decreases from i to i'. Thus, *an increase in the supply of money leads to a decrease in the interest rate.* The decrease in the interest rate increases the demand for money so that it equals the larger money supply.

Monetary Policy and Open Market Operations

We can get a better intuition for the results in Figures 4–5 and 4–6 by looking more closely at how the central bank actually changes the money supply and what happens when it does so.

Assume that the central bank changes the amount of money in the economy by buying or selling bonds in the bond market. If it wants to increase the amount of money in the economy, it buys bonds and pays for them by printing money. If it wants to decrease the amount of money in the economy, it sells bonds and removes from circulation the money it receives in exchange for the bonds. Such operations are called **open market operations**, so called because they take place in the "open market" for bonds. They are one of the standard methods central banks use to change the money stock in modern economies.

> The balance sheet of a bank (or firm or individual) is a list of its assets and liabilities. The assets are the sum of what the bank owns and what is owed to the bank; the liabilities are what the bank owes to others.

The balance sheet of the central bank is given in Figure 4–7. The assets of the central bank are the bonds that it holds in its portfolio. Its liabilities are the stock of money in the economy. Open market operations lead to equal changes in assets and liabilities. If the central bank buys, say, $1 million worth of bonds, the amount of bonds it holds is higher by $1 million, and so is the amount of money in the economy. If it sells $1 million worth of bonds, both the amount of bonds held by the central bank and the amount of money in the economy are lower by $1 million.

The other step we need to take is to look at the relation between bond prices and interest rates. We have focused so far on the interest rate on bonds. In fact, what is determined in bond markets is not interest rates but bond *prices*; the interest rate on a bond can then be inferred from the price of the bond. Understanding the relation between the interest rate and the price of a bond will prove useful both here and later in the book.

> What you get for the bond a year from now ($100) minus what you pay for the bond today ($$P_B$), divided by the price of the bond today, ($$P_B$).

Suppose the bonds in our economy are one-year bonds—bonds that promise a payment of a given number of dollars, say, $100, a year hence. In Canada, such bonds, when issued by government and promising payment in a year or less, are called **Treasury bills** or **T-bills.** You can think of the bonds in our economy as one-year T-bills. Let the price of a bond today be $$P_B$, where B stands for "bond." If you buy the bond today and hold it for a year, the rate of return on holding the bond for a year is equal to ($100 $-$ $$P_B$)/$$P_B$. Therefore, the interest rate on the bond is:

$$i = \frac{\$100 - \$P_B}{\$P_B}$$

If $$P_B$ is $95, the interest rate equals $5/$95 $=$ 0.053, or 5.3%. If $$P_B$ is $90, the interest rate is 11.1%. *The higher the price of the bond, the lower is the interest rate.*

Equivalently, if we are given the interest rate, we can infer the price of the bond. Reorganizing the formula above, the price today of a one-year bond paying $100 a year from today is given by:

$$\$P_B = \frac{\$100}{1 + i}$$

FIGURE **4–7**

The Balance Sheet of the Central Bank

The assets of the central bank are the bonds it holds. The liabilities are the stock of money in the economy. An open market operation in which the central bank buys bonds and issues money increases both assets and liabilities by the same amount.

The price of the bond is equal to the final payment divided by 1 plus the interest rate. If the interest rate is positive, the price of the bond is less than the final payment. The higher the

Assets	Liabilities
Bonds	Money (currency)

interest rate, the lower is the price today. When newspapers write that "bond markets went up today," they mean that *the prices of bonds went up* and therefore that *interest rates went down*.

We are now ready to return to the effects of an open market operation. Consider an **expansionary open market operation**—an operation in which the central bank increases the supply of money. In such a transaction, the central bank buys bonds in the bond market and pays for them by creating money. As the central bank buys bonds, the demand for bonds goes up, increasing the price of bonds. Equivalently, the interest rate on bonds goes down. When the central bank wants instead to decrease the supply of money—a **contractionary open market operation**—it sells bonds. This leads to a decrease in their price, an increase in the interest rate.

To summarize:

- The interest rate is determined by the equality of the supply of money and the demand for money.
- By changing the supply of money, the central bank can affect the interest rate.
- The central bank changes the supply of money through open market operations, which are purchases or sales of bonds for money.
- Open market operations in which the central bank increases money supply by buying bonds lead to an increase in the price of bonds—equivalently, a decrease in the interest rate.
- Open market operations in which the central bank decreases the money supply by selling bonds lead to a decrease in the price of bonds—equivalently, an increase in the interest rate.

Our economy with its two assets, money and bonds, is a much simplified version of actual economies with their many financial assets and many financial markets. But, as we will see later in the book, the basic lessons we have just seen apply very generally. The only change we will have to make is to replace "interest rate" in our conclusions by "short-term interest rate." We will see that the short-term interest rate is determined by the condition that money supply equals money demand; that the central bank can change the amount of money and the short-term interest rate.

The complication: The short-term interest rate—the rate directly affected by monetary policy—is ◀ not the only interest rate in the economy. The determination of other interest rates and asset prices (such as stock prices) is the topic of Chapter 19.

There is one dimension, however, in which our model must be extended. We have assumed that all money was currency, supplied by the central bank. In the real world, money includes not only currency but also chequable deposits. Chequable deposits are supplied not by the central bank, but by (private) banks. How the presence of banks, and of chequable deposits, changes our conclusions is the topic of the next section. The section is optional. For those of you who decide to skip it, let us state its basic conclusion. In an economy in which money includes both currency and chequable deposits, the central bank no longer controls the total amount of money directly. It does, however, control it indirectly. In particular, it can still use open market operations—purchases and sales of bonds—to increase or decrease the supply of money and affect the interest rate. The Bank of Canada can also use other methods as described in Chapter 25.

*4-3 | The Determination of the Interest Rate: II

To understand what determines the interest rate in an economy with both currency and chequable deposits, we must first look at what banks do.

What Banks Do

Modern economies are characterized by the existence of many types of **financial intermediaries**, institutions that receive funds from people and firms and use these funds to buy bonds or stocks or make loans to other people and firms. Their liabilities are the funds that they owe to the people and firms from whom they have received funds. Their assets are the stocks and bonds they own and the loans they have made.

---

*This section is optional.

Banks are one type of financial intermediaries. What makes banks special—and the reason we focus on banks here rather than financial intermediaries in general—is that their liabilities are money: People can pay for transactions by writing cheques up to the amount of their account balance. Let us look more closely at what they do.

Banks receive funds from depositors. They keep some of these funds as reserves and use the rest to make loans and purchase bonds. Their balance sheet is shown in Figure 4–8(a). Their liabilities consist of chequable deposits, the funds deposited by people and firms. Their assets consist of reserves, loans, and bonds.

Banks receive funds from people and firms who either deposit funds or have funds sent to their chequing account (their paycheque, for example). At any point in time, people and firms can write cheques or withdraw up to the full amount of their account balance. Thus, the liabilities of the banks are equal to the total value of *chequable deposits*.[1]

Banks keep as **reserves** some of the funds they have received. These reserves are reserves of central bank money; they are held partly in cash and partly on an account the banks have at the central bank, on which they can draw when they need to.

Why do banks hold reserves? For three reasons:

- On any given day, some depositors withdraw cash from their chequing account, while others deposit cash into their account. There is no reason for the inflows and outflows of cash to be equal, so the bank must keep some cash on hand.

- In the same way, on any given day, people with accounts at a bank, bank A, write cheques to people with accounts at other banks, and people with accounts at other banks write cheques to people with accounts at bank A. What bank A, as a result of these transactions, owes to other banks may be greater or less than what other banks owe to bank A. For this reason also, a bank needs to keep reserves. If, at the end of a business day, a bank is short of reserves, it must borrow these reserves from other banks or from the Bank of Canada. Banks keep reserves to avoid these costly loans.

- The first two reasons imply that banks would want to keep some reserves even if they were not required to. But, in addition, in some countries, the United States, for example, banks are subject to legal reserve requirements, which require them to hold reserves in some proportion to chequable deposits. In these countries, reserve requirements are set by their central banks and vary by size of deposits as well as over time. The actual **reserve ratio**, the ratio of bank reserves to chequable deposits, is about 1% in Canada today.

Leaving aside reserves, banks use the remainder of their funds to make loans to firms and consumers or to buy bonds. Loans represent roughly 80% of banks' assets. Bonds account for the rest, thus 20%. The distinction between bonds and loans is unimportant for our purpose—understanding the determination of money supply. So, in what follows, we will assume for simplicity that banks do not make loans and thus hold only reserves and bonds as assets. However, the distinction between loans and bonds is important for other purposes, from the likelihood of bank runs to the role of federal deposit insurance. These topics are explored in the Focus box "Bank Runs."

Figure 4–8(b) gives the balance sheet of the central bank in an economy with banks. It is very similar to the balance sheet in Figure 4–7. The asset side is the same as before: The assets

[1]**DIGGING DEEPER**. This description simplifies reality in two ways. First, banks also offer other types of deposits, such as savings and time deposits. These cannot be used directly in transactions, and so they are not money. We will ignore this part of the banks' activity, which is not central for our purposes. Also, banks are the main but not the only financial intermediary to offer chequable deposits; other savings institutions and credit unions also offer such deposits. We also ignore this complication here and use "banks" to denote all suppliers of chequable deposits.

Making a loan to a firm and buying a government bond are more similar than they may seem. In one case, one lends to a firm. In the other, one lends to government. This is why, for simplicity, we have ignored in the text the fact that banks both make bank loans and hold government bonds, and we have assumed that they hold only bonds.

But, in one respect, making a loan is very different from buying a bond. Bonds, especially government bonds, are very liquid; in case of need, they can be sold easily in the bond market. Loans are often not liquid at all. Calling them back may be impossible: The firm, which has used the loan to buy inventories or a new machine, no longer has the cash. Selling the loan itself to a third party may be very difficult because potential buyers know little about how reliable the firm is as a borrower.

This fact has one important implication. Take a healthy bank, a bank with a good portfolio of loans. Suppose rumours start that the bank is not doing well and some loans will not be paid back. Believing that the bank may fail, people with deposits at the bank will want to close their accounts and get cash. If enough people do so, the bank will run out of reserves. Given that the loans cannot be called back, the bank will not be able to satisfy the demand for cash, and it will have to close.

Therefore, the belief that a bank may close may lead it to close, even if all of its loans are good. The financial history of many countries is full of such **bank runs**. One bank fails for the right reason (that is, it has made bad loans), leading depositors at other banks to get scared and run on their own banks, thus forcing them to close, whether or not their loans are good. You may have seen *It's a Wonderful Life*, an old movie with James Stewart that runs on TV every year around Christmas. Because of the failure of another bank in town, depositors at the savings and loan bank, of which James Stewart is the manager, get scared and come to get their money back. It takes all of James Stewart's persuasion to avoid closure. The movie has a happy ending. In real life, most bank runs did not.

What can be done to avoid such runs? The way Canada has dealt with this problem is by creating, in 1967, a system of **federal deposit insurance** operated by the Canada Deposit Insurance Corporation (CDIC). You may have seen CDIC stickers on the doors of your bank. The Canadian government insures each account up to a ceiling of $60,000. There is no reason for depositors to panic and get their money out, and healthy banks do not fail.

However, federal deposit insurance leads to problems of its own. Depositors, who do not have to worry about their deposits, no longer look at the activities of the banks in which they have their deposits, and banks may misbehave. Banks may make risky loans they would not have made without the insurance.

An alternative solution is **narrow banking**. Narrow banking would restrict banks to holding liquid, safe, government bonds, such as T-bills. It would eliminate bank runs as well as the need for federal insurance. Loans to firms could be made by other financial intermediaries. Narrow banking has often been proposed around the world but, so far, never implemented.

of the central bank are the bonds that it holds. The liabilities of the central bank are the money it has issued, **central bank money**. The new feature is that not all of central bank money is held as currency by the public. Some of it is held as reserves by banks.

The Supply and Demand for Central Bank Money

The easiest way to think about the determination of the interest rate in this economy is by thinking in terms of the supply and the demand for central bank money. The demand for central bank money is equal to the demand for currency by people plus the demand for reserves

(a)

Banks

Assets	Liabilities
Reserves Loans Bonds	Chequable deposits

(b)

Central Bank

Assets	Liabilities
Bonds	Central bank money = reserves + currency

FIGURE   4–8

The Balance Sheet of Banks (a) and the Balance Sheet of the Central Bank Revisited (b)

FIGURE   4–9

Determinants of the Demand
and the Supply of Central
Bank Money

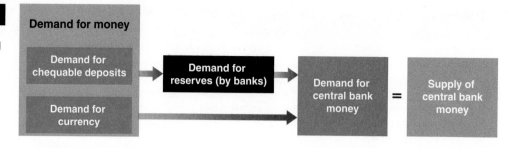

Demand for money

Demand for
chequable deposits

Demand for
currency

Demand for
reserves (by banks)

Demand for
central bank
money

=

Supply of
central bank
money

by banks. The supply of central bank money is under the direct control of the central bank. The
equilibrium interest rate is such that the demand and the supply for central bank money are
equal.

Figure 4–9 shows the structure of demand and supply in more detail. Start from the left
side. The demand for money is a demand for both chequable deposits and currency. Banks
have to hold reserves against chequable deposits: The demand for chequable deposits leads
to a demand for reserves by banks. The demand for central bank money is equal to the
demand for reserves by banks plus the demand for currency by people. The supply of central
bank money is determined by the central bank. The interest rate must be such that the demand
and the supply are equal.

Let us go through each of the steps in Figure 4–9 and ask: What determines the demand
for chequable deposits and the demand for currency? What determines the demand for
reserves by banks? How does the interest rate reconcile the demand and the supply of central bank money?

The Demand for Money. When people can hold both currency and chequable deposits, the
demand for money involves two decisions. First, people must decide how much money to
hold. Second, they must decide how much of this money to hold in currency and how much
to hold in chequable deposits.

It is reasonable to assume that the overall demand for money is given by the same factors
as before. The higher the level of transactions and the lower the interest rate on bonds, the
more money people will hold. So, we assume that overall money demand is given by the
same equation as before (equation [4.1]):

$$M^d = \$Y\,L(i) \qquad (4.4)$$
$$(-)$$

That brings us to the second decision. How do people decide how much to hold in currency and how much in chequable deposits? Currency is more convenient for small transactions. Cheques are more convenient for large transactions. Holding money in your
chequing account is safer than holding it in cash. We will simply assume here that people
hold a fixed proportion of their money in currency—call this proportion c—and, by implication, a fixed proportion $(1 - c)$ in chequable deposits. In Canada, people hold 40% of
their money in the form of currency; so, think of c as equal to 0.4.

Call the demand for currency CU^d (CU for currency, and d for demand). Call the demand for
chequable deposits D^d (D for deposits, and d for demand). The two demands are thus given by:

$$CU^d = cM^d \qquad (4.5)$$
$$D^d = (1 - c)M^d \qquad (4.6)$$

Equation (4.5) gives the first component of the demand for central bank money, the demand
for currency by the public. Equation (4.6) gives the demand for chequable deposits. This
demand for chequable deposits leads to a demand by banks for reserves, the second component
of the demand for central bank money. To see how, let us turn to the behaviour of banks.

The Demand for Reserves. The larger the amount of chequable deposits, the larger is the amount of reserves the banks must hold to allow customers to retrieve cash or to clear cheques between banks. Let θ (the Greek lowercase letter theta) be the reserve ratio, the amount of reserves banks hold per dollar of chequable deposits. Let R denote the dollar amount of reserves of banks. Let D denote the dollar amount of chequable deposits. Then, by the definition of θ, the following relation holds between R and D:

$$R = \theta D \qquad (4.7)$$

We saw earlier that in Canada today, the reserve ratio is roughly equal to 1%. Thus, θ is roughly equal to 0.01.

If people want to hold D^d in deposits, then, from equation (4.7) banks must hold θD^d in reserves. Combining equations (4.6) and (4.7), the second component of the demand for central bank money—the demand for reserves by banks—is given by:

$$R^d = \theta(1 - c)M^d \qquad (4.8)$$

The Determination of the Interest Rate. We are now ready to characterize the equilibrium. Let H be the supply of central bank money; H is directly controlled by the central bank, which can change the amount of H through open market operations. The demand for central bank money is equal to the sum of the demand for currency and the demand for reserves. The equilibrium condition is that the supply of central bank money be equal to the demand for central bank money:

◄ More on open market operations coming next.

$$H = CU^d + R^d \qquad (4.9)$$

Replace CU^d and R^d by their expressions from equations (4.5) and (4.8) to get:

$$H = cM^d + \theta(1 - c)M^d = [c + \theta(1 - c)]M^d$$

Finally, replace the overall demand for money, M^d, by its expression from equation (4.4) to get:

$$H = [c + \theta(1 - c)]\$Y L(i) \qquad (4.10)$$

The supply of central bank money (the left side) is equal to the demand for central bank money (the right side), which is equal to the term in brackets times the overall demand for money.

Look at the term in brackets more closely. Assume that people only hold currency: $c = 1$. Then, the term in brackets is equal to 1, and the equation is exactly the same as equation (4.3) in section 4-2 (with the letter H replacing the letter M on the left side, but both H and M standing for the supply of central bank money). In this case, people hold only currency, and banks play no role in the supply of money.

Assume, instead, that people do not hold currency at all but hold only chequable deposits. In this case, $c = 0$, and the term in brackets is equal to θ. Suppose for example that $\theta = 0.01$, and so the term in brackets equals 0.01. Then, the demand for central bank money is one-hundredth of the overall demand for money. This is easy to understand: People hold only chequable deposits. For every dollar they want to hold, banks need to have 1 cent in reserves. The demand for reserves is 1% of the overall demand for money.

Leaving aside these two extreme cases, note that as long as people hold some chequable deposits (so that $c < 1$), the term in brackets is less than 1: The demand for central bank money is less than the overall demand for money. This comes from the fact that the demand for reserves by banks is only a fraction of the demand for chequable deposits.

The equilibrium condition in equation (4.10) is represented graphically in Figure 4–10. The figure looks the same as Figure 4–4 but with central bank money rather than money on the horizontal axis. The interest rate is measured on the vertical axis. The demand for central bank money, $CU^d + R^d$, is drawn for a given level of nominal income. A higher interest rate implies a lower demand for central bank money for two reasons. The demand for currency

FIGURE 4-10

The Determination of the Interest Rate When Money Includes Both Currency and Chequable Deposits

The equilibrium interest rate is such that the supply of central bank money is equal to the demand for central bank money.

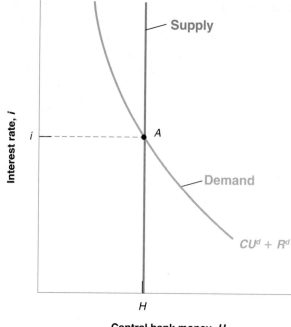

goes down; the demand for chequable deposits also goes down, leading to a decrease in the demand for reserves by banks. The supply of money is fixed and is represented by a vertical line at H. Equilibrium is at point A, with interest rate i.

The effects of either changes in nominal income or changes in the supply of central bank money are qualitatively the same as in the previous section. In particular, an increase in the supply of central bank money leads to a shift in the vertical supply line to the right. This leads to a lower interest rate. As before, an increase in central bank money leads to a decrease in the interest rate; symmetrically, a decrease in central bank money leads to an increase in the interest rate. The rest of this section is spent exploring this result further.

Two Alternative Ways of Looking at the Equilibrium

We have looked at the equilibrium through the condition that the supply and the demand of central bank money be equal. There are two alternative ways of looking at the equilibrium. One is through the condition that the supply and demand of *reserves* be equal. The other is through the condition that the supply and the demand of *money* be equal. Going through each will strengthen your intuition.

The Supply and Demand for Reserves. Take the equilibrium condition (4.9) and move the demand for currency to the left side to get:

$$H - CU^d = R^d$$

The left side gives the *supply of reserves* as the amount of central bank money minus what people hold as currency. The right side gives the *demand for reserves*. The equilibrium condition now reads: The supply of reserves must be equal to the demand for reserves.

This way of looking at the equilibrium is attractive because in Canada, there is, indeed, a market for reserves, in which the interest rate that reconciles the demand and the supply of reserves is determined. The market is called the **market for overnight funds**. Banks that have excess reserves at the end of the day lend them to banks that have insufficient reserves. In equilibrium, the total demand for reserves by all banks, R^d, must be equal to the supply of reserves, $H - CU^d$—the equilibrium condition above. The interest rate determined in that market is called the **overnight interest rate** (sometimes shortened to the "overnight rate"). Because the Bank of Canada can change the supply of central bank money, H, it can, in effect, choose the overnight rate. The Bank of Canada, as of the time of writing, announces a 0.5% range for the overnight rate approximately every six weeks. The **Bank Rate** is the highest value that the Bank of Canada will allow the overnight rate to attain. The lowest allowed value is the Bank Rate minus 0.5%. Announcements of the Bank Rate are indicators of Bank of Canada policy, reflecting the overnight rate desired by the Bank. The Bank Rate appears on the Bank of Canada Web site.

The Supply and Demand for Money. Yet another, but still equivalent, way of looking at the equilibrium is as the condition that the overall demand for money is equal to the overall supply of money. To see this, take equation (4.10) and divide both sides by $[c + \theta (1 - c)]$ to get:

$$\frac{1}{[c + \theta (1 - c)]} H = \$Y L(i) \qquad (4.11)$$

$$\text{Supply of money} = \text{Demand for money}$$

The right side of the equation gives the overall demand for money (currency plus chequable deposits). The left side gives the overall supply of money (currency plus chequable deposits). The equilibrium condition is that demand and supply be equal.

Note that the overall supply of money is equal to a constant term times central bank money. Note that because $c + \theta(1 - c)$ is less than 1, its inverse—the constant term on the left of the equation above—is greater than 1. This term is often called the **money multiplier**. Equation (4.11) then tells us that the overall supply of money is a multiple of the supply of central bank money, with the multiple given by the money multiplier. Suppose $c = 0.4$ and $\theta = 0.01$. Then $[c + \theta(1 - c)] = [0.4 + 0.01(0.6)] = 0.406$, and the multiplier equals $1/0.406$, or about 2.46. A multiplier of 2.46 implies that the overall money supply is equal to 2.46 times the supply of central bank money. To reflect the fact that the overall money supply in the end depends on central bank money, central bank money is often called **high-powered money** (this is where the letter H we used to denote central bank money comes from), or the **monetary base**.

The multiplier in equation (4.11) implies that a given change in central bank money has a larger effect on money supply—and, in turn, a larger effect on interest rates—in an economy with banks than in an economy without banks. In an economy without banks—the economy we studied in section 4-2—the effect of a change in central bank money on money supply is simply one for one, as central bank money and money are the same thing. Here, the effect is given by the multiplier: The effect on money supply is a multiple of the original change in central bank money. To give you more intuition for this result, the last subsection looks at the effects of an open market operation in an economy in which people hold chequable deposits.

"High-powered" because increases in H lead to more than one-for-one increases in the supply of money—the left side of equation (4.11): Increases in H are high-powered.

Open Market Operations Revisited

Consider the special case where people hold only chequable deposits; so, $c = 0$. In this case, the multiplier is $1/\theta$: An increase of one dollar of high-powered money leads to an increase of $1/\theta$ dollars in money supply. Assume further that $\theta = 0.01$ so that the multiplier equals $1/0.01 = 100$. The purpose of what follows is to get more intuition for where this multiplier comes from and, more generally, for how the initial increase in central bank money leads to a 10-fold increase in the overall money supply.

Suppose the Bank of Canada buys $100 worth of bonds in an open market operation. It pays the seller—call him seller 1—$100, creating $100 in central bank money. At this point, the increase in central bank money is $100. When we looked earlier at the effects of an open market operation in an economy in which there were no banks, this was the end of the story. Here, it is just the beginning:

There is a parallel between our interpretation of the money multiplier as the result of successive purchases of bonds and the interpretation of the goods market multiplier (Chapter 3) as the result of successive rounds of spending. Multipliers can often be derived as the sum of a geometric series and be interpreted as the result of successive rounds of decisions. This interpretation often gives a better intuition for the process at work.

- Seller 1 (who, we have assumed, does not want to hold any currency) deposits the $100 in a chequing account at his bank—call it bank A. This leads to an increase in chequable deposits of $100.
- Bank A keeps $100 × 0.01 = $1 in reserves and buys bonds with the rest, $100 × 0.99 = $99. It pays $99 to the seller of those bonds—call her seller 2.
- Seller 2 deposits $99 in a chequing account in her bank—call it bank B. This leads to an increase in chequable deposits of $99.
- Bank B keeps $99 × 0.01 = $0.99 in reserves and buys bonds with the rest, $99 × 0.99 = $98.01. It pays $98.01 to the seller of those bonds—call him seller 3.
- Seller 3 deposits $98.01 in a chequing account in his bank—call it bank C. And so on.

By now, the chain of events should be clear. What is the eventual increase in money supply? The increase in chequable deposits is $100 when seller 1 deposits the proceeds of his sale of bonds in bank A, plus $99 when seller 2 deposits the proceeds of her sale of bonds in bank B, plus $98.01 when seller 3 does the same, and so on. Let us write the sum as:

$$\$100 \, (1 + 0.99 + 0.99^2 + \cdots)$$

See Appendix 2 at the end of the book for a refresher on geometric series.

The series in parentheses is a geometric series, so its sum is equal to $1/(1 - 0.99) = 100$. Money supply increases by $10,000, 100 times the initial increase in central bank money.

This derivation gives us another way of thinking about the money multiplier: We can think of the ultimate increase in money supply as the result of *successive rounds of purchases of bonds*—the first by the Bank of Canada in its open market operation, the following ones by banks. Each successive round leads to an increase in money supply; eventually, the increase in money supply is equal to 100 times the initial increase in central bank money.

Work out the case where $c > 0$. In each round, take into account that not all money is deposited in a chequing account.

To summarize: When we take into account the fact that money is composed of both currency and chequable deposits, the best way to think about the determination of the interest rate is as the condition that the demand for central bank money equals the supply of central bank money. Changes in the supply of central bank money, carried out by the central bank through open market operations, affect the equilibrium interest rate. Increases in central bank money decrease the interest rate; decreases in central bank money increase the interest rate.

SUMMARY

- The demand for money depends positively on the level of transactions in the economy and negatively on the interest rate.

- Given the supply of money, an increase in income leads to an increase in the demand for money and an increase in the interest rate. An increase in money supply leads to a decrease in the interest rate.

- The central bank affects the interest rate through open market operations. Open market operations in which the central bank increases money supply by buying bonds lead to an increase in the price of bonds—equivalently, a decrease in the interest rate.

  Open market operations in which the central bank decreases money supply by selling bonds lead to a decrease in the price of bonds—equivalently, an increase in the interest rate.

- When people hold currency and chequable deposits, the central bank does not directly control money supply. But it controls the supply of central bank money. The interest rate must be such that the supply of central bank money is equal to the demand for central bank money, which is itself the sum of the demand for currency by people and of reserves by banks.

- In an economy where people hold both currency and chequable deposits, the effect of a given change in central bank money on money supply is given by the money multiplier. The larger the money multiplier, the larger is the effect of a given change in central bank money on money supply and, in turn, on the interest rate.

- Bank of Canada, 60
- Bank Rate, 75
- bank runs, 71
- bonds, 61
- central bank money, 71
- chequable deposits, 61
- contractionary open market operation, 69
- currency, 61
- expansionary open market operation, 69
- federal deposit insurance, 71
- financial intermediaries, 69
- financial investment, 61
- financial markets, 60
- financial wealth, 61
- flow, 61
- high-powered money, 75
- income, 61

- *LM* relation, 66
- *M*1, 64
- market for overnight funds, 74
- monetary base, 75
- money, 61
- money market funds, 62
- money multiplier, 75
- narrow banking, 71
- open market operation, 68
- overnight interest rate, 75
- reserve ratio, 70
- reserves, 70
- savings, 61
- stock, 61
- Treasury bills, or T-bills, 68
- velocity, 64
- wealth, 61

QUESTIONS AND PROBLEMS

An asterisk denotes a harder question. [Web] indicates that the question requires access to the Internet.

1. TRUE/FALSE/UNCERTAIN

a. Income and financial wealth are both examples of stock variables.

b. The demand for money does not depend on the interest rate because only bonds earn interest.

c. Given their financial wealth, if people are satisfied with the amount of money they hold, then they must also be satisfied with the amount of bonds they hold.

d. Financial innovations slowly change velocity.

e. In the past 25 years, the ratio of money to nominal income has moved in the same direction as the interest rate.

f. The central bank can increase the supply of money by selling bonds in the market for bonds.

g. By construction, bond prices and interest rates always move in opposite directions.

2. MONEY DEMAND

Suppose that a person's wealth is $50,000 and that her yearly income is $60,000. Also, suppose that her money demand function is given by:

$$M^d = \$Y(0.35 - i)$$

a. What is her demand for money and her demand for bonds when the interest rate is 5%? 10%?

b. Describe the effect of the interest rate on money demand and bond demand. Is it consistent with the theory in Chapter 4? Why?

c. Suppose that the interest rate is 10%. In percentage terms, what happens to her demand for money if her yearly income is reduced by 50%?

d. Suppose that the interest rate is 5%. In percentage terms, what happens to her demand for money if her yearly income is reduced by 50%?

e. Summarize the effect of income on money demand. How does it depend on the interest rate?

3. BONDS AND THE INTEREST RATE

A bond promises to pay $100 in one year.

a. What is the interest rate on the bond if its price today is $75? $85? $95?

b. What is the relation between the price of the bond and the interest rate?

c. If the interest rate is 8%, what is the price of the bond today?

4. FINANCIAL MARKETS EQUILIBRIUM

Suppose that money demand is given by:

$$M^d = \$Y(0.25 - i)$$

where $\$Y$ is $100. Also, suppose that the supply of money is $20. Assume equilibrium in financial markets.

a. What is the interest rate?

b. If the Bank of Canada wants to increase i by 10% (from, say, 2% to 12%), at what level should it set the supply of money?

5. BOND DEMAND

Suppose that a person's wealth is $50,000 and that her yearly income is $60,000. Also, suppose that her money demand function is given by:

$$M^d = \$Y(0.35 - i)$$

a. Derive the demand for bonds. What is the effect of an increase in the interest rate of 10% (from, say, 2% to 12%) on the demand for bonds?

b. What are the effects of an increase in wealth on money demand and on bond demand? Explain in words.

c. What are the effects of an increase in income on money and on bond demand? Explain in words.

d. "When people earn more money, they obviously want to hold more bonds." What is wrong with this statement?

6. THE MONEY MULTIPLIER

Suppose the following assumptions hold:
1. The public holds no currency.
2. The ratio of reserves to deposits is 0.1.
3. The demand for money is given by:

$$M^d = \$Y(0.8 - 4i)$$

Initially, the monetary base is $100 billion, and nominal income is $5 trillion.

a. What is the demand for high-powered money?

b. Find the equilibrium interest rate by setting the demand for high-powered money equal to the supply of high-powered money.

c. What is the overall supply of money? Is it equal to the overall demand for money at the interest rate you found in (b)?

d. What is the impact on the interest rate if high-powered money is increased to $300 billion?

e. If the overall money supply increases to $3000 billion, what will be the impact on i? (*Hint*: Use what you learned in d.)

7. ATMS AND CREDIT CARDS

In this problem, we examine the effect of the introduction of ATMs and credit cards on money demand. For simplicity, let us examine a person's demand for money over a period of four days.

Suppose ATMs and credit cards do not exist and a person goes to the bank once at the beginning of each four-day period and withdraws from his savings account all the money he needs for the next four days. He spends $4 per day.

a. How much does he withdraw each time he goes to the bank?

Compute the person's money holdings for days 1 through 4 (in the morning, before he spends any of the money he withdraws).

b. What is the amount of money he holds on average?

After the advent of ATMs, he now withdraws money once every two days.

c. How much does he withdraw each time he goes to the ATM?

d. What is the amount of money he holds on average?

Finally, with the advent of credit cards, the person pays for all his purchases using his card. He withdraws no money from his savings account until the fourth day, when he withdraws the whole amount necessary to pay for his credit card purchases over the previous four days.

e. Compute the person's money holdings for days 1 through 4.

f. What is the amount of money he holds on average?

g. On the basis of your answers to (b), (d), and (f), what has been the effect of ATMs and credit cards on money demand?

8. THE VELOCITY OF MONEY

Let money demand be given by:

$$M^d = \$Y L(i)$$

a. Derive an expression for velocity as a function of i. How does it depend on i?

b. Look at Figure 4-2. What has happened to the velocity of money from 1968 to 2005?

For a more detailed description of financial markets and institutions, you might want to look at a textbook on money and banking. An excellent Canadian text on this subject is by Pierre Siklos, *Money, Banking and Financial Institutions: Canada and the Global Environment* (Third Edition) (Toronto: McGraw-Hill).

A more recent book on Canadian monetary policy, *The Two Percent Target: Canadian Monetary Policy Since 1991*, David E.W. Laidler and William B.P. Robson. (C.D. Howe Institute) Chapters 2 and 3 discuss monetary policy mechanisms.

The Bank of Canada maintains a useful Web site (**www.bankofcanada.ca**) that contains data on financial markets as well as information on what the Bank of Canada is doing and the current announcement of the Bank Rate.

CHAPTER 5

GOODS AND FINANCIAL MARKETS: THE *IS-LM* MODEL

We looked at the goods market in Chapter 3 and at financial markets in Chapter 4. We now look at goods and financial markets together. By the end of this chapter, you will have a framework to think about how output and the interest rate are determined in the short run.

In developing this framework, we follow a path first traced by two economists, John Hicks and Alvin Hansen, in the late 1930s and the early 1940s. When Keynes's *General Theory* was published in 1936, there was much agreement that the book was both fundamental and nearly impenetrable. (Look at it, and you will agree.) There were many debates about what Keynes really meant. In 1937, John Hicks summarized what he saw as one of Keynes's main contributions: the joint description of goods and financial markets. His analysis was later extended by Alvin Hansen. Hicks and Hansen called their formalization the *IS-LM* model.

Macroeconomics has made substantial progress since the early 1940s. This is why the *IS-LM* model is treated in Chapter 5 rather than in the last chapter of this book. (Think of it: If you had taken this course 40 years ago, you would be nearly done.) But to most economists, the *IS-LM* model still represents an essential building block—one that, despite its simplicity, captures much of what happens in the economy in the short run. This is why the *IS-LM* model is still taught and used today.

5-1 | The Goods Market and the *IS* Relation

Let us first summarize what we learned in Chapter 3:

- We characterized equilibrium in the goods market as the condition that production, Y, be equal to the demand for goods, Z. We called this condition the *IS* relation because it can be reinterpreted as the condition that investment be equal to saving.
- We defined demand as the sum of consumption, investment, and government spending. We assumed that consumption was a function of disposable income (income minus taxes) and took investment spending, government spending, and taxes as given. The equilibrium condition was given by:

$$Y = C(Y - T) + \bar{I} + G$$

- Using this equilibrium condition, we then looked at the factors that changed equilibrium output. We looked, in particular, at the effects of changes in government spending and of shifts in consumption demand.

The exact relation, from Chapter 3:

$$Y = Z \Leftrightarrow$$
$$I = S + (T - G)$$

The two simplifications of this first model were that (1) the interest rate did not affect the demand for goods, and (2) exports, imports, and net exports were zero. Our first task in this chapter is to remove the first simplification, to introduce the interest rate in our model of goods–market equilibrium. For the time being, we will focus only on the effect of the interest rate on investment and take up a discussion of its effects on the other components of demand later. The task in the next chapter is to include exports and imports in our model.

We will do this in Chapter 20, where we will look at the effects of interest rates on both consumption and investment.

Investment, Sales, and the Interest Rate

In our first model of output determination, investment was left unexplained—we assumed investment was constant, even when output changed. Investment—spending on new machines and plants by firms—is, in fact, far from constant, and it depends primarily on two factors:

- *The level of sales.* A firm facing an increase in sales needs to increase production. To do so, it may need to buy additional machines or build an additional plant. A firm facing low sales will feel no such need and will spend little, if anything, on investment.
- *The interest rate.* Consider a firm deciding whether to buy a new machine. To buy the new machine, the firm must borrow, either by taking a loan from a bank or by issuing bonds. The higher the interest rate, the less likely the firm is to borrow and buy the machine. At a high enough interest rate, the additional profits from the new machine will not cover interest payments, and the new machine will not be worth buying.

To capture these two effects, we write the investment relation as follows:

$$I = I(Y, i) \tag{5.1}$$
$$(+, -)$$

Equation (5.1) states that investment depends on production, Y, and the interest rate, i. Although our discussion suggests that sales may be a more appropriate variable, we will assume that sales and production are equal—in other words, we will assume that inventory investment always equals zero—and use production instead. The positive sign under Y indicates that an increase in production leads to an increase in investment. The negative sign under the interest rate i indicates that an increase in the interest rate leads to a decrease in investment.

$$Y\uparrow \Rightarrow I\uparrow$$
$$i\uparrow \Rightarrow I\downarrow$$

The *IS* Curve

Taking into account the investment relation (5.1), the equilibrium condition in the goods market becomes:

$$Y = C(Y - T) + I(Y,i) + G \tag{5.2}$$

The supply of goods (the left side) must be equal to the demand for goods (the right side). Equation (5.2) is our expanded *IS* relation. We can now look at what happens to output when the interest rate changes.

Start with Figure 5–1. Demand (the right side of equation [5.2]) is measured on the vertical axis. Output (equivalently, production or income) is measured on the horizontal axis. The curve *ZZ* plots demand as a function of output for a given value of the interest rate, *i*. As output, and thus income, increases, so does consumption; we studied this relation in Chapter 3. As output increases, investment also increases; this is the relation between investment and production that we have introduced in this chapter. Through its effects on both consumption and investment, an increase in output leads to an increase in demand: *ZZ* is upward sloping.

Note that we have drawn *ZZ* so that it is flatter than the 45-degree line. Put another way, we have assumed that an increase in output leads to a less than one-for-one increase in demand. In Chapter 3, where investment was constant, this restriction naturally followed from the restriction that consumers spend only part of their additional income on consumption. But now that we allow investment to respond to production, this restriction may no longer hold. When output increases, the sum of the increase in consumption and the increase in investment could exceed the initial increase in output. Although this is a theoretical possibility, the empirical evidence suggests that it is not the case in practice. That is why we will assume the response of demand to output is less than one-for-one and draw *ZZ* flatter than the 45-degree line.

Equilibrium is reached at the point where demand equals production, at point *A*—the intersection of *ZZ* and the 45-degree line. The equilibrium level of output is given by *Y*.

We have drawn the demand relation, *ZZ*, for a given value of the interest rate. Suppose that the interest rate increases from its initial value *i* to a new higher value *i'*. At any level of output, investment decreases. The demand curve *ZZ* shifts down to *ZZ'*: At a given level of output, demand is lower. The new equilibrium is at the intersection of the lower demand curve *ZZ'* and the 45-degree line, at point *A'*. The equilibrium level of output is now *Y'*.

In words: An increase in the interest rate decreases investment. The decrease in investment leads to a decrease in output, which further decreases consumption and investment. In other words, the initial decrease in investment leads to a larger decrease in output through the multiplier effect.

Using Figure 5–1, we can find the equilibrium value of output associated with *any* value of the interest rate. The relation between equilibrium output and the interest rate is derived in Figure 5–2. Figure 5–2(a) reproduces Figure 5–1. The interest rate *i* implies a level of output

Remember that (1) production is a synonym for output, and (2) production and income are always equal.

Since we have not assumed that the consumption and investment relations in equation (5.2) are linear, *ZZ* is, in general, a curve rather than a line. Thus, we draw it as a curve in Figure 5–1.

Equilibrium in the goods market: *i* ↑ ⟹ *Y* ↓

FIGURE 5–1

The Effects of an Increase in the Interest Rate on Output

An increase in the interest rate decreases the demand for goods at any level of output. Because we have not assumed that the consumption and investment relations in equation (5.2) are linear, *ZZ* is, in general, a curve rather than a line, as shown. But all the arguments that follow would apply if we assumed that the consumption and investment relations were linear and that *ZZ* was a line instead.

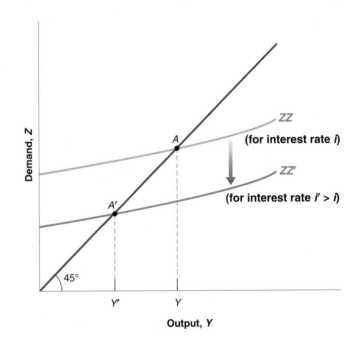

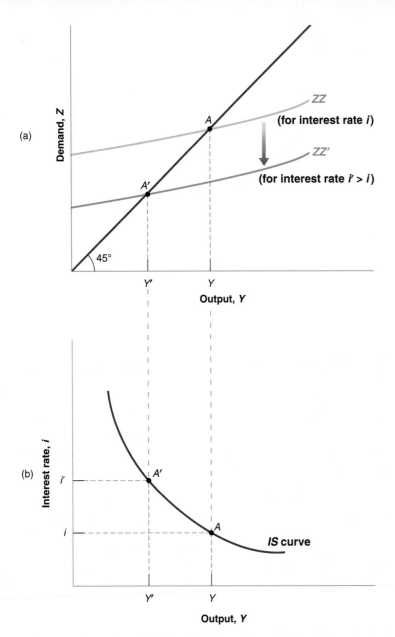

FIGURE 5-2

The Derivation of the IS Curve

Equilibrium in the goods market implies that output is a decreasing function of the interest rate. The IS curve is downward sloping.

equal to Y. The higher interest rate i' implies a lower level of output, Y'. Figure 5–2(b) plots equilibrium output Y on the horizontal axis against the interest rate on the vertical axis. Point A in Figure 5–2(b) corresponds to point A in Figure 5–2(a), and point A′ in Figure 5–2(b) corresponds to A′ in Figure 5–2(a). More generally, equilibrium in the goods market implies that the higher the interest rate, the lower is the equilibrium level of output. This relation between the interest rate and output is represented by the downward-sloping curve in Figure 5–2(b). This curve is called the **IS curve**.[1]

Equilibrium in the goods market implies that output is a decreasing function of the interest rate. This relation is represented by the downward-sloping IS curve.

[1]**DIGGING DEEPER**. Consider what happens to investment and saving as we move down the IS curve. As we move down, the interest rate decreases, and production increases; both factors increase investment. As we move down, income increases so that saving increases. Thus, as income increases and we move down the IS curve, both investment and saving increase; indeed, by the construction of the IS curve, they increase by the same amount so that investment remains equal to saving.

FIGURE 5-3

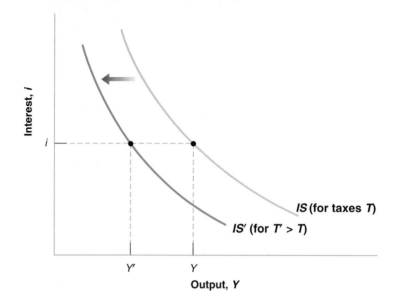

Shifts in the *IS* Curve

Note that we have derived the *IS* curve in Figure 5–2 for given values of taxes, *T*, and government spending, *G*. Changes in either *T* or *G* will shift the *IS* curve.

To see how, consider Figure 5–3. The *IS* curve gives the equilibrium level of output as a function of the interest rate. It is drawn for given values of taxes and spending. Now, consider an increase in taxes, from *T* to *T'*. At a given interest rate, say, *i*, consumption decreases, leading to a decrease in the demand for goods and, through the multiplier, to a decrease in equilibrium output. The equilibrium level of output decreases, say, from *Y* to *Y'*. Put another way, the *IS* curve shifts to the left: At any interest rate, the equilibrium level of output is lower than it was before the increase in taxes.

More generally, any factor that, for a given interest rate, decreases the equilibrium level of output, leads the *IS* curve to shift to the left. We have looked at an increase in taxes. But the same would hold for a decrease in government spending or a decrease in consumer confidence (which decreases consumption given disposable income). In contrast, any factor that, for a given interest rate, increases the equilibrium level of output—a decrease in taxes, an increase in government spending, an increase in consumer confidence—leads the *IS* curve to shift to the right.

Let us summarize:

- Equilibrium in the goods market implies that output is a decreasing function of the interest rate.
- This relation is represented by the downward-sloping *IS* curve.
- Changes in factors that decrease or increase the demand for goods given the interest rate shift the *IS* curve to the left or to the right.

> For a given *i*, $T\uparrow \Rightarrow Y\downarrow$

5-2 | Financial Markets and the *LM* Relation

> Left side: Money supply
> $M^s = M$
> Right side: Money demand
> $M^d = \$YL(i)$

Let us now turn to financial markets. We saw in Chapter 4 that the interest rate is determined by the equality of the supply of and the demand for money.

$$M = \$Y\,L(i)$$

The variable *M* on the left side is the nominal money stock. We will ignore here the details of the money-supply process and simply think of the central bank as controlling *M* directly. The right side gives the demand for money, which is a function of nominal income, $Y, and of the nominal interest rate, i; an increase in nominal income increases the demand for money; an increase in the interest rate decreases the demand for money. Equilibrium requires that money supply (the left side of the equation) be equal to money demand (the right side of the equation).

Real Money, Real Income, and the Interest Rate

The equation $M = \$Y L(i)$ gives a relation among money, nominal income, and the interest rate. It will be more convenient here to rewrite it as a relation among real money (that is, money in terms of goods), real income (that is, income in terms of goods), and the interest rate.

Recall that nominal income divided by the price level equals real income, Y. Dividing both sides of the equation by the price level P (which we take as given here) gives:

From Chapter 2:
$$\frac{\$Y}{P} = Y$$

$$\frac{M}{P} = Y L(i) \qquad (5.3)$$

Hence, we can restate our equilibrium condition as the condition that *real money supply*—that is, the money stock in terms of goods, not dollars—be equal to *real money demand*, which depends on real income Y and the interest rate i. The notion of a "real" demand for money may feel a bit abstract, so an example may help. Think not of your demand for money in general but just of your demand for coins. Suppose you like to have coins in your pocket to buy four cups of coffee during the day. If a cup costs 60 cents, you will want to keep about $2.40 in coins: This is your nominal demand for coins. Equivalently, you want to keep enough coins in your pocket to buy four cups of coffee. This is your demand for coins in terms of goods—here, in terms of cups of coffee.

From now on, we will refer to equation (5.3) as the *LM relation*. The advantage of writing things this way is that *real income*, Y, appears on the right side of the equation instead of *nominal income*, Y. And real income (equivalently real output) is the variable we focus on when looking at equilibrium in the goods market. To make the reading lighter, we will refer to the right and left sides of equation (5.3) simply as "money supply" and "money demand" rather than the more accurate but heavier "real money supply" and "real money demand." Similarly, we will refer to income rather than "real income."

The *LM* Curve

To see the relation between output and the interest rate implied by equation (5.3), let us start with Figure 5–4. Let the interest rate be measured on the vertical axis and (real) money be measured on the horizontal axis. Money supply is given by the vertical line at M/P and is denoted M^s. For a given level of income, Y, money demand is a decreasing function of the interest rate. It is drawn as the downward-sloping curve denoted M^d. Except for the fact that we measure real rather than nominal money on the horizontal axis, the figure is similar to Figure 4–4 in Chapter 4. The equilibrium is at point A, where money supply is equal to money demand, and the interest rate is equal to i.

Now, consider an increase in income from Y to Y', which leads people to increase their demand for money at any given interest rate. Money demand shifts to the right, to $M^{d'}$. The new equilibrium is at A', with a higher interest rate, i'. Why does an increase in income lead to an increase in the interest rate? When income increases, money demand increases. But money supply is a given. Thus, the interest rate must go up until the two opposite effects on the demand for money—the increase in income that leads people to want to hold more money and the increase in the interest rate that leads people to want to hold less money—cancel each other. At that point, the demand for money is equal to the unchanged money supply, and financial markets are again in equilibrium.

Equilibrium in financial markets: For a given M, $Y\uparrow \Rightarrow i\uparrow$

FIGURE 5-4

The Effects of an Increase in Income on the Interest Rate

An increase in income leads, at a given interest rate, to an increase in the demand for money. Given the money supply, this leads to an increase in the equilibrium interest rate.

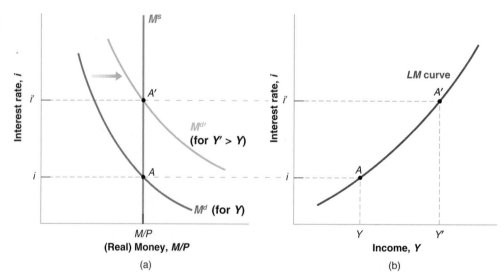

Using Figure 5-4, we can find out the value of the interest rate associated with *any* value of income for a given money stock. The relation is derived in Figure 5-5. Figure 5-5(a) reproduces Figure 5-4. When income is equal to Y, money demand is given by M^d and the equilibrium interest rate is equal to i. When income is equal to the higher value Y', money demand is given by $M^{d'}$ and the equilibrium interest rate is equal to i'. Figure 5-5(b) plots the equilibrium interest rate i on the vertical axis against income on the horizontal axis. Point A in Figure 5-5(b) corresponds to point A in Figure 5-5(a), and point A' in Figure 5-5(b) corresponds to point A' in Figure 5-5(a). More generally, equilibrium in financial markets implies that the higher the level of output, the higher is the demand for money and therefore the higher is the equilibrium interest rate. This relation between output and the interest rate is represented by the upward-sloping curve in Figure 5-5(b). This curve is called the **LM curve**. Economists sometimes characterize this relation by saying that "higher economic activity puts pressure on interest rates." Make sure you understand the steps behind this statement.

> Equilibrium in financial markets implies that for a given money stock, the interest rate is an increasing function of the level of income. This relation is represented by the upward-sloping *LM* curve.

FIGURE 5-5

The Derivation of the LM Curve

Equilibrium in financial markets implies that the interest rate is an increasing function of the level of income. The *LM* curve is upward sloping.

FIGURE 5-6

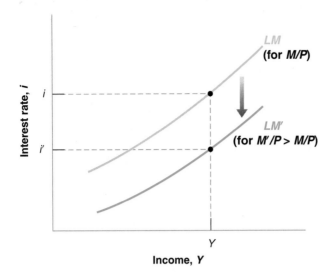

Shifts in the *LM* Curve

We have derived the *LM* curve in Figure 5–5 taking both the nominal money stock, *M*, and the price level, *P*—and, by implication, their ratio, the real money stock, *M/P*—as given. Changes in *M/P*, whether they come from changes in the nominal money stock, *M*, or from changes in the price level, *P*, will shift the *LM* curve.

To see how, consider Figure 5–6. The *LM* curve gives the interest rate as a function of the level of income. It is drawn for a given value of *M/P*. Now, consider an increase in nominal money supply, from *M* to *M'*, so that at an unchanged price level, real money supply increases from *M/P* to *M'/P*. At a given level of income, *Y*, this increase in money leads to a decrease in the equilibrium interest rate from *i* to *i'*. Put another way, the *LM* curve shifts down; at any level of income, an increase in money leads to a decrease in the equilibrium interest rate. By the same reasoning, at any level of income, a decrease in money leads to an increase in the interest rate. A decrease in money leads the *LM* curve to shift up.

Let us summarize:

- Equilibrium in financial markets implies that the interest rate is an increasing function of the level of income. This relation is represented by the upward-sloping *LM* curve.
- Increases in money shift the *LM* curve down; decreases in money shift the *LM* curve up.

5-3 | The *IS-LM* Model: Exercises

We can now put the *IS* and *LM* relations together. At any point in time, the supply of goods must be equal to the demand for goods. And the supply of money must be equal to the demand for money. Both the *IS* and *LM* relations must hold:

IS   relation $Y = C(Y - T) + I(Y,i) + G$

LM relation $\dfrac{M}{P} = Y L(i)$

Figure 5–7 plots both the *IS* curve and the *LM* curve on one graph. Output—equivalently production or income—is measured on the horizontal axis. The interest rate is measured on the vertical axis.

Any point on the downward-sloping *IS* curve corresponds to equilibrium in the goods market. Any point on the upward-sloping *LM* curve corresponds to equilibrium in financial markets. Only at point *A* are both equilibrium conditions satisfied. That means point *A*, with

◀ For a given *Y*, *M/P*↑ ⇒ *i*↓ An increase in money shifts the *LM* curve down.

◀ Why do we talk about shifts of the *IS* curve to the left and to the right but about shifts of the *LM* curve up or down?

We think of the goods market as determining *Y*, given *i*; so, we want to know what happens to *Y* when some exogenous variable changes. *Y* is measured on the horizontal axis and moves right or left.

We think of financial markets as determining *i*, given *Y*; so, we want to know what happens to *i* when some exogenous variable changes. *i* is measured on the vertical axis and moves up or down.

FIGURE 5-7

The *IS-LM* Model

Equilibrium in the goods market implies that output is a decreasing function of the interest rate. Equilibrium in financial markets implies that the interest rate is an increasing function of output. Only at point *A* are both goods and financial markets in equilibrium.

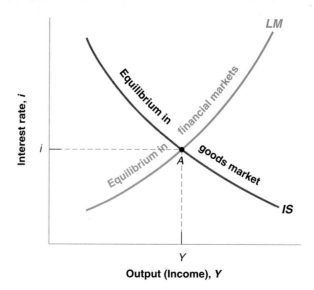

associated level of output *Y* and interest rate *i*, is the overall equilibrium, the point at which there is equilibrium in both the goods market and the financial markets.

The *IS* and *LM* relations that underlie Figure 5–7 contain a lot of information about consumption, investment, money demand, and equilibrium conditions. But you may ask, so what if the equilibrium is at point *A*? How does this fact translate into anything directly useful about the world? Do not despair: Figure 5–7 does, in fact, hold the answer to many questions in macroeconomics. Used properly, it allows us to study what happens to output and the interest rate when the central bank decides to increase the money stock, or when government decides to increase taxes, or when consumers become more pessimistic about the future, and so on.

Let us now see what the *IS-LM* model can do.

Fiscal Policy, Activity, and the Interest Rate

Decrease in $G - T \Leftrightarrow$ fiscal contraction $\Leftrightarrow$ fiscal consolidation

Increase in $G - T \Leftrightarrow$ fiscal expansion

Suppose government decides to reduce the budget deficit and does so by increasing taxes while keeping government spending unchanged. Such a policy, aimed at reducing the budget deficit, is often called a **fiscal contraction** or a **fiscal consolidation**. (An *increase* in the deficit, either due to an increase in spending or to a decrease in taxes, is called a **fiscal expansion**.) What are the effects of such a fiscal contraction on output, on its components, and on the interest rate?

In answering this or any question about the effects of changes in policy, always follow these three steps:

Step 1. Ask how this change affects goods and financial markets equilibrium relations, that is, how it shifts the *IS* or/and the *LM* curve.

Step 2. Characterize the effects of these shifts on the equilibrium.

Step 3. Describe the effects in words.

With time and experience, you will often be able to go directly to step 3; by then you will be ready to give an instant commentary on the economic events of the day. But until you achieve that level of expertise, go step by step.

Going through step 1, the first question is how the increase in taxes affects equilibrium in the goods market—that is, how it affects the *IS* curve.

Let us draw, in Figure 5–8(a) on page 90, the *IS* curve corresponding to equilibrium in the goods market before the increase in taxes. Take an arbitrary point, *B*, on this *IS* curve. By construction of the *IS* curve, output Y_B and the corresponding interest rate i_B are such that the supply of goods is equal to the demand for goods.

From the 1950s to the 1970s, the *IS-LM* model was the dominant model in macroeconomics. Nearly every question was recast in terms of whether the *IS* curve or the *LM* curve shifted and how this shift led to a change in output.

The dominance of the *IS-LM* model led Axel Leijonhufvud, an economist at the University of California, Los Angeles, to write a satire of macroeconomics. In "Life among the Econ," he pretended to be an "econologist"—an anthropologist studying a tribe called the Econ. He described the tribe as divided into castes, the "Micros" and the "Macros," each with "elders" and "grads," each making "models," and each with its own totems. Here is how he describes macro and the *IS-LM*:

> Consider the totems of the Micro and the Macro. Both could be roughly described as formed by two carved sticks joined together in the middle somewhat in the form of a pair of scissors. [See Figure 1.]

> Certain ceremonies connected with these totems are of great interest to us. . . . The following account of the "prospecting" ceremony among the Macro brings out several riddles that currently perplex econologists working in the area:

The elder grasps the LM *with his left hand and the* IS *with his right hand and, holding the totem out in front of himself, with elbows slightly bent, proceeds in a straight line—gazing neither left nor right, in the words of their ritual—out over the chosen terrain. . . . At long last, the totem vibrates, then oscillates more and more; finally, it points, quivering, straight down. The elder waits for the grads to gather around and then pronounces, with great solemnity: "Behold, the Truth and the Power of Macro." . . .*

The Macro maintain that they strike gold this way. Some travellers and investigators support the contention, others dismiss it as mere folklore. The issues are much the same as those connected with attempts to appraise the divining-rod method of finding water. Numerous people argue that it works—but no scientific explanation of why it would has ever been advanced.

Source: Axel Leijonhufvud, "Life among the Econ," *Western Economic Journal*, 1973, pp. 327–337.

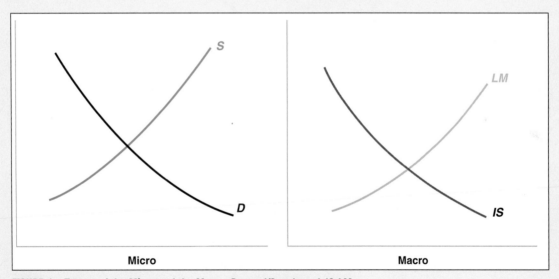

FIGURE 1 Totems of the Micro and the Macro. Demand/Supply and *IS-LM*

Now, at the interest rate i_B, ask what happens to output if taxes increase from T to T'. We saw the answer in section 5-1. Because people have less disposable income, the increase in taxes decreases consumption and, through the multiplier, decreases output. At interest rate i_B, output decreases from Y_B to Y_C. More generally, at *any* interest rate, higher taxes lead to lower output: The *IS* curve shifts to the left from *IS* to *IS'*.

Taxes appear in the *IS* relation ⟺
◀ taxes shift the *IS* curve.

Next, let us see if anything happens to the *LM* curve. Figure 5–8(b) on page 90 draws the *LM* curve corresponding to financial-markets equilibrium before the increase in taxes. Take an arbitrary point, F, on this *LM* curve. By construction of the *LM* curve, the interest rate i_F and income Y_F are such that the supply of money is equal to the demand for money.

FIGURE 5-8

The Effects of an Increase in Taxes

An increase in taxes shifts the *IS* curve to the left, and leads to a decrease in equilibrium output and the equilibrium interest rate.

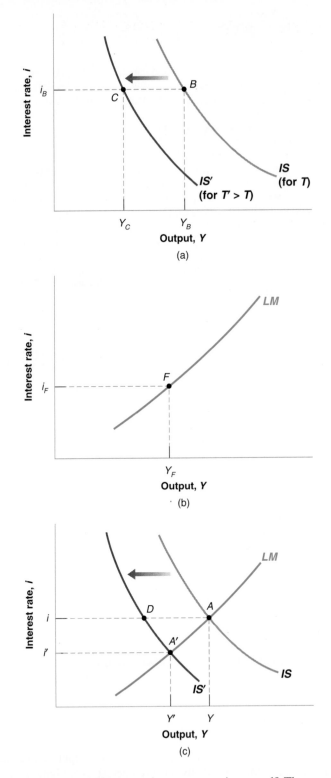

(a)

(b)

(c)

What happens to the *LM* curve when taxes are increased? The answer: nothing. At the given level of income Y_F, the interest rate at which the supply of money is equal to the demand for money is the same as before, namely, i_F. In other words, because taxes do not appear in the *LM* relation, they do not affect the equilibrium condition. They do not affect the *LM* curve.

Taxes do not appear in the *LM* relation $\Leftrightarrow$ taxes do not shift the *LM* curve.

Note the general principle here: *A curve shifts in response to a change in an exogenous variable only if this variable appears directly in the equation represented by that curve.* Taxes enter equation (5.2), so the *IS* curve shifts. But taxes do not enter equation (5.3), so the *LM* curve does not shift.

A reminder. Exogenous variables are variables we take as given, unexplained within the model.

Now let us consider the second step, the determination of the equilibrium. Let the initial equilibrium in Figure 5–8(c) on page 90 be at point *A*, at the intersection between the initial *IS* curve and the *LM* curve. After the increase in taxes, the *IS* curve shifts to the left, and the new equilibrium is at the intersection of the new *IS* curve and the unchanged *LM* curve, at point *A'*. Output decreases from *Y* to *Y'*. The interest rate decreases from *i* to *i'*. Thus, as the *IS* curve *shifts*, the economy *moves along* the *LM* curve, from *A* to *A'*. The reason these words are italicized is that it is very important to distinguish *shifts in* curves (here, the *IS* curve) and *movements along* a curve (here, the *LM* curve). Many mistakes result from not distinguishing between the two.

$T\uparrow \Rightarrow$ the *IS* curve shifts. The *LM* curve does not shift. The economy moves along the *LM* curve.

The third and final step is to tell the story in words: The increase in taxes leads to lower disposable income, which causes people to consume less. This leads, through the multiplier effect, to a decrease in output and income. The decrease in income reduces the demand for money, leading to a decrease in the interest rate. The decline in the interest rate reduces but does not completely offset the effect of higher taxes on the demand for goods.

If the interest rate did not decline, the economy would go from point *A* to point *D* in Figure 5–8(c), and output would be directly below point *D*. Because of the decline in the interest rate—which stimulates investment—the decline in activity is only to point *A'*.

What happens to the components of demand? By assumption, government spending remains unchanged: We have assumed that the reduction in the budget deficit takes place through an increase in taxes. Consumption surely goes down, both because taxes go up and because income goes down: Disposable income goes down on both counts. But what happens to investment? On the one hand, lower output means lower sales and lower investment. On the other hand, a lower interest rate leads to higher investment. Without knowing more about the exact form of the investment relation, equation (5.1), we cannot tell which effect dominates. If investment depends only on the interest rate, then investment surely increases; if investment depends only on sales, then investment surely decreases. In general, investment depends on both the interest rate and sales, so we cannot tell. Contrary to what is often stated by politicians, a reduction in the budget deficit does not necessarily lead to an increase in investment. (The Focus box "Deficit Reduction: Good or Bad for Investment?" discusses this at more length.) We will return to the relation between fiscal policy and investment many times in this book, and we will qualify this first answer in many ways. But the result that *in the short run, deficit reduction may decrease investment*, will remain.

FOCUS   Deficit Reduction: Good or Bad for Investment?

You may have heard the argument before: "Private saving goes toward either financing the budget deficit or financing investment. It does not take a genius to conclude that reducing the budget deficit leaves more saving available for investment, which increases investment."

This argument sounds simple and convincing. How do we reconcile it with what we just saw in the text, that deficit reduction may decrease rather than increase investment?

Remember from Chapter 3 that we can also think of the goods-market equilibrium condition as:

$$I \quad = \quad S \quad + \quad (T - G)$$
Investment   Private saving + Public saving

In equilibrium, investment is equal to private saving plus public saving. If public saving is positive, government is said to run a budget surplus; if public saving is negative, government

runs a budget deficit. So, it is true that given private saving, if government reduces its deficit—either by increasing taxes or reducing government spending so that $T - G$ goes up—investment must go up. Given *S*, $T - G$ going up implies that *I* goes up.

The crucial part of this statement, however, is "given private saving." And a fiscal contraction affects private saving as well: A fiscal contraction leads to lower output, that is, lower income; as consumption goes down by less than income, private saving also goes down. And it may go down by more than the reduction in the budget deficit, leading to a decrease rather than an increase in investment. In terms of the equation above: If *S* decreases more than $T - G$ increases, then *I* will decrease, not increase. To sum up, a fiscal contraction may decrease investment. Or, looking at the reverse case, a fiscal expansion—a decrease in taxes or an increase in spending—may actually increase investment.

Monetary Policy, Activity, and the Interest Rate

Increase in $M \Leftrightarrow$ monetary expansion.

Decrease in $M \Leftrightarrow$ monetary contraction $\Leftrightarrow$ monetary tightening. ▶

P fixed, M increases by 10% $\Rightarrow M/P$ increases by 10%. ▶

Money does not appear in the IS relation $\Leftrightarrow$ Money does not shift the IS curve. ▶

Money appears in the LM relation $\Leftrightarrow$ Money shifts the LM curve. ▶

$M \uparrow \Rightarrow$ The IS curve does not shift. The LM curve shifts down. The economy moves along the IS curve. ▶

An increase in the money supply is called a **monetary expansion**. A decrease in the money supply is called a **monetary contraction** or **monetary tightening**.

Let us take the case of a monetary expansion. Suppose that the central bank increases nominal money, M, through an open market operation. Given our assumption that the price level is fixed, this increase in nominal money leads to a one-for-one increase in real money, M/P. Let us denote the initial real money supply by M/P, the new higher one by M'/P, and trace the effects of money supply increase on output and the interest rate.

The first step is again to see whether and how the IS and the LM curves shift. Let us look at the IS curve first. Money supply does not affect directly either the supply of or the demand for goods. In other words, M does not appear in the IS relation. Thus, a change in M does not shift the IS curve.

Money enters the LM relation, however, so that the LM curve shifts when money supply changes. As we saw in section 5-2, an increase in money shifts the LM down: At a given level of income, an increase in money leads to a decrease in the interest rate.

Putting things together, a monetary expansion shifts the LM curve and does not affect the IS curve. Thus, in Figure 5–9, the economy moves along the IS curve, and the equilibrium moves from point A to point A'. Output increases from Y to Y', and the interest rate decreases from i to i'. In words: The increase in money leads to a lower interest rate. The lower interest rate leads to an increase in investment and, through the multiplier, to an increase in demand and output.

In contrast to the case of a fiscal contraction, we can tell exactly what happens to the different components of demand after a monetary expansion. With higher income and unchanged taxes, consumption goes up. With both higher sales and a lower interest rate, investment also unambiguously goes up. A monetary expansion is more investment friendly than a fiscal expansion.

To summarize:

- You should remember the method we have developed in this section to look at the effects of changes in policy on output and the interest rate. We will use it throughout the book.

- We have used this method to look at the effects of fiscal and monetary policies on output and the interest rate. Table 5–1 summarizes what we have learned. But you can use the same method to look at other changes as well. For example, you may want to trace

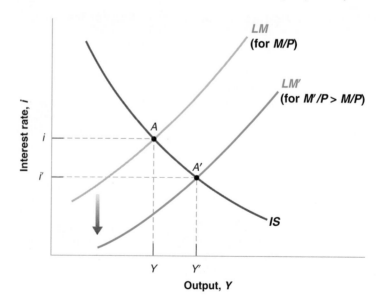

FIGURE   5-9

The Effects of a Monetary Expansion

A monetary expansion leads to higher output and a lower interest rate.

TABLE 5–1 The Effects of Fiscal and Monetary Policies

	Shift in *IS*	Shift in *LM*	Movement in Output	Movement in Interest Rate
Increase in taxes	left	none	down	down
Decrease in taxes	right	none	up	up
Increase in spending	right	none	up	up
Decrease in spending	left	none	down	down
Increase in money	none	down	up	down
Decrease in money	none	up	down	up

IN DEPTH   The Martin-Thiessen Policy Mix

When Jean Chretien's first term of office as Prime Minister began in 1993, Canada had come through some difficult macroeconomic times. As Table 1 shows, there had been a severe recession in 1991 and slow growth in 1992, and even in 1993 growth in real GDP was far below its normal level. Unemployment had been high for the past three years. Anger at the economic outcomes associated with the previous Conservative government was one important reason for the Liberal election victory in 1993. How could this government do better than its predecessor?

The second line of Table 1 shows the other macroeconomic problem faced by the new Liberal government. The federal government had an enormous budget deficit. Tax revenues were far short of federal government outlays. Finance Minister Paul Martin was clear that this deficit must be reduced. From the Budget Speech (February 27, 1995):

Canadians want more than temporary fiscal remission. They want full fiscal health. It is absolutely essential that once we meet our interim target we do not stall. We will continue to set firm, short-term deficit goals—rolling two-year targets, until the deficit is erased.

Two years later, the federal budget deficit was erased. This deficit was erased using some tax rate increases, some spending decreases, and the happy coincidence for Mr. Martin of a booming U.S. economy. The increase in American income led to increases in Canadian exports and higher GDP growth in Canada. Some of his success at deficit reduction was good luck. Some of his success was a good choice of policies by the Bank of Canada and the federal government. We can use the *IS-LM* framework to understand these choices.

Tax increases and expenditure reductions should, by themselves, shift the *IS* curve down. This is shown in Figure 1 as the movement from *IS* to *IS'*. Without further changes, the economy should experience a recession at *B*. But the Bank of Canada, as shown in the third row of Table 1, reduced interest rates in most years from 1991 to 1997 (with a one-year rise in rates in 1995). The reduction in interest rates is associated with a downward shift in the *LM* curve in Figure 1 from the curve labelled *LM* to the curve labelled *LM'*. The final outcome is represented as *A'*, a lower interest rate without adverse effects on output.

The combined effect of the policy actions by the federal Department of Finance to reduce the deficit and the Bank of

(continued)

Year	1991	1992	1993	1994	1995	1996	1997	1998	1999
(1)	–2.0	0.9	2.4	4.7	2.7	1.5	4.4	3.9	5.0
(2)	–5.4	–5.1	–5.4	–4.5	–3.9	–2.0	0.7	1.0	0.9
(3)	8.8	6.5	4.9	5.4	7.0	4.3	3.2	4.7	4.7

TABLE 1 Selected Macro Variables for Canada, 1991–1999

(1) Real GDP growth (percent) (*Source*: Using CANSIM II variable V1992259.)

(2) Budget surplus (percent of GDP) (*Source*: Table 46: *Fiscal Reference Tables 2001*. Department of Finance, Canada.)

(3) Interest rate (percent) (*Source*: Using CANSIM II variable V122484.)

Canada to lower interest rates allowed output to grow rapidly in 1994, 1995, 1997, 1998, and 1999. The rapid output growth, in turn, increased tax revenues to the federal government and helped turn the large deficit into a large surplus.

Our *IS-LM* model can even account for (in a crude way) the slowdown in real GDP growth in 1996. Section 5-5 in this chapter adds dynamics to the *IS-LM* model. In these dynamics, interest rates can rise rapidly with a monetary contraction as they did in 1995, while the effect of the monetary contraction on output is slower to develop. Although the interest rate increase takes place in 1995, the slowdown in growth takes place in 1996. This can be seen in Figure 5–11, on page 98.

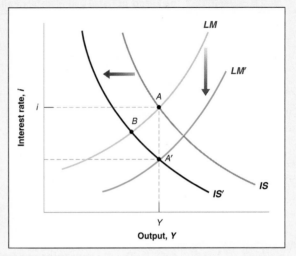

FIGURE 1 Deficit Reduction and Monetary Expansion
The right combination of deficit reduction and monetary expansion can achieve a reduction in the deficit without adverse effects on output.

the effects of a decrease in consumer confidence through its effect on consumption demand or of the introduction of new, more convenient credit cards through their effect on the demand for money.

5-4 | Using a Policy Mix

We have looked so far at fiscal and monetary policies in isolation. Our purpose was to show how each worked. In practice, the two are often used together. The combination of monetary and fiscal policies is known as the **monetary–fiscal policy mix**, or simply the **policy mix**.

Fiscal contraction ⇔ Reduction in budget deficit ▶

Sometimes, monetary and fiscal policies are used for a common goal. For example, expansionary monetary policy is used to offset the adverse effect on the demand for goods of a fiscal contraction. This was the case in Canada, where, used in combination, fiscal and monetary policies have delivered both sustained deficit reduction and output growth. How it was done and how much of the credit should go to Finance Minister Paul Martin and Bank of Canada Governor Gordon Theissen is described in the In Depth box "The Martin-Thiessen Policy Mix" on page 93.

See the boxes "German Unification, Interest Rates, and the EMS" in Chapter 8, and "Anatomy of a Crisis: The September 1992 EMS ▶ crisis" in Chapter 13.

Sometimes, the monetary–fiscal policy mix emerges from tensions or even disagreements between government (which is in charge of fiscal policy) and the central bank (which is in charge of monetary policy). A typical scenario is one in which the central bank, disagreeing with what it considers a dangerous fiscal expansion, embarks on a course of monetary contraction to offset some of the effects of the fiscal expansion on activity. An example of such a tension is what happened in Germany after unification in the early 1990s, described in the Global Macro box "German Unification and the German Monetary–Fiscal Tug-of-War."

5-5 | Adding Dynamics

In Chapter 3, we added dynamics to our description of the goods market and were able to describe the adjustment of output both more realistically and more intuitively. We do the same here.

Let us return first to the *IS* curve and examine the effects of a tax increase. As we have seen, a tax increase shifts the *IS* curve to the left. In Figure 5–10(a), the *IS* curve shifts from *IS* to *IS'*. At a given interest rate, say, i_A, the equilibrium level of output decreases from Y_A to Y_B.

In 1992, the U.S. economy embarked on a long expansion. For the rest of the decade, GDP growth was positive and high. In 2000, however, signs appeared that the expansion might be coming to an end. GDP growth was negative in the third quarter, although it turned positive again in the fourth quarter. In 2001, GDP growth remained negative for the first three quarters, before becoming positive again in the last quarter. (Figure 1 shows the growth rate of GDP for each quarter from 1999:1 to 2002:4, measured at an annual rate. The shaded area corresponds to the three quarters of negative growth in 2001.) The National Bureau of Economic Research (known as the NBER), a nonprofit organization that has traditionally dated U.S. recessions and expansions, concluded that the U.S. economy had, indeed, had a recession in 2001, starting in March 2001 and ending in December 2001. Canada did not experience a recession at this time.

What triggered the recession was a sharp decline in investment demand. Nonresidential investment—the demand for plants and equipment by firms—decreased by 4.5% in 2001. The cause was the end of what Alan Greenspan had dubbed a period of "irrational exuberance." During the second part of the 1990s, firms had been extremely optimistic about the future, and the rate of investment had been very high. The average yearly growth rate of investment from 1995 to 2000 exceeded 10%. This is very high. In 2001, however, it became clear to firms that they had been overoptimistic and had invested too much. This led them to cut back on investment, leading to a decrease in demand, and through the multiplier, a decrease in GDP.

The recession could have been much worse. But it was met by a strong macroeconomic policy response, which certainly limited the depth and the length of the recession.

Take monetary policy first. Starting in early 2001, the Federal Reserve, feeling that the economy was slowing down, started increasing the money supply and decreasing the federal funds rate aggressively. (Figure 2 shows the behaviour of the federal funds rate, from 1991:1 to 2002:4.) It continued to do so throughout the year. The funds rate, which stood at 6.5% in January, stood at less than 2% at the end of the year, a very low level by historical standards.

Turn to fiscal policy. During the 2000 campaign, then-presidential candidate George Bush had run on a platform of lower taxes. The argument was that the federal budget was in surplus and so there was room to reduce tax rates while keeping the budget in balance. When President Bush took office in 2001 and it became clear that the economy was slowing down, he had an additional rationale to cut tax rates, namely, the use of lower taxes to increase demand and fight the recession. Both the 2001 and the 2002 budgets included substantial reductions in tax rates. On the spending side, the events of September 11, 2001, led to an increase in spending, mostly on defence and homeland defence.

Figure 3 shows the evolution of federal government revenues and spending during 1999:1–2002:4, both expressed as ratios to GDP. Note the dramatic decrease in revenues, starting in the third quarter of 2001. Even without decreases in tax rates, revenues would have gone down during the recession: Lower output and lower income mechanically imply lower tax revenues. But, because of the tax cuts, the decrease in revenues in 2001 and 2002 was much larger than can be explained by the recession. Note also the smaller but steady increase in spending, starting around the same time. As a result, the budget surplus—the difference between revenues and spending—

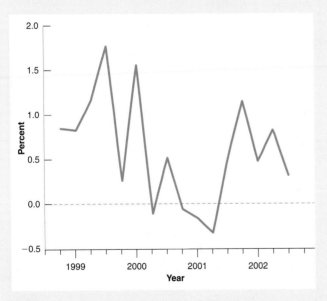

FIGURE 1 The U.S. Growth Rate, 1999: 1–2002:4

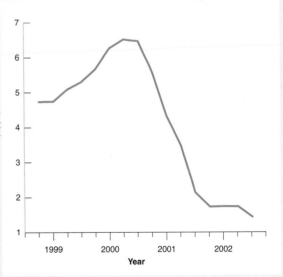

FIGURE 2 The Federal Funds Rate, 1999:1–2002:4

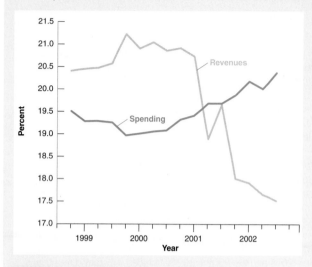

FIGURE 3 U.S. Federal Government Revenues and Spending (as ratios to GDP), 1999:1– 2002:4

went from positive up until 2000, to negative in 2001 and, much more so, in 2002.

The effects of the initial decrease in investment demand and the monetary and fiscal responses can be represented using the *IS–LM* model. In Figure 4, assume that the equilibrium at the end of 2000 is represented by point *A*, at the intersection of the initial *IS* and the initial *LM* curves. What happened in 2001 was the following:

● The decrease in investment demand led to a sharp shift of the *IS* curve to the left, from *IS* to *IS"*. Absent policy reactions, the economy would have been at point *A"*, with output *Y"*.

● The increase in the money supply led to a downward shift of the *LM* curve, from *LM* to *LM'*.

● The decrease in tax rates and the increase in spending both led to a shift of the *IS* curve to the right, from *IS"* to *IS'*.

As a result of the decrease in investment demand and of the two policy responses, the economy in 2001 ended up at point *A'*, with a decrease in output and a much lower interest rate. The output level associated with *A'* was lower than the output level associated with *A*—there was a recession—but it was much higher than the output level associated with *A"*, the level that would have prevailed in the absence of policy responses.

Let us end by taking up three questions you are probably asking at this point:

● Why weren't monetary and fiscal policy used to avoid rather than just to limit the recession?

The reason is that changes in policy affect demand and output only over time (more on this in section 5-5). Thus, by the time it became clear that the U.S. economy was entering a recession, it was already too late to use policy to avoid it. What the policy did was to reduce both the depth and the length of the recession.

● Weren't the events of September 11, 2001, also a cause of the recession?

The answer, in short, is no. As we have seen, the recession started long before September 11, 2001, and ended soon after. Indeed, GDP growth was positive in the last quarter of 2001. One might have expected—as, indeed, most economists did—the events of September 11 to have large adverse effects on output, leading, in particular, consumers and firms to delay spending decisions until the outlook was clearer. In fact, the drop in spending was short and limited. Decreases in the federal funds rate after September 11—and large discounts by automobile producers in the last quarter of 2001—are believed to have been crucial in maintaining consumer confidence and consumer spending during that period.

● Was the monetary–fiscal mix used to fight the recession a textbook example of how policy should be conducted?

On this, economists differ. Most economists give high marks to the Federal Reserve for strongly decreasing interest rates as soon as the economy slowed down. But most economists are worried that the tax cuts introduced in 2001 and 2002 have led to large and persistent budget deficits. They argue that the tax cuts should have been temporary, helping the U.S. economy get out of the recession, but stopping thereafter. Instead, the tax cuts were permanent, and despite the fact that the U.S. economy is now going through a strong expansion, budget deficits are still large and are projected to remain large at least for the rest of the decade.

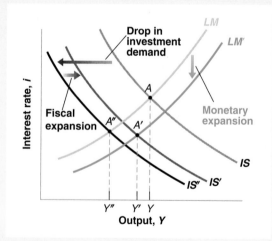

FIGURE 4   The U.S. Recession of 2001

Will output really decline instantaneously from Y_A to Y_B? No. We saw some reasons why not in Chapter 3: It may take a while for consumers to respond to the decrease in income. It takes a while for production to respond to the decrease in sales. Firms may initially accumulate inventories rather than cut production. We can now add to that list the fact that it may also take a while for firms to revise their investment plans in light of a decrease in sales. For all these reasons, the decline in output will occur only over time. In terms of Figure 5–10(a), output will decrease slowly from Y_A to Y_B.

Sources of dynamics in the goods market: (a) Production adjusts slowly to demand; (b) demand (consumption and investment) adjusts slowly to income (production).

More generally, it is reasonable to assume that when output is to the right of the equilibrium curve—which, in our case, after the tax increase, is IS'—output decreases slowly; when it is to the left of the equilibrium curve, output increases slowly. This basic conclusion is represented by the two large arrows on each side of IS' in Figure 5–10(a).

Now, let us look at the LM curve and the effects of a monetary contraction. As we have seen, a monetary contraction shifts the LM curve up. In Figure 5–10(b), the LM curve shifts from LM to LM': At a given level of income, say, Y_A, the interest rate increases from i_A to i_B. Will the interest rate increase instantaneously? In this case, the answer is yes. Interest rates adjust very quickly to changes in supply and demand. The market for government bonds is one of the most efficient markets in the world and clears within seconds of changes in demand or supply. If the Bank of Canada does an open market operation, selling bonds in the bonds market, the interest rate adjusts almost instantaneously. Therefore, the right assumption is that the decrease in money supply causes the interest rate to increase instantaneously from i_A to i_B in Figure 5–10(b). For the rest of the book, we will assume that the adjustment of the interest rate to any change in the demand or the supply of money is so fast that *the economy is always on the LM curve.*

Slow adjustment of Y in goods markets

Fast adjustment of i in financial markets

Equipped with these dynamics, let us re-examine the effects of a monetary contraction on activity and the interest rate. The adjustment is shown in Figure 5–11. Before the decrease in money supply, the economy is at point A, with output Y and interest rate i. At the moment at which the central bank decreases money supply, the LM curve shifts from LM to LM'. The economy jumps to point A'': Output does not change right away, and so the interest rate must do all the adjustment, increasing from i to i''. Over time, the higher interest rate leads to lower investment, a lower demand for goods, and lower output so that output slowly decreases from its initial level. The economy moves along LM' and eventually reaches point A'. At A', the interest rate is equal to i' and output is equal to Y'. Note that the eventual increase in the interest rate is smaller than the initial increase in the interest rate: This is because, as output contracts, so does the demand for money, which puts some pressure on the interest rate to decrease.

After a decrease in money: Interest rates initially increase and then decline, partially offsetting the initial increase. Output initially does not change, then declines over time.

In words: The monetary contraction leads initially to a sharp increase in the interest rate. Over time, this increase leads to a decrease in output. This time dimension is important, and

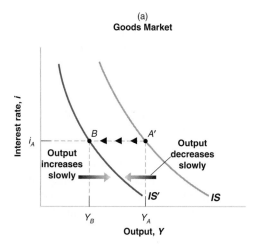

(a)
Goods Market

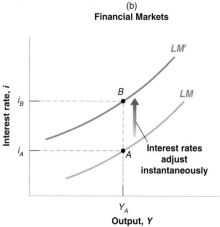

(b)
Financial Markets

FIGURE 5–10

Introducing Dynamics in the *IS-LM* Model

When output is above or below the level implied by the *IS* relation, it adjusts slowly to that level. In contrast, interest rates adjust quickly so that the *LM* relation is always satisfied.

FIGURE 5-11

The Dynamic Effects of a Monetary Contraction

A monetary contraction leads to an increase in the interest rate. The increase in the interest rate leads, over time, to a decline in output.

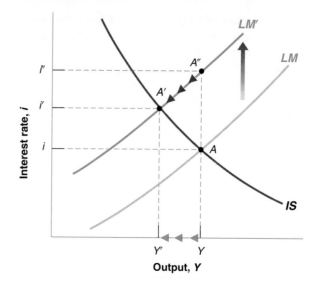

there is a general lesson about policy to be drawn from it. Monetary policy can affect the interest rate quickly but cannot affect output right away. So, the central bank must be careful not to be fighting the last battle. For example, there is no point in fighting a recession through a lower interest rate if the recession is already over when the lower interest rate starts affecting economic activity.

We will let you look at the dynamic effects of a change in fiscal policy on your own. And, from now on, we will often rely on these dynamics to tell more realistic stories of how changes in policy or behaviour affect economic activity.

5-6 | Does the *IS-LM* Model Actually Capture What Happens in the Economy?

The *IS-LM* model gives us a way of thinking about the determination of output and the interest rate. But it is a theory based on many assumptions and many simplifications. How do we know that we have made the right simplifications? How much should we believe the answers given by the *IS-LM* model?

These are the questions facing any theory, whether in macroeconomics or anywhere else. A theory must pass two tests.

- First, the assumptions and the simplifications must be reasonable. What "reasonable" means is not entirely clear. Surely assuming—as we have done—that there is only one type of good in the economy is factually wrong. But it may still be a reasonable simplification of reality if allowing for more than one type of good led to a more complicated model, but roughly the same results for aggregate activity, the interest rate, and so on. One assumption we have made in Chapters 3, 4, and 5 is factually wrong. We assumed net exports were zero and that exports and imports did not vary. In the next chapter, we will change that aspect of the model. This leads us to test theory against the American experience where exports and imports are less important.

- Second, the major implications of the theory must be consistent with what we actually see in the world. This is easier to check. Using econometrics, we can trace the effects of changes in monetary policy and fiscal policy in the United States and see how close the effects correspond to the predictions of the *IS-LM* model. And it turns out that the *IS-LM* model does quite well.

Figure 5–12 makes this point nicely. It shows the results of a recent econometric study of the effects of changes in monetary policy on activity, using data from the United States from 1960 to 1990. We use the U.S. economy to study the *IS-LM* model when exports and imports are less important. We add exports and imports in the next chapter. The study focuses on the effects of changes in the **federal funds rate**, the interest rate in the United States that is most directly affected by changes in monetary policy. It then traces the typical effects of such a change on activity.

We discussed the market for overnight funds and the ◀ overnight funds rate in Chapter 4, section 4-3.

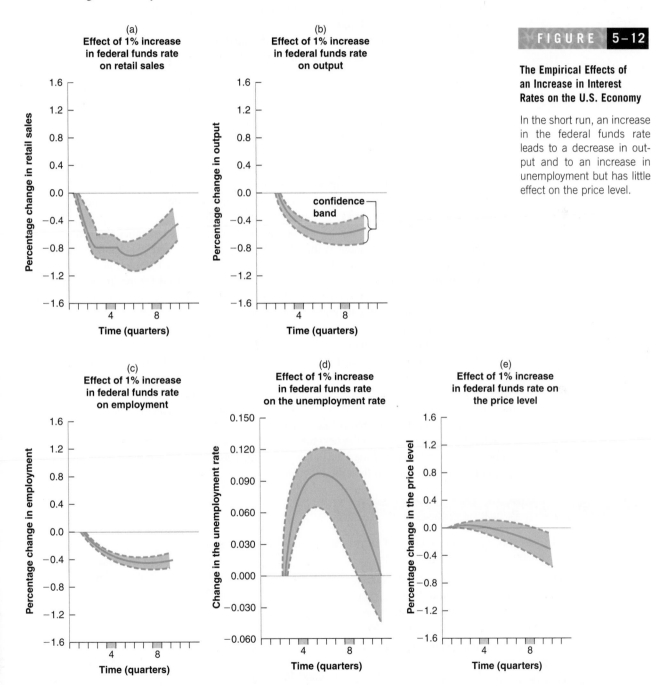

FIGURE 5–12

The Empirical Effects of an Increase in Interest Rates on the U.S. Economy

In the short run, an increase in the federal funds rate leads to a decrease in output and to an increase in unemployment but has little effect on the price level.

Source: Lawrence Christiano, Martin Eichenbaum, and Charles Evans, "The Effects of Monetary Policy Shocks: Evidence from the Flow of Funds," *Review of Economics and Statistics,* February 1996, Vol. 78, No. 1, pp. 16–34.

For an introduction to econometrics, see Appendix 3 at the end of the book.

Figure 5–12(a) shows the effects of an increase in the federal funds rate of 1% on retail sales over time. The percentage change in retail sales is plotted on the vertical axis and time, measured in quarters, on the horizontal axis. The figure plots three lines. The best estimate of the effect of the change in the interest rate on output is given by the solid line. But there is no such thing as learning the exact value of a coefficient or the exact effect of one variable on another. Rather, econometrics provides a best estimate—here, the solid line—and a measure of confidence we should have in the estimate. The true value of the effect lies within the two dotted lines with 60% probability. For this reason, the space between the two dashed lines is called a **confidence band**.

Focusing on the best estimate—the solid-colour line—we see that the increase in the federal funds rate leads to a decline in retail sales. The largest decrease, −0.9%, is achieved after five quarters.

Figure 5–12(b) shows how lower sales lead to lower output. In response to the decrease in sales, firms cut production, but initially by less than the decrease in sales. Put another way, firms accumulate inventories for some time. The adjustment of production is smoother and slower than the adjustment of sales. The largest decrease, −0.7%, is reached after eight quarters.

Figure 5–12(c) shows how lower output leads to lower employment: As firms cut production, they also cut employment. As with output, the decline in employment is slow and steady, reaching −0.5% after eight quarters. The decline in employment is reflected in an increase in the unemployment rate, shown in Figure 5–12(d).

Figure 5–12(e) looks at the behaviour of the price level. Remember that one of the *assumptions* of the *IS-LM* model is that the price level is given and so does not change in response to changes in demand. Figure 5–12(e) shows that this assumption is not a bad approximation in the short run. The price level is nearly unchanged for the first six quarters or so. Only after the first six quarters does the price level appear to decline. This gives a strong hint as to why the *IS-LM* model becomes less reliable as we look at the medium run: In the medium run, we can no longer assume that the price level is a given, and movements in the price level become important.

Figure 5–12 is comforting. It shows that the implications of the *IS-LM* model are consistent with what we observe in the economy. This does not *prove* that the *IS-LM* model is right. It may be that what we observe in the economy is the result of a completely different mechanism and that the fact that the *IS-LM* model fits well is a coincidence. But this seems unlikely. The *IS-LM* model looks like a solid basis on which to build to look at movements in activity in the short run. In the next three chapters, we look at the implications of openness in both goods and financial markets in the short run. Then, we return to what determines output in the medium run and then the long run.

SUMMARY

- The *IS-LM* model characterizes the implications of equilibrium in both the goods and the financial markets.

- The *IS* relation and the *IS* curve show the combinations of the interest rate and the level of output that are consistent with equilibrium in the goods market. An increase in the interest rate leads to a decline in output.

- The *LM* relation and the *LM* curve show the combinations of the interest rate and the level of output consistent with equilibrium in financial markets. Given the real money supply, an increase in output leads to an increase in the interest rate.

- A fiscal expansion shifts the *IS* curve to the right, leading to an increase in output and an increase in the interest rate. A monetary expansion shifts the *LM* curve down, leading to an increase in output and a decrease in the interest rate.

- The combination of monetary and fiscal policies is known as the monetary–fiscal policy mix, or simply policy mix. Sometimes monetary and fiscal policies are used for a common goal. Sometimes, the monetary–fiscal mix emerges from tensions or even disagreements between government (which is in charge of fiscal policy) and the central bank (which is in charge of monetary policy).

- The *IS-LM* model appears to describe the behaviour of the economy well in the short run. In particular, the effects of monetary policy appear to be similar to those implied by the *IS-LM* model once dynamics are introduced in the model. An increase in the interest rate due to a monetary contraction leads to a steady decrease in output, with the maximum effect taking place after about eight quarters.

QUESTIONS AND PROBLEMS

An asterisk denotes a harder question. [Web] indicates that the question requires access to the Internet.

1. TRUE/FALSE/UNCERTAIN

a. The main determinants of investment are the level of sales and the interest rate.

b. If all the exogenous variables in the *IS* relation are constant, then a higher level of output can be achieved only at a lower interest rate.

c. The *IS* curve is downward sloping because goods–market equilibrium implies that an increase in taxes leads to a lower level of output.

d. If both government spending and taxes increase by the same amount, the *IS* curve does not shift.

e. The *LM* curve is upward sloping because a higher level of money supply is needed to increase output.

f. An increase in government spending decreases investment.

g. An increase in output at a constant interest rate can only be achieved using a monetary–fiscal policy mix.

*2. INVESTMENT AND THE INTEREST RATE

The chapter argues that the reason investment depends negatively on the interest rate is the following: When the interest rate increases, the cost of borrowing funds also increases, and this discourages investment. However, firms often finance their investment projects using their own funds. Because no borrowing actually occurs, will higher interest rates discourage investment in this case? Explain. (*Hint*: Think of yourself as an owner of a firm who is consid-

ering financing new investment projects in your firm using the profits your firm just earned, or buying bonds. Will your decision to invest in new projects in your firm be affected by the interest rate?)

3. THE MULTIPLIER REVISITED

Consider first the goods market model with constant investment that we saw in Chapter 3:

$$C = c_0 + c_1(Y - T), \text{ and } I, G, \text{ and } T \text{ are given.}$$

a. Solve for equilibrium output. What is the value of the multiplier?

Now, let investment depend on both sales and the interest rate:

$$I = b_0 + b_1 Y - b_2 i$$

b. Solve for equilibrium output. At a given interest rate, is the effect of change in autonomous spending bigger than what it was in (a)? Why? (Assume $c_1 + b_1 < 1$).

Next, let us introduce the financial market equilibrium condition with real money demand equal to real money supply.

$$M/P = d_1 Y - d_2 i$$

c. Solve for equilibrium output. (*Hint*: Eliminate the interest rate in the *IS* equation using the expression from the *LM* equation.) Derive the multiplier (the effect of a one-unit change in b_0 on output).

d. Is the multiplier you obtained smaller or larger than the multiplier you derived in your answer to (a)? Explain how your answer depends on the behavioural equations for consumption, investment, and money demand.

4. THE RESPONSE OF INVESTMENT TO FISCAL POLICY

a. Using the *IS-LM* graph, determine the effects on output and the interest rate of a decrease in government spending. Why is the effect on investment ambiguous?

With more information on the parameters of the *IS* and *LM* relation, we may be able to determine, for example, whether deficit reduction is good or bad for *I* in the short run. Consider the following equations for consumption, investment, and money demand:

$$C = c_0 + c_1(Y - T)$$
$$I = b_0 + b_1 Y - b_2 i$$
$$M/P = d_1 Y - d_2 i$$

b. Solve for equilibrium output. (*Hint:* You may want to work through question 3 if you are having trouble with this step.)

c. Solve for the equilibrium interest rate. (*Hint:* Use the *LM* relation.)

d. Solve for investment.

e. Under what condition on the parameters of the model (for example, c_0, c_1, and so on) will investment increase when *G* decreases?

f. Explain the condition you derived in (e).

5. MONETARY AND FISCAL POLICIES: AN EXAMPLE

Consider the following *IS-LM* model:

$$C = 200 + 0.25Y_D$$
$$I = 150 + 0.25Y - 1000i$$
$$G = 250$$
$$T = 200$$
$$(M/P)^d = 2Y - 8000i$$
$$M/P = 1600$$

a. Derive the equation for the *IS* curve. (*Hint:* You want an equation with *Y* on the left hand side and all else on the right.)

b. Derive the equation for the *LM* curve. (*Hint:* It will be convenient for later use to write this equation with *i* on the left side and all else on the right.)

c. Solve for equilibrium real output. (*Hint:* Substitute the expression for the interest rate given by the *LM* equation into the *IS* equation, and solve for output.)

d. Solve for the equilibrium interest rate. (*Hint:* Substitute the value you obtained for *Y* in (c) into either the *IS* or the *LM* equation, and solve for *i*. If your algebra is correct, you should get the same answer from both equations.)

e. Solve for the equilibrium values of *C* and *I*, and verify the value you obtained for *Y* by adding up *C*, *I*, and *G*.

f. Now, suppose that money supply increases to $M/P = 1840$. Solve for *Y*, *i*, *C*, and *I*, and explain in words the effects of expansionary monetary policy.

g. Set *M/P* equal to its initial value of 1600. Now, suppose that government spending increases to $G = 400$. Summarize the effects of expansionary fiscal policy on *Y*, *i*, and *C*.

***h.** (Try this question only if you have already answered question 4.) Without solving for *Y* and *i*, can you tell whether contractionary fiscal policy will increase or decrease *I*? To verify your answer, set all exogenous variables back to their initial values, and solve for investment when government spending decreases to $G = 100$.

*6. THE LIQUIDITY TRAP

a. Suppose the interest rate on bonds was negative. Would people want to hold bonds or money? Explain.

b. Draw the demand for money as a function of the interest rate, for a given level of real income. How does your answer to (a) affect your answer? (*Hint:* Show that the demand for money becomes very flat as the interest rate gets very close to zero.)

c. Derive the *LM* curve. What happens to the *LM* curve as the interest rate gets very close to zero? (*Hint:* It becomes very flat.)

d. Take your *LM* curve. Suppose that the interest rate is very close to zero and that the central bank increases the supply of money. What happens to the interest rate at a given level of income?

e. Can an expansionary monetary policy increase output when the interest rate is already very close to zero?

This inability of the central bank to decrease the interest rate when it is already very close to zero is known as the "liquidity trap" and was first mentioned by Keynes in 1936 in his *General Theory*—which laid the foundations of the *IS-LM* model.

f. Keynes also mentioned that he was not aware of there ever having been a liquidity trap. Yet, in 1998, Japan's interest rate was almost zero, and output had barely changed even in the face of expansionary monetary policy by the central bank of Japan. Do you think that Japan was experiencing a liquidity trap?

g. Also, in 1998, the Japanese government pursued an expansionary fiscal policy in its effort to increase output. Do you agree with this course of action? Is fiscal policy more or less effective than monetary policy when there is a liquidity trap?

7. POLICY RECOMMENDATIONS

Suggest a policy or a policy mix to achieve the following objectives:

a. Increase Y while keeping i constant.

b. Decrease the deficit while keeping Y constant. What happens to i? To investment?

FURTHER READING

Paul Krugman, an economist at the Massachusetts Institute of Technology (MIT), regularly writes columns for several magazines, including *Fortune* and *Slate*. The columns are insightful and fun to read. You can find them on his home page (**http://web.mit.edu/krugman/www/**). One column, "Vulgar Keynesians," discusses the role of monetary policy in the U.S. economy. Read it, and try to see if you can restate his arguments in terms of the *IS-LM* model.

CHAPTER 6
OPENNESS IN GOODS AND FINANCIAL MARKETS

We have assumed so far that the economy was *closed*—that it did not interact with the rest of the world. We started this way, to keep things simple and build up your intuition for the basic macroeconomic mechanisms. We are now ready to open the economy. Understanding the macroeconomic implications of openness will occupy us in this and the next two chapters.

"Openness" has three distinct dimensions:

1. **Openness in goods markets**: the opportunity for consumers and firms to choose between domestic and foreign goods. In no country is this choice completely free of restrictions: Even the countries most committed to free trade have tariffs and quotas on at least some foreign goods. (**Tariffs** are taxes on imported goods; **quotas** are restrictions on the quantities of goods that can be imported.) At the same time, in most countries, average tariffs are low and getting lower.

2. **Openness in financial markets**: the opportunity for financial investors to choose between domestic and foreign financial assets. Until recently, even some of the richest countries, such as France and Italy, had **capital controls**, tight restrictions on the foreign assets their domestic residents could hold as well as on the domestic assets foreigners could hold. These restrictions are rapidly disappearing. As a result, world financial markets are becoming more and more closely integrated.

3. **Openness in factor markets**: the opportunity for firms to choose where to locate production and for workers to choose where to work and whether or not to migrate. Here also, trends are clear. More and more companies move their operations around the world to take advantage of low costs. Much of the debate about the **North American Free Trade Agreement (NAFTA)**, signed in 1993 by the United States, Canada, and Mexico, centred on its implications for the relocation of U.S. firms to Mexico. Immigration from low-wage countries to high-wage countries is a hot political issue in countries ranging from Germany to the United States.

In the short run and the medium run—the focus of this and the next two chapters—openness in factor markets plays much less of a role than openness in either goods or financial markets. Thus, we will ignore openness in factor markets and focus only on the first two dimensions of openness here. We return to openness in factor markets in Chapter 17. In this chapter, section 6-1 looks at the implications of openness in the goods market. Section 6-2 looks at the implications of openness in financial markets.

6-1 | Openness in Goods Markets

Figure 6–1 plots the evolution of Canadian exports and imports, as ratios to GDP, since 1961. ("Canadian exports" means exports *from* Canada; "Canadian imports" means imports *to* Canada.) What is striking is how these ratios have increased over time. Exports and imports, which were equal to around 12% of GDP as recently as the 1960s, now stand around 40% of GDP. Canada trades substantially more with the rest of the world than it did just 40 years ago.

A closer look at Figure 6–1 reveals two interesting patterns:

- For most of the last 40 years, in fact, in all years except 1989 to 1992, Canada ran a trade surplus, that is, exports of goods and services were larger than imports of goods and services. This feature of the data receives further consideration in Chapter 17, Economic Growth in the Open Economy.
- Although Canada usually has a trade surplus, the size of that trade surplus has varied over time. We have already noted that the trade surplus was negative from 1989 to 1992. The trade surplus from 1995 to 2000 was very large as was the trade surplus from 1961 to 1973. The trade surplus was smaller in the 1980s. We need a way to understand these variations over time.

> Recall from Chapter 3 that the trade balance is equal to the difference between exports and imports. If exports are larger than imports, then there is a trade surplus (equivalently, a positive trade balance). If exports are smaller than imports, then there is a trade deficit (equivalently, a negative ◄ trade balance).

Given the constant media talk about *globalization*, the data in Figure 6–1 are one aspect of the reality of globalization. Canada produces many goods and services consumed by people living in other countries. Canadians consume many goods and services produced in other countries. With exports around 40% of GDP, Canada has one of the largest ratios of exports to GDP among the rich countries of the world. Table 6–1 gives ratios for eight other OECD countries.

> For more on the OECD and for the list of member ◄ countries, see Chapter 1.

The United States and Japan are at the low end of the range of export ratios. The large European countries, such as Germany and the United Kingdom, have ratios that are two to three times larger. Germany is similar to Canada, and the smaller European countries have even larger ratios than does Canada, up to 105% for Belgium, and 228% for Luxembourg! (These two countries illustrate an odd possibility: Could a country have exports larger than its GDP—an export ratio greater than 1? The answer is yes. The reason is given in the Focus box "Can Exports Exceed GDP?")

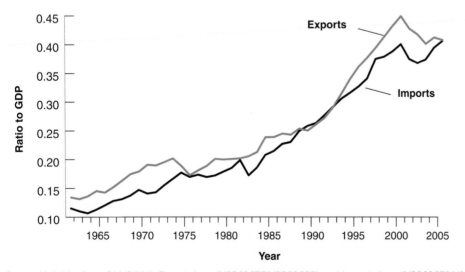

Source: Variables from CANSIM II: Export share (V3862675/V3862685) and import share (V3862679/V3862685).

FIGURE 6-1

Canadian Exports and Imports as Ratios of GDP, 1961–2005

Exports and imports, which were equal to 12% of GDP as recently as the 1960s, now stand around 40% of GDP.

TABLE   6-1   Ratios of Exports to GDP for Selected OECD Countries, 2003

Country	Export Ratio (%)	Country	Export Ratio (%)
United States	11	Switzerland	61
Japan	16	Austria	65
United Kingdom	46	Belgium	105
Germany	29	Luxembourg	228

Source: OECD National Accounts.

Do these numbers indicate that the United States or Japan has more trade barriers than, say, Belgium or Luxembourg? No. The main factors behind these differences are geography and size. Distance from other markets explains a good part of the low Japanese ratio. Size also matters: The smaller the country, the more it must specialize in only a few products, produce and export them, and rely on imports for the others. Luxembourg can hardly afford to produce the range of goods produced by the United States, a country with a GDP more than 300 times larger. Part of the reason Canada's exports-to-GDP ratio is so large is the full integration of automobile production across Canada and the United States.

> Iceland is both isolated and small. What would you expect its export ratio to be?

The Choice between Domestic and Foreign Goods

How does openness in goods markets force us to rethink the way we look at equilibrium in the *goods* market? When thinking about consumers' decisions in the goods market, we have focused so far on their decision to save or to consume. But when goods markets are open, domestic consumers face another decision: whether to buy domestic goods or foreign goods. Other domestic buyers (firms, government) and foreign buyers also face this decision. If they decide to buy more domestic goods, the demand for domestic goods increases, and so does domestic output. If they decide to buy more foreign goods, then foreign output increases instead.

> In a closed economy, consumers have to make one decision: save or buy (consume). In an open economy, consumers have to make two decisions: (1) save, or (2) buy domestic or foreign.

Central to consumers' and firms' decisions to buy foreign or domestic goods is the price of foreign goods in terms of domestic goods. We call this relative price the **real exchange rate**. The real exchange rate is not directly observable, and you will not find it in the newspapers. What you will find there are *nominal exchange rates*, the relative prices of currencies. Let us start by looking at nominal exchange rates, then see how we can use them to construct real exchange rates.

FOCUS   Can Exports Exceed GDP?

Can a country have exports larger than its GDP—an export ratio greater than 1?

At first, it would seem that countries cannot export more than they produce so that the export ratio must be less than 1. Not so. The trick is to realize that exports and imports may include exports and imports of intermediate goods.

For example, take a country that imports intermediate goods for $1 billion. Suppose it transforms them into final goods using only labour. Say that total wages equal $200 million and there are no profits. The value of final goods is thus equal to $1200 million. Assume that $1 billion worth of final goods is exported and the rest is consumed domestically.

Exports and imports therefore both equal $1 billion. What is GDP in this economy? Remember that GDP is value added *in* the economy (see Chapter 2). So, in this example, GDP equals $200 million, and the ratio of exports to GDP equals $1000/$200 = 5.

Hence, exports can exceed GDP. This is, indeed, the case for many small countries where most economic activity is organized around a harbour and import–export activities. Luxembourg and Belgium are examples of such countries.

Nominal Exchange Rates

Nominal exchange rates between two currencies are quoted in two ways: (1) the price of the domestic currency in terms of the foreign currency, or (2) the price of the foreign currency in terms of the domestic currency. In 2005, for example, the nominal exchange rate between the Canadian dollar and the American dollar could be quoted as either the price of a Canadian dollar in terms of American dollars ($1 C = $0.7685 US) or as the price of an American dollar in terms of Canadian dollars ($1 US = 1/0.7685 = $1.3012 C). It is annoying that both Canada and the United States call their unit of currency a dollar. In newspapers, exchange rates really are quoted to four decimal places. The extra places matter if the transaction involves billions of dollars, of either country!

In this book, we will define the **nominal exchange rate** as *the price of foreign currency in terms of domestic currency* and denote it by *E*. When, for example, looking at the exchange rate between Canada and the United States (from the viewpoint of Canada, the Canadian dollar is the domestic currency), *E* will denote the price of a U.S. dollar in terms of Canadian dollars—so, as of 2005, this is $1.3012.

◀ A definition to remember: *E* is the nominal exchange rate or the price of foreign currency in terms of domestic currency. (For example, from the point of view of Canada, it is the price of U.S. dollars in terms of Canadian dollars.)

Exchange rates between foreign currencies and the dollar change every day, every minute of the day. These changes are called *nominal appreciations* or *nominal depreciations*— appreciations or depreciations for short. An **appreciation** of the domestic currency is an increase in the price of the domestic currency in terms of a foreign currency. Given our definition of the exchange rate as the price of the foreign currency in terms of domestic currency, an appreciation of the domestic currency corresponds to a *decrease* in the exchange rate, *E*.

◀ A warning: Defining exchange rates as the price of foreign currency in terms of domestic currency is the convention in economic articles and books on the North American side of the Atlantic. On the other side of the Atlantic, however, economists more often use the alternative definition, defining exchange rates as the price of domestic currency in terms of foreign currency.

This is more intuitive than it seems: Consider the Canadian dollar and the American dollar (from the viewpoint of Canada). An *appreciation* of the Canadian dollar means that the price of the Canadian dollar in terms of the U.S. dollar goes up. Equivalently, the price of the American dollar in terms of Canadian dollars goes down, which is the same as saying that the exchange rate has decreased. A **depreciation** of the Canadian dollar means the price of the Canadian dollar in terms of American dollars goes down. Equivalently, the price of the American dollar in terms of Canadian dollars goes up, the same as saying that the exchange rate has increased.

That an appreciation corresponds to a decrease in the exchange rate and a depreciation to an increase in the exchange rate will almost surely be confusing to you at first—indeed, it confuses many professional economists—but it will eventually become familiar as your understanding of open-economy macroeconomics deepens. Until then, consult Figure 6–2, which summarizes the terminology. (You may have encountered two other words for movements in exchange rates: "revaluations" and "devaluations." These two terms are used when countries operate under **fixed exchange rates**—a system in which two or more countries maintain an unchanging exchange rate between their currencies. Under such a system, decreases in the exchange rate—infrequent, by definition—are called **revaluations** (rather than appreciations). Increases in the exchange rate are called **devaluations** (rather than depreciations). We discuss fixed exchange rates in Chapter 8.)

Keep in mind these definitions as we move on to Figure 6–3, which plots the nominal exchange rate between the American dollar and the Canadian dollar since 1970. The figure has four important features:

1. *The trend increase in the exchange rate*. In 2005, it cost about $1.20 Canadian to buy one American dollar. From 1970 to 1975, one American dollar cost a Canadian roughly one Canadian dollar. Over the last 30 years or so, there has been a sustained depreciation of the Canadian dollar.

◀ Remember,
Increase in the exchange rate ⇔ Depreciation
Decrease in the exchange rate ⇔ Appreciation

2. There was a significant period from 1988 to 1991 when the Canadian dollar appreciated. At the end of 1987, one American dollar cost $1.31 Canadian. At its most valuable recent level, October 1991, one American dollar cost only $1.13 Canadian.

3. A significant appreciation from 2002, where one U.S. dollar costs $1.50 Canadian to 2005, where one U.S. dollar costs $1.20 Canadian.

FIGURE 6-2

The Nominal Exchange
Rate, Appreciation, and
Depreciation: Canada and
the United States (from the
viewpoint of Canada)

**From the viewpoint of Canada
looking at the United States**

Nominal exchange rate *E*
Price of the American dollar in terms
of Canadian dollars

Appreciation of the Canadian dollar

Price of Canadian dollars in U.S. dollars
increases equivalently:
Price of U.S. dollars in Canadian dollars
decreases equivalently:
Exchange rate decreases: *E*↓

Depreciation of the Canadian dollar

Price of Canadian dollars in U.S. dollars
decreases equivalently:
Price of U.S. dollars in Canadian dollars
increases equivalently:
Exchange rate increases: *E*↑

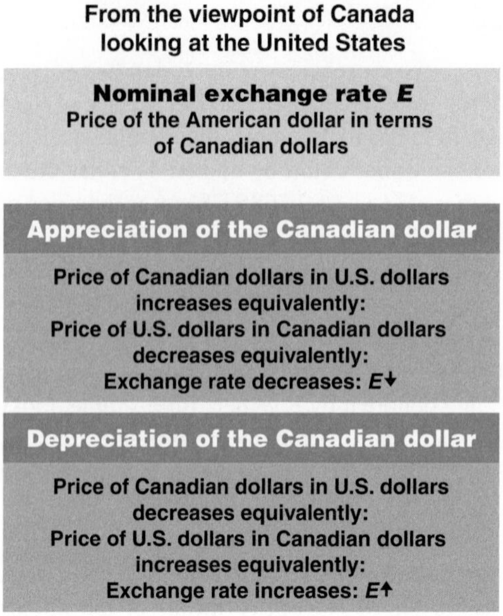

4. The nominal exchange exhibits a lot of movement or, to use another word, is very volatile. Figure 6–3 is drawn using a monthly average of daily observations. It would look more volatile if we had plotted the daily data. In macroeconomics, we are mostly interested in movements in the value of the Canadian dollar over longer periods, such as the average change over three months or even a year.

Figure 6–3 tells us only about movements in the relative price of the two currencies. To Canadian tourists thinking of visiting the United States, the question is not, however, how much one American dollar costs in terms of Canadian dollars but also how many goods their Canadian dollar will buy. It does them little good to get more American dollars per Canadian dollar if the American dollar prices of goods have increased in roughly the same proportion. This takes us closer to where we want to go—to the construction of real exchange rates.

Real Exchange Rates

How do we construct the real exchange rate between Canada and the United States—the price of American goods in terms of Canadian goods?

FIGURE 6-3

The Nominal Exchange Rate
between the American
Dollar and the Canadian
Dollar, 1970–2006

The trend depreciation of
the Canadian dollar from
1977 to 2001 is broken only
by a sharp appreciation
from 1988 to 1991. There
has been another large
appreciation since 2001.

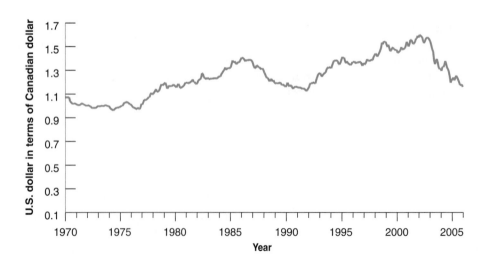

Source: Using CANSIM II variable V37426.

Suppose the United States produced only one good, an SUV (sport utility vehicle) (this is one of those completely counterfactual "Suppose" statements, but we will become more realistic shortly) and Canada also produced only one good, say, a minivan.

Constructing the real exchange rate, the price of this one American good in terms of that one Canadian good would be straightforward.

- The first step would be to take the price of the SUV in U.S. dollars and convert it to a price in Canadian dollars. Suppose the price of the SUV in the United States is $40,000 US. Suppose a U.S. dollar is worth 1.5 Canadian dollars. So, the price of the SUV in Canadian dollars is $40,000 \times 1.5 = \$60,000$.
- The second step would be to compute the ratio of the price of the SUV in Canadian dollars to the price of the minivan in Canadian dollars. The price of a minivan in Canada is $40,000. Thus, the price of the SUV in terms of minivans—that is, the real exchange rate between Canada and the United States—would be $60,000/$40,000 = 1.5.

◀

Computing the relative price of SUVs in terms of minivans:

SUV:
$40,000 US $\times$ 1.5
$\qquad = \$60,000$ C

Minivan: $= \$40,000$ C

Relative price of SUVs in terms of minivans:

$$\frac{\$60,000}{\$40,000} = 1.5$$

But Canada and the United States produce more than minivans and SUVs, and we want to construct a real exchange rate that reflects the relative price of *all* the goods produced in the United States in terms of *all* the goods produced in Canada. The computation we just went through tells us how to proceed. Rather than use the U.S. dollar price of an SUV and the Canadian dollar price of a minivan, we must use a U.S. dollar price index for all goods produced in the United States and a Canadian dollar price index for all goods produced in Canada. This is exactly what the GDP deflators we introduced in Chapter 2 do: They are, by definition, price indexes for the set of final goods and services produced in the economy.

So, let P be the GDP deflator for Canada, P^* be the GDP deflator for the United States (as a rule, we will denote foreign variables by an asterisk), and E be the U.S. dollar–Canadian dollar nominal exchange rate. Figure 6–4 shows the steps needed to construct the real exchange rate.

- The price of U.S. goods in U.S. dollars is P^*. Multiplying it by the exchange rate, E (the price of U.S. dollars in terms of Canadian dollars) gives us the price of U.S. goods in Canadian dollars, EP^*.
- The price of Canadian goods in Canadian dollars is P. The real exchange rate, the price of U.S. goods in terms of Canadian goods, which we shall call ϵ (the Greek lowercase epsilon), is thus given by

$$\epsilon = \frac{EP^*}{P} \qquad (6.1)$$

◀

Another definition to remember: ϵ is the real exchange rate or the price of foreign goods in terms of domestic goods. (For example, from the point of view of Canada, it is the price of U.S. goods in terms of Canadian goods.)

Note that unlike the price of an SUV in terms of a minivan, the real exchange rate is an index number: That is, its level is arbitrary and thus uninformative. This is because the GDP deflators used in the construction of the real exchange rate are themselves index numbers; as we saw in Chapter 2, they are equal to 1 (or 100) in whatever year is chosen as the base year. But while its level is uninformative, relative changes in the real exchange rate are informative: If, for example, the real exchange rate between the United States and Canada increases by 10%, this tells us Canadian goods are now 10% cheaper relative to U.S. goods than they were before.

An increase in the relative price of domestic goods in terms of foreign goods is called a **real appreciation**; a decrease is called a **real depreciation**. *Real* indicates that we are

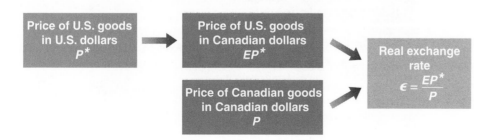

FIGURE 6-4

The Construction of the Real Exchange Rate

referring to changes in the relative price of *goods*, not the relative price of currencies. Given our definition of the real exchange rate as the price of foreign goods in terms of domestic goods, a real appreciation corresponds to a *decrease* in the real exchange rate, ϵ. Similarly, a real depreciation corresponds to an *increase* in ϵ. These definitions are summarized in Figure 6–5, which does for the real exchange rate what Figure 6–2 did for the nominal exchange rate.

Figure 6–6 plots the evolution of the real exchange rate between the United States and Canada from 1970 to 2005. For convenience, it also reproduces the evolution of the nominal exchange rate from Figure 6–3. Real and nominal exchange rates were both about 1 in 1976. But remember the units of the real exchange rate are arbitrary.

Figure 6–6 has three distinct sections:

- From 1970 to 1984, although the nominal exchange rate depreciated, the Canadian dollar price of an American dollar increased from about $1 C per $1 US to $1.25 C per $1 US. In spite of this nominal depreciation, the value of the real exchange rate in 1984 was roughly the same as in 1970.

    How can this be? Given the increase in the nominal exchange rate over the period, how come the real exchange rate has remained roughly the same? The answer: Although the Canadian dollar depreciated from 1970 to 1984 by 25%, the price level in Canada increased more than the price level in the United States. To see this more clearly, return to the definition of the real exchange rate:

$$\epsilon = \frac{EP^*}{P}$$

Two things happened between 1970 and 1984. First, E went up: The U. S. dollar cost more in terms of Canadian dollars—this is the nominal depreciation we saw earlier. Second, inflation was higher in Canada than in the United States, leading to a larger increase in the Canadian price level, P, than in the American price level, P^*. This has led to a decrease in P^*/P. The increase in E and the decrease in P^*/P roughly cancelled out between 1970 and 1984, leading to an unchanged real exchange rate.

To make this more concrete, return to our American tourists thinking of visiting Canada. They could buy 25% more Canadian dollars per American dollar in 1984 than in 1970. Does this imply their trip would be 25% cheaper? No. When they arrived in

From the viewpoint of Canada looking at the United States

Real exchange rate ϵ
Price of American goods in terms of Canadian goods

Real appreciation

Price of Canadian goods in terms of American goods increases
equivalently:
Price of American goods in terms of Canadian goods decreases
equivalently:
Real exchange rate decreases: $\epsilon\downarrow$

Real depreciation

Price of Canadian goods in terms of American goods decreases
equivalently:
Price of American goods in terms of Canadian goods increases
equivalently:
Real exchange rate increases: $\epsilon\uparrow$

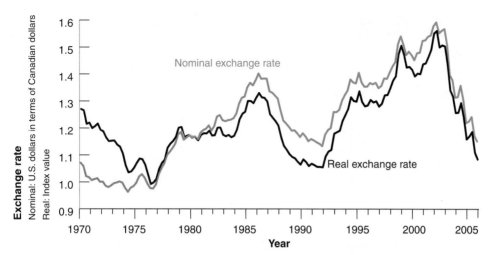

FIGURE 6-6

Real and Nominal Exchange Rates between Canada and the United States, 1970–2005

The nominal and the real exchange rates moved together for most of this period.

Source: Nominal exchange rate using CANSIM II variable V37426; the United States real GDP deflator using series GDPDEF from the Federal Reserve Bank of St. Louis FRED database; the Canadian GDP deflator using CANSIM II variable V19920677 divided by V498086. The real exchange rate is EP*/P.

Canada, they would have discovered that the prices of goods in Canada had increased by 25% more than the prices of goods in the United States, roughly cancelling the increase in the value of the American dollar in terms of Canadian dollars. Their trip would have been no cheaper in 1984 than it would have been in 1970.

There is a general lesson here. Over long periods of time, depending on differences in inflation rates across countries, nominal and real exchange rates can move quite differently. We will return to this issue in Chapter 13.

Can there be a real appreciation with no nominal appreciation? Can there be a nominal appreciation with no real appreciation?

- From 1992 to 2002, both the nominal and real exchange rates depreciated. The American dollar, which cost a Canadian about $1.25 C in 1984, cost a $1.57 C in 2002. This is the "dead duck" description of the loonie over the decade of the 1990s. Throughout most of the decade, the Canadian dollar fell in value or the U.S. dollar became more expensive for Canadians.

In the 1990s, Canada had a lower average inflation rate than did the United States. The ratio $P*/P$ actually increased. This can be seen in Figure 6–6, where the increase in the real exchange rate from 1997 to 2001 is substantially larger than the increase in the nominal exchange rate.

Between 1970 and 2001, the difference between the American inflation rate and the Canadian inflation rate was usually less than 1% in a given year. In other words, the change in $P*/P$ from one year to the next was usually 1% or less. In contrast, there have been several years when the nominal exchange rate has changed by much more than 5% within the year.

- The third and fourth observations to make concerning Figure 6–6 is to look at the periods of real exchange rate appreciation. The first period is from 1987 to 1991. In this period, as the Canadian dollar appreciated from $1.30 C per $1 US to $1.15 C per $1 US, American goods became 15% cheaper to Canadians, or Canadian goods became 15% more expensive for Americans (these are the same statements). Cross-border shopping became a major recreational activity for Canadians as they flocked across the American border in search of cheaper American goods. And Americans stopped shopping in Canada! We need to understand the source of this massive real and nominal appreciation of the Canadian dollar from 1987 to 1991. The second period is from 2002 to 2005. We return to this period in our discussion of long-run equilibrium real exchange rate in section 19–4 as well as in the general discussion of recent Canadian monetary policy in Chapter 25.

We have one last step to take. Canada trades mostly with the United States, as noted in Table 6–2. The numbers refer to **merchandise trade**—exports and imports of goods; they do not include exports and imports of services, such as travel services and tourism.

The United States accounts for 84% of Canada's merchandise exports and, a slightly smaller percentage, only 72%, of Canada's merchandise imports. The only exchange rate of

Countries	Exports to		Imports from	
	$ Billions	**Percent**	**$ Billions**	**Percent**
United States	351.9	81.8	250.0	68.8
Japan	10.0	2.3	10.0	2.8
United Kingdom	9.4	2.2	9.2	2.5
Other EEC Countries	17.7	4.1	27.1	7.4
Other OECD Countries	14.2	3.3	22.4	6.2
Other Countries	27.2	6.3	44.5	12.3
Total	**430.4**	**100.0**	**363.1**	**100.0**

Source: Statistics Canada, CANSIM II Tables 228-0001, 228-0002, 228-0003.

Bi- means two. *Multi-* means many.

The multilateral real U.S. exchange rate is also called the U.S. **trade-weighted real exchange rate**, and the U.S. **effective real exchange rate**.

vital interest to Canadians is the exchange rate with respect to the United States. Sometimes, this is called our **bilateral real exchange rate**; implicitly for Canada, we mean the exchange rate with the United States.

Canada, as Table 6–2 shows, also trades with Japan, the United Kingdom, the rest of Europe, and, indeed, the rest of the world. We could calculate a bilateral real exchange rate with Japan, the United Kingdom, and every other country. The **multilateral real exchange rate** is a weighted average of bilateral real exchange rates. The weights could be either export shares or import shares (or an average of these two shares). Canadians, because the United States accounts for 80% of trade, rarely bother to calculate a multilateral real exchange rate. If you planned a graduation trip to the United Kingdom, the rest of Europe, or more exotic destinations, you would have to make a multilateral real exchange rate calculation to calculate the cost of your trip around the world.

6-2 | Openness in Financial Markets

Openness in financial markets allows financial investors to hold both domestic and foreign assets, to diversify their portfolios, to speculate on movements in foreign versus domestic interest rates, exchange rates, and so on. And diversify and speculate they do. Given that buying or selling foreign assets implies, as part of the operation, buying or selling foreign currency (sometimes called **foreign exchange**), the size of transactions in foreign-exchange markets gives a sense of the importance of international financial transactions.

International financial markets are dominated by trades in assets. Here is an example. In 2001, the recorded *daily* volume of foreign-exchange transactions in the world was $2.6 trillion, of which 90% — about $2.4 trillion — involved dollars on one side of the transaction. To get a sense of the magnitude of these numbers, the sum of U.S. exports and imports in 2001 totalled $2.5 trillion for the year, or about $7 billion a day. If the only dollar transactions in foreign-exchange markets had been on one side by U.S. exporters selling their foreign currency earnings and on the other side by U.S. importers buying the foreign currency they needed to buy foreign goods, the volume of transactions would have been $7 billion a day, or about 0.3% of the actual daily volume of dollar transactions ($2.4 trillion) involving dollars in foreign-exchange markets. This computation yields a simple conclusion: Most of the transactions are associated not with trade but with purchases and sales of financial assets. The volume of transactions in foreign-exchange markets is not only high but also increasing rapidly. The volume of foreign-exchange transactions in New York is now more than 25 times what it was in 1980. Again, this activity reflects an increase in financial transactions rather than an increase in trade over the last 15 years.

For a country as a whole, openness in financial markets has an important implication. It allows the country to run trade surpluses and trade deficits. A country running a trade deficit is buying more from the rest of the world than it is selling to the rest of the world and must borrow the difference. It borrows by making it attractive for foreign financial investors to increase their holdings of domestic assets—in effect, to lend to the country. This lending from one country to another plays a key role in economic growth. We explore this feature of economic growth in Chapter 17. In the meantime, international forces also play an important role in the short-run macroeconomic outcome in Canada and in other countries. These forces are measured using a set of accounts called the balance of payments.

◄ Daily volume of foreign exchange transactions with U.S. dollars on one side of the transaction: $2 trillion.

Daily volume of trade of the United States with the rest of the world: $6 billion (0.3% of the volume of foreign exchange transactions).

The Balance of Payments

A country's transactions with the rest of the world are summarized by a set of accounts called the **balance of payments**. Table 6–3 presents the Canadian balance of payments for 2005.

In this presentation, the table has two parts, separated by a line. Transactions are referred to as either **above the line** or **below the line**.

The Current Account. The transactions above the line all record payments to and from the rest of the world. These are called **current account** transactions.

The first two lines record exports and imports of goods and services. Exports lead to payments from the rest of the world and imports to payments to the rest of the world. In 2005, exports exceeded imports, leading to a Canadian trade surplus of $53.4 billion. (Note that the numbers for exports and imports are different from those in Table 6–2; this is because the numbers in Table 6–2 refer only to goods, and the numbers here include both goods *and* services.)

Exports and imports are not the only sources of payments to and from the rest of the world. Canadian residents receive **investment income** on their holdings of foreign assets, and foreign residents receive investment income on their holdings of Canadian assets. In 2005, investment income received from the rest of the world was $44.6 billion and investment income paid to foreigners was $67.5 billion, for a **net investment income** balance of −$22.9 billion.

TABLE   6–3 The Canadian Balance of Payments, 2005, in Billions of Canadian Dollars

Current Account		
Exports	516.4	
Imports	463.0	
Trade balance (surplus = +) (1)		53.4
Investment income received	44.6	
Investment income paid	67.5	
Net investment income (2)		−22.9
Net transfers paid (3)		−0.3
Current account balance (surplus = +) (1) + (2) + (3)		30.2
Capital Account		
Increase in foreign holdings of Canadian assets	84.0	
Increase in Canadian holdings of foreign assets	−112.1	
Decrease in Canada's net foreign debts (or increase in Canada's net foreign assets)		−28.1
Statistical discrepancy		−2.1

Source: Statistics Canada, CANSIM II Tables 376-0001, 376-0002.

Finally, countries give and receive foreign aid and other transfers to or from foreigners; the net value of these payments is recorded as **net transfers paid**. In 2005, these amounted to +$0.3 billion paid by Canadians. This small transfer makes it seem as though Canada, a relatively rich country, gives almost no foreign aid. Be assured this is not the case. Canadians, both through their governments and privately through organizations, such as UNICEF or Mennonite Central Committee, do give money to aid in world development. Foreigners pay taxes to the Canadian government, and these taxes count as transfers to Canadians. More importantly, foreigners, as immigrants, become Canadians. Some immigrants bring assets with them. These assets are also treated as transfers to Canadians. This is a strange feature of the international accounts in Table 6–3.

Can a country have a trade deficit and no current account deficit? A current account deficit and no trade deficit?

Adding all payments to and from the rest of the world, net payments were equal to 53.4 – 22.9 – 0.3 = 30.2 billion. This total is the *current account balance*. So, in 2005, Canada ran a current account surplus of $30.2 billion, or about 2% of its GDP.

The Capital Account. The fact that Canada had a current account surplus of $30.2 billion in 2005 implies that it had to lend $30.2 billion to the rest of the world—equivalently, net foreign holdings of Canadian assets had to decrease by $30.2 billion. The numbers below the line describe the way this result was achieved. Transactions below the line are called **capital account** transactions.

The measured increase in Canadian holdings of foreign assets in 2005 was $112.1 billion. But at the same time, the increase in foreign holdings of Canadian assets was $84 billion. So, the net increase in Canadian assets abroad, which is also called **net capital flows** (in this case, it is an outflow, but in other years, it has been an inflow) from Canada, was $112.1 − $84 = $28.1 billion.

Shouldn't net capital flows be equal to the current account surplus? Yes. But the numbers for current and capital account transactions come from different sources; although they should give the same answers, they typically do not. In 2005, the difference between the two, the **statistical discrepancy**, was quite small, $2.1 billion.

Why does it have a negative sign? The increase in foreign holdings of Canadian assets in Table 6–3 has a positive sign, and we imagine Canadians receive foreign currency as foreigners buy factories in Canada. The increase in Canadian holdings of foreign assets has a negative sign as Canadians pay foreign currency to buy foreign assets. Above the line, Canadians earned $30.2 billion in foreign currency. Below the line, these $30.2 billion are spent. Using the first two lines of the capital account spends only $28.1 billion as Canadians are measured as buying $112.1 billion more in foreign assets than foreigners paid for assets in Canada (the $84 billion).

Here is a variant on the same statistical problem: The sum of the current account deficits of all countries should be equal to zero: One country's deficit should show up as a surplus for the other countries taken as a whole. This is not, however, the case in the data: If we added the published current account deficits of all the countries in the world, it would appear that the world is running a large current account deficit. Some economists speculate that the explanation is unrecorded trade with the Martians. Most others believe that mismeasurement is the explanation.

The statistical discrepancy in this case is –$2.1 billion. These are almost certainly purchases of foreign assets by Canadians that they did not report to their governments. Why are these not reported? Assets typically earn some income. For example, a Canadian may own a condominium in Florida and rent it out. If she does not want to report that rental income on her tax return, she would conceal her ownership of the condominium. In most countries, in most years, the statistical discrepancy is negative. It is often treated as an increase in domestic holdings of foreign assets.

Now that we have looked at the current account, we can return to an issue we touched on in Chapter 2, the difference between GDP, the measure of output we have used so far, and GNP, another measure of aggregate output. This is done in the Global Macro box "GDP versus GNP: The Example of Kuwait."

The Choice between Domestic and Foreign Assets

Why were Canadian investors willing, in 2005, to increase their holdings of foreign assets by $112.1 billion? To answer this question, we must look at the choice investors face in holding domestic versus foreign assets.

It might appear that we have to think about at least two new decisions: the choice of holding domestic versus foreign *money* and the choice of holding domestic versus foreign *interest-paying assets*. But remember why people hold money: to engage in transactions. For somebody who lives in Canada whose transactions are thus in Canadian dollars, there is little point in holding foreign currency: It cannot be used for transactions, and if the goal is to hold foreign assets, holding foreign currency is clearly less desirable than holding foreign bonds, which, at least, pay interest. Thus, the only new choice we have to think about is the choice between domestic and foreign interest-paying assets.

Let us think of them for now as domestic and foreign one-year bonds and consider the choice between Canadian and American one-year bonds.

There are two qualifications to this statement: Foreigners involved in illegal activities often hold American dollars in cash because such dollars can be exchanged easily and cannot be traced. Also, in times of very high inflation, people sometimes switch to the use of a foreign currency, often the American dollar, even for some domestic transactions. This is known as the dollarization of an economy. In Serbia, in the 1990s, citizens used German currency as a medium of exchange.

● Suppose you decide to hold Canadian bonds. Let i_t be the one-year Canadian nominal interest rate. Then, as Figure 6–7 shows, for every Canadian dollar you put in Canadian bonds, you will get $(1 + i_t)$ Canadian dollars next year.

● Suppose you decide instead to hold American bonds. To buy American bonds, you must first buy American dollars. Let E_t be the nominal exchange rate between the Canadian dollar and the American dollar. For every Canadian dollar, you get $(1/E_t)$ American dollars.

  Let i_t^* denote the one-year nominal interest rate on American dollar bonds. When the next year comes, you will have $\$(1/E_t)(1 + i_t^*)$ US. You will then have to convert your American dollars back into Canadian dollars. If you expect the nominal exchange rate next year to be E_{t+1}^e, you can expect to have $(1/E_t)(1 + i_t^*)E_{t+1}^e$ Canadian dollars next year for every Canadian dollar you invested. This set of steps is represented in the lower part of Figure 6–7. We will look at the expression we just derived in more detail soon. But note already its basic implication: In assessing the attractiveness of American dollar bonds, you cannot look just at the American and Canadian interest rates; you must also assess what you think will happen to the exchange rate between this year and the next.

Let us now make the simplest assumption concerning the choices made in financial markets. We will assume that you and other financial investors want only to hold the asset with the highest expected rate of return when held for the same length of time. The one-year interest rates we have been discussing are just that, assets held for one year. In that case, if both American dollar and Canadian dollar one-year bonds are to be held, they must have the same expected rate of return, so the following *arbitrage relation* must hold.

This is the simplest assumption. You and other investors in the financial markets also consider the riskiness of assets as well as the length of time you expect to hold the assets. Nonetheless, the expected rate of return is a major factor in your asset choices.

$$1 + i_t = \left(\frac{1}{E_t}\right)(1 + i_t^*)(E_{t+1}^e)$$

Or, reorganizing slightly,

$$1 + i_t = (1 + i_t^*)\left(\frac{E_{t+1}^e}{E_t}\right) \tag{6.2}$$

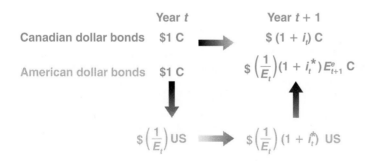

FIGURE 6–7

Expected Returns from Holding One-Year Canadian Dollar or American Dollar Bonds

Should value added in an open economy be defined as:

● The value added domestically (that is, within the country)?
● The value added by domestically owned factors of production?

The two definitions are not the same. Some domestic output is produced with capital owned by foreigners, while some foreign output is produced with capital owned by domestic residents.

The answer is that either definition is fine, and economists use both. **Gross domestic product (GDP)**, the measure we have used so far, corresponds to value added domestically. **Gross national product (GNP)** corresponds to the value added by domestically owned factors of production. To go from GDP to GNP, one must start from GDP, add factor payments received from the rest of the world, and subtract factor payments paid to the rest of the world. Put another way, GNP is equal to GDP plus net factor payments from the rest of the world. While GDP is now the measure most commonly mentioned, GNP was widely used until the early 1990s, and you will still encounter it in newspapers and academic publications.

For most countries, the difference between GNP and GDP is typically small because factor payments to and from the rest of the world roughly cancel one another. For the United States in 2003, the difference between GDP and GNP was $43 billion—about 0.4% of GDP. (This is an unusually small number, by historical standards. But, for the United States, the difference between the two has never exceeded 1% of GDP.)

There are a few exceptions. Among them is Kuwait. When oil was discovered in Kuwait, Kuwait's government decided that a portion of oil revenues would be saved and invested abroad, rather than spent, so as to provide future Kuwaiti generations

with investment income when oil revenues came to an end. Kuwait ran a large current account surplus, steadily accumulating large foreign assets. As a result, it now has large holdings of foreign assets and receives substantial investment income from the rest of the world. Table 1 gives GDP, GNP, and net factor payments for Kuwait, from 1989 to 1994.

Note how much larger GNP is compared with GDP throughout the period. Note also how net factor payments decreased after 1989. This is because Kuwait had to pay its allies for part of the cost of the 1990–1991 Gulf War and to pay for reconstruction after the war. It did so by running a current account deficit—that is, by decreasing its net holdings of foreign assets. This, in turn, led to a decrease in the income it earned from foreign assets and, by implication, a decrease in its net factor payments.

TABLE	1	GDP, GNP, and Net Factor Payments in Kuwait, 1989–1994

Year	GDP	GNP	Net Factor Payments
1989	7143	9616	2473
1990	5328	7560	2232
1991	3131	4669	1538
1992	5826	7364	1538
1993	7231	8386	1151
1994	7380	8321	941

Source: International Financial Statistics, IMF, All numbers are in millions of Kuwaiti dinars, with 1 dinar = $3.3 US (2003).

Equation (6.2) is called the **uncovered interest parity relation,** or simply the **interest parity condition.**[1]

The assumption that financial investors will hold only the bonds with the highest expected rate of return is obviously too strong, for two reasons:

● It ignores transaction costs: Going in and out of American dollar bonds requires three separate transactions, each with a transaction cost.

[1]**DIGGING DEEPER**. The word "uncovered" is to distinguish this relation from another relation called the *covered interest parity* condition. That condition is derived by looking at the following choice: Buy and hold Canadian dollar bonds for one year. Or buy an American dollar bond today, buy one-year American dollar bonds with the proceeds, and agree to sell the American dollars for Canadian dollars a year ahead at a predetermined price, called the *forward exchange rate*. The rate of return to these two alternatives, which can both be realized at *no risk today*, must be the same. The covered interest parity condition is a *riskless arbitrage condition.*

- It ignores risk: The exchange rate a year from now is uncertain; that means that holding American dollar bonds is more risky, in terms of Canadian dollars, than holding Canadian dollar bonds.[2]

But as a characterization of capital movements among the major world financial markets (New York, Frankfurt, London, Tokyo, and perhaps Toronto), it is not far off. Small changes in interest rates and rumours of impending appreciation or depreciation can lead to movements of tens of billions of dollars within minutes. For the rich countries of the world, the arbitrage assumption in equation (6.2) is a good approximation of reality. Other countries, whose capital markets are smaller and less developed or that have various forms of capital control, have more leeway in choosing their domestic interest rate than is implied by equation (6.2). We will return to this issue at the end of Chapter 13.

To get a better sense of what arbitrage implies, rewrite equation (6.2) as:

$$1 + i_t = (1 + i_t^*)\left(1 + \frac{E_{t+1}^e - E_t}{E_t}\right) \tag{6.3}$$

This gives a relation among the domestic nominal interest rate, the foreign nominal interest rate, and the expected rate of depreciation. Remember that an increase in E is a depreciation, so $(E_{t+1}^e - E_t)/E_t$ is the expected rate of depreciation of the domestic currency. (If the domestic currency is expected to appreciate, then this term is negative.) As long as interest rates or the expected rate of depreciation are not too large (say, below 20% a year) a good approximation to this equation is given by:

> This follows from proposition 3 in Appendix 2.

$$i_t \approx i_t^* + \frac{E_{t+1}^e - E_t}{E_t} \tag{6.4}$$

This is the relation you must remember: Arbitrage implies that *the domestic interest rate must be (approximately) equal to the foreign interest rate plus the expected depreciation rate of the domestic currency.*

Let us apply this equation to American dollar versus Canadian dollar bonds. Suppose the one-year nominal interest rate is 4% in Canada and 2.5% in the United States. Should you hold American dollar or Canadian dollar bonds? It depends on whether you expect the Canadian dollar to depreciate vis-à-vis the U.S. dollar by more or less than 4% − 2.5% = 1.5% over the coming year. If you expect the Canadian dollar to depreciate by more than 1.5%, then, despite the fact that the interest rate is lower in the United States than in Canada, investing in American bonds is more attractive than investing in Canadian bonds. By holding American bonds, you will get fewer American dollars a year from now, but the U.S. dollars will also be worth more in terms of Canadian dollars a year from now, making investing in American dollar bonds more attractive than investing in Canadian dollar bonds. However, if you expect the Canadian dollar to depreciate by less than 1.5% or even to appreciate, then the reverse holds, and Canadian dollar bonds are more attractive than American dollar bonds.

> An important relation to remember: Under the uncovered interest parity condition, the domestic interest rate must approximately equal the foreign interest rate plus the expected depreciation of the domestic currency.

In other words, the uncovered interest parity condition tells us that financial investors must be expecting, on average, a depreciation of the Canadian dollar with respect to the American dollar of about 1.5% over the coming year, and this is why they are willing to hold American dollar bonds despite their lower interest rate. (Another example is provided in the Global Macro box "Buying Brazilian Bonds.")

---

[2]**DIGGING DEEPER**. Whether holding American dollar or Canadian dollar bonds is more risky depends on which investors we are looking at. Holding American dollar bonds is more risky from the point of view of Canadian investors. Holding Canadian dollar bonds is more risky from the point of view of American investors. (Why?)

Put yourself back in September 1993 (the very high interest rate in Brazil at the time helps make the point we want to get across here). Brazilian bonds are paying a *monthly* interest rate of 36.9%. This seems very attractive compared with the *annual* rate of 3% on U.S. bonds—corresponding to a *monthly* interest rate of about 0.2%. Shouldn't you buy Brazilian bonds?

The discussion in this chapter tells you that to decide, you need one more crucial element, the expected rate of appreciation of the dollar vis-à-vis the cruzeiro (the name of the Brazilian currency at the time; the currency is now called the real). You need this information because (as Figure 6–7 makes clear) the return in dollars from investing in Brazilian bonds for a month is:

$$(1 + i_t^*) \frac{E_{t+1}^e}{E_t} = (1.369) \frac{E_{t+1}^e}{E_t}$$

What rate of cruzeiro depreciation should you expect over the coming month? Assume that the rate of depreciation next

month will be equal to the rate of depreciation last month. You know that 100,000 cruzeiros, worth $1.01 at the end of July 1993, were worth only $0.75 at the end of August 1993. If depreciation continues at the same rate, the return from investing in Brazilian bonds for a month is:

$$(1 + i_t^*) \frac{E_{t+1}^e}{E_t} = (1.369) \left(\frac{0.75}{1.01} \right) = 1.016$$

The expected rate of return in dollars from holding Brazilian bonds is only $(1.016 - 1) = 1.6\%$ per month, not the 36.9% per month that looked so attractive. Note that 1.6% per month is still much higher than the monthly interest rate on U.S. bonds (about 0.2%.) But think of the risk and the transaction costs—all the elements we ignored when we wrote the arbitrage condition. When these are taken into account, you may well decide to keep your funds out of Brazil.

The arbitrage relation between interest rates and exchange rates in equation (6.4) will play a central role in the following chapters. It suggests that unless financial markets expect large depreciations or appreciations, domestic and foreign interest rates are likely to move very much together. Take the extreme case of two countries that commit to maintaining their bilateral exchange rates at a fixed value. If markets have faith in this commitment, they will expect the exchange rate to remain constant, and the expected depreciation will be zero. In that case, the arbitrage condition implies that interest rates in the two countries will have to move together exactly. Most of the time, as we will see, governments do not make such absolute commitments, but they often do try to avoid large movements in the exchange rate.

FIGURE 6-8

Canadian and American One-Year Nominal Interest Rates, 1970–2005

Canadian and American one-year interest rates have moved together but are not identical. The lower line is the differential—Canadian interest rate minus U.S. interest rate. There are periods where there is a large gap.

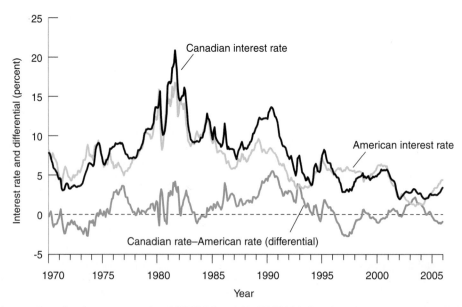

Source: Canadian interest rate using CANSIM II variable V122484; American interest rate using Federal Reserve Board variable RIFSGFSM03_N.M.

This puts sharp limits on how much they can allow their interest rate to deviate from interest rates elsewhere in the world.

How much do nominal interest rates actually move together between major countries? Figure 6–8 plots one-year nominal interest rates in Canada and the United States since 1970. The impression is, indeed, one of closely related but not identical movements. Interest rates were high (by historical standards) in both countries around 1980, lower in the late 1970s, and lower in the 1990s. At the same time, differences between the two are sometimes large. In 1989–1990, the Canadian interest rate was nearly 5% above the U.S. interest rate. More recently, by contrast, the Canadian interest rate has been both slightly above and slightly below the U.S. interest rate. In the coming chapters, we will return to why these differences emerged and what their implications were.

Meanwhile, do the following: Look at the back pages of a recent issue of *The Economist* for short-term interest rates in different countries relative to the United States. Which are the currencies against which the dollar is expected to depreciate?

6-3 | Conclusions and a Look Ahead

We have now set the stage for the study of the open economy. Openness in goods markets allows a choice between domestic and foreign goods. This choice depends primarily on the *real exchange rate* — the relative price of foreign goods in terms of domestic goods.

Openness in financial markets allows a choice between domestic and foreign assets. This choice depends primarily on their relative rates of return, which depend, in turn, on domestic and foreign interest rates and on the expected rate of depreciation of the domestic currency.

In the next chapter, Chapter 7, we look at the implications of openness in goods markets. Chapter 8 brings in openness in financial markets. Later, in Chapter 13, we look at the medium run in an open economy, and we discuss the pros and cons of different exchange rate regimes.

SUMMARY

- Openness in goods markets allows people and firms to choose between domestic and foreign goods. Openness in financial markets allows financial investors to choose between domestic or foreign financial assets.

- The nominal exchange rate is the price of foreign currency in terms of domestic currency. From the viewpoint of Canada, the nominal exchange rate between Canada and the United States is the price of the American dollar in terms of Canadian dollars.

- A nominal appreciation (an appreciation, for short) is an increase in the price of the domestic currency in terms of foreign currency; given the definition of the exchange rate, it corresponds to a decrease in the exchange rate. A nominal depreciation (a depreciation, for short) is a decrease in the price of the domestic currency in terms of foreign currency; it corresponds to an increase in the exchange rate.

- The real exchange rate is the relative price of foreign goods in terms of domestic goods. It is equal to the nominal exchange rate times the foreign price level divided by the domestic price level.

- A real appreciation is an increase in the relative price of domestic goods in terms of foreign goods; it corresponds to a decrease in the real exchange rate. A real depreciation is a decrease in the relative price of domestic

goods; it corresponds to an increase in the real exchange rate.

- The multilateral real exchange rate, or real exchange rate, for short, is a weighted average of bilateral real exchange rates, with weights equal to trade shares.

- The balance of payments records a country's transactions with the rest of the world. The current account balance is equal to the sum of the trade balance, net investment income, and net transfers received from the rest of the world. The capital account balance is equal to capital flows from the rest of the world minus capital flows to the rest of the world.

- The current account and the capital account are mirror images of each other. A current account deficit is financed by net capital flows from the rest of the world, thus by a capital account surplus. Similarly, a current account surplus corresponds to a capital account deficit.

- Uncovered interest parity, or interest parity, for short, is an arbitrage condition stating that the expected rates of return in terms of domestic currency on domestic and foreign bonds must be equal. Interest parity implies that the domestic interest rate approximately equals the foreign interest rate plus the expected depreciation rate of the domestic currency.

QUESTIONS AND PROBLEMS

An asterisk denotes a harder question. [Web] indicates that the question requires access to the Internet.

1. TRUE/FALSE/UNCERTAIN

a. Countries with net capital inflows must be running current account deficits.

b. Although the export ratio can be larger than one (as it is in Belgium and Luxembourg), the same cannot be true of the ratio of imports to GDP.

c. That a rich country such as Japan has such a small ratio of imports to GDP is clear evidence of an unfair playing field for exporters in other countries.

d. Uncovered interest parity implies that real interest rates must be the same across countries.

e. If the nominal exchange rate between the American dollar and the Canadian dollar is 0.70, it means that one American dollar is worth 70 Canadian cents.

f. If the real exchange rate between the United States and Canada is 2, this means that goods are twice as expensive in the United States as in Canada.

2. BALANCE OF PAYMENTS

Consider two fictional economies, one the "domestic country" and the other the "foreign country." Construct a balance of payments for each country given the following list of transactions:

The domestic country purchased $100 in oil from the foreign country.

Foreign tourists spent $25 on domestic ski slopes.

Domestic residents purchased $45 in life insurance in the foreign country.

Domestic residents purchased $5 in illegal substances from foreigners.

Foreign investors were paid $15 in dividends from their holdings of domestic equities.

Domestic residents sent $25 to foreign charities.

Foreign businessmen spent $35 in bribes to domestic government officials.

Domestic businesses borrowed $65 from foreign banks.

Foreign investors purchased $15 in domestic junk bonds.

Domestic investors sold off $50 in holdings of foreign government bonds.

3. UNCOVERED INTEREST PARITY

Consider the following prices for government bonds and foreign exchange in Canada and the United States. Assume that both government securities are one-year bonds, paying the face value of the bond one year from now. The exchange rate E stands at $1 US = $0.95 C.

The face values and prices on the two bonds are given by:

		Face Value	Price
Canada	1-year bond	$10,000 C	$9,615.38 C
United States	1-year bond	$13,333 US	$12,698.10 US

a. Compute the nominal interest rate on each of the bonds.

b. Compute the expected exchange rate next year consistent with uncovered interest parity.

c. If you expect the Canadian dollar to depreciate relative to the American dollar, which bond should you buy?

d. Assume you are a Canadian investor. You exchange your dollars for U.S. dollars and purchase the American bond. One year from now, it turns out E is actually 0.90 ($1 US = 0.90 Canadian dollars). What is your realized return in Canadian dollars compared with the realized return you would have made had you held the Canadian dollar bond?

e. Are the differences in returns in (d) consistent with the uncovered interest parity condition? Why, or why not?

*4. COVERED INTEREST PARITY

Assume that there exists a market for buying and selling foreign exchange one year in the future, at a price determined today. This price is called the forward exchange rate. Denote the forward price of $1 US in terms of dollars by F. In other words, you can enter into a contract today to sell $1 US for $$F$ C one year in the future.

a. Derive the following approximation to covered interest parity where i denotes expected nominal return and an asterisk denotes foreign variables:

$$i = i^* + \frac{F - E}{E}$$

b. Given the two government bonds and exchange rate from the previous problem, find the forward exchange rate of $1 US consistent with covered interest parity.

c. What should you do if the forward exchange rate is different from the value you just derived?

d. Suppose the forward exchange rate is as you computed it in (b). You buy U.S. dollars today, buy the American dollar bond today, and enter into a contract today to sell the American dollars you will receive in a year at the forward exchange rate. Does a surprise in the exchange rate between now and next year affect the returns on your investment? Why, or why not?

5. REAL EXCHANGE RATES

E units of domestic currency per unit of foreign currency
P, P^* are the domestic and foreign price index respectively

Year	E	P	P*	EP*/P
1	1.0	100	100	1.0
2	1.1	110	—	1.0
3	1.1	—	110	1.1
4	1.1	110	121	—
5	—	110	121	1.155

Fill in the missing elements of the table above and answer the following questions:

a. Between which years did the domestic nominal exchange rate change?

b. Between which years did the domestic real exchange rate change?

c. Did the domestic nominal exchange rate depreciate or appreciate between Year 1 and Year 5?

d. Did the domestic real exchange rate depreciate or appreciate between Year 1 and Year 5?

FURTHER READING

If you want to learn more about international trade and international economics, read the textbook by Paul Krugman and Maurice Obstfeld, *International Economics, Theory and Policy*, 6th ed. (New York: HarperCollins, 2002).

If you want to know current exchange rates between the Canadian dollar and any currency in the world, look at the "currency converter" at the Bank of Canada homepage (**www.bankofcanada.ca**).

CHAPTER 7
THE GOODS MARKET IN AN OPEN ECONOMY

Canada experienced strong economic growth from 1997 to 2000, then a slowdown in 2001. During the period of strong growth and falling unemployment, provincial and federal politicians claimed that their excellent policy choices made strong growth possible. During the slowdown, the same politicians noted how world and especially American economic events had a strong influence on Canada's economy. The slowdown was, to some degree, beyond their control.

Do foreign events dominate Canada's economy? If so, how much? To answer this question, we need to expand the treatment of the goods market from Chapter 3 to take into account openness. That is what we do in this chapter.

7-1 | The *IS* Relation in the Open Economy

When we were assuming that the economy was closed to trade, there was no need to distinguish between the domestic demand for goods and the demand for domestic goods: They were clearly the same. Now, we must distinguish between the two: Some domestic demand falls on foreign goods, and some of the demand for domestic goods comes from foreigners. Let us look at this distinction more closely.

The terms "the domestic demand for goods" and "the demand for domestic goods" may sound close. But, in an open economy, they need not be equal.

The Demand for Domestic Goods

In an open economy, the **demand for domestic goods** is given by:

$$Z \equiv C + I + G - \epsilon Q + X \tag{7.1}$$

The first three terms—consumption (C), investment (I), and government spending (G)—constitute the **domestic demand for goods**. If the economy were closed, $C + I + G$ would also be the demand for domestic goods. This is why, until now, we looked only at $C + I + G$. But now we have to make two adjustments.

- First, we must subtract imports, that part of domestic demand that falls on foreign goods. We must be careful here. Foreign goods are different from domestic goods, so we cannot just subtract the quantity of imports, Q; if we were to do so, we would be subtracting apples (foreign goods) from oranges (domestic goods). We must first express the value of imports in terms of domestic goods. This is what ϵQ in equation (7.1) stands for: As we saw in Chapter 6, ϵ is the real exchange rate, the price of foreign goods in terms of domestic goods. Thus, ϵQ (the price times the quantity of imports) is the value of imports in terms of domestic goods.

In Chapter 3, we ignored this and subtracted Q. This was wrong, but we did not want to have to talk about the real exchange rate and complicate matters so early in the book.

- Second, we must add exports, the demand for domestic goods that comes from abroad. This is captured by the term X in equation (7.1).

The Determinants of the Demand for Domestic Goods

Having listed the five components of demand, our next task is to specify their determinants. Let us start with the first three: C, I, and G.

The Determinants of C, I, and G. Now that we are assuming that the economy is open, how should we modify our earlier descriptions of consumption, investment, and government spending? The answer is not very much, if at all. How much consumers decide to spend still depends on their income and their wealth. Although the real exchange rate surely affects the *composition* of consumption spending between domestic and foreign goods, there is no obvious reason why it should affect the overall *level* of consumption. The same is true of investment: The real exchange rate may affect whether firms buy domestic or foreign machines, but it should not affect total investment.

Domestic demand for goods ($C + I + G$)
− domestic demand for foreign goods (imports, ϵQ)
+ foreign demand for domestic goods (exports, X)
= Demand for domestic goods ($C + I + G - \epsilon Q + X$)

This is good news because it implies that we can use the descriptions of consumption, investment, and government spending that we developed earlier. Therefore,

$$\text{Domestic demand:} \quad C + I + G = C(Y - T) + I(Y, i) + G$$
$$(\ +\ ) \quad (+,-)$$

We assume that consumption depends positively on disposable income ($Y - T$) and that investment depends positively on production (Y) and negatively on the interest rate (i). We continue to take government spending (G) as a given.

Domestic demand ($C + I + G$) depends on income (Y), the interest rate (i), taxes (T), and the level of government spending (G).

The Determinants of Imports. What does the quantity of imports, Q, depend on? Primarily on the overall level of domestic demand: The higher the level of domestic demand, the higher is the demand for all goods, both domestic and foreign. But Q also clearly depends on the real exchange rate: The higher the price of foreign goods relative to domestic goods, the lower is the relative domestic demand for foreign goods and the lower the quantity of imports.

Thus, we write imports as:

$$Q = Q(Y, \epsilon) \tag{7.2}$$
$$(+, -)$$

As ϵ goes up while Q goes down, what happens to ϵQ, the value of imports in terms of domestic goods, is ambiguous. We return to this point later. ▶

Imports depend on income (or, equivalently, output—the two are still the same in an open economy), Y: Higher income leads to higher imports.[1] Imports also depend on the real exchange rate. Recall that the real exchange rate, ϵ, is defined as the price of foreign goods in terms of domestic goods. A higher real exchange rate means that foreign goods are relatively more expensive, leading to a decrease in the quantity of imports, Q. This negative effect of the real exchange rate on imports is captured by the negative sign under ϵ in the import equation.

The volume of imports (Q) ▶ depends on the level of output (Y), and the real exchange rate (ϵ).

The Determinants of Exports. The export of one country is, by definition, the import of another. In thinking about what determines Canadian exports, we can ask, equivalently, what determines foreign imports. From our discussion of the determinants of imports in the preceding paragraph, we know that foreign imports are likely to depend on foreign activity and on the relative price of foreign goods. Thus, we can write exports as:

$$X = X(Y^*, \epsilon) \tag{7.3}$$
$$(+, +)$$

Recall that asterisks refer ▶ to foreign variables.

Y^* is income in the rest of the world, or simply *foreign* income (equivalently foreign output). An increase in foreign income leads to an increase in the foreign demand for all goods, some of which falls on Canadian goods, leading to higher Canadian exports. An increase in ϵ—an increase in the relative price of foreign goods in terms of Canadian goods—makes Canadian goods relatively more attractive, leading to an increase in exports.

Exports depend on the ▶ level of foreign income (Y^*) and the real exchange rate (ϵ).

For Canada, Y^* is usually real income in the United States and ϵ is usually the real exchange rate between Canada and the United States. Although we trade with other countries, as we saw in the previous chapter, the United States is our dominant trading partner.

We can represent what we have learned so far in Figure 7–1, which plots the various components of demand against output, keeping constant all other variables that affect demand (the interest rate, taxes, government spending, foreign output, and the real exchange rate).

In Figure 7–1(a), the line DD plots *domestic demand*, $C + I + G$, as a function of output, Y. This relation between demand and output is familiar from Chapter 3. Under our standard assumptions, the slope of the relation between demand and output is positive but less than 1: An increase in output (equivalently, in income) increases demand but less than one for one. (In the absence of good reasons to the contrary, we draw the relation between demand and output, as well as the other relations in this chapter, as lines rather than curves. This is purely for convenience, and none of the discussions that follow depend on that assumption.)

For a given real exchange rate ϵ, ϵQ (the value of imports in terms of domestic goods) moves exactly ▶ with Q (the volume of imports).

To arrive at the *demand for domestic goods*, we must first subtract imports. This is done in Figure 7–1(b) and gives us the line AA: The distance between DD and AA equals the value of imports, ϵQ. Because the quantity of imports increases with income, the distance between the two lines increases with income. We can establish two facts about line AA, which will be useful later in the chapter:

---

[1]**DIGGING DEEPER**. We cheat a bit here. Our discussion suggests that we should be using domestic demand, $C + I + G$, instead of income, Y. You might also dispute the assumption that imports depend on the sum of domestic demand and not on its composition: It may well be that the proportion of imports in investment differs from that of imports in consumption. For example, many poor countries import most of their capital equipment but consume mostly domestic goods. In that case, the composition of demand would matter for imports. We leave these complications aside. You may want to explore them on your own.

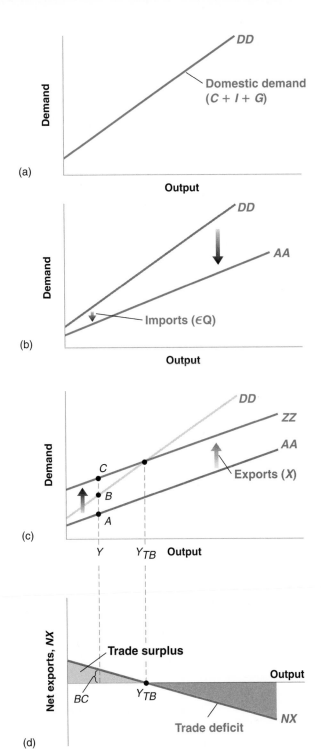

FIGURE 7-1

The Demand for Domestic Goods and Net Exports

The domestic demand for goods is an increasing function of income. The demand for domestic goods is obtained by subtracting the value of imports from domestic demand and then adding exports. The trade balance is a decreasing function of output.

1. *AA* is flatter than *DD*: As income increases, some of the additional domestic demand falls on foreign goods rather than on domestic goods. As income increases, the domestic demand for domestic goods increases less than does total domestic demand.

2. As long as some of the additional demand falls on domestic goods, *AA* has a positive slope: An increase in income leads to some increase in the demand for domestic goods.

Finally, we must add exports. This is done in Figure 7–1(c) and gives us the line ZZ, which is above AA. The distance between ZZ and AA equals exports. Because exports do not depend on domestic output, the distance between ZZ and AA is constant, so the two lines are parallel. Because AA is flatter than DD, ZZ is flatter than DD as well.

From the information in Figure 7–1(c) we can characterize the behaviour of net exports — the difference between exports and imports $(X − \epsilon Q)$ — as a function of output. At output level Y for example, exports are given by the distance AC and imports by the distance AB, so net exports are given by the distance BC.

Recall that *net exports* is ▶ synonymous with trade balance. Positive net exports correspond to a trade surplus, negative net exports to a trade deficit.

This relation between net exports and output is represented as the line denoted NX (for net exports) in Figure 7–1(d). Net exports are a decreasing function of output: As output increases, imports increase and exports are unaffected, leading to lower net exports. Call Y_{TB} (TB for trade balance) the level of output at which the value of imports is just equal to exports so that net exports are equal to zero. Levels of output above Y_{TB} lead to higher imports, leading to a trade deficit. Levels of output below Y_{TB} lead to lower imports and to a trade surplus.

7-2 | Equilibrium Output and the Trade Balance

Equilibrium in the goods market requires that domes- ▶ tic output be equal to the demand for domestic goods.

The goods market is in equilibrium when domestic output equals the demand for domestic goods:

$$Y = Z$$

FIGURE   7–2

Equilibrium Output and Net Exports

The goods market is in equilibrium when production is equal to the demand for domestic goods. At the equilibrium level of output, the trade balance may show a deficit or a surplus.

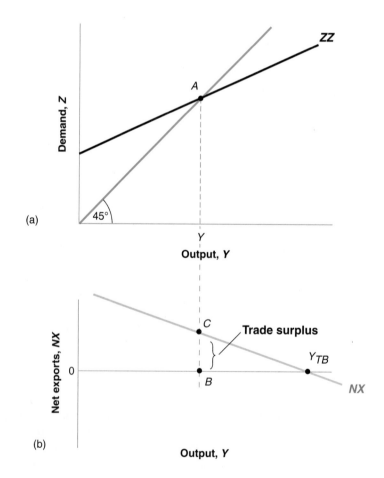

(a)

(b)

Collecting the relations we derived for the components of the demand for domestic goods, Z:

$$Y = C(Y - T) + I(Y, i) + G - \epsilon Q(Y, \epsilon) + X(Y^*, \epsilon) \qquad (7.4)$$

This equilibrium condition determines output as a function of all the variables we take as givens, from taxes to the real exchange rate to foreign output. This is not a simple relation; Figure 7–2 represents it in a more user-friendly way. In Figure 7–2(a), demand is measured on the vertical axis, output (equivalently, income) on the horizontal axis. The line ZZ plots demand as a function of output; this line just replicates the line ZZ in Figure 7–1; ZZ is upward sloping, but with slope less than 1.

Equilibrium output is at the point where demand equals output, at the intersection of the line ZZ and the 45-degree line, so at point A in the figure, with associated output level Y.

Figure 7–2(b) replicates Figure 7–1(d), drawing net exports as a decreasing function of output. There is, in general, no reason why the equilibrium level of output, Y, should be the same as the level of output at which trade is balanced, Y_{TB}. As we have drawn the figure, equilibrium output is associated with a trade surplus, equal to the distance BC.

We now have the tools needed to answer the questions we asked at the beginning of this chapter.

The equilibrium level of output is given by the condition $Y = Z$. The level of output at which there is trade balance is given by the condition $\epsilon Q = Y$. These are two different conditions.

7-3 | Increases in Demand, Domestic or Foreign

How do changes in demand affect output in an open economy? Let us start with a variation of what is by now an old favourite, an increase in government spending, and then turn to a new exercise, the effects of an increase in foreign activity.

Increases in Domestic Demand

Suppose the economy is in recession and government decides to increase government spending to increase domestic demand and output. What will be the effects on output and on the trade balance?

The answer is given in Figure 7–3. Before the increase in government spending, demand is given by ZZ in Figure 7–3(a), and the equilibrium is at point A, where output equals Y. Let us assume (though, as we have seen, there is no reason why this should be true in general) that trade is initially balanced, so, in Figure 7–3(b), $Y = Y_{TB}$.

What happens if government increases spending by ΔG? At any level of output, demand is higher by ΔG, shifting the demand relation up by ΔG from ZZ to ZZ'. The equilibrium point moves from A to A', and output increases from Y to Y'. The increase in output is larger than the increase in government spending: There is a multiplier effect.

So far, the story sounds like what happened in the closed economy earlier (see Chapter 3). However, let us look more closely: There is now an effect on the trade balance. Because government spending enters neither the exports relation nor the imports relation directly, the relation between net exports and output in Figure 7–3(b) does not shift. Thus, the increase in output from Y to Y' leads to a trade deficit equal to BC.

Not only does government spending now generate a trade deficit, but its effect on output is smaller than in the closed economy. Recall from Chapter 3 that the smaller the slope of the demand relation, the smaller is the multiplier (for example, if ZZ were horizontal, the multiplier would be 1). And recall from Figure 7–1 that the demand relation, ZZ, is flatter than the demand relation in the closed economy, DD. That means the multiplier is smaller in the open economy.

The trade deficit and the smaller multiplier arise from the same cause: An increase in demand now falls not only on domestic goods but also on foreign goods. Thus, when income increases, the effect on the demand for domestic goods is smaller than it would be in a closed economy, leading to a smaller multiplier. And because some of the increase in demand falls on imports—and exports are unchanged—the result is a trade deficit.

As in the core, we start by ignoring all markets other than the goods market; the conclusions we derive here will still apply when we introduce financial and labour markets later on.

Starting from trade balance, an increase in government spending leads to a trade deficit.

The smaller multiplier and the trade deficit have the same underlying cause: Some domestic demand falls on foreign goods, not on domestic goods.

THE GOODS MARKET IN AN OPEN ECONOMY

FIGURE 7-3

The Effects of Higher Government Spending

An increase in government spending leads to an increase in output and a trade deficit.

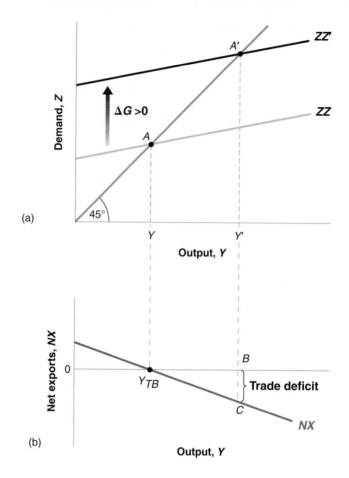

(a)

(b)

These two implications are important. In an open economy, an increase in domestic demand has a smaller effect on output than in a closed economy as well as an adverse effect on the trade balance. Indeed, the more open the economy, the smaller is the effect on output and the larger the adverse effect on the trade balance. For example, take Belgium, which has a ratio of imports to GDP close to 70%. This implies that when demand increases in Belgium, roughly 70% of this increased demand goes to higher imports and only 30% to an increase in the demand for domestic goods. The effect of an increase in government spending is thus likely to be a large increase in Belgium's trade deficit and only a small increase in its output, making domestic demand expansion a rather unattractive policy for Belgium. For the United States, which has an import ratio of only 13%, an increase in demand will be associated with some deterioration in the trade position. (This conclusion is discussed further in the Focus box "Multipliers: Canada versus the United States.") Canada's ratio of imports to GDP is about 40% (between those of Belgium and the United States).

Increases in Foreign Demand

Consider now an increase in foreign activity, an increase in Y^*. This could be due to an increase in foreign government spending, G^*—the policy change we just analyzed, but now taking place abroad. But we do not need to know where the increase comes from to analyze the effects on the Canadian economy.

Figure 7–4 shows the effects of an increase in foreign activity on domestic output and the trade balance. The initial demand for domestic goods is given by ZZ in Figure 7–4(a). The equilibrium is at point A, with output level Y. Let us assume trade is balanced so that in Figure 7–4(b) the net exports associated with Y equal zero.

It will be useful to refer to the line that gives the domestic demand for goods $C + I + G$ as a function of income. This line is drawn as *DD*. Recall from Figure 7–1 that *DD* is steeper than *ZZ*. The difference between *ZZ* and *DD* equals net exports so that if trade is balanced at point *A*, then *ZZ* and *DD* intersect at point *A*.

DD is the domestic demand for goods. *ZZ* is the demand for domestic goods.

Now, consider the effects of an increase in foreign output, ΔY^*. Higher foreign output means higher foreign demand, including higher foreign demand for Canadian goods. So, the direct effect of the increase in foreign output is to increase Canadian exports by some amount, call it ΔX. For a given level of output, this increase in exports leads to an increase in the demand for Canadian goods by ΔX, so the line giving the demand for domestic goods as a function of output shifts up by ΔX, from *ZZ* to *ZZ'*. As exports increase by ΔX at a given level of output, the line giving net exports as a function of output in Figure 7–4(b) also shifts up by ΔX, from *NX* to *NX'*.

$Y^* \uparrow \Rightarrow X = X(Y^*, \epsilon) \uparrow$

The new equilibrium is at point *A'*, with output level *Y'*. The increase in foreign output leads to an increase in domestic output. The reason is clear: Higher foreign output leads to higher exports of domestic goods, which increases domestic output and the domestic demand for goods through the multiplier.

Y^* directly affects exports and so enters the relation between the demand for domestic goods and output. An increase in Y^* leads to a shift in *ZZ*.

Y^* does not affect consumption, investment, or government spending directly and so does not enter the relation between the domestic demand for goods and output. An increase in Y^* does not lead to a shift in *DD*.

What happens to the trade balance? We know that exports go up. But could it be that the increase in domestic output leads to such a large increase in imports that the trade balance actually deteriorates? The answer is: No, the trade balance must improve. To see why, note that when foreign demand increases, the demand for domestic goods shifts up from *ZZ* to *ZZ'*; but the line *DD*, which gives domestic demand for goods as a function of output, does not shift. At the new equilibrium level of output *Y'*, domestic demand is given by the distance

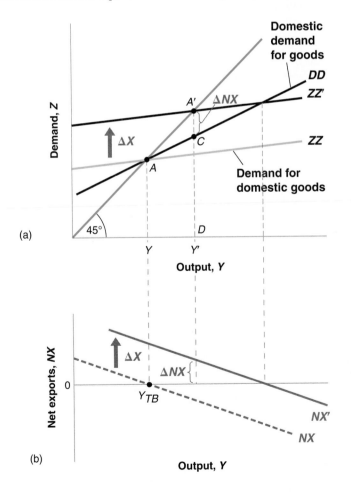

(a)

(b)

FIGURE 7–4

The Effects of Higher Foreign Demand

An increase in foreign demand leads to an increase in output and to a trade surplus.

If we assume that the various relations in equation (7.4) are linear, we can compute the effects of government spending, foreign output, and so forth, on both output and the trade balance. Here, we will focus on the differences between the effects of government spending in a large country, such as the United States, and in a small country, such as Canada.

Assume that consumption increases with disposable income and that investment increases with output and decreases with the real interest rate:

$$C = c_0 + c_1(Y - T)$$
$$I = d_0 + d_1 Y - d_2 r$$

For simplicity, ignore movements in the real exchange rate, and assume that the real exchange rate is equal to 1. Also, assume that imports are proportional to domestic output and exports are proportional to foreign output:

$$Q = q_1 Y$$
$$X = x_1 Y^*$$

In the same way we referred to c_1 as the marginal propensity to consume, q_1 is the **marginal propensity to import**.

The equilibrium condition is that output be equal to the demand for domestic goods:

$$Y = C + I + G - Q + X$$

(Recall that we are assuming that ϵ is equal to 1.) Replacing the components by the expressions from above gives:

$$Y = [c_0 + c_1(Y - T)] + (d_0 + d_1 Y - d_2 r) + G - q_1 Y + x_1 Y^*$$

Regrouping terms gives:

$$Y = (c_1 + d_1 - q_1)Y$$
$$+ (c_0 + d_0 - c_1 T - d_2 r + G + x_1 Y^*)$$

Bringing the terms in output together, and solving, gives:

$$Y = \frac{1}{1 - (c_1 + d_1 - q_1)}$$
$$\times (c_0 + d_0 - c_1 T - d_2 r + G + x_1 Y^*)$$

Output is equal to the multiplier times the term in parentheses, which captures the effect of all the variables we take as givens in explaining output.

Consider the multiplier. More specifically, consider the term $(c_1 + d_1 - q_1)$ in the denominator. As in the closed economy, $(c_1 + d_1)$ gives the effects of an increase in output on consumption and investment demand; $(-q_1)$ captures the fact that some of the increased demand falls not on domestic goods but on foreign goods. In the extreme case where all the additional demand falls on foreign goods—that is, when $q_1 = c_1 + d_1$—an increase in output has no effect back on the demand for domestic goods; in that case, the multiplier is equal to 1. In general, q_1 is less than $(c_1 + d_1)$ so that the mul-

tiplier is larger than 1. But it is smaller than it would be in a closed economy.

Using this equation, we can easily characterize the effects of an increase in government spending of ΔG. The increase in output is equal to the multiplier times the change in government spending, thus:

$$\Delta Y = \frac{1}{1 - (c_1 + d_1 - q_1)} \Delta G$$

The increase in imports that follows from the increase in output implies a change in net exports of:

$$\Delta NX = -q_1 \Delta Y$$
$$= -\frac{q_1}{1 - (c_1 + d_1 - q_1)} \Delta G$$

Let us see what these formulas imply by choosing numerical values for the parameters. Take $c_1 + d_1$ equal to 0.6. What value should we choose for q_1? We saw in Chapter 6 that in general, the larger the country, the more self-sufficient it is and the less it imports from abroad. So, let us choose two values of q_1—a small value, say, 0.1, for a large country, such as the United States, and a larger one, say, 0.3, for a small country, such as Canada. Note that we can think of $q_1/(c_1 + d_1)$ as the proportion of an increase in demand that falls on imports so that an equivalent way of stating our choices of q_1 is that in the large country, one-sixth of demand falls on imports, versus half in the small country.

For the large country, the effects on output and the trade balance are given by:

$$\Delta Y = \frac{1}{1 - (0.6 - 0.1)} \Delta G = 2.0 \, \Delta G$$

and

$$\Delta NX = -0.1 \, \Delta Y = \frac{-0.1}{1 - (0.6 - 0.1)} \Delta G = -0.2 \, \Delta G$$

For the small country, the effects are given by:

$$\Delta Y = \frac{1}{1 - (0.6 - 0.3)} \Delta G = 1.43 \, \Delta G$$

and

$$\Delta NX = -0.3 \, \Delta Y = \frac{-0.3}{1 - (0.6 - 0.3)} \Delta G = -0.43 \, \Delta G$$

These computations show how different the trade-offs faced by both countries are. In the large country, the effect of an increase in G on output is large and the effect on the trade balance is small. In the small country, the effect on output is small, and the deterioration of the trade balance is equal to one-third of the increase in government spending.

This example makes clear how drastically openness binds the hands of policy makers in small countries. We will see more examples of this proposition as we go along.

DC, and the demand for domestic goods is given by *DA'*. Net exports are thus given by the distance *CA'* — which, because *DD* is necessarily below *ZZ'*, is necessarily positive. Thus, although imports increase, the increase does not offset the increase in exports, and the trade balance improves.

An increase in foreign output increases output and improves the trade balance.

Games that Countries Play

We have derived two basic results so far:

- An increase in domestic demand leads to an increase in output but also to an increase in the trade deficit or a reduction in the trade surplus. (We looked at an increase in government spending, but the results would have been the same for a decrease in taxes, an increase in consumer spending, and so on.)
- An increase in foreign demand (which could come from the same types of changes taking place abroad) leads to an increase in domestic output and a trade surplus.

Governments do not like trade deficits, and for good reasons. The main reason is that a country that runs a trade deficit accumulates debt vis-à-vis the rest of the world and therefore has to pay higher interest payments to the rest of the world. Thus, it is no wonder that countries prefer increases in foreign demand (which lead to an improvement in the trade balance) to increases in domestic demand (which lead to a deterioration in the trade balance).

These preferences may have disastrous implications. Consider a group of countries, all trading a lot with each other so that an increase in demand in any one country falls largely on the goods produced in the other countries. Suppose all these countries are in recession and each has roughly balanced trade to start. Each country may be very reluctant to increase domestic demand: The result would be a small increase in output but also a large trade deficit. Each country may just wait for others to increase their own demand. But if they all wait, nothing happens, and the recession may endure.

Is there a way out of this situation? Yes, at least in theory. If all countries coordinate their macroeconomic policies to increase domestic demand simultaneously, each can expand without increasing its trade deficit (vis-à-vis the others; their combined trade deficit with respect to the rest of the world will still increase). The reason is clear: The coordinated increase in demand leads to increases in both exports and imports in each country. It is still true that domestic demand expansion leads to larger imports; but this increase in imports is offset by the increase in exports, which comes from the foreign demand expansions.

Coordination is a word that governments often invoke. The eight major countries of the world — the so-called **G-8** (the United States, Japan, France, Germany, the United Kingdom, Italy, Russia, and Canada) — meet regularly to discuss their economic situations; the communiqué at the end of the meeting rarely fails to mention coordination. But the evidence is that there is, in fact, very limited macrocoordination among countries. Here are some reasons why.

Coordination may imply that some countries have to do more than others. They may not want to do so:

- Suppose, in our example, that only some countries are in recession. Countries that are not in a recession will be reluctant to increase their own demand; but if they do not, the countries that expand will run a trade deficit vis-à-vis the countries that do not.
- Suppose instead that some countries are already running a large budget deficit. These countries will not want to cut taxes or increase spending further and will ask other countries to take on more of the adjustment. Those other countries may be reluctant to do so.

Another reason is that countries have a strong incentive to promise to coordinate and then not deliver on that promise. Once all countries have agreed, say, to an increase in spending, each country has an incentive not to deliver in order to benefit from the increase in demand elsewhere and thereby improve its trade position. But if each country cheats, or does not do everything it promised, there will be insufficient demand expansion to get out of the recession.

These are far from abstract concerns. Countries in the European Union, which are highly integrated with one another, have in the past 30 years often suffered from such coordination problems. In the late 1970s, a bungled attempt at coordination left most countries weary of trying again. In the early 1980s, an attempt by the French socialists to go at it alone led to a large French trade deficit and eventually to a change in policy. Thereafter, most countries decided that it was better to wait for an increase in foreign demand than to increase their own demand. There has been very little coordination of fiscal policy since then in Europe.

What happened in the late 1970s is that European countries embarked on fiscal expansion "too late." By the time they increased spending, their economies were already recovering, and there was no longer a need for higher government spending. ▶

7-4 | Depreciation, the Trade Balance, and Output

Suppose the Canadian government takes policy measures that lead to a depreciation of the dollar. (We shall see in Chapter 8 how it can do so using monetary policy; for the moment, we assume that government can simply choose the exchange rate.)

Recall that the real exchange rate is given by:

$$\epsilon \equiv \frac{EP^*}{P}$$

The real exchange rate, ϵ (the price of foreign goods in terms of domestic goods), equals the nominal exchange rate, E (the price of foreign currency in terms of domestic currency), times the foreign price level, P^*, divided by the domestic price level, P. Under our maintained assumption that the price levels are given, a nominal depreciation is thus reflected one for one in a real depreciation. More concretely, if the Canadian dollar depreciates vis-à-vis the American dollar by 5% (a 5% nominal depreciation), and if the price levels in Canada and the United States do not change, Canadian goods will be 5% cheaper compared with American goods (a 5% real depreciation).

Let us now ask what the effects of this real depreciation will be on the Canadian trade balance and on Canadian output.

A look ahead: In Chapter 13, after we understand the adjustment of the price level, we will have a second look at the effects of a nominal depreciation. We will see that a nominal depreciation leads to a real depreciation in the short run but not in the medium run. ▶

Depreciation and the Trade Balance: The Marshall–Lerner Condition

Return to the definition of net exports:

$$NX \equiv X - \epsilon Q$$

Replace X and Q by their expressions from equations (7.2) and (7.3):

$$NX = X(Y^*, \epsilon) - \epsilon Q(Y, \epsilon)$$

As the real exchange rate ϵ enters in three places, this equation makes clear that the real depreciation—an increase in ϵ—affects the trade balance through three channels.

If the Canadian dollar depreciates vis-à-vis the American dollar by 5%, Canadian goods will be cheaper in the United States, leading to a larger volume of Canadian exports to the United States. ▶

1. *X increases.* The real depreciation makes Canadian goods relatively cheaper abroad, leading to an increase in foreign demand for Canadian goods—an increase in Canadian exports.

American goods will be more expensive in Canada, leading to a smaller volume ▶ of imports of American goods to Canada.

2. *Q decreases.* The real depreciation makes foreign goods relatively more expensive in Canada, leading to a shift in domestic demand toward domestic goods, to a decrease in the quantity of imports.

American goods will be ▶ more expensive, leading to a higher import bill for a given volume of imports of American goods to Canada.

3. *The relative price of foreign goods, ϵ, increases.* This tends to increase the import bill, ϵQ. The same quantity of imports now costs more to buy (in terms of domestic goods).

For the trade balance to improve following a depreciation, exports must increase enough and imports must decrease enough to compensate for the increase in the price of imports. The condition under which a real depreciation leads to an increase in net exports is known as the **Marshall–Lerner condition**. (The condition is named for the two economists, Alfred

Figure 1 shows the evolution of U.S. exports and imports as ratios to GDP since 1990. It shows how, since the mid-1990s, exports and imports have steadily diverged. The import ratio has continued to increase, but the export ratio has decreased, going from 11.5% in 1997 to 9.5% in 2003. As a result, the U.S. trade deficit has steadily increased, and in 2003, it stood at 4.5%. The current account deficit (which, you will remember, is equal to the trade deficit plus transfers from the United States to the rest of the world minus net income payments from the rest of the world to the United States and tells us how much the United States has to borrow from the rest of the world) stood at an even higher 5% of GDP.

The 2003 trade and current account deficits were by far the largest (both absolutely and in proportion to GDP) in recorded U.S. history. And given the size of the U.S. economy, a current account deficit of 5% of GDP represents a very large amount—more than $500 billion—which the United States has to borrow from the rest of the world. This raises two main questions: Where do these deficits come from, and what do they imply for the future? Let us take up each question in turn.

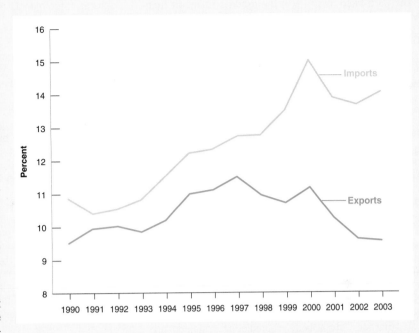

FIGURE 1   U.S. Exports and Imports as Ratios to U.S. GDP since 1990

Where Does the Trade Deficit, and by Implication, the Current Account Deficit, Come From?

Three factors appear to have played roughly equal roles.

The first is the high U.S. growth rate since the mid-1990s, relative to the growth rate of its trading partners. Table 1 gives the average annual growth rate for the United States, Japan, the European Union, and the world economy (excluding the United States) for three periods, 1991–1995, 1996–2000, and 2001–2003. From 1991 to 1995, growth in the United States was roughly in line with growth in the rest of the world. Since 1996, however, U.S. growth has been much higher than growth in the rest of the world. The U.S. performance from 1996 to 2000 reflects the "new economy" boom, which we have discussed at many points in the book. U.S. growth has decreased since 2000 (recall that the United States went through a recession in 2001), but growth in the rest of the world has slowed by even more.

Higher growth does not necessarily lead to a higher trade deficit. If the main source of the increase in demand and growth in a country is an increase in foreign demand, the country can grow fast and maintain trade balance or even sustain a trade surplus. In the case of the United States, since the mid-1990s, how-

ever, the main source of increased demand has been domestic demand, with high consumption and investment demand as the main factors behind the sustained expansion. Thus, higher growth has come with an increasing trade deficit.

The second factor is the steady real appreciation of U.S. goods—the increase in the real U.S. effective exchange rate. Even if, at a given real exchange rate, growth leads to an increase in the trade deficit, a real depreciation can help maintain trade balance by making domestic goods more competitive. But just the opposite happened to the U.S. real exchange rate in the late 1990s. The United States experienced a real appreciation, not a real depreciation. As shown in Figure 2, the multilateral real exchange rate (normalized to equal 1 in 2000) decreased from 1.5 in 1991 to 0.95 in 2002—a 20% real appreciation. Although the U.S. dollar has depreciated since 2002, the depreciation has so far

(continued)

TABLE 1	Average Annual Growth Rates in the United States, Japan, the European Union, and the World, 1991–2003 (percent per year)		
	1991–1995	**1996–2000**	**2001–2003**
United States	2.5	4.1	2.9
Japan	1.5	1.5	0.9
European Union	2.1	2.6	1.9
World (excluding U.S.)	3.2	2.8	1.5

been limited, and the real exchange rate remains lower than in the mid-1990s.

The third factor is shifts in the export and import functions, that is, changes in exports or in imports due neither to changes in activity nor to changes in the exchange rate. The evidence is that these shifts have played an important role as well, explaining up to one-half of the increase in the trade deficit. At a given level of income and a given exchange rate, U.S. consumers, for example, buy a higher proportion of foreign goods—say, more foreign cars, fewer domestic cars.

What Happens Next?

Should we expect the large trade deficit and current account deficit to naturally disappear in the future? At an unchanged real exchange rate, the answer is probably not.

If there were good reasons to expect U.S. trading partners to experience much higher growth than the United States over the coming decade, then we could expect to see the same process we saw in the 1990s, but this time in reverse. Lower growth in the United States than in the rest of the world would lead to a steady reduction in the trade deficit. There are few reasons, however, to expect such a scenario. Although the United States cannot expect to replicate the growth rates of the late 1990s, there is also no reason to expect much lower growth than average over the coming decade. And nobody is predicting sustained high growth in the European Union or in Japan.

Can we expect the shifts in exports and imports to reverse themselves, leading to an improvement in the trade balance without the need for a depreciation? The source of the shifts is poorly understood, so one must be careful in predicting what might happen. But there does not appear to be any particular reason to think that, for example, U.S. consumers will shift back from foreign cars to U.S. cars. Put another way, there is no particular reason to expect that the trade deficit will narrow by itself, without a depreciation of the dollar.

Can the United States afford to sustain a large trade deficit and a large current account deficit for many more years? The answer, again, is probably not. While financial investors have been willing to lend to the United States until now, it may be difficult for the United States to continue to borrow $500 billion per year or so in the future. And even if financial investors were willing to continue to lend, it is not clear that it would be a wise policy for the United States to accumulate such a large debt vis-à-vis the rest of the world.

These arguments have two implications:

■ The U.S. trade and current account deficits will need to be reduced.

■ This is unlikely to happen without a real depreciation. How large a depreciation? Estimates range from 20 to 40%—in short, a substantial real depreciation. When will this depreciation take place? This is a

much harder question to answer. It will take place when foreign investors become reluctant to lend to the United States at the rate of $500 billion or so a year.

Go back to the issues discussed in Table 7-1 in the text. A depreciation on such a scale will have major effects on the demand for goods both in the United States and abroad.

The depreciation will increase the demand for U.S. goods. If, when the depreciation takes place, U.S. output is already close to its natural level, the risk is that the depreciation will lead to too high a level of demand and too high a level of output. If this happens, the right policy will be a fiscal contraction, a reduction in the large budget deficits that the U.S. government currently runs. If the U.S. government succeeds in achieving a smooth depreciation and the appropriate fiscal contraction, the outcome may be sustained growth and a reduction of the trade deficit.

The depreciation will decrease the demand for foreign goods. By the same argument, this may require foreign governments to implement policies to sustain their own demand and output. This would ordinarily call for a fiscal expansion, but it might not be the right solution in this case. A number of countries, for example, France, Germany, and Japan, are already running large budget deficits. Further increasing these deficits may be difficult, even dangerous. If fiscal policy cannot be used to maintain demand and output, a strong dollar depreciation might therefore trigger a recession in those countries.

In short, a smooth reduction of the U.S. trade deficit will require the combination of a dollar depreciation and fiscal policy changes both in the United States and abroad. Many economists worry that this might not be easy to achieve.

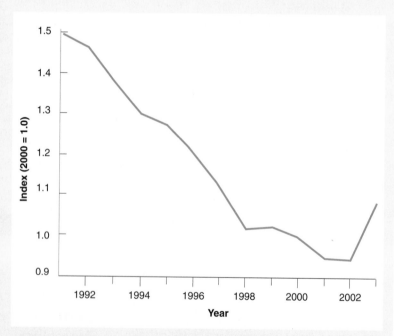

FIGURE 2   US Multilateral Real Exchange Rate 1991–2003

Source: OECD Effective Exchange Rates.

Marshall and Abba Lerner, who stated it first.) It is derived formally in this chapter's appendix. It turns out—with a caveat, which we will state when we introduce dynamics later in this chapter—that this condition is satisfied in reality. So, for the rest of this book, we will assume that an increase in ϵ, a real depreciation, leads to an increase in net exports.

The Effects of a Depreciation

We have looked so far only at the *direct* effects of a depreciation on the trade balance, that is, the effects *given Canadian and foreign outputs*. But the effects do not end there. The change in net exports changes domestic output, which affects net exports further.

Because the effects of a real depreciation are very much like those of an increase in foreign output, we can use Figure 7–4, the same figure that we used to show the effects of an increase in foreign output earlier.

Just like an increase in foreign output, a depreciation leads to an increase in net exports (assuming, as we do, that the Marshall–Lerner condition holds), at any level of output. Both the demand relation (ZZ in Figure 7–4a) and the net exports relation (NX in Figure 7–4b) shift up. The equilibrium moves from A to A'; output increases from Y to Y'. By the same argument we used earlier, the trade balance improves: The increase in imports induced by the increase in output is smaller than the direct improvement in the trade balance induced by the depreciation.

To summarize: The depreciation leads to a shift in demand, both foreign and domestic, toward domestic goods. This leads, in turn, both to an increase in domestic output and to an improvement in the trade position.

Although a depreciation and an increase in foreign output each have the same effect on domestic output and the trade balance, there is a subtle but important difference between the two. A depreciation works by making foreign goods relatively more expensive. But this means that given their income, people—who now have to pay more to buy foreign goods because of the depreciation—are worse off. This mechanism is strongly felt in countries that undergo a major depreciation. Governments that try to achieve a major depreciation often find themselves with strikes and riots, as people react to the much higher prices of imported goods. This was the case in Mexico, where the large depreciation of the peso in 1994–1995 (from 3.44 pesos per U.S. dollar in November 1994 to 5.88 pesos per dollar in May 1995) led to a large decline in workers' living standards and strong social tensions. A more recent example is that of Indonesia in 1998.[2] In Canada, a depreciation of the Canadian dollar does make purchases of American goods and services more expensive (especially trips to Florida in the winter. The recent appreciation has made these trips cheaper.).

Combining Exchange-Rate and Fiscal Policies

Suppose a government wants to reduce the trade deficit without changing the level of output. A depreciation alone will not do: It will reduce the trade deficit, but it also will increase output. Nor will a fiscal contraction do: It will reduce the trade deficit, but it will decrease output. What should that government do? The answer is to use the right combination of depreciation and fiscal contraction. Figure 7–5 shows what this combination should be.

The initial equilibrium in Figure 7–5(a) is at A, associated with output Y. The trade deficit is given by the distance BC in Figure 7–5(b). If government wants to eliminate the trade deficit without changing output, it must do two things:

● First, it must achieve a depreciation sufficient to eliminate the trade deficit at the initial level of output. So, the depreciation must shift the net exports relation from NX to

---

[2]**DIGGING DEEPER**. There is an alternative to strikes and riots: asking for and obtaining an increase in wages. But if wages increase, presumably the prices of domestic goods will increase as well, leading to a smaller real depreciation. To discuss this mechanism, we need to look at the supply side in more detail than we have done so far. We return to the dynamics of depreciation, wage movements, and price movements in Chapter 8.

FIGURE 7-5

Reducing the Trade Deficit without Changing Output

To reduce the trade deficit without changing output, government must achieve a depreciation and decrease government spending.

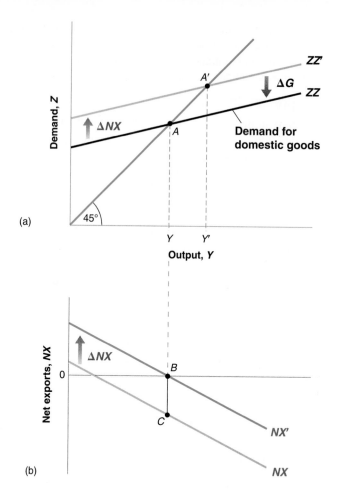

(a)

(b)

NX' in Figure 7–5(b). But this depreciation, and the associated increase in net exports, also shifts the demand relation in Figure 7–5(a) from *ZZ* to *ZZ'*. In the absence of other measures, the equilibrium would move from *A* to *A'*, and output would increase from *Y* to *Y'*.

- Second, to avoid the increase in output, government must reduce government spending so as to shift *ZZ'* back to *ZZ*. This combination of a depreciation and a fiscal contraction leads to the same level of output and an improved trade balance.

There is a general point behind this example. To the extent that governments care about *both* the level of output and the trade balance, they have to use *both* fiscal and exchange-rate policies. We just saw one such combination. Table 7–1 shows others, depending on the initial output and trade situation. Take, for example, the case represented in the top right corner of the table. Initial output is too low (put another way, unemployment is too high), and the economy has a trade deficit. A depreciation will help on both the trade and the output fronts: It reduces the trade deficit and increases output. But there is no reason for the depreciation to

TABLE 7–1	Exchange Rate and Fiscal Policy Combinations	
Initial Conditions	**Trade Surplus**	**Trade Deficit**
Low output	ϵ ? $G\uparrow$	$\epsilon\uparrow$ G?
High output	$\epsilon\downarrow$ G?	ϵ ? $G\downarrow$

achieve both the right increase in output and the elimination of the trade deficit. Depending on the initial situation and the relative effects of the depreciation on output and the trade balance, government may need to complement the depreciation with either an increase or a decrease in government spending. This ambiguity is captured by the question mark in the box. Make sure that you understand the logic behind each of the other three cases.

7-5 | Looking at Dynamics: The J-Curve

We have ignored dynamics so far in this chapter. It is time to reintroduce them. The dynamics of consumption, investment, sales, and production we discussed in Chapter 3 are as relevant to the open economy as they were to the closed economy. But there are additional dynamic effects as well, which come from the dynamics of exports and imports. We focus on these effects here.

Return to the effects of the exchange rate on the trade balance. We argued earlier that a depreciation leads to an increase in exports and to a decrease in imports. But these effects do not happen overnight. Think of the dynamic effects of, say, a 5% depreciation of the Canadian dollar. In the first few months following the depreciation, the effect of the depreciation is likely to be reflected much more in prices than in quantities. The price of imports to Canada goes up, the price of Canadian exports abroad goes down.[3] But the quantities of imports and exports are likely to adjust slowly: It takes a while for consumers to realize that relative prices have changed, it takes a while for firms to shift to cheaper suppliers, and so on. Thus, a depreciation may well lead to an initial deterioration of the trade balance; ϵ increases, but neither X nor Q adjusts very much initially, leading to a decline in net exports $(X - \epsilon Q)$.

As time passes, the effects of the change in the relative prices of both exports and imports become stronger. Exports increase, and imports decrease. If the Marshall–Lerner condition eventually holds—and we have argued that it does—the response of exports and imports eventually becomes stronger than the adverse price effect, and the eventual effect of the depreciation is to improve the trade balance.

Figure 7–6 captures this adjustment by plotting the evolution of the trade balance against time in response to a real depreciation. The trade deficit before the depreciation is OA. The depreciation initially *increases* the trade deficit to OB: ϵ goes up, but neither Q nor X changes

The response of the trade balance to the real exchange rate:

Initially:
◁ (X, Q) unchanged, $\epsilon \uparrow \Rightarrow$
$(X - \epsilon Q) \downarrow$

Eventually:
◁ $(X \uparrow, Q \downarrow, \epsilon \uparrow) \Rightarrow$
$(X - \epsilon Q) \uparrow$

The J-Curve

A real depreciation leads initially to a deterioration and then to an improvement of the trade balance.

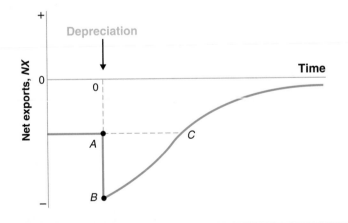

> [3]**DIGGING DEEPER**. The price of imported goods may not go up by 5%, however. The price would go up 5% if importers adjusted their dollar price fully for the dollar depreciation. To keep their market share, or because they are committed under previous contracts to deliver at a given dollar price, importers may decide instead to pass along only part of the dollar depreciation and take a reduction in their profit margins. This is what we observe in practice: Whereas import prices respond to a depreciation, they respond less than one for one. The same logic applies to the prices of exports. We stay away from these complications here.

right away. Over time, exports increase and imports decrease, reducing the trade deficit. Eventually, the trade balance improves beyond its initial level; this is what happens from point *C* on in the figure. Economists refer to this adjustment process as the **J-curve** because—admittedly, with a bit of imagination—the curve in the figure resembles a "J": first down, then up.

The importance of the effects of the real exchange rate on the trade balance can be seen from the evidence: Figure 7–7 plots the Canadian trade balance against the real exchange rate from 1970 to 2005. As we saw in the last chapter, the period from 1987 to 1991 was one of sharp real appreciation and the period from 1992 to 2002 one of sharp real depreciation. Turning to the trade balance, which is expressed as a proportion of GDP, it is clear that movements in the real exchange rate were reflected in parallel movements in net exports. The appreciation was associated with a large deterioration of the trade balance, and the later depreciation was associated with a large improvement in the trade balance. In the Canadian case, the J-curve effects are relatively weak and the response of net exports to the real exchange rate relatively swift. However, for other countries, particularly the United States, the slow effect of a real exchange rate change on trade is an important policy constraint.

In general, the statistical evidence on the dynamic relation among exports, imports, and the real exchange rate suggests that in rich countries, a real depreciation eventually leads to a trade balance improvement. But it also suggests that this process may take some time, typically between six months and a year. These lags have implications not only for the effects of a depreciation on the trade balance but also for the effects of a depreciation on output. If a depreciation initially decreases net exports, it also initially exerts a contractionary effect on output. Thus, if a government relies on a depreciation to both improve the trade balance and expand domestic output, the effects will go the "wrong" way for a while.

This effect is sometimes an issue in the developing countries. International organizations, such as the International Monetary Fund or the World Bank, recommend a devaluation to improve economic conditions. When the improvement is slow due to the J-curve, this can lead to considerable political unrest and a tendency to blame the international organizations involved.

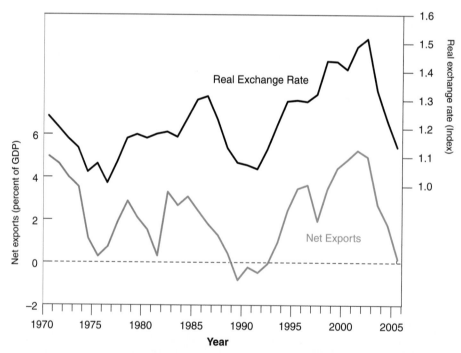

FIGURE 7–7

The Real Exchange Rate and the Ratio of Net Exports to GDP in Canada, 1970–2005

The level of the real exchange rate has a powerful influence on net exports. A real depreciation increases net exports, and a real appreciation reduces net exports. Net exports are measured as percent of GDP. The appreciation after 2002 did reduce net exports.

Source: Variables from CANSIM II: Export share (V3862675/V3862685) and import share (V3862674/V3862685); Nominal exchange rate using CANSIM II variable V37426; the United States real GDP deflator using series GDPDEF from the Federal Reserve Bank of St. Louis FRED database; the Canadian GDP deflator using CANSIM II variable V19920677 divided by V498086. The real exchange rate is EP*/P.

- In an open economy, the demand for domestic goods is equal to the domestic demand for goods (consumption plus investment plus government spending) minus imports plus exports.

- An increase in domestic demand leads to a smaller increase in output in an open economy than in a closed economy because some of the additional demand falls on imports. It also leads to a deterioration of the trade balance.

- An increase in foreign demand leads, as a result of increased exports, to an increase in domestic output and an improvement in the trade balance.

- Because increases in foreign demand improve the trade balance and increases in domestic demand worsen it, countries may be tempted to wait for increases in foreign demand to move them out of a recession. When a group of countries is in recession, coordination can help them get out of it.

- If the Marshall–Lerner condition is satisfied—and econometric evidence suggests that it is—a real depreciation leads to an improvement in net exports.

- The typical response of the trade balance to a real depreciation is first a deterioration and then an improvement. This adjustment process is known as the J-curve.

KEY TERMS

- coordination, 131
- demand for domestic goods, 123
- domestic demand for goods, 123
- G-8, 131

- J-curve, 138
- marginal propensity to import, 130
- Marshall–Lerner condition, 132

QUESTIONS AND PROBLEMS

An asterisk denotes a harder question. [Web] indicates that the question requires access to the Internet.

1. TRUE/FALSE/UNCERTAIN

a. Trade deficits generally reflect high investment.

b. Budget deficits cause trade deficits.

c. It is much easier for the government of a small open economy to maintain output at a given level than for the government of a large closed economy.

d. The only way a country can eliminate a trade surplus is through an appreciation of its currency.

e. A small open economy can reduce its trade deficit through fiscal contraction at a smaller cost in output than can a large economy.

f. If the trade deficit is equal to zero, the domestic demand for goods and the demand for domestic goods are the same.

g. The U.S. trade deficit in the last decade is a result of higher growth in the U.S. than in the rest of the world.

2. REAL EXCHANGE RATES AND THE BALANCE OF TRADE

a. Using the definition of the real exchange rate, verify that the following is true (you may want to use propositions 7 and 8 of Appendix 2 at the end of the book):

$$\frac{\Delta \epsilon}{\epsilon} = \frac{\Delta E}{E} + \frac{\Delta P^*}{P^*} - \frac{\Delta P}{P}$$

b. If domestic inflation is higher than foreign inflation but the domestic country has a fixed exchange rate, what happens to net exports over time? Assume that the Marshall–Lerner condition holds. Explain in words.

*3. COORDINATION AND FISCAL POLICY

Consider the following open economy. The real exchange rate is fixed and equal to one. Consumption, investment, government spending, and taxes are given by:

$$C = 10 + 0.8(Y - T) \quad I = 10 \quad G = 10 \quad T = 10$$

Imports and exports are given by:

$$Q = 0.3Y \qquad X = 0.3Y^*$$

where an asterisk denotes a foreign variable.

a. Solve for equilibrium income in the domestic economy, given Y^*. What is the multiplier in this economy? If we were to close the economy (so that exports and imports were equal to zero), what would the multiplier be? Why are the two multipliers different?

b. Assume the foreign economy has the same equations as the domestic economy (remove the asterisk from all the variables with an asterisk, and add an asterisk to all the variables without an asterisk). Use the two sets of equations to solve for the equilibrium income of each country. What is the multiplier for each country now? Why is it different from the open economy multiplier above?

c. Assume both countries have a target level of output of 125. What is the increase in G necessary in either of these countries, assuming that the other country does not change G, to achieve target output? Solve for net exports and the budget deficit in each country.

d. What is the common increase in G necessary to achieve target output?

e. Why is fiscal coordination (such as the common increase in G in (d)) difficult to achieve in practice?

*4. TARIFFS

Consider two open *IS-LM* economies.

a. Consider a domestic tax, at rate τ, on imports of foreign goods. How does this affect the import relation? The export relation?

b. What are the consequences of the tax on equilibrium output and net exports in the domestic country?

c. What are the consequences of the tax on equilibrium output and net exports in the foreign country?

d. Suppose that the foreign country retaliates by putting a tax on its imports. What is the additional effect of this foreign retaliation on equilibrium output in the domestic country and on the volume of trade? Assume identical economies and a foreign tax equal to the domestic one.

5. A U.S. RECESSION AND THE CANADIAN ECONOMY

a. The share of American spending on Canadian goods is about 80% of Canadian exports, which are themselves equal to about 45% of GDP. What is the share of American spending on Canadian goods relative to Canadian GDP?

b. Assume the multiplier in Canada is 2 and that a recession in the U.S. has reduced output by 5% (relative to its natural level). What is the impact of the U.S. slowdown on Canadian GDP?

c. If the U.S. recession also leads to a slowdown of the other economies which import goods from Canada, the effect could be larger. Assume exports fall by 5% (of themselves). What is the impact on the Canadian GDP?

d. Comment on the following statement from an economist on television: "Unless the U.S. recovers from recession quickly, growth will grind to a halt in Canada."

6. DYNAMICS OF A DEPRECIATION

Consider an economy with a fixed exchange rate. Assume that the price level is fixed.

a. What is the effect of a depreciation on equilibrium income and trade balance in the first six months after the depreciation?

b. What is the effect of the depreciation on equilibrium income and trade balance after the first six months?

*7. EXPORT RATIOS

Look at a recent issue of the *International Financial Statistics,* published monthly by the IMF. Find the list of countries in the table of contents. Make a list of five countries you would expect to have high ratios of exports to GDP. Then, go to the page corresponding to each country, and find the numbers for exports and for GDP for the most recent year available. (Make sure that you are comparing exports and GDP measured in the same units— either domestic currency or dollars. If one variable is in domestic currency and the other variable is in dollars, use the exchange rate to convert the two to the same currency.) Compute the export ratios. How good were your guesses?

DERIVATION OF THE MARSHALL–LERNER CONDITION

Start from the definition of net exports, $NX \equiv X - \epsilon Q$, and assume trade to be initially balanced so that $X = \epsilon Q$. The Marshall–Lerner condition is the condition under which a real depreciation, an increase in ϵ, leads to an increase in net exports.

To derive this condition, consider an increase in the real exchange rate of $\Delta\epsilon$. The change in the trade balance thus is given by:

$$\Delta NX = \Delta X - \epsilon\Delta Q - Q\Delta\epsilon$$

The first term on the right (ΔX) gives the change in exports, the second ($\epsilon\Delta Q$) the real exchange rate times the change in the quantity of imports, and the third ($Q\Delta\epsilon$) the quantity of imports times the change in the real exchange rate.

Divide both sides of the equation by X to get:

$$\frac{\Delta NX}{X} = \frac{\Delta X}{X} - \epsilon\frac{\Delta Q}{X} - \frac{Q\Delta\epsilon}{X}$$

Use the fact that $\epsilon Q = X$ to replace ϵ/X by $1/Q$ in the second term on the right and to replace Q/X by $1/\epsilon$ in the third term on the right. This substitution gives:

$$\frac{\Delta NX}{X} = \frac{\Delta X}{X} - \frac{\Delta Q}{Q} - \frac{\Delta\epsilon}{\epsilon}$$

This equation says that the change in the trade balance in response to a real depreciation, normalized by exports, is equal to the sum of three terms. The first is the proportional change in exports, $\Delta X/X$, induced by the real depreciation. The second term is equal to minus the proportional change in imports, $-\Delta Q/Q$, induced by the real depreciation. The third term is equal to minus the proportional change in the real exchange rate, $-\Delta\epsilon/\epsilon$, or equivalently, minus the rate of real depreciation.

The Marshall–Lerner condition is the condition that the sum of these three terms be positive. If it is satisfied, a real depreciation leads to an improvement in the trade balance.

A numerical example will help here. Suppose that a 1% depreciation leads to a relative increase in exports of 0.9% and to a relative decrease in imports of 0.8%. (Econometric evidence on the relation of exports and imports to the real exchange rates suggests that these are, indeed, reasonable numbers.) In that case, the right-hand side of the equation is equal to $0.9\% - (-0.8\%) - 1\% = 0.7\%$. Thus, the trade balance improves: The Marshall–Lerner condition is satisfied.

CHAPTER 8
OUTPUT, THE INTEREST RATE, AND THE EXCHANGE RATE

The Core: The Short Run

In Chapter 7, we treated the exchange rate as one of the policy instruments available to government. But the exchange rate is not a policy instrument. Rather, it is determined in the foreign-exchange market—a market where, as we saw in Chapter 6, there is an enormous amount of trading. This fact raises two obvious questions: What determines the exchange rate? How can government affect it?

These are the questions that motivate this chapter. More generally, we examine the implications of equilibrium in both the goods and financial markets, including the foreign exchange market. This allows us to characterize the joint movements of output, the interest rate, and the exchange rate in an open economy. The model we develop is an extension of the open economy of the *IS-LM* model we saw in Chapter 5 and is known as the **Mundell–Fleming model**, after the two economists Robert Mundell and Marcus Fleming, who first put it together in the 1960s. (The model presented here keeps the spirit but differs in its details from the original Mundell–Fleming model.)

Sections 8-1 and 8-2 look at equilibrium in the goods and financial markets, respectively. Section 8-3 puts the two equilibrium conditions together and looks at the determination of output, the interest rate, and the exchange rate. Section 8-4 looks at the role of policy under flexible exchange rates, and section 8-5 does the same under fixed exchange rates.

8-1 | Equilibrium in the Goods Market

Equilibrium in the goods market was the focus of Chapter 7, where we derived the following equilibrium condition:

$$Y = C(Y - T) + I(Y, i) + G - \epsilon Q(Y, \epsilon) + X(Y^*, \epsilon)$$
$$(\ + \ ) \quad (+, -) \qquad\qquad (+, -) \quad\ (+, +)$$

For the goods market to be in equilibrium, output (the left side of the equation) must be equal to the demand for domestic goods (the right side of the equation).

Demand, in turn, is equal to consumption plus investment plus government spending minus imports plus exports. Consumption depends positively on disposable income. Investment depends positively on output and negatively on the interest rate. Government spending is taken as a given. The volume of imports depends positively on output and negatively on the real exchange rate. Exports depend positively on foreign output and positively on the real exchange rate.

It will be convenient in what follows to regroup the last two terms under "net exports," defined as exports minus imports, $X - \epsilon Q$:

$$NX(Y, Y^*, \epsilon) \equiv X(Y^*, \epsilon) - \epsilon Q(Y, \epsilon)$$

It follows from our assumptions about imports and exports that net exports depend on domestic output, foreign output, and the real exchange rate. An increase in domestic output increases imports and thus decreases net exports. An increase in foreign output increases exports, thus increasing net exports. An increase in ϵ—a real depreciation—leads (under the Marshall–Lerner condition, which we will assume to hold throughout this chapter) to an increase in net exports. Using this definition of net exports, we can rewrite the equilibrium condition as:

$$Y = C(Y - T) + I(Y, i) + G + NX(Y, Y^*, \epsilon) \qquad (8.1)$$
$$(\ + \ ) \quad (+, -) \qquad\qquad (-, +, +)$$

> Goods-market equilibrium condition (*IS*): Output = Demand for domestic goods.

> A reminder: A real depreciation is represented by an increase in the real exchange rate—an increase in the price of foreign goods in terms of domestic goods.

For our purposes, the essential implication of equation (8.1) is the dependence of demand, and so of equilibrium output, on both the interest rate and the real exchange rate:

- An increase in the interest rate leads to a decrease in investment spending, and so to a decrease in the demand for domestic goods. This leads, through the multiplier, to a decrease in output.
- An increase in the exchange rate—a real depreciation—leads to a shift in demand toward domestic goods, and thus an increase in net exports. The increase in net exports increases demand and output.

In writing (8.1), we have assumed that the domestic price level, P, is fixed in the short run. We make a similar assumption about the foreign price level in the short run so that P^* is fixed. Extending this assumption to the foreign price level means the real exchange rate ($\epsilon = EP^*/P$) and the nominal exchange rate (E) move together. A nominal depreciation leads, one for one, to a real depreciation. If for notational convenience, we choose P and P^* so that $P = P^* = 1$ (and we can do so because they are index numbers), then $\epsilon = E$ and we can replace ϵ by E in equation (8.1).

> Simplification: $P = P^* = 1$, so $\epsilon = E$

With these simplifications, equation (8.1) becomes:

$$Y = C(Y - T) + I(Y, i) + G + NX(Y, Y^*, E) \qquad (8.2)$$

Output depends on both the nominal interest rate and the nominal exchange rate.

8-2 | Equilibrium in Financial Markets

When we looked at financial markets in the *IS-LM* model, we assumed that people chose between only two financial assets, money and bonds. Now that we look at a financially open economy, we must allow for a second choice—the choice between domestic bonds and foreign bonds. Let us consider each choice in turn.

Money versus Bonds

When looking at the determination of the interest rate in the *IS-LM* model, we wrote the condition that the supply of money be equal to the demand for money as:

$$\frac{M}{P} = Y L(i) \tag{8.3}$$

We took the real supply of money (the left side of equation [8.3]) as a given. We assumed that the real demand for money (the right side of equation [8.3]) depended on the level of transactions in the economy, measured by real output (Y), and on the opportunity cost of holding money rather than bonds, the nominal interest rate on bonds (i).

How should we change this characterization now that the economy is open? The answer is not very much, if at all.

In an open economy, the demand for domestic money is still mostly a demand by domestic residents. There is not much reason for, say, Canadians to hold American currency or American dollar–denominated demand deposits. They cannot use them for transactions in Canada—which require payment in Canadian money. If they want to hold American dollar-denominated assets, they are better off holding U.S. bonds, which at least pay a positive interest rate. And the demand for money by domestic residents still depends on the same factors as before: their level of transactions, that we proxy by domestic real output, and the opportunity cost of holding money, the nominal interest rate on bonds.[1]

Therefore, we can still use equation (8.3) to think about the determination of the nominal interest rate in an open economy. The interest rate must be such that the supply and the demand for money are equal. An increase in money supply leads to a decrease in the interest rate. An increase in money demand, say, as a result of an increase in output, leads to an increase in the interest rate.

Domestic Bonds versus Foreign Bonds

In looking at the choice between domestic bonds and foreign bonds, we will rely on the assumption we introduced in Chapter 6: Financial investors, domestic or foreign, go for the highest expected rate of return. This implies that in equilibrium, both domestic bonds and foreign bonds must have the same expected rate of return; otherwise, investors would be willing to hold only one or the other, but not both, and this could not be an equilibrium.

As we saw in Chapter 6, this assumption implies that the following arbitrage relation— the *interest parity condition*—must hold:

Recall from Chapter 6 that this is only an approximation (but a good one). For notational convenience, we replace the earlier approximation symbol ($\approx$) with an equal sign (=).

$$i_t = i_t^* + \frac{E_{t+1}^e - E_t}{E_t}$$

The domestic interest rate i_t must be equal to the foreign interest rate i_t^* plus the expected rate of depreciation of the domestic currency ($(E_{t+1}^e - E_t)/E_t$).

---

[1]**DIGGING DEEPER.** Given that domestic residents can now hold both domestic and foreign bonds, the demand for money should depend on the expected rates of return on both domestic and foreign bonds. But our next assumption—interest parity—implies that these two expected rates of return are equal so that we can write the demand for money directly as we did in equation (8.3).

For now, we will take the expected future exchange rate as given and denote it as $\overline{E}^e$ (we will relax this assumption in Chapter 13). Under this assumption, and dropping time indexes, the interest parity condition becomes:

$$i = i^* + \frac{\overline{E}^e - E}{E} \tag{8.4}$$

Multiplying both sides by E, bringing the terms in E to the left side, and dividing both sides by $(1 + i - i^*)$ give the current exchange rate as a function of the expected future exchange rate and the domestic and foreign interest rates:

$$E = \frac{\overline{E}^e}{1 + i - i^*} \tag{8.5}$$

Equation (8.5) implies a negative relation between the domestic interest rate and the exchange rate. Given the expected future exchange rate and the foreign interest rate, *an increase in the domestic interest rate leads to a decrease in the exchange rate—equivalently, to an appreciation of the domestic currency. A decrease in the domestic interest rate leads to an increase in the exchange rate—to a depreciation.*

◀ An increase in the domestic interest rate leads to an appreciation of the domestic currency. An increase in the foreign interest rate leads to a depreciation of the domestic currency.

This relation between the exchange rate and the domestic interest rate plays a central role in the real world and will play a central role in the rest of this chapter. To understand it further, think about the sequence of events that takes place in financial and foreign exchange markets after an increase in the Canadian interest rate above the American interest rate:

- Suppose that, to start with, the Canadian and American interest rates are equal so that $i = i^*$. This implies, from equation (8.5), that the current exchange rate equals the expected future exchange rate: $E = E^e$.
- Suppose, as a result of a Canadian monetary contraction, the Canadian interest rate increases. At an unchanged exchange rate, Canadian bonds become more attractive, so financial investors want to shift out of American bonds and into Canadian bonds. To do so, they must sell American bonds for American dollars, then sell American dollars for Canadian dollars, and then use the Canadian dollars to buy Canadian bonds. As investors sell American dollars and buy Canadian dollars, the Canadian dollar appreciates.
- That an increase in the Canadian interest rate leads to an appreciation of the Canadian dollar is intuitively straightforward: An increase in the demand for Canadian dollars leads to an increase in the price of Canadian dollars. What is less intuitive is *by how much* the Canadian dollar must appreciate. The important point here is that if financial investors do not change their expectation of the future exchange rate, then *the more the Canadian dollar appreciates today*, the more investors expect it to *depreciate in the future* (as they expect it to return to the same value in the future). Other things being equal, this expectation makes American dollar bonds more attractive: When the Canadian dollar is expected to depreciate, a given rate of return in American dollars means a higher rate of return in Canadian dollars.
- This gives us the answer: The initial Canadian dollar appreciation must be such that the expected future depreciation compensates for the increase in the Canadian interest rate. When this is the case, investors are again indifferent, and equilibrium prevails.

A numerical example will help. Assume one-year Canadian and American interest rates are both equal to 4%. Suppose the Canadian interest rate now increases to 10%. The Canadian dollar will appreciate by 6% today. Why? Because if the Canadian dollar appreciates by 6% today and investors do not change their expectation of the exchange rate one year ahead, the Canadian dollar is now expected to depreciate by 6% over the coming year. Put the other way, the American dollar is expected to appreciate by 6% relative to the Canadian dollar over the coming year so that holding American bonds yields an expected rate of return of 10%—the 4% rate of return in U.S. dollars plus the expected 6% appreciation of the U.S. dollar.

FIGURE 8–1

The Relation between the Interest Rate and the Exchange Rate Implied by Interest Parity

A lower domestic interest rate leads to a higher exchange rate—to a depreciation of the domestic currency. A higher domestic interest rate leads to a lower exchange rate—to an appreciation of the domestic currency.

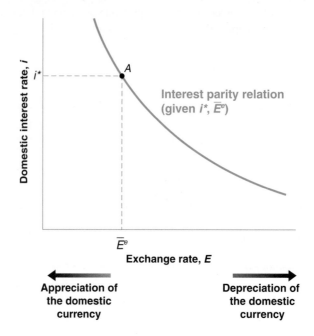

Appreciation of the domestic currency

Depreciation of the domestic currency

Make sure you understand the three steps in the argument: (1) The one-year interest rate on Canadian bonds increases by 6%. Investors then buy Canadian bonds and Canadian dollars. (2) The Canadian dollar appreciates until it is expected to depreciate by 6% during the coming year. (3) This happens when the Canadian dollar has appreciated today by 6%.

Holding Canadian bonds or holding American bonds both yield an expected rate of return of 10% in Canadian dollars. Financial investors are willing to hold either one, so there is equilibrium in the foreign exchange market. In terms of equation (8.4):

$$i = i^* + \frac{\overline{E}^e - E}{E}$$

$$10\% = 4\% + 6\%$$

The rate of return from holding Canadian dollar bonds (the left side) is equal to 10%. The expected rate of return from holding American dollar bonds, expressed in Canadian dollars, (the right side) is equal to the U.S. interest rate, 4%, plus the expected depreciation of the Canadian dollar, 6%.

Figure 8–1 plots the relation between the (domestic) interest rate and the exchange rate implied by equation (8.5)—the interest parity relation. It is drawn for a given expected future exchange rate, $\overline{E}^e$, and a given foreign interest rate, i^*. The lower the interest rate, the higher is the exchange rate: The relation is thus drawn as a downward-sloping curve. Equation (8.5) also implies that when the domestic interest rate is equal to the foreign interest rate, the exchange rate is equal to the expected future exchange rate: When $i = i^*$, then $E = \overline{E}^e$. This point is denoted A in the figure.[2]

What happens to the curve if i^* increases? If $\overline{E}^e$ increases?

[2]**DIGGING DEEPER**. The argument in the text relies heavily on the assumption that when the interest rate changes, the expected exchange rate remains unchanged. This implies that an appreciation today (a decrease in the current exchange rate) leads to an expected depreciation in the future (as the exchange rate is expected to return to the same, unchanged, value). We will relax the assumption that the future exchange rate is fixed in Chapter 19. But the two basic conclusions will remain: (1) An increase in the domestic interest rate leads to an appreciation. (2) An increase in the foreign interest rate leads to a depreciation.

8-3 | Putting Goods and Financial Markets Together

We now have all the elements we need to understand the movements of output, the interest rate, and the exchange rate.

Goods-market equilibrium implies that output depends, among other factors, on the interest rate and the exchange rate:

$$Y = C(Y - T) + I(Y, i) + G + NX(Y, Y^*, E)$$

The interest rate is determined by the equality of money supply and money demand:

$$\frac{M}{P} = Y L(i)$$

And the interest parity condition implies a negative relation between the domestic interest rate and the exchange rate:

$$E = \frac{\overline{E}^e}{1 + i - i^*}$$

Together, these three relations determine output, the interest rate, and the exchange rate. Working with three relations is not very easy. But we can easily reduce them to two by using the interest parity condition to eliminate the exchange rate in the goods-market equilibrium relation. Doing this gives us the following two equations, the open-economy versions of our old *IS* and *LM* relations:

IS:
$$Y = C(Y - T) + I(Y, i) + G + NX\left(Y, Y^*, \frac{\overline{E}^e}{1 + i - i^*}\right)$$

LM:
$$\frac{M}{P} = Y L(i)$$

Take the *IS* relation first, and consider the effects of an increase in the interest rate on output. An increase in the interest rate now has two effects:

- The first, which was already present in a closed economy, is the direct effect on investment. A higher interest rate leads to a decrease in investment, and so to a decrease in the demand for domestic goods and a decrease in output.
- The second, which is present only in the open economy, is the effect through the exchange rate. An increase in the domestic interest rate leads to an appreciation of the domestic currency. The appreciation, which makes domestic goods more expensive relative to foreign goods, leads to a decrease in net exports, and thus to a decrease in the demand for domestic goods and a decrease in output.

Both effects work in the same direction: An increase in the interest rate decreases demand directly, and indirectly—through the adverse effect of the appreciation. Note that the multiplier is smaller than in the closed economy. This is because part of demand falls on foreign goods rather than all on domestic goods.

The *IS* relation between the interest rate and output is drawn in Figure 8–2(a) for given values of all the other variables in the relation—namely, T, G, Y^*, i^*, and $\overline{E}^e$. The *IS* curve is downward sloping: An increase in the interest rate leads to a decrease in output. It looks very much the same as in the closed economy, but it hides a more complex relation than before: The interest rate affects output not only directly but also indirectly through the exchange rate.

The *LM* relation is exactly the same as in the closed economy. The *LM* curve is upward sloping. For a given value of the real money stock, (M/P), an increase in output leads to an increase in the demand for money and to an increase in the equilibrium interest rate.

Equilibrium in the goods and financial markets is attained at point A in Figure 8–2(a), with output level Y and interest rate i. The equilibrium value of the exchange rate cannot be

> An increase in the interest rate leads, both directly and indirectly (through the exchange rate), to a decrease in output.

FIGURE 8-2

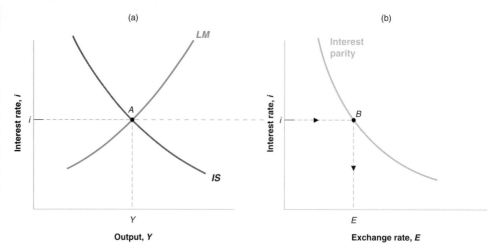

(a)

(b)

An increase in the interest rate reduces output both directly and indirectly (through the exchange rate): The *IS* curve is downward sloping. Given the real money stock, an increase in income increases the interest rate: The *LM* curve is upward sloping.

read directly from the graph. But it is easily obtained from Figure 8–2(b), which replicates Figure 8–1, and gives the exchange rate associated with a given interest rate. The exchange rate associated with the equilibrium interest rate i is equal to E.

To summarize: We have derived the *IS* and the *LM* relations for an open economy. The *IS* curve is downward sloping: An increase in the interest rate leads directly, and indirectly through the exchange rate, to a decrease in demand and a decrease in output. The *LM* curve is upward sloping: An increase in income increases the demand for money, requiring an increase in the equilibrium interest rate. Equilibrium output and the equilibrium interest rate are given by the intersection of the *IS* and the *LM* curves. Given the foreign interest rate and the expected future exchange rate, the equilibrium interest rate determines the equilibrium exchange rate.

8-4 | The Effects of Policy in an Open Economy

Having derived the *IS-LM* model for the open economy, we can now put it to use and look at the effects of policy.

The Effects of Fiscal Policy in an Open Economy

Let us look again at a change in government spending. Suppose that starting from budget balance, government decides to increase infrastructure spending and thus to run a budget deficit. What happens to the level of output and to its composition? To the interest rate? To the exchange rate?

The answers are given in Figure 8–3(a): The economy is initially at point A. An increase in government spending from G to G' increases output at a given interest rate, shifting the *IS* curve to the right, from *IS* to *IS'*. Because government spending does not enter the *LM* relation, the *LM* curve does not shift. The new equilibrium is at point A', with a higher level of output and a higher interest rate. As shown in Figure 8–3(b), the higher interest rate leads to a decrease in the exchange rate—an appreciation of the domestic currency. Thus, *an increase in government spending leads to an increase in output, an increase in the interest rate, and an appreciation.*

In words: An increase in government spending leads to an increase in demand, leading to an increase in output. As output increases, so does the demand for money, leading to upward pressure on the interest rate. The increase in the interest rate, which makes domestic bonds more attractive, also leads to an appreciation of the domestic currency. Both the higher interest rate and the appreciation decrease the domestic demand for goods, offsetting some of the effect of government spending on demand and output.

An increase in government spending shifts the *IS* curve to the right. It shifts ▶ neither the *LM* curve nor the interest parity curve.

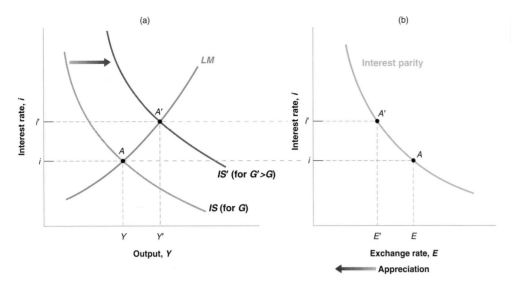

(a)   (b)

FIGURE 8-3

The Effects of an Increase in Government Spending

An increase in government spending leads to an increase in output, an increase in the interest rate, and an appreciation.

Can we tell what happens to the various components of demand?

- Clearly, both consumption and government spending go up—consumption goes up because of the increase in income, and government spending goes up by assumption.
- What happens to investment is ambiguous. Recall that investment depends on both output and the interest rate: $I = I(Y, i)$. On the one hand, output goes up, leading to an increase in investment. But on the other, the interest rate also goes up, leading to a decrease in investment. Depending on which of these two effects dominates, investment can go up or down.

  > The effect of a change in government spending on investment was ambiguous in the closed economy; it remains ambiguous in the open economy.

- Recall that net exports depend on domestic output, foreign output, and the exchange rate: $NX = NX(Y, Y^*, E)$. Thus, both the appreciation and the increase in output combine to decrease net exports: The appreciation decreases exports and increases imports, and the increase in output increases imports further. The budget deficit leads to a deterioration of the trade balance. If trade is balanced to start with, then the budget deficit leads to a trade deficit.

  > Note: Although an increase in the budget deficit increases the trade deficit, the effect is far from mechanical. It works through the effect of the budget deficit on output and on the exchange rate.

The Effects of Monetary Policy in an Open Economy

The effects of our other favourite policy experiment, a monetary contraction, are shown in Figure 8–4. At a given level of output, a decrease in the money stock, from M/P to M'/P, leads to an increase in the interest rate: The LM curve in Figure 8–4(a) therefore shifts up, from LM to LM'. Because money does not directly enter the IS relation, the IS curve does not shift. The equilibrium moves from point A to point A'. The increase in the interest rate leads to an appreciation of the domestic currency (Figure 8–4b).

> A monetary contraction shifts the LM curve up. It shifts neither the IS curve nor the interest parity curve.

Thus, *a monetary contraction leads to a decrease in output, an increase in the interest rate, and an appreciation.* The story is easy to tell. A monetary contraction leads to an increase in the interest rate, making domestic bonds more attractive and triggering an appreciation. The higher interest rate and the appreciation both decrease demand and output. As output decreases, money demand decreases, leading to a decrease in the interest rate, offsetting some of the initial increase in the interest rate and some of the initial appreciation.

> Can you tell what happens to consumption, investment, and net exports?

How well do the implications of this model fit the facts? To answer, one could hardly design a better experiment than the sharp monetary contraction in Canada from 1988 to 1991. This is described in the In Depth box "Monetary Contraction in Canada, 1989–1992." The Mundell–Fleming model and its predictions pass with flying colours.

> That these experiments were instructive for economists does not imply they were good for the Canadian economy. How costly the large budget deficits have turned out to be is taken up in Chapter 27.

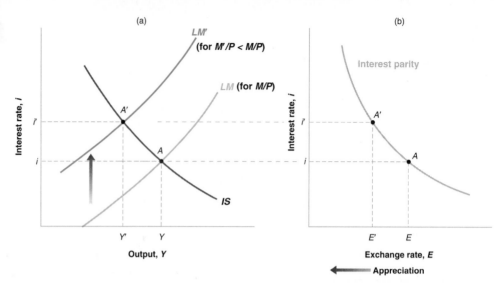

FIGURE 8-4

The Effects of a Monetary Contraction

A monetary contraction leads to a decrease in output, an increase in the interest rate, and an appreciation.

Monetary Contraction in Canada, 1989–1992

From 1988, the Bank of Canada decided to engage in a sharp monetary contraction. Its goal was to reduce inflation. We will consider that issue in detail in Chapters 9 through 13 when we adapt the *IS-LM* model to allow prices to adjust slowly. However, the monetary contraction is a "textbook example" of the effects of tight monetary policy in an open economy. Table 1 walks us through these effects.

First, the Bank of Canada policy was effective. Growth in real GDP declined sharply in 1989 and again in 1990. Growth in real GDP was negative 2% in 1991, the most severe recession in Canada since the Great Depression of the 1930s. With a lag of one year, the unemployment rate in Canada increased sharply. In both 1991 and 1992, more than 1 in 10 Canadians in the labour force were unemployed. What caused demand for Canadian-produced goods and services to fall?

The Bank of Canada raised interest rates from 9.4% in 1988 to over 12% in both 1989 and 1990. This reduced investment. It also generated a very large real appreciation of the Canadian dollar. The increase in Canadian interest rates was much larger than the increase in American interest rates. The gap between Canadian and American interest rates was 5.3% in 1990.

The real exchange rate appreciation greatly reduced Canada's net exports. Net exports of goods and services were 1.2% of GDP, a large surplus in 1987. Canada usually has a trade surplus. But in 1991 and 1992 (you can see a small J-curve effect in these data), Canada's trade balance was negative.

Monetary policy is a powerful tool to affect aggregate demand and output in an open economy. Canada, from 1990 to 1992, provides an excellent example of this fact.

TABLE 1   Some Major Canadian Macroeconomic Variables, 1987–1992

	1987	1988	1989	1990	1991	1992
GDP growth (%)	4.0	4.8	2.5	0.3	−2.0	1.0
Unemployment rate (%)	8.8	7.8	7.5	8.1	10.3	11.2
Canadian interest rate (%)	8.2	9.4	12.0	12.8	8.8	6.5
American interest rate (%)	5.8	6.7	8.1	7.5	5.4	3.4
Interest rate differential (%)	2.4	2.7	3.9	5.3	3.4	3.1
Real exchange rate	1.33	1.21	1.16	1.15	1.14	1.21
Trade surplus (Trade deficit if negative) as a % of GDP	1.2	0.8	0.0	0.1	−0.6	−0.4

Sources: Real GDP growth using CANSIM II variable V3862685; unemployment rate using CANSIM II variable V159752; Canadian one-year Treasury bill rate using CANSIM II; *U.S. one-year Treasury bill rate* using Federal Reserve Board variable RIFSGFSM03_N.M.; *real exchange rate:* Nominal exchange rate using CANSIM II variable V37426; United States GDP deflator using CANSIM II variable V122054/V149258; Canada GDP deflator using CANSIM II variable V498918/V1992259; *trade surplus* using CANSIM II variables (V646954–V646957)/V646937.

8-5 | Fixed Exchange Rates

We have assumed so far that the central bank chose money supply and let the exchange rate adjust in whatever manner was implied by equilibrium in the foreign-exchange market. In many or even most countries, this assumption does not reflect reality: Central banks act under implicit or explicit exchange-rate targets and use monetary policy to achieve those targets. The targets are sometimes implicit, sometimes explicit; they are sometimes specific values, sometimes bands or ranges. These exchange-rate arrangements come under many names. Let us first see what these various names mean.

Pegs, Crawling Pegs, Bands, the EMS, and the Euro

At one end of the spectrum, there are units with flexible exchange rates. These countries have no explicit exchange-rate targets. The largest economic units in the world operate under this arrangement, including the United States, Canada, Japan, the United Kingdom, and the collective of countries that jointly use the euro as their currency and unit of account. Although their central banks surely do not ignore movements in the exchange rate, they have shown themselves quite willing to let their exchange rates fluctuate considerably.

At the other end, there are countries that operate under fixed exchange rates. These countries maintain a fixed exchange rate in terms of some foreign currency. Some **peg** their currency to the U.S. dollar: The list ranges from the Bahamas to Oman. Canada did peg its currency to the U.S. from 1962 to 1970. Swaziland and Lesotho, two small countries adjacent to South Africa, peg their currencies to the South African rand. Others peg to a basket of currencies, with the weights reflecting the composition of their trade. The label "fixed" is a bit misleading: It is not the case that the exchange rates in countries with fixed exchange rates actually never change. But changes are rare. An extreme case is that of the African countries pegged to the French franc. When their exchange rates were readjusted in January 1994, this was the first adjustment in 45 years. Because these changes are rare, economists use specific words to distinguish them from the daily changes that occur under flexible exchange rates. They refer to an increase in the exchange rate under a fixed exchange rate regime as a *devaluation* rather than a depreciation and to a decrease in the exchange rate under a fixed exchange rate regime as a *revaluation* rather than an appreciation.

Between these extremes are the countries with various degrees of commitment to an exchange rate target. For example, some countries operate under a **crawling peg**. The name describes it well: These countries often have inflation rates that exceed the inflation rate in the United States. Since most of these countries peg their nominal exchange rate to the U.S. dollar, the more rapid increase in their domestic price level over the U.S. price level would lead to a steady real appreciation and rapidly make their goods noncompetitive. To avoid this effect, these countries choose a predetermined rate of depreciation against the U.S. dollar. They choose to "crawl" (move slowly) vis-à-vis the U.S. dollar.

Yet another arrangement is for a group of countries to maintain their bilateral exchange rates (the exchange rate between each pair of countries) within some bands. The most prominent example is the **European Monetary System (EMS)**—which determined the movements of exchange rates within the European Union from 1978 to 1998. Under the rules of this **exchange rate mechanism**, or **ERM**, member countries agreed to maintain their exchange rate vis-à-vis the other currencies in the system within narrow limits or **bands** around a **central parity**. Changes in the central parity and devaluations or revaluations of specific currencies could occur, but only by common agreement among member countries. After a major crisis in 1992, which forced several countries to drop out of the EMS altogether, exchange rate adjustments became more and more infrequent, leading several countries to move one step further and adopt a common currency, the *euro*. Conversion from domestic currencies to the euro started in earnest on January 1, 1999. Full conversion was achieved in 2002. We will return to the implications of the move to the euro in Chapter 13.

Recall the definition of the real exchange rate $\epsilon = EP^*/P$. If domestic inflation is higher than foreign inflation: P increases faster than P^*. Equivalently, P^*/P decreases. If the nominal exchange rate E is fixed, EP^*/P decreases; there is a steady real appreciation, and domestic goods become steadily more expensive relative to foreign goods. ◄

We look at the 1992 crisis ◄ in Chapter 13.

You can think of countries adopting a common currency as adopting an extreme form of fixed ◄ exchange rates: Their "exchange rate" is fixed at one to one between any pair of countries.

We will discuss the pros and cons of different exchange regimes in Chapter 13 as well. But first, we must understand how pegging the exchange rate affects the scope for and the effects of monetary and fiscal policies. This is what we do in the rest of this chapter.

Pegging the Exchange Rate and Monetary Control

Until now, we looked at macroeconomic policy under flexible exchange rates. We now look at policy under fixed exchange rates. ▶

Suppose a country decides to peg its exchange rate at some chosen value, call it $\overline{E}$. How does it actually achieve this? It cannot just announce the value of the exchange rate and do nothing further. Rather, it must take measures so that the chosen exchange rate will prevail in the foreign-exchange market. Let us look at the implications and mechanics of pegging.

Pegging or no pegging, under the assumption of perfect capital mobility, the exchange rate and the nominal interest rate must satisfy the interest parity condition:

$$i_t = i_t^* + \frac{E_{t+1}^e - E_t}{E_t}$$

Now, suppose the country pegs the exchange rate at $\overline{E}$, so the current exchange rate $E_t = \overline{E}$. If financial and foreign exchange markets believe that the exchange rate will remain pegged at this value in the future, their expectation of the future exchange rate, E_{t+1}^e, is also equal to $\overline{E}$, and the interest parity relation becomes:

$$i_t = i_t^* + \frac{\overline{E} - \overline{E}}{\overline{E}} = i_t^*$$

Under perfect capital mobility, fixing the exchange rate means giving up the freedom to choose the interest rate (which must equal the foreign interest rate). ▶

In words: If financial investors expect the exchange rate to remain fixed, they will require the same nominal interest rate in both countries. *Under a fixed exchange rate and perfect capital mobility, the domestic interest rate must be equal to the foreign interest rate.*

This condition has one further important implication. Return to the equilibrium condition that the supply of money and demand for money be equal. Now that $i = i^*$, this condition becomes:

$$\frac{M}{P} = Y L(i^*) \tag{8.6}$$

Suppose an increase in domestic output increases the demand for money. In a closed economy, the central bank could leave the money stock unchanged, leading to an increase in the equilibrium interest rate. In an open economy, and under flexible exchange rates, the central bank can still do the same: The result will be both an increase in the interest rate and an appreciation of the domestic currency. But under a fixed exchange rate, the central bank cannot keep the money stock unchanged. If it did, the domestic interest rate would increase above the foreign interest rate, leading to an appreciation of the domestic currency. To maintain the exchange rate, it must increase the supply of money in line with the increase in the demand for money so the equilibrium interest rate does not change. Given the price level, P, nominal money M must adjust so that equation (8.6) holds.

These results depend very much on the assumption of perfect capital mobility. The case of fixed exchange rates with imperfect capital mobility, which is more relevant for middle-income countries, such as those in Latin America or Asia, is treated in ▶ the appendix to this chapter.

To summarize: *Under fixed exchange rates, the central bank gives up monetary policy as a policy instrument.* A fixed exchange rate implies a domestic interest rate equal to the foreign rate. And the money supply must adjust to maintain that interest rate.

Fiscal Policy under Fixed Exchange Rates

If monetary policy can no longer be used under fixed exchange rates, what about fiscal policy? To answer, we use Figure 8–5.

Figure 8–5 starts by replicating Figure 8–3(a), which we used earlier to analyze the effects of fiscal policy under flexible exchange rates. In that case, we saw that a fiscal expansion shifted the *IS* curve to the right from *IS* to *IS′*. Under flexible exchange rates, the money stock remained unchanged, leading to a movement in the equilibrium from *A* to *B*, with an increase in output from Y_A to Y_B, an increase in the interest rate, and a decrease in the exchange rate—an appreciation of the domestic currency.

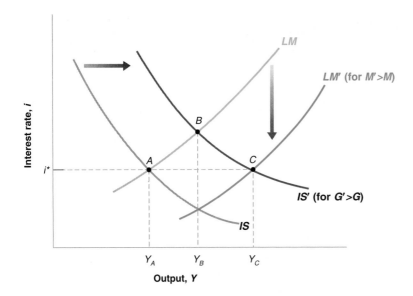

FIGURE 8-5

The Effects of a Fiscal Expansion under Fixed Exchange Rates

Under flexible exchange rates, a fiscal expansion increases output from Y_A to Y_B. Under fixed exchange rates, output increases from Y_A to Y_C.

However, under fixed exchange rates, the central bank cannot allow the currency to appreciate. As the increase in output leads to an increase in the demand for money, the central bank must accommodate this increased demand for money by increasing money supply. In terms of Figure 8–5, the central bank must shift the *LM* curve down as the *IS* curve shifts to the right so that the interest rate and, by implication, the exchange rate do not change. Therefore, the equilibrium moves from *A* to *C*, with higher output Y_C and unchanged interest and exchange rates. Thus, under fixed exchange rates, fiscal policy is more powerful than it is under flexible exchange rates. This is because fiscal policy triggers monetary accommodation.

As this chapter comes to an end, a question should have started to form in your mind. Why would a country choose to fix its exchange rate? We have seen several reasons why this appears to be a bad idea:

Is the effect of fiscal policy stronger in a closed economy or in an open economy with fixed exchange rates? (Hint: The answer is ambiguous.)

1. By fixing the exchange rate, a country gives up a powerful tool for correcting trade imbalances or changing the level of economic activity.

2. By committing to a particular exchange rate, a country also gives up control of its interest rate. It must match movements in the foreign interest rate, at the risk of unwanted effects on its own activity. This is what happened in the early 1990s in Europe. Because of the increase in demand due to reunification, Germany felt it had to increase its interest rate. To maintain their parity with the deutchmark (DM), other countries in the European Monetary System (EMS) also were forced to increase their interest rate, something that they would rather have avoided. (This is the topic of the Global Macro box "German Unification, Interest Rates, and the EMS.") This tension was the cause of a major exchange rate crisis within the EMS in 1992, which we study in Chapter 13.

3. While the country retains control of fiscal policy, one policy instrument is not enough. As we saw in Chapter 7, for example, a fiscal expansion can help the economy get out of a recession, but only at the cost of a larger trade deficit. And a country that wants to decrease its budget deficit cannot, under fixed exchange rates, use monetary policy to offset the contractionary effect of its fiscal policy on output.

So, why do some countries fix their exchange rates? Why have 12 European countries just adopted a common currency? To answer these questions, we must do some more work. We must look at what happens not only in the short run—which is what we did in this chapter—but also in the medium run, when the price level can adjust. Chapters 9, 10, 11, and 12 allow the price level to adjust in a closed economy. Once we have done this, we will then be able to give an assessment of the pros and cons of exchange rate regimes. These are the open economy topics we return to in Chapter 13.

Under a system of fixed exchange rates, such as the EMS (let us ignore here the degree of flexibility afforded by the bands), no individual country can change its interest rate if the others do not change theirs as well. So, how do interest rates actually change? Two arrangements are possible. One is for the member countries to coordinate all changes in their interest rates. Another is for one of the countries to take the lead and for the other countries to follow—this is what happened in the EMS, with Germany as the leader.

During the 1980s, most European central banks shared similar goals and were happy to let the Bundesbank (the German central bank) take the lead. But in 1990, German unification led to a sharp divergence in goals between the Bundesbank and the other EMS nations' central banks. Recall the macroeconomic implications of unification from Chapter 5: Both the need for large transfers to eastern Germany and an investment boom led to a large increase in demand in Germany. The Bundesbank's fear that this shift would generate too strong an increase in activity led it to adopt a restrictive monetary policy. The result was, as we saw, strong growth in Germany together with a large increase in interest rates.

This may have been the right policy mix for Germany. But for other countries, the effects of German unification were less appealing. The other countries had not experienced the same increase in demand, but to stay in the EMS, they had to match German interest rates. The net result was a sharp decrease in demand and in output in the other countries. These results are presented in Table 1, which gives nominal and real interest rates, inflation rates, and GDP growth from 1990 to 1992 for Germany and for two of its EMS partners, France and Belgium.

Note first how the high German nominal interest rates were matched by both France and Belgium. Nominal interest rates were actually higher in France than in Germany in all three years! This is because France needed higher interest rates than did Germany to maintain the DM/franc parity; the reason for this is that financial markets were not sure that France would actually keep the parity of the franc vis-à-vis the DM. Worried about a possible devaluation of the franc, they asked for a higher interest rate on French bonds than on German bonds.

Although they had to match—or, as we have just seen, more than match—German nominal rates, France and Belgium had lower inflation than Germany. The result was very high real interest rates, higher than in Germany. In both France and Belgium, average real interest rates from 1990 to 1992 were close to 7%. And in both countries, the period 1990 to 1992 was characterized by slow growth and rising unemployment. Unemployment in France in 1992 was 10.4%, up from 8.9% in 1990. Unemployment in Belgium in 1992 was 12.1%, up from 8.7%.

Although we have looked at only two of Germany's EMS partners, a similar story was unfolding for the others. Average unemployment in the European Union, which stood at 8.7% in 1990, had increased to 10.3% in 1992. The effects of high real interest rates on spending were not the only cause of this slowdown, but they were the main one.

By 1992, an increasing number of countries were wondering whether to keep defending their EMS parity or to give it up and lower their interest rates. Worried about the risk of devaluations, financial markets started to ask for higher interest rates in those countries where they thought devaluation was more likely. The result was two major exchange rate crises, one in the fall of 1992 and the other in the summer of 1993. By the end of these two crises, two countries, Italy and the United Kingdom, had left the EMS. We look at these crises, their origins and their implications, in Chapter 13.

TABLE 1	German Unification, Interest Rates, and Output Growth: Germany, France, and Belgium, 1990–1992					
	Nominal Interest Rates			**Inflation**		
	1990	1991	1992	1990	1991	1992
Germany	8.5	9.2	9.5	2.7	3.7	4.7
France	10.3	9.6	10.3	2.9	3.0	2.4
Belgium	9.6	9.4	9.4	2.9	2.7	2.4
	Real Interest Rates			**Real GDP Growth**		
	1990	1991	1992	1990	1991	1992
Germany	5.7	5.5	4.8	5.7	4.5	2.1
France	7.4	6.6	7.9	2.5	0.7	1.4
Belgium	6.7	6.7	7.0	3.3	2.1	0.8

The *nominal interest rate* is the short-term nominal interest rate. The *real interest rate* is the realized real interest rate over the year—that is, the nominal interest rate minus actual inflation over the year. All rates are annual.

Source: OECD Economic Outlook.

- In an open economy, the demand for goods depends on both the interest rate and the exchange rate. A decrease in the interest rate increases the demand for goods. An increase in the exchange rate—a depreciation—also increases the demand for goods.

- The interest rate is determined by the equality of money demand and money supply. The exchange rate is determined by the interest parity condition, which states that the domestic interest rate must equal the foreign interest rate plus the expected rate of depreciation.

- Given the expected future exchange rate and the foreign interest rate, increases in the domestic interest rate lead to a decrease in the exchange rate (an appreciation), and decreases in the domestic interest rate lead to an increase in the exchange rate (a depreciation).

- Under flexible exchange rates, an expansionary fiscal policy leads to an increase in output, an increase in the interest rate, and an appreciation. A contractionary monetary policy leads to a decrease in output, an increase in the interest rate, and an appreciation.

- There are many types of exchange-rate arrangements. They range from fully flexible exchange rates to crawling pegs, to pegs, to fixed exchange rates, to the adoption of a common currency. Under fixed exchange rates, a country maintains a fixed exchange rate in terms of a foreign currency or a basket of currencies.

- Under fixed exchange rates and perfect capital mobility, a country must maintain an interest rate equal to the foreign interest rate. Thus, the central bank loses the use of monetary policy as a policy instrument. Fiscal policy becomes more powerful, however, because fiscal policy triggers monetary accommodation and thus does not lead to offsetting changes in the domestic interest rate and exchange rate.

- bands, 151
- central parity, 151
- crawling peg, 151
- European Monetary System (EMS), 151
- exchange rate mechanism (ERM), 151
- foreign-exchange reserves, 156
- Mundell–Fleming model, 142
- peg, 151

An asterisk denotes a harder question. [Web] indicates that the question requires access to the Internet.

1. **TRUE/FALSE/UNCERTAIN**

a. Because the multiplier is smaller in an open economy than in a closed economy, fiscal policy is more effective in an open economy than in a closed economy.

b. Monetary policy is more effective in a closed economy than in an open economy with flexible exchange rates.

c. If financial investors expect the exchange rate to be higher next year, interest parity implies that it will be higher today.

d. If financial investors expect the American dollar to depreciate vis-à-vis the yen over the coming year, one-year interest rates will be higher in the United States than in Japan.

e. If the Japanese interest rate is equal to zero, foreigners will not want to hold Japanese bonds.

f. Under fixed exchange rates, the money stock must be constant.

2. **A CURRENCY CRISIS**

a. Consider an economy with fixed exchange rates. Suppose that government devalues unexpectedly and that investors believe that there will be no further devaluation. What will be the effects of the devaluation on output and on the interest rate?

b. Suppose instead that after the devaluation investors believe that another devaluation is likely to come soon. What will be the effects of the initial devaluation on output and on the interest rate?

3. FIXED EXCHANGE RATES AND MONETARY POLICY

Consider a group of open economies with perfect capital mobility among them.

a. Assume that there is a Leader country. All other countries (referred to as the Follower countries) fix their exchange rates to the Leader country. Discuss the effectiveness of monetary policy in the Follower countries.

b. If all the Follower countries fix their exchange rate vis-à-vis the Leader country, isn't the Leader country's exchange rate also fixed? What does this imply for the effectiveness of the Leader country's monetary policy?

c. If the Leader country reduces its money supply to fight inflation, what must the Follower countries do to enforce their fixed exchange rates? What is the effect on their economies? What would happen if the Follower countries did nothing?

4. THE EFFECTS OF CHANGES IN FOREIGN VARIABLES

Consider the *IS* and *LM* equations in section 8-3.

a. Show the effect of a decrease in foreign output Y^* on domestic output Y. Explain in words.

b. Show the effect of an increase in the foreign interest rate i^* on domestic output Y. Explain in words.

c. "A monetary contraction abroad is likely to lead to a recession at home." Discuss this statement.

5. ELIMINATING A TRADE DEFICIT UNDER FIXED EXCHANGE RATES

Consider a small, open *IS-LM* economy with a fixed exchange rate, where output is at its natural level but there is a trade deficit. What is the appropriate fiscal–monetary policy mix?

6. MONETARY POLICY AND THE COMPONENTS OF GDP

Consider a monetary expansion in an economy operating under flexible exchange rates. Discuss the effects on consumption, investment, and net exports.

FIXED EXCHANGE RATES, INTEREST RATES, AND CAPITAL MOBILITY

The assumption of perfect capital mobility is a good approximation to what happens in countries with highly developed financial markets and few capital controls, such as the United States, the United Kingdom, Japan, and Canada. But the assumption is more questionable in countries that have less developed financial markets or have a battery of capital controls in place. There, domestic financial investors may have neither the savvy nor the legal right to move easily into foreign bonds when domestic interest rates are low. The central bank may then be able both to decrease interest rates and to maintain a given exchange rate.

To look at these issues, let us start with the balance sheet of the central bank. In Chapter 4, we assumed the only asset held by the central bank was domestic bonds. In an open economy, the central bank actually holds two types of assets: (1) domestic bonds, and (2) **foreign-exchange reserves**, which we shall think of as foreign currency, although they also take the form of foreign bonds or foreign interest-paying assets. The balance sheet of the central bank is represented in Figure 8A–1. On the asset side are bonds and foreign currency reserves, and on the liability side is the monetary base. There are now two ways in which the central bank can change the monetary base: either by purchases or sales of bonds in the bond market or by purchases or sales of foreign currency in the foreign-exchange market.*

Perfect Capital Mobility and Fixed Exchange Rates

Consider first the effects of an open market operation under the assumptions of perfect capital mobility and fixed exchange rates (the assumptions we made in the last section of this chapter).

● Assume that the domestic and foreign nominal interest rates are initially equal so that $i = i^*$. Suppose the central bank embarks on an expansionary open-market operation, buying bonds in the bond market in amount ΔB

---

*__DIGGING DEEPER__. If you have not read section 4-3 in Chapter 4, substitute "monetary base" with "money supply," and you will get the sense of the argument. If you have read that section, recall that money supply is equal to the monetary base times the money multiplier. Take the money multiplier as a given, and our conclusions about the monetary base extend straightforwardly to money supply.

Assets	Liabilities
Bonds Foreign exchange reserves	Monetary base

FIGURE 8A–1

Balance Sheet of
the Central Bank

and creating money—increasing the monetary base—in exchange. This purchase of bonds leads to a decrease in the domestic interest rate, i. This is, however, only the beginning of the story.

● Now that the domestic interest rate is lower than the foreign interest rate, financial investors prefer to hold foreign bonds. To buy foreign bonds, they must first buy foreign currency. They go to the foreign exchange market and sell domestic currency for foreign currency.

● If the central bank did nothing, the price of domestic currency would fall, and the result would be a depreciation. Under its commitment to a fixed exchange rate, the central bank cannot allow the currency to depreciate. Thus, it must intervene in the foreign-exchange market and sell foreign currency for domestic currency. As it buys domestic money, the monetary base decreases.

● How much foreign currency must the central bank sell? It must keep selling until the monetary base is back to its pre–open-market operation level, so the domestic interest rate is again equal to the foreign interest rate. Only then are financial investors willing to hold domestic bonds.

How long do all these steps take? Under perfect capital mobility, all this may happen within minutes or so of the original open-market operation. After these steps, the balance sheet of the central bank looks as in Figure 8A–2. Bond holdings are up by ΔB, reserves of foreign currency are down by ΔB, and the monetary base is unchanged, having gone up by ΔB in the open-market operation and down by ΔB as a result of the sale of foreign currency in the foreign-exchange market.

To summarize: Under fixed exchange rates and perfect capital mobility, the only effect of the initial open-market operation is to change the *composition* of the central bank's balance sheet but not the monetary base.

Imperfect Capital Mobility and Fixed Exchange Rates

Let us now move away from the assumption of perfect capital mobility. Suppose it takes some time for financial investors to shift between domestic and foreign bonds.

An expansionary open market operation can now initially bring the domestic interest rate below the foreign interest rate. But over time, investors shift to foreign bonds, leading to an increase in the demand for foreign currency in the foreign-exchange market. To avoid a depreciation of the domestic currency, the bank must again stand ready to sell foreign currency and buy domestic currency. Eventually, the central bank buys enough domestic currency to offset the effects of the initial open-market operation. The monetary base is back to its pre–open-market operation level, and so is the interest rate. The central bank holds more bonds and smaller reserves of foreign currency.

The difference between this case and the preceding one is that by accepting a loss in foreign-exchange reserves, the central bank is now able to decrease interest rates *for some time*. If it takes just a few days for financial investors to adjust, the trade-off is rather unattractive—as many countries have discovered. But, if the central bank can affect the domestic interest rate for a few weeks or months, it may, in some circumstances, be willing to do so.

Now, let us move further from perfect capital mobility. Suppose, in response to a decrease in the domestic interest rate, financial investors are either unwilling or unable to move much of their portfolio into foreign bonds. This is the relevant case for many middle-income countries, from Latin America to Eastern Europe to Asia. After an expansionary open-market operation, the domestic interest rate decreases, making domestic bonds less attractive. Some domestic investors move into foreign bonds, selling domestic currency for foreign currency. To maintain the exchange rate, the central bank must buy domestic currency and

Assets		Liabilities	
Bonds:	ΔB	Monetary base $\Delta B - \Delta B$	
Reserves:	$-\Delta B$		$= 0$

FIGURE 8A–2

Balance Sheet of the Central
Bank after an Open Market
Operation and the Induced
Intervention in the Foreign-
Exchange Market

supply foreign currency. However, the foreign-exchange intervention may now be small compared with the initial open-market operation. And if capital controls truly prevent investors from moving into foreign bonds at all, there may be no need at all for such an intervention.

Even leaving this extreme case aside, the net effect is likely to be an increase in the monetary base, a decrease in the domestic interest rate, an increase in the central bank's bond holdings, and some (but smaller) loss in reserves of foreign currency. With imperfect capital mobility, a country has some freedom to move the domestic interest rate while maintaining its exchange rate. Its freedom to do so depends primarily on three factors:

- The degree of development of its financial markets, and how willing domestic and foreign investors are to shift between domestic and foreign assets.
- The degree of capital controls it is able to impose on both domestic and foreign investors.
- The amount of foreign-exchange reserves it holds: The higher the amount, the more it can afford the loss in reserves it is likely to sustain if it decreases the interest rate at a given exchange rate.

THE CORE: THE MEDIUM RUN

The next five chapters focus on the medium run.

CHAPTER 9

Chapter 9 looks at equilibrium in the labour market. It derives the natural rate of unemployment as the unemployment rate to which the economy tends to return in the medium run. Associated with the natural rate of unemployment is a natural level of output.

CHAPTER 10

Chapter 10 looks at equilibrium in all three markets—goods, financial, labour—together. It shows how, in the short run, output can deviate from its natural level and how it tends to return to this natural level in the medium run. The model developed in Chapter 10 is called the *AS-AD* model and is, like the *IS-LM* model, one of the workhorses of macroeconomics.

CHAPTER 11

Chapter 11 looks more closely at the relation between inflation and unemployment, a relation known as the Phillips curve. It shows that in Canada today, low unemployment leads to an increase in inflation and high unemployment to a decrease in inflation.

CHAPTER 12

Chapter 12 looks at the determination of output, unemployment and inflation, and the effects of money growth. In the short run, decreases in money growth can trigger a recession. In the medium run, however, they are neutral; they are reflected one for one in changes in the rate of inflation.

CHAPTER 13

Chapter 13 focuses on the implications of fixed and flexible exchange rates in the medium run. When prices can change, the real exchange rate can change even under a fixed exchange rate regime. This may trigger a foreign exchange rate crisis. The chapter ends by discussing the pros and cons of various exchange rate regimes, including the adoption of a common currency.

CHAPTER 9
THE LABOUR MARKET

Think about what happens when firms respond to an increase in demand by stepping up production:

- Higher production requires an increase in employment.
- Higher employment leads to lower unemployment.
- Lower unemployment puts pressure on wages.
- Higher wages increase production costs, forcing firms, in turn, to increase prices.
- Higher prices lead workers to ask for higher wages, and so on.

In the previous six chapters, for both closed and open economies, we ignored this sequence of events: We assumed that firms were able and willing to supply any level of output at a given price level. So long as our focus was on the *short run*, this was an acceptable simplification. As our attention turns to what happens in the *medium run*, we must now relax this assumption, explore how prices and wages adjust over time, and how this, in turn, affects the response of output. This will be our task in this and the next four chapters.

At the centre of the process described above is the *labour market*, the market in which wages are determined. This chapter starts with an overview of the labour market and takes a first pass at deriving equilibrium in the labour market. In particular, it derives the central notion of the *natural rate of unemployment*. The next three chapters then combine our earlier treatment of goods and financial markets with our newly acquired knowledge of the labour market. The fourth chapter in this section looks at an open economy in the medium run. When we are done, you will know how to think about movements in output and the price level, both in the short run and in the medium run.

9-1 | A Tour of the Labour Market

The total Canadian population in 2005 was 32.3 million. The relevant population available for civilian employment is the able-bodied population of working age (15 years of age or older). Specifically excluded are full-time members of the Canadian Armed Forces and inmates of institutions (penal institutions or long-term care facilities). Also excluded, for the most part because they are difficult to sample, are residents of the two territories and persons living on native reserves. Together, these excluded groups represent approximately 2% of the working-age population. In 2005, the over-15 population in Canada was 25.8 million (Table 9–1).

The **labour force**—the sum of those either working or looking for work—was, however, only 17.3 million. The other 8.5 million people were not in the labour force, neither working in the marketplace nor looking for work. (Work in the home, such as cooking or raising children, is not classified as work in official statistics. The reason is simply the difficulty of measuring these activities, not a value judgement as to what is work or not work.) The participation rate, defined as the ratio of the labour force to the noninstitutionalized population, was thus equal to 17.3/25.8 or 67.0%. The participation rate has steadily increased over time; it stood at only 61.5% in 1976. This increase reflects the steadily increasing participation rate of women.

Of those in the labour force, 16.2 million were employed, and 1.2 million were unemployed. The unemployment rate, defined as the ratio of the unemployed to the labour force in percentage terms, was thus equal to 1.2/17.3 = 6.9%. A convenient approximation to keep in mind is that a 1% increase in the Canadian unemployment rate corresponds roughly to 150,000 more people unemployed.

These numbers tell us where people were (whether they were employed, unemployed, or not in the labour force) at one point in time—in this case, 2005. But they do not tell us what typically happens to them over time. Do those out of the labour force stay out all the time, or do they go back and forth between participation and nonparticipation? How long do the unemployed remain unemployed? How long do the employed remain employed? To answer these questions, we must turn to the evidence on flows rather than stocks.

The Large Flows of Workers

To think further about unemployment, the following analogy will be helpful: Take an airport full of passengers. This may be because it is a busy airport with many planes taking off and landing. Many passengers are quickly moving in and out of the airport. Or it may be because bad weather is delaying flights and passengers are stuck, waiting for the weather to improve. The number of passengers in the airport may be the same in both cases, but their plight is quite different. In the same way, a given unemployment rate may reflect two very different realities. It may reflect an active labour market, with many **separations** (workers leaving or losing their jobs), many **hires**, and lots of workers entering and exiting unemployment; or it may reflect a sclerotic labour market, with few separations, few hires, and a stagnant unemployment pool.

Sclerosis, a medical term, means hardening of the arteries. In social sciences, it is used to describe institutions that do not adapt to changes in their environment, and, as a result, function less and less well over time.

TABLE 9–1	Population, Labour Force, Employment, and Unemployment (Millions) in Canada, 2005
Total population	32.3
Age 15 and over	25.8
Labour force	17.3
Employed	16.2
Unemployed	1.2

Source: Statistics Canada, CANSIM II Tables 282-0002, 282-0022.

FIGURE 9–1

Average Monthly Flows among Employment, Unemployment, and Nonparticipation in Canada, February 1976 to October 1991

(1) The flows of workers into and out of employment are large. (2) The flows into and out of unemployment are large in relation to the number of unemployed. (3) There are also large flows into and out of the labour force, much of it directly to and from employment.

Source: See footnote 1.

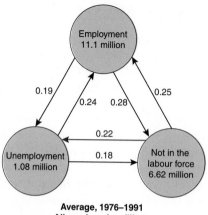

Average, 1976–1991
All numbers in millions.

Finding out what reality hides behind the aggregate unemployment rate requires data on the movements of workers. Such data are available in Canada from the Labour Force Survey (LFS). Average monthly flows, computed from the LFS for Canada from 1976 to 1991, are reported in Figure 9–1.[1] (For more on the ins and outs of the LFS, see the Focus box "The Labour Force Survey.")

Figure 9–1 has three striking features:

1. *The size of the flows into and out of employment:* The average monthly flow into employment is almost half a million: 0.24 million from unemployment plus 0.25 million from nonparticipation in the labour force. The average monthly flow out of employment is 0.47 million: 0.19 million to unemployment plus 0.28 million to nonparticipation in the labour force. Put another way, over this sample period, hires by firms and separations from firms equalled, respectively, 4.4% and 3.3% of employment *each month*.[2]

   Why are these flows so large? About half of separations (the flows from employment) are **quits**, workers leaving their jobs in search of better alternatives. The other half are **layoffs**. These come mostly from changes in employment levels across firms: The slowly changing aggregate employment numbers hide a reality of continual job destruction and job creation across firms. At any time, some firms are experiencing decreases in demand and decreasing their employment; others are experiencing increases in demand and increasing employment.

2. *The size of the flows into and out of unemployment in relation to the total number of unemployed.* The average monthly flow out of unemployment each month is 0.42 million: 0.24 million to employment plus 0.18 million to nonparticipation in the labour force. Put another way, the proportion of unemployed leaving unemployment is equal to 0.42/1.08, or 39% each month. Put yet another way, the average **duration of unemployment** is about three months.[3]

   This fact has an important implication. You should not think of unemployment in Canada as a stagnant pool of workers waiting indefinitely for jobs. For most of the unem-

Think of it this way. Suppose the number of unemployed is constant. If each unemployed person remains unemployed for *n* months, then it must be that a proportion 1/*n* is leaving unemployment each month (and, as the number of unemployed is constant, an equal number enters unemployment). More formally, the proportion of people leaving unemployment is the inverse of unemployment duration. Conversely, unemployment duration is the inverse of the proportion of people leaving unemployment.

[1]**DIGGING DEEPER**. The data used in Figure 9–1 are taken from Stephen R.G. Jones, "Cyclical and Seasonal Properties of Canadian Gross Flows of Labour," *Canadian Public Policy*, XIX:1 (1993).

[2]**DIGGING DEEPER**. This is actually an underestimate because it excludes movements of workers directly from one job to another.

[3]**DIGGING DEEPER**. For those who know statistics: If *p* is the probability of finding a job each month, the expected duration of unemployment is equal to 1/*p*. Here, p is equal to 39%, so the expected time—equivalently, the duration of unemployment—is 1/0.39, or 2.6 months.

Since its inception in 1945, the Labour Force Survey (LFS) is the main source of statistics on the labour force, employment, and participation in Canada.

The LFS has been a monthly survey since 1952. Its coverage has expanded over the years, and there were major redesigns of the survey content in 1976 and again in 1997. The most recent changes provide a number of improvements, including data on wages and union status and more detailed information on job status and hours worked. Since July 1995, a total of 52,350 households across Canada are surveyed each month; this amounts to over 100,000 respondents. The sample is not random, but it is chosen to obtain reasonably accurate estimates for different demographic groups (determined by age and gender) and at various geographic levels: national, provincial, census metropolitan areas (large cities), and employment insurance regions. The LFS follows a rotating panel design; each household stays in the survey for six months before it is replaced. From month to month, one-sixth of the survey is replaced. The initial interview is done through a personal visit, and a large amount of socio-demographic information for each person in the household is collected. Subsequent interviews are conducted by telephone. Since 1994, the data have been entered directly into a laptop computer to reduce processing time and transcription errors.

Although the survey is conducted monthly, labour force status is determined by looking at what happened during a single week, called the **reference week**, for that month. Persons are classified as employed if they do any work at all at a job or business during the reference week (including unpaid work for a family business) or if they had a job but were away because of illness, vacation, labour dispute, or similar reasons. The concept of being unemployed is a bit fuzzier. Anyone available for work is called unemployed when he or she is (a) on a temporary layoff, (b) without work and has been actively looking for work in the past four weeks, or (c) waiting to start a job at a future date. Full-time students looking for full-time work are not included in this list. Anyone not considered employed or unemployed is deemed to be not in the labour force. The notion of "actively looking for work" is a bit loose. In the United States, the criteria require the individual to actually contact potential employers; in Canada, it is enough to check the newspaper.

ployed, being unemployed is more a way-station between jobs: For the period 1976–1991, the proportion of unemployed getting a job was just over 20% (0.24/1.08) each month. In this respect, Canada resembles the United States more closely than Europe. Evidence from Western Europe indicates lower flows into and out of unemployment compared with the stock of unemployed, thus a longer average duration of unemployment.

◀ In the other direction, some unemployed may be unwilling to accept any job offered to them and should probably not be counted as unemployed (that is, looking for a job).

3. *The size of the flows into and out of the labour force.* One might have expected these flows to be small, composed on one side of those finishing school and entering the labour force for the first time and on the other side of workers going into retirement. But these groups actually represent a small fraction of the total flows. The fact is that many of those classified as not in the labour force are, in fact, willing to work and move back and forth between participation and nonparticipation. The flow from nonparticipation in the labour force to employment is larger than the flow from unemployment to employment.

This fact also has an important implication. The sharp focus on the unemployment rate by economists, policy makers, and newspapers is partly misdirected. Some of those classified as not in the labour force are, in fact, very much like the unemployed; they are in effect discouraged workers, and although they are not actively looking for a job, they will take it if they find it. This is why economists sometimes focus on the **employment rate**, the ratio of employment to population, rather than the unemployment rate. We will follow tradition and focus on the unemployment rate, but keep in mind that the unemployment rate typically underestimates the number of people available for work.

Differences across Workers

The aggregate picture is one of large flows among employment, unemployment, and nonparticipation. However, this picture conceals important differences across groups of workers. Table 9–2, based on evidence from the LFS, shows some of the differences in separation rates by age and gender, again for the period 1976–1991.

TABLE   9–2   Monthly Separation Rates for Different Groups, 1976–1991

Category	Monthly Separation Rate (%) (Quits and Layoffs)
Young (15–24 years old)	8.7
Older (25+)	2.9
Male	3.7
Female	4.9

The separation rate is defined as the monthly flow out of employment divided by the initial level of employment. The number is the average separation rate for the period 1976–1991.
Source: Statistics Canada; also see footnote 1.

On average, 8.7% of workers aged 15 to 24 leave their jobs each month. By contrast, the rate is only 2.9% among workers aged 25 and over. Slightly more women than men leave their jobs every month, 4.9% versus 3.7%; the difference is largely due to a higher rate of going from employment to nonparticipation in the labour force. These different separation rates are reflected in different unemployment rates for the different groups. In April 2005, when the aggregate unemployment rate was 6.8%, the rate of unemployment among young males aged 15 to 24 was 14.9%.

Where do these differences come from? Young people often hold low-paying jobs, the proverbial McJobs, which are often only marginally more attractive than unemployment. Young workers have little seniority and are often the first to be laid off when a firm needs to downsize its workforce. Thus, young workers frequently move among jobs, unemployment, and nonparticipation. Middle-aged males, in contrast, tend to keep the jobs they have. This is because the jobs are typically better and because family responsibilities make it much more difficult to give up the jobs they have for a chance at a better one.

The variations in labour-market experiences reflect, in part, life-cycle considerations, with the young going from one job to the next until they eventually find one they like and settle down. But they also reflect permanent differences among workers, including education level, skill, and race. Unskilled workers, whatever their age, typically have higher unemployment rates. So do workers in Newfoundland. In April 2005, the unemployment rate in Newfoundland was 16.1%, more than twice the national average.

These differences across jobs and workers have sometimes led macroeconomists and labour economists to model the labour market as a **dual labour market** that includes a **primary labour market**, where jobs are good, wages are high, and turnover is low, and a **secondary labour market**, where jobs are poor, wages are low, and turnover is high. This is not a distinction that we will pursue in this book.

9-2 | Movements in Unemployment

Let us now turn to movements in the unemployment rate over time. Figure 9–2 shows the average annual value of the unemployment rate for the years 1926 to 2005. Three different sources are cited because the methods used to count the unemployed vary slightly over time. However, the data are consistent since 1976 and reasonably consistent since 1953.

The most prominent feature of Figure 9–2 is the very high, over 20%, rate of unemployment in the 1930s, during the Great Depression. In this period, one in five Canadians was unemployed. This macroeconomic disaster led to the study of macroeconomics (see Chapter 27 for a brief discussion of Keynes). World War II ended unemployment as men and women entered the armed forces. Most economists believe that a combination of bad trade

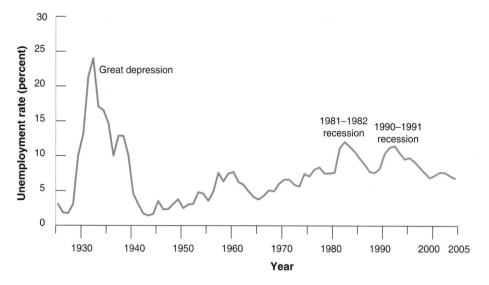

FIGURE 9-2

Movements in the Canadian Unemployment Rate, 1926–2004

The enormously high unemployment rate during the Great Depression is the most noticeable feature here. The two recessions in 1981–1982 and 1990–1991 also stand out as periods of high unemployment. There has been no severe recession in Canada since 1991. Finally, there appears to be an upward trend in the normal rate of unemployment in Canada since 1950.

Source: 1926–1952 using *Historical Statistics of Canada*; 1953–1975 using CANSIM I variable D767611; 1976–2004 using CANSIM II variable V159752.

policy, bad monetary policy, and bad fiscal policy in both Europe and North America had led to the Great Depression. We investigate this decade in more detail in Chapter 22.

The second feature of the data in Figure 9–2 is a trend increase in the unemployment rate in Canada. On average, unemployment has been higher from 1980 to 2004 than it was from 1950 to 1960. The 1970s were a period of steadily rising unemployment. We will return to this issue in Chapter 11.

The third prominent feature of Figure 9–2 are the two long periods of high unemployment associated with the 1981–1982 recession and the 1990–1991 recession. In both cases, Canadians experienced four consecutive years with unemployment rates exceeding 10%.

How do fluctuations in the *aggregate unemployment rate* affect *individual workers*? This is an important question for two reasons. The answer determines both the effect of movements in unemployment on the welfare of workers—and the effect of unemployment on wages.

◄ The average unemployment rate for the year 1982 was less than 10%. But in the month of November, the unemployment rate reached 10.8%.

Think about how firms can decrease their employment in response to a decrease in demand. They can hire fewer new workers, or they can lay off the workers they currently employ. Typically, firms prefer first to slow or stop the hiring of new workers, relying on quits and retirements to achieve a decrease in employment. But if the decrease in demand is large, this may not be enough, and firms may then have to lay off workers.

Now, think about the implications for workers, employed or unemployed. If the adjustment takes place through a decrease in hires, the effect is to decrease the chance that an unemployed worker will find a job. Fewer hires means fewer job openings; higher unemployment means more job applicants. Fewer openings and more applicants combine to make it harder for the unemployed to find jobs. If the adjustment takes place instead through higher layoffs, then the employed workers are at a higher risk of losing their jobs. In general, when firms use both margins of adjustment, the result is likely to be both a higher chance of losing a job if employed and a lower chance of finding a job if unemployed. The first effect can be seen in Table 9–3. When the overall unemployment rate is high, a much larger proportion of the unemployed are persons who are described as job losers (those who are fired or laid off). In sharp contrast, the proportion of the pool of unemployed who are job leavers (voluntarily leaving their current jobs) or those who are new entrants or re-entrants (those who are looking for a new job after finishing their education or after a period of time out of the labour force) both remain relatively constant over time.

TABLE 9-3 Decomposition of Unemployment by Reason, 1975–2003

		Reason for Job Loss		
	Unemployment Rate	**Job Losers (%)**	**Job Leavers (%)**	**New and Re-entrants (%)**
1976–1979	7.7	3.4	1.2	2.2
1980–1981	7.5	3.4	1.2	2.3
1982–1983	11.5	5.9	1.3	2.9
1984–1987	10.1	4.8	1.4	2.6
1988–1989	7.7	3.5	1.3	2.0
1990–1992	9.9	5.0	1.3	2.4
1993–1996	10.2	4.5	1.0	2.9
1997–2000	7.9	3.0	0.8	2.8
2001–2003	7.5	2.7	0.8	2.9

Source: Dwayne Benjamin, Morley Gunderson and W. Craig Riddell, *Labour Market Economics* (Toronto: McGraw-Hill Ryerson, 2001), p. 516. Updated from Statistics Canada, Labour Force Historical Review.

The second effect can be seen in Figure 9–3. There is a nearly exact relationship between the average unemployment rate and the average length of time (called duration) a person remains unemployed. The higher the unemployment rate, the higher is the average duration of unemployment.

To summarize: When unemployment is high, workers are worse off in two ways. The probability that they lose their jobs is higher. And if they become unemployed, the probability that they will find another job is lower; equivalently, they can expect to be unemployed for a longer period of time.

9-3 | Wage Determination

Having looked at the nature of unemployment, let us turn to wage determination and to the relation between wages and unemployment.

FIGURE 9-3

The Unemployment Rate and the Average Duration of Unemployment, 1976–2003

When unemployment is high, it takes a longer time for the unemployed to find a new job.

Source: Unemployment rate using CANSIM II variable V159752; and duration using column D3 of Table 17.3, Dwayne Benjamin, Morley Gunderson, and W. Craig Riddell, *Labour Market Economics* (Toronto: McGraw-Hill Ryerson, 2001), p. 518.

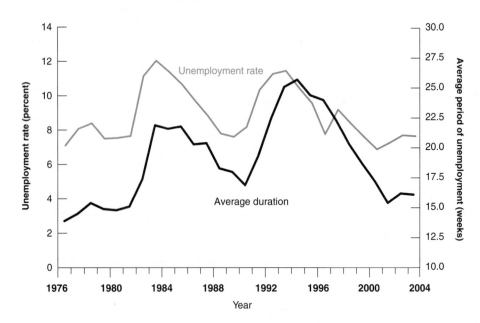

Wages are set in many ways. Sometimes, they are set by **collective bargaining**, that is, bargaining between firms and unions. In Canada, however, collective bargaining plays a limited role, especially outside the manufacturing and public sectors. Today, between 25 and 35% of workers are covered by collective bargaining agreements. For the rest, wages are set either by employers or by individual bargaining between the employer and the employee. The higher the skills needed to do the job, the more typical is individual bargaining. Wages offered for entry-level jobs at McDonald's are on a take-it-or-leave-it basis. New college graduates can typically negotiate a few aspects of their contract. CEOs and sports stars can negotiate a lot more.

There are also large differences across countries. In the United States, less than 15% of the labour force is involved in collective bargaining. In European countries, such as Germany and France, over 90% of the paid workers have wages determined by collective bargaining, although a smaller proportion of workers are actually members of unions. Negotiations may take place at the level of the firm, at the level of industry, or at the national level. Contract agreements sometimes apply only to those firms that have signed the agreement; sometimes, they are automatically extended to all firms and all workers in the sector or the economy.

Given these differences across workers and across countries, can we hope for anything like a general theory of wage determination? Yes. Although institutional differences play a role, there are common forces at work in all countries. Two sets of facts stand out:

1. Workers are typically paid a wage that exceeds their **reservation wage**, the wage that would make them indifferent to working or becoming unemployed. In other words, most workers are paid a high enough wage that they prefer to be employed rather than unemployed.
2. Wages typically depend on labour-market conditions: The lower the unemployment rate, the higher are the wages.

To think about these facts, economists have focused on two broad lines of explanation. The first is that even in the absence of collective bargaining, workers have some bargaining power, which they can and do use to obtain wages above their reservation wage. The second is that firms themselves may, for a number of reasons, want to pay wages higher than the reservation wage. Let us look at each explanation.

Bargaining

How much **bargaining power** a worker has depends on two factors. The first is how easy it would be for the firm to replace him, were he to leave the firm. The second is how easy it would be for him to find another job, were he to leave the firm. The harder it is for the firm to replace him, or the easier it is for him to find another job, the stronger he will be in bargaining.

This has two implications. First, how much bargaining power a worker has depends on the nature of his job. Replacing a worker at McDonald's is not very costly; the required skills can be taught quickly, and typically a large number of willing applicants have already filled out job application forms. In this situation, the worker is unlikely to have much bargaining power. If he asks for a higher wage, the firm can lay him off and find a replacement at minimum cost. In contrast, a highly skilled worker who has proven unusually good at his job may be very difficult to replace. This gives him more bargaining power. If he asks for a higher wage, the firm may decide that it is best to give it to him.

Second, how much bargaining power workers have depends on labour market conditions. When the unemployment rate is low, it is more difficult for firms to find acceptable replacements, and it is easier for workers to find other jobs. Under such conditions, workers are in a stronger bargaining position and may be able to obtain a higher wage. Conversely, when the unemployment rate is high, finding good replacements is easier for firms, whereas finding another job is harder for workers. Being in a weaker bargaining position, workers may have no choice but to accept a lower wage.

Efficiency Wages

Leaving aside workers' bargaining power, firms themselves may want to pay more than the reservation wage. Firms want their workers to be productive, and the wage can help them achieve that goal.

If, for example, it takes a while for workers to learn how to do a job correctly, firms will want their workers to stay. But if workers are paid just their reservation wage, they will be indifferent between staying or leaving. Many of them may quit, and turnover may be high. In such a situation, paying a wage above the reservation wage will make it financially attractive for workers to stay. It will decrease turnover and increase productivity.

Behind this example lies a more general proposition: Most firms want their workers to feel good about their jobs. Feeling good promotes good work, which leads to higher productivity. Paying a high wage is one instrument the firm can use to achieve these goals. (See the Focus box "Henry Ford and Efficiency Wages.") Economists call the theories that link the *productivity* or the *efficiency* of workers to the wage they are paid **efficiency wage theories**.

Like theories based on bargaining, efficiency wage theories suggest that wages depend both on the nature of the job and on labour-market conditions.

The evidence is that workers who operate more expensive machinery are typically paid more. Can efficiency wage theories explain this fact?

- Firms—such as high-tech firms—that see employees' morale and commitment as essential to the quality of their work will pay more than firms in sectors where workers' activity is more routine.

FOCUS   Henry Ford and Efficiency Wages

In 1914, Henry Ford—the builder of the most popular car in the world at the time, the Model T—made a stunning announcement. His company would pay all qualified employees a minimum of $5 a day for an eight-hour day. This was a very large salary increase for most employees, previously earning on average $2.34 for nine-hour days. Although company profits were substantial, this increase in pay was far from negligible—it represented about half of the company's profits at the time.

What Ford's motivations were is not entirely clear. Ford himself gave too many reasons for us to know which ones he actually believed. The reason was not that the company had a hard time finding workers at the previous wage. But the company clearly had a hard time retaining workers. There was a very high turnover rate as well as high dissatisfaction among workers.

Whatever the reasons behind Ford's decision, the results of the wage increase were astounding, as Table 1 shows.

The annual turnover rate (the ratio of separations to employment) plunged from a high of 370% in 1913 to a low of 16% in 1915. (An annual turnover rate of 370% means that on average 31% of the company's workers left each month, so that over the year the ratio of separations to employment was 31% × 12 ≈ 370%.) The layoff rate collapsed from 62% to nearly 0%. Other measures point in the same direction. The average rate of absenteeism (not shown in the table), which ran at 10% in 1913, was down to 2.5% a year later. There is little question that higher wages were the main source of these changes.

Did productivity at the Ford plant increase enough to offset the cost of increased wages? The answer to this question is less clear. Productivity was much higher in 1914 than in 1913; estimates of productivity increases range from 30% to 50%. Despite higher wages, profits were also higher in 1914 than in 1913. But how much of this increase in profits was due to changes in workers' behaviour and how much was due to the increasing success of Model-T cars is harder to establish.

Although the effects support efficiency-wage theories, it may be that the increase in wages to $5 a day was excessive, at least from the point of view of profit maximization. But Henry Ford probably had other objectives as well, from keeping the unions out—which he did—to generating publicity for himself and the company—which he surely did as well.

Source: Dan Raff and Lawrence Summers, "Did Henry Ford Pay Efficiency Wages?" *NBER Working Paper,* 2101, December 1986.

TABLE 1	Annual Turnover and Layoff Rates (%) at Ford, 1913–1915		
	1913	**1914**	**1915**
Turnover rate	370	54	16
Layoff rate	62	7	0.1

- Labour-market conditions will affect the wage. Lower unemployment makes it more attractive for employed workers to quit: Lower unemployment makes it easier to find another job. A firm that wants to avoid an increase in quits will have to counteract the effects of lower unemployment by increasing the wage it pays its workers. In short, lower unemployment will lead to higher wages.

Wages and Unemployment

The following equation captures the main conclusions of our discussion of wage determination:

$$W = P^e F(u, z) \qquad (9.1)$$
$$(-,+)$$

where W, the nominal wage, depends on three factors:

- The expected price level, P^e.
- The unemployment rate, u.
- A catchall variable, z, that stands for all other variables that affect the outcome of wage setting.

Let us look at each factor in turn.

The Expected Price Level. Leave aside first the difference between the expected and the actual price level, and ask: Why does the price level affect wages? Quite simply because workers and firms care about *real wages*, not nominal wages.

- Workers care not about how many dollars they receive but about how many goods they can buy with their wages. In other words, they care about their wage in terms of goods, about W/P.
- In the same way, firms care not about the nominal wages they pay workers but about the nominal wages they pay in terms of the price of the output they sell. So, firms also care about W/P.

If both workers and firms knew that the price level was going to double, they would agree to doubling the nominal wage. This relation between the wage and the expected price level is captured in equation (9.1). A doubling in the expected price level leads to a doubling of the nominal wage chosen in wage setting.

◄ $P^e\uparrow \Rightarrow W\uparrow$

Returning to the distinction we put aside at the start of the preceding paragraph: Why do wages depend on the *expected price level, P^e*, rather than the *actual price level, P*? Because wages are set in nominal (dollar) terms, when they are set, what the relevant price level will be is not yet known. For example, in many union contracts, nominal wages are set in advance for three years. Unions and firms have to decide what nominal wages will be over the following three years based on what they expect the price level to be over those three years. Even when wages are set by firms, or by bargaining between the firm and each worker, nominal wages are typically set for a year. If the price level goes up unexpectedly during the year, nominal wages are typically not re-adjusted. (How workers and firms form expectations of the price level will occupy us for much of the next three chapters; we leave this issue aside for the moment.)

The Unemployment Rate. Also affecting the aggregate wage in equation (9.1) is the unemployment rate. The minus sign under u indicates that an increase in the unemployment rate *decreases* wages.

This is one of the main implications of our earlier discussion of wage determination. If we think of wages as being determined by bargaining, higher unemployment weakens workers' bargaining power, forcing them to accept lower wages. If we think of wages as being determined by efficiency wage considerations, higher unemployment allows firms to pay lower wages and still keep workers willing to work.

◄ $u\uparrow \Rightarrow W\downarrow$

The Other Factors. The third variable in equation (9.1), z, is a catchall variable that stands for all the factors that affect wages given the expected price level and the unemployment rate. By convention, z is defined in such a way that an increase in z leads to an increase in the wage—hence the plus sign under z. Our earlier discussion suggests a long list of such factors. For instance:

- Unemployment insurance offers workers protection from a complete loss of income if they become unemployed. There are good reasons why society should provide at least partial insurance to workers who lose their jobs and find it difficult to find another. But there is little question that by making the prospects of unemployment less distressing, more generous unemployment benefits do increase wages. To take an extreme example, suppose unemployment insurance did not exist. Workers would then be willing to accept very low wages to avoid being unemployed. But unemployment insurance does exist, and it allows unemployed workers to hold out for higher wages. In this case, we can think of z as standing for the level of unemployment benefits: Higher unemployment benefits increase wages.
- Suppose the economy undergoes a period of structural change, so more jobs are created and more jobs are destroyed, leading to larger flows into and out of unemployment. This implies that at a given level of unemployment, there are more job openings and thus a better chance of finding a job while unemployed. If it is easier to get a job while unemployed, then unemployment is less of a threat to workers. At a given level of unemployment, workers are in a stronger bargaining position, and wages increase. In this case, we can think of z as standing for an increase in the rate of structural change in the economy.

It is easy to think of other examples, from changes in minimum-wage legislation to changes in restrictions on firing and hiring, and so on. We will explore the implications of some of these as we go along.

9-4 | Price Determination

Having looked at the determination of wages given expected prices, let us now look at the determination of prices given wages.

Prices depend on costs. Costs depend on the nature of the **production function**—the relation between the inputs used in production and the quantity of output produced. We will assume that firms produce goods using labour as the only factor of production, and according to the production function:

$$Y = AN$$

where Y is output, N is employment, and A is labour productivity. This implies that **labour productivity**—the ratio of output per worker—is constant and equal to A.

Using a term from micro-economics, this assumption implies *constant returns to labour in production*. If firms double the amount of labour they use, they can double the amount of output they produce.

It should be clear that this assumption is a drastic simplification of reality. Firms use other factors of production than labour. They use capital—machines and plants. They use raw materials—oil, for example. We know that there is technological progress so that labour productivity (A) is not constant but instead steadily increases over time. We will face these realities later. We will introduce raw materials in Chapter 10 when we discuss the oil crises of the 1970s. We will focus on the role of capital and technological progress when we turn to the determination of output in the *long run* in Chapters 14 to 17. For the moment, the simple relation between output and employment will make our lives easier and still serve our purposes.

Given the assumption that labour productivity, A, is constant, we can make one further simplification. We can choose the units for output so that one worker produces one unit of output—so that $A = 1$. (This way we do not have to carry the letter A around, and this will simplify notation.) With that choice, the production function becomes:

$$Y = N \tag{9.2}$$

The production function $Y = N$ implies that the cost of producing one more unit of output is the cost of employing one more worker, at wage W. Using the terminology introduced in your microeconomics course, the marginal cost of production is equal to W. Marginal cost is the extra cost to a firm of producing one more unit of output. If one more unit of output is produced using one more unit of labour, and a unit of labour is paid wage W, then one more unit of output costs W. If there were perfect competition in the goods market, the price of a unit of output would be equal to marginal cost: P would be equal to W. But many goods markets are not competitive, and firms charge a price higher than their marginal cost. A simple way of capturing this fact is to assume that firms set their price according to:

$$P = (1 + \mu)W \qquad (9.3)$$

where μ is the markup of price over cost. If goods markets were perfectly competitive, the price would simply equal the cost and μ would equal zero. To the extent that they are not competitive and that firms have market power, the price will be higher than the cost, and μ will be positive.

> If we had not put A equal to 1, then to produce one unit of goods, the firm would need $1/A$ units of labour, at cost W/A (the wage times the number of units of labour.) Thus, P would equal $(1 + \mu)W/A$.

9-5 | The Natural Rate of Unemployment

Let us now look at the implications of wage and price determination for unemployment. Let us do so under the assumption that in wage determination, nominal wages depend on the actual price level, P, rather than on the expected price level, P^e (why we assume this will become clear soon). Under this assumption, wage setting and price setting determine the equilibrium rate of unemployment. Let us see how.

> An important assumption for the rest of the chapter: $P^e = P$.

The Wage-Setting Relation

Given the assumption that nominal wages depend on the actual price level (P) rather than on the expected price level (P^e), equation (9.1), which characterizes wage determination, becomes:

$$W = P \, F(u,z)$$

Or, dividing both sides by the price level,

$$\frac{W}{P} = F(u, z) \qquad (9.4)$$
$$(-,+)$$

Wage determination implies a negative relation between the real wage, W/P, and the unemployment rate, u: *The higher the unemployment rate, the lower is the real wage chosen by wage setters.* The intuition is straightforward: The higher the unemployment rate, the weaker the workers are in bargaining, and so the lower the real wage.

This relation between the real wage and the rate of unemployment—let us call it the **wage-setting relation**—is drawn in Figure 9–4. The real wage is measured on the vertical axis. The unemployment rate is measured on the horizontal axis. The wage-setting relation is drawn as the downward-sloping curve WS (for wage setting): The higher the unemployment rate, the lower is the real wage.

> "Wage setters" means unions and firms if wages are set by collective bargaining; it means individual workers and firms if wages are set in bilateral bargaining; it means firms if wages are set on a take-it-or-leave-it basis.

The Price-Setting Relation

Turn now to the implications of price determination. If we divide both sides of the price-determination equation (9.3), by the nominal wage, we get:

$$\frac{P}{W} = 1 + \mu \qquad (9.5)$$

FIGURE 9-4

The Wage-Setting Relation, the Price-Setting Relation, and the Natural Rate of Unemployment

The real wage chosen in wage setting is a decreasing function of the unemployment rate. The real wage implied by price setting is constant, independent of the unemployment rate. The natural rate of unemployment is the unemployment rate such that the real wage chosen in wage setting is equal to the real wage implied by price setting.

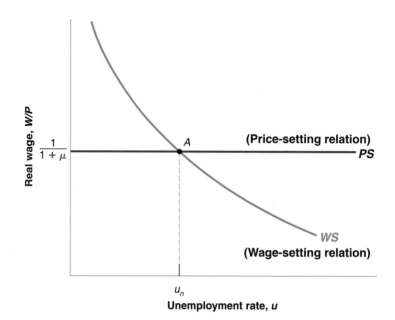

More help with the intuition: If the firm in which I work increases its markup and so increases the price of its products, my real wage does not change very much, if at all. I am still paid the same wage, and, even if one of the goods I buy is the good produced by the firm, it is at most a very small part of my consumption basket. But, if not only the firm I work for but all firms increase their markup and the price of their products, then the prices of all the goods I buy go up. My real wage goes down.

The ratio of the price level to the wage implied by the price-setting behaviour of firms equals 1 plus the markup. Now, invert both sides of this equation to get the implied real wage:

$$\frac{W}{P} = \frac{1}{1 + \mu} \tag{9.6}$$

Price-setting decisions determine the real wage paid by firms. An increase in the markup leads firms to increase prices given wages; equivalently, it leads to a decrease in the real wage.

The step from equation (9.5) to equation (9.6) is algebraically straightforward. But how price setting actually determines the real wage paid by firms may not be intuitively obvious. A numerical example will help. Suppose it takes one hour of work to produce one unit of output, firms pay a wage of $10 per hour, and the firms' markup is 20%, so they sell each unit of output for $10 × 1.2 = $12. The real wage—how many units of the good workers can buy if they work for an hour—is 10/12 = 0.83 units of the good. If firms increase their markup to 30%, the real wage falls to 10/13 = 0.76 units. By choosing their markup, firms in effect determine the real wage. This is what is captured in equation (9.6).

The **price-setting relation** in equation (9.6) is drawn as the horizontal line *PS* (for price setting) in Figure 9–4. The real wage implied by price setting is constant, equal to $1/(1 + \mu)$, and therefore independent of the unemployment rate.

Equilibrium Real Wages and Unemployment

Equilibrium in the labour market requires that the real wage chosen in wage setting be equal to the real wage implied by price setting. (This way of stating equilibrium may sound strange if you learned to think in terms of labour supply and labour demand in your microeconomics course. The relation between wage setting and price setting on the one hand and labour supply and labour demand on the other is closer than it looks at first and is explored further in the appendix at the end of this chapter.) In Figure 9–4, equilibrium is therefore given by point A, and the equilibrium unemployment rate is given by u_n.

We can also characterize the equilibrium unemployment rate algebraically; eliminating W/P between equations (9.4) and (9.6) gives:

$$F(u_n, z) = \frac{1}{1 + \mu} \tag{9.7}$$

The equilibrium unemployment rate, u_n, is such that the real wage chosen in wage setting—the left side of equation (9.7)—is equal to the real wage implied by price setting—the right side of equation (9.7).

The equilibrium unemployment rate (u_n) is called the **natural rate of unemployment** (which is why we used the subscript n to denote it). The terminology has become standard, so we will adopt it, but this is actually a bad choice of words. The word "natural" suggests a constant of nature, one that is unaffected by institutions and policy. As its derivation makes clear, however, the "natural" rate of unemployment is anything but natural. The positions of the wage-setting and price-setting curves, and thus the equilibrium unemployment rate, depend on both z and u. Consider two examples:

"Natural," in Webster's Dictionary, means "in a state provided by nature, without man-made changes."

- *An increase in unemployment benefits.* An increase in unemployment benefits can be represented by an increase in z. Because an increase in benefits makes the prospect of unemployment less painful, it increases the wage set by wage setters at a given unemployment rate. So, it shifts the wage-setting relation up, from WS to WS' in Figure 9–5. The economy moves along the PS line, from A to A'. The natural rate of unemployment increases from u_n to u_n'.

    In words: At a given unemployment rate, higher unemployment benefits lead to a higher real wage. A higher unemployment rate is needed to bring the real wage back to what firms are willing to pay.

An increase in unemployment benefits shifts the wage-setting curve up. The economy moves along the price-setting curve. Equilibrium unemployment increases.

This has led some economists to call unemployment a "discipline device." Higher unemployment is the device that returns wages to the level firms are willing to pay.

- *A less stringent enforcement of existing antitrust legislation.* To the extent that this allows firms to collude more easily and increase their market power, it leads to an increase in their markup—an increase in μ. The increase in μ implies a decrease in the real wage paid by firms, so it shifts the price-setting relation down, from PS to PS' in Figure 9–6. The economy moves along WS. The equilibrium moves from A to A', and the natural rate of unemployment increases from u_n to u_n'.

    In words: By letting firms increase their prices, given the wage, less stringent enforcement of antitrust legislation leads to a decrease in the real wage. Higher unemployment is required to make workers accept this lower real wage, leading to an increase in the natural rate of unemployment.

An increase in the markup shifts the price-setting curve (line in this case). The economy moves along the wage-setting curve. Equilibrium unemployment increases.

Such factors as the generosity of unemployment benefits or antitrust legislation can hardly be thought of as the result of nature. Rather, they reflect various characteristics of the

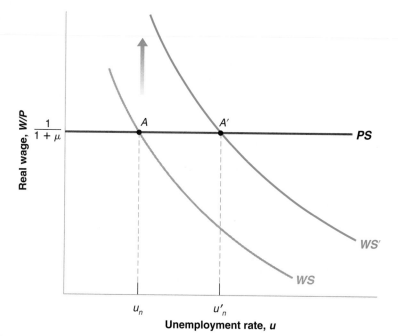

FIGURE 9–5

Unemployment Benefits and the Natural Rate of Unemployment

An increase in unemployment benefits leads to an increase in the natural rate of unemployment.

FIGURE 9-6

Markups and the Natural Rate of Unemployment

An increase in markups decreases the real wage and leads to an increase in the natural rate of unemployment.

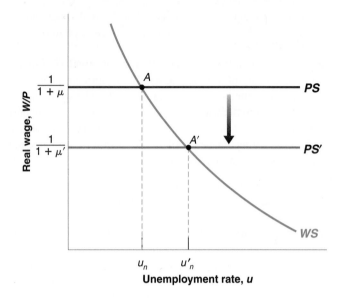

This name has been suggested by Edmund Phelps, from Columbia University.

structure of the economy. For that reason, a better name for the equilibrium rate of unemployment would be the **structural rate of unemployment**, but so far, the name has not caught on.

From Unemployment to Employment

Associated with the natural rate of unemployment is a **natural level of employment**, the level of employment that prevails when unemployment is equal to its natural rate.

Let us review the relation among unemployment, employment, and the labour force. Let U denote unemployment, N denote employment, and L the labour force. Then,

$$u \equiv \frac{U}{L} = \frac{L - N}{L} = 1 - \frac{N}{L}$$

The first step follows from the definition of the unemployment rate (u). The second follows from the fact that, from the definition of the labour force, the level of unemployment

$L = N + U \Rightarrow U = L - N$ (U), equals the labor force (L), minus employment (N). The third step follows from simplifying the fraction. Putting all three steps together, the unemployment rate u equals one minus the ratio of employment N to the labor force L.

Rearranging to get employment in terms of the labour force and the unemployment rate gives:

$$N = L\,(1 - u)$$

Employment N is equal to the labour force L, times one minus the unemployment rate u.

So, if the natural rate of unemployment is u_n, and the labour force is equal to L, the natural level of employment N_n is given by:

$$N_n = L\,(1 - u_n)$$

For example, if the labour force is 30 million and the natural rate of unemployment is 5%, then the natural level of employment is 28.5 million.

From Employment to Output

Finally, associated with the natural level of employment is the **natural level of output**, the level of production when employment is equal to the natural level of employment.

Given the production function we used in this chapter ($Y = N$), the natural level of output Y_n is easy to derive. It is given by:

$$Y_n = N_n = L\,(1 - u_n)$$

Using Equation (9.7) and the relations among the unemployment rate, employment, and the output we just derived, the natural level of output satisfies the following equation:

$$F\left(1 - \frac{Y_n}{L},\, z\right) = \frac{1}{1 + \mu} \tag{9.8}$$

The natural level of output (Y_n) is such that at the associated rate of unemployment $(u_n = 1 - Y_n/L)$, the real wage chosen in wage setting—the left side of equation (9.8)—is equal to the real wage implied by price setting—the right side of equation (9.8). Equation (9.8) will turn out to be very useful in the next chapter.

We have gone through many steps in this section. Let us summarize.

Assume that the expected price level is equal to the actual price level. Then,

- The real wage chosen in wage setting is a decreasing function of the unemployment rate.

- The real wage implied by price setting is constant.

- Equilibrium in the labour market requires that the real wage chosen in wage setting be equal to the real wage implied by price setting. This determines the unemployment rate.

- This equilibrium unemployment rate is known as the natural rate of unemployment.

- Associated with the natural rate of unemployment is a natural level of employment and a natural level of output.

9-6 | Where Do We Go from Here?

We have just seen how the equilibrium in the labour market determines the natural rate of unemployment, which then determines the natural level of output. So, what have we been doing in the previous three chapters? If our primary goal was to understand the determination of output, why did we spend so much time looking at the goods and financial markets? What about our earlier conclusions that the level of output was determined by such factors as monetary policy, fiscal policy, consumer confidence, and so on—all factors that do not enter equation (9.7) and thus do not affect the natural level of output?

The key to the answers is simple, yet important.

- We have derived the natural rate of unemployment and the associated levels of unemployment and output under two assumptions. We have assumed equilibrium in the labour market. We have assumed that the price level was equal to the expected price level.

- There is no reason for the second assumption to be true in the *short run*. The price level may turn out to be different from what was expected by wage setters when nominal wages were set. Hence, in the short run, there is no reason for unemployment to be equal to the natural rate or for output to be equal to its natural level. As we will see in the next chapter, the factors that determine movements in output *in the short run* are the factors we focused on in the preceding six chapters: monetary policy, fiscal policy, and so on. Your time (or ours) was not wasted.

- But expectations of the price level are unlikely to be systematically wrong forever (say, always too high or always too low). That is why, in the medium run, unemployment tends to return to the natural rate, and output tends to return to the natural level. *In the medium run*, the factors that determine unemployment and output are the factors that appear in equations (9.7) and (9.8).

These, in short, are the answers to the questions asked in the first paragraph. Developing these answers in detail will be our task in the next three chapters.

In the short run, the factors that determine movements in output are the factors we focused on in the preceding six chapters: monetary policy, fiscal policy, and so on.

In the medium run, output tends to return to the natural level, and the factors that determine output are the factors we have focused on in this chapter.

SUMMARY

- The labour force is composed of those who are working (employed) or looking for work (unemployed). The unemployment rate is equal to the ratio of the number of unemployed to the labour force. The participation rate is equal to the ratio of the labour force to the population of working age.

- The labour market is characterized by large flows between employment and unemployment and out of the labour force. Each month, on average, more than one-third of the unemployed move out of unemployment, either to take a job or to drop out of the labour force.

- Many people who are not actively searching for jobs and are therefore not counted as unemployed are, in fact, willing to work if they find a job. This is one reason why the unemployment rate is an imperfect measure of the number of people not working but willing to work.

- There are important differences across groups of workers in terms of their average unemployment rate and in terms of their average duration of unemployment. Unemployment rates are typically higher among the young, the low-skilled, and minorities.

- Unemployment is high in recessions and low in expansions. During periods of high unemployment, the probability of losing a job increases and the probability of finding a job if unemployed decreases.

- Wages depend negatively on the unemployment rate. Wages depend positively on expected prices. The reason why wages depend on expected rather than actual prices is that wages are typically set in nominal terms for some period of time. During that time, even if prices turn out to be different from what was expected, wages are typically not re-adjusted.

- Prices set by firms depend on wages and on the markup of prices over wages. The higher the markup chosen by firms, the lower is the real wage implied by price-setting decisions.

- Equilibrium in the labour market requires that the real wage chosen in wage setting be equal to the real wage implied by price setting. Under the additional assumption that the actual price level is equal to the expected price level, equilibrium in the labour market determines the unemployment rate. This unemployment rate is known as the *natural rate of unemployment*.

- In general, the actual price level may turn out to be different from what was expected by wage setters, and therefore the unemployment rate need not be equal to the natural rate. The coming chapters will show that in the short run, unemployment and output are determined by the factors we focused on in the preceding six chapters but that in the medium run, unemployment tends to return to the natural rate and output tends to return to its natural level.

KEY TERMS

An asterisk denotes a harder question. [Web] indicates that the question requires access to the Internet.

1. TRUE/FALSE/UNCERTAIN

a. Since 1950, the participation rate in Canada has remained roughly constant at 60%.

b. Each month, the flows in and out of employment are very small compared with the size of the labour force.

c. One-third of all unemployed workers exit the unemployment pool each year.

d. The unemployment rate tends to be high in recessions and low in expansions.

e. Most workers are typically paid their reservation wage.

f. Workers who do not belong to unions have very little bargaining power.

g. It may be in the best interests of employers to pay wages higher than their workers' reservation wage.

h. The natural rate of unemployment is unaffected by policy changes.

i. The natural rate of unemployment could equally be called the structural rate of unemployment.

2. LABOUR-MARKET NUMBERS

Answer the following questions using the information about Canada in Figure 9–1.

a. As a percentage of the employed workers, what is the size of the flows in and out of employment (that is, hires and separations) each month?

b. As a percentage of the unemployed workers, what is the size of the flows from unemployment into employment each month?

c. As a percentage of the unemployed, what is the size of the total flows out of unemployment each month? What is the average duration of unemployment?

d. As a percentage of the labour force, what is the size of the total flows in and out of the labour force each month?

e. New workers enter the labour force through gaining employment. Retirees (and others) leave the labour force without experiencing unemployment. Calculate this total flow as a percent of employment

3. THE LABOUR MARKET AT A GLANCE [WEB]

Go to the Web site maintained by Statistics Canada, **www.statcan.ca**. Look under the links Canadian Statistics, Latest Indicators, Labour, Labour Force Characteristics.

a. What are the latest monthly data on the size of the Canadian labour force, the number of unemployed people, and the unemployment rate?

b. How many people are employed?

c. Compute the change in the number of unemployed from the first available number to the most recent month in the table. Do the same for the number of employed workers. Is the decline in unemployment equal to the increase in employment? Explain in words.

*4. UNEMPLOYMENT SPELLS AND LONG-TERM UNEMPLOYMENT

According to the data presented in this chapter, about one of every three unemployed workers leaves unemployment each month.

a. What is the probability a worker will still be unemployed after one month? Three months? Six months?

b. What proportion of the unemployed has been unemployed for six months or more?

5. RESERVATION WAGES

In the mid-1980s, a famous supermodel once said that she would not get out of bed for less than $10,000 (presumably per day).

a. What is your own reservation wage?

b. Did your first job pay more than your reservation wage at the time?

c. Relative to your reservation wage at the time you accept each job, which job pays more: your first one or the one you expect to have in 10 years?

d. Explain your answers in terms of the efficiency wage theory.

6. BARGAINING POWER AND WAGE DETERMINATION

Even in the absence of collective bargaining, workers do have some bargaining power that allows them to receive a wage higher than their reservation wage. Each worker's bargaining power depends both on the nature of the job and on the economywide labour-market conditions. Let us consider each factor in turn.

a. Compare the job of a delivery person and the job of a computer network administrator. In which of these jobs does a worker have more bargaining power? Why?

b. For any given job, how do labour-market conditions affect the workers' bargaining power? Which labour-market variable would you look at to assess labour-market conditions?

7. THE NATURAL RATE OF UNEMPLOYMENT AND THE NATURAL LEVEL OF OUTPUT

Suppose that the firms' mark-up over costs is 5% and the wage-setting equation is $W = P(1 - u)$ where u is the unemployment rate.

a. What is the real wage as determined by the price-setting relationship?

b. Solve for the natural rate of unemployment, that is, the rate of unemployment at the real wage determined by the price-setting relationship. You will need to use further information scattered through the chapter.

c. Using the production function in expression (9.2), and the notation that the total labour force is equal to L when employment equals N, solve for the natural level of output. $Y_n = N$ where employment is at the natural rate $= (1 - u_n) * L$

d. Suppose the mark-up of prices over costs increases to 10%. What happens to the natural rate of unemployment? Explain the logic behind the answer and the sense in which there is nothing "natural" about the natural rate of unemployment

FURTHER READING

An in-depth discussion of unemployment along the lines of this chapter is given by Richard Layard, Stephen Nickell, and Richard Jackman in *The Unemployment Crisis* (Oxford University Press, 1994).

APPENDIX

WAGE- AND PRICE-SETTING RELATIONS VERSUS LABOUR SUPPLY AND LABOUR DEMAND

In your microeconomics course, you probably saw a representation of labour market equilibrium in terms of labour supply and labour demand. You may therefore be asking yourself: How does the representation in terms of wage setting and price setting relate to the representation of the labour market I saw in my microeconomics course?

In an important sense, the two representations are similar.

To see why, let us redraw Figure 9–6 in terms of the real wage and the level of *employment* (rather than the unemployment rate). We do this in Figure 9A–1.

Employment, N, is measured on the horizontal axis. The level of employment must be somewhere between zero and L, the labour force. Employment cannot exceed the number of people available for work, the labour force. For any employment level, N, unemployment is given by $U = L - N$.

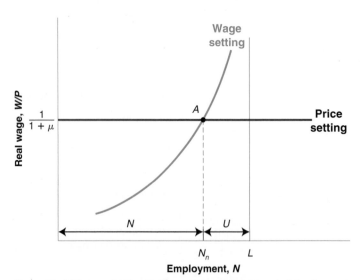

Figure 9A–1 Wage and Price Setting and the Natural Level of Employment

Knowing that, we can measure unemployment by starting from L and *moving to the left* on the horizontal axis. Unemployment is given by the distance between L and N. The lower employment, N, is, the higher unemployment is and, by implication, the higher the unemployment rate, u.

Let us now draw the wage-setting and price-setting relations and characterize the equilibrium:

- An increase in employment (a movement to the right along the horizontal axis) implies a decrease in unemployment, and therefore an increase in the real wage chosen in wage setting. Thus, the wage-setting relation is now *upward sloping*. Higher employment implies a higher real wage.

- The price-setting relation is still a horizontal line at $W/P = 1/(1 + \mu)$.

- The equilibrium is given by point A, with "natural" employment level N_n (and an implied natural unemployment rate equal to $u_n = [L - N_n]/L$).

In this figure, the wage-setting relation looks like a labour-supply relation. As the level of employment increases, the real wage paid to workers increases as well. For that reason, the wage-setting relation is sometimes called the "labour supply" relation (in quotes).

What we have called the price-setting relation looks like a flat labour-demand relation. The reason it is flat rather than downward sloping has to do with our simplifying assumption of constant returns to labour in production. Had we assumed, more conventionally, that there were decreasing returns to labour in production, our price-setting curve would, like the standard labour-demand curve, be downward sloping. As employment increased, the marginal cost of production would increase, forcing firms to increase their prices, given the wages they pay. In other words, the real wage implied by price setting would decrease as employment increased.

But, in a number of ways, the two approaches are different:

- The standard labour-supply relation gives the wage at which a given number of workers are willing to work.

The higher the wage, the larger is the number of workers who are willing to work.

In contrast, the wage corresponding to a given level of employment in the wage-setting relation is the result of a process of bargaining between workers and firms or unilateral wage setting by firms. Such factors as the structure of collective bargaining or the use of wages to deter quits affect the wage-setting relation. In the real world, they seem to play an important role. Yet they play no role in the standard labour-supply relation.

- The standard labour-demand relation gives the level of employment chosen by firms at a given real wage. It is derived under the assumption that firms operate in competitive goods and labour markets and therefore take wages and prices—and by implication, the real wage—as givens.

In contrast, the price-setting relation takes into account the fact that in most markets, firms actually set prices. Such factors as the degree of competition in the goods market affect the price-setting relation by affecting the markup. But these factors are not considered in the standard labour-demand relation.

- In the labour supply–labour demand framework, those unemployed are *willingly unemployed*. At the equilibrium real wage, they prefer to be unemployed rather than to work.

In contrast, in the wage-setting–price-setting framework, unemployment is likely to be involuntary. For example, if firms pay an efficiency wage—a wage above the reservation wage—workers would rather be employed than unemployed. Yet, in equilibrium, there is still involuntary unemployment. This also seems to capture reality better than does the labour supply–labour demand framework.

These are the three reasons why we have relied on the wage-setting and the price-setting relations rather than on the labour supply–labour demand approach to characterize equilibrium in this chapter.

CHAPTER 10
PUTTING ALL MARKETS TOGETHER: THE *AS-AD* MODEL

The Core: The Medium Run

We are now ready to think about the determination of output in both the short run and in the medium run. This requires taking into account equilibrium in *all* markets (goods, financial, and labour). We do so by deriving two relations:

- The aggregate supply relation captures the implications of equilibrium in the labour market; it builds on what we learned in Chapter 9.
- The aggregate demand relation captures the implications of equilibrium in both the goods and financial markets; it builds on what we learned in Chapter 5.

Using both relations, we can characterize the equilibrium level of output and prices over time. This is what we do in this and the next two chapters. This chapter develops a basic version of the model, called the *AS-AD* (for aggregate supply–aggregate demand) model. When confronted with macroeconomic questions, it is the model that we typically use to organize our thoughts. For some questions (in particular, for the study of inflation), however, it must be refined and extended. This is what we will do in Chapters 11 and 12. In Chapter 13, we will extend this model to the open economy in the medium run.

10-1 | Aggregate Supply

The **aggregate supply relation** captures the effects of output on the price level. It is derived from equilibrium in the labour market.

The Derivation of the Aggregate Supply Relation

Recall our characterization of wage and price determination in Chapter 9:

$$W = P^e F(u, z)$$
$$P = (1 + \mu)W$$

- The nominal wage (W), set by wage setters, depends on the expected price level (P^e), the unemployment rate (u), and the catchall variable (z) that stands for all the other factors that affect wage determination, from unemployment benefits to the form of collective bargaining.
- The price level (P) set by price setters is equal to the nominal wage (W), times 1 plus the markup (μ).

Combining these two equations by replacing the wage in the second equation by its expression from the first gives:

$$P = P^e(1 + \mu) F(u, z)$$

The price level is a function of the expected price level and the unemployment rate. It will be more convenient in this chapter to express the price level as a function of the level of output rather than as a function of the unemployment rate. To do this, recall from Chapter 9 the relation between the unemployment rate, employment, and output:

$$u \equiv \frac{U}{L} = 1 - \frac{N}{L} = 1 - \frac{Y}{L}$$

The first step follows from the definition of the unemployment rate, the second from the definition of unemployment ($U \equiv L - N$). The last follows from our specification of the production function, which says that one unit of output requires one worker so that $Y = N$.

Replacing u in the previous equation gives the aggregate supply relation among the price level, the expected price level, and output:

$$P = P^e(1 + \mu) F\left(1 - \frac{Y}{L}, z\right) \tag{10.1}$$

> A better name would be "the labour market equilibrium relation." But because the relation looks graphically like a supply curve (that is, a positive relation between output and the price), it has become traditional to call it "the aggregate supply relation." We will follow tradition.

Note two things about equation (10.1):

1. *A higher expected price level leads, one for one, to a higher actual price level.* For example, if the expected price level doubles, then the price level will also double. This effect works through wages: If wage setters expect higher prices, they set higher nominal wages. This, in turn, leads firms to set higher prices.

2. *An increase in output leads to an increase in the price level.* This is the result of four underlying steps:

   - An increase in output leads to an increase in employment.
   - The increase in employment leads to a decrease in unemployment, and therefore a decrease in the unemployment rate.
   - The lower unemployment rate leads to an increase in nominal wages.
   - The increase in nominal wages leads to an increase in costs, which leads firms to increase prices.

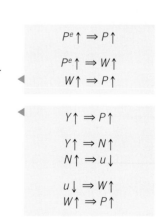

$P^e \uparrow \Rightarrow P \uparrow$

$P^e \uparrow \Rightarrow W \uparrow$
$W \uparrow \Rightarrow P \uparrow$

$Y \uparrow \Rightarrow P \uparrow$

$Y \uparrow \Rightarrow N \uparrow$
$N \uparrow \Rightarrow u \downarrow$

$u \downarrow \Rightarrow W \uparrow$
$W \uparrow \Rightarrow P \uparrow$

FIGURE 10–1

The Aggregate Supply Curve

(a) Given the expected price level, an increase in output leads to an increase in the price level. (b) An increase in the expected price level shifts the aggregate supply curve up.

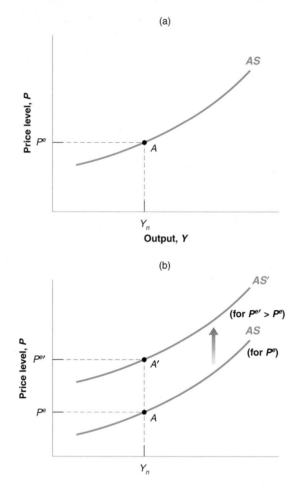

(a)

(b)

The aggregate supply relation between output and the price level is represented by the *aggregate supply curve AS* in Figure 10–1(a). This aggregate supply curve has two characteristics:

Here is an informal way of saying the same thing: High activity puts pressure on prices.

- It is upward sloping: For a given value of the expected price level, P^e, an increase in output leads to an increase in the price level.
- It goes through point A, where $Y = Y_n$ and $P = P^e$. That is, if output is equal to its natural level Y_n, then the price level is equal to the expected price level: $P = P^e$. We know this from the definition of the natural level of output in Chapter 9: We derived the natural rate of unemployment (and, by implication, the natural level of output) as the unemployment rate (and, by implication, the level of output) that prevails if the price level and the expected price level are equal.

These characteristics have, in turn, two implications; both will be useful when we trace movements in equilibrium output later in this chapter:

- When output is above its natural level, the price level is higher than expected: $P > P^e$. Conversely: When output is below its natural level, the price level is lower than expected: $P < P^e$. This is shown in Figure 10–1(a). To the left of A, the price level is lower than was expected. To the right of A, the price level is higher than was expected.
- An increase in the expected price level shifts the aggregate supply curve up. Conversely, a decrease in the expected price level shifts the aggregate supply curve down.

This second implication is shown in Figure 10–1(b). If the expected price level increases from P^e to $P^{e'}$, the aggregate supply curve shifts up: Instead of going through point A (where $Y = Y_n$ and $P = P^e$), it now goes through point A' (where $Y = Y_n$, $P = P^{e'}$).

To summarize: We have derived the *aggregate supply relation*, the first of the two relations we need to characterize the equilibrium. This relation is derived from equilibrium in the labour market. It says that the price level is an increasing function of the level of output and of the expected price level. It is represented by an upward sloping curve. Changes in the expected price level shift the curve up or down.

10-2 | Aggregate Demand

The **aggregate demand relation** captures the effect of the price level on output. It is derived from equilibrium in the goods and financial markets.

Borrowing from Chapter 5, the two equations that characterize equilibrium in goods and financial markets were:

(Goods market) $\quad IS: \quad Y = C(Y - T) + I(Y, i) + G$

(Financial markets) $\quad LM: \quad \dfrac{M}{P} = YL(i)$

Equilibrium in the goods market requires that the supply of goods equal the demand for goods—the sum of consumption, investment, and government spending. This is the *IS* relation.

Equilibrium in financial markets requires that the supply of money equal the demand for money; this is the *LM* relation. Note that what appears on the left side of the *LM* equation is the real money stock, M/P. We have focused so far on changes in the real money stock that came from changes in nominal money, M—monetary contractions or expansions implemented by the central bank. But changes in M/P also can come from changes in the price level. A 10% increase in the price level has the same effect on M/P as does a 10% decrease in the stock of nominal money: Both lead to a 10% decrease in the real money stock.

Figure 10–2 derives the relation between the price level and output implied by equilibrium in the goods and the financial markets. Figure 10–2(a) draws the *IS* and *LM* curves. The *IS* curve is downward sloping: An increase in the interest rate leads to a decrease in demand and in output. The *LM* curve is upward sloping: An increase in output increases the demand for money, and the interest rate must increase so as to maintain equality of money demand and the (unchanged) money supply. The initial equilibrium is at point A.

While still looking at Figure 10–2(a), consider an increase in the price level from P to P'. Given the stock of nominal money, M, the increase in the price level decreases the real money stock, M/P, and the *LM* curve shifts up: At a given level of output, the lower real money stock leads to an increase in the interest rate. The equilibrium moves from A to A′; the interest rate increases from i to i', and output decreases from Y to Y'. The increase in the price level leads to a decrease in output.

In words: As the price level increases, the demand for *nominal* money increases. Because the supply of nominal money is fixed, the interest rate must increase to induce people to decrease their demand for money, and re-establish equilibrium. The increase in the interest rate leads, in turn, to a decrease in the demand for goods and a decrease in output.[1]

The implied negative relation between output and the price level is drawn as the downward-sloping curve *AD* in Figure 10–2(b). Points A and A′ in Figure 10–2(b) correspond to points A and A′ in Figure 10–2(a). An increase in the price level from P to P' leads to a decrease in

A better name would be "the goods and financial markets equilibrium relation." But because this is a long name and because the relation looks graphically like a demand curve (that is, a negative relation between output and the price), it has become traditional to call it the "aggregate demand relation." Be aware, however, that the aggregate supply and aggregate demand relations are very different from regular supply and demand curves.

---

[1]**DIGGING DEEPER**. When we extend the model to the open economy, the increase in i causes an exchange rate appreciation. This is, given fixed prices, a real exchange rate appreciation. The price rise in Canada (P rising) adds to the real exchange rate appreciation and further reduces the demand for Canadian goods. Thus, the AD curve is also negatively sloped in the open economy. To keep things simple in this and the next two chapters, we will work in the closed economy. The open economy effects are not difficult to incorporate. It is more difficult in Chapters 18 through 21 to fully incorporate expectations of inflation into the model. When this task is complete, the *IS* relationship is written as: $Y = C(Y - T) + I(Y, i = \pi^e) + G$, where $i = \pi^e$ is the real interest rate.

output from Y to Y'. We will call this curve the aggregate demand curve and call the underlying negative relation between output and the price level the aggregate demand relation.

Any variable other than the price level that shifts either the IS curve or the LM curve in Figure 10–2(a) also shifts the aggregate demand curve in Figure 10–2(b). Take, for example, an increase in consumer confidence, which shifts the IS curve to the right and so leads to higher output. At the same price level, output is higher: The aggregate demand curve shifts to the right. Or take a contractionary open-market operation, which shifts the LM curve up and decreases output. At the same price level, output is lower: The aggregate demand curve shifts to the left.

Recall that a contractionary open market operation is a decrease in nominal money, M, implemented through the sale of bonds by the central bank.

We represent the aggregate demand relation by:

$$Y = Y\left(\frac{M}{P}, G, T\right) \tag{10.2}$$
$$(+,+,-)$$

Output is an increasing function of the real money stock, an increasing function of government spending, and a decreasing function of taxes. Other factors, such as consumer confidence, could be introduced in this equation but are omitted for simplicity. Given monetary and fiscal policies—that is, given M, G, and T—an increase in the price level, P, leads to a decrease in the real money stock, M/P, which leads to a decrease in output. This is the relation captured by the AD curve in Figure 10–2(b).

To summarize: We have derived the *aggregate demand relation*, the second of the two relations we need to characterize the equilibrium. This relation is derived from equilibrium

FIGURE 10–2

The Derivation of the Aggregate Demand Curve

An increase in the price level leads to a decrease in output. Any variable other than the price level that shifts either the IS curve or the LM curve in (a) also shifts the aggregate demand relation in (b).

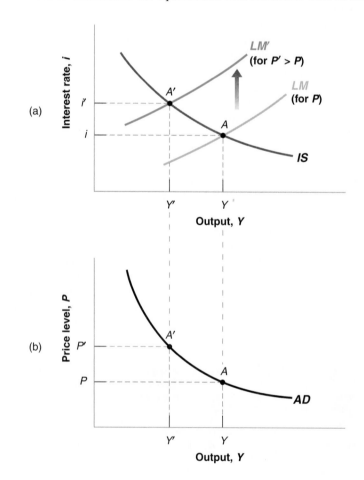

in the goods and financial markets. It says that the level of output is a decreasing function of the price level and is represented by a downward-sloping curve. Changes in monetary or fiscal policy—or more generally, in any factor that shifts the *IS* or the *LM* curves—shift the aggregate demand curve to the right or to the left.

10-3 | Equilibrium Output in the Short Run and the Medium Run

We now put the *AS* and the *AD* relations together. From sections 10-1 and 10-2, the two relations are given by:

$$AS \text{ relation} \qquad P = P^e(1 + \mu) F\left(1 - \frac{Y}{L}, z\right)$$

$$AD \text{ relation} \qquad Y = Y\left(\frac{M}{P}, G, T\right)$$

Figure 10–3 plots the two corresponding curves. The aggregate supply curve *AS*, drawn for a given value of P^e, is upward sloping. Recall from the derivation of the aggregate supply curve in section 10-1 that when output is equal to its natural level, the price level is equal to the expected price level. This implies that the aggregate supply curve goes through point *B*— if output is equal to Y_n, the price level is equal to the expected price level, P^e. The aggregate demand curve *AD* is downward sloping. Its position depends on the values of *M*, *G*, and *T*.

The equilibrium is given by the intersection of the two curves at point *A*. By construction, at point *A*, the goods, financial, and labour markets are *all* in equilibrium. The fact that the labour market is in equilibrium comes from the fact that point *A* is on the aggregate supply curve. The fact that the goods and financial markets are in equilibrium comes from the fact that point *A* is also on the aggregate demand curve. The equilibrium level of output and price level are given by *Y* and *P*.

Note that there is no reason why, in general, equilibrium output *Y* should be equal to the natural level of output Y_n. Equilibrium output depends on both the position of the aggregate supply curve—thus on the value of P^e—and the position of the aggregate demand curve— thus on the values of *M*, *G*, and *T*. As we have drawn the two curves, the equilibrium is such that *Y* is larger than Y_n: The economy is operating above its natural level of output. But we could clearly have drawn the *AS* and the *AD* curves so that equilibrium output was smaller than its natural level. It all depends on the specific values of the expected price level and the values of the variables affecting the position of aggregate demand.

◀ Equivalently, the unemployment rate is below the natural rate.

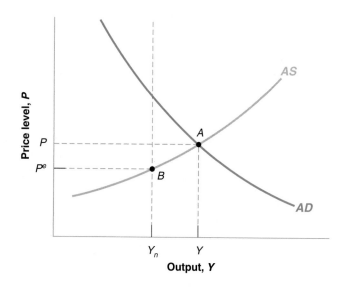

FIGURE 10–3

Equilibrium Output and Price Level

The equilibrium is given by the intersection of the aggregate supply and the aggregate demand curves. At point *A*, the labour, goods, and financial markets are all in equilibrium.

This gives us our first result: In the short run, there is no reason why output should equal its natural level. We can, however, go further and ask: What happens over time? More specifically, suppose that (as in Figure 10–3) output is above its natural level. Now, suppose that the economy is left to itself; that is, policy and other exogenous variables remain constant. What will happen to output over time? Will it return to its natural level? If so, how? These are the questions we take up in the rest of this section.

The Dynamics of Output and the Price Level

To study the movement of output over time, we must first specify how wage setters form expectations. In drawing Figure 10–3, we took the expected price level, P^e, as a given. But P^e is likely to change over time: If the price level last year turned out to be different from what they expected, wage setters are likely to take this into account when forming expectations of what the price level will be this year. We will assume in this chapter that wage setters always expect the price level this year to be equal to the price level last year. This assumption is too simple, and we will improve on it in the next two chapters. But starting with it will make it easier to understand the basic mechanisms at work.

As we now look at the evolution of output and other variables over time, the other thing we need to do is to introduce time indexes. So, P_t will refer to the price level in year t, P_{t-1} to the price level in year $t - 1$, P_{t+1} to the price level in year $t + 1$, and so on.

Using this notation, the assumption that the expected price level equals the price level last year is written as:

$$P_t^e = P_{t-1}$$

And the aggregate supply and demand relations must now be written as:

$$\text{AS relation} \qquad P_t = P_{t-1}(1 + \mu) F\left(1 - \frac{Y_t}{L}, z\right) \qquad (10.3)$$

$$\text{AD relation} \qquad Y_t = Y\left(\frac{M}{P_t}, G, T\right) \qquad (10.4)$$

Note that the parameters (μ, z) and the exogenous variables (L in the aggregate supply relation, M, G, and T in the aggregate demand relation) do not have a time subscript. This is because we will assume they remain constant, so there is no need for a time subscript.

With the help of Figure 10–4, we can now look at the evolution of output over time.

1. Assume that in year t, the equilibrium is the same as the equilibrium characterized in Figure 10–3. So, Figure 10–4(a), which gives the equilibrium for year t, replicates Figure 10–3; the only change is the presence of time indexes. Under our assumption that the expected price level is equal to last year's price level, $P_t^e = P_{t-1}$, and the aggregate supply curve goes through point B, where output is equal to Y_n and the price level equals P_{t-1}.

   Equilibrium is at point A, with output Y_t and price level P_t. Output Y_t is above its natural level Y_n. The price level P_t is higher than the expected price level P_t^e, hence higher than P_{t-1}.

2. Now, turn to year $t + 1$. Equilibrium in year $t + 1$ is shown in Figure 10–4(b). The curves AS and AD repeat the AS and AD for year t from Figure 10–4(a).

   To draw the aggregate supply curve for year $t + 1$, recall that *the aggregate supply curve always goes through the point where, if output is equal to its natural level, the price level is equal to the expected price level—which, under our assumptions, is itself equal to the price level the year before.* This implies, as we saw earlier, that the aggregate supply curve for year t goes through point B, where output equals Y_n and the price level is equal to P_{t-1}. Using the same logic, this implies that the aggregate supply curve for year $t + 1$ goes through point B', where output equals Y_n and the price level is equal to P_t. As P_t is higher than P_{t-1}, this implies that the aggregate supply shifts up from year t to year $t + 1$.

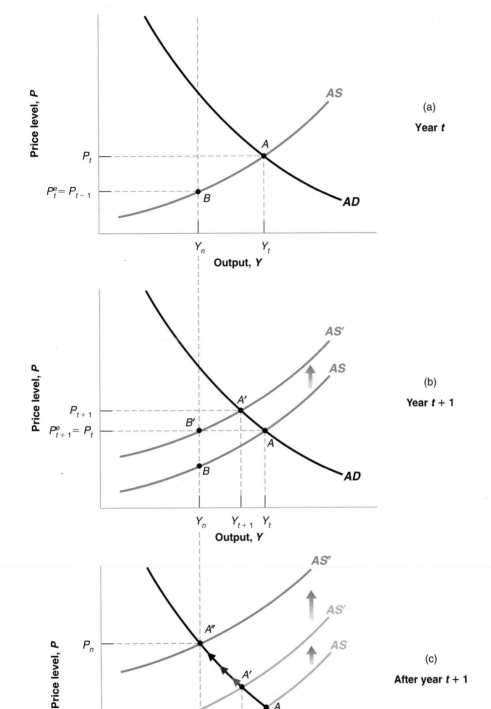

FIGURE 10-4

The Dynamics of Adjustment to the Natural Level of Output

(a) Output is above its natural level. The price level is higher than expected. (b) As wage setters revise their price expectations up, the aggregate supply curve shifts up. Output declines. The price level increases. (c) The aggregate supply curve keeps shifting up, until, in the medium run, output is equal to its natural level.

(a)

Year t

(b)

Year t + 1

(c)

After year t + 1

Make sure you understand the steps in the previous paragraph. But do not lose track of the basic intuition for why the aggregate supply curve shifts up. In year t, output is higher than its natural level, so prices turn out to be higher than expected. This leads wage setters in year $t + 1$ to increase their price expectations, leading the aggregate supply curve to shift up.

Turn to the aggregate demand curve. Note that it does not shift: The aggregate demand curve gives the relation between output and the price level from goods and financial markets equilibrium, for given values of M, G, and T. And by assumption, M, G, and T remain constant.

The shift in the aggregate supply curve implies that the economy moves from A in year t to A' in year $t + 1$. The price level P_{t+1} is higher than P_t. Output Y_{t+1} is lower than Y_t, thus closer to the natural level of output Y_n.

In words: Because output is above its natural level in year t, the price level in year t is higher than expected. This leads wage setters to increase their expectations of the price level in year $t + 1$, leading to a higher price level in year $t + 1$. Given nominal money, a higher price level leads to a lower real money stock in year $t + 1$. The lower real money stock leads to a higher interest rate. The higher interest rate leads to a lower demand for goods, and a lower level of output in year $t + 1$.

3. We have looked at what happens in year t and $t + 1$. What happens in the following years is now easy to describe and is shown in Figure 10–4(c). As long as output is higher than its natural level, the price level keeps increasing, and the aggregate supply curve keeps shifting up. Output keeps decreasing. The economy moves up along the AD curve, until it eventually reaches point A''. At point A'', the aggregate supply curve is given by AS'' and output is equal to its natural level. There is no longer any pressure on prices to increase, and the economy settles at Y_n, with associated price level P_n.[2]

This is the basic mechanism through which the economy returns to its natural level. We will use it in the next three sections to understand the dynamic effects of various shocks and changes in policy. But we already can draw two important lessons:

Short run $Y \neq Y_n$

- In the *short run*, output can be above or below its natural level. Changes in any of the variables that enter the aggregate supply or aggregate demand relation lead to changes in output and prices.

Medium run $Y \rightarrow Y_n$

- In the *medium run*, however, output eventually returns to its natural level. The adjustment process works through prices. When output is above its natural level, prices increase. Higher prices decrease demand and output. When output is below its natural level, prices decrease, increasing demand and output.

We can now use the model to look at the dynamic effects of changes in policy or in the economic environment. We will focus on three changes. The first two are old favourites by now: an open-market operation, which changes the stock of nominal money, and a decrease in the budget deficit. The third, which we could not examine until we had developed a theory of wage and price determination, is an increase in the price of oil. Each of these shocks is interesting in its own right. Monetary policy was responsible for the recession of 1990–1991. Budget deficit reduction made headlines throughout the 1990s in Canada. And increases in the price of oil were a major cause of the 1973–1975 recession in the United States. The recession in the United States led directly to a slowdown in growth in Canada.

[2]**DIGGING DEEPER.** What if the aggregate supply curve shifts up so much from one period to the next that equilibrium output ends up below its natural level? That may happen. If so, with output below the natural level, the price level is lower than the expected price level, and the aggregate supply curve starts shifting down. In short, the return to the natural level may involve oscillations of output rather than a smooth adjustment of output to Y_n. These oscillations are not important for our purposes, and we will not consider them further.

10-4 | The Effects of a Monetary Expansion

What are the short- and medium-run effects of an expansionary monetary policy, say, an increase in the level of nominal money from M to M'?

The Dynamics of Adjustment

Assume that before the change in nominal money, output is at its natural level. In Figure 10–5, aggregate demand and aggregate supply cross at point A, and the level of output at A equals Y_n.

Now consider an increase in nominal money. Recall the specification of aggregate demand from equation (10.4):

$$Y_t = Y\left(\frac{M}{P_t}, G, T\right)$$

For a given price level P_t, the increase in money leads to an increase in M/P_t, leading to an increase in output. The aggregate demand curve shifts to the right, from AD to AD'. The equilibrium moves from point A to A'. Output is higher, and so is the price level.

Over time, the adjustment of price expectations comes into play. Seeing higher prices, wage setters ask for higher nominal wages, which lead to higher prices. Prices keep rising. Equivalently, as long as output exceeds its natural level, the aggregate supply curve shifts up. The economy moves up along the aggregate demand curve AD'. The adjustment process stops when output has returned to its natural level. In the medium run, the aggregate supply curve is given by AS'', and the economy is at point A'': Output is back to its natural level, and the price level is higher.

We can pin down exactly the size of the eventual increase in the price level. If output is back to its natural level, the real money stock must also be back to its initial value. In other words, the proportional increase in prices must be equal to the proportional increase in the nominal money stock: If the initial increase in nominal money is equal to 10%, then the price level ends up 10% higher.

Looking Behind the Scene

It is useful to look behind the scene at what happens in terms of the underlying *IS-LM* model. This is done in Figure 10–6. Figure 10–6(a) reproduces Figure 10–5, showing the adjust-

We leave the more difficult question of the effects of a change in the rate of growth of money—rather than a change in the level of money—to the next two chapters.

We think of shifts in the aggregate demand curve as shifts to the right and the left. It is because we think of the aggregate demand relation as giving output, given the price level. We then ask: At a given price level, does output increase (a shift to the right) or decrease (a shift to the left)? We think of shifts in the aggregate supply curve as shifts up or down. It is because we think of the aggregate supply relation as giving the price level, given output. We then ask: At a given output level, does the price level increase (a shift up) or decrease (a shift down)?

If M/P is unchanged, it must be that M and P increase in the same proportion.

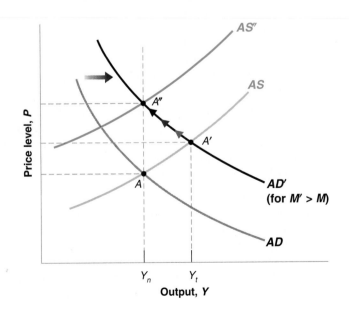

FIGURE 10–5

The Dynamic Effects of a Monetary Expansion

A monetary expansion leads to an increase in output in the short run but has no effect on output in the medium run.

FIGURE 10-6

The Dynamic Effects of a Monetary Expansion on Output and the Interest Rate

The increase in nominal money initially shifts the LM curve down, decreasing the interest rate and increasing output. Over time, the price level increases, shifting the LM curve back up until output is back at its natural level. Look back at Figure 10–5. There is a movement along AD' and a series of shifts in the AS curve from AS to AS'.

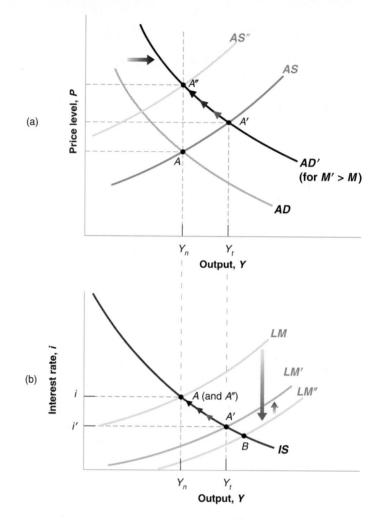

(a)

(b)

ment of output and the price level. Figure 10–6(b) shows the adjustment of output and the interest rate, by looking at the adjustment in terms of the *IS-LM* model.

Look at Figure 10–6(b). Before the change in money, the economy is at point *A* (which corresponds to point *A* in Figure 10–6(a)). Output is equal to its natural level, Y_n, and the interest rate is given by *i*. The short-run effect of the monetary expansion is to shift the *LM* curve down from *LM* to *LM'*, moving the equilibrium from *A* to *A'* (which corresponds to *A'* in Figure 10–6(a)). The interest rate is lower, output is higher. Note that there are two effects at work behind the shift in the *LM* curve:

- The increase in nominal money shifts the *LM* curve down to *LM''*. If the price level did not change—as was our assumption in Chapter 5—the economy would move to point *B*.
- But even in the short run, the price level increases with output as the economy shifts along the aggregate supply curve. So, this increase in the price level shifts the *LM* curve upward from *LM''* to *LM'*, partially offsetting the effect of the increase in nominal money.

Why only partially? Suppose the increase in the price level fully cancelled the increase in nominal money, leaving the real money stock unchanged. If the real money stock were unchanged, output ► would remain unchanged as well. But if output were unchanged, the price level would not increase, in contradiction with our premise.

Over time (after the first year), the price level increases further, reducing the real money stock and shifting the *LM* back up. The economy thus moves along the *IS* curve: The interest rate increases and output declines. Eventually, the *LM* curve returns to where it was before the increase in nominal money. The economy ends up at point *A*, which corresponds to point *A''* in Figure 10–6(a). The increase in nominal money is then exactly offset by a proportional increase in the price level, which leaves the real money stock unchanged. With the real money stock unchanged, output is back to its initial value, Y_n, and the interest rate also returns to its initial value, *i*.

The Neutrality of Money

Let us summarize what we have learned about the effects of monetary policy in this section:

- In the short run, a monetary expansion leads to an increase in output, a decrease in the interest rate, and an increase in the price level. How much of the initial effect falls on output and how much falls on prices depends on the slope of the aggregate supply curve. In Chapter 5, we assumed that the aggregate supply curve was flat so that the price level did not increase at all in response to an increase in output. This was a simplification, but empirical evidence shows that the initial effect of changes in output on prices is quite small. We saw this when we looked at estimated American responses to changes in the interest rate in Figure 5–12: Despite the movement in output, the price level remained practically unchanged for nearly a year.

- Over time, prices increase, and the effects of the monetary expansion on output and the interest rate disappear. In the medium run, the increase in nominal money is reflected entirely in a proportional increase in the price level; it has no effect on output or the interest rate. (How long it takes for the effects of money on output to disappear is the topic of the Focus box "How Long Lasting Are the Real Effects of Money?") Economists refer to the absence of medium-run effects of money on output and the interest rate by saying that money is *neutral in the medium run*.

> ◄ Actually, the way the proposition is typically stated is that money is neutral in the *long run*. This is because many economists use "long run" to refer to what we call in this book the "medium run."

The **neutrality of money** does not imply that monetary policy cannot or should not be used: An expansionary monetary policy can, for example, help the economy move out of a recession and return faster to its natural level. But it is a warning that monetary policy cannot sustain higher output forever.

F O C U S   How Long Lasting Are the Real Effects of Money?

How long lasting are the effects of an increase in money on output?

One way to answer is to turn to macroeconometric models. These models, which are used both to forecast activity and to look at the effects of alternative macroeconomic policies, are large-scale versions of the aggregate supply and aggregate demand model presented in the text. Figure 1 shows the effects in such a model—a model built by John Taylor of Stanford University—of a 3% permanent increase in nominal money. The increase in nominal money is assumed to take place over the

(continued)

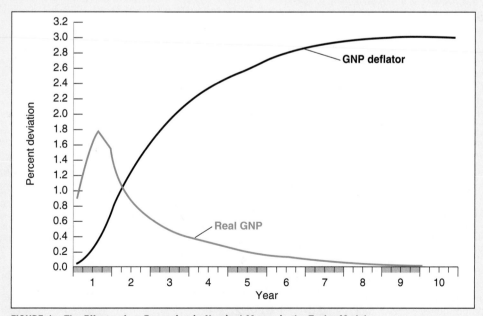

FIGURE 1   The Effects of an Expansion in Nominal Money in the Taylor Model

four quarters of year 1: 0.1% in the first quarter, another 0.6% in the second, another 1.2% in the third, and another 1.1% in the fourth. After these four-step increases, nominal money remains at its new higher level forever.

The effects of money on output reach a maximum after three quarters. By then, output is 1.8% higher than it would have been without the increase in nominal money. Over time, however, prices increase, and output returns to its natural level. In year 4, the price level is up by 2.5%, whereas output is up by only 0.3%. Therefore, the Taylor model suggests that it takes roughly four years for money to be neutral.

Some economists are skeptical of the results of simulations from such large models. Building such a model requires making decisions about which equations to include, which variables to include in each equation, and which ones to leave out. Some decisions are bound to be wrong. Because the models are so large, it is difficult to know how each of these decisions affects the outcome of a particular simulation. So, they argue, whenever possible, one should use simpler methods.

One such method is simply to trace out, using econometrics, the effects of a change in money on output. This method is not without its problems: A strong relation between money and output may not come from an effect of money on output but rather from an effect of output on the conduct of monetary policy and thus on nominal money (the econometric problems raised by such two-way causation are discussed further in Appendix 3 at the end of the book). But the method can provide a useful first pass. The results of such a study by Frederic Mishkin, building on earlier work by Robert Barro, are summarized in Table 1.

Following Barro, Mishkin first separates movements in nominal money into those movements that could have been predicted on the basis of the information available up to that time (a component he calls **anticipated money**) and those that could not (a component he calls **unanticipated money**). The motivation for this distinction should be clear from this chapter: If wage setters anticipate increases in money, they may expect the price level to be higher and ask for higher wages. Thus, to the extent that they are anticipated, changes in money may have a larger effect on prices and a smaller effect on output.

The results in Table 1 confirm that changes in money have stronger effects when they are unanticipated. Whether anticipated or unanticipated, the effects of changes in money on output peak after about two quarters. The effects are substantially larger than in the Taylor model (which looked at a 3% increase in nominal money; Table 1 looks at the effects of 1% increase). As in the Taylor model, the effects disappear after three to four years (12 to 16 quarters).

Zisimos Koustas has tested the validity of the proposition that money is neutral in the long run in Canada. He uses a third approach to the problem. He does not distinguish between anticipated and unanticipated money. He does allow lags of real output growth to cause money growth—remember from Chapter 4 that money is primarily bank deposits. If real output grows, then people with more income may take out more loans. In our language, money becomes endogenous. Thus, output may be changed in the short term by changes in the money stock, and over time, the money stock may be changed by real output in the short term. But our model predicts that in the long term, all of the effect of money on real output goes away, and the entire increase in the level of the money supply is taken up with higher prices. Real money M/P remains the same. Koustas does not test whether M/P remains the same. He does find that the increase in money has no long-run impact on the level of real output and infers that the impact of money is felt entirely on prices.

Paul DeGrauve and Claudia Costa Storti analyze the effect of monetary policy on prices and output using a "meta-analysis." They consider 43 published studies from more than 19 different countries. The key result, a monetary contraction reduces output in the short run. The effect on output goes away in the longer run.

Finally, George McCandless and Warren Weber have presented data on money growth (three different definitions of money) and inflation across 110 countries over 30 years. They find that money is neutral. Growth rates of money and growth rates of prices are highly correlated in the long run.

Although the results using the five approaches are not identical, they share a number of features. Money has a strong effect on output in the short run. But the effect is largely gone after four years. By then, the effect of higher nominal money is largely reflected in higher prices, not higher output.

Sources:

Figure 1 is reproduced from John Taylor, *Macroeconomic Policy in a World Economy* (New York: W.W. Norton, 1993), Figure 5–1A, p. 138.

Table 1 is taken from Frederic Mishkin, *A Rational Expectations Approach to Macroeconometrics* (Chicago: NBER and University of Chicago, 1983), Table 6.5, p. 122.

The study by Mishkin builds, in turn, on Robert Barro, "Unanticipated Money Growth in the United States," *American Economic Review*, March 1977, pp. 101–115.

Koustas's work, which is quite technical, is found in "Canadian Evidence on Long-Run Neutrality Propositions," *Journal of Macroeconomics*, Vol. 20, No. 2, Spring 1998, pp. 397–411.

Paul DeGrauve and Claudia Costa Storti, *The Effects of Monetary Policy: A Meta Analysis.* CESifo Working Paper No. 1224 February 2004.

The study by George McCandless and Warren Weber "Some Monetary Facts" is found in *The Federal Reserve Bank of Minneapolis Quarterly Review*, Vol. 19, No. 3, Summer 1995, pp. 2–11.

TABLE 1	The Effects of a 1% Increase in Nominal Money, Anticipated and Unanticipated on Output (Percent)					
Quarters	0	2	4	6	12	16
Effects on output of:						
Anticipated money	1.3	1.9	1.8	1.3	0.7	− 0.6
Unanticipated money	2.0	2.3	2.2	2.0	0.5	− 0.4

10-5 | A Decrease in the Budget Deficit

The policy we just looked at—a monetary expansion—led to a shift in aggregate demand coming from a shift in the *LM* curve. Let us now look at the effects of a shift in the *IS* curve.

Suppose that government was running a budget deficit and decides to eliminate it. It does so by decreasing government spending (*G*) while leaving taxes unchanged. How will this affect the economy in the short run and the medium run?

Assume that output is initially at its natural level so that the economy is at point *A* in Figure 10–7: Output equals Y_n. The decrease in government spending shifts the aggregate demand curve to the left, from *AD* to *AD'*: At a given price level, the demand for output is lower. The economy therefore moves from *A* to *A'*, leading to lower output and lower prices. The initial effect of deficit reduction is thus to trigger a recession. We first derived this result in Chapter 3 and confirmed it in Chapter 5, and it holds here as well.

What happens over time? As long as output is below its natural level, the aggregate supply curve keeps shifting down. The economy moves down along the aggregate demand curve *AD'* until the aggregate supply curve is given by *AS"* and the economy reaches point *A"*. By then, the initial recession is over, and output is back at Y_n.

So, just like an increase in nominal money, a reduction in the budget deficit does not affect output forever. Eventually, output returns to its natural level; unemployment returns to the natural rate. But there is an important difference between the effects of a change in money and the effects of a change in the deficit: At point *A"*, not everything is the same as before. Output is back to its natural level, but the price level and the interest rate are now lower than before the shift. The best way to see why is to look at the adjustment in terms of the underlying *IS-LM* model.

The Budget Deficit, Output, and the Interest Rate

Figure 10–8 shows the adjustment in terms of output and the interest rate. Figure 10–8(a) reproduces Figure 10–7. Figure 10–8(b) shows the adjustment in terms of the *IS-LM* model.

Look at Figure 10–8(b). The economy is initially at point *A* (which corresponds to *A* in Figure 10–8[a]). Output is equal to its natural level, Y_n, and the interest rate is equal to *i*. As the government reduces the budget deficit, the *IS* curve shifts to the left, to *IS'*. If the price level did not change, the economy would move from point *A* to point *B*. But because prices decline in response to the decrease in output, the real money stock increases, leading to a

That the price level decreases as the economy goes first from *A* to *A'* and then from *A'* to *A"* over time feels strange: We rarely observe deflation. This result comes, however, from our assumption that there is no money growth so that there is zero inflation in the medium run. In the real world, money growth is typically positive, and inflation is positive. Recessions generate a temporary decrease in inflation, not a decrease in the price level. We will explore the implications of positive money growth in the next two chapters.

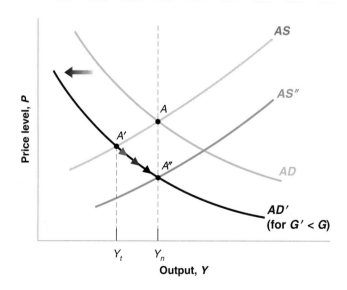

FIGURE 10–7

The Dynamic Effects of a Decrease in the Budget Deficit

A decrease in the budget deficit leads initially to a decrease in output. Over time, output returns to its natural level.

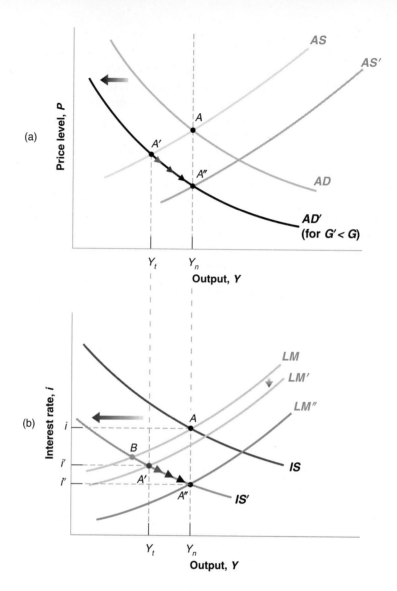

FIGURE 10-8

The Dynamic Effects of a Decrease in the Budget Deficit on Output and the Interest Rate

Deficit reduction leads in the short run to a decrease in output and in the interest rate. In the medium run, output returns to its natural level, whereas the interest rate declines further.

partly offsetting shift of the *LM* curve downward, to *LM'*. The initial effect of deficit reduction is thus to move the economy from *A* to *A'*; point *A'* corresponds to point *A'* in Figure 10–8(a). Both output and the interest rate are lower than before the fiscal contraction. Note, for later use, that whether investment increases or decreases in the short run is ambiguous: Lower output decreases investment, but the lower interest rate increases it.

Over time, output below the natural level—equivalently, unemployment above the natural rate—leads to a further decrease in prices. As long as output is below its natural level, prices decrease, and the *LM* curve shifts down. The economy moves down from point *A'* along *IS'* and eventually reaches *A"* (which corresponds to *A"* in Figure 10–8(a)). At *A"*, the *LM* curve is given by *LM"*. Output is back at its natural level. But the interest rate is now equal to *i"*, lower than it was before deficit reduction. The composition of output is now different. To see how and why, let us rewrite the *IS* relation, taking into account that at *A"*, output is back at its natural level so that $Y = Y_n$:

$$Y_n = C(Y_n - T) + I(Y_n, i) + G$$

Because neither income nor taxes have changed, consumption is the same as before deficit reduction. By assumption, government spending, G, is lower than before; therefore, investment, I, must be higher than before deficit reduction—higher by an amount exactly equal to the decrease in the budget deficit. Put another way, in the medium run, a reduction in the budget deficit unambiguously leads to a decrease in the interest rate and an increase in investment.

Budget Deficits, Output, and Investment

Let us summarize what we have learned about the effects of fiscal policy in this section:

1. In the short run, a budget deficit reduction, if implemented alone (that is, without an accompanying change in monetary policy) leads to a decrease in output and may lead to a decrease in investment. However, note the qualification "without an accompanying change in monetary policy": In principle, these adverse short-run effects on output can be avoided by using the right monetary–fiscal policy mix. What is needed is for the central bank to decrease interest rates enough to offset the adverse effects of the decrease in government spending on demand. As we saw in Chapter 5, this is what happened in Canada in the early 1990s: The Bank of Canada was able to ensure that even in the short run, deficit reduction did not lead to a recession and to a decrease in output.

2. In the medium run, output returns to its natural level, and the interest rate is lower. In the medium run, deficit reduction leads to an *increase* in investment. So far, we have not taken into account the effects of investment on capital accumulation and the effects of capital on production (we will do so from Chapter 14 on when we look at the long run). But it is easy to see how our conclusions would be modified if we did. In the long run, a lower budget deficit leads to higher investment. Higher investment leads to a higher capital stock, which leads to higher output.

> Effects of a deficit reduction:
>
> Short run: $Y\downarrow$ and $I\uparrow\downarrow$?
>
> Medium run:
> Y unchanged and $I\uparrow$
>
> ◀ Long run: $Y\uparrow$ and $I\uparrow$

Everything we have just said about the effects of deficit reduction would apply equally to measures aimed at increasing private saving. An increase in the saving rate increases output and investment in the medium run and long run. But it may also create a recession and a decrease in investment in the short run.

Disagreements among economists about the effects of measures aimed at increasing either public saving or private saving often come from differences in time frames. Those concerned with short-run effects worry that such measures may create a recession and decrease saving and investment for some time. Those who look beyond the short run see the eventual increase in saving and investment and emphasize the favourable medium- and long-run effects on output. We will return to these issues again in Chapter 27.

10-6 | Changes in the Price of Oil

In the 1970s, the price of oil increased dramatically. This was the result of the formation of the Organization of Petroleum Exporting Countries (OPEC), a cartel of oil producers. Behaving as a monopolist, OPEC reduced the supply of oil and, in doing so, increased its price. Figure 10–9 plots the U.S. dollar price of a barrel of crude oil since 1960. The price of petroleum, which had remained roughly constant throughout the 1960s, almost tripled between 1970 and 1982. This was the result of two particularly sharp increases in the price, the first in 1973–1975 and the second in 1979–1981.

From 1982 on, however, the cartel became unable to enforce the production quotas it had set for its members. Some member countries started to produce more than their assigned quota, and the supply of oil steadily increased, leading to a large decline in the price. As Figure 10–9 shows, the breakdown of OPEC has led to a steady decline in the relative price of crude petroleum. From a high of 37 dollars in 1981, the price index fell to 14 dollars in 1998. The price rose again from 2000 onward.

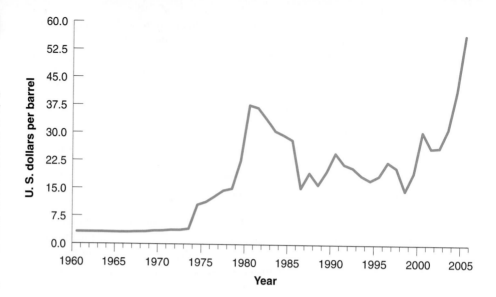

FIGURE 10–9

The Price of Crude Petroleum, 1960–2005

There were three large price increases in the U.S. dollar price of a barrel of oil: one in 1970, one in 1979, and a more recent run up in oil prices between 2000 and 2005. For a discussion and a more thoughtful look at oil prices, read Section 10–6 and the Global Macro box "Why Was There 'No' Oil Shock in the Period from 2000–2005?"

Source: Federal Reserve Bank of St. Louis, Spot Oil Price; West Texas Intermediate; U.S. dollars).

In thinking about the macroeconomic effects of an increase in the price of oil, we face an obvious problem: The price of oil appears neither in our aggregate supply relation nor in our aggregate demand relation! The reason is that we have assumed thus far that output was produced using only labour. One way of proceeding would be to relax this assumption, recognize explicitly that output is produced using labour and other inputs (including energy), and derive the implications for the relation of prices to wages and the price of oil. We will instead use a shortcut and capture the increase in the price of oil by an increase in μ, the markup of prices over wages. The justification is straightforward: Given wages, an increase in the price of oil increases the cost of production, forcing firms to increase prices.

We can then track the dynamic effects of an *increase in the markup* on output and prices. It is best here to work backward in time, to start by asking what happens in the medium run, and then working out the dynamics of adjustment.

Effects on the Natural Rate of Unemployment

Let us first ask what happens to the natural rate of unemployment as a result of the increase in the price of oil. Figure 10–10 reproduces the characterization of labour-market equilibrium from Chapter 9. The wage-setting curve is downward sloping. The price-setting relation

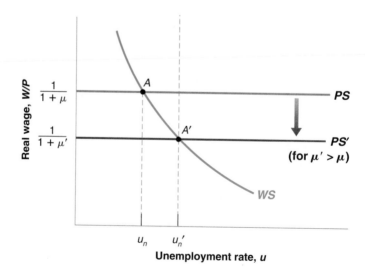

FIGURE 10–10

The Effects of an Increase in the Price of Oil on the Natural Rate of Unemployment

An increase in the price of oil leads to a lower real wage and a higher natural rate of unemployment.

is represented by the horizontal line at $W/P = 1/(1 + \mu)$. The initial equilibrium is at point A, and the initial natural unemployment rate is u_n.

An increase in the markup leads to a downward shift of the price-setting line, from PS to PS': The higher the markup, the lower is the real wage implied by price setting. The equilibrium moves from A to A'. The real wage is lower. The natural unemployment rate is higher: Getting workers to accept the lower real wage requires an increase in unemployment.

The increase in the natural rate of unemployment implies a decrease in the natural level of employment. If we assume that the relation between employment and output is unchanged—that is, that each unit of output still requires one worker, in addition to the energy input—then the decrease in the natural level of employment leads to an identical decrease in the natural level of output. In short, an increase in the price of oil leads to a decrease in the natural level of output.

The Dynamics of Adjustment

Let us now turn to dynamics. Suppose that before the increase in the price of oil, the economy is at point A in Figure 10–11, with output at its natural level, Y_n, and a constant price level (so that $P_t = P_{t-1}$). We have just established that the increase in the price of oil decreases the natural level of output from Y_n to, say, Y_n'. We now want to know what happens in the short run and how the economy moves from Y_n to Y_n'.

Recall that the aggregate supply relation is given by:

$$P_t = P_{t-1}(1 + \mu) F\left(1 - \frac{Y_t}{L}, z\right)$$

An increase in the markup leads to an increase in the price level (P_t) at a given level of output (Y_t). Thus, in the short run, the aggregate supply curve shifts up.

We can be more specific about the size of the shift, and this will be useful in what follows. We know from section 10-1 that the aggregate supply curve always goes through the point such that output equals its natural level and the price level equals the price level expected by wage setters. Before the increase in the price of oil, the aggregate supply curve goes through point A, where output equals Y_n and the price level is equal to P_{t-1} (as we are assuming that expectations of the price level are such that $P_t^e = P_{t-1}$). After the increase in the price of oil, the new aggregate supply curve goes through point B, where output equals the new lower natural level Y_n' and the price level equals the expected price level, P_{t-1}. Thus, the aggregate supply curve shifts from AS to AS'.

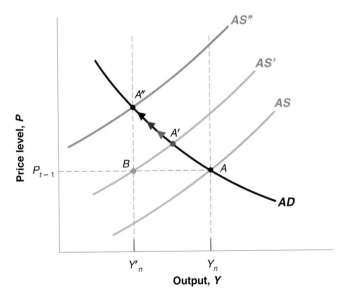

FIGURE 10–11

The Dynamic Effects of an Increase in the Price of Oil

An increase in the price of oil leads, in the short run, to a decrease in output and an increase in the price level. Over time, output decreases further, and the price level increases further.

Does the aggregate demand curve shift as a result of the increase in the price of oil? There are many channels through which demand might be affected at a given price level. The higher price of oil may lead firms to change their investment plans, cancelling some investment projects and/or shifting to less energy-intensive equipment. The increase in the price of oil also redistributes income from oil buyers to oil producers. Oil producers may have a higher propensity to save than oil buyers. Let us take the easy way here: Because some of the effects shift the aggregate demand curve to the right and others shift the aggregate demand curve to the left, let us assume simply that the effects cancel each other out and that aggregate demand does not shift.

This was the case in the 1970s. The OPEC countries realized that high oil revenues might not last forever. So, most of them saved a large proportion of their incomes. ▶

In the short run, therefore, the economy moves from A to A'. The increase in the price of oil leads firms to increase prices; the increase in prices decreases demand and output. Note the different effects of adverse demand and supply shocks: Adverse demand shocks (for example, the reduction in the budget deficit we looked at in section 10-5) lead to lower output and lower prices. Adverse supply shocks (in this case, an increase in the price of oil) lead to lower output and *higher* prices.

What happens over time? Although output has decreased, the natural level of output has decreased even more: At point A', the economy is still above the new natural level of output Y'_n. This leads to a further increase in prices. The economy therefore moves over time from A' to A''. At point A'' output is equal to its new natural level, and prices are higher than before the oil shock. Shifts in aggregate supply affect output not only in the short run but in the medium run as well.

How does our story compare to what actually happened in Canada and the United States after the first oil shock? Table 10–1 gives the basic macroeconomic facts for both countries.

From 1973 to 1975, the cumulative increase in petroleum prices (in American dollars) was 77.3%. The results in the United States were very much what our model predicts: a combination of a recession and large increases in prices. In 1974 and 1975, American GDP growth was negative. In both 1974 and 1975, inflation (as measured by the rate of change of the GDP deflator) was higher than the year before. At the time, this combination of negative growth and high inflation—which was named **stagflation** to capture the combination of *stag*nation and *inflation*—came as a surprise to economists. It was the trigger for a large amount of research on the effects of supply shocks for the rest of the decade. By the time of the second oil shock in the late 1970s, macroeconomists were better equipped to understand it.

TABLE 10–1 The Effects of the Increase in the Price of Oil, 1973–1975

	1973	1974	1975
Rate of change of petroleum price in the world (%)	10.4	51.8	15.1
United States			
Rate of change of GDP deflator (%)	5.6	9.0	9.4
Rate of real GDP growth (%)	5.8	−0.6	−0.4
Unemployment rate (%)	4.9	5.6	8.5
Canada			
Rate of change of GDP deflator (%)	9.0	13.7	9.7
Rate of real GDP growth (%)	7.0	4.0	2.1
Unemployment rate (%)	5.8	5.6	7.4

Source for U.S. variables: Economic Report of the President, 1997.

Source for Canadian variables: GDP deflator using CANSIM II variable (V646937/V3862685); real GDP using CANSIM II variable V3862685; unemployment rate using CANSIM I variable D767611.

A quick look back at Figure 10–9 suggests that there should be *three* oil price shocks. The text discusses the effect of the oil price shock in the period 1973–1975 on both Canada and the United States. There was a similar shock in 1979 with similar consequences. The model fits well for the United States and less well for Canada. However, a superficial look at Figure 10–9 suggests that there has been an oil price shock even in our lifetime. In December 1998, West Texas Intermediate (a specific type of crude oil often used to benchmark the price of crude oil) was a mere $11.28 US per barrel. Crude oil, as a world commodity, is priced in U.S. dollars. In November 2004, the same barrel of crude oil was priced at $53.13 US. You may even recall the increase in the price of gasoline. But this enormous increase in price did not induce the stagflation described in the previous section. Why?

There are two basic answers. In Figure 1, the nominal price of crude oil is presented, and so is a measure of the real price of oil. The U.S. consumer price index (1982–1984 = 100) is used to deflate the price of oil—reread Chapter 2 if you need to remember what a price index is. On average, from 1982–1984, the value of the U.S. CPI was 100. In 2004, the average value of the U.S. CPI was 189. Average prices for all commodities in the United States roughly doubled between 1982 and 2004. Thus, although the nominal price of crude oil in 2004 was a great deal higher than in 1973 and even slightly higher than in 1979, the real price of crude oil was much lower than in 1979 and about the same as in 1973. As we learned in Chapter 2, it is very important to look at variables in real terms. This is a useful example of how large the adjustment from nominal to real terms can be and how important it is to make the adjustment.

The second basic answer relates to the changes in the effects of higher real crude oil prices on the economy over time. The production function described in Chapter 9 and Chapter 10 was much too simple. We wrote that Y = AN and, for conve-nience, set A = 1. In fact, both capital and raw materials, like oil, are used to produce output. The more expensive oil becomes, the less oil is used. This process of switching out of expensive oil can be very slow. Only when you replace your delivery truck do you choose a truck with a more efficient engine. Only when your oil furnace wears out do you replace that furnace with a natural gas furnace. Only when your car wears out do you buy a new, more fuel-efficient hybrid vehicle. A car may take 5 to 10 years to wear out, a furnace even longer. How do we see this in the data? In the 1970s, crude oil was 13% of commodity imports of OECD countries. In the 1990s that share fell to 4%. In the United States, by far the biggest oil importer, a unit of GDP is produced with half as much oil in the 1990s as in the 1960s. In the language of our model, the size of the parameter "z" for the same increase in real oil prices is much smaller.

While oil prices are still important to the world economy, they are less important than they were in the 1970s when the really big oil shocks occurred. In the period 1998–2004, both the shock and the response of the economy to a given shock (the size of "z" related to oil) were smaller. This does not mean that an oil shock is impossible. It does mean that the increase in the oil price from 1998 to 2004 was not as big as it looked and did not have nearly as large an impact as the shocks in 1973 and 1979. If the nominal price of oil were to increase to $150 US a barrel in the period 2005–2008, we might well get a repeat of the period 1973–1980, the period of stagflation in the world economy. Oil prices did continue to rise through 2005 in both real and nominal terms. The effect on the economy was not known at the time of writing.

Source: *The Economist*, April 30, 2005, in a "Survey: Oil: In Troubled Waters" writes about the changes in the world economy due to changes in the price of oil. This box draws on that material. Your university or college library may have an electronic subscription to *The Economist* that includes the back issues if you want to read more.

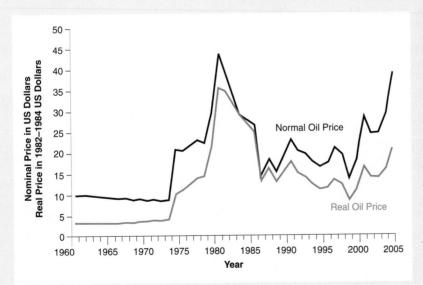

FIGURE 1 A Comparison of the Real and the Nominal Price Oil, 1960–2005

Notice that although the nominal price of oil rose a great deal from 1998 to 2005, the real price of oil in 2004 is not as high as it was in 1979 and just barely at its 1973 level. So the 2004 increases in oil prices were not as large a shock to the economy as the oil price increases in either 1973 or 1979.

Source: Oil Prices: Federal Reserve Bank of St. Lous spot oil price: West Texas Intermediate; Consumer Price Index: Federal Reserve Bank of St. Lous, 1982–1984 = 100.

The model does not seem to fit the Canadian facts as well. There was a large increase in inflation as the aggregate supply line shifted to the left. Real GDP growth slowed from a torrid 7% in 1973 to 4% in 1974 and then 2.1% in 1975. Unemployment finally increased in 1975. Why might the Canadian response be different from that in the United States? There is a variety of possibilities. The most likely explanation is that Canada, unlike the United States, is a large net exporter of energy, both crude oil and natural gas. Thus, the increases in oil prices led to an investment boom in Canada's energy sector as producers scrambled to find and produce more oil. It seems likely that for Canada, the *AD* curve, while shifting to the left with a decline in exports to the United States, would shift to the right as Canadian oil-producing areas increased investment. The oil-price shock has a less severe impact on Canada than on the United States.

Many questions still remain, however. One of the most intriguing is whether the effects of changes in oil prices are symmetric, that is, whether increases and decreases have symmetrical effects on output. The motivation for the question is the fact that the favourable effects on output of the large decrease in oil prices since 1982 appear to have been weaker than the negative effects of the increases in oil prices of the 1970s. Do lower oil prices actually reduce investment in Canada's oil patches, the "old" oil patch in Alberta and the new oil patch on the East Coast?

In the late 1990s, the price of oil had decreased further. One question is whether this decrease is one of the reasons the 1990s' expansion went on far longer than was forecast. ▶

We have focused in this section on the effects of an increase in the price of oil. But, like shifts in aggregate demand, shifts in aggregate supply can come in many forms. Anything that affects labour productivity or leads to changes in the markup of prices over wages can potentially act as an aggregate supply shift.

10-7 | Conclusions

This has been an important chapter. Let us repeat and develop some of the conclusions.

The Short Run versus the Medium Run

One message of this chapter is that changes in policy or, more generally, changes in the economic environment (from changes in consumer confidence to changes in the price of oil) typically have different short-run and medium-run effects. We looked at the effects of a monetary expansion, of a deficit reduction, and of an increase in the price of oil. The main results are summarized in Table 10–2. A monetary expansion, for example, affects output in

TABLE 10–2 Short- and Medium-Run Effects of a Monetary Expansion, a Budget Deficit Reduction, and an Increase in the Price of Oil on Output, the Interest Rate, and the Price Level

	Short Run			Medium Run		
	Output Level	Interest Rate	Price Level	Output Level	Interest Rate	Price Level
Monetary expansion	increase	decrease	increase (small)	no change	no change	increase
Deficit reduction	decrease	decrease	decrease (small)	no change	decrease	decrease
Increase in oil price	decrease	increase	increase	decrease	increase	increase

the short run but not in the medium run. In the short run, a decrease in the budget deficit decreases output and the interest rate and may therefore decrease investment. But in the medium run, the interest rate decreases, output returns to the natural rate, and investment increases. An increase in the price of oil decreases output not only in the short run but also in the medium run. And so it goes.

This difference between the short- and medium-run effects of policies is one of the main reasons economists disagree in their policy recommendations. Some economists believe that the economy adjusts quickly to its medium-run equilibrium, so they emphasize medium-run implications of policy. Others believe that the adjustment mechanism through which output returns to its natural level is a slow one at best, so they put more emphasis on the short-run effects of policy. They are more willing to use active monetary policy or budget deficits to get out of a recession, even if money is neutral in the medium run and budget deficits have adverse implications in the long run.

We will return to these issues many times in the book. See, in particular, Chapter 22, which focuses on periods of sustained high unemployment, such as the Great Depression, and Chapters 25 to 27, which look at macro-economic policy in more detail.

Shocks and Propagation Mechanisms

This chapter also gives you a general way of thinking about **output fluctuations** (sometimes called **business cycles**)—movements in output around its trend (a trend that we have ignored so far but will focus on in Chapters 14 to 17).

The economy is constantly buffeted by **shocks** to aggregate supply, or to aggregate demand, or to both. These shocks may be shifts in consumption coming from changes in consumer confidence, shifts in investment, shifts in portfolio behaviour, shifts in labour productivity, and so on. Or they may come from changes in policy—from the introduction of a new tax law, to a new program of infrastructure investment, to the decision by the central bank to fight inflation through tight money.

Each shock has dynamic effects on output and its components. These dynamic effects are called the **propagation mechanism** of the shock. Propagation mechanisms are different for different shocks. The effects on activity may be largest at the beginning and then may decrease over time. Or the effects may build up for a while and then decrease and eventually disappear. We saw, for example, that the effects of an increase in money on output peak after six to nine months and then slowly decline afterward, as prices eventually increase in proportion to the increase in money. Some shocks have effects even in the long run. This is the case for any shock that has a permanent effect on aggregate supply, such as a permanent change in the price of oil.

Fluctuations in output come from the constant appearance of new shocks, each with its own propagation mechanism. At times, some shocks are sufficiently bad or come in sufficiently bad combinations that they create a recession. The two recessions of the 1970s were due largely to increases in the price of oil; the recession of the early 1980s was due to a sharp change in monetary policy; the recession of the early 1990s was due primarily to a sudden decline in consumer confidence. What we call economic fluctuations are the result of these shocks and their dynamic effects on output.

Defining *shocks* is harder than it appears. Suppose a failed economic program in a foreign country leads to the fall of democracy in that country, which leads to an increase in the risk of nuclear war, which leads to a fall in domestic consumer confidence in our country, which leads to a drop in consumption. What is the "shock"? The failed program? The fall of democracy? The increased risk of nuclear war? Or the decrease in consumer confidence? In practice, we have to cut the chain of causation somewhere. Thus, we may refer to the drop in consumer confidence as "the shock," ignoring its underlying causes.

Output, Unemployment, and Inflation

In developing the model of this chapter, we made the assumption that the nominal money stock was constant. That is, although we considered the effects of a one-time change in the level of nominal money (in section 10-4), we did not allow for sustained nominal money growth. One implication of that assumption was that the price level was constant in the medium run so that there was no sustained inflation. We must now relax this assumption and allow for nominal money growth. Only by doing so can we explain why inflation is typically positive and think about the relation between economic activity and inflation. Movements in unemployment, output, and inflation are the topics of the next two chapters.

- The model of aggregate supply and aggregate demand describes the movements in output and prices when account is taken of equilibrium in the goods, financial, and labour markets.

- The aggregate supply relation captures the effects of output on the price level. It is derived from equilibrium in the labour market. It is a relation among the price level, the expected price level, and the level of output. An increase in output decreases unemployment, increases wages and, in turn, increases the price level. A higher expected price level leads, one for one, to a higher increase in the actual price level.

- The aggregate demand relation captures the effects of the price level on output. It is derived from equilibrium in the goods and financial markets. An increase in the price level decreases the real money stock, increases interest rates, and decreases output.

- In the short run, movements in output come from shifts in either aggregate demand or aggregate supply. In the medium run, output returns to its natural level, which is determined by equilibrium in the labour market.

- An expansionary monetary policy leads, in the short run, to an increase in the real money stock, a decrease in the interest rate, and an increase in output. Over time, the price level increases, leading to a decrease in the real money stock until output has returned to its natural level. In the medium run, money is neutral: It does not affect output, and changes in money are reflected in proportional increases in the price level.

- A decrease in the budget deficit leads, in the short run, to a decrease in the demand for goods and thus a decrease in output. Over time, the price level decreases, leading to an increase in the real money stock and a decrease in the interest rate. In the medium run, output is back to its natural level, but the interest rate is lower and investment is higher.

- An increase in the price of oil leads, in both the short run and the medium run, to a decrease in output. In the short run, it leads to an increase in prices, which decreases the real money stock and leads to a contraction of demand and output. In the medium run, it decreases the real wage paid by firms, increases the natural rate of unemployment, and, in turn, decreases the natural level of output.

- The difference between short- and medium-run effects of policies is one of the main reasons why economists disagree in their policy recommendations. Some economists believe that the economy adjusts quickly to its medium-run equilibrium and thus emphasize medium-run implications of policy. Others believe that the adjustment mechanism through which output returns to its natural level is a slow one at best and put more emphasis on short-run effects.

- Economic fluctuations are the result of a constant stream of shocks to aggregate supply or to aggregate demand and of the dynamic effects of each of these shocks on output. Sometimes, the shocks are sufficiently adverse, alone or in combination, that they lead to a recession.

An asterisk denotes a harder question. [Web] indicates that the question requires access to the Internet.

1. TRUE/FALSE/UNCERTAIN

a. The aggregate supply relation implies that an increase in output leads to an increase in the price level.

b. The natural level of output can be determined by looking only at the aggregate supply relation.

c. The aggregate demand relation implies that an increase in the price level leads to an increase in output.

d. In the absence of changes in fiscal and/or monetary policy, the economy will always remain at the natural level of output.

e. Expansionary monetary policy has no effect on the level of output in the medium run.

f. Fiscal policy cannot affect investment in the medium run because output always returns to its natural level.

g. In the medium run, prices and output always return to the same value.

2. SPENDING SHOCKS AND THE MEDIUM RUN

Using the *AS-AD* model developed in this chapter, show the effects of each of the following shocks on the position of the *IS*, *LM*, *AD*, and *AS* curves in the medium run. Then, show the effect on output, the interest rate, and the price level, also in the medium run. Assume that before the changes, the economy was at the natural level of output.

a. An increase in consumer confidence

b. An increase in taxes

3. SUPPLY SHOCKS AND THE MEDIUM RUN

Using the *AS-AD* model developed in this chapter, show the effects of each of the following shocks on the position of the *WS*, *PS*, *IS*, *LM*, *AD*, and *AS* curves in the medium run. Then state the effects on output, the interest rate, and the price level, also in the medium run. Assume that before the changes, the economy was at the natural level of output.

a. An increase in unemployment benefits

b. A decrease in the price of oil

4. THE NEUTRALITY OF MONEY

a. In what sense is money neutral? Why is monetary policy useful, even though money is neutral?

b. Fiscal policy, just like monetary policy, cannot change the natural level of output. Why then is monetary policy considered neutral but fiscal policy is not?

c. Discuss this statement: "Because neither fiscal nor monetary policy can affect the natural level of output, it follows that in the medium run, the natural level of output is independent of all government policies."

*5. WHAT IF THE INTEREST RATE HAD NO EFFECT ON INVESTMENT?

Suppose that investment is not responsive to the interest rate.

a. Can you think of a situation where that may happen?

b. What does this imply for the *IS* curve?

c. What does this imply for the *LM* curve?

d. What does this imply for the *AD* curve?

Now, suppose that the economy starts at the natural level of output and that due to a shock to the catchall variable *z*, the *AS* curve shifts up.

e. What is the short-run effect on prices and output?

f. What happens to output and prices over time? Explain in words.

6. WHAT IF MONEY DEMANDS ARE FLAT (AS IN THE CASE AT VERY LOW INTEREST RATES)?

a. What does this imply for the slope of the *LM* curve?

b. What does this imply for the slope of the *IS* curve?

c. What does this imply for the slope of the *AD* curve?

Draw the *AD* and *AS* curves, and assume that the equilibrium is at a point below the natural rate of output.

d. Suppose that the central bank increases the money stock. What will be the effects on output in the short run and in the medium run? Explain in words.

7. INVESTMENT AND MONETARY POLICY

Consider the following model of the economy (we ignore the role of G and T on demand; also, to simplify the algebra, we assume that output depends on the difference between M and P rather than on their ratio):

$$AD: \quad Y = c(M - P)$$
$$AS: \quad P = P^e + d(Y - Y_n)$$

where c and d are parameters.

a. What is the natural level of output? If nominal money is equal to M_0, what is the initial price level? Call this initial price level P_0.

Suppose that in an effort to increase investment, the Bank of Canada decides to pursue an expansionary monetary policy and doubles the nominal money stock: $M_1 = 2M_0$.

b. Solve for the equilibrium value of output in the short run.

c. What happens to investment behind the scene? Explain in words.

d. Solve for the equilibrium value of output in the medium run.

e. What happens to investment in the medium run? Explain in words.

CHAPTER 11
THE PHILLIPS CURVE

The Core: The Medium Run

In 1958, A. W. Phillips drew a diagram plotting the rate of inflation against the rate of unemployment in the United Kingdom for each year from 1861 to 1957. He found clear evidence of a negative relation between inflation and unemployment: When unemployment was low, inflation was high, and when unemployment was high, inflation was low, often even negative. As is common in the social sciences, the same experiment was repeated using the data from other countries.

Figure 11–1 shows the evidence that Phillips would have had for Canada. It plots the inflation rate, measured as the percent change in the consumer price index against the unemployment rate. There appears to be a negative relationship between inflation and unemployment in Canada also. In the three years in the heart of the Great Depression, unemployment is very high and the rate of inflation is negative.

This relation, which became known as the Phillips curve, rapidly became central to macroeconomic thinking and policy. It appeared to imply that countries could choose between different combinations of unemployment and inflation. They could achieve low unemployment if they were willing to tolerate higher inflation, or they could achieve price level stability—zero inflation—if they were willing to tolerate higher unemployment. Much of the discussion about macroeconomic policy became a discussion about which point to choose on the Phillips curve.

In the 1970s, however, the relation broke down. In Canada, the United States, and most OECD countries, there was both high inflation *and* high unemployment, clearly contradicting the original Phillips curve. A relation reappeared, but it was now a relation between the unemployment rate and the *change* in the inflation rate. Today, in both Canada and the United States, high unemployment leads not to low inflation but, instead, to a decrease in inflation.

The purpose of this chapter is to explore the mutations of the Phillips curve and, more generally, to understand the relation between inflation and unemployment. We will see that what Phillips discovered was the aggregate supply relation and that the mutations of the Phillips curve came from changes in the way people and firms formed expectations.

FIGURE 11-1

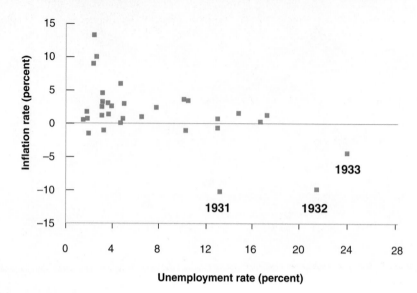

During the period 1927–1959 in Canada, low unemployment was typically associated with high inflation, and high unemployment was typically associated with low or negative inflation. The years 1931, 1932, and 1933 are notable for very high unemployment rates and large negative inflation rates.

Source: Inflation rate using CANSIM II variable V35319; unemployment rate 1927–1952 using *Historical Statistics of Canada*, and 1953–1975 using CANSIM I variable D7676.

We will from now on refer to the inflation rate as "inflation," and to the unemployment rate as "unemployment." ▶

After deriving this relation ▶ in Chapter 10, we replaced the unemployment rate by its expression in terms of output to obtain a relation among the price level, the expected price level, and output. It will be more convenient in this chapter to stay with the relation in terms of unemployment rather than output.

$P^e \uparrow \Rightarrow P \uparrow ; u \uparrow \Rightarrow P \downarrow$ ▶

$\pi^e \uparrow \Rightarrow \pi \uparrow ; u \uparrow \Rightarrow \pi \downarrow$ ▶

11-1 | Inflation, Expected Inflation, and Unemployment

Our first step will be to show that the aggregate supply relation we derived in Chapter 10 can be rewritten as a relation between *inflation* and *unemployment*, given *expected inflation*.

To do this, go back to the relation among the *price level*, the *expected price level*, and the *unemployment rate* we derived in Chapter 10:

$$P_t = P_t^e(1 + \mu) F(u_t, z)$$

Recall that the function F captures the effects on the wage of the unemployment rate, u_t, and of the other factors that affect wage setting, represented by the catchall variable, z. It will be convenient here to assume a specific form for the function F:

$$F(u_t, z) = 1 - \alpha u_t + z$$

This captures the notion that the higher the unemployment rate, the lower is the wage, and the higher z, the higher is the wage. The parameter α (the Greek lowercase letter alpha) captures the strength of the effect of unemployment on wages: The larger the α, the stronger is the (negative) effect of unemployment on wages.

Replacing in the earlier equation gives:

$$P_t = P_t^e(1 + \mu)(1 - \alpha u_t + z)$$

With a few manipulations, this relation can be rewritten as a relation among the *inflation rate*, the *expected inflation rate*, and the *unemployment rate*:

$$\pi_t = \pi_t^e + (\mu + z) - \alpha u_t \tag{11.1}$$

where π_t denotes the inflation rate, defined as the rate of change of prices from last year to this year, and π_t^e denotes the corresponding expected inflation rate—the rate of change of prices from last year to this year, expected by wage setters as of last year.

In short, equation (11.1) tells us that *inflation depends positively on expected inflation and negatively on unemployment.*

- *Higher expected inflation leads to higher inflation.* We saw in Chapter 10 how higher expected prices lead to higher nominal wages, which lead to higher prices. But note that given last year's prices, higher prices this year imply higher inflation this year; similarly, higher expected prices imply higher expected inflation. So, higher expected inflation leads to higher actual inflation.
- *Given expected inflation, the higher the markup chosen by firms, μ, or the higher the factors that affect wage determination, z, the higher is inflation.* We saw in Chapter 10 how a higher markup leads to higher prices, given expected prices. We can restate this proposition as follows: A higher markup leads to higher inflation, given expected inflation. The same argument applies to increases in any of the factors that affect wage determination.
- *Given expected inflation, the higher the unemployment, the lower is inflation.* We saw in Chapter 10 that given expected prices, a higher unemployment rate leads to lower prices. We can restate this proposition as follows: Given expected inflation, a higher unemployment rate leads to lower actual inflation.

With this reformulation of the aggregate supply relation, we can now return to the tribulations of the Phillips curve.

Going from the relation between the expected price level and the price level to a relation between inflation and expected inflation.

Start with:

$$P_t^e \uparrow \Rightarrow P_t \uparrow$$

Subtract P_{t-1} from both sides, and divide both sides by P_{t-1}:

$$(P_t^e - P_{t-1})/P_{t-1} \uparrow \Rightarrow (P_t - P_{t-1})/P_{t-1}$$

Recall the definitions of expected inflation ($\pi_t^e = (P_t^e - P_{t-1})/P_{t-1}$) and actual inflation ($\pi_t = (P_t - P_{t-1})/P_{t-1}$), and replace:

$$\pi_t^e \uparrow \Rightarrow \pi_t \uparrow$$

11-2 | The Phillips Curve

Let us start with the relation between unemployment and inflation as it was first discovered by Phillips, circa 1960.

The Early Incarnation

Think of an economy where inflation is positive in some years, negative in others, and on average equals zero. This is clearly not the way things are in Canada today: The last year during which inflation was negative—the last year during which there was **deflation**—was 1953, when inflation was -1%. But as we will see later in this chapter, average inflation *was* close to zero during much of the period that Phillips, Samuelson, and Solow were examining.

Think of wage setters choosing nominal wages for the coming year and thus having to forecast what inflation will be over the year. With the average inflation rate equal to zero in the past, it is reasonable for them to expect that inflation will be equal to zero over the next year as well. Assuming that $\pi_t^e = 0$ in equation (11.1) gives the following relation between unemployment and inflation:

$$\pi_t = (\mu + z) - \alpha u_t \tag{11.2}$$

This is precisely the negative relation between unemployment and inflation that Phillips found for the United Kingdom and that seems to be in the Canadian data in Figure 11–1. The story behind it is simple: Given expected prices, which workers simply take to be last year's prices, lower unemployment leads to higher nominal wages. Higher nominal wages lead to higher prices. Putting the steps together, lower unemployment leads to higher prices this year compared with last year's prices—that is, to higher inflation.

This mechanism has sometimes been called the **wage-price spiral**, and this phrase captures well the basic mechanism at work:

- Low unemployment leads to higher nominal wages.
- In response to higher wages, firms increase their prices.
- In response to higher prices, workers ask for higher nominal wages.
- Firms further increase prices, so workers ask for further increases in wages.
- And so on, with the result being steady wage and price inflation.

Mutations

The combination of an apparently reliable empirical relation, together with a plausible story to explain it, led to the adoption of the Phillips curve by macroeconomists and policy makers alike. Macroeconomic policy in the 1960s was aimed at maintaining unemployment in the range that appeared consistent with moderate inflation. And, throughout the 1960s, the negative relation between unemployment and inflation provided a reliable guide to the joint movements in unemployment and inflation. Figure 11–2 plots the combinations of inflation and unemployment in Canada for each year from 1960 to 1969. Note how well the relation held during the 1960s.

From 1970 on, however, the relation broke down. Figure 11–3 gives the combination of inflation and unemployment in Canada for each year from 1970 to 2001. The points are scattered in a roughly symmetric cloud: There is no relation between the unemployment rate and the inflation rate.

Why did the original Phillips curve vanish? There are two main reasons:

- As we saw in Chapter 10, in the 1970s, there were two periods where the price of oil increased rapidly. The effect of this increase in nonlabour costs was to force firms to increase their prices given wages, to increase μ. As shown in equation (11.1), an increase in μ leads to an increase in inflation, even at a given rate of unemployment, and this indeed happened twice in the 1970s. But the main reason for the breakdown of the Phillips curve relation was elsewhere.
- The main reason was that wage setters changed the way they formed expectations. This change came from a change in the process of inflation itself. Look at Figure 11–4, which plots the Canadian inflation rate for each year from 1927 to 2005. Starting around 1960 (indicated by the vertical bar in the figure), there was a clear change in the way the rate of inflation moved over time. First, rather than being sometimes positive and sometimes negative, as it had for the first part of the century, the rate of inflation became consistently positive. Second, inflation became more persistent. High inflation in one year became more likely to be followed by high inflation the next year.

The persistence of inflation led workers and firms to revise the way they formed their expectations. When inflation is consistently positive, expecting that prices this year will be the same as last year becomes systematically incorrect; indeed, it becomes foolish. People do not like to make the same mistake repeatedly. So, as inflation became consistently positive and more persistent, expectations started to take into account the

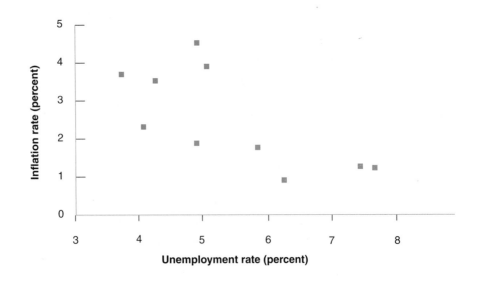

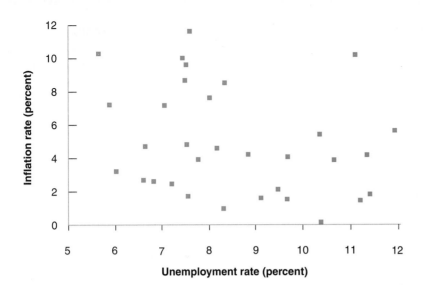

FIGURE 11-3

Inflation and Unemployment in Canada, 1970–2005

Beginning in 1970, the relation between the unemployment rate and the inflation rate disappeared in Canada.

presence of inflation. This change in expectation formation changed the nature of the relation between unemployment and inflation.

To understand what happened, suppose expectations are formed according to:

$$\pi_t^e = \theta \pi_{t-1} \tag{11.3}$$

The value of the parameter θ (the Greek lowercase letter theta) captures the effect of last year's inflation rate on this year's expected inflation rate. The higher the value of θ, the more last year's inflation leads workers and firms to revise their expectations of what inflation will be this year and so the higher is expected inflation.

We can then think of what happened from 1970 on as an increase in the value of θ over time. As long as inflation was low and not very persistent, it was reasonable for workers and firms to ignore past inflation and to assume that this year's price level would be roughly the same as last year's. For the period that Phillips had looked at, θ was close to zero, expectations were roughly given by $\pi_t^e = 0$, and the relation between the inflation and unemployment rates was given by equation (11.2).

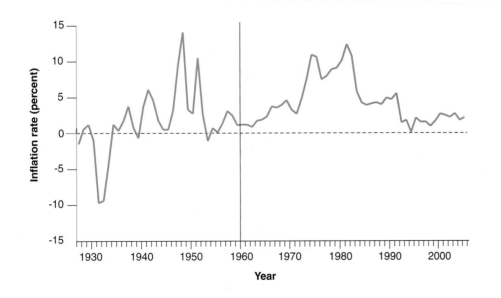

FIGURE 11-4

Canadian Inflation, 1927–2005

Since the 1960s, Canadian inflation has been consistently positive. Inflation has also become more persistent: High inflation in the current year is more likely to be followed by high inflation the following year. In the last decade, inflation has been very close to 2%, which is its target. We would anticipate that expected inflation has been near 2% as well.

But, as inflation became more persistent, workers and firms started changing the way they formed expectations. They started assuming that if inflation had been high last year, inflation was likely to be high this year as well. The parameter θ, the effect of last year's inflation rate on this year's expected inflation rate, steadily increased. By the 1970s, the evidence is that people formed expectations by expecting this year's inflation rate to be the same as last year's—in other words, that θ was now equal to 1.

To see the implications of different values of θ for the relation between inflation and unemployment, replace equation (11.3) in equation (11.1). Doing so gives:

$$\pi_t = \theta\pi_{t-1} + (\mu + z) - \alpha u_t$$

- When θ equals zero, we get the original Phillips curve, a relation between the inflation rate and the unemployment rate.
- When θ is positive, the inflation rate depends not only on the unemployment rate but also on last year's inflation rate.
- When θ equals 1, the relation becomes (moving last year's inflation rate to the left side of the equation):

$$\pi_t - \pi_{t-1} = (\mu + z) - \alpha u_t \qquad (11.4)$$

So, when $\theta = 1$, the unemployment rate affects not the inflation rate, but rather the *change* in the inflation rate: High unemployment leads to decreasing inflation; low unemployment leads to increasing inflation.

To distinguish equation (11.4) from the original Phillips curve (equation (11.2)), it is often called the **modified Phillips curve**, or the **expectations-augmented Phillips curve** (to indicate that the term π_{t-1} stands for expected inflation), or the **accelerationist Phillips curve** (to indicate that a low unemployment rate leads to an increase in the inflation rate and thus an *acceleration* of the price level). We will simply call equation (11.4) the Phillips curve and refer to the earlier incarnation, equation (11.2), as the *original* Phillips curve.

This discussion gives the key to what happened from 1970 on. As θ increased from 0 to 1, the simple relation between unemployment and inflation disappeared. This is what we saw in Figure 11–3. But equation (11.4) tells us what to look for: a relation between unemployment and the *change* in inflation. This relation is shown in Figure 11–5, which plots the

Original Phillips curve:

$$u_t\uparrow \Rightarrow \pi_t\downarrow$$

Modified Phillips curve:

$$u_t\uparrow \Rightarrow (\pi_t - \pi_{t-1})\downarrow$$

FIGURE 11–5

Change in Inflation versus Unemployment in Canada, 1970–2005

Since 1970, there has been a negative relation between the unemployment rate and the change in the inflation rate in Canada.

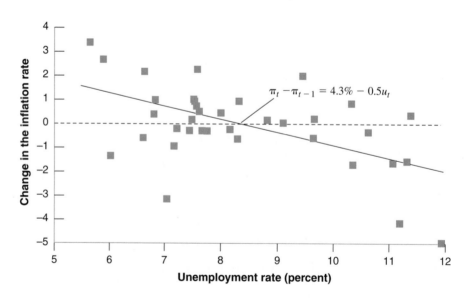

$$\pi_t - \pi_{t-1} = 4.3\% - 0.5u_t$$

Source: Inflation rate using CANSIM II variable V735319; unemployment rate 1927–1952 using *Historical Statistics of Canada*, 1953–1975 using CANSIM I variable D767611, and 1976–2005 using CANSIM II variable V2062815.

change in the inflation rate versus the unemployment rate for each year since 1970. It shows a negative relation between unemployment and the change in inflation. The line that best fits the scatter of points for the period 1970–2001 is:

$$\pi_t - \pi_{t-1} = 4.3\% - 0.5u_t \qquad (11.5)$$

This line is obtained using econometrics. (See Appendix 3 at the end of the book.) Note that the line does not fit the cloud of points very tightly. There are years when the change in inflation is much larger than implied by the line, years when the change in inflation is much less than implied by the line. We return to this point below.

The corresponding line is drawn in Figure 11–5. For low unemployment, the change in inflation is positive. For unemployment larger than 8.6% (2 times 4.3%), the change in inflation is negative.

Back to the Natural Rate of Unemployment

The history of the Phillips curve is closely related to the discovery of the concept of the natural unemployment rate that we developed in Chapter 9.

The original Phillips curve implied that there was no such thing as a natural unemployment rate: If policy makers were willing to tolerate a higher inflation rate, they could maintain a lower unemployment rate forever.

In the late 1960s, and even while the original Phillips curve still gave a good description of the data, two economists, Milton Friedman and Edmund Phelps, questioned the existence of such a trade-off between unemployment and inflation. They questioned it on logical grounds. They argued that such a trade-off could exist only if wage setters systematically underpredicted inflation and that they were unlikely to do so forever. They also argued that if government attempted to sustain lower unemployment by accepting higher inflation, the trade-off would ultimately disappear; the unemployment rate could not be sustained below a certain level, a level they called the "natural rate of unemployment." Events proved them right, and the trade-off between the unemployment rate and the inflation rate indeed disappeared. (See the Focus box "Theory Ahead of the Facts: Milton Friedman and Edmund Phelps.") Today, most economists accept the notion of a *natural rate of unemployment*—subject to the many caveats we state in the next section.

Let us make explicit the connection between the Phillips curve and the natural rate of unemployment. By definition, the natural rate of unemployment is that unemployment rate in which the actual price level turns out equal to the expected price level. Equivalently, and more conveniently here, the natural rate of unemployment is the unemployment rate in which the actual inflation rate is equal to the expected inflation rate. Denote the natural unemployment rate by u_n. Then, imposing the condition that actual inflation and expected inflation be the same ($\pi_t = \pi_t^e$) in equation (11.1) gives:

In Chapter 9, we derived the natural rate of unemployment as the rate of unemployment in which the expected and actual price level are the same. In Chapter 10, when drawing the aggregate supply curve, we emphasized that when output is equal to its natural level (hence unemployment is at the natural rate), the price level is equal to the expected price level.

$$0 = (\mu + z) - \alpha u_n$$

Solving for the natural rate u_n,

$$u_n = \frac{\mu + z}{\alpha} \qquad (11.6)$$

If $P_t^e = P_t$, then
$$\pi_t^e \equiv (P_t^e - P_{t-1})/P_{t-1}$$
$$= (P_t - P_{t-1})/P_{t-1} = \pi_t$$

Thus, the higher the markup, μ, or the higher the factors that affect wage setting, z, the higher is the natural rate.

From equation (11.6), $\alpha u_n = \mu + z$. Replacing ($\mu + z$) by αu_n in equation (11.1) and rearranging gives:

$$\pi_t - \pi_t^e = -\alpha(u_t - u_n) \qquad (11.7)$$

If the expected rate of inflation (π_t^e) is well approximated by last year's inflation rate (π_{t-1}), the relation finally becomes:

$$\pi_t - \pi_{t-1} = -\alpha(u_t - u_n) \qquad (11.8)$$

Economists are usually not very good at predicting major changes before they happen, and most of their insights are derived after the fact. Here is an exception.

In the late 1960s—precisely as the original Phillips curve relation was working like a charm—two economists, Milton Friedman and Edmund Phelps, argued that the appearance of a trade-off between inflation and unemployment was an illusion.

Here are a few quotes from Milton Friedman. Talking about the Phillips curve, he said,

Implicitly, Phillips wrote his article for a world in which everyone anticipated that nominal prices would be stable and in which this anticipation remained unshaken and immutable whatever happened to actual prices and wages. Suppose, by contrast, that everyone anticipates that prices will rise at a rate of more than 75% a year—as, for example, Brazilians did a few years ago. Then, wages must rise at that rate simply to keep real wages unchanged. An excess supply of labor will be reflected in a less rapid rise in nominal wages than in anticipated prices, not in an absolute decline in wages.

He went on to say,

To state [my] conclusion differently, there is always a temporary trade-off between inflation and unemployment; there is no permanent trade-off. The temporary trade-off comes not from inflation per se, but from a rising rate of inflation.

He then tried to guess how much longer the apparent trade-off between inflation and unemployment would last in the United States:

But how long, you will say, is "temporary"? . . . I can at most venture a personal judgment, based on some examination of the historical evidence, that the initial effect of a higher and unanticipated rate of inflation lasts for something like two to five years; that this initial effect then begins to be reversed; and that a full adjustment to the new rate of inflation takes as long for employment as for interest rates, say, a couple of decades.

Friedman could not have been more right. A few years later, the original Phillips curve started to disappear, in exactly the way Friedman had predicted.

Source: Milton Friedman, "The Role of Monetary Policy," March 1968, *American Economic Review*, Vol. 58, No. 1, pp. 1–17. (The article by Phelps, "Money-Wage Dynamics and Labor-Market Equilibrium," *Journal of Political Economy*, August 1968, part 2, pp. 678–711, made the same points more formally.)

Calling the natural rate "the nonaccelerating inflation rate of unemployment" is actually wrong. It should be called "the nonincreasing inflation rate of unemployment," or NIIRU. But NAIRU has now become so standard that it is too late to change it. ▶

Equation (11.8) gives us another way of thinking about the Phillips curve, as a relation among the actual unemployment rate, the natural unemployment rate, and the change in the inflation rate: *The change in inflation depends on the difference between the actual and the natural unemployment rates. When the actual unemployment rate is higher than the natural unemployment rate, inflation decreases; when the actual unemployment rate is lower than the natural unemployment rate, inflation increases.*

Equation (11.8) also gives us another way of thinking about the natural rate of unemployment: It is the rate of unemployment required to keep inflation constant. This is why the natural rate is also called the **nonaccelerating inflation rate of unemployment**, or **NAIRU**.

What has been the natural rate of unemployment in Canada since 1970? In other words, what is the unemployment rate such that, on average, inflation has been constant? We can find the answer by returning to the estimated equation (11.5). Putting the change in inflation equal to zero in equation (11.5) implies a value for the natural unemployment rate of $4.3\%/0.5 = 8.6\%$. In other words, the evidence suggests that since 1970, in Canada, the rate of unemployment required to keep inflation constant has been, on average, around 8.6%.

11-3 | A Summary and Many Warnings

To summarize: The aggregate supply relation is well captured in Canada today by the Phillips curve, which is a relation between the change in the inflation rate and the deviation of unemployment from its natural rate (equation (11.8)). When unemployment exceeds the natural rate, inflation decreases. When unemployment is below the natural rate, inflation increases.

This relation has held quite well since 1970. But its earlier history points to the need for several warnings. All of them point to one main fact: The relation can change, and it often has.

The Inflation Process and the Phillips Curve

Recall how the Canadian Phillips curve changed as inflation became more persistent and the way wage setters formed inflation expectations changed as a result. The lesson is a general one: The relation between unemployment and inflation is likely to change with the inflation process. Evidence from countries with high inflation confirms this lesson. Not only does the way in which workers and firms form expectations change, but institutional arrangements change as well.

When the inflation rate becomes high, inflation also tends to become more variable. Workers and firms become more reluctant to enter into labour contracts that predetermine nominal wages for a long period of time: If inflation turns out to be higher than expected, real wages may plunge and workers may suffer a large cut in their standard of living. If inflation turns out to be lower than expected, real wages may explode, and firms may go bankrupt.

More concretely, when inflation runs on average at 5% a year, wage setters can be confident the rate will be, say, between 3 and 7%. When inflation runs on average at 30% a year, wage setters can be confident the rate will be, say, between 20 and 40%. If they set a nominal wage, their real wage may vary in the first case by 2% up or down relative to what they expected; in the second case, it may vary by as much as 10% relative to what they expected. There is much more uncertainty in the second case.

For this reason, the form of wage agreements changes with the level of inflation. Nominal wages are set for shorter periods of time, down from a year to a month or even less. **Wage indexation**, a rule that increases wages automatically in line with inflation, becomes more prevalent.

These changes lead to a stronger response of inflation to unemployment. To see this, an example based on wage indexation will help. Think of an economy that has two types of labour contracts. A proportion λ (the Greek lowercase letter lambda) of labour contracts is indexed: Nominal wages in those contracts move one for one with variations in the actual price level. A proportion $1 - \lambda$ of labour contracts is not indexed: Nominal wages are set on the basis of expected inflation. Finally, assume expected inflation is equal to last year's inflation.

This assumption is actually too strong. Indexation clauses typically adjust wages not for current inflation (which is only known with a lag) but for inflation in the recent past, so there remains a short lag between inflation and wage adjustments. We ignore this lag here.

Under this assumption, equation (11.7) becomes:

$$\pi_t = [\lambda \pi_t + (1 - \lambda)\pi_{t-1}] - \alpha(u_t - u_n)$$

The term in square brackets on the right reflects the fact that a proportion λ of contracts responds to actual inflation (π_t), and a proportion $(1 - \lambda)$ responds to expected inflation, which we have assumed is equal to last year's inflation (π_{t-1}).

When $\lambda = 0$, all wages are set on the basis of expected inflation—which is equal to last year's inflation, π_{t-1}—and the equation reduces to equation (11.8). When λ is positive, however, a proportion λ of wages is set on the basis of actual rather than expected inflation.

Reorganizing the equation gives

$$\pi_t - \pi_{t-1} = -\frac{\alpha}{(1 - \lambda)}(u_t - u_n)$$

Indexation increases the effect of unemployment on inflation. The higher the proportion of indexed contracts—the higher the λ—the larger is the effect of the unemployment rate on the change in inflation—the higher is the coefficient $\alpha/(1 - \lambda)$.

The intuition is as follows: Without indexation, lower unemployment increases wages, which, in turn, increases prices. But because wages do not respond to prices right away, there is no further effect within the year. With wage indexation, however, an increase in prices leads to a further increase in wages within the year, which, in turn, leads to a further increase in prices, and so on, so the effect of unemployment on inflation within the year is higher.

If and when λ gets close to 1—when most labour contracts allow for wage indexation—small changes in unemployment can lead to very large changes in inflation. Put another way, there can be large changes in inflation with nearly no change in unemployment. This is, indeed, what happens in countries where inflation is very high: The relation between inflation and unemployment becomes more and more tenuous and eventually disappears altogether.

High inflation is the topic of Chapter 23.

Deflation and the Phillips Curve Relation

We have just looked at what happens to the Phillips curve when inflation is very high. Another issue is what happens when inflation is low, and possibly negative—when there is deflation.

The motivation for asking this question is given by an aspect of Figure 11–1 that we mentioned at the start of the chapter but then left aside. In that figure, note how the points corresponding to the 1930s (they are denoted by triangles) lie to the right of the others. Not only is unemployment unusually high—this is no surprise because we are looking at the years corresponding to the Great Depression—but given the high unemployment rate, the inflation rate may be surprisingly high in 1932 and 1933. In other words, given the very high unemployment rate, we would have expected not merely deflation, but a large rate of deflation. In fact, deflation was limited.

How do we interpret that fact? There are two potential explanations.

For more on the Great Depression, see Chapter 22.

One is that the Great Depression was associated with an increase not only in the actual unemployment rate but also in the natural unemployment rate. This seems unlikely. Most economic historians see the Great Depression primarily as the result of a large adverse shift in aggregate demand leading to an increase in the actual unemployment rate over the natural rate of unemployment rather than an increase in the natural rate of unemployment itself.

Consider two scenarios. In one, inflation is 4%, and your nominal wage goes up by 2%. In the other, inflation is 0%, and your nominal wage is cut by 2%. Which do you dislike most? You should be indifferent between the two. In both cases, your real wage goes down by 2%. There is some evidence, however, that most people find the first scenario less painful.

The other is it may be that when the economy starts experiencing deflation, the Phillips curve relation breaks down. One possible reason is the reluctance of workers to accept decreases in their nominal wages. Workers will unwittingly accept a cut in their real wages that occurs when their nominal wages increase more slowly than inflation does. However, they are likely to fight the same cut in their real wages if it results from an overt cut in their nominal wages. If this argument is correct, this implies that the Phillips curve relation between the change in inflation and unemployment may disappear or at least become weaker when the economy is close to zero inflation.

This issue is a crucial one at this stage because in many countries, inflation is now very low. As you saw in Chapter 1, Japan is actually having negative inflation. What happens to the Phillips curve relation in this environment of low inflation or even deflation is one of the developments closely watched by macroeconomists today.

This issue, as related to monetary policy, will be discussed in Chapter 26.

Differences in the Natural Rate Across Countries

Recall from equation (11.6) that the natural rate of unemployment depends on all the factors that affect wage setting, represented by the catchall variable, z; on the markup set by firms, μ; and on the response of inflation to unemployment, represented by α. To the extent that these factors differ across countries, there is no reason to expect different countries to have the same natural rate of unemployment. And, indeed, natural rates differ across countries. Consider the unemployment rates in Canada and the United States shown from 1950 to 2005 in Figure 11–6. Until the middle of the 1960s, the two rates were very similar. Remember that recessions in the United States nearly always cause recessions in Canada. From 1950 to 1969, average unemployment in Canada was 4.9%; in the United States, average unemployment was 4.6%. The situation changed dramatically after 1970. From 1970 to 2001, unemployment in Canada averaged 8.5%, while unemployment averaged 6.3% in the United States. In the five years 2001–2005, Canadian unemployment rates exceeded those in the United States by 1.9%.

What might account for this difference? The Global Macro box "Small Differences That Matter" explores this issue further.

Variations in the Natural Rate over Time

In estimating equation (11.6), we treated $\mu + z$ as a constant. But there is no reason to believe that μ and z are constant over time. The composition of the labour force, the structure of wage bargaining, the system of unemployment benefits, and so on are likely to change over time, leading to changes in the natural rate of unemployment.

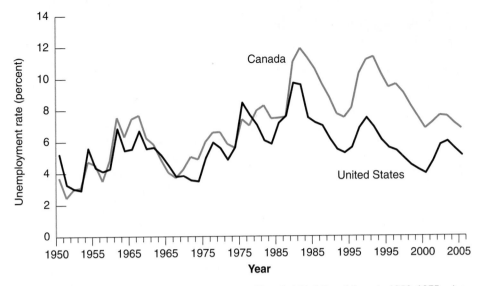

FIGURE 11-6

Unemployment Rates in Canada and the United States, 1950–2005

The impact of American recessions on Canadians seems clear. Higher unemployment in America raises unemployment in Canada. But the sharp decline in American unemployment in the 1990s to levels not seen for 30 years is striking, particularly when compared with Canadian unemployment rates that remained higher.

Source: Canadian unemployment rate 1950–1952 using *Historical Statistics of Canada*; 1953–1975 using CANSIM I variable D767611; and 1976–2004 using CANSIM II variable V12062815; United States unemployment rate using CANSIM II variable V122076.

Changes in the natural unemployment rate over time are hard to measure. Again, the reason is that we do not observe the natural rate, only the actual rate. But broad evolutions can be established by comparing average unemployment rates across decades. We see in Figure 11–6 that the natural rate of unemployment almost certainly increased in Canada. Many economists observe the sharp increase just after 1970. In 1971, the Canadian unemployment insurance system (now called Employment Insurance, or EI) was changed. A larger proportion of workers were included in coverage. The benefits were increased and the number of weeks of work required to qualify was reduced. Some of these changes were partially reversed in 1996. A very large number of labour economists have investigated the impact of these changes on the Canadian labour market.

The Limits of Our Understanding

The theory of the natural rate gives macroeconomists directions where to look for differences in natural rates across countries or for variations in the natural rate over time in a given country. But the truth is that macroeconomists' understanding of exactly which factors determine the natural rate of unemployment is still very limited. In particular, there is considerable uncertainty about the exact list of factors behind z and about the dynamic effects of each factor on the natural unemployment rate.

Let us return, for example, to an increase in the price of oil. When we examined its effects in the previous chapter—capturing it by an increase in the markup, μ—we concluded that an oil price increase would lead to an increase in the natural rate of unemployment. (The same conclusion holds in equation (11.6): An increase in μ increases the natural rate.)

But there is, in fact, more uncertainty about the effects of an increase in the price of oil than our discussion lets appear. Some of the bargaining models that underlie the wage-determination equation imply that workers may eventually accept a wage cut without a need for an increase in the unemployment rate. In terms of equation (11.6), these models suggest that when μ increases, z eventually decreases so that $\mu + z$, and thus the natural rate of unemployment $u_n = (\mu + z)/\alpha$, remains unchanged. Other models imply that although z may decrease in response to an increase in μ, the offset is only partial so that an increase in the price of oil has a permanent effect on the natural rate.

The two books on unemployment we mentioned in Chapter 9 reach different conclusions on this point. Layard and colleagues argue that such factors as the price of oil, indirect taxes, the real exchange rate, and the real interest rate have no permanent effect on the natural rate. Phelps argues that these factors can have permanent effects on the natural rate and explain a good part of the movements in unemployment in OECD countries over the last 20 years.

In a 1993 book with the wonderful title "Small Differences That Matter," a group of economists looked at various aspects of the labour market in Canada and the United States. From the title, you can guess the theme of the book. Small differences in the institutions related to labour markets were found to have substantial impacts on the lives of working Canadians and Americans.

The topics addressed included how wage inequality varies across the two countries, how the social safety net varies, and how immigration policies have differed. There are also the differences in the roles and sizes of unions. For this chapter, we want to learn why the natural rate of unemployment seems to be so much higher after 1970 in Canada than in the United States. Like in any good detective story, there are a number of suspects.

The usual suspect was already mentioned in the text: the more generous Canadian unemployment insurance system. This is quite clearly the case. Canada's unemployment system covers more workers, pays higher benefits, includes maternity benefits, and generally encourages labour force participation.

There are more unusual suspects as well. These measurement differences acoount for about 0.7% of the gap from 1993 to present day. In Canada, by definition, a full-time student cannot be considered unemployed. In the U.S. survey, a full-time student can state he or she is looking for a job and be considered unemployed. In the United States, a person is counted as unemployed only if he or she "actively searches," that is, takes action to find a job. In Canada, "passive search," even just look-ing at an ad, is sufficient to count as unemployed. Finally, there are differences in the treatment of those who are waiting for a known job to start. In Canada, these persons are unemployed, in the United States, they are not. There is the higher rate of incarceration in the United States. The prison population in the United States almost doubled between the mid-1980s and the mid-1990s. This removes from the labour force a large number of persons who would be likely to be counted as unemployed. There are also some differences in the way Aboriginal people are treated in the measurement of the unemployed. In both countries, Aboriginal people are more likely to be counted as unemployed.

Figure 1 replicates Figure 11–5 but with American data from 1970 to 2004. The estimated regression line in the graph is $\pi_t - \pi_{t-1} = 4.74 - 0.77u_t$. Using the methodology developed earlier, this line says that the natural rate of unemployment in the United States is 4.74/0.77 = 6.15%. This is, indeed, lower than the estimate for Canada using the data in Figure 11–5.

Sources:

Small Differences That Matter: Labor Markets and Income Maintenance in Canada and the United States. Edited by David Card and Richard B. Freeman (University of Chicago Press, 1993).

Craig W. Riddell, "Why is Canada's Unemployment Rate Persistently Higher than in the United States?" *Canadian Public Policy* 31, March 2005, pp. 93–100.

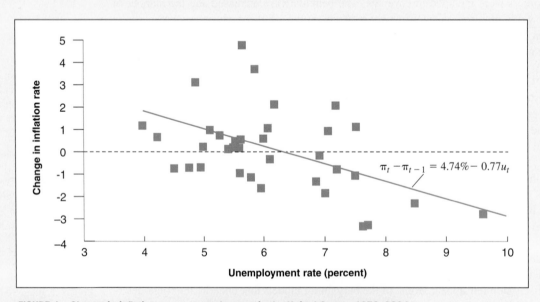

FIGURE 1   Change in inflation versus unemployment in the United States, 1970–2004

Source: U.S. consumer price index using Bureau of Labor Statistics **ftp://ftp.bls.gov/pub/special.requests/cpi/cpiai.txt**; U.S. unemployment rate using CANSIM II variable V122076.

The fact that different models lead to different conclusions is not unusual; the way to decide which model is most appropriate is to see which fits the data best. In this case, the data do not speak very clearly and have so far been unable to give us precise answers. Whether changes in the price of oil have a permanent effect on the natural rate of unemployment, for example, is still very much an open question.

The limits of our understanding are particularly clear and painful in the case of Europe today. Recall our discussion of the evolution of European unemployment in Chapter 1. The European unemployment rate, which until the early 1970s had been much lower than the unemployment rate of the United States or Canada, has steadily increased since.

As a matter of logic, this high unemployment rate could reflect a large deviation of the actual unemployment rate from the natural rate, or a high natural rate. How can we tell? By looking at the change in inflation. If inflation is decreasing fast, this is an indication that the actual unemployment rate is far above the natural rate. If inflation is stable, this is an indication that the actual and the natural rate are roughly equal and that the natural rate itself is high.

The EU countries have had slowly declining inflation over the second half of the 1990s. So, we can infer that the actual unemployment rate is above—but not far from—the natural rate. This point is made in Figure 11–7, which plots the change in the EU inflation rate against the unemployment rate for each year between 1961 and 2003. It is quite clear that in the euro area, the natural rate—the unemployment rate at which inflation remains constant—is now around 9%, much higher than it was two or three decades ago.

Why is the natural rate of unemployment so high in Europe today? The question is sufficiently important that we will spend a good part of Chapter 22 trying to answer it. But be warned: Although this is one of the major economic questions of our time, there is little agreement on the answer.

Looking at the change in inflation to infer whether high unemployment reflects a high natural rate, or unemployment above the natural rate. From equation (8.8):

$$\pi_t - \pi_{t-1} = -\alpha(u_t - u_n)$$

So, if $\pi_t - \pi_{t-1} < 0$, it must be that $u_t > u_n$. And if $\pi_t - \pi_{t-1} = 0$, it must be that $u_t = u_n$.

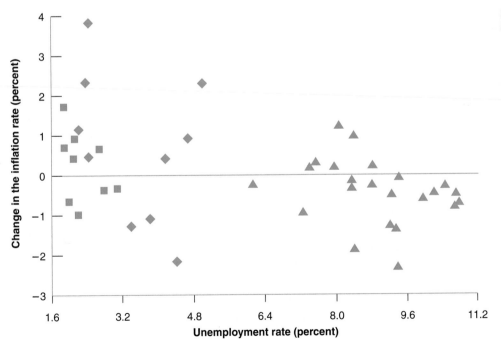

FIGURE 11–7

Change in Inflation versus Unemployment: Euro Area 1961–2003 (Squares denote the 1960s, diamonds the 1970s, triangles the dates since 1980)

The Phillips curve relation between the change in the inflation rate and the unemployment rate has shifted to the right over time, suggesting a steady increase in the natural unemployment rate in Europe since 1960.

- The aggregate supply relation can be expressed as a relation among inflation, expected inflation, and unemployment. The higher the expected inflation, the higher is actual inflation. The higher the unemployment, the lower is inflation.

- When inflation is not very persistent, expected inflation does not depend very much on past inflation. Thus, the aggregate supply relation becomes a relation between inflation and unemployment. This is what Phillips in the United Kingdom discovered when he looked in the late 1950s at the joint behaviour of unemployment and inflation.

- As inflation became more persistent in the 1970s and 1980s, expected inflation became increasingly dependent on past inflation. In Canada today, the aggregate supply relation takes the form of a relation between unemployment and the change in inflation. High unemployment leads to decreasing inflation; low unemployment leads to increasing inflation.

- The natural unemployment rate is the unemployment rate at which inflation remains constant. When the actual unemployment rate exceeds the natural rate, inflation decreases; when the actual unemployment rate is less than the natural rate, inflation increases.

- Changes in the way the inflation rate varies over time affect the way wage setters form expectations and how much they use wage indexation. When wage indexation is widespread, small changes in unemployment can lead to very large changes in inflation. At high rates of inflation, the relation between inflation and unemployment disappears altogether.

- The natural rate of unemployment depends on many factors that differ across countries and can change over time. Thus, the natural rate varies across countries: It is higher in Canada than in the United States. The natural rate may also vary over time. In Canada, the natural rate seems to have increased after 1970. In Europe, the natural rate has steadily increased since the 1960s.

- accelerationist Phillips curve, 210
- deflation, 207
- expectations-augmented Phillips curve, 210
- modified Phillips curve, 210

- nonaccelerating inflation rate of unemployment (NAIRU), 212
- wage indexation, 213
- wage-price spiral, 207

An asterisk denotes a harder question. [Web] indicates that the question requires access to the Internet.

1. **TRUE/FALSE/UNCERTAIN**

a. The original Phillips curve is the negative relation between unemployment and inflation first observed by Phillips for the United Kingdom.

b. The original Phillips curve relation has proven to be very stable across both countries and time.

c. The aggregate supply relation is consistent with the Phillips curve as observed before the 1970s, but not since.

d. Policy makers can only temporarily exploit the inflation-unemployment trade-off.

e. Before the 1970s, there was no natural rate of unemployment, and policy makers could achieve as low a rate of unemployment as they wanted.

f. The expectations-augmented Phillips curve is consistent with workers and firms adapting their expectations following the macroeconomic experience of the 1960s.

2. **THE PHILLIPS CURVE**

Discuss the following statements:

a. The Phillips curve implies that when unemployment is high, inflation is low, and vice versa. Therefore, we may experience either high inflation or high unemployment, but we will never experience both together.

b. As long as we do not mind having high inflation, we can achieve as low a level of unemployment as we want. All we have to do is increase the demand for goods and services by using, for example, expansionary fiscal policy.

3. MAINTAINING LOW UNEMPLOYMENT

Suppose that the Phillips curve is given by:

$$\pi_t = \pi_t^e + 0.1 - 2u_t$$

where

$$\pi_t^e = \theta\pi_{t-1}$$

Also, suppose that θ is initially equal to zero.

a. What is the natural rate of unemployment?

Suppose that the rate of unemployment is initially equal to the natural rate. In year t, the authorities decide to bring the unemployment rate down to 3% and hold it there forever.

b. Determine the rate of inflation in years t, $t + 1$, $t + 2$, $t + 10$, $t + 15$.

c. Do you believe the answer you gave in (b)? Why, or why not? (*Hint:* Think about how inflation expectations are formed.)

Now, suppose that in year $t + 5$, θ increases from 0 to 1.z.

d. Why might θ increase like this? What is the effect on u_n?

Suppose that government is still determined to keep u at 3% forever.

e. What will the inflation rate be in years $t + 5$, $t + 10$, and $t + 15$?

f. Do you believe the answer given in (e)? Why, or why not?

4. INDEXATION OF WAGES

Suppose that the Phillips curve is given by:

$$\pi_t - \pi_t^e = 0.1 - 2u_t$$

where

$$\pi_t^e = \pi_{t-1}$$

Suppose that inflation in year $t - 1$ is zero. In year t, the authorities decide to keep the unemployment rate at 4% forever.

a. Compute the rate of inflation for years t, $t + 1$, $t + 2$, and $t + 3$.

Now, suppose that half the workers have indexed labour contracts.

b. What is the new equation for the Phillips curve?

c. Repeat the exercise in (a).

d. What is the effect of indexation on the relation between π and u?

5. OIL SHOCKS, INFLATION, AND UNEMPLOYMENT

Suppose that the Phillips curve is given by:

$$\pi_t - \pi_t^e = 0.08 + 0.1\mu - 2u_t$$

where μ is the markup of prices over wages.

Suppose that μ is initially equal to 20% but that as a result of a sharp increase in oil prices, μ increases to 40% in year t and after.

a. Why would an increase in oil prices result in an increase in μ?

b. What is the long-run effect of the increase in μ on the natural rate of unemployment?

6. FAVOURABLE OIL SHOCKS, UNEMPLOYMENT, AND INFLATION

In sharp contrast to the oil shocks of the 1970s, the price of oil substantially declined in the early part of the 1990s.

a. Can this explain the good performance of both inflation and unemployment in the 1990s?

b. What has been the probable effect on the natural rate of unemployment?

7. USING THE NATURAL RATE OF UNEMPLOYMENT MODEL [WEB]

In the chapter, using data from 1970 to 2005, the equation $\pi_t - \pi_{t-1} = 4.3\% - 0.5u_t$ was found to best predict changes in inflation in Canada. You can check to see if the equation continues to describe changes in inflation after this book was written.

At the Statistics Canada Web site (**www.statcan.ca**), follow the links through Canadian Statistics, Economic Conditions, and then to Prices (here, you will find annual inflation rates for the last five calendar years under Consumer Prices). You will have to "go back" to Economic Conditions, and under the Labour Force and Unemployment Rates, you will find unemployment rates for the last five calendar years.

a. Calculate the change in inflation predicted by the equation $\pi_t - \pi_{t-1} = 4.3\% - 0.5u_t$ using the data from the five years listed. There will be four observations of $\pi_t - \pi_{t-1}$ and four matching observations of the corresponding value of u_t.

b. Graph your four observations. You could try to place these points on Figure 11–5 or draw your own graph.

c. Does it seem like the natural rate of unemployment is still 8.6%? Why, or why not?

FROM THE AGGREGATE SUPPLY RELATION TO THE PHILLIPS CURVE

The purpose of this appendix is to derive equation (11.1), expressing the relation among inflation, expected inflation, and unemployment.

The starting point is the aggregate supply relation among the price level, the expected price level, and the unemployment rate derived in Chapter 10:

$$P_t = P_t^e (1 + \mu)(1 - \alpha u_t + z)$$

Divide both sides by last year's price level, P_{t-1}:

$$\frac{P_t}{P_{t-1}} = \frac{P_t^e}{P_{t-1}} (1 + \mu)(1 - \alpha u_t + z) \quad (11A.1)$$

Rewrite the fraction P_t/P_{t-1} on the left side as:

$$\frac{P_t}{P_{t-1}} = 1 + \frac{P_t - P_{t-1}}{P_{t-1}} = 1 + \pi_t$$

where the first equality follows from adding and subtracting one, and the second from the definition of the inflation rate: $\pi_t \equiv (P_t - P_{t-1})/P_{t-1}$.

Do the same for the fraction P_t^e/P_{t-1} on the right side, using the definition of the expected inflation rate: $\pi_t^e \equiv (P_t^e - P_{t-1})/P_{t-1}$.

$$\frac{P_t^e}{P_{t-1}} = 1 + \frac{P_t^e - P_{t-1}}{P_{t-1}} = 1 + \pi_t^e$$

Replacing P_t/P_{t-1} and P_t^e/P_{t-1} in equation (11A.1) by the expressions we have just derived,

$$(1 + \pi_t) = (1 + \pi_t^e)(1 + \mu)(1 - \alpha u_t + z)$$

This gives us a relation among inflation (π_t), expected inflation (π_t^e), and the unemployment rate (u_t). The remaining steps make the relation look more friendly:

Divide both sides by $(1 + \pi_t^e)(1 + \mu)$:

$$\frac{(1 + \pi_t)}{(1 + \pi_t^e)(1 + \mu)} = 1 - \alpha u_t + z$$

As long as inflation, expected inflation, and the markup are not too large, a good approximation to this equation is given by (see propositions 3 and 6 in Appendix 2 at the end of the book):

$$1 + \pi_t - \pi_t^e - \mu = 1 - \alpha u_t + z$$

Rearranging gives:

$$\pi_t = \pi_t^e + (\mu + z) - \alpha u_t$$

This is equation (11.1) in the text. The inflation rate depends on the expected inflation rate and the unemployment rate, u_t. The relation depends on the markup, μ, on the factors that affect wage setting, z, and on the effect of the unemployment rate on wages, α.

CHAPTER 12
INFLATION, ACTIVITY, AND MONEY GROWTH

On January 8, 1988, Governor John Crow, head of the Bank of Canada at the time, used the Hanson lecture at the University of Alberta to lay out the agenda for monetary policy in Canada during his seven-year term. In 1987, inflation was 4.2% measured using the consumer price index (CPI) and 4.6% measured using the GDP deflator. The speech surprised Canadian economists because Governor Crow stated unequivocally, "Monetary policy should be conducted so as to achieve a pace of monetary expansion that promotes stability in the value of money. This means pursuing a policy aimed at achieving and maintaining stable prices." By 1992, both measures of inflation were less than 2%. Since then, inflation has remained less than 3%. The Bank of Canada achieved its goal of reducing inflation; however, the 1990–1991 recession was the largest economic downturn in Canada since the Great Depression. Governor Crow, whose term was up for renewal in 1994, did not receive a second term in office.

Why did Governor Crow decide to reduce inflation? How was it done? Why was there a recession? More generally, what are the effects of money growth on inflation and on activity? Our treatment of expectations in Chapter 10 was too simple to allow us to tackle these issues. But with our discussion of expectations and the introduction of the Phillips curve relation in Chapter 11, we now have what we need. In this chapter, we ask how inflation was reduced and model the recession that followed. In Chapter 26, we consider the choice of the optimal (best) rate of inflation.

The first section of this chapter looks at the links among output, unemployment, and inflation. The next several sections put these links together and discuss both the short-run and the medium-run effects of money growth on inflation and activity. The last section returns to the Canadian disinflation following the 1988 Hanson lecture.

12-1 | Output, Unemployment, and Inflation

In thinking about the interactions among output, unemployment, and inflation, you must keep in mind three relations:

1. Okun's law, which relates the change in unemployment to the deviation of output growth from normal.
2. The Phillips curve, which relates the change in inflation to the deviation of unemployment from the natural rate.
3. The aggregate demand relation, which relates output growth to the rate of growth of nominal money minus the rate of inflation.

This section looks at each relation on its own. The rest of the chapter looks at their joint implications.

Okun's Law: Output Growth and Changes in Unemployment

When we wrote the relation between output and unemployment in Chapter 9, we did so under two convenient but restrictive assumptions. We assumed that output and employment moved together, so changes in output led to equal changes in employment. And we assumed that the labour force was constant, so changes in employment were reflected one for one in opposite changes in unemployment.

We must now move beyond these assumptions. To see why, think about what they imply for the relation between the rate of output growth and the unemployment rate. As output and employment move together, a 1% increase in output leads to a 1% increase in employment. And because movements in employment are reflected in opposite movements in unemployment, a 1% increase in employment leads to a decrease of 1% in the unemployment rate.[1] Let g_{yt} denote the growth rate of output. Then, under these two assumptions, the following relation should hold:

$$u_t - u_{t-1} = -g_{yt} \tag{12.1}$$

The change in the unemployment rate should be equal to the negative of the growth rate of output. If output growth is, say, 4%, then the unemployment rate should decline by 4%.

Contrast this with the actual relation between output growth and the change in the unemployment rate, the relation known as Okun's law. Figure 12–1 plots the change in the unemployment rate against the rate of output growth for each year since 1962. It also plots the regression line that best fits the scatter of points. The relation corresponding to the line is given by:

$$u_t - u_{t-1} = -0.33(g_{yt} - 3.7\%) \tag{12.2}$$

Equation (12.2) differs in two ways from equation (12.1):

If $g_{yt} = 3.7\%$, then

$u_t - u_{t-1}$
$= -0.33(3.7\% - 3.7\%)$
$= 0$

▶ • Annual output growth has to be at least 3.7% to prevent the unemployment rate from rising. This is because of two factors we have neglected so far—both the labour force and the productivity of labour are growing over time.

---

[1]**DIGGING DEEPER**. This last step is only approximately correct. Remember the definition of the unemployment rate:

$$u \equiv U/L = 1 - N/L$$

If the labour force L is fixed,

$$\Delta u = \Delta U/L = -\Delta N/L = -(\Delta N/N)(N/L)$$

where the last equality follows from multiplying and dividing by N. If N/L is equal to, say, 0.95, then a 1% increase in employment leads to a decrease of 0.95% in the unemployment rate. The result in the text is based on approximating N/L by 1, so a 1% increase in employment leads to a decrease of 1% in the unemployment rate.

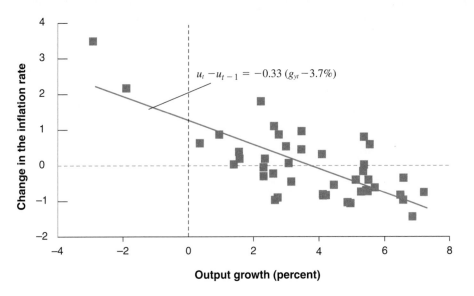

FIGURE 12–1

Changes in the Unemployment Rate versus Output Growth in Canada, 1962–2005

High output growth is associated with a reduction in the unemployment rate; low output growth is associated with an increase in the unemployment rate.

$$u_t - u_{t-1} = -0.33\,(g_{yt} - 3.7\%)$$

Output growth (percent)

Change in the inflation rate

Source: Real GDP using CANSIM II variable V3862685; unemployment rate 1976–2005 using CANSIM II variable V2062815 after 1976, 1961–1975 series D233, *Historical Statistics of Canada.*

Suppose the labour force grows at 2% a year. To maintain a constant unemployment rate, employment must grow at the same rate as the labour force, at 2% a year.

Suppose also that labour productivity—output per worker—is growing at 1.7% a year. If employment grows at 2% and labour productivity grows at 1.7%, output will grow at 1.7% + 2% = 3.7%. In other words, to maintain a constant unemployment rate, output growth must be equal to 3.7%. In Canada, the sum of the rate of labour-force growth and of labour-productivity growth has been equal to 3.7% on average since 1962, and this is why the number 3.7% appears on the right side of equation (12.2). We will call the rate of output growth needed to maintain a constant unemployment rate the **normal growth rate** in what follows.

● The coefficient on the deviation of output growth from the normal growth rate is −0.33 in equation (12.2), not −1 as in equation (12.1). Put another way, output growth of 1% in excess of the normal growth rate leads to only a 0.33% reduction in the unemployment rate rather than a 1% reduction. There are two reasons why:

1. Firms adjust employment less than one for one in response to deviations of output growth from the normal growth rate. More specifically, output growth that is 1% above normal for one year leads to only a 0.67% increase in the employment rate.

   One reason is that some workers are needed no matter what the level of output is. The accounting department of a firm, for example, needs roughly the same number of employees whether the firm is selling more or less than normal.

   Another reason is that training new employees is costly. That is why many firms prefer to keep current workers rather than lay them off when output is lower than normal and to ask them to work overtime rather than hire new employees when output is higher than normal. In bad times, firms, in effect, hoard labour; this behaviour is called **labour hoarding**.

2. An increase in the employment rate does not lead to a one-for-one decrease in the unemployment rate. More specifically, a 0.67% increase in the employment rate leads to only a 0.33% decrease in the unemployment rate.

   The reason is that labour participation increases. When employment increases, not all the new jobs are filled by the unemployed. Some of the jobs go to people who

Putting the two steps together:

1% increase in output above normal ⇒

0.67% increase in employment ⇒

0.33% decrease in the unemployment rate.

The coefficient β in Okun's law gives the effect on the unemployment rate of deviations of output growth from normal. A value of β of 0.4 tells us that output growth 1% above the normal growth rate for 1 year decreases the unemployment rate by 0.4%.

The coefficient β depends, in part, on how firms adjust employment in response to their fluctuations in their productions. This adjustment of employment depends, in turn, on such factors as the internal organization of firms and the legal and social constraints on hiring and firing. As these differ across countries, we would, therefore, expect the coefficient β to differ across countries, and, indeed, it does. Table 1 gives the estimated coefficient β for a number of countries.

The first column gives estimates of β based on data from 1960 to 1980. The United States has the highest coefficient (0.39), followed by Germany (0.20), the United Kingdom (0.15), and Japan (0.02).

The ranking in the first column fits well with what we know about the behaviour of firms and the structure of firing/hiring regulations across countries. As you saw in Chapter 8, Japanese firms offer a high degree of job security to their workers, so variations in Japan's output have little effect on employment and, by implication, little effect on unemployment. So, it is no surprise that β is smallest in Japan. It is no surprise that β is largest in the United States, where there are few social and legal constraints on firms' adjustment of employment. Legal restrictions on firing—from severance pay to the need for legal permission from the state to terminate employment—explain why the coefficients estimated for the two European countries are in-between those of Japan and the United States.

The second column gives estimates based on data from 1981 to 2003. The coefficient is unchanged for the United States, but it becomes higher for the other three countries. This again fits with what we know about firms and regulations. Increased competition in goods markets since the early 1980s has led firms in most countries to reconsider and reduce their commitment to job security. And at the urging of firms, legal restrictions on hiring and firing have been considerably weakened in many countries. Both factors have led to a larger response of employment to fluctuations in output, thus to a larger value of β.

TABLE 1	Okun's Law Coefficients Across Countries and Time	
Country	**1960–1980** β	**1981–2003** β
United States	0.39	0.39
United Kingdom	0.15	0.54
Germany	0.20	0.32
Japan	0.02	0.12

Source: Calculations by Olivier Blanchard.

Okun's law:
$$g_{yt} > \bar{g}_y \Rightarrow u_t < u_{t-1}$$

were classified as *out of the labour force*, meaning they were not actively looking for a job. And as labour-market prospects improve for the unemployed, some discouraged workers—who were previously classified as out of the labour force—decide to start actively looking for a job and become classified as unemployed. For both reasons, the decrease in unemployment is smaller than the increase in employment.

Using letters rather than numbers, let us write the relation between output growth and the change in the unemployment rate as:

$$u_t - u_{t-1} = -\beta(g_{yt} - \bar{g}_y) \tag{12.3}$$

where $\bar{g}_y$, is the normal growth rate of the economy (about 3.7% for Canada between 1962 and 2005), and β (the Greek lowercase letter beta) tells us how growth in excess of normal growth translates into decreases in the unemployment rate. In Canada, β equals 0.33. (The evidence for other countries is given in the Global Macro box "Okun's Law across Countries.")

The Phillips Curve: Unemployment and the Change in Inflation

We derived in Chapter 11 the following relation among inflation, expected inflation, and unemployment (equation [11.7]):

$$\pi_t = \pi_t^e - \alpha(u_t - u_n) \tag{12.4}$$

Inflation depends on expected inflation and on the deviation of unemployment from the natural rate.

We then argued that expected inflation appears to be well approximated by last year's inflation so that we can replace π_t^e by π_{t-1}. With this assumption, the relation between inflation and unemployment takes the form:

$$\pi_t - \pi_{t-1} = -\alpha(u_t - u_n) \tag{12.5}$$

Unemployment above the natural rate leads to a decrease in inflation; unemployment below the natural rate leads to an increase in inflation. The parameter α gives the effect of unemployment on the change in inflation. We saw in Chapter 11 that since 1970, in Canada, the natural unemployment rate has been on average equal to 8.6% and α roughly equal to 0.5. This value of α means that an unemployment rate of 1% above the natural rate for one year leads to a decrease in the inflation rate of about 0.5%. We will refer to equation (12.5) as the Phillips curve.

> Phillips curve:
> $u_t < u_n \Rightarrow \pi_t > \pi_{t-1}$

> We should call equation (12.5) the "Phillips relation" and reserve the expression "Phillips curve" for the curve that represents the relation. But the tradition is to use "Phillips curve" to denote equation (12.5). Tradition is respected here.

The Aggregate Demand Relation: Money Growth, Inflation, and Output Growth

In Chapter 10, we wrote the aggregate demand relation as a relation between output and the real money stock, government spending, and taxes (equation (10.2)). To focus on the relation between the real money stock and output, we will ignore changes in factors other than real money here and write the aggregate demand relation simply as:

$$Y_t = \gamma \frac{M_t}{P_t} \tag{12.6}$$

where γ (the Greek lowercase gamma) is a positive parameter. This equation states that the demand for goods, and thus output, is simply proportional to the real money stock. This simplification will make our life easier. You should keep in mind, however, that behind this relation hides the set of steps we saw in the *IS-LM* model:

- An increase in the real money stock leads to a decrease in the interest rate.
- The decrease in the interest rate leads to an increase in the demand for goods and to an increase in output.

> $M/P\uparrow \Rightarrow i\downarrow$
> $i\downarrow \Rightarrow Y\uparrow$
> Putting the two steps together: $M/P\uparrow \Rightarrow Y\uparrow$

For our purposes, we need to move from the relation between levels (the output level, the level of nominal money, and the price level) in equation (12.6) to a relation between growth rates (of output, nominal money, and prices). Let g_{yt} be the growth rate of output. Let g_{mt} be the growth rate of nominal money, and let π_t be the growth rate of prices—the rate of inflation. Then, from equation (12.6), it follows that:

$$g_{yt} = g_{mt} - \pi_t \tag{12.7}$$

> If a variable is the ratio of two variables, its growth rate is the difference between the growth rates of these two variables (proposition 8 in Appendix 2 at the end of the book). So, if $Y = \gamma M/P$, and γ is constant, $g_y = g_m - \pi$.

The growth rate of output is equal to the growth rate of nominal money minus the rate of inflation. Given money growth, high inflation leads to a decrease in the real money stock and a decrease in output; low inflation leads to an increase in the real money stock and an increase in output.

> Aggregate demand relation:
> $g_{mt} > \pi_t \Rightarrow g_{yt} > 0$

12-2 | The Medium Run

Let's collect the three relations among inflation, unemployment, and output growth we derived in section 12-1. Okun's law relates the change in the unemployment rate to the deviation of output growth from normal (equation (12.3)):

$$\underset{\text{unemployment rate}}{\underset{\text{Change in the}}{}} \qquad \underset{\text{growth from normal}}{\underset{\text{Deviation of output}}{}}$$

$$u_t - u_{t-1} = -\beta(g_{yt} - \bar{g}_y)$$

The Phillips curve relates the change in inflation to the deviation of the unemployment rate from its natural rate (equation (12.5)):

$$\underset{\text{inflation rate}}{\underset{\text{Change in the}}{}} \qquad \underset{\text{from the natural rate}}{\underset{\text{Deviation of unemployment}}{}}$$

$$\pi_t - \pi_{t-1} = -\alpha(u_t - u_n)$$

The aggregate demand relation relates output growth to the difference between nominal money growth and inflation (equation (12.7)):

$$\underset{\text{of output}}{\underset{\text{Rate of growth}}{}} \qquad \underset{\text{money minus rate of inflation}}{\underset{\text{Rate of growth of nominal}}{}}$$

$$g_{yt} = g_{mt} - \pi_t$$

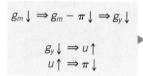

$$g_m \downarrow \Rightarrow g_m - \pi \downarrow \Rightarrow g_y \downarrow$$

$$g_y \downarrow \Rightarrow u \uparrow$$
$$u \uparrow \Rightarrow \pi \downarrow$$

Our task is now to see what these three relations imply for the effects of money growth on output, unemployment, and inflation. We can go some way already. Take, for example, a decrease in money growth:

- From the aggregate demand relation, given inflation, lower money growth implies a decrease in output growth.
- From Okun's law, this decrease in growth leads to an increase in unemployment.
- From the Phillips curve, higher unemployment implies a decrease in inflation.

We can already see that the initial effects of lower money growth are to slow output growth, increase unemployment, and decrease inflation. But what happens after this initial response is harder to tell: Does unemployment keep going up? What happens to inflation? The easiest way to answer these questions is to work backward in time, to start by looking at the medium run—that is, where the economy ends when all the dynamics have worked themselves out—and then to return to the dynamics. This section looks at the *medium run*. The following sections return to dynamics.

Assume that the central bank maintains a constant growth rate of nominal money, call it $\bar{g}_m$. What will be the values of output growth, unemployment, and inflation in the medium run?

- In the medium run, unemployment must be constant; unemployment cannot be increasing or decreasing forever. Putting $u_t = u_{t-1}$ in Okun's law implies that $g_{yt} = \bar{g}_y$. *In the medium run, output grows at its normal rate of growth, $\bar{g}_y$.*

Medium run: $g_y = \bar{g}_y$

- With money growth equal to $\bar{g}_m$ and output growth equal to $\bar{g}_y$, the aggregate demand relation implies that inflation is constant and satisfies:

$$\bar{g}_y = \bar{g}_m - \pi$$

Moving π to the left, and $\bar{g}_y$ to the right, gives

$$\underset{\text{of nominal money}}{\underset{\text{Rate of growth}}{}} \qquad \underset{\text{rate of output}}{\underset{\text{Normal growth}}{}}$$

Inflation rate

$$\pi = \bar{g}_m \qquad\qquad - \bar{g}_y \qquad\qquad (12.8)$$

Medium run: $\pi = \bar{g}_m - \bar{g}_y$

In the medium run, inflation is equal to nominal money growth minus normal output growth. It will be convenient to call nominal money growth minus normal output growth

adjusted nominal money growth so that this result can be stated as: *In the medium run, inflation equals adjusted nominal money growth.*

One way to think about this result is as follows: A growing level of output implies a growing level of transactions and thus a growing demand for real money. If output is growing at 3.7%, the real money stock must also grow at 3.7% per year. If the nominal money stock grows at a rate different from 3.7%, the difference must show up in inflation (or deflation). For example, if nominal money growth is 10%, then inflation must be equal to 6.3%.

- If inflation is constant, then $\pi_t = \pi_{t-1}$. Putting $\pi_t = \pi_{t-1}$ in the Phillips curve implies that $u_t = u_n$. *In the medium run, the unemployment rate must be equal to the natural rate.*

◀ Medium run: $u = u_n$

These results are the natural extension of the results we derived in Chapter 10. There, we saw that *changes in the level of money* were neutral in the medium run: They had no effect on either output or unemployment but were reflected one for one in changes in the price level. We see here that a similar neutrality result applies to *changes in the rate of growth of money.* Changes in nominal money growth have no effect on output or unemployment in the medium run but are reflected one for one in changes in the rate of inflation.

In the medium run, changes in money growth have no effect on output or on unemployment. ◀ They are reflected one for one in changes in the rate of inflation.

Another way to state this last result is that the only determinant of inflation in the medium run is adjusted money growth. Milton Friedman put it this way: *Inflation is always and everywhere a monetary phenomenon.* Unless they lead to higher nominal money growth, such factors as the monopoly power of firms, strong unions, strikes, fiscal deficits, the price of oil, and so on have no effect on inflation *in the medium run.*

The "unless" qualification ◀ is important. When we study episodes of very high inflation in Chapter 23, we will see that fiscal deficits often lead to money creation and to higher nominal money growth.

We can summarize the results of this section with the help of Figure 12–2, which plots the unemployment rate on the horizontal axis and the inflation rate on the vertical axis.

In the medium run, the unemployment rate is equal to the natural rate. The economy must thus be somewhere on the vertical line at $u = u_n$.

In the medium run, inflation must be equal to adjusted money growth—the rate of nominal money growth minus the normal rate of growth of output. This is represented by the horizontal line at $\pi = \bar{g}_m - \bar{g}_y$.

A decrease in nominal money growth from $\bar{g}_m$ to $\bar{g}'_m$ shifts the horizontal line downward, moving the equilibrium from point A to point B. The inflation rate decreases by the same amount as the decrease in nominal money growth. There is no change in the unemployment rate, which is still equal to u_n.

Having looked at what happens in the medium run, we can now return to the dynamics of adjustment. This is the focus of the next three sections.

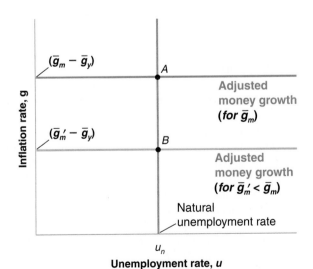

FIGURE 12–2

Inflation and Unemployment in the Medium Run

In the medium run, unemployment is equal to the natural rate, and inflation is equal to adjusted money growth.

12-3 | Disinflation: A First Pass

What is so bad about high inflation if growth is proceeding at a normal rate ▶ and unemployment is at its natural rate? To answer, we need to discuss the costs of inflation and why policy makers take steps to decrease inflation. We will do this in Chapters 23 and 26.

Suppose the economy is in medium-run equilibrium: Unemployment is at its natural rate, and the rate of growth of output is equal to the normal growth rate. But the inflation rate is high, and there is a general consensus that it must be reduced.

We know from the previous section that achieving lower inflation requires lowering money growth. But we also know that a decrease in money growth will slow output growth and increase unemployment, at least initially. Knowing this, how should the central bank achieve **disinflation**—that is, the decrease in inflation? Should it decrease money growth quickly or slowly? Let us see what our equations imply.

How Much Unemployment? And for How Long?

Start with the Phillips curve relation (equation (12.5)):

$$\pi_t - \pi_{t-1} = -\alpha(u_t - u_n)$$

This relation makes it clear that disinflation can be obtained only at the cost of higher unemployment. For the left side of the equation to be negative—that is, for inflation to decrease—the term $(u_t - u_n)$ must be positive: The unemployment rate must exceed the natural rate.

When should we use "percentage point" rather than "percent"? Suppose you are told that the unemployment rate, which was equal to 10%, has increased by 5%. Is it 5% of itself, in which case the unemployment rate is equal to $(1.05) \times 10\% = 10.5\%$? Or is it 5 ▶ percentage points, in which case it is equal to $10\% + 5\% = 15\%$? The use of "percentage point" rather than "percent" helps avoid the ambiguity. If you are told the unemployment rate has increased by 5 percentage points, this means that the unemployment rate is $10\% + 5\% = 15\%$.

The equation actually has a stronger and quite startling implication: The total amount of unemployment required for a given decrease in inflation does not depend on the speed at which disinflation is achieved. In other words, disinflation can be achieved quickly, at the cost of very high unemployment for a few years; or it can be achieved more slowly, with a smaller increase in unemployment spread over more years. In both cases, the total amount of unemployment, summing over the years, will be the same.

Let us now see why this is. Define first a **point-year of excess unemployment** as a difference between the actual and the natural unemployment rate of one percentage point for one year. For example, if the natural rate is 8.6%, an actual unemployment rate of 11% four years in a row corresponds to $4 \times (11 - 8.6) = 9.6$ point-years of excess unemployment.

Now, suppose a central bank wants to reduce inflation by x percentage points. To make things simpler, let us use specific numbers: Assume that the central bank wants to reduce inflation from 14% to 4% so that x is equal to 10 percentage points. Let us also assume that α equals 0.5.

Suppose it wants to achieve the reduction in inflation in just one year. Equation (12.5) tells us that what is required is one year of unemployment at 20 percentage points above the natural rate. In this case, the right side of the equation is equal to -10 percentage points, and the inflation rate decreases by 10 percentage points within a year.

Suppose it wants to achieve the reduction in inflation over a period of two years. Equation (12.5) tells us that two years of unemployment are required at 10 percentage points above the natural rate. During each of the two years, the right side of the equation is equal to -10 percentage points, so the inflation rate decreases by 5 percentage points each year, thus by 10 percentage points over two years.

By the same reasoning, reducing inflation over a period of five years requires five years of unemployment at 4 percentage points above the natural rate; reducing inflation over a period of 10 years requires 10 years of unemployment at 2 percentage points above the natural rate, and so on.

Note that in each case, the number of point-years of excess unemployment required to decrease inflation is the same, namely, 20: 1 year times 20 percentage points excess unemployment in the first scenario, 2 years times 10 percentage points in the second, 10 years times 2 percentage points in the last. The implication is straightforward: The central bank can choose the distribution of excess unemployment over time, but it cannot change the total number of point-years of excess unemployment.

Sacrifice ratio

$$= \frac{\text{Excess point-years}}{\text{Decrease in inflation}}$$ ▶

We can state this conclusion another way. Define the **sacrifice ratio** as the number of point-years of excess unemployment needed to achieve a decrease in inflation of 1 percentage point. Then, equation (12.5) implies that this ratio is independent of policy and simply equal to $(1/\alpha)$. If α roughly equals 0.5, as the estimated Phillips curve suggests, then the sacrifice ratio is roughly equal to two.

If the sacrifice ratio is constant, does this imply that the speed of disinflation is irrelevant? No. Suppose that the central bank tried to achieve the 10 percentage points decrease in inflation in one year. As we have just seen, this would require an unemployment rate of 20 percentage points above the natural rate for one year. With a natural unemployment rate of 8.6%, this would require increasing the actual unemployment rate to 28.6% for one year. From Okun's law, using a value of 0.33 for β and a normal output growth rate of 3.7%, output growth would have to satisfy:

$$u_t - u_{t-1} = -\beta \; (g_{yt} - \bar{g}_y)$$
$$28.6\% - 8.6\% = -0.33(g_{yt} - 3.7\%)$$

This implies a value for $g_{yt} = -(20\%)/0.33 + 3.7\% = -56.9\%$. In words, output growth would have to equal -56.9% for a year! For comparison, the largest negative growth rate in Canada this century was -12% in 1931, during the Great Depression. It is fair to say that macroeconomists do not know with great confidence what would happen if monetary policy were aimed at inducing such a large negative growth rate. But most would surely be unwilling to try. The increase in the overall unemployment rate would lead to extremely high unemployment rates for some groups—specifically the young and the unskilled. Not only would the welfare costs for these groups be large, but such high unemployment might leave permanent scars. The sharp drop in output would most likely also lead to a large number of bankruptcies, with long-lasting effects on economic activity. In short, the disruptions from a fast disinflation might be very large.

This suggests very high unemployment may have long-lasting effects on the natural rate itself. This will be one of the questions we take up when looking at European unemployment in Chapter 22.

Working Out the Required Path of Money Growth

Let us assume that based on the computations we just went through, the central bank decides to decrease the inflation rate from 14% to 4% in five years. Clearly, it does not control either inflation or unemployment directly. What it controls is money growth. Using our equations, we can solve for the path of money growth that will achieve the disinflation.

As we saw in Chapter 4, what the central bank actually controls is central bank money, not the money stock itself. We will ignore this complication here.

Let us make the same numerical assumptions as before. Normal output growth is 3.7%. The natural rate of unemployment is 8.6%. The parameter α in the Phillips curve is equal to 0.5; β in Okun's law is equal to 0.33. These are the values estimated from Canadian data over the past two chapters. Table 12–1 shows how to derive the path of money growth needed to achieve 10% disinflation over five years.

In year 0, before the disinflation, output growth is proceeding at its normal rate of 3.7%. Unemployment is at the natural rate, 8.6%; inflation is running at 14%; nominal money growth is equal to 17.7%. Real money growth equals $17.7\% - 14\% = 3.7\%$, the same as output growth.

The decision is then made to reduce inflation from 14% to 4% over five years, starting in year 1.

The easiest way to solve for the path of money growth is to start from the desired path of inflation, find the required path of unemployment and the required path of output growth, and, finally, derive the required path of money growth.

The way to read the rest of this section is first to follow the logic of the step-by-step computations; do not worry about understanding the broader picture. When you have done this, step back and look at the way the economy adjusts over time. Make sure you can tell the story in words.

- The first line of Table 12–1 gives the *target path of inflation*. Inflation starts at 14% before the change in monetary policy, decreases by 2 percentage points a year from year 1 to year 5, and then remains at its lower level of 4% thereafter.

◀ From the inflation path.

- The second line gives the required *path of unemployment* implied by the Phillips curve. If inflation is to decrease by 2 percentage points a year and $\alpha = 0.5$, the economy must accept five years of unemployment at 4 percentage points above the natural rate (5×2 percentage points = 10 percentage points, the required decrease in inflation). Thus, from year 1 to year 5, the unemployment rate must equal $8.6\% + 4\% = 12.6\%$.

To the path of unemployment.

TABLE 12–1 Engineering Disinflation

	Before	Year						After		
		Disinflation								
	0	1	2	3	4	5	6	7	8
Inflation (%)	14	12	10	8	6	4	4	4	4
Unemployment rate (%)	8.6	12.6	12.6	12.6	12.6	12.6	8.6	8.6	8.6
Output growth (%)	3.7	−8.42	3.7	3.7	3.7	3.7	15.82	3.7	3.7
Nominal money growth (%)	17.7	3.58	13.7	11.7	9.7	7.7	19.82	7.7	7.7

To the path of output growth. ▶ • The third line gives the required *path of output growth*. From Okun's law, we know that the initial increase in unemployment requires lower output growth. With β equal to 0.33, an initial increase in unemployment of 4 percentage points requires the rate of output growth to be lower than normal by 4% ÷ 0.33 = 12.12 percentage points. Given a normal growth rate of 3.7%, the economy must therefore have a growth rate of 3.7% − 12.12% = −8.42% in year 1. There must be a huge recession in year 1.

From years 2 to 5, growth must proceed at a rate sufficient to maintain the unemployment rate constant at 12.6%. Thus, output must grow at its normal rate, 3.7%. In other words, from years 2 to 5, the economy grows at a normal rate but has an unemployment rate that exceeds the natural rate by 4 percentage points.

Once disinflation is achieved, a burst of output growth in year 6 is needed to return unemployment to normal: To decrease the unemployment rate by 4 percentage points in a year, the rate of output growth must exceed normal growth by 4% ÷ 0.33, thus by 12.12%. The economy must therefore grow at 3.7% + 12.12% = 15.82% for one year.

To the path of nominal money growth. ▶ • The fourth line gives the implied path of *nominal money growth*. From the aggregate demand relation, (equation (12.7)), we know that output growth equals nominal money growth minus inflation or, equivalently, that nominal money growth equals output growth plus inflation. Adding the numbers for inflation in the first line and for output growth in the third gives us the required path for the rate of nominal money growth.

The path looks surprising at first: Money growth goes down sharply in year 1, then up again, then slowly down for three years, then up again in the year following disinflation, to finally reach its permanent lower level of 7.7%. But this is easy to explain: To start disinflation, the central bank must induce an increase in unemployment. This requires a sharp contraction in money growth in year 1. The decrease in nominal money growth—from 17.7% to 3.58%—is much sharper than the decrease in inflation—from 14% to 12%. The result is thus a sharp decrease in real money growth, decreasing demand and output, which increases the unemployment rate.

For the next four years, monetary policy is aimed at maintaining unemployment at 12.6%, not at increasing unemployment further. Nominal money growth is aimed at allowing demand and therefore output to grow at the normal growth rate. Put another way, nominal money growth is set equal to inflation plus the normal growth rate of 3.7%. And as inflation decreases—because of high unemployment—so does nominal money growth.

At the end of the disinflation, the central bank must allow unemployment to return to its natural rate (otherwise, inflation would continue to decrease.) This implies that it provides in year 6 a one-time increase in money growth before returning, from year 7 on, to the new lower rate of money growth.

FIGURE 12-3

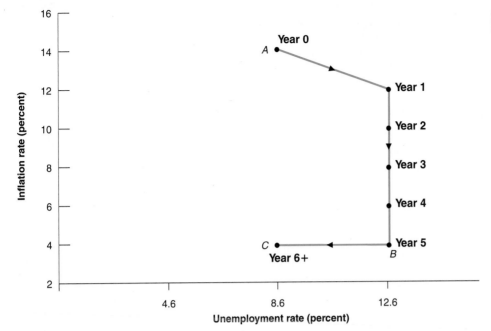

A Disinflation Path

Five years of unemployment above the natural rate lead to a permanent decrease in inflation.

Figure 12–3 shows the path of unemployment and inflation implied by this disinflation path. In year 0, the economy is at point *A*: The unemployment rate is 8.6%, and the inflation rate is 14%. Years 1 to 5 are years of disinflation, during which the economy moves from *A* to *B*. Unemployment is higher than the natural rate, leading to a steady decline in inflation. Inflation decreases until it reaches 4%. From year 6 on, the economy remains at point *C*, with unemployment back down to its natural rate and an inflation rate of 4%. *In the medium run, money growth and inflation are lower, and the unemployment rate and output growth are back to normal;* this is the neutrality result we obtained in section 12-2. *But the transition to lower money growth and lower inflation is associated with a period of higher unemployment.*

The disinflation path drawn in Figure 12–3 is one of many possible paths. We could have looked instead at a path that front-loaded the increase in the unemployment rate and allowed it to return slowly to the natural rate, avoiding the awkward increase in money growth that takes place at the end of our scenario (year 6 in Table 12–1). Or we could have looked at a path where the central bank decreased the rate of money growth from 17.7% to 7.7% at once, letting inflation and unemployment adjust over time.[2] But all the paths we would draw would share one characteristic: The total unemployment cost—that is, the number of point-years of excess unemployment—would be the same. Put another way, *unemployment has to remain above the natural rate by a large enough amount, and/or long enough, to achieve disinflation.*

The analysis we have just developed is very much the type of analysis economists at central banks were conducting in the late 1970s. The econometric model they used, as well as most econometric models in use at the time, shared our simple model's property that policy could change the timing, but not the number of point-years of excess unemployment. We will call this the *traditional approach* in what follows. This traditional approach was challenged by two groups of academic economists. The next section presents their arguments and the discussion that followed.

---

[2]**DIGGING DEEPER**. It would seem natural to look at a policy where the central bank permanently decreases the rate of money growth, say, from 17.7% to 7.7%. If you trace the effects of such a policy on output, unemployment, and inflation (solve for output, unemployment, and inflation for time *t*, then for *t* + 1, and so on), you will find that it leads to a complicated path of inflation and unemployment, with inflation actually being lower than its new medium-run value for some time.

12-4 | Expectations, Credibility, and Nominal Contracts

The focus of both groups of economists was the role of expectations and how changes in expectation formation might affect the unemployment cost of disinflation. But despite this common focus, they reached quite different conclusions.

Expectations and Credibility: The Lucas Critique

The conclusions of the first group were based on the work of Robert Lucas and Thomas Sargent of the University of Chicago.

In what has become known as the **Lucas critique**, Lucas pointed out that when trying to predict the effects of a major change in policy—such as the change considered by the Bank of Canada in 1988—it could be very misleading to take as given the relations estimated from past data.

In the case of the Phillips curve, taking equation (12.5) as a given was equivalent to assuming that wage setters would keep expecting inflation in the future to be the same as in the past, that the way wage setters formed expectations would not change in response to the change in policy. This was an unwarranted assumption, Lucas argued. Why shouldn't wage setters take policy changes into account? If they believed that the Bank of Canada was committed to lower inflation, they might well expect inflation to be lower in the future than in the past. If they lowered their expectations of inflation, then actual inflation would decline without the need for a protracted recession.

The logic of Lucas's argument can be seen by returning to equation (12.4):

$$\pi_t = \pi_t^e - \alpha(u_t - u_n)$$

If $\pi_t^e = \pi_{t-1}$, the Phillips curve is given by

$$\pi_t - \pi_{t-1} = -\alpha(u_t - u_n)$$

To achieve $\pi_t < \pi_{t-1}$, one must have $u_t > u_n$.

If wage setters kept forming expectations of inflation by looking at last year's inflation (if $\pi_t^e = \pi_{t-1}$), then the only way to decrease inflation would, indeed, be to accept higher unemployment for some time; we explored the implications of this assumption in the preceding section.

But if wage setters could be convinced that inflation was, indeed, going to be lower than in the past, they would decrease their expectations of inflation. This would, in turn, reduce actual inflation, without necessarily any change in the unemployment rate. For example, if wage setters were convinced that inflation, which had been running at 14% in the past, would be only 4% in the future, and if they formed expectations accordingly, then inflation would decrease to 4%, *even if unemployment remained at the natural rate*:

$$\pi_t = \pi_t^e - \alpha(u_t - u_n)$$
$$4\% = 4\% - \alpha(0\%)$$

Money growth, inflation, and expected inflation could all be reduced without the need for a recession. Put another way, decreases in money growth could be neutral not only in the medium run but also in the short run.

Lucas and Sargent did not believe that disinflation could really take place without some increase in unemployment. But Sargent, looking at the historical evidence on the end of several very high inflations, concluded that the increase in unemployment could be small. The sacrifice ratio—the amount of excess unemployment needed to achieve disinflation—might be much lower than suggested by the traditional approach. The essential ingredient of successful disinflation, he argued, was **credibility** of monetary policy—the belief by wage setters that the central bank was truly committed to reducing inflation. Only credibility would lead wage setters to change the way they formed expectations. Furthermore, he argued, a clear and quick disinflation program was much more likely to be credible than a protracted one that offered plenty of opportunities for reversal and political infighting along the way.

The credibility view: Fast disinflation is likely to be more credible than slow disinflation. Credibility decreases the unemployment cost of disinflation. Thus, the central bank should implement a fast disinflation.

Nominal Rigidities and Contracts

A contrary view was taken by Stanley Fischer, of the Massachusetts Institute of Technology, and John Taylor, then at Columbia University. Both emphasized the presence of **nominal rigidities**, meaning that in modern economies, many wages and prices are set in nominal terms for some time and are typically not re-adjusted when there is a change in policy.

Fischer argued that even with credibility, too rapid a decrease in money growth would lead to higher unemployment. Even if the Bank of Canada fully convinced workers and firms that money growth was going to be lower, the wages set before the change in policy would reflect expectations of inflation prior to the change in policy. In effect, inflation would already be built into existing wage agreements and could not be reduced costlessly and instantaneously. At the very least, Fischer said, a policy of disinflation should be announced sufficiently in advance of its actual implementation to allow wage setters to take it into account when setting wages.

Taylor's argument went one step further. An important characteristic of wage contracts, he argued, is that they are not all signed at the same time. Instead, they are staggered over time. He showed that this **staggering of wage decisions** imposed strong limits on how fast disinflation could proceed without triggering higher unemployment, even if the Bank of Canada's commitment to inflation was fully credible. Why the limits? If workers cared about relative wages—that is, cared about their wages relative to the wages of other workers—each wage contract would choose a wage not very different from wages in the other contracts in force at the time. Too rapid a decrease in nominal money growth would not lead to a proportional decrease in inflation. So, the real money stock would decrease, triggering a recession and an increase in the unemployment rate.

Taking into account the time pattern of wage contracts in the United States, which is similar to the time pattern of contracts in Canada, Taylor then showed that under full credibility of monetary policy, there *was* a path of disinflation consistent with no increase in unemployment. This path is shown in Figure 12–4.

Disinflation starts in quarter 1 and lasts for 16 quarters. Once it is achieved, the inflation rate, which started at 10%, is 3%. The striking feature is how slowly disinflation proceeds at the beginning. One year (four quarters) after the announcement of the change in policy,

The nominal rigidities view: Many wages are set in nominal terms, sometimes for many years. The way to decrease the unemployment cost of disinflation is to give wage setters time to take the change in policy into account. Thus, the central bank should implement a slow disinflation.

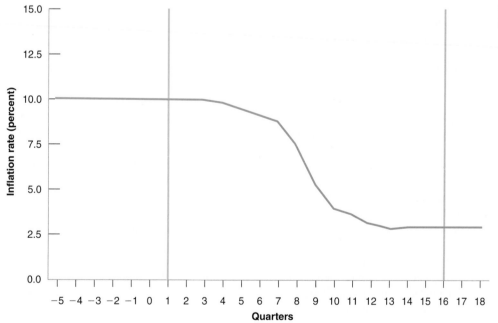

FIGURE 12–4

Disinflation without Unemployment in the Taylor Model

With staggering of wage decisions, disinflation must be phased in slowly to avoid an increase in unemployment.

inflation is still 9.9%. But then disinflation occurs faster. By the end of the third year, inflation is down to 4%, and by the end of the fourth year, the desired disinflation is achieved.

The reason for the slow decrease in inflation at the beginning—and, behind the scene, for the slow decrease in nominal money growth—is straightforward. Wages in force at the time of the policy change are the result of decisions made before the policy change so that the path of inflation in the near future is largely predetermined. If nominal money growth were to decrease sharply, inflation could not decrease very much right away, and the result would be a decrease in real money and a recession. Thus, the best policy is for the Bank of Canada to proceed slowly at the beginning, while announcing it will proceed faster in the future. This announcement leads new wage settlements to take the new policy into account. When most wage decisions in the economy come from decisions made after the change in policy, disinflation can proceed much faster. This is what happens in the third year following the policy change.

Like Lucas and Sargent, Taylor did not believe that disinflation really could be implemented without increasing unemployment. For one thing, he realized that the path of disinflation drawn in Figure 12–4 might not be credible. The announcement this year that money growth will be decreased two years from now is likely to run into a serious credibility problem. Wage setters are likely to ask themselves: If the decision has been made to disinflate, why should the central bank wait two years? Without credibility, inflation expectations might not change, defeating the hope of disinflation without an increase in the unemployment rate. But Taylor's analysis had two clear messages. First, like Lucas and Sargent's analysis, it emphasized the role of expectations. Second, it suggested that a slow but credible disinflation might have a cost lower than that implied by the traditional approach.

With this discussion in mind, let us end the chapter with a look at what happened in Canada from 1988 to 1993.

12-5 | The Canadian Disinflation, 1988 to 1993

In 1988, as shown in row 8 of Table 12–2, consumer price index inflation in Canada was 4%. The unemployment rate was 7.8%, below our estimate of the natural rate of 8.6%. Our model would predict an acceleration in inflation, which did occur; the next entry in the eighth row of Table 12–2 is 4.9%. The Bank of Canada's Governor Crow decided to publicly announce that the Bank of Canada had a new policy goal: price stability. The quote from the Hanson lecture that opened this chapter made this goal clear to Canadians. Did they believe Governor Crow, or in the language of section 12-4, was the disinflation credible?

If the disinflation was credible, then the reduction in inflation should have occurred without a significant increase in unemployment. Figure 12–5 reminds us that as monetary policy was tightened and Canadian interest rates rose higher than American rates, the Canadian real exchange rate appreciated. Table 12–2 shows that unemployment increased sharply, GDP growth was negative in 1991, and there is little evidence that the disinflation was credible. Our discussion of credibility in section 12-4 indicated that a second way to ask if Governor Crow was credible is to ask if this disinflation was less costly than predicted by the traditional model. We can answer this question by calculating the sacrifice ratio. You are also referred to the Focus box, "Was the Cost of the 1988–1993 Disinflation Higher than Expected by the Bank of Canada?"

The sacrifice ratio can be calculated using the data in Table 12–2. There is one complication. In this period, Canada was switching to make more extensive use of sales taxes to raise revenue at both the provincial and federal levels. In particular, on January 1, 1991, a "new" federal sales tax, the Goods and Services Tax (GST), was introduced. Because this tax fell on goods and services bought by consumers and the consumer price index (CPI) measures the cost of the things consumers buy, the CPI jumped from 1990 to 1991. You can see in row 8 how inflation jumped from 4.7% in 1990 to 5.5% in 1991. The introduction of the GST was responsible for 2.2 percentage points of the inflation in that year. The Bank of Canada calculates the rate of inflation after removing the effect of provincial and federal sales tax changes. These values are found in row 9. These are the correct values to use in calculation of the sacrifice ratio.

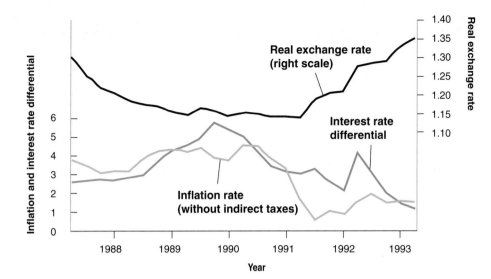

FIGURE 12-5

Monetary Policy and Inflation, 1988–1993

Here, we add the inflation rate (measured without indirect taxes) and the real exchange rate to the Canadin and American interest rate differential from Figure 6–8. The Bank of Canada raised interest rates in Canada relative to interest rates in the United States. The resulting real appreciation raised unemployment and lowered inflation.

Source: Real exchange rate using CANSIM II variables V37426, V122054, V149258, V498918, V1992259; interest rate differential using CANSIM II variable V122484, Federal Reserve Board RIFSGFSM03_N.M.

To calculate the sacrifice ratio in Table 12–2, we first need the cumulative number of point-years of excess unemployment (assuming a natural rate of 8.6%). This is calculated in line 10, starting in 1991, the first year where unemployment exceeds the natural rate. Row 10

TABLE 12–2 Inflation and Unemployment in Canada, 1988–1993

VARIABLE	1988	1989	1990	1991	1992	1993
1. GDP growth (%)	4.8	2.5	0.3	–2.0	1.0	2.4
2. Unemployment rate (%)	7.8	7.5	8.1	10.3	11.2	11.4
3. Canadian interest rate (%)	9.4	12.0	12.8	8.8	6.5	4.9
4. U.S. interest rate (%)	6.7	8.1	7.5	5.4	3.4	3.0
5. Interest rate differential (%)	2.7	3.9	5.3	3.4	3.1	1.9
6. Real exchange rate	1.21	1.16	1.15	1.14	1.21	1.3
7. Trade surplus (% of GDP)	0.8	0.0	0.1	–0.6	–0.4	0.0
8. CPI inflation	4.0	4.9	4.7	5.5	1.5	1.8
9. CPI inflation without indirect tax changes	3.2	4.2	4.2	3.3	1.0	1.6
10. Cumulative unemployment	—	—	—	1.7	4.3	7.1
11. Cumulative disinflation	—	—	—	0.9	3.2	2.6
12. Sacrifice ratio	—	—	—	1.9	1.34	2.7

The only new variable in Table 12–2 is found in row 9, CPI inflation without indirect tax changes. This variable is created by the Bank of Canada. Indirect taxes is a term used for sales taxes. Since consumers pay sales taxes, the CPI in row 8 includes the effects of sales-tax increases. The year 1991 saw the introduction of the federal consumer sales tax, the Goods and Services Tax (GST). In 1991, CPI inflation in row 8 is much larger than CPI inflation without indirect tax changes in row 9. The row 9 variable is the correct inflation rate to use to calculate the sacrifice ratio.

Cumulative unemployment is the sum of point-years of excess unemployment from 1991 on, assuming a natural rate of unemployment of 8.6%

Cumulative disinflation is the difference between CPI inflation without indirect tax changes in a given year and CPI inflation without indirect tax changes in 1990. The sacrifice ratio is the ratio of cumulative unemployment to cumulative disinflation.

The model assessment in section 12–5 was not quite a fair test of our understanding of disinflation. In physical sciences, like biology, we test a hypothesis with a controlled experiment. We hypothesize that there is a best amount of water. We take 10 seeds, put them in 10 flowerpots on the same windowsill, and give each pot a different amount of water at the same time each day. Both the plants that get too little water and those that get too much water die. We may even graph millilitres of water against biomass produced. We may even repeat the experiment one hundred times. In the 101st repetition, we may even make a prediction on the best amount of water per day. This kind of experiment is difficult to conduct in macroeconomics. To measure the sacrifice ratio, we would like to repeat the same experiment of reducing inflation many times. We cannot do this. In section 12-5, the comparison of the calculated sacrifice ratio using Table 12–2 with the estimated sacrifice ratio in section 12-2 is not quite right. We used the data from the 1988 to 1993 disinflation to estimate α, then checked our estimate of α with the data. Our reasoning, unlike the experiment with the plants, was quite circular.

One way out of this circularity is to estimate the sacrifice ratio with data up to 1988 and then use the model estimated with the pre-1988 data to predict the post-1988 behaviour of the economy. This predictive test is a much stronger test. Johnson and Gerlich (2002) did just such a predictive test for Canada. Fortunately for us, the Bank of Canada was very interested in the sacrifice ratio even before the 1988–1993 disinflation. Two Bank of Canada economists, Barry Cozier and Gordon Wilkinson, published estimates of the sacrifice ratio estimated

from the Canadian economy using data from 1964 to 1988. Using slightly different methodology from our methodology, they came up with three estimates of the sacrifice ratio—their estimates were scaled as the percent of GDP lost per unit decline in inflation. They estimated that a unit decline in inflation would require a 1 to 2% decline in output for one year. Using Okun's law, a 1 to 2% decline in output is 2.5 to 5 point-years of excess unemployment. These values are very close to the values Johnson and Gerlich (2002) estimated including all of the data from 1962 to 2001.[1]

It looks very much as though the traditional model of disinflation estimated with data before 1988 correctly predicts the cost of the disinflation after 1988. The Bank of Canada should not have been surprised that a reduction in Canada's inflation rate from 4% to 2% would involve a significant recession.

[1]Johnson and Gerlich (2002) also formally test the statistical hypothesis that the Cozier-Wilkinson model of inflation estimated with data from 1964 to 1988 continues to predict Canadian inflation from 1989 to 2001. This null hypothesis cannot be rejected.

Sources:
David Johnson and Sebastian Gerlich, "How Has Inflation Changed in Canada? A Comparison of 1989–2001 to 1964–1988," *Canadian Public Policy* 28, 2002, pp. 563–579.
Barry Cozier and Gordon Wilkinson, "Some Evidence on Hysteresis and the Costs of Disinflation in Canada," *Bank of Canada Technical Report No. 55*, 1991.

indicates that by 1993, Canada had experienced 7.1 point-years of excess unemployment. The cumulative fall in inflation from 1991 to 1993 was 2.6 percentage points. The sacrifice ratio calculated over that period was 2.7. Our model predicted a sacrifice ratio of about 2. The disinflation was even more costly than predicted by our estimate of α.

The large actual sacrifice ratio suggests that Canada's 1988–1993 disinflation was not credible. A whole host of other evidence also points to this conclusion. According to Laidler and Robson (1993), direct measures of expected inflation are slow to adjust. According to Johnson (1997), there is evidence that expected inflation began to fall only after actual inflation fell and not during the Bank of Canada's presentation of the case for lower inflation. Finally, Johnson (1990) made the argument that fiscal policy in Canada depended on inflation rate in excess of 3%, and monetary policy aimed at inflation less than 2%. This issue was not resolved until 1991. We will return to these issues in Chapters 25 and 26. There are three additional readings listed at the end of this chapter that are specific to the Canadian experience. The Canadian experience of disinflation was very similar to the disinflation experienced in other countries over the last 30 years.

In short, the Canadian disinflation from 1988 to 1993 was associated with a substantial increase in unemployment. The Phillips curve relation between the change in inflation and the deviation of the unemployment rate from the natural rate proved more robust than many economists anticipated. The Focus box "Was the Cost of the 1988–1993 Disinflation Higher than Expected by the Bank of Canada?" looks at what the Bank of Canada knew when the disinflation was started. Was this outcome due to a lack of credibility of the change in monetary policy or to the fact that credibility is not enough to reduce substantially the cost of disinflation? Laurence Ball, of Johns Hopkins University, estimated sacrifice ratios for

65 disinflation episodes in 19 OECD countries over the last 30+ years. He reaches three main conclusions:

- Disinflations typically lead to higher unemployment for some time. Put another way, even if it is neutral in the medium run, a decrease in money growth leads to an increase in unemployment for some time.
- Faster disinflations are associated with smaller sacrifice ratios. This conclusion provides some evidence to support the expectation and credibility effects emphasized by Lucas and Sargent.
- Sacrifice ratios are smaller in countries that have shorter wage contracts. This provides some evidence to support Fischer and Taylor's emphasis on the importance of the structure of wage settlements.

SUMMARY

- There are three relations linking inflation, output, and unemployment:

  The first is Okun's law, which relates the change in the unemployment rate to the deviation of the rate of growth of output from the normal growth rate. In Canada today, output growth of 1% above normal for a year leads to a decrease in the unemployment rate of about 0.33%.

  The second is the Phillips curve, which relates the change in the inflation rate to the deviation of the actual unemployment rate from the natural rate. In Canada today, an unemployment rate 1% below the natural rate for a year leads to an increase in inflation of about 0.5%.

  The third is the aggregate demand relation, which relates the rate of growth of output to the rate of growth of the real money stock. The growth rate of output is equal to the growth rate of nominal money minus the rate of inflation. Given nominal money growth, higher inflation leads to a decrease in output growth.

- In the medium run, the unemployment rate is equal to the natural rate, and output grows at its normal growth rate. Money growth determines the inflation rate: A 1% increase in money growth leads to a 1% increase in the inflation rate. As Milton Friedman put it, inflation is always and everywhere a monetary phenomenon.

- In the short run, a decrease in money growth leads to a slowdown in growth and an increase in unemployment for some time. Thus, disinflation (a decrease in the inflation rate) can be achieved only at the cost of more unemployment. How much unemployment is required is a controversial issue.

- The traditional approach assumes that people do not change the way they form expectations when monetary policy changes so that the relation between inflation and unemployment is unaffected by the change in policy. This approach implies that disinflation can be achieved by a short but large increase in unemployment or by a longer and smaller increase in unemployment. But policy cannot affect the total number of point-years of excess unemployment.

- An alternative view is that if the change in monetary policy is credible, expectation formation may change, leading to a smaller increase in unemployment than predicted by the traditional approach. In its extreme form, this alternative view implies that if policy is fully credible, it can achieve disinflation at no cost in unemployment. A less extreme form recognizes that although expectation formation may change, the presence of nominal rigidities is likely to imply some increase in unemployment, although less than implied by the traditional answer.

- The Canadian disinflation from 1988 to 1993, during which inflation decreased by approximately 2%, was associated with a large recession. The unemployment cost was close to the predictions of the traditional approach.

KEY TERMS

- adjusted nominal money growth, 227
- credibility, 232
- disinflation, 228
- labour hoarding, 223
- Lucas critique, 232
- nominal rigidities, 233
- normal growth rate, 223
- point-year of excess unemployment, 228
- sacrifice ratio, 228
- staggering of wage decisions, 233

An asterisk denotes a harder question. [Web] indicates that the question requires access to the Internet.

1. TRUE/FALSE/UNCERTAIN

a. The Canadian unemployment rate will remain constant as long as output growth is positive.

b. Many firms prefer to keep workers around when demand is low (rather than lay them off), even if the workers are underutilized.

c. The behaviour of Okun's law across countries and across decades is consistent with our knowledge of firm behaviour and labour market regulations.

d. There is a reliable negative relation between the rate of inflation and the growth rate of output.

e. In the medium run, the rate of inflation is equal to the rate of nominal money growth.

f. According to the Phillips curve relation, the sacrifice ratio is independent of the speed of disinflation.

g. Contrary to the traditional Phillips curve analysis, Taylor's analysis of staggered wage contracts made a case for a slow approach to disinflation.

h. Johnson and Gerlich's analysis showed that the recession associated with the 1988–1993 disinflation could have been predicted by the Bank of Canada before 1988.

2. OKUN'S LAW

As shown by equation (12.2) the estimated Okun's law for Canada is given by

$$u_t - u_{t-1} = -0.33(g_{yt} - 3.7\%)$$

a. What growth rate of output leads to an increase in the unemployment rate of 1% per year? How can the unemployment rate increase even though the growth rate of output is positive?

b. What rate of growth output do we need to decrease unemployment by 1 percentage points over the next four years?

c. Suppose that we experience a second baby boom. How do you expect Okun's law to change if the rate of growth of the labour force increases by 2 percentage points?

3. REDUCING THE INFLATION RATE IN THE UNITED STATES

Blanchard, in the American edition of this text, finds that the U.S. economy can be described by the following three equations:

$$u_t - u_{t-1} = -0.4(g_{yt} - 3\%) \quad \text{Okun's law}$$
$$\pi_t - \pi_{t-1} = -(u_t - 5\%) \quad \text{Phillips curve}$$
$$g_{yt} = g_{mt} - \pi_t \quad \text{aggregate demand}$$

a. What is the natural rate of unemployment for this economy? How is it different from that of Canada?

b. Suppose that the unemployment rate is equal to the natural rate and that the inflation rate is 8%. What is the growth rate of output? What is the growth rate of the money supply?

c. Suppose that conditions are as in (b), when the authorities use monetary policy to reduce the inflation rate to 4% in year t and keep it there. What must happen to the unemployment rate and output growth in years t, $t + 1$, and $t + 2$? What money growth rate in years t, $t + 1$, and $t + 2$ will accomplish this goal?

4. THE EFFECTS OF A PERMANENT DECREASE IN MONEY GROWTH

Suppose that the economy can be described by the following three equations:

$$u_t - u_{t-1} = -0.4(g_{yt} - 3\%) \quad \text{Okun's law}$$
$$\pi_t - \pi_{t-1} = -(u_t - 5\%) \quad \text{Phillips curve}$$
$$g_{yt} = g_{mt} - \pi_t \quad \text{aggregate demand}$$

a. Reduce the three equations to two by substituting g_{yt} from the aggregate demand equation into Okun's law.

Assume initially that $u_t = u_{t-1} = 5\%$, $g_{mt} = 13\%$, and $\pi_t = 10\%$. Now, suppose that this year's money growth is permanently reduced from 13% to 0%.

b. Compute the impact on unemployment and inflation this year and next year.

c. Compute the values of unemployment and inflation in the medium run.

5. POLICY RECOMMENDATIONS

Suppose that you are advising a government that wants to reduce its inflation rate. It is considering two options: a gradual reduction over several years and an immediate reduction.

a. Lay out the arguments for and against each option.

b. If the only criterion you were to consider was the sacrifice ratio, which option would you take? Why might you want to consider other criteria?

c. What particular features of the economy might you want to look at before giving your advice?

6. THE APPROPRIATE REACTION TO OIL SHOCKS

Suppose that the Phillips curve is given by:

$$\pi_t - \pi_{t-1} = -(u_t - 8.6\%) + 0.1\mu$$

where μ is the markup.

Suppose that unemployment is initially at its natural rate. Suppose now that an oil shock increases μ but that the monetary authority continues to keep the unemployment rate at its previous value.

a. What will happen to inflation?

b. What should the monetary authority do instead?

FURTHER READING

The Lucas critique was first presented by Robert Lucas in "Econometric Policy Evaluation: A Critique," in *The Phillips Curve and Labor Markets*, Carnegie Rochester Conference, Vol. 1, 1976, pp. 19–46.

The article by Stanley Fischer arguing that credibility would not be enough to achieve costless disinflation is "Long-Term Contracts, Rational Expectations, and the Optimal Money Supply Rule," *Journal of Political Economy*, 85, 1977, pp. 163–190.

The article that derived the path of disinflation reproduced in Figure 12–4 is by John Taylor, "Union Wage Settlements," *American Economic Review*, December 1983, pp. 981–993.

(All three preceding articles are relatively technical.)

A description of Canadian monetary policy in the 1988 to 1993 period is found in *The Great Canadian Disinflation: The Economics and Politics of Monetary Policy in Canada,*

1988–93, by David E.W. Laidler and William B.P. Robson. (Toronto: C.D. Howe Institute, 1993). The story told in this book extends into the material we discuss in Chapters 25 and 26.

Even more details on monetary policy in Canada in this period can be found in "An Evaluation of the Bank of Canada Zero Inflation Target: Do Michael Wilson and John Crow Agree?" *Canadian Public Policy*, Vol. 16, No. 3, September 1990, pp. 308–325; "Expected Inflation in Canada 1988–1995: An Evaluation of Bank of Canada Credibility and the Effect of Inflation Targets," *Canadian Public Policy*, September 1997, Vol. 23, No. 3: pp. 223–258; and "How Has Inflation Changed in Canada. A Comparison of 1989–2001 to 1964–1988" *Canadian Public Policy* 28, 2002, pp. 563–579. All three articles were written by David Johnson, one of the authors of this book. The last article was written jointly with Sebastian Cerlich.

CHAPTER 13
EXCHANGE RATES IN THE MEDIUM RUN: ADJUSTMENTS, CRISES, AND REGIMES

In Chapters 6, 7, and 8, we introduced open economy considerations into the short-run macro-economic model. We saw that the real exchange rate, the price of foreign goods in terms of domestic goods, is very important in an open economy. We saw that interest rate parity, the equalization of expected nominal returns, is a useful way to think about the links between financial markets across countries. These two concepts are used extensively in this chapter; you may need to review them as the analysis unfolds. We consider two choices available to policy makers in the open economy in the medium run. One choice: Should the nominal exchange rate be flexible, or should the nominal exchange rate be fixed in terms of the currency of your principal trading partner? In only one of the last five decades did Canada fix the value of the Canadian dollar in terms of U.S. dollars, from 1962 to 1970. For the remainder of the last half-century, the value of the Canadian dollar has been determined in the foreign exchange market. There have been serious suggestions, particularly in the years from 1995 to the present, that Canada should return to a fixed exchange rate. Which exchange rate system is better for Canada?

The same question has been faced by the international financial system over the years. The Bretton Woods agreement (Bretton Woods is a resort in New Hampshire, where a meeting was held in 1944 to consider whether exchange rates should be fixed or flexible when World War II was over) decided nominal exchange rates should be fixed. This agreement was implemented between the major trading countries in the world in the period 1950–1970. However, in 1973, the agreement fell apart, and since then, the major currencies in the world—the American dollar, the Japanese yen, and the major European currencies—have traded freely in financial markets. Their relative values, the various bilateral exchange rates, have been determined in those markets. Which exchange rate system is better for the world economy? You may have noticed that we said only the exchange rates between major countries have been freely determined in financial markets. For many smaller countries, nominal exchange rates were and still are fixed in value relative to the currency of their major trading partner. Thus, small European countries tended to fix their currency's value to the German Deutschemark (DM) or euro, and Latin American and Asian countries tended to fix the price of their currencies in terms of the U.S. dollar.

The second choice we consider is: If you do fix your nominal exchange rate in terms of the currency of your principal trading partner (and many countries do just that), are there circumstances in which you need to change the value of your currency? If there is never a reason to change the value of your nominal exchange rate, then logic suggests you should simply use the currency of another country or share currencies across nations. A few countries do use the currency of another country as their money. Examples include very small countries in Europe—Monaco used the French franc and San Marino the Italian lira, both before the creation of the euro. Many of you will know that as of January 1, 1999, most of the countries in Western Europe decided to replace their national currencies with a new shared currency, the euro. The creation of a new joint currency and a new joint central bank for this large an area and this many countries is an unprecedented experiment. We will discuss this experiment briefly at the end of the chapter. Both over time and across countries, there have been a variety of policy choices made to establish a value for the nominal exchange rate.

In section 13-1, we extend our medium run *AS-AD* model into a situation in which the nominal exchange rate is freely determined in financial markets. The main lesson: If a country chooses a flexible nominal exchange rate and chooses a higher inflation rate than the inflation rate in its principal trading partner, then the nominal exchange rate will continuously depreciate. The choice to have a flexible exchange rate is intimately linked to the choice to have an inflation rate different from that of your trading partner. This same point is explored in a different way in section 13-2. Here, we analyze the medium run in an open economy under fixed exchange rates. Remember, a fixed exchange rate is a fixed nominal exchange rate. In the short run, both domestic and foreign price levels are fixed, so the fixed nominal exchange rate implies a fixed real exchange rate as well. But in the medium run, price levels adjust, and even if the nominal exchange rate is fixed, the real exchange rate may change. We see this is indeed the case. However, we now have to provide an adjustment path to the "right" real exchange rate. This adjustment path, particularly the path of real output, can be quite different depending on whether it is the nominal exchange rate that is adjusted or the price level that is adjusted. In section 13-3, we look at exchange rate crises. Countries that fix their exchange rate often face serious crises. This was the case in 1973 for the countries that had operated under the Bretton Woods system when that system collapsed. It was the case in Europe in 1992 for countries operating within the European fixed exchange rate system. It was the case for many Asian countries in 1997 and 1998. Exchange rate crises typically start when participants in financial markets conclude the current nominal exchange rate is not sustainable and that the country will soon devalue its currency. To compensate investors for the perceived risk of devaluation, the central bank must increase the domestic interest rate, often to very high levels. The country is faced with a tough choice: maintain the interest rate at a very high level, which decreases the demand for goods and may trigger a recession, or give up the parity value of the nominal exchange rate and devalue the currency. Understanding such crises helps us assess one of the major problems associated with a fixed exchange rate.

Building on what we have done in sections 13-1, 13-2, and 13-3, the chapter closes in section 13-4 with a discussion of the pros and cons of flexible and fixed exchange rate regimes.

13-1 | Flexible Exchange Rates and the Adjustment of the Nominal Exchange Rate in the Medium Run

In this section, we present a country that operates with a flexible exchange rate and a positive rate of inflation. That rate of inflation will be constant at 5% throughout the following extensive example. The foreign country that is this country's major trading partner will have a zero rate of inflation. It is crucial that the two countries have a *different* rate of inflation but not crucial that one rate of inflation happens to be zero. Zero inflation in the foreign country simplifies the example just a little bit. The analysis is still quite complicated.

Our analysis in the last two chapters has shown us that an economy can operate with a sustained positive rate of inflation. We wrote that:

$$\pi_t = \pi_t^e - \alpha(u_t - u_n) \tag{13.1}$$

where inflation equalled expected inflation if the rate of unemployment were at the natural rate of unemployment. The evidence supporting this model is presented in Chapters 11 and 12. If expected inflation is equal to actual inflation, it follows that the expected price level equals the actual price level in each period. We use this fact below.

Aggregate Supply

The aggregate supply relation is the relation between the price level and the output level implied by equilibrium in the labour market. In Chapter 10 (equation 10.1), we wrote:

$$P_t = P_t^e(1 + \mu) F\left(1 - \frac{Y_t}{L}, z\right) \tag{13.2}$$

The price level depends on the expected price level for this year and the level of output. Recall the mechanisms at work:

- The price level expected to prevail in year t, P_t^e, affects the nominal wage in year t, which affects the actual price level in year t, P_t.
- Higher real output this year (Y_t) leads to lower unemployment which leads to higher wages which leads to a higher price level in this year.

We are now dealing in a world where expected inflation is positive. If π_t^e is the expected rate of inflation (written as a decimal so that 10% equals 0.10), then we can rewrite our aggregate supply relationship as:

$$P_t = (1 + \pi_t^e)P_{t-1}(1 + \mu) F\left(1 - \frac{Y_t}{L}, z\right) \tag{13.3}$$

This aggregate supply curve is placed in Figure 13-1 so that when output is at Y_n, the price level P_t is at its expected level P_t^e. Y_n is the full employment or natural level of output. This is point A in Figure 13–1.

With aggregate supply in place, we need to review the elements of aggregate demand in the open economy.

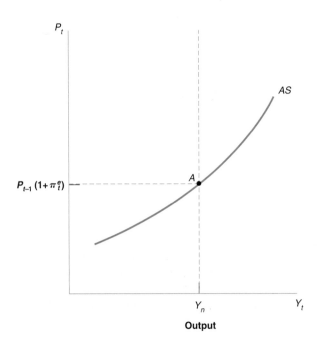

Aggregate Demand

The aggregate demand relationship defines an equilibrium in the goods market between the goods people are willing to buy and those that are produced. From section 8-3 in Chapter 8, we write:

$$Y_t = C(Y_t - T) + I(Y_t, i_t) + G + NX\,(Y_t, Y^*, \frac{E_t P^*}{P_t}) \tag{13.4}$$
$$\quad\;\; +\quad - \qquad + \;\; - \quad + \qquad\quad - \;\; + \qquad +$$

Because the price level varies in the medium run, the real exchange rate replaces the nominal exchange rate in the aggregate demand relation. For the goods-market equilibrium, the output produced, the left side of equation (13.4), must equal the output demanded, the right side of equation (13.4).

The signs below the variables, positive or negative, indicate how the variables in equation (13.4) affect demand. Let us review the influence of these variables:

- G (+) represents the increase in the demand for domestic goods with higher government spending.
- T (–) represents the decrease in demand for domestic goods with higher taxes.
- Y_t (+) is the indirect influence of more domestic output on both consumption (C) and investment (I).
- The domestic nominal interest rate, i_t (–), has a negative influence on aggregate demand. This effect was stressed in Chapter 5. Strictly speaking, now that expected inflation is positive, this variable should be the real interest rate. The discussion of the interaction among expected inflation, the nominal interest rate, and the real interest rate is deferred to Chapters 18 through 21. In this chapter, we want to focus only on the open economy interactions of prices and exchange rate. This is quite enough to do!
- Y^* (+) represents the influence of foreign output on the demand for domestic goods. Higher foreign output means more net exports (NX) from Canada. Y_t (–) in the NX expression is the effect of more domestic output on imports (not exports).
- ϵ_t, the real exchange rate, has a negative effect (+) on imports and a positive effect (+) on exports. A real exchange rate depreciation, an increase in ϵ_t, means that imports fall and exports rise. This increases net exports (NX). The Marshall-Lerner conditions discussed in Chapter 7 are assumed to hold.

In a world where the price level moves, we recognize that the value of the real exchange rate $\epsilon_t = E_t P^*/P_t$ changes. Such changes may occur because of any combination of movements in E_t, the nominal exchange rate; P^*, the foreign price level; and P_t the domestic price level. It is these movements that we must understand and follow through the analytical exercise below.

There are two further equilibrium conditions in the financial market of the open economy. The first:

$$\frac{M_t}{P_t} = Y_t L(i_t) \tag{13.5}$$

is the financial market equilibrium condition that characterized the LM curve. Here, real money demand equals real money supply at the domestic interest rate, i_t.

The second condition is uncovered interest parity, where:

$$i_t = i^* + (\frac{E^e_{t+1} - E_t}{E_t}) \tag{13.6}$$

means that expected returns on one-year bonds denominated in either currency are equal. The expected rate of depreciation of the domestic currency:

$$\frac{E^e_{t+1} - E_t}{E_t}$$

equals the interest rate difference between the domestic country and the foreign country. If bonds denominated in either currency earn equal expected returns, they will be held by the participants in either financial market.

You may have noticed time subscripts on some variables in equations (13.4), (13.5), and (13.6). We are going to allow these variables the possibility that they vary over time (but not all these variables will vary over time). Time will begin in period t, then move to period $t + 1$, period $t + 2$, period $t + 3$, and so on. Some variables will never vary over time, specifically the foreign interest rate and foreign income, as well as domestic government spending and taxes. There are no subscripts on these variables. In addition to the four variables above, we are going to work in the situation where the foreign price level P^* is held constant. This means the foreign inflation rate is zero. However, the analysis does generalize to the situation where the foreign country simply has a different inflation rate from the domestic country.

A Full Employment Open Economy with Positive Inflation in the Medium Run

Figure 13–2 and Table 13–1 are used to illustrate a sequence of *AS-AD* points that this economy could experience in a medium-run equilibrium. At each point in this example, actual inflation equals expected inflation.[1] Table 13–1 opens with four rows of foreign variables that are constant over time, that is, take the same value in each period. The next four rows are the values of the domestic variables, which are predetermined for us in this analysis. Domestic inflation is 5% each year (row (6)). The actual price level (row (5)) and the expected domestic price level (row (7)) simply reflect the expected and actual inflation of 5% in each year. Because actual prices always equal expected prices, output is always at full employment, Y_n (row (8)). Whatever happens on the demand side of this economy, in each period, the level of domestic prices rises by 5%, the *AS* curve shifts up by 5%, and output remains at full employment. These shifts are illustrated in Figure 13–2 for periods t, $t + 1$ and $t + 2$. More periods could be added, but the diagram would simply get more cluttered. Figure 13–2 shows aggregate demand curves that also shift up each period so that the intersection of *AS* and *AD* remains at Y_n. How do we ensure this result?

FIGURE **13–2**

Aggregate Demand and Aggregate Supply in an Open Economy with Expected Inflation

As the price level increases, the nominal exchange rate depreciates. At the same real exchange rate (points *A*, *B*, and *C*), demand for domestic output remains the same.

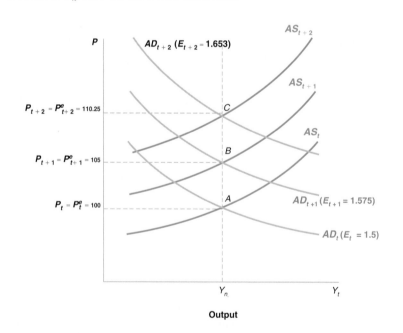

[1]**DIGGING DEEPER**. Implicitly, we have already considered various aspects of the situation in which actual inflation need not equal expected inflation in Chapters 6, 7, and 8, as well as in Chapters 10, 11, and 12.

244   THE CORE   THE MEDIUM RUN

TABLE 13–1 An Open Economy Under Flexible Exchange Rates: An Example

Row	Symbol	Variable	t	$t+1$	$t+2$	$t+3$	$t+4$
(1)	P^*	Foreign prices (index)	100	100	100	100	100
(2)	π^*	Foreign inflation (%)	0	0	0	0	0
(3)	i^*	Foreign interest rate (%)	5	5	5	5	5
(4)	Y^*	Foreign output (index)	100	100	100	100	100
(5)	P_t	Domestic prices (index)	100	105	110.25	115.76	121.55
(6)	π_t	Domestic inflation	5	5	5	5	5
(7)	P_t^e	Expected domestic price level	100	105	110.25	115.76	121.55
(8)	Y_t	Output	Y_n	Y_n	Y_n	Y_n	Y_n
(9)	E_t	Nominal exchange rate (domestic currency per foreign currency)	1.5	1.575	1.653	1.736	1.823
(10)	ϵ_t	Real exchange rate (index)	1.5	1.5	1.5	1.5	1.5
(11)	$\frac{(E_{t+1}^e - E_t)}{E_t}$	Expected rate of depreciation (%)	5	5	5	5	5
(12)	i_t	(%)	10	10	10	10	10
(13)	M_t	Money supply (dollars)	1000	1050	1102.5	1115.76	1215.5
(14)	M_t/P_t	Real money supply (period t dollars)	1000	1000	1000	1000	1000

The data in this box are used in section 13–1 as an example of how an open economy can function when the domestic country chooses a different inflation rate from the inflation rate in its principal trading partner.

If output is to remain at Y_n, then total aggregate demand in equation (13.4) cannot change between period t and period $t + 1$. We have kept some of these elements constant in equation (13.4) constant in this problem, that is, G, T, and Y^* are all constant. We need to calculate what will happen to i_t, the domestic interest rate, and ϵ_t, the real exchange rate. Here is the methodology: We are going to propose a solution, a sequence of choices for i_t, and ϵ_t and then ask if our proposed choices make sense.

Rows (9), (10), and (11) of Table 13–1 are the first step. In these rows, a nominal depreciation of 5% between each period exactly offsets 5% domestic inflation (when foreign prices are fixed) so that the real exchange rate ϵ_t never changes. The domestic price level in period t is 100. The nominal exchange rate in period t is 1.5. The foreign price level in period t is 100. (Remember these are index numbers where the initial values are arbitrary.) The real exchange rate in period t is 1.5. If, in period $t + 1$, the domestic price level moves to 105, a depreciation of the nominal exchange rate to 1.575 will leave the real exchange rate ϵ_t equal to the real exchange rate ϵ_{t+1} where both are equal to the period t value of 1.5. The same logic repeats from period $t + 2$ to $t + 3$ and so on. The proposed solution has no variation in the real exchange rate and thus no variation in the demand for domestic goods from this source. Exports and imports remain unchanged in equation (13.4). This seems a promising first step to keeping the level of aggregate demand constant, that we should keep the real exchange rate constant. The next step is to deal with the domestic interest rate.

The variables needed for the analysis of interest rate parity (13.6) appear in rows (11) and (12), as well as in row (3). In the proposed solution, the uncovered interest parity condition, equation (13.6), holds between each period. Note the exchange rate in period $t + 1$ (1.575 domestic currency units per unit of foreign currency), is the exchange rate expected in period $t + 1$ as of period t. The same relationship holds in Table 13–1 between each set of periods. In each period, a 5% depreciation of the domestic currency is expected and which occurs. In each period, the domestic nominal interest rate is 5% higher than the foreign interest rate. In Table 13–1, the domestic interest rate is constant and equal to 10%. There is no variation in aggregate demand from variation in the domestic interest rate. Thus, all of the variables that determine aggregate demand are constant over time, and the solution we propose seems to be a viable solution. In each period, the aggregate demand curve shifts up to intersect the aggregate supply curve at Y_n. This shift is represented in Figure 13–2 by denoting that each aggregate demand curve is drawn for a different value of the nominal exchange rate.

An aside: A very astute reader might notice that this is not the only possible solution, simply the most sensible solution. For example, suppose that between each period, a nominal exchange rate depreciation of less than 5% was expected and which occurred. To be concrete, suppose the expected and actual depreciation from period t to $t + 1$ was only 4%. There would be two consequences: (1) The lower domestic interest rate (9%) would increase the demand for domestic goods. (2) The real exchange rate in period t would have to be lower (an appreciation), which would decrease the demand for domestic goods. Then, in period $t + 1$, because domestic prices had risen 5% and the nominal exchange rate had depreciated by only 4%, the real exchange rate in period $t + 1$ would be even lower than in period t. To balance demand and supply at Y_n in period $t + 1$, the domestic interest rate would have to fall again. The lower domestic interest rate implies a smaller nominal depreciation and an even larger real appreciation from period $t + 1$ to $t + 2$. This would repeat indefinitely except that at some point, the domestic nominal interest rate is zero or the real exchange rate becomes infinite. This means that eventually it would take an unlimited amount of the domestic good to buy one unit of the foreign good or zero units of the foreign good to buy one unit of the domestic good. Neither value makes any economic or common sense, thus we rule out any solution that requires zero prices for goods or a zero or negative interest rate. In Chapter 15, there is a brief discussion of stock market bubbles. In a bubble, the proposed path of the price of a common share finds that common share to be infinitely valuable at some point in the future. For example, you might believe that your one share of Microsoft, if held long enough with a fast enough percent increase in price, would eventually trade for the value of all other assets in the world. This makes no economic sense, although such a path is mathematically possible. It thus makes no economic sense to propose a solution in which the real exchange rate constantly appreciates and the domestic interest rate must constantly fall, even to a negative value. Further discussion of this problem is left to a more advanced macroeconomics course.

The last step in this quite complicated analysis is to be certain that our solution allows the domestic financial market to be in equilibrium. Look again at equation (13.5). The right side of equation (13.5), the demand for real money, is constant in Table 13–1. Y_n is the constant level of output (row (8)) and i_t is the constant domestic interest rate equal to 10% (row (12)). If the right side of equation (13.5) is constant, the left side of equation (13.5) must be constant as well. Rows (13) and (14) that finish Table 13–1 show that as the domestic price level rises by 5% and the domestic nominal money supply also rises by 5%, then the real money supply, the very last row of Table 13–1, remains constant. This entire analysis is the open economy analogue of the analysis in Chapter 10. In Chapter 10, as long as prices rose in proportion to an increase in the money stock, money was neutral. In this analysis, the money stock continues to rise in proportion to prices, but in the open economy, the nominal exchange rate must also depreciate in proportion to the increase in domestic prices. When these conditions hold, as they do in the numerical example of Table 13–1, then the increase in the money stock is neutral in the open economy as well as in the closed economy.

Conclusions

This exercise teaches us an important lesson. If the domestic country wants to have a higher inflation rate in the medium run than its principal foreign trading partner, then it must also undergo a nominal depreciation of its currency relative to its trading partner. To put this another way, higher inflation countries will experience a constantly declining value of their currency. The Global Macro box "What Makes the Canadian Dollar (and Other Currencies) Fall in Value?" tests this proposition using the data from 1973 to 1998, the long period in which major currencies floated against the United States dollar. Countries that chose to have

This box looks at the change in nominal exchange rates over a large number of years. In the analysis in section 13-1, we suggested that if a country had a higher rate of inflation than its trading partner, then it would need to depreciate its currency so that the real exchange rate stayed constant. Here, we look at the evidence from 22 countries over the most recent period of flexible exchange rates, 1973–1998. The end date, 1998, is chosen because many of these countries adopted the euro on January 1, 1999. Because the euro countries share one currency, we no longer have seperate observations on their nominal exchange rates to the U.S. dollar. The list of countries used are: Australia, Austria, Belgium, Canada, Denmark, Finland, France, Germany, Greece, Iceland, Ireland, Italy, Japan, Korea, the Netherlands, New Zealand, Norway, Portugal, Spain, Sweden, Switzerland, and the United Kingdom.

In each case, the average annual rate of inflation in the consumer price index (CPI) was calculated from the data for the years 1973–1998. There is wide variation in the inflation outcome across countries. The highest inflation country was Iceland at 22% per year; the lowest inflation country was a tie—both Switzerland and Germany with average inflation of 3.1% per year. The United States was then treated as the principal trading partner of all these countries, that is, the average annual rate of depreciation in the bilateral exchange rates between each country and the United States dollar was calculated. Average inflation in the United States was 5.2% over the sample. Using our analysis in section 13-1, we would predict that countries with inflation less than 5.2% would experience an appreciation against the U.S. dollar, and countries with an inflation rate higher than 5.2% should experience a depreciation against the U.S. dollar.

Figure 1 and Table 1 show the results of these calculations. The horizontal axis in Figure 1 is the inflation in that country minus the inflation in the United States. The vertical axis is the average annual percent depreciation (a negative value is an appreciation) against the U.S. dollar. If the analysis in section 13-1 were exactly correct, then all of these points in the scatter would lie on a 45-degree line through the centre of Figure 1. They are not exactly on such a line, but the fit is remarkably close. Differences in inflation rates account for most of the nominal exchange rate change between the United States and these 22 countries from 1973 to 1998. For example, in every country in which the inflation rate was lower than the American inflation rate, there is a nominal appreciation of that country's currency against the U.S. dollar. The opposite holds true for the countries with higher inflation than in the United States.

What of Canada? The Canadian average annual inflation rate from 1973 to 1988 was 0.22% higher than the inflation rate in the United States. All of this difference was early in this sample. Since 1991, Canada has had a lower inflation rate than has the United States. The Canadian dollar depreciated from 1973 to 1998 by an average of 1.59%. The Canadian dollar depreciated "too much," that is, we experienced a real depreciation. Canada is actually one of the countries that does not fit the model very well. Canada is labelled in Figure 1. You can use the data in the table to locate the points in the figure for the other countries.

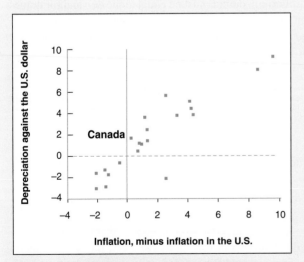

FIGURE 1   Inflation Differences and Nominal Exchange Rate Change

Countries with high inflation rates—in this case, higher inflation rates than the United States—see their currencies fall in value against the U.S. dollar.

TABLE 1

Country	Inflation rate (%)	Inflation rate – U.S. inflation rate	Average depreciation (%) against the U.S. dollar
Australia	6.3	1.1	3.5
Austria	3.9	–1.3	–1.8
Belgium	4.6	–0.6	–0.7
Canada	5.4	0.2	1.59
Denmark	5.8	0.6	0.40
Finland	6.5	1.3	1.3
France	6.0	0.8	1.1
Germany	3.1	–2.1	–1.7
Greece	14.7	9.5	9.2
Iceland	22.5	17.3	17.5
Ireland	7.7	2.5	–2.2
Italy	9.3	4.1	4.3
Japan	3.7	–1.5	–2.9
Korea	9.2	4.0	5.0
Netherlands	3.7	–1.5	–1.4
New Zealand	8.4	3.2	3.7
Norway	6.0	0.8	1.1
Portugal	13.7	8.5	8.0
Spain	9.4	4.2	3.8
Sweden	6.5	1.3	2.4
Switzerland	3.1	–2.1	–3.1
United Kingdom	7.7	2.5	5.6
United States	5.2	—	—

Source for data: International Financial Statistics Yearbook. International Monetary Fund, 2001.

a higher inflation rate than the United States also chose to have a currency that constantly depreciated against the United States dollar. We will see in section 13-2 that if a country chooses to have a fixed exchange rate, it must eventually adopt the inflation rate chosen by its principal trading partner. If it does not do so, then the conditions for an exchange rate crisis are set up, conditions discussed in section 13-3.

13-2 | Fixed Exchange Rates and the Adjustment of the Real Exchange Rate

Take a country operating under a fixed exchange rate regime. Suppose its currency is *overvalued*: At the real exchange rate implied by the fixed nominal exchange rate and the current domestic and foreign price levels, domestic goods are very expensive relative to foreign goods. As a result, the demand for domestic goods is low, and so is output: The country is in a recession.

To get out of the recession, the country has several options. Among them:

Remember that under fixed exchange rates, a change in the exchange rate is called a devaluation ▶ (not a depreciation) or a revaluation (not an appreciation).

- Devalue: By making domestic goods cheaper relative to foreign goods, a devaluation leads to an increase in the demand for domestic goods, and thus to an increase in output and an improvement in the trade balance.
- Do nothing: Keep the nominal exchange rate fixed, and rely instead on the adjustment of the price level over time.

In this section, we compare the macro implications of these two options, both in the short run and in the medium run. To begin, we focus again on the aggregate demand and aggregate supply relations for an open economy under fixed exchange rates.

Aggregate Demand under Fixed Exchange Rates

Warning: The understanding of the next paragraphs depends on what you learned in earlier chapters. Make sure you remember the definitions, the real exchange rate (Chapter 6), and the interest rate parity condition (Chapter 6).

Go back to the condition for goods-market equilibrium, equation (13.7) rewritten below:

$$Y = C(Y - T) + I(Y, i) + G + NX(Y, Y^*, \epsilon) \tag{13.7}$$

For the goods market to be in equilibrium, output must be equal to the demand for domestic goods — the sum of consumption, investment, government spending, and net exports.

Recall that under fixed exchange rates, the nominal exchange rate is fixed. Denote by $\overline{E}$ the value at which it is fixed so that:

$$E = \overline{E}$$

Recall, finally, that under fixed exchange rates and perfect capital mobility, the domestic interest rate must be equal to the foreign interest rate:

$$i = i^*$$

Use these two relations to rewrite equation (13.4) when the exchange rate is fixed:

$$Y = C(Y - T) + I(Y, i^*) + G + NX\left(Y, Y^*, \frac{\overline{E}P^*}{P}\right)$$

This is a rich — if complicated — equilibrium condition. It tells us that in an open economy with fixed exchange rates equilibrium output (or, more precisely, the level of output implied by equilibrium in the goods, financial, and foreign exchange markets) depends on the variables we saw in section 13-1:

- *Government spending (G) and taxes (T)*. An increase in government spending increases output, as does a decrease in taxes.
- *The domestic interest rate, which is equal to the foreign nominal interest rate (i*)*. An increase in the domestic interest rate decreases output.

- *Foreign output (Y*).* An increase in foreign output increases exports and increases domestic output.
- *The real exchange rate, equal to the fixed nominal exchange rate ($\overline{E}$) times the foreign price level (P*) divided by the domestic price level (P).* An increase in the real exchange rate, equivalently a real depreciation, leads to an increase in net exports, increasing output.

We will focus here on the effects of only three of these variables: the real exchange rate, government spending, and taxes. It will be convenient to write the relation between these three variables and output simply as:

$$Y = Y\left(\frac{\overline{E}P^*}{P}, G, T\right) \tag{13.8}$$

$$= \quad (+\ ,+,-\ )$$

An increase in the real exchange rate—a real depreciation—increases output. So does an increase in government spending or a decrease in taxes. All the other variables that affect output in equation (13.7) are taken as givens and, to simplify notation, we simply omit them from equation (13.8).

Equation (13.8) gives us our *aggregate demand relation*, the relation between output and the price level implied by equilibrium in the goods market and in financial markets. This aggregate demand relation implies a negative relation between the price level and output: Given the fixed nominal exchange rate ($\overline{E}$) and the foreign price level (P*), an increase in the domestic price level (P) leads to a decrease in the real exchange rate $\overline{E}P^*/P$—equivalently, a real appreciation. This real appreciation leads to a decrease in net exports and a decrease in Y.

In words, an increase in the price level makes domestic goods more expensive, decreasing the demand for domestic goods and, in turn, decreasing output.

Although the sign of the effect of the price level on output is the same as in the closed economy, the channel is quite different. In a closed economy, the price level affects output through its effect on the real money stock and, in turn, on the interest rate. In an open economy under fixed exchange rates, the interest rate is fixed—pinned down by the foreign interest rate. The way the price level affects output is, instead, through its effect on the real exchange rate.

In a closed economy:
$P\uparrow \Rightarrow M/P\downarrow \Rightarrow i\uparrow \Rightarrow Y\downarrow$

In an open economy with fixed exchange rates:
$P\uparrow \Rightarrow \overline{E}P^*/P\downarrow$
$\quad\quad \Rightarrow NX\downarrow \Rightarrow Y\downarrow$

Aggregate Demand and Aggregate Supply

Rewrite the aggregate demand relation, equation (13.8), with time indexes—which will be needed as we look at dynamics later:

$$Y_t = Y\left(\frac{\overline{E}P^*}{P_t}, G, T\right) \tag{13.9}$$

Note that we have put time indexes only on output and the price level. Given our assumption that the country operates under fixed exchange rates, the nominal exchange rate is fixed and does not need a time index. And, for convenience, we assume that the foreign price level and government spending and taxes are constant as well.

The aggregate demand curve implied by equation (13.9) is drawn as the *AD* curve in Figure 13–3. The aggregate demand curve is downward sloping: An increase in the price level decreases output. As always, the relation is drawn for given values of all other variables, in particular for a given value of the nominal exchange rate.

Turn now to aggregate supply and the determination of the price level. Recall from Chapter 10 that the aggregate supply relation is the relation between the price level and output implied by equilibrium in the labour market. We will rely here on the simple version of the *aggregate supply relation* we derived in Chapter 10, equation (10.1):

This equation was derived in Chapter 10 assuming that expected prices are equal to last year's prices. While we refined the assumption in later chapters, this assumption will do here as we focus on the dynamics around a misaligned fixed exchange rate.

$$P_t = P_{t-1}(1 + \mu)\, F\left(1 - \frac{Y_t}{L}, z\right) \tag{13.10}$$

FIGURE 13–3

Aggregate Demand and Aggregate Supply in an Open Economy under Fixed Exchange Rates

An increase in the price level leads to a real appreciation and a decrease in output: The aggregate demand curve is downward sloping. An increase in output leads to an increase in the price level: The aggregate supply curve is upward sloping.

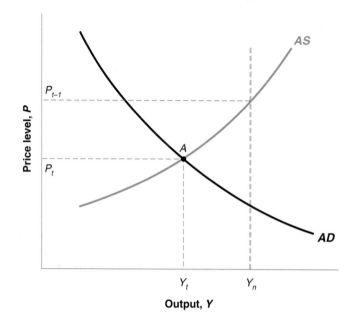

The price level depends on the price level last year and on the level of output (this year). Recall the mechanisms at work:

- Last year's price level matters because it affects expectations of the price level this year, which affect nominal wages this year, which affect the price level this year.
- Higher output matters because it leads to higher employment, which leads to lower unemployment, which leads to higher wages, which lead to a higher price level.

The aggregate supply curve is drawn as the AS curve in Figure 13–3, for a given value of last year's price level. It is upward sloping: Higher output leads to a higher price level.

The short-run equilibrium we want to consider is given by the intersection of the aggregate demand curve and the aggregate supply curve, point A in Figure 13–3. This equilibrium is at A, where output is below the natural level of output Y_n. The economy is in a recession. The rationale for looking at such a situation was given at the beginning of the section. We want to understand what will happen over time if government decides to either maintain the exchange rate or devalue.

Thinking about aggregate supply and aggregate demand can explain how this economy may have arrived at such a situation. P_{t-1} is marked on Figure 13–3. It is where the AS curve (equation (13.9)) crosses Y_n. Something must have happened to reduce aggregate demand. In the AD curve (equation (13.9)), an increase in taxes or a decrease in government spending would cause AD to shift left. Taking advantage of other terms in equation (13.4), AD could shift to the left if Y^* were lower, that is, there was a recession in your trading partner. Whatever the source of the reduction in output, Y_t is now less than Y_n, and government must decide how to act.

Adjustment without a Devaluation. Suppose, first, government does not devalue. What will happen over time is shown in Figure 13–4.

Need a refresher? Reread Chapter 10, section 10-1.

Recall that as long as output is below its natural level, the aggregate supply curve keeps shifting down. That is, at a given level of output, the price level in a given year will be below the price level the year before. In the absence of a change in the nominal exchange rate, the aggregate demand curve does not shift. Thus, starting from A, the economy will move over time along the aggregate demand curve, until it reaches B. At B, output is equal to its natural level. The price level is lower; by implication the real exchange rate is higher.

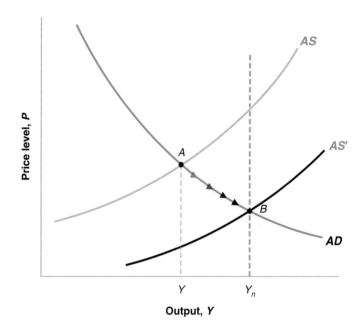

FIGURE 13-4

**Adjustment without
a Devaluation**

The aggregate supply shifts
down, leading to a decrease in
the price level, a real depreciation, and an increase in output over time. The process
ends when output has
returned to its natural level.

In words, the steady decrease in the price level over time will lead to a steady real depreciation. This real depreciation will lead to an increase in output until output has returned to
its natural level.

This is an important conclusion. In the medium run, despite the fact that the nominal
exchange rate is fixed, the economy achieves the real depreciation needed to return output to
its natural level. This is an important qualification to the conclusions we reached in the previous chapter—where we were focusing only on the short run:

- In the short run, a fixed nominal exchange rate implies a fixed real exchange rate.
- In the medium run, a fixed nominal exchange rate is consistent with an adjustment of
  the real exchange rate. The adjustment is achieved through movements in the price
  level.[2]

Adjustment with a Devaluation. Now, suppose that instead of letting the economy adjust
over time along the path AB, government decides to give up the existing parity and devalue.

For a given price level, a devaluation (an increase in the nominal exchange rate) leads to
a real depreciation (an increase in the real exchange rate), and thus to an increase in output.
In other words, a devaluation shifts the aggregate demand curve to the right: The demand for
domestic output is higher at a given price level. We saw this in Figure 13–2: As the flexible
currency depreciated in value, the AD curve shifted to the right.

This has a straightforward implication. A devaluation of the right size can take the economy directly back to the natural level of output. In terms of Figure 13–5, the right size revaluation can take the economy from point A to point C. The economy is initially at A, the same
point A as in Figure 13–3. The right size depreciation shifts the aggregate demand curve from

[2]**DIGGING DEEPER**. Note that along the path of adjustment, the price level *decreases*. This would
seem implausible, as we rarely observe countries going through deflation. (Japan in the late 1990s is
a recent exception.) But this is the result of our assumption that the foreign price level is constant so
that for domestic goods to become relatively cheaper, the domestic price level must *decrease*. If,
instead, we had assumed that the foreign price level was increasing through time, the domestic price
level would have to increase by less than the foreign price level or, put another way, domestic inflation
would have to be lower than foreign inflation for some time.

FIGURE 13–5

Adjustment with a Devaluation

The right size devaluation can shift aggregate demand to the right, moving the economy from point *A* to point *C*. At point *C*, output is back at its natural level.

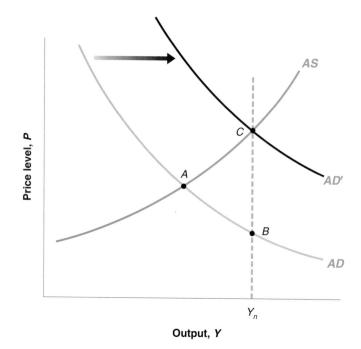

AD to *AD'*, moving the equilibrium from *A* to *C*. At *C*, output is equal to its natural level Y_n. The real exchange rate is the same as at *B*. (We know this because output is the same at points *B* and *C*. From equation (13.9), and without changes in *G* or *T*, this implies that the real exchange rate must also be the same.)

That the "right size" devaluation can return output to its natural level right away — rather than over time, as was the case without the devaluation — sounds too good to be true, and in practice, it is. Achieving the "right size" devaluation — the devaluation that takes output to Y_n right away — is easier to achieve in a graph than in the real world:

See section 7-5 on the ▶ J-curve.

- In contrast to our simple aggregate demand relation (equation (13.9)), the effects of a real depreciation on output do not happen right away: Indeed, as we saw in Chapter 7, the initial effects of a depreciation on output may be contractionary, as people pay more for imports, and the quantities of imports and exports have not yet adjusted.

- Also, in contrast to our simple aggregate supply relation (13.10), there is likely to be a direct effect of the devaluation on the price level: As the price of imported goods increases, the price of a consumption basket increases. This is likely to lead workers to ask for higher nominal wages, forcing firms to increase their prices as well.

But these complications do not affect the basic conclusion: Allowing the nominal exchange rate to adjust can help output return to its natural level, if not right away, at least much faster than without a devaluation.

To summarize: We have learned that we must qualify some of the conclusions we had reached in Chapter 8. Even under fixed *nominal* exchange rates, countries can adjust their *real* exchange rate in the medium run. They can do so by relying on adjustments in the price level. Nevertheless, the adjustment may be long and painful.

Thus, whenever an exchange rate appears overvalued — be it because output is too low or the trade deficit too large — there is sure to be a debate about whether the country should devalue or, instead, stick to the existing parity.

- Those who want faster adjustment argue for devaluation. Perhaps the most forceful presentation of this view was made more than 70 years ago by Keynes, who argued against Winston Churchill's 1925 decision to return the English pound to its pre–World War I

In 1925, Britain decided to return to the **gold standard**. The gold standard was a system in which each country fixed the price of its currency in terms of gold and stood ready to exchange gold for currency at the stated parity. This system implied fixed nominal exchange rates between countries.

The gold standard had been in place from 1870 until World War I. Because of the need to finance the war, and to do so, in part, by money creation, Britain had suspended the gold standard in 1914. In 1925, Winston Churchill, then Britain's Chancellor of the Exchequer (the British equivalent of the Minister of Finance in Canada), decided to return to the gold standard, and to do so at the prewar parity—that is, at the prewar value of the pound in terms of gold. But because prices had increased faster in Britain than in many of its trading partners, returning to the prewar parity implied a large real appreciation: At the same nominal exchange rate as before the war, British goods were now more expensive relative to foreign goods.

Keynes severely criticized the decision to return to the prewar parity. In *The Economic Consequences of Mr. Churchill*, a book he published in 1925, Keynes argued as follows: If Britain was going to return to the gold standard, it should have done so at a higher price of gold in terms of currency, at a nominal exchange rate higher than the prewar nominal exchange rate. In a newspaper article, he articulated his views as follows:

> There remains, however, the objection to which I have never ceased to attach importance, against the return to gold in actual present conditions, in view of the possible consequences on the state of trade and employment. I believe that our price level is too high, if it is converted to gold at the par of exchange, in relation to gold prices elsewhere; and if we consider the prices of those articles only which are not the subject of international trade, and of services, i.e., wages, we shall find that these are materially too high—not less than 5%, and probably 10%. Thus, unless the situation is saved by a rise of prices elsewhere, the Chancellor is committing us to a policy of forcing down money wages by perhaps 2 shillings in the Pound.
>
> I do not believe that this can be achieved without the gravest danger to industrial profits and industrial peace. I would much rather leave the gold value of our currency where it was some months ago than embark on a struggle with every trade union in the country to reduce money wages. It seems wiser and simpler and saner to leave the currency to find its own level for some time longer rather than force a situation where employers are faced with the alternative of closing down or of lowering wages, cost what the struggle may.
>
> For this reason, I remain of the opinion that the Chancellor of the Exchequer has done an ill-judged thing—ill judged because we are running the risk for no adequate reward if all goes well.

Keynes's prediction turned out to be right. While other countries were growing, Britain was in a recession for the rest of the decade. Most economic historians attribute a good part of the blame to the initial overvaluation.

Source: The Nation and Athenaeum, May 2, 1925.

parity. His arguments are presented in the Global Macro box "The Return of Britain to the Gold Standard: Keynes versus Churchill." Most economic historians believe that history proved Keynes right and that overvaluation of the pound was one of the main reasons for Britain's poor economic performance after World War I.

- Those who oppose a devaluation argue that there are good reasons to choose fixed exchange rates and that too much willingness to devalue defeats the purpose of adopting a fixed exchange rate regime in the first place. They also argue that too much willingness on the part of governments to consider a devaluation may lead to an increased likelihood of exchange rate crises. To understand their arguments, we now turn to a discussion of these crises: what triggers them and what their implications might be.

13-3 | Exchange Rate Crises

Take a country operating under fixed exchange rates. Suppose that participants in financial markets start believing there may soon be an exchange rate adjustment—either a devaluation or a shift to a flexible exchange rate regime accompanied by a depreciation. Why might this be the case?

- The domestic currency may be overvalued. A real depreciation is called for. While this can be achieved without a devaluation, financial investors may conclude that government will take the quickest way out and devalue. Such an overvaluation often happens in countries that fix the nominal exchange rate while having an inflation rate higher than the inflation rate in the country they are pegging to. Higher relative inflation implies a steadily increasing price of domestic goods relative to foreign goods, a steady real appreciation, and so a steady worsening of the trade position. As time passes, the need for an adjustment of the real exchange rate steadily increases, and financial investors become more and more nervous.

- Internal conditions may call for a decrease in the domestic interest rate. A decrease in the domestic interest rate cannot be achieved under fixed exchange rates. But it can be achieved if the country is willing to shift to a flexible exchange rate regime. If a country lets the exchange rate float and then decreases its domestic interest rate, we know from Chapter 8 that this will trigger an increase in the nominal exchange rate—a nominal depreciation.

Whatever the reason, suppose financial markets believe a devaluation may be imminent. For the central bank to maintain the exchange rate requires an increase, often a large one, in the domestic interest rate. To see this, return to the interest parity condition we derived in Chapter 6 and used earlier in this chapter:

$$i_t = i_t^* + \frac{(E_{t+1}^e - E_t)}{E_t}$$

(13.11)

More precisely, the necessary interest rate differential is $(1.02)^{24} - 1 = 26.8\%$.

In Chapter 6, we interpreted this equation as a relation between the *one-year* domestic and foreign nominal interest rates, the current exchange rate and the expected exchange rate a year hence. But the choice of one year as the period was arbitrary. The relation holds over a day, a week, a month. If financial markets expect the exchange rate to be 2% higher a month from now, they will hold domestic bonds only if the one-month domestic interest rate exceeds the one-month foreign interest rate by 2% (or, if we express interest rates at an annual rate, if the domestic interest rate exceeds the foreign interest rate by approximately $2\% \times 12 = 24\%$).

Under fixed exchange rates, the current exchange rate E_t is fixed at some level, say, $\bar{E}$. If markets expect the parity will be maintained over the period, then $E_{t+1}^e = \bar{E}$, and the interest parity condition simply states that the domestic and the foreign interest rates must be equal.

Suppose, however, that participants in financial markets start anticipating a devaluation—an increase in the exchange rate. Suppose that they believe that over the coming month, there is a 50% chance the parity will be maintained and a 50% chance there will be a 10% devaluation. Thus, the term $(E_{t+1}^e - E_t)/E_t$ in the interest parity equation (13.11), which we assumed equal to zero earlier, now equals $0.5 \times 0\% + 0.5 \times 10\%$ (a 50% chance of no change plus a 50% chance of a devaluation of 10%), thus equals 5%.

This implies that if the central bank wants to maintain the existing parity, it must now offer a monthly interest rate 5% higher—that is, $12 \times 5\% = 60\%$ higher at an annual rate! Sixty percent is the "annual" interest differential needed to convince investors to hold domestic bonds in view of the risk of a devaluation!

What, then, are the choices confronting government and the central bank?

In most countries, government is formally in charge of choosing the parity and the central bank formally in charge of defending it. In practice, choosing and defending the parity are joint responsibilities of government and the central bank.

- First, government and the central bank can try to convince markets they have no intention of devaluing. This is always the first line of defence: Communiqués are issued, and prime ministers appear on TV to reiterate their absolute commitment to the existing parity. But words are cheap, and they rarely convince financial markets.

In the summer of 1998, Boris Yeltsin announced that the Russian government had no intention of devaluing the ruble. Two weeks later, the ruble collapsed.

- Second, the central bank can increase the interest rate, but by less than needed to satisfy equation (13.11)—in our example, by less than 60%. Although domestic interest rates are high, they are not high enough to fully compensate for the perceived risk of devaluation. This action typically leads to a large capital outflow, as financial investors still see foreign bonds are more attractive. To maintain the parity, the central bank must buy domestic currency and sell foreign currency in the foreign exchange market. In doing so, it often loses most of its reserves of foreign currency. (The mechanics of central bank intervention were described in the appendix to Chapter 8.)

- Eventually—after a few hours or a few months—the choice for the central bank becomes either to increase the interest rate enough to satisfy equation (13.11) or to validate the market's expectations and devalue. Setting a very high short-term domestic interest rate can have a devastating effect on demand and on output. This course of action makes sense only if (1) the perceived probability of a devaluation is small, so the interest rate does not have to be too high, and (2) government believes markets will soon become convinced that no devaluation is coming, allowing domestic interest rates to decrease. Otherwise, the only option is to devalue.

To summarize: Expectations that a devaluation may be on the way can trigger an exchange rate crisis. Faced with such expectations, government has two options: (1) give in and devalue, or (2) fight and maintain the parity, at the cost of very high interest rates and a potential recession. Fighting may not work anyway: The recession may force government to change policy later on or force government out of office.

An interesting twist here is that a devaluation may occur even if the belief that a devaluation was imminent was initially groundless. Even if government initially had no intention of devaluing, it may be forced to devalue if financial markets believe that it will devalue: The cost of maintaining the parity would be a long period of high interest rates and a recession so, government prefers to devalue instead. Some economists believe that the exchange rate crises that hit many Asian countries in 1997 had such a self-fulfilling element; we will return to this issue in Chapter 24. In the rest of the section, we focus on the exchange rate crisis which shook the European Monetary System in the early 1990s.

Crises in the European Monetary System

At the start of the 1990s, the European Monetary System (EMS) appeared to work well. Started in 1979, it was an exchange rate system based on fixed parities with bands: Each member country (among them, France, Germany, Italy, and [starting in 1990] the United Kingdom) had to maintain its exchange rate vis-à-vis all other member countries within narrow bands. The first few years had been rocky, with many **realignments**—adjustment of parities—among member countries, but from 1987 to 1992, there were only two realignments. There was increasing talk about narrowing the bands further and even moving to the next stage—to a common currency.

In 1992, however, financial markets became increasingly convinced that more realignments were soon to come. The reason was one we have seen already, namely, the implications of German reunification. Because of the pressure on demand coming from reunification, the Bundesbank was maintaining high interest rates to try to avoid too large an increase in output and an increase in inflation in Germany. Although Germany's trading partners needed lower interest rates to reduce a growing unemployment problem, they had to match the German interest rates to maintain their EMS parities. To financial markets, the position of Germany's partners looked increasingly untenable. Lower interest rates outside Germany, and thus devaluations of many currencies vis-à-vis the Deutchmark (DM), appeared increasingly likely.

Throughout 1992, the perceived probability of a devaluation forced several of Germany's trading partners to maintain higher nominal interest rates than Germany. But the first major crisis did not come until September 1992. The day-by-day story is told in the Global Macro box "Anatomy of a Crisis: The September 1992 EMS Crisis." The belief, in early September, that a number of countries were soon going to devalue led to speculative attacks on several currencies, with financial investors selling in anticipation of an oncoming devaluation. All the lines of defence described earlier were used. First, solemn communiqués were issued, but with

See the Global Macro box in Chapter 5 "German Unification and the German Monetary–Fiscal Tug-of War" and the Global Macro box in Chapter 8 "German Unification, Interest Rates, and the EMS."

- **September 5–6**. The Ministers of Finance of the European Union meet in Bath, England. The official communiqué at the end of the meeting reaffirms their commitment to maintaining existing parities within the exchange rate mechanism (ERM) of the European Monetary System (EMS).

- **September 8: The first attack**. The attack comes not against one of the currencies in the EMS but rather against the currencies of Scandinavian countries, which are also pegged to the DM. The Finnish authorities give in and decide to let their currency, the markka, **float**—that is, be determined in the foreign exchange market without central bank intervention. The markka depreciates by 13% vis-à-vis the DM. Sweden decides to maintain its parity and increases its overnight interest rate to 24% (at an annual rate). Two days later, it increases it further to 75%.

- **September 10–11: The second attack**. The Bank of Italy intervenes heavily to maintain the parity of the lira, leading the bank to sustain large losses of foreign exchange reserves. But on September 13, the lira is devalued by 7% vis-à-vis the DM.

- **September 16–17: The third and major attack**. Speculation starts against the British pound, leading to large losses in reserves by the Bank of England. The Bank of England increases its overnight rate from 10% to 15%. However, speculation continues against both the pound and (despite the previous devaluation) the lira. Both the United Kingdom and Italy announce they are temporarily suspending their participation in the ERM.

Over the following weeks, both currencies depreciate by roughly 15% vis-à-vis the DM.

- **September 16–17**. With the pound and the lira out of the ERM, the attack turns against the other currencies. To maintain its parity, Sweden increases its overnight rate to 500%! Ireland increases its overnight rate to 300%. Spain decides to stay in the ERM but to devalue by 5%.

- **September 20**. French voters narrowly approve the Maastricht treaty (the treaty that sets the timing for the transition to a common currency) in a referendum. A negative vote would surely have amplified the crisis. The narrow, but positive, vote is seen as the sign that the worst may be over and that the treaty will eventually be accepted by all EU members.

- **September 23–28**. Speculation against the franc forces the Banque de France to increase its short-term interest rate by 2½ percentage points. To defend their parity without having to resort to very high short-term interest rates, both Ireland and Spain reintroduce capital controls.

- **End of September**. The crisis ends. Two countries, the United Kingdom and Italy, have left the ERM and let their currency depreciate. Spain remains within the ERM, but only after a devaluation. The other countries have maintained their parity, but, for some of them, at the cost of large reserve losses.

Source: *World Economic Outlook*, October 1993.

---

no discernible effect. Then, interest rates were increased, up to 500% for the overnight interest rate (the rate for lending and borrowing overnight) in Sweden (expressed at an annual rate). But they were not increased enough to prevent capital outflows and large losses of foreign exchange reserves by the central banks under pressure. Next, different courses of action were followed in different countries: Spain devalued its exchange rate, Italy and the United Kingdom suspended their participation in the EMS, and France decided to tough it out through higher interest rates until the storm was over.

By the end of September, financial markets believed no further devaluations were imminent. Some countries were no longer in the EMS, others had devalued but remained in the EMS, and those that had maintained their parity had shown their determination to stay in the EMS, even if this meant very high interest rates. But the underlying problem—the high German interest rates—was still there, and it was only a matter of time until the next crisis. In November 1992, further speculation forced a devaluation of the Spanish peseta, the Portuguese escudo, and the Swedish krona. The peseta and the escudo were further devalued in May 1993. In July 1993, after yet another large speculative attack, the EMS countries decided to adopt large bands of fluctuations (plus or minus 15%) around central parities, in effect moving to a system that allowed for very large exchange rate fluctuations. This system with wider bands was kept until the introduction of the euro in January 1999.

13-4 | Choosing between Exchange Rate Regimes

Let us return to one of the questions that started the chapter: Should countries choose flexible or fixed exchange rates? Are there circumstances when flexible rates dominate and others when fixed rates dominate?

On macroeconomic grounds, everything we have seen so far would seem to favour flexible exchange rates. The analysis in section 13-1 in this chapter showed that in the medium run, a flexible exchange rate allows a country to choose its own inflation rate. This seems to give countries more choices and favour flexible exchange rates. But governments also care about what happens in the short run, and in the short run, flexible exchange rates also clearly dominate: Under fixed exchange rates, a country gives up control not only of its exchange rate but also—at least under perfect capital mobility—of its interest rate. The open economy macroeconomic model developed in Chapters 6, 7, and 8 assumed exchange rates were flexible. In the open economy, monetary policy works through both the interest rate and the real and nominal exchange rate. The Bank of Canada is firmly in favour of a flexible exchange rate for Canada. Canada has had a flexible exchange rate since 1970, about three years before flexible exchange rates became common in the rest of the world. Canada also had a flexible exchange rate throughout the 1950s when very few countries had flexible exchange rates. Between 1962 and 1970, the Canadian dollar was fixed at $1.08 Canadian per U.S. dollar. How can it ever be a good idea to give up monetary policy in the short run? How can some economists still favour fixed exchange rates? There are three reasons:

- Flexible exchange rates are not without their own problems.
- In some cases, the costs of fixed exchange rates may not be that high.
- In some cases, the benefits of fixed exchange rates may be large.

Let us look at each of these arguments.

The Problems of Flexible Exchange Rates

In the model we developed in Chapter 8, there was a simple relation between the interest rate and the exchange rate: The lower the interest rate, the higher is the exchange rate. This implied that a country that wanted to maintain a stable exchange rate simply had to maintain its interest rate close to the foreign interest rate. A country that wanted to achieve a given depreciation simply had to decrease its interest rate by the right amount.

◄ See Figure 8–1.

In the real world, the relation between the interest rate and the exchange rate is not so simple. Exchange rates often move even in the absence of movements in interest rates. The size of the effect of a given decrease in the interest rate on the exchange rate is often hard to predict, making it much harder for monetary policy to achieve its desired outcome. To see why, let us go back to the interest parity condition:

$$1 + i_t = \left(\frac{1}{E_t}\right)(1 + i_t^*)(E_{t+1}^e)$$

Rewrite it as:

$$E_t = \frac{1 + i_t^*}{1 + i_t} E_{t+1}^e \tag{13.12}$$

Think of the time period as one year. The exchange rate this year depends on the domestic interest rate, the foreign interest rate, and the exchange rate expected for next year. We assumed in Chapter 8 that the expected exchange rate next year (E_{t+1}^e) was constant. But this was a simplification. The exchange rate expected one year hence is not constant. Using equation (13.12), but now for the next year, it is clear that the exchange rate one year hence will depend on the domestic and foreign interest rates expected for next year, on the expected exchange rate two years from now, and so on. Thus, any change in

Note the similarity with stock prices: The stock price depends on the current dividend and interest rate and on the expected stock price next year. The expected price next year depends on next year's expected dividend and interest rate, as well as on the expected stock price two years from now. And so on. This similarity is no coincidence: Exchange rates, like stock prices, depend on current and expected future conditions. Stock prices and interest rates are further explored ◄ in Chapter 19.

expectations of *current and future* domestic and foreign interest rates, as well as changes in the expected exchange rate in the far future, will affect the exchange rate today. This argument is further explored in Chapter 19, which looks at expectations in financial markets and focuses on exchange rate movements under flexible exchange rates. But, if the details are better left to later study, the two basic conclusions are simple:

- The exchange rate can move for many other reasons than changes in the current domestic interest rate.
- The effect of a change in the current domestic interest rate on the exchange rate depends very much on how this change in the interest rate affects expectations of future interest rates.

In short, under flexible exchange rates, the exchange rate may move for many reasons, creating large changes in the real exchange rate and large fluctuations in output. Stabilizing the exchange rate may require large movements in the interest rate; these large interest movements may themselves lead to large fluctuations in output. Thus, controlling the economy under flexible exchange rates is much harder than we made it look in Chapter 8. Put another way, the benefits of a flexible exchange rate regime may be smaller than our previous arguments suggested.

The Limited Costs of Fixed Exchange Rates

The costs of a fixed exchange rate regime may also be smaller than our previous arguments suggested. True, countries that operate under a fixed exchange rate regime are constrained to have the same interest rate. But how costly is that constraint? If they face roughly the same macroeconomic problems and the same shocks, they would have chosen similar policies in the first place. Forcing them to have the same monetary policy may not be much of a constraint.

This is the same Mundell who put together the Mundell–Fleming model we saw in Chapter 8.

This argument was explored by Robert Mundell, who looked at the conditions under which a set of countries might want to operate under fixed exchange rates or even adopt a common currency. For countries to constitute an **optimal currency area**, Mundell argued, they need to satisfy one of two conditions:

- They have to experience similar shocks. We just saw the rationale for this: If they have similar shocks, then they would have chosen roughly the same policy anyway.
- Or, if they experience different shocks, they must have high factor mobility. For example, if workers are willing to move from countries doing poorly to countries doing well, factor mobility rather than macroeconomic policy can allow countries to adjust to shocks. The exchange rate is not needed.

Each province could have its own currency that freely floated against other provincial currencies. But this is not the case: Canada is a common currency area, with one currency, the Canadian dollar.

Following Mundell's analysis, many economists have asked if a country or a group of countries is an optimal currency area. The 10 provinces (and three territories) of Canada are a common currency area. The first condition above is clearly not satisfied; provinces ("regions" is a better choice) do not suffer from the same shock. British Columbia has a large forestry sector, Manitoba and Saskatchewan a large grain sector, Ontario and Quebec large manufacturing sectors. The Atlantic provinces depend more heavily than other regions on forestry and fishery. Alberta is much more affected by oil prices than are other provinces. But the second condition is partly satisfied. There is considerable labour mobility among English-speaking provinces; many people from the rest of Canada have moved to both Alberta and British Columbia in the past 30 years. Quebec, with language variation, is a special case. The Further Reading in this chapter includes various discussions of whether Canada and the United States together form an optimal currency area.

The Benefits of Fixed Exchange Rates

Finally, fixed exchange rate systems have several potential benefits:

- First, operating under fixed exchange rates simplifies things for firms. They can think about where to locate plants and how to increase sales without having to worry about potentially large fluctuations in the exchange rate. These advantages are very clear when countries decide not only to fix their bilateral exchange rates but also to go all the way and adopt a common currency. The benefits of having a common currency for all provinces within a country for firms and consumers are obvious; think of how complicated life would be if you had to change currency every time you crossed a provincial line.

This is true also of the major new common currency area, the euro zone. (The Focus box "The Euro: A Short History" gives you a short history of the euro and a discussion of current issues in that zone.) A report by the European Commission estimates that the adoption of the euro, which will eliminate foreign exchange transactions within the euro zone, will save 0.5% of the combined GDP of these countries. The benefits of the euro in terms of improved efficiency are likely to be much larger than just lower transaction costs. When prices are quoted in the same currency, it becomes much easier for buyers to compare prices, and competition between firms increases, benefiting consumers. There is already some evidence that this is happening in Europe. When shopping for cars, for example, European consumers now are looking for the lowest price anywhere in the euro zone. This already has led to a decline in the price of cars in several countries.

- Second, there may be cases where a country may actually want to limit its ability to use monetary policy. We will look at this argument in more detail in Chapter 23—where we look at the dynamics of hyperinflation—and in Chapter 26—where we look at monetary policy in general—but the essence of the argument is simple:

Take a country that has had very high inflation in the recent past. This may be, for example, because it was unable to finance its budget deficit by any other means than through money creation, resulting in high money growth and high inflation. Suppose the country decides to reduce money growth and inflation. One way of convincing financial markets that it is serious about reducing money growth is to fix its exchange rate: The need to use money supply to maintain the parity then constrains the monetary authority. To the extent that financial markets expect the parity to be maintained, they will stop worrying about money growth being used to finance the budget deficit.

Note the qualifier *to the extent that financial markets expect the parity to be maintained*. Fixing the exchange rate is not a magic solution. The country needs to convince participants in financial markets that not only is the exchange rate fixed today, it will remain fixed in the future. This has two implications: (1) Fixing the exchange rate must be part of a more general macroeconomic package. (2) Fixing the exchange rate while continuing to run a large budget deficit will only convince financial markets that money growth will start again and that a devaluation is soon to come.

◄ This is what happened in Russia in 1998. (More on this in Chapter 24.)

Making it symbolically or technically harder to change the parity may also be useful. With this aim, several countries have adopted an exchange rate regime known as a **currency board**. Under a currency board, a central bank stands ready to buy or sell foreign currency at the official exchange rate; furthermore, it cannot engage in open market operations, that is, buy or sell government bonds. Currency boards have been quite popular in the 1990s. From 1991 to 2001, Argentina, for example, ran a currency board, with a highly symbolic parity of one U.S. dollar for one Argentinian peso. Giving up the currency board in 2001 and allowing the peso to float was a major defeat for government. The Argentine experience with a currency board is described in the Focus box "Argentina's Currency Board".

To summarize:

- For countries that are highly integrated, adopting fixed exchange rates can yield large benefits. If so, it makes sense for these countries to go all the way and adopt a common currency. Not only does it increase the benefits of fixed exchange rates but it also eliminates the risk of exchange rate crises. Remember, however, if Mundell's conditions are not satisfied, the macroeconomic costs may be large.

- As the European Union celebrated its 30th birthday in 1988, a number of governments decided that the time had come to plan a move to a common currency. They asked Jacques Delors, the President of the European Union, to prepare a report, which he presented in June 1989.

  The Delors report suggested moving to a European Monetary Union (EMU) in three stages: Stage I was the abolition of capital controls. Stage II was the choice of fixed parities, to be maintained except for "exceptional circumstances." Stage III was the adoption of a single currency.

- Stage I was implemented in July 1990.

- Stage II started in 1994, after the exchange rate crises of 1992–1993 had subsided. A minor but symbolic decision involved choosing the name of the new common currency. The French liked "Ecu" (European currency unit), which is also an old French currency name. But its partners preferred **euro**, and the name was adopted in 1995.

- In parallel, EU countries held referendums on whether they should adopt the **Maastricht treaty**. The treaty, negotiated in 1991, set three main conditions for joining the EMU: low inflation, a budget deficit below 3%, and a public debt below 60%. The treaty was not very popular, and in many countries, the outcome of the popular vote was close. In France, the treaty passed with only 51% of the votes. In Denmark, the treaty was rejected.

- In 1996–1997, it looked as if few European countries would satisfy the Maastricht conditions. But a number of countries took drastic measures to reduce their budget deficit. When the time came to decide, in May 1998, which countries would be members of the EMU, 11 countries made the cut: Austria, Belgium, Finland, France, Germany, Italy, Ireland, Luxembourg, the Netherlands, Portugal, and Spain. The United Kingdom, Denmark, and Sweden decided to stay out, at least at the beginning. Greece did not qualify.

- Stage III started in January 1999. Parities between the 11 currencies and the euro were "irrevocably" fixed. The new **European Central Bank (ECB)** based in Frankfurt became responsible for monetary policy for the euro area. In 2001, Greece finally qualified and joined.

  From 1999 to 2002, the euro existed as a unit of account, but euro coins and bank notes did not exist. In effect, the euro area was still functioning as an area with fixed exchange rates. The next and final step was the introduction of euro coins and bank notes in January 2002. For the first few months of 2002, national currencies and the euro then circulated side by side, before national currencies were taken out of circulation later in the year.

  Today, the euro is the only currency used in the euro area. The euro area, as the group of member countries is called, has become a common currency area.

  For more on the euro, go to **http://www.euro. ecb.int/.**

  There is, however, less agreement on whether Europe constitutes an optimal common currency area. This is because neither of the two Mundell conditions appears to be satisfied. While the future may be different, European countries have experienced very different shocks in the past; recall German reunification and how differently it has affected Germany and the other European countries. Furthermore, labour mobility is very low in Europe and likely to remain low. Workers move much less within European countries than they do within the United States or Canada. Given the language and cultural differences among European countries, mobility between countries is likely to be even lower. The risk is, therefore, that at some time now or in the future, one or more euro members may suffer from a large decline in demand and output and will not be able to use either the interest rate or the exchange rate to increase activity. As we saw in section 13-3, the adjustment will still take place in the medium run. But, as you also saw there, this adjustment may be long and painful. There is some evidence in the period around 2005 that Germany, with very high unemployment, must undergo precisely such an adjustment. Germany may yet wish it had never joined the euro group.

The situation in Europe, as discussed in the Focus box "The Euro: A Short History," is unclear.

- For countries that have to establish or re-establish a reputation for responsible macroeconomic policy, a fixed exchange rate regime may also be useful. In this case, it may make sense to use a highly symbolic regime, such as the currency board.
- For other countries, it probably makes more sense to float. This does not imply ignoring the exchange rate altogether in the setting of monetary policy. But it means being willing to let the exchange rate move over time and to use the interest rate and the exchange rate to reduce output fluctuations.

When Carlos Menem became President of Argentina in 1989, he inherited an economic mess. Inflation was running at more than 30% a month. Output growth was negative.

Menem and his economic minister, Domingo Cavallo, quickly came to the conclusion that under these circumstances, the only way to bring money growth—and by implication, inflation—under control was to peg the peso (Argentina's currency) to the U.S. dollar, and to do this through a very hard peg. So, in 1991, Cavallo announced that Argentina would adopt a currency board. The central bank would stand ready to exchange pesos for dollars, on demand. Furthermore, it would do so at the highly symbolic rate of 1 U.S. dollar for 1 peso.

Both the creation of a currency board and the choice of a symbolic exchange rate had the same objective: to convince financial markets that government was serious about the peg and to make it more difficult for future governments to give up the parity and devalue. And so, by making the fixed exchange rate more credible in this way, they could decrease the risk of a foreign-exchange crisis.

For a while, the currency board appeared to work extremely well. Inflation, which had exceeded 2300% in 1990, was down to 4% by 1994! This was clearly the result of the tight constraints the currency board put on money growth. Even more impressive, this large decrease in inflation was accompanied by strong output growth. Output growth averaged 5% a year from 1991 to 1999.

Starting in 1999, however, growth turned negative, and Argentina went into a long and deep recession. Was the recession due to the currency board? Yes and no:

- Throughout the second half of the 1990s, the dollar steadily appreciated vis-à-vis other major world currencies. Because the peso was pegged to the dollar, the peso also appreciated. By the late 1990s, it was clear that the peso was overvalued, leading to a decrease in demand for goods from Argentina, a decline in output, and an increase in trade deficit.

- Was the currency board fully responsible for the recession? No—there were other causes. But the currency board made it much harder to fight it. Lower interest rates and a depreciation of the peso would have helped the economy recover; but under the currency board, this was not an option.

In 2001, the economic crisis turned into a financial and exchange rate crisis, along the lines we described in section 13-2:

- Because of the recession, the fiscal deficit had increased, leading to an increase in government debt. Worried that

government might default on its debt, financial investors started asking for very high interest rates on government debt, making the fiscal deficit even larger and, by doing so, further increasing the risk of default.

- Worried that government would give up the currency board and devalue in order to fight the recession, financial investors started asking for very high interest rates in pesos, making it more costly for government to sustain the parity with the dollar, and so making it more likely that the currency board would be abandoned.

In December 2001, government defaulted on part of its debt. In early 2002, it gave up the currency board and let the peso float. The peso sharply depreciated, reaching 3.75 pesos for 1 U.S. dollar by June 2002! People and firms that, given their earlier confidence in the peg, had borrowed in dollars found themselves with a large increase in the value of their debts in pesos. Many went bankrupt. The banking system collapsed. Despite the sharp real depreciation, which should have helped exports, GDP fell by 11% in 2002, and unemployment increased to nearly 20%. Output growth turned positive in 2003, but it will take some time before GDP gets back to its 1999 level.

Does this mean that the currency board was a bad idea? Economists still disagree:

- Some argue that it was a good idea, but it did not go far enough. Argentina should have simply dollarized, that is, adopted the U.S. dollar as the currency, and eliminated the peso altogether. By eliminating the domestic currency, this solution would have eliminated the risk of a devaluation. The lesson, they argue, is that even a currency board does not provide a sufficiently hard peg for the exchange rate. Only dollarization will do.

- Others argue that the currency board may have been a good idea at the start but that it should not have been kept for so long. Once inflation was under control, Argentina should have moved from a currency board to a floating exchange rate regime. The problem was that Argentina kept the fixed parity with the dollar for too long, to the point where the peso was overvalued, and an exchange rate crisis was inevitable.

The debate is likely to go on. Meanwhile, Argentina has to reconstruct its economy.

(For more on Argentina, go to Nouriel Roubini's Web site at www.stern.nyu.edu/globalmacro/ and go to the country page on Argentina.)

- Even under a fixed exchange rate regime, countries can adjust their *real* exchange rate in the medium run by relying on adjustments in the price level. Nevertheless, the adjustment may be long and painful. Nominal exchange rate adjustments can, in principle, allow the economy to adjust faster and reduce the pain.

- Exchange rate crises typically start when participants in financial markets believe a currency may soon be devalued. Defending the parity then requires very high interest rates, with potentially large adverse macroeconomic effects. These adverse effects may force the country to devalue, even if there were no plans for such a devaluation in the first place.

- In thinking about flexible versus fixed exchange rates, you must keep in mind four sets of arguments:

  1. Flexible exchange rates allow the central bank to use both the interest rate and the exchange rate for macroeconomic purposes. Fixed exchange rates and perfect capital mobility eliminate the scope for using either the exchange rate or the interest rate.

  2. Flexible exchange rates are often associated with large fluctuations in the exchange rate, making it difficult for the central bank to stabilize the economy.

  3. Fixed exchange rates may not be very costly if one of two conditions is satisfied: The countries that are pegging their exchange rate face largely the same shocks. Or there is high labour mobility between them.

  4. Fixed exchange rates also have benefits. They reduce transaction costs and improve efficiency. These benefits are even larger if countries adopt not only fixed exchange rates but also a common currency. Fixed exchange rates may also help governments establish or re-establish their reputation for responsible macroeconomic policy.

- currency board, 259
- euro, 260
- European Central Bank (ECB), 260
- float, 256

- gold standard, 253
- Maastricht treaty, 260
- optimal currency area, 258
- realignments, 255

An asterisk denotes a harder question. [Web] indicates that the question requires access to the Internet.

1. **TRUE/FALSE/UNCERTAIN**

a. Britain's return to the gold standard caused years of high unemployment.

b. If in a country committed to a fixed exchange rate, investors suddenly fear a severe devaluation, they may well trigger an exchange rate crisis.

c. Because speculative behaviour by foreign investors can cause currency crises, small countries would be better off not allowing foreigners to hold domestic assets.

d. The countries of Southeast Asia should form a common currency area as they produce similar goods and are subject to largely similar shocks.

e. The large number of immigrants from Mexico to the United States every year indicates there is substantial labour mobility between the two countries, and thus they constitute an optimal currency area.

2. **A CLOSER LOOK AT AGGREGATE DEMAND**

Consider the specification of the aggregate demand relation in an open economy with fixed exchange rates given in the text:

$$Y = C(Y - T) + I(Y, i^*) + G$$
$$+ NX\left(Y, Y^*, \frac{\bar{E}P^*}{P}\right)$$

a. Discuss the effects on output, given the domestic price level, of an increase in the foreign price level.

b. Discuss the effects on output, given the domestic price level, of an increase in expected inflation.

c. Discuss the effects on output of an increase in foreign interest rates. If the country wishes to keep its exchange rate fixed, how can it keep output constant?

3. EXCHANGE RATE CHANGES WITH DOMESTIC AND FOREIGN INFLATION

a. Use the data below to calculate nominal exchange rates in period $t + 1$, $t + 2$ and $t + 3$ that keep the real exchange rate constant.

b. If the foreign rate of interest is 8% each period and the expected exchange rate in period t is the actual exchange rate in period $t + 1$ (and similarly for periods $t + 2$ and $t + 3$), what is the domestic rate of interest when uncovered interest parity holds?

c. If you observed that during the 1970s Germany usually had a lower rate of interest than the United Kingdom, what would you expect of the exchange rate between the German mark and the British pound over this decade?

4. SHORT-RUN AND MEDIUM-RUN EFFECTS OF CHANGES IN GOVERNMENT SPENDING

Consider a country operating under fixed exchange rates, with aggregate demand and aggregate supply given by:

$$Y_t = Y\left(\frac{\bar{E}P^*}{P_t}, G, T\right)$$

and

$$P_t = P_{t-1}(1 + \mu) \, F\left(1 - \frac{Y_t}{L}, z\right)$$

Assume the economy is initially in medium-run equilibrium, with constant prices and output equal to its natural level.

a. Describe the short-run and the medium-run effects of an increase in government spending on output, the real exchange rate, and the interest rate.

b. Describe the short-run and medium-run effects of an increase in government spending on the components of spending: consumption, investment, and net exports.

c. Budget deficits lead to trade deficits. Discuss.

5. EAST GERMANY AND REUNIFICATION

When East Germany and West Germany were reunited in 1990, the exchange rate between the two countries was irrevocably fixed. In a symbolic gesture of equality between the two countries, it was decreed that one East German mark would be worth the same as one West German mark, even though the currency of the East was in reality worth much less.

a. Think of East Germany as the domestic economy. Suppose East Germany is initially in medium-run equilibrium before reunification (obviously a counterfactual assumption here, but one has to start somewhere . . .) and suppose that the exchange rate (vis-à-vis West Germany) is set much too low. Discuss the impact of that decision on equilibrium output and unemployment using *AS-AD* analysis.

b. What happens over time?

c. Suppose that prices in Western Germany are constant—there is no inflation. What has to happen to prices and wages in Eastern Germany?

6. THE BRAZILIAN DEVALUATION OF JANUARY 1999

In January 1999, Brazil was forced to devalue its currency, the real, by 8% against the U.S. dollar despite receiving a multibillion-dollar package from the IMF in November 1998 to defend the currency. In the week before the devaluation, Brazilian stock prices decreased by nearly half. But after the devaluation was announced, the stock market indexes returned to their pre-crisis levels.

Symbol	Variable	t	$t + 1$	$t + 2$	$t + 3$
E	Nominal exchange rate (domestic currency per unit of foreign currency)	1.5	—	—	—
π_t	Domestic inflation (%)	3	3	3	3
π_t^e	Foreign inflation (%)	5	5	5	5

Can you explain these movements in stock prices, assuming arbitrage in financial markets?

(To learn more about events leading up to the crisis, you may want to read an editorial by Rudiger Dornbusch, from MIT, written in November at the time of the IMF package. You can find it at **http://web.mit.edu/rudi/Editorials.html**. In order to read more about the crisis itself, check out the January 16–22, 1999, issue of *The Economist*.)

7. THE PRESSURE ON CHINA TO REVALUE DURING 2005

Between 2004 and 2005, there was a tremendous pressure on China to revalue the yuan. The reasons are fairly clear. As the Chinese economy modernized and joined the world economy, it did so with a fixed exchange rate of 8.25 yuan per U.S. dollar. Over this period, China had a very large trade surplus, particularly with the United States. The American policy response is to ask the Chinese to abandon a decade-long fixed exchange rate to the U.S. dollar.

a. If the yuan were to be revalued by 20%, calculate what its new value would be.

b. If both the price level in China and in the United States did not change when the yuan was revalued, what would be the percentage change in the real exchange rate?

c. Explain why, if the Chinese economy is booming and above full employment, the Chinese would favour a revaluation.

d. Explain how the proposed revaluation of the yuan affect the U.S. economy already at full employment.

FURTHER READING

The issue of whether or not Canada and the United States form an optimal currency area and thus should either share the same currency or at least have fixed exchange has been an active policy issue in Canada over the past 50 years. The debate is summarized in "The W. Irwin Gillespie Round Table on Public Policy: Canadian Exchange Rate Policy," *Canadian Public Policy*, Vol. 25(3), September 1999, pp. 307–324. A history of the early flexible exchange rate regime in Canada and of the movement to a fixed rate in 1962 is found in Paul Wonnacott's book *The Canadian Dollar, 1948–1962* (Toronto: University of Toronto Press, 1961).

THE CORE: THE LONG RUN

The next four chapters focus on the long run. In the long run, what dominates is not fluctuations, but growth. The basic question now is, what determines growth?

CHAPTER 14

Chapter 14 looks at the facts of growth. Looking first at the OECD countries over the past 50 years, it documents the large increase in output, the convergence of output per capita across countries, and the slowdown in growth that has taken place since the mid-1970s. Taking a wider look, both across time and space, it shows that on the scale of human history, growth is a recent phenomenon and that convergence is not a worldwide phenomenon: Many countries are both poor and not growing.

CHAPTER 15

Chapter 15 focuses on the role of capital accumulation in growth. It shows that capital accumulation cannot by itself sustain output growth but that it does affect the level of output. A higher saving rate typically leads to lower consumption initially but more consumption in the long run.

CHAPTER 16

Chapter 16 turns to the role of technological progress. It shows how in the long run, the growth rate of an economy is determined by the rate of technological progress. It then returns to the facts of growth presented in Chapter 14 and shows how to interpret them in light of the theory we have developed.

CHAPTER 17

Chapter 17 shows how growth in an open economy occurs. In an open economy, capital, labour, and technology may be imported from or exported to the rest of the world.

CHAPTER 14
THE FACTS OF GROWTH

Our perceptions of how the economy is doing tend to be dominated by year-to-year fluctuations in activity. A recession leads to gloom, an expansion to optimism. But if we step back to get a look at activity over longer periods of time—say, over the course of many decades—we see a different picture. Fluctuations fade in importance. **Growth**—the steady increase in aggregate output over time—dominates the picture.

Figure 14–1 shows the evolution of Canadian GDP (in 1997 dollars) since 1926. The years after 1930 correspond to the large decrease in output during the Great Depression, and the years 1981–1982 and 1990–1991 correspond to the two largest postwar recessions. Note how small these two episodes appear compared with the steady increase in output since 1926.

Our focus so far in the book has been on fluctuations. In this and the next three chapters, we focus instead on growth. Put another way, we turn from the study of the determination of output in the *short run* and *medium run*—where fluctuations dominate—to the determination of output in the *long run*—where growth dominates.

This chapter presents the facts of growth from Canada, the United States, and elsewhere, from the recent as well as the not so recent past, and introduces the framework economists use to think about growth. The framework is developed in the next two chapters. Chapter 15 focuses on the role of capital accumulation in growth. Chapter 16 focuses on the role of technological progress. Chapter 17 shows how we integrate the open economy into discussions of long-term growth.

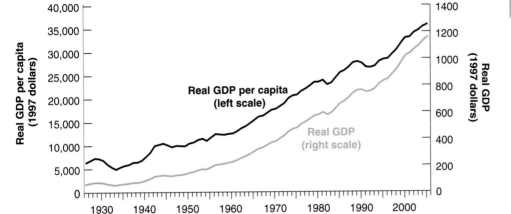

FIGURE 14-1

Real GDP and Real GDP per Capita in Canada, 1926–2005

Aggregate real output has increased by a factor of 19 in Canada since 1926. Per capita real output has increased by a factor of 5.5 times. The latter shows that the average Canadian was much better off in 2005than in 1926.

Source: Real GDP using CANSIM I variable D14442 and CANSIM II variable V3862685; population using CANSIM II variables.

The scale used to measure $GDP on the right-hand vertical axis in Figure 14–1 is called a **logarithmic scale**. It differs from the standard linear scale in the following way:

Take a variable that grows over time at a constant growth rate, say, 3% per year. Then, the larger the variable, the larger will be its increase from one year to the next. When GDP was $60 billion (in 1997 dollars) in 1926, a 3% increase meant an increase of $1.8 billion; in 2001, with GDP at $1,027 billion (in 1997 dollars), a 3% increase meant an increase of $30.8 billion. If we were to plot GDP using a linear vertical scale, the increments would become larger and larger over time. Using a logarithmic scale, the same proportional increase is represented by the same vertical distance on the scale. Put another way, the behaviour of a variable that grows at a constant rate is represented by a curve that becomes steeper and steeper when a linear scale is used but is represented by a straight line when a logarithmic scale is used. The slope of the line is equal to the rate of growth: If a variable grows at 3% per year, the slope of the line is 0.03.

Even when a variable has a growth rate that varies from year to year—as is the case for GDP—the slope at any point in time still gives the growth rate of the variable at that point in time. The slope of the line between two points at two different dates gives the average growth rate from the first to the second date. This is the reason for using a logarithmic scale to plot variables that grow over time: By looking at the slope, we can easily see what is happening to the growth rate.

Check that you have understood how to use a logarithmic scale. Look at Figure 14–1. In which 10-year period was output growth highest? Has average growth since 1970 been lower or higher than average growth from 1950 to 1970?

14-1 | Growth in Rich Countries since 1950

Table 14–1 gives the evolution of **output per capita** (GDP divided by population) for Canada, France, Japan, the United Kingdom, and the United States since 1950. We have chosen these five countries not only because they are the world's major economic powers but because their experience is broadly representative of that of the advanced countries (the countries that are members of the OECD) over the last half century or so.

There are two reasons for looking here at the numbers for output *per capita* rather than the numbers for total output. The evolution of the standard of living is given by the evolution of output per capita, not total output. And, when comparing countries with different populations, output numbers must be adjusted to take into account these differences in population size. This is exactly what output per capita does.

The growth in incomes in Figure 14–1 gives practice in both thinking about growth and using the logarithmic scale. Where the slope of the line measuring total real GDP (the lower line) is steeper, its growth rate is faster. This makes perfect sense. In 1926, there were only

The Organization for Economic Cooperation and Development (OECD) is an international organization that includes most of the world's rich economies. (See Chapter 1.)

Output: GDP

Output per capita: GDP divided by population

9.5 million Canadians, in 2001, there were 31 million Canadians. Total real output in Canada went up by a factor of over 17 times. Real output per capita went up by a factor of only five times. It is important to adjust to per capita values.

Before discussing the table, we should discuss the way the output numbers are constructed. So far, in constructing output numbers for other countries, we have used the straightforward method of taking that country's GDP expressed in that country's currency, then multiplying it by the current exchange rate to express it in terms of U.S. dollars (see Chapter 1). But this simple computation will not do here, for two reasons.

First, exchange rates can vary a lot as we have already seen. The Canadian dollar depreciated from 1.35 Canadian dollars to 1.58 Canadian dollars per U.S. dollar, a depreciation of 17% between 1997 and 2001. It then appreciated to 1.25 Canadian dollars per U.S. dollar in 2005, an appreciation of 20%. But the standard of living in Canada neither decreased by 17% nor increased by 20%. Most people lived in the same houses, wore similar clothes, and consumed similar food. Yet, if we compared GDP per capita using current exchange rates, we would conclude that Canadians had become 17% poorer in four years or 20% richer in three years.

The second reason goes well beyond fluctuations in exchange rates. In 1997, GDP per capita in India, using the current exchange rate, was $362, compared with $29,800 in the United States. Surely nobody could live on $362 a year in the United States. But people live on it—admittedly, not very well—in India, where the prices of basic goods, those goods needed for subsistence, are much lower than in the United States. The level of consumption of the average consumer in India, who consumes mostly basic goods, is not 82 times smaller than that of his or her U.S. counterpart. This pattern applies to other countries besides the United States and India: In general, the lower a country's income, the lower are the prices of food and basic services in that country.

Thus, when our focus is on comparing standards of living, either across time or across countries, we get more meaningful comparisons by correcting for the effects just discussed. This is what the numbers in Table 14–1 do. The details of construction are complicated, but the principle is simple: The numbers for GDP in Table 14–1 are constructed using a common set of prices for the goods and services produced in each economy. Such adjusted real GDP numbers, which you can think of as measures of **purchasing power** across time or across countries, are called **purchasing power parity (PPP)** numbers. Further discussion is given in the Focus box "The Construction of PPP Numbers."

At this point, the "Penn World Tables" project (described in the accompanying Focus box) has constructed PPP numbers only up to the early 1990s. In Table 14–1, We extended those numbers to 2000 for the five major OECD countries.

When looking, however, at larger sets of countries later in this chapter, extending the numbers would be too much work. So, we look at evolutions of output per capita only up to the latest year available in the data set (1992 for most countries).

TABLE 14–1 The Evolution of Output per Capita in Five Rich Countries since 1950

	Annual Growth Rate Output per Capita (%)		Real Output per Capita (1996 dollars)		
	1950–1973	1974–2000	1950	2000	Ratio of Real Output per Capita, 2000/1950
Canada	2.5	1.8	9,023	26,922	3.0
France	4.0	1.8	5,519	22,371	4.1
Japan	7.4	2.3	2,417	24,671	10.2
United Kingdom	2.4	1.8	7,641	22,188	2.9
United States	2.4	2.1	10,601	33,308	3.1
Average	**3.7**	**2.0**	**7,040**	**25,892**	**4.7**

Source: Penn World Tables, Version 6–1, constructed by Robert Summers, Alan Heston, and Bettina Aten (http://pwt.econ.upenn.edu). The numbers for output per capita are in 1996 dollars. The average in the last line is a simple (unweighted) average.

Let us consider two countries—say, the United States and Russia—but without attempting to fit the facts of these two countries very closely.

In the United States, annual consumption per capita equals $20,000. Individuals buy two goods. Every year, they buy a new car for $10,000, and spend the rest on food. The price of a yearly bundle of food is $10,000.

In Russia, annual consumption per capita equals 12,000 rubles. People keep their cars for 15 years. The price of a car is 60,000 rubles, so individuals spend, on average, 4000 rubles— 60,000/15—a year on cars. They buy the same yearly bundle of food as their U.S. counterparts, at a price of 8000 rubles.

Russian and U.S. cars are of identical quality, and so are Russian and U.S. foods. (You may dispute the realism of these assumptions. Whether a car in country X is the same as a car in country Y is very much the type of problem confronting economists constructing PPP measures.) The exchange rate is such that one U.S. dollar is equal to six rubles. What is consumption per capita in Russia relative to consumption per capita in the United States?

One way to answer is by taking consumption per capita in Russia and converting it into dollars using the exchange rate. Using that method, Russian consumption per capita in dollars is $2000 US (12,000 rubles divided by the exchange rate, six rubles to the dollar), thus 10% of U.S. consumption.

Does this answer make sense? True, Russians are poorer, but food is relatively much cheaper in Russia. A U.S. consumer spending all of his $20,000 on food would buy ($20,000/ $10,000) = 2 bundles of food. A Russian consumer spending all of the 12,000 rubles on food would buy (12,000 rubles/8000 rubles) = 1.5 bundles of food. In terms of food bundles, the difference between U.S. and Russian consumption per capita looks much smaller. And given that one-half of consumption in the United States and two-thirds of consumption in Russia go to spending on food, this seems like a relevant computation.

Can we improve on our initial answer? Yes. One way is to use the same set of prices for both countries and then measure the quantities of each good consumed in each country using this common set of prices. Suppose we use U.S. prices. In terms of U.S. prices, annual consumption per capita in the United States is obviously still $20,000. What is it in Russia? Every year, the average Russian buys approximately 0.07 car (one car every 15 years) and one bundle of food. Using U.S. prices—specifically, $10,000 for a car and $10,000 for a bundle of food—gives Russian consumption per capita: [(0.07 × $10,000) + (1 × $10,000)] = ($700 + $10,000] = $10,700. This puts annual Russian consumption per capita at $10,700/ $20,000 = 53.5% of annual U.S. consumption per capita, a better estimate of relative standards of living than we obtained using our first method (which gave only 10%).

This type of computation, namely, the construction of variables across countries using a common set of prices, underlies PPP estimates. Rather than using U.S. dollar prices as in our example (why use U.S. prices rather than Russian or, for that matter, French prices?), these estimates use average prices across countries; these prices are called international dollar prices. The estimates we use in Table 14–1 and elsewhere in this chapter are the result of an ambitious project known as the "Penn World Tables." Led by three economists—Irving Kravis, Robert Summers, and Alan Heston— over more than 15 years, this project has constructed PPP series not only for consumption (as we just did in our example) but more generally for GDP and its components, going back to 1950, for most countries in the world.

In Canada, we are very concerned that an accurate comparison of GDP per capita between Canada and the United States is made. Each year, Statistics Canada cooperates with the OECD to construct a PPP estimate using the goods and services typical of North America, not those used in the Penn World Tables. These estimates are available from 1981 to the present. A description of the methods used to construct these estimates is found in Statistics Canada catalogue 13-001-XPB, third quarter, 1999, National Income and Expenditure Accounts.

Further Reading

For more on the construction of PPP numbers, read Robert Summers and Alan Heston, "The Penn World Table Mark 5: An Expanded Set of International Comparisons, 1950–1988," *Quarterly Journal of Economics*, 2, 1991: pp. 327–368.

The differences between PPP numbers and the numbers based on current exchange rates can be substantial. Take the comparison between India and the United States. Using PPP numbers, GDP per capita in the United States is roughly equal to 17 times GDP per capita in India. This is still a large difference, but less than the 82 times difference we derived using the current exchange rate. Or consider the ranking of rich countries by output per capita. In 1997, using current exchange rates, U.S. GDP per capita was only 90% of Japan's output per capita; using PPP numbers, it was 130%. Using PPP numbers, the United States still has the highest GDP per capita among the world's major countries.

Bottom line: When comparing standards of living across countries, use PPP numbers.

We can now turn to the numbers in Table 14–1. You should draw three main conclusions from the table:

1. First and foremost is how strong growth has been in all five countries and how much the standard of living has improved since 1950. Growth from 1950 to 2000 has increased real output per capita by a factor of 3.0 in Canada, and 3.1 in the United States, by a factor of 4.1 in France, and by a factor of 10.2 in Japan.

   These numbers show what is sometimes called the *force of compounding*. In a different context, you probably have heard how saving even a little while you are young will build to a large amount by the time you retire. For example, if the interest rate is 5.1% a year, an investment of one dollar, with the proceeds reinvested every year, leads to about 11 dollars 48 years later ($[1 + 0.051]^{48} = 10.9$ dollars). The same logic applies to the Japanese growth rate from 1950 to 2000. The average annual growth rate in Japan over the period was equal to 5.1%, leading to a 12-fold increase in real output per capita. Clearly, a better understanding of growth, if it leads to the design of policies that stimulate growth, can have a very large effect on the standard of living. A policy measure that increased the growth rate from, say, 2% to 3%, would lead, after 40 years, to a standard of living 100% higher than it would have been without the policy.

Needless to say, policy measures with such magic results have proven difficult to discover. ▶

2. Growth rates have decreased since the mid-1970s.

   The first two columns of Table 14–1 show growth rates of output per capita for both pre- and post-1973. Pinpointing the exact date of the decrease in growth is difficult; 1973, the date used to split the sample in the table, is as good as any date in the mid-1970s.

   Growth has decreased in all five countries. The decrease has been stronger in the countries that were growing fast pre-1973, such as France, and especially Japan, with the result that the differences in growth rates across countries are smaller post-1973 than they were pre-1973.

   If it continues, this decline in growth will have profound implications for the evolution of income per capita in the future. At a growth rate of 3.7% per year—the average growth rate across our five countries from 1950 to 1973—it takes only 19 years for the standard of living to double. At a growth rate of 2% per year—the average from 1973 to 2000—it takes 35 years. Expectations of fast growth in individual income that had developed in the 1950s and 1960s have had to confront the reality of lower growth since 1973. For some socioeconomic groups, lower growth of income per capita for the economy as a whole, together with a decline in their income relative to the average, has led to an absolute decline in their income. Those who have been affected the most have typically been the least skilled workers.

The "rule of 70": If a variable grows at *x*% a year, then it will take approximately 70/*x* years for the variable to double. If ▶ *x* = 3.7, it will take about 19 years (70/3.7) for the variable to double. If *x* = 2.0, it will take about 35 years (70/2.0).

3. Levels of output per capita across the six countries have converged over time. Put another way, those countries that were behind have grown faster, reducing the gap between them and the United States.

   In 1950, output per capita in Canada and the United States was around twice the level of output per capita in the United Kingdom, France, and more than six times that of Japan. Looking from Japan and Europe, North America was seen as the land of plenty, where everything was bigger and better. Today, these perceptions have faded, and the numbers explain why. Using PPP numbers, North American output per capita is still the highest, but in 2000, it was only about 25% above output per capita in the other four countries, a much smaller difference than in the 1950s.

This **convergence** of levels of output per capita across countries extends to the set of OECD countries. This is shown in Figure 14–2, which plots the average annual growth rate of output per capita from 1950 to 2000 against the initial level of output per capita in 1950 for the set of countries that are members of the OECD today. There is a clear negative

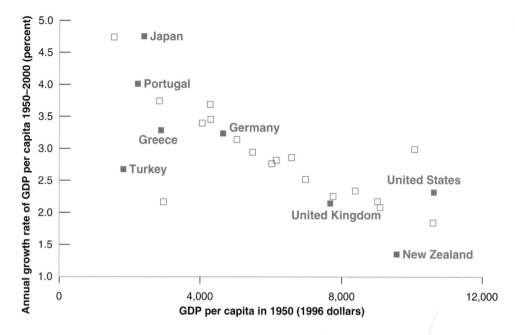

FIGURE 14-2

Growth Rate of GDP per Capita since 1950 versus GDP per Capita in 1950; OECD Countries

Countries with lower levels of output per capita in 1950 have typically grown faster. *Source: See Table 14-1. South Korea, the Czech Republic, Hungary, and Poland are not included because of missing data.*

relation between the initial level of output per capita and the growth rate since 1950: Countries that were behind in 1950 have typically grown faster. The relation is not perfect: Turkey, which had roughly the same low level of output per capita as Japan in 1950, has had a growth rate equal to only about half that of Japan. But the relation is clearly there.

The issue of convergence of output per capita has been a hot topic of macroeconomic research over the past decade. Some have pointed to a potential flaw in such graphs as Figure 14-2. By looking at the set of countries that are members of the OECD today, what we have done, in effect, is to look at a club of economic winners: OECD membership is not officially based on economic success, but economic success is surely an important determinant of membership. But when you look at a club whose membership is based on economic success, you will find that those who came from behind had the fastest growth: This is precisely why they made it to the club. Thus, the finding of convergence could come, in part, from the way we selected the countries in the first place.

Thus, a better way of looking at convergence is to define the set of countries we look at not on the basis of where they are today—as we did in Figure 14-2 by looking at today's OECD members—but on the basis of where they were in, say, 1950. For example, we can look at all countries that had an output per capita of at least one-fourth of U.S. output per capita in 1950, then look for convergence within that group. It turns out that most of the countries in that group have, indeed, converged, and therefore convergence is not solely an OECD phenomenon. However, a few countries—Uruguay, Argentina, and Venezuela among them—have not converged. Perhaps the most striking case is Argentina. Output per capita in Argentina, which was $5120 (in 1992 dollars) in 1950—similar to that of France then—was only $5976 (in 1992 dollars) in 1990, a meager 17% increase in 40 years and far below the 1990 French level of $17,658.

As explained earlier, at this time, 1992 (and, in some cases, 1991 or 1990) is the latest year for which we have PPP numbers for most countries in the world.

1990 is the latest year for which PPP numbers are available for Argentina.

14-2 | A Broader Look across Time and Space

The three basic facts we will keep in mind and try to explain as we go along are:

- The large increase in the standard of living since 1950.
- The decrease in growth since the mid-1970s.
- The convergence of output per capita among rich countries.

Economists take for granted that higher output per capita means higher utility and increased happiness. The evidence on direct measures of happiness, however, points to a more complex picture.

Looking across Countries

Figure 1 shows the results of a study of happiness in 81 countries in the late 1990s. In each country, a sample of people was asked two questions. The first one was: "Taking all things together, would you say you are very happy, quite happy, not very happy, not at all happy?" The second was: "All things considered, how satisfied are you with your life as a whole these days?" Answers were rated on a scale ranging from 1 (dissatisfied) to 10 (satisfied). The measure on the vertical axis is constructed as the average of the percentage of people declaring themselves very happy or happy in answer to the first question, and the percentage of people answering 6 or more to the second question. The measure of output per capita on the horizontal axis is the level of output per capita, measured at PPP prices, in 1999 dollars. (The levels of output per capita in the figure are constructed by the World Bank and are somewhat different from the numbers from the Penn World Tables we have used in the rest of the chapter.) The figure suggests three conclusions.

First, most of the countries with very low happiness levels are the Eastern European countries, which, in the 1990s, were suffering from the collapse of the communist regimes and the difficult transition to capitalism.

Second, and leaving those countries aside, there appears to be a positive relation between happiness and the level of output per capita. Happiness is lower in poor countries than in rich ones.

Third, looking at rich countries—the countries with PPP output per capita above $20,000 (in 1999 dollars), there

appears to be no relation between the level of output per capita and happiness. (To see that, cover the left side of the figure, and just look at the right side.) For this set of countries, higher output per capita does not seem to yield greater happiness.

Looking over Time

One may reasonably argue that comparing happiness across countries is difficult. Different cultures may have different notions of what happiness is. Some countries may be chronically happier or unhappier than others. For this reason, it may be more informative to look at what happens to happiness over time in a given country. This can be done for the United States, where the General Social Survey has asked the following question since the early 1970s: "Taken all together, how would you say things are these days—would you say you are very happy, pretty happy, or not too happy?" Table 1 gives the proportion of answers in each category given in 1975 and in 1996. The numbers in the table are striking. During those 21 years, output per capita increased by more than 60%, but there was basically no change in the distribution of happiness. In other words, a higher standard of living was not associated with an increase in self-reported happiness. Evidence from Gallup polls over the last 60 years confirms the finding. The proportion of people defining themselves as "very happy" is the same as it was in the early 1950s.

Looking over Individuals

Does this mean that "money" (more properly "income") does not bring happiness? The answer is no. If one looks across individuals at any point in time, rich people are more likely to report themselves as being happy than are poor people. This is shown in Table 2, which is again constructed using the answers to the

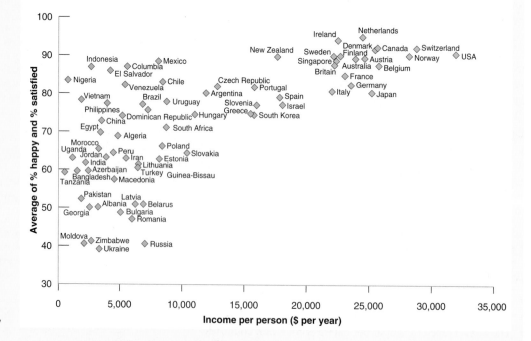

FIGURE 1
Happiness and Output per Capita across Countries

Source: "World Values Survey, 1999–2000 Wave."

 **TABLE** **1**	Distribution of Happiness in the United States over Time (percent)	
	1975	**1996**
Very happy	32	31
Pretty happy	55	58
Not too happy	13	11

TABLE **2**	Distribution of Happiness in the United States across Income Groups (percent)	
Income Level	Top Quarter	Bottom Quarter
Very happy	37	16
Pretty happy	57	53
Not too happy	6	31

General Social Survey and gives the distribution of happiness for different income groups in the United States in 1998.

The results are again striking. The proportion of "very happy" people is much higher among the rich (the people in the top quarter of the income distribution) than among the poor (the people in the bottom quarter of the income distribution). And the reverse holds for the proportion of "not too happy" people. The proportion is much lower among the rich than among the poor.

What conclusions can we draw from all this evidence? At low levels of output per capita, say, up to $15,000 or about half of the current U.S. level, increases in output per capita lead to increases

in happiness. At higher levels, however, the relation appears much weaker. Happiness appears to depend more on people's relative incomes. If this is, indeed, the case, this has important implications for economic policy, at least in rich countries. Growth, and therefore policies that stimulate growth, may not be the key to happiness.

Source: This box is based on the Lionel Robbins Memorial Lectures on *"Happiness. Has Social Science a Clue?"* given by Richard Layard, April 2003 (**cep.lse.ac.uk/events/lectures/layard/RL30303.pdf**). (These three fascinating lectures review both the psychological and medical research on the topic, present more facts, and discuss implications for economic policy.)

Before we do so, however, it is useful to put them in a broader perspective. This is what we do in this section, by looking at the evidence over both a much longer time span and a wider set of countries.

Looking across Two Millennia

Has output per capita in the currently rich economies always grown at growth rates similar to those in Table 14–1? The answer is no. To see why, you do not even need to look at history, just do a simple computation. Suppose that the annual growth rate in the five countries of Table 14–1 had been as small as 0.5% per year since year 0 of the Christian calendar (clearly an arbitrary date here). Working backward, this implies that output per capita in year 0 would have been 0.005% of output per capita today. This is an absurdly small number.

An examination of history confirms this conclusion. Estimates of growth are clearly harder to construct as we look further back in time. But there is agreement among economic historians about the main evolutions over the last 2000 years.

From the end of the Roman Empire to roughly the year 1500 A.D., there was essentially no growth of output per capita in Europe: Most workers were employed in agriculture, in which there was little technological progress. Because agriculture's share of output was so large, inventions with applications outside agriculture could contribute little to overall production and output. Although there was some output growth, it was reflected in a roughly proportional increase in population, leading to rough constancy of output per capita.

In the years 1500 to 1700, growth of output per capita turned positive but small, around 0.1% per year, increasing to 0.2% per year from 1700 to 1820.

Even during the Industrial Revolution, growth rates were not high by current standards. The growth rate of output per capita from 1820 to 1950 in the United States was only 1.5% per year.

On the scale of human history, therefore, growth of output per capita is a recent phenomenon. In light of the growth record of the last 200 years or so, what appears unusual is the high growth rate achieved in the 1950s and the 1960s rather than the lower growth rate since 1973.

History also puts into context the convergence of the OECD countries to the level of U.S. output per capita since 1950. The United States was not always the world's economic leader. History looks more like a long-distance race in which one country assumes leadership for

◄ If the growth rate had been 0.5% per year, output per capita today would be equal to $1.005^{2006} =$ approximately 22,000 times output per capita in year 0. Equivalently, output in year 0 would have been equal to approximately $1/22,000 = 0.004\%$ of output today.

some time, only to lose it to another and return to the pack or disappear from sight. For much of the first millennium, and until the fifteenth century, China probably had the world's highest level of output per capita. For a couple of centuries, leadership moved to the cities of northern Italy. It was then assumed by the Netherlands until around 1820, and then by the United Kingdom from 1820 to around 1870. Since then, the United States has been in the lead. Seen in this light, history looks more like **leapfrogging** (in which countries get close to the leader and then overtake it) than like convergence (in which the race becomes closer and closer). If history is any guide, the United States will not remain in the lead forever.

Looking across Countries

We have seen how output per capita has converged among the OECD countries. But what about the other countries? Are the poorest countries also growing faster? Are they converging towards the United States, even if they are still far behind?

The answer is given in Figure 14–3, which plots the annual growth rate of output per capita from 1960 to 1992 against output per capita for the year 1960 for 99 countries.

Figure 14–3 shows no clear pattern. Over the last 30+ years, convergence has not been the rule. Countries that were relatively poorer in 1960 have not in general grown faster.

However, the cloud of points hides several interesting subpatterns, which appear when we put countries into different groups. We identify three groups in Figure 14–4. The diamonds represent the OECD countries we looked at earlier. The squares represent African countries. The triangles represent Asian economies: Singapore, Taiwan, Hong Kong, and South Korea. To avoid cluttering, Figure 14–4 leaves out all other countries that show less obvious patterns.

The figure yields three main conclusions:

1. The picture for OECD countries is much the same as in Figure 14–2, which looked at a slightly longer period of time (from 1950 on rather than from 1960 on here). Nearly all start at relatively high levels of output per capita (say, at least one-third of the U.S. level in 1960), and there is clear evidence of convergence.

2. Convergence is also evident in the case of the Asian economies. Whereas Japan (represented by a diamond as a member of the OECD) was the first of the Asian economies

The numbers for 1950 are missing for too many countries to use 1950 as the initial year, as we did in Figure 14–2. Figure 14–3 ▶ includes all the countries for which PPP estimates of GDP per capita exist for both 1960 and 2000 or near 2000. There are some notable absences, such as China and several Eastern European countries, for which the numbers for 1960 are not available.

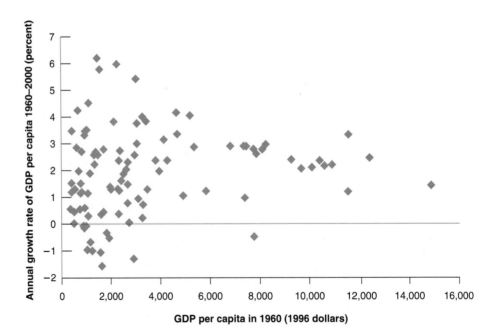

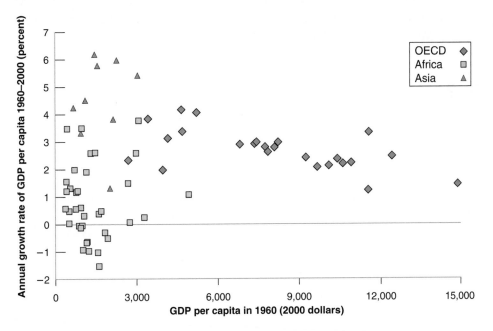

FIGURE 14–4

Growth Rate of GDP per Capita, 1960–2000, versus GDP per Capita in 1960: OECD, Africa, and Asia

Asian countries are converging to OECD levels. There is no evidence of convergence for African countries.

Source: See Table 14–1.

These numbers cover only 1960 to 1992 and do not include recent years and the decrease in growth due to the "Asian crisis" discussed in Chapter 1. But including the lower growth numbers for the late 1990s would make no difference. Put another way, the current output decline in some Asian economies does not ◄ change the fact that they have done extremely well since 1960.

◄ At current exchange rates, Chinese real GDP is only 12% of U.S. real GDP. Can you explain why?

◄ The distinction between *growth theory* and *development economics* is fuzzy. A rough distinction: Growth theory takes many institutions (for example, the legal system, the form of government) as givens. Development economics asks what institutions are needed to sustain steady growth.

to grow rapidly and now has the highest level of output per capita in Asia, several other Asian economies are trailing it closely. Singapore, Taiwan, Hong Kong, and South Korea—sometimes called the **four tigers**—have had average annual growth rates of GDP per capita in excess of 6% over the last 30 years. In 1960, their average output per capita was about 16% of the U.S. number; by 2000, it had increased to 65% of U.S. output. Not far behind (in terms of growth rates) is China, with an average growth rate of 4.2%. With rapidly rising output per capita and a population of 1.3 billion people, China is rapidly becoming a world economic power. At PPP prices, Chinese real GDP now stands at 50% of U.S. real GDP.

3. The picture is very different for African countries. Convergence is certainly not the rule in Africa. Most African countries were very poor in 1960, and many have experienced negative growth of output per capita—an absolute decline in their standard of living— since then. Even in the absence of major wars, output per capita has declined at the rate of 1.3% annually in Chad and Madagascar since 1960; output per capita in these two countries stands at 67% of its 1960 level. Why so many African countries are not growing is one of the main questions facing development economists today.

We shall not take on the wider challenges raised by the facts presented in this section. Doing so would take us too far into economic history and development economics. But they put in perspective the three basic facts we discussed earlier for the OECD:

1. Growth is not a historical necessity. There was little growth for most of human history, and in many countries today, growth remains elusive. Theories that explain growth in the OECD today must also in principle be able to explain the absence of growth in the past and its absence in much of Africa today.

2. Convergence of OECD countries to the United States may well be the prelude to leap-frogging, a stage when economic leadership slips from one country to another. Theories that explain convergence must therefore also allow for the possibility that convergence will be followed by leapfrogging and the appearance of a new economic leader.

3. Finally, in a longer historical perspective, it is not so much the lower growth since 1973 in the OECD that is puzzling. More puzzling is the earlier period of exceptionally fast

growth. Finding the explanation for lower growth today may come from understanding what factors contributed to fast growth post–World War II, and whether these factors have disappeared.

14-3 | Thinking about Growth: A Primer

Solow's article, "A Contribution to the Theory of Economic Growth," appeared in the *Quarterly Journal of Economics*, February 1956, pp. 65–94. Solow received the Nobel prize in 1987 for his work on growth.

How do we explain the facts we saw in sections 14-1 and 14-2? What determines growth? What is the role of capital accumulation? What is the role of technological progress? To think about and answer these questions, economists use a framework developed originally by Robert Solow, from the Massachusetts Institute of Technology, and Trevor Swan from the Australian National University in the late 1950s. The framework has proven sturdy and useful, and we will use it here. This section provides an introduction. Chapters 15 and 16 provide a more detailed analysis, first of the role of capital accumulation and then of the role of technological progress in the process of growth. Chapter 17 extends the analysis to the open economy.

The Aggregate Production Function

The starting point of any theory of growth is the **aggregate production function**, the relation between aggregate output and the inputs in production.

The aggregate production function we introduced in Chapter 9 to study the determination of output in the short and the medium run took a particularly simple form. Output was simply proportional to employment (equation (9.2)). This assumption was acceptable so long as our focus was on fluctuations in output and employment. But now that our focus shifts to growth, it will no longer do: It implies that output per worker is constant, ruling out growth (or at least growth of output per worker) altogether.

It is time to relax it. So, from now on, we will assume that aggregate output is produced using two inputs, capital and labour:

$$Y = F(K, N) \tag{14.1}$$

The aggregate production function is:

$$Y = F(K, N)$$

Aggregate output (Y) depends on the aggregate capital stock (K) and aggregate employment (N).

As before, Y is aggregate output; K is capital—the sum of all the machines, plants, office buildings, and housing in the economy; N is labour—the number of workers in the economy. The function F, which tells us how much output is produced for given quantities of capital and labour, is the aggregate production function. This way of thinking about aggregate production is clearly an improvement on our treatment in Chapter 9. It is still a drastic simplification of reality. Surely, machines and office buildings play very different roles in the production of aggregate output and should be treated as separate inputs. Surely, workers with Ph.D.s are different from high-school dropouts; yet, by constructing the labour input as simply the *number* of workers in the economy, we treat all workers as identical. We will relax some of these simplifications later. For the time being, equation (14.1), which emphasizes the role of both labour and capital in production, will do.

What does the aggregate production function F itself depend on? In other words, how much output can be produced for given quantities of capital and labour? This depends on the **state of technology**. A country with a more advanced technology will produce more output from the same quantities of capital and labour than will an economy with only a primitive technology.

The function F depends on the state of technology. The higher the state of technology, the higher is $F(K, N)$ for a given K and a given N.

What do we mean by the state of technology? In a narrow sense, we can think of the state of technology as the list of blueprints defining both the range of products that can be produced in the economy as well as the techniques available to produce them. We can also think of the state of technology in a broader sense: How much output is produced in an economy also depends on how well firms are run, on the organization and sophistication of markets, on the system of laws and their enforcement, on the political environment, and so on. We shall think of the state of technology in the narrow sense for most of the next two chapters.

We will return at the end of Chapter 16 to what we know about the role of the other factors, from the system of laws to the form of government.

Returns to Scale and Returns to Factors.
Now that we have introduced the aggregate production function, what restrictions can we reasonably impose on this function?

Consider a thought experiment in which we doubled both the number of workers and the amount of capital in the economy. It is reasonable to guess that output would roughly double as well: In effect, we would have cloned the original economy, and the clone economy could produce output in the same way as the original economy. This property is called **constant returns to scale**: If the scale of operation is doubled—that is, if the quantities of capital and labour are doubled—then output will also double:

$$2Y = F(2K, 2N)$$

Or more generally, for any number *x:*

$$xY = F(xK, xN) \tag{14.2}$$

Constant returns to scale refers to what happens to production when *both* capital and labour are increased. What should we assume when only *one* input—say, capital—is increased?

It is surely reasonable to assume that output will increase as well. It is also reasonable to assume that a given increase in capital will lead to smaller and smaller increases in output as the level of capital increases. Why? Think, for example, of a secretarial pool, composed of a given number of secretaries. Think of capital as computers. The introduction of just one computer will substantially increase the pool's production, as the computer assumes some of the more time-consuming tasks. As the number of computers increases and more secretaries in the pool get their own PCs, production will further increase, although by less per additional computer than was the case when the first one was introduced. Once each secretary has a PC, increasing the number of computers further is unlikely to increase production very much, if at all. Additional computers may simply remain unused and left in their shipping boxes and lead to no increase in output whatsoever.

Increases in capital lead to smaller and smaller increases in output as the level of capital increases. We will refer to this property as **decreasing returns to capital** (a property that will be familiar to those who have taken a course in microeconomics). A similar property holds for the other input, labour: Increases in labour, given capital, lead to smaller and smaller increases in output as the level of labour increases. (Return to our previous example, and think of what happens as you increase the number of secretaries for a given number of computers.) There are **decreasing returns to labour** as well.

Output and Capital per Worker.
The aggregate production function we have written and the two properties we have just assumed imply a simple relation between output per worker and capital per worker.

To derive the relation between output per worker and capital per worker, we let $x = 1/N$ in equation (14.2) so that:

$$\frac{Y}{N} = F\left(\frac{K}{N}, 1\right) \tag{14.3}$$

Note that Y/N is output per worker, and K/N is capital per worker. So, equation (14.3) says that the amount of output per worker depends on the amount of capital per worker. This relation between output per worker and capital per worker is drawn in Figure 14–5.

Output per worker (Y/N) is measured on the vertical axis and capital per worker (K/N) on the horizontal axis. The relation between the two is given by the upward-sloping curve. As capital per worker increases, so does output per worker. But because of decreasing returns to capital, increases in capital lead to smaller and smaller increases in output. At point *A*,

Following up on growth versus development economics: Think of growth theory as focusing on the role of technology in the narrow sense and development economics as focusing on the role of technology in the broader sense.

You may question this assumption: Doubling the economy requires double the space. What about the fact that a country has a given size? This objection is right in theory, but not very important in practice, except for economies where agriculture plays a central role. For example, Hong Kong, with very little land, has a thriving economy. For modern economies, constant returns to scale seems to be a good approximation to reality.

Even under constant returns to scale, there are decreasing returns to each factor, keeping the other factor constant:
- Given labour, there are decreasing returns to capital: Increases in capital lead to smaller and smaller increases in output as the level of capital increases.
- Given capital, there are decreasing returns to labour: Increases in labour lead to smaller and smaller increases in output as the level of labour increases.

where capital per worker is low, an increase in capital per worker equal to the distance *AB* leads to an increase in output per worker of *A'B'*. At point *C*, where capital per worker is larger, the same increase in capital per worker, *CD* (the distance *CD* is equal to the distance *AB*), leads to a much smaller increase in output per worker, only *C'D'*. This is just as in our example of the secretarial pool, where additional computers led to less and less effect on total output.

Increases in capital per worker lead to smaller and smaller increases in output per worker as the level of capital per worker increases. ▶

The Sources of Growth

We are now ready to return to growth. Where does growth come from? Why does output per worker—or output per capita, if we assume the ratio of workers to the population as a whole remains roughly constant over time—go up over time? Equation (14.3) gives a simple answer:

Increases in capital per worker: Movements along the production function. ▶

- Increases in output per worker (Y/N) can come from increases in capital per worker (K/N). This is the relation we just looked at in Figure 14–5. As (K/N) increases—as we move to the right on the horizontal axis—(Y/N) increases.

- Or they can come from improvements in the state of technology, which shift the production function, *F*, and lead to more output per worker *given* capital per worker. This is shown in Figure 14–6. An improvement in the state of technology shifts the production function from *F* to *F'*. For a given level of capital per worker, the improvement in technology leads to an increase in output per worker. For example, for the level of capital per worker corresponding to point *A*, output per worker increases from *A'* to *B'*.

Improvements in the state of technology: Shifts of the production function. ▶

Hence, we can think of growth as coming from **capital accumulation** and from **technological progress**—the improvement in the state of technology. We shall see, however, that these two factors play very different roles in the growth process:

- Capital accumulation by itself cannot sustain growth. A formal argument will have to wait until Chapter 15. But we can derive the basic intuition for this answer from Figure 14–5. Because of decreasing returns to capital, sustaining a steady increase in output per worker would require larger and larger increases in the level of capital per worker. At some stage, society will not be willing to save and invest enough to further increase capital. At that stage, output per worker will stop growing.

    Does this mean that an economy's **saving rate**—the proportion of income that is saved—is irrelevant? No. It is true that a higher saving rate cannot permanently increase the *growth rate* of output. But it can sustain a higher *level* of output. Let us state this in a slightly different way. Take two economies that differ only in their saving rate. The

FIGURE 14–5

Output and Capital per Worker

Increases in capital per worker lead to smaller and smaller increases in output per worker.

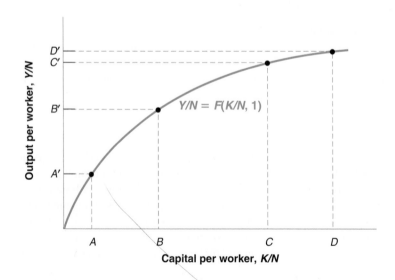

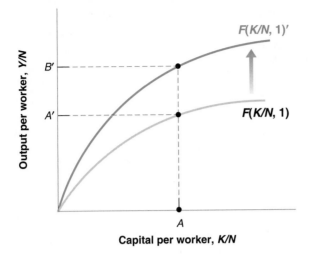

FIGURE 14-6

The Effects of an Improvement in the State of Technology

An improvement in the state of technology shifts the production function up, leading to an increase in output per worker for a given level of capital per worker.

two economies will grow at the same rate; but at any point in time, the economy with the higher saving rate will have a higher level of output per capita than the other. How and how much the saving rate affects the level of output and whether such a country as Canada or the United States (both have a very low saving rate) should try to increase its saving rate will be one of the topics we take up in Chapter 15.

● Sustained growth requires sustained technological progress. This really follows from the first proposition: Given that the two factors that can lead to an increase in output per capita are capital accumulation and technological progress, if capital accumulation cannot sustain growth forever, then technological progress must be key—and it is. We will see in Chapter 16 that the rate of growth of output per capita is eventually determined by the rate of technological progress.

This has a strong implication. In the long run, an economy that sustains a higher rate of technological progress will eventually overtake all other economies. This raises the question of what determines the rate of technological progress. What we know about the determinants of technological progress—from the role of spending on fundamental and applied research, to the role of patent laws, to the role of education and training—will be one of the topics taken up in Chapter 16.

SUMMARY

● Over long periods of time, fluctuations in output are dwarfed by growth, the steady increase of aggregate output over time.

● Looking at growth in five rich countries (Canada, France, Japan, the United Kingdom, and the United States) since 1950, three main facts emerge:

1. All five countries have experienced strong growth and a large increase in the standard of living. Growth from 1950 to 2000 increased real output per capita by a factor of 3.1 in the United States, 3 in Canada, by a factor of 4.1 in France, and by a factor of 10.2 in Japan.

2. Growth has decreased since the mid-1970s. The average growth rate of output per capita has gone from 2.5% per year in Canada from 1950 to 1973 to 1.8% from 1974 to 2000.

3. The levels of output per capita across the five countries have converged over time. Put another way, those countries that were behind have grown faster, reducing the gap between them and the current world economic leader, the United States.

● Looking at the evidence across a broader set of countries and a longer period of time, the following facts emerge:

1. On the scale of human history, sustained output growth is a recent phenomenon. From the end of the Roman Empire to roughly year 1500 A.D., there was essentially no growth of output per capita in Europe. Even during the Industrial Revolution, growth rates were not high by current standards. The growth rate of output per capita from 1820 to 1950 in the United States was 1.5%.

2. Convergence of levels of output per capita is not a worldwide phenomenon. Many Asian countries are rapidly catching up, but most African countries have both very low levels of output per capita and low growth rates.

- To think about growth, economists start from an aggregate production function relating aggregate output to two factors of production: capital and labour. How much output is produced given these inputs depends on the state of technology.

- Under the assumption of constant returns, the aggregate production function implies that increases in output per worker can come either from increases in capital per worker or from improvements in the state of technology.

- Capital accumulation by itself cannot permanently sustain growth of output per capita. Nevertheless, how much a country saves is very important because the saving rate determines the *level* of output per capita, if not its growth rate.

- Sustained growth of output per capita is ultimately due to technological progress. Perhaps the most important question in growth theory is what the determinants of technological progress are.

KEY TERMS

- aggregate production function, 276
- capital accumulation, 278
- constant returns to scale, 277
- convergence, 270
- decreasing returns to capital, 277
- decreasing returns to labour, 277
- four tigers, 275
- growth, 266
- leapfrogging, 274
- logarithmic scale, 267
- output per capita, 267
- purchasing power, 268
- purchasing power parity (PPP), 268
- saving rate, 278
- state of technology, 276
- technological progress, 278

QUESTIONS AND PROBLEMS

An asterisk denotes a harder question. [Web] indicates that the question requires access to the Internet.

1. TRUE/FALSE/UNCERTAIN

a. Despite the Great Depression, Canadian output was higher in 1940 than in 1929.

b. On a log scale, a variable that increases at 5% a year will move along an upward-sloping line, with slope 0.05.

c. If Japan had continued to grow at the same rate during 1974 to 2000 as it had during 1950 to 1973, its output per capita in 2000 would have been more than twice U.S. output per capita.

d. The price of food is higher in poor countries than in rich countries.

e. Output per capita in most countries in the world is converging to the level of output per capita in the United States.

f. Capital accumulation does not affect the level of output in the long run. Only technological progress does.

g. The aggregate production function is a relation among output, labour, and capital.

h. Because eventually we will know everything, technological progress will end, and growth will eventually end as well.

2. THE DECREASE IN GROWTH SINCE 1973

Use Table 14–1 to answer the following questions:

a. Compute what output per capita would have been in 2000 for each of the five rich countries if the growth rate from 1973 to 2000 for each country had remained the same as during 1950 to 1973.

b. What would have been the ratio of output per capita in Japan relative to output per capita in the United States?

c. Did convergence continue during the growth slowdown from 1973 to 2000?

3. PURCHASING POWER PARITY

Assume that the typical consumers in Mexico and Canada buy the quantities and pay the prices indicated in the accompanying table:

	Bread		Car Services	
	Price	Quantity	Price	Quantity
Mexico	1 peso	400	7 pesos	300
Canada	$1	1000	$2	2000

a. Compute Canadian consumption per capita in Canadian dollars.

b. Compute Mexican consumption per capita in pesos.

c. Suppose a peso is worth 20 cents ($0.20). Compute Mexican consumption per capita in dollars.

d. Using the purchasing power parity method and Canadian prices and quantities, compute Mexican consumption per capita in dollars.

e. Under each of the methods used in (c) and (d), how much lower is the standard of living in Mexico than in Canada? Does the choice of method make a difference?

4. THE PRODUCTION FUNCTION AND CONSTANT RETURNS TO SCALE

Consider the production function $Y = \sqrt{K}\sqrt{N}$.

a. Compute output when $K = 49$ and $N = 81$.

b. If both capital and labour double, what happens to output?

c. Is this production function characterized by constant returns to scale? Explain.

d. Write this production function as a relationship between output per worker and capital per worker.

e. Let $K/N = 4$. What is Y/N? Now, double K/N to 8. Does Y/N more or less than double?

f. Does the relation between output per worker and capital per worker exhibit constant returns to scale?

g. Is your answer in (f) the same as your answer in (c)? Why, or why not?

h. Plot the relation between output per worker and capital per worker. Does it have the same general shape as the relation in Figure 14–5? Explain.

5. GROWTH AND TECHNOLOGICAL PROGRESS

Between 1950 and 1973, France, Germany, and Japan all experienced growth rates that were at least 2 percentage points higher than those in Canada or the United States. Yet, the most important technical advances of that period were made in North America. How can this be?

6. CONVERGENCE OVER TIME [WEB]

In Table 14–1, we saw that the levels of output per capita in the United Kingdom, France, Japan, Canada, and the United States were much closer in 2000 than they were in 1950. Here, we will examine convergence for another set of countries. At some point over the lifetime of this edition, data beyond 2000 may become available. The Penn World Tales get updated from time to time.

Go to <**pwt.econ.upenn.edu/**>. It contains the Penn World Tables (see Table 14–1 and the Focus box "The Construction of PPP Numbers").

a. At the Web site's menu, select Real GDP per capita (Constant Prices: Laspoyres) for France, Belgium, Italy, and the United States, for 1950 to 2000.

b. Once the numbers appear on your Web browser, save them as a text file, and import them to your favourite spreadsheet program. Define for each country for each year the ratio of its real GDP to that of the United States for that year (so that this ratio will be equal to one for the United States for all years).

c. Graph the ratios for France, Belgium, and Italy over the period 1950 to 2000 (all on the same graph). Does your graph support the notion of convergence among the four countries listed in (a)?

d. Repeat the same exercise for Argentina, Venezuela, Chad, Madagascar, and the United States. Does your new graph support the notion of convergence among this group of countries?

FURTHER READING

Brad deLong has a number of fascinating articles on growth on his Web page (**http://econ161.berkeley.edu/**). Read, in particular, "Berkeley Faculty Lunch Talk: Main Themes of Twentieth Century Economic History," which covers many of the themes in this chapter.

A broad presentation of facts about growth is given by Angus Maddison in *The World Economy. A Millenium Perspective* (Paris: OECD, 2001). The associated site

www.theworldeconomy.org has a large number of facts and data on growth over the last two millenia.

Chapter 3 in *Productivity and American Leadership* by William Baumol, Sue Anne Batey Blackman, and Edward Wolff (Cambridge, MA: MIT Press, 1989) gives a vivid description of how life has been transformed by growth in the United States since the mid-1880s.

CHAPTER 15
SAVING, CAPITAL ACCUMULATION, AND OUTPUT

Since 1950, the Canadian saving rate—the ratio of saving to GDP—has averaged only 22%, compared with 25% in Germany and 34% in Japan. Can this explain why the Canadian growth rate has been lower than in most OECD countries in the last 50 years? Would increasing the Canadian saving rate lead to sustained higher Canadian growth in the future?

We have already given the basic answer to these questions at the end of Chapter 14: The answer is no. Over the long run (an important qualification to which we will return), an economy's growth rate does not depend on its saving rate. Lower Canadian growth in the last 50 years is not due to the low saving rate. Nor should we expect that an increase in the saving rate would lead to sustained higher Canadian growth.

This conclusion does not imply, however, that we should not be concerned about the low Canadian saving rate. Even if the saving rate does not permanently affect the growth rate, it does affect the level of output and the standard of living. An increase in the saving rate would lead to higher growth for some time and eventually to a higher standard of living in Canada. In addition, as we will see in Chapter 17, a higher saving rate may pay off some foreign debts and allow higher future consumption.

The effects of the saving rate on capital and output are the topics of this chapter. The first two sections look at the interactions between output and capital accumulation and the effects of the saving rate. The third section plugs in numbers to give a better sense of the magnitudes involved. The fourth section extends the initial model to allow not only for physical capital but also for human capital.

15-1 | Interactions between Output and Capital

To understand the determination of output in the long run, you must keep in mind two relations between output and capital.

- The amount of capital determines the amount of output being produced.
- The amount of output determines the amount of saving and investment, and thus the amount of capital being accumulated.

Together, these two relations, which are represented in Figure 15–1, determine the evolution of output and capital over time. We now look at each relation in turn.

The Effects of Capital on Output

We started discussing the first of these two relations, the effect of capital on output, in section 14-3. There, we introduced the aggregate production function and saw that under the assumption of constant returns to scale, we can write the following relation between output and capital per worker:

$$\frac{Y}{N} = F\left(\frac{K}{N}, 1\right)$$

Output per worker (Y/N) is an increasing function of capital per worker (K/N). Under the assumption of decreasing returns to capital, the effects of an increase in capital per worker become smaller, the larger the initial ratio of capital per worker. When capital per worker is already very high, further increases have only a small effect on output.

To simplify notation, we rewrite this relation between output and capital per worker simply as:

$$\frac{Y}{N} = f\left(\frac{K}{N}\right)$$

where the function f represents the same relation between output and capital per worker as the function F:

$$f(K/N) \equiv F(K/N, 1)$$

In this chapter, in order to focus on the role of capital accumulation, we will make two further assumptions:

- The first is that employment, N, is constant. Let us be more specific here. Start with the relations we saw in Chapter 2 (and again in Chapter 9) among population, the labour force, and employment. Employment is equal to the labour force times one minus the unemployment rate. The labour force, in turn, is equal to population times the participation rate. In this chapter, we will assume that population, the participation rate, and the unemployment rate are all constant. Constant population and a constant participation rate imply that the labour force is constant. A constant labour force and a constant unemployment rate imply that the level of employment, N, is constant. Note that under these assumptions, output per worker (output divided by employment), output per capita

Suppose the function F has the following "double square root" form:

$$F(K, N) = \sqrt{K}\,\sqrt{N}$$

Then,

$$Y/N = F(K/N, 1)$$
$$= \sqrt{K/N}\,\sqrt{N/N}$$
$$= \sqrt{K/N}$$

So, the function f is simply the square root function:

$$f(K/N) = \sqrt{K/N}$$

◀

Labour force (L) = Population × Participation rate

Employment (N) = Labour force (L) × [1 – unemployment rate (u)]

◀ If population, the participation rate, and the unemployment rate are constant, population, the labour force, and employment will be constant.

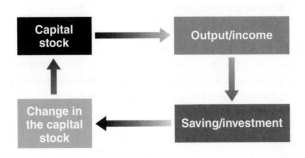

FIGURE 15–1

Capital, Output, and Saving/Investment

If the participation rate is 60% and the unemployment rate is 10%, then employment is 60% times $(1 - 0.10) = 54\%$ of the population. Output per capita is 54% of output per worker.

(output divided by population), and output itself all move proportionately. Although we will usually refer to movements in output or capital *per worker*, to lighten the text we will sometimes just talk about movements in output or capital, leaving out the "per worker" or "per capita" qualification, where it is completely obvious.

The reason for assuming that N is constant is to make it easier to focus on the role of capital accumulation in growth: If N is constant, the only factor of production that changes over time is capital. The assumption is not very realistic, however, and we will relax it in the next two chapters. In Chapter 16, we will allow for steady population and employment growth. In Chapter 17, we will integrate the open economy into our analysis of the long run. But both steps are better left for later.

- The second assumption is that there is no technological progress, so the production function f (or, equivalently, F) does not change through time. Again, the reason for making this—obviously counterfactual—assumption is to focus on the role of capital accumulation. In Chapter 16, we will introduce technological progress and see that the basic conclusions we derive here about the role of capital in growth also hold when there is technological progress. Again, this step is better left for the next chapter.

With these two assumptions, our first relation between output and capital per worker, from the production side, can be written as:

From the production side: The level of capital per worker determines the level of output per worker.

$$\frac{Y_t}{N} = f\left(\frac{K_t}{N}\right) \tag{15.1}$$

where we have introduced time indexes for output and capital (but not for labour, N, which we assume to be constant and so does not need a time index). In short, higher capital per worker leads to higher output per worker.

As we will see in Chapter 17, saving and investment need not be equal in an open economy. A country may save more than it invests and lend the difference to the rest of the world. This has been the case for Japan, which has been running a large trade surplus, lending part of its saving to the rest of the world. We will ignore this possibility here and use saving and investment interchangeably.

The Effects of Output on Capital Accumulation

To derive the second relation, between output and capital accumulation, we proceed in two steps. First, we derive the relation between output and investment. Then, we derive the relation between investment and capital accumulation.

Output and Investment. To derive the relation between output and investment, we make three assumptions:

- We continue to assume that the economy is closed. As we saw in Chapter 3, this implies that investment is equal to saving, private and public:

$$I = S + (G - T)$$

- To focus on the behaviour of private saving, we ignore both taxes and government spending, so $G = T = 0$, and by implication public saving $(G - T) = 0$. (We will relax this assumption later when we focus on the implications of fiscal policy on growth.) Replacing in the equation above gives:

$$I = S$$

Investment is equal to private saving.

You have now seen two specifications of saving behaviour (equivalently consumption behaviour): one for the short run in Chapter 3 and one for the long run in this chapter. You may wonder how the two specifications relate to each other and whether they are consistent. The answer is yes. A full discussion is given in Chapter 20.

- We assume that private saving is proportional to income, so:

$$S = sY$$

The parameter s is the saving rate, and has a value between 0 and 1. This assumption captures two basic facts about saving. The saving rate does not appear systematically to increase or decrease as a country becomes richer. And richer countries do not appear to have systematically higher or lower saving rates than poorer ones.

Combining the two relations above and introducing time indexes gives:

$$I_t = sY_t$$

Investment is proportional to output: The higher the level of output, the higher is the level of investment.

Investment and Capital Accumulation. The second step relates investment, which is a flow (the new machines produced and new plants built during a given period), to capital, which is a stock (the existing machines and plants in the economy at a point in time).

Think of time as measured in years, so t denotes year t, $t + 1$ denotes year $t + 1$, and so on. Think of capital as being measured at the beginning of each year, so K_t refers to the capital stock at the beginning of year t, K_{t+1} to the capital stock at the beginning of year $t + 1$, and so on.

Assume that capital depreciates at rate δ (the lowercase Greek letter delta) per year: That is, from one year to the next, a proportion δ of the capital stock breaks down and becomes useless. The parameter δ is called the **depreciation rate**.

The evolution of the capital stock is then given by:

$$K_{t+1} = (1 - \delta)K_t + I_t$$

The capital stock at the beginning of year $t + 1$, K_{t+1}, is equal to the capital stock at the beginning of year t, K_t, adjusted for depreciation—thus multiplied by $(1 - \delta)$—plus investment during year t, I_t.

We can now combine the relation between output and investment and the relation between investment and capital accumulation to obtain the second relation we need to think about growth, namely, the relation between output and capital accumulation.

Replacing investment by saving in the previous equation and dividing both sides by N (the number of workers in the economy) gives:

$$\frac{K_{t+1}}{N} = (1 - \delta)\frac{K_t}{N} + s\frac{Y_t}{N}$$

In words: Capital per worker at the beginning of year $t + 1$ is equal to capital per worker at the beginning of year t, adjusted for depreciation, plus investment per worker during year t. Investment per worker is, in turn, equal to the saving rate times output per worker during year t.

Moving K_t/N to the left and reorganizing:

$$\frac{K_{t+1}}{N} - \frac{K_t}{N} = s\frac{Y_t}{N} - \delta\frac{K_t}{N} \tag{15.2}$$

In words: The change in the capital stock per worker—the term on the left—is equal to saving per worker (the first term on the right) minus depreciation per worker (the second term on the right.) This equation gives us the second relation between output and capital per worker.

15-2 | Implications of Alternative Saving Rates

We have derived two relations. From the production side, equation (15.1) shows how capital determines output. From the saving side, equation (15.2) shows how output, in turn, determines capital accumulation. Let us now put them together and see what they imply for the behaviour of output and capital over time.

Dynamics of Capital and Output

Replacing output per worker (Y_t/N) in equation (15.2) by its expression in terms of capital per worker from equation (15.1) gives:

$$\frac{K_{t+1}}{N} - \frac{K_t}{N} = sf\left(\frac{K_t}{N}\right) - \delta\frac{K_t}{N} \tag{15.3}$$

$$\begin{array}{ccc} \text{change in capital} & = & \text{investment} & - & \text{depreciation} \\ \text{from year } t \text{ to year } t + 1 & & \text{during year } t & & \text{during year } t \end{array}$$

Recall that flows are variables that have a time dimension (that is, they are defined per unit of time); stocks are variables that do not have a time dimension (they are defined at a point in time). Output, saving, and investment are flows. Employment and the capital stock are stocks.

From the saving side: The level of output per worker determines the change in the level of capital per worker over time.

This relation describes what happens to capital per worker. The change in capital per worker from this year to next year depends on the difference between two terms:

$K_t/N \Rightarrow Y_t/N = f(K_t/N)$
$f(K_t/N) \Rightarrow sf(K_t/N)$ ▶

$K_t/N \Rightarrow \delta K_t/N$ ▶

- Investment per worker, the first term on the right. The level of capital per worker this year determines output per worker this year. Given the saving rate, output per worker determines the amount of saving per worker, and thus of investment per worker this year.
- Depreciation per worker, the second term on the right. The capital stock per worker determines the amount of depreciation per worker this year.

If investment per worker exceeds depreciation per worker, the change in capital per worker is positive. Capital per worker increases. If investment per worker is less than depreciation per worker, the change in capital per worker is negative. Capital per worker decreases.

Given capital per worker, output per worker is then given by equation (15.1):

$$\frac{Y_t}{N} = f\left(\frac{K_t}{N}\right)$$

Equations (15.3) and (15.1) contain all the information we need to understand the dynamics of capital and output over time. The easiest way to interpret them is to use a graph. We do this in Figure 15–2, where output per worker is measured on the vertical axis, capital per worker on the horizontal axis.

In Figure 15–2, look first at the curve representing output per worker, $f(K_t/N)$, as a function of capital per worker. The relation is the same as in Figure 14–5. Output per worker increases with capital per worker, but the higher the level of capital per worker, the smaller is the effect.

Now, look at the two curves representing the two components on the right of equation (15.3).

To make the graph easier ▶ to read, we have assumed an unrealistically high saving rate. (Can you tell roughly what value we have assumed for s? What would be a plausible value for s?)

The relation representing investment per worker, $sf(K_t/N)$, has the same shape as the production function, except that it is lower by a factor s. At the level of capital per worker K_0/N, for example, output per worker is given by the distance AB, and investment per worker is given by the distance AC, which is equal to s times the distance AB. Thus, investment increases with capital, but by less and less as capital increases. When capital is already very high, the effect of a further increase in capital on output, and thus, in turn, on investment, is very small.

The relation representing depreciation per worker, $\delta K_t/N$ is represented by a line. Depreciation per worker increases in proportion to capital per worker, so the relation is rep-

FIGURE 15–2

Capital and Output Dynamics

When capital and output are low, investment exceeds depreciation, and capital increases. When capital and output are high, investment is less than depreciation, and capital decreases.

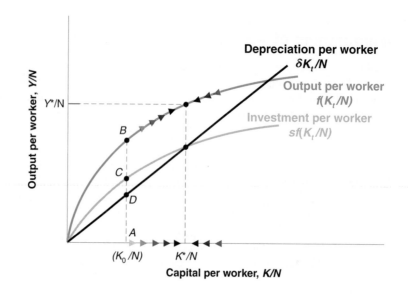

resented by a straight line with slope equal to δ. At the level of capital per worker given by K_0/N, depreciation is given by the distance AD.

The change in capital per worker is given by the difference between investment per worker and depreciation per worker. At K_0/N, the difference is positive and given by the distance $CD = AC - AD$. As we move to the right along the horizontal axis and look at higher and higher levels of capital per worker, investment increases by less and less, while depreciation keeps increasing in proportion to capital. For some level of capital per worker, K^*/N in Figure 15–2, investment is just enough to cover depreciation, and capital per worker remains constant. To the left of K^*/N, investment exceeds depreciation, and capital per worker increases. This is indicated by the arrows pointing to the right along the curve representing the production function. To the right of K^*/N, depreciation exceeds investment, and capital per worker decreases. This is indicated by the arrows pointing to the left along the curve representing the production function.

Characterizing the evolution of capital per worker and output per worker over time is now easy. Consider an economy that starts with a low level of capital per worker—say, K_0/N in Figure 15–2. Because investment exceeds depreciation, capital per worker increases. And because output moves with capital, output per worker increases as well. Capital per worker eventually reaches K^*/N, the level at which investment is equal to depreciation. Once the economy has reached the level of capital K^*/N, output and capital per worker remain constant at Y^*/N and K^*/N, their long-run equilibrium levels.

When capital per worker is low, capital per worker and output per worker increase over time. When capital per worker is high, capital per worker and output per worker decrease over time.

For example, think of a country that loses part of its capital stock, perhaps as a result of a war. The mechanism we have just seen suggests that if it has suffered much larger capital losses than population losses, it will come out of the war with a low level of capital per worker, and so at a point to the left of K^*/N. It will then experience a large increase in both capital per worker and output per worker for some time. This appears to describe quite well what happened after World War II to countries that had proportionately larger destructions of capital than of human lives (see the Global Macro box "Capital Accumulation and Growth in France in the Aftermath of World War II").

If a country starts instead from a high level of capital per worker, from a point to the right of K^*/N, then capital per worker and output per worker will decrease: The initial level of capital per worker is too high to be sustained given the saving rate. This decrease in capital per worker will continue until the economy again reaches the point where investment is equal to depreciation, where capital per worker is equal to K^*/N. From then on, capital and output per worker will remain constant.

What does the model predict for postwar growth if a country suffers roughly proportional losses in population and in capital? Do you find this answer convincing? What elements may be missing from the model?

Steady-State Capital and Output

Let us characterize the levels of output per worker and capital per worker to which the economy converges in the long run. This will be useful to us later. The state in which output per worker and capital per worker are no longer changing is called the **steady state** of the economy. Putting the left side of equation (15.3) equal to zero (in steady state, by definition, the change in capital per worker is zero), the steady-state value of capital per worker, K^*/N, is given by:

$$sf\left(\frac{K^*}{N}\right) = \delta \frac{K^*}{N} \tag{15.4}$$

The steady-state value of capital per worker is such that the amount of saving (the left side) is just sufficient to cover depreciation of the existing capital stock (the right side).

Given steady-state capital per worker (K^*/N), the steady-state value of output per worker (Y^*/N), is given by the production function:

$$\frac{Y^*}{N} = f\left(\frac{K^*}{N}\right) \tag{15.5}$$

Capital Accumulation and Growth in France in the Aftermath of World War II

When World War II ended in 1945, France had suffered some of the heaviest losses among all European countries. The losses in lives were large; more than 550,000 people had died, out of a population of 42 million. The losses in capital were much larger. Estimates are that the French capital stock in 1945 was about 30% below its prewar value. A more vivid picture of the destruction of capital is provided by the numbers in Table 1.

The model of growth we have just seen makes a clear prediction about what will happen to a country that loses a large part of its capital stock: The country will experience fast capital accumulation and output growth for some time. In terms of Figure 15–2, a country with capital per worker initially far below K^*/N will grow rapidly as it converges to K^*/N and output converges to Y^*/N.

This prediction fares well in the case of postwar France. There is plenty of anecdotal evidence that small increases in capital led to large increases in output. Minor repairs to a major bridge would lead to the reopening of a bridge. Reopening the bridge would lead, in turn, to large reductions in the travel time between two cities, leading to a large reduction in transport costs. A large reduction in transport costs would then allow a plant to receive much needed inputs and increase production and so on.

The more convincing evidence, however, comes directly from the numbers on growth of aggregate output itself. From 1946 to 1950, the annual growth rate of French real GDP was a very high 9.6% per year, leading to an increase in real GDP of about 60% over five years.

Was all the increase in French GDP due to capital accumulation? The answer is no. There were other forces in addition to the mechanism in our model. Much of the remaining capital stock in 1945 was old. Investment had been low in the 1930s (a decade dominated by the Great Depression) and nearly nonexistent during the war. Much of the postwar capital accumulation was associated with the introduction of more modern capital and the use of more modern production techniques. This was another reason for the high growth rates of the postwar period.

Source: Gilles Saint-Paul, "Economic Reconstruction in France, 1945–1958," in Rudiger Dornbusch, Willem Nolling, and Richard Layard, eds., *Postwar Economic Reconstruction and Lessons for the East Today* (Cambridge, MA: MIT Press, 1993), pp. 83–114.

TABLE 1	Proportion of the French Capital Stock Destroyed at the End of World War II		
Railways		Rivers	
Tracks	6%	Waterways	86%
Stations	38%	Canal locks	11%
Engines	21%	Barges	80%
Hardware	60%	Buildings	
Roads		Dwellings	1,229,000
Cars	31%	Industrial	246,000
Trucks	40%		

Source: See source note for this box.

We now have the elements we need to discuss the effects of the saving rate on output per worker, both over time and in steady state.

The Saving Rate and Output

We can now return to the question asked at the beginning of the chapter: What are the effects of the saving rate on the growth rate of output per worker? Our analysis leads to a three-part answer:

1. *The saving rate has no effect on the long-run growth rate of output per worker, which is equal to zero.*

This result is rather obvious: We have seen that eventually, the economy converges to a constant level of output per worker. In other words, in the long run, the growth rate of the economy is equal to zero, whatever the value of the saving rate.

There is, however, a way of thinking about this result that will be useful when we introduce technological progress in Chapter 16. Think of what would be needed to sustain a constant positive growth rate of output per worker in the long run. Capital per worker would have to increase. And because of decreasing returns to capital, it would have to increase faster than output per worker. This implies that each year the economy would have to save a larger and larger fraction of output and put it toward capital accumulation. At some point, the fraction of output that it would need to save would be greater than one: This is clearly not possible. This is why it is impossible to sustain a constant positive growth rate forever. In the long run, capital per worker must be constant and so must be output per worker.

2. Nonetheless, *the saving rate determines the level of output per worker in the long run.* Other things being equal, countries with a higher saving rate will achieve higher output per worker in the long run.

   Figure 15–3 illustrates this point. Consider two countries with the same production function, the same level of employment, and the same depreciation rate, but different saving rates, say, s_0 and $s_1 > s_0$. Figure 15–3 draws their common production function, $f(K_t/N)$, and the functions giving saving/investment as a function of capital for each of the two countries, $s_0 f(K_t/N)$ and $s_1 f(K_t/N)$. In the long run, the country with saving rate s_0 will reach the level of capital per worker K_0/N and output Y_0/N. The country with saving rate s_1 will reach the higher levels K_1/N and Y_1/N.

3. *An increase in the saving rate will lead to higher growth of output per worker for some time, but not forever.*

   This conclusion follows from the two propositions we just discussed. From the first, we know that an increase in the saving rate does not affect the long-run *growth rate of output per worker*, which remains equal to zero. From the second, we know that an increase in the saving rate leads to an increase in the long-run *level of output per worker*. It follows that as output per worker increases to its new higher level in response to the increase in the saving rate, the economy will go through a period of positive growth. This period of growth will come to an end when the economy reaches its new steady state.

   We can use Figure 15–3 again to illustrate this point. Consider a country that has an initial saving rate of s_0. Assume that capital per worker is initially equal to K_0/N, with associated output per worker Y_0/N. Now, consider the effects of an increase in the saving rate from s_0 to s_1. (You can think of this increase as coming from tax changes that make it more attractive to save or from reductions in the budget deficit; the origin of the increase in the saving rate does not matter here.) The function giving saving/investment per worker as a function of capital per worker shifts upward from $s_0 f(K_t/N)$ to $s_1 f(K_t/N)$.

Some economists argue that the relatively high growth rate achieved by the Soviet Union from 1950 to 1990 was the result of such a steady increase in the saving rate over time and so could not be sustained forever. Paul Krugman has used the term "Stalinist growth" to denote this type of growth—growth resulting from a higher and higher saving rate over time.

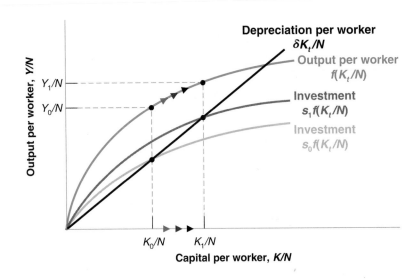

FIGURE 15–3

The Effects of Different Saving Rates

A country with a higher saving rate achieves a higher level of output in steady state.

FIGURE 15-4

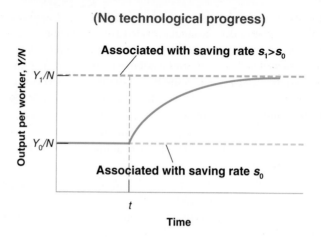

The Effects of an Increase in the Saving Rate on Output per Worker

An increase in the saving rate leads to a period of positive growth until output reaches its new higher steady-state level.

At the initial level of capital per worker, K_0/N, investment now exceeds depreciation, so capital per worker increases. As capital per worker increases, so does output per worker, and the economy goes through a period of positive growth. When capital eventually reaches K_1/N, investment is again equal to depreciation and growth ends. The economy remains from then on at K_1/N, with associated output per worker Y_1/N. The movement of output per worker is plotted against time in Figure 15–4. Output per worker is initially constant at level Y_0/N. After the increase in the saving rate at, say, time t, output per worker increases for some time until it reaches the higher level Y_1/N and the growth rate returns to zero.

We have derived these three results under the assumption of no technological progress and thus no growth of output in the long run. But, as we will see in Chapter 16, the three results extend directly to an economy in which there is technological progress. Let us briefly indicate how.

An economy where there is technological progress has a positive growth rate of output per worker even in the long run. This growth rate is independent of the saving rate—the extension of the first result just discussed. The saving rate affects the level of output per worker, however—the extension of the second result. And an increase in the saving rate leads to growth greater than the steady-state growth rate for some time until the economy reaches its new higher path—the extension of our third result.

These three results are illustrated in Figure 15–5, which extends Figure 15–4 by plotting the effect of an increase in the saving rate in an economy with positive technological

FIGURE 15-5

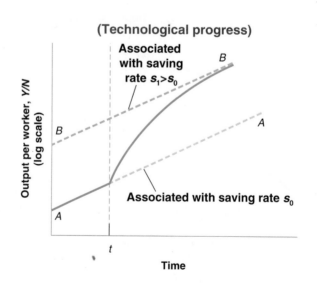

The Effects of an Increase in the Saving Rate on Output per Worker in an Economy with Technological Progress

An increase in the saving rate leads to a period of higher growth until output reaches a new, higher path.

progress. The figure uses a logarithmic scale to measure output per worker so that an economy where output per worker grows at a constant rate is represented by a line with slope equal to that growth rate. At the initial saving rate, s_0, the economy moves along AA. If, at time t, the saving rate increases to s_1, the economy experiences higher growth for some time until, eventually, it reaches its new higher path, BB. On path BB, the growth rate is again the same as before the increase in the saving rate (that is, the slope of BB is the same as the slope of AA). But the level of output per worker is permanently higher than before.

See the sidebar on logarithmic scales in Chapter 14.

The Saving Rate and the Golden Rule

Governments can use various instruments to affect the saving rate. They can run budget deficits or surpluses. They can give tax breaks to saving, making it more attractive for people to save. What saving rate should governments aim for? To think about this question, we must shift our focus from the behaviour of *output* to the behaviour of *consumption*. What matters to people is not output per se but how much they consume.

It is clear that an increase in saving must come initially at the expense of lower consumption. (Except when we think it helpful, we will drop the "per worker" in this subsection and refer just to consumption rather than consumption per worker, capital rather than capital per worker, and so on.) A change in the saving rate this year has no effect on capital this year, and thus no effect on output and income *this year*. Therefore, an increase in saving comes initially with an equal decrease in consumption.[1]

Given the definition of K_t as the capital stock at the beginning of year t, investment this year does not affect the capital stock this year: I_t affects K_{t+1}, not K_t.

Does an increase in saving lead to an increase in consumption in the long run? Not necessarily. Consumption may decrease not only initially but also in the long run. You may find this surprising. After all, we know from Figure 15–3 that an increase in the saving rate always leads to an increase in the level of *output* per worker. But output is not the same as consumption. To see why not, consider what happens for two extreme values of the saving rate:

- An economy in which the saving rate is (and has always been) zero is an economy in which capital is equal to zero. In this case, output is also equal to zero, and so is consumption. A saving rate equal to zero implies zero consumption in the long run.

- Now, consider the opposite extreme: an economy in which the saving rate is equal to 1. People save all of their income. The level of capital, and thus output, will be very high. But because people save all of their income, consumption is equal to zero. What happens is that the economy is carrying an excessive amount of capital: Simply maintaining that level requires that all output be devoted to replacing depreciation! A saving rate equal to 1 also implies zero consumption in the long run.

These two extreme cases suggest that there must be some value of the saving rate between 0 and 1 at which the steady-state level of consumption reaches a maximum value. Increases in the saving rate *below* this value lead to a decrease in consumption initially but to an increase in consumption in the long run. Increases in the saving rate *beyond* this value decrease consumption not only initially but also in the long run. This happens because the increase in capital associated with the increase in the saving rate leads to only a small increase in output, an increase that is too small to cover the increased depreciation: The economy carries too much capital. The level of capital associated with the value of the saving rate that yields the highest level of consumption in steady state is known as the **golden-rule level of capital**. Increases in capital beyond the golden-rule level reduce steady-state consumption.

---

[1]**DIGGING DEEPER**. Because we assume that employment is constant, we are ignoring the short-run effect of an increase in the saving rate on output we focused on in Chapter 3. In the short run, not only does an increase in the saving rate reduce consumption given income, but it may also create a recession and decrease income further. We will return to a discussion of short- and long-run effects of changes in saving at various points in the book. See, for example, Chapter 26.

FIGURE 15-6

The Effects of the Saving
Rate on Consumption per
Worker in Steady State

An increase in the saving
rate leads to an increase,
then to a decrease in consumption per worker in
steady state.

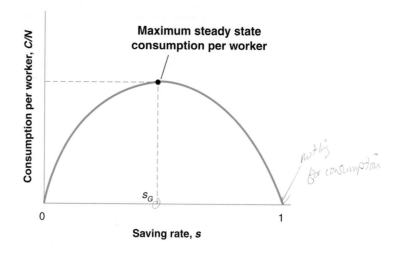

This argument is illustrated in Figure 15–6, which plots consumption per worker in steady state against alternative values of the saving rate. A saving rate equal to zero implies a capital stock per worker equal to zero, a level of output per worker equal to zero and, by implication, a level of consumption per worker equal to zero. For s between 0 and s_G, (G for golden rule) higher values of the saving rate imply higher values for capital per worker, output per worker, and consumption per worker. For s larger than s_G, increases in the saving rate still lead to higher values of capital per worker and output per worker; but they lead to lower values of consumption per worker: This is because the increase in output is more than offset by the increase in depreciation due to the larger capital stock. For $s = 1$, consumption per worker is equal to zero. Capital per worker and output per worker are high, but all of output is used just to replace depreciation, leaving nothing for consumption.

If an economy already has so much capital that it is operating beyond the golden rule, then increasing saving further will decrease consumption not only now but also later. Is this a relevant worry? Do some countries actually have too much capital? The empirical evidence indicates that most OECD countries are actually far below their golden-rule level of capital. If they were to increase the saving rate, it would lead to higher consumption in the future.

This conclusion implies that in practice, governments face a trade-off: An increase in the saving rate implies lower consumption initially but higher consumption later. What should governments do? How close to the golden rule should they try to get? That depends on how much weight they put on the welfare of current generations—who are more likely to lose from policies aimed at increasing the saving rate—versus the welfare of future genera-tions—who are more likely to gain. However, future generations do not vote now. This implies that governments are unlikely to ask current generations for large sacrifices, which, in turn, means that capital is likely to stay far below its golden-rule level. These intergenerational issues are very much in evidence in the current debate on Social Security reform; this is explored in the In Depth box "Old Age Pensions and Capital Accumulation in Canada."

15-3 | Getting a Sense of Magnitudes

How large is the effect of a change in the saving rate on output in the long run? For how long and by how much would an increase in the saving rate affect growth? What does the golden-rule level of capital look like? To get a better sense of the answers to these questions, let us now make more specific assumptions, plug in some numbers, and see what comes out.

Assume the production function is:

$$Y = \sqrt{K}\,\sqrt{N} \qquad (15.6)$$

The Canadian federal government has three programs that make significant payments to the elderly (those over 65) in Canada. They are **Old Age Security (OAS)**, **Guaranteed Income Supplement (GIS)**, and the **Canada Pension Plan (CPP)**. The latter has a separate plan for Quebec known as the **Quebec Pension Plan (QPP)**. In 2005, there were almost four million Canadians (13% of 32.3 million Canadians) over 65. This number and percentage is forecast to increase rapidly over the next 30 years.

One can think of two ways to set up and fund retirement incomes:

- One is to tax workers and distribute the tax contributions as benefits to retirees. Such a system is called a **pay-as-you-go** system: The system pays benefits out "as it goes," that is, as it collects them in contributions.

- The other is to tax workers, invest the contributions in financial assets, and pay back the principal plus the interest to workers when they retire. Such a system is called **fully funded**: At any time, the system has funds equal to the accumulated contributions of workers, and from which it will be able to pay out benefits when those workers retire.

From the point of view of retirees, the two systems feel similar, but they are not identical. What the retirees receive in a pay-as-you-go system depends on demographics—the ratio of retirees to workers—and on the evolution of the tax rate set by the system; what they receive in a fully funded system depends on the rate of return on the financial assets held by the fund. But, in both cases, they pay contributions when they are employed and receive benefits later.

From the point of view of the economy, the two systems are very different, however: In a pay-as-you-go system, the contributions are redistributed, not invested; in a fully funded system, they are invested, leading to a higher capital stock. So, a fully funded social security system leads to a higher capital stock.

You may notice that in both systems above, the word "tax" is used to refer to the contribution made by workers. This implies membership in government-operated retirement systems is mandatory. This is indeed the case. There are private retirement pensions as well. In Canada, about 30% of pension incomes comes from OAS or GIS. This is a government-operated plan, where there are no financial assets—the contributions are collected as your federal income tax and paid as benefits to those over 65. In Canada, about 30% of retirement income comes from the Canada and Quebec Pension Plans. Here, there are some financial assets but not enough to consider these plans fully funded. Finally, about 40% of retirement income is provided by privately operated fully funded private plans. These plans contribute to Canada's capital stock.

As noted above, the Canada Pension Plan and its Quebec counterpart are partly pay-as-you-go and partly funded public pension plans. Contributions from workers were used to pay benefits to the retirees; for the first few decades of the system, retirees received benefits without having contributed or without having contributed for very long. This gift to the initial retirees was widely perceived as fair: These were the generations that had suffered during the Great Depression and World War II. It also was not very costly: The number of eligible retirees was small at the beginning, so the contribution tax rate required to finance benefits was low.

The CPP and the QPP came into trouble in the 1990s because of demographic changes. Life expectancy and the average length of retirement have steadily increased. The large baby-boom generation is approaching retirement. As a result, the ratio of workers to retirees has steadily decreased and will continue to decrease over the next 50 years. By 2026, Statistics Canada projects that 21% of Canada's population will be over 65 years of age. If CPP (and QPP) contributions were not increased, there would have been a growing imbalance between benefits and contributions. However, contribution rates were increased over the 1990s. Contributions are higher than benefits for the time being. In a change in policy, some of the excess of contributions over benefits is being invested in private sector financial instruments. This part is called the Canada Pension Plan Investment Board, and as of 2005, it held about $60 billion in various stocks, bonds, and real estate. Some CPP assets (around $30 billion in 2005) were held in the form of provincial government bonds. The $90 billion in assets as well as the higher contribution rate is projected to maintain a balance between CPP benefits and CPP contributions over the near future. The Canada Pension Plan is now a combination of pay-as-you-go and fully funded systems. However, the Old Age Security and Guaranteed Income Supplement remain completely pay-as-you-go systems. These systems are not small. In 2001–2004, the federal government projected that about $25 billion a year (or 2.5% of GDP) would be paid out in these programs.

In this context, some economists and politicians argue that the goal should be a shift to a fully funded system. Their argument is that the saving rate is too low and that a fully funded system would increase it. Martin Feldstein, an advocate of such a shift, has concluded that it could lead to a 34% increase of the capital stock in the long run.

How should we think about such a proposal? It might have been a good idea to fully fund the system at the start. Canada would have a higher saving rate. The Canadian capital stock would be higher and output and consumption would also be higher. But we cannot rewrite history. The existing system has promised benefits to retirees, and these promises have to be honoured. This means that if we wanted to shift to a fully funded system, current workers would have, in effect, to contribute twice: once to finance the benefits owed to retirees, and then again to fund the system and finance their own retirement. This would be good for Canada in the long run but would impose a disproportionate cost on current workers. The practical implication is that, if it is to happen, the move to a fully funded system will have to be very slow so that the burden of adjustment does not fall too much on one generation relative to the others.

Further Readings

Two books that review recent pension policy in Canada are:
  The Future of Pension Policy: Individual Responsibility and State Support, British-North American Committee 41, by William B.P. Robson (1997) and *When We're 65: Reforming Canada's Retirement Income System*, by John P. Burbidge et al. (C.D. Howe Institute, 1996).
There are many other books written on this subject. The federal Department of Finance Web site (**www.fin.gc.ca**) also leads to many other sites describing the federal government's role in the provision of retirement income.

Output equals the product of the square root of capital and the square root of labour. Note that this production function exhibits both constant returns to scale, and decreasing returns to either capital or labour.[2]

Dividing both sides by N (because we are interested in output per worker) gives:

$$\frac{Y}{N} = \frac{\sqrt{K}\sqrt{N}}{N} = \frac{\sqrt{K}}{\sqrt{N}} = \sqrt{\frac{K}{N}}$$

Output per worker equals the square root of capital per worker. Put another way, the production function f relating output per worker to capital per worker is given by:

$$f(K_t/N) = \sqrt{K_t/N}.$$

Now, go back to equation (15.3), which is repeated here for convenience:

$$\frac{K_{t+1}}{N} - \frac{K_t}{N} = sf\left(\frac{K_t}{N}\right) - \delta\frac{K_t}{N}$$

Replace $f(K_t/N)$ by $\sqrt{K_t/N}$:

$$\frac{K_{t+1}}{N} - \frac{K_t}{N} = s\sqrt{\frac{K_t}{N}} - \delta\frac{K_t}{N} \qquad (15.7)$$

This equation describes the evolution of capital per worker over time. Let us now look at what it implies.

The Effects of the Saving Rate on Steady-State Output

How large is the effect of an increase in the saving rate on the steady-state level of output per worker?

Start with equation (15.7). In steady state, the amount of capital per worker is constant, so the left side of the equation equals zero.

This implies:

$$s\sqrt{\frac{K}{N}} = \delta\frac{K}{N}$$

(We have dropped time indexes, which are no longer needed because in steady state K/N is constant.) Square both sides:

$$s^2\frac{K}{N} = \delta^2\left(\frac{K}{N}\right)^2$$

Divide both sides by (K/N), and reorganize:

$$\frac{K}{N} = \left(\frac{s}{\delta}\right)^2 \qquad (15.8)$$

---

[2]**DIGGING DEEPER**. A more general specification for the production function would be:

$$Y = K^\alpha N^{1-\alpha}$$

where α is a number between 0 and 1.

The production function we use in the text assumes $\alpha = 0.5$, giving equal weights to capital and labour. (Taking the square root of a variable is the same as raising it to the power 0.5.) A more realistic production function would give more weight to labour and less to capital, for example $\alpha = 0.3$.

There are two reasons why we use $\alpha = 0.5$: The first is that it makes the algebra much simpler. The second is based on a broader interpretation of capital than just physical capital. As we will see in section 15-4, we can think of the accumulation of skills, say, through education or on-the-job training, as a form of capital accumulation as well. Under this broader view of capital, a coefficient of 0.5 for capital is roughly appropriate.

This gives us an equation for steady-state capital per worker. From equations (15.6) and (15.8), steady-state output per worker is given by:

$$\frac{Y}{N} = \sqrt{\frac{K}{N}} = \sqrt{\left(\frac{s}{\delta}\right)^2} = \frac{s}{\delta} \qquad (15.9)$$

Output per worker is equal to the ratio of the saving rate to the depreciation rate; capital per worker is equal to the square of that ratio. A higher saving rate and a lower depreciation rate both lead to higher capital per worker and output per worker in the long run.

Suppose the depreciation rate is 10% per year, and take the saving rate to be 10% as well. Then, using equations (15.8) and (15.9), we see that capital per worker and output per worker in steady state are both equal to 1. Now, suppose that the saving rate doubles, from 10% to 20%. It follows from equation (15.8) that in the new steady state, capital per worker increases from 1 to 4. And from equation (15.9), output per worker doubles, from 1 to 2. Thus, doubling the saving rate leads, in the long run, to doubling output: This is a large effect.

The Dynamic Effects of an Increase in the Saving Rate

After an increase in the saving rate, how long does it take for the economy to reach the new higher level of output? Put another way, by how much and for how long does an increase in the saving rate affect the growth rate?

To answer these questions, we must use equation (15.7) and solve it for capital in year 0, year 1, and so on.

Suppose that the saving rate, which had always been equal to 0.1, increases in year 0 from 0.1 to 0.2 and remains at this higher value forever after. In year 0, nothing happens to the capital stock (recall that it takes one year for higher saving and higher investment to show up in higher capital). So, capital per worker remains equal to the steady-state value associated with a saving rate of 0.1. From equation (15.8), $K_0/N = (0.1/0.1)^2 = 1^2 = 1$.

In year 1, equation (15.7) gives:

$$\frac{K_1}{N} - \frac{K_0}{N} = s \sqrt{\frac{K_0}{N}} - \delta \frac{K_0}{N}$$

With a depreciation rate equal to 0.1 and a saving rate now equal to 0.2, this equation implies that $K_1/N - 1 = [(0.2)(\sqrt{1})] - [(0.1)1]$ so that $K_1/N = 1.1$.

In the same way, we can solve for K_2/N, and so on. Once we have the values of capital per worker in year 0, year 1, and so on, we can then use equation (15.6) to solve for output per worker in year 0, year 1, and so on. The results of this computation are presented in Figure 15–7(a), which plots the *level* of output per worker against time. (Y/N) increases over time from its initial value of 1 in year 0 to its steady-state value of 2 in the long run. Figure 15–7(b) gives the same information in a different way, plotting instead the *growth rate* of output per worker against time. Growth of output per worker is highest at the beginning and then decreases over time. As the economy reaches its new steady state, growth of output per worker returns to zero.

Figure 15–7 clearly shows that the adjustment to the new, higher, long-run equilibrium takes a long time. It is only 40% complete after 10 years and is 63% complete after 20 years. Put another way, the increase in the saving rate increases the growth rate of output per worker for a long time. The average annual growth rate is 3.1% for the first 10 years, and 1.5% for the next 10. Although changes in the saving rate have no effect on growth in the long run, they do lead to higher growth for quite some time.

To return to the question raised at the beginning of the chapter, can the lower saving/investment rate in Canada and the United States explain why the North American growth rate has been lower relative to other OECD countries since 1950? The answer would be yes, if North America had had a higher saving rate in the past and *if this saving rate had decreased substantially in the last 50 years*. If this were the case, this could explain the period of lower growth in North America in the last 50 years along the lines of the mechanism in Figure 15–7 (with the

FIGURE 15-7

Dynamic Effects of an Increase in the Saving Rate from 10% to 20% on the Level and the Growth Rate of Output per Worker

It takes a long time for output to adjust to its new higher level after an increase in the saving rate. Put another way, an increase in the saving rate leads to a long period of higher growth.

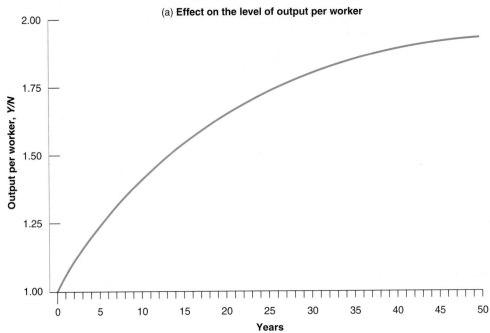

(a) Effect on the level of output per worker

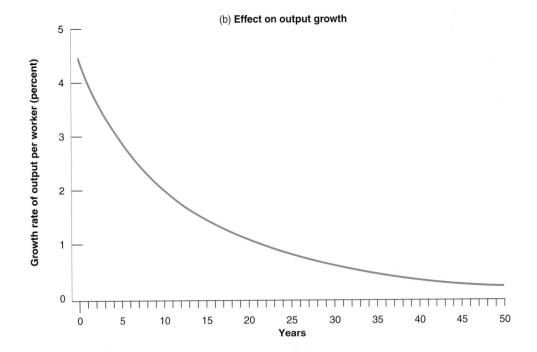

(b) Effect on output growth

sign reversed, as we would be looking at a decrease, not an increase, in the saving rate). But this is not the case: The North American saving rate has been low for a long time. Low saving cannot explain the poor North American growth performance over the last 50 years.

The Canadian Saving Rate and the Golden Rule

Let us now turn to the third question we asked at the beginning of this section. <u>What is the saving rate that would maximize steady-state consumption?</u>

Saving Rate, s	Capital per Worker, K/N	Output per Worker, Y/N	Consumption per Worker, C/N
0.0	0.0	0.0	0.0
0.1	1.0	1.0	0.9
0.2	4.0	2.0	1.6
0.3	9.0	3.0	2.1
0.4	16.0	4.0	2.4
0.5	25.0	5.0	2.5
0.6	36.0	6.0	2.4
...	...	...	...
1.0	100.0	10.0	0.0

In steady state, consumption per worker is equal to output per worker minus depreciation per worker:

$$\frac{C}{N} = \frac{Y}{N} - \delta \frac{K}{N}$$

Using equations (15.8) and (15.9) for the steady-state values of output per worker and capital per worker, consumption per worker is thus given by:

$$\frac{C}{N} = s/\delta - \delta(s/\delta)^2$$
$$= s(1 - s)/\delta$$

Using this equation together with equations (15.8) and (15.9), Table 15–1 gives the steady-state values of capital per worker, output per worker, and consumption per worker for different values of the saving rate (and for a depreciation rate equal to 10%).

Steady-state consumption is largest when $s(1 - s)$ is largest; this occurs when s equals one-half: The golden-rule level of capital is associated with a saving rate of 50%. Below that level, increases in the saving rate lead to an increase in long-run consumption. Above that level, they lead to a decrease. Few economies in the world today have saving rates above 40%, and (as we saw at the beginning of the chapter) the Canadian saving rate is about 22%. As rough as it is, our computation suggests that in most economies, an increase in the saving rate would increase both output and consumption levels in the long run.

Check your understanding of the issues: Using the equations in this section, argue the pros and cons of policy measures aimed at increasing the Canadian saving rate from its current value of about 25% to, say, 35%.

15-4 | Physical versus Human Capital

We have concentrated so far on physical capital—on machines, plants, office buildings, and so on. But economies have another type of capital: the set of skills of the workers in the economy, what economists call **human capital**. An economy with many highly skilled workers is likely to be much more productive than an economy in which most workers cannot read or write.

The increase in human capital has been as dramatic as the increase in physical capital over the last two centuries. At the beginning of the Industrial Revolution, only 30% of the population knew how to read. Today, the literacy rate in the OECD countries is above 95%. Schooling was not compulsory prior to the Industrial Revolution. Today it is, usually until the age of 16. Still, there are large differences across countries. Today, in the OECD countries, nearly 100% of children get a primary education, 90% get a secondary education, and 38% get a higher education. The corresponding numbers in poor countries, countries with GDP per capita below $400 in 1985, are 95%, 32%, and 4%, respectively.

How should we think about the effect of human capital on output? How does the introduction of human capital change our earlier conclusions? These are the questions we take up in this last section.

Extending the Production Function

The most natural way of extending our analysis to allow for human capital is to modify the production function relation (15.1) to read:

$$\frac{Y}{N} = f\left(\frac{K}{N}, \frac{H}{N}\right) \tag{15.10}$$

$$(+, +)$$

The level of output per worker depends on both the level of physical capital per worker, K/N, and the level of human capital per worker, H/N. As before, an increase in capital per worker (K/N) leads to an increase in output per worker. And an increase in the average level of skill (H/N) also leads to more output per worker. More skilled workers can use more complex machines; they can deal more easily with unexpected complications; they can adapt faster to new tasks. All of these lead to higher output per worker.

We assumed earlier that increases in physical capital per worker increased output per worker but that the effect became smaller as the level of capital per worker increased. The same assumption is likely to apply to human capital per worker. Think of increases in H/N as coming from increases in the number of years of education. The evidence is that the returns to increasing the proportion of children acquiring a primary education are very large. At the very least, the ability to read and write allows workers to use more sophisticated equipment. For rich countries, however, primary education—and, for that matter, secondary education—are no longer the relevant margins: Most children now get both. The relevant margin is higher education. The evidence here—and we are sure this will come as good news to most of you—is that higher education increases skills, at least as measured by the increase in wages for those who acquire it. But, to take an extreme example, it is not clear that forcing everybody to acquire a Ph.D. would increase aggregate output very much. Many people would end up overqualified and probably more frustrated rather than more productive.

How should we construct the measure for human capital, H? The answer is very much the same way we construct the measure for physical capital, K. In constructing K, we just add the values of the different pieces of capital so that a machine that costs $2000 gets twice the weight of a machine that costs $1000. Similarly, we construct the measure of H such that workers who are paid twice as much get twice the weight.[3] Take, for example, an economy with 100 workers, half of them unskilled and half of them skilled. Suppose the relative wage of skilled workers is twice that of unskilled workers. We can then construct H as [(50 × 1) + (50 × 2)] = 150. Human capital per worker, H/N, is equal to 150/100 = 1.5.

---

[3] **DIGGING DEEPER.** The logic for using relative wages as weights is that they are supposed to capture the relative marginal products of different workers so that a worker who is paid three times as much as another has a marginal product that is three times higher.

This would be correct if labour markets were perfectly competitive: Recall from your microeconomics course that in a perfectly competitive labour market, each worker is paid a wage equal to his or her marginal product. But as we discussed in Chapter 9, labour markets are not perfectly competitive, and you may question whether relative wages accurately reflect relative marginal products. To take one, very controversial, example: In the same job, with the same seniority, women still often earn less than men. Does this fact reflect that their marginal product is lower? Should they be given a lower weight than men in the construction of human capital?

Even this comparison may be misleading. The quality of education may be quite different across countries.

Note that we are using the same symbol, H, to denote the monetary base in Chapter 4, and human capital in this chapter. Both uses are traditional. Do not be confused.

We look at the relation between skills and relative wages in more detail in Chapter 16.

Human Capital, Physical Capital, and Output

How does the introduction of human capital change the analysis of the previous sections?

Our conclusions about *physical capital accumulation* remain valid: An increase in the saving rate increases steady-state physical capital per worker and therefore increases output per worker. But our conclusions now extend to *human capital accumulation* as well. An increase in how much society "saves" in the form of human capital—through education and on-the-job training—increases steady-state human capital per worker, which leads to an increase in output per worker.

Our extended model gives us a richer picture of the determination of output per worker. In the long run, it tells us, output per worker depends both on how much society saves and on how much it spends on education.

What is the relative importance of human and physical capital in the determination of output per worker? To answer this question, we can start by comparing how much is spent on formal education and how much is invested in physical capital. In Canada, spending on formal education is about 8% of GDP. This number includes both government and private expenditures. This number is between one-third and one-half of the gross investment rate for physical capital (which is around 20%). But this comparison is only a first pass. Consider the following complications:

- Education, especially higher education, is partly consumption—done for its own sake—and partly investment. We should include only the investment part for our purposes. However, the 8% number in the preceding paragraph includes both.
- At least for postsecondary education, the opportunity cost of a person's education is also forgone wages while one is acquiring the education. Spending on education should include not only the actual cost of education but also the opportunity cost. The 8% number does not include the opportunity cost.
- Formal education is only part of education. Much of what we learn comes from on-the-job training, formal or informal. Both the actual costs and the opportunity costs of on-the-job training should also be included. The 8% number does not include either cost.
- We should compare investment rates net of depreciation. Depreciation of physical capital, especially of machines, is likely to be higher than depreciation of human capital. Skills deteriorate but do so slowly. And, unlike physical capital, the more the skills are used, the more slowly they deteriorate.

◀ How large is your opportunity cost relative to your tuition?

For all these reasons, it is difficult to come up with reliable numbers for investment in human capital. The bulk of the evidence from recent research suggests that increases in physical capital and increases in human capital may have played roughly equal roles in the increase in output per worker over time. The implication is clear: Countries that save more and/or spend more on education can achieve substantially higher steady-state levels of output per worker.

Endogenous Growth

Note what the conclusion we just reached did and did not say. It did say that a country that saves more or spends more on education will achieve a *higher level* of output per worker in steady state. It did not say that by saving or spending more on education a country can sustain permanent *higher growth* of output per worker.

This conclusion, however, has been challenged in the past decade. Following the lead of Robert Lucas and Paul Romer, researchers have explored the possibility that the combination of physical and human capital accumulation may actually be enough to sustain growth. They have asked the following question: Given human capital, increases in physical capital will run into decreasing returns. And given physical capital, increases in human capital will also run into decreasing returns. But what if both physical and human capital increase in tandem? Can't an economy grow forever just by having steadily more capital and more skilled workers?

◀ We have mentioned Lucas once already, in connection with the Lucas critique in Chapter 12.

There are models where the answer to this question is yes—growth can continue forever. The simplest such model begins by assuming that population growth has stopped. To simplify the presentation, we set $N = 1$. Then, the more complicated production function (15.1) becomes:

$$Y_t = AK_t \qquad (15.11)$$

where A is a constant value over time. For obvious reasons, this is sometimes called the "AK" model. Equation (15.11) is rearranged so that:

$$K_t = \frac{Y_t}{A}$$

The accumulation of capital in this economy follows (15.3):

$$K_{t+1} - K_t = sY_t - \delta K_t$$

and when we substitute for K_{t+1} and K_t, this yields:

$$\frac{Y_{t+1}}{A} - \frac{Y_t}{A} = sY_t - \delta \frac{Y_t}{A}$$

Now, factor out 1 over A from the right-hand side, divide both sides by Y_t and multiply both sides by A to yield the basic growth equation in this economy:

$$\frac{Y_{t+1} - Y_t}{Y_t} = sA - \delta \qquad (15.12)$$

In thinking about growth, even in this simplest model, this equation is very interesting. Why? Growth continues forever as long as $sA > \delta$. In stark contrast, go back and look at Figure 15–7. In the model presented earlier in the chapter, when the saving rate rises, after many years, the growth rate of output per person falls to zero.

The model is also called a **model of endogenous growth** because s, the saving rate, is a choice or is endogenous. The choice can be interpreted quite broadly. It can be a choice to accumulate more human capital as described in the previous section. A high value of s could be a large amount of educational spending. A higher value of s could be interpreted as a choice to spend more current income in creating technology, for example, by paying a lot of people to do basic research in physics or biology. Technology is explored in more detail in the next chapter. However, the contrast to the model presented in this chapter arises because capital does not encounter diminishing returns in equation (15.11). As long as sA is larger than s, then growth is positive and can continue forever. The jury is still out, but the indications so far are that the conclusions we drew earlier need to be qualified but not abandoned. There is no evidence that countries can sustain higher growth just from capital accumulation and skill improvements.

To end this chapter, let us state our earlier conclusions, modified to take into account human capital: Output per worker depends on the level of both physical capital per worker and human capital per worker. Both forms of capital can be accumulated, one through physical investment, the other through education and training. Increasing either the saving rate or the fraction of output spent on education and training can lead to much higher levels of output per worker in the long run. However, for a given rate of technological progress, such measures are unlikely to lead to a permanently higher growth rate.

Note the qualifier in the last proposition: *for a given rate of technological progress*. But is technological progress unrelated to the level of human capital in the economy? Can't a better-educated labour force lead to a higher rate of technological progress? These questions take us to the topic of the next chapter, the sources and the effects of technological progress.

- In the long run, the evolution of output is determined by two relations. (To make the reading of this summary easier, we will omit "per worker" in what follows.) First, the level of output depends on the amount of existing capital. Second, capital accumulation depends, in turn, on the level of output, which determines saving and investment.

- These interactions between capital and output imply that starting from any level of capital (and ignoring technological progress, the topic of Chapter 16), an economy converges in the long run to a steady-state (constant) level of capital. Associated with this level of capital is a steady-state level of output.

- The steady-state level of capital and thus the steady-state level of output depend positively on the saving rate. A higher saving rate leads to a higher steady-state level of output; during the transition to the new steady state, a higher saving rate leads to positive output growth. But (again ignoring technological progress) in the long run, the growth rate of output is equal to zero and is thus independent of the saving rate.

- An increase in the saving rate requires an initial decrease in consumption. In the long run, the increase in the saving rate may lead to an increase or to a decrease in consumption, depending on whether the economy is below or above the golden-rule level of capital, the level of capital at which steady-state consumption is highest.

- Most countries appear to have a level of capital below the golden-rule level. Thus, an increase in the saving rate will lead to an initial decrease in consumption followed by an increase in the long run. In thinking about whether to take policy measures aimed at changing the saving rate, policy makers must decide how much weight to put on the welfare of current generations versus the welfare of future generations.

- Although most of the analysis of this chapter focuses on the effects of physical capital accumulation, output depends on the levels of both physical *and* human capital. Both forms of capital can be accumulated, one through investment and the other through education and training. Increasing the saving rate and/or the fraction of output spent on education and training can lead to large increases in output in the long run.

- In the model of endogenous growth, an increase in the saving rate can increase the growth rate.

- Canada Pension Plan (CPP), 293
- Cobb-Douglas production function, 303
- depreciation rate, 285
- fully funded old age security system, 293
- golden-rule level of capital, 291
- Guaranteed Income Supplement (GIS), 293
- human capital, 297
- models of endogenous growth, 300
- Old Age Security (OAS), 293
- pay-as-you-go social security system, 293
- Quebec Pension Plan (QPP), 293
- steady state, 287

An asterisk denotes a harder question. [Web] indicates that the question requires access to the Internet.

1. **TRUE/FALSE/UNCERTAIN**

a. The saving rate is always equal to the investment rate.

b. A higher investment rate can sustain growth of output forever.

c. If capital never depreciated, growth could go on forever.

d. The higher the saving rate, the higher is consumption in steady state.

e. Output per capita in Canada is roughly equal to 60% of output per worker.

f. We should fully fund payments to the aged. This would increase consumption, now and in the future.

g. The Canadian capital stock is far below the golden-rule level. Government should give tax breaks for saving.

2. THE GROWTH RATE AND THE SAVING RATE

"The Japanese growth rate of output per worker will remain higher than that of Canada for as long as the Japanese saving rate exceeds that of Canada." Do you agree with this statement? Why, or why not?

3. THE PARADOX OF SAVING REVISITED

In Chapter 3, we saw that an increase in the saving rate can lead to a recession in the short run. You now can examine the effects beyond the short run. If the saving rate increases permanently, what will be the effect on the growth rate after 1 year, 10 years, 50 years? Explain in words.

4. THE DETERMINANTS OF OUTPUT PER WORKER IN STEADY STATE

Discuss the likely impact of the following changes on the level of output per worker in the long run:

a. The right to exclude saving from income when paying the income tax

b. A higher rate of female participation (but constant population)

*5. GROWTH WITH A MORE GENERAL PRODUCTION FUNCTION, PART I

Suppose that the economy's production function is given by $Y = K^{\alpha}N^{1-\alpha}$. (This production function is called the Cobb-Douglas production function.) In section 15-3, we took α to be 1/2. Assume now that $\alpha = 1/3$.

a. Is this production function characterized by constant returns to scale? Explain.

b. Are there decreasing returns to capital?

c. Are there decreasing returns to labour?

d. Transform the production function into a relation between output per worker and capital per worker.

e. For a given saving rate (s) and a depreciation rate (δ), give an expression for capital per worker in the steady state.

f. Give an expression for output per worker in the steady state.

g. Solve for the steady state level of output per worker when $\delta = 0.08$ and $s = 0.32$.

h. Suppose that the depreciation rate remains constant at $\delta = 0.08$, whereas the saving rate is reduced by half to $s = 0.16$. What happens to the steady state level of output per worker?

*6. GROWTH WITH A MORE GENERAL PRODUCTION FUNCTION, PART II

Suppose that the economy's production function is $Y = K^{1/3}N^{2/3}$ and that both the saving rate (s) and the depreciation rate (δ) are equal to 0.10.

a. What is the steady-state level of capital per worker?

b. What is the steady-state level of output per worker?

Suppose that the economy has reached its steady state in period t, and then, in period $t + 1$, the depreciation rate doubles to 0.20.

c. Solve for the new steady-state levels of capital per worker and output per worker.

d. Compute the path of capital per worker and output per worker over the first three periods after the change in the depreciation rate.

7. SEARCHING FOR THE GOLDEN RULE

Suppose that the production function is given by $Y = 0.5\sqrt{K}\sqrt{N}$.

a. Derive the steady-state levels of K/N and Y/N in terms of the saving rate (s) and the depreciation rate (δ).

b. Derive the equation for steady-state output per worker and steady-state consumption per worker in terms of s and δ.

c. Suppose that $\delta = 5\%$. With your favourite spreadsheet software, compute steady-state output per worker and steady-state consumption per worker for $s = 0, 0.1, 0.2, \ldots, 1.0$. Explain.

d. Use your software to graph the steady-state level of output per worker and consumption per worker as a function of the saving rate (that is, measure the saving rate on the horizontal axis of your graph and the corresponding values of output per worker and consumption per worker on the vertical axis).

e. Does the graph show that there is a value of s that maximizes output per worker? Does the graph show that there is a value of s that maximizes consumption per worker? If so, what is this value?

FURTHER READING

The classic treatment of the relation between the saving rate and output is provided by Robert Solow in *Growth Theory: An Exposition* (New York: Oxford University Press, 1970).

APPENDIX: THE COBB–DOUGLAS PRODUCTION FUNCTION AND THE STEADY STATE

In 1928, Charles Cobb (a mathematician) and Paul Douglas (an economist, who went on to become a U.S. senator) concluded that the following production function gave a very good description of the relation among output, physical capital, and labour in the United States from 1899 to 1922:

$$Y = K^{\alpha}N^{1-\alpha} \tag{15.A1}$$

with α being a number between zero and one. Their findings proved surprisingly robust. Even today, the production function (15.A1), now known as the **Cobb–Douglas production function**, still gives a good description of the relation among output, capital, and labour in the United States, and it has become a standard tool in the economist's toolbox. (Verify for yourself that it satisfies the two properties we discussed in the text: constant returns to scale and decreasing returns to capital and to labour.)

The purpose of this appendix is to characterize the steady state of an economy when the production function is given by (15.A1). (All you need to follow the steps is a knowledge of the properties of exponents.)

Recall that in steady state, saving per worker must be equal to depreciation per worker. Let us see what this implies:

- To derive saving per worker, we must derive first the relation between output per worker and capital per worker implied by equation (15.A1). Divide both sides of equation (15.A1) by N:

$$Y/N = K^{\alpha}N^{1-\alpha}/N$$

Using the properties of exponents:

$$N^{1-\alpha}/N = N^{1-\alpha}N^{-1} = N^{-\alpha}$$

so, replacing in the preceding equation, we get:

$$Y/N = K^{\alpha}N^{-\alpha} = (K/N)^{\alpha}$$

Output per worker Y/N is equal to the ratio of capital per worker K/N raised to the power α.

Saving per worker is equal to the saving rate times output per worker, so using the previous equation, it is equal to:

$$s(K^*/N)^{\alpha}$$

- Depreciation per worker is equal to the depreciation rate times capital per worker:

$$\delta(K^*/N)$$

- The steady-state level of capital, K^*, is determined by the condition that saving per worker be equal to depreciation per worker, so:

$$s(K^*/N)^{\alpha} = \delta(K^*/N)$$

To solve this expression for the steady-state level of capital per worker K^*/N, divide both sides by $(K^*/N)^{\alpha}$:

$$s = \delta(K^*/N)^{1-\alpha}$$

Divide both sides by δ, and change the order of the equality:

$$(K^*/N)^{1-\alpha} = s/\delta$$

Finally, raise both sides to the power $1/(1-\alpha)$:

$$(K^*/N) = (s/\delta)^{1/(1-\alpha)}$$

This gives us the steady-state level of capital per worker.

From the production function, the steady-state level of output per worker is then equal to:

$$(Y^*/N) = (K/N)^{\alpha} = (s/\delta)^{\alpha/(1-\alpha)}$$

Let us see what this last equation implies:

- In the text, we actually worked with a special case of equation (15.A1), the case where $\alpha = 0.5$. (Taking a variable to the power 0.5 is the same as taking the square root of this variable). If $\alpha = 0.5$, the preceding equation means:

$$Y^*/N = s/\delta$$

Output per worker is equal to the ratio of the saving rate to the depreciation rate. This is the equation we discussed in the text. A doubling of the saving rate leads to a doubling in steady-state output per worker.

- The empirical evidence suggests, however, that if we think of K as physical capital, α is closer to one-third than to one-half. Assuming $\alpha = 1/3$, then $\alpha(1-\alpha) = (1/3)/(1-(1/3)) = (1/3)/(2/3) = 1/2$, and the equation for output per worker yields

$$Y^*/N = (s/\delta)^{1/2} = \sqrt{s/\delta}$$

This implies smaller effects of the saving rate on output per worker than was suggested by the computations in the text. A doubling of the saving rate, for example, means that output per worker increases by a factor of $\sqrt{2}$, or only about 1.4 (put another way, a 40% increase in output per worker).

- There is, however, an interpretation of our model in which the appropriate value of α is close to one-half, so the computations in the text are applicable. If, along the lines of section 15-4, we take human capital into account as well as physical capital, then a value of α around one-half for the contribution of this broader definition of capital to output is, indeed, roughly appropriate. Thus, one interpretation of the numerical results in section 15-3 is that they show the effects of a given saving rate, but that saving must be interpreted to include saving in both physical capital and in human capital (more machines and more education).

CHAPTER 16
TECHNOLOGICAL PROGRESS AND GROWTH

Our conclusion in Chapter 15 that capital accumulation cannot, by itself, sustain growth has a straightforward implication: Sustained growth *requires* technological progress. This chapter looks at the relation between technological progress and growth.

Section 16-1 looks at the respective role of technological progress and capital accumulation in growth. It shows how, in steady state, the rate of growth of output per capita is simply equal to the rate of technological progress. This does not mean, however, that the saving rate is irrelevant: The saving rate affects the level of output per capita, if not its rate of growth. Section 16-2 turns to the determinants of technological progress, focusing in particular on the role of research and development (R&D). Section 16-3 returns to the facts of growth presented in Chapter 14 and interprets them in light of what we have learned in this and the preceding chapters.

16-1 | Technological Progress and the Rate of Growth

In an economy in which there is both capital accumulation and technological progress, at what rate will output grow? To answer this question, we need to extend the model developed in Chapter 15 to allow for technological progress. To do so, we must first revisit the aggregate production function.

Technological Progress and the Production Function

Technological progress has many dimensions:

- It may mean larger quantities of output for given quantities of capital and labour. For example, think of a new type of lubricant that allows a machine to run at a higher speed.
- It may mean better products. For example, think of the steady improvement in car safety and comfort over time.
- It may mean new products. For example, think of the introduction of the CD player and the fax machine.
- It may mean a larger variety of products. For example, think of the steady increase in the types of breakfast cereals available at your local supermarket.

These dimensions are more similar than they may appear. If we think of consumers as caring not about the goods themselves but about the services these goods provide, then all these examples have something in common. In each case, consumers receive more services. A better car provides more safety, a new product such as the fax machine provides more communication services, and so on.

If we think of output as the set of underlying services provided by the goods produced in the economy, we can think of technological progress as leading to increases in output for given amounts of capital and labour. We can then think of the *state of technology* as a variable that tells us how much output can be produced from capital and labour at any time. Let us denote the state of technology by A and rewrite the production function as:

$$Y = F(K, N, A)$$

$$(+, +, +)$$

This is our extended production function. Output depends on both capital and labour (K and N) and on the state of technology (A): Given capital and labour, an improvement in the state of technology, A, leads to an increase in output.

It will prove convenient to use a slightly more restrictive form of the preceding equation, namely:

$$Y = F(K, AN) \qquad (16.1)$$

This equation states that production depends on capital and on labour multiplied by the state of technology. This way of introducing the state of technology makes it easier to think about the effect of technological progress on the relation among output, capital, and labour.[1] Equation (16.1) implies that we can think of technological progress in two equivalent ways:

1. Given the existing capital stock, technological progress reduces the number of workers needed to achieve a given amount of output. A doubling of A allows the economy to produce the same quantity of output with only half the original number of workers, N.

---

[1]**DIGGING DEEPER**. This way of writing the production function implies that technological progress is *labour augmenting*: It *augments* (that is, multiplies) labour in the production function. We could assume instead that technological progress is *capital augmenting* (that is, multiplies capital) or that it is both labour and capital augmenting. The justification for the assumption made here is convenience: It leads to a simpler characterization of growth in the long run.

In Chapter 15, we assumed that technology did not change, but only the amount of capital used in production. In this chapter, we take into account that technology itself changes over time, that there is technological progress.

The average number of items carried by a supermarket increased from 2200 in 1950 to 17,500 in 1985. To get a sense of what this means, watch Robin Williams (who plays an immigrant from the Soviet Union) in the supermarket scene in the movie *Moscow on the Hudson*.

For simplicity, we will ignore human capital here.

AN is also sometimes called **labour in efficiency units**. The use of "efficiency" for "efficiency units" here and of "efficiency wages" in Chapter 9 is a coincidence: The two notions are unrelated.

2. Technological progress increases AN, the amount of **effective labour** in the economy. If the state of technology doubles, it is as if the economy had twice as many workers. In other words, we can can think of output being produced by two factors: capital (K) on the one hand and effective labour (AN) on the other.

What restrictions should we impose on the extended production function, equation (16.1)? We can build directly here on our discussion in Chapter 14.

It is again reasonable to assume constant returns to scale: *For a given state of technology* (A), doubling both the amount of capital (K) and the amount of labour (N) is likely to lead to a doubling of output:

$$2Y = F(2K, 2AN)$$

More generally, for any number x:

$$xY = F(xK, xAN)$$

It is also reasonable to assume decreasing returns to each of the two factors, capital and effective labour. Given effective labour, an increase in capital is likely to increase output, but at a decreasing rate. Symmetrically, given capital, an increase in effective labour is likely to increase output, but at a decreasing rate.

Per worker: divided by the number of workers (N).

Per effective worker: divided by the number of effective workers (NA)—the number of workers, N, times the state of technology, A.

It was convenient in Chapter 15 to think in terms of output and capital *per worker*. That was because the steady state of the economy was a state where output and capital *per worker* were constant. It is convenient here to look at output and capital *per effective worker*. The reason is the same: As we shall soon see, in steady state, output and capital *per effective worker* are constant.

To get a relation between output per effective worker and capital per effective worker, take $x = 1/AN$ in the preceding equation. This gives:

$$\frac{Y}{AN} = F\left(\frac{K}{AN}, 1\right)$$

Suppose that F has the "double square root" form:

$$Y = F(K, AN) = \sqrt{K}\sqrt{AN}$$

Then,

$$Y/AN = \sqrt{K/AN}\sqrt{AN/AN}$$
$$= \sqrt{K/AN}$$

So, the function f is simply the square root function:

$$f(K/AN) = \sqrt{K/AN}$$

Or, if we define the function f so that $f(K/AN) \equiv F(K/AN,1)$:

$$\frac{Y}{AN} = f\left(\frac{K}{AN}\right) \qquad (16.2)$$

Output per effective worker   Capital per effective worker

Equation (16.2) gives us a relation between *output per effective worker* and *capital per effective worker*. Output per effective worker increases if and only if capital per effective worker increases. The relation between output per effective worker and capital per effective worker is drawn in Figure 16–1. It looks very much the same as the relation we drew in Figure 15–2 between output per worker and capital per worker in the absence of technological progress: Increases in K/AN lead to increases in Y/AN, but at a decreasing rate.

FIGURE   **16–1**

Output per Effective Worker versus Capital per Effective Worker

Increases in capital per effective worker lead to smaller and smaller increases in output per effective worker.

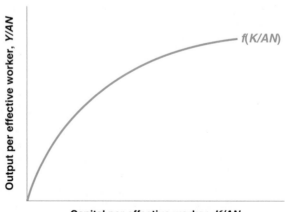

Output per effective worker, Y/AN

$f(K/AN)$

Capital per effective worker, K/AN

Interactions between Output and Capital

We now have the elements we need to think about the determinants of growth. Our analysis will parallel the analysis of Chapter 15. There we looked at *output and capital per worker*. Here, we look at the dynamics of *output and capital per effective worker*.

In Chapter 15, we characterized the dynamics of output and capital per worker using Figure 15–2. In that figure, we drew three relations:

Here is the key to understanding the results in this chapter: The results we derived for *output per worker* in Chapter 15 still hold in this chapter, but now for *output per effective worker*. For example, in Chapter 15, we saw that output per worker was constant in steady state. In this chapter, we will see that output per effective worker is constant in steady state.

- The relation between output per worker and capital per worker.

- The implied relation between investment per worker and capital per worker.

- The relation between depreciation per worker—the investment per worker needed to maintain a constant level of capital per worker—and capital per worker.

The dynamics of capital per worker and, by implication, of output per worker were determined by the relation between investment per worker and depreciation per worker. Depending on whether investment per worker was greater or smaller than depreciation per worker, capital per worker increased or decreased over time, and so did output per worker.

We follow exactly the same approach here in building Figure 16–2. The difference is that we focus on output, capital, and investment per effective worker, rather than per worker.

1. The relation between output per effective worker and capital per effective worker was derived in Figure 16–1. This relation is repeated in Figure 16–2. Output per effective worker increases with capital per effective worker, but at a decreasing rate.

2. Under the same assumptions as in Chapter 15—investment is equal to private saving, and the private saving rate is constant—investment is given by:

$$I = S = sY$$

Divide both sides by the number of effective workers, AN, to get:

$$\frac{I}{AN} = s\frac{Y}{AN}$$

Substituting output per effective worker Y/AN by its expression from equation (16.2) gives:

$$\frac{I}{AN} = sf\left(\frac{K}{AN}\right)$$

The relation between investment per effective worker and capital per effective worker is drawn as the lower curve in Figure 16–2. It is equal to the upper curve—the relation between output per effective worker and capital per effective worker—multiplied by the saving rate, s (which is less than one).

3. Finally, we need to derive the level of investment per effective worker needed to maintain a given level of capital per effective worker.

In Chapter 15, the answer was simple; for capital to be constant, investment had to be equal to the depreciation of the existing capital stock. Here, the answer is slightly more complicated. The reason is as follows: Now that we allow for technological progress, the number of effective workers (AN) is increasing over time. Thus, maintaining the same ratio of capital to effective workers (K/AN) requires an increase in the capital stock (K) proportional to the increase in the number of effective workers (AN). Let us look at this condition more closely.

In Chapter 15, we were assuming both g_A and g_N were equal to zero. Our main focus in this chapter is on the implications of technological progress, $g_A > 0$. But, once we allow for technological progress, introducing population growth $g_N > 0$ is straightforward. Thus, we allow for both.

Assume that population is growing at annual rate g_N. If we assume that the ratio of employment to the total population remains constant, the number of workers (N) also grows at annual rate g_N. Assume also that the rate of technological progress equals g_A. Together, these two assumptions imply that the growth rate of effective labour (AN) equals $g_A + g_N$. If

The growth rate of the product of two variables is the sum of the growth rates of the two variables. See proposition 7 in Appendix 2 at the end of the book.

the number of workers is growing at 1% per year and the rate of technological progress is 2% per year, then the growth rate of effective labour is equal to 3%.

Let δ be the depreciation rate of capital. Then the level of investment needed to maintain a given level of capital per effective worker is given by:

$$\delta K + (g_A + g_N)K$$

An amount δK is needed just to keep the capital stock constant. If the depreciation rate is 10%, then investment must be equal to 10% of the capital stock just to maintain the same level of capital. And an additional amount $(g_A + g_N)K$ is needed to ensure that the capital stock increases at the same rate as effective labour. If effective labour increases at 3% a year, then capital must increase by 3% a year to maintain the same level of capital per effective worker. Putting δK and $(g_A + g_N)K$ together in this example, if the depreciation rate is 10% and the growth rate of effective labour is 3%, then investment must equal 13% of the capital stock to maintain a constant level of capital per effective worker.

Grouping the terms in K in the preceding expression and dividing by the number of effective workers to get the amount of investment per effective worker needed to maintain a constant level of capital per effective worker gives:

$$(\delta + g_A + g_N)\frac{K}{AN}$$

The level of investment per effective worker needed to maintain a given level of capital per effective worker is represented by the upward-sloping line, "Required investment" in Figure 16–2. The slope of the line equals $\delta + g_A + g_N$.

Dynamics of Capital and Output

We can now give a graphical description of the dynamics of capital per effective worker and output per effective worker. Consider in Figure 16–2 a given level of capital per effective worker, say, $(K/AN)_0$. At that level, output per effective worker equals the distance AB. Investment per effective worker is equal to AC. The amount of investment required to maintain that level of capital per effective worker is equal to AD. Because actual investment exceeds the investment level required to maintain the existing level of capital per effective worker, K/AN increases.

Hence, starting from $(K/AN)_0$, the economy moves to the right, with the level of capital per effective worker increasing over time. This goes on until investment is just sufficient to

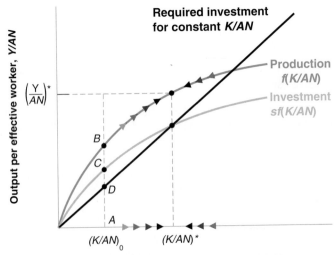

FIGURE 16–2

Dynamics of Capital and Output per Effective Worker

Capital and output per effective worker converge to constant values in the long run.

Capital per effective worker, *K/AN*

maintain the existing level of capital per effective worker, until capital per effective worker reaches $(K/AN)^*$. In the long run, capital per effective worker reaches a constant level, and so does output per effective worker. Put another way, the steady state of this economy is such that *capital per effective worker and output per effective worker are constant and equal to* $(K/AN)^*$ *and* $(Y/AN)^*$, *respectively*.

Note what this conclusion implies: *In steady state, in this economy, what is constant is not output but rather output per effective worker*. This implies that in steady state, output (Y) is growing at the same rate as effective labour (AN) (so that the ratio of the two is, indeed, constant). Because effective labour grows at rate $(g_A + g_N)$, output growth in steady state must also equal $(g_A + g_N)$. The same reasoning applies to capital. Because capital per effective worker is constant in steady state, capital is also growing at rate $(g_A + g_N)$.

These conclusions give us our first important result. *In steady state, the growth rate of output equals the rate of population growth (g_N) plus the rate of technological progress, (g_A). By implication, the growth rate of output is independent of the saving rate.*

The best way to strengthen your intuition for this result is to go back to the argument we used in Chapter 15 to show that without technological progress and population growth, the economy could not sustain positive growth forever. The argument went as follows: Suppose the economy tried to achieve positive output growth. Because of decreasing returns to capital, capital would have to grow faster than output. The economy would have to devote a larger and larger proportion of output to capital accumulation. At some point, there would be no more output to devote to capital accumulation. And growth would come to an end.

Exactly the same logic is at work here. Effective labour grows at rate $(g_A + g_N)$. Suppose the economy tried to achieve output growth in excess of $(g_A + g_N)$. Because of decreasing returns to capital, capital would have to increase faster than output. The economy would have to devote a larger and larger proportion of output to capital accumulation. At some point, this would prove impossible. Thus, the economy cannot permanently grow faster than $(g_A + g_N)$.

We have focused on the behaviour of aggregate output. To get a sense of what happens, not to aggregate output but rather to the standard of living over time, we must look instead at the behaviour of output per worker (not output per *effective worker*). Because output grows at rate $(g_A + g_N)$ and the number of workers grows at rate g_N, output per worker grows at rate g_A. In other words, *in steady state, output per worker grows at the rate of technological progress*.

Because output, capital, and effective labour all grow at the same rate $(g_A + g_N)$ in steady state, the steady state of this economy is also called a state of **balanced growth**: In steady state, output and the two inputs, capital and effective labour, grow in balance (at the same rate). The characteristics of balanced growth will be helpful later in the chapter and are summarized in Table 16–1.

If the number of effective workers is constant, then constant output per effective worker implies constant output. This was the case in Chapter 15, where we assumed there was neither population growth nor technological progress. But this is not the case here.

If Y/AN is constant, Y must grow at the same rate as AN. So, it must grow at rate $g_A + g_N$.

The standard of living is given by the level of output per worker (or, more accurately, the level of output per capita), not the level of output per effective worker.

The growth rate of Y/N is equal to the growth rate of Y minus the growth rate of N (see proposition 8 in Appendix 2 at the end of the book). So, the growth rate of Y/N is given by $(g_Y - g_N) = (g_A + g_N) - g_N = g_A$.

TABLE 16–1 The Characteristics of Balanced Growth

		Growth Rate
1.	Capital per effective worker	0
2.	Output per effective worker	0
3.	Capital per worker	g_A
4.	Output per worker	g_A
5.	Labour	g_N
6.	Capital	$g_A + g_N$
7.	Output	$g_A + g_N$

On the balanced growth path (equivalently, in steady state; equivalently, in the long run):

- Capital per effective worker and output per effective worker are constant; this is the result we derived in Figure 16–2.
- Equivalently, capital per worker and output per worker are growing at the rate of technological progress, g_A.
- Or, in terms of labour, capital, and output: Labour is growing at the rate of population growth, g_N; capital and output are growing at a rate equal to the sum of population growth and the rate of technological progress, $(g_A + g_N)$.

The Effects of the Saving Rate

Note an important implication of our results so far: In steady state, the growth rate of output depends *only* on the rate of population growth and the rate of technological progress. Changes in the saving rate do not affect the steady-state growth rate. This does not mean, however, that the saving rate is irrelevant: Changes in the saving rate do affect the steady-state level of output per effective worker.

This result is best seen in Figure 16–3, which shows the effect of an increase in the saving rate from s_0 to s_1. The increase in the saving rate shifts the investment relation from $s_0 f(K/AN)$ to $s_1 f(K/AN)$. It follows that the steady-state level of capital per effective worker increases from $(K/AN)_0$ to $(K/AN)_1$, with a corresponding increase in the level of output per effective worker from $(Y/AN)_0$ to $(Y/AN)_1$.

Figure 16–4 is the same as Figure 15–5, which anticipated the derivation presented here.

Following the increase in the saving rate, capital per effective worker and output per effective worker increase for some time as they converge to their new higher level. Figure 16–4 plots the evolution of output and capital against time. Both output and capital are measured on logarithmic scales. The economy is initially on the balanced growth path AA: Capital and output are growing at rate $(g_A + g_N)$—the slope of AA is equal to $(g_A + g_N)$. After the increase in the saving rate at time t, output and capital grow faster for some time. Eventually, capital and output end up at higher levels than they would have without the increase in saving. But their growth rate returns to $g_A + g_N$. In the new steady state, the economy grows at the same rate, but on a higher growth path, BB—BB, which is parallel to AA, also has a slope equal to $(g_A + g_N)$.

For a description of logarithmic scales, see the margin note in Chapter 14.

When a logarithmic scale is used, a variable growing at a constant rate moves along a straight line. The slope of the line is equal to the rate of growth of the variable.

To summarize: In an economy with technological progress and population growth, output grows over time. In steady state, output *per effective worker* and capital *per effective worker* are constant. Put another way, output *per worker* and capital *per worker* grow at the rate of technological progress. Put yet another way, output and capital grow at the same rate

FIGURE 16–3

The Effects of an Increase in the Saving Rate: Part I

An increase in the saving rate leads to an increase in the steady-state levels of output and capital per effective worker.

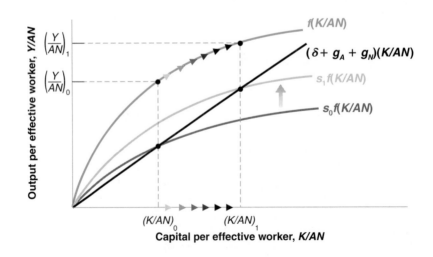

FIGURE 16-4

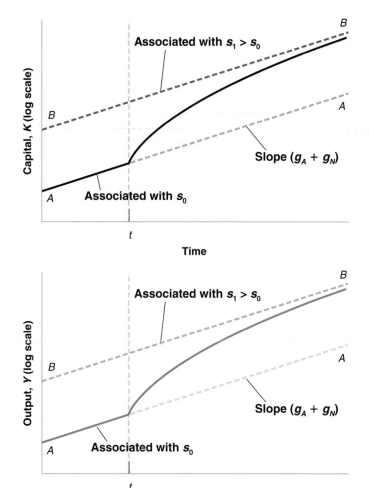

The Effects of an Increase in the Saving Rate: Part II

The increase in the saving rate leads to higher growth until the economy reaches its new, higher, balanced growth path.

as effective labour, and thus at a rate equal to the growth rate of the number of workers plus the rate of technological progress. When the economy is in steady state, it is said to be on a balanced growth path.

The rate of output growth in steady state is independent of the saving rate. The saving rate affects the steady-state level of output per effective worker, however. And increases in the saving rate lead, for some time, to an increase in the growth rate above the steady-state growth rate.

16-2 | The Determinants of Technological Progress

We have just seen that the growth rate of output per worker is ultimately determined by the rate of technological progress. But what, in turn, determines the rate of technological progress? This is the question we take up in this section.

Technological progress brings to mind images of major discoveries: the invention of the microchip, the discovery of the structure of DNA, and so on. These discoveries suggest a process driven largely by scientific research and chance rather than by economic forces. But the truth is that most technological progress in modern economies is the result of a humdrum process: the outcome of firms' **research and development (R&D)** activities. Industrial R&D expenditures account for between 2 and 3% of GDP in each of the five major rich countries we looked at in Chapter 14 (Canada, the United States, France, Japan, and the United

Kingdom). About 75% of the roughly one million U.S. scientists and researchers working in R&D are employed by firms. U.S. firms' R&D spending equals more than 20% of their spending on gross investment and more than 60% of their spending on net investment. In Canada, about 1.7% of GDP was used each year for research and development purposes. There is slightly more public sector activity than in the United States: 30% of research funding passes through institutions of higher education, and 12% is done directly by government, leaving 58% of R&D spending in the hands of industry. Canadian industry does the smallest share of R&D spending among Canada, France, Germany, Japan, the United Kingdom, and the United States. This is a matter of some concern for policy, since many consider the most creative and most interesting jobs are associated with the R&D process.

Firms spend on R&D for the same reason they buy new machines or build new plants: to increase profits. By increasing spending on R&D, a firm increases the probability that it will discover and develop a new product. (We will use "product" as a generic term to denote new goods or new techniques of production.) If the new product is successful, the firm's profits will increase. There is, however, an important difference between purchasing a machine and spending more on R&D. The difference is that the outcome of R&D is fundamentally ideas. And, unlike a machine, an idea potentially can be used by many firms at the same time. A firm that has just acquired a new machine does not have to worry that another firm will use that particular machine. A firm that has discovered and developed a new product can make no such assumption.

This last point implies that the level of R&D spending depends not only on the *fertility* of the research process, but also on the *appropriability* of research results. Let us look at each aspect in turn.

The Fertility of the Research Process

Fertility of research refers to how spending on R&D translates into new ideas and new products. If research is very fertile—if R&D spending leads to many new products—then, other things being equal, firms will have more incentives to do R&D; R&D and technological progress will be higher. The determinants of the fertility of research lie largely outside the realm of economics. Many factors interact here:

In Chapter 15, we looked at the role of human capital as an input in production: More educated people can use more complex machines or handle more complex tasks. Here, we see a second role of human capital: better researchers and scientists and, by implication, a higher rate of technological progress. ▷

- The fertility of research depends on the successful interaction between basic research (the search for general principles and results) and applied research and development (the application of these results to specific uses and the development of new products). Basic research does not lead, by itself, to technological progress. But the success of applied research and development depends ultimately on basic research. Much of the computer industry's development can be traced to a few breakthroughs, from the invention of the transistor to the invention of the microchip.

- Some countries appear more successful at basic research; others are more successful at applied research and development. Studies point to the relevance of the education system. For example, it is often argued that the French higher education system, with its strong emphasis on abstract thinking, produces researchers that are better at basic research than at applied research and development. Studies also point to the importance of a "culture of entrepreneurship," in which a big part of technological progress comes from the entrepreneurs' ability to organize the successful development and marketing of new products.

- It takes many years, and often many decades, for the full potential of major discoveries to be realized. The usual sequence is one in which a major discovery leads to the exploration of potential applications, then to the development of new products, then to the adoption of these new products. The Focus box "The Diffusion of New Technology: Hybrid Corn" shows the results of one of the first studies of this process of diffusion of ideas. Closer to us is the example of personal computers. Twenty years after the commercial introduction of the personal computer, it often feels as if we have just started discovering its potential.

An age-old worry is that most major discoveries have already been made and that technological progress will now slow down. This fear may come from thinking about mining, where

New technologies are not developed or adopted overnight. One of the first studies of the diffusion of new technologies was carried out in 1957 by Zvi Griliches, who looked at the diffusion of hybrid corn in different states in the United States.

Hybrid corn is, in the words of Griliches, "the invention of a method of inventing." Producing hybrid corn entails crossing different strains of corn to develop a type of corn adapted to local conditions. Introduction of hybrid corn can increase the corn yield by up to 20%.

Although the idea was first developed at the beginning of the twentieth century, the first commercial application of hybridization on a substantial scale did not take place until the 1930s in the United States. Figure 1 shows the rate at which hybrid corn was adopted in five U.S. states from 1932 to 1956.

Figure 1 shows two dynamic processes at work. One is the process through which appropriate hybrid corns were discov-ered for each state. Hybrid corn became available in the southern states (Texas, Alabama) many years after it had become available in the northern states (Iowa, Wisconsin, Kentucky). The other is the speed at which hybrid corn was adopted within each state. Within eight years of introduction, practically all corn in Iowa was hybrid corn. The process was much slower in the south. More than 10 years after its introduction, hybrid corn accounted for only 60% of total acreage in Alabama.

Why was the speed of adoption higher in Iowa than in the south? Griliches' article showed that the reason was an economic one: The speed of adoption in each state was a function of the profitability of introducing hybrid corn. And profitability was higher in Iowa than in the southern states.

Source: Zvi Griliches, "Hybrid Corn: An Exploration in the Economics of Technological Change," *Econometrica*, October 1957, Vol. 25, No 1.

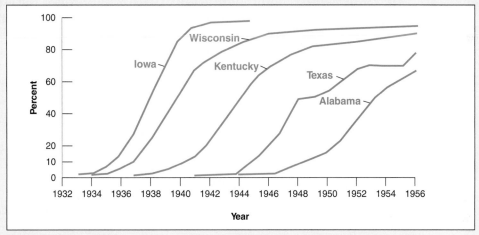

FIGURE 1   **Percentage of total corn acreage planted with hybrid seed, selected U.S. states, 1932–1956**

Source: See source note for this box.

high-grade mines were exploited first and where we have had to turn to lower-and-lower-grade mines as resources are depleted. But this is only an analogy, and so far there is no evidence that it applies.

The Appropriability of Research Results

The second determinant of the level of R&D and of technological progress is the degree of **appropriability** of research results, the extent to which firms benefit from the results of their own R&D. If firms cannot appropriate the profits from the development of new products, they will not engage in R&D and technological progress will be slow. Many factors are also at work here:

● One is the nature of the research process itself. For example, if it is widely believed that the discovery of a new product will quickly lead to the discovery of an even better product, there may be little payoff to being first. Thus, a highly fertile field of research may not generate high levels of R&D. This example is extreme but revealing.

- Probably most important is the degree of protection given to new products by the law. Without legal protection, profits from developing a new product are likely to be small. Except in rare cases where the product is based on a trade secret (such as Coca-Cola), it generally will not take long for other firms to produce the same product, eliminating any advantage the innovating firm may have had initially. This is why countries have patent laws. **Patents** give a firm that has discovered a new product—usually a new technique or device—the right to exclude anyone else from the production or use of the new product for some time.

How should governments design patent laws? On the one hand, protection is needed to provide firms with the incentives to spend on R&D. On the other, once firms have discovered new products, it would be best for society if the knowledge embodied in those new products were made available to other firms and to people without restrictions. Take biogenetic research, for example. The prospect of large profits is what leads bioengineering firms to embark on expensive research projects. Once a firm has created a new product that can save many lives, it clearly would be best to make it available to all potential users at a price equal to the cost of production. But if such a policy was systematically followed, it would eliminate incentives for firms to do research in the first place. Patent law must strike a difficult balance: Too little protection will lead to little R&D. Too much protection will make it difficult for new R&D to build on the results of past R&D and may also lead to little R&D.

> This type of dilemma is known as "time inconsistency." We will see other examples and discuss the issue at length in Chapter 25.

Countries that are less technologically advanced often have poorer patent protection. For example, China is a country with poor enforcement of patent rights. Our discussion helps explain why. Poorer countries are typically users rather than producers of new technologies. Much of their improvement in productivity comes not from inventions within the country but from the adaptation of foreign technologies. In this case, the costs of weak patent protection are small because there would be few domestic inventions anyway. But the benefits of low patent protection are clear: They allow domestic firms to use and adapt foreign technology without having to pay royalties to the foreign firms that developed the technology.

16-3 | The Facts of Growth Revisited

In Chapter 14, we looked at growth in five rich countries since 1950, and we identified three main facts:

- Sustained growth, especially from 1950 to the mid-1970s
- A slowdown in growth since the mid-1970s
- Convergence: Countries that were further behind now growing faster

Let us now use the theory we have developed to see what light it sheds on these facts.

Capital Accumulation versus Technological Progress

Suppose we see an economy growing unusually fast—either in relation to its own growth in the past or in relation to growth in other countries. Our theory suggests that this fast growth may be due to one of two causes:

- It may be due to a higher rate of technological progress so that faster output growth reflects faster balanced growth. In other words, if g_A is higher, balanced output growth ($g_A + g_N$) will also be higher.
- Or it may reflect the adjustment to a higher level of capital per effective worker, K/AN. As we saw in Figure 16–4, such an adjustment leads to a period of higher growth, even if the rate of technological progress has not increased.

How can we tell which is the cause? If high growth reflects high balanced growth, output per worker should be growing at a rate *equal* to the rate of technological progress (see Table 16–1, line 4). If, instead, high growth reflects the adjustment to a higher level of capital per effective worker, this adjustment should be reflected in a growth rate of output per worker that exceeds the rate of technological progress.

This discussion suggests a simple strategy, that of computing the growth rate of output per worker and the rate of technological progress for our five countries since 1950 and then comparing the two numbers. Angus Maddison implemented this strategy; his results are summarized in Table 16–2. (What Maddison has computed, and thus what is reported in Table 16–2, is the growth rate of output *per capita* rather than the growth rate of output *per worker*. If the ratio of employment to population had remained constant, the growth rates of output per capita and of output per worker would be identical. They are not, but they are close, so we can ignore the difference here.)

Columns 1 and 2 correspond to the first two columns of Table 14–1. (There are minor differences between the two tables due to differences in sources and in time periods.) They give the average annual growth rates of output per capita during 1950–1973 and 1973–2000, respectively. The Canadian data start in 1962. Column 3 gives the change in the growth rate from the first to the second period.

Columns 4 and 5 give the average annual rates of technological progress during 1950 to 1973 and 1973 to 2000, respectively. Column 6 gives the change in the rate of technological progress from the first period to the second. (The method of construction of the rate of technological progress—which is not directly observable—is presented in the appendix at the end of this chapter.)

Let us now return to our three main facts. The table suggests the following conclusions:

1. *The period of high growth of output per capita, from 1950 to 1973, was due to rapid technological progress, not to unusually high capital accumulation.*

   Look at columns 1 and 4 of the table. In all five countries, the growth rate of output per capita from 1950 to 1973 was roughly equal to the rate of technological progress. This is what we would expect when countries are growing along their balanced growth path; the main source of high growth from 1950 to 1973 was a high rate of technological progress.

   This is an important conclusion because it rejects one hypothesis for the reason growth was so high from 1950 to 1973. The hypothesis is that fast growth was the result of the destruction of capital during World War II, leading to rapid rates of capital

In the United States, for example, the ratio of employment to population increased from 55% in 1950 to 62.5% in 1994. This represents an increase of 0.17% per year. Thus, in the United States, output per capita increased by 0.17% more per year than output per worker—a small difference, relative to the numbers in the table.

| TABLE | 16–2 | Average Annual Rates of Growth of Output per Worker and Technological Progress in Five Rich Countries, 1950–2000 |

	Growth of Output per Worker(%)			Rate of Technological Progress(%)		
	1950–1973 (1)	1973–2000 (2)	Change (3)	1950–1973 (4)	1973–2000 (5)	Change (6)
France	4.8	2.1	−2.7	5.3	1.6	−3.7
Japan	7.1	2.1	− 5.0	7.0	1.4	− 5.6
United Kindom	3.4	1.7	− 1.7	3.7	1.9	− 1.8
United States	2.7	1.2	− 1.5	2.9	1.4	− 1.5
Canada	2.7	1.0	− 1.7	2.5	0.7	− 1.8
Average	4.1	1.6	− 2.5	4.3	1.4	− 2.9

Source: 1950–1960: Angus Maddison, *Dynamic Forces in Capitalist Development,* New York: Oxford University Press, 1991. 1960–2000: OECD Economic Outlook Database. "Average" is a simple average of the growth rates in each column.

Canadian values refer to periods 1962–1973 and 1974–2000. *Output*—nonagricultural business sector using CANSIM II variable V716153; *number of jobs*—nonagricultural business sector using CANSIM II variable V716375; *multifactor productivity growth* from Table 2, Productivity Growth in Canada, Statistics Canada 15-204-XPE.

growth after the war. As we saw in the Global Macro box in Chapter 15, this does explain some of the high growth in the immediate postwar period in France and probably in other countries as well. But it is not the reason for the sustained growth of the 1950s and 1960s in the five countries we are looking at.

2. *The slowdown in growth of output per capita since 1973 has come from a decrease in the rate of technological progress, not from unusually low capital accumulation.*

    This conclusion comes from looking at columns 3 and 6 of Table 16–2. If lower capital accumulation were to blame for the growth slowdown, we would see a larger decline in the growth rate of output per capita than in the rate of technological progress. But this is not what the table shows. In all five countries, the decrease in technological progress has been roughly equal to the decrease in the growth rate of output per capita.

    Thus, contrary to some popular beliefs, the slowdown in growth since the mid-1970s is not due to a sharp drop in the saving rate, to the "disappearance of thrift." It is due to the decrease in the rate of technological progress, which declined from an average of 4.3% per year during 1950–1973 to only 1.4% per year 1973–2000. This is potentially bad news for the future. In contrast to a decline in the saving rate—which, as we have seen, leads only to a temporary decline in growth—lower technological progress implies a permanently lower rate of growth.

3. *Convergence of output per capita across countries has come from higher technological progress, rather than from faster capital accumulation, in the countries that started behind.*

    Look at column 4 of Table 16–2. During 1950–1973, the annual rate of technological progress in Japan was 3.3% higher than that in the United States. The French rate was 2.4% higher. During 1973–2000, the differences narrowed to 0% between Japan and the United States.

These facts yield an important conclusion: One can think, in general, of two sources of convergence between countries. The first is that the poorer countries are poorer because they have less capital to start with. Over time, they accumulate capital faster than the others, generating convergence. The second is that the poorer countries are poorer because they are less technologically advanced than the others. But, over time, they become more sophisticated, either by importing technology from advanced countries or developing their own. As technological levels converge, so does output per capita. The conclusion we can draw from Table 16–2 is that the more important source in this case has clearly been the second one. For example, Japan's output per worker has increased relative to that of the United States not so much because Japan has accumulated capital extremely quickly but rather because the state of technology has improved very quickly in Japan over the last 40 years.

Fluctuations in the Pace of Technological Progress

The conclusions we reached in the preceding section raise an obvious question: Why did technological progress slow in the mid-1970s?

The truth is that despite a large amount of research, this slowdown remains largely a mystery. The decrease in technological progress has been widespread, affecting most sectors. This suggests the need to look for a general rather than for a sector-specific explanation. A natural hypothesis would be that there was a general decline in R&D, which led to lower technological progress across the board. But it turns out that the facts do not support this hypothesis. In the five countries we have been looking at, spending on R&D as a share of GDP has remained constant or increased since the early 1960s.

This leaves, by default, another hypothesis. The decline in the rate of technological progress in the mid-1970s was not in the amount but in the fertility of R&D. This is, indeed, the explanation preferred by a number of economists. They argue that, once in a while, some inventions have wide applicability across many sectors of the economy. Going back in time, think of the discovery of the steam engine, of electricity, and of the transistor, as examples of such inventions. As these inventions are adopted and implemented, economies experience fast

Average annual productivity growth in the United States from 1996 to 2002 was 2.1%—a high number relative to the anemic 1.1% average achieved from 1973 to 1995.

Is it a sign, as proponents of the "New Economy" argue, that the U.S. economy has entered an era of high productivity growth? Research, to date, gives reasons both for optimism and for caution.

It suggests that a sharp distinction must be drawn between what is happening in the information technology (IT) sector—the sector that produces computers, computer software, software services, and communications equipment—and the rest of the economy that uses this information technology:

- In the IT sector, technological progress has, indeed, been proceeding at an extraordinary pace.

  In 1965, researcher Gordon Moore, who later founded Intel Corporation, predicted that the number of transistors in a chip would double every 24 months, allowing for steadily more powerful computers. As shown in Figure 1, the relation showing a doubling every 18–24 months—now known as **Moore's law**—has held extremely well over time. The first logic chip produced in 1971 had 2300 transistors; the Pentium IV, released in 2000, had 42 million.

  Although at a less extreme pace, technological progress in the rest of the IT sector has also been very high. And the share of the IT sector in GDP is steadily increasing, from 3% of GDP in 1980 to 7% today. This combination of high technological progress in the IT sector and of an increasing IT share has led to a steady increase in the economywide rate of technological progress. This is one of the factors behind the high productivity growth in the United States since the mid-1990s.

  In the non-IT sector—the "old economy," which still accounts for more than 90% of the U.S. economy—however, there is little evidence of a parallel technological revolution.

- On the one hand, the steady decrease in the price of IT equipment (reflecting technological progress in the IT sector) has led firms in the non-IT sector to increase their stock of IT capital. This has led to an increase in the ratio of capital per worker and an increase in productivity growth in the non-IT sector.

  Let us go through this argument a bit more formally. Go back to equation (16.2), which shows the relation of output per effective worker to the ratio of capital per effective worker:

  $$Y/AN = f(K/AN)$$

  Think of this equation as giving us the relation between output per effective worker and capital per effective worker in the non-IT sector. The evidence is that the decrease in the price of IT capital has led firms to increase their stock of IT capital and, by implication, their overall capital stock. In other words, K/AN has increased in the non-IT sector, leading to an increase in Y/AN.

- On the other hand, the IT revolution does not appear to have had a major direct effect on the pace of technological progress in the non-IT sector. You have surely heard claims that the information technology revolution was forcing firms to drastically reorganize, leading to large gains in productivity. Firms may be reorganizing, but so far, there is no evidence that this is leading to large gains in productivity. Measures of technological progress show only a small rise in the rate of technological progress in the non-IT sector from the post-1973 average.

In terms of the production function relation we just discussed, there is no evidence that the technological revolution has led to a higher rate of growth of A in the non-IT sector.

Are there reasons to expect productivity growth to be higher in the future than in the last 25 years? The answer is yes. The factors we have just discussed are here to stay. Technological progress in the IT sector is likely to remain high, and the share of IT is likely to continue to increase. Moreover, firms in the non-IT sector are likely to further increase their stock of IT capital, leading to further increases in productivity.

How high can we expect productivity growth to be in the future? Probably not as high as it was during 1996–2002. Much of that was the result of a strong expansion in the second half of the 1990s. But, according to some estimates, it may go perhaps 0.5 percentage points higher than its post-1973 average. This may not be the miracle some have claimed, but if sustained, it is an increase that will make a substantial difference to the U.S. standard of living in the future.

For more on these issues, read "Information Technology and the U.S. Economy," by Dale Jorgenson, *American Economic Review*, March 2001, pp. 1–32.

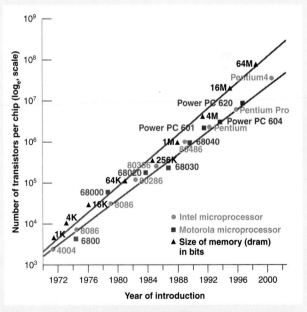

FIGURE 1   Moore's law. Number of transistors per chip, 1970–2000

Source: *Dale Jorgenson*,
http://post.economics.harvard.edu/faculty/jorgenson/papers/aea5.ppt.

technological progress. Eventually, however, the process of adoption and implementation comes to an end, and technological progress slows until the next major invention, and so on. This hypothesis is particularly interesting in the light of the recent increase in the rate of productivity growth in the United States that we saw in Chapter 1. It raises the possibility that we have just entered another wave of faster technological progress, driven by the development of information technologies. The evidence, to date, is reviewed in the Focus box "The New Economy and Productivity Growth" on page 317. The basic conclusion at this point: The claims made by the proponents of a "New Economy" are too strong; but there is, indeed, some basis for optimism.

16-4 | Institutions and Growth

We have focused on the role of capital accumulation and of technological progress in explaining productivity growth in a given country or in explaining differences in productivity levels across countries. But capital accumulation and technological progress depend on more fundamental factors, on what economists refer to as "institutions."

To get a sense of the issues, let us go beyond the set of rich countries we have focused on, and compare Kenya and the United States. In 2000, PPP GDP per capita in Kenya was about one-twentieth of PPP GDP per capita in the United States. Part of the difference was due to a much lower level of capital per worker in Kenya. The other part of the difference was due to a much lower technological level in Kenya. It is estimated that A, the state of technology in Kenya, is about one-tenth of the U.S. level. Why is the state of technology in Kenya so low? After all, Kenya, like most poor countries, has access to most of the technological knowledge in the world. What prevents it from simply adopting much of the advanced countries' technologies, and quickly closing much of its technological gap with the United States?

One can think of a number of potential answers, ranging from Kenya's geography and climate to its culture. Most economists believe, however, that the main source of the problem, for poor countries in general and for Kenya in particular, lies in their poor institutions.

What institutions do economists have in mind? At a broad level, the protection of propert rights may well be the most important. Few individuals are going to create firms, introduce new technologies, and invest, if they expect that profits will be either appropriated by the state, extracted in bribes by corrupt bureaucrats, or stolen by other people in the economy. Figure 16–5 plots PPP GDP per capita in 1995 (using a logarithmic scale) for 90 countries, against an index measuring the degree of protection from expropriation, constructed for each of these countries by an international business organization. The positive correlation between the two is striking (the figure also plots the regression line). Low protection is associated with a low GDP per capita (at the extreme left of the figure are Zaire and Haiti); high protection is associated with a high GDP per capita (at the extreme right are the United States, Luxembourg, Norway, Switzerland, and the Netherlands).

What does "protection of property rights" mean in practice? It means a good political system, in which those in charge cannot expropriate or seize the property of the citizens. It means a good judicial system, where disagreements can be resolved efficiently and rapidly. Looking at an even finer degree of detail, it means laws against insider trading in the stock market so that people are willing to buy stocks and thus provide financing to firms; it means clearly written and well-enforced patent laws so that firms have incentive to do research and develop new products. It means good antitrust laws so that competive markets do not turn into monopolies with few incentives to introduce new methods of production and new products. And the list goes on. (A particularly clear example of the role of institutions is given in the Focus box "The Importance of Institutions: North and South Korea.")

This still leaves one essential question: Why don't poor countries adopt these good institutions? The answer is that it is hard! Good institutions are complex and difficult for poor countries to put in place. Surely, causality runs both ways in Figure 16-5. Low protection

The importance of property rights for growth was also painfully obvious during the transition of Eastern European countries from central planning to a market economy in the early 1990s. In many of these countries, poorly defined property rights, poorly enforced laws, and corrupt public officials severely constrained the growth of new firms and led to a decline in output. ▶

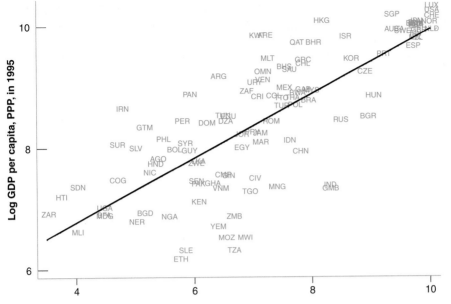

Protection from Expropriation and GDP per Capita

There is a strong positive relation between the degree of protection from expropriation and the level of GDP per capita.

Source: Daron Acemoglu, "Understanding Institutions," Lionel Robbins Lectures, 2004.

against expropriation leads to low GDP per capita. But it is also the case that low GDP per capita leads to worse protection against expropriation. Poor countries are often too poor to afford a good judicial system or to maintain a good police force, for example. Thus, improving institutions, and starting a virtuous cycle of higher GDP per capita and better institutions, is often very difficult. The fast-growing countries of Asia have succeeded in doing this. So far, much of Africa has been unable, however, to start such a virtuous cycle.

◀ This is where we move from the realm of growth theory to the—fascinating—realm of development economics.

FOCUS   The Importance of Institutions: North and South Korea

Following the surrender of Japan in 1945, Korea formally acquired its independence but became divided at the 38th parallel into two zones of occupation, with the Soviet armed forces occupying the North, and the U.S. armed forces occupying the South. Attempts by both sides to claim jurisdiction over all of Korea triggered the Korean War, which lasted from 1950 to 1953. At the armistice in 1953, Korea became formally divided into two countries, the "Democratic People's Republic of North Korea" and the "Republic of Korea" in the south.

An interesting feature of Korea before separation was its ethnic and linguistic homogeneity. The North and the South were inhabited by essentially the same people, with the same culture and the same religion. Economically, the two regions were also highly similar at the time of separation. PPP GDP per capita, in 1996 dollars, was roughly the same, about $700 in both the North and the South.

Yet, 50 years later, as shown in Figure 1, GDP per capita was 10 times higher in South Korea than in North Korea— $12,000 versus $ 1100! On the one hand, South Korea had

joined the OECD, the club of rich countries. On the other, North Korea had seen its GDP per capita decrease by nearly two-thirds from its peak of $3000 in the mid-1970s and was facing famine on a large scale.

What happened? Institutions and the organization of the economy were dramatically different during that period in the South and in the North. South Korea relied on a capitalist organization of the economy, with strong state intervention, but also private ownership and legal protection of private producers. North Korea relied on central planning. Industries were quickly nationalized. Small firms and farms were forced to join large cooperatives so that they could be supervised by the state. There were no private property rights for individuals. The result was the decline of the industrial sector and the collapse of agriculture. The lesson is sad but transparent: Institutions matter very much for growth.

Source: Daron Acemoglu, "Understanding Institutions," Lionel Robbins Lectures, 2004.

(continued)

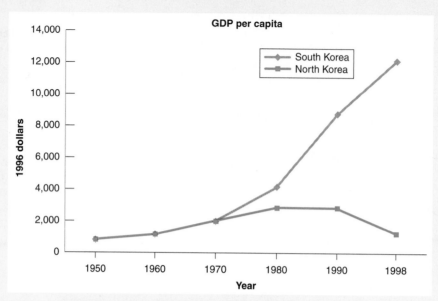

Figure 1   PPP GDP per capita, North and South Korea, 1950–1998

16-5 │ Epilogue: The Secrets of Growth

Why the rate of technological progress has declined since the mid-1970s is not the only unanswered question in the economics of growth. Many other questions remain.

We understand the basic mechanisms of growth in rich countries. But we are not very good at answering more specific questions: for example, what specific measures could be taken to increase growth? Are governments spending the right amount on basic research? Should patent laws be modified? Is there a case for an **industrial policy**, a policy aimed at helping specific sectors of the economy (for example, those sectors with the potential for high technological progress, and thus the potential for large spillovers for the rest of the economy)? What can we expect in terms of additional growth from increasing the average number of years of education by another year?

Turning from growth in rich countries since 1950 to growth over a longer time span or across a broader set of countries, our knowledge is even more limited. For example, consider the fact that many countries in the world have a level of output per worker that is less than one-tenth the North American level of output per worker. The framework developed in this chapter and the previous one gives us a way of approaching this fact. If we think of output per worker as depending on physical capital per worker, human capital per worker, and the state of technology, we can ask: Are these countries poorer because they have less physical and human capital or because the state of their technology is lower?

See Robert Hall and Charles Jones, "Why Do Some Countries Produce So Much More Output per Worker Than Others?" NBER working paper 6564, May 1998.

The answer turns out that much of the difference comes from differences in the measured level of technology across countries. Compare, for example, the United States and China. GDP per worker (Y/N) is 16 times higher in the United States than in China. If this ratio reflected only differences in the level of physical capital and human capital per worker between the two countries, then we would find that adjusting for differences in physical and human capital, the two economies had the same value of A: The level of technology would be the same in both countries. Existing estimates imply that A is, in fact, 10 times higher in the United States than in China. In short, even if China suddenly acquired the same levels of physical capital and education per worker as the United States, output per worker would still be only a small fraction of what it is in the United States.

This answer is a useful first step, but it raises another question. Poor countries have access to most of the technological knowledge in the world. What prevents these countries from simply adapting much of the advanced countries' technologies, quickly closing a good part of their **technology gap**? It is clear that the answer to that question requires us to take a broader interpretation of technology than we have so far in this chapter and to look at many of the factors we left aside in thinking about the determinants of the production function in Chapter 14. These include poorly established property rights, political instability, the lack of entrepreneurs, and poorly developed financial markets. The importance of these factors has been particularly obvious in the transition from central planning to a market economy in the countries of Eastern Europe during the 1990s. In many of these countries, poorly defined property rights, poorly enforced laws, and corruption of public officials have severely constrained the growth of new firms. The list is easy to make. But the specific role of each of these factors is hard to pinpoint. And solving these problems is not easy: Many of them are as much the result of low income as they are the cause of low income.

For more on transition, see Chapter 24.

Looking at the poor countries that have grown rapidly in the last 20 years (such as the "four tigers": Hong Kong, Taiwan, Singapore, and South Korea) or at the even more recent fast growers (such as China, Indonesia, Malaysia, and Thailand) would seem the best way of uncovering the secrets of growth. But here again, the lessons are not proving simple. In all these countries, growth has come with the rapid accumulation of both physical and human capital. And in all these countries, growth has also come with an increase in the importance of foreign trade: an increase in exports and imports. But beyond these two factors, clear differences emerge. Some countries, such as Hong Kong, have relied mostly on free markets and limited government intervention. Others, such as Korea and Singapore, have relied instead on government intervention and an industrial policy aimed at fostering the growth of specific industries. (The cases of Hong Kong and Singapore are discussed in detail in the In Depth box "Hong Kong and Singapore: A Tale of Two Cities.") The bottom line is clear: We have not yet fully unravelled the secrets of growth.

For example, political instability and ethnic conflicts are at the source of output stagnation in several African countries. And, in turn, output stagnation contributes to political instability and exacerbates ethnic conflicts.

IN DEPTH   Hong Kong and Singapore: A Tale of Two Cities

Between 1960 and 1985, the average growth rate of output in both Hong Kong and Singapore was 6.1% per year.* How did both Hong Kong and Singapore grow so fast? On close inspection, one is struck both by the similarities and by the differences in their economic evolutions.

The Similarities

Hong Kong and Singapore have much in common. Both are former British colonies. Both are essentially cities that served initially as trading ports with little manufacturing activity. The postwar populations of both countries were composed primarily of immigrant Chinese from southern China. During the course of their rapid growth, they have gone through a similar sequence of industries, with Singapore starting later than Hong Kong by 10 to 15 years. The respective sequences are summarized in Table 1.

The Differences

A closer look, however, shows major differences in the way the two countries have grown.

Hong Kong has grown under a policy of minimal government intervention. For the most part, government has limited its

TABLE 1	The Sequence of Activities in Hong Kong and Singapore Since the Early 1950s
Hong Kong	
Early 1950s	Textiles
Early 1960s	Clothing, Plastics
Early 1970s	Electronics
1980s	Trade, Banking
Singapore	
Early 1960s	Textiles
Late 1960s	Electronics, Petroleum refining
Early 1970s	Electronics, Petroleum refining, Textiles, Clothing
1980s	Banking, Electronics

Source: See source note for this box.

*These numbers are computed using PPP measures of GDP, from Heston and Summers (see the Focus box on PPP measures in Chapter 14).

(continued)

intervention to providing infrastructure and selling land as it became required for further growth. In contrast, growth in Singapore has been dominated by government intervention. Through budget surpluses, as well as forced saving through pension contributions, government has achieved a very high national saving rate. Singapore's share of gross investment in GDP increased from 9% in 1960 to 43% in 1984, one of the highest investment rates in the world. The development of specific industries has been the result of systematic government targeting, implemented through large tax incentives for mostly foreign investors.

These differences in strategies are reflected in the relative roles of capital accumulation and technological progress. In Hong Kong, the annual growth rate of output per worker from 1970 to 1990 was 2.4%; the growth rate of technological progress over the same period was 2.3%. Using the interpretation provided by the model we developed in this chapter, growth in Hong Kong has been roughly balanced. In Singapore, the growth rate of output per worker from 1971 to 1990 was 1.5%. In the article on which this box is based, Alwyn Young, an economist at the University of Chicago, concludes that the rate of technological progress during that period was a surprisingly low 0.1%. If his computation is right (and, after an intense controversy triggered by his article, it appears to be

largely so), this implies that Singapore has grown nearly entirely through unusually high capital accumulation, not through technological progress. Singapore's growth has been very much unbalanced.

Why has Singapore achieved so little technological progress? Alwyn Young argues that, in effect, Singapore has gone too fast from one industry to the next. By going so fast, it has not had time to learn how to produce any of them very efficiently. And by relying largely on foreign investment, it has not allowed a class of domestic entrepreneurs to learn and replace foreign investment in the future.

If Alwyn Young is right, what lies in store for Singapore? The model we have developed in this chapter suggests that a slowdown in growth is inevitable. High saving and investment rates can lead to high growth only for a while. The numbers appear brighter for Hong Kong, which seems to be growing on a balanced growth path. But major changes are in store for Hong Kong as well: In 1997, Hong Kong again became part of China; whether this will help or hinder its growth remains to be seen.

Source: Alwyn Young, "A Tale of Two Cities: Factor Accumulation and Technical Change in Hong Kong and Singapore," *NBER Macroeconomics Annual*, 1992, pp. 13–63.

SUMMARY

- When looking at the implications of technological progress for growth, it is useful to think of technological progress as increasing the amount of effective labour available in the economy (that is, labour multiplied by the state of technology). We can then think of output as being produced with capital and effective labour.

- In steady state, output *per effective worker* and capital *per effective worker* are constant. Put another way, output *per worker* and capital *per worker* grow at the rate of technological progress. Put yet another way, output and capital grow at the same rate as effective labour, thus at a rate equal to the growth rate of the number of workers plus the rate of technological progress. When the economy is in steady state, it is said to be on a balanced growth path.

- The rate of output growth in steady state is independent of the saving rate. However, the saving rate affects the steady-state level of output per effective worker. And increases in the saving rate lead, for some time, to an increase in the growth rate above the steady-state growth rate.

- Technological progress depends on both (1) the fertility of research and development, and (2) the appropriability of the results of R&D (that is, the extent to which firms benefit from the results of their R&D).

- In designing patent laws, governments must trade off protection for future discoveries with a desire to make existing discoveries available to potential users without restrictions.

- Canada, France, Japan, the United Kingdom, and the United States have had roughly balanced growth since 1950. The slowdown in growth since the mid-1970s is the result of a decrease in the rate of technological progress. Convergence of output appears to have come primarily from a convergence in technology levels.

- There is no good explanation for the decline in the rate of technological progress since the mid-1970s. More generally, our understanding of the determinants of technological progress and its relation to such factors as the legal system or the political system remains limited.

- appropriability, 313
- balanced growth, 309
- effective labour, or labour in efficiency units, 306
- fertility of research, 312
- industrial policy, 320
- Moore's law, 317

- patents, 314
- rate of growth of multifactor productivity, 325
- research and development (R&D), 311
- Solow residual, 325
- technology gap, 321

An asterisk denotes a harder question. [Web] indicates that the question requires access to the Internet.

1. TRUE/FALSE/UNCERTAIN

a. Writing the production function in terms of capital and effective labour implies that as the level of technology increases by a certain percentage, the number of workers required to achieve the same level of output decreases by the same percentage.

b. Because our production function exhibits constant returns to capital and effective labour, output per effective worker also exhibits constant returns to capital per effective worker.

c. If the rate of technological progress increases, investment must increase to keep capital per effective worker constant must increase.

d. In steady state, output per effective worker grows at the rate of population growth.

e. In steady state, output per worker grows at the rate of technological progress.

f. A higher saving rate implies a higher level of capital per effective worker in the steady state, and thus a higher rate of growth of output per effective worker in steady state.

g. Even if the potential returns from R&D spending are identical to the potential returns from investing in a new machine, R&D spending is much riskier for firms than investing in new machines.

h. The fact that one cannot patent a theorem implies that private firms will not engage in basic research.

2. R&D SPENDING

Why is the amount of R&D spending important for growth? How do the appropriability and fertility of research affect the amount of R&D spending?

For each of the following policy proposals, determine how the appropriability and fertility of research are affected and what you expect the long-run effect to be on R&D and on output:

a. An international treaty that ensures that each country's patents are legally protected all over the world.

b. Tax credits for each dollar of R&D spending.

c. A decrease in funding of government-sponsored conferences between universities and corporations.

d. The elimination of patents on breakthrough drugs so that the drugs can be sold at low cost as soon as they are available.

3. PATENTS AND GROWTH

Where does technological progress come from for the economic leaders of the world? Where does it come from in the developing countries? Do you see any reasons why the developing countries may choose to have poor patent protection? Are there any dangers in such a policy (for the developing countries)?

4. DIFFUSION OF INVENTIONS

Use the medical and automobile industries to provide examples of technological advances that have not yet fully diffused in the economy. Can you think of some advances in those industries whose diffusion is relatively more important than that of others for society? Name a policy that would accelerate the diffusion process. Would such a policy also have disadvantages for society? Explain.

5. THE SLOWDOWN IN PRODUCTIVITY GROWTH

Consider the following two scenarios:
i. The rate of technological progress declines forever.
ii. The saving rate declines forever.

a. What is the impact of each of these scenarios on economic growth over the next five years?

b. Over the next five decades?

In both cases, make sure to consider the effects on both the growth rate and the level of output.

6. STEADY STATE OUTPUT AND TECHNOLOGICAL PROGRESS

Suppose that the economy's production function is:

$$Y = \sqrt{K} \sqrt{NA}$$

and that the saving rate (s) is equal to 16% and the rate of depreciation (δ) is equal to 10%. Further, suppose that the number of workers grows at 2% per year and the rate of technological progress is 4% per year.

a. Find the steady state values of:
   The capital stock per effective worker.
   Output per effective worker.
   The growth rate of output per effective worker.
   The growth rate of output per worker.
   The growth rate of output.

b. Suppose that the rate of technological progress doubles to 8% per year. Recompute the answers to (a). Explain.

c. Now, suppose that the rate of technological progress is still equal to 4% per year but the number of workers now grows at 6% per year. Recompute the answers to (a). Are people better off in (a) or in (c)? Explain.

*7. GROWTH ACCOUNTING [WEB]

In the appendix to this chapter, it is shown how data on output, capital, and labour can be used to construct estimates of the rate of growth of technological progress. Consider the following production function, which gives a good description of production in rich countries:

$$Y = K^{1/3}(NA)^{2/3}$$

Following the same steps as in the appendix, you can show that:

$$\text{Residual} = [g_Y - \tfrac{1}{3}g_K - \tfrac{2}{3}g_N]$$

or reorganizing:

$$\text{Residual} = [(g_Y - g_N) - \tfrac{1}{3}(g_K - g_N)]$$

The rate of technological progress is then obtained by dividing the residual by the share of labour, which, given the production function we have assumed, is equal to two-thirds:

$$g_A = \text{Residual}/(2/3) = (3/2)\,\text{Residual}$$

Using the instructions provided in Chapter 14, problem 6, download the series "Real GDP per worker" and "Non-residential capital stock per worker" for both Japan and the United States for the period 1965–2000 from the Penn World Tables. (Unfortunately, the series on K/N is not available for years prior to 1965.)

Input the series into your favourite spreadsheet program.

a. Compute the growth rate of Y/N, $(g_Y - g_N)$, and K/N, $(g_K - g_N)$, for each year and for each country.

b. For each country, calculate the average growth rate of Y/N and K/N for the sub-periods 1965–1973 and 1974–2000.

c. Using the equations above, compute the rate of technological progress for both sub-periods for both countries.

d. Do you find evidence of a slowdown? For which period?

e. The U.S. was the technological leader in both periods. So, why is it that Japan's growth rate of technological progress is so much higher than that of the U.S. in both periods? Why does the difference become smaller in the later sub-period?

f. Does the difference in g_A explain all the difference in $(g_Y - g_N)$? If not, where does the rest come from?

FURTHER READING

For an issue we have not explored in the text, growth and the environment, read *Development and the Environment, World Development Report* (New York: World Bank; Oxford University Press, 1992).

For more on growth, both theory and evidence, read Charles Jones, *Introduction to Economic Growth* (New York: Norton, 2nd ed., 2002). Jones' Web page (**http://emlab.berkeley.edu/users/chad/**) is a useful portal to the research on growth.

For more on institutions and growth, read Daron Acemoglu, *Understanding Institutions*, 2004 (**http://cep.lse.ac.uk/events/lionel_robbins.asp**). Read also "The Tiger in Front," a survey of growth in India and China in *The Economist*, March 3, 2005.

For more on what the future may hold, read "The Next Society. A Survey of the Near Future," *The Economist*, November 3, 2001.

CONSTRUCTING A MEASURE OF TECHNOLOGICAL PROGRESS

In 1957, Robert Solow suggested a way of constructing an estimate of the rate of technological progress. The method, still used today, relies on one important assumption: Each factor of production is paid its marginal product.

Under this assumption, it is easy to compute the contribution of an increase in any factor of production to the increase in output. For example, if a worker is paid $30,000 a year, the assumption implies that her contribution to output is equal to $30,000. Now, suppose that this worker increases the amount of hours she works by 10%. The increase in output coming from the increase in her hours will therefore be equal to $30,000 × 10%, or $3000.

Let us write this more formally. Denote output by Y, labour by N, and the real wage by W/P. Then, as we just established, the change in output is equal to the real wage multiplied by the change in labour:

$$\Delta Y = \frac{W}{P} \Delta N$$

Divide both sides of the equation by Y, divide and multiply the right side by N, and reorganize:

$$\frac{\Delta Y}{Y} = \frac{WN}{PY} \frac{\Delta N}{N}$$

Note that the first term on the right (WN/PY) is equal to the share of labour in output—the total wage bill in dollars divided by the value of output in dollars. Denote this share by α. Note that $\Delta Y/Y$ is the rate of growth of output, and denote it by g_Y. Note similarly that $\Delta N/N$ is the rate of change of the labour input, and denote it by g_N. Then, the previous relation can be written as:

$$g_Y = \alpha g_N$$

More generally, this reasoning implies that the part of output growth attributable to growth of the labour input is equal to α times g_N.

Similarly, we can compute the part of output growth attributable to growth of the capital stock. As there are only two factors of production, labour and capital, and as the share of labour is equal to α, the share of capital in income must be equal to $(1 - \alpha)$. If the growth rate of capital is equal to g_K, then the increase in output attributable to growth of capital is equal to $(1 - \alpha)$ times g_K.

Putting the contributions of labour and capital together, the growth in output attributable to growth in both labour and capital is equal to $(\alpha g_N + (1 - \alpha)g_K)$.

We can then measure the effects of technological progress by computing what Solow called the residual, the excess of actual growth of output over the growth attributable to growth in labour and capital $(\alpha g_N + (1 - \alpha)g_K)$.

$$\text{residual} \equiv g_Y - [\alpha g_N + (1 - \alpha)g_K]$$

actual growth attributable to
growth growth of labour and capital

This measure is called the **Solow residual**. It is easy to compute: All we need to know to compute it are the growth rates of output, labour, and capital, as well as the shares of labour and capital.

The Solow residual is sometimes called the **rate of growth of multifactor productivity**. This is to distinguish it from the *rate of growth of labour productivity*, which is defined as $(g_Y - g_N)$, the rate of output growth minus the rate of labour growth.

The Solow residual is related to the rate of technological progress in a simple way. The residual is equal to the share of labour times the rate of technological progress:

$$\text{residual} = \alpha g_A$$

We will not derive this result here. But the intuition for this relation comes from the fact that what matters in the production function $Y = F(K, AN)$, equation (16.1), is the product of labour times the state of technology, AN. We saw that to get the contribution of labour growth to output growth, we must multiply the growth rate of labour by its share. Because N and A enter in the same way in the production function, it is clear that to get the contribution of technological progress to output growth, we must also multiply it by the share of labour.

If the Solow residual is equal to zero, so is technological progress. To construct an estimate of g_A, one must construct the Solow residual and then divide it by the share of labour. This is how the estimates of g_A presented in the text are constructed.

Table 1 presents updated estimates of multifactor productivity growth in Canada. The source is *Productivity Growth in Canada* as cited below. In this very extensive project by Statistics Canada, a great deal of energy was put into constructing more accurate estimates of multifactor productivity growth. The slowdown in the growth of productivity in the period 1980–1989 is very clear. There is a partial recovery 1990–1999 which is encouraging. Table 1 presents data for the production of goods and the production of services. It is easier to both measure and increase productivity in goods-producing industries. However, services are playing a larger and larger role in the Canadian economy. Thus, the slower growth of productivity in the services sector is a matter of particular concern.

Sources: Robert Solow, "Technical Change and the Aggregate Production Function," *Review of Economics and Statistics*, 1957, pp. 312–320. Statistics Canada, *Productivity Growth in Canada*, Catalogue No. 15-204-XPE, February 2001.

Keep straight the definitions of productivity growth we have seen in this chapter. The two important ones are:

(1) labour productivity growth: $g_Y - g_N$

and

◄ (2) rate of technological progress: g_A

In steady state, labour productivity growth ($g_Y - g_N$) equals the rate of technological progress g_A. Outside of steady state, they need not be equal. An increase in the ratio of capital per effective worker due, for example, to an increase in the saving rate, increases $g_Y - g_N$ over g_A for some time.

The rate of technological progress is not directly observable. To construct it, we start from:

(3) the Solow residual: $g_Y - (\alpha g_N + (1 - \alpha)g_K)$

The Solow residual is also called the rate of growth of total factor productivity. The rate of technological progress equals the Solow residual divided by the labour share: $g_A = $ residual$/\alpha$.

TABLE 1	**Estimates of Multifactor Productivity Growth in Canada, 1962–1999 (percent)**		
	Business Sector Excluding Agriculture	**Business Sector Goods Industries**	**Business Sector Services Industries**
1962–1969	2.2	3.0	1.6
1970–1979	1.6	1.4	1.7
1980–1989	0.2	0.6	0.1
1990–1999	0.8	1.5	0.3

Source: Appendix 5, Statistics Canada, *Productivity Growth in Canada*, Catalogue No. 15-204-XPE.

CHAPTER 17
ECONOMIC GROWTH IN THE OPEN ECONOMY

To this point in our discussion of growth, we have dealt only with a closed economy, that is, an economy that does not trade with countries in the rest of the world. We need to modify this assumption. Other countries play a huge role in the growth of almost every national economy. We live in an interconnected world. In this chapter, we look at three different ways in which the international economy affects growth. They are:

- The migration of people across international borders plays a large role in the growth of total output. In Canada's case, net immigration will provide the largest source of population growth in the next few decades. The level of immigration is an important policy choice.

- There is a great deal of lending and borrowing across international borders. A substantial portion of the capital stock in Canada is owned by foreigners. Residents of Canada sell their bonds to nonresidents. Residents of Canada take out loans from residents of other countries. Residents of other countries own shares in Canadian corporations. Canadians typically own some physical assets in foreign countries. Canadians frequently lend money to nonresidents and buy shares of corporations resident in other countries. We need to understand why international borrowing and lending in all these forms occurs; and we need to understand how to measure these flows of assets and incomes.

- It is clear that technology and knowledge flow across international borders. This means that technology is an international good. We touched on this issue in Chapter 16 but there is more to say. There are important policy issues around trade in technology.

In the appendix to this chapter, the issue of an optimal current account deficit is addressed. We show such an optimal deficit exists. If a country takes advantage of its interconnections with the rest of the world, growth takes place at a more rapid pace.

17-1 | Growth in the Labour Input to Production in Canada

The production function in the three previous chapters made use of a variable we called N. N meant total employment. In the last chapter, N grew at g_N percent per year. g_N was exogenous with its value determined outside of any choices that are part of the economic or political policy process. N has been measured as the number of workers. In this section, we want to be more precise about the measurement of N and the sources of its growth over time. There is at least one important policy choice to be made by Canadians. There are three variables leading to the final value of g_N, one unique to the open economy and two variables common to both open and closed economies.

The Ratio of Employment to Population and Average Hours of Work

Thus far, the variable N has been total employment, representing the number of workers. If we wanted to be more precise about N as a measure of the labour input to production, we should measure N in terms of number of hours of work and not simply the number of workers. Statistics Canada reports that Canadians worked 530,382,600 hours in the year 2004, an incomprehensibly large number. We need to break this number down into its components.

First, realize that many people in the total population of Canada do not work. They are too young, too old, in school, or simply choose to remain out of paid employment for other reasons. Even if the total population of Canada remained constant, N, the number of persons working could vary as more or fewer people are at work. Figure 17–1 shows the variation in the percentage of Canadians over 15 years of age who were employed. The data begin in 1976 and end in 2005. Values are presented for the total population, both male and female. These variables are called the **employment-to-population ratio**, the number of employed workers divided by the population 15 years of age and over.

The employment-to-population ratio in Canada has been roughly constant since 1976, about 60% of Canadians over the age of 15 have a job of some type. There are significant short-term fluctuations. In the large recessions of 1982 and 1991, a smaller proportion of Canadians were employed. We considered these fluctuations in the short-run and medium-run analyses in the preceding chapters. The small variation in the employment-to-population

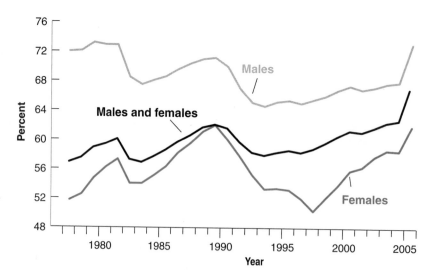

Source: Using CANSIM II variable V2461266, V2461476, and V2461687.

ratio for the total of all Canadians does mask some interesting differences between men and women. The employment-to-population ratio for males declined slightly from 1976 to 2004, while the employment-to-population ratio for females rose quite steadily from 1976 to about 1990. The increase in female labour force activity was one of the largest social and economic changes in the twentieth century. There are a variety of reasons why the male employment-to-population ratio has fallen recently. Longer life expectancy creates a longer period of retirement and, therefore given the same retirement age, more retired people. There is a very slow movement toward earlier retirement in Canada. There is a longer period of postsecondary education for both men and women. These factors lower the employment-to-population ratio. These long-term forces that change the employment-to-population ratio are slow to act. Dramatic variation in the growth of hours of work in the Canadian economy is not likely to come from fluctuations in the employment-to-population ratio.

The Labour Force Survey also calculates the number of hours worked per employed person. Figure 17–2 shows the **average** number of **hours** per week per employed worker in Canada. Again, the recessions of 1982 and 1991 stand out. Those who remained employed did work fewer hours. You will notice a slight decline in average hours of work for the period of the data (the scale of this diagram varies by a very small range—less than two hours. Although the labour input into production could rise if each worker in Canada worked a few more hours, this is very unlikely to be a large source of an increased labour input. As Canadians get richer, they are likely to want more leisure time, not less. Many people work part time by choice in order to have more time for family or schooling. These people do not want more hours of work.

We can write what we have learned as an equation:

$$\text{Total hours} = \text{Average hours per employee} \times \frac{\text{Number of employees}}{\text{Population}} \times \text{Population}$$

If we accept that the first two variables in the equation above (the employment-to-population ratio and the average hours worked per employed person) are very slow to change, then the labour input into the production process in Canada will grow only if the Canadian population grows. How can the total population of Canada grow?

FIGURE 17–2

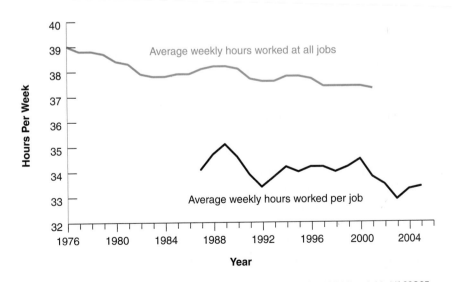

Average Weekly Hours Worked by Canadians, 1976–2005

Average weekly hours worked by Canadians at all jobs has declined slightly but steadily from 1976 to 2001. After 2001, Statistics Canada no longer measured this variable. Instead, Statistics Canada now calculates a measure of average hours per week per job. Average hours per week per job is now about 33 hours per week. It has also fallen slightly between 1987 and 2004. The figure makes it clear that some people have more that one job.

Source: Average weekly hours worked at all jobs 1976–2001 using CANSIM II variable V163865; average weekly hours per job from 1987– 2004 using CANSIM II variable V2641490 divided by CANSIM II variable V2641481.

FIGURE 17-3

Sources of Population Growth in Canada, 1950–2004

Population growth can come from an excess of births over deaths or from net immigration. Net immigration played a large but variable role in Canada's population growth throughout the last half-century. The bulge of the baby boom stands out. In the 1950s births greatly exceeded deaths. In the 1990s, net immigration took over from natural increase as the dominant source of population growth in Canada.

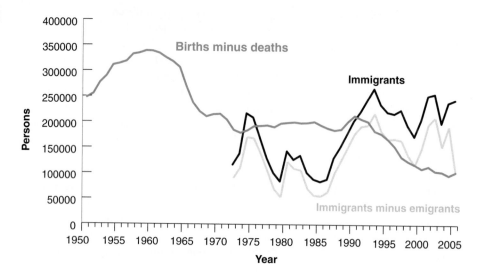

Source: Births using CANSIM I variable V62; deaths using CANSIM II variable V77; *immigrants* using CANSIM II variable V391099; and *emigrants* using CANSIM II variable V391114.

Natural Population Growth

In a closed economy, a country without international interaction, the identity:

$$\text{Population change} = \text{number of births} - \text{number of deaths}$$

completely describes population change. One of the few countries in the world that would look much like this equation would be North Korea. In North Korea, both immigration and emigration are very small. This equation describes only part of population growth in Canada. Figure 17–3 plots births minus deaths in Canada over the last half-century. The baby boom of the 1950s stands out. As the generation born in the late 1950s passed through the population structure, there were first more children, then more working-age adults, and finally there will be more retired and aged adults. The children of the baby boom create a small "echo" of this pattern. We are not primarily concerned with the consequences of the baby boom (fascinating though they are). We want to use Figure 17–3 to make the point that in the near term, **natural population growth** from the excess of births over deaths in Canada is declining. From 1989, natural population growth drops rapidly from 200,000 to 100,000 persons per year. At current birth rates, given an aging population and the subsequent rise in the death rate, natural population growth will become negative. Europe and Japan are also close to or at negative natural population growth. As these countries became richer and more females participated in the workforce, the number of births dropped below the number of deaths. Net immigration will be the source of population growth in Canada for the foreseeable future.

Immigration and Emigration in Canada

Canada is a nation of immigrants. Many of the users of this book are immigrants or the children of immigrants. Given the discussion above, it will not surprise you to learn that the growth in labour inputs in Canada now depends primarily on **net immigration**. Table 17–1 fills in the values for the identity:

$$\text{Population change} = \text{number of births} - \text{number of deaths} + \text{net immigration}$$

as much as possible. The identity is the correct description of population change in Canada. In fact, we do not have complete knowledge of emigration from Canada. Emigration is

TABLE 17-1 Components of Population Growth in Canada, 1950–2004

The source of Canada's population growth has shifted in the past sixty years. In the early part of the twentieth century, population growth was dominated by natural increase, an excess of births over deaths. In the latter part of the century, net immigration became the dominant component of population growth.

Period	Population at End of Period	Change in Population	Births	Deaths	Births – Deaths	Immigration	Emigration	Net Immigration
1950–1954	15,444	1637	2011	629	1382			
1955–1959	17,624	1790	2312	672	1640			
1960–1964	19,420	1411	2343	718	1625			
1965–1969	21,111	1334	1911	757	1154			
1970–1974	22,907	1507	1776	806	969			
1975–1979	24,279	1039	1806	838	968	696	158	538
1980–1984	25,678	1074	1866	867	999	596	130	466
1985–1989	27,408	1493	1888	931	956	633	137	496
1990–1994	29,095	1281	1980	996	984	1171	205	966
1995–1999	30,495	1098	1772	1077	696	1031	277	754
2000–2004	32,040	1253	1653	1123	530	1153	251	902

Units: thousands of persons

Source: Births using CANSIM II variable V62; *deaths* using CANSIM II variable V77; *immigrants* using CANSIM II variable V391099; and *emigrants* using CANSIM II variable V391114.

discussed further in the In Depth box "Canada: Brain Drain or Brain Gain?" Table 17–1 makes it clear that both in the immediate past and for the indefinite future, net immigration will be the major source of population growth in Canada. In Figure 17–3, lines are plotted to measure births minus deaths since 1950 and then net annual immigration for the period after 1975. You can see that while there is emigration from Canada, it is much smaller than immigration. You can also see that after 1995, net immigration is a larger component of population growth in Canada than natural population growth.

The dominant role of immigration in population and labour force growth in Canada leads to two macroeconomic questions: (1) Do immigrants cause unemployment? (2) How much immigration is the "right" amount?

First, it should be absolutely obvious that immigration cannot itself "cause" the unemployment rate to be higher. We have had massive net immigration in the last 40 years into Canada. Average unemployment rates have been more or less stable since 1970, while immigration has been large, both in absolute terms and relative to the population. Common sense tells us that immigrants, like the native-born, have to be housed, fed, educated, and clothed. This is an increase in aggregate demand. Immigrants are productive and thus increase aggregate supply. Over the long term, immigration leads to equal increases in aggregate supply and aggregate demand. There are numerous studies that find that the unemployment rates of immigrants and native-born Canadians are similar. In fact, immigrants use Employment Insurance and other forms of social assistance less not more than do native-born Canadians. With a little thought, this fact may not be that surprising. Immigrants are, for the most part, persons with enough talents, ability, and courage to leave their own cultures and go to a new country. Such characteristics are likely to lead to economic success.

The second question asked was: How much net immigration is the "right" amount? This is a much harder question to answer. It is a cause of much social tension in some developed countries. It seems to cause less social tension in Canada. It is clearly wrong to assert that immigration raises the unemployment rate. But how fast a society wants population growth

In statistical studies, this is sometimes called sample-selection bias. You might think random samples of the native-born and immigrants are comparable. But these random samples draw on different pools of persons. The pool of immigrants has the characteristics of persons willing to leave their own cultures and go to another culture on a permanent basis. These are not going to be a random sample of persons from their countries of origin. The sample of the native-born will be much closer to a random sample of persons born in Canada. The only persons missing from the draw of the native-born will be those who left Canada, a relatively small group.

In the 1990s, Canadians heard much about the "**brain drain**." This expression referred to the increased emigration of Canadians to the United States. Most emigration from Canada is to the United States. The data in Table 17–1 show a sharp increase in the five-year period from 1995–1999 in emigration, from an average of 41,000 per year 1990–1994 to an average of 55,000 per year in the years from 1995–1999. In all years in Table 17–1, including the period 1995–1999, the total number of immigrants far exceeded the number of emigrants. The quantity of net immigration is not the issue.

But emigration did become a serious policy issue in the late 1990s. Those who saw a problem claimed that it was not the number of emigrants to the United States during the 1995–1999 period that was the problem. Rather, it was the quality of the emigrants. Put simply: Canada was losing its best and brightest to the United States. It was argued that a disproportionate number of medical workers, both doctors and nurses as well as engineers (particularly in the computer and technology sector) left Canada for better opportunities in the United States. It is clear that there was some truth in this, that persons in these fields did leave Canada for better economic opportunities in the United States. Table 1 presents available numbers for one year—1996—when persons who left Canada and filed income tax returns for the year of departure identified their industry of employment. You can see that the industries with the largest number of emigrants are precisely health, education, and high technology. Persons emigrated from these industries in numbers well out of proportion to total employment in these industries in Canada. Much as we might all want the job of a university professor, it is not the second most numerous profession in Canada. Thus, a disproportionate number of professors did leave Canada in 1996.

Some commentators pointed out that many of the jobs in medicine and research are primarily funded by the public sector in Canada. The overall reduction in government spending in the 1990s (discussed more in Chapter 26) may have contributed to the decisions of some to leave Canada.

There was a huge discussion about lower income tax rates in the United States being a primary motivation in the decisions of emigrants to move from the higher income tax rates in Canada. The question was not settled. Not all U.S. states have lower income taxes than all Canadian provinces. Some services paid for by taxes in Canada are paid for privately in the United States. The most careful empirical work finds a role for the pull of lower taxes in the United States but an equally strong pull from both better job opportunities and higher before-tax salaries. If higher income taxes in Canada had been the sole factor in the "brain drain," then a logical conclusion would be that lower income taxes would reduce the "brain drain." This seems overly simplistic. In fact, to keep Canadian "brains" in Canada requires a variety of policy tools. Some of these policy tools have been used. There was a significant increase in health-care funding and funding in health research. There was a significant increase in other research funding, particularly in the sciences. The federal government has funded more capital expenditures at universities through the Canadian Foundation for Innovation. The Canada Research Chairs, federally funded research chairs at Canadian universities, were put in place partly to combat the "brain drain." Whether these policies are successful will only be known with time.

Further Reading

"The Brain Drain: Myth and Reality" in *Choices*, Vol. 7, NO. 6, November 2001, Institute for Research in Public Policy is an issue of one of Canada's policy journals devoted entirely to discussing the brain drain. There are many other references to brain-drain studies in that issue of *Choices*.

TABLE 1 Tax Filers Leaving Canada for All Destinations by Industry of Employer, 1996	
Industry	**Number of Movers in 1996**
Hospitals	1060
University education	910
Elementary and secondary education	690
Architectural, engineering, and other scientific and technical services	660
Computer and related services	580
Banks, trust companies, and credit unions	520
Food services	440
Federal government services	420
Communication and other electronic equipment	360
Other business services	290
All remaining industries	10,640

Source: Ross Finnie, "The Brain Drain: Myth and Reality—What It Is and What Should Be Done," in *Choices*, Volume 7, number 6, Institute for Research in Public Policy, November 2001, p. 12.

to occur is not obvious. For example, most immigrants end up in one of Canada's three largest cities: Toronto, Vancouver, or Montreal. Do we want these cities to continue to grow into their surrounding agricultural areas? Are there congestion and other environmental consequences of further urban growth in these three cities? Is it possible to encourage immigrants to settle elsewhere? Most Canadians seem to recognize that if net immigration were zero, then the population of Canada would both fall and certainly become older on average. The discussion of old age pensions in Chapter 15 in the In Depth box "Old Age Pensions and Capital Accumulation in Canada" told us that without net immigration, fewer and fewer workers will be supporting the average retired person in the public pay-as-you-go pension arrangements that are already in place. This would be a problem. It is the policy of the Government of Canada that immigration average about 1% of the population over the next five years. These immigrants will be the primary source of growth in the labour force in Canada. With these immigrants there will be significant growth in N, whether measured as the total number of workers or as the total number of hours. Whatever the number of immigrants finally is, they need to be equipped with capital to work with. In the closed economy, capital can only come from a reduction in current consumption. In the open economy, new capital can come from two sources, a reduction in current consumption or from foreign borrowing. We investigate these sources next.

17-2 | Equipping Workers with Capital in an Open Economy

A Closed Economy Review

Before we actually ask how we equip workers with capital in an open economy, we need to review the creation of new physical capital in a closed economy. If there is no government sector (we will add the government sector to this analysis in Chapter 26), then we wrote in Chapter 15 that:

$$I_t = S_t = Y_t - C_t \tag{17.1}$$

where I_t is new capital formation, the amount of physical investment, S_t is savings, Y_t is total output, and C_t is total consumption. The second equation to review:

$$K_{t+1} = (1 - \delta)K_t + I_t \tag{17.2}$$

kept track of the level of the capital stock at the beginning of period $t + 1$, denoted K_{t+1}. The total capital stock in the country increases only if investment was large enough to replace the amount of capital depreciating (wearing out). δ is the depreciation rate. Using these two equations, we found the steady-state level of output, looked at the short-term and longer-term effects of changing the savings rate and chose a value of the savings rate to maximize C in the long run. While these are all interesting issues to address, we did not emphasize the most difficult issue these two equations raise. That issue: If you want more capital stock in the future, equation (17.2) says you must invest more today, and then equation (17.1) says that if you invest more today, you *must* consume less today. This is an unpleasant choice. No one wants to give up consumption. In the open economy, there is a little more freedom to choose. But that freedom does come at a cost.

Consumption and Investment Choices in an Open Economy

When international trade is possible, equation (17.1) is re-written as:

$$C_t + I_t = Y_t + Q_t - X_t = Y_t - NX_t \tag{17.3}$$

In writing equation (17.3), the real exchange rate ϵ is set equal to unity in every period. This means that the units we are using to measure domestic production are the same units we use to measure exports and imports. This saves some notation without changing the basic analysis. Q_t is imports and X_t is exports, NX_t is net exports.

The total of consumption and investment in any period can now be different from the total amount of domestic production. In particular, this country can now increase investment in period t and thus its capital stock in period $t + 1$ *without* reducing consumption in period t. How? Rearrange equation (17.3) so that:

$$I_t = Y_t - C_t + Q_t - X_t = Y_t - C_t - NX_t$$

Suppose this country wants to increase investment and leave consumption unchanged. This can occur if net exports (NX_t) become more negative. To be absolutely clear on this vital point, let us consider a numerical example. Suppose we start with $Y_t = 100$, $C_t = 70$, and $I_t = 30$ and set both exports and imports to zero. We can then increase I_t (investment) by $10 and leave consumption unchanged only if this country imports the additional investment goods. The first lesson learned: If the use of goods and services ($C_t + I_t$) is greater than the production of goods (Y_t) in any period t, then net exports in that period must be negative. This sounds like a great situation; this country can now increase its future capital and hence its future production and not reduce its consumption today. But as we warned you before, there is a catch.

The Accumulation of Foreign Debts in an Open Economy

Foreign aid is the giving of additional resources from one country to another. Foreign aid would allow additional consumption or investment without incurring foreign debts. That is the point of foreign aid. This equation ignores foreign aid. Foreign aid is a small part of providing additional resources. Most international transfers of resources take place through borrowing and lending, not gifts. Canadian taxpayers do make gifts to other countries through the Canadian International Development Agency (CIDA). The private sector in Canada makes gifts to other countries through both Canadian nongovernmental organizations (NGOs), such as Mennonite Central Committee (MCC), and through international NGOs, such as UNICEF and OXFAM. The total value of gifts from Canada to other countries is quite small. The official goal for gifts from the Canadian taxpayer to other countries is 0.7% of GDP. This goal has not been achieved since it was set in 1995.

The catch is quite straightforward. The foreign countries do not typically make a gift of the extra resources needed for the additional investment spending, which are the imports we use to install the new capital goods. Rather, they lend us those goods or they lend us the money to buy those goods. When you are lent money, the lender expects to be repaid and usually to be repaid with interest. Foreign lenders are no different from any other type of lender. To keep track of our loans from foreigners (and our loans to foreigners), we need one more equation and two more pieces of notation. B_t^f is going to measure the amount of foreign bonds people in the domestic country hold at the beginning of period t. B stands for bonds and f for foreign. B_t^f is positive if Canadians have net foreign assets and is negative if Canadians have net foreign debts. We will see in the data that the units of B_t^f can be quite complicated. We are simply going to measure them in units of real output (the same units used for Y_t and its components). This once again sets the real exchange rate ϵ equal to one for simplicity. The equations below use bonds as a shorthand for all possible types of international financial instruments. We are going to have one interest rate on all loans made to or taken from foreigners with these bonds. That real interest rate is denoted r. r is not going to vary over time. r is a real interest rate (a concept fully explored in the next chapter). For now r (in decimal form) means that if we lend one dollar of output to a foreigner in period t, they will repay $(1 + r)$ dollars of output in period $t + 1$. If we borrow one dollar of output in period t from a foreigner in period t, then we will repay $(1 + r)$ dollars of output in period $t + 1$.

These are inflation-adjusted or real dollars throughout this chapter. We keep track of our net foreign assets (or our net foreign debts) using:

$$B_{t+1}^f - B_t^f = rB_t^f + Y_t - (C_t + I_t) \tag{17.4}$$

Equation (17.4) says that the money foreigners owe to us (our foreign assets) increases ($B_{t+1}^f - B_t^f$ is positive) when the sum of the interest we earn on our foreign assets (rB_t^f) and our production (Y_t) exceeds our use of resources ($C_t + I_t$). Equation (17.4) is a version of Canada's international budget constraint.[1] The left-hand side of equation (17.4) is Canada's **current account balance**.

Equation (17.4) has a perfect analogy to your own finances. Think of yourself as a country (and everyone else is now the rest of the world). Start off your year in debt, so B_t^f is negative. In this example, $B_t^f = -\$1500$; you have a debt outstanding on your credit card. Suppose this year, the sum of your consumption (the food you eat—denote this C_t and set this equal to \$9000) and your investment (a stove you buy—denote this I_t and set this equal to \$500) is exactly the earnings you make from your job (Y_t—your earnings from your job were \$9500). You might ask why we treat the stove purchase as a physical investment. A stove lasts through many years of productive use. A stove is used to produce other goods and services rather than being directly consumed. Thus, in this example, the stove stands in for physical investment. You are already in debt and must also pay the interest on existing debt, that is,

---

[1] **DIGGING DEEPER.** There is no government spending in (17.4). This is added in Chapter 26.

rB_t^f is negative in your version of equation (17.4). If the interest rate on your credit card is 10%, then $rB_t^f = 0.10 \times -\$1500 = -\$150$. Your assets at the beginning of period t were negative. Since you spent more exactly what you earned, you could not have paid off any of your debts and, in fact, must borrow a bit more. The new borrowing is rB_t^f, which is used to "pay" the interest on your debt. Now you owe even more—the original debt plus the interest you did not pay. Your total financial assets at the end of the year will be negative $1650. This is called "rolling over" your debt. You reborrowed the money you had owed at the beginning of the period, and you borrowed the interest you owed on that money. It is like having a credit card bill where you pay nothing on the bill, not even the minimum payment. The next month the bill has the same debt plus the interest that you did not pay last month, even when you did not use the card. Thus, your debt would rise by exactly the amount of the interest. In the numerical example above $B_{t+1}^f - B_t^f = rB_t^f$ because Y_t was exactly equal to $C_t + I_t$.

Countries can "roll over" their debt as well. As long as the lenders are willing to allow the interest to be added to the debt outstanding, the country can use its entire production for consumption and investment. This is not typical, either for you or for a country. A lender usually wants the interest paid and perhaps some of the debt repaid, if for no other reason than to believe that some day all of the debt will be repaid. There is a minimum payment on a credit card for this reason. Similarly, countries are expected to make a minimum payment on their foreign debts. It is very important for you and for a country to keep track of debts. How can we tell if a country experiences increasing or decreasing foreign debts?

We can rewrite equation (17.4) as:

$$B_{t+1}^f - B_t^f = rB_t^f + Q_t - X_t = rB_t^f + NX_t \qquad (17.5)$$

using the identity $Y_t = C_t + I_t + X_t - Q_t$. This equation calculates a country's current account balance. We have seen a version of this equation in Chapter 6 in Table 6–3. In Table 6–3, we used the middle portion of equation (17.5). Equation (17.5) presents the current account balance in a second way. On the far left, the current account balance is written as the change in the country's foreign assets. If this is positive, then this country could be acquiring foreign assets, that is, increasing its wealth in the form of foreign assets. These foreign assets earn interest and will allow higher consumption in the future. If the value of $B_{t+1}^f - B_t^f$ on the far left of (17.5) is negative, then either foreign assets become a smaller positive value or your foreign debts take on a more negative value (that would mean foreign debts are increasing). When a current account balance is negative, then either more of the future output of this country must be devoted to paying the interest on these debts and eventually repaying these debts or less interest will be earned in the future on that country's net foreign assets.

The middle and right sides of equation (17.5) are also the current account balance, written as it appeared in Table 6–3, as the sum of the trade balance (net exports) and the net value of investment income received and investment income paid. Hence, the change in a nation's foreign indebtedness is the sum of the trade balance and the investment income balance.

There is a third way to look at the accumulation of international debt. Rewriting (17.4) as:

$$B_{t+1}^f - B_t^f = (rB_t^f + Y_t) - (C_t + I_t) = GNP_t - (C_t + I_t) \qquad (17.6)$$

emphasizes the fact (as we said in Chapter 6) that GNP (gross national product) is slightly different from GDP (gross domestic product), that is, $GNP_t = rB_t^f + GDP_t$. Most of the time, we do not get very excited about the difference between GDP and GNP because in studying the behaviour of GDP, we learn about employment, unemployment, and the difference between actual output and the natural rate of output as the main source of inflationary pressure. These are the variables we care most about. But the difference between GNP and GDP is precisely the net interest received from or paid to foreigners. If GNP is less than GDP, then your income available to consume or invest is less than your production because part of your production must be used to pay interest on existing debts. If we want to keep careful track of foreign debts, we must make the distinction between GNP and GDP.

If this is positive, this country could also be repaying net foreign debts, that is, both B_{t+1}^f and B_t^f are negative but B_{t+1}^f is smaller in absolute value. Then less interest will be paid on net debt in the future.

The catch to using foreign resources to increase your capital stock without reducing consumption is now understood. If your income (GNP *not* GDP) is less than your expenditures, including expenditures on new capital, you must borrow. The foreigners you borrow from expect to be repaid with interest. If your income (GNP *not* GDP) is more than your expenditures, then you are able to lend, and you expect to be repaid by foreigners with interest. There is a huge amount of international borrowing and lending. Canada has been one of the largest participants in international financial markets over the past century. Canada has been a large-scale international borrower for most its existence as a nation.

Canada's International Portfolio

Table 17–2 presents Canada's international portfolio as of the end of 2004. A portfolio is a collection of your assets and your debts. International refers to the debts you owe to foreigners and the debts foreigners owe to you. International also refers to the assets foreigners own in Canada and the assets Canadians own in other countries. Table 17–2 shows Canadians own some $955.4 billion in foreign assets. $40.3 billion of those assets are called **official international reserves**. These particular assets are primarily bonds issued by the governments of other countries and owned by our federal government. These are the assets used for the foreign exchange market intervention we discussed in Chapter 13. As you can see, these assets are a relatively "small" amount of money. We have simplified the rest of the data and divided the remaining assets and liabilities into three other categories.

The largest category within Canadian assets is "Direct investment abroad," $445 billion. This category refers to a situation in which a corporation located in a foreign country has a controlling interest of its shares owned by Canadians. The usual situation is a foreign subsidiary of a Canadian firm, for example, Canadian Pacific Railways owns a variety of railway lines in the United States, and the Bank of Montreal owns a number of banks in the United States. A quick look at the lower half of Table 17–2 shows a large number of foreign firms also own controlling interest in Canadian firms (often as wholly owned subsidiaries). **Foreign direct investment** in Canada totals $365.6 billion. Foreign direct investment in Canada can be seen in nearly any industrial park in Canada, where a look at the names on the buildings tells you that at least one firm is foreign controlled. Direct investment is an important method through which new foreign capital enters Canada and Canadians provide capital to residents of other countries. Why is it so useful to have this form of foreign lending? The

TABLE 17–2	Canada's International Investment Position, 2004 (in billions of Canadian dollars)		
Foreign Assets of Canadians	**Total**	**955.4**	
Direct investment abroad		445.0	
Portfolio foreign stocks		186.6	
All other assets		283.5	
Official international reserves		40.3	
Foreign Liabilities of Canadians	**Total**	**1,136.5**	
Foreign direct investments in Canada		365.6	
Portfolio foreign stocks		108.6	
All other liabilities		662.3	
Canada's net international investment position		**–181.1**	

Source: CANSIM II Table 376-0037.

This table presents Canada's international assets, international debts, and net foreign assets at the end of 2004. It is updated annually by Statistics Canada.

usual reason is that these firms are in a business where the most straightforward way to enter another country's market is to set up a subsidiary. This can occur if the product has specialized service needs, for example, heavy equipment built by multinational firms, such as Caterpillar or Komatsu. This often occurs if the product or service is associated partly or entirely with patented information—the best way to ensure quality and retain absolute control of the information is to set up a subsidiary. Coca-Cola with its protected formula is an example of this type of foreign investment. Pharmaceutical firms also fall into this category as do various forms of copyrighted entertainment. Foreign direct investment can occur if the production processes within a firm are heavily integrated across borders. The most obvious example in Canada is the various foreign-owned automobile-manufacturing facilities. The individual plants in both Canada and the United States produce all versions of the particular model for all of North America. It is clear from the data in Table 17–2 that foreign direct investment is a huge part of international lending and borrowing.

The second category in each half of Table 17–2 is labelled "Portfolio foreign stocks" followed by "All other assets (liabilities)." Both categories fit into a general category **foreign portfolio investment**, where Canadians and nonresidents own assets outside their own countries as part of investment portfolios, that is, without voting control. These assets can be stocks or in the form of bonds or other loans. On the asset side, these are Canadian holdings of foreign stocks where Canadians do not have voting control of the foreign company in question. Canadians hold these stocks to receive their share of any profits these companies might earn. Canadians do choose to hold a lot of foreign equity in this form; $186.6 billion in 2004. Foreigners hold fewer Canadian shares without voting control: only $108.6 billion. This makes complete sense. Both Canadians and foreigners hold shares without control to diversify risk across stock markets. If times are bad in Canada, Canadians can hope that their foreign shares will have a high payoff. Foreigners want a similar performance from their holdings of Canadian shares. Because Canada is so small compared with the rest of the world, it makes sense that foreigners only want a relatively small holding of Canadian stocks for diversification purposes. The same logic suggests Canadians would want a lot of foreign stocks to diversify their portfolio across many countries.

The last category is labelled "All other assets" and "All other liabilities." It is this category that corresponds most closely to the simple idea of foreign bonds in equations (17.4) through (17.6). These financial instruments are mixtures of long-term bonds, short-term bonds, and bank loans as well as bank accounts—all financial instruments that pay a rate of interest. There are no voting rights attached to these financial instruments. You will notice that Canada owes a lot of international debt in this form, $662.3 billion at the end of 2004. Canadians are owed relatively little debt in this form, only $283.5 billion. Thus, Canada has borrowed a lot of money from foreign countries exactly in the form of equation (17.4) through (17.6).

The bottom line in Table 17–2 presents Canada's **net international investment position**. Canadians owe $181.1 billion more to foreigners than foreigners owe to us. This is our net foreign debt. This means, with a population of 32 million, the average Canadian owed $5606 to the rest of the world at the end of 2004. This is the debt on which interest must be paid, and eventually, if Canadians want to, this debt may be repaid. Both the payment of interest and the repayment of principal involve a reduction in consumption in the future. Was it a good thing for Canadians to take on this debt in the past?

When Is International Debt Good for an Economy?

Canada is not the only economy in the world with a significant international debt. In the past 20 years, the United States has moved from being a net international creditor to a net international debtor. We saw in Chapter 6 that Kuwait was a large lender to the rest of the world,

You now realize that the real interest rate in equations (17.4) through (17.6) is a very complex weighted average of returns on all the financial instruments in Table 17–2. This will include interest rates on bank loans, bonds, dividends on shares, and capital gains.

that is, for Kuwait, B_t^f is a large positive value. Many developing countries, including many of the former communist countries in transition to market economies, are taking on foreign debt. We have already seen the main reason for such activity. If a country wants to install some more physical capital and does not want to reduce consumption now, it must borrow from the rest of the world to install the new physical capital. Equations (17.3) and (17.4) make this clear. Borrowing from the rest of the world is not a problem as long as the new capital installed is productive enough to pay the interest on the debt. This seems likely to be the case in many circumstances. First, if this is a country with a small amount of capital per worker, then the marginal product of capital will be high, and it will be relatively easy to pay the interest on the foreign loan. There will be many profitable opportunities for lending in a country that is short of capital. Second, many foreign loans are for specific projects, such as the development of a new mine, oilfield, or railway where the need for the new capital is well defined. In the appendix to this chapter, we look in more detail at how international debts can make a country better off. The analysis in the appendix makes precise the idea of an optimal amount of foreign borrowing. The precision comes with some complexity. We look at Canada's international debts in a broader sense below and ask if Canada's net foreign debt is too large.

Figures 17–4 and 17–5 are different ways of answering that question: Is Canada's net foreign debt too large? Figure 17–4 looks at the size of Canada's debt relative to total production in Canada. This is like looking at the debts owed by your family relative to your family's income. If your family owes $10,000 but makes $100,000, there is no problem. If the debt is $100,000 and family income is $10,000 per year, there is a problem. Net foreign debt in Canada as a percent of GDP has two peaks, 41% in 1961 and 45% in 1993. These two peaks are probably different. The first peak followed very large foreign investments that enlarged Canada's physical capital stock in the 1950s. Specific projects in the 1950s included the oil and gas pipelines that crossed Canada from Alberta to Ontario as well as the building of the St. Lawrence Seaway. The peak in 1993 seems to be due to large public sector borrowing during the 1980s. We will discuss this issue further in Chapter 26 under the heading "Twin Deficits." One startling aspect of Figure 17–4 is the enormous growth in both foreign assets and foreign debts after 1993. Canadians appear to be diversifying into foreign assets. Foreigners are diversifying into Canadian assets. This graph shows a clear effect of globalization in international financial markets.

FIGURE 17–4

Canada's International Debts and Canada's International Assets, 1950–2004

Canada's international debts are large relative to its GDP. In the early 2000s, Canada's international debt was greater than 100% of GDP but fell back down to 92% in 2003. In 2003, Canada's foreign assets were approximately 75% of GDP, down from nearly 85% in 2002. Both assets and debts grew sharply during the 1990s as Canadians diversified and purchased foreign assets for their portfolios. Canada's net foreign debts fell sharply in the 1990s after peaking in 1993. An earlier peak in Canada's net foreign debt in 1961 was associated with large foreign investments in the Canadian economy through the 1950s.

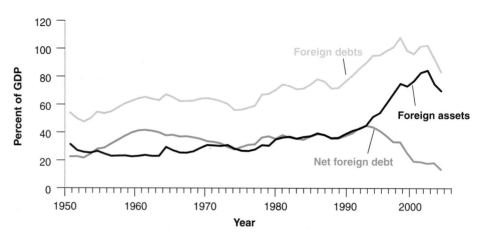

Source: Total foreign assets, using CANSIM II variable V235395; total foreign debt, using CANSIM II variable V235411; net foreign debt, using CANSIM II variable V235422; nominal GDP 1926–1960, using CANSIM II variable V500633, 1961–2001 using CANSIM II variable V646937.

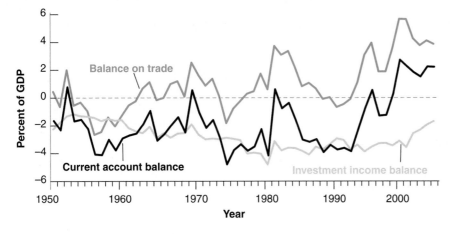

Source: Current account balance using CANSIM II variable V113713; investment income balance using CANSIM II variable V113723; balance on trade using CANSIM II variable, V113714; nominal GDP 1926–1960 using CANSIM II variable V500633, 1961–2001 using CANSIM II variable V646937.

FIGURE 17–5

Canada's Interaction with the Rest of the World

The current account balance shows the change in Canada's net foreign debt. A negative value indicates an increase in net foreign debts. For most of the period after 1950, Canadians borrowed from the rest of the world. Only from 1999 to 2004 do we observe consecutive years where the current account balance is positive. The negative investment income balance is the interest paid on Canada's foreign debts. It is the difference between GNP and GDP. Finally, the positive balance on trade shows that Canadians export goods and services to other countries to pay the interest on their foreign debts.

A second way to look at the data is found in Figure 17–5. The current account balance tells us if Canada's net foreign debt is increasing or decreasing. In almost every year since 1950, Canada's current account balance has been negative and about 2% of GDP. Why didn't Canada's debts as a percentage of GDP grow very much? During the early period in which the debt was increasing, GDP or production, partly from the new capital, was also increasing quickly. Thus, for most of the period before 1975, net foreign debts did not grow faster than the ability to service that debt. The entirely negative line in Figure 17–5 is the percentage of GDP used to service Canada's net foreign debt. The value of this gap is, to recall Chapter 6, the difference between GDP and GNP. In the 1950s about 1.5% of GDP was used to pay the interest on Canada's debts. This number increased to 2.4% in the 1960s to 3% in the 1970s, and then to 4% in the 1980s. By the late 1980s, Canada's international debts were looking like a problem. A growing proportion of Canada's production was claimed by foreigners. However, the 1990s saw a sharp reversal (0.5% of GDP is about $5 billion), and an average of 3.4% of GDP was used to service foreign debt over that decade. In 2001, only 2.5% of GDP was used to pay interest on foreign debt. This change resulted from a dramatic swing in the current account balance from negative to positive in the late 1990s. From 1999 to 2004, Canadians repaid foreign debt or ran a current account surplus.

From this brief look at the data, it seems like international borrowing was clearly good for Canada in the 1950s. It allowed a large expansion of the Canadian capital stock and Canadian output without a large drop in consumption. There was a gradual decline in net foreign debts as a percentage of GDP throughout the 1960s and even into the 1970s. The period of the 1980s and early 1990s saw an expansion of foreign debts and an increase in the percentage of GDP used to service those debts. Canadians took on foreign debt from 1980 to 1998 without a proportional increase in output to service those debts. This is a concern that we discuss further in Chapter 26.

There is absolutely no doubt that over the history of Canada borrowing from foreigners played a significant role in the creation of the Canadian capital stock. Many profitable investment opportunities were financed from abroad. The same story can be told for many other countries in the world.

17-3 | The Import and Export of Technology

The Flows

We have presented evidence that Canada imports labour inputs from the rest of the world through net immigration. We have presented evidence that Canada's growth is partly due to the import of physical and the associated financial capital from the rest of the world. Canada has frequently run current account deficits. Common sense tells us that the import of technology from the rest of the world is also an important part of the growth process in any country. Canada is no exception. If a Canadian or a Canadian firm creates a new product, it often moves to export that product. If it does so in the form of a foreign subsidiary, it exports its technology to another country. This is only one form of the export of technology. However, it is also possible that a Canadian inventor registers a patent in another country and receives payments for the use of that idea. Similarly foreign inventors will register patents and copyrights in Canada. Canadians do make payments to nonresidents for the rental of their technology.

The OECD presents some numbers of the **technology balance of payments**. These numbers for Canada are summarized in Table 17–3. They clearly do not cover all aspects of technology transfers. For example, if part of the profits remitted to a parent from a Canadian subsidiary are payments for the use of the parent's technology, this is a substantial undercounting. The OECD tries to capture licence fees and copyright fees paid across borders. The values in Table 17–3 begin in 1977 and end in 1998. What is striking is the growth in these values and the increase in both Canadian exports and Canadian imports of technology over the period. It is also striking that the numbers in Table 17–3 are quite small relative to the values in Figure 17–5. Note that 2.5% of GDP in Figure 17–5 (the difference between GNP and GDP in Canada in 2001) is about $25 billion. This is income produced in Canada and paid to foreigners on their previous investments in Canada. The values in Table 17–3 are measured in millions of dollars. In 1998, net payments from Canada on the technology balance as measured by the OECD are negligible. However, the transfer of technology across borders takes place in thousands of unmeasured ways: books, the Internet, education, conferences, subsidiaries, the migration of knowledgeable people, and probably many other ways we cannot even think of.

Policy Implications of the Transfer of Technology

In Chapter 16, we discussed how the appropriability of research results is one determinant of the rate of technological progress and thus of growth. The argument is made that with a strong

TABLE 17–3	Canada's Technology Balance of Payments (millions of Canadian dollars)	
Year	**Receipts**	**Payments**
1977–1983	219	447
1984–1988	670	761
1989–1993	1,057	1,022
1994–1998	1,983	1,472

Source: OECD Main Science and Technology Indicators, various issues.

For several years, the OECD has operated a project to look at trade in technology. Part of the interest in this type of data comes out of the difficult issues raised by intellectual property rights in international trade negotiations.

set of laws protecting the use of new innovations and the generation of monetary returns from intellectual property, there will be more new innovations. This is the justification for patent and copyright laws. There are always problems in the enforcement of such laws even within a country. How different does an innovation have to be before you are allowed a new patent? How much effort goes into the enforcement of copyright laws? Most of us have personal experience at the photocopying machine or with downloading material from the Internet. We know little effort is expended in enforcing copyright laws on individuals. But we also observe lawsuits filed for patent and copyright infringements at a corporate level.

Problems related to appropriability of ideas are magnified in the international setting. In the World Trade Organization (WTO), the organization that creates and enforces international trade agreements, payments across borders for the use of intellectual property has been one of the most difficult issues to settle. In particular, there have been huge problems with the piracy of software across international borders. There has been much concern about very poor countries making large payments for drugs that are needed to stave off the spread of AIDS (acquired immune deficiency syndrome) and stabilize the lives of AIDS sufferers. These drugs are developed in rich countries by private drug companies that view them as their corporate property and wish to be paid for their development costs. They are happy to put these drugs up for sale to poor countries, but the poor countries feel that they cannot afford the payments the companies want and want to pay a much smaller fee for the use of these drugs. They often want to make and use generic copies of these drugs. It is almost impossible to stop a poor country that is determined to use these drugs without paying licence fees. This issue remains very much unsettled in the WTO. Even in Canada, a rich country, drug patents have been a controversial issue. Until 1987, Canadian generic drug manufacturers were allowed to make generic copies of patented drugs after 10 years for a relatively small licensing fee. After 1987, the generic drug companies were forced to wait 17 years for the same opportunity. This did make new drugs created in other countries more expensive for Canadians. This change may also have created a stronger incentive for Canadian as well as foreign drug companies to develop new drugs. In the United States, there has been a periodic pressure on Congress to shorten the period of monopoly granted to a new drug from 20 years to 10 years, the period of the pre-1987 law in Canada. Should such legislation be ever passed, Canada then may return to its pre-1987 drug patent laws to match those in the United States. These examples are among many where the need to consider the international aspect of intellectual property laws arises.

17-4 | Growth in the Open Economy: A Summary

This chapter has emphasized that growth in the open economy makes extensive use of international inputs. There has been substantial migration of labour among countries. In Canada's case, net immigration is the numerically dominant component of overall population growth. This is likely to be the case for nearly all developed countries in the next few decades. There have been enormous international capital flows. Canada is a net debtor because of previous inflows of foreign capital. This has not created severe problems in the Canadian economy where production has increased, partly with the use of foreign capital, enough to pay the interest on the foreign loans. We will see in Chapter 24 when we discuss the East Asian crisis that this is not always the case. Finally, we know that technology and knowledge flow across international borders. We know that this flow is quite difficult to measure in any accurate way. However, it must be the case that in any open economy, knowledge from all sources, both foreign and domestic, is used to create economic progress.

- In an open economy, growth in total output can come from both domestic and international sources. More output requires more labour, more capital, or more technology. Any of the three inputs to production may come from the rest of the world.

- Labour inputs to the production process are best measured by total hours of work. Total hours of work are the product of average hours of work and the number of workers. The number of workers depends on both total population and the employment-to-population ratio. Neither the employment-to-population ratio nor average hours of work change rapidly over time. Thus, a larger population will be the major source of the growth in the labour input in Canada.

- In Canada, natural population growth, the excess of births over deaths, has declined steadily since the 1950s' baby boom. Net immigration, the excess of immigrants over emigrants, is the main source of population in Canada.

- Increasing the capital stock in either a closed or open economy means physical investment must be larger than depreciation. If a society wants more capital in a closed economy, current consumption must be reduced.

- In an open economy, more capital can be created without a reduction in current consumption by increasing foreign borrowing. A current account deficit (the term for foreign borrowing), increases your foreign debt and thus future payments of interest on that debt.

- Canada has engaged in extensive international borrowing since 1950. It appears that for the first 25 years after 1950, this international borrowing was used to increase Canada's physical capital stock and output. More recent international borrowing, after 1975, did increase Canada's net debts as a percent of GDP and the percentage of GDP used to service that debt. This issue is further addressed in Chapter 26.

- There are substantial flows of technology across international borders. These flows create particular difficulties in international trade agreements as countries and companies try to enforce intellectual property laws across borders.

- average hours, 329
- brain drain, 332
- current account balance, 334
- employment-to-population ratio, 328
- foreign direct investment, 336
- foreign portfolio investment, 337

- natural population growth, 330
- net immigration, 330
- net international investment position, 337
- official international reserves, 336
- technology balance of payments, 340

An asterisk denotes a harder question. [Web] indicates that the question requires access to the Internet.

1. **TRUE/FALSE/UNCERTAIN**

a. Total population in a country increases only if there is an excess of births over deaths.

b. Canadians owned no foreign assets in 2004.

c. Average hours of work in Canada have declined over the past decade.

d. In an open economy, the capital stock can be expanded without a decrease in consumption.

e. Payments across international borders for intellectual property are an important part of Canada's trade.

2. **IMMIGRATION POLICY IN CANADA**

Look at Table 17–1 in detail.

a. In which five-year period is the excess of births over deaths the largest value? In which five-year period is the excess of births over deaths the smallest value? What are the implications of your findings if there is no net immigration into Canada after 2005?

b. In which five-year period is net immigration the largest value? In which five-year period is net immigration the smallest value? What are the implications of your findings for population growth in Canada after 2004?

c. Use an estimate of the employment-to-population ratio and the average hours per week to estimate the percent increase in total labour input available to Canada if net immigration had been 100,000 larger in each year between 2000 and 2004.

3. AN INCREASE IN CAPITAL AND INTERNATIONAL DEBTS

Fill in the missing values in the table below.

CA_t is notation for the current account balance. All other notations are in the text. The stock variable B_t^f is calculated at the end of the period using equation (17.4). The stock variable K_t is calculated as of the beginning of the period using equation (17.2). At the end of period 1 (the beginning of period 2) B_t^f is zero. K_t equals 300 at the beginning of period 2. The interest rate earned on foreign assets or paid on foreign debt is 10%.

a. What is the value of the depreciation rate δ? Why is the capital stock unchanged from year 4 to year 5?

b. What is the value of B_t^f at the end of period 2? Is there a current account deficit in period 2? Explain the source of the current account deficit in year 3. Calculate net foreign debts at the end of year 3.

c. There is a sharp fall in consumption in year 5. What is the effect of that drop in consumption in the current account? What is the effect of that drop in consumption in this country's net foreign debts at the end of year 5?

4. THE INTERNATIONAL DEBTS OF THE UNITED STATES [WEB]

The international debts of the United States are of direct concern to Canadians. The United States is our largest trading partner. A very useful source of basic American economic data is the Appendix Tables to the *Economic Report of the President*. This can be accessed through any search engine under "economic report of the President." The statistical tables are even available as a spreadsheet at **http://w3.access.gpo.gov/usbudget/**.

a. Use the table titled "U.S. International Transactions," and find a decade in which there is only one current account surplus. From 1992 to 2004, there is an unbroken string of current account deficits. Explain what this string does to the U.S. international asset position. Explain why the column "balance on income" remains positive to 1998, while the current account balance is negative after 1992. What is the significance of the "balance on income" switching from positive to negative?

b. Find the table entitled "International investment position of the United States." This will list U.S. international assets and debts for approximately 10 years. During the 1990s, according to this table, is the United States a net debtor to the rest of the world? What is the form of the largest U.S. foreign asset? What is the form of the largest U.S. foreign debt?

c. The first table in the *Economic Report of the President* usually presents GDP numbers. Calculate, for the years of net foreign debt available, the ratio of net international debts to U.S. GDP. Is the U.S. international debt becoming a problem? Why, or why not? Suppose that the U.S. national debt becomes a problem for U.S. policy makers. They want to reduce imports and increase exports. How would this impact Canada?

Year	Y_t	C_t	I_t	X_t	Q_t	CA_t	B_t^f	Trade Balance	K_t
2	100	70	30	20	20		0		300
3	100	65	40		25		−5		
4	105	73	31	21	20				310
5	105	68	31		20				310

APPENDIX

THE OPTIMAL AMOUNT OF FOREIGN BORROWING

This appendix uses a two-period framework to ask and answer the following question: How much international borrowing is optimal? This is a difficult question. It involves making the correct choice of physical investment and then the best choice of consumption over time. International financial markets are used to allow a country to expand its choice set and make the very best of its opportunities. Using the two-period analysis helps us see the nature of the best choice. We can also answer the question: "How much international borrowing is optimal?" when there are many periods of time. However, the mathematics required for the many-period problem is beyond the scope of this book. The key lessons can be learned from the two-period example below.

▲

Optimal means making the best decision from the set of available decisions.

An Improvement Using Only International Borrowing and Lending

We will start our country at the beginning of period 1 without either foreign debts or foreign assets. In the notation of the body of the chapter, $B^f = 0$. The real interest rate available to our country on the international capital market is 7%. Figure 17A–1 shows what this country is able to do when only international borrowing and lending are used to make an improvement. This is our first step to understanding the optimal current account choice. We will then build gradually. On the horizontal axis is dollars in period 1, representing choices made *now*. On the vertical axis is dollars in period 2, representing choices made in the *future*. We will simply call these period 1 and period 2. This country, without any physical investment in period 1 (we add physical investment shortly), produces 50 dollars of output in period 1 and then 40 dollars of output in period 2. You could think of this country as Kuwait. We looked at Kuwait's balance of payments in Chapter 6. In Kuwait, oil reserves are falling over time so that existing wells will produce less in the second period. Kuwait expects its production (its GDP) to be lower in the second period. We start our analysis at point A in Figure 17A–1. If there is neither international

▲

This material is very closely related to the material in Appendix A to Chapter 20. In Chapter 20, we use a similar two-period model to represent a multi-period consumption problem.

borrowing nor international lending and no physical investment in period 1, then point A must also represent the consumption choices in this country. Using equations and the notation from the body of the chapter, we write:

$$C_1 = Y_1 = 50 \text{ and } C_2 = Y_2 = 40$$

where C is consumption and Y is GDP or output. This choice says this country simply consumes its production in each period. Is there a better choice?

The Appendix A to Chapter 20 introduces the concept of indifference curves, a concept you may have used in a microeconomics course. This concept helps identify a better choice. We could add indifference curves on consumption in period 1 and period 2 to Figure 17A–1. However, we will use a simpler idea here. We are going to state that if consumption can be made exactly equal between period 1 and

FIGURE 17A–1

An Improvement Using Only International Borrowing and Lending

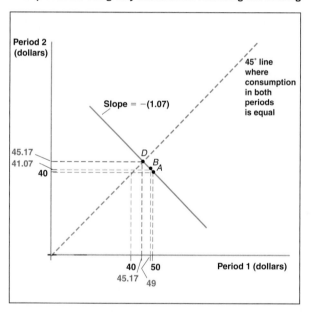

Without international lending and borrowing, consumption in period 1 must equal production in period 1, and consumption in period 2 must equal production in period 2. Point A with 50 dollars of consumption in period 1 and 40 dollars of consumption in period 2 represents this choice. Point B shows the effect of lending one dollar to nonresidents in period 1 and consuming the repayment of that loan in addition to production in period 2. Point D shows the situation where consumption is equal in period 1 and period 2. The country lends 4.83 dollars in period 1, thus reducing consumption in period 1 to 45.17 dollars. The loan is repaid with 7% interest in period 2 allowing period 2, consumption to rise to 40 + (1.07 x 4.83) = 45.17 dollars.

period 2, then this society will be happier. We appeal to the idea that persons generally prefer a smoother path of consumption. We see households saving for retirement to smooth consumption. Most of us do not want to eat like a glutton one month and then starve the next month or be homeless one month and live in a palace the next month. We see Kuwait and other resource-rich societies saving today to build up their foreign assets. These assets enable future consumption to be equal to current consumption even after the oil runs out. Note that consumption in period 1 at point A is not equal to consumption in period 2 at point A. This is not the best choice for this society. We are going to consider two ways for this country to equalize consumption between period 1 and period 2. The first way involves lending dollars to the rest of the world in period 1 and then adding the repayment of those loans to consumption in period 2.

Figure 17A–1 first explores the idea of taking one dollar from period 1 output and lending it to a nonresident. Starting from point A, consumption in period 1 is reduced to 49 dollars at point B. This money is lent to a nonresident on the international capital market. That nonresident repays the one-dollar loan with 7% interest in period 2. Consumption in period 2 at point B is increased to 41.07 dollars, the 40 dollars of income already available in period 2 and the repayment of the loan made to the nonresident in period 1. Point B is "better" than point A because consumption is now more equal. How much lending to nonresidents is required to equalize consumption across the two periods? We can solve the equation:

$$50 - L_1 = 40 + 1.07(L_1)$$

for the size of the period 1 loan (denoted L_1) that will equalize consumption in the two periods. The left side of the equation above is consumption in period 1, income minus the loan to the nonresident. The right side of the equation above is consumption in period 2, income plus the repayment of the loan made to the nonresident in period 1. Solving this equation yields $L_1 = 4.83$ dollars. If this country saves 4.83 dollars in period 1, this reduces period 1 consumption to $50 - 4.83 = 45.17$ dollars. When the loan made by this country to a nonresident is repaid in period 2 with interest, period 2 consumption rises to $40 + 1.07(4.83) = 45.17$ dollars. In Figure 17A–1, this is a movement from point A to point D. D is a point of equal consumption. In our simplified model, equal consumption is the most desirable consumption choice. There is no reason for this country to save in period 2—this is a two-period model, and there is no further activity after the second period. This disadvantage of the two-period model ends if the problem is extended to a multi-period framework.

We have learned two important lessons. International lending and borrowing can be used to equalize consumption over time. International financial markets have allowed this country to be better off because consumption is now more equal than it would be without international financial markets. We can use the equations from the body of this chapter to note that this country has a current account surplus in period 1 in Figure 17A–1. The current account surplus is $Y_1 - C_1 = 50 - 45.17 = 4.83$. There is no physical investment up to this point in the example. Physical investment is introduced immediately below.

An Improvement in Well Being from Physical Investment Activity Only

Figure 17A–2 introduces the possibility of using physical investment to make consumption more equal across the two periods. Physical investment means taking some period 1 output and using it to install more physical capital in period 1 rather than consuming those resources in period 1.

An Improvement Using Only Physical Investment

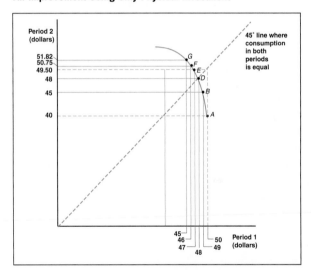

Without any physical investment in new capital in period 1 (and without international borrowing and lending), consumption in period 1 must equal production in period 1 and consumption in period 2 must equal production in period 2. Point A with 50 dollars of consumption in period 1 and 40 dollars of consumption in period 2 represents this choice. The first dollar invested in physical capital increases period 2 production and consumption by five dollars while only reducing period 1 consumption by one dollar. This decision is represented in moving from point A to point B. If a second dollar is spent on physical investment in period 1, then consumption in period 1 is 48 dollars, but consumption and production in period 2 is also 48 dollars. This is the movement from point B to point D. Further investment in period 1 continues to increase production and consumption in period 2 but only at the cost of reduced consumption in period 1. Such a decision is represented in moving from point D to points E, F, or G.

Consumption in period 1 must be reduced to allow that physical investment to take place. Most countries do have some physical investment opportunities. To continue with the Kuwait example, there may be new oilfields to discover and put into production. If more physical capital is installed in period 1, then there is more production in period 2. Investment in physical capital can also be used to equalize consumption because investment reduces consumption in period 1 and increases consumption in period 2.

Table 17A–1 shows how much extra production will occur in period 2 when different amounts of physical capital (measured in dollars) are installed in this country in period 1. This table shows that capital has decreasing returns. This assumption was also made in Chapter 14. The first dollar of new capital installed in period 1 increases period 2 output by five dollars. This is shown by moving from point A to point B in Figure 17A–2. The second dollar of new physical capital (a total of two dollars of investment spending) increases output in period 2 by three more dollars, a movement from point B to point D in Figure 17A–2. At point D, consumption in period 1 equals consumption in period 2. Both are equal to 48 dollars. Figure 17A–2 is now a bit trickier to read. From point A, as more physical capital is installed, there is less consumption in period 1. You are moving to the left from point A to keep track of the reduction in consumption. The distance left from point A measures the reduction in consumption from 50 dollars. The distance from the origin measures consumption in period 1. But there is more output and more consumption in period 2. Point D is the best choice for this country if the only available option to move consumption from period 1 to period 2 is physical investment in period 1.

We can compare Figures 17A–1 and 17A–2. Note that point D in Figure 17A–2 is clearly better than point D in Figure 17A–1. In Figure 17A–2, consumption in both periods is equal to 48 dollars. In Figure 17A–1, the equal consumption available in both periods is only 45.17 dollars. We can see why this is the case. The first dollar of investment into physical capital is much more productive (it earned five dollars) than the first dollar lent to foreigners (which only earned 1.07 dollars). Both returns are gross rates of return. The second dollar of physical investment is also more productive than a dollar lent to foreigners; it repays three dollars, the second dollar lent to foreigners pays only 1.07 dollars. For this country, it is better to use its first two dollars of physical investment opportunities than it is to lend to nonresidents. The rate of return is higher.

Let us continue in Figure 17A–2 to use physical investment opportunities to try to generate changes in consumption opportunities. If we invest a third dollar in physical capital, then period 1 consumption is 47 dollars and period 2 consumption is 49.5 dollars. This is point E. Moving from point D to point E still looks like a good rate of return on physical investment. One dollar invested in new capital yielded 1.5 dollars in period 2 income, a gross rate of return of 1.5 or a net rate of return of 50%. But we have a problem! Consumption in the two periods becomes less equal in moving from point D to point E in Figure 17A–2. In moving from point E to point F, we invest an additional dollar (the fourth dollar) in physical capital to yield a gross return of 1.25 or a net return of 25%. This seems to create more of a problem as consumption in period 1 continues to fall and consumption in period 2 continues to rise. Finally, the fifth dollar of physical capital (moving from point F to point G) yields a gross return of 1.07 or a net return of 7%. As we undertook more physical investment, at point G, with five dollars invested in physical capital, then consumption becomes more unequal. At point G period 1

| TABLE | 17A–1 | Investment and Consumption without International Borrowing |

Point in Figure 17A-2	Production in Period 1	Physical Investment in Period 1	Consumption in Period 1*	Production in Period 2	Marginal Product of Dollar of New Capital	Consumption in Period 2**
A	50	0	50	40	—	40
B	50	1	49	45	5	45
D	50	2	48	48	3	48
E	50	3	47	49.5	1.5	49.5
F	50	4	46	50.75	1.25	50.75
G	50	5	45	51.82	1.07	51.82
H	50	6	44	52.82	1	52.82

*This consumption choice in period 1 reflects the fact that if investment is increased, then consumption must decrease.

**This consumption choice in period 2 reflects the fact that production in period 2 and consumption in period 2 are identical in the absence of international borrowing and lending.

consumption is only 45 dollars (the 50 dollars in period 1 income less the five dollars invested in new physical capital) and period 2 consumption is 51.82 dollars at point G. We have failed miserably to organize the country to have equal consumption in the two periods. The best we can do, if we are only using physical investment to equalize consumption, is point D. This is quite odd: There seems to be very good investment opportunities with very high rates of return at E and F, 50% and 25%, respectively. These rates of return are much higher than the 7% rate of return on international investments available in Figure 17A–1. We return to this fact later.

We are trapped by equation (17.1), repeated:

$$I_t = S_t = Y_t - C_t \qquad (17.1)$$

Equation (17.1) says that only if we reduce consumption today can we increase investment and increase consumption tomorrow. Equation (17.1) must be true in a closed economy. But all is not lost. We are in an open economy. We learned that equation (17.3) can sidestep equation (17.1), repeated :

$$C_t + I_t = Y_t + Q_t - X_t = Y_t - NX_t \qquad (17.3)$$

Now, we can increase both consumption and investment in period 1 if we are willing to borrow from the rest of the world. Making use of international capital markets will allow us to exploit all good physical investment opportunities and equalize consumption. It will be the best of Figures 17A–1 and 17A–2.

An Improvement Using Both Physical Investment and International Borrowing and Lending

The problem with point G in Figure 17A–2 is that we have too much production and consumption in period 2 and too little consumption in period 1. This is the opposite problem to that faced at point A in Figure 17A–1, where we had too much consumption in period 1 and not enough consumption in period 2. We found that lending to the rest of the world would solve the problem in Figure 17A–1. We use that insight to solve our new problem, that of too little consumption in period 1 and too much consumption in period 2 at point G in Figure 17A–2. From point G, we need to borrow in period 1 and then repay the loan in period 2. How large a loan will exactly equalize consumption from point G in Figure 17A–2? Let the value of the borrowing in period 1 be L_G. L_G is the solution to the following equation:

$$51.82 - 1.07(L_G) = 50 - 5 + L_G$$

The left side of the equation above is consumption in period 2: production in period 2 minus the repayment of the loan. The right side is consumption in period 1: production

minus investment plus the value of the loan. The two values of consumption are set equal. Solving yields $L_G = 3.29$ dollars. Substituting that value finds $C_1 = C_2 = 48.29$. This is marked as point G^* on Figure 17A–3. This is the very best point this country can attain. How do we know this?

First, note that it is better than either point D in Figure 17A–1 or point D in Figure 17A–2. International borrowing and lending makes this country even better off. From point

An Improvement Using Both Physical Investment and International Borrowing and Lending: The Optimal Current Account Choice

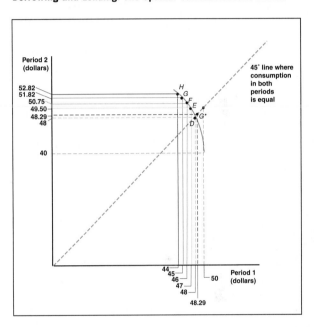

Without any physical investment in new capital in period 1 (and without international borrowing and lending), consumption in period 1 must equal production in period 1, and consumption in period 2 must equal production in period 2. Point A represents this choice. The first dollar invested (point A to point B) in physical capital increases period 2 production and consumption by 5 dollars while only reducing period 1 consumption by one dollar. The second dollar is spent on physical investment in period 1, then without international borrowing and lending) consumption in both period 1 and period 2 would be 48 dollars. This is the movement from point B to point D. Further investment in period 1 continues to increase production in period 2. The third, fourth, and fifth dollar of physical investment yield a return greater than or equal to the 7% cost of borrowing a dollar from a nonresident. Thus, if these physical investments take place, the economy moves through points E, F, and G. At G, consumption in period 1 and period 2 are not equal. However, if this economy borrows 3.29 dollars in period 1 to move itself from point G to point G*, then consumption in the two periods is equalized at 48.29 dollars. This is the best equal-consumption point available; 3.29 dollars is the optimal current account deficit.

G, point G^* is the largest amount of most equal consumption available, that is, 48.29 dollars is larger than 48 dollars. We need to "prove" that G in Figure 17A–3 is the best physical investment choice. There is a clear argument that this country should not invest in the sixth dollar of physical capital, that is, move period 2 production from point G to point H in either Figure 17A–3 or Table 17A–1. Why? One more dollar invested in physical capital from point G to point H yields a gross return of one dollar or a net return of 0%. If the country took that dollar and lent that dollar to a foreigner instead of investing in more physical capital, that dollar would earn a gross return of 1.07 dollars or a net return of 7%. Lending the extra dollar to a foreigner is better than an additional unit of physical investment. The physical investment from G to H is worse than simply lending on the international capital market. This is what Kuwait has found. Investment opportunities in other countries are better than investment opportunities in Kuwait itself. Now, consider the possibility that this country did not make the fourth dollar of investment into physical capital. That dollar earned 25% invested in physical capital but could only earn 7% invested on international markets. This is a good physical investment. You can borrow at 7% and make 25% by installing the fourth dollar of capital. Finally, the movement from F to G, the fifth dollar of investment in physical capital, is the dollar of investment that yields exactly the same rate of return, 7%, that it would earn if the dollar had been placed in the international capital market. Here, you are exactly indifferent about installing the fifth dollar of capital. We play the usual game in microeconomics. Since it does no harm to install the fifth dollar of physical capital, we do so. It is now clear that the best plan for new physical investment is to invest until the gross marginal product of capital equals the gross rate of return available on the world capital market. Point G is the best physical investment choice. It dominates both point H and point F.

Now, consider the possibility that this country will lend a dollar to a foreigner from point G. This is completely silly. Such a loan would take the country away from point G^* and make consumption in period 1 even lower and consumption in period 2 even higher. The borrowing of 3.29 dollars to move from G to G^* is the very best choice this country can make. Note that point G^* in Figure 17A–3 is actually a little bit better than point D in Figure 17A–2. At G^*, consumption in each period is 48.29 dollars. You might not think that is very much of a difference. It is "only" 0.81% more consumption in each period. But 0.81% of GDP is quite a large number, and the second period in this model represents many future periods. The movement from point D in Figure 17A–2 to point G^* in Figure 17A–3 could be a substantial improvement. The source of the improvement is due to the fact that the international capital market allowed this country to borrow at a 7% rate of interest to invest in physical capital that produced a higher than 7% rate of return. This gap between the cost of borrowing and the return on physical capital allows a little more consumption in both periods.

Putting the Analysis in the Language of the Current Account

The last step is to put the graphical analysis into the language of the current account. Using Figure 17A–3, in period 1 and working from points G and G^*:

$$Y_1 = 50 \quad C_1 = 48.29 \quad I_1 = 5$$

Thus:

$$Q_1 = Y_1 - C_1 - I_1 = CA_1 = -3.29$$

The current account deficit in period 1 is simply the trade balance because there are no initial foreign assets or debts in this example. Imports are large enough to make up for the gap between the sum of consumption and investment ($C_1 + I_1$) and production (Y_1).

In period 2:

$$Y_2 = 51.82 \quad C_2 = 48.29 \quad I_2 = 0$$

There is no physical investment in period 2 because it makes no sense to install more capital to produce output in a nonexistent third period. This is a limitation of the two-period model. The current account surplus in period 2 is:

$$X_2 + rB_1^f = 3.53 + (0.07)(-3.29) = Y_2 - C_2 = 3.29$$

Since $B_1^f = -3.29$, we can use equation (17.4) and know that the value of net foreign debt at the end of period 2 is zero. Exports (the gap between production and consumption) are large enough in period 2 to fully repay the period 1 loan with interest. The current account surplus in period 2 is exactly the correct amount to repay the optimal current account deficit in period 1.

SUMMARY

This appendix makes two points. First, with a world capital market there is an optimal amount of physical investment in an open economy. All physical investment opportunities that yield a return higher than the cost of borrowing on the world market should be undertaken. They yield a profit and add to the country's consumption opportunities. Second, after an optimal physical investment plan is identified, a country has an optimal current account deficit as well.

Given the best choice of physical investment using the rule above, a country can borrow and lend to generate a smooth or smoother consumption path. This will yield a clear value for the optimal current account deficit (or surplus) in period 1 and a plan to repay and service that debt in the future. This plan will create benefits from international borrowing and lending for all countries.

The appendix should close with both a cautionary note and a note of optimism. In the example above, the country involved repays its foreign debt smoothly. We often read of situations where this does not occur. Argentina and several other Latin American countries had difficulty repaying debts in the last decade, but there will be others because many other countries have had difficulty repaying or servicing foreign debts in the past. A failure to repay or service foreign debts is a fairly regular occurrence. The reasons are many and varied. There can be war or natural disaster. There can be fraud—it has been the case that promised physical investments in period 1 did not take place. Rather, the rulers of the country involved embezzle the international loan. There can be revolution and political turmoil. Sometimes, these events are combined together. Although the international bankruptcies make the headlines, there are many years when countries do exactly what we have described in this chapter and in this appendix. They make use of international capital markets to borrow. This allows the installation of new physical capital and the creation of future output without large reductions in current consumption. Other countries, with poorer investment opportunities at home, are happy to lend to the countries in need of such loans. Loans are smoothly repaid. This process has gone on at a large scale for the past 250 or more years all over the world. It is not likely to stop anytime in the near future.

EXTENSIONS: EXPECTATIONS

The next four chapters represent the first major extension of the core. They look at the role of expectations in fluctuations.

CHAPTER 18

Chapter 18 introduces two important tools. The first is the distinction between the real interest rate and the nominal interest rate. The second is the concept of expected present discounted value. The chapter ends by deriving and discussing the "Fisher hypothesis," the proposition that in the medium run, nominal interest rates fully reflect inflation and money growth.

CHAPTER 19

Chapter 19 focuses on the role of expectations in financial markets. It first looks at the determination of bond prices and bond yields. It shows how we can learn about the course of expected future interest rates by looking at the yield curve. It then turns to stock prices, and shows how they depend on expected future dividends and interest rates. It discusses whether stock prices always reflect fundamentals or may instead contain bubbles or fads. Expectations of future policy play a role in the determination of the exchange rate today.

CHAPTER 20

Chapter 20 focuses on the role of expectations in consumption and investment decisions. It argues that consumption depends partly on current income and partly on wealth defined as the sum of financial, housing, and human wealth—the expected present value of labour income. It argues that investment depends partly on current cash flow and partly on the expected present value of future profits.

CHAPTER 21

Chapter 21 puts the pieces together and looks at the role of expectations in fluctuations. It modifies our previous description of goods market equilibrium (the *IS* relation) to reflect the effect of expectations on spending. It then revisits the effects of monetary and fiscal policies on output. It shows, in particular, that in contrast to the results derived in the core, a fiscal contraction may increase output, even in the short run.

CHAPTER 18
EXPECTATIONS: THE BASIC TOOLS

Extensions: Expectations

The consumer considering whether to buy a new car must ask: Can I safely take a new car loan? How much of a wage raise can I expect over the next few years? How safe is my job?

The manager who observes an increase in current sales must ask: Is this a temporary boom that I should meet with the existing production capacity? Or does this upswing reflect a permanent increase in sales, in which case I should order new machines? How much additional profit can I expect if I buy a new machine?

The pension fund manager who observes a boom in the stock market must ask: Are stock prices going to increase further, or is the boom likely to fizzle? Does this increase in prices reflect expectations of higher profits by firms in the future? Do I share those expectations? Should I reallocate some of my funds between stocks and bonds?

These examples make clear that many economic decisions depend not only on what is happening today but also on expectations of what will happen in the future. Indeed, some decisions should depend very little on what is happening today. For example, why should an increase in sales today, if that increase is not accompanied by expectations of higher sales in the future, lead a firm to alter its investment plans? The new machines may not be in operation before sales have returned to normal. Till then, they might sit idle, gathering dust.

Until now, we have not paid much attention to the role of expectations in goods and financial markets. We have ignored them in our construction of both the *IS-LM* model and the aggregate demand component of the *AS-AD* model that builds on the *IS-LM*. When looking at the goods market, we assumed that consumption depended on current income and that investment depended on current sales. When looking at financial markets, we lumped assets together and called them "bonds"; we then focused on the choice between bonds and money and ignored the choice between bonds and stocks, short-term bonds and long-term bonds, and so on. Only in the foreign exchange market did the expected exchange rate next year play a role. But if next year's expected exchange rate matters, so does the expectation of the exchange rate in the following year. We ignored this. We introduced these simplifications to build the intuition for the basic mechanisms at work. It is now time to think about the role and the determination of expectations in fluctuations. This is our task in this and the next three chapters.

In this chapter, we lay the groundwork by introducing two key concepts: The first is the distinction between the *nominal* and the *real* interest rates. The second is the concept of *expected present discounted value*. We then show, in the last two sections of the chapter, how the distinction between real and nominal interest rates sheds light on the relation between interest rates and inflation in the short run and the medium run. The next three chapters build on this groundwork. Chapter 19 looks at the role of expectations in financial markets. It looks in particular at the determination of the term structure of interest rates, and the determination of stock prices. Chapter 20 looks at the role of expectations in consumption and investment decisions. Chapter 21 puts the pieces together: It extends the analysis of the *IS-LM* model we developed in the core to allow for the presence of expectations. It then takes another look at the role and the limits of policy in an economy in which expectations play a major role in affecting decisions.

18-1 | Nominal versus Real Interest Rates

In 1980, the *annual T-bill rate*—the interest rate on one-year government bonds—was 17.5%. In 2005, the annual T-bill rate was only 3%. Although most of us cannot borrow at the same interest rate as government can, the interest rates we face as consumers were also substantially lower in 2005 than in 1980. Borrowing was clearly much cheaper in 2005 than it was in 1980.

Or was it? In 1980, inflation was around 10%. In 2005, inflation was around 2%. This information would seem very relevant: The interest rate tells us how many dollars we will have to pay in the future in exchange for having one more dollar today. But we do not consume dollars; we consume goods. When we borrow, what we really want to know is how many goods we shall have to give up in the future in exchange for the goods we get today. Likewise, when we lend, we want to know how many goods—not how many dollars—we will get in the future for the goods we give up today. The presence of inflation makes the distinction important. What is the point of receiving high interest payments in the future if inflation between now and then is so high that we are able to buy only a few goods with the proceeds?

To examine this further, let us introduce two definitions. Let us refer to interest rates in terms of dollars (or, more generally, in units of the national currency) as **nominal interest rates**. The interest rates printed in the financial pages of newspapers are nominal interest rates. For example, when we say that the one-year T-bill rate is 4.5%, we mean that for every dollar that government borrows by issuing one-year T-bills, it promises to pay 1.045 dollars a year from now. More generally, if the nominal interest rate for year t is i_t, borrowing one dollar this year requires you to pay $1 + i_t$ dollars next year. This relation is represented in Figure 18–1(a): one dollar this year corresponds to $1 + i_t$ dollars next year.

Let us refer to interest rates expressed *in terms of a basket of goods* as **real interest rates**. Thus, if we denote the real interest rate for year t by r_t, then, by definition, borrowing the equivalent of one basket of goods this year requires you to pay the equivalent of $1 + r_t$ baskets of goods next year. This relation is represented in Figure 18–1(b): 1 basket of goods this year corresponds to $1 + r_t$ baskets of goods next year.

Computing the Real Interest Rate

Let us look at the relation between the nominal and the real interest rates. Suppose the nominal interest rate is i_t. What is the real interest rate r_t, and how can we construct it? To start,

> Nominal interest rate: the interest rate in terms of dollars.

> We will substitute "this year" for "today" and "next year" for "one year from today."

> Real interest rate: the interest rate in terms of a basket of goods.

FIGURE 18-1

Nominal and Real Interest Rates

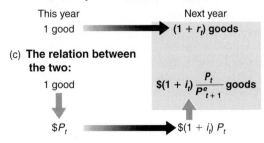

(a) Definition:
The one-year nominal interest rate

This year   Next year
$1 ⟶ $(1 + i_t)

(b) Definition:
The one-year real interest rate

This year   Next year
1 good ⟶ $(1 + r_t)$ **goods**

(c) **The relation between the two:**

1 good $(1 + i_t) \dfrac{P_t}{P^e_{t+1}}$ **goods**

P_t ⟶ $(1 + i_t) P_t$

assume there is only one good in the economy, say, bread (we will add jam and other goods later). If you borrow enough to eat one more kilogram of bread this year, how much will you have to repay, in terms of kilograms of bread, next year?

Figure 18–1(c) helps us derive the answer.

- If the price of a kilogram of bread this year is P_t dollars, to eat one more kilogram of bread, you must borrow P_t dollars. This is represented by the arrow pointing down in Figure 18–1(c).
- Let i_t be the one-year nominal interest rate, the interest rate in terms of dollars. If you borrow P_t dollars, you will have to repay $(1 + i_t)P_t$ dollars next year. This is represented by the arrow from left to right at the bottom of Figure 18–1(c).
- What you care about is not dollars, but kilograms of bread. Thus, the last step involves converting dollars to kilograms of bread next year. Let P^e_{t+1} be the price of bread you expect for next year. (The superscript "e" indicates this is an expectation: You do not know yet what the price of bread will be next year.) How much you expect to repay next year, in terms of kilograms of bread, is therefore equal to $(1 + i_t)P_t/P^e_{t+1}$. This is represented by the arrow pointing up in Figure 18–1(c).

Putting together parts (b) and (c) of Figure 18–1, it follows that one plus the one-year real interest rate, r_t, is defined by:

$$1 + r_t = (1 + i_t) \frac{P_t}{P^e_{t+1}} \tag{18.1}$$

This looks intimidating. Two simple manipulations make it look friendlier.

Denote expected inflation by π^e_t. Given there is only one good—bread—the expected rate of inflation equals the expected change in the dollar price of bread between this year and next year, divided by the dollar price of bread this year:

$$\pi^e_t = \frac{(P^e_{t+1} - P_t)}{P_t} \tag{18.2}$$

Using equation (18.2), rewrite P_t/P^e_{t+1} in equation (18.1) as $1/(1 + \pi^e_t)$. Replace in (18.1) to get:

$$(1 + r_t) = \frac{1 + i_t}{1 + \pi^e_t} \tag{18.3}$$

One plus the real interest rate equals the ratio of one plus the nominal interest rate, divided by one plus the expected rate of inflation.

Add one to both sides in equation (18.2):

$$1 + \pi^e_t = 1 + \frac{(P^e_{t+1} - P_t)}{P_t}$$

Reorganize:

$$1 + \pi^e_t = \frac{P^e_{t+1}}{P_t}$$

Take the inverse on both sides:

$$\frac{1}{1 + \pi^e_t} = \frac{P_t}{P^e_{t+1}}$$

Replace in (18.1):

$$1 + r_t \equiv \frac{1 + i_t}{1 + \pi^e_t}$$

Equation (18.3) gives us the *exact* definition of the real interest rate. However, when the nominal rate and expected inflation are not too large—say, less than 20% per year—a close approximation to this equation is given by the simpler relation:

$$r_t = i_t - \pi_t^e \qquad (18.4)$$

Equation (18.4) is simple, and you should remember it. It says that *the real interest rate is (approximately) equal to the nominal interest rate minus expected inflation*. It has several implications:

- When expected inflation equals zero, the nominal and the real interest rates are equal.
- Because expected inflation is typically positive, the real interest rate is typically lower than the nominal interest rate.
- For a given nominal interest rate, the higher the expected rate of inflation, the lower is the real interest rate.

The case where expected inflation happens to be equal to the nominal rate is worth looking at more closely. Suppose the nominal interest rate and expected inflation both equal 10%, and you are the borrower. For every dollar you borrow, you will have to repay 1.10 dollars next year, but dollars will be worth 10% less in terms of goods next year. Thus, if you borrow the equivalent of one good, you will have to repay the equivalent of one good next year: The real cost of borrowing—the real interest rate—is equal to zero. Now, suppose you are the lender: For every dollar you lend, you will receive 1.10 dollars next year. This looks attractive, but dollars next year will be worth 10% less in terms of goods. If you lend the equivalent of one good, you will get the equivalent of one good next year: Despite a 10% nominal interest rate, the real interest rate is equal to zero.

We have assumed so far that there was only one good, bread. But what we have done generalizes easily. All we need to do is to substitute the *price level*—the price of a basket of goods—for the price of bread. If we use the consumer price index (the CPI) to measure the price level, the real interest rate tells us how much consumption we must give up next year in order to consume more today.

Nominal and Real Interest Rates in Canada since 1975

Let us return to the question with which we started this section. We can now restate it as follows: Was the *real interest rate* lower in 2005 than it was in 1980? More generally, what has happened to the real interest rate in Canada since 1975?

The answer is given in Figure 18–2, which plots both nominal and real interest rates since 1975. For each year, the nominal interest rate is the one-year T-bill rate at the beginning of the year. To construct the real interest rate, we need a measure for expected inflation—more precisely, the rate of inflation expected as of the beginning of each year. The source line for Figure 18–2 gives details. Here, expected inflation in the next calendar year is the average forecast over a group of private-sector forecasters. These forecasters were surveyed by three different firms over the period 1975–2005.

Figure 18–2 shows how important the adjustment for expected inflation is. The nominal interest rate in 1980 was 17.5%. It fell to 5.9% in the year 2000 and to 2.5% in 2005. Both are annual averages of daily rates. However, the measure of the real rate of interest in Figure 18–2 fell from 6.9% in 1980 to 3.7% in the year 2000 to 1% in 2005. The much smaller decline in real rates follows from the fact that both inflation and expected inflation have steadily declined since the early 1980s.

18-2 | Expected Present Discounted Values

Let us now turn to the second key concept we introduce in this chapter, that of expected present discounted value.

This approximation is derived in proposition 6, Appendix 2. To see how close the approximation is, suppose the nominal interest rate is 10% and expected inflation is 5%. Using the exact formula (18.3) gives $r_t = 4.8\%$. The approximation given by equation (18.4) is 5%, which is close enough. The approximation is not nearly as good when nominal interest rates and expected inflation are very high, say, equal to 100% and 80% respectively—the exact formula gives a real interest rate of 11%, whereas the approximation yields 20%.

The real interest rate $(i - \pi^e)$ is based on expected inflation, not actual inflation. If actual inflation turns out to be different from expected inflation, the realized real interest rate $(i - \pi)$ will turn out to be different from the real interest rate.

To reflect this distinction, the real interest rate is sometimes called the *ex-ante* real interest rate ("*ex-ante*" means "before the fact"; here, before inflation is known), and the realized real interest rate is called the *ex-post* real interest rate ("*ex-post*" means "after the fact"; here, after inflation is known).

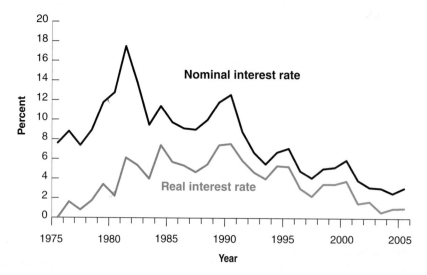

FIGURE 18–2

Nominal and Real T-Bill Rates in Canada, 1975–2004

Although both nominal and real interest rates declined from peaks in 1980 and 1990, the decline in nominal interest rates has been much larger than the decline in expected inflation. Real interest rates in 2003 and 2004 were quite low.

Sources: The *nominal interest rate* plotted from 1975–1986 is the six-month T-bill rate using CANSIM II, variable V122552; after 1987, the nominal interest rate is the one-year T-bill rate using CANSIM, variable V122498. The *real rate* is the nominal rate minus expected inflation. In 1984–2000, expected inflation is the average next-year inflation rate from Consensus Forecast. In 1975–1983, expected inflation is the average next-year forecast from the Conference Board of Canada Survey of Forecasters. From 2001–2005, expected inflation is the average forecast reported in the January issue of *The Economist* in that year.

To see why this concept is helpful, let us return to the example of the manager considering whether to buy a new machine. On the one hand, buying and installing the machine involves a cost today. On the other, the machine allows for higher production, higher sales, and thus higher profits in the future. The question facing the manager is whether the value of these expected profits is higher than the cost of buying and installing the machine. This is where the concept of expected present discounted value comes in handy: The **expected present discounted value** of a sequence of future payments is the value today of this expected sequence of payments. Once the manager has computed the expected present discounted value of the sequence of profits, her problem becomes simple. If this value exceeds the initial cost, she should go ahead and buy the machine. If it does not, she should not.

As in the case of the real interest rate in section 18-1, the practical problem is that expected present discounted values are not directly observable. They must be constructed from information on the sequence of expected payments and interest rates. Let us first look at the mechanics of construction.

Computing Expected Present Discounted Values

If the one-year nominal interest rate is i_t, lending one dollar this year yields $1 + i_t$ dollars next year. Equivalently, borrowing one dollar this year implies paying back $1 + i_t$ dollars next year. In that sense, one dollar this year is worth $1 + i_t$ dollars next year. This relation is represented graphically in Figure 18–3(a).

Turn the argument around and ask: One dollar *next year* is worth how many dollars this year? The answer, shown in Figure 18–3(b), is $1/(1 + i_t)$ dollars. Think of it this way: If you lend $1/(1 + i_t)$ dollars this year, you will receive $1/(1 + i_t) \times (1 + i_t) = 1$ dollar next year. Equivalently, if you borrow $1/(1 + i_t)$ dollars this year, you will have to repay exactly one dollar next year.

Thus, one dollar next year is worth $1/(1 + i_t)$ dollars this year. More formally, we say that $1/(1 + i_t)$ is the *present discounted value* of one dollar next year. The term "present" comes from the fact that we are looking at the value of a payment next year in terms of dollars *today*. The term "discounted" comes from the fact that the value next year is discounted, with $1/(1 + i_t)$ being the **discount factor** (the one-year nominal interest rate, i_t,

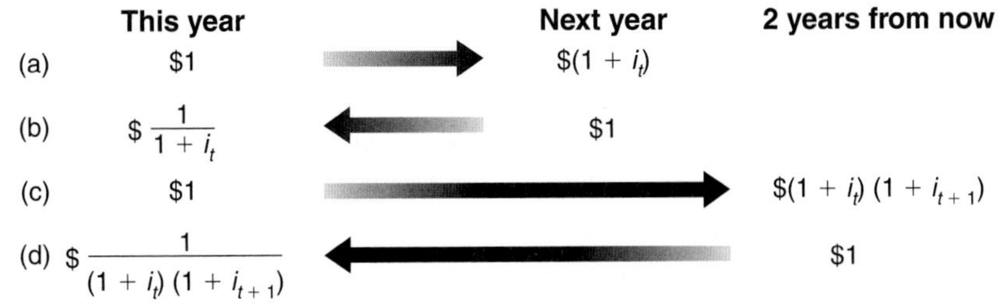

FIGURE 18-3

	This year		Next year	2 years from now
(a)	$1	→→→	$(1 + i_t)	
(b)	$\dfrac{1}{1 + i_t}$	←←←	$1	
(c)	$1	→→→		$(1 + i_t)(1 + i_{t+1})$
(d)	$\dfrac{1}{(1 + i_t)(1 + i_{t+1})}$	←←←		$1

Computing Present Discounted Values

is sometimes called the **discount rate**). Note that because the nominal interest rate is always positive, the discount factor is always less than 1: A dollar next year is worth less than a dollar this year. The higher the nominal interest rate, the lower is the value this year of a dollar next year. If $i = 5\%$, the value this year of a dollar next year is $1/1.05 \approx 95$ cents. If $i = 10\%$, the value this year of a dollar next year is $1/1.10 \approx 91$ cents.

Now, apply the same logic to the value this year of a dollar two years from now. For the moment, assume that current and future one-year nominal interest rates are known with certainty. Let i_t be the nominal interest rate for this year, and i_{t+1} be the one-year nominal interest rate next year.

If you lend one dollar for two years, you will get $(1 + i_t)(1 + i_{t+1})$ dollars two years from now. Put another way, one dollar this year is worth $(1 + i_t)(1 + i_{t+1})$ dollars two years from now. This relation is represented in Figure 18–3(c).

What is one dollar two years from now worth this year? By the same logic as before, the answer is $1/[(1 + i_t)(1 + i_{t+1})]$ dollars: If you lend $1/[(1 + i_t)(1 + i_{t+1})]$ dollars this year, you will get exactly one dollar in two years. More formally, the *present discounted value of a dollar two years from now* is equal to $1/[(1 + i_t)(1 + i_{t+1})]$ dollars. This relation is shown in Figure 18–3(d). If, for example, the one-year nominal interest rate is the same this year and next, and equal to 5%, so $i_t = i_{t+1} = 5\%$, then the present value of a dollar in two years is equal to $1/(1.05)^2$ or about 91 cents this year.

A General Formula. Having gone through these steps, it is easy to derive the present discounted value for the general case.

Consider a sequence of payments in dollars, now and in the future. Assume for the moment that these future payments are known with certainty. Denote the current payment by z_t, the payment next year by z_{t+1}, the payment two years from now by z_{t+2}, and so on.

The present discounted value of this sequence of payments—the value in this year's dollars of the sequence of payments, which we shall call V_t—is given by:

$$V_t = z_t + \frac{1}{(1 + i_t)} z_{t+1} + \frac{1}{(1 + i_t)(1 + i_{t+1})} z_{t+2} + \cdots$$

Each payment in the future is multiplied by its respective discount factor. The more distant the payment, the smaller is the discount factor, and thus the smaller the value of the payment this year. In other words, future payments are discounted more heavily, so their present value is lower.

We have assumed so far that both future payments and future interest rates were known with certainty. Actual decisions, however, have to be based on expectations of future payments rather than on actual values for these payments. In our earlier example, the manager cannot be sure of how much profit the new machine will actually bring; nor can she be sure of what interest rates will be. The best she can do is to get the best forecasts she can, and then compute the *expected present discounted value* of profits, based on these forecasts.

How do we compute the expected present discounted value when future payments or interest rates are uncertain? Basically in the same way as before, but replacing the *known* future payments and *known* interest rates in the expression above by *expected* future

Discount rate: i_t

Discount factor: $1/(1 + i_t)$

◄ If the discount rate goes up, the discount factor goes down.

payments and *expected* interest rates.[1] Formally, denote expected payments next year by $\$z_{t+1}^e$, expected payments two years from now by $\$z_{t+2}^e$, and so on. Similarly, denote the expected one-year nominal interest rate next year by i_{t+1}^e, and so on (the one-year nominal interest rate this year, i_t, is known today, so it does not need a superscript "e"). The expected present discounted value of this expected sequence of payments is given by:

$$\$V_t = \$z_t + \frac{1}{(1 + i_t)}\,\$z_{t+1}^e + \frac{1}{(1 + i_t)(1 + i_{t+1}^e)}\,\$z_{t+2}^e + \cdots \tag{18.5}$$

"Expected present discounted value" is a heavy expression to carry; we will often use, for short, just **present value**. Also, it will be convenient to have a shorthand way of writing equations, such as equation (18.5). To denote the present value of an expected sequence for $\$z$, we will write $V(\$z_t)$, or just $V(\$z)$.

Using Present Values: Examples

Equation (18.5) has two important implications:

$\$z$ or future $\$z^e \uparrow \Rightarrow V\uparrow$ ▶ ● The present value depends positively on current and expected future payments. An increase in either $\$z$ or any future $\$z^e$ leads to an increase in the present value.

i or future $i^e \uparrow \Rightarrow V\downarrow$ ▶ ● The present value depends negatively on current and expected future interest rates. An increase in either i or in any future i^e leads to a decrease in the present value.

Equation (18.5) is not simple, however, and intuition for these effects is best built by going through some examples.

Constant Interest Rates. To focus on the effects of the sequence of payments on the present value, assume that interest rates are expected to be constant over time so that $i_t = i_{t+1}^e = \ldots$, and denote their common value by i. The present value formula—equation (18.5)—becomes:

$$\$V_t = \$z_t + \frac{1}{(1 + i)}\,\$z_{t+1}^e + \frac{1}{(1 + i)^2}\,\$z_{t+2}^e + \cdots \tag{18.6}$$

The weights correspond to the terms of a geometric series. See geometric series in Appendix 2. ▶ In this case, the present value is a *weighted sum* of current and expected future payments: The weights decline *geometrically* through time. The weight on a payment this year is 1, the weight on the payment n years from now is $[1/(1 + i)]^n$. With a positive interest rate, the weights get closer and closer to zero as we look further and further into the future. For example, with an interest rate equal to 10%, the weight on a payment in 10 years is equal to $1/(1 + 0.10)^{10} = 0.386$ so that a payment of $1000 in 10 years is worth $386 this year; the weight on a payment in 30 years is $1/(1 + 0.10)^{30} = 0.057$ so that a payment of $1000 in 30 years is worth only $57 this year!

Constant Interest Rates and Payments. In some cases, the sequence of payments for which we want to compute the present value is simple. For example, a fixed-rate 30-year mortgage requires constant dollar payments over 30 years. Consider a sequence of equal payments—

---

[1]**DIGGING DEEPER.** This statement glosses over a difficult issue. If people dislike risk, the value of a risky payment, now or in the future, will be lower than that of a riskless payment, even if both have the same expected value. We will ignore this effect here, assuming implicitly that people in the economy are **risk neutral** (they are indifferent to risk). Studying what happens when people are **risk averse** (when they dislike risk) would take us too far afield. It would require a whole course, namely, a course in finance theory.

call them z without a time index—over n years including the current year. In this case, the present value formula in equation (18.6) simplifies to:

$$\$V_t = \$z \left[1 + \frac{1}{(1 + i)} + \cdots + \frac{1}{(1 + i)^{n-1}} \right]$$

Because the terms in the expression in brackets represent a geometric series, we can compute the sum of the series and get:

$$\$V_t = \$z \frac{1 - [1/(1 + i)^n]}{1 - [1/(1 + i)]}$$

By now, geometric series should not hold any secret, and you should have no problem deriving this relation. But if you do, see Appendix 2.

Suppose you have just won a million dollars in the lottery and have been presented with a two-metre-long $1,000,000 cheque on TV. Afterwards, you are told that to protect you from your worst spending instincts as well as from your many new "friends," the province will pay you the million dollars in equal yearly instalments of $50,000 over the next 20 years. What is the present value of your prize? Taking, for example, an interest rate of 6%, the equation above gives $V = \$50{,}000\ (0.688)/(0.057) = $ or about $608,000. Not bad, but winning the prize did not make you a millionaire.

What is the present value if i equals 4%? 8%? (Answers: $706,000; $530,000)

Constant Interest Rates and Payments, Going on Forever. Let us go one step further and assume that payments are not only constant but also go on forever. Real world examples are harder to come by for this case, but one comes from nineteenth-century England, when government issued *consols*, bonds paying a fixed yearly amount forever. In Canada, the Canadian Pacific Railway issued similar consols for a period of time. These bonds were repurchased and retired by the company. Let z be the constant payment. Assume that payments start next year rather than right away as in the previous example (this makes for simpler algebra). From equation (18.6), we have:

Many consols were bought back by the British government at the end of the nineteenth and early twentieth centuries. But some are still around.

$$\$V_t = \frac{1}{(1 + i)} \$z + \frac{1}{(1 + i)^2} \$z + \cdots$$

$$= \frac{1}{(1 + i)} \left[1 + \frac{1}{(1 + i)} + \cdots \right] \$z$$

where the second line follows by factoring out $1/(1 + i)$. The reason for factoring out $1/(1 + i)$ should be clear from looking at the term in brackets: It is an infinite geometric sum, so we can use the property of geometric sums to rewrite the present value as:

$$\$V_t = \frac{1}{1 + i} \frac{1}{(1 - [1/(1 + i)])} \$z$$

Or simplifying (the steps are given in the application of proposition 2 in Appendix 2):

$$\$V_t = \frac{\$z}{i}$$

The present value of a constant sequence of payments z is equal to the ratio of z to the interest rate i. If, for example, the interest rate is expected to be 5% forever, the present value of a consol that promises $10 per year forever equals $10/0.05 = $200. If the interest rate increases and is now expected to be 10% forever, the present value of the consol decreases to $10/0.10 = $100.

Zero Interest Rates. Because of discounting, computing present discounted values typically requires the use of a calculator. There is, however, a special case worth keeping in mind where computations simplify. This is the case where the interest rate is equal to zero. Because the interest rate is, in fact, positive, this is only an approximation, but it is a very useful one

How bad an approximation it is depends on how far the interest rate is from zero. Go back to the lottery example. The sum of payments is $1,000,000. If the interest rate is 1%, the present value of payments is $911,000. The approximation is not too bad. If the interest rate is 2%, the expected present value is $834,000. The approximation quickly gets worse.

for back-of-the-envelope computations. The reason is obvious from equation (18.6): If $i = 0$, then $1/(1 + i)$ equals 1, and so does $1/(1 + i)^n$ for any power n. For that reason, the present discounted value of a sequence of expected payments at zero interest rate is then just the *sum* of those expected payments.

Nominal versus Real Interest Rates, and Present Values

We have so far computed the present value of a sequence of dollar payments by using interest rates in terms of dollars—nominal interest rates. Specifically, we have written equation (18.5):

$$\$V_t = \$z_t + \frac{1}{(1 + i_t)} \$z_{t+1}^e + \frac{1}{(1 + i_t)(1 + i_{t+1}^e)} \$z_{t+2}^e + \cdots$$

where i_t, i_{t+1}^e, $\ldots$ is the sequence of current and expected future nominal interest rates, and $\$z_t$, $\$z_{t+1}^e$, $\$z_{t+2}^e$, $\ldots$ is the sequence of current and expected future dollar payments.

Suppose we want to compute instead the present value of a sequence of *real* payments, that is, payments in terms of a basket of goods rather than in terms of dollars. Following the same logic as before, what we need to do is to use the right interest rates for this case, namely, interest rates in terms of the basket of goods—*real interest rates*. Specifically, we can write the present value of a sequence of real payments as:

$$V_t = z_t + \frac{1}{(1 + r_t)} z_{t+1}^e + \frac{1}{(1 + r_t)(1 + r_{t+1}^e)} z_{t+2}^e + \cdots \tag{18.7}$$

where r_t, r_{t+1}^e, $\ldots$ is the sequence of current and expected future real interest rates, z_t, z_{t+1}^e, z_{t+2}^e, $\ldots$ is the sequence of current and expected future real payments, and $V_t \equiv \$V_t/P_t$ is the real present value of future payments.

The proof that they are equivalent is given in the appendix to this chapter. Go through it to test your understanding of the two tools introduced in this chapter: real versus nominal rates, and expected present values.

These two ways of writing the present value are equivalent. That is, we can compute the present value as (1) the present value of the sequence of payments expressed in dollars, discounted using nominal interest rates, or (2) the present value of payments expressed in real terms, discounted using real interest rates.

Do we need both formulas? Yes. Which one is more helpful depends on the context. Take bonds, for example. Bonds typically are claims to a sequence of nominal payments over a period of years. For example, a 10-year bond may promise $50 a year for 10 years, plus a final payment of $1000 in the last year. So, when we look at the pricing of bonds in Chapter 19, we shall rely on equation (18.5) rather than on equation (18.7).

But sometimes, we have a better sense of future expected real values than of future expected dollar values. You may have little idea of what your dollar income will be in 20 years: Its value depends very much on what happens to inflation between now and then. But you may be confident that your nominal income will increase at least as much as inflation—equivalently, that your real income will not decrease. In this case, using equation (18.5), which requires you to form expectations of future dollar income, may be difficult; using equation (18.7), which requires you to form expectations of future real income, will be easier. For that reason, when we discuss consumption and investment decisions in Chapter 20, we will rely on equation (18.7) rather than on equation (18.5).

18-3 | Nominal and Real Interest Rates, and the IS-LM Model

In the next three chapters, using the tools we have just developed, we will explore the role of expectations in determining activity. In the rest of this chapter, we take a first step, introducing the distinction between real and nominal interest rates in the *IS-LM* model, and then exploring the relation among money growth, inflation, and real and nominal interest rates.

In the *IS-LM* model we developed in the core (Chapter 5), the interest rate entered in two places: It affected investment in the *IS* relation, and it affected the choice between money and bonds in the *LM* relation. Which interest rate—nominal or real—were we talking about in each case?

Take the *IS* relation first. Our discussion earlier in this chapter should make it clear that in deciding how much investment to undertake, firms care about the *real interest rate*: Firms produce goods. They want to know how much they will have to repay, not in terms of dollars but in terms of goods. So, what belongs in the *IS* relation is the real interest rate. Let *r* denote the real interest rate. The *IS* relation therefore must be rewritten as:

$$Y = C(Y - T) + I(Y, r) + G$$

Investment spending, and thus the demand for goods, depends on the real interest rate.

Now, turn to the *LM* relation. In deriving the *LM* relation, we argued that the demand for money depends on the interest rate. Were we referring to the nominal interest rate or the real interest rate?

The answer is the *nominal interest rate*. Remember why the interest rate affects the demand for money. When thinking about whether to hold money or bonds, people take into account the opportunity cost of holding money rather than bonds—what they give up by holding money rather than bonds. Money pays a zero nominal interest rate. Bonds pay a nominal interest rate of *i*. Hence, the opportunity cost of holding money is equal to the difference between the two interest rates, $i - 0 = i$, which is just the nominal interest rate. Therefore, the *LM* relation is still given by:

$$\frac{M}{P} = YL(i)$$

Collecting the two equations and the relation between the real and the nominal interest rates, the extended *IS-LM* model is given by:

IS: $\qquad Y = C(Y - T) + I(Y, r) + G$

LM: $\qquad M/P = Y L(i)$

Real interest rate: $\quad r \approx i - \pi^e$

Note an immediate implication of these three equations. The interest rate directly affected by monetary policy (the interest rate that enters the *LM* equation) is the nominal interest rate. The interest rate that affects spending and output (the rate that enters the *IS* relation) is the real interest rate. The effects of monetary policy on output therefore depend on the relation between the movements in the nominal interest rate and the real interest rate. To explore this implication further, the next section looks at the effects of an increase in money growth on the nominal interest rate and the real interest rate, both in the short run and in the medium run.

> We will ignore time subscripts here; they are not needed for the rest of the chapter.

> Interest rate in the *IS* relation: Real interest rate, *r*
> Interest rate in the *LM* relation: Nominal interest rate, *i*

18-4 | Money Growth, Inflation, and Nominal and Real Interest Rates

The Bank of Canada's decision to allow for higher money growth is the main factor behind the decline in interest rates in the last six months.
(Imaginary quote, circa 2001)

The nomination of David Dodge as Governor of the Bank of Canada, perceived to be softer on inflation than an appointment from inside the Bank of Canada, has led financial markets to worry about higher money growth, higher inflation, and higher interest rates in the future.
(Imaginary quote, circa 2001)

▶

These two quotes are made up, but they are composites of what was written at the time. Which one is correct? Does higher money growth lead to lower interest rates, or does it lead to higher interest rates? The answer is: Both! There are two keys to this answer. The first is the distinction we just introduced between the real and the nominal interest rates. The second is the distinction we developed in the core between the short run and the medium run. As we shall see, the full answer is:

- Higher money growth leads to lower nominal interest rates in the short run but to higher nominal interest rates in the medium run.
- Higher money growth leads to lower real interest rates in the short run but has no effect on real interest rates in the medium run.

The purpose of this section is to develop this answer and draw its implications.

Nominal and Real Interest Rates in the Short Run

We could eliminate the nominal interest rate and keep the real interest rate. r would enter the IS relation; $(r + \pi^e)$ would enter the LM relation. The graphical analysis would look a bit different, but the conclusions would be the same. ▶

To look at the short run, it is convenient to reduce the three equations we derived in the last section—the IS relation, the LM relation, and the relation between the real and the nominal interest rates—to two, by replacing the real interest rate in the IS relation by the nominal interest rate minus expected inflation. This gives

$$IS: \quad Y = C(Y - T) + I(Y, i - \pi^e) + G$$

$$LM: \quad M/P = Y L(i)$$

These two equations are the same as in Chapter 5, with just one difference: Spending in the IS relation depends on the real interest rate, which is equal to the nominal interest rate minus expected inflation.

If $r = i - \pi^e$, then
$$\Delta r = \Delta i - \Delta \pi^e.$$
If π^e is constant,
$$\Delta \pi^e = 0,$$
so,
$$\Delta r = \Delta i.$$

▶

The associated IS and LM curves are drawn in Figure 18–4, for given values of P, M, π^e, G, and T.

- For a given expected rate of inflation (π^e), the nominal interest rate and the real interest rate move together. Hence, a decrease in the nominal interest rate implies an equal decrease in the real interest rate, leading to an increase in spending and in output: The IS curve is downward sloping.

FIGURE 18–4

Equilibrium Output and Interest Rates

The equilibrium level of output and the equilibrium nominal interest rate are given by the intersection of the IS and the LM curves. The real interest rate equals the nominal interest rate minus expected inflation.

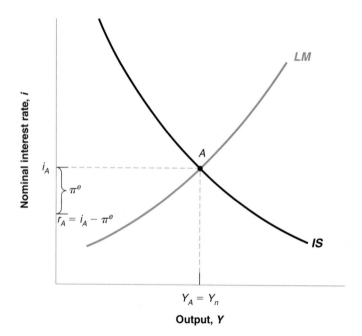

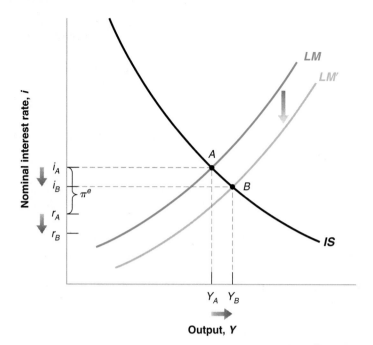

FIGURE 18–5

The Short-Run Effects of an Increase in Money Growth

An increase in money growth increases the real money stock in the short run. This increase in real money leads to an increase in output and a decrease in both the nominal and the real interest rates.

- The *LM* curve is upward sloping: An increase in output leads to an increase in the demand for money, putting pressure on the nominal interest rate.
- The equilibrium is at the intersection of the *IS* and *LM* curves, point *A*, with output level Y_A, nominal interest rate i_A. Given the nominal interest rate i_A the real interest rate r_A is given by $r_A = i_A - \pi^e$.

Assume the economy initially is at the natural level of output, so $Y_A = Y_n$. Now, suppose that the central bank increases the rate of growth of money. What happens to output, to the nominal interest rate, and to the real interest rate in the short run?

One of the lessons from our analysis of monetary policy in the core is that in the short run, the faster increase in nominal money will not be matched by an equal increase in the price level. In other words, the higher rate of growth of nominal money will lead, in the short run, to an increase in the real money stock, (*M/P*). This is all we need to know for our purposes. What happens to output and to interest rates in the short run is shown in Figure 18–5.

The increase in the real money stock leads to a downward shift in the *LM* curve, from *LM* to *LM'*: For a given level of output, the increase in the real money stock leads to a decrease in the nominal interest rate. The *IS* curve does not shift: Given expected inflation, a given nominal interest rate corresponds to the same real interest rate and to the same level of spending and output. The equilibrium moves from *A* to *B*: Output is higher. The nominal interest rate is lower, and given expected inflation, so is the real interest rate.

To summarize: In the short run, the increase in nominal money growth leads to an increase in the real money stock. This increase in real money leads to an increase in output, and to a decrease in both the nominal and the real interest rates.[2] Return to our first quote: The goal of the Bank of Canada in the fall of 2001 and through 2002 was precisely to achieve

In the short run, when the rate of money growth increases, *M/P* increases. Both *i* and *r* decrease.

[2]**DIGGING DEEPER.** Even in the short run, there may be a second effect at work—in addition to the increase in *M/P*. As money growth increases, so does inflation—although, initially, by less than money growth. As inflation increases, expected inflation may also increase. The implications of an increase in expected inflation are explored in problem 8 at the end of the chapter. In short, the increase in expected inflation leads to an even larger decrease in the real interest rate in the short run.

this outcome. Worried that the recession might get worse, the Bank of Canada increased money growth in order to decrease the real interest rate and increase output.

Nominal and Real Interest Rates in the Medium Run

Turn now to the medium run. Suppose the central bank increases the rate of money growth permanently. What will happen to output, nominal, and real interest rates in the medium run?

To answer that question, we rely on two of the central propositions we derived in the core. The two propositions were derived in a model that did not make a distinction between real and nominal rates, but they still hold here:

In the medium run: $Y = Y_n$ ▶
- In the medium run, output returns to its natural level.

    As we saw in Chapter 9, this is because in the medium run, the unemployment rate must return to the natural unemployment rate. The natural level of output is simply the level of output associated with the natural unemployment rate.

    Although we spent chapters 14 to 17 looking at growth of output over time, we will, for simplicity, ignore output growth here. Thus, we will assume that Y_n, the natural level of output, is constant over time.

- In the medium run, the rate of inflation is equal to the rate of money growth minus the rate of growth of output.

    We derived this conclusion in Chapter 12. The intuition for it is simple: A growing level of output implies a growing level of transactions and thus a growing demand for real money. If output is growing at 3%, the real money stock must also grow at 3% per year. If the nominal money stock grows at a rate different from 3%, the difference must show up in inflation (or deflation). For example, if nominal money growth is 10%, then inflation must be equal to 7%.

In the medium run,
(if $g_y = 0$) $\pi = g_m$ ▶

    If, as we assume here, output growth is equal to zero, this proposition takes an even simpler form: In the medium run, the rate of inflation is equal to the rate of nominal money growth.

The implications of these two propositions for the behaviour of the real and the nominal interest rates in the medium run are then straightforward:

- Take the real interest rate first. For convenience, let us rewrite the *IS* equation:

$$Y = C(Y - T) + I(Y, r) + G$$

    One way of thinking about the *IS* relation is that it tells us, for given values of G and T, what real interest rate r is needed to sustain a given level of spending, and so a given level of output Y. If, for example, output is equal to its natural level Y_n, then, for given values of G and T, the real interest rate must be such that:

$$Y_n = C(Y_n - T) + I(Y_n, r) + G$$

    By analogy with our use of the word "natural" to denote the level of output in the medium run, call this value of the real interest rate the *natural real interest rate*, and denote it by r_n. Then, our earlier proposition that in the medium run, output returns to its natural level Y_n, has a direct implication: For given G and T, in the medium run, the real interest rate returns to the natural interest rate, r_n. In other words, in the medium run, both output *and* the real interest rate are unaffected by the rate of money growth.

- Turn to the nominal interest rate. Recall the relation between the nominal and the real interest rate:

$$i = r + \pi^e$$

    We have just seen that in the medium run, the real interest rate equals the natural interest rate, r_n. This means:

$$i = r_n + \pi^e$$

In the medium run, expected inflation is equal to actual inflation (people do not have incorrect expectations of inflation forever), so:

$$i = r_n + \pi$$

In the medium run, inflation is equal to money growth (recall we are assuming that the rate of growth of output equals zero), so:

$$i = r_n + g_m$$

In words: In the medium run, an increase in money growth leads to an equal increase in the nominal interest rate.

To summarize: In the medium run, money growth does not affect the real interest rate but affects both inflation and the nominal interest rate one for one. A permanent increase in nominal money growth of, say, 10%, is eventually reflected in a 10% increase in the inflation rate and a 10% increase in the nominal interest rate—leaving the real interest rate unchanged.

The result that in the medium run, nominal interest rates increase one for one with inflation is known as the **Fisher effect**, or the **Fisher hypothesis**, after Irving Fisher, an economist at Yale University, who first stated it at the beginning of the twentieth century. This result underlies the second quote at the beginning of the section: If financial investors were, indeed, worried that replacing John Crow as Governor of the Bank of Canada in 1994 might lead to higher money growth, they were right to expect higher nominal interest rates in the future.

Irving Fisher, *The Rate of Interest* (New York: Macmillan, 1906).

In this case, their fears turned out to be unfounded. The Bank of Canada remained committed to low inflation throughout the 1990s.

From the Short Run to the Medium Run

We have now shown how to reconcile the two quotes at the beginning of the section: An increase in monetary growth (a monetary expansion) is likely to lead to a *decrease* in nominal interest rates in the short run but to an *increase* in nominal interest rates in the medium run.

What happens between the short run and the medium run? A complete characterization of the movements of real and nominal interest rates over time would take us beyond what we can do here. But the basic features of the adjustment process are easy to describe.

In the short run, real and nominal interest rates go down. Why don't they stay down forever? As long as the real interest rate is below the natural real interest rate (the value corresponding to the natural level of output), output is higher than the natural level. Equivalently, unemployment is below the natural rate. From the Phillips curve relation, we know that as long as unemployment is below the natural rate, inflation increases.

In the short run: $i \downarrow r \downarrow$

$$r < r_n \Rightarrow Y > Y_n$$
$$Y > Y_n \Rightarrow u < u_n$$
$$u < u_n \Rightarrow \pi \uparrow$$

As inflation increases, it eventually becomes higher than nominal money growth, leading to negative real money growth. When real money growth turns negative, the nominal interest rate starts increasing. And, given expected inflation, so does the real interest rate.

Over time: $\pi \uparrow$
Eventually $\pi > g_m'$
$$g_m' - \pi < 0 \Rightarrow i \uparrow$$

In the medium run, the real interest rate increases back to its initial value. Output is then back to its natural level, unemployment is back to its natural rate, and inflation is no longer changing. As the real interest rate converges back to its initial value, the nominal interest rate converges to a new higher value, equal to the real interest rate plus the new, higher rate of nominal money growth.

In the medium run:

$$r = r_n$$
$$Y = Y_n,$$
$$u = u_n, \pi \text{ constant}$$
$$\pi = g_m'$$
$$i = r_n + g_m'$$

Figure 18–6 summarizes these results by showing the adjustment over time of the real and the nominal interest rates to an increase in nominal money growth from, say, 0% to 10%, starting at time *t*. Before time *t*, both interest rates are constant and equal to each other. The real interest rate is equal to r_n. The nominal interest rate is also equal to r_n (as inflation and expected inflation are equal to zero).

At time *t*, the rate of money growth increases from 0% to 10%. The increase in the rate of nominal money growth leads, for some time, to an increase in real money and to a decrease in the nominal interest rate. As expected inflation increases, the decrease in the real interest rate is larger than the decrease of the nominal interest rate.

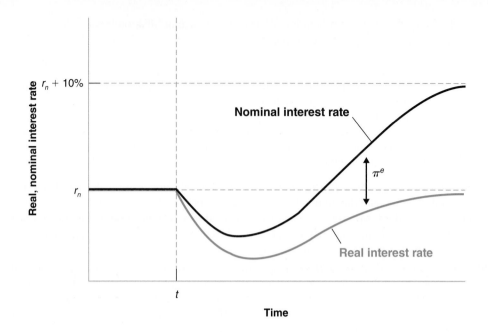

FIGURE   18-6

The Adjustment of the Real and the Nominal Interest Rates to an Increase in Money Growth from 0% to 10%

An increase in money growth leads initially to a decrease in both the real and the nominal interest rates. Over time, the real interest rate returns to its initial value. The nominal interest rate converges to a new higher value. This new higher value is equal to the initial value plus the increase in money growth.

Eventually, the nominal and the real interest rates start increasing. In the medium run, the real interest rate returns to its initial value. Inflation and expected inflation converge to the new rate of money growth, thus 10%. The nominal interest rate converges to a value equal to the real interest rate plus 10%.

Evidence on the Fisher Hypothesis

There is plenty of evidence that a monetary expansion decreases nominal interest rates in the short run (see, for example, section 5-5). But how much evidence is there for the Fisher hypothesis, the proposition that in the medium run, increases in inflation lead to one-for-one increases in nominal interest rates?

Economists have tried to answer this question by looking at two types of evidence. The first is the relation between nominal interest rates and inflation *across countries*. Because the relation holds only in the medium run, we should not expect inflation and nominal interest rates to be close to each other in any one country at any one time, but the relation should hold on average. This approach is explored further in the Global Macro box "Nominal Interest Rates and Inflation across Latin America," which looks at Latin American countries in the early 1990s and finds substantial support for the Fisher hypothesis.

The second type of evidence is the relation between the nominal interest rate and inflation over time for one country. Again, the Fisher hypothesis does not suggest that the two should move together from year to year. But it does suggest that the long swings in inflation should eventually be reflected in similar swings in the nominal interest rate. To see these long swings, we need to look at as long a period of time as we can. Figure 18–7 looks at the nominal interest rate and inflation in Canada since 1950. The nominal interest rate is the three-month Treasury bill rate, and the inflation rate is the rate of change of the CPI.

Figure 18–7 has several interesting features.

● The steady increase in inflation from the early 1950s to the early 1980s was associated with a roughly parallel increase in the nominal interest rate. The decrease in inflation since the mid-1980s has been associated with a decrease in the nominal interest rate. These evolutions support the Fisher hypothesis.

Figure 1 plots nominal interest rates and inflation for eight Latin American countries (Argentina, Bolivia, Chile, Ecuador, Mexico, Peru, Uruguay, and Venezuela) for both 1992 and 1993. (Because the Brazilian numbers would dwarf those from other countries, they are not included here. In 1992, Brazil's inflation rate was 1008% and its nominal interest rate was 1560%. In 1993, inflation was 2140% and the nominal interest rate was 3240%.) The numbers for inflation refer to the rate of change of the consumer price index. The numbers for nominal interest rates refer to the "lending rate." The exact definition of this term varies with each country, but you can think of it as corresponding to the prime interest rate in Canada—the rate charged to borrowers with the best credit rating.

Note the wide range of inflation rates, from 10% to about 100%. This is precisely why we have chosen to present num-bers from Latin America in the early 1990s. With this much variation in inflation, we can learn a lot about the relation between nominal interest rates and inflation. And Figure 1, indeed, shows a clear relation between inflation and nominal interest rates. The line drawn in the figure plots what the nominal interest rate should be under the Fisher hypothesis, assuming an underlying real interest rate of 10% so that $i = 10\% + \pi$. The slope of the line is one: Under the Fisher hypothesis, a 1% increase in inflation should be reflected in a 1% increase in the nominal interest rate.

As you can see, the line fits well; roughly half of the points are above the line, the other half below. The Fisher hypothesis appears roughly consistent with the evidence from Latin America in the early 1990s.

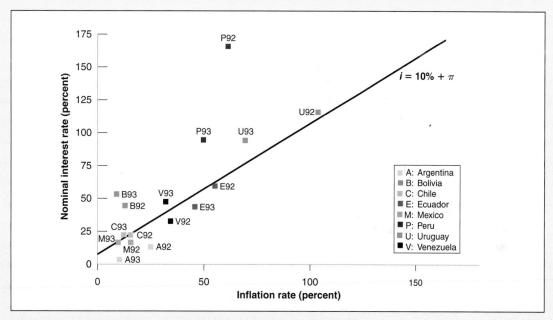

FIGURE 1   Nominal Interest Rates and Inflation: Latin America, 1992 and 1993

Brazil is not shown; its four-digit nominal interest rate and inflation rate would be way off the scale.

- Evidence of the short-run effects that we discussed earlier is also easy to see. The nominal interest rate lagged behind the increase in inflation in the 1970s, whereas the disinflations of the early 1980s and early 1990s were associated with an initial *increase* in the nominal rate, followed by a much slower decline in the nominal interest rate than in inflation.
- There is a very sharp inflation spike in 1951. This spike underlines the "medium run" qualifier in the Fisher hypothesis. In 1951, inflation was high, over 10%, but short-lived. And it disappeared before it had time to be reflected in a higher nominal interest rate. It took sustained higher inflation to generate a higher nominal interest rate.

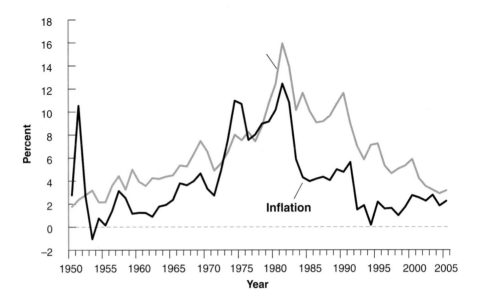

The 1–3-Year Bond Yield and Inflation, 1950–2005

The increase in inflation from the 1950s to the early 1980s was associated with an increase in the nominal interest rate. The decrease in inflation since 1982 has been associated with a decrease in the nominal interest rate.

Sources: Inflation using CANSIM II variable V735319; *nominal interest rate* using CANSIM II variable V122558.

More careful studies confirm our basic conclusion. The Fisher hypothesis that in the medium run increases in inflation are reflected in a higher nominal interest rate appears to fit the data quite well. But the adjustment takes a long time. The data confirm the speculation by Milton Friedman, which we quoted in Chapter 11, that it typically takes a "couple of decades" for nominal interest rates to reflect the higher inflation rate.

SUMMARY

- The nominal interest rate tells us how many dollars one has to repay in the future in exchange for one dollar today.

- The real interest rate tells us how many goods one has to repay in the future in exchange for one good today.

- The real interest rate is approximately equal to the nominal interest rate minus expected inflation.

- The expected present discounted value of a sequence of payments is the value this year of the expected sequence of payments. It depends positively on current and future expected payments. It depends negatively on current and future expected interest rates.

- In discounting a sequence of current and expected future nominal payments, one should use current and expected future nominal interest rates. In discounting a sequence of current and expected future real payments, one should use current and expected future real interest rates.

- Investment decisions depend on the real interest rate. The choice between money and bonds depends on the nominal interest rate. Thus, the real interest rate enters the *IS* relation, whereas the nominal interest rate enters the *LM* relation.

- In the short run, an increase in money growth typically leads to a decrease of both the nominal interest rate and the real interest rate. In the medium run, an increase in money growth has no effect on the real interest rate and increases the nominal interest rate one for one.

- The proposition that in the medium run, changes in inflation are reflected one for one in changes in the nominal interest rate is known as the Fisher effect, or the Fisher hypothesis. The empirical evidence suggests that although it takes a long time, changes in inflation are eventually reflected in changes in the nominal interest rate.

QUESTIONS AND PROBLEMS

An asterisk denotes a harder question. [Web] indicates that the question requires access to the Internet.

1. TRUE/FALSE/UNCERTAIN

a. As long as inflation remains roughly constant, the movements in the real interest rate are equal to the movements in the nominal interest rate.

b. If inflation turns out to be higher than expected, then the realized real cost of borrowing turns out to be lower than expected.

c. Looking across countries, the real interest rate is likely to vary much less than the nominal interest rate.

d. The real interest rate is equal to the nominal interest rate divided by the price level.

e. In the medium run, the real interest rate is not affected by money growth.

f. The Fisher effect states that in the medium run, the nominal interest rate is not affected by money growth.

g. The experience of Latin American countries in the early 1990s supports the Fisher hypothesis.

h. The value today of a nominal payment in the future cannot be greater than the nominal payment itself.

i. The real value today of a real payment in the future cannot be greater than the real payment itself.

2. REAL AND NOMINAL INTEREST RATES: PART I

For each of the following problems, would you use real payments and real interest rates or nominal payments and nominal interest rates to compute the expected present discounted value? In each case, explain why.

a. Estimating the present discounted value of the profits from purchasing a new machine.

b. Estimating the present value of a 20-year government bond.

c. Deciding whether to lease or buy a car.

3. REAL AND NOMINAL INTEREST RATES: PART II

For each of the following, compute the real interest rate using the exact formula and the approximation formula.

a. $i = 4\%$; $\pi^e = 2\%$

b. $i = 15\%$; $\pi^e = 11\%$

c. $i = 54\%$; $\pi^e = 46\%$

4. REAL AND NOMINAL INTEREST RATES: PART III

a. Can the nominal interest rate ever be negative? Explain.

b. Can the real interest rate ever be negative? Under what circumstances? If so, why not just hold cash instead?

c. What are the effects of a negative real interest rate on borrowing and lending?

d. Find a recent issue of *The Economist* and look at the tables in the back ("Economic Indicators" and "Financial Indicators"). Use the three-month money-market rate as the nominal interest rate and the most recent three-month rate of change in consumer prices as the expected rate of inflation (both are in annual terms). Which countries have the lowest nominal interest rates? Which countries have the lowest real interest rates? Are some of these real interest rates negative?

5. EARLY VERSUS LATE TAX CREDITS

You want to save $2000 today for retirement in 40 years. You have to choose between two plans:

i. Pay no taxes today, put the money in an interest-yielding account, and pay taxes equal to 25% of the total amount withdrawn at retirement. (This is similar to most RRSPs.)

ii. Pay taxes equivalent to 20% of the investment amount today, put the remainder in an interest-yielding account, and pay no taxes when you withdraw your funds at retirement.

a. What is the expected present discounted value of each of these options if the interest rate is 1%? 10%?

b. Which alternative would you pick in each case? Under what circumstances would you pick the other policy? (*Hint:* Think of the tax rates.) This is the structure of an RRSP in some countries, including Canada and the United States.

6. CONSOLS

The present value of an infinite stream of dollar payments of $z (that starts next year) is $z/i when the nominal interest rate, i, is constant. This formula gives the price of a consol. It also is a good approximation for the present discounted value of a stream of constant payments over long but not infinite periods. Let us examine how close the approximation is. Suppose that $i = 10\%$.

a. Let $z = 100$. What is the present value of the consol?

b. What is the expected present discounted value for a bond that pays $z over the next 10 years? 20 years? 30 years? 60 years? (*Hint:* Use the formula from Chapter 18, but remember to adjust for the first payment.)

c. Repeat the exercise with $i = 2\%$ and $i = 5\%$.

7. THE FISHER HYPOTHESIS

a. What is the Fisher hypothesis?

b. Does the experience of Latin American countries in the 1990s support or refute the Fisher hypothesis? Explain.

c. Look at the figure in the Global Macro box on Latin America. Note that the line drawn through the scatter of points does not go through the origin. Does the Fisher effect suggest that it should go through the origin? Explain.

d. "If the Fisher hypothesis is true, then changes in the growth rate of the money stock translate one for one into changes in i, and the real interest rate is left unchanged. Thus, there is no room for monetary policy to affect activity." Discuss.

*8. THE SHORT-RUN EFFECTS OF AN INCREASE IN MONEY GROWTH REVISITED

When looking at the short run in section 18-4, we concentrated on the effects of higher nominal money growth on the real money stock. We saw how this led to higher output and lower nominal and real interest rates.

Starting from the analysis in the text (as summarized in Figure 18–5), assume that as a result of higher money growth, expected inflation increases by $\Delta \pi^e$.

a. Show the effect of the increase in π^e on the *IS* curve. Explain in words.

b. Show the effect of the increase in π^e on the *LM* curve. Explain in words.

c. Show the combined effects of the increase in the real money stock and of the increase in expected inflation on output and on the nominal interest rate. Could the nominal interest rate end up higher, not lower, than before the change in money growth? Why?

d. Even if what happens to the nominal interest rate is ambiguous, can you tell what happens to the real interest rate? (*Hint:* What happens to output? What does this imply for what happens to the real interest rate?)

DERIVING THE EXPECTED PRESENT DISCOUNTED VALUE USING REAL OR NOMINAL INTEREST RATES

This appendix shows that the two ways of expressing present discounted values, equations (18.5) and (18.7), are equivalent.

Let us first rewrite these two equations.

Equation (18.5) gives the present value as the sum of current and future expected *nominal payments*, discounted using current and future expected *nominal interest rates*:

$$\$V_t = \$z_t + \frac{1}{1 + i_t} \$z_{t+1}^e$$

$$+ \frac{1}{(1 + i_t)(1 + i_{t+1}^e)} \$z_{t+2}^e + \cdots \quad (18.5)$$

Equation (18.7) gives the present value as the sum of current and future expected *real payments*, discounted using current and future expected *real interest rates*:

$$V_t = z_t + \frac{1}{1 + r_t} z_{t+1}^e$$

$$+ \frac{1}{(1 + r_t)(1 + r_{t+1}^e)} z_{t+2}^e + \cdots \quad (18.7)$$

Divide both sides of equation (18.5) by the current price level, P_t. The left side becomes $\$V_t/P_t = V_t$, the real present discounted value, the same as the left-hand side of equation (18.7).

Now, consider each term on the right of equation (18.5):

- The first becomes $\$z_t/P_t = z_t$, the current payment in real terms. This term is the same as the first term on the right of equation (18.7).

- The second is given by $[1/(1 + i_t)](\$z^e_{t+1}/P_t)$. Multiplying the numerator and the denominator by P^e_{t+1}, the price level expected for next year, gives:

$$\frac{1}{1 + i_t} \frac{P^e_{t+1}}{P_t} \frac{\$z^e_{t+1}}{P^e_{t+1}}$$

The third fraction, $\$z^e_{t+1}/P^e_{t+1}$, is the expected real payment at time $t + 1$. Consider the second fraction. Note that P^e_{t+1}/P_t can be rewritten as $1 + [(P^e_{t+1} - P_t)/P_t]$, thus, using the definition of expected inflation, as $(1 + \pi^e_t)$. This gives:

$$\frac{(1 + \pi^e_t)}{(1 + i_t)} z^e_{t+1}$$

Finally, using the definition of the real interest rate in equation (18.3), $[1 + r_t = (1 + i_t)/(1 + \pi^e_t)]$ gives:

$$\frac{1}{(1 + r_t)} z^e_{t+1}$$

This is the same as the second term on the right-hand side of equation (18.7).

- The same method applies to the other terms; make sure that you can derive the next one.

It follows that equations (18.5) and (18.7) are equivalent ways of stating and deriving the expected present discounted value of a sequence of payments.

CHAPTER 19
FINANCIAL MARKETS
AND EXPECTATIONS

In our first look at financial markets in the core (back in Chapter 4), we assumed there were only two assets, money and just one type of bond—so that we could easily focus on the choice between money and all other assets. We are now ready to relax this assumption. In this chapter, we look at the choices among nonmoney assets—between short-term and long-term bonds, between bonds and stocks, and so on.

Section 19-1 looks at the determination of bond prices and the yield curve. It shows in particular how we can use the yield curve to infer what financial markets expect to happen to short-term interest rates in the future. Section 19-2 looks at the determination of stock prices. It shows how stock prices depend on current and expected future profits, as well as on current and expected future interest rates. It then discusses the relation between movements in stock prices and movements in economic activity. Section 19-3 looks at fads and bubbles in the stock market—episodes when stock prices appear to move for reasons unrelated to either profits or interest rates—and discusses their macroeconomic implications. Finally, section 19-4 applies these ideas to the fluctuations in the value of the Canadian dollar as determined in foreign exchange markets.

19-1 | Bond Prices and the Yield Curve

Bonds differ in two basic dimensions:

- **Default risk**, the risk that the issuer of the bond will not pay back the full amount promised by the bond.

- **Maturity**, the length of time over which it promises to make payments to the holder. A bond that promises to make one payment of $1000 in six months has a maturity of six months; a bond that promises $100 per year for the next 20 years and a final payment of $1000 at the end of those 20 years has a maturity of 20 years. Maturity is the more important dimension for our purposes, and we will focus on it here.

Bonds of different maturities each have a price and an associated interest rate called the *yield to maturity*, or simply the *yield*. By looking on any given day at the yields on bonds of different maturities, we can graphically trace the relation between yields and maturity. This relation is called the **yield curve**, or the **term structure of interest rates** (the word "term" is synonymous with maturity).

◄ Term structure ⇔
Yield curve

Figure 19–1 gives the term structure on Canadian government bonds in June 1990 and January 1997. The choice of the two dates is not accidental; why we chose them will be clear shortly.

◄ To find out what the term structure is at the time you read this chapter, look in the *Report on Business* in *The Globe and Mail*.

Note the yield curve is upward sloping in January 1997. The three-month rate (the interest rate on a three-month T-bill) was only 2.9%, whereas the long-term rate (the interest rate on bonds with more than 10 years to maturity) was 7.4%. Note the yield curve in June 1990 slopes down. The three-month rate was 13.5%, and the long-term rate was 10.5%.

Why did the yield curve slope up in 1997 and down in 1990? What does a yield curve tell us about expectations in financial markets? To answer these questions, we proceed in two steps. First, we look at the relation among the *prices of bonds* of different maturities. Second, we show the relation among *yields of bonds* of different maturities and examine the determinants of the shape of the yield curve.

Two steps: (1) the determination of bond prices, and (2) the determination of bond yields.

Bond Prices as Present Values

Consider two bonds: a one-year bond that promises one payment of $100 in one year, and a two-year bond that promises one payment of $100 in two years. Let their prices today be $\$P_{1t}$ and $\$P_{2t}$, respectively. How will these two prices be determined?

Note both bonds are *discount bonds* (see the ◄ Focus box).

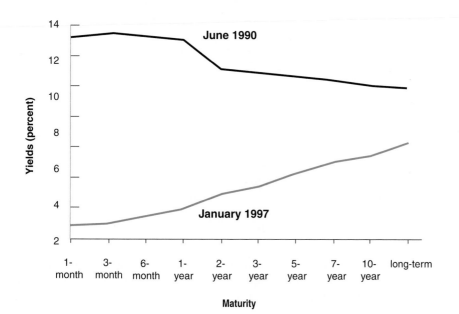

FIGURE 19–1

Canadian Yield Curves, June 1990 and January 1997

In January 1997, the Canadian yield curve sloped upward. In June 1990, it sloped downward.

Source: Various benchmark bond and Treasury bill yields from CANSIM II Table 1760043 were used to construct these curves.

Understanding the basic vocabulary of financial markets will help make them less mysterious. Here is a basic vocabulary review.

- Bonds are issued by government to finance its deficit or by firms to finance their investment. If issued by government or by government agencies, the bonds are called **government bonds**. If issued by firms, they are called **corporate bonds**.

- In the United States and Canada, bonds are rated for their default risk (the risk they will not be repaid) by two private firms, the Standard and Poor's Corporation (S&P) and Moody's Investors Service. Moody's **bond ratings** range from *Aaa* for bonds with nearly no risk of default, such as U.S. or Canadian federal government bonds, to *C* for bonds whose default risk is high. A lower rating typically implies that the bond has to pay a higher interest rate. The difference between the interest rate paid on a bond and the interest rate paid on the bond with the highest (best) rating is called the **risk premium**.

    Bonds with high default risk are known as **junk bonds**. Because they promised a very high interest rate, they became very popular with financial investors in the 1980s. After a few well-publicized defaults, they have become less popular today.

- Bonds that promise a single payment at maturity are called **discount bonds**. The single payment is called the **face value** of the bond.

- Bonds that promise multiple payments before maturity and one payment at maturity are called **coupon bonds**. The payments before maturity are called **coupon payments**. The final payment is called the face value of the bond. The ratio of coupon payments to the face value is called the **coupon rate**. The **current yield** is the ratio of the coupon payment to the price of the bond.

    For example, a bond with coupon payments of $5 each year, a face value of $100, and a price of $80 has a coupon rate of 5% and a current yield of 6.25%. From an economic viewpoint, neither the coupon rate nor the current yield are interesting measures. The correct measure of the interest rate on a bond is its *yield to maturity*, or simply *yield*; you can think of it as roughly the average annual interest rate paid by the bond over its life (we will define it more precisely later in this chapter).

- **Short-term**, **medium-term**, and **long-term bonds** typically refer to bonds with maturity of 1 year or less, 1 to 10 years, and 10 years or more, respectively.

- Government bonds range in maturity from a few days to 30 years. Bonds with a maturity of up to a year when they are issued are called Treasury bills, or T-bills. They are discount bonds, making only one payment at maturity. Bonds with a maturity of one to 30 years when they are issued are called **Canada bonds**. These are coupon bonds.

- Bonds are typically nominal bonds: They promise a sequence of fixed nominal payments—payments in terms of domestic currency. However, there are other types of bonds. Among them are **indexed bonds**, bonds that promise not fixed nominal payments but rather payments adjusted for inflation. Instead of promising to pay, say, 100 dollars in a year, a one-year indexed bond promises to pay $100 (1 + \pi)$ dollars, where π is the rate of inflation that will take place over the coming year. Because they protect bondholders against the risk of inflation, indexed bonds are popular in many countries. They play a particularly important role in the United Kingdom, where, over the last 20 years, people have increasingly used them to save for retirement. By holding long-term indexed bonds, they can make sure that the payments they receive when they retire will be protected from inflation. In Canada, indexed bonds are called **real return bonds**. Such bonds have been sold in Canada since 1991. They are used to help measure expected inflation. They are held mostly by pension plans that offer pensions that increase with the price level.

Take the *one-year bond* first. Let the current one-year nominal interest rate be i_{1t}. Note that we now denote the one-year interest rate in year t by i_{1t}, rather than simply by i_t as we did in earlier chapters. This is to make it easier to remember that it is the *one-year* interest rate.

The price of the one-year bond today is the present value of $100 next year. So:

$$\$P_{1t} = \frac{\$100}{1 + i_{1t}} \tag{19.1}$$

The price of a one-year bond varies inversely with the current one-year nominal interest rate. We already saw this relation in Chapter 4. Indeed, we saw that what actually is determined in the bond market is the price of one-year bonds, and the one-year interest rate is then inferred from the price according to equation (19.1). Reorganizing equation (19.1), it follows that if the price of one-year bonds is $\$P_{1t}$, then the current one-year interest rate equals $(\$100 - \$P_{1t})/\$P_{1t}$.

Turn now to the *two-year bond*. Its price is the present value of $100 in two years:

$$\$P_{2t} = \frac{\$100}{(1 + i_{1t})(1 + i_{t+1}^e)} \tag{19.2}$$

where i_{1t} denotes the one-year interest rate this year and i_{t+1}^e denotes the one-year rate expected by financial markets for next year. The price of a two-year bond depends on both the current one-year rate and the one-year rate expected for next year.

In the same way, we could write the price of an *n*-year bond—a bond that promises to pay, say, $100 in *n* years—as depending on the sequence of one-year rates expected by financial markets over the next *n* years.

Before exploring further the implications of equations (19.1) and (19.2), let us look at an alternative derivation of equation (19.2) based on the notion of *arbitrage*. This alternative derivation will prove useful at many points in the book.

Arbitrage and Bond Prices

Suppose you have the choice between holding one-year bonds or two-year bonds. You care about how much you will have one year from now. Which bonds should you hold?

- For every dollar you put in one-year bonds, you will get $(1 + i_{1t})$ dollars next year. This relation is represented in the first line of Figure 19–2.
- Because the price of a two-year bond is $\$P_{2t}$, every dollar you put in two-year bonds buys you $\$1/\$P_{2t}$ bonds today. When next year comes, the bond will have only one more year before maturity and thus will have become a one-year bond. Therefore, the price at which you can expect to sell it next year is $\$P_{1t+1}^e$, the expected price of a one-year bond next year. Thus, for every dollar you put in two-year bonds, you can expect to receive $(\$P_{1t+1}^e/\$P_{2t})$ dollars next year. This is represented in the second line of Figure 19–2.

Which bonds should you hold? Suppose that you, and other financial investors, care *only* about the expected return and choose to hold only the bond with the higher expected return.[1]

Under this assumption, and if there are positive amounts of one-year and two-year bonds in the economy, it follows that the two bonds must offer the same expected one-year return. To see why, suppose this condition were not satisfied. For example, suppose that the one-year return on one-year bonds were lower than the expected one-year return on two-year bonds. Nobody would want to hold the existing supply of one-year bonds, and the market for one-year bonds would not be in equilibrium. Only if the expected one-year return is the same will financial investors be willing to hold both one-year bonds and two-year bonds.

	Year *t*	Year *t* + 1
One-year bonds	$1	$1 $(1 + i_{1t})$
Two-year bonds	$1	$1 $\dfrac{\$P_{1t+1}^e}{\$P_{2t}}$

FIGURE 19–2

Returns from Holding One-Year and Two-Year Bonds for One Year

[1]**DIGGING DEEPER.** The return from holding one-year bonds for one year is known with certainty. The return from holding two-year bonds for one year depends on the price of one-year bonds next year and is therefore uncertain. The assumption that financial investors care only about expected return is another way of saying they are indifferent to risk—in other words, they are risk neutral. This is the same assumption we made to derive expected present discounted values in Chapter 18. In the context of the choice between bonds of different maturities, it is called the **expectations hypothesis**—to capture the notion that the choice only depends on expected returns.

If the two bonds offer the same expected one-year return, it follows from Figure 19–2 that:

$$1 + i_{1t} = \frac{\$P^e_{1t+1}}{\$P_{2t}} \tag{19.3}$$

The left side gives the return per dollar from holding a one-year bond for one year; the right side gives the expected return per dollar from holding a two-year bond for one year. We will call such equations as (19.3)—equations that state that the expected returns on two assets have to be equal—**arbitrage** relations.

Rewrite equation (19.3) as:

$$\$P_{2t} = \frac{\$P^e_{1t+1}}{1 + i_{1t}} \tag{19.4}$$

Arbitrage implies that the price of a two-year bond today is the present value of the expected price of the bond next year. This raises the question: What does the expected price of one-year bonds next year ($\$P^e_{1t+1}$) depend on?

The answer is straightforward. Just as the price of a one-year bond this year depends on this year's one-year interest rate, the price of a one-year bond next year will depend on the one-year interest rate next year. Writing equation (19.1) for next year (year $t + 1$) and denoting expectations in the usual way:

$$\$P^e_{1t+1} = \frac{\$100}{(1 + i^e_{1t+1})}$$

The price of the bond next year is expected to equal the final payment, $100, discounted by the one-year rate expected for next year.

Replacing $\$P^e_{1t+1}$ in equation (19.4) gives:

$$\$P_{2t} = \frac{\$100}{(1 + i_{1t})(1 + i^e_{1t+1})} \tag{19.5}$$

This expression is the same as equation (19.2). What we have shown is that *arbitrage* between one- and two-year bonds implies that the price of the two-year bond is the *present value* of the payment in two years, namely, $100, discounted using current and next year's expected one-year rates. We could have used the same approach to derive the price of three-year bonds and so on; you may want to make sure you can do it. The relation between arbitrage and present value is important; we will use it again in this and later chapters.

From Bond Prices to Bond Yields

We have derived bond prices. We now move to bond yields.

To begin, we need a definition of the yield to maturity. The **yield to maturity** on an *n*-year bond, or equivalently the *n*-**year interest rate**, is defined as that constant annual interest rate that makes the bond price today equal to the present value of future payments on the bond.

This definition is simpler than it sounds. For example, take the two-year bond we introduced earlier. Denote its yield by i_{2t}, where the subscript 2 reminds us that this is the yield to maturity on a two-year bond, or equivalently the two-year interest rate. This yield is defined as the constant annual interest rate that would make the present value of $100 in two years equal to the price of the bond today:

$$\$P_{2t} = \frac{\$100}{(1 + i_{2t})^2} \tag{19.6}$$

Suppose the bond sells for $90 today. Then, the two-year rate i_{2t} is given by $\sqrt{100/90} - 1$, or 5.4%. In other words, holding the bond for two years—until maturity—yields an interest rate of 5.4% per year.

What is the relation of the two-year rate to the current one-year rate and the expected one-year rate? To answer this question, we simply compare equation (19.6) with equation (19.5). Eliminating $\$P_{2t}$ between the two gives:

$$\frac{\$100}{(1 + i_{2t})^2} = \frac{\$100}{(1 + i_{1t})(1 + i_{1t+1}^e)}$$

Rearranging:

$$(1 + i_{2t})^2 = (1 + i_{1t})(1 + i_{1t+1}^e)$$

This gives the exact relation between the two-year rate and the current and expected one-year rates. A useful approximation to this relation is given by:

$$i_{2t} < \frac{1}{2}(i_{1t} + i_{1t+1}^e) \qquad (19.7)$$

We used a similar approximation when we looked at the relation between nominal and real interest rates in Chapter 18. See proposition 3 in Appendix 2.

Equation (19.7) is intuitive and important. It says that the two-year rate is (approximately) the average of the current one-year rate and next year's expected one-year rate. The relation extends to interest rates on bonds of higher maturity. *The n-year rate is (approximately) equal to the average of current and expected one-year rates over this and the next (n − 1) years*:

$$i_{nt} < \frac{1}{n}(i_{1t} + i_{1t+1}^e + \cdots + i_{1t+n-1}^e)$$

These relations give us the key we need to interpret the yield curve. *An upward-sloping yield curve tells us that financial markets expect short-term rates to increase in the future. A downward-sloping yield curve tells us that financial markets expect short-term interest rates to decrease in the future.*

An example will make this clear. Return to the January 1997 yield curve in Figure 19–1. We can infer from it what the financial markets expected the one-year interest rate to be one year hence—namely, in January 1998. To do so, multiply both sides of equation (19.7) by 2, and reorganize to get:

$$i_{1t+1}^e = 2i_{2t} - i_{1t} \qquad (19.8)$$

In January 1997, i_{1t} (the one-year rate, the interest rate for 1997) was 3.64%. The two-year rate was 4.44%. The expected one-year rate for January 1998 was therefore equal to $(2 \times 4.44\%) - 3.64\% = 5.24\%$, thus 1.6% above the January 1997 one-year rate.[2]

The Yield Curve and Economic Activity

Why was the yield curve so steep in January 1997? Equivalently, why did financial markets expect short-term interest rates to increase in the near future? The short answer is because the Canadian economy was growing quite rapidly after the recession of the early 1990s. To see why, let us use the *IS-LM* we developed in the core (Chapter 5). Also, to concentrate on the difference between interest rates of different maturities, let us leave aside the distinction between nominal and real interest rates we introduced in Chapter 18. More specifically, let

---

[2]**DIGGING DEEPER**. Back to risk: Bonds of higher maturity are more risky to hold because if they are sold before maturity, variations in their price can lead to large gains or losses. Contrary to our assumption that people are indifferent to risk, participants in bond markets are, in fact, risk averse and require a risk premium for bonds of higher maturity. Thus, a mildly upward-sloping yield curve—such as the yield curve in January 1998—is more likely to reflect a risk premium that increases with maturity rather than expectations of higher short-term rates in the future. The computation in the text does not take this risk premium into account.

In Chapter 21, we will▶
extend the *IS-LM* model to
take explicitly into account
what we have learned
about the effects of expectations on decisions. For
the moment, the basic *IS-
LM* will do.

us assume that expected inflation is equal to zero so that real and nominal rates are the same. Figure 19-3 draws the *IS-LM*, with the (nominal) interest rate on the vertical axis and output on the horizontal axis.

In June 1990, the Canadian economy was slipping into a recession. The Bank of Canada, concerned about inflation, had made a concerted effort to constrain the money supply. In terms of Figure 19–3, monetary policy had shifted the *LM* curve from its usual position to *LM'*. Interest rates were driven up to *i'* in early 1990, but market participants expected that the recession would lead the Bank to return to a less restrictive policy stance and future interest rates would be lower. In mid-1990, the U.S. economy also slipped into a recession. What had been a modest slowdown in growth in Canada turned into a much deeper and prolonged recession than most had foreseen. For a variety of reasons, the recovery that began in 1992 was extremely weak, both by historical standards and by comparison with the robust recovery enjoyed by our southern neighbours. Both governments worked to improve their finances by cutting expenditures and raising revenues. The labour market underwent a good deal of churning as governments and many large firms were forced to "downsize" in order to adapt to changes in the economic environment. Increases in interest rates around the world and political uncertainty about the Quebec referendum made borrowing in Canada more expensive. The recovery stalled in 1995, and the economy grew well below trend in 1996.

By early 1997, however, it looked as though the Canadian economy was finally on the verge of some rapid growth. The U.S. economy was booming. The Bank of Canada was pleased with the low and stable rate of inflation and did its best to jump-start the economy. Look at Figure 19–4. The various shocks to the Canadian economy since 1990 had left us with a leftward shift of the *IS* curve to *IS"*. The expansionary monetary policy of the Bank had shifted the *LM* curve to *LM"*. Market participants realized that these shifts were transitory and that over time these curves would shift back to their usual levels and interest rates would return to *i*. The interest rate at *i"* looked lower than its future value.

Our discussion suggests a more general proposition: When short-term interest rates move, whether down (as in the 1990–1991 recession) or up, long-term interest rates are likely to move in the same direction, but by less. This is because financial markets are likely to assume that part of the movement in short-term interest rates will not last. Figure 19–5 shows how well this proposition, indeed, characterizes movements in Canadian short- and long-term interest rates.

Figure 19–5 plots monthly changes in the three-month interest rate on the horizontal axis and in the long-term interest rate (here the average yield on bonds of 10 or more years' maturity) on the vertical axis since 1960. The figure has three main features:

**On the Brink of the
1990–1991 Recession**

Tight money in the early
1990s led to above-average
short-term interest rates.

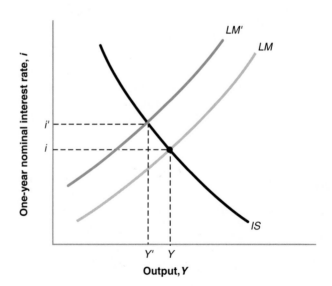

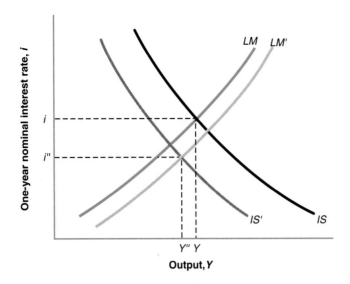

FIGURE 19-4

The Expected Path of Recovery as of Early 1997

The market expected the recovery to bring higher interest rates.

- First, monthly changes in the short-term interest rate range from –3.1 to 3.4%, while monthly changes in the long-term interest rate range only from –2.3 to 2%. Long-term rates move less than short-term rates.
- Second, most of the points lie in the northeast or the southwest quadrants of the diagram. Most of the time, short- and long-term interest rates move in the same direction.
- Third, the typical response of movements in the long-term interest rate to movements in the short-term interest rate is less than one for one. The diagram plots the regression line. The equation associated with this regression is:

$$\Delta i_L = 0.00 + 0.21\Delta i_S$$

where i_L (L for long) denotes the long-term interest rate, i_S (S for short) denotes the three-month rate, and Δ denotes the change in a rate from one month to the next. This equation tells us that an increase in the short-term interest rate of 1 percentage point is typically associated with an increase in the long-term interest rate of only 0.21 percentage points.

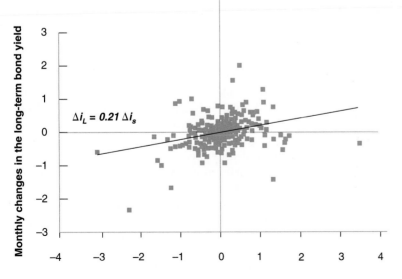

$$\Delta i_L = 0.21\,\Delta i_s$$

Monthly changes in three-month T-bill yield

FIGURE 19-5

Monthly Changes in the Canadian Three-Month and Long-Term Interest Rates, 1960–2005

Movements in the short-term interest rate are typically associated with smaller movements in the long-term interest rate in the same direction.

Source: Long-term bond yield using CANSIM II variable V122487; three-month Treasury bill yield using CANSIM II variable V122484.

This section has covered a lot of ground. Let us briefly summarize the main points:

- Arbitrage between bonds of different maturities implies that the price of a bond is the present value of the payments on the bond, discounted using current and expected short-term interest rates. Thus, higher current or expected short-term interest rates lead to lower bond prices.
- The yield to maturity on a bond with a maturity of n years (or equivalently, the n-year rate) is approximately equal to the average of current and expected future one-year interest rates.
- The slope of the yield curve tells us what financial markets expect to happen to short-term interest rates in the future. A downward-sloping yield curve implies that the market expects a decrease in short-term rates in the future; an upward-sloping yield curve implies that the markets expect an increase in short-term rates in the future.

19-2 | The Stock Market and Movements in Stock Prices

We have so far focused on bonds. But while government finances itself primarily by issuing bonds, the same is not true of firms. Firms raise funds in two ways: through **debt finance**—bonds and loans—and through **equity finance**, through issues of **shares**—or stock, as shares are also called. Instead of paying predetermined amounts as bonds do, stocks pay **dividends** in an amount decided by the firm. Dividends are paid from the firm's profits. They are typically less than profits, as firms retain some of their profits to finance their investment. But dividends move with profits: When profits increase, so do dividends.

Our focus in this section is on the determination of stock prices. As a way of introducing the issues, Figure 19–6 shows the behaviour of an index of stock prices, the *TSE 300 Composite Index* from 1960 to 2005. Movements in the index measure movements in the average stock price of 300 large companies based in Canada. Many of the companies in the TSE 300 also list their shares on the stock exchanges in the United States. And many Canadians purchase shares listed on American stock exchanges. Two American stock price indexes are the *Standard and Poor's 500 Composite Index* (average prices of 500 large companies) and the *Dow Jones Industrial Index* (average prices of only 30 large industrial companies). Similar indexes exist for other countries. (The *Nikkei Index* reflects movements in stock prices in Tokyo, and the *FT* and *CAC* indexes reflect stock-price movements in London and Paris, respectively.)

Figure 19–6 plots two lines. The upper line gives the evolution of the index as it was published in newspapers or flashed on the evening news. The index shows near constancy until 1980 and a rapid increase since. It rose from 2000 in 1980 to more than 4000 in 1989, and to 11,000 in September 2000.

This index, however, is nominal—that is, it gives the evolution of stock prices in terms of dollars. Of more interest to us is the evolution of the index in real terms (that is, adjusted for inflation). The evolution of that index, constructed by dividing the nominal index by the CPI for each year, is shown by the lower line in Figure 19–6. By construction, the CPI is equal to 1 in 1980, so the nominal and real indexes are equal by construction in 1980.

The plot of the real index shows a somewhat different picture. It shows a real stock price index that fluctuated in a narrow range, from 1500 to 2000 over the whole period from 1960 until 1995. Then, from 1995 to 2000, real stock prices grew very rapidly so that a stock portfolio worth $100 in 1995 (index value 2200) was worth over $200 in 2000 (index value over 4400). This doubling over five years is measured in constant dollars. Truly, these were amazing returns on holding stocks. However, through 2001 and 2002 stock values fell sharply. There was a recovery in 2004 and 2005.

Why do stock prices move so much over brief periods of time? While we do not offer a complete answer (if we could, we would be making our fortunes on the stock market, not teaching and researching macroeconomics), we ask in the next section how stock prices respond to changes in the economic environment and in macroeconomic policy.

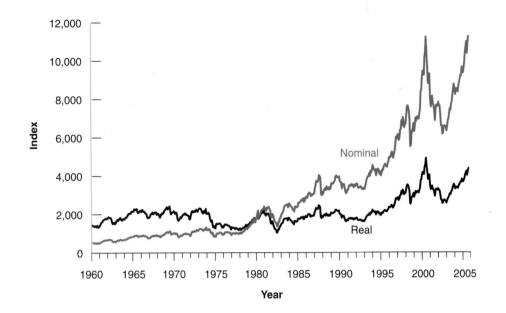

FIGURE 19–6

The TSE 300 Composite Index in Nominal and Real Terms, 1960–2005

Nominal stock prices in 2005 were more than 21 times their value in 1960. Real stock prices, on the other hand, have increased only by a factor of 3 over the same time period. Real stock prices were essentially level until 1994, grew rapidly in the early 1990s, and peaked in 2000. The slump and recovery to 2005 left real stock prices in 2005 slightly below their level in 2000.

Source: TSE 300 Composite using CANSIM II variable V122620; consumerprice index using CANSIM II variable V735319.

Stock Prices as Present Values

What determines the price of a stock that promises a sequence of dividends in the future? By now, we are sure the material in Chapter 18 has become familiar, and you already know the answer: The stock price must equal the present value of future expected dividends.

Let $\$Q_t$ be the price of the stock. Let $\$D_t$ denote the dividend this year, $\$D_{t+1}^e$ the dividend expected for next year, $\$D_{t+2}^e$ the dividend expected for two years from now, and so on.

Suppose we look at the price of the stock just after the dividend has been paid this year—this price is known as the *ex-dividend price*—so that the first dividend to be paid after the purchase of the stock is next year's dividend. (This is just a matter of convention; alternatively, we could look at the price before this year's dividend has been paid.) The price of the stock is then given by:

$$\$Q_t = \frac{\$D_{t+1}^e}{1 + i_{1t}} + \frac{\$D_{t+2}^e}{(1 + i_{1t})(1 + i_{1t+1}^e)} + \cdots \tag{19.9}$$

The price of the stock is equal to the present value of the dividend next year, discounted using the current one-year interest rate, plus the present value of the dividend two years from now, discounted using both this year's one-year interest rate and next year's expected one-year interest rate, and so on.

As in the case of long-term bonds, the present value relation in equation (19.9) can be derived from arbitrage, from the assumption that the expected return per dollar from holding a stock for one year must be equal to the return from holding a one-year bond. The derivation is given in Appendix A at the end of this chapter. (Going through it will improve your understanding of the relation between arbitrage and present value, but it can be skipped.)[3]

[3]**DIGGING DEEPER**. Two complications: (1) The assumption we have maintained throughout this and the previous chapter that financial investors are risk neutral and require equal expected rates of returns on all assets is definitely not right here. Holding stocks for one year is much more risky than holding one-year bonds for one year, and historically, financial investors have required a *risk premium*—a higher expected rate of return—for holding stocks relative to bonds. How to modify both the arbitrage equation and the present value formula to take account of a risk premium is discussed in the Appendix A at the end of this of this chapter. (2) That arbitrage implies that the price of a stock is the present value of dividends is true except in the presence of speculative bubbles, which we discuss in section 19-3.

Equation (19.9) gives the stock price as the present value of *nominal* dividends, discounted by *nominal* interest rates. From Chapter 18, we know we can rewrite it to get the *real* stock price as the present value of *real* dividends, discounted by *real* interest rates. So, we can rewrite the real stock price as:

$$Q_t = \frac{D_{t+1}^e}{(1 + r_{1t})} + \frac{D_{t+2}^e}{(1 + r_{1t})(1 + r_{1t+1}^e)} + \cdots \tag{19.10}$$

Q_t and D_t, without a dollar sign, denote the real price and real dividends at time t. *The real stock price is the expected present value of future real dividends, discounted by the sequence of one-year real interest rates.*

This relation has two important implications. Higher expected future real dividends lead to a higher stock price. Higher current and expected future one-year real interest rates lead to a lower stock price. Let us now see what light this relation sheds on movements in the stock market.

The Stock Market and Economic Activity

Figure 19–6 showed the large movements in stock prices over the last 40 years. It is not unusual for the index to go up or down by large amounts within a year. In 1974, the stock market went down by 37% (in real terms); in 1983, it went up by 22%. Daily movements of 2% or more also are not unusual. What causes these movements?

The first point to be made is that these movements are, for the most part, unpredictable. The reason is best understood by thinking in terms of the choice people have between stocks and bonds. If it were widely believed that a year from now, the price of a stock was going to be 20% higher than today's price, holding the stock for a year would be unusually attractive, much more attractive than holding short-term bonds. There would be a very large demand for the stock. Its price would increase *today* to the point where the expected return from holding the stock was back in line with the expected return on other assets. In other words, the expectation of a high stock price next year would lead to a high stock price today.

There is, indeed, a saying in economics that it is a sign of a well-functioning stock market that movements in stock prices are unpredictable. The saying is too extreme: A few financial investors may, indeed, have better information or simply be better at reading the future. If they are only a few, they may not buy enough of the stock to bid its price all the way up today. Thus, they may get large expected returns. But the basic idea is, nevertheless, right. The financial market gurus who regularly predict large imminent movements in the stock market over the next few months are quacks. Major movements in stock prices cannot be predicted.

If movements in the stock market cannot be predicted, if they are the result of news, where does this leave us? We can still do two things:

- We can do Monday-morning quarterbacking, looking back and identifying the news to which the market reacted.
- We can ask "what if" questions. For example, What would happen to the stock market if the Bank of Canada was going to embark on a more expansionary policy or if consumers were to become more optimistic and increase spending?

Let us look at two "what if" questions. To do so, let us use the *IS-LM* model. To simplify things, let us assume, as we did earlier, that expected inflation equals zero so that real and nominal interest rates are equal.

A Monetary Expansion and the Stock Market. Suppose the economy is in a recession (output is below its natural level) and the Bank of Canada decides to adopt a more expansionary monetary policy. The increase in money shifts the *LM* curve down in Figure 19–7. Equilibrium output moves from A to A'. How will the stock market react? The answer depends on what the stock market expected monetary policy to be before the Bank of Canada's move.

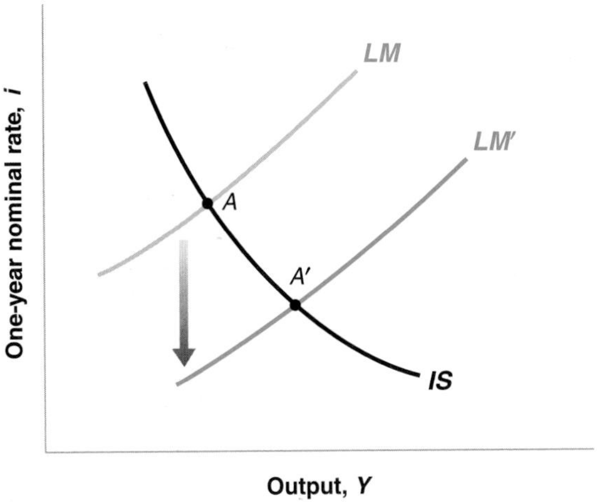

FIGURE 19-7

An Expansionary Monetary Policy and the Stock Market

A monetary expansion decreases the interest rate and increases output. What it does to the stock market depends on whether financial markets anticipated the monetary expansion.

If the stock market fully anticipated the expansionary policy, then the stock market will not react: Neither its expectations of future dividends nor its expectations of future interest rates are affected by a move it had already anticipated. Thus, in equation (19.9) nothing changes, and stock prices will remain the same.

Suppose, instead, that the Bank of Canada's move is at least partly unexpected. In that case, stock prices will increase. There are two reasons for this. First, a more expansionary monetary policy implies lower interest rates for some time. Second, a more expansionary monetary policy also implies higher output for some time (until the economy returns to the natural level of output), and so higher dividends. As equation (19.9) tells us, both lower interest rates and higher dividends, current and expected, will lead to an increase in stock prices.

An Increase in Consumer Spending and the Stock Market. Now, consider an unexpected shift of the *IS* curve to the right, resulting, for example, from stronger-than-expected consumer spending. As a result of the shift, equilibrium output in Figure 19–8(a) increases from *A* to *B*. Will stock prices go up? One is tempted to say yes: A stronger economy means higher profits and higher dividends for some time. But this answer is incomplete, for at least two reasons.

First, it ignores the effect of higher activity on interest rates: The movement along the *LM* curve from *A* to *B* also implies an increase in interest rates. Higher interest rates decrease stock prices. Which of the two effects—higher profits or higher interest rates—dominates? The answer depends on the slope of the *LM* curve. As drawn in Figure 19–8(b), a very steep *LM* curve implies large increases in interest rates, small increases in output, and so a fall in stock prices. As drawn in Figure 19–8(c), a very flat *LM* curve leads to small increases in interest rates, large increases in output, and so an increase in stock prices.

Second, it ignores the effect of the shift in the *IS* curve on the Bank of Canada's behaviour. In practice, this is the effect that financial investors often care about the most. When receiving the news of unexpectedly strong economic activity, the main question in the stock market is: How will the Canadian and American central banks react?

- Will the central bank accommodate the shift in the *IS* curve—that is, increase money supply in line with money demand to avoid an increase in the interest rate? This case is shown in Figure 19–8(d). **Accommodation** corresponds to a downward shift of the *LM* curve, from *LM* to *LM'*. In this case, the economy will go from point *A* to point *B'*. Stock prices will increase: Output is expected to be higher, and interest rates are not expected to increase.
- Will the central bank instead keep the same monetary policy, leaving the *LM* curve unchanged? This is the case we saw in Figure 19–8(a); the economy will go from *A* to

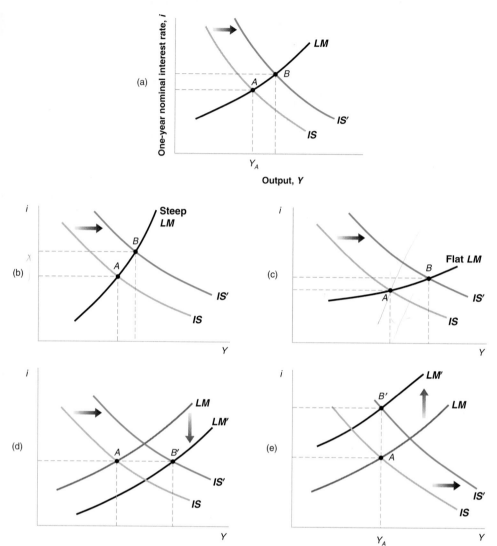

FIGURE 19–8

An Increase in Consumption Spending and the Stock Market

(a) The increase in consumption spending leads to a higher interest rate and a higher level of output. What happens to the stock market depends on the slope of the *LM* curve and on the central bank's behaviour. (b) Steep *LM* curve: The interest rate increases a lot, and output increases little. Stock prices go down. (c) Flat *LM* curve: The interest rate increases little, and output increases a lot. Stock prices go up. (d) The central bank accommodates: The interest rate does not increase, but output does. Stock prices go up. (e) The central bank decides to keep output constant: The interest rate increases, but output does not. Stock prices go down.

B. As we saw earlier, what happens to stock prices is ambiguous. The economy will have higher profits, but the interest rate will be higher as well.

● Or will the central bank worry that an increase in output above Y_A may lead to an increase in inflation? This will be the case if the economy is already close to the natural level of output, if Y_A is close to Y_n. This case is shown in Figure 19–8(e). In this case, a further increase in output would lead to an increase in inflation, something that the central bank wants to avoid. The central bank decides to counteract the rightward shift of the *IS* curve with a monetary contraction, an upward shift of the *LM* curve from *LM* to *LM′* so that output does not change. In that case, stock prices will surely go down: There is no change in expected profits, but the interest rate is now likely to be higher for some time.

To summarize: Changes in output may or may not be associated with changes in stock prices in the same direction. Whether they are depends on (1) what the market expected in the first place, (2) the source of the shocks, and (3) how the market expects the central bank to react to the output change.

Here are some quotes from *The Wall Street Journal*. Try to make sense of them, using what you have just learned.

● April 1997. Good news on the economy, leading to an increase in stock prices:

Bullish investors celebrated the release of market-friendly economic data by stampeding back into stock and bond markets, pushing the Dow Jones industrial Average to its second-largest point gain ever and putting the blue-chip index within shooting distance of a record just weeks after it was reeling.

● September 1998. Bad news on the economy, leading to a decrease in stock prices:

NASDAQ stocks plummeted as worries about the strength of the U.S. economy and the profitability of U.S. corporations prompted widespread selling.

● December 1999. Good news on the economy, leading to a decrease in stock prices:

Good economic news was bad news for stocks and worse news for bonds . . . The announcement of stronger-than-expected November retail-sales-numbers was not welcome. Economic strength creates inflation fears and sharpens the risk that the Federal Reserve will raise interest rates again.

● August 2001. Bad news on the economy, leading to an increase in stock prices:

Investors shrugged off more gloomy economic news and focused instead on their hope that the worst is now over for both the economy and the stock market. The optimism translated into another 2% gain for the NASDAQ Composite Index.

19-3 | Bubbles, Fads, and Stock Prices

Do all movements in stock prices come from news about future dividends or interest rates? Many economists doubt it. They point to such times as Black October in 1929, when the U.S. stock market fell by 23% in two days, or to October 19, 1987, when the Dow Jones index fell by 22.6% in a single day. They point to the amazing rise of Japanese stock prices in the 1980s, followed by a sharp fall in the 1990s. They point to the rise of high-tech stocks from 1995 to 2000. As we saw in Chapter 1 (see Figure 1–6), the Nikkei increased from around 13,000 in 1985 to around 35,000 in 1989, only to decline to around 16,000 in 1992. In each case, they point to the lack of obvious news, or at least news important enough to justify such enormous movements.

They argue that stock prices are not always equal to their **fundamental value**, defined as the present value of expected dividends given in equation (19.10) and that stocks are sometimes underpriced or overpriced. Overpricing eventually ends, sometimes with a crash as in October 1987, or with a long slide as has occurred in Japan. Most feel the fall in stock prices since 2000 was a correction to overpricing.

Under what conditions can such mispricing occur? The surprising answer is that it can occur even when investors are rational and when arbitrage holds. To see why, consider the case of a truly worthless stock (that is, a stock of a company that all financial investors know will never make profits and will never pay dividends). Putting D_{t+1}^e, D_{t+2}^e, and so on, equal to zero in equation (19.10) yields a simple and unsurprising answer: The fundamental value of such a stock is equal to zero.

Might you, nevertheless, be willing to pay a positive price for such a stock? Yes. You might if you expect the price at which you can sell the stock next year to be higher than this year's price. And the same applies to a buyer next year: She may be willing to buy at a high price if she expects to sell at an even higher price in the following year. This process suggests that stock prices may increase just because investors expect them to increase. Such movements in stock prices are called **rational speculative bubbles**. Financial investors may be behaving rationally as the bubble inflates. Even those investors who hold the stock at the time

In a speculative bubble, the price of a stock is higher than its fundamental value. Investors are willing to pay a high price for the stock in anticipation of ▶ being able to resell the stock at an even higher price.

of the crash, and therefore sustain a large loss, may also have been rational. They may have realized there was a chance of a crash but also a chance that the bubble would keep growing and they could sell at an even higher price.

To make things simple, our example assumed the stock to be fundamentally worthless. But the argument is general and applies to stocks with a positive fundamental value as well. People might be willing to pay more than the fundamental value of a stock if they expect its price to increase more in the future. And the same argument applies to other assets, such as housing, gold, and paintings. Two such bubbles are described in the Global Macro box, "Famous Bubbles: From Tulipmania in Seventeenth-Century Holland to Russia in 1994."

GLOBAL macro — Famous Bubbles: From Tulipmania in Seventeenth-Century Holland to Russia in 1994

Tulipmania in Holland

In the seventeenth century, tulips became increasingly popular in western European gardens. A market developed in Holland for both rare and common forms of tulip bulbs.

The episode called the "tulip bubble" took place from 1634 to 1637. In 1634, the price of rare bulbs started increasing. The market went into a frenzy, with speculators buying tulip bulbs in anticipation of even higher prices later. The price of a bulb called "Admiral Van de Eyck," for example, increased from 1500 guineas in 1634 to 7500 guineas in 1637, the equivalent of the price of a house at the time. There are stories about a sailor mistakenly eating some bulbs, only to realize the cost of

his "meal" later. In early 1637, prices increased faster. Even the price of more common bulbs skyrocketed, rising by a factor of up to 20 in January. But, in February 1637, prices collapsed. A few years later, bulbs were trading for roughly 10% of their value at the peak of the bubble.

The MMM Pyramid in Russia

In 1994, a Russian "financier," Sergei Mavrody, created a company called MMM and proceeded to sell shares, promising shareholders a rate of return of at least 3000% per year!

The company was an instant success. The share price increased from 1600 rubles (then $1) in February to 105,000 rubles ($51) in July. And by July, according to company claims, the number of shareholders had increased to 10 million.

The trouble was that the company was not involved in any type of production and held no assets, except for its 140 offices in Russia. The shares were intrinsically worthless. The company's initial success was based on a standard pyramid scheme: MMM used the funds from the sale of new shares to pay the promised returns on the old shares. Despite repeated warnings by government officials, including Boris Yeltsin, that MMM was a scam and that the increase in the price of shares was a bubble, the promised returns were just too attractive to many Russian people, especially in the midst of a deep economic recession.

The scheme could work only as long as the number of new shareholders—and thus new funds to be distributed to existing shareholders—increased fast enough. By the end of July 1994, the company could no longer make good on its promises, and the scheme collapsed. The company closed. Mavrody tried to blackmail government into paying the shareholders, claiming that not doing so would trigger a revolution or a civil war. Government refused, leading many shareholders to be angry at government rather than at Mavrody. Later that year, Mavrody actually ran for Parliament, as a self-appointed defender of the shareholders who had lost their savings. He won!

Source: The account of "Tulipmania in Holland" is taken from Peter Garber, "Tulipmania," *Journal of Political Economy*, June 1989, pp. 535–560.

Anthony Claesz (1592–1635), *Tulips, Lilies, Irises, & Roses.* Around the time this painting was painted, some tulip bulbs in Holland were selling for the same price as a house.

Are all deviations from fundamental values in financial markets rational bubbles? Probably not. Many financial investors are not rational. An increase in stock prices in the past, say, due to a succession of good news, often creates excessive optimism. If investors simply extrapolate from past returns to predict future returns, a stock may become "hot" (high priced) for no reason other than the fact that its price has increased in the past. Such deviations of stock prices from their fundamental value are called **fads**. We are all aware of the existence of fads outside of the stock market; there are good reasons to believe that they exist in the stock market as well.

How much of the movement in stock prices is due to movements in the fundamental value of stocks and how much to fads and bubbles? As of 1999, that question was very much on the minds of many economists and financial investors. They wondered whether the large increase in the stock market since the early 1990s was not, in part, a bubble. The In Depth box "Was the Stock Market Overvalued?" looks at the evidence and concludes that the

In the context of the U.S. stock market, Alan Greenspan has called it "irrational exuberance."

IN DEPTH   Was the Stock Market Overvalued?*

At the end of 1998, U.S. stock prices stood in real terms at nearly three times their 1990 level. Canadian stock prices were 2.5 times their 1990 levels. This large increase has led a number of economists, financial investors, and policy makers to worry that the stock market might be overvalued and that a large market correction (as large declines in stock prices are euphemistically called) may be in store.

That stock prices have increased in the 1990s is not by itself a puzzle. Since the 1990–1991 recession, the North American economy has undergone a long expansion, one lasting much longer than most economists and financial investors had anticipated. With the long expansion have come high profits and high dividends—higher than could have been expected

in 1990. These higher-than-expected dividends should have led to higher-than-expected stock prices—and, indeed, they have!

The question is whether the strong performance of stock prices can be fully explained by the strong performance of dividends. The evidence here suggests that it cannot. If higher dividends fully accounted for higher prices, stock prices should have increased roughly in line with dividends. Put another way, the dividend-price ratio (also called the dividend yield) should have remained roughly constant. Figure 1 plots the evolution of the dividend–price ratio for the stocks in the S&P index since 1990. The message is clear: the dividend–price ratio declined a lot, from 3.6% in 1990 to 1.4% in 1998—a historical low. Prices have increased much more than dividends.

(continued)

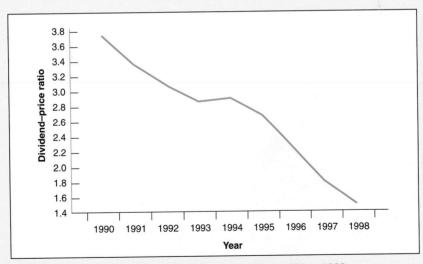

FIGURE 1   The Evolution of the Dividend–Price Ratio from 1990 to 1998

*Campbell and Shiller's article was written in mid-1999. As you read it and have the benefit of hindsight, see how it has stood the test of time.

That stock prices are high relative to current dividends does not prove the stock market is overvalued, for at least three reasons:

- High stock prices may reflect anticipations of much higher dividends in the future. Return to equation (19.10): The higher the future expected dividends, the higher is the stock price, even given the current dividend.
- High stock prices may reflect a decrease in real interest rates since 1990. Again, return to equation (19.10): Given current and expected dividends, the lower the current and future expected real interest rates, the higher is the stock price.
- High stock prices may reflect a factor we have ignored in this chapter, a decrease in the risk premium associated with stocks relative to bonds. To the extent that investors perceive stocks as less risky than before, they may be willing to pay a higher price for stocks than before. (Appendix A at the end of this chapter shows how a decrease in the risk premium leads to an increase in the stock price.)

Whether these factors together can explain the full increase in stock prices is the subject of much current research and is far from settled. John Campbell, from Harvard, and Robert Shiller, from Yale, have shown that based on historical evidence, there are good reasons to worry. Whenever the dividend-price ratio has been low in the past, stock prices have done poorly over the following 10 years, leading to a much lower return on holding stocks than holding bonds.

To reach this conclusion, Campbell and Shiller compute two variables for each year from 1927 to 1987: (1) the dividend-price ratio, and (2) the rate of change of real stock prices over the following 10 years. They then plot the rate of change of real stock prices against the dividend-price ratio. The scatter plot they obtain is shown in Figure 2.

The plot clearly shows that historically a low dividend-price ratio has been followed by a poor performance of the stock market over the following 10 years. (For example, on the eve of the stock market crash of 1929, the dividend-price ratio was the lowest it had been in decades; the rate of return over the next 10 years, 1929 to 1938, was a dismal −46%.) The figure plots the regression line, the line that fits the scatter of points best. According to this line, a dividend–price ratio of 1.4% (the value of the ratio in 1998) is followed on average by a decrease in real stock prices of more than 50% over the following 10 years! The relation is not very tight, and things well may be different this time; but it is a serious warning, nevertheless.

The Bank of Canada cares about the valuation of stocks. As we will see in the next chapter, consumers who feel wealthier spend more. At the peak of the stock market boom in the year 2000, economist Bob Hannah of the Financial Markets Department wrote: "Market values (measured at the end of February 2000) could be sustained only by rapid growth of dividends in the future or by the continued assumption of an uncharacteristically low risk premium on equity ... explaining high stock market valuation requires assumptions that are outside historical experience." The Bank of Canada was concerned a bubble was a possibility. They appear to have been correct.

Perhaps you know people who made or lost money in the recent gyrations of the stock market.

Sources: John Campbell and Robert Shiller, "Valuation Ratios and the Long-Run Stock Market Outlook," *Journal of Portfolio Management*, Winter 1998, pp. 11–26. Bob Hannah, "Approaches to Current Stock Market Valuations," *Bank of Canada Review*, Summer 2000, pp. 27–36.

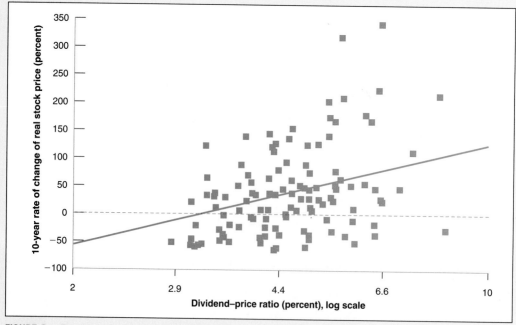

FIGURE 2   **Ten-Year Change in the Real Stock Price versus Dividend–Price Ratio, 1927–1987**

current level of the stock market seems, indeed, high relative to fundamentals. The general question of what determines stock prices — fundamentals only, or also fads and bubbles — is an important question not only for finance but also for macroeconomics. The stock market is more than just a sideshow: As we will see in the next two chapters, not only are stock prices affected by economic activity, but they also affect it through their effect on both consumption and investment spending. Many economists believe the stock market crash of 1929 was one of the sources of the Great Depression. And, as was illustrated way back in Figure 1–8, the long and large decline of the Nikkei after what was probably, in large part, a speculative bubble in the 1980s is one of the causes of the slump in Japan since the early 1990s.

◀ See Chapter 22.

19-4 | Exchange Rate Movements and Expectations*

We saw in Chapter 6 and again in Chapter 13 how the interest parity condition led to a relation between the short-term domestic nominal interest rate and the foreign nominal interest rate on the one hand, and the current nominal exchange rate and the expected future nominal exchange rate on the other.

The same condition can be used to derive a relation between the long-term domestic real interest rate and the long-term foreign real interest rate on the one hand, and the current real exchange rate and the expected future real exchange rate on the other. This seems like a mouthful, but do not worry: It is simpler than it sounds. And this relation will provide us with a way of thinking about movements of the exchange rate.

Real Interest Rates and the Real Exchange Rate

Consider, as in Chapter 6, the choice between one-year Canadian and one-year U.S. bonds. But instead of expressing the two rates of return in Canadian dollars as we did there, let us express both of them in terms of Canadian goods. Suppose you decide to invest the equivalent of one Canadian good, to "invest one Canadian good," for short, in what follows:

- Suppose you decide to hold Canadian bonds. Let r_t be the one-year Canadian real interest rate, the interest rate on one-year Canadian bonds in terms of Canadian goods. By the definition of the real interest rate, you will get $(1 + r_t)$ Canadian goods next year. This is represented by the top line in Figure 19–9.

- Suppose you decide instead to hold U.S. bonds. This involves exchanging Canadian dollars for U.S. dollars, holding U.S. bonds for a year, and selling U.S. dollars for Canadian dollars a year from now.

Let ϵ_t be the real exchange rate, the relative price of U.S. goods in terms of Canadian goods. A real exchange rate of ϵ_t means you get $(1/\epsilon_t)$ U.S. goods for every Canadian good you invest.

Let r_t^* be the one-year U.S. real interest rate, the interest rate on one-year U.S. bonds in terms of U.S. goods. Let the expected real exchange rate a year from now be ϵ_{t+1}^e. Then, for every Canadian good you invest in one-year U.S. bonds, you can expect to get

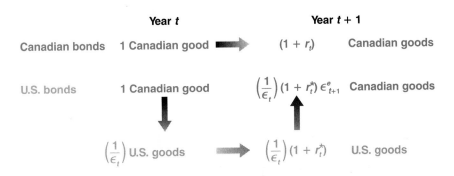

	Year t	Year $t + 1$	
Canadian bonds	1 Canadian good ➡	$(1 + r_t)$	Canadian goods
U.S. bonds	1 Canadian good	$\left(\frac{1}{\epsilon_t}\right)(1 + r_t^*)\,\epsilon_{t+1}^e$	Canadian goods
	$\left(\frac{1}{\epsilon_t}\right)$ U.S. goods	$\left(\frac{1}{\epsilon_t}\right)(1 + r_t^*)$	U.S. goods

FIGURE 19–9

Expected Returns, in Terms of Canadian Goods, from Holding Canadian or U.S. Bonds

*This material can be skipped without loss of continuity.

$(1/\epsilon_t)(1 + r_t^*)\,\epsilon_{t+1}^e$ Canadian goods next year. The three steps involved in the transaction are represented in the bottom part of Figure 19–9.

If we assume that expected returns expressed in the same units (here, Canadian goods) must be equal in equilibrium (the interest parity condition), the following condition must hold:

$$(1 + r_t) = \left(\frac{1}{\epsilon_t}\right)(1 + r_t^*)(\epsilon_{t+1}^e) \qquad (19.11)$$

This equation gives us a relation between the domestic and the foreign real interest rates on the one hand, and the current and expected future real exchange rates on the other.

You may wonder whether this differs from the condition derived in terms of nominal interest rates and nominal exchange rates, contained in equation (6.2). The answer is no. The two conditions are equivalent and we can derive one from the other. (It is presented as an exercise at the end of this chapter. The derivation is not much fun, but it is good practice and a useful way of brushing up on the relation between nominal and real interest rates, and nominal and real exchange rates.)

The basic reason why they are equivalent is that the interest parity condition states that the expected returns *when expressed in common units*—whatever these units are, as long as they are common—must be equal. Until now, we took the common unit to be the Canadian dollar. Here, we take the common unit to be a Canadian good.

Long-Term Real Interest Rates and the Real Exchange Rate

We have just looked at the choice of holding domestic versus foreign bonds *for one year*. But we can apply the same logic to the choice of holding domestic and foreign bonds *for many years*. Suppose you decide to invest the equivalent of one Canadian good—to invest one Canadian good, for short—for n years in either n-year Canadian bonds or n-year U.S. bonds (think of n as, say, 10 years).

- Suppose you decide to hold n-year Canadian bonds. Let r_{nt} be the n-year Canadian real interest rate. Recall that by the definition of an n-year interest rate, r_{nt} is the average annual interest rate you can expect to get if you hold the n-year bond for n years. So, by the definition of the n-year real interest rate, you can expect to get $(1 + r_{nt})^n$ goods in n years. This is represented in the top line of Figure 19–10.
- Now, suppose you decide to hold n-year U.S. bonds instead. Let ϵ_t be the real exchange rate. Let r_{nt}^* be the n-year U.S. real interest rate. Let the expected real exchange rate n years from now be ϵ_{t+n}^e. Then, for every Canadian good you invest in n-year U.S. bonds, you can expect to get $(1/\epsilon_t)(1 + r_{nt}^*)^n\epsilon_{t+n}^e$ Canadian goods in n years. This set of steps is represented in the bottom part of Figure 19–10.

If we assume again that expected returns have to be the same, then the following condition must hold:

$$(1 + r_{nt})^n = \left(\frac{1}{\epsilon_t}\right)(1 + r_{nt}^*)^n(\epsilon_{t+n}^e) \qquad (19.12)$$

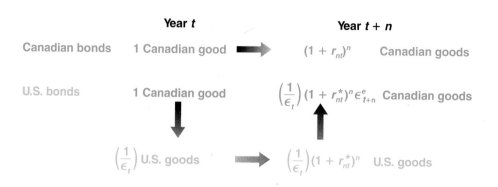

FIGURE 19–10

Expected Returns, in Terms of Canadian Goods, from Holding *n*-year Canadian or U.S. Bonds for *n* Years

Year *t* | **Year *t + n***

Canadian bonds   1 Canadian good   ➡ $(1 + r_{nt})^n$ Canadian goods

U.S. bonds   1 Canadian good $\left(\frac{1}{\epsilon_t}\right)(1 + r_{nt}^*)^n \epsilon_{t+n}^e$ Canadian goods

$\left(\frac{1}{\epsilon_t}\right)$ U.S. goods   ➡ $\left(\frac{1}{\epsilon_t}\right)(1 + r_{nt}^*)^n$ U.S. goods

A good approximation (derived as an application of proposition 5 in Appendix 2 at the end of the book) is given by:

$$n \, r_{nt} = n \, r_{nt}^* + \frac{(\epsilon_{t+n}^e - \epsilon_t)}{\epsilon_t}$$

Rewriting the equation so that the current exchange rate is on the left:

$$\epsilon_t = \frac{\epsilon_{t+n}^e}{1 + n(r_{nt} - r_{nt}^*)} \tag{19.13}$$

This relation says that the real exchange rate today depends on the expected future real exchange rate n years from now and on the differential between n-year domestic and foreign real interest rates. Let us look at it more closely.

The Real Exchange Rate, Trade, and Interest Rate Differentials

The first determinant of the current real exchange rate in equation (19.13) is the expected future real exchange rate, ϵ_{t+n}^e. If we take the number of years, n, to be large, we can think of ϵ_{t+n}^e as the exchange rate that financial market participants expect to prevail in the *medium run* or the *long run*. For simplicity, we will now call it the *long-run real exchange rate*.

How should we think of the long-run real exchange rate? In the long run, we can assume the current account will be roughly balanced. No country can run a current account deficit each and every year; this means their foreign debt increases without limit. Just as a person cannot have unlimited personal debt because lenders will stop lending to him, a country faces a limit on its total foreign debt. Similarly, a country does not want its foreign assets to increase forever. Eventually, the foreign assets should be used for consumption purposes. Most individuals do not want to keep working to accumulate personal wealth forever; they want to eventually retire and spend most of their assets on an enjoyable retirement. If the current account is to be zero, then the trade balance is negative for a country with positive foreign assets. Kuwait was the example in Chapter 6. In Canada's case, our existing foreign assets are negative, that is, we are indebted to foreigners. For a zero current account balance, our long-run real exchange rate must generate a trade surplus equal to the difference between GDP and GNP.[4]

The second determinant of the current real exchange rate is the difference between domestic and foreign long-term real interest rates. *An increase in the domestic long-term real interest rate over the foreign long-term real interest rate leads to a decrease in the real exchange rate—a real appreciation.* We focused on this mechanism when discussing a similar relation between the nominal interest rate and the nominal exchange rate in Chapter 8. Let us go through its logic again.

Suppose the long-term domestic real interest rate goes up, making domestic bonds more attractive than foreign bonds. As investors try to shift out of foreign bonds into domestic bonds, they sell foreign currency and buy domestic currency so that the domestic currency appreciates. Because the exchange rate is expected to return eventually to its long-run value, the more the domestic currency appreciates today, the more it is expected to depreciate in the future. Therefore, the domestic currency appreciates today to the point at which the expected future depreciation exactly offsets the fact that the long-term domestic real interest rate is higher than the long-term foreign real interest rate. At that point, financial investors are again indifferent to holding domestic bonds or holding foreign bonds.

We now have a way of thinking about exchange rate movements. Let us use this approach first to look at the movements of the Canadian dollar in the 1990s and then, more generally, to look at the effects of monetary policy and the relation between interest rates and exchange rates.

---

[4]**DIGGING DEEPER**. This is not quite right. An increase in population or productivity may allow a constant ratio of foreign debt to GDP, while the current account remains in deficit. We ignore growth in population and technology above.

The Canadian Dollar from 1998 to 2005

Remember the large movements in the Canadian dollar from 1998 to 2005, a real depreciation, followed by a substantial real appreciation. In light of the theory we just developed, we can ask: Were these movements due more to movements in long-term real interest rates in Canada relative to the United States or more to movements in the long-run real exchange rate?

Note from equation (19.13) that if the long-run real exchange rate were constant, there would be an exact negative relation between the difference between the domestic and the foreign long-term real interest rates $(r_{nt} - r_{nt}^*)$, and the real exchange rate, ϵ_t.

This statement suggests the following approach to interpreting movements in the real exchange rate: Construct for each year the difference between the long-term domestic real interest rate and the foreign long-term real interest rate. Then, plot the real exchange rate against this difference. If the two series move closely together, differences in long-term real interest rates must be the dominant factor in explaining movements in the real exchange rate. If they do not, changes in the long-run real exchange rate must play an important role.

Figure 19–11 implements this approach. It focuses on the bilateral real exchange rate between the United States and Canada from 1998 to 2005. As we saw in Chapter 6, movements in this bilateral real exchange rate are the movements that matter to Canada.

The real exchange rate is defined and constructed in the same way as in Figure 6–6. It is given by $(E_t P_t^*/P_t)$, where E_t is the Canadian Dollar/U.S. Dollar exchange rate, and P_t and P_t^* are the GDP deflators in Canada and the United States, respectively. The evolution of the real exchange rate is given by the upper line in the figure. It is measured on the scale at the right of the figure.

The gap between the long-term Canadian and U.S. real interest rate for each year using yields on inflation-indexed bonds is plotted in Figure 19–11. The lower line in the figure plots the difference between the U.S. and the Canadian real interest rates. This difference is measured in percentage on the scale at the left of the figure.

The fit between the two series requires some interpretation. The depreciated level of the Canadian dollar in the early part of the period is associated with higher real interest rates in Canada. This repeats our analysis of Chapter 6. However, the size of the appreciation after 2002 seems more mysterious.

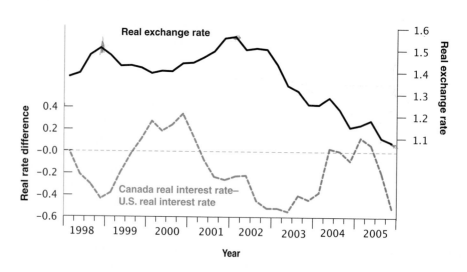

The Real Exchange Rate and the Difference between Long–Term Real Interest Rates in Canada and the United States

There is a relationship between the gap between Canadian and U.S. long-term real interest rates $r_{nt} - r_{nt}^*$, and the real exchange rate, C_t, While other factors do affect the value of the real exchange rate, the figure does show that the larger the gap, the more depreciated the Canadian currency during much of the period between 1998 and 2005.

Source: Real exchange rate—see Figure 6–6. The long-term real interest rate in Canada is measured using CANSIM II variable V122553. The long-term real interest rate in the United States is measured using Series ID TP 30A28 Federal Reserve Bank of St. Louis. Both real interest rates are yields on inflation-indexed bonds issued by the federal governments of the respective countries.

Our equation (19.13) gives a hint. If ϵ^e_{t+n} is smaller (a real appreciation), then ϵ_t will also be larger. Where might a movement in ϵ^e_{t+n} come from? We saw in Chapter 17 that since 1999, Canada's foreign debts decreased rapidly. Thus, to pay the interest on these foreign debts would require a smaller trade balance, which would require a real appreciation.

Where, in turn, did these movements in long-term real exchange rates come from? The main reason lies in the fiscal policy mix followed by the United States under George W. Bush. Since Bush's election, U.S. fiscal policy has been very loose, leading to higher U.S. foreign debt and a long-term real appreciation of the currencies of its trading partners, including Canada.

Monetary Policy, Interest Rates, and Exchange Rates

Let us now return to how monetary policy works in an open economy with flexible exchange rates. Let us start with a blatantly unrealistic case. It is easier to analyze, yet it provides a good base on which to build a more realistic discussion.

Assume there is no inflation, here or abroad, current or expected; so, we do not need to distinguish between nominal and real interest rates or between nominal and real exchange rates. Suppose further that initially, domestic and foreign interest rates are expected to be constant and equal to each other.

Now, suppose the central bank unexpectedly announces that in order to increase output, it has decided to decrease interest rates. The central bank announces that one-year interest rates will be 2 percentage points lower for each of the next five years, after which they will return to normal. Financial markets fully believe this announcement.

What happens at the time of the announcement? Short-term interest rates go down by 2%, and so do rates on bonds with maturities less than or equal to five years. Yields on bonds with longer maturity go down, but by less.

What is the effect on the exchange rate today? To answer, work backward in time.

- Start five years in the future. The exchange rate five years from now depends on what is expected to happen to interest rates thereafter, as well as on the long-run exchange rate. Because the announcement does not change expectations of interest rates beyond the first five years and presumably does not change the long-run exchange rate either, there is no change in the expected real exchange rate five years from now.

- What happens between today and five years hence? The interest parity condition tells us that for each of the next five years, there must be an expected appreciation of the domestic currency of 2% per year so that the expected rates of return on holding domestic and foreign bonds are equal. That means there must be an expected cumulative appreciation of $5 \times 2\% = 10\%$ over the next five years.

- As the expected exchange rate five years hence is unchanged, to generate the expected appreciation of 10% over the next five years, there must therefore be a depreciation today of 10%. In other words, if the domestic currency *depreciates by 10% today* and then is expected to *appreciate by 2% a year for the next five years*, financial investors will be willing to hold domestic bonds although the domestic interest rate is 2% lower than the foreign interest rate.

The expected paths of one-year interest rates and the exchange rate are shown in Figure 19–12. Before the announcement, the domestic interest rate is expected to be the same as the foreign interest rate forever. After the announcement, the domestic interest rate is expected to be 2 percentage points lower than the foreign interest rate for five years. The effect of the announcement is an increase in the exchange rate of 10% at the time of the announcement (a 10% depreciation), followed by a decrease of 2% a year (an expected appreciation of 2% a year) over the next five years. Note how much the exchange rate initially moves and overshoots its long-run value—increasing first, only to decrease back to its initial value five years later. For that reason, this exchange rate adjustment is often referred to as **overshooting**.

FIGURE 19–12

The Effects of Monetary Policy on the Interest Rate and the Exchange Rate

A decrease in interest rates expected to last for five years leads to a depreciation today, followed by expected appreciation over the next five years.

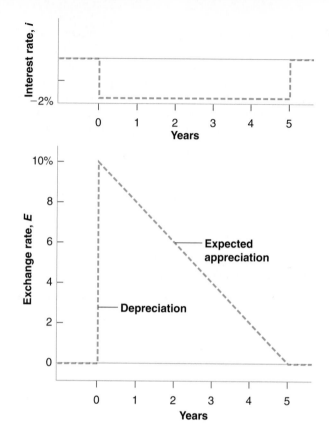

This result is an important one. When, in the early 1970s, countries moved from fixed to flexible exchange rates, the large fluctuations in exchange rates that followed came as a surprise to most economists. For a long time, these fluctuations were thought to be the result of irrational speculation in foreign exchange markets. It was not until the mid-1970s that economists realized that these large movements could be explained, as we have done here, by the rational reaction of financial markets to differences in future interest rates.

Policy and Expectations

In the example we just looked at, we dismissed many complications. We assumed, in particular, that the central bank announced what it was going to do over the next five years and that financial markets fully believed the announcement. In practice, this is not the way things happen.

When the central bank cuts interest rates, financial markets have to assess whether this action signals a major shift in monetary policy and is just the first of many such cuts or whether this cut is just a temporary movement in interest rates. Announcements by the central bank itself may not be very useful: The central bank itself may not know what it will do in the future. Typically, it will be reacting to early signals, which may be reversed later. Financial markets also have to assess how foreign central banks will react, whether they will stay put or follow suit and cut their interest rates.

To summarize: How a change in the short-term interest rate affects the exchange rate is more complex than it appeared in Chapter 6. The response of the exchange rate depends very much on the effect of the change in the interest rate on expectations of future domestic and foreign interest rates. Sometimes, a small decrease in short-term interest rates may convince markets that monetary policy has substantially changed, resulting in a large decrease in long-term interest rates and a large depreciation. But if markets anticipated a large cut and the central bank announces a smaller cut than was anticipated, the effect may actually be an appreciation, not a depreciation. The reaction of foreign exchange, stock, and bond markets to policy news is the topic of the Focus box "News and Movements in Foreign Exchange, Stock, and Bond Markets."

Remember the game we played earlier in the chapter: "Why did the stock market go up/down today?" Now we can play the advanced version of the game. Why did the domestic/foreign stock/bond markets go up/down today, and why did the dollar also go up/down?

The game is a good way for you to test your understanding of the various mechanisms at work. It can be played every day. Listen to the news and try to predict what happened to the various markets and why. (This is not an easy game to play. If you are like me, you will be more often wrong than right. But it gives you a sense of the difficulties faced by policy makers when they try to predict the effects of a change in policy.)

Here is one example: In the fall of 1998, many economists started to worry that the long expansion of the 1990s may have been slowing down. Participants in financial markets started anticipating a cut in interest rates by the Federal Reserve Board to avoid a potential recession. On October 15, the Federal Reserve Board lowered its target federal funds rate—the short-term interest rate that the Federal Reserve Board affects most directly—by 0.25%.

The effect in the United States was very much as you would have predicted after reading this chapter. In anticipation of lower

U.S. short-term rates now and in the future, long-term interest rates went down by 0.05%. For the same reason, the Dow Jones index—an index of stock prices—went up by 330 points, an increase of more than 3%. And the U.S. dollar depreciated by 2% against both the DM and the yen. (Do the magnitudes of the adjustment in long-term rates, the exchange rate, and the stock market strike you as reasonable?)

On November 17, the Federal Reserve Board again cut the federal funds rate by 0.25%. That time, there was basically no reaction in financial markets! Long-term interest rates remained unchanged. The Dow Jones dropped by 24 points, or about 0.3%. And the dollar remained stable against both the DM and the yen.

Why was the second time so different from the first? For a simple reason: Whereas the first cut was unexpected, the second was widely expected. Whatever effect the second cut had on stock prices, bond prices, and on the dollar, it had it in the days preceding November 17—when participants in financial markets started anticipating it, not *on* November 17 when it was actually implemented.

SUMMARY

- Arbitrage among bonds of different maturities implies that the price of a bond is the present value of the payments on the bond, discounted using current and expected short-term interest rates. Hence, higher current or expected short-term interest rates lead to lower bond prices.

- The yield to maturity on a bond with a maturity of n years (or equivalently, the n-year interest rate) is approximately equal to the average of current and expected future one-year interest rates over this and the next $n - 1$ years.

- The slope of the yield curve (equivalently, the term structure) tells us what financial markets expect to happen to short-term interest rates in the future. A downward-sloping yield curve implies that the markets expect a decrease in short-term rates; an upward-sloping yield curve implies that the markets expect an increase in short-term rates.

- The fundamental value of a stock is the present value of expected future real dividends, discounted using current and future expected one-year real interest rates. In the absence of bubbles or fads, the price of a stock is equal to its fundamental value.

- An increase in expected dividends leads to an increase in the fundamental value of stocks; an increase in current and expected one-year interest rates leads to a decrease in the fundamental value.

- Changes in output may or may not be associated with changes in stock prices in the same direction. Whether they are depends on (1) what the markets expected in the first place, (2) the source of the shocks, and (3) how the markets expect the central bank to react to the output change.

- Stock prices can be subject to bubbles or fads that lead a stock price to differ from its fundamental value. Bubbles are episodes when financial investors buy a stock for a price higher than its fundamental value in anticipation of reselling the stock at an even higher price. "Fad" is a general term for times when, for reasons of fashion or overoptimism, financial investors are willing to pay more than the fundamental value of the stock.

- The real exchange rate today depends both on the long-run real exchange rate and on the difference between domestic and foreign long-term real interest rates. An increase in the domestic long-term real interest rate over the corresponding foreign interest rate leads to a real appreciation and a decrease to a real depreciation.

- Movements in Canadian interest rates relative to U.S. interest rates explain some of the movements in the Canadian real exchange rate in the 1990s. However, the real depreciation over the whole period reflects higher Canadian foreign debts.

- When account is taken of expectations, changes in monetary policy may lead to large variations in the exchange rate. An increase in interest rates leads to a large initial appreciation, followed by a slow depreciation over time. This large initial movement of the exchange rate is known as overshooting.

KEY TERMS

- accommodation, 383
- arbitrage, 376
- bond ratings, 374
- Canada bonds, 374
- corporate bonds, 374
- coupon bonds, 374
- coupon payments, 374
- coupon rate, 374
- current yield, 374
- debt finance, 380
- default risk, 373
- discount bonds, 374
- dividends, 380
- equity finance, 380
- equity premium, 399
- expectations hypothesis, 375
- face value, 374

- fads, 387
- fundamental value, 385
- government bonds, 374
- indexed bonds, 374
- junk bonds, 374
- maturity, 373
- overshooting, 393
- random walk, 382
- rational speculative bubbles, 385
- real return bonds, 374
- risk premium, 374
- shares, 380
- short-term, medium-term, and long-term bonds, 374
- yield curve, or term structure of interest rates, 373
- yield to maturity, or *n*-year interest rate, 376

QUESTIONS AND PROBLEMS

An asterisk denotes a harder question. [Web] indicates that the question requires access to the Internet.

1. TRUE/FALSE/UNCERTAIN

a. Junk bonds are bonds nobody wants to hold.

b. The price of a one-year bond decreases when the nominal one-year interest rate increases.

c. Given the Fisher hypothesis (see Chapter 18), an upward-sloping yield curve may indicate that financial markets are worried about inflation in the future.

d. Long-term interest rates typically move more than short-term interest rates.

e. An equal increase in expected inflation and nominal interest rates at all maturities should have no effect on the stock market.

f. A monetary expansion will lead to an upward-sloping yield curve.

g. A rational investor should never pay a positive price for a stock that will never pay dividends.

h. The strong performance of the U.S. stock market of the 1990s reflects the strong performance of the U.S. economy.

2. THE YIELD TO MATURITY

Determine the yield to maturity of each of the following bonds:

a. A discount bond with a face value of $1000, a maturity of three years, and a price of $800.

b. A discount bond with a face value of $1000, a maturity of four years, and a price of $800.

c. A discount bond with a face value of $1000, a maturity of four years, and a price of $850.

3. THE YIELD CURVE

Suppose that the interest rate this year is 5% and financial markets expect the interest rate to increase by 0.5 percentage point each year for the following three years. Determine the yield to maturity on a:

a. one-year bond.

b. two-year bond.

c. three-year bond.

*4. THE EQUITY PREMIUM, DIVIDENDS, AND STOCK PRICES

A share is expected to pay a dividend of $1000 next year, and the real value of dividend payments is expected to increase by 3% per year forever after. Determine the current price of the stock if the real interest rate is expected to remain constant at:

a. 5%.

b. 8%.

Now, suppose that people require a risk premium to hold stocks (as described in the first appendix to this chapter).

c. Repeat (a) and (b) with the required risk premium at 8%.

d. Repeat (a) and (b) with the required risk premium at 4%.

e. What happens to stock prices if the risk premium decreases? Explain in words.

5. MACROECONOMICS AND STOCK PRICES

Using the *IS-LM* model, determine the impact of each of the following on stock prices. If the effect is ambiguous, explain what additional information would be needed to reach a conclusion.

a. An unexpected expansionary monetary policy with no change in fiscal policy.

b. A fully expected expansionary monetary policy with no change in fiscal policy.

c. A fully expected expansionary monetary policy with expansionary fiscal policy.

6. EXPANSIONARY MONETARY POLICY AND THE YIELD CURVE

In the previous chapter, we examined the effects of an increase in the growth rate of money on interest rates and inflation.

a. Draw the path of the nominal interest rate following an increase in growth rate of money.

Suppose that the lowest point in the path is reached after one year and that the long-run value is achieved after three years.

b. Draw the yield curve, just after the increase in the growth rate of money, one year later, three years later.

7. DERIVING THE INTEREST PARITY CONDITION IN TERMS OF REAL INTEREST RATES

This problem helps you derive (19–11) in the text. Start from the interest parity condition:

$$(1 + i_t) = (1 + i_t^*) \frac{E_{t+1}^e}{E_t}$$

Recall the definition of the (domestic) real interest rate:

$$(1 + r_t) = \frac{1 + i_t}{1 + \pi_t^e}$$

where $\pi_t^e = (P_{t+1}^e - P_t)/P_t$ is the expected rate of inflation. Similarly, the foreign real interest rate is given by:

$$(1 + r_t^*) = \frac{1 + i_t^*}{1 + \pi_t^{*e}}$$

where $\pi_t^{*e} = (P_{t+1}^{*e} - P_t^*)/P_t^*$ is the expected foreign rate of inflation. Recall that the real exchange rate is defined as:

$$\epsilon_t = E_t P_t^*/P_t$$

So, the expected real exchange rate is given by:

$$\epsilon_{t+1}^e = E_{t+1} P_{t+1}^{*e}/P_{t+1}^e$$

Derive equation (19–11) in the text. (*Hint:* Use the two interest rate relations to eliminate nominal interest rates in the interest parity condition. Then, rewrite to get from nominal exchange rates to real exchange rates.)

8. EXPECTED NOMINAL AND REAL DEPRECIATIONS

Assume that the nominal interest rate on 10-year bonds is 10% at home and 6% abroad. Further, assume inflation is expected to be 6% at home and 3% abroad.

a. What is the expected annual real depreciation consistent with interest parity?

b. What is the expected annual nominal depreciation consistent with interest parity?

c. If you expected a nominal appreciation of the domestic currency over the next 10 years, which bond would you purchase?

There are many bad books written about the stock market. A good one, and one that is fun to read, is Burton Malkiel, *A Random Walk Down Wall Street*, 6th ed. (New York: Norton, 1995).

An account of historical bubbles is given by Peter Garber in "Famous First Bubbles," *Journal of Economic Perspectives*, Spring 1990, pp. 35–54.

ARBITRAGE AND STOCK PRICES

This appendix shows that in the absence of rational speculative bubbles, arbitrage between stocks and bonds implies that the price of a stock is equal to the expected present value of dividends.

Suppose you face the choice of investing either in one-year bonds or in stocks for a year. What should you choose?

Suppose you decide to hold one-year bonds. Then, for every dollar you put in one-year bonds, you will get $(1 + i_{1t})$ dollars next year. This payoff is represented in the upper line of Figure 19A–1.

Suppose, instead, you decide to hold stocks for a year. This implies buying a stock today, receiving a dividend next year, and then selling the stock. As the price of a stock is $\$Q_t$, every dollar you put in stocks buys you $\$1/\$Q_t$ stocks. And for each stock you buy, you expect to receive $(\$D_{t+1}^e + \$Q_{t+1}^e)$, the sum of the expected dividend and the stock price next year. So, for every dollar you put in stocks, you expect to receive $(\$D_{t+1}^e + \$Q_{t+1}^e)/\$Q_t$ dollars next year. This payoff is represented in the lower line of Figure 19A–1.

Let us use the same arbitrage argument we used for bonds earlier. If financial investors care only about expected rates of return, then equilibrium requires that the expected rate of return from holding stocks for one year be the same as the rate of return on one-year bonds:

$$\frac{(\$D_{t+1}^e + \$Q_{t+1}^e)}{\$Q_t} = 1 + i_{1t}$$

Rewrite this equation as:

$$\$Q_t = \frac{\$D_{t+1}^e}{(1 + i_{1t})} + \frac{\$Q_{t+1}^e}{(1 + i_{1t})} \qquad (19A.1)$$

Arbitrage implies that the price of the stock today must be equal to the present value of the expected dividend plus the present value of the expected stock price next year.

The next step is to think about what determines $\$Q_{t+1}^e$, the expected stock price next year. Next year, financial investors will again face the choice between stocks and one-year bonds. Thus, the same arbitrage relation will hold. Writing the previous equation, but now for time $t + 1$, and taking expectations into account gives:

$$\$Q_{t+1}^e = \frac{\$D_{t+2}^e}{(1 + i_{1t+1}^e)} + \frac{\$Q_{t+2}^e}{(1 + i_{1t+1}^e)}$$

The expected price next year is simply the present value next year of the sum of the expected dividend and price two years from now. Replacing the expected price $\$Q_{t+1}^e$ in equation (19A.1) gives:

$$\$Q_t = \frac{\$D_{t+1}^e}{(1 + i_{1t})} + \frac{\$D_{t+2}^e}{(1 + i_{1t})(1 + i_{1t+1}^e)}$$
$$+ \frac{\$Q_{t+2}^e}{(1 + i_{1t})(1 + i_{1t+1}^e)}$$

The stock price is the present value of the expected dividend next year plus the present value of the expected dividend two years from now plus the expected price two years from now.

If we replace the expected price in two years as the present value of the expected price and dividends in three years, and so on for n years, we get:

$$\$Q_t = \frac{\$D_{t+1}^e}{(1 + i_{1t})} + \cdots + \frac{\$D_{t+n}^e}{(1 + i_{1t}) \cdots (1 + i_{1t+n-1}^e)}$$
$$+ \frac{\$Q_{t+n}^e}{(1 + i_{1t}) \cdots (1 + i_{1t+n-1}^e)}$$

Look at the last term, which is the present value of the expected price in n years. As long as people do not expect the stock price to explode in the future, then, as we keep replacing Q_{t+n}^e, and n increases, this term will go to zero. To see why, suppose the interest rate is constant and equal to i, and people expect the price of the stock to converge to some value, call it $\$\overline{Q}$ in the far future. Then, the last term

---

*DIGGING DEEPER. When prices are subject to rational bubbles as discussed in section 19-3, the condition that the expected stock price does not explode is not satisfied. When there are bubbles, the stock price need not be equal to the present value of expected dividends.

	Year t		Year $t + 1$
One-year bonds	$1	→	$1 (1 + i_{1t})$
Stocks	$1	→	$1 \dfrac{\$D^e_{t+1} + \$Q^e_{t+1}}{\$Q_t}$

FIGURE 19A–1

Returns from Holding One-Year Bonds or Stocks for One Year

becomes $\$\overline{Q}/(1 + i)^n$. If the interest rate is positive, the term goes to zero as n becomes large.* The previous expression reduces to equation (19.9) in the text: The price today is the present value of expected future dividends.

An Extension to the Present Value Formula to Take Risk into Account

If people perceive stocks as more risky than bonds, and people dislike risk, they will require a risk premium to hold stocks rather than bonds. In the case of shares, this risk premium is called the **equity premium**. Denote it by θ (the Greek lowercase letter theta). If θ is, for example, 5%, then people will hold stocks only if the expected rate of return on stocks exceeds the expected rate of return on short-term bonds by 5 percentage points a year.

In that case, the arbitrage equation between stocks and bonds becomes:

$$\frac{\$D^e_{t+1} + \$Q^e_{t+1}}{\$Q_t} = 1 + i_{1t} + \theta$$

The only change is the presence of θ on the right side of the equation. Going through the same steps as above, the stock price equals:

$$\$Q_t = \frac{\$D^e_{t+1}}{(1 + i_{1t} + \theta)} + \cdots$$

$$+ \frac{\$D^e_{t+n}}{(1 + i_{1t} + \theta) \cdots (1 + i^e_{1t+n-1} + \theta)} + \cdots$$

The stock price is still equal to the present value of expected future dividends. But the discount rate here equals the interest rate plus the equity premium. Note that the higher the premium, the lower is the stock price. Over the last 100 years, in the United States, the average equity premium has been equal to roughly 5%. But (in contrast to our assumption above) it is not constant. The equity premium appears, for example, to have decreased since the early 1950s, from around 7% to less than 3% today. Variations in the equity premium are another source of fluctuations in stock prices.

APPENDIX B

THE REAL EXCHANGE RATE, AND DOMESTIC AND FOREIGN REAL INTEREST RATES

We derived in section 19-3 a relation between the current nominal exchange rate, current and expected future domestic and foreign nominal interest rates, and the expected future nominal exchange rate (equation (19.5)). This appendix derives a similar relation, but in terms of real interest rates and the real exchange rate. It then briefly discusses how this alternative relation can be used to think about movements in the real exchange rate.

Deriving the Real Interest-Parity Condition

Start from the nominal interest-parity condition, equation in Chapter 6:

$$(1 + i_t) = (1 + i^*_t) \frac{(E_t)}{E^e_{t+1}}$$

Recall the definition of the real interest rate from Chapter 18, equation (18.3):

$$(1 + r_t) \equiv \frac{(1 + i_t)}{(1 + \pi^e_t)}$$

where $\pi^e_t \equiv (P^e_{t+1} - P_t)/P_t$ is the expected rate of inflation. Similarly, the foreign real interest rate is given by:

$$(1 + r_t^*) = \frac{(1 + i_t^*)}{(1 + \pi_t^{*e})}$$

where $\pi_t^{*e} \int (P_{t+1}^{*e} - P_t^*)/P_t^*$ is the expected foreign rate of inflation.

Use these two relations to eliminate nominal interest rates in the interest-parity condition, so:

$$(1 + r_t) = (1 + r_t^*)\left[\frac{E_t}{E_{t+1}^e} \frac{(1 + \pi_t^{*e})}{(1 + \pi_t^e)} \right] \qquad (19.A1)$$

Note from the definition of inflation that $(1 + \pi_t^e) = P_{t+1}^e/P_t$ and, similarly, $(1 + \pi_t^{*e}) = P_{t+1}^{*e}/P_t^*$.
Using these two relations in the term in brackets gives:

$$\frac{E_t}{E_{t+1}^e} \frac{(1 + \pi_t^{*e})}{(1 + \pi_t^e)} = \frac{E_t P_{t+1}^{*e} P_t}{E_{t+1}^e P_t^* P_{t+1}^e}$$

Reorganizing terms:

$$\frac{E_t P_{t+1}^{*e} P_t}{E_{t+1}^e P_t^* P_{t+1}^e} = \frac{E_t P_t / P_t^*}{E_{t+1}^e P_{t+1}^e / P_{t+1}^{*e}}$$

Using the definition of the real exchange rate:

$$\frac{E_t P_t / P_t^*}{E_{t+1}^e P_{t+1}^e / P_{t+1}^{*e}} = \frac{\epsilon_t}{\epsilon_{t+1}^e}$$

Replacing in equation (19.A1) gives:

$$(1 + r_t) = (1 + r_t^*) \frac{\epsilon_t}{\epsilon_{t+1}^e}$$

Or, equivalently:

$$\epsilon_t = \frac{1 + r_t}{1 + r_t^*} \epsilon_{t+1}^e \qquad (19.A2)$$

The real exchange rate today depends on the domestic and foreign real interest rates this year and the expected future real exchange rate next year. This equation corresponds to equation (19.11) in the text, but now in terms of the real rather than nominal exchange and interest rates.

Solving the Real Interest-Parity Condition Forward

The next step is to solve equation (19.A2) forward, in the same way as we did for equation (19.4) in the text. The equation above implies that the real exchange rate in year $t + 1$ is given by:

$$\epsilon_{t+1} = \frac{1 + r_{t+1}}{1 + r_{t+1}^*} \epsilon_{t+2}^e$$

Taking expectations, as of year t:

$$\epsilon_{t+1}^e = \frac{1 + r_{t+1}^e}{1 + r_{t+1}^{*e}} \epsilon_{t+2}^e$$

Replacing in the previous relation:

$$\epsilon_{t1} = \frac{(1 + r_t)(1 + r_{t+1}^e)}{(1 + r_t^*)(1 + r_{t+1}^{*e})}$$

Solving for ϵ_{t+2}^e and so on gives:

$$\epsilon_t = \frac{(1 + r_t)(1 + r_{t+1}^e)\ldots(1 + r_{t+n}^e)}{(1 + r_t^*)(1 + r_{t+1}^{*e})\ldots(1 + r_{t+n}^{*e})} \epsilon_{t+n}^e$$

This relation gives the current real exchange rate as a function of current and expected future domestic real interest rates, of current and expected future foreign real interest rates, and of the expected real exchange rate in year $t + n$.

The advantage of this relation over the relation we derived in the text between the nominal exchange rate and nominal interest rates, equation (6.2), is that it is typically easier to predict the future real exchange rate than to predict the future nominal exchange rate. If, for example, the economy suffers from a large trade deficit, we may be fairly confident that there will have to be a real depreciation—that ϵ_{t+n}^e will have to be higher. Whether there will be a nominal depreciation—what happens to E_{t+n}^e—is harder to tell. That depends on what happens to inflation, both at home and abroad over the next n years.

CHAPTER 20
EXPECTATIONS, CONSUMPTION, AND INVESTMENT

Having looked at the role of expectations in financial markets, we now turn to their role in determining the two main components of spending—consumption and investment. This description of consumption and investment will be the main building block of the expanded *IS-LM* model we will develop in Chapter 21.

Section 20-1 looks at consumption and shows how consumption decisions depend not only on current income but also on expected future income as well as on financial wealth. Section 20-2 turns to investment and shows how investment decisions depend on current and expected profits and current and expected interest rates. Finally, section 20-3 looks at the movements of consumption and investment over time and shows how we can interpret them in light of the theories developed in this chapter.

20-1 | Consumption

How do people decide how much to consume and how much to save? In our first pass at the answer in the core (Chapter 3), we made the simple assumption that consumption and saving depended on current income. By now, you do not need to be convinced that they depend on much more, particularly on expectations of the future. We now explore how those expectations affect the consumption decision.

The theory of consumption on which this section is based was developed independently in the 1950s by Milton Friedman of the University of Chicago, who called it the **permanent income theory of consumption**, and by Franco Modigliani, of the Massachusetts Institute of Technology (MIT), who called it the **life cycle theory of consumption**. Each chose his label carefully. Friedman's "permanent income" emphasized that consumers look beyond current income. Modigliani's "life cycle" emphasized that consumers' natural planning horizon is their entire lifetime.

Friedman received the ▶ Nobel prize in economics in 1976 and Modigliani in 1985.

The behaviour of aggregate consumption has remained a hot area of research ever since, for two reasons. The first is simply the sheer size of consumption in GDP and therefore the need to understand movements in consumption. The second is the increasing availability of large surveys of individual consumers, such as the Panel Study of Income Dynamics described in the Focus box "Up Close and Personal: Learning from Panel Data Sets." These surveys, which were not available when Friedman and Modigliani developed their theories, have allowed economists to steadily improve their understanding of how consumers actually behave. What follows summarizes what we know today.

The Very Foresighted Consumer

Let us start with an assumption that will surely—and rightly—strike you as extreme but will serve as a convenient benchmark. We will call it the theory of the *very foresighted consumer*. How would a very foresighted consumer decide how much to consume? He would proceed in two steps.

FOCUS   Up Close and Personal: Learning from Panel Data Sets

Panel data sets are data sets that give the value of one or more variables for many individuals or many firms over time. We described one such survey, the *Labour Force Survey*, in Chapter 9. Another is the Panel Study of Income Dynamics, or PSID. This data is available only in the United States. Canada has a panel data set for income and unemployment called SLID (Survey of Labour Income Dynamics), which tracks individuals for as long as six years. But SLID asks only about labour market experiences and not about consumption.

The PSID was started in 1968, with approximately 4800 families. Interviews of these families have been conducted every year since and are still continuing. The survey has grown as new individuals have joined the original families, either by marriage or by birth. Each year, the survey asks people about their income, wage rate, number of hours worked, health, and food consumption. (The focus on food consumption is because one of the survey's initial aims was to better understand the living conditions of poor families. The survey would be more useful if it asked about all of consumption rather than food consumption.

Unfortunately, it does not.)

By using over 30 years of information about individuals and about extended families, the survey has allowed economists to ask and answer questions for which there was previously only anecdotal evidence. Among the many questions for which the PSID has been used in the recent past are the following:

- How much does (food) consumption respond to transitory movements in income? For example, to the loss of income from becoming unemployed?

- How much risk-sharing is there within families? For example, when a family member becomes sick or unemployed, how much help does he or she get from other family members?

- How much do people care about staying geographically close to their families? When somebody becomes unemployed, for example, how does the probability that he will migrate to another city depend on how many family members live in the city in which he currently lives?

- First, he would add up the value of the stocks and bonds he owns, the value of his chequing and savings accounts, the value of the house he owns minus the mortgage still due, and so on. This would give him a notion of his financial wealth and his **housing wealth**.

  He would also estimate what his after-tax labour income was likely to be over his working life and compute the present value of expected after-tax labour income. This would give him an estimate of what economists call his **human wealth**—to contrast it with his **nonhuman wealth**, defined as the sum of financial and housing wealth.

- Adding his human and nonhuman wealth, he would have an estimate of his **total wealth**. He would then decide how much to spend out of this total wealth. A reasonable assumption is that he would decide to spend a proportion of total wealth such as to maintain roughly the same level of consumption each year throughout his life. If that level of consumption was higher than his current income, he would then borrow the difference. If it was lower than his current income, he would instead save the difference.

With a slight abuse of language, we will use "housing wealth" to refer not only to housing but also to the other goods that the consumer may own, from cars to paintings and so on.

Human wealth (= Present value of expected after-tax labour income) + Non-human wealth (= Housing wealth + Financial wealth) = Total wealth

Let us write this formally. What we have described is a consumption decision of the form:

$$C_t = C\,(\text{total wealth}_t) \tag{20.1}$$

where C_t is consumption, and (total wealth$_t$) is the sum of nonhuman wealth (financial plus housing wealth) and human wealth (the expected present value of after-tax labour income).

This description contains much truth: Like the foresighted consumer, we surely do think about our wealth and our expected future labour income in deciding how much to consume today. But one cannot help thinking that it assumes too much computation and foresight on the part of the typical consumer.

To get a better sense of what the description implies and what is wrong with it, let us apply this decision process to the problem facing a typical university student.

Because each of us is a consumer, we can use introspection as a way of checking on the plausibility of a particular theory. Alas, introspection is not without potential pitfalls: Economists perhaps do not think like other people. . . .

An Example

Let us assume you are 21 years old, with three more years of university before you take your first job. Some of you may be in debt today, having borrowed to go to university; some of you may own a car and a few other worldly possessions. For simplicity, let us assume your debt and your possessions roughly offset each other so that your nonhuman wealth is equal to zero. Your only wealth is your human wealth, the present value of your expected after-tax labour income.

Based on what we know today, you can expect your starting salary in three years to be around $40,000 (in year 2000 dollars) and to increase by an average of 3% a year in real terms, until your retirement at age 60. About 25% of your income will go to taxes.

You are welcome to use your own numbers, and see where the computation takes you.

Building on what we saw in Chapter 18, let us compute the present value of your labour income as the value of *real* expected after-tax labour income, discounted using *real* interest rates (equation (18.7)). Let Y_{Lt} denote real labour income in year t. Let T_t denote real taxes (net of transfers). Let $V(Y_{Lt}^e - T_t^e)$ denote your human wealth, that is, the expected present value of your after-tax labour income. To make the computation simple, assume the real interest rate equals zero—so the expected present value is simply the sum of expected after-tax labour income over your working life and is therefore given by:

$$V(Y_{Lt}^e - T_t^e) = 0.75[1 + (1.03) + (1.03)^2 + \cdots + (1.03)^{36}](\$40,000)$$

The first term (0.75) comes from the fact that because of taxes you keep only 75% of what you earn. The second term $[1 + (1.03) + (1.03)^2 + \cdots + (1.03)^{36}]$ reflects the fact that you expect your real income to increase by 3% a year for 37 years (you will start earning income at age 24 and work until age 60). The third term ($40,000) is the initial level of labour income, in year 2000 dollars. Using the properties of geometric series to solve for the sum in brackets gives:

$$V(Y_{Lt}^e - T_t^e) = 0.75(66.2)(\$40,000) = \$1,986,000$$

Your wealth today, the expected value of your lifetime after-tax labour income, is around $2 million.

How much should you consume? You can expect to live about 16 years after retirement, so your expected remaining life today is 56 years. If you want to consume the same amount every year, the constant level of consumption that you can afford equals your total wealth divided by your expected remaining life, or $1,986,000/56 = $35,464 a year. Given that your income until you get your first job is equal to zero, this implies borrowing $35,464 a year for the next three years and starting to save when you get your first job.

Toward a More Realistic Description

Your first reaction to this computation may be that this is a stark and slightly sinister way of summarizing your life prospects. Your second reaction may be that while you agree with most of the ingredients that went into the computation, you surely do not intend to borrow $35,464 \times 3 = $106,392 over the next three years.

The computation of what consumption level you can sustain is made easier by our assumption that the real interest rate equals zero. In this case, if you consume one fewer good today, you can consume exactly one more good next year, and the condition you must satisfy is simply that the sum of consumption over your lifetime is equal to your wealth. If you want to consume a constant amount each year, then, to find how much you can consume each year, you need to divide your wealth by the remaining number of years in your life.

1. You may not want to plan for constant consumption over your lifetime and may be quite happy with deferring higher consumption until later. Student life usually does not leave much time for expensive activities. You may want to defer memberships in golf clubs and trips to the Galápagos islands to later in life. You also have to think about the additional expenses that will come with having children, sending them to nursery school, summer camp, postsecondary education, and so on.

2. You may find that the amount of computation and foresight involved in the computation we just went through far exceeds the amount you use in your own decisions. You may never have thought until now about exactly how much income you are going to make, and for how many years. You may feel that most consumption decisions are made in a simpler, less forward-looking fashion.

3. The computation of total wealth is based on forecasts of what can reasonably be expected to happen. But things can turn out better or worse. What happens if you are unlucky and you become unemployed or sick? How will you pay back what you borrowed? You may well want to be prudent, making sure that you can adequately survive even the worst outcomes and thus borrow much less than $106,392.

4. Even if you decided to borrow $106,392, you are likely to find the bank from which you try to borrow that amount to be unreceptive. Why? The bank may worry that you are taking on a commitment you will not be able to afford if times turn bad and that you may not be able or willing to repay the loan.

These reasons, all good ones, imply that to characterize consumers' actual behaviour, we must modify the description we gave earlier. The last three reasons in particular suggest consumption depends not only on total wealth but also on current income.

Take the second reason. You may, because it is a simple rule, decide to let your consumption follow your income and not think about what your wealth might be. In that case, consumption will depend on current income, not on your wealth. Now, take the third reason. It implies that a safe rule may be to consume no more than your current income. This way, you do not run the risk of accumulating debt that you could not repay if times were to turn bad. Or take the fourth reason. It implies that you may have little choice anyway. Even if you wanted to consume more than your current income, you may be unable to do so because no bank will make you a loan.

If we want to allow for a direct effect of current income on consumption, what measure of current income should we use? A convenient variable is after-tax labour income, introduced earlier when defining human wealth. This leads to a consumption function of the form:

$$C_t = C(\text{Total wealth}_t, Y_{Lt} - T_t) \tag{20.2}$$
$$(\qquad + \qquad , \quad + \quad)$$

The plus sign under "Total wealth" indicates that an increase in total wealth increases consumption. The same holds for $Y_{Lt} - T_t$.

In words: *Consumption is an increasing function of total wealth and of current after-tax labour income. Total wealth is the sum of nonhuman wealth—financial wealth plus housing wealth—and of human wealth—the present value of expected after-tax labour income.*

The practical issue then becomes how much consumption depends on total wealth (and thus on expectations of future income) and how much on current income. Some consumers, especially those who have temporarily low income and poor access to credit, are likely to consume their current income regardless of what they expect will happen to them in the future. A worker who becomes unemployed and has no financial wealth may have a hard time borrowing to maintain her level of consumption, even if she is fairly confident that she will soon find another job. Consumers who are richer and have easier access to credit are more likely to give more weight to the expected future and to try to maintain roughly constant consumption through time.

The relative importance of wealth and income on consumption can be settled only by looking at the empirical evidence. This is not easy to do, and the In Depth box "How Much Do Expectations Matter? Looking for Natural Experiments" explains why. But even if some details still need to be filled in, the basic evidence is clear and unsurprising: Both total wealth and current income affect consumption.

Tiff Macklem of the Bank of Canada did an exhaustive study of consumption in Canada as part of the Bank's research effort to model behaviour in the Canadian economy. Canadian

◄ How expectations of higher output in the future affect consumption today:

Future output ↑ ⇒
Future labour income ↑ ⇒
Human wealth ↑ ⇒
Consumption today ↑

Future output ↑ ⇒
Future dividends ↑ ⇒
Stock prices ↑ ⇒
Nonhuman wealth ↑ ⇒
Consumption today ↑

IN DEPTH　　How Much Do Expectations Matter? Looking for Natural Experiments

How much does consumption depend on current income versus expected future income? This is not an easy question to answer because, most of the time, expectations of future income move very much with current income. If we get promoted and receive a raise, not only does our current income go up but, typically, so does the income we can expect to receive in future years. Whether or not we are very foresighted, our consumption will typically move closely with our current income.

What can economists do to disentangle the effects of current income versus future income? They must look for times and events where current income and expected future income move in different ways and then look at what happens to consumption. Such events are called **natural experiments**. "Experiments" in the sense that, like laboratory experiments, these events allow us to test a theory or to get a better estimate of an important parameter. "Natural" meaning that, unlike researchers in the physical sciences, economists typically cannot run experiments themselves. They must rely on experiments given by nature—or, as we will see in our second example below, created by policy makers.

Here are three examples from recent research on consumption:

(1) Retirement

Retirement implies a large, predictable change in labour income: Labour income drops to zero. By looking at how people save for retirement, we can, in principle, find out whether, when, and by how much people take into account the predictable decline in their future labour income.

A recent U.S. study, based on a panel data set called the *Survey of Income and Program Participation*, sheds some light

on retirement behaviour. Table 1, taken from the study, shows the mean level and the composition of total wealth for people between 65 and 69 years in 1991.

A mean wealth of $313,807 is substantial (U.S. per capita personal disposable income was $16,205 in 1991), suggesting an image of forward-looking individuals making careful saving decisions and retiring with enough wealth to enjoy a comfortable retirement.

A closer look at the table, and at differences between individuals, suggests two caveats.

- The largest component of wealth is the present value of Social Security benefits, an amount over which workers have no control. Indeed, one of the main motivations behind the introduction of the Social Security program in the United States was to make sure people contributed to their retirement, whether or not they would have done so on their own. The third largest component is an employer-provided pension—another component over which workers have limited control. The only components that clearly reflect individual saving decisions (personal retirement assets + other financial assets) account only for $53,010, or about 17% of total wealth. Thus, one also can read the evidence as suggesting that people save enough for retirement because they are forced to, through social security and other contributions.

- The numbers in the table are averages and hide substantial differences across individuals. The same study shows that most people retire with little more than their Social Security pensions. More generally, studies of retirement saving give the following picture: Most people appear to

(continued on the next page)

---

give little thought to retirement saving until some time during their 40s. At that point, many start saving for retirement. But many also save little and rely mostly on Social Security benefits when they retire.

(2) Announced tax cuts

In 1981, the Reagan administration designed a fiscal package with phased-in tax cuts over 1981 to 1983. Income tax rates were to be reduced in three steps: 5% in 1981, 10% in 1982, and 8% in 1983, implying a cumulative reduction of 23%, a very large amount, indeed. Congress passed the package in July 1981, and it became law in August 1981.

This period of U.S. history provides us with a natural experiment. The experiment is a change in expected future after-tax labour income coming from an anticipated decrease in taxes. And the question we want to answer is simple: Did consumers react in 1981 to the expected decrease in taxes in 1982 and 1983, and if so, by how much?

This is exactly the question asked by James Poterba, from MIT, in a 1988 article. Using econometrics, Poterba looked for evidence of an unusual increase in consumption, given disposable income, in the summer of 1981 (the time when Congress passed the package). He found no evidence of such an increase.

Is this conclusive evidence that consumers do not take into account changes in expected future income in their consumption decision? Not necessarily. There are at least two alternative interpretations of the facts. People may have believed that Congress would change its mind, leading them to take a wait-and-see attitude and wait for the actual decreases in taxes to adjust their consumption. Or maybe people do not take into account expected changes in taxes but take into account other expected changes in their income (say, an expected promotion or the coming of retirement). These arguments cannot be dismissed. But what can be safely said is that the evidence from that particular natural experiment does not provide evidence for a strong effect of expected future tax changes on consumption.

Canada had a recent experience with announced tax cuts. In an *Economic Statement* (October 18, 2000) just prior to the federal election of November 27, 2000, Finance Minister Paul Martin promised to substantially reduce federal income taxes over the next five years. Mr. Martin's party was expected to win the election and did. In 2001, when economic growth slowed in both Canada and the United States, the tax cuts in 2001 and those promised in future years were credited with maintaining strong consumer demand. However, without a panel data set, such as the PSID, further testing of this hypothesis is difficult.

(3) The effects of increases in real estate prices on consumption

A key macroeconomic concern in the last decade has been the effect of increases in house prices on consumption. The mechanism is quite clear, as the value of houses rises relative to the overall price level, consumers feel wealthier and consume more. Banks are very willing to allow consumers to borrow against the value of their house in the form of mortgage-backed lines of credit. From 1997 to 2004, house prices rose by 41% in Canada; by 52% in New Zealand; by 65% in the United States; by 113% in Australia; by 147% in Britain; and by 195% in South Africa. It is unclear if the rise in values of houses is a fundamental, that is, a rise in the present discounted value of the rental stream to the house, or a bubble in house prices. We discussed bubbles in Chapter 19. Because real interest rates fell over this period (see Figure 18–2), the value of houses "should have" risen if the fundamentals model described housing prices. House price rises in excess of that predicted by fundamentals would be a bubble, and people buy houses only to resell at a higher price. It is very difficult to detect if a bubble is occurring as it occurs. Regardless of the source of the increase in house prices, the macroeconomic question is whether consumers responded to the increase in wealth by increasing consumption. The way to test this hypothesis is to ask whether consumption rose more in countries and states where house prices increased more. That is precisely what Karl Case, John Quigley, and Robert Shiller did. They studied 14 countries and a panel of U.S. states during the 1980s and 1990s. There was a large effect of housing wealth on consumption. So, if housing prices fall, we would predict a decline in consumption.

Sources:

On retirement: Steven Venti and David Wise, "The Wealth of Cohorts: Retirement and Saving and the Changing Assets of Older Americans," mimeo, Kennedy School, Harvard University, October 1993.

On the Reagan tax cuts: James Poterba, "Are Consumers Forward Looking? Evidence from Fiscal Experiments," *American Economic Review*, May 1988, pp. 413–418.

On the increases in real estate prices: Karl E. Case, John N. Quigley, and Robert J. Shiller "Comparing Wealth Effects: The Stock market versus the Housing Market," *Advances in Macroeconomics*, Volume 5, No 1, Article 1, 2005.

TABLE 1	Mean Wealth of People in the United States, Age 65–69, in 1991 (in Current Dollars)

Social Security pension	$ 99,682
Employer-provided pension	62,305
Personal retirement assets	10,992
Other financial assets	42,018
Home equity	64,955
Other equity	33,855
Total	$313,807

Source: Venti and Wise, Table A1. (The first two items are expected present values of future payments.)

consumption fits equation (20.2)—fluctuations in both wealth and in current disposable income after taxes explain fluctuations in consumption.

Putting Things Together: Current Income, Expectations, and Consumption

Let us go back to what motivates this chapter, the importance of expectations in the determination of spending. Note first that with consumption behaviour described by equation (20.2), expectations affect consumption in two ways:

- They affect it directly through human wealth: To compute their human wealth, consumers have to form their own expectations of future labour income, real interest rates, and taxes.
- They affect it indirectly, through nonhuman wealth—stocks, bonds, housing. Consumers do not need to do any computation here and can take the value of these assets as a given. But as we saw in Chapter 19, the computation is, in effect, done for them by financial markets. The price of their stocks, for example, depends itself on expectations of future dividends and interest rates.

This dependence of consumption on expectations has, in turn, two main implications.

First, *consumption is likely to respond less than one for one to fluctuations in current income.* In thinking about how much they should consume, consumers look at more than current income. If they conclude that a decrease in income is permanent, they may decrease consumption one for one with the decrease in income. But if they conclude that the decrease in current income is transitory, they will adjust their consumption by less. In a recession, consumption adjusts less than one for one to decreases in income. This is because consumers know that recessions typically do not last for more than a few quarters and that the economy will eventually return to its natural output level. The same is true during expansions. Faced with an unusually rapid increase in income, consumers are unlikely to increase consumption by as much. They are likely to assume that the boom is transitory and that things will return to normal.

Second, *consumption may move even if current income does not change.* The election of a charismatic leader who articulates the vision of an exciting future may lead people to become more optimistic about the future in general and about their own future income in particular, leading them to increase consumption even if their current income does not change. We know that "consumer confidence" appears in the news as a key economic variable. It measures optimism about future income prospects among households. Optimistic consumers increase their consumption, and pessimistic consumers decrease their consumption and can even "cause" a recession.

> Go back to the two consumption functions we used in the core:
> Looking at the short run (Chapter 3), we assumed $C = c_0 + c_1 Y$. (Ignore taxes for simplicity here.) This implied that when output increased, consumption increased less than proportionately (C/Y goes down). This was appropriate, as our focus was on output fluctuations—on transitory movements in output.
> Looking at the long run (Chapter 15), we assumed that $S = sY$, or, equivalently, $C = (1 - s)Y$. This implied that when output increases, consumption increases proportionately (C/Y is constant). This was appropriate, as our focus was on permanent—long run—movements in output.

> What does this suggest happens to the saving rate in a recession?

20-2 | Investment

How do firms make investment decisions? In our first pass at the answer in the core (Chapter 5), we took investment to depend on the current interest rate and the current level of sales. We improved on that answer in Chapter 18 by pointing out that what mattered was the real interest rate, not the nominal interest rate. It is clear that these answers underplayed the role of expectations. We will now look at their role more closely.

Think of the decision by a firm about buying a new machine. What will matter is the present value of profits the firm expects from having this machine, compared with the cost of buying the machine. If the present value exceeds the cost, the firm should buy the machine, that is, invest; if the present value is less than the cost, then the firm should not buy the machine, that is, not invest. This, in a nutshell, is the theory of investment. Let us look at it in more detail.

Investment and Expectations of Profit

Let us go through the steps a firm must take to determine whether to buy a new machine. (Although we refer to a machine, the same reasoning applies to the other components of investment, the building of a new factory, the renovation of an office complex, and so on.)

1. To compute the present value of expected profits, the firm first must estimate how long the machine will last. Most machines are like cars. They can last nearly forever; but as time passes, they become more and more expensive to maintain and less and less reliable.

   Let us assume a machine loses its usefulness at rate δ (the Greek lowercase letter delta) per year. A machine that is new this year is worth only $(1 - \delta)$; machines next year, $(1 - \delta)^2$; machines in two years, and so on. The *depreciation rate*, δ, measures how much usefulness the machine loses from one year to the next. What are reasonable values for δ? This is a question that the statisticians in charge of computing how the capital stock changes over time have had to answer. On the basis of their studies of depreciation of specific machines and buildings, they use numbers between 4 and 15% per year for machines and between 2 and 4% per year for buildings and factories. There are direct measures of the Canadian physical capital in the National Balance Sheets.

2. The firm must then compute the present value of expected profits. To capture the fact that it takes some time to put machines in place (and even more time to build a factory or an office building), let us assume that a machine bought in year t becomes operational—and starts depreciating—only one year later, in year $t + 1$.

   Denote profit per machine in real terms by Π (this is an uppercase pi as opposed to the lowercase pi, which we use to denote inflation). If the firm purchases a machine in year t, the machine generates its first expected profit in year $t + 1$; denote this expected profit by Π^e_{t+1}. The present value, in year t, of this expected profit in year $t + 1$, is given by

$$\frac{1}{1 + r_t} \Pi^e_{t+1}$$

This computation is represented by the arrow pointing left in the upper line of Figure 20–1. Because we are measuring profit in real terms, we are using real interest rates to discount future profits. This is one of the lessons we learned in Chapter 18.

   Denote expected profit per machine in year $t + 2$ by Π^e_{t+2}. Because of depreciation, only $(1 - \delta)$ of the machine bought in year t is left in year $t + 2$, so the expected profit from the machine is equal to $(1 - \delta)\Pi^e_{t+2}$. The present value of this expected profit as of year t is equal to:

$$\frac{1}{(1 + r_t)(1 + r^e_{t+1})} (1 - \delta)\Pi^e_{t+2}$$

This computation is represented by the arrow pointing left in the lower line of Figure 20–1.

   The same reasoning applies to expected profit in following years. Putting the pieces together gives us *the present value of expected profits* from buying the machine in year t, call it $V(\Pi_t^e)$:

$$V(\Pi_t^e) = \frac{1}{1 + r_t} \Pi^e_{t+1} + \frac{1}{(1 + r_t)(1 + r^e_{t+1})} (1 - \delta)\Pi^e_{t+2} + \cdots \tag{20.3}$$

Computing the Present Value of Expected Profits

Present Value in Year t	Expected Profit in: Year $t + 1$	Year $t + 2 \ldots$
$\frac{1}{1 + r_t} \Pi^e_{t+1}$	Π^e_{t+1}	
$\frac{1}{(1 + r_t)(1 + r^e_{t+1})} (1 - \delta)\Pi^e_{t+2}$		$(1 - \delta)\Pi^e_{t+2}$

The expected present value is equal to the discounted value of expected profit next year plus the discounted value of expected profit two years from now (taking into account the depreciation of the machine) and so on.

3. The firm must then decide whether to buy the machine. This decision depends on the relation between the present value of expected profits and the price of the machine. To simplify notation, let us assume that the real price of a machine—that is, the machine's price in terms of the basket of goods produced in the economy—equals one. What the firm must then do is compare the present value of profits to one.

   If the present value is less than one, the firm should not buy the machine: If it did, it would be paying more for the machine than it expects to get back in profits later. If the present value exceeds one, the firm has an incentive to buy the new machine.

Let us now jump from this one-firm, one-machine example to investment in the economy as a whole. Let I_t denote aggregate investment. Denote profit per machine, or more generally profit per unit of capital (where capital includes machines, factories, office buildings, and so on), for the economy as a whole by Π_t. Denote the expected present value of profit per unit of capital by $V(\Pi_t^e)$, defined as in equation (20.3). Our discussion suggests an investment function of the form:

$$I_t = I(V(\Pi_t^e)) \qquad (20.4)$$
$$(\ +\ )$$

In words: Investment depends positively on the expected present value of future profits (per unit of capital). The higher the current or expected profits, the higher is the expected present value and the higher the level of investment. The higher the current or expected real interest rates, the lower is the expected present value, and thus the lower the level of investment.

If the present value computation the firm has to make strikes you as quite similar to the present value computation we saw in Chapter 19 for the fundamental value of a stock, you are right. This relation was first explored by James Tobin, from Yale University, who argued that there, indeed, should be a tight relation between investment and the value of the stock market. His argument and the evidence are presented in the Focus box "Investment and the Stock Market." ◀ Tobin received the Nobel prize in economics in 1981.

A Convenient Special Case

Before exploring further implications and extensions of equation (20.4), it is useful to go through a special case, where the relation among investment, profit, and interest rates becomes very simple.

Suppose firms expect both future profits (per unit of capital) and future interest rates to remain at the same level as today so that $\Pi_{t+1}^e = \Pi_{t+2}^e = \cdots = \Pi_t$, and $r_{t+1}^e = r_{t+2}^e = \cdots = r_t$. Under these assumptions, equation (20.3) becomes:

$$V(\Pi_t^e) = \frac{\Pi_t}{r_t + \delta} \qquad (20.5)$$

(The derivation is given in appendix B of this chapter.) The present value of expected profits is simply the ratio of profit to the sum of the real interest rate and the depreciation rate.

Replacing (20.5) in equation (20.4), investment is:

$$I_t = I\left(\frac{\Pi_t}{r_t + \delta}\right) \qquad (20.6)$$

Look more closely at the fraction in parentheses. The denominator—the sum of the real interest rate and the depreciation rate—is called the **user cost** or the **rental cost of capital**. To see why, suppose the firm, instead of buying the machine, rented it by the year from a rental agency. How much would the rental agency charge? Even if the machine did not ◀ Such arrangements exist: Many firms lease cars and trucks from leasing companies.

Suppose a firm has 100 machines and 100 shares outstanding—one share per machine. Suppose the price per share is $2, and the purchase price of a machine is only $1. Obviously the firm should invest—buy a new machine—and finance it by issuing a share. Each machine costs the firm $1 to purchase, but stock market participants are willing to pay $2 for a share corresponding to this machine when it is installed in the firm.

This is an example of a more general argument made by Tobin that there should be a tight relation between the stock market and investment. When deciding whether or not to invest, he argued, firms might not need to go through the type of complicated computation you saw in the text. In effect, the stock price tells firms how much the stock market values each unit of capital already in place. The firm then has a simple problem. Compare the purchase price of an additional unit of capital with the price the stock market is willing to pay for it. If the stock market value exceeds the purchase price, the firm should buy the machine; otherwise, it should not.

Tobin then constructed a variable corresponding to the value of a unit of capital in place relative to its purchase price and looked at how closely it moved with investment. He used the symbol "q" to denote the variable, and the variable has become known as **Tobin's q.** Its construction is as follows:

1. Take the total value of U.S. corporations, as assessed by financial markets. That is, compute the sum of their stock market value (the price of a share times the number of shares). Compute also the total value of their bonds outstanding (firms finance themselves not only through stocks but also through bonds). Add together the value of stocks and bonds.

2. Divide this total value by the value of the capital stock of U.S. corporations at replacement cost (the price firms would have to pay to replace their machines, their plants, and so on).

The ratio gives us, in effect, the value of a unit of capital in place relative to its current purchase price. This ratio is Tobin's q. Intuitively, the higher the q, the higher the value of capital relative to its current purchase price, and the higher investment should be. (In the example at the start of the box, Tobin's q is equal to two, so the firm should definitely invest.)

How tight is the relation between Tobin's q and investment? The answer is given in Figure 1, which plots two variables for each year from 1960 to 1999 for the United States.

Measured on the left vertical axis is the rate of change of the ratio of investment to capital.

Measured on the right vertical axis is the rate of change of Tobin's q. This variable has been lagged once. For 1987, for example, the figure shows the change in the ratio of investment to capital for 1987 and the change in Tobin's q for 1986—that is, a year earlier. The reason for presenting the two variables this way is that the strongest relation in the data appears to be between investment this year and Tobin's q last year. Put another way, movements in investment this year are more closely associated with movements in the stock market last year rather than with movements in the stock market this year; a plausible explanation is that it takes time for firms to make investment decisions, build new factories, and so on.

The figure shows that there is a clear relation between Tobin's q and investment. This is probably not because firms blindly follow the signals from the stock market, but because investment decisions and stock market prices depend very much on the same factors—expected future profits and expected future interest rates.

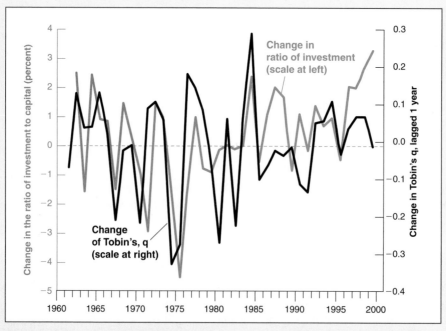

FIGURE 1   Tobin's q versus the Ratio of Investment to Capital: Annual Rates of Change, 1960–1999

depreciate, the agency would have to charge an interest rate equal to r_t times the price of the machine (we have assumed the price of a machine to be 1 in real terms, so r_t times 1 is just r_t): The agency has to get at least as much from buying and then renting the machine as it would from, say, buying bonds. In addition, the rental agency would have to charge for depreciation, δ times the price of the machine, 1. The rental price would therefore be equal to $(r_t + \delta)$. Even though firms typically do not rent their machines, $(r_t + \delta)$ still captures the implicit cost—sometimes called the *shadow cost*—to the firm of using the machine for one year.

The investment function given by equation (20.6) then has a simple interpretation: *Investment depends on the ratio of profit to the user cost.* The higher the profit compared with the user cost, the higher is the level of investment. The higher the real interest rate, the higher is the user cost and the lower the level of investment.

This relation among profit, the real interest rate, and investment relies on a strong simplifying assumption: The future is expected to be the same as the present. It is nevertheless a useful relation to remember, and a relation macroeconomists keep handy in their toolbox.

If the future is expected to be the same as the present, investment depends on the ratio of profit to the user cost—the sum of the real interest rate and the depreciation rate.

Profit ↑ ⟹ investment ↑
Real interest rate ↑
　　　⟹ investment ↓

Current versus Expected Profits

Let us now return to the general case. Equations (20.3) and (20.4) imply that investment should be forward looking and depend primarily on *expected future profits*. (Under our assumption that new capital starts being operational only one year after purchase, current profit does not even appear in equation (20.3).) One striking empirical fact about investment, however, is how strongly it moves with fluctuations in *current profit*.

This relation is shown in Figure 20–2, which plots investment and profit since 1961 for the Canadian economy. Investment is measured as *investment in nonresidential structures and equipment* in 1997 dollars. Profit is constructed as the ratio of the sum of *after-tax profits of corporations* divided by GDP. After-tax profits is total profits of corporations and government business enterprises minus direct taxes paid by corporations deflated using the GDP deflator. Figure 20–2 shows this measure of after-tax profit varies substantially as a percent of GDP. The 1981–1982 and 1990–1991 recessions coincide with very sharp reductions in profits.

The positive relation between investment, also as a percentage of GDP, and current profit is clear in Figure 20–2. Is this relation inconsistent with the theory we have just developed, which holds that investment should be related to the present value of expected future profits

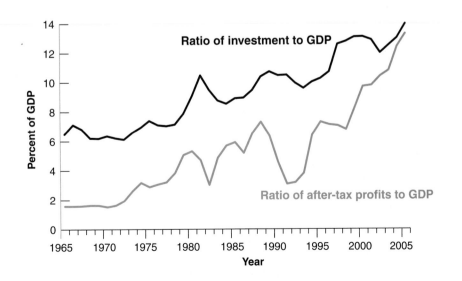

FIGURE 20-2

Investment and Profits in Canada, 1965–2005

Investment and after-tax profits move together. Over this time period, the average percent of GDP in gross investment has increased. Gross investment, which includes housings, is a larger percentage of GDP than are profits.

Source: Investment to GDP using CANSIM II variables V3862666, V3862685; *after-tax profits to GDP* using CANSIM II variables V647065, V647066, V647073, V386 2685.

rather than to current profit? It need not be: If firms expect future profits to move very much like current profit, then the present value of profits will move very much like current profit, and so will investment.

Economists who have looked at the question more closely have concluded, however, that the effect of current profit on investment is stronger than the theory we have developed so far would predict. (How they have gathered some of the evidence is described in the Focus box "Profitability versus Cash Flow.") On the one hand, some firms with highly profitable investment projects but low current profit appear to be investing too little. On the other hand, some firms that have high current profit sometimes appear to invest in projects of doubtful profitability. In short, current profit appears to affect investment, even after controlling for the expected present value of profits.

Why does current profit play a role in the investment decision? The answer lies in our discussion in section 20-1 of why consumption also depends directly on current income. Many of the reasons we used to explain the behaviour of consumers also apply to firms:

1. If its current profit is low, a firm that wants to buy new machines can get the funds it needs only by borrowing. It may be reluctant to borrow: Although expected profits may look good, things may turn bad, leaving the firm unable to repay the debt. But if current

---

FOCUS   Profitability versus Cash Flow

How much does investment depend on the expected present value of profits, and how much does it depend on current profit? Economists often refer to the question as the relative importance of **profitability** (the expected present discounted value of profits) versus **cash flow** (current profit, the net flow of cash the firm is receiving) in investment decisions.

The difficulty in answering this question is similar to the problem of identifying the relative importance of current and expected future incomes on consumption—a problem we discussed in the first Focus box in this chapter: Most of the time, cash flow and profitability are likely to move together. Firms that do well typically have both large cash flows and good future prospects. Firms that suffer losses often also have poor future prospects.

As in the case for consumption, the best way to isolate the effects of cash flow and profitability is to identify times or events when cash flow and profitability move in different directions and then look at what happens to investment. This is the approach taken by Owen Lamont, an economist at the University of Chicago. An example will help you understand Lamont's strategy.

Think of two firms, A and B. A is involved only in steel production. B is composed of two parts, one part steel production, the other part petroleum exploration.

Suppose there is a sharp drop in the price of oil, leading to losses in oil exploration. This shock decreases firm B's cash flow. If the losses in oil exploration are large enough to offset the profits from steel production, firm B may show an overall loss.

The question we can now ask is: As a result of the decrease in the price of oil, will firm B invest less in its steel operation than firm A does? If only *profitability* in steel production matters, there is no reason for firm B to invest less in its steel operation than firm A does. But if current *cash flow* also matters, the fact that firm B has a lower cash flow may prevent it from investing as much as firm A does in its steel operation. Looking at invest-

ment in the steel operations of the two firms can tell us how much investment depends on cash flow versus profitability.

This is the empirical strategy followed by Lamont. He focuses on what happened in 1986 when the price of oil in the United States dropped by 50%, leading to large losses in oil-related activities. He then looks at whether firms that had substantial oil-activities cut investment in their non-oil-activities relatively more than other firms in the same non-oil-activities. He concludes that they did. He finds that for every $1 decrease in cash flow due to the decrease in the price of oil, investment spending in non-oil activities was reduced by 10 to 20 cents. In short, current cash flow matters.

Huntley Schaller, from Carleton University, uses another strategy to estimate the impact of cash flows on Canadian investment. He compares firms that belong to a tightly knit web of corporate directorships, a sort of Canadian analogue to the Japanese Keiretsu, with those that are large, independent, and on their own. He estimates that one dollar of after-tax cash flow can have very different impacts on the investment decisions of the two kinds of firms. For firms that are members of an industrial group, the increase may be as little as 5 cents, while for firms that are largely on their own, the impact may be as large as 60 cents.

Sources:
Owen Lamont, "Cash Flow and Investment: Evidence from Internal Capital Markets," *Journal of Finance*, March 1997.
A general review of studies along these lines is given by R. Glenn Hubbard, "Capital-market Imperfections and Investment," *Journal of Economic Literature*, 1995.
Huntley Schaller, "Asymmetric Information, Liquidity Constraints and Canadian Investment," *Canadian Journal of Economics*, August 1993.

---

profit is high, the firm may be able to finance its investment by retaining some of its earnings and without having to borrow. The bottom line is that higher current profit may lead the firm to invest more.

2. Even if the firm wants to invest, it may find it difficult to borrow. Potential lenders may not be convinced the project is as good as the firm says, and they may worry the firm will be unable to repay. If the firm has large current profits, it does not have to borrow and so does not need to convince potential lenders. It can proceed and invest as it pleases and is more likely to do so.

In summary, to fit the investment behaviour we observe, the investment equation is better written as:

$$I_t = I(V(\Pi_t^e), \Pi_t)$$

$$(\quad + \quad , \quad +)$$

(20.7)

Investment depends both on the expected present value of profits and on the current level of profit.

Profit and Sales

We have argued that investment depends on both current and expected profit. One last step is to ask: What, in turn, determines profit? The answer is: primarily two factors—(1) the level of sales, and (2) the existing capital stock. If sales are low relative to the capital stock, profits per unit of capital are likely to be depressed as well.

Let us write this more formally. Ignore the distinction between sales and output, and let Y_t denote output or, equivalently, sales. Let K_t denote the capital stock at time t. Our discussion suggests the following relation:

$$\Pi_t = \Pi\left(\frac{Y_t}{K_t}\right)$$

$$(+)$$

(20.8)

Profit per unit of capital is an increasing function of the ratio of sales to the capital stock. Given the capital stock, the higher the sales, the higher is profit. Given sales, the higher the capital stock, the lower is profit.

How does this relation hold in practice? Figure 20–3 plots yearly changes in profit per unit of capital and changes in the ratio of output to capital since 1965. As in Figure 20–2, profit is

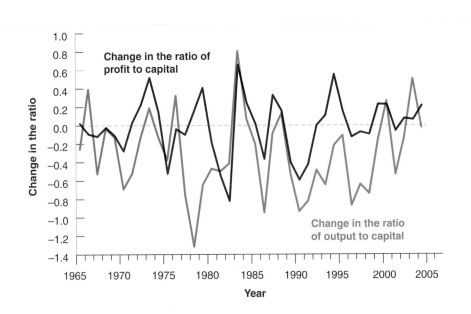

FIGURE 20–3

Changes in the Ratio of After-Tax Profit to Capital and Changes in the Ratio of Output to Capital in Canada, 1965–2004

Profit and the ratio of output to capital do move together over time.

Source: After-tax profits to capital using CANSIM II variables V647065, V647066, V647073, V31690; output to capital using CANSIM II variables V646937, V31690.

defined as after-tax profits now divided by total assets, measured at replacement cost. The ratio of output to capital is constructed as the ratio of GDP to total assets of corporations and government business enterprises.

The figure shows a relation between changes in profit and changes in the ratio of output to capital. Given that most of the year-to-year changes in the ratio of output to capital come from movements in output (capital moves slowly over time; even large swings in investment lead to slow changes in capital), we can state the relation as follows: Profit decreases in recessions and increases in expansions.

Why is this relation between output and profit relevant here? Because it implies a link between *current output* and *expected output* on the one hand and *investment* on the other. For example, the anticipation of a long, sustained economic expansion leads firms to expect high profits, now and for some time in the future. These expectations, in turn, lead to higher investment. The effect of current and expected output on investment, together with the effect of investment back on demand and output, will play a crucial role when we return to the determination of output in Chapter 21.

High expected output ⇒
High expected profit ⇒
High investment today.

20-3 | The Volatility of Consumption and Investment

You surely will have noticed the similarities between our treatment of consumption and of investment behaviour in sections 20-1 and 20-2:

- Whether consumers perceive current movements in income to be transitory or permanent affects their consumption decisions.
- In the same way, whether firms perceive current movements in sales to be transitory or permanent affects their investment decisions. The less they expect a current increase in sales to last, the less they revise their assessment of the present value of profits, and thus the less likely they are to buy new machines or build new factories. This is why, for example, the boom in sales that happens every year over Christmas does not lead to a boom in investment every year in December. Firms understand that this boom is transitory.

But there are also important differences between consumption and investment decisions:

- The theory of consumption we developed implies that when faced with an increase in income consumers perceive as permanent, they respond with *at most* an equal increase in consumption. The permanent nature of the increase in income implies that they can afford to increase consumption now and in the future by the same amount as the increase in income. Increasing consumption more than one for one would require cuts in consumption later, and there is no reason for consumers to want to plan consumption this way.
- Now, consider the behaviour of firms faced with an increase in sales they believe to be permanent. The present value of expected profits increases, leading to an increase in investment. In contrast to consumption, there is no implication that the increase in investment should be no greater than the increase in sales. Rather, once a firm has decided that an increase in sales justifies the purchase of a new machine or the building of a new factory, it may want to proceed quickly, leading to a large but short-lived increase in investment spending. This increase may exceed the increase in sales.

  More concretely, take a firm that has a ratio of capital to its annual sales of, say, three. An increase in sales of $10 million this year, if expected to be permanent, requires the firm to spend $30 million on additional capital if it wants to maintain the same ratio of capital to output. If the firm buys the additional capital right away, the increase in investment spending this year will be equal to *three times* the increase in sales. Once the capital stock has adjusted, the firm will return to its normal pattern of investment. This example is extreme because firms are unlikely to adjust their capital stock right away.

In North America, retail sales are, on average, 24% higher in December than in other months. In France and Italy, sales are 60% higher in December. (These numbers and other facts about such seasonal cycles come from J. Joseph Beaulieu and Jeffrey Miron, "A Cross Country Comparison of Seasonal Cycles and Business Cycles," *Economic Journal*, July 1992, pp. 772–778.)

But even if they do adjust their capital stock more slowly, say, over a few years, the increase in investment may still exceed the increase in sales for a while.

We can tell the same story in terms of equation (20.8). As we make no distinction here between output and sales, the initial increase in sales leads to an equal increase in output, Y, so that Y/K (the ratio of the firm's output to its existing capital stock) also increases. The result is higher profit, which leads the firm to undertake more investment. Over time, the higher level of investment leads to a higher capital stock, K, so that Y/K decreases, returning to normal. Profit per unit of capital returns to normal, and so does investment. Thus, in response to a permanent increase in sales, investment may increase a lot initially and then return to normal over time.

These differences suggest that investment should be more volatile than consumption. How much more volatile? The answer from the data is given in Figure 20–4, which plots yearly rates of change in consumption and investment since 1961. To make the figure easier to interpret, both rates of change are plotted as deviations from the average rate of change so that they are, on average, equal to zero.

You can see two things in the figure:

- Consumption and investment usually move together: Recessions, for example, are typically associated with decreases in *both* investment and consumption. Given our discussion, which has emphasized that consumption and investment depend largely on the same determinants, this should not come as a surprise.
- Investment is, indeed, much more volatile than consumption. Relative movements in investment range from −18 to +15%, whereas relative movements in consumption range only from −6 to +4%.
- Another way of stating the same fact is that whereas the level of investment is much smaller than the level of consumption (recall, investment accounts for about 15% of GDP versus about 60% for consumption) the range of changes in the level of investment from one year to the next is roughly the same as the range of changes in the level of consumption from one year to the next. Both components contribute roughly equally to fluctuations in output over time.

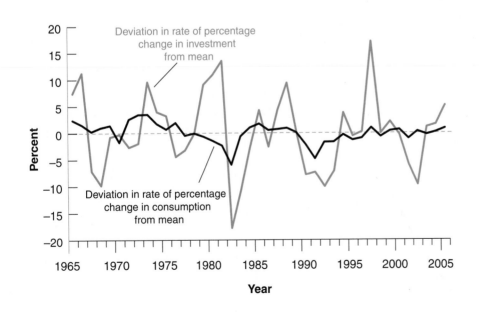

FIGURE 20–4

Rates of Change of Consumption and Investment in Canada, 1965–2005

Relative movements in investment are much larger than relative movements in consumption.

Source: Consumption using CANSIM II variable V3862655; *investment* using CANSIM II variable V3862666.

- Consumption depends on both current income and wealth. Wealth is the sum of nonhuman wealth (financial and housing wealth) and human wealth (the present value of expected after-tax labour income).

- The response of consumption to changes in income depends on whether consumers perceive these changes as transitory or permanent.

- Consumption is likely to respond less than one for one to movements in income, and consumption may move even if current income does not change.

- Investment depends on both current profit and the present value of expected future profits.

- Under the simplifying assumption that firms expect future profits and interest rates to be the same in the future as they are today, we can think of investment as depending on the ratio of profit to the user cost of capital, where the user cost is the sum of the real interest rate and the depreciation rate.

- Movements in profit are closely related to movements in output. Hence, we can think of investment as depending indirectly on current and future expected output movements. Firms that anticipate a long output expansion, and thus a long sequence of high profits, will invest. Movements in output that are not expected to last will have a small effect on investment.

- Investment is much more volatile than consumption.

- cash flow, 412
- housing wealth, 403
- human wealth, 403
- life cycle theory of consumption, 402
- natural experiment, 405
- nonhuman wealth, 403
- panel data sets, 402

- permanent income theory of consumption, 402
- profitability, 412
- Tobin's q, 410
- total wealth, 403
- user cost or rental cost of capital, 409

An asterisk denotes a harder question. [Web] indicates that the question requires access to the Internet.

1. TRUE/FALSE/UNCERTAIN

a. For the typical university student, human wealth and nonhuman wealth are approximately equal.

b. Natural experiments, such as retirement and announced tax cuts, do not suggest that expectations of future income are major factors affecting consumption.

c. Buildings and factories depreciate much faster than machines do.

d. A high value for Tobin's q indicates the stock market believes that capital is overvalued and thus investment should be lower.

e. Economists have found that the effect of current profit on investment can be fully explained by the effect of current profit on expectations of future profits.

f. Data from the past three decades suggest that corporate profits are closely tied to the business cycle.

g. Changes in consumption and investment are typically of the same sign and are roughly of the same magnitude.

2. PDV COMPUTATIONS AND RETIREMENT

A consumer has nonhuman wealth equal to $100,000. She earns $40,000 this year and expects her salary to rise by 5% in real terms each year for the following two years. She will then retire. The real interest rate is equal to 0% and is expected to remain at 0% in the future. Labour income is taxed at the rate of 25%.

a. What is this consumer's human wealth?

b. What is her total wealth?

c. If she expects to live for another seven years after retirement and wants her consumption to remain the same (in real terms) every year from now on, how much can she consume this year?

d. If she were given a bonus of $20,000 in the current year only, with all future salary payments remaining as stated earlier, by how much could she increase consumption now and in the future?

e. Now, suppose that at retirement, the Canada Pension Plan will start paying each year benefits equal to 60% of the consumer's earnings during her last working year. (Assume benefits are not taxed.) How much can she consume this year (and still maintain constant consumption)?

3. INVESTMENT DECISIONS IN THE PRETZEL INDUSTRY

A pretzel manufacturer is considering buying a pretzel-making machine that costs $100,000. The machine will depreciate by 8% per year. It will generate real profits equal to $18,000 next year, $18,000 $(1-0.08\%)$ two years from now (that is, the same real profits, but adjusted for depreciation), $18,000 $(1-0.08\%)^2$ three years from now, and so on. Determine whether the manufacturer should buy the machine if the real interest rate is assumed to remain constant at:

a. 5%.   **b.** 10%.   **c.** 15%.

4. INVESTING IN EDUCATION

Suppose that at age 22, you have just finished university and have been offered a starting salary of $40,000. Your salary will remain constant in real terms. However, you have also enrolled in a professional school. The school takes two years to complete, and upon graduation, you expect your starting salary to be 10% higher in real terms and remain constant in real terms thereafter. The tax rate on labour income is 40%.

a. If the real interest rate is zero and you expect to retire at age 60 (that is, if you do not go to professional school, you expect to work for 38 years in total), what is the maximum you should be willing to pay in tuition to attend this professional school?

b. What should you pay in tuition for professional school if you expect to pay 30% of your income in taxes?

*5. WEALTH ACCUMULATION

Suppose that every consumer is born with zero financial wealth and lives through three periods: youth, middle age, and retirement age. Consumers work in the first two periods and retire in the last one. Their income is $5 in the first period, $25 in the second, and $0 in the last one. Inflation and expected inflation are zero, and the real interest rate is also zero.

a. What is the present discounted value of future labour income at the beginning of life? What is the highest sustainable level of consumption such that consumption is equal in all three periods?

b. For each age group, what is the amount of saving that allows consumers to maintain the constant level of consumption you found in (a)? (*Hint*: Saving can be a negative number, if the consumer needs to borrow in order to maintain a certain level of consumption.)

c. Suppose there are N people born each period. What is the total saving? (*Hint*: Compute the total amount saved by the generations that save and subtract the total amount dissaved by the generations that dissave.) Explain.

d. What is the total financial wealth in the economy? (*Hint*: Compute the financial wealth of people at the beginning of the first period of life, the second period of life, and the third period of life. Remember that people can be in debt, so financial wealth can be negative. Add them up.)

Suppose now that restrictions on borrowing do not allow young consumers to borrow. At each age group, consumers once again compute their total wealth and then determine their desired level of consumption as the highest level that allows their consumption to be equal in all three periods. However, if that is greater than their income plus their financial wealth, then they are constrained to consuming exactly their income plus their financial wealth.

e. Derive consumption in each period of life. Explain the difference from your answer to (a).

f. Derive total saving. Explain the difference, if any, from your answer to (c).

g. Derive total financial wealth. Explain the difference from your answer to (d).

h. "Financial liberalization may be good for people, but it is bad for overall capital accumulation." Discuss.

6. MOVEMENTS IN CONSUMPTION AND INVESTMENT [WEB]

For this exercise, you will need annual data on real consumption and real investment. Many of you will have access to the CANSIM II database from Statistics Canada at your university. You may have to ask a librarian for the sequence of steps to get to the database. You can then retrieve to a spreadsheet variable V3862655 (personal expenditure or consumer goods and services) and variable V3862666 (nonresidential structures and equipment).

Both these variables are measured in 1997 dollars. Use your spreadsheet to carry out the following exercises:

a. On average, how much bigger is consumption than investment?

b. Compute the change in the levels of consumption and investment from one year to the next, and graph them for the period 1962–2004. Are the year-to-year changes in consumption and investment of the same magnitude?

c. What do your answers in (a) and (b) imply about the volatility of consumption and investment? Is this implication consistent with Figure 20–4?

d. The last major recessions were in 1981–1982 and 1990–1991. Using your graph from part (b), which component played the largest role in each of these recessions, consumption or investment? Is this consistent with what we have learned so far about these recessions?

FURTHER READING

A technical description of how wealth, disposable income, and consumption interact in Canada is found in Tiff Macklem, "Wealth, Disposable Income and Consumption: Some Evidence for Canada," *Bank of Canada Working Paper*, November 1994. This paper can be found, along with many others, at the Bank of Canada Web site (**www.bankofcanada.ca**).

APPENDIX A

USING GRAPHS TO ILLUSTRATE CONSUMPTION DECISIONS WHEN EXPECTATIONS ARE IMPORTANT[1]

It is useful to represent the material in section 20-1 using graphs. Many of us are visual in our learning strategy. Using graphs, the consumer has only two periods in his planning horizon. We will call these periods 1 and 2; you can think of these two periods as the present and the future. With only two periods, we can apply the methods familiar to many students of a microeconomics course. We start with the choices available to the consumer when making consumption decisions over time. These are the consumer's budget lines. We then add indifference curves to this diagram, these curves represent how the consumer compares different points available for consumption. Finally we address various macroeconomic events already discussed in section 20-1.

What Choices Are Available to the Consumer?

In the text, we denoted after-tax labour income in period t as $Y_{Lt} - T_t$. In period 1, this is known to the consumer and denoted $Y_{L1} - T_1$. In period 2, as of period 1, you expect after-tax labour income of $Y^e_{L2} - T^e_2$. Both are measured in real dollars. Real dollars represent baskets of goods that a consumer can buy. Taxes in both periods are usually zero in this appendix. For simplicity, we will measure everything in

dollars where these are understood to represent baskets of goods consumers can buy. In the two-period case, there is one real interest rate, denoted r. Thus, if you lend 1 dollar (1 basket of goods) in period 1, you receive $(1 + r)$ dollars (baskets of goods) in period 2. If you borrow 1 dollar in period 1, you repay $(1 + r)$ dollars in period 2. Borrowing and lending rates are frequently different in the marketplace. For our purposes, this distinction is not important.

Figure 20A–1 shows a consumer with 40 dollars of after-tax labour income in period 1 and 60 dollars of expected after-tax labour income in period 2. This consumer expects an increase in labour income from now to the future, that is, an increase in after-tax income from period 1 to period 2. We will assume this consumer has no nonhuman wealth (later, we relax this assumption). The real interest rate is 7% from period 1 to period 2. The two incomes are marked as point A on Figure 20A–1. What consumption choices can the consumer make from point A?

One choice is simply to consume their incomes in the period in which they are earned. Consumption would be 40 dollars in period 1 and 60 dollars in period 2. This is point A on the diagram. This is not the only choice available to this consumer. They can certainly save 1 dollar of income in period 1. This means they consume only 39 dollars in period 1 but are then able to consume 61.07 dollars in period 2. The one dollar they saved in period 1 earns 7 cents in interest and increases their consumption by 1.07 dollars. They also consume the principal on their savings in period 2. This is point B. They could save 2 dollars in period 1 and consume $2 \times (1.07) = 2.14$ more dollars in period 2.

---

[1]This material can be omitted without loss of continuity.

Consumption Choices in a Two-Period Model

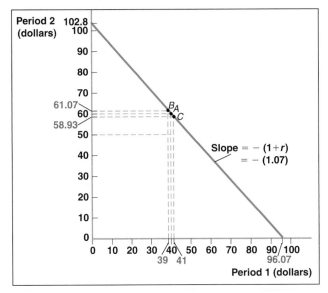

Point *A* represents the after-tax labour income measured in real terms. This consumer earns $40 in period 1 and expects to earn $60 in period 2. The real interest rate, paid on loans and earned on savings, is 7%. The budget line shows how the consumer can save to reduce period 1 consumption and increase period 2 consumption. This is a movement from point *A* to point *B*. The budget line also shows how the consumer can borrow to increase period 1 consumption but only at the cost of reduced period 2 consumption. This is a movement from point *A* to point *C*.

Note that the slope of the budget line is $-(1.07)$ or $-(1 + r)$, where the interest rate is written in decimal form. Thus, if the consumer makes the unlikely decision to consume nothing in period 1, the maximum possible consumption in period 2 is $60 + (1.07) \times 40 = 102.8$ dollars. This is the intercept of the vertical axis. The more interesting intercept is the intercept on the horizontal axis. From point *A*, the consumer could consume one more dollar in period 1. But he must borrow that dollar. If he borrows a dollar and increases consumption to 41 dollars, then he must repay that dollar with interest, and consumption in the second period is reduced $60 -((1.07) \times 1) = 58.93$ dollars. This is point *C* on the diagram. If he wants 42 dollars of consumption in period 1, then he must borrow 2 dollars in period 1 and repay $2 \times 1.07 = 2.14$ dollars in period 2. This leaves only $60 - 2.14 = 57.86$ dollars to consume in period 2. What is the maximum amount this consumer could consume in period 1? Suppose he promises a lender to repay a loan with all 60 dollars of expected period 2 income. He cannot borrow 60 dollars in period 1, as the lender would also want interest on the loan. The maximum amount he can borrow in period 1 is 60 divided by 1.07, or 56.07 dollars. The

horizontal intercept, the maximum consumption possible in period 1 is:

$$40 + 60/1.07 = 40 + 56.07 = 96.07$$

This is an exact two-period representation of the expression (20.1) on page 403 in section 20-1, where the interest rate is positive and there are only two periods needed to calculate this person's human wealth. The more general formula is:

$$\text{Human wealth} = Y_{L1} + Y^e{}_{L2}/(1 + r) \qquad (20A.1)$$

Human wealth is the present discounted value of expected after-tax labour income. Human wealth has a visual representation as the maximum consumption available in period 1 (using only after-tax labour income), where consumption in period 2 is zero. This concept generalizes so that wealth is the maximum consumption in the current period, consumption in period 1, when you plan to have zero consumption in all future periods. To fully generalize the concept, we also need to add nonhuman wealth to the diagram.

Adding nonhuman wealth to the diagram is quite straightforward. Suppose the nonhuman wealth of this consumer is 20 dollars, perhaps a bond or a mutual fund. It is denoted F_1, the subscript indicating this is nonhuman (financial) wealth in period 1. In Figure 20A–2, point *A* is at 60 dollars of consumption in period 2 and at 60 dollars of consumption in period 1. Point *A* is our label for a point where

Financial Wealth and Consumption Choices in the Two-Period Model

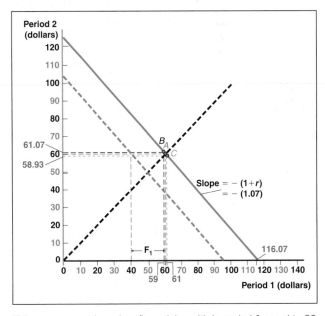

If the consumer above has financial wealth in period 1 equal to 20 dollars, then his consumption choices are enlarged. The budget line moves out horizontally by the amount of financial wealth.

there is no lending or borrowing based on after-tax labour incomes. Why? If our consumer chooses to consume 60 dollars in period 1, this uses 40 dollars of after-tax labour income and the 20 dollars of financial wealth. This exhausts their financial wealth. They have no debts and no assets entering period 2 and simply consume all of their after-tax labour income in period 2. We now use the same method as above to represent variation around point A.

Suppose that our consumer chooses to consume only 59 dollars in period 1. Then, the one dollar not consumed remains in financial wealth and earns 7% interest. Consumption in period 2 can rise to 60 + 1.07 dollars, marked as point B. Suppose that our consumer wants more than 60 dollars of consumption in period 1. Point C shows 61 dollars of consumption in period 1. To obtain that much consumption in period 1, our consumer spends all of his after-tax labour income, all of his financial wealth, and borrows one dollar. That dollar must be repaid with interest so consumption in period 2 at point C must be 60 − 1.07 or 58.93 dollars. We have now learned the slope of the choice line, the budget line, remains at −1.07 or –(1 + r). What is the value of the horizontal intercept, the maximum possible consumption in period 1 if consumption in period 2 is zero? It is:

$$20 + 40 + 60/1.07 = 116.07$$

Using the formula developed above and calling this intercept wealth because it is the maximum consumption available in period 1, we write:

$$\text{Wealth} = \text{Nonhuman wealth} + \text{Human wealth}$$

or in symbols:

$$W_1 = F_1 + Y_{L1} + Y^e_{L2}/(1 + r) \qquad (20A.2)$$

If you substitute the values in the example above into the formula, you should get 116.07. Now that we have a graphical representation of the choices available to our consumer, we need a way to represent the choice actually made. Equation 20A.2 is the equation for the *budget line*. This line is the maximum amount of consumption available in period 2 for each choice of consumption in period 1 (or vice versa). With the budget line, we use another tool from microeconomics, indifference curves.

▲

Budget line: In a diagram of consumer choice, the budget line represents the choices available to the consumer. For a given value of consumption in period 1, the budget line is the largest value of consumption available in period 2.

Representing Choices Using Indifference Curves

In Figure 20A–3, three indifference curves have been drawn. Each represents combinations of consumption in period 1 and period 2 where our consumer is indifferent, that is, does not have a preference between the points that are

Indifference Curves in the Two-Period Model

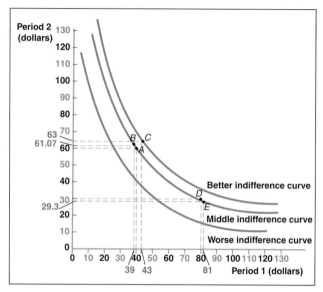

Indifference curves are combinations of points where the consumer is equally happy with either of the consumption choices. Along the middle indifference curve, the consumer finds points A and B equally satisfactory. Along the same curve, the consumer finds points D and E equally satisfactory. The "bowed to the origin shape" and the negative slope along a line implies that consumers generally prefer more equal consumption. Finally, any point on the indifference curve with the point C (a point clearly better than either point A or point B because there are more of both goods) are superior to all the points on the middle indifference curve.

on the same indifference curve. Points A, B, D, and E are four such points on the middle curve in the figure. Moving from A to B, our consumer willingly gives up one dollar of consumption in period 1 to receive 1.07 dollars of consumption in period 2 and is equally happy. The slope of the indifference curve is −1.07. If consumers tend to prefer relatively equal amounts of consumption in both periods, then the indifference curves are "bowed in" to the origin. This is shown along the middle indifference curve by using two more points, points D and E. Note that this is a place where the consumer has a lot of period 1 consumption and not much period 2 consumption at point D. Thus, to move from D to E, one more dollar of period 1 consumption will only occur if very little (in the diagram only 0.3 dollars) period 2 consumption is lost. Another way to say this is that the negative slope of the indifference curve is steepest where period 1 consumption is relatively low and flattest where period 1 consumption is relatively high. The slope is negative throughout. In order to be just as happy (indifferent), if you give up consumption in period 1, you require more consumption in period 2. An indifference curve that is further from the origin is one where the consumer is better off, that is, has more consumption in both periods. Moving from either point A or point B to point C is clearly an improvement, there is more consumption in both periods. An indifference curve where all points are worse is closer to the origin than the middle indifference curve. We think of an infinite number of *indifference curves* (although we only drew three) so that the consumer can rank every point in the diagram.

▲
Indifference curve: In the diagram of consumer choice, an indifference curve represents combinations of consumption in period 1 and consumption in period 2 that the consumer likes equally. Moving along an indifference curve does not increase or reduce the well being of the consumer. If the consumption of both goods increases, the well being of the consumer must improve and move the consumer to a higher indifference curve.

There is a useful special case of indifference curves. These are drawn in Figure 20A–4. These are right-angled indifference curves, where the right angle passes through the 45-degree line. These "curves" say that this consumer strongly prefers equal consumption in the two periods, so much so that this consumer is *only* better off if he gets more consumption in both periods, that is, point B is better than point A, but point C, where there is more con-

sumption in period 1 but the same amount of consumption in period 2 as at point A, is, from the point-of-view of this rather peculiar consumer, just the same as point A. These are quite silly indifference curves; most of us would think point C is clearly better than point A. At C, we have more consumption in period 1 than at point A and the same amount of period 2 consumption as at point A. But we actually used this kind of indifference curve in section 20-1 when we found "the constant level of consumption that you can afford" as the best choice. Using these peculiar indifference curves means that if equal consumption in each period of your life is a choice available, this is the choice that will be made. The case of equal consumption in all periods of your life is a choice where an algebraic solution is particularly easy. We will make this assumption when it is useful. We can put together the indifference curves for either the general case or the special case with the budget line to determine the consumer's choices. Then, we can conduct a series of macroeconomic experiments.

Making the Best Available Choice

The general case is illustrated in Figure 20A–5. Using our first budget constraint from Figure 20A–1 (after-tax labour income in period 1 = 40 dollars, after-tax labour income in period 2 = 60 dollars, zero nonhuman wealth, real interest

FIGURE 20A–4

Peculiar Indifference Curves

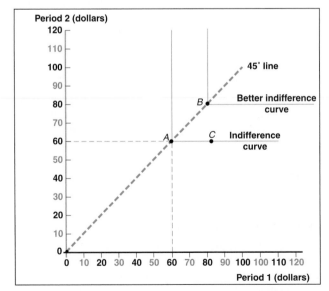

These indifference curves will lead consumers to always (if at all possible) choose equal consumption in both periods. These are useful in getting analytical solutions to our consumer problem. They are not very realistic; most of us would actually like point C better than point A, not the same as point A.

FIGURE 20A–5

The Best Consumption Choice Using General Indifference Curves

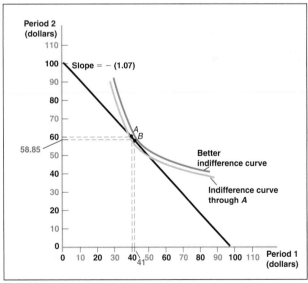

From point A, the consumer borrows. This increases period 1 consumption and reduces period 2 consumption. However, the activity of borrowing moves the consumer to an indifference curve that represents a higher level of well being; borrowing makes the consumer better off. Point B is on a better indifference curve than point A.

rate = 7%), if the consumer neither borrows nor lends, then consumption in period 1 is 40 dollars and consumption in period 2 is 60 dollars. This is unlikely to be the best choice because if at all possible, most of us prefer fairly equal consumption across the periods of our life. Most people, for example, your parents, are saving for retirement. They are reducing consumption now and moving consumption to the future when after-tax labour income will be lower. Persons who win large lottery prizes usually spread the spending of their winnings over the rest of their lifetime. In Figure 20A–5, this desire to have more equal consumption is revealed. At point A, the slope of the indifference curve is clearly shown as −1.15. This consumer will give up, from point A, 1.15 dollars of consumption in period 2 to get one more dollar of consumption in period 1 and be just as happy. The cost to this consumer (the slope of the budget line) of an extra dollar of consumption in period 1 is 1.07 dollars of consumption in period 2. When this consumer actually gives up 1.07 dollars in period 2 consumption, he is able to move to an indifference curve that is farther from the origin. Thus, this consumer will borrow from point A because the action of borrowing moves him to a higher indifference curve at B. At point B the slope of the indifference curve and the slope of the budget line are both −1.07, and this is the highest indifference curve this consumer can attain. This consumer borrowed in period 1 and repaid the loan in period 2 in order to make his consumption more equal between the two periods. Note that consumption in period 1 can be higher because the relatively high expected after-tax labour income in period 2 allows this consumer to borrow and then repay the loan.

Figure 20A–6 reworks this problem for the right-angle indifference curves in Figure 20A–4. These are convenient indifference curves because we know these curves will lead to our consumer choosing exactly equal consumption in the two periods. We also add financial wealth in period 1 to the problem. The best available consumption choice solves the equation:

$$C_1 + C^e_2/(1 + r) = [(2 + r)/(1 + r)] \, C$$
$$= F_1 + (Y_{L1} + Y^e_{L2}/(1 + r)) \quad (20A.3)$$

so that:

$$C = [((1 + r)/(2 + r))] \, [F_1 + (Y_{L1} + Y^e_{L2}/(1 + r))]$$
$$(20A.4)$$

C is the choice of consumption in both periods. This is an exact formula in the two-period case for the words in section 20-1, that is, that consumption could be written as a function of wealth:

Consumption = C (Total Wealth)
= $[((1 + r)/(2 + r))] \times$ Total Wealth

The Solution When Consumption Is Equal in Each Period

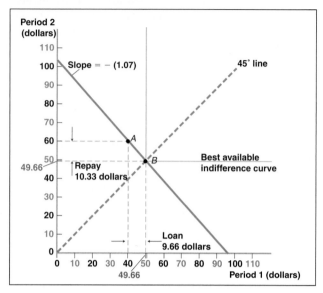

The right-angle indifference curve in Figure 20A–4 allows the analytical solution to the consumer's problem illustrated in this figure. Equal consumption means the choice made is along the 45-degree line. The consumer borrows in period 1 and repays the loan in period 2. The size of the loan is just enough to equalize consumption.

If we solve this for the following values: $F_1 = 0$; $r = 0.07$; $Y_{L1} = 40$; $Y^e_{L2} = 60$, then $C_1 = C_2 = C = 49.66$. A loan of 9.66 dollars is taken out in period 1 and 1.07 × 9.66 = 10.33 dollars is repaid in period 2. This is illustrated in Figure 20A–6. You might notice that when the interest rate is zero, this formula says consume half your wealth in period 1 and half your wealth in period 2. We used this result in section 20-1. We are now going to use graphs and this formula to consider the various macroeconomic events already considered in section 20-1.

Higher Expected Future income

Let us start from Figure 20A–1. Suppose that expected after-tax labour income in period 2 increases from 60 dollars to 80 dollars. This is represented in Figure 20A–7 by a shift out in the budget line. The original budget line is dotted. An increase in expected future after-tax labour income could occur because of an expected tax cut, an increase in "consumer confidence" (you believe your income will increase as a recession comes to an end), or the introduction of the Canada Pension Plan in the 1960s. In that plan, discussed in Chapter 15, consumers believed they would get higher pension income on retirement. We will see that higher expected future income leads to more consumption now, which is a lower saving rate now, the effect predicted by the introduction of a pay-as-you-go national pension plan. All of these scenarios are actual macroeconomic events.

Comparing Figure 20A–7 with Figure 20A–1 or Figure 20A–6, we see that the increase in expected future income moves the budget line out. On the vertical axis, the budget line moves out by 20 dollars. On the horizontal axis, the budget line does not move out by 20 dollars, but by 20/(1.07) dollars because the maximum increase in consumption in period 1 must take into account repaying a loan used to increase period 1 consumption. Thus, human wealth and total wealth increase only by the discounted present value of the increase in expected future income. Nonetheless, if we assume right-angle indifference curves represent preferences and allocate the increase in expected future income so that consumption is expected to be equal in the two periods, consumption in period 1 rises from 49.66 to 59.32 dollars. To arrange this increase in period 1 consumption, this consumer must borrow even more in period 1. We have learned two crucial facts. Consumption today will rise if income is expected to rise in the future.

We have also learned that consumption today will not rise by the full increase in expected future income.

The Effect of a Change in Nonhuman Wealth

We will use the same special case to explore the effect of a decrease in financial or nonhuman wealth. We will start from Figure 20A–2 and construct Figure 20A–8. In Figure 20A–2, our consumer had 40 dollars of after-tax income in period 1, 60 dollars of after-tax income expected in period 2, and 20 dollars of financial wealth in period 1. Point A was the point where there was neither lending nor borrowing in period 1. It happens to be the point of equal consumption and, for the family of right-angled indifference curves, the best choice available. Suppose there is a stock-market crash so that as stock values fall, nonhuman wealth falls from 20 dollars to 10 dollars. This will shift in the budget line by 10 dollars. The original budget line is dotted. Total wealth will also fall by 10 dollars. But consumption in period 1 will not fall by 10 dollars. Using equation 20A–4, we find that consumption in both period 1 and period 2 (they are always equal) falls from 60 dollars to 54.83

FIGURE   20A–8

The Effect of a Reduction in Financial Wealth

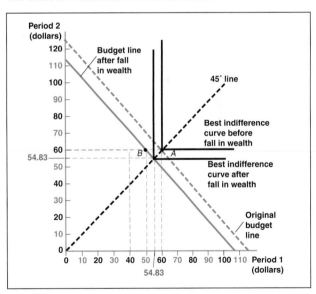

There are large fluctuations in financial wealth as stock prices and housing prices move. This figure explores the effect of such fluctuations on period 1 consumption. When financial wealth falls, so does period 1 consumption. The decrease in consumption is less than the decrease in financial wealth. Consumers try to maintain equal consumption in the two periods of their live. If the second period represents a large number of future periods, then the effect of a fall in financial wealth on period 1 consumption may be quite small.

FIGURE   20A–7

The Effect of an Increase in Expected Future Income

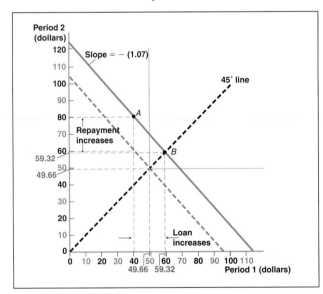

An increase in expected future income in period 2 will lead to an increase in consumption in period 1. This requires even more borrowing in period 1 and a larger loan repayment in period 2. The consumer is acting to equalize consumption across the two periods in this example using the right-angled indifference curves. The borrowing leads to a higher level of well being for the typical consumer.

dollars. Our consumer, faced with a decline in financial wealth, acts such that consumption remains constant over the two periods. Note that this plan still requires our consumer to borrow 4.83 dollars in period 1, repay $1.07 \times 4.83 = 5.17$ dollars in period 2, and consume $60 - 5.17 = 54.83$ dollars in period 2.

This exercise teaches us a second important lesson. Fluctuations in financial wealth should lead to fluctuations in consumption, but not on a one-for-one basis. If we take period 2 to represent many future periods together, a large change in financial wealth may have only a small effect on consumption in period 1.

When Our Consumer Cannot Borrow against Future Income

It is frequently the case that a consumer cannot borrow against her future after-tax labour income. Most loans to consumers that are of any size (that is beyond the loan in a credit card balance) are backed by some kind of physical collateral. Furthermore, the value of the loan is usually less than the value of the physical collateral. Buying a car requires a substantial downpayment so that the balance of the loan is less than the resale value of the car. In this case, the lender is protected against the borrower losing his job or having a car accident. Purchasing a house requires a downpayment so that the mortgage outstanding is less likely to exceed the value of the home. This arrangement puts the risk of house price fluctuations onto the borrower, not the lender. You or your friend may have a student loan outstanding. A student loan is truly a loan against expected future after-tax labour income. However, this loan market does not work without government intervention. Government steps in and guarantees at least the principal on your student loan. The bank or other lender has no other guarantee that you will not simply leave for a world tour after graduation and refuse to repay your loan. Thus, there are many persons in society who cannot borrow against future income and have no significant financial wealth available for current consumption.[2] The two-period diagram is very helpful in representing this situation.

Figure 20A–9 illustrates the following case: After-tax income in period 1 is quite low, only 25 dollars; but expected after-tax income in period 2 is much higher, 80 dollars. Current financial wealth is zero. This may be similar to your plans after graduation. Clearly, this consumer

[2]Many middle-aged persons do have significant financial wealth in the form of a future pension. However, this form of financial wealth cannot be reduced for current consumption. Many of you will find that quite early in your career, you will be required to join a pension plan. This forces you to have positive financial wealth even at a time in your life when you might not choose to be saving.

The Two-Period Model When the Consumer Cannot Borrow against Expected Future After-Tax Labour Income

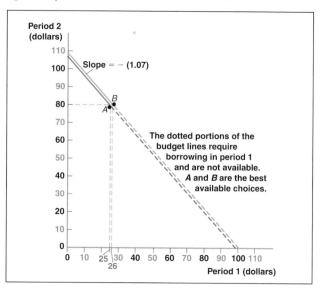

Many consumers cannot easily borrow against after-tax expected future income. If expected future income is high and current income low and the consumer cannot borrow against high expected future income, a common situation for many in society, then the best consumption plan available is to consume all period 1 income in period 1 and all period 2 income in period 2. The budget line is truncated so that it is only possible to increase period 2 consumption. Period 1 consumption cannot be increased. If one more dollar of period 1 income becomes available, then it will all be spent. This is illustrated in moving from point A to point B. This consumer's marginal propensity to consume out of additional period 1 income is 1.

would like to be able to borrow against expected after-tax labour income with nearly any shape of indifference curve you would draw. For equal expected consumption in the two periods with our usual 7% interest rate, this would require a loan of 26.57 dollars in period 1. This loan would be in excess of our consumer's period 1 income, and unless the bank shared this person's knowledge and optimism about her future income, in all likelihood, this loan would be refused. While a small loan might be granted, perhaps at a prohibitive rate, to keep the analysis simple, assume no loan is available to this consumer in period 1. In Figure 20A–9, this means while the consumer can save from her period 1 income and increase her consumption in period 2, she cannot borrow to increase the period 1 consumption. The dotted portion of the budget line is no longer available to her. The best choice available to this consumer is to consume all of the period 1 income in period 1 and all of the period 2 income in period 2. She can do no better. Many of us have been or are in exactly this situation. Why is this situation important to macroeconomists?

The consumer in Figure 20A–9, if given one additional dollar in period 1 income, will consume all of that additional dollar in period 1. In Chapter 3, we made the argument that the average person in society, if given an extra dollar of after-tax income, will consume part of that extra dollar and save part of that extra dollar. This analysis tells us that some people in society, those who would like to borrow but cannot, will, in fact, consume all of the extra dollars in income as consumption. This is illustrated in Figure 20A–9. This analysis tells us that the marginal propensity to consume in a society depends partly on the proportion of consumers who are *liquidity constrained*.

The concept of a liquidity-constrained consumer has very important practical implications. Who in society actually gets an increase in after-tax labour income matters! If a tax cut comes in the form of a tax credit for low-income parents of young children, these consumers are very likely to be liquidity constrained. A $500 million dollar tax cut in the form of such a tax credit might lead to an increase in aggregate demand of close to $500 million. If a tax cut comes in the form of a cut in taxes on capital gains earned on high-tech shares, then the persons holding these shares are very unlikely to be liquidity constrained. A $500 million capital gains tax cut may only lead to a $100 million boost in consumption. In recent years, in Canada, we have had both kinds of personal income tax reductions.

▲

Liquidity constrained: A liquidity-constrained consumer would like to borrow against future labour income but cannot obtain such a loan. The consequence of being liquidity constrained is: if such a consumer receives an extra dollar of after-tax income now, he increases consumption by one full dollar. Equivalently, if a liquidity constrained consumer expects to receive more income in the future, consumption now is not affected.

SUMMARY

This appendix explores the use of graphs to illustrate consumption decisions when expectations matter. The graphs clarify the definition of wealth—wealth is consumption in period 1 of your life when consumption in all other periods is zero. The graphs show that an increase in expected future income will increase consumption immediately. A reduction in financial wealth will reduce consumption immediately. Both effects are smaller than the change in expected income or the change in financial wealth respectively. Both effects occur because consumers try to equalize consumption between periods. Finally, the graphs illustrate the behaviour of a liquidity-constrained consumer. Such a consumer would like to borrow but cannot borrow. If he receives one extra dollar of after-tax income now, he increases consumption by one dollar immediately. These consumers play an important role in the transmission of aggregate demand changes.

QUESTIONS AND PROBLEMS

An asterisk denotes a harder question. [Web] indicates that the question requires access to the Internet.

1. TRUE/FALSE/UNCERTAIN

a. An increase in expected future after-tax labour income in period 2 usually leads to an increase in consumption in period 1.

b. An increase in period 1 after-tax labour income never leads to an equal increase in period 1 consumption.

c. An increase in the real interest rate must reduce human wealth and thus period 1 consumption.

d. An increase in financial wealth leads to an increase in period 1 consumption.

2. WHEN BORROWING AND LENDING RATES DIFFER

Start from Figure 20A–1. After-tax labour income in period 1 is 40 dollars and after-tax labour income in period 2 is 60 dollars. Draw the budget line when the consumer can borrow at 10% but receives only 7% return on his savings from period 1 to period 2.

a. For the case of the right-angled indifference curves, work out the amount of borrowing when consumption is equal in period 1 and period 2.

b. Suppose there is more competition in the banking industry and the borrowing rate falls to 8%. Calculate the effect on period 1 consumption.

3. WHEN CONSUMERS ARE IMPATIENT

The case where consumption is equal in the two periods is an extreme case. Many of us are impatient and want our fun now. We can represent this by saying the period 1 consumption is always 5% larger than period 2 consumption.

a. Draw the right-angled indifference curves that are consistent with period 1 consumption being 5% higher than period 2 consumption.

b. For the case where the borrowing and lending rate are both equal to 7%, create the appropriate consumption function for period 1 consumption:

$$C_1 = C \text{ (Total Wealth)} = \alpha \times \text{Total Wealth}$$

c. How does the value of the parameter α compare with its value in equation (20A.4)?

d. If a society becomes even more impatient, in the way suggested above, what happens to the value of the marginal propensity to consume out of period 1 after-tax labour income?

DERIVATION OF THE EXPECTED PRESENT VALUE OF PROFITS WHEN FUTURE PROFITS AND INTEREST RATES ARE EXPECTED TO BE THE SAME AS TODAY

We saw that the expected present value of profits is given by:

$$V(\Pi_t^e) = \frac{1}{1 + r_t} \Pi_{t+1}^e$$
$$+ \frac{1}{(1 + r_t)(1 + r_{t+1}^e)} (1 - \delta)\Pi_{t+2}^e + \cdots \quad (20B.1)$$

If firms expect both future profits (per unit of capital) and future interest rates to remain at the same level as today so that $\Pi_{t+1}^e = \Pi_{t+2}^e = \cdots = \Pi_t$, and $r_{t+1}^e = r_{t+2}^e = \cdots = r_t$, the equation becomes:

$$V(\Pi_t^e) = \frac{1}{1 + r_t} \Pi_t + \frac{1}{(1 + r_t)^2} (1 - \delta)\Pi_t + \cdots$$

Factoring out $[1/(1 + r_t)]\Pi_t$:

$$V(\Pi_t^e) = \frac{1}{1 + r_t} \Pi_t \left(1 + \frac{1 - \delta}{1 + r_t} + \cdots\right)$$

The term in parentheses in this equation is a geometric series, a series of the form $1 + x + x^2 + \cdots$ where x equals $(1 - \delta)/(1 + r_t)$. Thus, its sum is given by $1/(1 - x) = (1 + r_t)/(r_t + \delta)$. Replacing it in the equation above, we get:

$$V(\Pi_t^e) = \frac{1}{1 + r_t} \Pi_t \left(\frac{1 + r_t}{r_t + \delta}\right)$$

Simplifying gives the equation we use in the text:

$$V(\Pi_t^e) = \frac{\Pi_t}{(r_t + \delta)} \quad (20B.2)$$

CHAPTER 21
EXPECTATIONS, OUTPUT, AND POLICY

In Chapter 19, we saw how expectations affected the determination of bond and stock prices. In Chapter 20, we saw how expectations affected consumption and investment decisions. Now, in this chapter, we put the pieces together and take another look at the effects of monetary and fiscal policies.

Section 21-1 draws the major implication of what we have learned, namely, that expectations of both future income and future interest rates affect current spending and therefore affect current output. Section 21-2 looks at monetary policy. It shows how the effects of monetary policy depend crucially on how expectations respond to policy: Monetary policy affects only the current interest rate. What happens to spending and output then depends on how changes in the current interest rate lead people and firms to change their expectations of future interest rates and of future income and, by implication, lead them to change their investment and consumption decisions. Section 21-3 turns to fiscal policy. It shows that in sharp contrast to the simple model we discussed in the core, a fiscal contraction may, under the right circumstances, lead to an increase in output, even in the short run. Again, how expectations respond to policy is at the centre of the story.

21-1 | Expectations and Decisions: Taking Stock

Let us start by reviewing what we have learned and discuss how we should modify the characterization of goods and financial markets—the *IS-LM* model—we developed in the core.

Expectations and the *IS* Relation

The theme of Chapter 20 was that both consumption and investment decisions very much depend on expectations of future income and interest rates. The channels through which expectations affect consumption and investment spending are summarized in Figure 21–1.

A model that gave a detailed treatment of consumption and investment along the lines shown in Figure 21–1 could be very complicated, and although this can be done—and, indeed, is done in the large empirical models that macroeconomists build to understand the economy and analyze policy—this is not the place to try. We want to capture the essence of what we have learned so far—the dependence of consumption and investment on expectations of the future—without getting lost in the details.

To do so, we make a major simplification that we also made in the appendix to Chapter 20. We reduce the present and the future to only two periods: (1) a *current* period, which you can think of as the current year, and (2) a *future* period, which you can think of as all future years lumped together. This way we do not have to keep track of expectations about each future year.

Having made this assumption, how should we then write the *IS* relation for the current period? Let us go back to the *IS* relation we wrote down before thinking about the role of expectations in consumption and investment decisions:

$$Y = C\,(Y - T) + I\,(Y, r) + G$$

Goods-market equilibrium requires that output be equal to aggregate spending—the sum of consumption spending, investment spending, and government spending. Before we introduce expectations into this equation, it will prove convenient to rewrite it in more compact form, but without changing its content. Let us define:

$$A\,(Y, T, r) \equiv C\,(Y - T) + I\,(Y, r)$$

where *A* stands for **aggregate private spending**, or, simply, *private spending*. With this notation we can rewrite the *IS* relation as:

$$Y = A(Y,\ T,\ r) + G \tag{21.1}$$
$$(+,\ -,\ -)$$

> This way of dividing time between "today" and "later" is the way many of us organize our own life: Think of "things to do today" versus "things that can wait."

> This is the equation we saw in Chapter 18, where we introduced the distinction between real and nominal interest rates.

> The reason for doing so is to regroup the two components of demand, *C* and *I*, which both depend on expectations. We continue to treat *G*, government spending, as exogenous—unexplained within our model.

FIGURE 21–1

Expectations and Spending: The Channels

Expectations affect consumption and investment decisions, both directly and through asset prices.

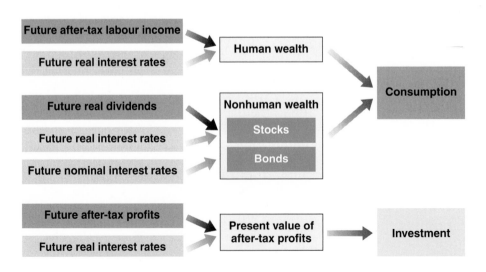

The properties of aggregate private spending, A, follow from the properties of consumption and investment that we laid down in earlier chapters:

- Aggregate private spending is an increasing function of income, Y: Higher income (equivalently, output) increases consumption and investment.
- It is a decreasing function of taxes, T: Higher taxes decrease consumption.
- It is a decreasing function of the real interest rate, r: A higher real interest rate decreases investment.

All we have done so far is simplify notation. Now, we need to extend equation (21.1) to reflect the role of expectations. The natural extension is to allow spending to depend not only on current variables but also on their expected values in the future period, thus:

$$Y = A(Y, T, r, Y'^e, T'^e, r'^e) + G \qquad (21.2)$$
$$(+, -, -, +, \ -, \ -)$$

Primes denote future values and the superscript e denotes an expectation, so Y'^e, T'^e, and r'^e denote expected future income, expected future taxes, and the expected future real interest rate, respectively. The notation is a bit heavy, but what it captures is straightforward:

- Increases in either current or expected future income increase private spending.
- Increases in either current or expected future taxes decrease private spending.
- Increases in either the current or expected future real interest rate decrease private spending.

With goods-market equilibrium now given by equation (21.2), Figure 21–2 shows the new IS curve. As usual, to draw the curve, we take all variables other than current output, Y, and the current real interest rate, r, as given. Thus, the IS curve is drawn for given values of current and future expected taxes, T and T'^e, for given values of expected future output, Y'^e, and for given values of the expected future real interest rate, r'^e.

The new IS curve is still downward sloping, and the reason is the same as before: A decrease in the current real interest rate leads to an increase in spending, which leads, through a multiplier effect, to an increase in output. We can say more, however: The new IS curve is much steeper than the IS curve we drew in earlier chapters. Put another way, a large decrease in the current interest rate is likely to have only a small effect on equilibrium output.

Notation: Primes stand for values of the variables in the future period. The superscript e stands for "expected."

$$Y \text{ or } Y'^e \uparrow \Rightarrow A \uparrow$$
$$T \text{ or } T'^e \uparrow \Rightarrow A \downarrow$$
$$r \text{ or } r'^e \uparrow \Rightarrow A \downarrow$$

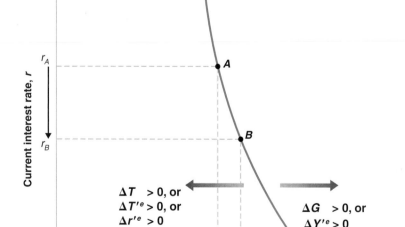

Current interest rate, r

$\Delta T > 0$, or
$\Delta T'^e > 0$, or
$\Delta r'^e > 0$

$\Delta G > 0$, or
$\Delta Y'^e > 0$

$Y_A \longrightarrow Y_B$

Current output, Y

FIGURE 21–2

The New IS Curve

Given expectations, a decrease in the real interest rate leads to a small increase in output. Increases in government spending, or in expected future output, shift the IS curve to the right. Increases in taxes, in expected future taxes, or in the expected future real interest rate shift the IS curve to the left.

To see why, take point A on the IS curve in Figure 21–2, and consider the effects of a decrease in the real interest rate. The effect of the decrease in the real interest rate on output depends on the strength of two effects: (1) the effect of the real interest rate on spending, given income, and (2) the size of the multiplier. Let us examine each one.

In terms of derivatives, A_r is small (in absolute value). ▶

- A decrease in the current real interest rate, *given unchanged expectations of the future real interest rate*, does not have much effect on spending. We saw why in the previous chapters: A change in only the current real interest rate does not lead to large changes in present values and so does not lead to large changes in spending. For example, firms are not likely to change their investment plans very much in response to a decrease in the current real interest rate if they do not expect future real interest rates to be lower as well.

In terms of derivatives, A_Y is small. ▶

- The multiplier is likely to be small. Recall that the size of the multiplier depends on the size of the effect of a change in current income (output) on spending. But a change in current income, *given unchanged expectations of future income*, is unlikely to have a large effect on spending. The reason is that changes in income that are not expected to last have only a limited effect on both consumption and investment. Consumers who expect their income to be higher only for a year will increase consumption, but by much less than the increase in income. Firms expecting sales to be higher only for a year are unlikely to change their investment plans very much.

Putting things together, a large decrease in the current real interest rate, from r_A to r_B in Figure 21–2, leads to only a small increase in output, from Y_A to Y_B. The IS curve, which goes through points A and B, is steeply downward sloping.

Changes in current taxes (T) or in government spending (G) shift the IS curve. An increase in current government spending increases spending at a given interest rate, shifting the IS curve to the right; an increase in taxes shifts the IS curve to the left. These shifts are represented in Figure 21–2.

Changes in expected future variables also shift the IS curve. An increase in expected future output, Y'^e, shifts the IS curve to the right: Higher expected future income leads consumers to feel wealthier and consume more. Higher expected future output implies higher expected profits, leading firms to invest more. By a similar argument, an increase in expected future taxes leads consumers to decrease current spending and shifts the IS curve to the left. And an increase in the expected future real interest rate decreases current spending, shifting the IS curve to the left. These shifts are also represented in Figure 21–2.

The *LM* Relation Revisited

The LM relation we derived in Chapter 4 and have used until now was given by:

$$\frac{M}{P} = Y L(i) \tag{21.3}$$

where M/P is the supply of money and $Y L(i)$ is the demand for money. Equilibrium in financial markets requires that the supply of money be equal to the demand for money. The demand for money depends on real income and on the short-term nominal interest rate—the opportunity cost of holding money. We derived this demand for money before thinking about expectations. Now that we have, the question is: Should we modify equation (21.3)? The answer—we are sure this will be good news—is no.

Think of your own demand for money. How much money you want to hold today depends on your *current* level of transactions, not on the level of transactions you expect next year or the year after; there will be time to adjust your money balances to your transaction level if it changes in the future. And the opportunity cost of holding money today depends on the *current* nominal interest rate, not on the expected nominal interest rate next year or the year after. If short-term interest rates were to increase in the future, increasing the opportunity cost of holding money, the time to reduce your money balances would be not now.

So, in contrast to the consumption decision, the decision about how much money to hold is myopic, depending primarily on current income and the current short-term nominal interest rate. We can still think of the demand for money as depending on the current level of output and the current nominal interest rate and use equation (21.3) to describe the determination of the nominal interest rate in the current period.

To summarize: We have seen that expectations about the future play a major role in spending decisions. This implies that expectations enter the *IS* relation: Private spending depends not only on current output and the current real interest rate but also on expected future output and the expected future real interest rate. In contrast, the decision about how much money to hold is largely myopic: The two variables entering the *LM* relation are still current income and the current nominal interest rate.

21-2 | Monetary Policy, Expectations, and Output

In the basic *IS-LM* model, there was only one interest rate, *i*, which entered both the *IS* relation and the *LM* relation. When the Bank of Canada expanded the money supply, "the" interest rate went down and spending increased. From the previous three chapters, we have learned that there are, in fact, many interest rates and that we must keep two distinctions in mind:

- The distinction between the nominal interest rate and the real interest rate
- The distinction between current and expected future interest rates

The interest rate that enters the *LM* relation, and thus the interest rate that the Bank of Canada affects directly, is the *current nominal interest rate*. In contrast, spending in the *IS* relation depends on both *current and expected future real interest rates*. Economists sometimes state this distinction even more starkly by saying that although the Bank of Canada controls the *short-term nominal interest rate*, what matters for spending and output is the *long-term real interest rate*.

Let us look at this more closely. Recall from Chapter 18 that the real interest rate is approximately equal to the nominal interest rate minus expected current inflation—inflation expected, as of today, for the current period:

$$r = i - \pi^e$$

Similarly, the expected future real interest rate is approximately equal to the expected future nominal interest rate minus expected future inflation—inflation expected, as of today, for the future period.

$$r'^e = i'^e - \pi'^e$$

When the Bank of Canada increases money supply, therefore decreasing the current nominal interest rate, *i*, the effect on the current and the expected future real interest rates depends on two factors:

- Whether the increase in money supply leads financial markets to revise their expectations of the future nominal interest rate, i'^e, as well.
- Whether the increase in money supply leads financial markets to revise their expectations of current and future inflation, π^e and π'^e. If for example, the change in money leads them to expect more inflation in the future, the expected future real interest rate, r'^e will decrease by more than the expected future nominal interest rate, i'^e.

We will leave aside the second factor, the role of changing expectations of inflation, and focus on the first, the role of changing expectations of the future nominal interest rate. Thus, we will assume that expected current and future inflation are both equal to zero. In this case, we need not distinguish between the nominal and the real interest rates, as they are equal, and we can use the same letter to denote both.

We explored the role of changing expectations of inflation on the relation between the nominal interest rate and the real interest rate in Chapter 18. Leaving changes in expected inflation aside will keep the analysis simpler here. You have, however, all the elements you need to think through what would happen if we also allowed expectations of current inflation and future inflation to adjust in response to an increase in money supply. How would these expectations adjust? Would this lead to a larger or a smaller effect on output in the current period?

Let r and r'^e denote the current and expected future real (and nominal) interest rates. With this simplification, we can rewrite the *IS* and *LM* relations in equations (21.2) and (21.3) as:

$$IS: \quad Y = A(Y, T, r, Y'^e, T'^e, r'^e) + G \tag{21.4}$$

$$LM: \quad \frac{M}{P} = Y\,L(r) \tag{21.5}$$

The corresponding *IS* and *LM* curves are drawn in Figure 21–3(a). The vertical axis measures the current interest rate, r; the horizontal axis measures current output, Y. The *IS* curve is downward sloping and steep. We saw the reason earlier: For given expectations, a change in the current interest rate has a limited effect on spending, and the multiplier is small. The *LM* is upward sloping. An increase in income leads to an increase in the demand for money; given the supply of money, the result is an increase in the interest rate.

Now, suppose that at point A, the economy is in a recession, and the Bank of Canada decides to increase money supply. Assume for the moment this expansionary monetary policy does not change expectations of either the future interest rate or future output. In

FIGURE 21–3

The Effects of an Expansionary Monetary Policy

(a) The equilibrium is determined by the intersection of the *IS* and the *LM* curves. (b) The effects of monetary policy on output depend very much on whether and how monetary policy affects expectations.

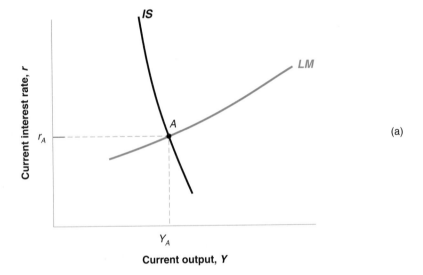

(a)

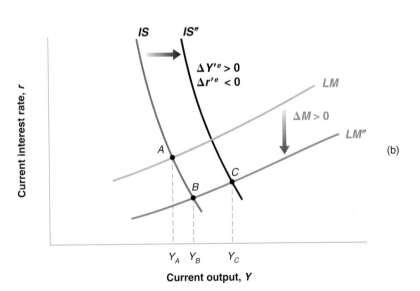

(b)

Figure 21–3(b), the *LM* shifts down, from *LM* to *LM"*. (Because we already use primes to denote future values of the variables, we will use double primes [such as in *LM"*] to denote shifts in curves in this chapter.) The equilibrium moves from point *A* to point *B*, with higher output and a lower interest rate. The steep *IS* curve, however, implies that the increase in money has only a small effect on output: Changes in the current interest rate, unaccompanied by changes in expectations, have only a small effect on spending and, in turn, on output.

But is it reasonable to assume that expectations are unaffected by an expansionary monetary policy? Isn't it likely that as the Bank of Canada decreases the current interest rate, financial markets anticipate lower interest rates in the future as well, along with higher future output stimulated by this lower future interest rate? What happens if they do? At a given current interest rate, prospects of a lower future interest rate and of higher future output both increase spending and output; they shift the *IS* curve to the right, from *IS* to *IS"*. The new equilibrium is given by point *C*. Thus, although the direct effect of the expansion in money on output is limited, the full effect, once changes in expectations are taken into account, is much larger.

Given expectations, an increase in money supply leads to a shift in the *LM* and a movement down the steep *IS*. This leads to a large decrease in *r*, a small increase in *Y*.

If the increase in money supply leads to an increase in Y^e and a decrease in r^e, the *IS* curve shifts to the right, leading to a larger increase in *Y*.

To summarize: We have just learned something important. The effects of monetary policy (of any type of macroeconomic policy for that matter) depend crucially on their effect on expectations. If a monetary expansion leads financial investors, firms, and consumers to revise their expectations of future interest rates and output, then the effects of the monetary expansion on output may be very large. But if expectations remain unchanged, the effects of the monetary expansion on output will be small.

Saying that the effect of policy depends on its effect on expectations is not the same as saying that anything can happen. Expectations are not arbitrary. A fund manager deciding whether to invest in stocks or bonds, a firm thinking about whether to build a new plant, a consumer thinking about how much he should save for retirement—all give a lot of thought to what may happen in the future. We can think of them as forming expectations about the future by assessing the likely course of future policy and then working out the implications for future activity. If they do not do it themselves—surely most of us do not spend our time solving macroeconomic models before making decisions—they do so indirectly by watching TV and reading newsletters and newspapers, which themselves rely on the forecasts of public and private forecasters. Economists refer to expectations formed in this forward-looking manner as **rational expectations**. The introduction of the assumption of rational expectations is one of the most important developments in macroeconomics in the last 25 years and is discussed further in the Focus box "Rational Expectations."

We could go back and think about the implications of rational expectations in the case of the monetary expansion we have just studied. It will be more fun to do this in the context of a change in fiscal policy, and this is what we now turn to.

21-3 | Deficit Reduction, Expectations, and Output

Recall the conclusions we reached in the core about the effects of a budget deficit reduction:

- In the medium run and the long run, a budget deficit reduction is likely to be beneficial for the economy. In the medium run, a lower budget deficit leads to higher investment. In the long run, higher investment translates into higher output.
- In the short run, however, unless it is offset by a monetary expansion, a reduction of the budget deficit leads to a reduction in spending, and thus to a contraction in output.

See section 10-5 for the analysis of short- and medium-run effects, and section 15-2 for the analysis of long-run effects—through the effect on the saving rate and, in turn, on capital accumulation.

It is this adverse short-run effect that—in addition to the unpopularity of increases in taxes or reductions in transfers or in other government programs—has often deterred governments from tackling their budget deficit: Why take the risk of a recession now for benefits that will accrue only in the future?

In the past 10 years, however, several economists have questioned this conclusion and have argued that a deficit reduction may actually increase output even in the *short run*. Their

Most macroeconomists today routinely solve their models under the assumption of rational expectations. But this was not always the case. Indeed, the last 25 years in macroeconomic research are often called the "rational expectations" revolution.

The importance of expectations is an old theme in macroeconomics. But until the early 1970s, macroeconomists thought of expectations in one of two ways:

1. One was as **animal spirits** (from an expression Keynes introduced in the *General Theory* to refer to movements in investment that could not be explained by movements in current variables): Shifts in expectations were considered important but largely unexplained.

2. The other was as simple, backward-looking rules. For example, people were often assumed to have **adaptive expectations**, to assume that if their income had grown fast in the past it would continue to do so in the future, to revise their expectations of future inflation upward if they had underpredicted in the past, and so on.

In the early 1970s, a group of macroeconomists led by Robert Lucas and Thomas Sargent argued that these assumptions did not do justice to the way people form expectations. (Robert Lucas received the Nobel prize in 1995 for his work on expectations.) They argued that in thinking about the effects of alternative policies, economists should assume that people have rational expectations, that people look to the future and do the best job they can in predicting it. This is not the same as assuming that people know the future but rather that they use the information they have in the best possible way.

Using the popular macroeconomic models of the time, Lucas and Sargent showed how replacing traditional assumptions about expectations formation by the assumption of rational expectations could fundamentally alter the results. We saw, for example, in Chapter 12 how Lucas challenged the notion that

disinflation necessarily required an increase in unemployment for some time. Under rational expectations, he argued, a credible disinflation policy might decrease inflation without any increase in unemployment. More generally, Lucas and Sargent's research showed the need for a complete rethinking of macroeconomic models under the assumption of rational expectations, and this is what has happened since.

Most macroeconomists today use the assumption of rational expectations as a working assumption in their models and in their analyses of policy. This is not because they believe that people always have rational expectations. Surely, there are times when people, firms, or financial market participants lose sight of reality and become too optimistic or too pessimistic. But these are more the exception than the rule, and it is not clear that economists can say much about those times anyway. In thinking about the likely effects of a particular economic policy, the best assumption to make seems to be that financial markets, people, and firms will do the best they can to work out its implications. Designing a policy on the assumption that people will make systematic mistakes in responding to it is unwise.

So, why did it take until the 1970s for rational expectations to become a standard assumption in macroeconomics? Largely because of technical problems. Under rational expectations, what happens today depends on expectations of what will happen in the future. But what happens in the future depends on what happens today. The success of Lucas and Sargent in convincing most macroeconomists to use rational expectations comes not only from the strength of their case but also from showing how it could actually be done. Much progress has been made since in developing solution methods for larger and larger models. Today, several large macroeconometric models are solved under rational expectations. (We presented a simulation from such a model in Chapter 10. We will see another example in Chapter 25.)

---

basic argument is simple: If people take into account the future beneficial effects of deficit reduction, their expectations about the future may improve enough to lead to an increase rather than a decrease in current spending and so an increase in current output. This section presents their argument more formally. The Global Macro box "Can a Budget Deficit Reduction Lead to an Output Expansion? The Example of Ireland in the 1980s" reviews some of the supporting evidence (page 436).

Assume the economy is described by equation (21.4) for the *IS* relation and equation (21.5) for the *LM* relation. Now, suppose that government announces a program to reduce the deficit, through decreases both in current spending, G, and in future spending, G'^e. What will happen to output during *this period*?

The Role of Expectations about the Future

Suppose first that expectations of future output (Y'^e) and of the future interest rate (r'^e) do not change. In this case, the decrease in government spending in the current period leads to a shift in the *IS* curve to the left, and thus to a decrease in equilibrium output. The crucial question therefore is: What happens to expectations? To answer, let us go back to what we learned in the core about the effects of a deficit reduction in the medium run and the long run:

- In the medium run, a deficit reduction has no effect on output. It leads, however, to a lower interest rate and to higher investment. These were two of the main lessons of Chapter 10. Let us review the logic behind each one.

    Recall that when we look at the medium run, we ignore the effects of capital accumulation on output. Thus, in the medium run, the natural level of output depends on the level of productivity (taken as given) and on the natural level of employment. The natural level of employment depends on the natural rate of unemployment. If spending by government on goods and services does not affect the natural rate of unemployment —and there is no obvious reason why it should—then changes in spending will not affect the natural level of output. Thus, deficit reduction has no effect on the level of output in the medium run.

    Now, recall that output must be equal to spending, which itself is the sum of public and private spending. Given that output is unchanged and that public spending is lower, private spending must be higher. This requires a lower interest rate: A lower interest rate leads to higher investment, and thus to higher private spending, which offsets the decrease in public spending and leaves output unchanged.

In the medium run: Y does not change, $I\uparrow$

- In the long run—that is, taking into account the effects of capital accumulation on output —higher investment leads to a higher capital stock, and thus to a higher level of output.

In the long run,
$I\uparrow \Rightarrow K\uparrow \Rightarrow Y\uparrow$

    This was the main lesson of Chapter 15. The higher the proportion of output saved (or invested; the two must be equal for the goods market to be in equilibrium), the higher is the capital stock, and thus the higher the level of output in the long run.

If people, firms, and financial market participants have rational expectations, then, in response to the announcement of a deficit reduction, they will expect these developments to take place in the future. Thus, they will revise their expectation of future output (Y'^e) up and their expectation of the future interest rate (r'^e) down.

Back to the Current Period

We can now return to the question of what happens during *this period* in response to the announcement and start of the deficit reduction program. Figure 21–4 draws the *IS* and *LM* curves for the current period. In response to the announcement of the deficit reduction, there are now three factors shifting the *IS* curve:

- Current government spending (G) goes down, leading to a shift of the *IS* curve to the left. At a given interest rate, the decrease in government spending leads to a decrease in spending and in output.

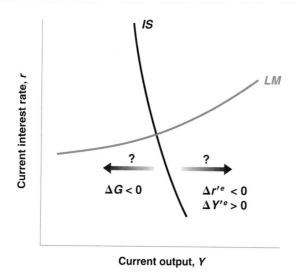

FIGURE **21-4**

The Effects of Deficit Reduction on Current Output

When account is taken of its effect on expectations, the decrease in government spending need not lead to a decrease in output.

- Expected future output (Y'^e) goes up, leading to a shift of the *IS* curve to the right. At a given interest rate, the increase in expected future output leads to an increase in private spending, thus increasing output.
- The expected future interest rate goes down, leading to a shift of the *IS* curve to the right. At a given current interest rate, a decrease in the expected future interest rate stimulates spending and increases output.

What is the net effect of these three shifts in the *IS* curve? Can the effect of expectations on consumption and investment spending offset the decrease in government spending? Without much more information about the exact form of the *IS* and *LM* relations and about the details of the deficit reduction program, we cannot tell which shifts will dominate and whether output will go up or down. But our analysis tells us that both cases are possible, that output may go up in response to the deficit reduction. And it gives us a few hints about when this might happen.

Note that the smaller the decrease in current government spending (G), the smaller is the adverse effect on spending today. Note also that the larger the decrease in expected future

---

GLOBAL macro

Can a Budget Deficit Reduction Lead to an Output Expansion? The Example of Ireland in the 1980s

Ireland underwent two major deficit reduction programs in the 1980s.

- The first program began in 1982. In 1981, the budget deficit had reached a very high 13% of GDP.

  Government debt, the result of the accumulation of current and past deficits, stood at 77% of GDP, also a very high level. Government clearly had to regain control of its finances. Over the next three years, it embarked on a program of deficit reduction, based mostly on tax increases. This was an ambitious program: Had output continued to grow at its normal rate, the program would have reduced the deficit by 5% of GDP.

  The results were dismal. As shown in line 2 of Table 1, output growth was low in 1982 and negative in 1983. Low growth was associated with a major increase in unemployment, from 9.5% in 1981 to 15% in 1984 (line 3). Because of low output growth, tax revenues, which depend on the level of activity, were lower than anticipated. The actual deficit reduction, shown in line 1, was only 3.5% of GDP. And the result of continuing high deficits and low GDP growth was a further increase in the ratio of debt to GDP to 97% in 1984.

- A second attempt was made starting in February 1987. The economy was still in very bad shape. The 1986 deficit was 10.7% of GDP; debt stood at 116% of GDP, a record high in Europe at the time. This new program of deficit reduction was different from the first. The focus was more on a reduction of the role of government and a decrease in government spending rather than on an increase in taxes. The tax increases in the program were achieved through a tax reform widening the tax base and without an increase in the marginal tax rate (the highest tax rate) on income. The program was again very ambitious: Had output grown at its normal rate, the reduction

in the deficit would have been 6.4% of GDP.

The results could not have been more different from those of the first program. The years 1987 to 1989 marked a period of strong growth, with average GDP growth exceeding 5%. The unemployment rate was reduced by 2%. Because of strong output growth, tax revenues were stronger than anticipated, and the deficit was reduced by nearly 9% of GDP.

Several economists have argued that the striking difference between the results of the two programs can be traced to the different reaction of expectations in each case. The first package, they argue, focused on tax increases and did not change what many saw as too large a role of government in the economy. The second, with its focus on cuts in spending and on tax reform, had a much more positive impact on expectations, and thus on output.

Are they right? One variable, the household saving rate (defined as disposable income minus consumption divided by disposable income) strongly suggests that expectations are, indeed, an important part of the story. To interpret the behaviour of the saving rate, recall the lessons from Chapter 20 about consumption behaviour. When disposable income grows unusually slowly or goes down—as it does in a recession—consumption typically slows down or declines by less than disposable income, as people expect things to improve in the future. Put another way, when the growth of disposable income is unusually low or negative, the saving rate typically comes down. Now, look at line 4 of the table at what happened from 1981 to 1984: Despite low growth throughout the period and a recession in 1983, the household saving rate actually increased a little. Put another way, people reduced their consumption by more than the reduction in disposable income. To do so, they must have been very pessimistic about the future.

(continued)

Now, turn to 1986 to 1989. During that period, the economy was growing unusually strongly. By the same argument as in the previous paragraph, we would have expected consumption to increase less strongly, and thus the saving rate to increase. Instead, it decreased very strongly, from 15.7% in 1986 to 12.6% in 1989. Consumers must have become much more optimistic about the future to increase their consumption by more than the increase in disposable income in such a way.

Can this difference in the adjustment of expectations over the two episodes be fully attributed to the differences in the two fiscal programs? The answer is: It almost surely cannot. Monetary policy was not identical during the two episodes. More importantly, Ireland was changing in many ways at the time of the second fiscal program. Productivity was increasing much faster than real wages, reducing the cost of labour for firms. Attracted by tax breaks, low labour costs, and an educated labour force, many foreign firms were coming to Ireland to create new plants: These factors played a major role in the expansion of the late 1980s. Irish growth has been very strong ever since, with average output growth exceeding 6% since 1990. Surely, this long expansion is due to other factors besides fiscal policy. Nevertheless, the change in fiscal policy in 1987 probably played a role in convincing people, firms (including foreign firms), and financial markets that government was regaining control of its finances. In any case, the fact remains that the substantial deficit reduction of 1987 to 1989 was accompanied by a strong output expansion, not by the recession predicted by the basic *IS-LM* model.

Further Reading

For a more detailed discussion, look at Francesco Giavazzi and Marco Pagano, "Can Severe Fiscal Contractions be Expansionary? Tales of Two Small European Countries," *NBER Macroeconomics Annual*, 1990, pp. 75–110.

A recent survey of what we have learned by looking at programs of deficit reduction around the world is given in John McDermott and Robert Wescott, "An Empirical Analysis of Fiscal Adjustments," IMF working paper, June 1996.

TABLE 1	Fiscal and Other Macroeconomic Indicators, Ireland, 1981–1984 and 1986–1989							
	1981	**1982**	**1983**	**1984**	**1986**	**1987**	**1988**	**1989**
1. Budget deficit (% of GDP)	−13.0	−13.4	−11.4	−9.5	−10.7	−8.6	−4.5	−1.8
2. Output growth rate (%)	3.3	2.3	−0.2	4.4	−0.4	4.7	5.2	5.8
3. Unemployment rate (%)	9.5	11.0	13.5	15.0	17.1	16.9	16.3	15.1
4. Household saving rate (% of disposable income)	17.9	19.6	18.1	18.4	15.7	12.9	11.0	12.6

Source: OECD Economic Outlook, June 1998.

government spending (G'^e), the larger is the effect on expected future output and interest rates, and thus the larger the favourable effect on spending today. This suggests that *backloading* (the tilting of the deficit reduction toward the future), with small cuts today and larger cuts in the future, is more likely to lead to an increase in output.

On the other hand, backloading raises other issues. If government announces the need for painful cuts in spending but then defers the required measures to some time in the future, its credibility—the perceived probability that government will actually do what it has promised—may well decrease. Government must perform a delicate balancing act: There have to be enough cuts in the current period to show a commitment to deficit reduction and enough cuts left to the future to reduce the adverse effects on the economy in the short run.

More generally, our analysis suggests that anything in a deficit reduction program that improves expectations of how the future will look is likely to make the short-run effects of deficit reduction less painful. Let us give two examples.

Measures that are perceived by firms and financial markets as reducing some of the existing distortions in the economy may improve expectations and make it more likely that output increases in the short run. Take, for example, unemployment benefits. We saw in Chapter 9 that lower unemployment benefits lead to a decline in the natural rate of unemployment, and thus a higher natural level of output. Thus, a reform of the social insurance system, which includes a reduction in the generosity of unemployment benefits, is likely to have two effects on spending, and thus on output in the short run. The first is the adverse effect on the

An important caveat: Even if a reduction in unemployment benefits increases output, this surely does not imply that unemployment benefits should be eliminated. Even if aggregate income goes up, we must worry about distribution effects: The consumption of the unemployed goes down, and the pain associated with being unemployed goes up.

As we will see in Chapter 23, a very large deficit often leads to very high money creation and, soon after, to very high inflation. Very high inflation leads not only to economic trouble but also to political instability.

Note how far we are from the results of Chapter 3, where by choosing spending and taxes wisely, government could achieve any level of output it wanted. Here, even the direction of the effect of a deficit reduction on output may be hard to predict.

consumption of the unemployed: Lower unemployment benefits will reduce their income and their consumption. The second is a positive effect on spending through expectations: The anticipation of a lower unemployment rate and of a higher level of output in the future may lead to both higher consumption and higher investment. If the second effect dominates, the effect may be an increase in overall spending, increasing output not only in the medium run but also in the short run.

Another example is that of an economy where government has, in effect, lost control of its budget: Government spending is high, tax revenues are low, and the deficit is very large. In such an environment, a credible deficit reduction program is also more likely to increase output in the short run. Before the announcement of the program, people may have expected major political and economic trouble in the future. The announcement of a program of deficit reduction may well reassure people that government has regained control and that the future is less bleak than they anticipated. This decrease in pessimism about the future may lead to an increase in spending and output, even if taxes are increased as part of the deficit reduction program.

To summarize: A program of deficit reduction may increase output even in the short run. Whether it does depends on many factors, in particular:

- The credibility of the program: Will spending be cut or taxes increased in the future as announced?
- The timing of the program: How large are spending cuts in the future relative to current spending cuts?
- The composition of the program: Does the program remove some of the distortions in the economy?
- The state of government finances in the first place: How large is the initial deficit? Is this a "last chance" program? What will happen if it fails?

This gives you a sense of both the importance of expectations in determining the outcome and of the difficulty of predicting the effects of fiscal policy in such a context.

SUMMARY

- Spending in the goods market depends on current and expected future output and on the current and the expected future real interest rate. Changes in expected future output or in the expected future real interest rate lead to changes in spending and in output today.

- By implication, the effects of any policy on spending and output depend on whether and how policy affects expectations of future output and the real interest rate.

- The assumption of rational expectations is that people, firms, and participants in financial markets form expectations of the future by assessing the course of future expected policy and then working out the implications for future output, interest rates, and so on. Although it is clear that most people do not go through this exercise themselves, we can think of them doing so indirectly by watching TV and reading newspapers, which in turn rely on the predictions of public and private forecasters.

- Although there surely are cases where people, firms, or financial investors do not have rational expectations, the assumption seems to be the best benchmark to evaluate the potential effects of alternative policies. Designing a policy on the assumption that people will make systematic mistakes in responding to it is surely unwise.

- Changes in money supply affect the short-term nominal interest rate. Spending, however, depends on the current and the expected future real interest rates. Thus, the effect of monetary policy on activity depends crucially on whether and how changes in the short-term nominal interest rate lead to changes in the current and the expected future real interest rate.

- When account is taken of its effect on expectations, a budget deficit reduction may lead to an increase rather than a decrease in output. This is because expectations of higher output and lower interest rates may more than offset the direct effect of the deficit reduction on spending.

- adaptive expectations, 434
- aggregate private spending, 428
- animal spirits, 434
- rational expectations, 433

An asterisk denotes a harder question. [Web] indicates that the question requires access to the Internet.

1. TRUE/FALSE/UNCERTAIN

a. Changes in expected future one-year real interest rates have a much larger effect on spending than changes in the current one-year real interest rate.

b. The introduction of expectations implies that the *IS* curve is still downward sloping but is now much flatter.

c. Current real money demand is inversely related to the future nominal interest rate.

d. The rational expectations assumption implies that consumers take into account the effects of future fiscal policy on output.

e. Future monetary policy affects future economic activity but not current economic activity.

f. Depending on its effect on expectations, a fiscal contraction may actually lead to an economic expansion.

g. The very different effects of Ireland's deficit reduction programs in 1982 and in 1987 provide little support for a single theory of expectations.

2. POLICY EXPERIMENTS

For each of the following, determine whether the *IS* curve, the *LM* curve, neither curve, or both shift. In each case, assume that expected current inflation and future inflation are equal to zero and that no other exogenous variable is changing.

a. A decrease in the expected future real interest rate.

b. A steeper yield curve.

c. An increase in the current money supply.

d. An increase in the expected future money supply.

e. An increase in expected future taxes.

f. A decrease in expected future income.

3. RATIONAL EXPECTATIONS

"The rational expectations assumption is unrealistic, because it essentially amounts to the assumption that every consumer has perfect knowledge of the economy." Discuss this statement.

4. FISCAL POLICY

A new prime minister, who promised during her campaign that she would cut taxes, has just been elected. People trust that she will keep her promise but that the tax cuts will be implemented only in the future. Determine the impact of the election result on current output, the current interest rate, and current private spending under each of the following assumptions. (In each case, indicate what you think will happen to Y'^e, r'^e, and T'^e, and then how these changes in expectations affect output today.)

a. The Bank of Canada will not change its policy.

b. The Bank of Canada will act to prevent any change in future output.

c. The Bank of Canada will act to prevent any increase in the future interest rate.

5. PAUL MARTIN'S DEFICIT REDUCTION PLAN

When the Liberals were first elected in 1993, the federal deficit in fiscal year 1992–1993 was $40.4 billion. Finance Minister Paul Martin toured Canada making it clear that the federal deficit would be reduced.

a. What does deficit reduction imply for output in the medium run and the long run? What are the advantages of reducing the deficit?

In February 1995, Finance Minister Martin committed to deficit reductions. The projected maximum deficits: 1994–1995, $37.9 billion; 1995–1996, $32.7 billion; 1996–1997, $24.3 billion. Deficits would be even lower if tax revenues grew faster than expected.

b. Why was the deficit reduction package backloaded? Are there any advantages and disadvantages to this approach?

From 1994 through 1997, the Canadian dollar depreciated.

c. Explain why the Bank of Canada might allow the Canadian dollar to depreciate in the short run, while the federal government was reducing the deficit.

6. PAUL MARTIN'S DEFICIT REDUCTION PLAN (CONTINUED) [WEB]

a. You can go to the Web site of the Bank of Canada (**www.bankofcanada.ca**) under "Rates and Statistics," "Selected Historical Interest Rates." Using the three-month Treasury Bill Auction, the five-year Government of Canada Benchmark Bond Yield, and the Long-term Government of Canada Benchmark Bond Yield, plot the yield curve for January 1993 and January 1996. Does the yield curve reveal a change in expectations in financial markets from 1993 to 1996?

b. Figure 1–2 shows Canada's unemployment rate. Did unemployment rise or fall after 1993? Did the economy go into a recession as the deficit was reduced?

c. Go to the Statistics Canada Web site (**www.statcan.ca**). Under "Canadian Statistics/Government/Revenues, Expenditures and Debt/Federal general government revenue and expenditure," you can find a report of the federal deficit in the last five fiscal years. Was Mr. Martin's plan to stabilize the deficit successful?

*d. Are there any reasons to think that factors other than the deficit reduction package may have helped reduce the deficit in the 1990s? (*Hint*: Look at the growth rate of real GDP in the late 1990s relative to the early 1990s.)

EXTENSIONS: PATHOLOGIES

Sometimes, (macroeconomic) things go very wrong: There is a sharp drop in output. Or unemployment remains high for very long. Or inflation increases to very high levels. These pathologies are the focus of the next two chapters.

CHAPTER 22

Chapter 22 looks at depressions and slumps, periods during which output drops far below and stays far below the natural level of output. The chapter discusses the adverse effects of deflation and what happens when an economy is caught in a liquidity trap. It looks at the Great Depression, what triggered it, what made it so bad, and what eventually led to the recovery. It then turns to the Japanese economic slump, a slump which started in the early 1990s and from which Japan is slowly emerging today. It shows that many of the factors which contributed to the Great Depression have also operated in Japan in the 1990s.

CHAPTER 23

Chapter 23 looks at episodes of high inflation, from Germany in the early 1920s to Latin America in the 1980s. It shows the role of both fiscal and monetary policies in generating high inflation. Budget deficits can lead to high nominal money growth, and high nominal money growth leads to high inflation. It then looks at how high inflations end and at the role and the nature of stabilization programs.

CHAPTER 22
DEPRESSIONS AND SLUMPS

Amajor theme of this book so far has been that while economies go through fluctuations in the short run, they tend to return to normal in the medium run. An adverse shock may lead to a recession but, fairly quickly, the economy turns around and output returns to its natural level.

Most of the time, this is what happens. But once in a while, things go wrong. Output remains far below its natural level for many years. Unemployment remains stubbornly high. Simply put, the economy appears to be stuck, unable to return to normal. The most infamous case is surely that of the Great Depression, which affected most of the world from the late 1920s to the start of World War II. (Although there is no agreed-upon definition, economists use the term **depression** to describe a deep and long-lasting recession.) A more recent case is the Japanese slump that started in the early 1990s, from which Japan is slowly emerging. (Again, while there is no agreed-upon definition, most economists use **slump** to denote a long period of low or no growth, longer than a typical recession, but less deep than a depression.)

What goes wrong during such episodes? Are the shocks particularly bad? Do the usual adjustment mechanisms break down? Or are macroeconomic policies particularly misguided? These are the questions we take up in this chapter.

- Section 22-1 looks at two of the mechanisms that have played a central role during both the Great Depression and the Japanese slump: the adverse effects of deflation, and the liquidity trap.

- Section 22-2 then gives an account of the Great Depression in Canada and the United States.

- Section 22-3 does the same for the Japanese slump.

22-1 | Disinflation, Deflation, and the Liquidity Trap

Let us go back to the argument we developed earlier for why output tends to return to its natural level in the medium run. The easiest way to present the argument is in terms of the *IS–LM* graph in Figure 22–1, with the nominal interest rate on the vertical axis and output on the horizontal axis.

The argument we developed in Chapter 10 went like this:

- Suppose an adverse shock leads to a decrease in output, so the economy is at point *A*, and the level of output, *Y*, is below the natural level of output, Y_n. The nature of the shock is not important here. It could be a decrease in spending by consumers or a decrease in investment spending by firms. What is important is that output is now below the natural level of output.

  Recall that the natural level of output is the level of output that prevails when the unemployment rate is equal to the natural unemployment rate. See Chapter 9.

- The fact that output is below the natural level of output leads, in turn, to a decrease in the price level over time. Given the nominal money stock, the decrease in the price level increases the real money stock. This increase in the real money stock shifts the *LM* curve down, leading to a lower interest rate and higher output. After some time, the economy is, for example, at point *B*, with output equal to Y'.

- So long as output remains below its natural level, the price level continues to fall, and the *LM* curve continues to shift down. The economy moves down the *IS* curve until it reaches point *C*, where output is equal to Y_n. In short: Output below the natural level of output leads to a decrease in the price level, which goes on until the economy has returned to normal.

The argument in Chapter 10 was based on the strong simplifying assumption that the nominal money stock was constant. This implied that in the medium run, the price level was also constant—that there was no inflation. It also implied that if output was below the natural level of output, the adjustment of output back to its natural level was achieved through a decrease in the price level—something we rarely observe in practice.

Chapters 11 and 12 presented a more realistic version of the model, where we allowed for positive nominal money growth—and so for positive inflation in the medium run. This model gave a richer description of the adjustment of output and inflation to shocks. It delivered, however, the same basic result as the simpler version of the model presented in Chapter 10: The economy tends to return to the natural level of output over time. The argument went as follows:

- Suppose that, as in Figure 22–1 (next page), output is below the natural level of output—equivalently, the unemployment rate is higher than the natural rate of unemployment.

- With the unemployment rate above the natural rate, inflation falls over time. Suppose nominal money growth and inflation were initially equal to each other, so real money growth (the difference between nominal money growth and inflation) was initially equal to zero. With inflation falling, and therefore becoming smaller than the rate of nominal money growth, real money growth now turns positive. Equivalently, the real money stock increases. This increase in the real money stock shifts the *LM* curve down, leading to an increase in output.

  This follows from the Phillips curve relation, equation (8.10): $u > u_n \Rightarrow \pi_t > \pi_{t-1}$.

- As long as output is below its natural level, inflation falls, and the *LM* curve continues to shift down. This goes on until, eventually, output is back to the natural level of output.

It would, therefore, appear that economies have a strong built-in stabilizing mechanism to get out of recessions:

- Output below the natural level of output leads to lower inflation.
- Lower inflation leads, in turn, to higher real money growth.

FIGURE 22-1

The Return of Output to Its Natural Level

Low output leads to a decrease in the price level. The decrease in the price level leads to an increase in the real money stock. The LM curve shifts down and continues to shift down until output has returned to the natural level of output.

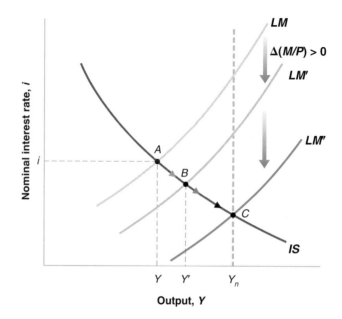

- Higher real money growth leads to an increase in output over time.

The study of depressions and slumps tells us, however, that this built-in mechanism is not foolproof, and that things can go wrong in a number of ways. We now look at some of them.

The Nominal Interest Rate, the Real Interest Rate, and Expected Inflation

When we looked at the adjustment of output in Figure 22–1, we ignored the distinction between the nominal interest rate and the real interest rate. This distinction turns out to be important here, so we need to reintroduce it. Recall from Chapter 18 that:

- What matters for spending decisions, and thus what enters the IS relation, is the real interest rate—the interest rate in terms of goods.

- What matters for the demand for money, and thus what enters the LM relation, is the nominal interest rate—the interest rate in terms of dollars.

Let r be the real interest rate, i be the nominal interest rate, and π^e be expected inflation. Then, from equation (14.4): $r = i - \pi^e$.

Recall also the relation between the two interest rates: The real interest rate is equal to the nominal interest rate minus expected inflation.

What this distinction between the two interest rates implies is shown in Figure 22–2. Suppose the economy is initially at A. Output is initially below the natural level of output. Because output is below the natural level of output, inflation falls. The decrease in inflation now has two effects:

The decrease in inflation leads to an increase in the real money stock. This shifts the LM curve down.

- The first effect is to increase the real money stock and shift the LM curve down, from LM to LM′. The shift of the LM curve—due to the increase in M/P—is the shift we saw in Figure 22–1. This shift of the LM curve tends to increase output. If this was the only shift, the economy would go from A to B.

The decrease in expected inflation leads to an increase in the real interest rate for a given nominal interest rate. It shifts the IS curve to the left.

- There is, however, now a second effect at work. Suppose the decrease in inflation leads to a decrease in expected inflation. Then, for a given nominal interest rate, the decrease in expected inflation increases the real interest rate. The higher real interest rate leads, in turn, to lower spending and lower output. So, at a given nominal interest rate, the level of output implied by equilibrium in the goods market is lower. The IS curve shifts to the left, from IS to IS′. The shift in the IS curve—due to the decrease in π^e—tends to decrease output. If this was the only shift, the economy would go from A to B′.

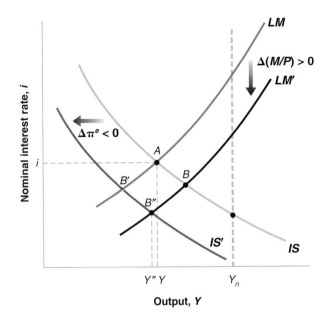

FIGURE 22-2

The Effects of Lower Inflation on Output

When inflation decreases in response to low output, there are two effects. (1) The real money stock increases, leading the *LM* curve to shift down. (2) Expected inflation decreases, leading the *IS* curve to shift to the left. The result may be a further decrease in output.

Does output go up or down as a result of these two shifts? The answer: We cannot tell. The combined effect of the two shifts is to move the economy from *A* to *B″*, with output *Y″*. Whether *Y″* is greater or smaller than *Y* depends on which shift dominates, and is, in general, ambiguous.

As we have drawn the figure, *Y″* is smaller than *Y*. In this case, rather than returning to its natural level, output declines further away from it. Things get worse rather than better. A numerical example will help you keep straight the two effects of inflation:

- Suppose that nominal money growth, inflation, and expected inflation are all equal to 5% initially. Suppose that the nominal interest rate is equal to 7%, so the real interest rate is equal to 7% − 5% = 2%.

- Suppose that, because output is lower than the natural level of output, inflation decreases from 5% to 3% after a year. Real money growth—nominal money growth minus inflation—is now equal to 5% − 3% = 2%. Equivalently, the real money stock increases by 2%. Suppose that this increase in the real money stock leads to a decrease in the nominal interest rate from, say, 7% to 6%. This is the first effect you saw above. Lower inflation leads to a higher real money stock and a lower nominal interest rate.

- Suppose that the decrease in inflation leads people to expect that inflation this year will be 2% lower than it was last year, so expected inflation decreases from 5% to 3%. This implies that at any given nominal interest rate, the real interest rate increases by 2%. This is the second effect you saw earlier. At a given nominal interest rate, lower expected inflation leads to an increase in the real interest rate.

- Combining the two effects: The nominal interest rate decreases from 7% to 6%. Expected inflation decreases from 5% to 3%. So, the real interest rate moves from 7% − 5% = 2% to 6% − 3% = 3%. The net effect of lower inflation is an increase in the real interest rate.

We have just looked at what happens at the start of the adjustment process. It is easy to describe a scenario in which things go from bad to worse over time. The decrease in output from *Y* to *Y″* leads to a further decrease in inflation, and so to a further decrease in expected inflation. This leads to a further increase in the real interest rate, which further decreases output, and so on. In other words, the initial recession can turn into a full-fledged depression,

In Chapter 9, you saw that in the medium run, inflation is equal to nominal money growth minus normal output growth. The example assumes, for simplicity, that normal output growth is zero, so inflation and nominal money growth are equal.

with output continuing to decline rather than returning to the natural level of output. The stabilizing mechanism we described in earlier chapters simply breaks down.

The Liquidity Trap

One reaction to the scenario we just saw is to conclude that while we should worry about it, it can easily be avoided with the appropriate use of monetary policy. The scenario was derived under the assumption that monetary policy (in our case, the rate of growth of nominal money) remained unchanged. But if the central bank was worried about a decrease in output, it would seem that all it would need to do is to embark on an expansionary monetary policy. In terms of Figure 22–2, all the central bank needs to do is to increase the stock of nominal money in order to shift the *LM* curve down far enough to increase output.

This is clearly the right prescription. But there is a limit to what the central bank can do. It cannot decrease the nominal interest rate below zero. If expected inflation is low or even negative (if people expect a deflation), the implied real interest rate may still not be low enough to get the economy out of a recession. This issue has been at the centre of discussions about the Japanese slump. Let us now look at it more closely.

Go back first to our characterization of the demand and the supply of money in Chapter 4. There we drew the demand for money, for a given level of income, as a decreasing function of the nominal interest rate. The lower the nominal interest rate, the larger is the demand for money—equivalently, the smaller the demand for bonds. What we did not ask in Chapter 4 is what happens when the interest rate goes down to zero. The answer is: Once people hold enough money for transaction purposes, they are then indifferent as to whether they hold the rest of their financial wealth in the form of money or in the form of bonds. The reason they are indifferent is: Both money and bonds pay the same nominal interest rate, namely, zero. Thus, the quantity of money demanded is as shown in Figure 22–3:

Look at Figure 4–1. We avoided the issue by not drawing the demand for money for interest rates close to zero.

- As the nominal interest rate decreases, people want to hold more money (and, thus, less bonds). The quantity of money demanded, therefore, increases.

- As the nominal interest rate becomes equal to zero, people want to hold an amount of money at least equal to the distance *OB*: This is what they need for transaction purposes. But they are willing to hold even more money (and, therefore, hold fewer bonds) because they are indifferent between money and bonds. Therefore, the demand for money becomes horizontal beyond point *B*.

Now, consider the effects of an increase in money supply:

- Consider the case where money supply is M^s, so the nominal interest rate consistent with financial market equilibrium is positive and equal to *i*. (This is the case we considered in Chapter 4.) Starting from that equilibrium in Figure 22–3, an increase in the money supply—a shift of the M^s line to the right—leads to a decrease in the nominal interest rate.

- Now, consider the case where money supply is $M^{s'}$, so the equilibrium is at point *B*; or the case where the money supply is $M^{s''}$, so the equilibrium is given at point *C*. In either case, the initial nominal interest rate is zero. And, in either case, an increase in money supply has no effect on the nominal interest rate at this point. Think of it this way.

From Chapter 4: The central bank changes the money stock through open-market operations, in which it buys or sells bonds in exchange for money.

Suppose that the central bank increases money supply. It does so through an open-market operation in which it buys bonds and pays for them by creating money. As the nominal interest rate is zero, people are indifferent as to how much money or bonds they hold, so they are willing to hold fewer bonds and more money at the same nominal interest rate, namely, zero. Money supply increases, but with no effect on the nominal interest rate—which remains equal to zero.

In short: Once the nominal interest rate is equal to zero, expansionary monetary policy becomes powerless. Or to use the words of Keynes, who was the first to point out the problem, the increase in money falls into a **liquidity trap**. People are willing to hold more money (more liquidity) at the same nominal interest rate.

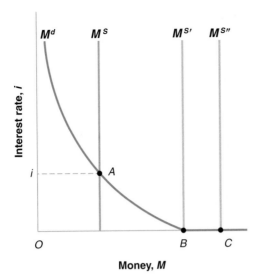

FIGURE 22-3

Money Demand, Money Supply, and the Liquidity Trap

When the nominal interest rate is equal to zero and once people have enough money for transaction purposes, they become indifferent as to whether they hold money or bonds. The demand for money becomes horizontal. This implies that when the nominal interest rate is equal to zero, further increases in money supply have no effect on the nominal interest rate.

Having looked at equilibrium in the financial markets, let us now turn to the *IS–LM* model and see how it must be modified to take into account the liquidity trap.

The derivation of the *LM* curve is shown in the two panels of Figure 22–4. Recall that the *LM* curve gives, for a given real money stock, the relation between the nominal interest rate and the level of income implied by equilibrium in financial markets. To derive the *LM* curve, panel (a) looks at equilibrium in the financial markets for a given value of the real money stock and draws three money demand curves, each corresponding to a different level of income:

- M^d shows the demand for money for a given level of income Y. The equilibrium is given by point A, with nominal interest rate equal to i. This combination of income Y and nominal interest rate i gives us the first point on the *LM* curve, point A in panel (b).

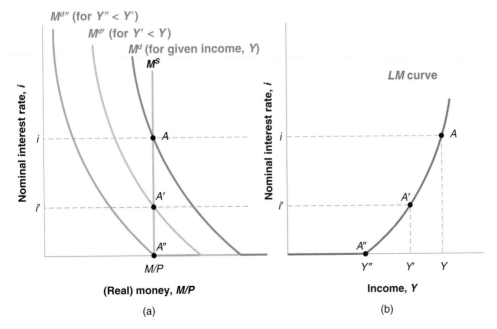

FIGURE 22-4

The Derivation of the *LM* Curve in the Presence of a Liquidity Trap

For low levels of output, the *LM* curve is a flat segment, with a nominal interest rate equal to zero. For higher levels of output, it is upward sloping. An increase in income leads to an increase in the nominal interest rate.

(a)

(b)

- $M^{d'}$ shows the demand for money for a lower level of income, $Y' < Y$. Lower income means fewer transactions and, therefore, a lower demand for money at any interest rate. In this case, the equilibrium is given by point A', with nominal interest rate equal to i'. This combination of income Y' and nominal interest rate i' gives us the second point on the LM curve, point A' in panel (b).

- $M^{d''}$ gives the demand for money for a still lower level of income $Y'' < Y'$. In this case, the equilibrium is given by point A'' in panel (a), with nominal interest rate equal to zero. Point A'' in panel (b) corresponds to A'' in panel (a).

- What happens if income decreases below Y'', shifting the demand for money further to the left in panel (a)? The intersection between the money supply curve and the money demand curve takes place on the horizontal portion of the money demand curve. The equilibrium remains at A'', and the nominal interest rate remains equal to zero.

So far, the derivation of the *LM* curve is exactly the same as in Chapter 5. It is only when income is lower than Y'' that things become different.

Let us summarize: In the presence of a liquidity trap, the LM curve looks as drawn in Figure 22–4, panel (b). For values of income greater than Y'', it is upward sloping—just as it was in Chapter 5 when we first characterized the LM curve. For values of income less than Y'', it is flat at $i = 0$. Intuitively: The nominal interest rate cannot go below zero.

Having derived the LM curve in the presence of a liquidity trap, we can look at the properties of the IS–LM model modified in this way. Suppose that the economy is initially at point A in Figure 22–5, at the intersection of the IS curve and the LM curve, with output Y and nominal interest rate i. And suppose that this level of output is far below the natural level of output Y_n. The question is: Can monetary policy help the economy return to Y_n?

Suppose that the central bank increases money supply, shifting the LM curve from LM to LM'. The equilibrium moves from point A down to point B. The nominal interest rate decreases from i to zero, and output increases from Y to Y'. Thus, to this extent, expansionary policy can, indeed, increase output.

What happens, however, if, starting from point B, the central bank increases money supply further, shifting the LM curve from LM' to, say, LM''?

The intersection of IS and LM'' remains at point B, and output remains equal to Y'. Expansionary monetary policy no longer has an effect on output; therefore, it cannot help output return to Y_n.

FIGURE 22-5

The *IS*–*LM* Model and the Liquidity Trap

In the presence of a liquidity trap, there is a limit as to how much monetary policy can increase output. Monetary policy may not be able to increase output back to its natural level.

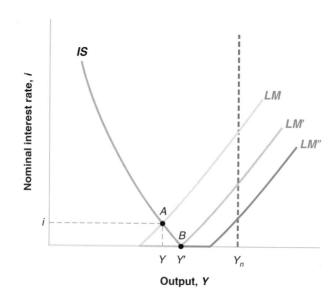

In words: When the nominal interest rate is equal to zero, the economy falls into a "liquidity trap." The central bank can increase "liquidity"—that is, increase money supply. But this "liquidity" falls into a "trap." The additional money is willingly held by financial investors at an unchanged interest rate, namely, zero. If, at this zero nominal interest rate, the demand for goods is still too low, then there is nothing further monetary policy can do to increase output.

Putting Things Together: The Liquidity Trap and Deflation

Just as you may have been skeptical when we were discussing the adverse effects of lower inflation earlier, you may well remain skeptical that the liquidity trap is a serious issue. After all, a zero nominal interest rate is a very low interest rate. Shouldn't a zero nominal interest rate be enough to strongly stimulate spending and avoid a recession?

The answer is no. The key to the answer is again the distinction between the real interest rate and the nominal interest rate. What matters for spending is the real interest rate. What the real interest is, corresponding to a zero nominal interest rate, depends on expected inflation:

- Suppose that the rate of inflation, actual and expected, is high, say, equal to 10%. Then, a zero nominal interest rate corresponds to a real interest rate of –10%. At such a negative real interest rate, consumption and investment spending are likely to be very high, probably high enough to make sure that demand is sufficient to return output to the natural level of output. So, at high inflation, the liquidity trap is unlikely to be a serious problem.

◀ $r = i - \pi^e = 0\% - 10\%$
$= -10\%$

Revisit our discussion of investment decisions in Chapter 16. Why is investment likely to be very high if firms can borrow at a real interest rate of −10%? (Hint: With what do firms compare the real interest rate?)

- Suppose that the rate of inflation, actual and expected, is negative—the economy is experiencing deflation. Say, the rate of inflation is –5% (equivalently, the rate of deflation is 5%). Then, even if the nominal interest rate was equal to zero, the real interest rate would still be equal to 5%. This real interest rate may still be too high to stimulate spending enough, and, in this case, there is nothing monetary policy can do to increase output.

◀ $r = i - \pi^e = 0\% - (-5\%)$
$= 5\%$

You can now see how the two mechanisms—the effects of expected inflation on the real interest rate, and the liquidity trap we described in this section—can come together to turn recessions into slumps or depressions:

- Suppose that the economy has been in a recession for some time, so inflation has steadily decreased and turned into deflation.
- Suppose that monetary policy has decreased the nominal interest rate down to zero. Even at this zero nominal interest rate, expected deflation implies that the real interest rate is still positive.
- Suppose that as a result, the economy is at a point such as A in Figure 22–6, at the intersection of the IS and the LM curves. The nominal interest rate is equal to zero, and output Y is below the natural level of output Y_n.
- There is clearly nothing monetary policy can do in this case to increase output. And things are likely to get worse over time.
- Because output is below the natural level of output, the rate of deflation, actual and expected, is likely to increase (inflation is likely to become more negative).
- At a given nominal interest rate, higher expected deflation leads to an increase in the real interest rate; the IS curve shifts to the left in Figure 22–6, from IS to, say IS', leading to a further decrease in output, from Y down to Y'.
- This leads to further deflation, which leads to a further increase in the real interest rate, a further decrease in output, and so on.

In words: The economy gets into a vicious cycle. Low output leads to more deflation. More deflation leads to a higher real interest rate and even lower output, and there is nothing monetary policy can do about it. The scenario might sound far-fetched, but, as we will now see when we look first at the Great Depression and then at the Japanese slump, it is far from impossible.

FIGURE 22-6

The Liquidity Trap and Deflation

Suppose the economy is in a liquidity trap and there is deflation. Output below the natural level of output leads to more deflation over time, which leads to a further increase in the real interest rate, and leads to a further shift of the *IS* curve to the left. This shift leads to a further decrease in output, which leads to more deflation, and so on.

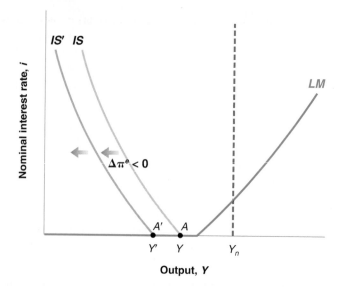

22-2 | The Great Depression in North America

No matter how often we look at it, the **Great Depression** of the 1930s inspires both awe and fear. From 1929 to 1933, real GDP in Canada fell by almost 30%, and output per capita did not recover until well past the onset of World War II. Over the same period, corporate profits fell from $400 million to *negative* $100 million. The decade saw double-digit unemployment rates in all but perhaps the last years, peaking at over 20% in 1933. The Great Depression was a worldwide phenomenon. (While there is no agreed-upon precise definition, economists use the word depression to describe a deep and long-lasting recession.) The average unemployment rate from 1930 to 1938 was 13.3% in Canada, 16.5% in the United States, 15.4% in the United Kingdom, 10.2% in France, and 21.2% in Germany. Being unemployed is never pleasant, but the lot of those unemployed in the 1930s appears to have been exceptionally mean.

A warning: The quality of the unemployment statistics is much lower for the pre–World War II period than it is for post–World War II numbers. Comparisons across countries are particularly perilous. ►

Such a cataclysmic event should inspire great study. You may be surprised to learn that the flow of research on the Great Depression in Canada is a very modest trickle. One thing seems certain, however. Canada did not create the Great Depression. We imported it. The 1930s stand as a potent reminder that to understand economic developments in Canada, we often must look elsewhere.

Soon after World War I, the United States replaced the United Kingdom as both our largest export market and our largest source of investment finance. While the United Kingdom still played an important role in Canadian economic life at the time, if we want to understand the Great Depression in Canada, we must turn our gaze south. Table 22–1 gives the evolution of the unemployment rate, the growth rate of output, the price level, and money supply, for both Canada and the United States, from 1929 to 1942. Although there are some interesting differences, the most striking impression that emerges from Table 22–1 is the similarity in the experiences of the two countries. Output fell dramatically from the peak, and by 1933, the rate of unemployment had increased sevenfold. Both economies grew quickly after 1933, but unemployment did not return to 1929 levels until well after each of the two countries had entered World War II. There is no contradiction here, just an application of Okun's law: A long period of high growth was needed to steadily decrease the high unemployment rate.

From section 12-1: Okun's law relates the change in the unemployment rate to the deviation of output growth from normal. ►

In what follows, we will first examine the main sources of the Great Depression in the United States. We will see that the episode is well explained by a sharp decline in aggregate demand coming first from a sharp decline in spending that was then aggravated by a steep fall in money supply. We will then contrast the U.S. experience with that of Canada and discuss how the downturn in the United States was transmitted to Canada and the rest of the world.

Year	Unemployment Rate (%)		Output Growth Rate (%)		Price Level		Nominal Money Supply	
	Canada	U.S.	Canada	U.S.	Canada	U.S.	Canada C$ millions	U.S. US$ billions
1929	2.9	3.2	0.9	-9.8	100.0	100.0	787.8	26.4
1930	9.1	8.7	-3.3	-7.6	96.7	97.4	722.0	25.4
1931	11.6	15.9	-11.2	-14.7	90.1	88.8	683.6	23.6
1932	17.6	23.6	-9.3	-1.8	81.8	79.7	605.8	19.4
1933	19.3	24.9	-7.2	9.1	80.2	75.6	603.6	21.5
1934	14.5	21.7	10.4	9.9	81.8	78.1	633.3	25.5
1935	14.2	20.1	7.2	13.9	82.6	80.1	704.2	29.2
1936	12.8	16.9	4.6	5.3	85.1	80.9	757.3	30.3
1937	9.1	14.3	8.8	-5.0	87.6	83.8	851.1	30.0
1938	11.4	19.0	1.4	8.6	86.8	82.2	857.0	30.0
1939	11.4	17.2	7.5	8.5	86.8	81.0	929.6	33.6
1940	9.2	14.6	13.3	16.1	90.9	81.8	1146.6	39.6
1941	4.4	9.9	13.3	12.9	97.5	85.9	1453.6	46.5
1942	3.0	4.7	17.6	13.2	102.5	95.1	1844.9	55.3

Sources: *For Canada: Unemployment rate* using Statistics Canada, CANSIM Series D31253 and D31254; *output growth, GDP growth,* using CANSIM Series D14442; *price level, GDP deflator* (1929=100) using CANSIM Series D14476; *money supply,* M1 from C. Metcalf, A. Redish, R. Shearer, "New Estimates of the Canadian Money Stock, 1871–1967," *Canadian Journal of Economics,* 1998.

For U.S.: Unemployment rate: Historical Statistics of the United States using U.S. Department of Commerce, Series D85-86; *output growth, GNP growth* using Series F31; *price level, CPI* (1929=100) using Series E135; *money stock,* M1 using Series X414; *Historical Statistics of the United States,* U.S. Department of Commerce.

The Fall in Spending in the United States

Popular accounts often say that the Great Depression was caused by the stock market crash of 1929. This is an overstatement. A recession had started before the crash in the United States, and other factors played an important role later in the Depression.

Nevertheless, the crash was important. The stock market had boomed from 1921 to 1929. Stock market prices had increased much faster than the dividends paid by firms, and as a result, the dividend/price ratio had decreased from 6.5% in 1921 to 3.5% in 1929. On October 28, 1929, the stock market price index dropped from 298 to 260. The next day, it dropped further to 230. This was a fall of 23% in just two days, and a drop of 40% from the peak of early September. By November, the index was down to 198. A stock market recovery in early 1930 was followed by a steady decline as the size of the depression became increasingly clear. The U.S. Stock Market is illustrated in Figure 22–7.

> Note the parallel between the evolution of stock prices during the 1920s and during the 1990s. The dividend/price ratio was 3.2% in 1991 and 1.4% at the end of 1998. (See Chapter 19.)

Was the October crash caused by the sudden realization that a depression was coming? The answer is no. There is no evidence of major news in October. The source of the crash was almost surely the end of a speculative bubble. Stockholders who had purchased stocks at high prices in the anticipation of further increases in prices got scared and attempted to sell their stocks, leading to further large price declines.

> Revisit the discussion of dividends and prices, as well as bubbles and crashes, in section 19-3.

The effects of the crash were to decrease consumers' wealth, increase uncertainty, and decrease demand. Unsettled by the crash and now uncertain about the future, consumers and firms decided to see how things evolved and to postpone purchases of durable goods and investment goods. For example, there was a large decrease in car sales—the type of pur-

FIGURE 22–7

The S&P Composite Index, 1920–1950

From September 1929 to June 1932, the stock market index fell from 313 to 47, before it slowly recovered.

chase that can easily be deferred—in the months just following the crash. In terms of the *IS-LM* model in Figure 22–8, the effect of the crash was to shift the *IS* curve to the left, from *IS* to *IS'*, leading to a sharp decrease in output from *Y* to *Y'*. (Note that we have the real interest rate, *r*, rather than the nominal interest rate, *i*, on the vertical axis in Figure 22–8. We will discuss the reason a bit later in this chapter.) Industrial production, which had declined by 1.8% from August to October 1929, declined by 9.8% from October to December and by another 24% from December 1929 to December 1930.

The focus in section 10-5 was on the effects of a reduction in government spending. The conclusions would have been the same had we looked instead at the effects of a reduction in consumption, due to a drop in wealth or in consumer confidence.

The Contraction in the U.S. Nominal Money

When we described the effects of a decrease in aggregate demand in Chapter 10, we showed how the economy would, after the initial recession, eventually return to the natural level of output. The mechanism was the following: Low output led to high unemployment. High unemployment led to lower wages. Lower wages led to lower prices. Lower prices led to an increase in the real money supply, steadily shifting the *LM* curve down until output returned to its natural level.

FIGURE 22–8

The Great Depression and the *IS-LM*: Part I

The effect of the stock market crash was to decrease wealth and increase uncertainty, leading the *IS* curve to shift to the left.

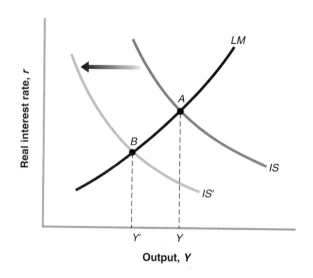

You can see from Table 22–1 that low output did, indeed, lead to lower prices in the years following 1929. The consumer price index decreased from 100 in 1929 to 75.6 in 1933, a 24% decrease in the price level in four years. But the rest of the mechanism failed, for two reasons. First, there was a large decrease in nominal money, leaving real money roughly unchanged. Second, the deflation itself had perverse effects, leading to a deeper decline in output.

Let us focus on the decrease in nominal money first. Table 22–2 gives the evolution of nominal money—both the money stock (measured by $M1$) and the monetary base (H)—from 1929 to 1933. It also shows the evolution of the money multiplier ($M1/H$) and of the real money stock ($M1/P$), where P is the consumer price index. From 1929 to 1933, nominal money, $M1$, *decreased* by 27%. To understand what happened, let us recall the basic mechanics of money creation.

Nominal money, $M1$ (the sum of currency in circulation and chequable deposits), is equal to the monetary base, H (currency plus banks' reserves), which is under the central bank's control, times the money multiplier:

$$M1 = H \times \text{money multiplier}$$

The money multiplier, in turn, depends both on how much reserves banks keep in proportion to their deposits and what proportion of money people keep in the form of currency as opposed to demand deposits.

Note that from 1929 to 1933, the monetary base, H, increased from \$7.1 to \$8.2 billion. Thus, the decrease in $M1$ did not come from a decrease in the monetary base. Rather, it came from a decrease in the money multiplier, $M1/H$, which went from 3.7 in 1929 to 2.4 in 1933.

This decrease in the multiplier was the result of bank failures. With the large decline in output, more and more borrowers found themselves unable to repay their loans to banks, and more and more banks became insolvent and closed down. Bank failures increased steadily from 1929 until 1933, when the number of failures reached a peak of 4000, out of about 20,000 banks in operation at the time.

Bank failures had a direct effect on money supply; chequable deposits at the failed banks became worthless. But the major effect on money supply was an indirect one. Worried that their banks might also fail, many people shifted from deposits to currency. The increase in the ratio of currency to deposits led to a decrease in the money multiplier, and thus to a decrease in money supply.

Think of the mechanism this way. If people had liquidated *all* their deposits and asked banks for currency in exchange, the multiplier would have decreased to one, and $M1$ would have been just equal to the monetary base. The shift was less dramatic than that. Nevertheless, the multiplier went down from 3.7 in 1929 to 2.4 in 1933, leading to a decrease

The classic treatment is by Milton Friedman and Anna Schwartz, *A Monetary History of the United States, 1867–1960* (Princeton, NJ: Princeton University Press, 1963).

| TABLE | 22–2 | U.S. Money Supply, Nominal and Real, 1929–1933 |

Year	M1	H	$\dfrac{M1}{H}$	$\dfrac{M1}{P}$
1929	26.4	7.1	3.7	26.4
1930	25.4	6.9	3.7	26.0
1931	23.6	7.3	3.2	26.5
1932	20.6	7.8	2.6	25.8
1933	19.4	8.2	2.4	25.6

Source: M1 using Series X414; *H* using Series X422 plus series X423; *P* using Series E135, *Historical Statistics of the United States*, U.S. Department of Commerce.

CHAPTER 22   DEPRESSIONS AND SLUMPS   **453**

in money supply despite an increase in the monetary base. (Some economists have argued that the shift from chequable deposits to currency had implications that went beyond the effect on the money multiplier. Their argument is presented in the Focus box titled "Money versus Bank Credit.")

With a decrease in the nominal money supply from 1929 to 1933 roughly proportional to the decrease in prices, the real money supply remained roughly constant, eliminating one of the mechanisms that could have led to a recovery. In other words, the *LM* curve remained roughly unchanged—it did not shift down as it would have if the real money supply had increased. Indeed, Milton Friedman and Anna Schwartz have argued that the Federal Reserve Board was responsible for the depth of the Great Depression—that it should have expanded the monetary base even more than it did to offset the decrease in the money multiplier.

The Adverse Effects of Deflation

See section 18-3.

In addition to the decrease in nominal money, deflation (the decrease in the price level) itself was a further source of decline in output during the Great Depression. Building on section 18-3, we can use the *IS-LM* diagram to see why, keeping in mind the distinction between the real interest rate and the nominal interest rate.

In Figure 22–9, think of the precrash equilibrium as given by point *A*. We argued earlier that the effect of the crash was, through its effects on wealth and uncertainty, to shift the *IS* curve to *IS'*, taking the economy from point *A* to point *B*. We then argued that from 1929 to 1933, the combined effects of the decrease in prices and the decrease in nominal money left the *LM* curve roughly unchanged.

Now, consider the effects of deflation on the difference between nominal and real interest rates. Recall that the real interest rate is equal to the nominal interest rate minus the expected rate of inflation (equivalently, plus the expected rate of deflation). By 1931, the rate of deflation exceeded 10% a year, and by then, the evidence is that people expected deflation to con-

FOCUS   Money versus Bank Credit

We have focused in this text on the effects of the shift from chequable deposits to currency on the money multiplier. A number of economists have argued that this shift had implications beyond those for the money multiplier. Faced with a decrease in deposits, banks had to call existing loans. Those who had borrowed from the banks were unable to find other sources of borrowing, and this was a further source of output contraction.

The argument has been developed by Ben Bernanke, now chairman of the U.S. Federal Reserve, from Princeton University. He starts from the observation that banks play a special role in credit markets. Banks make loans to borrowers who are typically too small, or not known well enough, to be able to issue bonds. Before making a loan to a firm, a bank acquires knowledge about the firm and, once the loan has been made, monitors the firm's decisions closely. If, for whatever reason, a bank decides to decrease its volume of loans, those who lose their loans cannot borrow elsewhere. Other banks do not have the first bank's specialized knowledge, and neither do bond markets. Thus, the borrower may be forced to cancel investment plans, curtail production, or close altogether. (Note that, in writing the investment equation as $I = I(i, Y)$ so far in this book,

we have implicitly assumed that firms could borrow as much as they wanted at the given interest rate i; we have therefore implicitly excluded the effect we are looking at now.)

By putting together many pieces of evidence, Bernanke builds a strong case that the **credit channel** was, indeed, important in first deepening and then prolonging the Great Depression. One citation from a large survey of firms, carried out in 1934–1935, puts it clearly: "[We find that there is] a genuine unsatisfied demand for credit by solvent borrowers, many of whom could make economically sound use of capital. The total amount of this unsatisfied demand for credit is a significant factor, among many others, in retarding business recovery."

Source: Ben Bernanke, "Nonmonetary Effects of the Financial Crisis in the Propagation of the Great Depression," *American Economic Review*, 1983, pp. 257–276.

Further Reading

For more on the role of banks and the credit channel of monetary policy, read Anil Kashyap and Jeremy Stein, "Monetary Policy and Bank Lending," in *Monetary Policy*, N. Gregory Mankiw, ed. (Chicago: University of Chicago Press and NBER, 1994), pp. 221–262.

tinue. This expectation implied that even low nominal rates—in 1931, the U.S. three-month Treasury-bill rate stood at only 1.4%—implied high real interest rates. When expected deflation is 10%, even a nominal rate of 0% implies a real interest rate of 0% − (−10%) = 10%!

In terms of Figure 22–9, the effect of the increase in expected deflation was to shift the LM curve up by an amount equal to the increase in expected deflation. At a given level of income, the nominal interest rate consistent with financial markets was unchanged; thus, the real interest rate was higher by an amount equal to the increase in expected deflation. The result of this shift from LM to LM′ was to move the economy from point B to point C and to decrease output further and deepen the depression.

Given i,
$$\pi^e \downarrow \Rightarrow r\,(\equiv i - \pi^e) \uparrow$$
$$\Rightarrow Y \downarrow$$
The LM curve shifts left.

The U.S. Recovery

The recovery started in 1933. Except for another sharp decrease in the growth rate of output in 1937 (see Table 22–1), growth was consistently high, running at an average of 7.7% for the period 1933–1941. Macroeconomists and economic historians have studied the recovery much less than they studied the initial decline. And many questions remain.

One of the factors that contributed to the recovery is clear. Following the election of Franklin Roosevelt in 1932, there was a dramatic increase in nominal money growth. From 1933 to 1936, nominal money increased by 50%, and the real money stock increased by 40%. From 1933 to 1941, nominal money increased by 140% and real money by 100%. These increases were due to increases in the monetary base, not in the money multiplier. In a controversial article, Christina Romer has argued that if monetary policy had been unchanged from 1933 on, output would have been 25% lower than it actually was in 1937 and 50% lower than it was in 1942. These are very large numbers, indeed. Even if one believes that these numbers overestimate the effect of monetary policy, the conclusion that money played an important role in the recovery is still surely warranted.

Christina Romer, "What Ended the Great Depression?" *Journal of Economic History*, December 1992, pp. 757–784.

The role of other factors, from budget deficits to the **New Deal**—the set of programs put in place by the Roosevelt administration to get the U.S. economy out of the Great Depression—is much less clear.

One New Deal program was aimed at improving the functioning of banks by creating the *Federal Deposit Insurance Corporation (FDIC)* to insure demand deposits, and thus to avoid bank runs and bank failures. And, indeed, there were few bank failures after 1933.

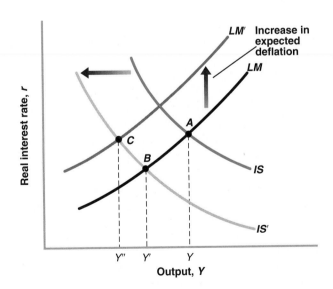

FIGURE 22–9

The Great Depression and the *IS-LM*: Part II

The effect of expected deflation was to shift the LM curve up, leading to a further decline in output.

The Great Depression in Canada

Canada entered the Great Depression at almost the same time as the United States did. How was the downturn in the United States transmitted so quickly? What were the differences and similarities in monetary and fiscal responses to the downturn in the two countries?

The western parts of Canada and the United States suffered a drought in 1929. The effects were felt in both countries but played a larger role in explaining the Canadian downturn. Wheat production peaked at 567 million bushels in 1928 and then, largely because of the drought, fell to 302 million bushels in 1929. Even so, wheat and wheat flour still managed to account for 35% of Canada's exports in 1929. Prices in 1929 did not reflect the downturn, but by 1930, wheat prices had fallen by half and stayed low until the end of the decade. What had been a *quantity* shock in 1929 became an adverse *terms of trade* shock in 1930 as the Great Depression spread to Europe. Not only was wheat affected: About 80% of Canada's exports in 1929 were based on natural resources or agricultural products. The prices of these primary commodities were particularly hard hit by the worldwide slump.

In 1928, 38% of Canada's exports went to the United States. It is not surprising that the sharp drop in income in the United States was transmitted to Canada. The decline in exports could account for a leftward shift of the *IS* curve in Canada, just as shown in Figure 22–1. But other factors were also at work in reducing aggregate demand. Canada had a large external debt in 1928, 70% of which was held by U.S. residents. Direct foreign ownership of Canadian firms was extremely high. The same forces that made American entrepreneurs reluctant to invest in their U.S. enterprises after the stock market crash of 1929 also reduced investment in Canada. Nor could Canadian entrepreneurs remain unaffected by what was going on around them. From 1929 to 1933, gross domestic investment fell from 22.1% to 8.6% of GDP, while real GDP itself was falling. Consumers in Canada reacted much like their American cousins. Automobile manufacturing had been one of the important sources of growth in the 1920s, but this changed with the onset of the Depression. Automobiles were viewed by many as a luxury and were either kept longer or not replaced. By 1932, the number of automobiles registered in Canada actually declined.

The decline in money supply in Canada was not as dramatic as in the United States. Canada had early on adopted a branch banking system, so there were only 31 active chartered banks in 1900. Canada's banking system underwent a number of crises; failures and mergers reduced that number to 11 by 1929, with the largest three controlling over 70% of chartered bank assets. Although there was further consolidation, bank failures played no role in reducing money supply. The last chartered bank to fail in Canada was the Home Bank that closed its doors in 1923. Not a single bank failed in Canada during the Great Depression. Another important difference to keep in mind is that Canada had no central bank until 1935. The Department of Finance had a monopoly on notes in amounts under five dollars, but private banks also issued their own notes. Rather than keep deposits at a central bank as reserves, the Canadian banks kept deposits in large New York banks. So, in Canada, not only was the multiplier determined by the private sector, so was the monetary base!

The introduction of deposit insurance in the 1960s and changes in the rules governing trust companies brought in a number of new trust companies in the 1970s. A few of these companies did go bankrupt.

You might ask: What pinned down the level of money supply? From the late nineteenth century until World War I, Canada, along with the United States and most of the countries of Europe, was on the gold standard. Among other things, the gold standard was a fixed-exchange-rate system. Each country fixed the value of its currency in terms of gold—that is, it stood ready to exchange its currency for gold on demand. By arbitrage, this determined the relative values of any two currencies. The gold standard also provided a limit to the growth of the domestic money supply. Banks in Canada were allowed to issue notes, but these had to be redeemable in gold or other legal tender, such as Dominion of Canada notes (the ability to redeem bank notes in gold was called *convertibility*). Canada had returned to the gold standard in 1926, but convertibility was suspended in 1928. Nonetheless, many market participants anticipated a return to convertibility, and this appears to have restrained private note issue. This expectation changed rather abruptly when the United Kingdom formally abandoned the gold standard in 1931, and Canada quickly followed suit. For the next four years, the chartered banks were literally licensed to print money. But they did not.

The gold standard is widely viewed as the mechanism by which the Great Depression in the United States was spread throughout the world. The decline in the U.S. money supply and the falling prices that ensued put pressure on other countries to deflate as well in order to maintain convertibility. The abandonment of the gold standard allowed currencies to float and to insulate their economies from the U.S. downturn. The Canadian dollar depreciated vis-à-vis the American dollar after 1931, and this helped speed up our recovery.

One of the more interesting stories of the Great Depression in Canada was the Social Credit Party. Among other things, they proposed simply printing money and giving it to private citizens as a way out of the Depression.

Canada's fiscal response to the Great Depression was also very passive. Although towns and the provinces greatly increased their relief payments, these levels of government were constrained by their constitutional restriction to raise revenue only through direct taxes. The federal government had access to larger sources of revenue, but, for the most part, tried to balance its budget and allow market forces to restore output and employment. By 1935, Prime Minister Bennett seemed open to some radical changes and proposed his own "New Deal" for Canada. But he lost the election to Mackenzie King. Just as Canada had imported the Great Depression, it waited for foreign forces to pull it out.

22-3 | The Japanese Slump

From the end of World War II to the beginning of the 1990s, Japan's economic performance was spectacular. From 1950 to 1973, the average growth rate was 7.4% per year. As in other OECD countries, the average growth rate decreased after 1973. But, from 1973 to 1991, it was still a very respectable 4% per year, a rate higher than in most other OECD countries. As a result of this growth, Japanese output per capita (measured in PPP terms), which was equal to only 22% of the U.S. level in 1950, had climbed to 84% of the U.S. level in 1990.

See the discussion of the post-1973 growth slowdown in major OECD countries in Chapter 12.

This growth came to an abrupt end in the early 1990s. Table 22–3 shows the evolution of the growth rate of GDP, the unemployment rate, and the inflation rate since 1990.

The table suggests the following conclusions:

Forgotten the definition of GDP in PPP terms? See Chapter 10.

- Output growth has been extremely low.

    From 1992 to 2002, the growth rate was either positive and small or negative. The average growth rate was 1%—far below what it had been in earlier decades. This long period of low growth has been termed the Japanese slump. This slump was obviously not as sharp and as deep as the Great Depression (recall from Table 22–1 that the average annual growth rate in the United States from 1929 to 1932 was −8.6%), but it was still substantial. Think of it this way. If average output growth between 1992 and 2002 had been the same as during 1973–1991, output in Japan would have been roughly 30% higher in 2002 than it actually was.

    Since 2003, there have been signs that the slump may be coming to an end. Output growth was higher from 2003 to 2005 and was projected to be higher again in 2006. Previous hopes of a recovery, in 1996 and again in 2000, had been dashed when higher growth rates did not last. Since 2004, most economists are a bit more optimistic. In the best of cases, however, it will still take many years for the Japanese economy to return to normal.

- Low output growth had led to a steady increase in unemployment until 2004. There was a slight fall in 2005. Looking at the evolution of the unemployment rate since 1990 in the second column of Table 22–3, you might conclude that Japan had not done so badly. True, the unemployment rate has increased, from 2.1% in 1990 to 5% in 2004. But 5% is still lower than the average unemployment rate in the United States over the last 40 years, and it is a rate that many European countries can only dream of achieving. This conclusion would be wrong, however. An unemployment rate of 5% in Japan is the sign of an extremely depressed labour market.

Year	Output Growth rate (%)	Unemployment Rate (%)	Inflation Rate (%)
1990	5.2	2.1	2.4
1991	3.4	2.1	3.0
1992	1.0	2.2	1.7
1993	0.2	2.5	0.6
1994	1.1	2.9	0.1
1995	1.9	3.1	−0.4
1996	3.4	3.4	−0.8
1997	1.9	3.4	0.4
1998	−1.1	3.4	−0.1
1999	0.1	4.1	−1.4
2000	2.8	4.7	−1.6
2001	0.4	5.0	−1.6
2002	−0.3	5.4	−1.2
2003	2.5	5.3	−2.5
2004*	3.0	4.8	−2.0
2005	2.4	4.4	−1.1

Source: OECD Economic Outlook.

To see why, we need to consider the organization of firms and of the labour market in Japan. Japanese firms offer substantial employment protection to their workers. So, when Japanese firms experience a decrease in production, they tend to keep their workers, leading to a small effect of the decrease in output on employment. As a result, unemployment does not rise much.

A useful way to think about the evolution of unemployment in Japan is in terms of Okun's law, the relation between output growth and unemployment that we saw in Chapter 11. In the United States, the Okun coefficient is equal to 0.4 and in Canada 0.33. A decrease in the growth rate of 1% for 1 year leads to an increase in the unemployment rate of 0.4% in the United States and 0.33% in Canada. In Japan, the Okun coefficient is equal to 0.1. A decrease in the growth rate of 1% for 1 year leads to an increase in the unemployment rate of only 0.1%. As cumulative output growth in Japan since 1992 has been roughly about 30% below normal, this has resulted in an increase in the unemployment rate of $0.1 \times 30\% = 3\%$. In the United States, the same shortfall in growth would have led to an increase in unemployment of $0.4 \times 30\% = 12\%$, a much larger increase. In Canada, the increase would have been 10%.

See the **Focus** box: "Okun's Law across Countries," in ▶ Chapter 11.

● Low growth and high unemployment (by Japanese standards) have led to a steady fall in the inflation rate in Japan over time.

As shown in Table 22–3, the inflation rate was already low at the start of the 1990s. Since 1995, inflation has turned into deflation, something that had not been observed in the OECD countries since the Great Depression. Despite higher output growth since 2003, unemployment is still high in Japan, and deflation has continued.

The numbers in Table 22–3 raise an obvious set of questions: What triggered Japan's slump? Why did it last so long? Were monetary and fiscal policies misused, or did they fail? What are the factors behind the current recovery? These are the questions we take up in the rest of this section.

The Rise and Fall of the Nikkei

The 1980s were associated with a stock market boom in Japan. The Nikkei index, a broad index of Japanese stock prices, increased from 7000 in 1980 to 35,000 at the end of 1989—a fivefold increase. Then, within two years, the index fell sharply—down to 16,000 at the end of 1992. Since then, it has declined further, and at the end of 2003, it stood slightly above 10,000, less than one-third of its value at the peak.

Why did the Nikkei rise so much in the 1980s and then fall so quickly in the early 1990s? Recall from Chapter 15 that there can be two reasons for a stock price to increase:

- A change in the fundamental value of the stock price, coming, for example, from an increase in current or future expected dividends. Knowing that the stock will pay higher dividends either now or in the future, investors are willing to pay more for the stock today. Consequently, its price goes up.

- A speculative bubble. Investors buy at a higher price simply because they expect the price to go even higher in the future.

Recall from Chapter 19 that in the absence of a speculative bubble, the price of a stock is equal to the expected present value of future dividends.

Figure 22–10 gives the evolution of dividends and stock prices in Japan since 1980. The upper line shows the evolution of the stock price index (the Nikkei); the lower line shows the evolution of the corresponding index for dividends. For convenience, both variables are normalized to one in 1980. A look at the figure yields a simple conclusion. While the stock price index increased in the 1980s, the dividends remained flat. This is not necessarily proof that the increase in the Nikkei was a bubble. Investors might have expected large increases in future dividends, even if current dividends were not increasing. But it strongly suggests that the increase in the Nikkei had a large bubble component and that the fall later was largely a bursting of that bubble.

Whatever its origin, the rapid fall in stock prices had a major impact on spending and, in turn, a big impact on output. Table 22–4 shows the evolution of GDP growth, consumption growth, and investment growth from 1988 to 1993. Investment, which had been very strong

See the discussion on the effects of stock prices on consumption and investment in Chapters 16 and 17.

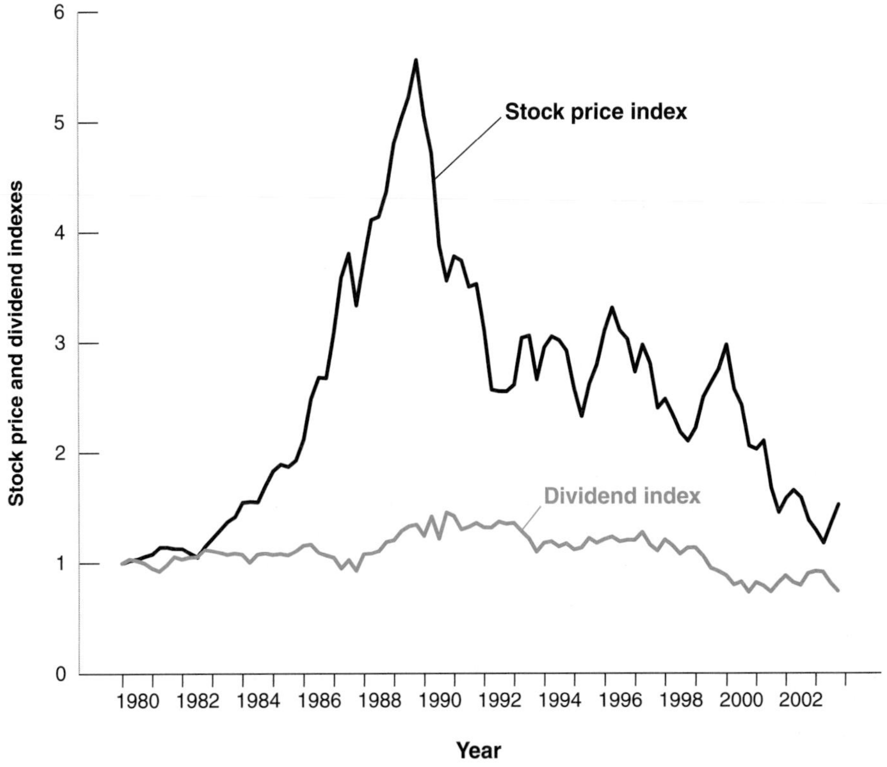

FIGURE 22–10

Stock Prices and Dividends: Japan (1980–2003)

The increase in stock prices in the 1980s and the subsequent decrease have not been associated with a parallel movement in dividends.

Year	GDP (%)	Consumption (%)	Investment (%)
1988	6.5	5.1	15.5
1989	5.3	4.7	15.0
1990	5.2	4.6	10.1
1991	3.4	2.9	4.3
1992	1.0	2.6	−7.1
1993	0.2	1.4	−10.3

TABLE 22-4 GDP, Consumption, and Investment Growth: Japan, 1988–1993

Source: *OECD Economic Outlook*, December 2001 and June 2004.
Investment is private, fixed, nonresidential investment.

during the rise of the Nikkei, collapsed. In contrast to the Great Depression—where consumption fell sharply after the stock market crash—consumption was less affected. But the strength in consumption was not enough to avoid a sharp decline in total spending and in GDP growth, from 6.5% in 1999 to 0.2% in 1993.

In short, there is no mystery as to how the Japanese slump started. The more difficult question to answer is why it continued for more than a decade. After all, perhaps the main lesson from the Great Depression was that macroeconomic policies could and should be used to help the economy recover. Were they used in Japan? If so, why did they fail? These are the next two questions we take up.

The Failure of Monetary and Fiscal Policies

● Monetary policy was used, but it was used too late. When it was eventually used, it faced the twin problems of the liquidity trap and deflation we discussed in section 22-1.

The point is made in Figure 22–11, which shows the evolution of the nominal interest rate and the real interest rate in Japan since 1990. (Because we do not observe expected inflation, we construct the real interest rate as the nominal interest rate minus actual—rather than expected—inflation.)

Recall that the stock price depends positively on current and expected future dividends and negatively on current and future interest rates. ▶

The nominal interest rate was high in 1990, close to 8%. This was, in part, because the Bank of Japan (often refered to as the BoJ), worried about the rise of the Nikkei, had tried to decrease stock prices by increasing the interest rate. With inflation around 2%, this nominal interest rate implied a real interest rate of about 6%. As growth slowed, the BoJ cut the nominal interest rate. But, it was done too slowly, and by 1996, when the nominal interest rate was down to less than 1%, the cumulative effect of low growth was such that inflation had turned to deflation. As a result, the real interest rate was higher than the nominal interest rate. Since the mid-1990s, Japan has been in a liquidity trap. The nominal short-term interest rate has been very close to zero. At the same time, unemployment has remained high, leading to deflation, and therefore to a positive real interest rate.

A joke circulating in Japan is that by the time the slump is over, the entire shoreline of the Japanese archipelago will be covered in concrete. ▶

● Fiscal policy was used as well. Figure 22–12 shows what happened to tax revenues and to government spending as a proportion of GDP, since 1990. It shows both the steady decrease in taxes—a decrease of close to 4% of GDP—and the steady increase in spending—an increase of close to 6%—since the start of the slump. Much of the increased spending has taken the form of public work projects, many of them of doubtful usefulness. But from the point of view of increasing demand, one project is as good as another, and so this increase in government spending should have contributed to an overall increase in demand.

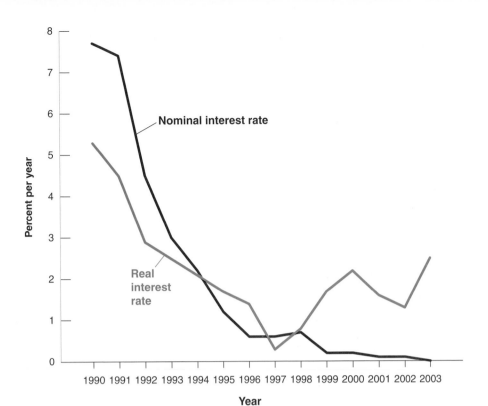

FIGURE 22-11

The Nominal Interest Rate and the Real Interest Rate in Japan, 1990–2003

Japan has been in a liquidity trap since the mid-1990s. The nominal interest rate has been close to zero, and the inflation rate has been negative. Even at a zero nominal interest rate, the real interest rate has been positive.

Has it? The economists who have looked at this question have concluded that it has, but just not enough to increase spending and output. Put another way, in the absence of increased government spending, output would have declined even more. Could the Japanese

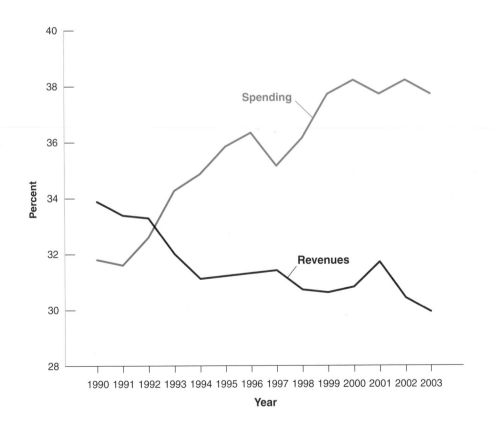

FIGURE 22-12

Government Spending and Revenues (as a percentage of GDP), in Japan, 1990–2003

Government spending increased and government revenues decreased steadily throughout the 1990s, leading to steadily larger deficits.

government have done more? Probably not. High government spending and low taxes have led to a long string of government deficits and a steady accumulation of government debt. The ratio of government debt to GDP has increased from 61% of GDP in the early 1990s to, depending on how it is measured, over 17% of GDP in 2005 (*source: CIA Factbook*). With a near-zero interest rate on government bonds, interest payments on the debt are small. But if the interest rate were to increase in the future, interest payments might represent a very heavy burden on the government budget. A more expansionary policy would have led to even higher levels of debt, something the Japanese government became increasingly reluctant to do as the slump continued.

The Recovery

Output growth has been higher since 2003, and most economists cautiously predict that the recovery will continue. This raises the last set of questions. What are the factors behind the current recovery? There appear to be two main factors.

A Regime Change in Monetary Policy. In the strange world of the liquidity trap, higher expected inflation is good. At a zero nominal interest rate, higher expected inflation implies a lower real interest rate. A lower real interest rate stimulates spending. Higher spending leads to higher output and lower unemployment.

This suggests that even if the nominal interest rate is already equal to zero, and thus cannot be reduced further, the central bank might still be able to lower the real interest rate by affecting inflation expectations. This may not be easy to do. Suppose that the central bank announces an *inflation target*, a rate of inflation it will try to achieve over the next few years. If people believe the announcement, then expected inflation will, indeed, increase, helping the economy get out of the slump. But, if people do not believe the announcement and continue to expect deflation, then deflation will continue.

Therefore, the advice given to the BoJ by many economists during the second half of the 1990s was that it should try to influence and increase inflation expectations. At worst, this would not work; at best, this might get the economy out of the slump. In 2003, the new Chairman of the BoJ decided to follow this advice. He announced that the BoJ was now committed to keeping the nominal interest rate equal to zero until there was strong evidence of sustained inflation. Just like in 1933 in the United States, this statement was perceived as a signal of regime change in monetary policy, and it appears to have changed inflation expectations. Although the current inflation rate is still negative, inflation is now expected to become positive in the future, and the long-term real interest rate has fallen. This appears to be one of the factors behind the strong increase in investment spending since 2003.

The Cleanup of the Banking System. It became clear in the 1990s that the banking system in Japan was in trouble. Largely as a result of the slump in output, many firms were doing poorly, and banks carried on their books many bad loans, loans the borrowers were not able to repay. (Why and how it happened are discussed in the Focus box "The Japanese Banking Problem.") Many "bad firms"—firms that were incurring losses and should have closed—continued to be financed by the banks and so continued to operate. At the same time, as a large proportion of bank financing continued to go to the firms with bad loans, "good firms"—firms with good prospects and good investment projects—could not find financing and thus could not invest. In short, bad loans further depressed investment spending.

In such a case, the appropriate policy is clear. Banks that have made too many bad loans should be forced to either close down or restructure. Firms that cannot pay their loans should be forced to do the same. These measures achieve two goals. First, they eliminate the bad firms, leading eventually—as these firms are replaced by more productive ones—to higher productivity and to a higher natural level of output. Second, they allow firms with good investment projects to find the funds they need to invest, leading to an increase in investment spending, and therefore to an increase in demand and output.

It is equally clear, however, that such a policy is politically very risky. Restructuring or closing down firms and banks leads initially to layoffs, a politically unpopular outcome, espe-

Like the Great Depression in the United States, the sharp decrease in output growth in Japan in the early 1990s left many firms unable to repay their bank loans.

The situation was made worse by two facts: (1) In the 1980s, the banks had started losing their best borrowers—the large Japanese firms. These large firms increasingly financed themselves by issuing bonds rather than by borrowing from banks. As a result, banks had made loans to more risky borrowers, some of whom would have a hard time repaying them, even in the absence of a slump. (2) To make things worse, many of the firms had used land as collateral ("collateral" stands for any asset that the borrower promises to give to the bank if the loan is not repaid). The problem is that land prices collapsed along with the stock market in the early 1990s. As a result, the value of that collateral collapsed as well.

During the Great Depression, bad bank loans had led to a series of bank failures and bank runs (see the Focus box "Bank Runs" in Chapter 4). Indeed, one of the lessons of the Great Depression was that to prevent such bank runs, governments should provide insurance to the depositors. Federal deposit insurance was introduced in 1934 in the United States, and similar insurance systems were later put into place in most countries, including Japan.

Deposit insurance solves one problem: It eliminates the risk of bank runs. But it creates other problems, which have been in evidence in Japan in the 1990s. To understand what these problems are, think of a bank that has the balance sheet described in Figure 1:

- On the asset side, it has one loan for $100.
- On the liability side, it has $50 in deposits.
- The net worth of the bank, the difference between assets and liabilities, is therefore $100 − $50 = $50.

(Note two differences with the balance sheets we studied in Chapter 4. First, we ignore reserves. They were important for the arguments developed in Chapter 4; they are not important here. Second, we assumed in Chapter 4 that assets were equal to liabilities—in other words, that net worth was zero. In reality, net worth is typically positive, and this plays an important role here.)

Assets	Liabilities
Loan: $100	Deposits: $50 Net worth: $50

FIGURE 1   The Bank's Balance Sheet

Now, suppose that the loan goes bad. The firm to which the loan was made cannot pay any of it back. What should happen?

- The value of the loan is now zero. The bank should write the loan off. The bank still owes $50 in deposits but cannot pay them back. Thus, deposit insurance should pay $50 to the depositors, and the bank should close down.

- But that is unlikely to happen. To keep his job, the manager of the bank might pretend that nothing has happened and that the loan is still good. Indeed, he might decide to lend even more to the firm so that the firm can repay the old loan. This way, it looks like business as usual. This is clearly throwing good money after bad, but by doing so, the manager buys time and keeps his job, at least for some time.

- Even the owners of the bank might go along. If the bank closes down now, they lose everything (net worth is clearly equal to zero). If there is the slightest chance that the firm will recover and be able to pay the loan back, the bank may end up with positive net worth. (This is known as "gambling for resurrection.") So, even if the odds of the firm repaying the loan are very low, the bank may continue to lend to the firm.

- Depositors do not care what the bank does. Their deposits are insured, whatever the bank does. Even the bank's regulator, if there is one, might prefer to close his eyes: Acknowledging the existence of bad loans, and the fact that the bank must be closed down, might reflect badly on him—again, better to wait.

The result: Banks are likely to renew the bad loans, or even make new loans to the bad firms, at the expense of the good firms. And so, as time passes, the problem of bad loans becomes worse.

This is exactly what has happened in Japan in the 1990s. Until 1993, Japanese banks did not disclose any information about their bad loans. Beginning in 1993, they reluctantly acknowledged the presence of bad loans on their books. The total amount of bad loans (self-reported by banks) steadily increased, from 12 trillion yen in 1993 to 30 trillion yen in 1998, to 44 trillion yen in 2001. But even that amount is far below the true number. An estimate by the OECD puts the total value of bad loans at 237 trillion yen, or close to 45% of Japan's GDP. Progress is now being made, but it will still take a long time for Japan to solve its banking problem.

cially when unemployment is already high. For this reason, not much was done to solve the banking problem in Japan in the 1990s. Banks continued to lend to bad firms, and the proportion of bad loans steadily increased. Since 2002, however, government has put increasing pressure on banks to reduce bad loans, and banks, in turn, have put increasing pressure on bad firms to restructure or close down. The proportion of bad loans has begun to fall, and good firms have been increasingly able to finance investment. This is another factor behind the strong increase in investment spending since 2003.

A number of other factors are also helping Japan's economy recover. In particular, strong output growth in the rest of Asia, particularly in China, has led to strong export growth in Japan. Even if export growth were to fall, however, the regime change in monetary policy, coupled with the cleanup of the banking system, implies that domestic spending might increase enough to sustain growth in the future. This is why most economists are now more optimistic about future growth in Japan than they have been for a decade.

22-4 | Conclusions

It is not clear that there is a unique "high unemployment pathology." The two major episodes of high unemployment in the twentieth century appear similar, both in their causes and in their symptoms.

The Great Depression was a case of a sharp decrease in activity followed by a long period of recovery. The decline in activity clearly had its origin on the demand side. Once the economy reached the bottom, recovery was strong, largely because of an increase in the money supply and the resulting demand expansion.

High unemployment in Japan in the 1990s appears to have a similar pattern. There was a substantial negative demand shock, a deflation, and a slow recovery.

SUMMARY

- In general, a recession leads to a decrease in inflation. Given nominal money growth, the decrease in inflation leads to an increase in real money growth, a decrease in the nominal interest rate, and a return of output to its natural level.

- One reason why this adjustment mechanism may fail is that the decrease in inflation may lead to an increase in the real interest rate. If the decrease in expected inflation is larger than the decrease in the nominal interest rate, the real interest rate will increase. Because spending depends on the real interest rate, the increase in the real interest rate will lead to a further decrease in output.

- Monetary policy can be used to decrease the nominal interest rate further, which helps increase output. Monetary policy, however, cannot decrease the nominal interest rate below zero. When this happens, the economy is said to be in a liquidity trap.

- The combination of the liquidity trap and deflation can transform a recession into a slump or a depression. If the nominal interest rate is zero, and the economy is experiencing a deflation, the real interest rate is positive, and it may be too high to lead to an increase in spending and output. Output may continue to decline, leading to higher deflation, a higher real interest rate, and so on.

On the Great Depression in the United States:

- The unemployment rate increased from 3.2% in 1929 to 24.9% in 1933.

- The initial cause of this increase in unemployment was a large adverse shift in demand, brought about by the stock market crash of 1929 and the resulting increase in uncertainty about the future.

- The result of high unemployment was a large deflation from 1929 to 1933.

- The favourable effect of the decrease in the price level on the real money stock was offset, however, by a roughly equal decrease in nominal money. This decrease in nominal money was due to bank failures and a decrease in the money multiplier. The main effect of deflation was a large increase in the real interest rate, leading to a further decrease in demand and output.

- Recovery started in 1933. Average output growth from 1933 to 1941 was high, 7.7% per year. Unemployment decreased, but it was still equal to 9.9% in 1941. In contrast to the predictions of the Phillips curve, deflation turned into inflation from 1934 on, despite a very high unemployment rate.

- Many questions remain about the recovery. What is clear is that high nominal money growth, leading to high real money growth, was an important factor in the recovery.

On the Great Depression in Canada:

- The unemployment rate increased from 2.9% in 1929 to 19.3% in 1933.

- The origins of the Great Depression in Canada can be linked to poor weather, a decline in the relative prices of exports, and a large adverse shift in demand. The Prairie provinces suffered a severe drought in 1929 that sharply reduced Canada's wheat exports. After 1929, the world price of wheat and other commodities that Canada exported dropped sharply. The United States, our largest export market and an important source of investment finance, slumped because of the stock market crash of 1929 and the resulting uncertainty. Canadian entrepreneurs and consumers behaved similarly to their American counterparts.

- Both the United States and Canada experienced deflation from 1929 to 1933. The favourable effects of deflation on real money balances were offset, however, by roughly equal decreases in nominal money stocks. In the United States, the decline in the money stock can be linked to bank failures. But no banks failed in Canada.

- The Canadian recovery began in 1933. The abandonment of the gold standard allowed the Canadian dollar to depreciate and helped exports. Fiscal policy did not play an active role until government sharply increased its spending as Canada entered World War II.

- Japan experienced deflation from 1995 to 2005.

- As in the Great Depression in North America, deflation in Japan was accompanied by high unemployment.

- Neither monetary nor fiscal policy was able to end the slump in Japan.

KEY TERMS

- credit channel, 454
- depression, 442
- Great Depression, 450

- liquidity trap, 446
- New Deal, 455
- slump, 442

QUESTIONS AND PROBLEMS

An asterisk denotes a harder question. [Web] indicates that the question requires access to the Internet.

1. TRUE/FALSE/UNCERTAIN

a. The stock market crash of 1929 reflected the realization by financial investors that the Great Depression was coming.

b. The Bank of Canada could have done more—if not to prevent, then at least to limit the scope of the Great Depression.

c. We have learned how to use fiscal and monetary policies to avoid another Great Depression.

d. The Japanese slump in the 1990s was triggered by the sharp fall of Japanese stock prices at the end of the 1980s.

e. The Japaese central bank can help the Japanese economy recover by keeping inflation very low.

*2. THE LIQUIDITY TRAP AND ROLE OF POLICY

Consider an economy in a recession and with a nominal interest rate very close to zero. (Think of Japan in 1998.) Assume that there are only two relevant periods for economic decision making, corresponding to the current and the future period.

a. Draw the *IS-LM* for the current period. (Draw it so that the equilibrium interest rate is very close to zero.)

b. Can current monetary policy increase current output? (*Hint*: Can the *LM* curve cross the horizontal axis?)

c. Can expected future monetary policy increase current output? How? under what conditions?

d. If you were the central bank, how would you convince people, firms, and financial investors that you will implement this monetary policy in the future?

e. Can we infer how successful the central bank is in convincing people that it will implement this monetary policy in the future by looking at what happens to term structure of interest rates today?

(For more discussion in the context of Japan, look at Krugman's discussion at **web.mit.edu/krugman/www/japtrap2.html**)

3. LONG-TERM UNEMPLOYMENT AND THE NATURAL RATE

Suppose that price setting is given by

$$\frac{W}{P} = \frac{1}{1 + 0.1}$$

And wage setting is given by

$$\frac{W}{P} = 1 - (u_s + 0.5u_L)$$

where u_S is the ratio of the number of short-term unemployed to the labour force and u_L is the ratio of the number of long-term unemployed to the labour force. Suppose further that the proportion of unemployed who are long-term unemployed is equal to β, so $u_L = \beta u$, and $u_S = (1 - \beta)u$.

a. According to the wage-setting equation, which type of unemployment has a greater impact on wages—long-term or short-term? Explain.

b. Derive the natural rate (*Hint*: Substitute $u_L = \beta u$ and $u_S = (1 - \beta)u$ in the wage-setting equation. The natural rate will depend on β.)

c. Compute the natural rate if $\beta = 0$; 0.4; 0.8. Explain.

4. LONG-TERM UNEMPLOYMENT AND DISINFLATION

Recall equation (11.4) in Chapter 11:

$$\pi - \pi_{t-1} = (\mu + z) - \alpha u$$

a. Interpret the equation. Why does higher unemployment lead to lower inflation given past inflation? Draw the change in inflation against the unemployment rate.

Write the overall unemployment rate u as $u = u_S + u_L$, with u_S the short-term unemployment rate (the ratio of the short-term unemployed to the labour force), and u_L the long-term unemployment rate (the ratio of the long-term unemployed to the labour force).

b. Now, assume that the long-term unemployed have no effect on wage bargaining. Show how the equation above should be modified.

c. Suppose the proportion of long-term unemployed in unemployment increases (for a given u, u_L increases, and u_S decreases). Show what happens to the curve relating the change in inflation to the overall unemployment rate.

d. "Disinflation may lead to high unemployment for some time. High unemployment leads to a higher proportion of long-term unemployed. If the long-term unemployed play no role in bargaining, the unemployment cost of disinflation will be higher than the cost derived in Chapter 11." Discuss.

5. THE JAPANESE SLUMP

Fiscal and monetary policy in Japan could have prevented the Japanese slump in the 1990s. Discuss.

FURTHER READING

For more on the Great Depression in Canada, see Kenneth, Norrie, and Douglas, *A History of the Canadian Economy* (Toronto: Harcourt Brace, 1996), Chapter 17, which gives the basic facts.

Ed Safarian's book, *The Canadian Economy in the Great Depression* (Toronto: University of Toronto Press, 1959) is the classic reference.

A description of the Great Depression through the eyes of those who suffered through it is given by Barry Broadfoot's *Ten Lost Years 1929–1939* (Toronto: McClelland and Stewart, 1997). This book, which has been turned into both a play and a video, is a moving account of the Great Depression in Canada.

For more on the Great Depression in the United States, see Lester Chandler's *America's Greatest Depression* (New York: Harper and Row, 1970), which gives the basic facts. So does the book by John A. Garraty, *The Great Depression* (New York: Harcourt Brace Jovanovich, 1986).

Peter Temin's *Did Monetary Forces Cause the Great Depression?* (New York: W.W. Norton, 1976) looks more specifically at the macroeconomic issues. So do the articles presented in a symposium on the Great Depression in the *Journal of Economic Perspectives*, Spring 1993.

A good book on the Japanese economy, although a bit out of date, is *The Japanese Economy* by Takatoshi Ito (Cambridge, MA: MIT Press, 1992).

Restoring Japan's Economic Growth, (Washington, D.C.: Institute for International Studies, 1998), by Adam Posen, discusses the Japanese slump.

An Empirical Assessment of Monetary Policy Alternatives at the Zero Bound (Washington, D.C.: Brookings Papers on Economic Activity, 2004), by Ben Bernake, Vincent Reinhart, and Brian Sack, discusses what monetary policy can and cannot do when the economy is in a liquidity trap.

CHAPTER 23
HIGH INFLATION

Extensions: Pathologies

In 1913, the value of all currency circulating in Germany was six billion marks. Ten years later, in October 1923, six billion marks were barely enough to buy a one-kilo loaf of rye bread in Berlin. A month later, the price had increased to 428 billion marks.

The German hyperinflation of the early 1920s is probably the most famous hyperinflation. (**Hyperinflation** simply means very high inflation.) But it is not the only one. Table 23−1 summarizes the seven major hyperinflations that followed World War I and World War II. They share several features. They were all short (lasting for a year or so) but intense, with monthly inflation running at about 50% or more. In all, the increase in the price level was staggering. As you can see, the largest price increase was actually not reached during the German hyperinflation, but in Hungary after World War II. What cost one Hungarian pengö in August 1945 cost 3800 trillions of trillions of pengös less than a year later.

TABLE 23−1 Seven Hyperinflations of the 1920s and 1940s

Country	Beginning	End	P_T/P_0	Average Monthly Inflation rate (%)	Average Monthly Money Growth (%)
Austria	Oct. 1921	Aug. 1922	70	47	31
Germany	Aug. 1922	Nov. 1923	1.0×10^{10}	322	314
Greece	Nov. 1943	Nov. 1944	4.7×10^6	365	220
Hungary I	Mar. 1923	Feb. 1924	44	46	33
Hungary II	Aug. 1945	Jul. 1946	3.8×10^{27}	19,800	12,200
Poland	Jan. 1923	Jan. 1924	699	82	72
Russia	Dec. 1921	Jan. 1924	1.2×10^5	57	49

P_T/P_0: Price level in the last month of hyperinflation divided by the price level in the first month.

Source: Philip Cagan, "The Monetary Dynamics of Hyperinflation," in Milton Friedman, ed., *Studies in the Quantity Theory of Money* (Chicago: University of Chicago Press, 1956), Table 1.

With an inflation rate of 40% per month, the price level at the end of 21 months is $(1 + 0.4)^{21} = 1171$ times the price level ▶ at the beginning.

Such rates of inflation had not been seen before, nor have they been seen since. The closest case in the recent past occurred in Bolivia. From January 1984 to September 1985, Bolivian inflation averaged 40% per month, implying a roughly 1000-fold increase in the price level over 21 months. But many countries, especially in Latin America, have struggled with prolonged bouts of high inflation. Both Argentina and Brazil had monthly inflation rates in excess of 10% for more than a decade. All four countries have now returned to low inflation—nearly zero inflation, in the case of Argentina.

What causes hyperinflations? We saw in Chapter 12 that *inflation ultimately comes from money growth.* This relation between money growth and inflation is confirmed by the last two columns of Table 23–1: Note how in each country, high inflation was associated with correspondingly high nominal money growth. This raises the next question: *Why* was money growth so high? The answer turns out to be common to all hyperinflations: Money growth is high because the budget deficit is high. The budget deficit is high because the economy is affected by major shocks that make it difficult or impossible for government to finance its expenditures. In this chapter, we look at this answer in more detail, relying on examples from various hyperinflations.

- Section 23-1 looks at the relation between the budget deficit and money creation.
- Section 23-2 looks at the relation between inflation and real money balances.
- Section 23-3 puts the two together and shows how a large budget deficit can lead to high and increasing inflation.
- Section 23-4 looks at how hyperinflations end.
- Section 23-5 draws conclusions from our two chapters on pathologies—depressions and slumps in Chapter 22, and high inflation in this chapter.

23-1 | Budget Deficits and Money Creation

A government can finance its deficit in one of two ways:

- It can borrow, the way any of us would. We would take a loan. Government borrows by issuing bonds.
- It can do something that none of us can do. It can, in effect, finance the deficit by creating money. We say "in effect" because, as you will remember from Chapter 4, government does not create money; the central bank does. But with the central bank's cooperation, government can, in effect, finance itself by money creation: It can issue bonds and ask the central bank to buy them. The central bank then pays government with the money it creates, and government uses that money to finance its deficit. This process is called **debt monetization**.

Most of the time and in most countries, deficits are financed primarily through borrowing rather than through money creation. But at the start of hyperinflations, two changes usually take place.

The first is a budget crisis. The source is typically a major social or economic upheaval:

- It may come from a civil war or a revolution, which destroys the state's ability to collect taxes, as in Nicaragua in the 1980s.
- It may come, as in the case of the hyperinflations in Table 23–1, from the aftermath of a war, which leaves government with both smaller tax revenues and the large expenditures needed for reconstruction. This is what happened in Germany in 1922 and 1923.

Burdened with payments for the war (called "war reparations") it had to pay to Allied forces, Germany had a budget deficit equal to more than two-thirds of its expenditures.

- It may come from a large adverse economic shock—for example, a large decline in the price of a raw material that is both the country's major export and its main source of revenues. As we will see in the Focus box on Bolivian hyperinflation (page 478), this is what happened in Bolivia in the 1980s. The decline in the price of tin, Bolivia's principal export, was one of the main causes of the Bolivian hyperinflation.

The second change is government's increasing unwillingness or inability to borrow from the public or from abroad to finance its deficit. The reason is the size of the deficit itself. Worried that government may not be able to repay the debt in the future, potential lenders start asking government for higher and higher interest rates. Sometimes, foreign lenders decide to stop lending to government altogether. As a result, government increasingly turns to the other source of finance—money creation. Eventually, most of the deficit is financed by money creation.

How large is the rate of money growth needed to finance a given deficit? To answer, let us assume the deficit is financed entirely by money creation:

$$\Delta M = \$ \text{ deficit}$$

This equation tells us that government (through the central bank) must create enough new money to cover the nominal deficit. M is the nominal money stock, measured, say, at the end of each month. (In the case of hyperinflation, variables change quickly enough that it is useful to divide time into months, rather than quarters or years.) ΔM is the change in the nominal money stock from the end of last month to the end of this month—nominal money creation during this month. "$ deficit" is the budget deficit, measured in nominal terms.

If we divide both sides of the equation by the price level during the month, P, and denote the real deficit by "deficit" without a dollar sign, we get:

$$\frac{\Delta M}{P} = \text{deficit} \qquad (23.1)$$

We are taking a shortcut here. What should be on the left-hand side of the equation is H, the monetary base—the money created by the central bank—not M, the money stock. We ignore the distinction here, as it does not play an important role in the argument that follows.

The revenues from money creation, $\Delta M/P$, are called **seignorage**. The word is revealing: The right to issue money was a precious source of revenues for the "seigneurs" of the past: They could buy the goods they wanted by issuing their own money and using it to pay for the goods. Equation (23.1) says that government must create enough money so that seignorage is enough to finance the real deficit.

By multiplying top and bottom of $\Delta M/P$ by M, we can rewrite seignorage as:

$$\underbrace{\frac{\Delta M}{P}}_{\text{Seignorage}} = \underbrace{\frac{\Delta M}{M}}_{\text{Money growth}} \times \underbrace{\frac{M}{P}}_{\text{Real money balances}} \qquad (23.2)$$

Seignorage is the product of money growth ($\Delta M/M$) times real money balances (M/P). The larger the real money balances held in the economy, the larger is the amount of seignorage corresponding to a given rate of money growth.

To think about relevant magnitudes, it is convenient to divide both sides of equation (23.2) by real income, Y (measured at a monthly rate):

$$\frac{\Delta M/P}{Y} = \frac{\Delta M}{M}\left(\frac{M/P}{Y}\right) \qquad (23.3)$$

Remember that income is a flow. Y here is real income per month.

This equation says that the ratio of seignorage to real income [($\Delta M/P)/Y$] is equal to the rate of money growth ($\Delta M/M$) times the ratio of real money balances to real income

[(M/P)/Y]. Suppose government is running a budget deficit equal to 10% of real income. If it finances the deficit through money creation, then seignorage must be equal to 10% of real income as well. Suppose that people hold real balances equal to two months of income so that $(M/P)/Y = 2$. Then, as equation (23.3) tells us, the monthly growth rate of money must be equal to $10\%/2 = 5\%$.

To summarize: The revenues from money creation are called seignorage. Seignorage is equal to the product of money growth and real money balances. For given real money balances, higher seignorage requires higher money growth.

Does this imply that government can finance a deficit equal to 20% of real income through a money growth rate of 10%, a deficit of 40% of real income through money growth of 20%, and so on? No. As money growth increases, so does inflation. And, as inflation increases, the opportunity cost of keeping money increases, leading people to reduce their real money balances. In terms of equation (23.2), an increase in $\Delta M/M$ leads to a decrease in M/P so that an increase in money growth does not generate a proportional increase in seignorage. What is crucial here is how much people adjust their real money balances in response to inflation, and it is the issue to which we turn next.

23-2 | Inflation and Real Money Balances

What determines the amount of real money balances that people are willing to hold?

Recall the *LM* relation we have used so far:

$$\frac{M}{P} = Y L(i)$$
$$(-)$$

Higher real income leads people to hold larger real money balances. A higher nominal interest rate increases the opportunity cost of holding money rather than bonds and leads people to reduce their real money balances.

This characterization holds in both stable economic times and times of hyperinflations. But in times of hyperinflation, we can simplify it further. Here is how. First, rewrite the *LM* relation using the relation between the nominal and the real interest rate, $i = r + \pi^e$:

See the discussion of nominal and real interest rates in section 18-1.

$$\frac{M}{P} = Y L(r + \pi^e)$$

Real money balances depend on real income, Y, on the real interest rate, r, and on expected inflation, π^e. All three variables move during a hyperinflation, but expected inflation moves much more than do the other two variables: During a typical hyperinflation, actual inflation—and presumably expected inflation—may move from close to 0 to 50% a month or more. Thus, it is not a bad approximation to assume that both income and the real interest rate are constant and focus just on the movements in expected inflation. So, we write:

$$\frac{M}{P} = \bar{Y} L(\bar{r} + \pi^e) \tag{23.4}$$

where the bars over Y and r mean that we now take both income and the real interest rate as constant. In times of hyperinflation, as equation (23.4) tells us, we can think of real money balances as depending primarily on expected inflation. As expected inflation increases and it becomes more and more costly to hold money, people will reduce their real money balances.

Indeed, during a hyperinflation, people find many ways of reducing their real money balances. When the monthly rate of inflation is 100%, for example, keeping currency for a month implies losing half of its real value (because things cost twice as much a month later). **Barter**, the exchange of goods for other goods rather than for money, increases. Payments for wages become much more frequent—often twice weekly. Once people are paid, they rush to stores to buy goods. Although government often makes it illegal to use other currencies than the one it is printing, people shift to foreign currencies as stores of value. And even if it is illegal, an increasing proportion of transactions takes place in foreign currency. During the Latin American hyperinflations of the 1980s, people shifted to U.S. dollars. The shift to dollars has become so widespread in the world that a new term has been coined: **dollarization** (the use of dollars in another country's domestic transactions).

By how much do real money balances actually decrease as inflation increases? Figure 23–1 examines the evidence from the Hungarian hyperinflation of the 1920s and provides some insights.

Figure 23–1(a) plots real money balances and the monthly inflation rate from November 1922 to February 1924. Note how movements in inflation are reflected in opposite movements in real money balances. The short-lived decline in Hungarian inflation from July to October 1923 is reflected in an equally short-lived increase in real money balances. At the

In describing the Austrian hyperinflation of the 1920s, Keynes noted, "In Vienna, during the period of collapse, mushroom exchange banks sprang up at every street corner, where you could change your krone into Zurich francs within a few minutes of receiving them, and so avoid the risk of loss during the time it would take you to reach your usual bank." (J. M. Keynes, *Tract on Monetary Reform* [New York: Harcourt Brace and Company, 1924], p. 51)

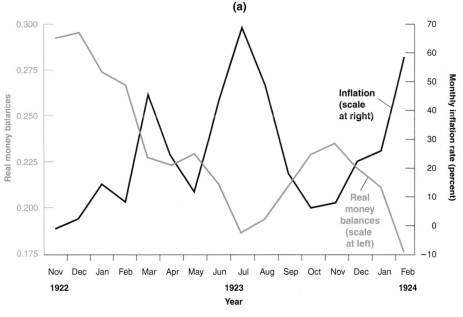

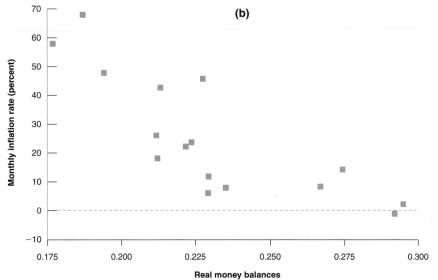

FIGURE 23–1

Inflation and Real Money Balances in Hungary, November 1922 to February 1924

At the end of the Hungarian hyperinflation, real money balances stood at roughly half their prehyperinflation level.

end of the hyperinflation in February 1924, real money balances stand at a little more than half their level at the beginning.

Figure 23–1(b) presents the same numbers, but in the form of a scatter diagram. It plots monthly real money balances on the horizontal axis against inflation on the vertical axis. (We do not observe expected inflation, which is clearly the variable we would like to plot, so we use actual inflation instead.) Note how the points nicely describe a downward-sloping demand for money: As actual inflation—and presumably expected inflation, as well—increases, the demand for money strongly decreases.

To summarize: Increases in inflation lead people to decrease their demand for money, leading, in turn, to a decrease in real money balances.

23-3 | Deficits, Seignorage, and Inflation

We have looked at the relation among seignorage, money growth, and real money balances (equation (23.2)), and the relation between real money balances and inflation (equation (23.4)). Combining them gives:

$$\text{seignorage} = \left(\frac{\Delta M}{M}\right)\left(\frac{M}{P}\right)$$

$$= \left(\frac{\Delta M}{M}\right)[\bar{Y}L(\bar{r} + \pi^e)] \tag{23.5}$$

The first line repeats equation (23.2): Seignorage equals the rate of money growth times real money balances. And the second line incorporates what we learned in equation (23.4): Real money balances depend negatively on expected inflation.

Using this relation, we can now show how the need to finance a large budget deficit can lead not only to *high inflation* but also, as is the case during hyperinflations, *high and increasing inflation*.

The Case of Constant Money Growth

Suppose that government chooses a *constant* rate of money growth and maintains that rate forever. (Clearly, this is not what happens during hyperinflations, where the rate of money growth typically increases over the course of the hyperinflation; we shall get more realistic later.) How much seignorage will this constant rate of money growth generate?

If money growth is constant forever, then inflation and expected inflation must eventually be constant as well. Assume output growth equals zero. Then, actual and expected inflation must equal money growth:

$$\pi^e = \pi = \frac{\Delta M}{M}$$

Replacing π^e by $\Delta M/M$ in equation (23.5) gives:

$$\text{Seignorage} = \frac{\Delta M}{M}\left[\bar{Y}L\left(\bar{r} + \frac{\Delta M}{M}\right)\right] \tag{23.6}$$

Note that money growth has two opposite effects on seignorage.

- On one hand, given real money balances, money growth increases seignorage. This is reflected by the first term on the right of equation (23.6): An increase in $\Delta M/M$ increases seignorage.
- On the other hand, an increase in money growth increases inflation and thus decreases real money balances. This is reflected by the presence of $\Delta M/M$ in the second term on the right of equation (23.6).

Thus, the net effect of money growth on seignorage is ambiguous. The empirical evidence is that the relation between seignorage and money growth is hump-shaped, as seen in Figure 23–2: At low rates of money growth, such as those we observe in Europe or the United States today, an increase in money growth leads to a small reduction in real money balances. Thus, it leads to an increase in seignorage. When money growth (and therefore inflation) becomes very high, however, the reduction in real money balances induced by higher money growth becomes larger and larger. Eventually, there is a rate of money growth—point A in Figure 23–2—beyond which further increases in money growth *decrease* seignorage.

The shape of the relation in Figure 23–2 may look familiar to those of you who have studied the economics of taxation. Income tax revenues equal the *tax rate on income* times income—the *tax base*. At low tax rates, the tax rate has little influence on how much people work, and tax revenues increase with the tax rate. But as tax rates increase further, some people start working less or stop declaring part of their income, and the tax base decreases. As the income tax reaches very high levels, increases in the tax rate lead to a decline in tax revenues. Obviously, tax rates of 100% lead to no tax revenue at all: Why work if government takes all of your income? This relation between tax revenues and the tax rate is often called the **Laffer curve**, after the economist Arthur Laffer, who argued in the early 1980s that a cut in U.S. tax rates would lead to more tax revenues. He was clearly wrong about where the United States was on the curve: The effect of the decrease in tax rates was to lower tax revenues, not increase them. But the general point still stands: When tax rates are high enough, a further increase in the tax rate can, indeed, lead to a decrease in tax revenues.

There is more than a simple analogy here. Inflation can be thought of as a tax on money balances. The tax rate is the rate of inflation, π, which reduces the real value of money holdings. The tax base is real money balances, M/P. The product of these two variables, $\pi(M/P)$, is called the **inflation tax**. There is a subtle difference with other forms of taxation: What government receives from money creation at any point in time is not the inflation tax but

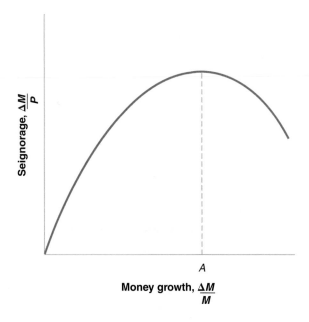

FIGURE 23–2

Seignorage and Money Growth

Seignorage is first an increasing function, followed by a decreasing function of money growth.

rather seignorage: $(\Delta M/M)(M/P)$. However, the two are closely related. When money growth is constant, inflation must eventually be equal to money growth so that:

$$\text{Inflation tax} = \pi \left(\frac{M}{P}\right)$$

$$= \left(\frac{\Delta M}{M}\right)\left(\frac{M}{P}\right)$$

$$= \text{Seignorage}$$

What rate of money growth leads to the *most seignorage*, and how much seignorage does it generate? These are the questions that Philip Cagan asked in a classic paper on hyperinflations written in 1956. In one of the earliest uses of econometrics, Cagan estimated the relation between the demand for money and expected inflation (equation (23.4)) during each of the hyperinflations in Table 23−1. Then, using equation (23.6), he computed the rate of money growth that maximized seignorage, and thus the associated amount of seignorage. The answers he obtained are given in the first two columns of Table 23−2. The third column repeats the actual money growth numbers from Table 23−1.

This table shows something very interesting: In all seven hyperinflations, actual average money growth (column 3) far exceeded the rate of money growth that maximizes seignorage (column 1). Compare the actual rate of money growth in Hungary after World War II, 12,200%, with the rate of money growth that would have maximized seignorage, 32%. This would seem to be a serious problem for the story we have developed so far. If the reason for money creation was to finance the budget deficit, why was the actual rate of money growth so much higher than the number that maximizes seignorage? The answer lies in the dynamics of the economy's adjustment to high money growth. We now turn to it.

The Dynamics of Increasing Inflation

Return to the argument we just developed: *If maintained forever*, a higher rate of money growth will *eventually* lead to a proportional increase in both actual and expected inflation and thus lead to a decrease in real money balances. If money growth is higher than the amount that maximizes seignorage, the increase in money growth will lead to a decrease in seignorage.

The crucial words in the argument are "if maintained forever" and "eventually." Consider a government that needs to finance a suddenly much larger deficit and decides to do so by creating money. As the rate of money growth increases, it may take a while for inflation and expected inflation to adjust. Even as expected inflation increases, it will take a while longer

TABLE 23−2	Money Growth and Seignorage		
	Monthly Rate of Money Growth Maximizing Seignorage (%)	**Implied Seignorage (% of output)**	**Actual Monthly Rate of Money Growth (%)**
Austria	12	13	31
Germany	20	14	314
Greece	28	11	220
Hungary I	12	19	33
Hungary II	32	6	12,200
Poland	54	4.6	72
Russia	39	0.5	49

Source: Philip Cagan, "The Monetary Dynamics of Hyperinflation," in *Studies in the Quantity Theory of Money*, Milton Friedman, ed. (Chicago: University of Chicago Press, 1956).

for people to fully adjust their real money balances: Creating barter arrangements takes time, the use of foreign currencies in transactions develops slowly, and so on.

Let us state this conclusion more formally. Recall our equation for seignorage:

$$\text{Seignorage} = \left(\frac{\Delta M}{M}\right)\left(\frac{M}{P}\right)$$

In the short run, an increase in the rate of money growth ($\Delta M/M$) may lead to little change in real money balances (M/P). Put another way, if it is willing to increase money growth sufficiently, a government will be able, *in the short run*, to generate nearly any amount of seignorage that it wants, far in excess of the numbers in the second column of Table 23–2. But over time, as prices adjust and real money balances decrease, this government will find that the same rate of money growth yields less and less seignorage. So, if government keeps trying to finance a deficit larger than that shown in the second column of Table 23–2 (for example, if Austria tries to finance a deficit that is more than 13% of GDP), it will find that it cannot do so with a constant rate of money growth. The only way it will succeed is by continually *increasing* the rate of money growth. This is why actual money growth exceeds the numbers in the first column and why hyperinflations are nearly always characterized by increasing money growth and inflation.

There is also another effect at work, which we have ignored until now, that goes in the same direction. We have taken the deficit as a given. But as inflation becomes very high, the budget deficit typically becomes larger. Part of the reason has to do with lags in tax collection. This effect is known as the **Tanzi–Olivera effect**, for Vito Tanzi and Julio Olivera, two economists who have emphasized its importance. As taxes are collected on past nominal income, their real value goes down with inflation. For example, if income taxes are paid this year on income received last year, and if the price level is 10 times higher than last year's, the actual tax rate is only one-tenth that of the official tax rate. Thus, high inflation typically decreases real government revenues, making the deficit problem worse. The problem is often compounded by other effects on the expenditure side: Governments often try to slow inflation by prohibiting firms under state control from increasing their prices, although costs are increasing with inflation. The direct effect on inflation is small at best, but the firms then run a deficit that must, in turn, be financed by the government, further increasing the budget deficit. As the budget deficit increases, so does the need for more seignorage and the need for even higher money growth.

Hyperinflations and Economic Activity

We have focused so far on movements in money growth and inflation—which clearly dominate the economic scene during a hyperinflation. But hyperinflations affect the economy in many other ways as well.

Initially, higher money growth leads to an *increase* in output. The reason is that it takes some time for increases in money growth to be reflected in inflation, and during that time, the effects of higher money growth are expansionary: As we saw in Chapter 18, the initial effects of an increase in nominal money growth are actually to *decrease* nominal and real interest rates, leading to an increase in demand and an increase in output.

But as inflation becomes very high, the adverse effects of hyperinflation dominate:

- The transaction system becomes less and less efficient. One famous example of inefficient exchange is the story of people using wheelbarrows to carry the currency needed for transactions at the end of the German hyperinflation.
- Price signals become less and less useful. Because prices change so often, it is difficult for consumers and producers to assess the relative prices of goods and to make informed decisions. The evidence shows that the higher the rate of inflation, the higher is the variation in the relative prices of different goods. Thus, the price system, which is crucial to the functioning of a market economy, also becomes less and less efficient.

Here is a joke told in Israel during the high inflation of the 1980s: "Why is it cheaper to take the taxi rather than the bus? Because in the bus, you have to pay the fare at the beginning of the ride. In the taxi, you pay only at ◄ the end."

We have discussed here the costs of very high inflation. The discussion today in the OECD countries is about the costs of, say, 5% inflation versus 0%. The issues are quite different in that case, and we return to it in Chapter 25. ▶

- Swings in the inflation rate also become larger. It becomes harder to predict what the inflation rate will be in the near future, whether it will be, say, 500% or 1000% over the next year. Borrowing at a given nominal interest rate becomes more and more of a gamble. If you borrow at, say, 1000% for a year, you may end up paying a real interest rate of 500% or 0%: A large difference! The result is that borrowing and lending typically come to a near stop in the last months of hyperinflation, leading to a large decline in investment.

So, as inflation increases and its costs become larger, there is typically an increasing consensus that it should be stopped. This takes us to the last section of this chapter, how hyperinflations actually end.

23-4 How Do Hyperinflations End?

Hyperinflations do not die a natural death. Rather, they have to be stopped through a **stabilization program**.

The Elements of a Stabilization Program

What needs to be done to end a hyperinflation follows from our analysis of the causes of hyperinflation.

- There must be a fiscal reform and a credible reduction of the budget deficit. This reform must take place both on the expenditure side and on the revenue side.

  On the expenditure side, reform typically implies reducing the subsidies that have often mushroomed during the hyperinflation. Obtaining a temporary suspension of interest payments on foreign debt also helps decrease expenditures. An important component of stabilization in Germany in 1923 was the reduction in reparation payments—precisely those payments that had triggered the hyperinflation in the first place.

  On the revenue side, what is required is not so much an increase in overall taxation than a change in the composition of taxation. This is important: During a hyperinflation, people are in effect paying a tax, the inflation tax. Stabilization implies replacing the inflation tax with other taxes. The challenge is to put in place and collect these other taxes. This cannot be done overnight, but it is essential that people become convinced that it will be done and that the budget deficit will be reduced.

This is what Argentina did in 1991, adopting a currency board and fixing the exchange rate at one dollar for one Argentinian peso. See the discussion of currency boards in ▶ Chapter 13.

- The central bank must make a credible commitment that it will no longer automatically monetize the government debt. This credibility may be achieved in several ways. The central bank can be prohibited, by decree, from buying any government debt so that no monetization of the debt is possible. Or the central bank can peg the exchange rate to the currency of a country with low inflation. An even more drastic step is to officially adopt dollarization, to make a foreign currency the country's official currency. This step is drastic because it implies giving up seignorage altogether and is often perceived as a decrease in the country's independence.

An Israeli finance minister ▶ was fired in the 1980s for proposing such a measure as part of a stabilization program. His proposal was perceived as an attack on the sovereignty of Israel.

- Are other measures needed as well? Some economists believe that **incomes policies**—that is, wage and price guidelines or controls—should be used, in addition to fiscal and monetary measures, to help the economy reach a new lower rate of inflation. Incomes policies, they argue, help coordinate expectations around a new lower rate of inflation. If firms know that wages will not increase, they will not increase prices. If workers know that prices will not increase, they will not ask for wage increases, and inflation can be eliminated more easily.

  Others believe credible deficit reduction and central bank independence are all that is required. They argue that the appropriate policy changes, if credible, can lead to drastic changes in expectations, and thus to the elimination of expected and actual inflation nearly overnight. They point to the potential dangers of wage and price controls. Governments may end up relying on the controls and may not take the painful but needed fiscal policy measures, leading ultimately to failure. Also, if the structure of relative prices is distorted to start with, price controls run the risk of maintaining these distortions.

Stabilization programs that do not include incomes policies are called **orthodox**; those that do are called **heterodox** (because they rely on both monetary–fiscal changes and incomes policies). The hyperinflations of Table 23–1 were all ended through orthodox programs. Many of the more recent Latin American stabilizations have relied on heterodox programs.

Can Stabilization Programs Fail?

Can stabilization programs fail? Yes. They can fail, and they often do. Argentina went through five stabilization plans from 1984 to 1989 before succeeding in 1990. Brazil succeeded only in 1995, in its sixth attempt in 12 years.

Sometimes, failure results from a botched or half-hearted effort at stabilization. A government puts wage controls in place but does not take the measures needed to reduce the deficit and money growth. Wage controls cannot work if money growth continues, and the stabilization program eventually fails.

Sometimes failure results from political opposition. If social conflict was at the root of the hyperinflation, it still may be present and just as hard to resolve at the time of stabilization. Those who lose from the fiscal reform needed to decrease the deficit will oppose the stabilization program and may force the government to retreat. Often, workers who see an increase in the price of public services or an increase in taxation, but who do not fully perceive the decrease in the inflation tax, strike or even riot, leading to failure of the stabilization plan.

Failure can also result from the anticipation of failure. Suppose that the exchange rate is fixed to the dollar as part of the stabilization program. Also, suppose that participants in financial markets anticipate that government will soon be forced to devalue. To compensate for the risk of devaluation, they require very high interest rates to hold domestic rather than U.S. bonds. These very high interest rates cause a large recession. The recession, in turn, forces government to devalue, validating the markets' initial fears. If, instead, markets had believed that government would maintain the exchange rate, the risk of devaluation would have been lower, interest rates would have been lower, and government would have been able to proceed with stabilization. To many economists, the successes and failures of stabilization plans appear to have such an element of self-fulfilling prophecy. Even well-conceived plans work only if they are expected to work. In other words, luck and good public relations both play a role.

The Costs of Stabilization

We saw in Chapter 12 how a disinflation is associated with a large recession and a large increase in unemployment. We might therefore expect the much larger disinflations associated with the end of a hyperinflation to be associated with very large recessions or even depressions. This is typically not the case.

To understand why, recall our discussion of disinflation in section 12-3. We argued that there were three reasons why inflation might not decrease as fast as money growth, leading to a recession. First, wages are typically set in nominal terms for some period of time (up to three years in Canada), and as a result, many of them are already determined when the decision to disinflate is made. Second, wage contracts are typically staggered, making it difficult to implement a slowdown in all wages at the same time. The third reason is credibility.

Hyperinflation eliminates the first two problems. During hyperinflation, wages and prices are changed so often that both nominal rigidities and the staggering of wage decisions become nearly irrelevant.

But the issue of credibility remains. The fact that even coherent programs may not succeed implies that no program is fully credible from the start. If, for example, government

This argument was particularly relevant in the stabilizations in Eastern Europe in the early 1990s, where because of central planning, the initial structure of relative prices was very different from that in a market economy. Imposing wage or price controls would have prevented relative prices from adjusting to their appropriate market values.

This is a variation on the theme of self-fulfilling exchange rate crises discussed in Chapter 19.

Remember that the rate of real money growth equals the rate of nominal money growth minus the rate of inflation. If inflation decreases by less than nominal money growth, this implies negative real money growth. This decrease in the real money stock then leads to high interest rates, which can trigger a recession.

In the 1970s, Bolivia achieved strong output growth, in large part because of high world prices for its exports: tin, silver, cocoa, oil, and natural gas. But by the end of the decade, the economic situation started deteriorating. The price of tin declined. Foreign lending, which had financed a large part of Bolivian spending in the 1970s, was sharply curtailed as foreign lenders started worrying about repayment. Partly as a result of this, and partly because of long-running social conflicts, political chaos ensued. From 1979 to 1982, the country had 12 presidents: nine military and three civilian.

When the first freely elected president in 18 years came to power in 1982, he faced a nearly impossible task. U.S. commercial banks and other foreign lenders were running scared. They surely did not want to make new loans to Bolivia, and they wanted the previous loans to be repaid. Net private (medium- and long-term) foreign lending to the Bolivian government had decreased from 3.5% of GDP in 1980 to −0.3% in 1982, and decreased to −1% in 1983. Because government felt it had no other choice, it turned to money creation to finance the budget deficit.

Inflation and Budget Deficits. The next three years were characterized by the interaction of steadily higher inflation and budget deficits.

Table 1 gives the budget numbers for the period 1981–1986. Because of the lags in tax collection, the effect of rising inflation was to dramatically reduce real tax revenues. And government's attempt to maintain low prices for public services was the source of large deficits for state-run firms. As these deficits were financed by subsidies from the state, the result was a further increase in the budget deficit. In 1984, the budget deficit reached a staggering 31.6% of GDP.

The result of higher budget deficits and the need for higher seignorage was to increase money growth and inflation. Inflation, which had run at an average 2.5% a month in 1981, increased to 7% in 1982 and to 11% in 1983. As shown in Figure 1, which gives Bolivia's monthly inflation rate from January 1984 to April 1986 (the vertical line indicates the beginning of stabilization), inflation kept increasing in 1984 and 1985, reaching 182% in February 1985.

Stabilization. There were many attempts at stabilization along the way. Stabilization programs were launched in November 1982, November 1983, April 1984, August 1984, and February 1985. The April 1984 package was an orthodox program involving a large devaluation, an announcement of tax reform, and an increase in public-sector prices. But the opposition from trade unions was too strong, and the program was abandoned.

After the election of a new president, yet another attempt at stabilization was made in September 1985. This one proved successful. It was an orthodox stabilization plan, organized around the elimination of the budget deficit. Its main features were:

- *Fiscal policy*: Public-sector prices were increased; food and energy prices were increased; public-sector wages were frozen; and a tax reform, aimed at re-establishing and broadening the tax base, was announced.
- *Monetary policy*: The official exchange rate of the peso was adjusted to what the black market rate had been prior to stabilization. The exchange rate was set at 1.1 million pesos to the dollar, up from 67,000 pesos to the dollar the month before (a 1600% devaluation). The exchange rate was then left to float, within limits.
- *Re-establish international creditworthiness*: Negotiations were started with international organizations and commercial banks to restructure the debt. An agreement with foreign creditors and the IMF was reached nine months later, in June 1986.

As in the previous attempt at stabilization, the unions called a general strike. In response, government declared a state of siege, and the strike was quickly terminated. After hyperinflation and so many failed attempts to control it, public opinion was clearly in favour of stabilization.

The effects on inflation were dramatic. For a few weeks, the inflation rate was actually negative! Inflation did not remain negative for very long, but the average monthly rate of inflation was below 2% during 1986–1989. As the table shows, the budget deficit was drastically reduced in 1986, and the average deficit was below 5% of GNP for the rest of the decade.

TABLE 1	Revenues, Expenditures, and the Deficit, as a Percentage of Bolivian GDP					
	1981	**1982**	**1983**	**1984**	**1985**	**1986**
Revenues	9.4	4.6	2.6	2.6	1.3	10.3
Expenditures	15.1	26.9	20.1	33.2	6.1	7.7
Budget balance (−: deficit)	−5.7	−22.3	−17.5	−31.6	−4.8	2.6

Revenues and expenditures of the central government.

Source: Jeffrey Sachs, "The Bolivian Hyperinflation and Stabilization," *National Bureau of Economic Research*, working paper No. 2073, November 1986, Table 3.

Did stabilization have a negative effect on output? It probably did. Real interest rates remained very high for more than a year after stabilization. The full effect of these high real interest rates on output is hard to establish, however. While stabilization was being implemented, Bolivia was hit with further large declines in the price of tin and natural gas. In addition, a major campaign against narcotics had the effect of disrupting cocoa production. How much of the Bolivian recession of 1986 was due to stabilization and how much was due to these other factors is difficult to assess.

Source: The material in this box draws largely from Jeffrey Sachs, "The Bolivian Hyperinflation and Stabilization," NBER working paper, 1986. Sachs was one of the architects of the stabilization program.

Further Reading

See also Juan Antonio Morales, "The Transition from Stabilization to Sustained Growth in Bolivia," in Michael Bruno et al., eds., *Lessons of Economic Stabilization and Its Aftermath,* (Cambridge, MA: MIT Press, 1991).

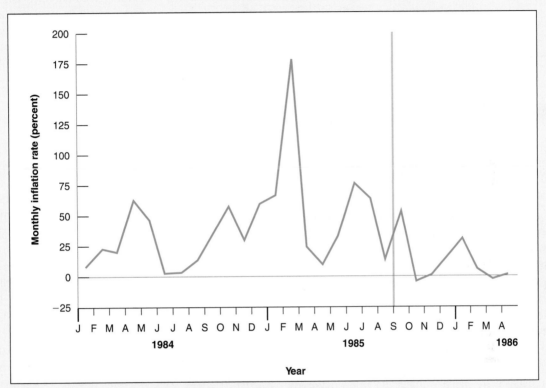

FIGURE 1   Bolivian Monthly Inflation Rate, January 1984–April 1986

decides to fix the exchange rate, a high interest rate may be needed initially to maintain the parity. Those programs that turn out to be successful are those in which government maintains the program and where increased credibility leads to lower interest rates over time. But even in that case, the initial high interest rate often leads to a recession. Overall, the evidence is that most, but not all, hyperinflations involve some cost in output. Much of the current research focuses on how stabilization packages should be designed to reduce this cost: orthodox versus heterodox, restrictions on money growth versus fixing of the exchange rate, and so on.

23-5 | Conclusions

We looked at the high unemployment pathology in Chapter 22. We characterized the Great Depression as a sharp decrease in activity followed by a long and strong recovery. There was a deflation. There is a similar pattern to the recent Japanese experience. This chapter shows that there is a clear hyperinflation pathology. High inflation has the feel of an intense but short-lived illness. Its causes are largely common across episodes: Hyperinflations come from governments' inability to control their budgets in the face of major shocks, economic or political. In addition, their symptoms are largely common across episodes: Accelerating inflation and progressively larger real costs until stabilization is attempted and eventually achieved.

An underlying theme of the core of this book was that, although output fluctuates around its natural level in the short run, it tends to return to this natural level in the medium run. And, if the adjustment was too slow, fiscal and monetary policy could be used to help shape the adjustment. Most of the time, this is, indeed, what happens. But as the last two chapters tell us, it does not always happen.

SUMMARY

- Hyperinflations are periods of high inflation. The most extreme took place after World War I and World War II in Europe. Latin America has had episodes of high inflation as recently as the early 1990s.

- High inflation comes from high money growth. High money growth comes from the combination of large budget deficits and the inability to finance them through borrowing, either from the public or from abroad.

- The revenues from money creation are called seignorage. Seignorage is equal to the product of money growth and real money balances. The smaller the real money balances, the higher is the required rate of money growth, and therefore the higher the rate of inflation required to generate a given amount of seignorage.

- Hyperinflations are typically characterized by increasing inflation. There are two reasons for this. One is that higher money growth leads to higher inflation, inducing

people to reduce real money balances, requiring even higher money growth (and thus leading to even higher inflation) to finance the same real deficit. The other is that higher inflation often increases the deficit, which requires higher money growth, and even higher inflation.

- Hyperinflations are ended through stabilization programs. To be successful, stabilization programs must include fiscal measures aimed at reducing the deficit and monetary measures aimed at reducing or eliminating money creation as a source of financing for the deficit. Some stabilization plans also include wage and price guidelines or controls.

- A stabilization program that imposes wage and price controls without changes in fiscal and monetary policies will fail. But even coherent and well-conceived programs do not always succeed. Anticipation of failure may lead to failure of even a coherent plan.

KEY TERMS

- barter, 470
- debt monetization, 468
- dollarization, 471
- heterodox stabilization program, 477
- hyperinflation, 467
- incomes policies, 476

- inflation tax, 473
- Laffer curve, 473
- orthodox stabilization program, 477
- seignorage, 469
- stabilization program, 476
- Tanzi–Olivera effect, 475

An asterisk denotes a harder question. [Web] indicates that the question requires access to the Internet.

1. TRUE/FALSE/UNCERTAIN

a. In the short run, governments can finance a deficit of any size through money growth.

b. The inflation tax is always equal to seignorage.

c. Hyperinflations may distort prices but have no effect on real output.

d. The solution to ending hyperinflations is simple: Institute a wage and price freeze, and inflation will stop.

e. As inflation is generally good for those who borrow money, hyperinflations are the best times in which to take out large loans.

f. Budget deficits usually shrink during hyperinflations.

2. SEIGNORAGE

Assume that money demand takes the following form:

$$\frac{M}{P} = Y[1 - (r + \pi^e)]$$

where $Y = 1000$ and $r = 0.1$.

a. Assume that in the short run, π^e is constant and equal to 25%. Compute the amount of seignorage if the rate of money growth, $\Delta M/M$, equals

   i. 25%.   **ii.** 50%.   **iii.** 75%.

b. In the medium run, $\pi^e = \pi = \Delta M/M$. Compute the amount of seignorage associated with the three rates of money growth in question (a). Explain why the answers differ from those in (a).

*c. In the medium run, what is the rate of money growth that maximizes seignorage?

3. THE TANZI–OLIVERA EFFECT

How would each of the following change the Tanzi–Olivera effect?

a. Requiring monthly instead of yearly tax payments by households.

b. Assessing greater penalties for under-withholding of taxes from monthly paycheques.

c. Decreasing the income tax and increasing the sales tax.

4. STABILIZATION

You are an economic advisor to a country suffering from a hyperinflation. Discuss the following statements made by politicians debating the proper course for stabilization:

a. "This crisis will not end until workers begin to pay their fair share of taxes."

b. "The central bank has demonstrated that it cannot responsibly wield its power to create money, so we have no choice but to adopt a currency board."

c. "Price controls are necessary to end this madness."

d. "Stabilization will require a large recession and substantial increase in unemployment."

e. "Let us not blame the central bank, the problem is fiscal policy not monetary policy." Discuss.

FURTHER READING

For more on the German hyperinflation, read Steven Webb, *Hyperinflation and Stabilization in the Weimar Republic* (New York: Oxford University Press, 1989).

Two good reviews of what economists know and do not know about hyperinflation are Rudiger Dornbusch, Federico Sturzenegger, and Holger Wolf, "Extreme Inflation: Dynamics and Stabilization," *Brookings Papers on Economic Activity*, 2, 1990, pp. 1–84; and Pierre Richard Agenor and Peter Montiel, *Development Macroeconomics* (Princeton, NJ: Princeton University Press, 1995), Chapters 8 to 11. Chapter 8 makes for easy reading; the other chapters are more difficult.

The experience of Israel, which underwent high inflation and stabilization in the 1980s, is described in Michael Bruno, *Crisis, Stabilization and Economic Reform* (New York: Oxford University Press, 1993), especially Chapters 2 to 5. Michael Bruno was the head of Israel's central bank for most of that period.

Much recent research has focused, in particular, on how to end hyperinflations. One of the classic articles is: "The Ends of Four Big Inflations," by Thomas Sargent, in Robert Hall, ed., *Inflation: Causes and Effects* (Chicago: NBER and the University of Chicago, 1982), pp. 41–97. In that article, Sargent argues that a credible program can lead to stabilization at little or no cost in terms of activity.

Rudiger Dornbusch and Stanley Fischer, "Stopping Hyperinflations, Past and Present," *Weltwirtschaftlichers Archiv*, 1, 1986, pp. 1–47, gives a very readable description of the end of hyperinflations in Germany, Austria, Poland, and Italy in 1947, Israel in 1985, and Argentina in 1985.

BACK TO POLICY

Nearly every chapter of this book has looked at the role of policy. The next three chapters put it all together.

CHAPTER 24

Chapter 24 asks two questions: Given the uncertainty about the effects of macroeconomic policies, wouldn't it be better not to use policy at all? And even if policy potentially can be useful, can we trust policy makers to carry out the right policy? Bottom line: Uncertainty limits the role of policy; policy makers do not always do the right thing. But with the right institutions, policy can help and should be used.

CHAPTER 25

Chapter 25 looks at monetary policy. It reviews what we have learned, chapter by chapter, and then focuses on two issues. The first is the optimal rate of inflation: High inflation is bad, but how low a rate of inflation should the cen-

tral bank aim for? The second is the design of policy: Given a target rate of inflation, how much should the central bank be willing to deviate from the target to stabilize output? The chapter ends with a description of the way monetary policy is conducted in Canada today.

CHAPTER 26

Chapter 26 looks at fiscal policy. Again, it reviews what we have learned and then looks more closely at the mechanics of debt, taxes, and spending implied by the government budget constraint. Having done so, it considers several issues, from how wars should be financed, to the dangers of high debt levels. It ends with a description of the current budget situation in Canada and a discussion of the problems on the horizon.

CHAPTER 24
SHOULD POLICY MAKERS BE RESTRAINED?

A recurrent theme of this book has been that macroeconomic policy has an important role to play. The right mix of fiscal and monetary policies can, we have argued, help a country out of a recession, improve its trade position without increasing activity and igniting inflation, slow down an overheating economy, stimulate investment and capital accumulation, and so on.

This theme, however, is clearly at odds with growing demands that policy makers be tightly restrained. In the European Union, countries that have adopted the euro are required to keep their budget deficit under 3% of GDP. The Mike Harris Conservative government in Ontario passed legislation requiring a balanced budget. There are, however, various escape clauses in this legislation that might allow the continued use of fiscal policy as an instrument of stabilization policy. Should such legislation be passed at a federal level? Some argue the case for such legislation, that we would not want to repeat the unbroken string of federal budget deficits from 1970 to 1997. Some central banks, notably the European Central Bank (ECB) as well as the central bank of New Zealand, are constrained by law to have one and only one goal, price stability. Should the Bank of Canada face a similar constraint? For a brief period during the drafting of the Charlottetown Accord, a proposal was made to incorporate a goal of price stability for the operation of the Bank of Canada into Canada's constitution. The proposal (and the Charlottetown Accord itself) was not implemented.

Arguments for restraints on policy fall in two general categories:

1. Policy makers may have good intentions, but they end up doing more harm than good.
2. Policy makers do what is best for themselves, which is not necessarily what is best for the country.

This chapter develops and examines these arguments in the context of macroeconomic policy in general. Chapters 25 and 26 then examine monetary policy and fiscal policy in more detail.

24-1 | Uncertainty and Policy

A blunt way of stating the first argument in favour of policy restraints is that those who know little should do little. The argument has two parts: First, macroeconomists and, by implication, the policy makers who rely on their advice know little; and, second, they should therefore do little.

How Much Do Macroeconomists Actually Know?

Macroeconomists are like doctors treating cancer. They know a lot, but there is also a lot they do not know.

Take an economy with high unemployment, where the central bank is considering the use of monetary policy to increase economic activity. Think of the sequence of links between an increase in money and an increase in output—all the questions the central bank faces when deciding whether and by how much to increase money supply:

- Is the current high rate of unemployment a sign that unemployment is above the natural rate or a sign that the natural rate has increased (Chapters 9, 10, and 22)? If the economy is too close to the natural rate, isn't there a risk that monetary expansion will lead to a decrease in unemployment below the natural rate and an increase in inflation (Chapters 11 and 12)?
- By how much will the change in money supply decrease the short-term interest rate (Chapter 4)? What will be the effect of the decrease in the short-term interest rate on the long-term interest rate (Chapter 19)? By how much will stock prices increase (Chapter 19)? By how much will the currency depreciate (Chapters 8, 13, and 19)?
- How long will it take for lower long-term interest rates and higher stock prices to affect investment and consumption spending (Chapter 20)? How long will it take for the J-curve effects to work themselves out and for the trade balance to improve (Chapter 7)? What is the danger that the effects come too late, when the economy has already recovered?

When assessing these questions, central banks—or macroeconomic policy makers, in general—do not operate in a vacuum. They rely, in particular, on macroeconometric models. The equations in these models give estimates of how these individual links have looked in the past. But different models give different answers. This is because they have different structures, different lists of equations, and different lists of variables.

Figure 24–1 shows an example of this diversity. This example comes from a study commissioned in the early 1990s by the Brookings Institution—a research institute in Washington, D.C.—asking the builders of the 12 main macroeconometric models each to answer a similar set of questions. (The models are described in the Focus box "Twelve Macroeconometric Models of the U.S. Economy and a Note on Canadian Forecasts") The goal was to see how different the answers would be across models. One question was:

> Consider a case where the U.S. economy is growing at its normal growth rate and where unemployment is at its natural rate; call this the baseline case. Suppose now that over the period of a year, the Federal Reserve Board increases money faster than in the baseline so that after a year, nominal money is 4% higher than it would have been in the baseline case. From then on, nominal money grows at the same rate as in the baseline case so that the level of nominal money remains 4% higher than it would have been without the change in monetary policy. Suppose further that interest rates in the rest of the world remain unchanged. What will happen to U.S. output?

A description of the models and of the study is given in Ralph Bryant et al., *Empirical Macroeconomics for Interdependent Economies* (Washington, DC: Brookings Institution, 1988). The study shows the effects not only of monetary policy, but also of fiscal policy. (The simulation described in the text is simulation E in the supplemental volume.)

Figure 24–1 shows the deviation of output from the baseline predicted by each of the 12 models. All 12 models predict that output will increase for some time after the increase in money. After one year, the average deviation of output from the baseline is positive. But the range of

FIGURE 24-1

The Response of Output to a Monetary Expansion: 12 Predictions from 12 Models

Although all 12 models predict that output will increase for some time in response to a monetary expansion, the range of answers regarding the size and the length of the output response is large.

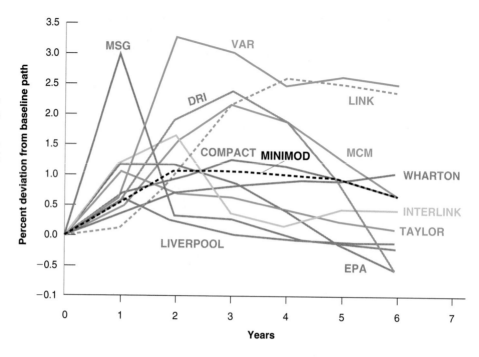

FOCUS   Twelve Macroeconometric Models of the U.S. Economy and a Note on Canadian Forecasts

Together, the set of models used in the Brookings project is representative of the different types of macroeconomic models used for forecasting and policy in the world today:

- Two, DRI (Data Resources Incorporated) and WHARTON, are commercial models. They are used regularly to generate and sell economic forecasts to firms and financial institutions.
- Five are used for forecasting and help in the design of policy. MCM (MultiCountry Model) is used by the Federal Reserve Board in Washington in the conduct of monetary policy; INTERLINK is used by the OECD in Paris; COMPACT is used by the Commission of the European Union in Brussels; EPA is used by the Japanese Planning Agency. Each of these four models was constructed by one team of researchers doing all the work, that is, building submodels for countries or groups of countries and linking them through trade and financial flows. In contrast, the fifth, LINK, is composed of individual country models—models constructed in each country by researchers from that country and then linked together by trade and financial relations.
- Four models incorporate rational expectations explicitly: the LIVERPOOL model, based in England; MINIMOD, used at the International Monetary Fund; MSG, developed by Warwick McKibbin and Jeffrey Sachs at Harvard

University; and the TAYLOR model—which we saw in section 10-4—developed by John Taylor of Stanford University. These are typically smaller models, with less detail than those listed above. But they are better at capturing the expectation effects of various policies.

- The last one, VAR (Vector AutoRegression, the technique of estimation used to build the model), developed by Christopher Sims and Robert Litterman at Minnesota, is very different from the others. It is not a structural model but rather a statistical summary of the relations between the different variables, without an explicit economic interpretation. Its strength is in its fit of the data. Its weakness is that it is, essentially, a (very big) black box.
- Canada, as a smaller economy, does not get the same amount of attention from modellers. Forecasts of the path of the Canadian economy are made by the IMF, the OECD, and by both the federal Department of Finance and the Bank of Canada. The forecast made by the Department of Finance, along with the budget, used to be made available to the public. However, the federal government has taken to simply reporting the average of a sample of private forecasts in recent budgets. In the Bank of Canada's semiannual *Monetary Policy Report*, a graph is presented with a range of estimates of the current and forecast output gaps.

answers is large, from nearly 0% to close to 3%; even leaving out the most extreme prediction, the range is still more than 1%. Two years later, the average deviation is 1.2%; again leaving out the most extreme prediction, the range is still 2%. And six years later, the average deviation is 0.6%, and the answers range from −0.5 to 2.5%. In short, if we measure uncertainty by the range of answers from this set of models, there is substantial uncertainty about the effects of policy.

Should Uncertainty Lead Policy Makers to Do Less?

Should uncertainty about the effects of policy lead policy makers to do less? In general, the answer is yes. Consider the following example, which builds on the simulation we just looked at.

Suppose that the Canadian economy is in recession. The unemployment rate is 9%, and the Bank of Canada is considering using monetary policy to expand output. To concentrate on uncertainty about the effects of policy, let us assume that the Bank of Canada knows everything else for certain. On the basis of its forecasts, it *knows* that without changes in monetary policy, unemployment will still be 9% next year. It knows that the natural rate of unemployment is 7%, and therefore the unemployment rate is 2 percentage points above the natural rate. And it knows, from Okun's law, that 1% more output growth for a year leads to a reduction in the unemployment rate of 0.4%.

> In the real world, of course, the Bank of Canada does not know any of these things with certainty. It can only make forecasts. It does not know the exact value of the natural rate, or the exact coefficient in Okun's law. Introducing these sources of uncertainty would reinforce our basic conclusion.

Under these assumptions, the Bank of Canada knows that if it could achieve 5% more output growth over the coming year, the unemployment rate a year from now would be lower by 0.4 times 5% = 2%, thus down to its natural rate of 5%. By how much should the Bank of Canada increase money supply?

Taking the average of the responses from the different models in Figure 24–1, an increase in money supply of 4% leads to a 0.85% increase in output in the first year. Equivalently, a 1% increase in money supply leads to a 0.85/4 = 0.21% increase in output.

Suppose that the Bank of Canada takes this average relation as holding with *certainty*. What it should then do is straightforward. To return the unemployment rate to the natural rate in one year requires 5% more output growth. And 5% output growth requires the Bank of Canada to increase money by 5%/0.21 = 23.8%. The Bank of Canada should therefore increase money supply by 23.8%. If the economy's response is equal to the average response from the 12 models, this increase in money supply will return the economy to the natural rate of unemployment within a year.

Suppose that the Bank of Canada actually increases money supply by 23.8%. But let us now take into account uncertainty, as measured by the range of responses of the different models in Figure 24–1. We will assume the range of uncertainty in models of the Canadian economy is similar to that in Figure 24–1 for models of the American economy. Recall that the range of responses of output to a 4% increase in money supply after one year varies from 0% to 3%; equivalently, a 1% increase in money supply leads to a range of increases in output from 0% to 0.75%. These ranges imply that an increase in money supply of 23.8% leads, across models, to an output response anywhere between 0% and (23.8% × 0.75) = 17.9%. These output numbers, in turn, imply a decrease in unemployment anywhere between 0 and 7 percentage points, or values of the unemployment rate a year hence anywhere between 9% and 2%!

The conclusion is clear: Given the range of uncertainty about the effects of monetary policy on output, increasing money supply by 23.8% would be irresponsible. If the effects of money supply on output are as strong as suggested by one of the 12 models, unemployment by the end of the year could be 5 percentage points below the natural rate, leading to enormous inflationary pressures. Given this uncertainty, the Bank of Canada should increase money supply by much less than 23.8%. For example, increasing money supply by 10% leads to a range for unemployment a year hence of 7% to 4%, clearly a safer range of outcomes.[1]

---

[1]**DIGGING DEEPER.** This example relies on the notion of *multiplicative uncertainty*—because the effects of policy are uncertain, more active policies lead to more uncertainty. See William Brainard, "Uncertainty and the Effectiveness of Policy," *American Economic Review*, May 1967, pp. 411–425.

Uncertainty and Restraints on Policy Makers

Let us summarize what we have learned so far. There is substantial uncertainty about the effects of macroeconomic policies. This uncertainty should lead policy makers to be more cautious, to use less active policies. Policies should be aimed broadly at avoiding prolonged recessions, slowing down booms, and avoiding inflationary pressure. The higher unemployment or inflation, the more active the policies should be. But they should stop well short of **fine tuning**, of trying to achieve constant unemployment or constant output growth.

Friedman and Modigliani are the same two economists who independently developed the modern ► theory of consumption (Chapter 20).

These conclusions would have been controversial 20 years ago. Back then, there was a heated debate between two groups of economists. One group, headed by Milton Friedman from Chicago, argued that because of long and variable lags, activist policy was likely to do more harm than good. The other group, headed by Franco Modigliani from Massachusetts Institute of Technology, had just built the first generation of large macroeconometric models and believed that economists' knowledge of the economy was becoming good enough to allow for increasingly fine tuning the economy. Today, most economists recognize there is substantial uncertainty about the effects of policy. They also accept the implication that this uncertainty should lead to less active policies.

Note that what we have developed so far is an argument for *self-restraint by* policy makers, not for *restraints on* policy makers. If policy makers understand the implications of uncertainty—and there is no reason to think they do not—they will, on their own, follow less active policies. There is no reason to impose further restraints, such as the requirement that money growth be constant or that the budget be balanced. Let us now turn to arguments for restraints on policy makers.

24-2 | Expectations and Policy

One reason the effects of macroeconomic policy are uncertain is the interaction of policy and expectations. How a policy works, and sometimes whether it works at all, depends not only on how it affects current variables but also on how it affects expectations about the future (the main theme of Chapter 21). However, the importance of expectations for policy goes beyond uncertainty about the effects of policy. This brings us to a discussion of games.

Until the 1970s, macroeconomic policy was seen in the same way as the control of a complicated machine. Methods of **optimal control**, developed initially to control and guide rockets, were increasingly being used to design macroeconomic policy. Economists no longer think this way. It has become clear that the economy is fundamentally different from a machine, even a very complex one. Unlike a machine, the economy is composed of people and firms that try to anticipate what policy makers will do and react not only to current policy but also to expectations of future policy. Hence, macroeconomic policy must be thought of as a **game** between policy makers and the economy. So, when thinking about policy, what we need is not **optimal control theory** but rather **game theory**.

Game theory is becoming an important tool in all branches of economics. The 1994 Nobel prize in economics was awarded to the three game theorists John Nash from Princeton, John Harsanyi from Berkeley, and Reinhard Selten from Germany. You ► may have seen the film about John Nash, *A Beautiful Mind.*

Let us clarify semantics. When economists say "game," they do not mean "entertainment," they mean **strategic interactions** between **players**. In the context of macroeconomic policy, the players are the policy makers and "the economy"—more concretely, the people and the firms in the economy. The strategic interactions are clear: What people and firms do depends on what they expect policy makers to do. In turn, what policy makers do depends on what is happening in the economy.

Game theory has given economists many insights, often explaining how some apparently strange behaviour makes sense when one understands the nature of the game being played. One of these insights is particularly important for our discussion of restraints here: Sometimes you can do better in a game by giving up some of your options. To see why, let us start with an example from outside economics, governments' policies concerning hijackers.

Hijackings and Negotiations

Most governments have a stated policy that they will not negotiate with plane hijackers. The reason for this stated policy is clear: to deter hijacking by making it not worthwhile to hijack planes.

Suppose, despite the stated policy, a hijacking takes place. Now that the hijacking has taken place anyway, why not negotiate? Whatever compensation the hijackers demand is likely to be less costly than the alternative—the likelihood that lives will be lost if the plane has to be taken back by force. So, the best policy would appear to be: Announce that you will not negotiate, but if a hijacking happens, negotiate nevertheless.

Upon reflection, it is clear this would, in fact, be a very bad policy. Hijackers' decisions do not depend on the stated policy but on what they expect will actually happen if they hijack a plane. If they know that negotiations will actually take place, they will rightly consider the stated policy as irrelevant. And hijackings will take place.

So, what is the best policy? Despite the fact that once hijackings have taken place, negotiations typically lead to a better outcome, the best policy is for governments to commit *not* to negotiate. By giving up the option to negotiate, they are likely to prevent hijackings in the first place.

Let us now turn to a macroeconomic example, based on the relation between inflation and unemployment. As you will see, exactly the same logic is involved.

Inflation and Unemployment Revisited

Recall the relation between inflation and unemployment we derived in Chapter 11 (equation (11.7), with the time indexes omitted):

$$\pi = \pi^e - \alpha(u - u_n) \tag{24.1}$$

Inflation (π) depends on expected inflation (π^e) as embodied in wages set in labour contracts and on the difference between the actual unemployment rate and the natural unemployment rate ($u - u_n$). The coefficient α captures the effect of unemployment on inflation, given expected inflation: When unemployment is above the natural rate, inflation is lower than expected; when it is below the natural rate, inflation is higher than expected.

Suppose the Bank of Canada announces it will follow a monetary policy consistent with zero inflation. On the assumption that wage setters believe the announcement, expected inflation (π^e) as embodied in wage contracts is equal to zero, and the Bank of Canada faces the following relation:

$$\pi = -\alpha(u - u_n) \tag{24.2}$$

If the Bank of Canada follows through on its announced policy of zero inflation, expected and actual inflation will both be equal to zero, and unemployment will be equal to the natural rate.

Zero inflation and unemployment equal to the natural rate is not a bad outcome. But it would seem that the Bank of Canada can actually do even better. Recall from Chapter 11 that α was a critical parameter. In Canada, we estimated α as 0.5. So, equation (24.2) implies that by accepting just 1% inflation, the Bank of Canada can achieve an unemployment rate of 0.5 percentage point below the natural rate. Suppose that the Bank of Canada—and everybody else in the economy—finds the trade-off attractive and decides to decrease unemployment by 0.5 percentage point in exchange for an inflation rate of 1%. This incentive to deviate from the announced policy once the other player has moved—in this case, once wage setters have set the wage—is known in game theory as the **time inconsistency** of optimal policy. In our example, the Bank of Canada can improve the outcome for this period by deviating from its announced policy of zero inflation: By accepting some inflation, it can achieve a substantial reduction in unemployment.

Unfortunately, this is not the end of the story. Seeing that the Bank of Canada has increased money by more than it announced it would, wage setters are likely to wise up and begin to expect positive inflation of 1%. If the Bank of Canada still wants to achieve an unemployment

A refresher: Given labour market conditions and given their expectations of what prices will be, firms and workers set nominal wages. Given the nominal wages they have to pay, firms then set prices. Thus, prices depend on expected prices and labour market conditions. Equivalently, price inflation depends on expected price inflation and labour market conditions. This is what is captured in equation (24.1).

For simplicity, we assume that the Bank of Canada can choose the rate of inflation exactly. In doing so, we ignore uncertainty about the effects of policy (the topic of section 24-1, but not a central issue here).

The natural rate of unemployment, despite its name, has no claim to being natural or best in any sense (see Chapters 9 and 11). It may be perfectly reasonable for the Bank of Canada and everyone else in the economy to prefer an unemployment rate lower than the natural rate.

rate 0.5 percentage point below the natural rate, it now has to accept 2% inflation. However, if it does, wage setters are likely to increase their expectations of inflation further, and so on.

The eventual outcome is likely to be high inflation. Because wage setters understand the Bank of Canada's motives, expected inflation catches up with actual inflation, and the Bank of Canada will eventually be unsuccessful in its attempt to achieve unemployment below the natural rate. In short, attempts by the Bank of Canada to make things better lead, in the end, to things being worse. The economy ends up with the *same unemployment rate* as would have prevailed if the Bank of Canada had followed its announced policy, but with *much higher inflation*.

How relevant is this example? Very relevant. Reread Chapter 11. We can see the history of the Phillips curve and the increase in inflation in the 1970s around the world as coming precisely from central bank attempts to maintain unemployment below the natural rate, leading to higher and higher expected and actual inflation. In that light, the shift of the original Phillips curve can be seen as the adjustment of wage setters' expectations to the central bank's behaviour.

So, what is the best policy in this case? It is for the Bank of Canada to make a credible commitment that it will not to try to decrease unemployment below the natural rate. By giving up the option of deviating from its announced policy, the Bank of Canada can achieve unemployment equal to the natural rate and zero inflation. The analogy with the hijacking example is clear: By credibly committing not to do something that would appear desirable at the time, policy makers can achieve a better outcome: no hijackings in our earlier example, no inflation here.

Establishing Credibility

How can a central bank credibly commit not to deviate from its announced policy?

One way to establish its credibility is for the central bank to give up—or to be stripped, by law, of—its policy-making power. For example, the mandate of the bank can be defined by law in terms of a simple rule, such as setting money growth at 0% forever.

Such a law surely takes care of the problem of time inconsistency. But such a tight restraint comes close to throwing the baby out with the bathwater. We want to prevent the central bank from pursuing too high a rate of money growth in an attempt to lower unemployment below the natural rate. But—subject to the restrictions discussed in section 24-1— we still want the central bank to be able to expand money supply when unemployment is far above the natural rate and contract money supply when unemployment is far below the natural rate. Such actions become impossible under a constant-money-growth rule. There are, indeed, better ways to deal with time inconsistency. In the case of monetary policy, our discussion suggests one way this can be done:

1. Make the central bank independent. Appointing central bankers for longer terms and making it harder to fire them will make them more likely to resist political pressure to decrease unemployment below the natural rate.

2. Then, choose a "conservative" central banker, somebody who dislikes inflation and is unwilling to accept more inflation in exchange for less unemployment when unemployment is at the natural rate. When the economy is at the natural rate, such a central banker simply will not be tempted to embark on a monetary expansion. Thus, the problem of time inconsistency will disappear altogether.

Appointing as the head of the central bank someone who does not have the same preferences as the general public might seem like a solution that only game theorists would concoct. But this is actually the way many countries have been responding to the problem of time consistency in monetary policy. In many countries, in the last two decades, central banks have been given more independence. And governments typically have appointed central bankers who are more "conservative" than the governments themselves—central bankers who appear to care more about inflation and less about unemployment than governments. (See the Focus box "Was Alan Blinder Wrong in Speaking the Truth?")

In the summer of 1994, President Clinton appointed Alan Blinder, an economist from Princeton, vice-chairman (in effect, second in command) of the Federal Reserve Board. (The Federal Reserve Board is the American central bank.) A few weeks later, Blinder, speaking at an economic conference, indicated his belief that the Federal Reserve Board has both the responsibility and the ability, when unemployment is high, to use monetary policy to help the economy recover. This statement was badly received. Bond prices decreased, and most newspapers ran editorials critical of Blinder.

Why was the reaction of markets and newspapers so negative? It was surely not that Blinder was wrong. There is no doubt that monetary policy can and should help the economy out of a recession. Indeed, the Federal Reserve Bank Act of 1978 requires the Federal Reserve Board to pursue full employment as well as low inflation.

The reaction was negative because, in terms of the argument we developed in the text, Blinder revealed by his words that he was not a conservative central banker, that he cared about unemployment as well as about inflation. With the unemployment rate equal to 6.1%, close to what was thought to be the natural rate at the time, markets interpreted Blinder's statements as suggesting that he might want to decrease unemployment below the natural rate. Interest rates increased because of higher expected inflation, so bond prices decreased.

The moral of the story is clear. Whatever views central bankers may hold, they should try to look and sound conservative. . . . This is why many heads of central banks are reluctant to admit, at least in public, the existence of any trade-off between unemployment and inflation, even in the short run.

Figure 24–2 suggests that this approach has been quite successful. The vertical axis gives the average annual inflation rate in 18 OECD countries for the period 1960–1992. The horizontal axis gives the value of an index of "central bank independence," constructed by looking at several legal provisions in the bank's charter—for example, whether and how government can remove the head of the bank. There is a striking inverse relation between the two variables, as summarized by the regression line: More central bank independence is systematically associated with lower inflation.

One can reasonably argue this does not prove that central bank independence leads to lower inflation. It may be that countries that dislike inflation tend to both give more independence to their central bankers and have lower inflation. (This is another example of the difference between correlation and causality, discussed in Appendix 3 at the end of the book.)

Time Inconsistency and Restraints on Policy Makers

Let us summarize what we have learned in this section: We have examined arguments for putting restraints on policy makers, based on the issue of time inconsistency. We have looked

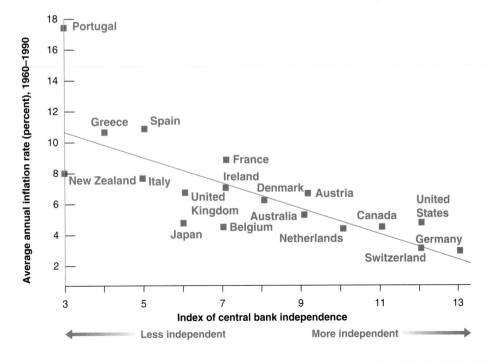

FIGURE 24–2

Inflation and Central Bank Independence, 1960–1992

Across the OECD countries, the higher the degree of central bank independence, the lower is the rate of inflation.

Source: Vittorio Grilli, Donato Masciandaro, and Guido Tabellini, "Political and Monetary Institutions and Public Financial Policies in the Industrial Countries," Economic Policy, October 1991, pp. 341–392.

at the case of monetary policy. But similar issues arise in the context of fiscal policy as well, for example, in the case of debt repudiation, an issue we will discuss in Chapter 26.

When issues of time inconsistency are relevant, tight restraints on policy makers—such as a fixed-money-growth rule in the case of monetary policy—can provide a coarse solution. But the solution may have large costs if it prevents the use of macroeconomic policy altogether. Better ways typically involve designing better institutions (such as an independent central bank) that can reduce the problem of time inconsistency without eliminating monetary policy as a macroeconomic policy tool.

24-3 | Politics and Policy

We have assumed so far that policy makers are *benevolent*—that they try to do what is best for the economy. However, much public discussion challenges that assumption: Politicians or policy makers, the argument goes, do what is best for themselves, and this is not always what is best for the country.

You have heard the arguments: Politicians avoid hard decisions, they pander to the electorate, partisan politics leads to gridlock, and nothing ever gets done. Discussing the flaws of democracy goes far beyond the scope of this book. What we can do here is to review briefly how these arguments apply to macroeconomic policy, then look at the empirical evidence, and see what light it sheds on the issue of policy restraints.

Games between Policy Makers and Voters

Many macroeconomic measures involve trading off short-run losses against long-run gains—or, symmetrically, short-run gains against long-run losses.

Take, for example, tax cuts. By definition, tax cuts lead to lower taxes today. They are also likely to lead to an increase in activity, and so to an increase in pretax income, for some time. But unless they are matched by equal decreases in government spending, they lead to a larger budget deficit and to the need for an increase in taxes in the future. If voters are shortsighted, the temptation for politicians to cut taxes may prove irresistible. Politics may lead to systematic deficits, at least until the level of government debt has become so high that politicians are scared into action.

Now, move on from taxes to macroeconomic policy in general. Again, suppose that voters are shortsighted. If the politicians' main goal is to please voters and get re-elected, what better policy than to expand aggregate demand before an election, leading to higher growth and lower unemployment? True, growth in excess of the normal growth rate cannot be sustained, and eventually the economy must return to the normal level of output: Higher growth must be followed by lower growth later. But with the right timing and shortsighted voters, higher growth can win the elections. Thus, we might expect a clear **political business cycle**, with higher growth, on average, before elections than after elections.

The arguments we have just laid out are familiar; in one form or another, you surely have heard them before. And their logic is convincing. So, it may come as a surprise that they do not fit the facts very well.

For example, our discussion of taxes might lead you to expect that budget deficits and high government debt have always been and will always be with us. Figure 24–3, which gives the evolution of the ratio of government debt to GDP in Canada since 1926, shows this is not the case. The first two buildups in debt happened in very special circumstances. The Great Depression, with a large reduction in both output and tax revenue, led to a sharp increase in the ratio of debt to GDP. World War II, in which Canada was a principal combatant for six long years, was financed by an enormous buildup of debt. After World War II ended, rapid growth in real GDP led to a long reduction in the ratio of debt to GDP. The lowest value is seen in 1976, 30.9%.

The tax cuts both decrease tax rates and increase activity. But they also lead to a long sequence of deficits, which may take considerable time to eliminate. We will look at the relation between current and future taxes more formally when we examine the implications of the government budget constraint ▶ in Chapter 26.

From Okun's law, output growth in excess of normal growth leads to a decline in the unemployment rate below the natural rate. In the medium run, we know that the unemployment rate must increase back to the natural rate. This, in turn, requires output growth below normal growth for some time. (See Chapter 12, in particular, Table 12–1).

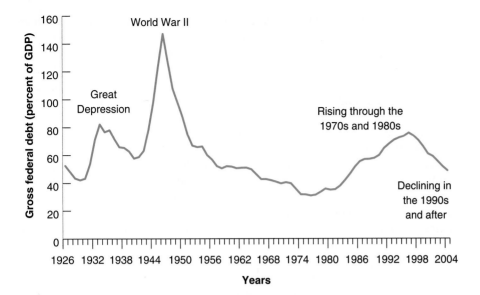

Source: Gross federal debt using CANSIM II variable V151537; nominal GDP using CANSIM II variables V500633 and V646925.

FIGURE 24-3

The Evolution of the Ratio of Government Debt to GDP, 1926–2004

There have been three major buildups in federal government debt in Canada. The Great Depression, by reducing GDP and tax revenue, increased the ratio of debt to GDP. World War II, with monumental government spending on the war effort, massively increased Canada's national debt. But national debt as a percent of GDP fell rapidly until 1976. From 1976 to 1994, an unbroken string of federal deficits raised the ratio of debt to GDP. Then, an unbroken string of surpluses lowered the ratio of debt to GDP.

Source: Gross federal debt using CANSIM II variable V151537; nominal GDP using CANSIM II variables V500633 and V646925.

The relation between the deficit, debt, and GDP is explored in detail in ◄ Chapter 26.

◄ Chapter 26 will examine alternative—and empirically more successful—explanations for the evolution of government debt, both over time and across countries.

The long increase in the debt-to-GDP ratio from 1976 to 1996, a period of 20 years, seems to fit the argument of shortsighted politicians well. But after 1996, the Liberal government did reverse the previous 20 years of fiscal policy (where both Liberal and Conservative governments had been in power), and the ratio of debt to GDP has fallen from 75% to 50%.

The Debt-to-GDP Ratio Is Falling

The deficit turned to a surplus. Explaining the behaviour of debt over a period of 20 years through the behaviour of shortsighted politicians raises the issue of why things were different before 1976 and also after 1996. The broader historical record suggests that by itself, shortsightedness does not explain much of the past evolution of deficits and debt.

Let us return to the political-business-cycle argument that policy makers try to get high output growth before the elections so that they will be re-elected. We can only look at the American evidence on this point. An American president knows when he (or she) is elected, exactly when the next election will occur. Election dates are fixed in advance, and thus an American president could try to generate an economic boom just before the next election. In Canada, the prime minister selects the election date already knowing the state of the economy. To date, only Ontario and British Columbia have experimented with fixed election dates. We cannot distinguish between booms "caused" by an upcoming election and elections that are "caused" by a previous boom. In the United States, if the political business cycle were important, we would expect to see faster growth before elections than after. Table 24–1 gives GDP growth rates for each of the four years of each U.S. administration since President Truman in 1948. It is, indeed, the case that growth has been highest on average in the last year of an administration. But the average difference across years is small: 3.7% in the last year of an administration versus 3.3% in the first year.

Games between Policy Makers

Another line of argument focuses not on games between politicians and voters, but rather on games between political parties. For example, take the issue of budget deficit reduction in Canada. When first elected, the Conservative government of Brian Mulroney had a clear mandate to reduce the deficit. It did not succeed in reducing the deficit. Some of its failure was part of the normal electoral and political process. Deficit reductions involve making painful decisions, either reducing spending or raising taxes. But other factors seemed to be at work as well. Some of the Conservatives were small "c" conservatives from Western Canada who clearly wanted less government spending. Some of the Conservatives were Quebec nationalists who did not want less government spending. Each side of this rather uneasy coalition wanted to set government's priorities. Perhaps as a result, neither issue was resolved. Each side may have hoped their issue would be resolved as first priority, with other issues being dealt with later.

Game theorists refer to these situations as **wars of attrition**. The hope that the other side will give in leads to long and often costly delays. Such wars of attrition are endemic in fiscal policy. Deficit reduction often takes place long after it would be best. This is particularly visible during episodes of hyperinflation. As we saw in Chapter 23, hyperinflations come from monetary finance of large budget deficits. Although the need to reduce those deficits is usually recognized early on, support for stabilization programs—which include the elimination of those deficits—typically comes only when inflation has reached such high levels that economic activity is severely affected.

Another example of a game between political parties is the movements in economic activity brought about by the alternation of parties in power. Republicans typically worry more than Democrats about inflation and less than Democrats about unemployment. So, we would expect Democratic administrations to show stronger growth—and thus less unem-

> Wars of attrition are not limited to fiscal policy: You may remember strikes in both basketball and baseball where all or part of the season was cancelled because owners and players could not reach an agreement.

TABLE 24–1	Growth During Democratic and Republican Administrations (Percent per Year)			
	Year			
	First	**Second**	**Third**	**Fourth**
Democratic				
Truman	0.0	8.5	10.3	3.9
Kennedy/Johnson	2.6	5.3	4.1	5.3
Johnson	5.8	5.8	2.9	4.1
Carter	4.7	5.3	2.5	−0.2
Clinton I	2.7	4.0	2.7	3.6
Clinton II	4.4	4.3	4.1	4.1
Average: Democratic	3.4	5.5	4.4	3.5
Republican				
Eisenhower	4.0	−1.3	5.6	2.1
Nixon	2.4	−0.3	2.8	5.0
Nixon/Ford	5.2	−0.5	−1.3	4.9
Reagan I	1.9	−2.5	3.6	6.4
Reagan II	3.6	3.0	2.7	3.0
Bush (George H.)	2.5	1.2	−0.7	2.6
Bush (George W.)	0.5	2.2	3.1	—
Average: Republican	2.9	0.3	2.2	4.0
Average	3.1	2.7	3.2	3.7

Source: Alberto Alesina, "Macroeconomics and Politics," *NBER Macroeconomics Annual*, 1988, pp. 13–61, Table 4. Updated.

ployment and more inflation—than Republican administrations. This prediction appears to fit the facts quite well. Look at Table 24–1 again. The most striking contrast in growth rates is in the second year of each administration. During the second year of each Democratic administration since Truman, growth has been very high. During the second year of each Republican administration, growth has been very low. In four out of seven Republican administrations, growth in the second year has been negative.

An intriguing question: Why is the effect so much stronger in the administration's *second* year? The theory of unemployment and inflation we developed in Chapter 12 suggests a plausible answer. There are lags in the effects of policy, so it takes about a year for a new administration to affect the economy. And sustaining higher growth than normal for too long would lead to increasing inflation, so even a Democratic administration would not want to sustain higher growth throughout its term. Thus, growth rates tend to be much closer to each other during the second halves of Democratic and Republican administrations than during first halves.

Back to a Balanced-Budget Law

Let us end this chapter with one of the issues we started with, the case for and against a balanced-budget law. What have we learned?

First, despite common beliefs, the picture of politicians pandering to shortsighted voters does not entirely fit the facts. Large peacetime deficits in Canada persisted with all parties from 1970 to 1995. Fiscal policy at a federal level was plagued with chronic deficits. Figure 24–4 portrays the evolution of per capita provincial debt in Ontario, measured in 1992 dollars per capita, from 1970 to 2003. You observe debt rising in most years. Elections are marked by vertical lines. If the simple political model were correct, tax cuts and spending increases should always be timed to raise the debt just before each election. There are nine elections. Debt falls before two elections (March 1981 and October 2003); is flat before two elections (September 1981 and September 1990); and does rise before every other Ontario election. There is some evidence that parties are unwilling to go to the polls just after tax increases or spending cuts. Thus, in Ontario politics, a balanced-budget law may help.

Such a balanced-budget law was passed in 1999. Similar laws are in place in Manitoba, British Columbia, and Alberta. In Ontario, the Cabinet is allowed to run a planned deficit

FIGURE 24–4

Debt per Capita in Ontario, 1970–2004

The evolution of provincial debt in Ontario does provide some support for the hypothesis of short-sighted politicians. In nine elections, real debt per capita fell only twice just before an election. However, the growth in provincial debt is quite steady over time and does not accelerate before elections. Elections are marked with vertical lines. The names of premiers are found between elections.

Sources: Ontario's net assets using CANSIM II variable VI51723; Ontario's population using CANSIM II variable V12; consumer price index using CANSIM II variable V735319.

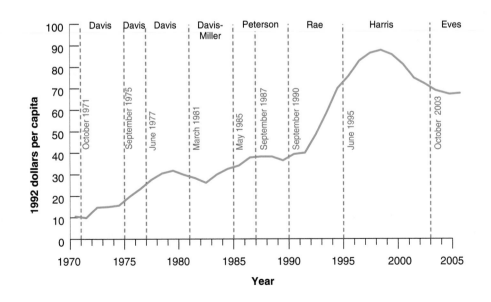

equal to 1% of revenue, only if they plan to run an equal or greater surplus in the following year. If the law is violated, Cabinet members are required to donate up to 50% of their extra pay back to the province. However, the law does not apply for a natural or other disaster, if there is war, or if revenues decline for reasons other than a reduction in a statutory tax rate. The revenue decline at the same tax rate must be at least 5% of the previous year's revenue. These loopholes are enormous and would certainly allow for fiscal policy to be used to fight a major recession or depression.

Nonetheless, most economists do not favour balanced-budget laws. Their arguments are presented below.

The Case against a Balanced-Budget Law. A balanced-budget law might (only might) eliminate the problem of deficits. In the Ontario law described above, there are many loopholes, and the actual consequences of breaking the law are quite trivial. The political consequences of openly breaking the law might be more substantial. If the law is broken freely through creative definitions of a natural or other disaster, then the credibility of a government to actually tackle the problem of the debt and deficit could be severely impaired. But it is very difficult to write a balanced-budget law without such loopholes.

Although using fiscal policy to stabilize the Ontario economy is not an important job of the Ontario government, it is an important job of the federal government. If such a law was in force at the federal level, it could be very awkward to manage fiscal policy. Most economists would argue that in the case of a severe recession, it is an important role of government to be able to run a deficit, increase the national or provincial debt, and stabilize the economy.

These economists are also skeptical of any rules that a legislature may impose upon itself but can undo by a vote later on. The balanced-budget laws passed by Ontario and other provinces could be repealed by subsequent governments. Proponents of these laws recognize that fact. They argue the law is useful in any case because of the increased political cost of the action to actually repeal the balanced-budget law. It brings the issue of the budget deficit and increased debt directly in front of the public. Proponents of such a law look at Figure 24–4 and make the argument that the government from 1990 to 1995, the Rae government, would not have as easily increased Ontario's debt if the balanced-budget law had been in place.

It is hard to argue balanced-budget laws are needed to reduce a deficit and stabilize debt. After all, Figure 24–3 shows how the Canadian federal government did just that without a balanced-budget law. It is also worth noting that the Harris government passed its balanced-budget law in 1999, four years after its election victory. In three of those four years, Ontario's debt continued to increase. The law was passed only after Ontario's deficits were substantially reduced. This suggests quite a bit of flexibility by a small "c" conservative government on the need to balance the budget. In the box "The Gowth and Stability Pact," the European experiences suggest international treaties to implement balanced budget laws are no more effective. In the end, balancing a budget and deciding on the appropriate level of government spending and taxation remain decisions made in the political arena. Economists can try to assess the consequences of alternative approaches. Simply creating a law seems overly simplistic.

The Case for a Balanced-Budget Law. To some economists, however, the answer is yes, a balanced-budget law is necessary. These economists are typically more skeptical of the usefulness of macroeconomic policy in general and of fiscal policy in particular. They worry that running deficits during recessions may have adverse effects on financial markets, hindering rather than helping the recovery (a potentially perverse effect of policy we discussed in Chapter 21). So, they are willing to give up fiscal policy as a macroeconomic instrument.

The Maastricht Treaty, negotiated by the countries of the European Union (EU) in 1991, set a number of convergence criteria that countries had to meet in order to qualify to join the Euro area. (For more on the history of the Euro area, see the Focus box "The Euro: A Short History" in Chapter 13.) Among them were two restrictions on fiscal policy. First, the ratio of a country's budget deficit to GDP had to be below 3%. Second, the ratio of its debt to GDP had to be below 60%, or, at least "approaching this value at a satisfactory pace."

In 1997, would-be members of the Euro area agreed to make some of these criteria permanent. The Stability and Growth Pact (SGP), signed in 1997, required members of the Euro area to follow the following fiscal rules:

- That countries commit to balance their budget in the medium run—that they present programs to the European authorities, specifying their objectives for the current and following three years in order to show how they are making progress toward their medium-run goal.

- That countries avoid excessive deficits, except under exceptional circumstances. Following the Maastricht Treaty

criteria, excessive deficits were defined as deficits in excess of 3% of GDP. Exceptional circumstances were defined as declines of GDP larger than 0.75%.

- That sanctions be imposed on countries that ran excessive deficits. These sanctions could range from 0.2 to 0.5% of GDP—so, for a country like France, up to roughly 10 billion dollars!

Figure 1 plots the evolution of budget deficits since 1990 for the Euro area as a whole. Note how from 1993 to 2000, budget balances went from a deficit of 5.8% of Euro area GDP to a surplus of 0.1%. The performance of some of the member countries was particularly impressive: Greece reduced its deficit from 13.4% of GDP to 1.4% of GDP (although we learned in 2004 that the Greek government had cheated in reporting its deficit numbers and that the actual improvement, although impressive, was less than reported); Italy eliminated its deficit, going from a deficit of 10.3% of GDP in 1993 to a surplus of 0.7% in 2000.

Can all the improvement be attributed to the Maastricht criteria and the SGP rules? Just as in the case of deficit

(continued)

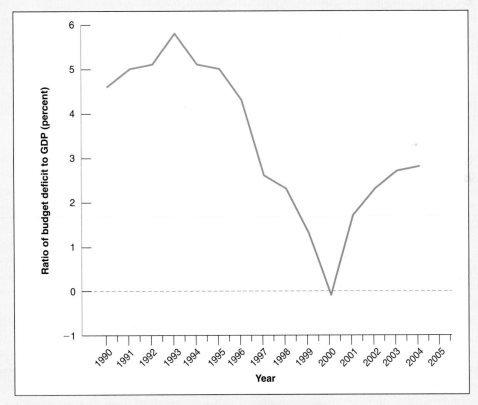

FIGURE 1   Euro Area Budget Deficits as a Percentage of GDP since 1990

Source: OECD *Economic Outlook*, December 2004.

reduction in the United States over the same period, the answer is no. The decrease in nominal interest rates, which decreased the interest payments on the debt, and the strong expansion of the late 1990s both played important roles. But, again as in the United States, the fiscal rules also played a significant role. The carrot—the right to become a member of the Euro area—was attractive enough to lead a number of countries to take tough measures to reduce their deficits.

Things turned around, however, in 2000. Since 2000, deficits have increased. The ratio of the deficit to GDP for the Euro area was back up to 2.3% in 2003 and is forecast to reach 2.7% in 2004. The main reason is low output growth since 2001, which has led to low tax revenues. Although the deficit for the Euro area as a whole is below the 3% limit, this is not the case for a number of individual countries. The first country to break the limit was Portugal in 2001, with a deficit of 4.4%. The next two were France and Germany, both with deficits in excess of 3% of GDP since 2002 and all the years following to date. In each case, the government of the country decided it was more important to avoid a fiscal contraction that could lead to even slower output growth than to satisfy the rules of the SGP.

Faced with clear "excessive deficits" (and without the excuse of exceptional circumstances because output growth in each these countries was low but positive), European authorities found themselves in a quandary. Starting the excessive deficit procedure against Portugal, a small country, might have been politically feasible, although it is doubtful that Portugal would have ever been willing to pay the fine. Starting the same procedure against the two largest members of the Euro area, France and Germany, proved politically impossible. After an internal fight between the two main European authorities, the European Commission and the European Council—the European Commission wanted to proceed with the excessive deficit procedure, while the European Council, which represents the states, did not—the procedure was suspended.

Since 2003, the legal status of the SGP has been in limbo, and the credibility of the Pact has been severely affected. This crisis has made clear that the rules were too inflexible. Romano Prodi, the head of the European Commission, admitted to that much. In an interview in October 2002, he stated, "I know very well that the Stability Pact is stupid, like all decisions that are rigid." And the attitudes of both France and Germany have shown that the threat to impose large fines on countries with excessive deficits was simply not credible.

The European Commission has therefore explored ways to improve the rules so as to make them more flexible and, by implication, more credible. The current proposals are to keep the 3% deficit and 60% debt numbers as desirable goals but to focus less on the numbers for a particular year and focus more on the path of debt forecast for the medium run. Fines are not viewed as credible, so the plan is to rely on early and very public warnings as well as on peer pressure from other Euro area countries. We already saw the potential problems with such proposals earlier in the chapter. Flexible rules are harder to interpret and more prone to disagreements of interpretation. And public warnings and peer pressure only go so far. Finding the right rules is hard, and it is not clear whether or how the SGP will survive.

SUMMARY

- There is substantial uncertainty about the effects of macroeconomic policies. This uncertainty should lead policy makers to be more cautious and to use less active policies. Policies must be broadly aimed at avoiding prolonged recessions, slowing down booms, and avoiding inflationary pressure. The higher the level of unemployment or inflation, the more active the policies should be. But they should stop short of fine tuning, of trying to maintain constant unemployment or constant output growth.

- Using macroeconomic policy to control the economy is fundamentally different from controlling a machine. Unlike a machine, the economy is composed of people and firms that try to anticipate what policy makers will do and react not only to current policy but also to expectations of future policy. In this sense, macroeconomic policy can be thought of as a game between policy makers and the economy.

- When playing a game, it is sometimes better for a player to give up some of his options. For example, when a hijacking occurs, it is best to negotiate with hijackers. But a government that credibly commits to not negotiating with hijackers—that gives up the option of negotiation—is actually more likely to deter hijackings in the first place.

- The same argument applies to various aspects of macroeconomic policy. By credibly committing to not using monetary policy to decrease unemployment below its natural rate, a central bank can alleviate fears that money growth will be high and in the process decrease both expected and actual inflation. When issues of time inconsistency are relevant, tight restraints on policy makers—such as a fixed-money-growth rule in the case of monetary policy—can, indeed, provide a coarse solution. But the solution may have large costs if it prevents the use of macroeconomic policy altogether. Better methods typically involve designing better institutions (such as an independent central bank) that can reduce the problem of time inconsistency without eliminating monetary policy as a macroeconomic policy tool.

- Another argument for putting restraints on policy makers is that they may play games either with the public or among themselves, and these games may lead to undesirable outcomes. Politicians may try to fool a shortsighted electorate by choosing policies with short-run benefits but large long-term costs—for example, large budget deficits. Political parties may delay painful decisions, hoping that the other party will make the adjustment and take the blame. These problems exist, although they are less prevalent than is usually perceived. In such cases, tight restraints on policy, such as a law to balance the budget, provide a partial solution. Better ways typically involve better institutions and better ways of designing the process through which policy and decisions are made.

KEY TERMS

- fine tuning, 488
- game, 488
- game theory, 488
- optimal control, 488
- optimal control theory, 488
- players, 488
- political business cycle, 492
- strategic interactions, 488
- time inconsistency, 489
- wars of attrition, 494

QUESTIONS AND PROBLEMS

An asterisk denotes a harder question. [Web] indicates that the question requires access to the Internet.

1. TRUE/FALSE/UNCERTAIN

a. There is so much uncertainty about the effects of monetary policy that we would be better off not using it.

b. Elect a Liberal government if you want low unemployment.

c. There is clear evidence of political business cycles in the United States: low unemployment around elections, higher unemployment the rest of the time.

d. Rules are ineffective in reducing budget deficits.

e. It would be good to put a device on planes that would prevent all communications with the outside in the event of a hijacking.

f. Once a central bank announces a target inflation rate, it has no incentive to deviate from the target.

2. TIME CONSISTENCY

Has the problem of "time consistency" ever arisen in your personal life? Who were the players in that "game"?

3. DESIGNING POLICY TO WIN ELECTIONS

You are an advisor to a newly elected prime minister. She will face new elections four years from now. Inflation last year was 3%, and the unemployment rate was equal to the natural rate. The Phillips curve is given by:

$$\pi_t = \pi_{t-1} - \alpha(u_t - u_n)$$

a. Assume you can use fiscal and monetary policies to achieve any unemployment rate you want for each of the next four years. Write a short memo to the prime minister indicating what unemployment and inflation rates she should try to achieve.

b. How would you change the content of your memo if the Phillips curve is given by:

$$\pi_t = \pi_t^e - \alpha(u_t - u_n)$$

and the evidence is that people form rational expectations?

4. THE NEW ZEALAND EXAMPLE

New Zealand rewrote the charter of its central bank in the early 1990s to make steady, low inflation its only goal. Why would New Zealand want to do this?

5. LIBERALS AND CONSERVATIVES

There are two parties: the Liberals, who care a lot more about unemployment than about inflation, and the Conservatives, who care a lot more about inflation than about unemployment.

The Phillips curve is given by:

$$\pi_t = \pi_t^e - \alpha(u_t - u_n)$$

where π_t^e denotes expectations held in year $t - 1$ for inflation in year t.

There are elections at the end of this year. Liberals and Conservatives have an equal chance of winning and being in power next year.

a. Describe how people will form expectations of inflation for next year.

b. Given these expectations, describe what happens to inflation and unemployment next year if the Liberals win.

c. Given these expectations, describe what happens to inflation and unemployment next year if the Conservatives win.

d. Suppose now that everybody expects Liberals to win the elections. Suppose the Liberals indeed win. What happens to inflation and unemployment next year? Explain.

*6. CUTTING THE BUDGET: THE PRISONER'S DILEMMA

Suppose there is a budget deficit in the United States. It can be reduced by cutting defence spending or by cutting welfare programs or by cutting both.

The Democrats have to decide whether to support cuts in welfare programs. The Republicans have to decide whether to support cuts in defence spending. Each party has to decide what to do, without knowing the decision of the other party.

The possible outcomes can be represented in the table to the right.

To understand how to read this table, look at the bottom left corner. If Democrats vote for welfare cuts, and Republicans vote against cuts in defence spending, the outcome is that the Republicans are very happy and the Democrats are unhappy. The Republicans get 3 (a high positive number), and the Democrats get -2. Make sure you understand each of the four outcomes.

		Welfare cuts	
		Yes	No
Defence cuts	**Yes**	(R = 1, D = 1)	(R = -2, D = 3)
	No	(R = 3, D = -2)	(R = -1, D = -1)

a. If the Republicans decide to cut defence spending, what is the best response of the Democrats? Given this response, how much will the Republicans get?

b. If the Republicans decide not to cut defence spending, what is the best response of the Democrats? Given this response, how much will the Republicans get?

c. What will the Republicans do? What will the Democrats do? Will the budget deficit be reduced? Why, or why not? (This is an example of a game known as the prisoner's dilemma in game theory.) Is there a way to improve the outcome?

FURTHER READING

A leading proponent of the view that governments misbehave and should be tightly restrained is James Buchanan, from George Mason University. Buchanan received the Nobel prize in 1986 for his work on public choice. Read his book co-authored with Richard Wagner, *Democracy in Deficit: The Political Legacy of Lord Keynes* (New York: Academic Press, 1977).

The argument that time consistency is a central issue for policy was first developed by Finn Kydland, from Carnegie Mellon, and Edward Prescott, from Minnesota, in "Rules Rather Than Discretion: The Inconsistency of Optimal Plans," *Journal of Political Economy*, 85(3), June 1977, pp. 473–492.

For a survey of the politics of fiscal policy, read Alberto Alesina and Roberto Perotti, "The Political Economy of Budget Deficits," *IMF Staff Papers*, 1995. Look also at James Poterba, "Do Budget Rules Work?" in Alan Auerbach, ed., *Fiscal Policy. Lessons from Economic Research* (Cambridge: MIT Press, 1997).

For more on the politics of monetary policy, read Alberto Alesina and Lawrence Summers, "Central Bank Independence and Macroeconomic Performance: Some Comparative Evidence," *Journal of Money, Credit and Banking*, May 1993, pp. 289–297.

For an interpretation of the increase in inflation of time inconsistency, see "Did Time Consistency Contribute to the Great Inflation?" by Henry Chappell (**dmsweb.moore. sc.edu/Chappel/Papers/Book/File10_Ch10.pdf**).

CHAPTER 25
MONETARY POLICY:
A SUMMING UP

Nearly every chapter has had something to say about monetary policy. This chapter puts it all together and ties up the remaining loose ends.

Let us first briefly review what we have learned (the Focus box "Monetary Policy: What We Have Learned and Where" gives a more detailed summary):

● In the short run, monetary policy affects the level of output as well as its composition: An increase in money leads to a decrease in interest rates and a depreciation of the currency. These lead to an increase in the demand for goods and an increase in output.

● In the medium run and the long run, monetary policy is neutral: Changes in the level of money eventually lead to proportional increases in prices, leaving output and unemployment unaffected. Changes in the rate of money growth lead to corresponding changes in the inflation rate.

We therefore can think of monetary policy as involving two basic decisions. The first is deciding what the average rate of money growth, and by implication the average inflation rate, should be. The second is deciding how much to deviate from this average rate of money growth to reduce fluctuations in output. In this context, this chapter explores two issues:

1. The optimal inflation rate. There is no question that very high inflation is costly. But how low should inflation be? Should central banks aim for an average inflation rate of, say, 2% or 4%, aim for price stability, or even aim for deflation (negative inflation)?

2. The design of monetary policy. Once the central bank has decided what rate of inflation it wants to achieve, how should it design monetary policy? Given that it directly controls money growth, should it announce a target rate for money growth? Or should it announce a target rate of inflation and try to hit it as best as it can? In the short run, how much should it be willing to deviate from whatever target it has announced if, say, the economy goes into recession?

Having explored these issues, the chapter ends by looking at what the Canadian central bank—the Bank of Canada—actually does, how it designs and carries out monetary policy, and how well it has done in the recent past.

- In Chapter 4, we looked at the determination of money demand and money supply and the effects of monetary policy on the interest rate.

  We saw how an increase in money supply (achieved through an open market operation) leads to a decrease in the interest rate.

- In Chapter 5, we looked at the short-run effects of monetary policy on output.

  We saw how an increase in money leads, through a decrease in the interest rate, to an increase in spending and to an increase in output.

- In Chapter 8, we looked at the effects of monetary policy in an economy with open goods and financial markets.

  We saw how, in an open economy, monetary policy affects spending and output not only through interest rates but also through the exchange rate. An increase in money leads to both a decrease in the interest rate and a depreciation and that they, in turn, increase spending and output.

- In Chapter 10, we looked at the effects of changes in money on output and prices, not only in the short run but also in the medium run.

  We saw that in the medium run, money is neutral: Changes in money are fully reflected in changes in prices.

- In Chapter 12, we looked at the relation among money growth, inflation, and unemployment.

  We saw that in the medium run, money growth is reflected one for one in inflation, leaving the unemployment rate unaffected. We looked at alternative disinflation strategies. On the basis of the Canadian disinflations in the early 1980s and early 1990s and other disinflations around the world, we concluded that disinflations typically come at a cost of higher unemployment for some time.

- In Chapter 13, we discussed the pros and cons of different monetary policy regimes, of flexible versus fixed exchange rates. We discussed the pros and cons of adopting a common currency, such as the euro.

  In the appendix, we looked further at the effects of monetary policy on interest rates and exchange rates, taking into account the role of expectations in financial and foreign-exchange markets.

- In Chapter 18, we introduced a distinction between the nominal interest rate and the real interest rate.

  We saw how higher money growth leads to a lower nominal interest rate in the short run but to a higher nominal interest rate—and an unchanged real interest rate—in the medium run.

- In Chapter 21, we returned to the short-run effects of monetary policy on output, taking into account the effects of monetary policy on expectations.

  We saw that monetary policy affects the short-term nominal interest rate, but that spending depends primarily on both current and expected future short-term real interest rates. We saw how, as a result, the effects of monetary policy on output depend on how expectations respond to policy.

- In Chapter 22, we looked at monetary policy during the Great Depression. We saw how a contraction in nominal money, bank failures, and deflation were all important sources of the large decline in output from 1929 to 1933. We also saw that the deflation in Japan in the 1990s was associated with high unemployment and slow growth.

- In Chapter 23, we studied hyperinflations and looked at the conditions under which such episodes arise and eventually end.

  We focused on the relation among budget deficits, money growth, and inflation. We saw how large budget deficits can lead to high money growth rates and to hyperinflation.

- In Chapter 24, we looked at the problems facing macroeconomic policy in general and monetary policy in particular.

  We saw that uncertainty about the effects of policy should lead to more cautious policies. We saw that even well-intentioned policy makers may sometimes not do what is best and that there is a case for restraints on policy makers. We also looked at the case for making the central bank independent and appointing a conservative central banker.

- In this chapter, we discuss the issues of the optimal inflation rate, the choice and the use of targets for monetary policy. We conclude the chapter by looking at how the Bank of Canada actually conducts monetary policy in Canada today.

25-1 | The Optimal Inflation Rate

Table 25–1 shows that inflation has steadily gone down in rich countries since the early 1980s. In 2003, average inflation in the OECD was 2%, down from 10.5% in 1981. Twenty-seven countries (out of 30) had an inflation rate below 5%; there were only two in 1981.

Does this imply that most central banks have now achieved their goal? Or should they aim for an even lower rate, perhaps 0%? The answer depends on the costs and benefits of inflation.

The Costs of Inflation

We saw in Chapter 23 how very high inflation, say, 30% a month or more, can thoroughly disrupt economic activity. The debate in the OECD countries today, however, is not about the costs of inflation rates of 30% a month or more. Rather, it centres on the advantages of, say, 0% versus 2% or 4% inflation a year. Within that range, economists identify four main costs of inflation: shoe-leather costs, tax distortions, money illusion, and inflation variability.

Shoe-Leather Costs. In the medium run, a higher inflation rate leads to a higher nominal interest rate, and thus to a higher opportunity cost of holding money. As a result, people decrease their money balances by making trips to the bank more often—thus the expression **shoe-leather costs**. These trips would be avoided if inflation were lower, and people could be doing other things instead, working more or enjoying more leisure.

> In the medium run, the real interest rate is not affected by inflation. Thus, an increase in inflation is reflected one for one in an increase in the nominal interest rate (Chapter 18).

During hyperinflations, shoe-leather costs can become quite large. But their importance in times of moderate inflation is limited. If an inflation rate of 4% leads people to go to the bank one more time every month or to do one more transaction between their money market fund and their chequing account every month, this hardly qualifies as a major cost of inflation.

Tax Distortions. The second cost of inflation comes from the interaction between the tax system and inflation. Consider, for example, the taxation of capital gains. Taxes on capital gains are typically based on the change in the dollar price of the asset between the time it was purchased and the time it is sold. This implies that the higher the rate of inflation, the higher is the tax. An example will make this clear.

Suppose that inflation has been running at π a year for the last 10 years. Suppose that you bought a cottage for $50,000 ten years ago, and you are selling it today for $50,000 times $(1 + \pi)^{10}$—so its real value is unchanged. If the capital-gains tax is 30%, the *effective tax rate* on the sale of your cottage—defined as the ratio of the tax you pay to the price for which you sell your house—is:

$$(30\%) \frac{50,000(1 + \pi)^{10} - 50,000}{50,000(1 + \pi)^{10}}$$

> The numerator of the fraction equals the sale price minus the purchase price. The denominator is the sale price.

Because you are selling your cottage for the same real price for which you bought it, your real capital gain is zero, and you should not be paying any tax. Indeed, if $\pi = 0$—if there has been no inflation—then the effective tax rate is 0%. But if $\pi = 4\%$, then the effective

---

TABLE 25–1 Inflation Rates in the OECD, 1981–2003

Year	1981	1985	1990	1995	2005
OECD average[1]	10.5%	6.5%	5.9%	5.1%	2.2%
Number of countries with inflation below 5%[2]	2	10	15	21	28

[1]Average of GDP deflator inflation rates, using relative GDPs as weights.
[2]Out of 30 countries.

Some economists argue that the costs of bracket creep were, in fact, much larger. As tax revenues steadily increased, there was little pressure on government to control spending. The result, they argue, was an increase in the size of government in the 1960s and 1970s far ▶ beyond what would have been desirable.

tax rate is 9.7%: Despite the fact that your real capital gain is zero, you end up paying a high tax. In Canadian tax law, your principal residence (but not a second residence) is exempt from capital-gains tax partly for this very reason.

The problems extend beyond capital-gains taxes on cottages. There are inflation-induced capital gains on shares as well. Although the real rate of return on an asset is the real interest rate, not the nominal interest rate, income for the purpose of income taxation includes nominal interest payments, not real interest payments. Or, to take yet another example, the income levels corresponding to different income-tax rates may not increase automatically with inflation. As a result, people could be pushed into higher tax brackets as their nominal income—but not necessarily their real income—increased over time, an effect known as *bracket creep*. Bracket creep was removed from the Canadian tax system from 1974 to 1986. In 1986, tax brackets were increased only by inflation in excess of 3% in each year. Economists C. G. Ruggieri, D. Van Wart, and R. Howard at the Alberta Treasury estimated that between 1986 and 1993, federal and provincial governments took in 2% more of GDP because of the cumulative effects of bracket creep. In 1999, Finance Minister Paul Martin announced that for federal income taxes, brackets would be fully indexed for inflation and bracket creep would end.

You may argue this cost is not a cost of inflation per se but rather the result of a badly designed tax system. In the example of the cottage we just discussed, government could eliminate the problem if it *indexed* the purchase price to the price level—that is, it adjusted the purchase price for inflation since the time of purchase—and computed the tax on the difference between the sale price and the adjusted purchase price. Under that computation, there would be no capital gains and therefore no capital-gains tax to pay. But because tax codes rarely allow for such systematic adjustment, the inflation rate matters and leads to distortions.

Money Illusion. The third cost comes from *money illusion*, the notion that people appear to make systematic mistakes in assessing nominal versus real changes. Many computations that would be simple under price stability become more complicated when there is inflation. In comparing their income this year to their income in the past, people have to keep track of the history of inflation. In choosing between different assets or deciding how much to consume or save, they have to keep track of the difference between the real interest rate and the nominal interest rate. Casual evidence suggests that many people find these computations difficult and often fail to make the relevant distinctions. Economists and psychologists have gathered more formal evidence, and it suggests that inflation often leads people and firms to make incorrect decisions (see the Focus box "Money Illusion.") If this is the case, then a simple solution is to have no inflation.

Inflation Variability. The last cost comes from the fact that higher inflation is typically associated with *more variable inflation*. And more variable inflation means that financial assets such as bonds, which promise fixed nominal payments in the future, become riskier.

Take a bond that pays $1000 in 10 years. With constant inflation over the next 10 years, the real value of the bond in 10 years is known with certainty. But with variable inflation, the real value of $1000 in 10 years becomes uncertain. Saving for retirement becomes more difficult. For those who have invested in bonds, lower inflation than expected means a better retirement; but higher inflation may mean poverty. This is one of the reasons retirees, for whom part of income is fixed in dollar terms, typically worry more about inflation than other groups in the population.

You may argue, as in the case of taxes, that these costs are not due to inflation per se but rather to the financial markets' inability to provide assets that protect their holders against inflation. Rather than issuing only nominal bonds (bonds that promise a fixed nominal amount in the future), governments or firms could also issue *indexed bonds*—bonds that promise a nominal amount adjusted for inflation so that people do not have to worry about the real value of the bond when they retire. Indeed, as we saw in Chapter 19, several

There is a lot of anecdotal evidence that many people fail to adjust properly for inflation in financial computations. Recently, economists and psychologists have started looking at money illusion more closely. In a recent study, two psychologists, Eldar Shafir from Princeton and Amos Tversky from Stanford, and one economist, Peter Diamond from the Massachusetts Institute of Technology, designed a survey aimed at finding the presence and the determinants of money illusion. Among the many questions they asked of people in various groups (people at the Newark International Airport, people at two New Jersey shopping malls, and a group of Princeton undergraduates) is the following:

Suppose that Adam, Ben, and Carl each received an inheritance of $200,000 and each used it immediately to purchase a house. Suppose that each sold his house one year after buying it. Economic conditions were, however, different in each case:

- During the time Adam owned his house, there was a 25% deflation—the prices of all goods and services decreased by approximately 25%. A year after Adam bought the house, he sold it for $154,000 (23% less than he had paid).
- During the time Ben owned his house, there was no inflation or deflation—the prices of all goods and services did not change significantly during the year. A year after Ben bought the house, he sold it for $198,000 (1% less than he had paid).

- During the time Carl owned his house, there was a 25% inflation—the prices of all goods and services increased by approximately 25%. A year after Carl bought the house, he sold it for $246,000 (23% more than he had paid).

Rank Adam, Ben, and Carl in terms of the success of their house transactions. Assign "1" to the person who made the best deal and "3" to the person who made the worst deal.

It is clear that in nominal terms, Carl clearly made the best deal, followed by Ben, followed by Adam. But what is relevant is how they did in real terms—adjusting for inflation. And in real terms, the ranking is reversed: Adam, with a 2% real gain, made the best deal, followed by Ben (with a 1% loss), followed by Carl (with a 2% loss).

The survey's answers were the following:

Carl was ranked first by 48% of the respondents, and Adam was ranked third by 53% of the respondents. These answers are very suggestive of money illusion. In other words, people have a hard time adjusting for inflation.

Rank	Adam	Ben	Carl
1st	37%	17%	48%
2nd	10%	73%	16%
3rd	53%	10%	36%

governments have now introduced such bonds. Indexed bonds now play an important role in the United Kingdom, where, over the last 20 years, people increasingly have used them to save for retirement. Canada has a small market in indexed federal government bonds. Indexed bonds were introduced in the United States only in 1997. They account for only a small proportion of U.S. government bonds at this point. We used returns on Canadian and American indexed bonds to construct Figure 19–11.

The Benefits of Inflation

Inflation is actually not all bad. One can identify three benefits of inflation: (1) seignorage, (2) the option of negative real interest rates for macroeconomic policy, and (3) (somewhat paradoxically) the use of the interaction between money illusion and inflation in facilitating real wage adjustments.

Seignorage. Money creation—the ultimate source of inflation—is one of the ways in which government can finance its spending. Put another way, money creation is an alternative to borrowing from the public or raising taxes.

Typically, government does not "create" money to pay for its spending. Rather, it issues and sells bonds and spends the proceeds. But if the bonds are bought by the central bank, which then creates money to pay for them, the result is the same: Other things being equal, the revenues from money creation—that is, *seignorage*—allow government to borrow less from the public or to lower taxes.

How large is seignorage in practice? When looking at hyperinflation in Chapter 23, we saw that seignorage is often an important source of government finance in countries with very high inflation rates. But its importance in the OECD economies today, and for the range of inflation rates we are considering, is much more limited. Take the case of Canada: The ratio of the monetary base—the money issued by the Bank of Canada (see Chapter 4)—to GDP is about 4%. An increase in money growth of 4% per year (which eventually leads to a 4% increase in inflation) would therefore lead to an increase in seignorage of 4% × 4%, or 0.16% of GDP. This is a small amount of revenues to get in exchange for 4% more inflation.

Therefore, while the seignorage argument is sometimes relevant (for example, in economies that do not yet have a good fiscal system in place), it seems hardly relevant in the discussion of whether OECD countries today should have, say, 0% versus 4% inflation.

The Option of Negative Real Interest Rates. A positive inflation rate allows the monetary authority to achieve *negative real interest rates*, an option that may be very useful for macro-economic policy when an economy is in recession. Let us look at this more closely.

The nominal interest rate on a bond cannot be negative. If it were, bondholders would be better off holding money rather than bonds. Thus, the lowest possible nominal interest rate is zero.

The real interest rate equals the nominal rate minus expected inflation (see Chapter 18). If inflation and expected inflation are positive, then the real interest rate can be negative. But if they are equal to zero, the lowest value the real interest rate can take is zero. And if there is actual and expected deflation, the real interest rate must remain positive. So, the lower the rate of inflation, the higher is the floor on the real interest rate and the more limited the role of monetary policy in increasing demand and ending a recession.

As we discussed in Chapter 22, this was, indeed, one of the adverse implications of deflation during the Great Depression: Expected deflation implied high real interest rates, despite low nominal interest rates. And today, because inflation is very low in many countries, the issue is resurfacing. Indeed, this is one of the issues facing Japan today. Faced with a sharp decrease in economic activity, the central bank has decreased short-term nominal interest rates to nearly zero. But with the decrease in activity, inflation has turned into deflation, leading to positive real interest rates. The Japanese economy would benefit from lower real interest rates. But this is not an option: the Japanese central bank cannot decrease nominal interest rates below zero.

Money Illusion Revisited. Paradoxically, the presence of money illusion provides at least one argument for having a positive inflation rate.

To see why, consider two situations. In the first, inflation is 4% and somebody's wage increases by 1% in dollar terms. In the second, inflation is 0%, and the wage is decreased by 3% in dollar terms. Both lead to the same decrease in the real wage, namely, 3%. There is some evidence, however, that many people will accept the real wage cut more easily in the first case than in the second.

Why is this example relevant to our discussion? The constant process of change that characterizes modern economies means some workers must sometimes take a real pay cut. Thus, the argument goes, the presence of inflation allows for these downward real-wage adjustments more easily than no inflation. This argument is plausible. Economists have not established its importance; but because so many economies now have very low inflation, we soon may be in a position to test it.

The Optimal Inflation Rate: The Current Debate

At this stage, the debate in the OECD countries is between those who think some inflation (say, 4%) is fine—a number of countries, including Canada, near 2% think that is fine—and those who want to achieve price stability—that is, 0% inflation.

Those who are happy with an inflation rate around 4% emphasize that the costs of 4% versus 2% or 0% inflation are small and that the benefits of some inflation are worth keeping. They argue some of the costs of inflation could be avoided by indexing the tax system and issuing more indexed bonds. They also say that going from current rates of inflation to a lower rate of inflation would require some increase in unemployment for some time and that this transition cost may well exceed the eventual benefits.

Those who want to aim for 0% argue that if inflation is bad, it should be eliminated and that there is no reason to stop at 4% or even 2% inflation just because we happen to be there. They make the point that 0% is a very different target rate from all others: It corresponds to price stability. This is desirable in itself. Knowing the price level will be the same in 10 or 20 years as it is today simplifies several complicated decisions and eliminates the scope for money illusion. Also, given the time consistency problem facing central banks (discussed in Chapter 24), credibility and simplicity of the target inflation rate are important. Price stability may achieve these goals better than a target inflation rate of 4%.

The debate is not settled. For the time being, most central banks, including Canada's, appear to be aiming for low but positive inflation—that is, inflation rates of about 2%.

The Optimal Rate of Inflation: The Canadian Debate

It may seem that the discussion of the optimal rate of inflation takes place in a theoretical vacuum. In Canada, this debate took place from 1988 to 1994. John Crow was appointed Governor of the Bank of Canada in 1987. In February of 1988, in a speech at the University of Alberta, known as the Hanson Lecture, he announced that the role of the Bank of Canada was to conduct monetary policy "so as to achieve a pace of monetary expansion that promotes stability in the value of money." Governor Crow's policy goal was clear; zero or close to zero inflation was to be the Bank's objective while he was Governor. The time period for the achievement of the goal of price stability was not made clear in the Hanson Lecture. However, later in the Hanson Lecture, Crow did make a clear statement about why price stability was to be the Bank's goal. Crow believed that lower inflation and eventually zero inflation would promote predictability in the inflation rate: "In my view, the notion of a high, yet stable rate of inflation is simply unrealistic." Crow believed that a lower rate of inflation and a predictable rate of inflation would increase real output growth: "Because inflation creates distortions, output will be higher over time in conditions of price stability than in those of inflation." He also believed price stability was the only feasible goal:

> ...an attempt to mimic price stability by achieving a stable inflation rate depends on strong public confidence that the authorities would not accept a further acceleration in the rate of inflation. However, if the authorities were unwilling to act to get the rate of inflation down from, for example, 4 percent, why should anyone believe they would be any more willing to get it back to 4 percent if for one reason or another upward pressures on prices led the inflation rate to rise to 5 percent? And so on. This is why a commitment to a steady inflation rate is ultimately not credible. To my mind, the only realistic policy we can pursue that will generate and warrant confidence in the future value of money is to work toward price stability. And ensuring that Canada has a money its citizens can trust is the most durable contribution monetary policy can make to our standard of living. (All quotations are from the Hanson Lecture as reprinted in the *Bank of Canada Review*, February 1988, pages 3–17.)

Crow's belief that lower inflation would lead to higher productivity growth was supported by evidence produced at the Bank of Canada. Peter Jarrett and Jack Selody (two Bank of Canada economists) had estimated that a permanent 1% decrease in the rate of inflation would increase productivity growth of labour by three-tenths of a percentage point. Governor Crow's position that a lower inflation rate would lead to a higher standard of living for Canadians was immediately and extensively debated. The benefits of lower inflation were thought to arrive from three sources: the ability of firms and consumers to respond more accurately to clearer relative price signals; lower tax rates on interest earnings and capital gains; and the fact that a lower rate of inflation was a more predictable rate of inflation. We discussed these sources above.

There was a volume of papers on the issue, *Zero Inflation: The goal of price stability* edited by Richard G. Lipsey, (Toronto: C.D. Howe Institute, March 1990). This volume contains contributions from most of Canada's prominent macroeconomists. The volume was generally supportive of the move ◄ to a lower inflation rate.

Three arguments were also made that measured inflation rates should not be driven to zero, that is, that price stability was not the best goal for monetary policy. First, it is widely known among economists that inflation as measured by the percent change in a consumer price index is overstated by somewhere between 1 and 2%, that is, when measured inflation is 1%, actual inflation may actually be zero. Thus, a policy to produce price stability as zero measured inflation may actually produce falling prices. The central bank needs to explain this issue carefully so that the public understands measured inflation of 1% is price stability. The other two arguments against measured price stability do not depend on the details of the construction of price indexes. They are also the arguments we made above, that two important prices may contain important nominal downward rigidities. One such price is the money wage. If workers strongly resist cuts in their money wages, a small positive inflation rate may allow real wages to fall as needed to allow for more effective adjustment in labour markets. The second price with an important rigidity is the nominal interest rate, which cannot fall below zero. It could be useful to have a negative real interest rate at times. In the end, economists and commentators in Canada and around the world did not agree on the benefits of price stability.

On February 27, 1991, for the first time in the history of Canadian monetary policy, the Minister of Finance in the Conservative government and the Governor of the Bank of Canada made a joint policy announcement. The announcement contained an explicit timetable for the reduction of inflation. The targets contained a specific plan to reduce inflation: inflation of 3% or less by the end of 1992; 2.5% inflation or less by the middle of 1994; and 2% or less inflation by the end of 1995 with "further progress to price stability thereafter." Targets were defined as plus or minus 1% from the number above. The "further progress" statement meant that the announcement also included, for the first time, a definition of price stability— inflation of less than 2% per year—and a time for its achievement—after 1995. It appeared that for Canada, the optimal rate of inflation was to be less than 2%. The 1991 target announcement assumes further measures would be taken to lower the rate of inflation below 2%. The optimal rate of inflation was, in this official policy document, less than 2%. Was this the "optimal rate" established forever?

In October 1993, the Liberals won the federal election, in which the management of monetary policy had been an important issue. The 1990–1991 recession had Canadians hoping for better things. The Opposition Liberals had severely criticized the Conservative government for its management of the economy and Governor Crow for his rigid anti-inflation policies. Bruce Little, of *The Globe and Mail* (Canada's leading newspaper), reported: "Just before the campaign began, Mr. Chrétien [leader of the Opposition Liberals] caused a stir when he said he would tell the Bank to end its fixation on inflation and pay more attention to job creation" (reported October 11, 1993). Stronger words were used by Mr. Chrétien, who denounced the Bank of Canada as "obsessed with inflation."

Crow's policy announcements in 1993 prior to the campaign (no significant announcements were made during the actual campaign itself because such action would be inappropriate) continued to stress that price stability was the goal and that goal had not yet been achieved. In the Bank of Canada's *Annual Report* for 1992, published March 1993, Crow titled the section on inflation "Progress toward price stability" and made clear the Bank's "fundamental monetary policy commitment to return to price stability." In another important policy announcement made in the spring of 1993, Crow mentioned "the great improvement in our inflation situation" but also indicated it was the Bank's goal that "money's purchasing power is itself maintained" (opening Statement before the House Standing Committee on Finance, *Bank of Canada Review*, Summer 1993).

The Conservatives were soundly defeated in the election of October 1993, reduced from a majority government to a mere two seats in the House of Commons. Paul Martin, the new Liberal Minister of Finance, had to decide whether or not to appoint John Crow to a second term as Governor of the Bank. Governor Crow's first term would expire on February 1, 1994.

Editorial opinion on the retention of John Crow was split. *The Toronto Star* wrote: "Find a New Governor for the Central Bank" (December 18, 1993). But the leading business columnist for *The Globe and Mail*, Terrence Corcoran, and for the *Financial Post* (the Canadian equivalent of the *Wall Street Journal*), William Watson, both argued in similar terms for the retention of John Crow. On December 13, 1993, there was a day-long round table organized by the Department of Finance. Vancouver economist Michael Walker surveyed 38 of 40 private sector and academic participants and announced that of those polled, 23 favoured Crow's reappointment, 6 were against, and 9 abstained (reported in the *The Globe and Mail*, December 14, 1993). Those in favour of reappointment argued that the costs of reducing inflation had already been borne by Canadians and that the benefits were still to be reaped. Some economists also argued that John Crow's personal credibility was necessary to maintain a low rate of inflation.

In fact, Paul Martin announced that John Crow was not going to be reappointed as Governor of the Bank of Canada. In February 1994, a new inflation target agreement between the Bank of Canada and the Department of Finance was announced. That agreement, since renewed in 1998 and 2001, no longer contains the phrase "further progress to price stability thereafter." Rather, the inflation target is set to a band at 1–3% per year. This 1–3% target for inflation was set in place to 2006.

A conference entitled "Issues in Inflation Targeting" was held at the Bank of Canada in November 2005. The debate rotated around leaving the target band at 1–3% or lowering the target band to 0–2% when the target agreement is renewed, likely in 2006. That renewal will have occurred by the time this book is in print. The new agreement can be found at the Bank of Canada Web site. The debate at the conference was no different than the debate outlined in the previous few pages of this book.

There was no concensus that reducing the target from 1–3% to 0–2% would confer great benefits to the Canadian economy. There was concern for transition costs, a recession, if the actual rate of inflation were lowered. Such a recession would be predicted by the analysis in Chapter 12. Finally, considerable concern was expressed over the increased probability of deflation (negative inflation) if the inflation target were lowered to 0–2%.[1]

Japan's recent experience with deflation, described in Chapter 22, was prominent in the discussion: high positive real rates of interest when the nominal rate of interest is zero and inflation is negative. High positive real rates of interest when the economy is in a recession are a problem. The most likely outcome in 2006 would be: 1–3% inflation will remain "optimal" for Canada and continue to be the target rate of inflation for the Bank of Canada.

25-2 | The Design of Monetary Policy

Once a central bank has decided what rate of inflation it wants to achieve, it still faces two issues:

- What target should it announce? Should it announce a target rate for money growth (which it controls), or should it announce a target for inflation (which is what it cares about, but does not control directly)?
- Once it has chosen a target, how closely should it try to meet it? For example, in the short run, how much weight should it put on meeting the target versus getting the economy out of a recession?

[1]**DIGGING DEEPER**. A few economists argue in favour of a price level target, that is, that the average rate of inflation should be zero. Periods of positive inflation would have to be followed by periods of negative inflation. The argument has not been accepted by the Bank of Canada, partly because in Japan, negative inflation has been very difficult to handle.

Money Growth and Inflation Revisited

Consider the following two propositions: (1) In the medium run and the long run, inflation is determined by the growth rate of the money stock. (2) The central bank controls the growth rate of the money stock.

Together, the two propositions suggest a simple rule for monetary policy: Compute the growth rate of the money stock consistent with the desired rate of inflation, and announce this growth rate as the target. By meeting its money growth target, the central bank will then achieve its desired rate of inflation.

As appealing as this rule sounds, it runs into a serious problem: It does not work! Even over long periods of time, it turns out that there is no tight relation between the rate of growth of the money stock and the rate of inflation. Sure, the two generally move together: If money growth is high, inflation will also be high; and if money growth is low, inflation will be low. Recall how much inflation and money growth move together during episodes of hyperinflation (Chapter 23). But the relation is not tight enough that by choosing a rate of money growth, the central bank can achieve precisely its desired rate of inflation.

This proposition is shown in Figure 25–1, which plots five-year averages of the inflation rate (using the CPI as the price index) against five-year averages of the growth rate of the money stock (*M*1B) from 1972 to 2004 (for example, the value of the inflation rate for 2000 is the average inflation rate for 1996–2000). The reason for using five-year averages should be clear: In the short run, changes in money growth affect mostly output, not inflation. It is only in the medium run that a relation between money growth and inflation should emerge. Taking five-year averages of both money and inflation is a way of looking for the presence of such a medium-run relation. Figure 25–1 shows that in Canada, since 1972, the relation between *M*1B growth and inflation has not been very tight. True, both went up at the beginning of the period, but inflation started declining in the early 1980s, whereas money growth measured using *M*1B actually increased. In the latter part of the period, after 1992, money growth was larger than inflation.

From Money to Monetary Aggregates

Why is there no tight relation between money growth and inflation? The answer is because of *shifts in the demand for money*. An example will help here. Suppose that as the result of the introduction of credit cards, people decide to hold only half the amount of money they

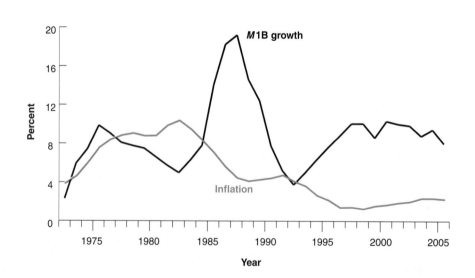

used to hold before; in other words, the real demand for money decreases by half. In the medium run, the real money stock must also decrease by half. For a given nominal money stock, the price level must double. So, even if the nominal money stock is constant, there will be a period of inflation as the price level doubles. During this period, there will be no tight relation between money growth (which is zero) and inflation (which is positive).

The reason the demand for money shifts over time goes beyond the introduction of credit cards. To understand why, we must challenge an assumption we have maintained until now, namely, that there was a sharp distinction between money and other assets. In fact, there are many financial assets that are close to money. They cannot be used for transactions—at least not without substantial restrictions—but they can be exchanged for money at little cost. In other words, they are very **liquid**; this makes them potentially attractive substitutes for money. Shifts between money and these assets are the main factor behind shifts in the demand for money.

Take, for example, *money market funds*. Money market funds are financial intermediaries that hold as assets short-maturity securities (typically, Treasury bills) and have deposits (or shares, as they are called) as liabilities. The funds pay depositors an interest rate close to the T-bill rate minus the administrative costs of running the fund. Deposits can be exchanged for money on notice and at little cost. Most money market funds allow depositors to write cheques but only above a certain amount, typically $500. Because of this restriction, money market funds are not included in $M1B$. When these funds were introduced in the mid-1970s, people were able, for the first time, to hold a very liquid asset while receiving an interest rate close to that on T-bills. Money market funds quickly became very attractive. Many people reduced the balances on their bank accounts and moved to money market funds. In other words, there was a large negative shift in the demand for money.

However, with lower inflation in the 1990s and lower nominal interest rates, it is entirely possible that some deposits shifted out of money market funds and back into chequable accounts.

The presence of shifts between money and other liquid assets have led central banks to construct measures that include not only money but also other liquid assets. These aggregates are called **monetary aggregates**, and typically come under the names $M2$, $M3$, and so on. $M2$—which is also sometimes called **broad money**—includes $M1B$ (currency and chequable deposits), plus all chequable notice deposits and personal term deposits. There is no reason to stop at $M2$; there is an $M2+$ (including bank-like institutions) and so on.

The construction of $M2$ and other monetary aggregates would appear to offer a solution to our earlier inflation targeting problem. If most of the shifts in the demand for money are between $M1B$ and other assets within $M2$, the demand for $M2$ should be more stable than the demand for $M1B$, so there should be a tighter relation between $M2$ growth and inflation than between $M1B$ growth and inflation. Thus, the central bank should target $M2$ growth. Although this is the approach taken by many central banks, it is not without problems:

- The relation between $M2$ growth and inflation is tighter than between $M1B$ growth and inflation; but it is still not very tight. This is shown in Figure 25–2, which plots five-year averages of the inflation rate and of the rate of growth of $M2$. The evolution of $M2$ growth is closer to that of inflation than was the case for $M1B$ growth. But the fit is still not perfect. Note, for example, how $M2$ growth was nearly 5% above inflation in the 1970s, and how this difference has disappeared over time. Put another way, a given rate of $M2$ growth is associated with 5% more inflation in the 1970s than now. The fit between $M2$ growth and inflation appears weaker again at the end of the figure's time period.

- There is a problem with $M2$. $M2$ is even more difficult for the Bank of Canada to control than is $M1B$. If people switch from chartered banks to trust companies, then $M2$ falls. There is nothing the Bank of Canada can do about these shifts. Thus, $M2$ (and to a lesser degree $M1B$) is a strange target for policy. The Bank of Canada does not have perfect control of or care directly about $M1B$ or $M2$. It actually cares about inflation and unemployment.

From Chapter 5, equation (5.3) (the *LM* equation): The real money supply (the left side) must be equal to the real demand for money (the right side):

$$\frac{M}{P} = YL(i)$$

If, as a result of the introduction of credit cards, the real demand for money halves, then:

$$\frac{M}{P} = \frac{1}{2}\,YL(i)$$

For a given level of output and a given interest rate, M/P must also halve. Given M, this implies that P must double.

For comparison, chequable deposits were equal to $560 billion in 1989.

First to adopt inflation targeting was New Zealand in 1990, which set a target range for inflation of 0% to 2%, later extended to 0% to 3%. Next was Canada in 1991, setting a target range for inflation of 1% to 3%. Since then, some form of inflation targeting has been adopted by, among others, the United Kingdom, Sweden, Israel, and Spain. The euro area countries, whose monetary policy is set by the European Central Bank, have an inflation target of "below 2%". The central bank of the United States, the Federal Reserve, does not explicitly target inflation.

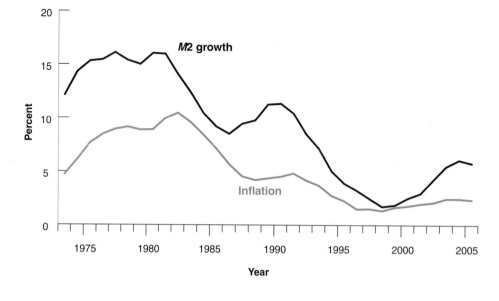

FIGURE 25-2

M2 Growth and Inflation: Five-Year Averages, 1973–2005

Although the relation between M2 growth and inflation is tighter than the relation between M1B growth and inflation, it is still not perfect.

Source: Inflation using CANSIM II variable V735319; *M2* using CANSIM II variable V37128.

These two problems have led an increasing number of central banks to shift from the targeting of some monetary aggregate to inflation targeting.

Interest Rate Rules or Taylor Rules

Once the central bank has chosen and announced a target, say, an inflation target, how closely should it try to meet that target?

Suppose that the target for inflation is 2%, but the current inflation rate is 5%. Should the central bank try to decrease inflation to 2% as fast as it can, or should it decrease it slowly? The fact that in the short run, money growth affects both output and inflation suggests that the answer should be: not too fast. Decreasing inflation quickly is likely to require a sharp recession, something the central bank should try to avoid. How slowly or how fast should the central bank go toward the target? In answer to this question, John Taylor from Stanford University has suggested a rule that the central bank may want to follow. **Taylor's rule** is as follows:

Let π be the rate of inflation, and π^* be the target rate of inflation. Let i be the nominal interest rate, and i^* be the target nominal interest rate—the nominal interest rate associated with the target rate of inflation π^* in the medium run. Let u be the unemployment rate, and u_n be the natural unemployment rate.

As we saw in Chapter 10: In the medium run, the real interest rate is given, so the nominal interest rate moves one for one with the inflation rate: If $r = 3\%$ and the target inflation rate $\pi^* = 2\%$, then the target nominal interest rate $i = 3\% + 2\% = 5\%$ If the target inflation rate π is 0% then $i^* = 3\% + 0\% = 3\%$.

Think of the central bank as choosing the nominal interest rate, i (recall from Chapter 5 that by controlling the money stock, the central bank can achieve any short-term nominal interest rate it wants). Then, Taylor argued, the central bank should follow this rule:

$$i = i^* + a(\pi - \pi^*) - b(u - u_n)$$

where a and b are positive coefficients. Let us look at what the rule says:

- If inflation is equal to target inflation ($\pi = \pi^*$), and the unemployment rate is equal to the natural rate ($u = u_n$), then the central bank should set the nominal interest rate i equal to its target value i^*. This way, the economy can stay on the same path, with inflation equal to the target and unemployment equal to the natural rate.
- If inflation is higher than the target ($\pi > \pi^*$), the central bank should increase the nominal interest rate above i^*. This higher interest rate will increase unemployment, and this increase in unemployment will lead to a decrease in inflation.

The coefficient *a* should therefore reflect how much the central bank cares about unemployment versus inflation. The higher the *a*, the more the central bank will increase the interest rate in response to inflation; the more the economy will slow down; the faster the inflation will return to the target.

In any case, Taylor pointed out, *a* should be larger than 1. Why? Because what matters for spending is the real interest rate, not the nominal interest rate. When inflation increases, the central bank, if it wants to decrease spending and output, must increase the *real* interest rate. In other words, it must increase the nominal interest rate more than one for one with inflation.

This ignores the difference between expected inflation and actual inflation. A more precise statement is that the nominal interest rate must increase more than one for one with expected inflation:

$$i\uparrow \; > \; \pi^e\uparrow \;\Rightarrow r(\equiv i - \pi^e)\uparrow$$

- If unemployment is higher than the natural rate ($u > u_n$), the central bank should decrease the nominal interest rate. The lower nominal interest rate will increase activity, leading to a decrease in unemployment. Like the coefficient *a*, the coefficient *b* should reflect how much the central bank cares about unemployment relative to inflation. The higher the *b*, the more the central bank will be willing to deviate from target inflation to keep unemployment close to the natural rate.

What values of *a* and *b* would a central bank choose if it cared only about inflation?

In stating this rule, Taylor did not argue that it should be followed blindly: Many other events, such as an exchange rate crisis or the need to change the composition of spending and thus the mix between monetary and fiscal policy, justify changing the nominal interest rate for reasons other than those included in the rule. But, he argued, the rule provides a useful way of thinking about monetary policy: Choose a target rate of inflation, and then try to achieve it taking into account not only current inflation but also current unemployment.

Since it was first introduced, The Taylor Rule has generated a lot of interest, from both researchers and central banks:

- Interestingly, researchers looking at the behaviour of both the Federal Reserve in the United States and the Bundesbank in Germany have found that although neither of these two central banks thought of itself as following the Taylor rule, this rule actually describes their behaviour over the last 15–20 years quite well.

- Other researchers have explored whether it is possible to improve on this simple rule: for example, whether the nominal interest rate should be allowed to respond not only to current inflation but also to expected future inflation.

- Yet other researchers have discussed whether central banks should adopt an explicit interest rate rule and follow it closely or whether they should use the rule more informally and feel free to deviate from the rule when appropriate. We will return to this issue in discussing the behaviour of the Federal Reserve in the next section.

- In general, most central banks have now shifted from thinking in terms of nominal money growth to thinking in terms of an interest rate rule. Whatever happens to nominal money growth as a result of following such a nominal interest rate rule is increasingly seen as unimportant, both by the central banks and by financial markets. The Bank of Canada is certainly one of the "most central banks" in this sense.

Inflation Targeting

In many countries, central banks have defined as their primary goal the achievement of a low inflation rate, both in the short run and in the medium run. This is known as **inflation targeting**. The logic is simple: Inflation may not be under the control of the central bank but it is what the central bank and the public care about.

- Trying to achieve a given inflation target in the medium run would seem, and indeed is, a clear improvement over trying to achieve a nominal money growth target. After all, in the medium run, the primary goal of monetary policy is to achieve a given rate of inflation. Better to have an inflation rate as the target than a nominal money growth target, which, as you have seen, may not lead to the desired rate of inflation.

- Trying to achieve a given inflation target in the short run would appear to be much more controversial. Focusing exclusively on inflation would seem to eliminate any role monetary policy could play to reduce output fluctuations. But, in fact, this is not the case. To see why, return to the Phillips curve relation between inflation, π_t, lagged inflation, π_{t-1}, and the deviation of the unemployment rate u_t from the natural rate of unemployment, u_n, [Equation (8.10)]:

$$\pi_t = \pi_{t-1} - \alpha(u_t - u_n)$$

Let the inflation rate target be π^*. Suppose the central bank could achieve its inflation target exactly in every period. Then, the relation would become:

$$\pi^* = \pi^* - \alpha(u_t - u_n)$$

<aside>
$0 = -\alpha(u_t - u_n)$
$\Rightarrow u_t = u$
</aside>

The unemployment rate u_t would always equal u_n, the natural rate of unemployment; by implication, output would always be equal to the natural level of output. In effect, inflation targeting would lead the central bank to act in such a way as to eliminate all deviations of output from its natural level.

The intuition: If the central bank saw that an adverse demand shock was going to lead to a recession, it would know that absent a monetary expansion, the economy would experience a decline in inflation below the target rate of inflation.

To maintain stable inflation, the central bank would then rely on a monetary expansion to avoid the recession. The converse would apply to a favourable demand shock. Fearing an increase in inflation above the target rate, the central bank would rely on a monetary contraction to slow the economy and keep output at the natural level of output. As a result of this active monetary policy, output would remain at the natural level of output all the time.

The result we have just derived—that inflation targeting eliminates deviations of output from its natural level—is too strong, however, for two reasons:

- The central bank cannot always achieve the rate of inflation it wants in the short run. So, suppose that, for example, the central bank was not able to achieve its desired rate of inflation last year, so π_{t-1} is higher than π^*. Then, it is not clear that the central bank should try to hit its target this year, and achieve $\pi_t = \pi^*$. The Phillips curve relation implies that such a decrease in inflation would require a potentially large increase in unemployment. We return to this issue below.

- Like all other macroeconomic relations, the Phillips curve relation above does not hold exactly. For example, inflation will increase even when the unemployment is at the natural rate of unemployment. In this case, the central bank will face a more difficult choice: whether to keep unemployment at the natural rate and allow inflation to increase or to increase unemployment above the natural rate, to keep inflation in check.

These qualifications are important, but the general point remains. Inflation targeting makes good sense in the medium run and allows for monetary policy to stabilize output around its natural level in the short run.

25–3 | The Bank of Canada in Action

<aside>
The Bank of Canada's Web site (**www.bankofcanada.ca**) gives a lot of information about how the Bank of Canada is organized and what it does.
</aside>

Let us end this chapter by looking at how the Bank of Canada actually designs and carries out monetary policy.

The Bank's Mandate

<aside>
A brief (and very reasonable) history of the Bank is available on its Web page.
</aside>

The Bank was formed in 1935. The **Bank of Canada Act** has been amended many times since then, but the preamble still gives the Bank the responsibility: *to regulate credit and currency in the best interests of the economic life of the nation, to control and protect the external value of the national monetary unit and to mitigate by its influence fluctuations in the general level of production, trade, prices, and employment, so far as may be possible within the scope of monetary action, and generally to promote the economic and financial welfare of Canada.*

Such a vague mandate leaves a lot of room for interpretation. What are the best interests of the nation? Should the Bank focus on obtaining stable income growth and high employment, low and stable inflation, some particular value for the Canadian dollar, low interest rates, or some undetermined combination of all? Since its founding, the Bank has, at one time or another, focused on each of these goals. During the constitutional debate that led up to the Meech Lake Accord of 1987, some economists, including the governor of the Bank of Canada, pressed for a statement in the new Constitution that would narrow the Bank's mandate to maintaining price stability. Although interesting, this suggestion was quickly shunted to the side by more pressing issues for renewing the Confederation. Undaunted, the Bank has, since 1988, chosen to focus almost exclusively on controlling inflation. The Bank has adopted this position because it has determined (largely by trial and error) that providing price stability is the best thing it can do to encourage a well-functioning economy.

The Instruments of Monetary Policy

In Chapter 4, we emphasized the link between money and reserves so that the supply of money equalled the demand for money (equation (4.11)). Using the equality of the demand and supply of money in equilibrium, equation (4.11) is written as:

$$\frac{1}{c + \theta (1 - c)} = \frac{M}{H} \tag{25.1}$$

M is money supply, the sum of currency and chequable deposits. H is the monetary base—the sum of currency and reserves held by banks. In some countries, such as the United States, and Canada before 1994, banks must hold reserves that equal a certain fraction of their deposits. In Canada, since 1994, reserves (the commercial banks' deposits at the Bank of Canada) are not held to meet legal requirements but to facilitate the clearing of cheques and other transfers between commercial banks; that is why they are often called **settlement balances**. The parameter c is the ratio of currency to chequable deposits; θ denotes the ratio of settlement balances held by commercial banks to chequable deposits. The expression $1/[c + \theta (1 - c)]$ is called the money multiplier. The main influence on monetary policy is on H, the quantity of high-powered money, and thus on M, the overall quantity of money.

Only a small number (currently 13) of the financial institutions in Canada hold deposits at the Bank of Canada. Strictly speaking, we should refer to them as "direct clearers" rather than banks, but we will stick with the simpler label. Every night, transfers drawn on these banks are matched up, and the balance is settled by transferring deposits at the Bank of Canada. For example, suppose bank A holds claims, such as cheques drawn on bank B, of $10 billion, while bank B holds claims on bank A of $11 billion. The difference of $1 billion is paid by transferring that amount from bank A's account held at the Bank of Canada to the account held by bank B. Deposits at the Bank of Canada pay only a low rate of interest, 50 basis points less than the Bank Rate. So, the banks have an incentive to minimize these balances. What if bank A doesn't have enough in its account to cover this transfer? It can borrow the necessary amount from either the Bank of Canada or from another commercial bank that has extra money in its account. These loans are for one day only or "overnight." The Bank of Canada fixes a band of 50 basis points (one-half of 1%) for such overnight loans. The Bank of Canada announces it will make overnight loans at the highest interest rate in that band. This interest rate is called the Bank Rate. Thus, the overnight rate on one-day loans between the commercial banks is never higher than the Bank Rate because any commercial bank offered a loan by another commercial bank at a rate higher than the Bank Rate will choose to borrow from the Bank of Canada instead because its rate is lower. Thus, the Bank of Canada effectively sets a maximum interest rate in the large market for overnight loans.

On the Bank of Canada Web page, both the **target for the overnight rate** (always 25 basis points less than the Bank Rate) and the Bank Rate are posted. Changes in the target for the overnight rate and thus in the Bank Rate are announced using a predetermined schedule, about every four to six weeks. The schedule is also posted on the Bank's Web site.

Beginning in late 1998, large-value transfers (amounts of over $50,000) have been cleared in real time. Large-value items represent a very small fraction of the settlements exchanged but account for over 90% of their value. Same-day settlement of large-value items allows the banks to more accurately estimate their settlement needs and allows them to reduce their balances held at the Bank.

From March 1980 to February 1996, the Bank Rate was set equal to the average interest rate, established at the auction of three-month Government of Canada Treasury bills, plus 25 basis points. The new definition of the Bank Rate went into effect February 22, 1996.

In a world of perfect certainty, it would not matter if the Bank of Canada fixed the level of reserves to achieve a given market-clearing interest rate in the overnight market or if it fixed the market-clearing interest rate to obtain a given level of reserves. In practice, because of uncertainties in the links between its actions and the subsequent path of output and prices, the Bank follows the second strategy. Having determined a desired path for the Bank Rate (following a procedure to be described below), the Bank of Canada then adjusts reserves in order to keep the overnight interest rate in its band. The main tool in managing reserves is transfers of federal government accounts. The federal government maintains fairly large cash balances to finance its activities. These balances are held in accounts at the Bank of Canada and private banks. Managing these balances provides an effective way to change the supply of reserves. For example, a transfer of $1 billion from government's account at the Bank of Canada to bank A creates an increase of $1 billion in the reserves held by bank A.

The Bank also makes loans called *Purchase and Resale Agreements (PRA)*. While an SPRA is made on ▶ the initiative of the Bank, a PRA is made on the initiative of a qualified borrower, such as an investment dealer.

An opposite transfer reduces reserves by the same amount. Other tools for influencing the interest rate in the overnight market are open-market operations, such as short-term loans called *Special Purchase and Resale Agreements (SPRA)* and short-term borrowing called *Sale and Repurchase Agreements (SRA)*. Since 1985, traditional open-market operations involving the purchase or sale of Treasury bills have rarely been used to "fine-tune" the quantity of reserves. However, the Bank uses purchases of Treasury bills to expand its asset holdings and determine the trend in monetary expansion.

The Practice of Policy

How does the Bank decide what policy to follow?

Because the actions of the monetary authority feed into the growth of nominal income and prices with long and variable lags, the Bank of Canada needs to keep its sights on what it expects will happen to the economy six months to several years ahead. The Bank goes through a cycle. Each time the Bank Rate needs to be announced, the Bank's staff prepares forecasts and simulations of the effects of different monetary policies. A path for the Bank Rate is sketched out for the next few years that will generate inflation consistent with the Bank's goals. Within this cycle, the Bank frequently updates its estimates of the path of the economy and reassesses its desired path for the Bank Rate. Information about the path of short-term interest rates plays a role. If short-term rates are lower than what the Bank expected, it is often a signal that aggregate demand in the economy has not grown as quickly as the Bank had forecast. The Bank takes this as a signal that it should reduce the Bank Rate in order to stimulate growth in aggregate demand. Because of the importance of international trade, the Bank also keeps an eye on the exchange rate; it views sharp declines in the exchange rate as stimulating aggregate demand and as a potential signal to raise the Bank Rate. Of course, both interest rates and the exchange rate can move in response to shocks that have no consequence for inflation. The Bank tries to use a variety of information sources to isolate the source of the shocks that appear and to determine if any response is warranted. Since November 2000, the Bank of Canada has preset a schedule, one-year ahead, for the announcement of policy decisions with respect to interest rate changes. A press release, explaining the reasons behind the decision to raise, lower, or maintain the interest rate is part of any announcement. A committee of senior Bank of Canada officials makes the interest rate decision. It is thought that a preset schedule is a better way to operate monetary policy in Canada. In particular, having a Canadian schedule that is distinct from a similar schedule in the United States is a useful way to emphasize the separation of Canadian and American monetary policies under a flexible exchange rate and with a distinct inflation target as the focus of Canadian monetary policy.

The Role of Target Ranges

Since 1991, the Bank of Canada has announced explicit targets for the rate of inflation. The target was set at 3% for 1992 and was reduced slowly to 2% in 1995, where it has remained since. In fact, the Bank announces a range that is its target, plus or minus 1%. How close has the Bank come to hitting its **inflation targets**? The answer is given in Figure 25–3, which plots the rate of inflation for each year since 1993 and gives the Bank's target range since 1992. The Bank prefers to use a measure of the CPI that excludes volatile components, such as food, energy, and the effect of indirect taxes. Although the Bank does not always hit its target, the number of errors since 1992 has been on the low side. That is, either inflation has been in the Bank's target range or it has fallen below.

Why should the Bank announce such a range? There are two reasons:

1. The target serves as a signal of the Bank's intentions. By adopting a target of gradually declining inflation after 1992, the Bank tried to signal its commitment to achieving a lower inflation rate.

2. The target serves as a benchmark for judging the Bank's behaviour. If actual inflation ends up higher than the Bank's range, then the Bank has some explaining to do. Similarly, raising the Bank Rate when inflation is below its target range (as the Bank did in January 1998) forces the Bank to explain its actions. As already noted, the Bank of Canada cut its target interest rate during 2001 from 5.75% to 2.25%. Inflation was not below its target. Rather, as the Bank explained, Canada's economy was slowing and world events on September 11, 2001, caused a further slowdown and even more uncertainty. Cutting interest rates to increase demand in Canada was an appropriate response. Unless it can provide a convincing explanation, the Bank risks losing its credibility and leaves financial markets worrying about how to interpret monetary policy.

With these two functions in mind, the Bank sets the target ranges for inflation and then adjusts monetary policy during the year. The width of the range indicates the degree of flexibility that the Bank thinks it may need. The Bank then tries to keep inflation within these bounds. But, when faced with either unexpectedly large special factors or macroeconomic shocks, the Bank is willing to tolerate a rate of inflation outside its range. It knows that as long as it can convince the markets that such a deviation is justified it will not lose credibility.

Does this way of running monetary policy work? The answer is that it has worked very well since 1992. The decline in the Bank's targets has been accompanied by a similar decline in inflation around the OECD, although Canada's performance on inflation has been better than average. During 2001, aggressive interest rate cuts seem to have prevented a severe recession. It remains to be seen how well the Bank's monetary policy process will work if inflation starts to challenge the upper bound of its target range.

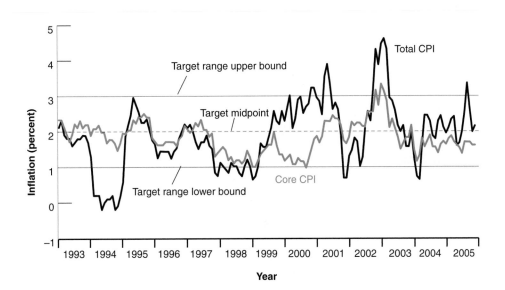

FIGURE 25–3

Inflation in Canada, 1993–2005: Realized Inflation Rate and Target Inflation Range

Inflation has been on the low side of the target range since 1992 and has fallen below the target range on several occasions.

Source: Total Inflation using CANSIM II variable V735319; *Core Inflation* using CAMSIM II variable V36398.

On the Optimal Rate of Inflation

- Inflation is down to very low levels in most OECD countries. One question facing central banks is whether they should try to achieve zero inflation—that is, price stability.

- The main arguments for zero inflation are the following:
  —Inflation, together with an imperfectly indexed tax system, leads to tax distortions.
  —Because of money illusion, inflation leads people and firms to make incorrect decisions.
  —Higher inflation typically comes with higher inflation variability, creating more uncertainty and making it more difficult for people and firms to make the right decisions about the future.
  —As a target, price stability has a simplicity and a credibility that a positive inflation target does not have.

- There are also arguments for maintaining low but positive inflation.
  —Revenues from money growth (seignorage) allow for lower taxes elsewhere. However, this argument is quantitatively unimportant when comparing inflation rates of 0% and, say, 4%.
  —Positive actual and expected inflation allow the central bank to achieve negative real interest rates, an option that can be useful when fighting a recession.
  —Positive inflation allows firms to achieve real wage cuts when needed without requiring nominal wage cuts.
  —A further decrease from the current positive rate of inflation to zero would imply an increase in unemployment for some time, and this transition cost may exceed whatever benefits come from zero inflation.

On the Design of Monetary Policy

- Once a central bank has decided what rate of inflation it wants to achieve, it faces two issues. First, should it choose a target for money growth or for inflation? Second, how closely should it try to meet the target?

- Because of shifts in the demand for money, the relation between $M1B$ growth and inflation is not tight. Thus, targeting $M1B$ growth would lead to large movements in inflation.

- Growth rates of monetary aggregates that include money and other liquid assets, such as $M2$, move more closely with inflation. But the relation is still not very tight. And more importantly, these larger aggregates are not under the control of the central bank.

- These problems have led several central banks to shift to inflation targeting. The issue then is how close the central bank should try to stay to the target.

- Taylor's rule gives a useful way of thinking about how the central bank should operate. The central bank should move its interest rate in response to two main factors: the deviation of the inflation rate from its target and the deviation of the unemployment rate from the natural rate. A central bank that follows this rule will stabilize activity and achieve its target inflation rate in the medium run.

On the Bank of Canada

- The Bank of Canada was founded in 1935 *"to regulate credit and currency in the best interests of the economic life of the nation."* The Bank influences the level of short-term interest rates by controlling reserves. Since 1994 (and in practice for several years before that), these reserves have been deposits held to settle transfers between the direct clearers. The main instrument of monetary policy is the transfer of federal government balances between the Bank and the direct clearers. The Bank also acts to influence interest rates directly in the overnight market through loans and borrowings that go by the acronyms SPRA and SRA, respectively.

- The Bank sketches out the path for its Bank Rate that will allow it to hit its inflation targets approximately six months to several years ahead. Within the six-month cycle, the Bank constantly monitors its assumptions and forecasts. On a week-to-week basis, the Bank pays particular attention to the movements in short-term interest rates and the multilateral exchange rate. Unexpected movements in these variables sometimes prompt a change in the Bank Rate.

- Every few years, the Bank announces a target range for inflation. Since 1995, the target has been 2% with a band of ±1%.

- The Bank has done a good job of hitting its inflation targets since 1992, although inflation has sometimes fallen below the target range.

QUESTIONS AND PROBLEMS

1. TRUE/FALSE/UNCERTAIN

a. The most important argument for a positive rate of inflation in the OECD countries is seignorage.

b. The Bank of Canada should target *M2* growth.

c. Fighting inflation should be the Bank's only purpose.

d. Announcing target ranges for money growth would limit the flexibility and therefore the usefulness of monetary policy.

e. We would do just as well if we replaced the Governor of the Bank of Canada with Taylor's rule.

f. The higher the inflation rate, the higher is the effective tax rate on income.

2. MONEY DEMAND SHIFTS

How would each of the following affect the demand for *M1B* and *M2*?

a. Banks reduce penalties on early withdrawal from time deposits.

b. Government forbids the use of money market funds for cheque-writing purposes.

c. Government legislates a tax on all ATM transactions.

d. The federal government decides to impose a tax on all transactions in short-term government securities.

3. NOMINAL INTEREST RATES, INFLATION, AND TAXES

Suppose you have a mortgage of $50,000. Consider two cases:

i. Expected inflation is 0%; the nominal interest rate on your mortgage is 4%.

ii. Expected inflation is 10%; the nominal interest rate on your mortgage is 14%.

a. What is the real interest rate you are paying on your mortgage in each case?

b. Suppose that you can deduct nominal mortgage interest payments from your income before paying the income tax (as is the case in the United States). Assume that the tax rate is 25%. Thus, for each dollar you pay in mortgage interest, you pay 25 cents less in taxes, in effect getting a subsidy from government for your mortgage costs. Compute, in each case, the real interest rate you are paying on your mortgage, taking into account this subsidy.

c. "In Canada, inflation is good for homeowners." Discuss this statement.

4. *M2* AND *M1B*

Suppose that *M1B* growth is very high but *M2* growth is equal to zero. Should you worry about inflation? Explain.

5. MONETARY POLICY IN ACTION

Using equation (25.1), show three ways in which monetary policy can decrease the interest rate, given the level of output. In each case, explain how it works.

6. NEGATIVE REAL INTEREST RATES

"The worry that with deflation real interest rates cannot be negative is misplaced. Fiscal policy can decrease the cost of borrowing as much as it wants, by offering subsidies to borrowers." Discuss this statement.

7. THE BANK OF CANADA [WEB]

Access the Web site of the Bank of Canada (**www.bankofcanada.ca**).

a. Find the most recent targeting agreement and identify the target for inflation.

b. Read the most recent press release concerning a change in interest rates and ask, "Does the Bank seem to be more worried about a slowdown in growth or a pickup in the pace of inflation?"

c. What is happening to the target interest rate?

8. INFLATION TARGETS AND TAYLOR RULES

Many countries around the world have set explicit inflation targets for the central bank. Suppose the inflation target is π^* and the Phillips curve looks like the one described in the chapter:

$$\pi_t = \pi_{t-1} + \alpha(u_t - u_n)$$

a. If the central bank is able to keep the inflation rate equal to the target inflation rate every period, does this imply that there will be dramatic fluctuations in unemployment?

b. Given your answer to (a), should all countries adopt inflation targets?

c. Explain how the Taylor rule implements an inflation target both directly and indirectly.

FURTHER READING

For evidence of nominal wage rigidity and the scope for inflation to facilitate real wage adjustments, see the results of a survey of managers by Alan Blinder and Don Choi, in "A Shred of Evidence on Theories of Wage Rigidity," *Quarterly Journal of Economics*, 1990, pp. 1003–1016.

For a discussion of the pros and cons of low inflation, look at George Akerlof, William Dickens, and George Perry, "The Macroeconomics of Low Inflation," *Brookings Papers on Economic Activity*, Vol. 1, 1996.

For more details on how the Bank of Canada operates, download "The Transmission of Monetary Policy in Canada" from the Bank of Canada's Web site. It contains articles from the *Bank of Canada Review* that outline the details of monetary policy during the first half of the 1990s.

It is a measure of the controversial nature of the 1990s disinflations in both Canada and the United States that books that dealt with the optimal rate of inflation and other macroeconomic issues became bestsellers. In Canada, Linda McQuaig's *Shooting the Hippo: Death by Deficit and Other Canadian Myths* (Viking Press, 1995) is popular. In the United States, Paul Krugman's book *The Age of Diminished Expectations* (The MIT Press, 1992) dealt with similar issues. Both books are nontechnical and lively.

"Modern Central Banking," written by Stanley Fischer for the 300th anniversary of the Bank of England, published in *The Future of Central Banking*, edited by Forrest Capie, Stanley Fischer, Charles Goodhart, and Norbert Schnadt (Cambridge: Cambridge University Press, 1995), provides a very interesting discussion of the current issues in central banking. Read also "What Central Bankers Could Learn from Academics—and Vice Versa," by Alan Blinder, in *Journal of Economic Perspectives*, Spring 1997, pp. 3–19.

On inflation targeting, read "Inflation Targeting: A New Framework for Monetary Policy?" by Ben Bernanke and Frederic Mishkin, in *Journal of Economic Perspectives*, Spring 1997, pp. 97–116.

For more on the Taylor rule, read John Taylor, "Discretion versus Policy Rules in Practice," in *Carnegie Rochester Conference Series on Public Policy 39* (Amsterdam: North-Holland, 1993), pp. 195–214.

A Bank of Canada conference volume, *Issues in Inflation Targeting*, will be published sometime in 2006. The paper by Christopher Ragan "The Road Ahead for Canadian Inflation Targeting," is a nontechnical summary. Finally, David E.W. Laidler and William B.P. Robson's book *Two Percent Target: Canadian Monetary Policy Since 1991* (C.D. Howe Institute, Policy Study 37, 2004) contains a detailed history of Canadian monetary policy from 1991 to 2004.

CHAPTER 26
FISCAL POLICY: A SUMMING UP

In this chapter, we do for fiscal policy what we did for monetary policy in Chapter 25—review what we have learned and tie up remaining loose ends.

Let us first briefly review what we have learned (the Focus box "Fiscal Policy: What We Have Learned and Where" gives a more detailed summary).

- In the short run, a budget deficit (triggered, say, by a decrease in taxes) increases demand and output. What happens to investment is ambiguous.

- In the medium run, output returns to its natural level. The interest rate and the composition of spending are different, however. The interest rate is higher; investment is lower.

- In the long run, lower investment implies a lower capital stock, and therefore a lower level of output.

In deriving these conclusions, however, we did not pay close attention to the government budget constraint, that is, to the relation among debt, deficits, government spending, and taxes. This chapter's first task is to do just that: to look at government's budget constraint and its implications. Having done so, we examine several fiscal policy issues where this constraint plays an important role, from the proposition that deficits do not really matter to the dangers of accumulating very high levels of public debt. Finally, we return to the history of Canadian government budget issues in the last 30 years.

- In Chapter 3, we looked at the role of government spending and taxes in determining demand and output in the short run. We saw how in the short run, increases in government spending and decreases in taxes both increase output.

- In Chapter 5, we looked at the short-run effects of fiscal policy on output and the interest rate. We saw how a fiscal contraction leads to decreases in both output and the interest rate. We also saw how fiscal and monetary policies can be used to affect both the level and the composition of output.

- In Chapter 7, we looked at the effects of fiscal policy when the economy is open to trade. We saw how fiscal policy affects both output and the trade balance and examined the relation between budget deficits and trade deficits. We saw how fiscal policy and exchange-rate adjustments can be used to affect both the level and the composition of output.

- In Chapter 8, we looked at the role of fiscal policy in an economy with open goods and financial markets. We saw how in the presence of international capital mobility, the effects of fiscal policy depend on the exchange-rate regime. Fiscal policy has a much stronger effect on output under fixed exchange rates than under flexible exchange rates.

- In Chapter 10, we looked at the effects of fiscal policy in the short run and the medium run. We saw that in the medium run (taking the capital stock as given), changes in fiscal policy have no effect on output and are simply reflected in a different composition of spending.

- In Chapter 15, we looked at how saving and thus budget deficits affect the level of capital accumulation and the level of output in the long run. We saw how once capital accumulation is taken into account, larger deficits decrease capital accumulation, leading to a lower level of output in the long run.

- In Chapter 21, we looked at the short-run effects of fiscal policy, taking into account not only its direct effects through taxes and government spending but also its effects on expectations. We saw how the effects of a deficit reduction on output depend on expectations of future fiscal and monetary policies. We also saw how a deficit reduction may, in some circumstances, be expansionary, even in the short run.

- In Chapter 23, we looked at the relation among fiscal policy, money growth, and inflation. We saw how budget deficits must be financed either by borrowing or by money creation. When money creation becomes the main source of finance, the result of large deficits is high money growth and hyperinflation.

- In Chapter 24, we looked at the problems facing fiscal policy makers, from uncertainty about the effects of policy to issues of time consistency and credibility. We discussed the pros and cons of restraints on the conduct of fiscal policy, such as a constitutional amendment to balance the budget.

- In this chapter, we look further at the implications of the budget constraint facing government and discuss current issues of fiscal policy in Canada.

26-1 | The Government Budget Constraint

Suppose that starting from a balanced budget, government cuts taxes, creating a deficit. What will happen to debt over time? Will government need to increase taxes later? If so, by how much?

To answer these questions, we must start with the definition of the budget deficit. We can write the budget deficit in year t as:

$$\text{deficit}_t = rB_{t-1} + G_t - T_t \tag{26.1}$$

All variables are in real terms. B_{t-1} is government debt at the end of year $t - 1$, or equivalently, at the beginning of year t; r is the real interest rate, which we will take to be constant here. Thus, rB_{t-1} equals the real interest payments on the existing government debt. G_t is government spending on goods and services during year t. T_t is taxes minus transfers during year t. In words: The budget deficit equals spending, including interest payments on the debt, minus taxes net of transfers.

Do not confuse the words "deficit" and "debt." (Many journalists and politicians do.) Debt is a *stock*, what government owes as a result of past deficits. The deficit is a flow, how much government borrows in a given year.

Note two characteristics of equation (26.1):

- We measure interest payments as real interest payments—the product of the *real* interest rate times existing debt—rather than as actual interest payments—the product of the nominal interest rate times existing debt. As we discuss in the Focus box "Inflation Accounting and the Measurement of Deficits," this is the correct way of measuring interest payments. However, official measures of the deficit include actual (nominal) interest payments and are therefore incorrect. The correct measure of the deficit is sometimes called the **inflation-adjusted deficit**.

- For consistency with our definition of G as spending on goods and services earlier, G does not include transfer payments. Transfers are instead subtracted from taxes so that T stands for taxes minus transfers. Official measures of government spending add transfers to spending on goods and services and define revenues as taxes, not taxes net of transfers. These are only accounting conventions. Whether transfers are added to spending or subtracted from taxes makes a difference to the measurement of G and T but clearly does not affect the measure of the deficit.

◀ Let G denote spending on goods and services, Tr denotes transfers, and Tax denotes total taxes. Then,

$Deficit = G + Tr - Tax$

This can be rewritten in two (equivalent) ways:

$Deficit = G - (Tax - Tr)$

The deficit is equal to spending on goods and services, minus net taxes—total taxes minus transfers. This is the way we write it in the text:

$Deficit = (G + Tr) - Tax$

The deficit is equal to total spending—spending on goods and services plus transfers—minus total taxes. This is the way government reports spending and revenues.

The **government budget constraint** then simply states that the *change in government debt during year t* is equal to the *deficit during year t*:

$$B_t - B_{t-1} = \text{deficit}_t$$

If government runs a deficit, government debt increases. If government runs a surplus, government debt decreases.

Using the definition of the deficit, we can rewrite the government budget constraint as:

$$B_t - B_{t-1} = rB_{t-1} + G_t - T_t \qquad (26.2)$$

The government budget constraint links the change in debt to the initial level of debt (which affects interest payments) and to current government spending and taxes.

It is often convenient to decompose the deficit into the sum of two terms:

- Interest payments on the debt,
- The difference between spending and taxes, This second term is called the **primary deficit** (equivalently, is called the **primary surplus**).

Using this decomposition, we can rewrite equation (26.2) as:

$$\underbrace{B_t - B_{t-1}}_{\text{Change in the debt}} = \underbrace{rB_{t-1}}_{\text{Interest payments}} + \underbrace{G_t - T_t}_{\text{Primary deficit}}$$

Or, moving to the right and reorganizing:

$$B_t = (1 + r)B_{t-1} + \underbrace{G_t - T_t}_{\text{Primary deficit}} \qquad (26.3)$$

Debt at the end of year t equals $(1 + r)$ times debt at the end of year $t - 1$, plus the primary deficit during year t, $(G_t - T_t)$. This relation will prove very useful in what follows.

Current versus Future Taxes

Let us look at the implications of a one-year decrease in taxes for the path of debt and future taxes. Start from a situation where, until year 1, government has balanced its budget, so that debt is equal to zero. During year 1, government decreases taxes by 1 for one year. Thus, debt at the end of year 1, B_1, is equal to 1. What happens thereafter? Let us consider different cases.

Official measures of the budget deficit are constructed as nominal interest payments, iB, plus spending on goods and services, G, minus taxes net of transfers, T (we have dropped the time indexes, which are not needed here):

$$\text{official measure of the deficit} = iB + G - T$$

This is an accurate measure of the *change in nominal debt*. If it is positive, government is spending more than it receives and must therefore issue new debt. If it is negative, government buys debt back.

But it is not an accurate measure of the *change in real debt*, the change in how much government owes, expressed in terms of goods rather than dollars. To see why not, suppose the official measure of the deficit is equal to zero, so government neither issues nor buys back debt, and the amount of nominal debt remains the same. Suppose inflation is positive and equal to 10%. Then, at the end of the year, the real value of the debt has decreased by 10%. If we define—as we should—the deficit as the change in the real value of the debt of government, government is, in fact, running a budget surplus equal to 10% times the initial level of debt.

More generally, if B is debt and π is inflation, the official measure of the deficit overstates the correct measure by an amount equal to πB. Put another way, the correct measure of the deficit is obtained by subtracting πB from the official measure:

$$\begin{aligned}
\text{correct measure of the deficit} &= iB + G - T - \pi B \\
&= (i - \pi)B + G - T \\
&= rB + G - T
\end{aligned}$$

where $r = i - \pi$ is the real interest rate. The correct measure of the deficit is thus equal to real interest payments plus government spending minus taxes net of transfers, the measure we have used in the text. (Note that r is equal here to the nominal interest rate minus *actual* inflation and should be more accurately called the "realized real interest rate," to distinguish it from the real interest rate, which is equal to the nominal interest rate minus *expected* inflation.)

The difference between the official and correct measures of the deficit equals πB. So, the higher the rate of inflation, π, or the higher the level of debt, B, the more inaccurate the official measure is. In countries in which both inflation and debt are high, the official measure may record a very large budget deficit, when, in fact, real government debt is actually decreasing. This is why you should always do the inflation adjustment before deriving conclusions about the position of fiscal policy.

Figure 1 plots the official measure and an inflation-adjusted measure of the federal budget deficit in Canada from 1970 to 2004. The official measure shows a substantially higher deficit (and a smaller surplus) in all years. There is positive debt outstanding in all years and inflation is positive in all years. From 1970 to 1975, although the actual deficit is positive, the inflation-adjusted deficit is negative. These are years of high inflation. With lower inflation in the 1990s, the two measures become more similar.

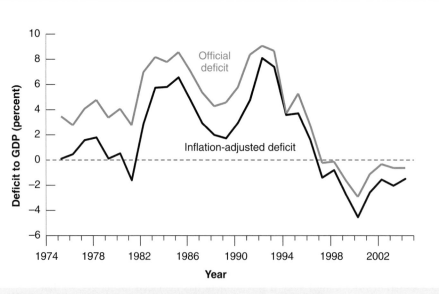

FIGURE 1   Official and Inflation-Adjusted Budget Deficits for Canada, 1970–2004

Source: Deficit from Table 45, *Fiscal Reference Tables*, October 2004. Inflation adjustment is consumer price index inflation multiplied by the ratio of gross federal debt to GDP from Figure 24–3.

Full Repayment in Year 2. Suppose that government decides to repay the debt fully during year 2. From equation (26.3), the budget constraint for year 2 is given by:

$$B_2 = (1 + r) B_1 + (G_2 - T_2)$$

If the debt is fully repaid during year 2, then debt at the end of year 2 is equal to zero: $B_2 = 0$. Replacing B_1 by 1 and B_2 by 0 in the preceding equation gives:

$$T_2 - G_2 = (1 + r)$$

To repay the debt fully during year 2, government must run a primary surplus equal to $(1 + r)$. It can do so in one of two ways: a decrease in spending or an increase in taxes. We will assume here and in what follows that the adjustment comes through taxes so that the path of spending is unaffected. It follows that the decrease in taxes by 1 below normal during year 1 must be offset by an increase in taxes by $(1 + r)$ above normal during year 2. The path of taxes and debt corresponding to this case is given in Figure 26–1(a) (assuming a value for r of 10%). The black bars represent taxes during each year—as deviations from their initial level, and the green lines represent the level of debt at the end of each year.

Full repayment in year 2:
$T_1 \downarrow$ by 1
$\Rightarrow T_2 \uparrow$ by $(1 + r)$

Full Repayment in Year _t_. Now, suppose that government decides to wait until year t to increase taxes and repay the debt. So, from year 2 to year $t - 1$, the primary deficit is equal to zero. Let us work out what this implies for the level of debt at the beginning of year t (equivalently, the end of year $t - 1$).

During year 2, the primary deficit is zero. So, from equation (26.3), debt at the end of year 2 is:

$$B_2 = (1 + r) B_1 + 0 = (1 + r)$$

where the second equality follows from the fact that $B_1 = 1$.

With the primary deficit still equal to zero during year 3, debt at the end of year 3 is:

$$B_3 = (1 + r) B_2 + 0 = (1 + r) (1 + r) = (1 + r)^2$$

Solving for debt at the end of year 4 and so on, it is clear that as long as government keeps a primary deficit equal to zero, debt grows at a rate equal to the interest rate, and thus debt at the end of year $t - 1$ is given by:

$$B_{t-1} = (1 + r)^{t-2} \tag{26.4}$$

Despite the fact that taxes are cut only in year 1, debt keeps increasing over time, at a rate equal to the interest rate. The reason is simple: Although the primary deficit is equal to zero, debt is now positive, and so are interest payments on the debt. Each year, government must issue more debt to pay the interest on existing debt.

In year t, the year in which government decides to repay the debt, the budget constraint is:

$$B_t = (1 + r) B_{t-1} + (G_t - T_t)$$

If debt is fully repaid during year t, then B_t (debt at the end of year t) is zero. Replacing B_t by zero, and B_{t-1} by its expression from equation (26.4), gives:

$$0 = (1 + r)(1 + r)^{t-2} + (G_t - T_t)$$

Reorganizing and bringing $G_t - T_t$ to the right implies:

$$T_t - G_t = (1 + r)^{t-1}$$

Add exponents:
$(1 + r)(1 + r)^{t-2} =$
$(1 + r)^{t-1}$ (see Appendix 2).

To pay back the debt, government must run a primary surplus equal to $(1 + r)^{t-1}$ during year t. If the adjustment is done through taxes, the initial decrease in taxes of 1 during year 1 leads to an increase in taxes of $(1 + r)^{t-1}$ during year t. The path of taxes and debt corresponding to this case is given in Figure 26–1(b).

Full repayment in year t:
$T_1 \downarrow$ by 1
$\Rightarrow T_t \uparrow$ by $(1 + r)^{t-1}$

FIGURE 26-1

Tax Cuts, Debt Repayment, and Debt Stabilization

(a) If debt is fully repaid during year 2, the decrease in taxes of 1 in year 1 requires an increase in taxes equal to $(1 + r)$ in year 2. (b) If debt is fully repaid during year t, the decrease in taxes of 1 in year 1 requires an increase in taxes equal to $(1 + r)^{t-1}$ during year t. In this case, $t = 60$. (c) If debt is stabilized from year 2 on, then taxes must be permanently higher by r from year 2 on.

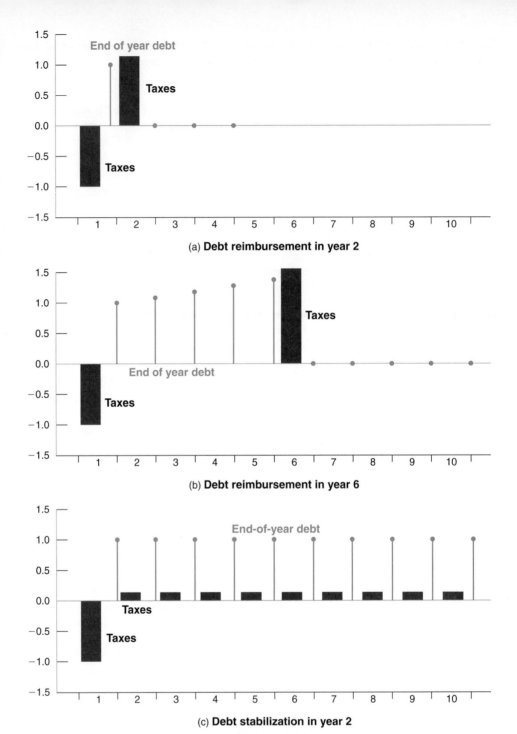

(a) **Debt reimbursement in year 2**

(b) **Debt reimbursement in year 6**

(c) **Debt stabilization in year 2**

This example yields our first basic conclusion. If spending is unchanged, a decrease in taxes must eventually be offset by an increase in taxes in the future. The longer government waits to increase taxes or the higher the real interest rate, the higher the eventual increase in taxes.

Debt and Primary Surpluses

We have assumed so far that government fully repays the debt. Let us now look at what happens to taxes if government only stabilizes the debt. (Stabilizing the debt means changing taxes or spending so that debt remains constant.)

Suppose that government decides to stabilize the debt from year 2 on. Stabilizing the debt from year 2 on means that debt at the end of year 2 and thereafter remains at the same level as at the end of year 1.

From equation (26.3), the budget constraint for year 2 is:

$$B_2 = (1 + r)B_1 + (G_2 - T_2)$$

Under our assumption that debt is stabilized in year 2, $B_2 = B_1 = 1$. Replacing in the preceding equation:

$$1 = (1 + r) + (G_2 - T_2)$$

Bringing $G_2 - T_2$ to the left side and reorganizing:

$$T_2 - G_2 = (1 + r) - 1 = r$$

To avoid a further increase in debt during year 1, government must run a primary surplus equal to real interest payments on the existing debt. It must do so in following years as well: Each year, the primary surplus must be sufficient to cover interest payments and thus to leave the debt level unchanged. The path of taxes and debt is shown in Figure 26–1(c): Debt remains at 1 from year 1 on. Taxes are permanently higher from year 1 on, by an amount equal to r; equivalently, from year 1 on, government runs a primary surplus equal to r.

The logic of this argument extends directly to the case where government waits until year t to stabilize. Whenever government stabilizes, it must from then on run a primary surplus sufficient to pay interest on the debt.

This example yields our second basic conclusion. The legacy of past deficits is higher government debt. To stabilize the debt, government must eliminate the deficit. To do so, it must run a primary surplus equal to the interest payments on the existing debt.

Stabilizing the debt from year 2 on:

$T_1 \downarrow$ by 1
$\Rightarrow T_2, T_3, \ldots \uparrow$ by r

The Evolution of the Debt-to-GDP Ratio

We have focused so far on the evolution of the level of debt. But in an economy in which output grows over time, it makes more sense to focus instead on the ratio of debt to output. To see how this change in focus modifies our conclusions, we need to go from equation (26.3) to an equation that gives the evolution of the **debt-to-GDP ratio**—the **debt ratio** for short.

To do this, first divide both sides of equation (26.3) by real output, Y_t, to get:

$$\frac{B_t}{Y_t} = (1 + r)\frac{B_{t-1}}{Y_t} + \frac{G_t - T_t}{Y_t}$$

Next, rewrite B_{t-1}/Y_t, as $(B_t/Y_{t-1})(Y_{t-1}/Y_t)$ (in other words, multiply top and bottom by Y_{t-1}):

$$\frac{B_t}{Y_t} = (1 + r)\left(\frac{Y_{t-1}}{Y_t}\right)\frac{B_{t-1}}{Y_{t-1}} + \frac{G_t - T_t}{Y_t}$$

We are nearly where we want to be: All the terms in the equation are now in terms of ratios to GDP$_t$ (Y_t). We can simplify further. Assume that output growth is constant, and denote the growth rate of output by g, so Y_{t-1}/Y_t can be written as $1/(1 + g)$. Use the approximation $(1 + r)/(1 + g) = 1 + r - g$. We can then rewrite the equation as:

$$\frac{B_t}{Y_t} = (1 + r - g)\frac{B_{t-1}}{Y_{t-1}} + \frac{G_t - T_t}{Y_t}$$

Finally, move B_{t-1}/Y_{t-1} to the left to get:

$$\frac{B_t}{Y_t} - \frac{B_{t-1}}{Y_{t-1}} = (r - g)\frac{B_{t-1}}{Y_{t-1}} + \frac{G_t - T_t}{Y_t} \qquad (26.5)$$

Start from:
$Y_t = (1 + g)Y_{t-1}$.
Divide both sides by:
Y_t
to get:
$1 = (1 + g)Y_{t-1}/Y_t$.
Reorganize to get:
$Y_{t-1}/Y_t = 1/(1 + g)$

This approximation is derived as proposition 6 in Appendix 2 at the end of the book.

The change in the debt ratio is equal to the sum of two terms. The first is the difference between the real interest rate and the growth rate times the initial debt ratio. The second is the ratio of the primary deficit to GDP.

If two variables (here, debt and GDP) grow at rates r and g, respectively, then their ratio (here, the ratio of debt to GDP) will grow at rate $(r - g)$. See proposition 8 in Appendix 2. ▶

Compare equation (26.5), which gives the evolution of the ratio of debt to GDP, with equation (26.2), which gives the evolution of debt itself. The difference is the presence of $r - g$ with equation (26.5) compared to r in equation (26.2). The reason for the difference is simple: Suppose the primary deficit is zero. Debt will then increase at a rate equal to the real interest rate, r. But if GDP is growing as well, the ratio of debt to GDP will grow more slowly; it will grow at a rate equal to the real interest rate minus the growth rate of output, $r - g$.

Equation (26.5) shows that the debt-to-GDP ratio increases more quickly:

- the higher is the real interest rate;
- the lower the growth rate of output;
- the higher the initial debt ratio; and
- the higher the ratio of the primary deficit to GDP.

All four factors have played a role in the evolution of the debt-to-GDP ratio over the last four decades in the OECD countries shown in Table 26–1:

1960s:
high g, low r $\Rightarrow B/Y\downarrow$ ▶

- The 1960s were a decade of strong growth, so strong that the average growth rate exceeded the average real interest rate in most countries. As a result, $(r - g)$ was negative, and most countries were able to decrease their debt ratios without having to run large primary surpluses.

1970s:
lower g, very low r
            $\Rightarrow B/Y\downarrow$

- The 1970s were a period of lower growth but of very low (often negative) real interest rates. (Nominal interest rates were high in the 1970s. But inflation was even higher, leading to negative real interest rates.) Thus, $(r - g)$ was again negative on average, and the result was a further decrease in the debt ratio in most OECD countries.

1980s:
low g, high r $\Rightarrow B/Y\uparrow$

- The situation changed drastically in the early 1980s. Real interest rates increased, and growth rates decreased. To avoid an increase in their debt ratios, the OECD countries would have had to run large primary surpluses. They did not, and the debt ratios increased rapidly.

1990s:
low g, high r, primary
surplus > 0 $\Rightarrow B/Y\rightarrow$

- In the 1990s, real interest rates remained high, and growth rates remained low. It became increasingly clear that most countries had no alternative to stabilize their debt ratios than to run larger primary surpluses. Most OECD countries have now done so. At the end of the 1990s, most countries are now running a primary surplus sufficient to imply a steady decline in their debt ratios.

Table 26–1 gives the evolution of the ratio of debt to GDP for Canada, the United States, and the euro area, as well as for Italy, Belgium, and Greece, from 1990 to 2005. These values do not match the values presented for Canada in Figure 26–2. In the OECD data, the OECDs are gross financial liabilities. The deficit in Table 26-1 is the primary deficit, not the

TABLE 26–1	Debt and Primary Surpluses for Canada, the United States, the European Union, and Selected Countries, 1990–2005 (Percent of GDP)				
	Debt/GDP				**2005**
Country	**1990**	**1995**	**2000**	**2005**	**Primary Surplus/GDP**
Canada	74.5	100.8	82.7	69.3	2.7
United States	66.6	74.2	58.1	63.8	–1.8
Italy	—	125.5	124.9	125.4	0.0
Belgium	126.2	135.2	113.4	98.5	4.2
Greece	79.6	108.7	114.0	108.1	0.5
Total OECD	56.9	72.8	70.8	76.9	–1.3

Source: Tables 29, 32. *OECD Economic Outlook*, December 2005.

overall deficit plotted in Figure 1 in the Focus box earlier in this chapter. The advantage of the OECD numbers is that the statisticians at the OECD work very hard to generate comparable numbers across countries.

Note how much the debt ratio has decreased in Canada since 1995. As shown in the last column, the reason for the turnaround is that Canada is running a primary surplus. In the United States, the primary deficit suggests the debt-to-GDP ratio will rise over time.

Note also how high the debt ratio has been in Italy, Belgium, and now in Greece. These countries have debt ratios among the highest in the OECD. In Belgium, things have turned around, and primary surpluses are also leading to a steady decline in the debt ratio. In Italy, debt reamins high. Part of the debt in Greece is due to the 2004 Olympics.

For more on the reduction of deficits in Europe, see the discussion of the Maastricht treaty—which puts a ceiling on deficits in the euro area countries—in Chapter 13. For more on the reduction of debt in Canada, see Chapter 24.

To summarize: We have looked at the government budget constraint. We have seen that the change in the ratio of debt to GDP can be expressed as the sum of the primary deficit to GDP plus the ratio of debt to GDP times the real interest rate minus the growth rate. In the 1980s, high interest rates, low growth, and primary deficits all contributed to an increase in debt in most OECD countries. In the 1990s, countries reacted by running large primary surpluses, and the debt-to-GDP ratio is now falling in most OECD countries.

26-2 Five Issues in Fiscal Policy

Having looked at the mechanics of the government budget constraint, we can now take up four issues in which this constraint plays an important role.

Ricardian Equivalence

How does taking into account the government budget constraint affect the way we should think of the effects of deficits on output?

One extreme view is that once this constraint is taken into account, neither deficits nor debt has an effect on economic activity! This argument is known as the **Ricardian equivalence** proposition. David Ricardo, a nineteenth-century English economist, was the first to articulate its logic. His argument was further developed and given prominence in the 1970s by Robert Barro, then at Chicago, now at Harvard University. For this reason, the argument is also known as the **Ricardo–Barro proposition**.

Although Ricardo stated the logic of the argument, he believed there were many reasons why it would not hold in practice. In contrast, Barro argues that the argument is not only logically correct but is also a good description of reality.

The best way to understand the proposition's logic is to use the example of tax changes from section 26-1. Suppose that government decreases taxes by 1 this year. And at the same time, it announces that to repay the debt, it will increase taxes by $(1 + r)$ next year.

What will be the effect of the initial tax cut on consumption? A plausible answer is that it will have no effect at all. Why? Because consumers realize that the tax cut is not much of a gift: Lower taxes this year are exactly offset, in present value, by higher taxes next year. Put another way, their human wealth—the present value of after-tax labour income—is unaffected. Current taxes go down by 1, but the present value of next year's taxes goes up by $(1 + r)/(1 + r) = 1$, and the net effect of the two changes is exactly equal to zero.

See Chapter 20 for a definition of human wealth and a discussion of its role in consumption.

We can look at the same result another way, by looking at saving rather than consumption. To say that consumers do not change consumption in response to the tax cut is the same as saying that *private saving increases one for one with the deficit*. Thus, the Ricardian equivalence proposition says that if a government finances a given path of spending through deficits, private saving will increase one for one with the decrease in public saving, leaving total saving unchanged. The total amount left for investment will not be affected. Over time, the mechanics of the government budget constraint imply that government debt will increase. But this increase will not come at the expense of capital accumulation.

Under the Ricardian equivalence proposition, the long sequence of deficits and the increase in government debt that characterized the OECD for most of the last 20 years are no cause for worry. As governments were dissaving, the argument goes, people were saving more in anticipation of the higher taxes to come. The decrease in public saving was offset by an equal increase in private saving. Total saving was therefore unchanged, and so was investment. OECD economies have the same capital stock today that they would have had if there had been no increase in debt. High debt is thus no cause for concern.

How seriously should you take the Ricardian equivalence proposition? Most economists would answer, "Seriously, but not seriously enough to think that deficits and debt are irrelevant." A major theme of this book has been that expectations matter, that consumption decisions depend not only on current income but also on future income. If it were widely believed that a tax cut this year is going to be followed by an offsetting increase in taxes *next year*, the effect on consumption probably would be small. Many consumers would save most or all of the tax cut in anticipation of higher taxes next year. (Replace "year" by "month" or "week" and the argument becomes even more convincing.)

Tax cuts rarely come, however, with the announcement of tax increases a year later. Consumers have to guess when and how taxes will eventually be increased.

The increase in taxes in year t is $(1 + r)^{t-1}$. The discount factor for a dollar in year t is $1/(1 + r)^{t-1}$. Thus, the value of the increase in taxes in year t as of today is:

$(1 + r)^{t-1}/(1 + r)^{t-1} = 1$. ▶

This fact does not by itself invalidate the Ricardian equivalence argument: No matter when taxes will be increased, the government budget constraint still implies that the present value of future tax increases must always be equal to the decrease in taxes today. Take the second example we looked at in section 26-1 (see Figure 26–1b) in which government waits t years to increase taxes and thus increases them by $(1 + r)^{t-1}$. The present value in year 0 of this expected tax increase is $(1 + r)^{t-1}/(1 + r)^{t-1} = 1$—exactly equal to the original tax cut. The change in human wealth from the tax cut is still zero.

But insofar as future tax increases appear more distant and their timing more uncertain, consumers are more likely to ignore them. This may be the case because they expect to retire before taxes go up or, more likely, because they just do not think that far into the future. In either case, Ricardian equivalence is likely to fail. In addition, liquidity-constrained consumers (see Chapter 20) who receive a larger government transfer with the increased deficit will spend it.

So, it is safe to conclude that budget deficits have an important effect on activity. In the short run, larger deficits are likely to lead to higher demand and higher output. In the long run, higher government debt lowers capital accumulation and thus lowers output.

Deficits, Output Stabilization, and the Cyclically Adjusted Deficit

Note the analogy with monetary policy: The fact that higher money growth leads in the long run to more inflation does not imply higher money growth should never be used for output stabilization. ▶

Ignore output growth in ▶ this section and thus the distinction between stabilizing the debt and stabilizing the debt-to-GDP ratio. (If you want, check that the arguments here extend in a straightforward way to the case where output is growing.)

The fact that deficits have long-run adverse effects on capital accumulation and output does not imply deficits should not be used for output stabilization. Rather, it implies that deficits during recessions should be offset by surpluses during booms, so as not to lead to a steady increase in debt.

To help assess whether fiscal policy is on track, economists have constructed deficit measures that tell them what the deficit would be, under existing tax and spending rules, if output were at its natural level. Such measures come under many names, from **full-employment deficit**, to **mid-cycle deficit**, to **standardized employment deficit**, to **structural deficit** (the term used by the OECD). We will use **cyclically adjusted deficit**, the term we find the most intuitive. Such a measure gives a simple benchmark by which to judge the direction of fiscal policy: If the actual deficit is large but the cyclically adjusted deficit is equal to zero, then current fiscal policy is consistent with no systematic increase in debt over time. Debt will increase as long as output is below its natural level; but as output returns to its natural level, deficits will disappear and the debt will stabilize.

This does not imply that the goal should be to maintain a cyclically adjusted deficit equal to zero at all times. In a recession, government may want to run a deficit large enough that even the cyclically adjusted deficit is positive. In that case, the fact that the cyclically adjusted deficit is positive provides a clear warning: The return of output to its natural level will not be enough to stabilize the debt, and government will have to take specific measures to decrease the deficit at some point in the future.

The theory underlying the cyclically adjusted deficit is simple. The practice has proven tricky. To see why, we need to look at how measures of the cyclically adjusted deficit are constructed. Construction requires two steps. First, establish how much lower the deficit would be if output were, say, 1% higher. Second, assess how far away output is from its natural level.

The first step is straightforward. A reliable rule of thumb is that a 1% decrease in output leads automatically to an increase in the deficit of 0.5% of GDP. This increase occurs because most taxes are proportional to output, whereas most government spending does not depend on the level of output. That means a decrease in output, which leads to a decrease in revenues and not much change in spending, naturally leads to a larger deficit. If output is, say, 5% below its natural level, the deficit as a ratio to GDP will be about 2.5% larger than it would be if output were at its natural level. (This effect of activity on the deficit has been called an **automatic stabilizer**: A recession naturally generates a deficit, and therefore a fiscal expansion that partly counteracts the recession.)

The second step is more difficult. Recall from Chapter 9 that the natural level of output is the output level that would be produced if the economy were operating at the natural rate of unemployment. Too low an estimate of the natural rate of unemployment will lead to too high an estimate of the natural level of output, and therefore to too optimistic a measure of the cyclically adjusted deficit. This explains, in part, what happened in Europe in the 1980s. Based on the assumption of an unchanged natural unemployment rate, the cyclically adjusted deficits did not look bad in the 1980s. If European unemployment had returned to its level of the 1970s, the increase in output would have been sufficient to re-establish budget balance in most countries. But, it turned out, much of the increase in unemployment reflected an increase in the natural unemployment rate, and unemployment remained very high throughout the 1980s. As a result, most of the decade was characterized by high deficits and a large increase in debt-to-GDP ratios.

Look at our earlier discussion of the evolution of the debt ratio in the OECD.

Figure 26–2 presents, using values from the federal Department of Finance, actual and cyclically adjusted deficits in Canada. In the two major recessions, 1982–1983 and 1991–1992, the recessions account for a substantial portion of the actual deficit, more than 1% of GDP for the actual deficit. Automatic stabilizers are an important part of Canadian fiscal policy. Figure 26–2 makes it very clear that Canada's deficit problem from 1970 to 1995 was not due to a string of recessions. There was a decision to run a string of actual deficits and substantially increase Canada's national debt.

See the discussion of high unemployment in Chapter 22.

Wars and Deficits

Wars typically bring about large budget deficits. As we saw in Chapter 24, the largest increases in Canadian government debt in the twentieth century occurred during World War

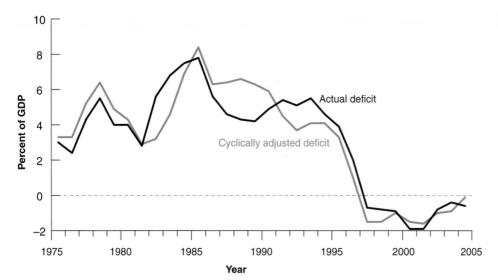

FIGURE 26-2

Actual and Cyclically Adjusted Deficits in Canada, 1975–2004

The federal Department of Finance reports both the actual deficit and a value for the cyclically adjusted deficit. This figure shows how the cyclically adjusted deficit is less than the actual deficit in a recession. The figure also reveals that Canada's deficit problem ran over two decades and both Liberal and Conservative governments.

Source: Table 46, *Fiscal Reference Tables*, Department of Finance, October 2004.

FISCAL POLICY: A SUMMING UP

In 1938, the share of Canadian government spending on goods and services in GDP was 9.7%, and the federal government's share was just 2.7%. By 1944, the figures were 40.8% and 36.9%, respectively. Not surprisingly, the bulk of the increase was due to increased spending on national defence, which went from 0.7% of GDP in 1938 to 35.6% in 1944.

Faced with such a massive increase in spending, the federal government reacted with large tax increases. For the first time in Canadian history, income taxes became a major source of revenue; income tax revenues which were less than 1% of GDP in 1938 increased to 7.2% in 1944. But the tax increase was still far less than the increase in expenditures. The increase in federal revenues, from 7.4% of GDP in 1938 to 35.6% in 1944, was only about two-thirds of the increase in expenditures.

The result was a sequence of large deficits. By 1944, the federal deficit reached 22% of GDP. The ratio of debt to GDP, already high at 65% in 1938 because of the deficits government had run during the Great Depression, climbed to almost 150% by the end of the war.

Was the increase in government spending achieved at the expense of consumption or private investment? (In principle, it could have come from higher imports and a current account deficit [see Chapter 6]. But Canada's trading partners were in no better shape than it was; net exports remained about 6% of GDP throughout the war.)

The 30% increase in the share of GDP going to government purchases was met, in large part, by a 19% drop in consumption's share of GDP from 70.3% to 51.9%. Part of the decrease in consumption may have been in anticipation of higher taxes after the war; part was also the result of the unavailability of many consumer durables; and patriotism probably played a role in leading people to save more and buy the war bonds issued by government to finance the war. But the increase in government purchases was also met by a 3% decrease in the share of (private) investment in GDP—a decrease from 10% to 7%. Thus, part of the burden of the war was, indeed, passed on in the form of lower capital accumulation to those living after the war.

Look at the peak associated with World War II in Figure 24–3.

II. We examine this case at greater length in the Focus box entitled "Deficits, Consumption, and Investment in Canada during World War II."

Is it right for governments to rely so much on deficits to finance wars? After all, war economies are usually operating at low unemployment, so the output stabilization reasons for running deficits we examined earlier are irrelevant. The answer, nevertheless, is yes. In fact, there are two good reasons to run deficits during wars. The first is distributional: Deficit finance is a way to pass some of the burden of the war to those alive after the war, and it seems only fair for future generations to share in the sacrifices a war requires. The second is more narrowly economic: Deficit spending helps reduce tax distortions. Let us look at each reason in turn.

Passing on the Burden of the Debt. Wars lead to large increases in government spending. Consider the implications of financing this increased spending either through increased taxes or through higher deficits. To distinguish this case from our earlier discussion of output stabilization, let us also assume that output is fixed at its natural level.

Suppose that government relies on deficit finance. With government spending sharply up, there will be a very large increase in the demand for goods. Given our assumption that output cannot increase, interest rates will have to increase enough so as to maintain equilibrium. Investment, which depends on the interest rate, will thus decrease sharply.

Assume that the economy is closed so that $Y = C + I + G$. Suppose that G goes up, and Y remains the same. Then, $C + I$ must go down. If taxes are not increased, most of the decrease comes from a decrease in I. If taxes are increased, most of the decrease comes from a decrease in C.

Suppose, instead, that government finances the spending increase through an increase in taxes. Consumption will decline sharply. Exactly how much depends on consumers' expectations. The longer they expect the war to last, the more they will decrease consumption and the less they will decrease saving. In any case, the increase in government spending will be partly offset by a decrease in consumption. Interest rates will increase by less than they would have under deficit spending. Investment will thus decrease by less.

In short, for a given output, the increase in government spending requires either a decrease in consumption and/or a decrease in investment. Whether government relies on tax increases or deficits determines whether consumption or investment does more of the adjustment.

How does all this affect who bears the burden of the war? The more the government relies on deficits, the smaller will be the decrease in consumption during the war and the larger the decrease in investment. Lower investment means a lower capital stock after the war, and thus lower output after the war. By reducing capital accumulation, deficits become a way of passing some of the burden of the war onto future generations.

Reducing Tax Distortions. There is another argument for running deficits, not only during wars but, more generally, in times when government spending is exceptionally high. Think, for example, of reconstruction after an earthquake or of the costs involved in the reunification of Germany in the early 1990s.

The argument is as follows: If government were to increase taxes in line with the increase in spending, tax rates would have to be very high. Very high tax rates can lead to very high distortions. Faced with very high income tax rates, people work less or engage in illegal, untaxed activities. Rather than moving the tax rate up and down to maintain a balanced budget, it is better (from the point of view of reducing distortions) to maintain a relatively constant tax rate, to *smooth taxes*. **Tax smoothing** implies running large deficits when government spending is exceptionally high and small surpluses the rest of the time.

The Dangers of Very High Debt

We now have seen two costs of high government debt—lower capital accumulation and higher tax rates and higher distortions. The recent experience of a number of countries points to yet another cost: High debt can lead to vicious circles and makes the conduct of fiscal policy extremely difficult.

To see why this is so, return to equation (26.5), which gives the evolution of the debt ratio over time:

$$\frac{B_t}{Y_t} - \frac{B_{t-1}}{Y_{t-1}} = (r - g)\frac{B_{t-1}}{Y_{t-1}} + \frac{(G_t - T_t)}{Y_t}$$

Take a country with a high debt ratio, say, 100%. Suppose that the real interest rate is 3% and the growth rate 2%. The first term on the right is $(3\% - 2\%) \times 100\% = 1\%$ of GDP. Suppose further that government is running a primary surplus of 1%, thus just enough to keep the debt ratio constant [the right side of the equation equals $1\% + (-1\%) = 0\%$].

Now, suppose financial investors start requiring a higher interest rate to hold government bonds. This may be because they are not sure government will be able to keep the deficit under control and repay the bonds in the future. The specific reason does not matter here. For concreteness, suppose the domestic interest rate increases from 3% to, say, 6%.

Now, assess the fiscal situation: $r - g$ is now $6\% - 2\% = 4\%$. With the increase in $r - g$ from 1% to 4%, government must increase its primary surplus from 1% to 4% of GDP just to keep the debt-to-GDP ratio constant. Now come the potential vicious circles.

Suppose that government takes steps to avoid an increase in the debt ratio. The spending cuts or tax increases are likely to prove politically costly, generating even more political uncertainty and the need for an even higher interest rate. Also, the sharp fiscal contraction is likely to lead to a recession, decreasing the growth rate. Both the increase in the interest rate and the decrease in growth further increase $r - g$, making it even harder to stabilize the debt ratio.

Alternatively, suppose that government proves unable or unwilling to increase the primary budget surplus by 3% of GDP. Debt then starts increasing, leading financial markets to become even more worried and require an even higher interest rate. The higher interest rate leads to even larger deficits, an even faster increase in the debt ratio, and so on.

In short, the higher the ratio of debt to GDP, the larger the potential for explosive debt dynamics. Even initially unfounded fears that government may not fully repay the debt can easily become self-fulfilling: By increasing the interest rate government must pay on its debt, these fears can lead government to lose control of its budget and lead to an increase in debt to a level such that government is unable to repay the debt, validating initial fears.

If this reminds you of our discussion of exchange rate crises and the possibility of self-fulfilling crises, you are right. Very much the same mechanisms are at work: Expectations that a problem may arise lead to the emergence of the problem, validating initial expectations.

◀ Exchange rate crises were studied in Chapter 19.

Indeed, in some crises, both mechanisms are at work. In the Brazilian crisis of 1998, fears of a devaluation of the *real* (the Brazilian currency) forced Brazil to increase interest rates to very high levels. These interest rates led to much larger budget deficits, raising questions about whether the Brazilian government could repay its debt, further increasing interest rates. Eventually, Brazil had no choice but to devalue. It did so in early 1999.

If a government decides that the debt ratio is too high, how and how fast should it reduce it? The answer is through many years, even many decades, of surpluses. The historical reference here is to England in the nineteenth century. By the end of its war against Napoleon in the early 1800s, England had run up a debt ratio in excess of 200% of GDP. It spent most of the nineteenth century reducing the ratio so that by 1900, the ratio stood at only 30% of GDP.

The prospect of many decades of fiscal austerity is unpleasant. Thus, when debt ratios are very high, an alternative solution keeps coming up—**debt repudiation**. The argument is a simple one. Repudiating the debt—cancelling it in part or in full—is good for the economy. It allows for a decrease in taxes and thus a decrease in distortions. It decreases the risk of vicious circles. The problem with repudiation, however, is the problem of time inconsistency that we studied in Chapter 24. If government reneges on its promises to repay the debt, it may find it very difficult to borrow again for a long time in the future; financial markets will remember what happened and be reluctant to lend again. What seems best today may be unappealing in the long run. Debt repudiation is very much a last resort, to be used when everything else has failed.

The Twin Deficits

To consider our last problem associated with a large government deficit, we need to return to the open economy. Many economists argue there is a link between the current account deficit (discussed in Chapters 6 and 17) and the government deficit. These are sometimes called the **twin deficits**.

We begin by reminding ourselves that all of GDP (Y_t) (GDP) created in a country must go somewhere. Thus, in a year:

$$Y_t = C_t + I_t + G_t + X_t - Q_t$$

Remember X_t is exports and Q_t is imports. We neglect real exchange rate effects and measure everything in units of domestic output. Rearranging the equation above by adding and subtracting T_t yields:

$$(Y_t - T_t - C_t) + (T_t - G_t) = I_t + (X_t - Q_t)$$

Finally, we add rB^f_t to both sides and label the items in parentheses as:

$$(rB^f_t + Y_t - T_t - C_t) + (T_t - G_t) = I_t + (rB^f_t + X_t - Q_t)$$

private sector saving	primary government surplus	current account surplus

r is the real interest rate paid or earned on net foreign assets, denoted B^f_t as in Chapter 17. Two groups in society can engage in saving on the left-hand side. The private sector saves by not consuming part of Gross National Product (GNP $= rB^f_t - Y_t$) after they have paid their taxes, T_t. The public or government sector can run a primary surplus if $T_t - G_t$ is positive or a primary deficit if $T_t - G_t$ is negative. The right-hand side shows that society can save in one of two forms. New physical capital (I_t) can be installed. Society can then accumulate more net foreign assets or repay foreign debts if the item in parentheses labelled current account surplus is positive.

The "twin deficits" observation notes that if government runs a primary deficit *and* the private sector does not increase its savings by the same amount, the sum of new investment and the current account surplus must fall. In practice, both are likely to fall. In a very open economy, such as Canada's, it seems very likely that a government deficit will lead to a current account deficit very quickly. Why?

Suppose that you are a Canadian with some savings. If you see a profitable investment opportunity, I_t will be positive. You take your savings and buy a new factory. Now, government runs a deficit and needs to borrow. It sells you a bond. You no longer have the savings to build your new factory but the investment opportunity still exists. You simply take out a loan from a foreigner (thus running a current account deficit) and continue to hold the government bond. The additional government borrowing "crowded" you into the international financial market. In a simpler scenario, one that does occur in Canada, government may sell its bonds directly to foreigners. This is the favoured route of many Canadian provinces but not the federal government. In either case, because total private sector saving did not expand as the government sector went into deficit, the most likely result of an increased government deficit is an increased current account deficit. These are the "twin deficits."

Figure 26–3 shows some evidence that larger primary deficits for all governments in Canada are associated with a larger current account deficit. As the primary deficits turned to primary surpluses, the current account moved into surplus.

Are the "twin deficits" a problem? It really depends, as it did in Chapter 17, on why government is borrowing. We argued in Chapter 17 that international borrowing was a useful source of physical capital when it is used to increase future production, which then repays the international loan. There is no reason why public sector primary deficits could not be used to build new public sector capital, roads, airports, and other infrastructure. It may even pay to borrow for education. However, the argument above does not avoid repaying the foreign loan. And if the foreign loan is not used to increase future production, then a higher current account deficit today does mean larger repayments of foreign debt in the future. A government deficit, in contributing to a current account deficit, can reduce the welfare of future generations in this way.

To summarize: We have looked at five issues that directly involve the government budget constraint:

1. Ricardian equivalence—the proposition that a larger deficit is offset by an equal increase in private saving, so deficits have no effect on demand and output. We have concluded that Ricardian equivalence does not usually hold and that deficits decrease capital accumulation and output in the long run.

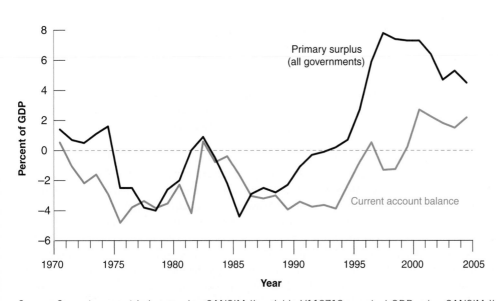

Source: Current account balance using CANSIM II variable V113713; nominal GDP using CANSIM II variable V646937; primary surplus, which is cyclically adjusted, comes from Table 46, *Fiscal Reference Tables,* Department of Finance, September 2005 and September 2001.

FIGURE 26–3

Twin Deficits

When Canada increased its government deficits from 1970 to 1985, the current account deficit also increased. As the primary government surplus switched from negative to positive, so did the current account surplus. If governments run deficits, they contribute to net foreign debts.

2. The use of cyclically adjusted deficits—measures that tell us what the deficit would be, under existing tax and spending rules, if output were at its natural level. If the cyclically adjusted deficit is positive, this signals that sooner or later, changes will have to be made to tax and spending rules.

3. The use of deficit finance in times of wars. We have seen how running a deficit during a war shifts some of the burden of the war from people living during the war to those living after the war. Deficits also help smooth taxes and reduce tax distortions.

4. The dangers of very high debt ratios. We have seen how high debt ratios increase the risk of fiscal crises, with high interest rates leading to large deficits, and large deficits leading, in turn, to higher interest rates.

5. The possibility that a large government deficit leads directly to a large current account deficit. These international debts must be repaid, which reduces future consumption.

26-3 | A Decade of Canadian Federal Fiscal Policy, 1993–2005: Facing the Twin Deficits

The Minister of Finance of Canada, through control of both taxation and spending, is the most important economic decision maker in the federal government. After the Liberal election victory in October 1993, new Finance Minister Paul Martin had to formulate both a short-term plan and a long-term plan for federal fiscal policy. Large federal deficits over the past 20 years had left the federal government deeply in debt. In addition, throughout the 1970s and 1980s foreign debts of all Canadians, both government and private, had skyrocketed. What fiscal plan could successfully lead Canada out of the twin deficits?

In 1993, the year of Paul Martin's appointment, the national debt of Canada staggers the mind: None of us can conceive of owing anyone $408.2 billion. Figure 26–3 showed the steady increase in federal debt as a percent of Canada's GDP to 1995. How could Martin reduce the debt-to-GDP ratio and reduce the deficit?

His first problem was to convince Canadians that the deficit and the debt were serious problems. He toured the country explaining this to Canadians. What effect does the national debt have on the Canadian economy? First, the existence of such a large national debt puts a severe constraint on federal fiscal choices. The interest on the federal debt must be paid, or government must declare bankruptcy. At the very least, the federal government must raise the tax revenue from Canadians to service the debt. More and more of GDP and tax revenue was simply being used to service Canada's national debt. The proportion of total GDP in Canada devoted to paying the interest on the national debt steadily increased from 2% in 1970 to 5.3% in 1993. If the national debt were entirely owned by Canadians, then raising the taxes to pay the interest on the debt would take money from one group of Canadians, the "average" taxpayer, and give money to another group of Canadians, the "average" bond owner. The "cost" of the national debt to the economy would be the costs of collecting these taxes. These costs have two components: the actual cost of the tax collection and the welfare of economic costs of the distortions associated with tax collection. The actual costs of tax collection are the costs of hiring the tax collectors, the taxpayers filling in forms, and the enforcement of tax laws. While these costs are significant, they will be incurred at any level of taxation, that is, at either a high tax rate or a low tax rate. Tax distortion costs increase when tax rates are higher.

Here are several examples of tax distortions. Suppose that there is an increase in the income tax rate and Canadians respond by working less and taking more time off as holidays. This would reduce total GDP. We could look at this reduction in production as a result of a tax distortion. But part of the tax distortion is offset by the enjoyment of the extra holiday time. Any other tax creates a similar distortion. If gasoline is taxed more heavily, then Canadians would drive a little less. If a payroll is taxed, then employers will hire fewer new workers. If there is a general increase in the sales tax rate, then Canadians consume less and

In fact, other measures indicate that the federal government may owe even more money. The federal government owes money in the form of future pensions promised to its employees. It owes money in the form of future payments out of the Canada Pension Plan, where the current assets are not sufficient to pay future liabilities. It owes money in the form of guarantees on bonds issued by agencies of the federal government.

save a little more. All taxes that exist create some kind of distortion, a change in the decision made by you or me, whether as households or firms. When more interest on the national debt increases tax rates, these distortions increase. This is a cost of the national debt, even if all the national debt is held by residents of Canada. But not all the national debt is held by Canadians. This both complicates and simplifies the analysis of the effect of the national debt on Canadians.

The simplification is that if the taxes raised to pay interest on federal government debt held by foreigners, then these taxes represent a direct reduction in the incomes of Canadians and a direct increase in the incomes of foreigners. We saw in Figure 26–3 that Canada's foreign debts increased with Canada's national debt. This is a clear-cut reduction in the welfare of Canadians when the national debt is held by foreigners.

The complicated effects relate to the analysis of interest rates in Canada. Usually, when the federal government runs a deficit and has to sell more bonds, it must offer higher interest rates to attract purchasers for those bonds. Increases in interest rates would reduce spending on new houses and new machinery, and this is a cost to the Canadian economy. There is less capital to produce output in the future. However, if the Government of Canada can induce foreigners to hold the bonds associated with the deficit, this may mean that the increases in Canadian interest rates usually associated with a deficit may be quite small. Canada's interest rate just stays at or near the foreign interest rate. This same argument can be made for any country in the world that has the option of selling its national debt to foreigners. But there are two other effects to consider.

The government deficit may increase the borrowing by other Canadians from foreigners. Here is an example. Suppose that a Canadian business wishes to sell some bonds to undertake an investment, perhaps an expansion of their factory. If there is no Canadian resident who will buy those bonds, then the Canadian business tries to sell those bonds abroad. Perhaps there are no Canadian residents willing to purchase those bonds because all of the savings of Canadian residents have been used up to buy government bonds created by the deficit. Then, part of the profits from the new factory are promised to foreigners and the future incomes of Canadians are smaller. The higher federal deficit increased Canada's other, nongovernment, foreign debts. The increase in Canadian foreign debts, government or private, may have one other effect in international capital markets.

It may be that the foreigners will only buy more Canadian bonds, either government or private, if the interest rate on Canadian bonds rises. This could occur as private Canadian firms or Canadian provincial governments sell more of their debt abroad. It could also occur if Canadians do not want to buy all the federal government bonds on offer in a given year, then nonresidents may only be willing to buy those bonds at a high interest rate. In 1993, an editorial in the *Wall Street Journal* took note of Canada's large foreign and national debt in suggesting to its readers that this debt was getting riskier and should only be held at a higher interest rate. To quote after the headline "Bankrupt Canada?":

> *Mexico isn't the only U.S. neighbor flirting with the financial abyss. Turn around and check out Canada, which has now become an honorary member of the Third World in the unmanageability of its debt problem. If dramatic action isn't taken in next month's federal budget, it's not inconceivable that Canada could hit the debt wall....*

> *Canada has the second-highest ratio of debt to GDP of any industrialized country, only Italy surpasses it. But Italy finances most of its debt through domestic borrowing, while Canada ran a $30 billion-dollar balance-of-payments deficit last year. About 40 percent of Canada's provincial debt is held by foreigners. They should worry that 35 percent of all federal revenues now go to service the debt.* (Wall Street Journal, January 12, 1993)

It seemed that the combination of domestic and foreign factors made Canadians ready in 1994 to tackle the issue of the federal deficit. How could this be done?

On November 17, 1993 Paul Martin announced that the actual budgetary deficit for the 1992–1993 **fiscal year** was \$40.5 billion. This was the last deficit completely under Conservative control. This number for the deficit was considerably larger than the \$27.5 billion for that fiscal year predicted in the Conservative Budget Speech of February 25, 1992, and considerably larger than the \$35.5 billion predicted in the Budget Speech of April 26, 1993. Some of the increase in the deficit to \$40.5 billion was accomplished with accounting tricks. Martin shifted some spending into the 1992–1993 fiscal year and shifted some revenue out of the 1992–1993 fiscal year. Some of the increase in the deficit occurred because the Conservatives, in February 1992, had considerably overestimated GDP growth, and thus revenue growth, to take place in the 1992–1993 fiscal year.

There was some external pressure on Canada to face its deficit issue as well. The day of the announcement of the \$40.5 billion deficit, the Canadian dollar exchange rate to the U.S. dollar fell by one-half a cent. In February 1993, the C.D. Howe Institute ran a workshop on Canada's national and foreign debts. Canada was compared with both Sweden and Italy. In these two countries, the inability to continue to finance a government deficit through foreign borrowing had led to a dramatic reduction in old age pensions and other social spending. Canadian provinces had their foreign debt downgraded by credit rating agencies. In 1992, both Alberta and Saskatchewan experienced debt downgrades. The stage was set. Martin's approach in his first formal budget was cautious and gradual.

The First Liberal Budget, February 1994

On page 1 of the budget, the strongest possible language was used; the consultation process, Martin said, had made it clear that Canadians wanted a Canada where "our public finances are in order, not in ruin." Martin was careful to make the path to fiscal order clear:

> *We are undertaking a major effort to build a responsible social security system that is fair, compassionate, and affordable.*
>
> *This means making fundamental changes to our unemployment insurance system.*
>
> *It means overhauling the structure of federal–provincial transfers for social programs....*
>
> *It is now time for the government to get its fiscal house in order. For years, governments have been promising more than they can deliver and delivering more than they can afford. That has to end. We are ending it. The actions taken in this budget will reduce the deficit from \$45.7 billion this year to \$39.7 billion in 1994–95 and \$32.7 billion the year after.*

(The Budget Speech, February 1994, page 2)

On the spending side, in his first budget, Martin only started to identify what programs he would reduce. There was a planned reduction in expenditures on Unemployment Insurance. This is a large federal program (now called **Employment Insurance**) that provides income support to the unemployed. Martin's planned reduction depended on a projected fall in the unemployment rate (reducing the cyclical portion of the budget deficit) and the reduction of benefits to the unemployed, particularly repeat users of the unemployment insurance system. Second, Martin reduced federal transfer payments to the provinces from \$27.1 billion in fiscal year 1993–1994 to \$26.4 billion in fiscal year 1995–1996. This was significant: These programs had been projected to grow rapidly. It is also significant that the planning horizon for these reductions was quite far ahead, one or two fiscal years. Although friction between the federal government and the provincial governments in Canada is common, this reduction in **transfers to the provinces** was not a surprise. There were no immediate cuts to transfers to the provinces, but transfers to the provinces were to be reduced in the future. The other two categories of federal spending are interest on the debt and then all other spending. Spending to service the debt was projected to rise through the three fiscal years. Part of this increase reflected a continued positive deficit, which leads to more debt outstanding. Because much of the debt is in the form of Treasury bills that roll over every three months, the interest rate projected to hold over three fiscal years can change the outlay on this item substantially.

A second strategy was used to further ensure that actual spending on all other items would fall and Martin's deficit targets would be achieved. In the category of "All other spending" Martin greatly enlarged a spending line called "Reserves net of lapse." Later, this line came to be called contingency spending. This line was $2.4 billion in fiscal year 1994–1995 and $3 billion in fiscal year 1995–1996. This is spending that Martin did not expect to incur, spending for emergencies, such as floods and ice storms, and extra military spending in the event of a second Gulf War. If the money was not spent, then the unspent money would be part of the reduced deficit and then the deficit target would be more easily met.

The Second Liberal Budget, February 1995

The budget of February 1995 again addressed the deficit first and foremost. This budget was the turning point. It pointed out that the modest target for the 1994–1995 deficit set in the 1994 Budget had been more than achieved. Instead of the $39.7 billion forecast for the 1994–1995 fiscal year, the Budget Speech claimed the actual budget deficit would be about $35.3 billion, about $4 billion less than forecast. Martin claimed there were three reasons for this success:

> The first is Canada's strong economic growth—which offset the increase in interest rates.

> The second is that when interest rates began to rise last spring, we reacted immediately by slamming the door shut on new spending initiatives.

> This, together with reductions in unemployment insurance, enabled us to keep program spending $1.9 billion below our expectations last February.

> Finally, the third reason we have done better than projected is that our overall economic assumptions were prudent. This means despite an unexpected rise in interest rates, we did not need to touch the contingency reserve we put in place.

> (The Budget Speech, February 27, 1995, page 3)

Deficit reduction and reduction in the ratio of debt to GDP took to the forefront of the 1995 Budget. To quote the Budget Speech again:

> By 1996–97 our financial requirements—which is the amount of new money we will have to borrow on financial markets—will be down to $13.7 billion or 1.7 percent of GDP....

> Perhaps more importantly, in that same year, the debt will no longer be growing faster than our economy. The debt-to-GDP ratio will have begun to decline. That is the key to fiscal sustainability....

> We will continue to set firm short-term deficit goals—rolling two year targets, until the deficit is erased. Short-term targets are the surest way to get to zero. They are the most effective spending control anyone could impose on governments. They keep our feet to the fire. They make it impossible to

postpone needed action. And they prevent fanciful, foolish forecasts—the escapism of wishful targets.

This government wants Canadians to be able to judge it not on its rhetoric, but on its results; not on promises made, but on real progress secured.

(The Budget Speech, February 27, 1995, pages 4–5)

The Finance Minister laid his credibility on the line in the clearest possible way. He had also been careful to cultivate public support of deficit reduction. An extensive public education program, highlighted by his own presentations, had taken place through 1994. The **Department of Finance** co-produced a document "Canada's Economy: What Path? What Future?" for use in teaching and to make more submissions to the Finance Minister. This document stressed the instability of the current fiscal path, the explosion in the debt-to-GDP ratio, and the dominant role of interest payments in the federal budget, a role so dominant that the federal government was not going to be able to continue to provide the social programs in health and support for the elderly that Canadians so clearly wanted.

In the 1995 Budget, other federal spending was to fall substantially over the next two fiscal years. Program spending, spending excluding debt service costs, was expected to fall from $120.9 billion in fiscal year 1994–1995, the fiscal year nearly complete in this budget, to $107.9 billion in fiscal year 1996–1997, a drop of more than $10 billion in just two fiscal years. The brunt of expenditure reduction was in four programs. We saw two in the 1994 Budget. First, expenditures to support the unemployed continued to fall by $1.6 billion. Second, cash transfers to the provinces took the biggest hit, as they were scheduled to fall by $3.6 billion. Third, subsidies to business were to fall by $1.9 billion. The new Liberal government had found the political courage to reduce several long-standing federal programs to subsidize the transportation sector in particular. These programs were on both the east and west coasts of Canada. Fourth, there was a substantial cut in defence spending, from $10.8 billion to $9.7 billion. There were other program spending cuts as well throughout government. The Liberals did not reduce either transfers to the elderly (the biggest single federal spending item) nor transfers to Canada's Aboriginal people. No other groups were exempt. The reserve for contingency spending continued to be built into both fiscal years in the projection, $2.5 billion in 1995–1996 and $3 billion in 1996–1997.

The Budget of 1995 contained only one significant tax-rate increase: The federal tax on gasoline was raised 1.5 cents per litre to increase revenues by $500 million. There were small symbolic tax increases on large corporations and on bank capital. Total tax revenue was forecast to rise rapidly with growth in the economy. There was no overall increase in statutory income tax or sales-tax rates. Revenue was forecast to rise from $125 billion in fiscal year 1994–1995 to $137.4 billion in fiscal year 1996–1997. However, this was not an increase in revenue as a percent of GDP. The deficit reduction projected to take place as of February 1995 was primarily a function of expenditure and transfer reductions, not of tax increases. The Liberals had been converted to fiscal conservatives.

The Fourth (Pre-election) Budget, February 1997

Let us skip a budget and move to February 1997. By this point, government was facing the next election. This budget was the pre-election budget. And while there were a few, very few, pre-election "goodies"on the spending side, this was only relative to the austerity of the previous three budgets. The Budget Speech opened with a summary of government's achievement:

This budget will show that our effort to restore health to the nation's finances is very clearly on track, that we are well ahead of our [deficit] target, and that we are staying the course on deficit reduction....

In fact, during 1996, our current account has moved into the black for the first time in 12 years. The sharp improvement in the current account means more of the income generated in Canada, stays in Canada, rather than being sent abroad....

Furthermore, we are clearly on track to meeting our deficit targets for the following two years—2 percent of GDP for 1997–98 and 1 percent for 1998–99....

Over the past two decades, our debt-to-GDP ratio has been rising relentlessly. In other words, the debt of Canada's government has been rising faster than the income of the country. Mr. Speaker, this had to be stopped. And we are stopping it.

(The Budget Speech, February 1997, pages 4–7)

Deficit targets had been met. The deficit-to-GDP ratio had been sharply reduced. The debt-to-GDP ratio had been stabilized. The Liberals ran for re-election as the fiscal saviours of Canada. As the balancers of the budget, they were easily re-elected to a second term.

From 1997, the federal budget was in surplus. The debt-to-GDP ratio continued to fall. The current account continued to be in surplus. There was tension between the left- and right-wing factions of the Liberal Party. The left wing wanted a larger role for government in Canadian society. This faction wanted to see, for example, a national program to pay for prescription drugs from tax revenue or a heavily subsidized national day care program similar to public education programs operated by the provinces. The right-wing faction in the Liberal party wanted to see little or no growth in the role of government in Canadian society. This dispute was resolved, at least temporarily with the November 2, 1999, *Economic and Fiscal Update*. This entire document, as well as all other budget material, is available on the Web site of the Department of Finance (**www.fin.gc.ca**). In the *Update*, which served as the Liberal platform for the 2000 election, it was clear that no new major spending programs were part of the long-term plan. Some spending increases were planned primarily related to the knowledge economy, education, and research: areas the federal government saw as priorities. However, the bulk of the fiscal plan was a reduction over a number of years in federal taxes. Some of these reductions were reduction in federal tax rates. Some were increases in federal tax brackets. Some were decreases in Employment Insurance premiums. And some were changes in the indexation of income tax brackets so that tax increases that would have taken place with inflation would not take place. Overall, the ratio of federal tax revenue to GDP was forecast to fall. Projections for total revenues, program spending, public debt charges, and the projected net public debt, all as a percent of GDP are found in Table 26–2.

TABLE 26–2 Fiscal Plans in the 2001 Federal Budget

Fiscal Year	2000–2001	2001–2002	2002–2003	2003–2004
Budgetary revenues	16.9	15.8	15.9	15.5
Program spending	11.3	12.0	12.4	12.1
Public debt charges	4.0	3.6	3.3	3.3
Projected surplus	1.6	0.2	0.2	0.2
Net public debt	51.8	50.5	49.9	47.1

All values are as a percent of GDP.

The federal budget includes projections for revenues and expenditures over a number of years into the future. This table summarizes plans presented in 2001 for the 2000–2001 fiscal year (then almost over) and the next three fiscal years. This was Paul Martin's last budget. It held the line on spending as a ratio of GDP and incorporated future tax reductions as promised in the November 1999 *Economic Update* that served as the Liberal campaign platform.

Source: Table 7.5, The Budget Plan 2001, Department of Finance.

It shows a small increase in program spending from 2000–2001 to 2001–2002 (as the Liberal government restored some funding to the provinces it had previously taken away) and then flat spending to GDP in future years. It shows a decline in both public debt charges as a per-cent of GDP with that decline used to reduce tax revenues as a percent of GDP. The projected budget deficit is expected to be close to zero (the contingency reserve accounts for the gap between a zero deficit and the projected deficit). The debt-to-GDP ratio continued to fall as GDP grew and the debt (with a zero projected deficit) remained constant. With this plan, Canada seemed to have returned to fiscal stability with a medium term plan. However, the election of the minority Liberal government in June 2004 introduced a new dimension to Canadian fiscal policy.

Fiscal Policy in a Minority Government

In a minority government, although the party with the most seats in the House of Commons forms the government, fiscal policy becomes more complicated. Budget legislation, includ-ing any bill that establishes or changes tax rates or authorizes expenditures, is a matter of "confidence." If the minority government is defeated on a confidence-related bill (usually a bill related to taxes or expenditure), then a new government must be formed. Most of the time, there will be an election to create a new House of Commons, and then a new govern-ment is formed. Occasionally, the Governor-General will call upon another party in the exist-ing House to attempt to form a government. The bottom line is that budget bills must achieve the support of the majority of the members of the House of Commons.

In February 2005, the Paul Martin minority Liberal government presented its first Budget to the House. It seemed, on its introduction, that the 2005 Budget had achieved its goal of maintaining the Liberal government in power. It did so by appealing to the members of the second largest party in the House, the Conservative Party of Canada led by Stephen Harper. The Liberal Budget was designed to appeal to the Conservatives. First, the budget offered (mostly future) tax relief both to individuals and corporations of all sizes. The Conservatives, being the party more to the right wing of Canadian politics, traditionally favour a smaller government sector than do the Liberals. If a balanced budget over time (we will discuss that issue shortly) is required, then voting for lower tax rates implies voting for lower spending. The second element of the February 2005 budget designed to appeal to the Conservatives was a significant increase in defence expenditure, which was also a Conservative priority. Even with the tax cuts and the defence spending increases, the February 2005 federal budget was projected to have neither a surplus nor a deficit in the period 2005–2006 to 2009–2010. Is this an exact projection? No. It is a statement that balancing the actual Budget is a policy prior-ity. In addition, an amount of $3 billion dollars is included as a contingency reserve in each year and thus as projected expenditure. If not spent, it would become a surplus and reduce the debt. Stephen Harper commented on Budget Day:

> "Let me just be clear, there's nothing in this Budget that would justify an election at this time. In fact, I'm a lot happier than I thought I'd be. The major priorities in this Budget are Conservative priorities; the major announcements are a tax reduction and national defence spending increases. (Toronto Star, February 24, 2005, p. A1)

With a statement like that, there was every expectation on Budget Day that the Liberals and Conservatives, the two largest parties in the House would pass the Budget and any elec-tion would be a year in the future. The New Democratic Party (NDP) and the Bloc Quebecois would vote against the Budget. However, politics in a minority Parliament can be, to say the least, fluid.

The Conservatives intended to support the Budget as written in February 2005 and allow the minority government to continue in power, at least for some period of time. But in the fol-lowing months, the Liberals became further enmeshed in the federal sponsorship scandal, which had triggered an investigation into the corruption in the sale and purchase of federal government advertising in Quebec. The led the Conservatives to believe that if the Liberal government were to be defeated in a confidence motion, there would be an election that the Conservatives might win. It became apparent that the Liberal government budget would be defeated and the fiscal program proposed by the Liberals would not, in fact, be carried out. However, the NDP, the left-wing party that prefers a larger government sector, stepped into this situation. The NDP offered to vote for a modified Budget. If the portion of the corporate tax reductions directed to large corporations were to be delayed and more federal spending on child care and support of postsecondary education and municipal infrastructure were to be added, then the NDP would support the Budget and Conservative support would not be needed. An amendment to the Budget was tabled. As some of you may well remember, even with the New Democrats, the Liberals did not have the 50% needed to pass the amended Budget. Days before the scheduled vote, one Conservative member, Belinda Stronach, crossed the floor to become a Liberal Cabinet Minister. Even then, in one of the more dramatic moments in recent Canadian political history, a crucial independent member, Chuck Cadman, stood up to vote with the Liberal government on the Budget amendment. With these two additional votes for the Liberal–NDP Budget, the vote on the bill to amend the Budget was tied at 152–152. The Speaker of the House cast the deciding vote to maintain the minority government in power. A possible election was deferred to the winter of 2006. Prime Minister Paul Martin had previously promised to call an election within 60 days of the release of the final report on the sponsorship corruption scandal. What were the fiscal issues in the upcoming campaign?

Canada had recorded a federal budget surplus since the 1998–1999 fiscal year. Will this continue? We have already seen that this string of budget surpluses has resulted in a steep decline in the ratio of government debt to GDP in Canada. This policy is frequently justified on demographic grounds. To quote:

> "This Budget reaffirms the Government's objective set out in the 2004 Budget to reduce the federal debt-to-GDP ratio to 25 per cent by 2014–15. As a result, debt-servicing costs will absorb a smaller share of revenues, placing the Government in a better position to deal with the fiscal pressures of an aging population." (The Budget in Brief, 2005, p. 21)

As the average age of the Canadian population increases, the direct financial responsibility of the federal government for old-age pensions and its indirect financial responsibility to transfer federal revenues to the provinces for health care expenditure involve an increase in expenditures related to the elderly when measured as a percentage of GDP. To make room for these expenditures, at the same tax rate, other government outlays must fall. The Liberals argued that a budget surplus would now reduce the share of revenue used to service government debt in the future and allow for planned increases in expenditure on the elderly and on health care at the same tax rate. There is a fairly strong consensus in Canada among all three political parties—the Liberals, the Conservatives, and the NDP—that the federal government budget should remain balanced, at least over the business cycle. No party is proposing a return to the deficits of the 1970s and 1980s. The Liberal–NDP plans for the fiscal years from June 2005 to October 2009 did not include any deficits. The amended Budget that was passed also presented a plan where there was neither a surplus nor a deficit. A balanced budget was part of the amended plan as it was of the original plan. Remember that an actual balanced budget implies a primary budget surplus and, with sufficient economic growth and a low real interest rate, offers a plan to reduce the debt-to-GDP ratio using equation (26.5).

The three major parties do vary in their preferences regarding the size of the balanced-budget government sector. The NDP prefers the state to have a larger role in the economy than do the Liberals. The Conservatives prefer the smallest size of government. To partner with the NDP, the Liberals had to increase government spending slightly. Since the Conservatives formed the next minority government beginning in 2006, we might expect a slight decline in the size of the government sector. There is an ongoing policy debate on the overall size of the government sector. You observe this debate working itself out in the role of private expenditures in health care, in the size of the national defence establishment needed for Canada's role in the world, in the trade-off between private and public costs of education, and in the role of public sector expenditures to preserve the environment.

One final policy issue that arose in the election campaign is the relationship of the federal budget surplus to the business cycle. Canada has not had a significant recession since 1991. If a recession were to occur, we have learned that revenues would fall and expenditures would rise. The 2005 federal budget contains estimates of the size of this effect, if real GDP growth were 1% lower than expected, than revenues are projected to fall by $2 billion and expenses to rise by $0.5 billion. The deficit would increase (or the surplus fall) by $2.5B. From a balanced budget, the actual budget would move into deficit. One question asked during the campaign: Which party would be most likely to allow the budget to go into actual deficit during a recession? Some economists, and certainly the New Democrats, would be inclined to allow an actual deficit during a recession. The Conservatives and even the Liberals would be less inclined in this direction. Neither party wanted to be associated with a return to deficit financing on a large scale. The experience of large deficits and large debts in the 1970s and 1980s has removed this option from the current politically acceptable menu for fiscal policy. The first Conservative Budget, presented on May 2, 2006, did project a balanced budget through to 2009–2010. What else did this budget contain?

The Conservative Budget of 2006

Stephen Harper campaigned on a promise to reduce the Goods and Services Tax (GST) rate by one percentage point for two consecutive years. The first percentage point drop, from 7 percent to 6 percent, took effect July 1, 2006. That promise was kept. The reduction in the GST rate will reduce federal government tax revenues and is fully consistent with a smaller government sector usually favoured by the more conservative party. The Conservative budget included the Universal Child Care Benefit (UCCB), a payment of $100 per month per child less than five years of age to all Canadian families with such children. This payment is a transfer, a negative tax, and replaces a Liberal plan to provide public sector daycare in partnership with the provinces. The UCCB is also part of a smaller role in the economy for the government. The other parts of the May 2006 Conservative budget are less clear. Federal outlays are projected to fall from 12.2% of GDP in fiscal year 2004–2005 to 11.9% in the fiscal years from 2005–2006 to 2009–2010. Some program expenditures will have to fall. The Budget did not identify these programs. The budget and subsequent announcements did make it clear that defence spending will rise. Although reducing the waiting time for medical procedures was one of the Conservative's five priorities, no funds for this purpose and no mechanism to achieve this goal was contained in the Budget. Indeed, since health care is primarily a provincial responsibility, it is unclear how the federal government could budget for shorter waiting times. The Bloc Quebecois supported the budget because of implicit promises in the budget of larger future transfers to the provinces, including Quebec. These larger transfers are intended to rectify Canada's "fiscal imbalance." This term refers to the idea that the provinces have too little revenue to meet the programs they are responsible for while the federal government has too much revenue. But the exact mechanism for the proposed increases in transfers from the federal government to the provincial governments remains to be decided. This is a matter of great controversy, particular since the provincial governments representing the two largest contributors to federal tax revenue, the taxpayers of Alberta and Ontario, do not want to see increases in equalization payments as the main mechanism to redress the fiscal imbalance. Equalization payments are payments from the federal government that are made only to Canada's poorer provinces. These payments are intended to "equalize" the level of services for all Canadian citizens. Recently Ontario and

Alberta have not received any equalization payments as "rich" provinces. Ontario, and to a lesser extent, Alberta, want the federal government to increase transfers to **all** provinces where a payment is made per person living in the province. Provinces with a larger population (noticeably Ontario) would receive more money from the federal government using this method to redress the "fiscal imbalance." The smaller provinces that receive equalization payments would like to see equalization payments increase rather than payments per person increase. That describes the state of play between the federal government and provincial governments as of the summer of 2006. The issue, an important issue for federal fiscal policy, remains to be resolved. It is unlikely that it will be resolved by lowering overall federal spending on transfers to the provinces. To summarize the Conservative fiscal plan as of May 2006: there is a planned reduction in the proportion of GDP to be raised as tax revenue; the overall budget is projected to be balanced; and there are significant proposed increases in defence spending and almost certain increases in transfers to the provinces. The conclusion, other federal spending must fall as a proportion of GDP. It remains to be seen which spending will be reduced.

SUMMARY

- The government budget constraint gives the evolution of government debt as a function of spending and taxes. One way of expressing the constraint is that the change in debt (the deficit) is equal to the primary deficit plus interest payments on the debt. The primary deficit is the difference between government spending on goods and services, *G*, and taxes net of transfers, *T*.

- If government spending is unchanged, a decrease in taxes must be offset by an increase in taxes in the future. The longer the government waits to increase taxes or the higher the real interest rate, the higher is the eventual increase in taxes.

- The legacy of past deficits is higher debt. To stabilize the debt, government must eliminate the deficit. To do so, it must run a primary surplus equal to the interest payments on the existing debt.

- Under the Ricardian equivalence proposition, a larger deficit leads to an equal increase in private saving. Thus, deficits have no effect on demand and output. The accumulation of debt does not affect capital accumulation. In reality, Ricardian equivalence fails, and larger deficits lead to higher demand and higher output in the short run. The accumulation of debt leads to lower capital accumulation, and thus to lower output in the long run.

- To stabilize the economy, government should run deficits during recessions and surpluses during booms. The cyclically adjusted deficit tells what the deficit would be, under existing tax and spending rules, if output were at its natural level.

- Deficits are justified in times of high spending, such as a war. Relative to an increase in taxes, they lead to higher consumption and lower investment during the war. They therefore shift some of the burden of the war from people living during the war to those living after the war. They also help smooth taxes and reduce tax distortions.

- Several European countries have very high debt-to-GDP ratios. In addition to reducing capital and requiring higher taxes and thus tax distortions, high debt ratios increase the risk of fiscal crises.

- Finance Minister Paul Martin engineered a series of federal budgets from 1994 to 1998 that significantly reduced the federal deficit and, indeed, moved that deficit to a substantial surplus. In November 1999, the *Economic and Fiscal Update* had to choose among three paths: a continued large surplus with similar tax and spending plans; similar tax rates with an increase in spending and a decline in the surplus; or similar spending plans with a reduction in tax rates and a smaller surplus. The third path was taken as the Liberals campaigned and won an election by promising a long-term reduction in taxes.

- The May 2006 Conservative minority budget proposes that the federal government collect less revenue and spend less as a proportion of GDP while increasing defence spending and transfers to the provinces. Since the federal budget is projected to remain balanced, other federal spending must fall as a proportion of GDP.

FISCAL POLICY: A SUMMING UP

QUESTIONS & PROBLEMS

1. TRUE/FALSE/UNCERTAIN

a. Tax smoothing and deficit finance help spread the burden of war across generations.

b. Government can never have a negative debt position.

c. The current budget surpluses for Canada will not last.

d. If Ricardian equivalence holds, an increase in income taxes will affect neither consumption nor saving.

e. The ratio of debt to GDP cannot exceed 100%. If it did, more than GDP would be needed to pay interest on the debt.

2. BUDGET NUMBERS

Consider an economy where the official budget deficit is 4% of GDP; the debt-to-GDP ratio is 100%; the nominal interest rate is 10%; and the inflation rate is 7%.

a. What is the primary deficit/surplus?

b. What is the inflation-adjusted deficit/surplus?

c. Suppose that the unemployment rate is 2% above the natural rate. What is the cyclically adjusted, inflation-adjusted deficit/surplus?

d. Suppose that the unemployment rate is equal to the natural rate. Suppose that the normal growth rate is 2%. Is the debt-to-GDP ratio going up or down?

e. If things continue as in (d), what will be the debt-to-GDP ratio in 10 years?

3. FISCAL CRISES

Suppose that in the economy described in the previous problem, financial investors worry that the level of debt is too high and that a devaluation may come. They start expecting a devaluation of 20%, with probability of 0.5, within a year.

a. If the foreign interest rate remains equal to 10%, what happens to the domestic interest rate?

b. Suppose that inflation remains the same. What happens to the domestic real interest rate? What is likely to happen to the growth rate?

c. What happens to the official budget deficit? To the inflation-adjusted deficit?

d. Suppose that the growth rate decreases from 2% to −2%. What happens to the change in the debt ratio?

e. Were the investors right to worry?

4. WARS AND DEFICITS

"A deficit during a war can be a good thing. First, the deficit is temporary; so, after it is over, government can go right back to its old level of spending and taxes. Second, given that the evidence supports Ricardian equivalence proposition, the deficit will stimulate the economy during wartime, helping keep the unemployment rate low." Identify four distinct mistakes in this reasoning.

The modern statement of the Ricardian equivalence proposition is provided in Robert Barro, "Are Government Bonds Net Wealth?" *Journal of Political Economy*, December 1974, pp. 1095–1117.

The Web site of the federal Department of Finance contains all kinds of material related to federal budget issues. The Centre for Policy Alternatives (**www.policyalternatives.ca**) provides alternative (left-wing) commentary on budget issues, both federal and provincial.

CHAPTER 27
EPILOGUE: THE STORY OF MACROECONOMICS

In the preceding 26 chapters, we presented the framework that most economists use to think about macroeconomic issues and the major conclusions they draw, as well as the issues on which they disagree. How this framework has been built over time is a fascinating story. It is the story told in this chapter.

27-1 | Keynes and the Great Depression

The history of modern macroeconomics starts in 1936, with the publication of Keynes's *General Theory of Employment, Interest, and Money*. As he was writing *General Theory*, Keynes confided to a friend: "I believe myself to be writing a book on economic theory which will largely revolutionize—not, I suppose, at once but in the course of the next 10 years—the way the world thinks about economic problems."

John Maynard Keynes

Keynes was right. The book's timing was one of the reasons for its immediate success. The Great Depression was not only an economic catastrophe but also an intellectual failure for the economists working on **business cycle theory**—as macroeconomics was then called. Few economists had a coherent explanation for the Depression, for either its depth or its length. Governments around the world, including Canada and the United States, had no framework for what few policy measures were taken to combat the Great Depression. *General Theory* offered an interpretation of events, an intellectual framework, and a clear argument for government intervention.

The *General Theory* emphasized **effective demand**—what we now call *aggregate demand*. In the short run, Keynes argued, effective demand determines output. Even if output eventually returns to its natural level, the process is, at best, slow. Indeed, one of Keynes's most famous quotes is, "In the long run, we are all dead."

In the process of deriving effective demand, Keynes introduced many of the building blocks of modern macroeconomics:

- The multiplier, which explains how shocks to demand can be amplified and lead to larger shifts in output.
- **Liquidity preference** (the term Keynes gave to the demand for money), which explains how monetary policy can affect interest rates and effective demand.
- The importance of expectations in affecting consumption and investment; and the idea that *animal spirits* (shifts in expectations) are a major factor behind shifts in demand and output.

Finally, *General Theory* was more than a treatise for economists. It offered clear policy implications, and they were in tune with the times. Waiting for the economy to return by itself to its natural level was irresponsible. In the midst of a depression, trying to balance the budget was not only stupid, it was also dangerous. Active use of fiscal policy was essential to return the country to high employment.

27-2 | The Neoclassical Synthesis

Within a few years, *General Theory* had transformed macroeconomics. Not everybody was converted, and few agreed with all of it. But most discussions became organized around it.

By the early 1950s, a large consensus had emerged, based on an integration of many of Keynes's ideas and the ideas of earlier economists. This consensus was called the **neoclassical synthesis**. To quote from Paul Samuelson in the 1955 edition of his textbook, *Economics*, the first modern economics textbook:

> *In recent years, 90 per cent of American economists have stopped being "Keynesian economists" or "anti-Keynesian economists." Instead, they have worked toward a synthesis of whatever is valuable in older economics and in modern theories of income determination. The result might be called neoclassical economics and is accepted, in its broad outlines, by all but about five per cent of extreme left-wing and right-wing writers.*

The neoclassical synthesis was to remain the dominant view for another 20 years. Progress was astonishing, and the period from the early 1940s to the early 1970s can be called the golden age of macroeconomics.

Franco Modigliani

James Tobin

Robert Solow

Progress on All Fronts

The first order of business after the publication of *General Theory* was to formalize mathematically what Keynes meant. Although Keynes knew mathematics, he had avoided using math in *General Theory*. One result was endless controversies about what Keynes meant and whether there were logical flaws in some of his arguments.

The *IS-LM* Model. Several formalizations of Keynes's ideas were offered. The most influential one was the *IS-LM* model, developed by John Hicks and Alvin Hansen in the 1930s and early 1940s. The initial version of the *IS-LM* model—which was actually very close to the version presented in Chapter 5 of this book—was criticized for emasculating many of Keynes's insights: Expectations played no role, and the adjustment of prices and wages was altogether absent. Yet, the *IS-LM* model provided a basis on which to start building, and as such, it was immensely successful. Discussions became organized around the slopes of the *IS* and *LM* curves: what variables were missing from the two relations, what equations for prices and wages should be added to the model, and so on.

Theories of Consumption, Investment, and Money Demand. Keynes had emphasized the importance of consumption and investment behaviour and of the choice between money and other financial assets. Major progress was soon made along all three fronts.

In the 1950s, Franco Modigliani (then at Carnegie Mellon and later at the Massachussetts Institute of Technology [MIT]) and Milton Friedman (then at the University of Chicago and now at the Hoover Institute at Stanford) independently developed the theory of consumption we discussed in Chapter 20. Both insisted on the importance of expectations in determining current consumption decisions.

James Tobin, at Yale, developed the theory of investment, based on the relation between the present value of profits and investment. The theory was further developed and tested by Dale Jorgenson, at Harvard. We discussed this theory in Chapter 20.

Tobin also developed the theory of the demand for money and, more generally, the theory of the choice between different assets based on liquidity, return, and risk. His work has become the basis not only for an improved treatment of financial markets in macroeconomics but also for the theory of finance in general.

Growth Theory. In parallel with the work on fluctuations, there was a renewed focus on growth. In contrast to the stagnation in the pre–World War II era, most countries were growing fast in the 1950s and 1960s. Even if they experienced fluctuations, their standard of living was increasing rapidly. The growth model developed by MIT's Robert Solow in 1956, which we discussed in Chapters 15 and 16, provided a framework to think about the determinants of growth. It was followed by an explosion of work on the roles of saving and technological progress in growth.

Macroeconometric Models. All of these contributions were integrated in larger and larger macroeconometric models. The first U.S. macroeconometric model, developed by Lawrence Klein, at the University of Pennsylvania, in the early 1950s, was an extended *IS* relation, with 16 equations. With the development of the National Income and Product Accounts (making better data available) and the development of econometrics and computers, the models quickly grew in size. The most important effort was the construction of the MPS model (MPS stands for MIT–Penn–SSRC, for the two universities and the research institution—the Social Science Research Council—involved in its construction), developed during the 1960s by a group of people led by Franco Modigliani. Both models were an expanded version of the *IS-LM* model, plus a Phillips curve mechanism. The Bank of Canada's first model, RDX2, was developed at the same time. But its components—consumption, investment, and money demand—all reflected the tremendous theoretical and empirical progress made since Keynes.

Lawrence Klein

Keynesians versus Monetarists

With such rapid progress, many macroeconomists came to believe that the future was bright. The nature of fluctuations was increasingly well understood; the development of models allowed for a better use of policy. The time when the economy could be fine-tuned and recessions all but eliminated seemed not far in the future.

This optimism was met with skepticism by a small but influential minority, the **monetarists**. Their intellectual leader was Milton Friedman. Although Friedman saw much progress being made—and was himself the father of one of the major contributions, the theory of consumption—he did not share in the general enthusiasm. He believed that the understanding of the economy remained very limited. He questioned the motives of governments as well as the notion that they actually knew enough to improve macroeconomic outcomes.

In the 1960s, debates between "Keynesians" and "monetarists" dominated the economic headlines. The debates centred around three issues: the effectiveness of monetary versus fiscal policy, the Phillips curve, and the role of policy.

Milton Friedman

Monetary versus Fiscal Policy. Keynes had emphasized *fiscal* rather than *monetary* policy as the key to fighting recessions. And this had remained the prevailing wisdom. The *IS* curve, many argued, was quite steep: Changes in the interest rate had little effect on demand and output. Thus, monetary policy did not work very well. Fiscal policy, which affects demand directly, could affect output faster and more reliably.

Friedman strongly challenged this conclusion. In a 1963 book titled *A Monetary History of the United States, 1867–1960*, Friedman and Anna Schwartz painstakingly reviewed the evidence on monetary policy and the relation between money and output in the United States over a century. Their conclusion was not only that monetary policy was very powerful but also that movements in money did explain most of the fluctuations in output. They interpreted the Great Depression as the result of a tragic mistake in monetary policy, a decrease in money supply due to bank failures—a decrease that the Federal Reserve Board could have avoided by increasing the monetary base but had not. (We discussed this interpretation in Chapter 22.)

Friedman and Schwartz's challenge was followed by a vigorous debate and by intense research on the respective effects of fiscal and monetary policies. In the end, a consensus was, in effect, reached. Both fiscal and monetary policies clearly had effects. And if one cared about the composition of output and took into account the openness of the economy, the best policy was typically a mix of the two.

The Phillips Curve. The second debate focused on the Phillips curve. The Phillips curve was not part of the initial Keynesian model. But because it provided such a convenient (and apparently reliable) way of explaining the movement of wages and prices over time, it had become part of the neoclassical synthesis. In the 1960s, based on the empirical evidence up to then, many Keynesian economists believed that there was a reliable trade-off between unemployment and inflation, even in the long run.

Milton Friedman and Edmund Phelps (at Columbia University) strongly disagreed. They argued that the existence of such a long-run trade-off flew in the face of basic economic theory. They argued that the apparent trade-off would quickly vanish if policy makers actually tried to exploit it—that is, if they tried to achieve low unemployment by accepting higher inflation. As we saw in Chapter 11, when we studied the evolution of the Phillips curve, Friedman and Phelps were most definitely right. By the mid-1970s, the consensus was, indeed, that there was no long-run trade-off between inflation and unemployment.

Edmund Phelps

The Role of Policy. The third debate centred on the role of policy. Much less certain that economists knew enough to stabilize output and that policy makers could be trusted to do the right thing, Friedman argued for the use of simple rules, such as steady money growth (a rule we discussed in Chapter 25). Here is what he said in 1958:

A steady rate of growth in the money supply will not mean perfect stability even though it would prevent the kind of wide fluctuations that we have experienced from time to time in the past. It is tempting to try to go farther and to use monetary changes to offset other factors making for expansion and contraction. . . . The available evidence casts grave doubts on the possibility of producing any fine adjustments in economic activity by fine adjustments in monetary policy—at least in the present state of knowledge. There are thus serious limitations to the possibility of a discretionary monetary policy and much danger that such a policy may make matters worse rather than better.

Political pressures to "do something" in the face of either relatively mild price rises or relatively mild price and employment declines are clearly very strong indeed in the existing state of public attitudes. The main moral to be drawn from the two preceding points is that yielding to these pressures may frequently do more harm than good.

(Milton Friedman, "The Supply of Money and Changes
in Prices and Output," Testimony to Congress, 1958.)

As we saw in Chapter 24, this debate on the role of macroeconomic policy has not been settled. The nature of the arguments has changed somewhat, but these arguments are still with us today.

Robert Lucas

27-3 | The Rational Expectations Critique

Despite the battles between Keynesians and monetarists, macroeconomics around 1970 looked like a successful and mature field. It appeared successful at explaining events and at guiding policy choices. Most debates were framed within a common intellectual framework. But, within a few years, the field was in crisis. The crisis had two sources.

One was events. By the mid-1970s, most countries were experiencing *stagflation*, a word created at the time to denote the simultaneous existence of high unemployment and high inflation. Macroeconomists had not predicted stagflation. After the fact and after a few years of research, a convincing explanation was provided, based on the effects of adverse supply shocks on both prices and output. (We discussed the effects of such shocks in Chapter 10.) But it was too late to undo the damage to the discipline's image.

The other was ideas. In the early 1970s, a small group of economists—Robert Lucas at Chicago; Thomas Sargent, then at Minnesota and now at Chicago; and Robert Barro, then at Chicago and now at Harvard—led a strong attack against mainstream macroeconomics. They did not mince words. In a 1978 paper, Lucas and Sargent stated:

Thomas Sargent

That the predictions [of Keynesian economics] were wildly incorrect, and that the doctrine on which they were based was fundamentally flawed, are now simple matters of fact, involving no subtleties in economic theory. The task which faces contemporary students of the business cycle is that of sorting through the wreckage, determining what features of that remarkable intellectual event called the Keynesian Revolution can be salvaged and put to good use, and which others must be discarded.

("After Keynesian Economics," in *After the Phillips Curve*:
Persistence of High Inflation and High Unemployment
[Boston: Federal Reserve Bank of Boston, 1978].)

The Three Implications of Rational Expectations

Lucas and Sargent's main argument was that Keynesian economics had ignored the full implications of the effect of expectations on behaviour. The way to proceed, they argued, was

Robert Barro

to assume that people formed expectations as rationally as they could, on the basis of the information they had. Thinking of people as having *rational expectations* had three major implications, all highly damaging to Keynesian macroeconomics.

The Lucas Critique. The first implication was that existing macroeconomic models could not be used to help design policy. Although these models recognized that expectations affect behaviour, they did not incorporate expectations explicitly. All variables were assumed to depend on current and past values of other variables, including policy variables. Thus, what the models captured was the set of relations among economic variables as they had held in the past, under past policies. Were these policies to change, Lucas argued, the way people formed expectations would change as well, making estimated relations—and, by implication, simulations generated using existing macroeconometric models—poor guides to what would happen under these new policies. This critique of macroeconometric models became known as the **Lucas critique**. To take, again, the history of the Phillips curve as an example, the data up to the early 1970s had suggested a trade-off between unemployment and inflation. As policy makers tried to exploit that trade-off, it disappeared.

Rational Expectations and the Phillips Curve. The second implication was as follows: When rational expectations were introduced in Keynesian models, these models actually delivered the very un-Keynesian conclusion that deviations of output from its natural level were short-lived, much more so than Keynesian economists claimed. This argument was based on a re-examination of the aggregate supply relation.

In Keynesian models, the slow return of output to its natural level came from the slow adjustment of prices and wages through the Phillips curve mechanism. An increase in money, for example, led first to higher output and lower unemployment. Lower unemployment then led to higher nominal wages and higher prices. The adjustment continued until wages and prices had increased in the same proportion as did nominal money, until unemployment and output were back at their natural levels.

This adjustment, Lucas pointed out, was highly dependent on wage setters' backward-looking expectations of inflation. In the MPS model, for example, wages responded only to current and past inflation and to current unemployment. But once the assumption that wage setters had rational expectations was made, the adjustment was likely to be much faster. Changes in money, to the extent that they were anticipated, might have no effect on output: For example, anticipating an increase in money of 5% over the coming year, wage setters would increase the nominal wages set in contracts for the coming year by 5%. Firms would, in turn, increase prices by 5%. The result would be no change in the real money stock and no change in demand or output.

Within the logic of the Keynesian models, Lucas therefore argued that only *unanticipated changes in money* should affect output. Predictable movements in money should have no effect on activity. More generally, if wage setters had rational expectations, shifts in demand were likely to have effects on output for only as long as wages were set in nominal terms, a year or so. Even on its own terms, the Keynesian model did not deliver a convincing theory of the long-lasting effects of demand on output.

Optimal Control versus Game Theory. The third implication of rational expectations was as follows: If people and firms had rational expectations, it was wrong to think of policy as the control of a complicated but passsive system. Rather, the right way was to think of policy as a game between policy makers and the economy. The right tool was not *optimal control*, but *game theory*. And game theory led to a different vision of policy. A striking example was the issue of *time inconsistency*, discussed by Finn Kydland and Edward Prescott (then at Carnegie Mellon, now at the University of Minnesota), an issue that we discussed in Chapter 24: Good intentions on the part of policy makers could actually lead to disaster.

Robert Hall

Rudiger Dornbusch

Stanley Fischer

John Taylor

To summarize: When rational expectations were introduced, (1) Keynesian models could not be used to determine policy, (2) Keynesian models could not explain long-lasting deviations of output from its natural level, and (3) the theory of policy needed to be redesigned using the tools of game theory.

The Integration of Rational Expectations

As you might guess from the tone of Lucas and Sargent's quote, the intellectual atmosphere in macroeconomics was tense in the early 1970s. But within a few years, a process of integration (of ideas, not people, because tempers remained high) had started, and it was to dominate the 1970s and the 1980s.

Fairly quickly, the idea that rational expectations was the right working assumption gained wide acceptance. This did not happen because all macroeconomists believe that people, firms, and participants in financial markets always form expectations rationally. But rational expectations appear to be a natural benchmark, at least until economists have made more progress in understanding whether and how actual expectations systematically differ from rational expectations.

Work then started on the challenges raised by Lucas and Sargent.

The Implications of Rational Expectations. First, there was a systematic exploration of the role and the implications of rational expectations in goods, financial, and labour markets. Much of what was discovered has been presented in this book already. Here are two examples:

- Robert Hall, then at MIT and now at Stanford, showed that if consumers were very foresighted (in the sense defined in Chapter 20), then changes in consumption should be unpredictable: The best forecast of consumption next year would be consumption this year! Put another way, changes in consumption should be very hard to predict. This result came as a surprise to most macroeconomists at the time, but it is, in fact, based on a simple intuition: If consumers are very foresighted, they will change their consumption only when they learn something new about the future. But by definition, such news cannot be predicted. This consumption behaviour, known as the **random walk of consumption**, has served as a benchmark in consumption research ever since.

- Rudiger Dornbusch, at MIT, showed that the large swings in exchange rates under flexible exchange rates, which had previously been thought of as the result of speculation by irrational investors, were fully consistent with rationality. We discussed his analysis in Chapter 19: Changes in monetary policy can lead to long-lasting changes in interest rates; changes in current and expected interest-rate differentials between two countries can lead to large changes in the exchange rate. Dornbusch's model, known as the *overshooting* model of exchange rates, has become the benchmark in discussions of exchange-rate movements.

Wage and Price Setting. Second, there was a systematic exploration of the determination of wages and prices, going far beyond the Phillips curve relation. Two important contributions were made by MIT's Stanley Fischer and John Taylor, then at Columbia University and now at Stanford. Both showed that the adjustment of prices and wages in response to changes in unemployment can be slow *even under rational expectations.*

They pointed to an important characteristic of both wage and price setting, the **staggering** of wage and price decisions. In contrast to the simple story we told earlier, where all wages and prices increased simultaneously in anticipation of an increase in money, actual wage and price decisions are staggered over time. So, there is not one sudden synchronized adjustment of all wages and prices to an increase in money. Rather, the adjustment is likely to be slow, with wages and prices adjusting to the new level of money through a process of leapfrogging over time. Fischer and Taylor thus showed that the second issue raised by the rational-expectations critique could be resolved and that a slow return of output to its natural level is consistent with rational expectations in the labour market.

The Theory of Policy. Third, thinking about policy in terms of game theory led to an explosion of research on the nature of the games being played, not only between policy makers and the economy but also between policy makers—between political parties, between the central bank and the government, or between governments of different countries. One of the major achievements of this research has been the development of a way of thinking more rigorously about such fuzzy notions as "credibility," "reputation," and "commitment." At the same time, there has been a distinct shift in focus from "what governments should do" to "what governments actually do," and thus a focus on the political constraints that economists should take into account when advising policy makers.

To summarize: By the end of the 1980s, the challenges raised by the rational-expectations critique had led to a complete overhaul of macroeconomics. The basic structure had been extended to take into account the implications of rational expectations or, more generally, of forward-looking behaviour by people and firms. Indeed, what we have presented in this book is what we see as the synthesis that has emerged and that now constitutes the common framework of macroeconomics. In the last section of this chapter, we will summarize what we see as the basic set of propositions on which most macroeconomists agree. But before we do so, we want to turn briefly to current research. Much of it is still too speculative to have made it in more detail into the book, but no doubt some of it will make the next edition.

27-4 | Current Developments

Today, three groups dominate the research headlines: the new classicals, the new Keynesians, and the new growth theorists. (Note the generous use of the word "new." Unlike producers of laundry detergents, economists stop short of using "new and improved." But the subliminal message is the same.)

New Classical Economics and Real Business Cycle Theory

The rational-expectations critique was more than just a critique of Keynesian economics. It also offered its own interpretation of fluctuations. Instead of relying on imperfections in labour markets, on the slow adjustment of wages and prices, and so on, to explain fluctuations, Lucas argued, macroeconomists should see how far they could go in explaining fluctuations as the effects of shocks in competitive markets with fully flexible prices and wages.

This is the research agenda that has been pursued by the **new classicals**. The intellectual leader is Edward Prescott, and the models he and his followers have developed are known as **real business cycle (RBC) models**. These models assume that output is always at its natural level. Thus, all fluctuations in output are movements of the natural level of output, as opposed to movements away from the natural level of output.

Where do these movements come from? The answer proposed by Prescott is technological progress. As new discoveries are made, productivity increases, leading to an increase in output. The increase in productivity leads to an increase in the wage, which makes it more attractive to work, leading workers to work more. Productivity increases therefore lead to increases in both output and employment, as we, indeed, observe in the real world.

The RBC approach has been criticized on many fronts. As we discussed in Chapter 16, technological progress is the result of very many innovations, each of which takes a long time to diffuse. It is hard to see how this process could generate anything like the large short-run fluctuations in output that we observe in practice. It is also hard to think of recessions as times of technological *regress*, times in which productivity and output both go down. Finally, as we have seen, there is very strong evidence that changes in money, which have no effect on output in RBC models, have, in fact, strong effects on output in the real world.

At this point, most economists do not believe that the RBC approach provides a convincing explanation of major fluctuations in output. The approach has nevertheless proved useful. It has drilled in the correct point that not all fluctuations in output are deviations of

Edward Prescott

output from its natural level. At a more technical level, it has provided several new techniques for solving complex models, which are widely used in research today. It is likely to evolve rather than disappear. Already, some recent RBC models have started introducing nominal rigidities, allowing for the effects of money on output.

New Keynesian Economics

The term **New Keynesians** denotes a loosely connected group of researchers who share a common belief that the synthesis that has emerged in response to the rational-expectations critique is basically correct. But they also share the belief that much remains to be learned about the nature of imperfections in different markets, and about the implications of those imperfections for macroeconomic evolutions.

George Akerlof

One line of research has focused on the determination of wages in the labour market. We discussed in Chapter 6 the notion of *efficiency wages*—the idea that wages, if perceived by workers as being too low, may lead to shirking by workers on the job, to problems of morale within the firm, to difficulties in recruiting or keeping good workers, and so on. One influential researcher in this area has been George Akerlof, at Berkeley, who has explored the role of "norms," the rules that develop in any organization—in this case, the firm—to assess what is fair or unfair. This research has led him and others to explore issues previously left to research in sociology and psychology and to examine their macroeconomic implications.

Another line of new Keynesian research has explored the role of imperfections in credit markets. Except for a discussion of the role of banks in the Great Depression and in the current Japanese recession, we have typically assumed in this book that the effects of monetary policy worked through interest rates, and that firms could borrow as much as they wanted at the market interest rate. In practice, many firms can borrow only from banks. And banks often turn down potential borrowers, despite the willingness of these borrowers to pay the interest rate charged by the bank. Why this happens and how it affects our view of how monetary policy works have been the subject of much research, in particular, by Ben Bernanke (at Princeton, and currently the chair of the Board of Governors of the Federal Reserve).

Ben Bernanke

Yet another direction of research is **nominal rigidities**. As we saw earlier in this chapter, Fischer and Taylor have shown that with the staggering of wage or price decisions, output can deviate from its natural level for a long time. This conclusion raises a number of questions. If staggering of decisions is responsible, at least in part, for fluctuations, why don't wage setters/price setters synchronize decisions? Why aren't prices and wages adjusted more often? Why aren't all prices and all wages changed, say, on the first day of each week? In tackling these issues, Akerlof and N. Gregory Mankiw (at Harvard University) have derived a surprising and important result often referred to as the **menu cost** explanation of output fluctuations.

Each wage setter or price setter is largely indifferent as to when and how often he changes his own wage or price (for a retailer, changing the prices on the shelf every day versus every week does not make much of a difference to the store's overall profits). Therefore, even small costs of changing prices—like the costs involved in printing a new menu, for example—can lead to infrequent and staggered price adjustment. This staggering leads to slow adjustment of the price level and to large aggregate output fluctuations in response to movements in aggregate demand. In short, decisions that do not matter much at the individual level (how often to change prices or wages) lead to large aggregate effects (slow adjustment of the price level, and shifts in aggregate demand that have a large effect on output).

New Growth Theory

After being one of the most active topics of research in the 1960s, growth theory went into an intellectual slump. Since the late 1980s, however, growth theory has made a strong comeback. The set of new contributions goes under the name of **new growth theory**.

Paul Romer

Two economists, Robert Lucas (the same Lucas who spearheaded the rational-expectations critique) and Paul Romer, then at Berkeley and now at Stanford, have played an important role in defining the issues. When growth theory faded in the late 1960s, two issues were left largely unresolved. One issue was the determinants of technological progress. The other was the role of increasing returns to scale—whether, say, doubling capital and labour can actually cause output to more than double. These are the two major issues on which new growth theory has focused. The discussions of the effects of R&D on technological progress, and of the interaction between technological progress and unemployment, reflect some of the advances economists have made on this front. One example is the work of Philippe Aghion (at Harvard University) and Peter Howitt (at Brown University), who have developed a theme first explored by Joseph Schumpeter in the 1930s, the notion that growth is a process of *creative destruction*, in which new products are constantly introduced, making old ones obsolete.

Philippe Aghion

To summarize, current research is proceeding mainly on three fronts:

1. The New Classical approach: Identifying how much of the fluctuations can be thought of as movements in the natural level of output and in the natural unemployment rate.
2. The New Keynesian approach: Identifying the precise nature of market imperfections and nominal rigidities that give rise to deviations of output from its natural level.
3. The New Growth theory: Identifying the factors responsible for technological progress and growth in the long run.

Increasingly, these three fronts overlap, and the borders are becoming fuzzier. Some models use the techniques developed by the New Classical approach, but they allow for some of the imperfections emphasized by the New Keynesian approach. Other models focus on the short-run effects on output of the process of creative destruction emphasized by new growth models, thus integrating the New Growth and the New Classical approaches. For the time being, synthesis, rather than major intellectual battles, dominates the field.

Peter Howitt

27-5 | Common Beliefs

As we come to the end of this book, let us state the basic set of propositions on which most macroeconomists agree:

- In the short run, shifts in aggregate demand affect output. Higher consumer confidence, a larger budget deficit, and faster growth of money are all likely to increase output and employment and to decrease unemployment.
- In the medium run, output returns to its natural level. This natural level depends on the natural rate of unemployment (which, together with the size of the labour force, determines the level of employment), on the capital stock, and on the state of technology.
- In the long run, two main factors determine the evolution of the level of output. The first is capital accumulation and the second the rate of technological progress.
- Monetary policy affects output in the short run, but not in the medium or the long run. A higher rate of money growth eventually translates one for one into a higher rate of inflation.
- Fiscal policy has short-run, medium-run, and long-run effects on activity. Higher deficits are likely to increase output in the short run. Higher deficits lead to current account deficits in the medium run. They are likely to decrease capital accumulation and output in the long run.

These propositions leave room for disagreement:

- One is the length of the short run, the period over which aggregate demand affects output. At one extreme, real business cycle theorists start from the assumption that output is always at its natural level: The short run is very short. On the other hand, the high levels of unemployment explored in Chapter 22 imply that the effects of demand may be extremely long-lasting, that the short run may really be very long.

- Another is the role for policy. Although conceptually distinct, it is largely related to the first. Those who believe that output returns quickly to its natural level are typically willing to impose tight rules on both monetary and fiscal policy, from constant money growth to the requirement of a balanced budget. Those who believe that the adjustment is slow typically believe in the need for more flexible stabilization policies.

But, behind these disagreements, there is a largely common framework in which most research is conducted and organized. The framework gives us a way of interpreting events and discussing policy. This is what we have done in this book.

SUMMARY

- The history of modern macroeconomics starts in 1936, with the publication of Keynes's *General Theory of Employment, Interest and Money*. Keynes's contribution was formalized in the *IS-LM* model by John Hicks and Alvin Hansen in the 1930s and early 1940s.

- The period from the early 1940s to the early 1970s can be called the golden age of macroeconomics. Among the major developments were the development of the theories of consumption, investment, money demand, and portfolio choice; the development of growth theory; and the development of large macroeconometric models.

- The main debate during the 1960s was between Keynesians and monetarists. Keynesians believed that developments in macroeconomic theory allowed for better control of the economy. Monetarists, led by Milton Friedman, were more skeptical of the ability of governments to stabilize the economy.

- In the 1970s, macroeconomics experienced a crisis. There were two reasons. The first was the appearance of stagflation, which came as a surprise to most economists. The second was a theoretical attack led by Robert Lucas. Lucas and his followers showed that when rational expectations were introduced, (1) Keynesian models could not be used to determine pol-

icy, (2) Keynesian models could not explain long-lasting deviations of output from its natural level, and (3) the theory of policy needed to be redesigned using the tools of game theory.

- Much of the 1970s and 1980s was spent integrating rational expectations into macroeconomics. As is reflected in this book, macroeconomists are now much more aware of the role of expectations in determining the effects of shocks and policy and of the complexity of policy than they were two decades ago.

- Current research in macroeconomic theory is proceeding along three lines. New classical economists are exploring the extent to which fluctuations can be explained as movements in the natural level of output, as opposed to movements away from the natural level of output. New Keynesian economists are exploring the role of market imperfections in fluctuations. New growth theorists are exploring the role of R&D and of increasing returns to scale in growth.

- Despite the differences, there exists a set of propositions on which most macroeconomists agree. The main two are: In the short run, shifts in aggregate demand affect output. In the medium run, output returns to its natural level.

KEY TERMS

- business cycle theory, 549
- effective demand, 549
- liquidity preference, 549
- Lucas critique, 553
- menu cost, 556
- monetarists, 551
- neoclassical synthesis, 549

- new classicals, 555
- new growth theory, 556
- New Keynesians, 556
- nominal rigidities, 556
- random walk of consumption, 554
- real business cycle (RBC) models, 555
- staggering, 554

The two classics are J. M. Keynes, *The General Theory of Employment, Money and Interest* (London: Macmillan Press, 1936), and Milton Friedman and Anna Schwartz, *A Monetary History of the United States, 1867–1960* (Princeton, NJ: Princeton University Press, 1963). Be warned: The first makes for hard reading, and the second is a heavy volume.

For an account of macroeconomics in textbooks since the 1940s, read Paul Samuelson's "Credo of a Lucky Textbook Author," *Journal of Economic Perspectives*, Spring 1997, pp. 153–160.

In the introduction to *Studies in Business Cycle Theory* (Cambridge, MA: MIT Press, 1981), Robert Lucas develops his approach to macroeconomics and gives a guide to his contributions.

The paper that launched real business cycle theory is by Edward Prescott, "Theory Ahead of Business Cycle Measurement," *Federal Reserve Bank of Minneapolis Review*, Fall 1986, pp. 9–22. It is not particularly easy reading.

For more on new Keynesian economics, read David Romer, "The New Keynesian Synthesis," *Journal of Economic Perspectives*, Winter 1993, pp. 5–22.

For more on new growth theory, read Paul Romer, "The Origins of Endogenous Growth," *Journal of Economic Perspectives*, Winter 1994, pp. 3–22. A more complete treatment is given in Charles Jones, *An Introduction to Economic Growth* (New York: W.W. Norton, 1997).

In a lighter mode, for a well-written set of essays on many economists and their ideas, read David Warsh, *Economic Principles: Masters and Mavericks of Modern Economics* (New York: Free Press, 1993).

For more on how macroeconomists, from Robert Solow to Robert Lucas, view macroeconomics, read Brian Snowdown and Howard Vane, *Conversations with Leading Economists, Interpreting Modern Macroeconomics* (Northampton, MA: Edward Elgar, 1999).

For macroeconomic and political news from around the world, *The Economist* is a wonderful source.

In Canada, relatively student-friendly articles on macroeconomics appear in *Canadian Public Policy* and in *Policy Options*.

If you want to learn more about macroeconomic issues and theory:

- Most economics journals are heavy on mathematics and are hard to read. But a few make an effort to be more friendly. *The Journal of Economic Perspectives*, in particular, has nontechnical articles on current economic research and issues. *The Brookings Papers on Economic Activity*, published twice a year, analyze current macroeconomic problems. So does *Economic Policy*, published in Europe, which focuses more on European issues.

- Most central banks, including the Bank of Canada, also publish reviews with easy-to-read articles; these reviews are available on the Web site of the Bank of Canada and those of other central banks. A large number are in English, even from non–English-speaking countries.

- More advanced treatments of current macroeconomic theory—roughly at the level of a first graduate course in macroeconomics—are given by David Romer, *Advanced Macroeconomics* (New York: McGraw-Hill, Third Edition, 2005) and by Olivier Blanchard and Stanley Fischer, *Lectures on Macroeconomics* (Cambridge, MA: MIT Press, 1989).

APPENDICES

Appendix 1: An Introduction to National Income and Expenditure Accounts

The purpose of this appendix is to introduce the basic structure as well as the terms used in the national income and expenditure accounts. The basic measure of aggregate activity is gross domestic product, or GDP. The **national income and expenditure accounts** (or simply **national accounts**) are organized around two decompositions of GDP. The first looks at *income:* Who receives what? The other looks at *expenditures:* What is produced, and who buys it?

The Income Side

Table A1–1 looks at the income side of GDP, at who receives what. The top half of the table (lines 1 to 10) goes from GDP to national income, the sum of the incomes received by the different factors of production.

■ The starting point, in line 1, is gross domestic product, or GDP. It is defined *as the market value of the final goods and services produced by labour and property located in Canada*. (Alternatively, it is the value of the income *produced* in Canada.)

■ The next two lines take us from GDP to GNP, the gross national product (line 3). GNP is an alternative measure of aggregate output. It is defined as *the market value of the final goods and services produced by labour and property supplied by Canadian residents* (alternatively, it is the income *accruing* to Canadian residents).

  For many years, most countries used GNP rather than GDP as the main measure of aggregate activity. The emphasis in the Canadian national accounts shifted from GNP to GDP in 1986. The difference between the two comes from the distinction between "located in Canada" (used to define GDP) and "supplied by Canadian residents" (used to define GNP). For example, profit from a Canadian-owned plant in the United States is not included in Canadian GDP but is included in Canadian GNP. Thus, to go from GDP to GNP, we must first add the difference between factor payments received from foreign residents and factor payments made to foreign residents. In the national accounts this is called net investment income received from non-residents and appears on line 2 (net factor payments to labour are small and are ignored). In 2005, payments to the rest of the world exceeded receipts from the rest of the world by about $23 billion, so GNP was smaller than GDP by the same amount.

■ The next step takes us from GNP to the net natural income at basic prices (line 7), where **capital consumption allowances** are subtracted. This is the Statistics Canada estimate of the economic depreciation of corporate and public sector capital. In a sense, part of gross income is the result of using up

TABLE A1–1	GDP: The Income Side, 2005 (Millions of Dollars)

From gross domestic product to net domestic income at basic prices:

1	Gross domestic product (GDP) at market prices	1,368,726
2	Add: Net investment income received from non-residents	−22,824
3	Equals: Gross national product (GNP) at market prices	1,345,902
4	Deduct: Capital consumption allowances	181,427
5	Deduct: Taxes less subsidies on products	94,750
6	Deduct: Statistical discrepancy	−658
7	Equals: Net national income at basic prices	1,070,383
8	Deduct: Net investment income paid to non-residents	−22,824
9	Equals: Net domestic product at basic prices	1,093,207
10	Wages, salaries, and supplementary labour income	678,925
11	Corporate profits before taxes	193,936
12	Government business enterprise profits before taxes	13,370
13	Interest and miscellaneous investment income	61,240
14	Accrued net income of farm operators from farm production	1,551
15	Net income of non-farm unincorporated business including rent	84,666
16	Inventory valuation adjustment	−442
17	Taxes less subsidies on factors of production	59,961
18	Net domestic product at basic prices (sum of rows 10 through 17)	1,093,207

Sources: The national accounts are kept up to date on the Statistics Canada Web site (**www.statcan.ca**) and on the CANSIM II database which should be available at your university. In paper form, a quarterly publication *National Income and Expenditure Accounts* (Catalogue No 13-001) gives commentary and details.

capital. The other adjustments are more complicated. Market prices incorporate sales taxes and subsidies (line 5) which are deducted from gross sales to get a measure of incomes. Finally, there is a statististical discrepency which follows from the measurement of national income.

National income measures are actually constructed in two independent ways in most countries. One way, from the top down, adds up all of the expenditures on goods and services produced in Canada. This exercise is presented in Table A1–3 in the next section. The other way to construct national income measures is presented in Table A1–1, the table we are working with. This can be thought of as from the bottom up. The lower portion of Table A1–1 adds up the different incomes earned by factors in Canada (wages and salaries, profits, and so on) to get a measure of net domestic product at basic prices (line 18 and line 9). The sum of all incomes earned by factors does not typically equal the sum of the values of all goods sold, although in theory and in practice, this must be the case. It is impossible for me to sell you $100 worth of services, for example, if I clean your apartment, without my also earning $100 worth of income. If one of us does not report either the purchase of services or the earning of income, or there is simply an accounting mistake, the two measures of national income will not be identical. This difference, between the sum of incomes reported to Statistics Canada and the sum of all purchases reported to Statistics Canada, is split roughly equally between the two measures of national income and creates the statistical discrepancy. In 2005, the measure of gross domestic product computed from the top down (from the expenditure side) was smaller by $658 million than the measure of gross domestic product computed from the bottom up (the income side) ($658 million is not a large error on $1,000 billion of income and many more dollars of transactions). To make the two measures of GDP equal, $658 million is subtracted from the income-side measure and $657 million is added to the expenditure-side measure. To recover the measure of income that corresponds to factor incomes earned by Canadians (net national income at basic prices) line 6 is subtracted from line 5. Line 7, net national income at basic prices, is the total of all incomes earned on both labour and capital by Canadian residents.

■ Finally, to look at all incomes earned inside the boundaries of Canada, we must add back the net investment income paid to nonresidents (line 8). Line 9 is **net domestic product at basic prices**, the sum of all incomes earned within the borders of Canada.

Various keywords appear in the national accounts often enough that it pays to discuss them briefly. The words "at basic prices" means that the prices used do not include the indirect taxes on products (GST and other sales taxes) which are included in market prices. Aggregates that have been adjusted for depreciation are given the modifier *net*; otherwise they are called *gross*. Aggregates that refer to Canadian residents are called *national*; if an aggregate refers to something that took place in Canada, it is called *domestic*. Using these distinctions, you can construct your own aggregates rather easily (or at least quickly see how to get from some published number to what you want). For example, we can compute gross domestic income at market prices by starting with line 7 and adding back lines 4 and 5.

Statistics Canada produces monthly estimates of GDP at basic prices, including the contributions by industry, with a lag of about 60 days. The monthly estimates are based on a number of clever tricks to proxy for unavailable data. Although useful, they tend to be rather inaccurate. Estimates of GDP at market prices (both income and expenditure accounts) are available on a quarterly basis and on an annual basis. The quarterly estimates arrive with a lag of about two months and are updated regularly for several years as better data become available. Some historical data are also available on an annual basis, but in December 1997, Statistics Canada announced that it would shift its emphasis to its quarterly series and many annual series would no longer be updated.

The bottom half of Table A1–1 (lines 10 to 17) decomposes net domestic product at basic prices into different types of income:

■ Wages, salaries, and supplementary labour income (line 10) is by far the largest component, accounting for 62% of net domestic product.

■ **Corporate profits** before taxes (line 11) is a highly volatile component of net domestic income. In 2005, it accounted for almost 18%.

■ Government business enterprise profits before taxes (line 12) constituted 1.2% of net domestic product in 2005. In Canada, some businesses are owned and operated by the government sector. These are primarily generators of electricity and the telephone systems in some provinces as well as some other smaller operations.

■ Interest and miscellaneous investment income (line 13) is the interest paid by firms minus the interest received by firms plus interest received from the rest of the world. In 2005, this component was approximately equal to 5.4% of net domestic income.

- The income of farm operators (line 14) is now a very small component of domestic income. It is measured on an accrued basis (rather than a cash flow basis). That is, the value of farm production is counted in the year in which it is produced, rather than the year in which it is sold.

- The income of other small businesses (line 15) accounted for about 7.7% of net domestic income. Rental income includes the rents received by landlords and an imputed value for owner-occupied housing. Owner-occupied housing generates a flow of services. To capture the value of this flow in domestic income, Statistics Canada estimates how much homeowners would have to pay themselves to rent their own homes and adds this into line 15.

- The inventory valuation adjustment (line 16) measures capital gains (or losses) from business inventories. These show up in corporate profits, but because they do not reflect economic production, they are subtracted before arriving at domestic income.

- Some taxes are levied directly on factors of production. These are primarily payroll taxes paid by employers. Net of any subsidies, these taxes add to the cost of the goods produced and thus to their basic prices. These must be added as though they were earned by a factor of production (line 17) to generate the total of all incomes earned by factors of production resident in Canada at basic prices (line 18).

Table A1–2 shows how to construct **personal disposable income**, the income available to consumers after they have received transfers and paid taxes.

- **Personal income**, the sum of income earned by households and transfers received from the other sectors in the economy, totalled $1017 billion in 2005. Many of the components of personal income are already familiar from our discussion of Table A1–1. Wages, salaries, and supplementary labour income (line 2) is by far the largest component of personal income. Unincorporated business net income (line 3) is just the sum of lines 14 and 15 in Table A1–1. Line 4 in Table A1–2 is obtained by adding the value of the dividends received from corporations to line 13 in Table A1–1. In addition to their earnings from supplying labour and capital, households also receive transfers, such as employment insurance benefits. In 2005, transfers amounted to 13.6% of personal income.

- From personal income, we subtract direct taxes (income taxes) and other transfers to government (some small things including fines).

- The net result is personal disposable income (line 7), the amount of income households have to spend after controlling for taxes and transfers. In 2004, personal disposable income was $777 million, or about 57% of GDP.

The Expenditure Side

Table A1–3 looks at the expenditure side of the national accounts, at who buys what. Let us start with the

TABLE A1–2	Personal Income and Personal Disposable Income, 2005 (Millions of Dollars)

Line	Short Name	Value
1	Personal income	1,017,885
2	Wages, salaries, and supplementary income	678,925
3	Unincorporated business income	86,217
4	Interest, dividends, and miscellaneous investment receipts	113,315
5	Transfers from government, corporations, and non-residents	139,428
6	Less: Income taxes and other transfers to governments	240,201
7	Equals: Personal disposable income	777,684

Source: See Table A1-1.

TABLE A1–3	GDP: The Expenditure Side, 2005 (Millions of Dollars)

Line	Short Name	Value
1	Gross domestic product	1,368,726
2	Personal expenditure on consumer goods and services	761,962
3	Durable goods	100,289
4	Semidurable goods	64,526
5	Nondurable goods	189,213
6	Services	407,934
7	Business investment in fixed capital	244,887
8	Residential construction	89,595
9	Non-residential construction	63,938
10	Machinery and equipment	91,354
11	Government purchases	297,525
12	Net exports	54,226
13	Exports	518,256
14	Imports	464,030
15	Changes in business inventories	9,469
16	Statistical discrepancy	657

Source: See Table A1-1.

three components of domestic demand: consumption, investment, and government spending.

■ Consumption, called **personal expenditure on consumer goods and services** (line 2), is by far the largest component of demand, accounting for 55% of GDP. It is defined as *the sum of goods and services purchased by persons resident in Canada*.

In the same way as they include rental income on the income side, the national accounts include imputed housing services as part of consumption. Owners of a house are assumed to consume housing services, for a price equal to the imputed rental income.

Consumption is decomposed into four components: purchases of **durable goods**, such as cars (line 3), semidurable goods, such as shoes (line 4), nondurable goods, such as strawberries (line 5), and services (line 6). **Nondurable goods** and **services** account for just over three-quarters of total consumption.

■ Investment is called business investment in fixed capital. It is the sum of two very different components: (1) residential construction (line 8) is the purchase of new houses or apartments by persons; (2) nonresidential construction (line 9) and machinery and equipment (line 10) are the investment decisions of firms related to plant and equipment.

■ **Government purchases** of goods and services (line 11) are mostly current expenditures but also include government investment (e.g., buildings) and a very small component for changes in government inventories.[1] They do not include transfers to persons (such as employment insurance or Canada Pension Plan payments) or interest on the public debt. In 2005, government purchases accounted for almost 22% of GDP.

■ The sum of consumption, investment, and government purchases gives the demand for goods by Canadian firms, Canadian persons, and Canadian governments. If Canada were a closed economy, this would be the same as the demand for Canadian goods. But because Canada is open, the two numbers are different. To get to the demand for Canadian goods, we must first add the foreign purchases of domestic goods, exports (line 13). Second, we must subtract Canadian purchases of foreign

goods, imports (line 14). In 2005, exports exceeded imports by just over $54 billion. Thus, net exports (or, equivalently, the trade balance) was equal to $54 billion (line 12).

■ Adding consumption, investment, government purchases, and net exports gives the total purchases of Canadian goods. However, production may be less than those purchases if firms satisfy the difference by decreasing inventories; or production may be greater than purchases, in which case firms accumulate inventories. Thus, line 15 in Table A1–3 gives **changes in business inventories**, also called (rather misleadingly) "business investment in inventories." This term is defined as the value of the change in the physical volume of inventories held by business. The change in business inventories can be positive or negative. In 2005, it was positive: Canadian production was more than total purchases of Canadian goods by $9.4 billion. Although relatively small, the change in business inventories is one of the most cyclically sensitive components of aggregate expenditure.

A Warning

National accounts give an internally consistent description of aggregate activity. But underlying these accounts are many choices of what to include and what not to include, where to put some types of income or spending, and so on. Here are three examples:

■ Work within the home is not counted in GDP. Thus, to take an extreme example, if two women decide to babysit each other's child and pay each other for the babysitting services, measured GDP will go up, while true GDP clearly does not change. The solution would be to count work within the home in GDP, in the same way that we impute rents for owner-occupied housing. But so far, this has not been done.

■ The purchase of a house is treated as an investment, and housing services are then treated as part of consumption. Contrast this with the treatment of automobiles. Despite the fact that they provide services for a long time—although not as long a time as houses do—purchases of automobiles are not treated as investment. They are treated as consumption and appear in the national accounts only in the year in which they are bought.

---

[1]Government investment in physical capital is quite large, $35 billion in 2005.

■ Physical investment and education are treated asymmetrically. Firms' purchases of machines are treated as investment. The purchase of education is treated as consumption of education services. But education is clearly, in part, an investment: People acquire it, in part, to increase their future income.

The list goes on. However, the purpose of these examples is not to make you conclude that national accounts are wrong. Most of the choices we just saw were made for good reasons, often because of data availability or for simplicity of treatment. Rather, the point is that to use the national accounts in the best way, you should understand not only their logic but also their choices and thus their limitations.

FURTHER READING

For more details on national income accounting, see Statistics Canada, *Guide to Income and Expenditure Accounts*, Catalogue No. 13-603E, No. 1, 1990.

Appendix 2:
A Math Refresher

This appendix presents the mathematical tools and the mathematical results that are used in the book.

Geometric Series

Definition. A geometric series is a sum of numbers of the form:

$$1 + x + x^2 + \cdots + x^n$$

where x is a number that may be greater or smaller than one, and x^n denotes x to the power n, that is, x times itself n times.

Examples of such series are:

- The sum of spending in each round of the multiplier (Chapter 3). If c is the marginal propensity to consume, then the sum of increases in spending after n rounds is given by:

$$1 + c + c^2 + \cdots + c^{n-1}$$

- The present discounted value of a sequence of payments of 1 each year for n years (Chapter 18), when the interest rate is equal to i:

$$1 + \frac{1}{1+i} + \frac{1}{(1+i)^2} + \cdots + \frac{1}{(1+i)^{n-1}}$$

We usually have two questions we want to answer when encountering such a series. The first one is what the sum is. The second is whether the sum explodes as we let n increase, or reaches a finite limit. The following propositions tell you what you need to know to answer these questions.

Proposition 1 tells you how to compute the sum:

Proposition 1:

$$1 + x + x^2 + \cdots + x^n = \frac{1 - x^{n+1}}{1 - x} \quad \text{(A.1)}$$

The proof is as follows. Multiply the sum by $(1 - x)$, and use the fact that $x^a x^b = x^{a+b}$ (that is: one has to add exponents when multiplying):

$$
\begin{aligned}
(1 + x + &x^2 + \cdots + x^n)(1 - x) \\
&= 1 + x + x^2 + \cdots + x^n \\
&\quad - x - x^2 - \cdots - x^n - x^{n+1} \\
&= 1 \hspace{4.5cm} - x^{n+1}
\end{aligned}
$$

All the terms on the right except for the first and the last cancel. Dividing both sides by $(1 - x)$ gives equation (A.1).

This formula can be used for any x and any n. If, for example, x is 0.9 and n is 10, then the sum is equal to 6.86. If x is 1.2 and n is 10, then the sum is equal to 32.15.

Proposition 2 tells you what happens as n gets large:

Proposition 2: If x is less than 1, the sum goes to $1/(1 - x)$ as n gets large. If x is equal to or greater than one, the sum explodes as n gets large.

The proof is as follows: If x is less than 1, then x^n goes to zero as n gets large. Thus, from equation (A.1), the sum goes to $1/(1 - x)$. If x is greater than 1, then x^n becomes larger and larger as n increases, $1 - x^n$ becomes a larger and larger negative number, and the ratio $(1 - x^n)/(1 - x)$ becomes a larger and larger positive number. Thus, the sum explodes as n gets large.

Application from Chapter 18: Consider the present value of a payment of $1 forever, starting next year, when the interest rate is equal to i. The present value is given by:

$$\frac{1}{(1+i)} + \frac{1}{(1+i)^2} + \cdots \quad \text{(A.2)}$$

Factoring out $1/(1 + i)$, rewrite this present value as:

$$\frac{1}{(1+i)}\left[1 + \frac{1}{(1+i)} + \cdots\right]$$

The term in brackets is a geometric series, with $x = 1/(1 + i)$. As the interest rate i is positive, x is less than 1. Applying proposition 2, when n gets large, the term in brackets is thus equal to:

$$\frac{1}{1 - \dfrac{1}{(1+i)}} = \frac{(1+i)}{(1+i-1)} = \frac{(1+i)}{i}$$

Replacing the term in brackets in the previous equation by $(1 + i)/i$ gives:

$$\frac{1}{(1+i)}\left[\frac{(1+i)}{i}\right] = \frac{1}{i}$$

The present value of a sequence of payments of $1 a year forever, starting next year, is thus equal to 1 over the interest rate. If i is equal to 5%, the present value is equal to $20.

Useful Approximations

Throughout the book, we use several approximations that make computations easier. These approximations are most reliable when the variables x, y, z below are small, say, between 0% and 10%. The numerical examples in propositions 3 through 10 that follow are based on the values $x = 0.05$ and $y = 0.03$.

Proposition 3:

$$(1 + x)(1 + y) < (1 + x + y) \qquad \text{(A.3)}$$

The proof is as follows: Expanding $(1 + x)(1 + y)$ gives $(1 + x)(1 + y) = 1 + x + y + xy$. If x and y are small, then the product xy is very small and can be ignored as an approximation (for example, if $x = 0.05$ and $y = 0.03$, then $xy = 0.0015$). So $(1 + x)(1 + y)$ is approximately equal to $(1 + x + y)$.

For the values x and y above, for example, the approximation gives 1.08 compared to an exact value of 1.0815.

Application from Chapter 6: Arbitrage between domestic and foreign bonds leads to the following relation:

$$(1 + i_t) = (1 + i_t^*)\left(1 + \frac{(E_{t+1}^e - E_t)}{E_t}\right)$$

Using proposition 3 on the right-hand side of the equation gives:

$$(1 + i_t^*)\left(1 + \frac{(E_{t+1}^e - E_t)}{E_t}\right)$$

$$< \left(1 + i_t^* + \frac{(E_{t+1}^e - E_t)}{E_t}\right)$$

Replacing in the arbitrage equation gives:

$$(1 + i_t) < \left(1 + i_t^* + \frac{(E_{t+1}^e - E_t)}{E_t}\right)$$

Subtracting 1 from both sides gives:

$$i_t < i_t^* + \frac{(E_{t+1}^e - E_t)}{E_t}$$

The domestic interest rate is approximately equal to the foreign interest rate plus the expected rate of depreciation of the domestic currency.

Proposition 4:

$$(1 + x)^2 < 1 + 2x \qquad \text{(A.4)}$$

The proof follows directly from proposition 3, with $y = x$. For the value of $x = 0.05$, the approximation gives 1.10, compared with an exact value of 1.1025.

Application from Chapter 19: From arbitrage, the relation between the two-year interest rate and the current and expected one-year rates is given by:

$$(1 + i_{2t})^2 = (1 + i_{1t})(1 + i_{1t+1}^e)$$

Using proposition 4 for the left-hand side of the equation gives:

$$(1 + i_{2t})^2 < 1 + 2\,i_{2t}$$

Using proposition 3 for the right-hand side of the equation gives:

$$(1 + i_{1t})(1 + i_{1t+1}^e) < 1 + i_{1t} + i_{1t+1}^e$$

Replacing in the original relation gives:

$$1 + 2\,i_{2t} = 1 + i_{1t} + i_{1t+1}^e$$

Or, reorganizing:

$$i_{2t} = \frac{(i_{1t} + i_{1t+1}^e)}{2}$$

The two-year rate is approximately equal to the average of the current and expected one-year rates.

Proposition 5:

$$(1 + x)^n < 1 + nx \qquad \text{(A.5)}$$

The proof follows by repeated application of propositions 3 and 4. For example, $(1 + x)^3 = (1 + x)^2(1 + x) \approx (1 + 2x)(1 + x)$ by proposition 4, $\approx (1 + 2x + x) = 1 + 3x$ by proposition 3.

The approximation becomes worse as n increases, however. For example, for $x = 0.05$ and $n = 5$, the approximation gives 1.25, compared to an exact value of 1.2763. For $n = 10$, the approximation gives 1.50, compared to an exact value of 1.63.

Application: In Chapter 19, we saw that arbitrage between n-year Canadian bonds and n-year American bonds implies:

$$(1 + r_{nt})^n = \left(\frac{1}{\epsilon_t}\right)(1 + r_{nt}^*)^n(\epsilon_{t+n}^e)$$

From proposition 5, it follows that:

$$(1 + r_{nt})^n < (1 + nr_{nt})$$

and:

$$(1 + r_{nt}^*)^n < (1 + nr_{nt}^*)$$

Note also that we can rewrite the two terms in ϵ on the right in the arbitrage equation as:

$$\frac{\epsilon_{t+n}^e}{\epsilon_t} = 1 + \frac{(\epsilon_{t+n}^e - \epsilon_t)}{\epsilon_t}$$

Replacing these three expressions in the arbitrage relation gives:

$$(1 + nr_{nt}) < (1 + nr_{nt}^*)\left(1 + \frac{(\epsilon_{t+n}^e - \epsilon_t)}{\epsilon_t}\right)$$

From proposition 3, it follows that:

$$(1 + nr_{nt}) < \left(1 + nr^*_{nt} + \frac{(\epsilon^e_{t+n} - \epsilon_t)}{\epsilon_t}\right)$$

Or, simplifying:

$$n(r_{nt} - r^*_{nt}) < \frac{(\epsilon^e_{t+n} - \epsilon_t)}{\epsilon_t}$$

The expected rate of real dollar depreciation over the next n years is approximately equal to n times the difference between the nth year Canadian and American real interest rates.

Proposition 6:

$$\frac{(1 + x)}{(1 + y)} \approx (1 + x - y) \qquad \text{(A.6)}$$

The proof is as follows: Consider the product of $(1 + x - y)(1 + y)$. Expanding this product gives $(1 + x - y)(1 + y) = 1 + x + xy - y^2$. If both x and y are small, then xy and y^2 are very small, so $(1 + x - y)(1 + y) \approx (1 + x)$. Dividing both sides of this approximation by $(1 + y)$ gives the proposition above.

For the values of $x = 0.05$ and $y = 0.03$, the approximation gives 1.02, while the correct value is 1.019.

Application from Chapter 18: The real interest rate is defined by:

$$(1 + r_t) \equiv \frac{(1 + i_t)}{(1 + \pi^e_t)}$$

Using proposition 6 gives:

$$(1 + r_t) \approx (1 + i_t - \pi^e_t)$$

Simplifying:

$$r_t \approx i_t - \pi^e_t$$

This gives us the approximation we use at many points in the book: The real interest rate is approximately equal to the nominal interest rate minus expected inflation.

These approximations are also very convenient when dealing with *growth rates*. Define the rate of growth of x by $g_x \equiv \Delta x/x$, and similarly for z, g_z and for y, g_y. The numerical examples below are based on the values $g_x = 0.05$ and $g_y = 0.03$.

Proposition 7: If $z = xy$, then:

$$g_z \approx g_x + g_y \qquad \text{(A.7)}$$

The proof is as follows. Let Δz be the increase in z when x increases by Δx and y increases by Δy. Then, by definition:

$$z + \Delta z = (x + \Delta x)(y + \Delta y)$$

Divide both sides by z so that:

$$\frac{(z + \Delta z)}{z} = \frac{(x + \Delta x)}{x}\frac{(y + \Delta y)}{y}$$

where we have used on the right hand side the fact that dividing by z is the same as dividing by xy. Simplifying gives:

$$\left(1 + \frac{\Delta z}{z}\right) = \left(1 + \frac{\Delta x}{x}\right)\left(1 + \frac{\Delta y}{y}\right)$$

Or, equivalently:

$$(1 + g_z) = (1 + g_x)(1 + g_y)$$

From proposition 3, $(1 + g_z) \approx (1 + g_x + g_y)$, or, equivalently, $g_z \approx g_x + g_y$.

For the values of g_x and g_y above, the approximation gives $g_z = 8\%$, while the correct value is 8.15%.

Application from Chapter 16: Let a production function be of the form $Y = NA$, where Y is production, N is employment, and A is productivity. Denoting the growth rates of Y, N, and A by g_Y, g_N, and g_A respectively, proposition 7 implies $g_Y \approx g_N + g_A$: The rate of output growth is approximately equal to the rate of employment growth plus the rate of productivity growth.

Proposition 8: If $z = x/y$, then:

$$g_z \approx g_x - g_y \qquad \text{(A.8)}$$

The proof is as follows: Let Δz be the increase in z, when x increases by Δx and y increases by Δy. Then, by definition:

$$z + \Delta z = \frac{x + \Delta x}{y + \Delta y}$$

Dividing both sides by z and using the fact that $z = x/y$ gives:

$$1 + \Delta z/z = \frac{1 + (\Delta x/x)}{1 + (\Delta y/y)}$$

Or, substituting:

$$1 + g_z = \frac{1 + g_x}{1 + g_y}$$

From proposition 6, $(1 + g_z) \approx (1 + g_x - g_y)$, or, equivalently, $g_z \approx g_x - g_y$.

For the values of $g_x = 0.05$ and $g_y = 0.03$, the approximation gives $g_z = 2\%$, while the correct value is 1.9%.

Application from Chapter 12: Let aggregate demand be given by $Y = \gamma M/P$, where Y is output, M is nominal money, P is the price level, and γ is a constant parameter. It follows from propositions 7 and 8 that:

$$g_y \approx g_\gamma + g_M - \pi$$

where π is the rate of growth of prices, equivalently the rate of inflation. As γ is constant, g_γ is equal to zero. Thus:

$$g_y \approx g_M - \pi$$

The rate of output growth is approximately equal to the rate of growth of nominal money minus the rate of inflation.

Functions

We use functions informally in the book, as a way of denoting how a variable depends on one or more other variables.

In some cases, we look at how a variable Y moves with a variable X. We write this relation as:

$$Y = f(X)$$
$$+$$

A plus sign below X indicates a positive relation: An increase in X leads to an increase in Y. A minus sign indicates a negative relation: An increase in X leads instead to a decrease in Y.

In some cases, we allow the variable Y to depend on more than one variable. For example, we allow Y to depend on X and Z:

$$Y = f(X, Z)$$
$$(+, -)$$

The signs indicate that an increase in X leads to an increase in Y holding the value of Z constant, and that an increase in Z leads to a decrease in Y holding the value of X constant.

An example of such a function is the investment function in Chapter 5:

$$I = I(Y, i)$$
$$(+, -)$$

This equation says that investment, I, increases with production, Y, and decreases with the interest rate, i.

In some cases, it is reasonable to assume that the relation between two or more variables is a linear relation. A given increase in X always leads to the same increase in Y. In that case, the function is given by:

$$Y = a + bX$$

The parameter a is called the **intercept**: It gives the value of Y when X is equal to zero. The parameter b is called the **slope**: It tells us by how much Y increases when X increases by one.

The simplest linear relation is the relation $Y = X$, which is represented by the 45-degree line and has a slope of one. Another example of a linear relation is the consumption function introduced in Chapter 3:

$$C = c_0 + c_1 Y_D$$

where C is consumption and Y_D is disposable income. The parameter c_0 tells us what consumption would be if disposable income were equal to zero. The parameter c_1 tells us by how much consumption increases when income increases by 1 unit; c_1 is called the propensity to consume.

KEY TERMS

- intercept, A9
- slope, A9

Appendix 3:
An Introduction to Econometrics

How do we know that consumption depends on disposable income? How do we know the value of the propensity to consume? To answer these questions and, more generally, to estimate behavioural relations and find out the values of the relevant parameters, economists use *econometrics*—the set of statistical techniques designed for use in economics. Econometrics can get fairly mathematical, but the basic principles behind econometric techniques are simple. This appendix shows you these basic principles.

To do so, we will use as an example the consumption function introduced in Chapter 3, and we will concentrate on estimating c_1, the propensity to consume out of disposable income.

Changes in Consumption and Changes in Disposable Income

The propensity to consume tells us by how much consumption changes for a given change in disposable income. A natural first step is simply to plot changes in consumption versus changes in disposable income and see how the relation between the two looks. This is done in Figure A3–1.

The vertical axis in Figure A3–1 measures the annual change in consumption minus the average annual change in consumption since 1962. More precisely, let C_t denote consumption in year t. Let ΔC_t denote

$C_t - C_{t-1}$, the change in consumption from year $t - 1$ to year t. Let $\overline{\Delta C}$ denote the average annual change in consumption since 1962. The variable measured on the vertical axis is constructed as $\Delta C_t - \overline{\Delta C}$. A positive value of the variable represents an increase in consumption larger than average, a negative value an increase in consumption smaller than average.

Similarly, the horizontal axis measures the annual change in disposable income, minus the average annual change in disposable income since 1962, $\Delta Y_{Dt} - \overline{\Delta Y_D}$.

A particular square in the figure gives the deviations of the change in consumption and disposable income from their respective means for a particular year between 1962 and 2004. In 1982, for example, the change in consumption was lower than average by $19.9 billion, the change in disposable income was lower than average by $9.9 billion dollars. (For our purposes, it is not important to know which year each square refers to, just what the set of points in the diagram looks like. So, except for 1982, the years are not indicated in Figure A3–1.)

Figure A3–1 suggests two main conclusions:

- First, there is a clearly positive relation between changes in consumption and changes in disposable income. Most of the points lie in the upper-right and lower-left quadrants of the figure: When disposable income increases by more than average, consumption also typically increases by more than

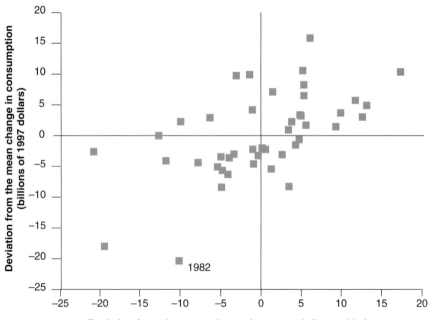

Source: Consumption (1997 dollars) using CANSIM II variable V3862655; consumption (current dollars) using CANSIM II variable V646938; current dollar personal disposable income using CANSIM II variable V647037 deflated by ratio of current dollar to constant dollar consumption.

FIGURE A3–1

Changes in Consumption versus Changes in Disposable Income, 1962–2005

There is a clearly positive relation between changes in consumption and changes in disposable income.

Deviation from the mean change in consumption (billions of 1997 dollars)

1982

Deviation from the mean change in personal disposable income (billions of 1997 dollars)

average; when disposable income increases by less than average, typically so does consumption.

- Second, the relation between the two variables is good but not perfect. In particular, there is only one point in the upper-left quadrant: This is a year where a smaller-than-average change in disposable income was associated with a larger-than-average change in consumption.

Econometrics allows us to state these two conclusions more precisely and to get an estimate of the propensity to consume. Using an econometrics software package, we can find the line that fits the cloud of points in Figure A3–1 best. This line-fitting process is called **ordinary least squares (OLS)**. (The term "least squares" comes from the fact that the line has the property that it minimizes the sum of the squared distances of the points to the line—thus it gives the "least" "squares." The word "ordinary" comes from the fact that this is the simplest method used in econometrics.) The estimated equation corresponding to the line is called a **regression**, and the line itself is called the **regression line**.

In our case, the estimated equation is given by:

$$(\Delta C_t - \overline{\Delta C}) = 0.47(\Delta Y_{Dt} - \overline{\Delta Y_D}) + \text{residual}$$
$$\overline{R}^2 = 0.33 \quad (A3.1)$$

The regression line corresponding to this estimated equation is drawn in Figure A3–2. Equation (A3.1) reports two important numbers (econometrics packages give more information than reported above; a typical printout, together with further explanations, is given in the Focus box "A Guide to Understanding Econometric Results"):

- The first is the estimated propensity to consume. The equation tells us that an increase in disposable income of $1 billion above normal is typically associated with an increase in consumption of $0.43 billion above normal. In other words, the estimated propensity to consume is 0.47. It is positive but smaller than 1.

- The second important number is $\overline{R}^2$, which is a measure of how well the regression line fits.

Having estimated the effect of disposable income on consumption, we can decompose the change in consumption for each year into that part that is due to the change in disposable income— the first term on the right in equation (A3.1)—and the rest, which is called the **residual**. For example, the residual for 1982 is indicated in Figure A3–2 by the vertical distance from the point representing 1982 to the regression line.

If all the points in Figure A3–2 were exactly on the estimated line, all residuals would be equal to zero; all changes in consumption would be explained by changes in disposable income. As you can see, however, this is not the case. $\overline{R}^2$ is a statistic that tells us how well the line fits. $\overline{R}^2$ is always between 0 and 1. A value of 1 would imply

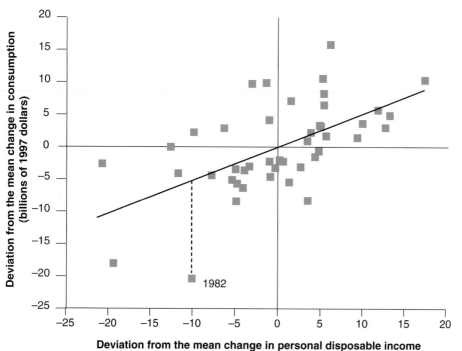

FIGURE A3–2

Changes in Consumption and Changes in Disposable Income: The Regression Line

The regression line is the line that fits the scatter of points best.

Source: Consumption (1997 dollars) using CANSIM II variable V3862655; consumption (current dollars) using CANSIM II variable V646938; current dollar personal disposable income using CANSIM II variable V647037 deflated by ratio of current dollar to constant dollar consumption.

that the relation between the two variables is perfect, that all points are exactly on the regression line. A value of 0 would imply that the computer can see no relation between the two variables. The value of $\bar{R}^2$ of 0.33 in equation (A3.1) is quite high, but not 1. It confirms the message from Figure A3–2: Movements in disposable income clearly affect consumption, but there is still quite a bit of movement in consumption that cannot be explained by movements in disposable income.

Correlation versus Causality

What we have established so far is that consumption and disposable income typically move together. More formally, we have seen that there is a positive **correlation**—the technical term for "co-relation"—between annual changes in consumption and annual changes in disposable income. And we have interpreted this relation as showing **causality**—that an increase in disposable income causes an increase in consumption.

We need to think again about this interpretation. A positive relation between consumption and disposable income may reflect the effect of disposable income on consumption. But it may also reflect the effect of consumption on disposable income. Indeed, the model we developed in Chapter 3 tells us that if, for any reason, consumers decide to spend more, then output, thus income, and, in turn, disposable income will increase. If part of the relation between consumption and disposable income comes from the effect of consumption on disposable income, interpreting equation (A3.1) as telling us about the effect of disposable income on consumption is not right.

An example will help here: Suppose that consumption does not depend on disposable income so that the true value of c_1 is equal to zero. (This is not very realistic, but it will make the point most clearly.) So, draw the consumption function as a horizontal line (a line with a slope of zero) in Figure A3–3. Next, suppose that disposable income is equal to Y_D so that the initial combination of consumption and disposable income is given by point A.

Now, suppose that because of improved confidence, consumers increase their consumption so that the consumption line shifts up. If demand affects output, then income, and, in turn, disposable income increase so that the new combination of consumption and disposable income will be given by, say, point B. If, instead, consumers become more pessimistic, the consumption line shifts down, and so does output, leading to a combination of consumption and disposable income given by point D.

If we look at that economy, we observe points A, B, and D. If, as we did earlier, we then draw the best-fitting line through these points, we estimate an upward-sloping line, such as CC', and so estimate a positive value for the propensity to consume, c_1. Remember, however, that the true value of c_1 is zero. Why do we get the wrong answer—a positive value for c_1 when the true value is zero? That is because we interpret the positive relation between disposable income and consumption as showing the effect of disposable income on consumption, where, in fact, the relation reflects the effect of consumption on disposable income: Higher consumption leads to higher demand, higher output, and so higher disposable income.

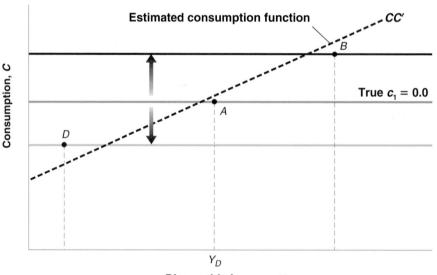

FIGURE A3–3

A Misleading Regression

The relation between disposable income and consumption comes from the effect of consumption on income rather than from the effect of income on consumption.

Estimated consumption function

CC'

B

True $c_1 = 0.0$

A

D

Consumption, C

Disposable income, Y_D

Y_D

In your readings, you may run across results of estimation using econometrics. Here is a guide, which uses the slightly simplified, but otherwise untouched computer output for the equation (A3.1):

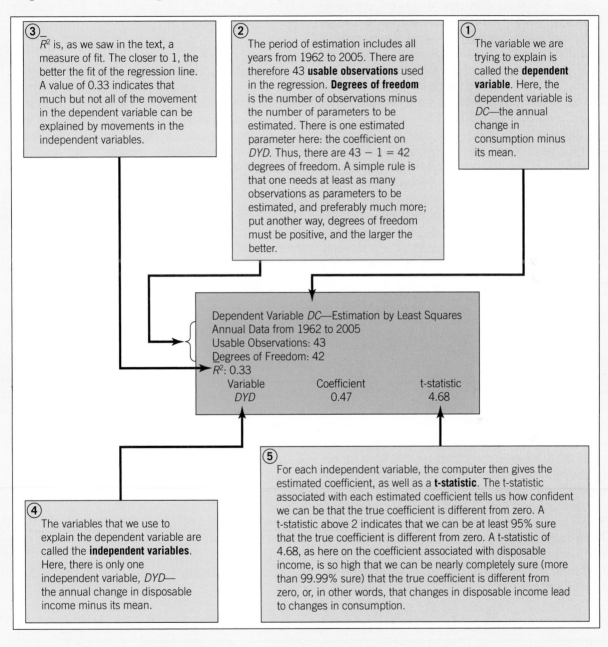

③ R^2 is, as we saw in the text, a measure of fit. The closer to 1, the better the fit of the regression line. A value of 0.33 indicates that much but not all of the movement in the dependent variable can be explained by movements in the independent variables.

② The period of estimation includes all years from 1962 to 2005. There are therefore 43 **usable observations** used in the regression. **Degrees of freedom** is the number of observations minus the number of parameters to be estimated. There is one estimated parameter here: the coefficient on *DYD*. Thus, there are 43 − 1 = 42 degrees of freedom. A simple rule is that one needs at least as many observations as parameters to be estimated, and preferably much more; put another way, degrees of freedom must be positive, and the larger the better.

① The variable we are trying to explain is called the **dependent variable**. Here, the dependent variable is *DC*—the annual change in consumption minus its mean.

Dependent Variable *DC*—Estimation by Least Squares
Annual Data from 1962 to 2005
Usable Observations: 43
Degrees of Freedom: 42
R^2: 0.33

Variable	Coefficient	t-statistic
DYD	0.47	4.68

④ The variables that we use to explain the dependent variable are called the **independent variables**. Here, there is only one independent variable, *DYD*— the annual change in disposable income minus its mean.

⑤ For each independent variable, the computer then gives the estimated coefficient, as well as a **t-statistic**. The t-statistic associated with each estimated coefficient tells us how confident we can be that the true coefficient is different from zero. A t-statistic above 2 indicates that we can be at least 95% sure that the true coefficient is different from zero. A t-statistic of 4.68, as here on the coefficient associated with disposable income, is so high that we can be nearly completely sure (more than 99.99% sure) that the true coefficient is different from zero, or, in other words, that changes in disposable income lead to changes in consumption.

There is an important lesson here, *the difference between correlation and causality*. The fact that two variables move together does not imply that movements in the first variable cause movements in the second variable. Perhaps the causality runs the other way: Movements in the second variable cause movements in the first variable. Or perhaps, as is likely to be the case here, the causality runs both ways: Disposable income affects consumption, *and* consumption affects disposable income.

Is there a way out of the correlation-versus-causality problem? If we are interested—and we are—in the effect of disposable income on consumption, can we still learn that from those data? The answer is yes, but only by using more information.

Suppose that we *knew* that a specific change in disposable income was not caused by a change in consumption. Then, by looking at the reaction of consumption to *this* change in disposable income, we could learn how consumption responds to disposable income; we could estimate the propensity to consume.

This answer would seem to simply assume away the problem: How can we know that a change in disposable income is not due to a change in consumption? In fact, sometimes, we can. Suppose, for example, that government embarks on a major increase in defence spending, leading to an increase in demand and, in turn, an increase in output. In that case, if we see both disposable income and consumption increase, we can safely assume that the movement in consumption reflects the effect of disposable income on consumption and thus estimate the propensity to consume.

This example suggests a general strategy:

- Find exogenous variables—that is, variables that affect disposable income but are not, in turn, affected by it.

- Look at the change in consumption in response not to all changes in disposable income—as we did in our earlier regression—but to those changes in disposable income that can be explained by changes in these exogenous variables.

By doing so, we can be confident that what we are estimating is the effect of disposable income on consumption, and not the other way around.

The problem of finding such exogenous variables is known as the **identification problem** in econometrics. These exogenous variables, when they can be found, are called **instruments**. Methods of estimation that rely on the use of such instruments are called **instrumental variable methods**.

When equation (A3.1) is estimated using an instrumental variable method (using changes in lagged U.S. real GDP, changes in lagged exports to the United States, and the contemporary change in the U.S. interest rates as instruments), the estimated equation becomes:

$$(\Delta C_t - \overline{\Delta C}) = 0.52(\Delta Y_{Dt} - \overline{\Delta Y_D}) + \text{residual}$$
$$\overline{R}^2 = 0.34 \quad \text{(A3.2)}$$

Note that the coefficient on disposable income, 0.52, is about the same as the coefficient 0.47 in equation (A3.1). Our earlier estimate in equation (A3.1) reflected not only the effect of disposable income on consumption but also the effect of consumption back on disposable income. The use of instruments eliminates this second effect. We would conclude in Canada's case the second effect is quite small.

This short introduction to econometrics is no substitute for a course in econometrics. But it gives you a sense of how economists use data to estimate relations and parameters and to identify causal relations between economic variables.

KEY TERMS

- causality, A12
- correlation, A12
- degrees of freedom, A13
- dependent variable, A13
- identification problem, A14
- independent variable, A13
- instruments, A14
- instrumental variable methods, A14
- ordinary least squares (OLS), A11
- regression, A11
- regression line, A11
- residual, $\overline{R}^2$, A11
- t-statistic, A13
- usable observations, A13

Appendix 4: Symbols Used in This Book

Symbol	Term	Introduced in Chapter
$(\ )^d$	Superscript d means demanded	
$(\ )^e$	Superscript e means expected	
A	Aggregate private spending	21
	Also: labour productivity/state of technology	9, 16
α	Effect of unemployment rate on inflation rate, given expected inflation	11
B	Bonds	4
B^f	Net foreign assets	17
β	Effect of an increase in output growth on the unemployment rate	12
C	Consumption	3
CA	Current account balance	17
CU	Currency	4
c	Proportion of money held as currency	4
c_0	Consumption when disposable income equals zero	3
c_1	Propensity to consume	3
D	Chequable deposits	4
	Also: real dividend on a stock	19
$\$D$	Nominal dividend on a stock	19
δ	Depreciation rate	15
E	Nominal exchange rate (price of foreign currency in terms of domestic currency)	6
$\overline{E}$	Fixed nominal exchange rate	8
E^e	Expected future exchange rate	6
ϵ	Real exchange rate	6
G	Government spending	3
g_A	Growth rate of technological progress	16
g_K	Growth rate of capital	16
g_m	Growth rate of nominal money	12
g_N	Growth rate of population	16
g, g_y	Growth rate of output	12
$\overline{g}_y$	Normal rate of growth of output	12
H	High-powered money/monetary base/central bank money	4
	Also: human capital	15
I	Fixed investment	3
$\overline{I}$	Investment, taken as exogenous	3
I_S	Inventory investment	3
i	Nominal interest rate	4
i_1	One-year nominal interest rate	19
i_2	Two-year nominal interest rate	19
i^*	Foreign nominal interest rate	6

Symbol	Term	Introduced in Chapter
K	Capital stock	14
L	Labour force	2
M	Money stock (nominal)	4
M^d	Money demand (nominal)	4
M^s	Money supply (nominal)	4
μ	Markup of prices over wages	9
N	Employment	2
N_n	Natural level of employment	9
NX	Net exports	7
P	GDP deflator/CPI/price level	2
P^*	Foreign price level	6
π	Inflation	2
Π	Profit per unit of capital	20
Q	Imports	3
	Also: real stock price	19
$\$Q$	Nominal stock price	19
R	Bank reserves	4
r	Real interest rate	18
S	Private saving	3
s	Private saving rate	15
T	Net taxes (taxes paid by consumers minus transfers)	3
Tr	Government transfers	26
θ	Reserve ratio of banks	4
U	Unemployment	2
u	Unemployment rate	2
u_n	Natural rate of unemployment	9
V	Present value of a sequence of real payments z	18
$\$V$	Present value of a sequence of nominal payments $\$z$	18
W	Nominal wage	9
Y	Real GDP/output/supply of goods	2
$\$Y$	Nominal GDP	2
Y_D	Disposable income	3
Y_L	Labour income	20
Y_n	Natural level of output	9
Y^*	Foreign output	7
X	Exports	3
Z	Demand for goods	3
z	Factors that affect the wage, given unemployment	9
	Also: real payment	18
$\$z$	Nominal payment	18

GLOSSARY

above the line, below the line In the balance of payments, the items in the *current account* are above the line drawn to divide them from the items in the *capital account,* which appear below the line.

accelerationist Phillips curve See *modified Phillips curve.*

accommodation A change in the money supply by the central bank to maintain a constant interest rate in the face of changes in money demand or in spending.

adaptive expectations A backward-looking method of forming expectations by adjusting for past mistakes.

adjusted nominal money growth Nominal money growth minus normal output growth.

aggregate demand relation The demand for output at a given price level. It is derived from equilibrium in goods and financial markets.

aggregate output Total amount of output produced in the economy.

aggregate private spending The sum of all non-government spending. Also called *private spending.*

aggregate production function The relation between the quantity of aggregate output produced and the quantities of inputs used in production.

aggregate supply relation The price level at which firms are willing to supply a given level of output. It is derived from equilibrium in the labour market.

animal spirits A term introduced by Keynes to refer to movements in investment that could not be explained by movements in current variables.

anticipated money Movements in nominal money that could have been predicted based on the information available at some time in the past.

appreciation An increase in the price of the domestic currency in terms of a foreign currency. Corresponds to a decrease in the exchange rate.

appropriability (of research results) The extent to which firms benefit from the results of their research and development efforts.

arbitrage The proposition that the expected rates of return on two financial assets must be equal. Also called *risky arbitrage* to distinguish it from *riskless arbitrage,* the proposition that the actual rates of return on two financial assets must be the same.

automatic stabilizer The fact that a decrease in output leads, under given tax and spending rules, to an increase in the budget deficit. This increase in the budget deficit in turn increases demand and thus stabilizes output.

autonomous spending That component of the demand for goods that does not depend on the level of output.

average hours The average hours per week worked by Canadians who are employed either full-time or part-time.

balance of payments A set of accounts that summarizes a country's transactions with the rest of the world.

balanced budget A budget in which taxes are equal to government spending.

balanced growth The situation in which output, capital, and effective labour all grow at the same rate.

bands (for exchange rates) The limits within which the exchange rate is allowed to move under a fixed exchange rate system.

Bank of Canada Canada's central bank.

Bank of Canada Act The Act of Parliament that describes the responsibilities and structure of the Bank of Canada.

Bank Rate The top of the 50 basis point target band for the overnight rate as set by the Bank of Canada.

bank run Simultaneous attempts by depositors to withdraw their funds from a bank.

bargaining power The relative strength of each side in a negotiation or a dispute.

barter The exchange of goods for other goods rather than for money.

base year When constructing real GDP by evaluating quantities in different years using a given set of prices, the year to which this given set of prices corresponds.

behavioural equation An equation that captures some aspect of behaviour.

bilateral real exchange rate The real exchange rate between two countries.

bond A financial asset that promises a stream of known payments over some period of time.

bond rating The assessment of a bond based on its default risk.

brain drain A term used to describe the emigration of highly educated workers from one country to another.

broad money See *M2.*

budget deficit The excess of government expenditures over government revenues.

business cycle theory The study of macroeconomic fluctuations.

business cycles See *output fluctuations.*

Canada bond A bond issued by the Canadian federal government with a maturity of 1 to 30 years.

Canada Pension Plan (CPP) One of the ways in which the federal government provides pensions to elderly persons in Canada. The CPP is partly a pay-as-you-go plan and partly a funded plan. The Quebec Pension Plan (QPP) is the equivalent plan for Quebecers.

capital account In the balance of payments, a summary of a country's asset transactions with the rest of the world.

capital accumulation Increase in the capital stock.

capital consumption allowances The estimated amount of the economic depreciation (wearing out) of corporate and public sector capital.

capital controls Restrictions on the foreign assets domestic residents can hold and on the domestic assets foreigners can hold.

capital depreciation See capital consumption allowances.

cash flow The net flow of cash a firm is receiving.

causality A relation between cause and effect.

central bank money Money issued by the central bank. Also known as the *monetary base* and *high-powered money.*

central parity The reference value of the exchange rate around which the exchange rate is allowed to move under a fixed exchange rate system. The centre of the *band.*

changes in business inventories In the national income and product accounts, the change in the physical volume of inventories held by businesses.

chequable deposits Deposits at banks and other financial institutions against which cheques can be written.

Cobb–Douglas production function A frequently used functional relationship among output, capital input, and labour input where there are constant returns to scale.

collective bargaining Bargaining about wages between firms and unions.

confidence band When estimating the dynamic effect of one variable on another, the range of values where we can be confident the true dynamic effect lies.

constant returns to scale The proposition that a proportional increase (or decrease) of all inputs leads to the same proportional increase (or decrease) in output.

consumer price index (CPI) The cost of a given list of goods and services consumed by a typical consumer.

consumption (*C*) Goods and services purchased by consumers.

consumption function A function that relates consumption to its determinants.

contractionary open market operation An open market operation in which the central bank sells bonds to decrease the money supply.

convergence The tendency for countries with lower output per capita to grow faster, leading to convergence of output per capita across countries.

coordination (of macroeconomic policies between two countries) The joint design of macroeconomic policies to improve the economic situation in the two countries.

corporate bond A bond issued by a corporation.

corporate profits In the national income and product accounts, firms' revenues minus costs (including interest payments) and minus depreciation.

correlation   A measure of the way two variables move together. A positive correlation indicates that the two variables tend to move in the same direction. A negative correlation indicates that the two variables tend to move in opposite directions. A correlation of zero indicates that there is no apparent relation between the two variables.

cost of living index   The average price of a consumption bundle.

coupon bond   A bond that promises multiple payments before maturity and one payment at maturity.

coupon payments   The payments before maturity on a coupon bond.

coupon rate   The ratio of the coupon payment to the face value of a coupon bond.

crawling peg   An exchange rate mechanism in which the exchange rate is allowed to move over time according to a pre-specified formula.

credibility   The degree to which people and markets believe that a policy announcement will actually be implemented and followed through.

credit channel   The channel through which monetary policy works by affecting the amount of loans made by banks to firms.

currency   Coins and bills.

currency board   An exchange rate system in which: (i) the central bank stands ready to buy or sell foreign currency at the official exchange rate; (ii) it cannot engage in open market operations, that is buying or selling government bonds.

current account   In the balance of payments, the summary of a country's payments to and from the rest of the world.

current account balance   The change in a country's net foreign assets or debts.

current yield   The ratio of the coupon payment to the price of a coupon bond.

cyclically adjusted deficit   A measure of what the government deficit would be under existing tax and spending rules, if output were at its natural level. Also called a *full-employment deficit, mid-cycle deficit, standardized employment deficit,* or *structural deficit.*

debt finance   Financing based on loans or the issuance of bonds.

debt monetization   The printing of money to finance a deficit.

debt ratio   See *debt-to-GDP ratio.*

debt repudiation   A unilateral decision by a debtor not to repay its debt.

debt-to-GDP ratio   The ratio of debt to gross domestic product. Also called simply the *debt ratio.*

decreasing returns to capital   The property that increases in capital lead to smaller and smaller increases in output as the level of capital increases.

decreasing returns to labour   The property that increases in labour lead to smaller and smaller increases in output as the level of labour increases.

default risk   The risk that the issuer of a bond will not pay back the full amount promised by the bond.

deflation   Negative inflation.

degrees of freedom   The number of usable observations in a *regression* minus the number of parameters to be estimated.

demand deposit   A bank account that allows depositors to write cheques or get cash on demand, up to an amount equal to the account balance.

demand for domestic goods   The demand for domestic goods by people, firms, and governments, both domestic and foreign. Equal to the domestic demand for goods plus net exports.

Department of Finance   The ministry of the federal government responsible for the broad outline of fiscal policy in Canada. The Minister of Finance is usually the federal politician most closely linked to presentation of the federal budget.

dependent variable   A variable whose value is determined by one or more other variables.

depreciation   A decrease in the price of the domestic currency in terms of a foreign currency. Corresponds to an increase in the exchange rate.

depreciation rate   A measure of how much usefulness a piece of capital loses from one period to the next.

depression   A deep and long-lasting recession.

devaluation   An increase in the exchange rate in a fixed exchange-rate system.

discount bond   A bond that promises a single payment at maturity.

discount factor   The value today of a dollar (or other national currency unit) at some time in the future.

discount rate   The interest rate used to discount a sequence of future payments. Equal to the nominal interest rate when discounting future nominal payments, to the real interest rate when discounting future real payments.

discouraged worker   A person who has given up looking for employment.

disinflation   A decrease in inflation.

disposable income (Y_D)   The income that remains once consumers have received transfers from the government and paid their taxes.

dividends   The portion of a corporation's profits that the firm pays out each period to shareholders.

dollar GDP   See *nominal GDP.*

dollarization   The use of U.S. dollars in domestic transactions in a country other than the United States.

domestic demand for goods   The sum of consumption, investment, and government spending.

dual labour market   A labour market that combines a *primary labour market* and a *secondary labour market.*

durable goods   Commodities that can be stored and have an average life of at least three years.

duration of unemployment   The period of time during which a worker is unemployed.

dynamics   Movements of one or more economic variables over time.

econometrics   Statistical methods applied to economics.

effective demand   Synonym for *aggregate demand.*

effective labour   The number of workers in an economy times the state of technology.

effective real exchange rate   See *multilateral exchange rate.*

efficiency wage   The wage at which a worker is performing a job most efficiently or productively.

efficiency wage theories   These theories of wage determination link an increase in the wage paid to workers to an increase in the efficiency or productivity.

Employment Insurance   This is the federal program that provides benefits to workers who become unemployed through layoffs or financial failures of firms. It also provides maternity, paternity, and adoption benefits.

employment rate   The percentage of the population that could work that are employed.

employment-to-population ratio   This is the employment rate in ratio form, the proportion of the population over 15 years of age and able to work that are employed.

endogenous variable   A variable that depends on other variables in a model and is thus explained within the model.

equilibrium   The equality between demand and supply.

equilibrium condition   The condition that supply be equal to demand.

equilibrium in the goods market   The condition that the supply of goods be equal to the demand for goods.

equity finance   Financing based on the issuance of shares.

equity premium   Risk premium required by investors to hold stocks rather than short-term bonds.

euro   The new European currency, which replaced national currencies in 12 countries in 2002.

European Central Bank (ECB)   The central bank, located in Frankfurt, in charge of determining monetary policy in the Euro zone.

European Monetary System (EMS)   A fixed exchange rate system in place in most of the countries of the European Union, from 1978 to 1999.

European Union (EU)   A political and economic organization of 15 European nations. Formerly called the European Community.

exchange rate mechanism (ERM)   The rules that determined the bands within which the member countries of the European Monetary System had to maintain their bilateral exchange rate.

exogenous variable   A variable that is not explained within a model but rather is taken as given.

expansion   A period of positive GDP growth.

expansionary open market operation   An open market operation in which the central bank buys bonds to increase the money supply.

expectations hypothesis The hypothesis that financial investors are risk neutral, which implies expected returns on all financial assets have to be equal.

expectations-augmented Phillips curve See *modified Phillips curve*.

expected present discounted value The value today of an expected sequence of future payments. Also called *present discounted value* or *present value*.

exports (X) The purchases of domestic goods and services by foreigners.

face value (on a bond) The single payment at maturity promised by a discount bond.

fad A period of time during which, for reasons of fashion or overoptimism, financial investors are willing to pay more than the fundamental value of a stock.

federal deposit insurance This federal program provides insurance for depositors against the financial failure of the bank where the deposits are held. The banks must pay a premium for this service and follow some regulations about the distributions of their loans.

federal funds rate The interest rate determined by equilibrium in the federal funds market. The interest rate affected most directly by changes in monetary policy.

Federal Open Market Committee (FOMC) A committee composed of the seven governors of the Fed, plus five District Bank presidents. The FOMC directs the activities of the *Open Market Desk*.

Federal Reserve Bank (the Fed) The U.S. central bank.

fertility of research The degree to which spending on research and development translates into new ideas and new products.

financial intermediary A financial institution that receives funds from people and/or firms, and uses these funds to make loans or buy financial assets.

financial investment The purchase of financial assets.

financial markets The markets in which financial assets are bought and sold.

financial wealth The value of all of one's financial assets minus all financial liabilities. Sometimes called *wealth* for short.

fine tuning A macroeconomic policy aimed at precisely hitting a given target, such as constant unemployment or constant output growth.

fiscal consolidation See *fiscal contraction*.

fiscal contraction A policy aimed at reducing the budget deficit through a decrease in government spending or an increase in taxation. Also called *fiscal consolidation*.

fiscal expansion An increase in government spending or a decrease in taxation, which leads to an increase in the budget deficit.

fiscal policy A government's choice of taxes and spending.

fiscal year An accounting period of 12 months. In Canada, the fiscal year of most provincial gov-

ernments and the federal government runs from April 1 of previous calendar year to March 31 of the next calendar year. Thus, fiscal year 2002–2003 refers to the period from April 1, 2002 to March 31, 2003. Corporations and other accounting units also declare fiscal years, which may not correspond to calendar years.

Fisher effect The proposition that in the long run an increase in nominal money growth is reflected in an identical increase in both the nominal interest rate and the inflation rate, leaving the real interest rate unchanged. Also called *Fisher hypothesis*.

Fisher hypothesis See *Fisher effect*.

fixed exchange rate An exchange rate between the currencies of two or more countries that is fixed at some level and adjusted only infrequently.

fixed investment See *investment (I)*.

flexible exchange rate See *floating exchange rate*.

float The exchange rate is said to float when it is determined in the foreign exchange market, without central bank intervention.

floating exchange rate An exchange rate determined in the foreign-exchange market without central bank intervention.

flow A variable that can be expressed as a quantity per unit of time (such as income).

foreign direct investment The purchase of existing firms or the development of new firms by foreign investors.

foreign exchange Foreign currency; all currencies other than the domestic currency of a given country.

foreign-exchange reserves Foreign assets held by the central bank.

foreign portfolio investment Foreign portfolio investment is foreign holdings of Canadian stocks without majority control of the firms. It also includes foreign holdings of bank loans to Canadians or bonds issued by Canadians.

four tigers The four Asian economies of Singapore, Taiwan, Hong Kong, and South Korea.

full-employment deficit See *cyclically adjusted deficit*.

fully funded social security system Retirement system in which the contributions of current workers are invested in financial assets, with the proceeds (principal and interest) given back to the workers when they retire.

fundamental value (of a stock) The present value of expected dividends.

G-8 The eight major economic powers in the world: the United States, Japan, France, Germany, the United Kingdom, Italy, Russia, and Canada.

game *Strategic interactions* between *players*.

game theory The prediction of outcomes from *games*.

GDP adjusted for inflation See *real GDP*.

GDP deflator The ratio of nominal GDP to real GDP; a measure of the overall price level. Gives

the average price of the final goods produced in the economy.

GDP growth The growth rate of real GDP in year t; equal to $(Y_t - Y_{t-1})/Y_{t-1}$.

GDP in 1997 dollars See *real GDP*.

GDP in constant dollars See *real GDP*.

GDP in current dollars See *nominal GDP*.

GDP in terms of goods See *real GDP*.

general equilibrium A situation in which there is equilibrium in all markets (goods, financial, and labour).

geometric series A mathematical sequence in which the ratio of one term to the preceding term remains the same. A sequence of the form $1 + c + c^2 + \cdots + c^n$.

gold standard A system in which a country fixed the price of its currency in terms of gold and stood ready to exchange gold for currency at the stated parity.

golden-rule level of capital The level of capital at which long-run consumption is maximized.

government bond A bond issued by a government or a government agency.

government budget constraint The budget constraint faced by the government. The constraint implies that an excess of spending over revenues must be financed by borrowing, and thus leads to an increase in debt.

government purchases In the national income and product accounts, the sum of the purchases of goods by the government plus compensation of government employees.

government spending (G) The goods and services purchased by federal, provincial, and local governments.

government transfers Payments made by the government to individuals that are not in exchange for goods or services. Example: Canada Pension Plan payments or welfare payments.

Great Depression The severe worldwide depression of the 1930s.

gross domestic product (GDP) A measure of aggregate output in the national income accounts. (The market value of the goods and services produced by labour and property located in Canada.)

gross national product (GNP) Income accruing to factors of production, both labour and capital, owned by Canadian residents.

growth The steady increase in aggregate output over time.

Guaranteed Income Supplement (GIS) This is a major federal government program of transfers to the elderly who are also poor and have no other support. Your income must fall below a certain threshold to receive the GIS.

hedonic pricing An approach to calculating real GDP that treats goods as providing a collection of characteristics, each with an implicit price.

heterodox stabilization program A stabilization program that includes incomes policies.

high-powered money See *central bank money*.

hires Workers newly employed by firms.

housing wealth The value of the housing stock.

human capital The set of skills possessed by the workers in an economy.

human wealth The labour-income component of wealth.

hyperinflation Very high inflation.

hysteresis In general, the proposition that the equilibrium value of a variable depends on its history. With respect to unemployment, the proposition that a long period of sustained actual unemployment leads to an increase in the equilibrium rate of unemployment.

identification problem In econometrics, the problem of finding whether correlation between variables X and Y indicates a causal relation from X to Y, or from Y to X, or both. This problem is solved by finding exogenous variables, called *instruments*, that affect X and do not affect Y directly, or affect Y and do not affect X directly.

identity An equation that holds by definition, denoted by the sign ≡.

imports (*Q*) The purchases of foreign goods and services by domestic consumers, firms, and the government.

income The flow of revenue from work, rental income, interest, and dividends.

incomes policies Government policies that set up wage and/or price guidelines or controls.

independent variable A variable that is taken as given in a relation or in a model.

index number A number, such as the GDP deflator, that has no natural level and is thus set to equal some value (typically 1 or 100) in a given period.

indexed bond A bond that promises payments adjusted for inflation. These are also called *real return bonds.*

indirect taxes Taxes on goods and services, primarily sales taxes.

industrial policy A policy aimed at helping specific sectors of an economy.

inflation A sustained rise in the general level of prices.

inflation rate The rate at which the price level increases over time.

inflation targeting The conduct of monetary policy so as to achieve a given inflation rate over time.

inflation targets If a central bank uses inflation targets it sets a public target, usually a band, for the desired rate of inflation. In Canada, the inflation target is 1–3%.

inflation tax The product of the rate of inflation and real money balances.

inflation-adjusted deficit The correct economic measure of the budget deficit: the sum of the *primary deficit* and real interest payments.

instrumental variable methods In econometrics, methods of estimation that use *instruments* to estimate causal relations between different variables.

instruments In econometrics, the exogenous variables that allow the identification problem to be solved.

intercept In a linear relation between two variables, the value of the first variable when the second variable is equal to zero.

interest parity condition See *uncovered interest parity relation.*

intermediate good A good used in the production of a final good.

International Monetary Fund (IMF) The principal international economic organization. Publishes the *World Economic Outlook* annually and the *International Financial Statistics (IFS)* monthly.

inventory investment (I_S) The difference between production and sales.

investment (*I*) Purchases of new houses and apartments by people, and purchases of new capital goods (machines and plants) by firms.

investment income In the current account, income received by domestic residents from their holdings of foreign assets.

IS curve A downward-sloping curve relating output to the interest rate. The curve corresponding to the *IS relation,* the equilibrium condition for the goods market.

IS relation An equilibrium condition stating that the demand for goods must be equal to the supply of goods, or equivalently that investment must be equal to saving. The equilibrium condition for the goods market.

J-curve A curve depicting the initial deterioration in the trade balance caused by a real depreciation, followed by an improvement in the trade balance.

junk bond A bond with a high risk of default.

labour force The sum of those employed and those unemployed.

Labour Force Survey (LFS) A large monthly survey of Canadian households used in particular to compute the unemployment rate.

labour hoarding The practice of retaining workers during a period of low product demand rather than laying them off.

labour in efficiency units See *effective labour.*

labour market rigidities Restrictions on firms' ability to adjust their level of employment.

labour productivity The ratio of output to the number of workers.

Laffer curve A curve showing the relation between tax revenues and the tax rate.

lagged value The value of a variable in the preceding time period.

layoffs Workers who lose their jobs either temporarily or permanently.

leapfrogging Advancing on and then overtaking the leader. Used to describe the process by which economic leadership passes from country to country.

life cycle theory of consumption The theory of consumption, developed initially by Franco Modigliani, that emphasizes that the planning horizon of consumers is their lifetime.

linear relation A relation between two variables such that a one-unit increase in one variable always leads to an increase of n units in the other variable.

liquid An asset is "liquid" when it can be sold for cash quickly and without significant transactions costs. Thus, Treasury bill is very liquid. A house is not a liquid asset: Although it can be converted into cash, it may take some time and involve large transactions costs. Assets vary in their liquidity.

liquid asset An asset that can be sold easily and at little cost.

liquidity preference The term introduced by Keynes to denote the demand for money.

liquidity trap The case where nominal interest rates are close to zero, and monetary policy cannot therefore decrease them further.

LM curve An upward-sloping curve relating the interest rate to output. The curve corresponding to the *LM relation,* the equilibrium condition for financial markets.

LM relation An equilibrium condition stating that the demand for money must be equal to the supply of money. The equilibrium condition for financial markets.

logarithmic scale A scale in which the same proportional increase represents the same distance on the scale so that a variable that grows at a constant rate is represented by a straight line.

long run A period of time extending over decades.

long-term bond A bond with maturity of 10 years or more.

long-term unemployment A situation in which an individual remains unemployed for a long time, usually more than one year.

Lucas critique The proposition, put forth by Robert Lucas, that existing relations between economic variables may change when policy changes. An example is the apparent trade-off between inflation and unemployment, which may disappear if policy makers try to exploit it.

M1 The sum of currency, traveller's cheques, and chequable deposits—assets that can be used directly in transactions. Also called *narrow money* and *denoted M1B.*

M2 M1 plus money market mutual fund shares, money market and savings deposits, and time deposits. Also called *broad money,* sometimes *denoted M2+.*

Maastricht treaty A treaty signed in 1991 that defined the steps involved in the transition to a common currency for the European Union.

macroeconomics The study of aggregate economic variables, such as production for the economy as a whole, or the average price of goods.

marginal propensity to import The effect on imports from an additional dollar in income.

market for overnight funds This is the financial market in which banks and other financial institutions lend money to each other for one day "overnight."

Marshall–Lerner condition The condition under which a real depreciation leads to an increase in net exports.

maturity The length of time over which a financial asset (typically a bond) promises to make payments to the holder.

medium run A period of time between the *short run* and the *long run*.

medium-term bond A bond with maturity of one to 10 years.

menu cost The cost of changing a price.

merchandise trade Exports and imports of goods.

microeconomics The study of production and prices in specific markets.

mid-cycle deficit See *cyclically adjusted deficit*.

models of endogenous growth Models in which accumulation of physical and human capital can sustain growth even in the absence of technological progress.

modified Phillips curve The curve that plots the change in the inflation rate against the unemployment rate. Also called an *expectations-augmented Phillips curve* or an *accelerationist Phillips curve*.

monetarism, monetarists A group of economists in the 1960s, led by Milton Friedman, who argued that monetary policy had powerful effects on activity.

monetary aggregate The market value of a sum of liquid assets. *M*1 is a monetary aggregate that includes only the most liquid assets.

monetary base See *central bank money*.

monetary contraction A change in monetary policy, which leads to an increase in the interest rate. Also called *monetary tightening*.

monetary expansion A change in monetary policy, which leads to a decrease in the interest rate.

monetary–fiscal policy mix The combination of monetary and fiscal policies in effect at a given time.

monetary tightening See *monetary contraction*.

money Those financial assets that can be used directly to buy goods.

money market funds Financial institutions that receive funds from people and use them to buy short-term bonds.

money multiplier The increase in the money supply resulting from a one-dollar increase in central bank money.

multilateral exchange rate (multilateral real exchange rate) The real exchange rate between a country and its trading partners, computed as a weighted average of bilateral real exchange rates. Also called the *trade-weighted real exchange rate* or *effective real exchange rate*.

multiplier The ratio of the change in an *endogenous variable* to the change in an *exoge-nous variable* (for example, the ratio of the change in output to a change in autonomous spending).

Mundell-Fleming model A model of simultaneous equilibrium in both goods and financial markets for an open economy.

narrow banking Restrictions on banks that would require them to hold only short-term government bonds.

narrow money See *M*1.

national accounts See *national income and expenditure accounts*.

national income and expenditure accounts The system of accounts used to describe the evolution of the sum, the composition, and the distribution of aggregate output.

natural experiment A real-world event that can be used to test an economic theory.

natural level of employment The level of employment that prevails when unemployment is equal to its natural rate.

natural level of output The level of production that prevails when employment is equal to its natural level.

natural population growth The excess of births over deaths in a given period of time.

natural rate of unemployment The unemployment rate at which price and wage decisions are consistent.

neoclassical synthesis A consensus in macroeconomics, developed in the early 1950s, based on an integration of Keynes's ideas and the ideas of earlier economists.

net capital flows Capital flows from the rest of the world to the domestic economy minus capital flows to the rest of the world from the domestic economy.

net domestic product at basic prices Domestic product is produced within the borders of a country. "Net" indicates depreciation has been subtracted. "At basic prices" indicates that to move to market prices, indirect taxes less subsidies must be added.

net exports (X – Q) The difference between exports and imports. Also called the *trade balance*.

net immigration Immigration minus emigration in a given period of time.

net international investment position A measure of Canada's net foreign assets or debts.

net investment income Receipts of factor income from abroad minus payments of factor income to non-residents. This item measures service payments or Canada's net foreign debts.

net national income at basic prices Gross national product minus depreciation and taxes less subsidies on products.

net transfers received In the current account, the net value of foreign aid received minus foreign aid given.

neutrality of money The proposition that an increase in nominal money has no effect on output or the interest rate but is reflected entirely in a proportional increase in the price level.

new classicals A group of economists who interpret fluctuations as the effects of shocks in competitive markets with fully flexible prices and wages.

New Deal The set of programs put in place by the Roosevelt administration to get the U.S. economy out of the Great Depression.

new growth theory Recent developments in growth theory that explore the determinants of technological progress and the role of increasing returns to scale in growth.

New Keynesians A group of economists who believe in the importance of nominal rigidities in fluctuations, and are exploring the role of market imperfections in explaining fluctuations.

nominal exchange rate The price of foreign currency in terms of domestic currency. The number of units of domestic currency you can get for one unit of foreign currency.

nominal GDP The sum of the quantities of final goods produced in an economy times their current price. Also known as *dollar GDP* and *GDP in current dollars*.

nominal interest rate Interest rate in terms of the national currency (in terms of dollars in Canada). Tells us how many dollars one has to repay in the future in exchange for one dollar today.

nominal rigidities The slow adjustment of nominal wages and prices to changes in economic activity.

nonaccelerating inflation rate of unemployment (NAIRU) The unemployment rate at which inflation neither decreases nor increases. See *natural rate of unemployment*.

nondurable goods Commodities that can be stored but have an average life of less than three years.

nonhuman wealth The financial and housing component of wealth.

non-residential investment The purchase of new capital goods by firms: *structures* and *producer durable equipment*.

normal growth rate The rate of output growth needed to maintain a constant unemployment rate.

North American Free Trade Agreement (NAFTA) An agreement signed by the United States, Canada, and Mexico in which the three countries agreed to establish all of North America as a free-trade zone.

not in the labour force Number of people who are neither employed nor looking for employment.

n-year interest rate See *yield to maturity*.

official international reserves Holdings of foreign assets by the federal government. These are held to allow intervention in foreign exchange markets.

Okun's law The relation between GDP growth and the change in the unemployment rate.

Old Age Security (OAS) A major federal program that transfers funds to older Canadians. Every

Canadian over the age of 65 receives an OAS payment. Higher-income older Canadians repay a portion of this payment through their income taxes.

open market operation The purchase or sale of government bonds by the central bank for the purpose of increasing or decreasing the money supply.

openness in factor markets The opportunity for firms to choose where to locate production and for workers to choose where to work and whether or not to migrate.

openness in financial markets The opportunity for financial investors to choose between domestic and foreign financial assets.

openness in goods markets The opportunity for consumers and firms to choose between domestic and foreign goods.

optimal control The control of a system (a machine, a rocket, an economy) by means of mathematical methods.

optimal control theory The set of mathematical methods used for *optimal control*.

optimal currency area Two regions that share the same currency are a currency union or currency area. If they are in an optimal currency area, then they either experience similar economic shocks or share complete labour mobility.

ordinary least squares A statistical method to find the best fitting relation between two or more variables.

Organization for Economic Cooperation and Development (OECD) An international organization that collects and studies economic data for many countries. Most of the world's rich countries belong to the OECD.

orthodox stabilization program A stabilization program that does not include incomes policies.

output fluctuations Movements in output around its trend.

output per capita A country's gross domestic product divided by its population.

overnight interest rate The interest rate charged for lending and borrowing overnight.

overshooting The large movement in the exchange rate triggered by a monetary expansion or contraction.

panel data set A data set that gives the values of one or more variables for many individuals or many firms over some period of time.

paradox of saving The result that an attempt by people to save more may lead both to a decline in output and to unchanged saving.

parameter A coefficient in a behavioural equation.

participation rate The ratio of the labour force to the noninstitutional civilian population.

patent The legal right granted to a person or firm to exclude anyone else from the production or use of a new product or technique for a certain period of time.

pay-as-you-go social security system Retirement system in which the contributions of current workers are used to pay benefits to retirees.

peg The exchange rate to which a country commits under a fixed exchange rate system.

permanent income theory of consumption The theory of consumption, developed by Milton Friedman, that emphasizes that people make consumption decisions based not on current income, but on their notion of permanent income.

personal disposable income Personal income minus personal tax and nontax payments. The income available to consumers after they have received transfers and paid taxes.

personal expenditure on consumer goods and services In the national income and product accounts, the sum of goods and services purchased by persons resident in Canada.

personal income The income actually received by persons.

Phillips curve The curve that plots the relation between (1) movements in inflation and (2) unemployment. The original Phillips curve captured the relation between the inflation rate and the unemployment rate. The modified *Phillips curve* captures the relation between (1) the change in the inflation rate and (2) the unemployment rate.

players The participants in a *game*. Depending on the context, players may be people, firms, governments, and so on.

point-year of excess unemployment A difference between the actual unemployment rate and the natural unemployment rate of one percentage point for one year.

policy mix See *monetary–fiscal policy mix*.

political business cycle Fluctuations in economic activity caused by the manipulation of the economy for electoral gain.

present value See *expected present discounted value*.

price level The general level of prices in an economy.

price liberalization The process of eliminating subsidies, decontrolling prices and allowing them to clear markets.

price-setting relation The relation between the price chosen by firms, the nominal wage, and the markup.

primary deficit Government spending, excluding interest payments on the debt, minus government revenues. (The negative of the *primary surplus*.)

primary labour market A labour market where jobs are good, wages are high, and turnover is low. Contrast to the *secondary labour market*.

primary surplus Government revenues minus government spending, excluding interest payments on the debt.

private saving (S) Saving by consumers. The value of consumers' disposable income minus their consumption.

production function The relation between the quantity of output and the quantities of inputs used in production.

profitability The expected present discounted value of profits.

propagation mechanism The dynamic effects of a *shock* on output and its components.

propensity to consume (c_1) The effect of an additional dollar of disposable income on con-

sumption. Also called *marginal propensity to consume*.

propensity to save The effect of an additional dollar of disposable income on saving (equal to one minus the propensity to consume). Also called *marginal propensity to save*.

public saving ($T - G$) Saving by the government; equal to government revenues minus government spending. Also called the *budget surplus*. (A *budget deficit* represents public dissaving.)

purchasing power Income in terms of goods.

purchasing power parity (PPP) A method of adjustment used to allow for international comparisons of GDP.

Quebec Pension Plan (QPP) The major way in which the Quebec government provides pensions to elderly persons in Quebec. The QPP is partly a pay-as-you-go plan and partly a funded plan. The Canada Pension Plan (CPP) is the equivalent plan for the rest of Canada.

quits Workers who leave their jobs in search of better alternatives.

quotas Restrictions on the quantities of goods that can be imported.

$\overline{R}^2$ A measure of fit, between zero and one, from a *regression*. An $\overline{R}^2$ of zero implies that there is no apparent relation between the variables under consideration. An $\overline{R}^2$ of 1 implies a perfect fit: All the *residuals* are equal to zero.

random walk The path of a variable whose changes over time are unpredictable.

random walk of consumption The proposition that if consumers are foresighted, changes in their consumption should be unpredictable.

rate of growth of multifactor productivity See *Solow residual*.

rational expectations The formation of expectations based on rational forecasts, rather than on simple extrapolations of the past.

rational speculative bubble An increase in stock prices based on the rational expectation of further increases in prices in the future.

real appreciation An increase in the relative price of domestic goods in terms of foreign goods. A decrease in the real exchange rate.

real business cycle (RBC) models Economic models that assume that output is always at its natural level. Thus all output fluctuations are movements of the natural level of output, as opposed to movements away from the natural level of output.

real depreciation A decrease in the relative price of domestic goods in terms of foreign goods. An increase in the real exchange rate.

real exchange rate The relative price of foreign goods in terms of domestic goods.

real GDP A measure of aggregate output. The sum of quantities produced in an economy times their price in a base year. Also known as *GDP in terms of goods, GDP in constant dollars, GDP adjusted for inflation*. The current measure of real GDP in Canada is called *GDP in (chained) 1997 dollars*.

real GDP in chained (1997) dollars See *real GDP.*

real interest rate Interest rate in terms of goods. Tells us how many goods one has to repay in the future in exchange for one good today.

real return bond A bond issued by the federal government that pays a real rate of interest and repays a principal that is indexed to the Consumer Price Index.

realignment Adjustment of parities in a fixed exchange-rate system.

recession A period of negative GDP growth. Usually refers to at least two consecutive quarters of negative GDP growth.

reference week The particular week in the month when the Labour Force Survey is taken.

regression The output of *ordinary least squares.* Gives the equation corresponding to the estimated relation between variables, together with information about the degree of fit and the importance of the different variables.

regression line The best-fitting line corresponding to the equation obtained by using *ordinary least squares.*

rental cost of capital See *user cost of capital.*

research and development (R & D) Spending aimed at discovering and developing new ideas and products.

reservation wage The wage that would make a worker indifferent to working or becoming unemployed.

reserve ratio The ratio of bank reserves to chequable deposits.

reserves These are deposits held by chartered banks and other financial institutions at the Bank of Canada. It is another term for *settlement balances.*

residential investment The purchase of new homes and apartments by people.

residual The difference between the actual value of a variable and the value implied by the *regression line.* Small residuals indicate a good fit.

revaluation A decrease in the exchange rate in a fixed exchange-rate system.

Ricardian equivalence The proposition that neither government deficits nor government debt have an effect on economic activity. Also called the *Ricardo–Barro proposition.*

Ricardo–Barro proposition See *Ricardian equivalence.*

risk averse A person is risk averse if he/she prefers to receive a given amount for sure to an uncertain amount with the same expected value.

risk neutral A person is risk neutral if he/she is indifferent between receiving a given amount for sure or an uncertain amount with the same expected value.

risk premium The difference between the interest rate paid on a bond and the interest rate paid on a given bond with the highest rating.

sacrifice ratio The number of point-years of excess unemployment needed to achieve a decrease in inflation of 1%.

saving The sum of private and public saving, denoted by *S.*

saving rate The proportion of income that is saved.

savings The accumulated value of past saving. Also called *wealth.*

scatter diagram A graphic presentation that plots the value of one variable against the value of another variable.

secondary labour market A labour market where jobs are poor, wages are low, and turnover is high. Contrast to the *primary labour market.*

seignorage The revenues from the creation of money.

separations Workers who are leaving or losing their jobs.

services Commodities that cannot be stored and thus must be consumed at the place and time of purchase.

settlement balances These are deposits held by chartered banks and other financial institutions at the Bank of Canada. It is another term for *reserves.*

severance payments Payments made by firms to laid-off workers.

share A financial asset issued by a firm that promises to pay a sequence of payments, called dividends, in the future. Also called *stock.*

shocks Movements in the factors that affect aggregate demand and/or aggregate supply.

shoe-leather costs The costs of going to the bank to take money out of a chequing account.

short run A period of time extending over a few years at most.

short-term bond A bond with maturity of one year or less.

slope In a linear relation between two variables, the amount by which the first variable increases when the second increases by one unit.

slump A long period of no growth.

Solow residual The excess of actual output growth over what can be accounted for by the growth in capital and labour.

stabilization program A government program aimed at stabilizing the economy (typically stopping high inflation).

stagflation The combination of stagnation and inflation.

staggering of wage decisions The fact that different wages are adjusted at different times, making it impossible to achieve a synchronized decrease in nominal wage inflation.

standardized employment deficit See *cyclically adjusted deficit.*

state of technology The degree of technological development in a country or industry.

statistical discrepancy A difference between two numbers that should be equal, based on differences in sources or methods of construction.

Statistics Canada The federal government agency that collects and publishes statistics that describe the economic and social activities of Canadians.

steady state In an economy without technological progress, the state of the economy where output and capital per worker are no longer changing. In an economy with technological progress, the state of the economy where output and capital per effective worker are no longer changing.

stock A variable that can be expressed as a quantity at a point in time (such as wealth). Also a synonym for *share.*

stocks An alternative term for *inventories.*

strategic interactions An environment in which the actions of one player depend on and affect the actions of another player.

structural deficit See *cyclically adjusted deficit.*

structural rate of unemployment See *natural rate of unemployment.*

Tanzi-Olivera effect The adverse effect of inflation on tax revenues and in turn on the budget deficit.

target for overnight rate The Bank of Canada announces a target range for the overnight funds rates and acts to keep the actual overnight funds rate within the bounds of their announced target.

tariffs Taxes on imported goods.

tax smoothing The principle of keeping tax rates roughly constant so that the government runs large deficits when government spending is exceptionally high and small surpluses the rest of the time.

Taylor's rule A rule, suggested by John Taylor, telling a central bank how to adjust the nominal interest rate in response to deviations of inflation from its target, and of the unemployment rate from the natural rate.

T-bill See *Treasury bill.*

technological progress An improvement in the state of technology.

technology balance of payments An estimate of the value of exports of technology minus the value of imports of technology.

technology gap The differences between states of technology across countries.

term structure of interest rates See *yield curve.*

time inconsistency In game theory, the incentive for one player to deviate from his previously announced course of action once the other player has moved.

Tobin's q The ratio of the value of the capital stock, computed by adding the stock market value of firms and the debt of firms, to the replacement cost of capital.

total wealth The sum of human wealth and nonhuman wealth.

trade balance The difference between exports and imports. Also called *net exports.*

trade deficit A negative trade balance; that is, imports exceed exports.

trade surplus A positive trade balance; that is, exports exceed imports.

trade-weighted real exchange rate See *multilateral exchange rate.*

transfers See *government transfers.*

transfers to the provinces Federal government tax revenues that are then given to the provinces.

Treasury bill A government bond with a maturity of up to one year. Both the U.S. and Canadian governments issue such bills. Also called the *T-bill*.

t-statistic A statistic associated with an estimated coefficient in a regression that indicates the level of confidence that the true coefficient differs from zero.

twin deficits A positive relationship sometimes observed in which a large government debt is associated with a large current account or trade deficit.

unanticipated money Movements in nominal money that could not have been predicted based on the information available at some time in the past.

uncovered interest parity relation An arbitrage relation stating that domestic and foreign bonds must have the same expected rate of return, expressed in terms of the domestic currency.

underground economy That part of a nation's economic activity that is not measured in official statistics, either because the activity is illegal or because people and firms are seeking to avoid taxes.

unemployment rate The ratio of the number of unemployed to the labour force.

union density The proportion of the work force that is unionized.

usable observation An observation for which the values of all the variables under consideration are available for *regression* purposes.

user cost of capital The cost of using capital over a year, or a given period of time. The sum of the real interest rate and the depreciation rate. Also called the *rental cost of capital*.

value added The value a firm adds in the production process, equal to the value of its production minus the value of the intermediate inputs it uses in production.

velocity The ratio of nominal income to money; the number of transactions for a given quantity of money, or the rate at which money changes hands.

wage indexation A rule that automatically increases wages in response to an increase in prices.

wage-price spiral The mechanism by which increases in wages lead to increases in prices, which lead in turn to further increases in wages, and so on.

wage-setting relation The relation between the wage chosen by wage setters and the unemployment rate.

war of attrition Occurs when both parties to an argument hold their grounds, hoping that the other party will give in.

wealth See *financial wealth*.

yield curve The relation between yield and maturity for bonds of different maturities. Also called the *term structure of interest rates*.

yield to maturity The constant interest rate that makes the price of an *n*-year bond today equal to the present value of future payments. Also called the *n-year interest rate*.

INDEX

Notes: Text in boldface identifies a definition; "f" following a page number indicates a figure or table.